The American Presidency

Contributors

Barber, James D. James B. Duke Professor of Political Science, Duke University.
Carter, Ralph G. Visiting Assistant Professor, Political Science, Texas Christian University.
Ciboski, Kenneth N. Associate Professor, Political Science, Wichita State University.
Cronin, Thomas. Professor, Political Science, Colorado College.
Cutler, Lloyd. Former Counselor to Jimmy Carter.
Donovan, Hedley. Former Editor-in-Chief, *Time* magazine, and former Senior Adviser to President Carter.
Edwards, George C. III. Professor, Political Science, Texas A & M University.
Farnsworth, David N. Professor, Political Science, Wichita State University.
Fesler, James W. Professor Emeritus, Political Science, Yale University.
Fisher, Louis. Specialist in American National Government at the Congressional Research Service, Library of Congress.
Hartman, Robert W. Policy Analyst, Congressional Budget Office.
Keagel, James. Associate Professor, Political Science, Air Force Academy.
Klotz, Frank, Jr. Formerly of the U.S. Air Force Academy, and 1982-83 White House Fellow.
Koenig, Louis W. Professor, Politics, New York University.
Kozak, David C. Professor, Department of Domestic Studies, National War College, National Defense University.
Ladd, Everett C. Professor, Political Science, University of Connecticut.
Lammers, William. Associate Professor, Political Science, University of Southern California.
Loevy, Robert D. Professor, Political Science, Colorado College.
McKenney, James W. Associate Professor and Chairperson, Political Science, Wichita State University.
Meese, Edwin III. Counselor to President Reagan.
Mueller, John E. Professor, Political Science, University of Rochester.
Murphy, Arthur B. Presidential Historian and Coordinator, Graduate School of Public Affairs, University of Colorado.
Natoli, Marie D. Associate Professor, Political Science, Emmanuel College.
Neustadt, Richard E. Professor, Government, Harvard University.
Pious, Richard M. Associate Professor, Political Science, Barnard College.
Polsby, Nelson W. Professor, Political Science, University of California at Berkeley.
Reedy, George E. Professor, Journalism, Marquette University.
Reinhard, Gregor. Professor, Political Science, and Director of Public Administration, Gannon University.
Relyea, Harold. Research Analyst, Library of Congress, and Book Review Editor, *Presidential Studies Quarterly*.
Rockman, Bert A. Professor, Political Science, University of Pittsburgh.

The American Presidency
A Policy Perspective from Readings and Documents

edited by *David C. Kozak*
and *Kenneth N. Ciboski*

with a Foreword by
Ambassador L. Bruce Laingen

The Nelson-Hall Series in Political Science
Consulting Editor: **Samuel G. Patterson**
The Ohio State University

Disclaimer: This collection, edited and written in part by a U.S. Air Force officer, was prepared for academic purposes and does not necessarily reflect the views of the Department of Defense, the U.S. Air Force, or National Defense University.

Library of Congress Cataloging in Publication Data

Main entry under title:

The American Presidency

Includes bibliographies.
1. Presidents—United States. 2. Presidents—United States—History—Sources. 3. United States—Politics and government—1981– . 4. United States—Politics and government—Sources. I. Kozak, David C. II. Ciboski, Kenneth N.
JK516.P654   1985   353.03'1   84–16587
ISBN 0–8304–1053–8

Copyright © 1985 by David C. Kozak and Kenneth N. Ciboski.

Reprinted 1987

All rights reserved. No part of this book may be reproduced in any form without permission in writing from the publisher, except by a reviewer who wishes to quote brief passages in connection with a review written for broadcast or for inclusion in a magazine or newspaper. For information address Nelson-Hall Inc., Publishers, 111 North Canal Street, Chicago, Illinois 60606.

Manufactured in the United States of America

10 9 8 7 6 5 4 3 2

To Professor *Nelson W. Polsby,* a friend,
teacher, writer, editor,
and humorist.

Thanks for everything, Nelson!

About the Editors

Ciboski, Kenneth N. (B.A., M.A., University of Kansas; Ph.D., University of Washington). Ken Ciboski has contributed articles on Soviet political leadership to several scholarly journals and has published "The Bureaucratic Connection: Explaining the Skybolt Decision" in *American Defense Policy*. He participated in a National Endowment for the Humanities seminar on the presidency chaired by Professor Louis Koenig at New York University in 1981. He is an Associate Professor of Political Science at Wichita State University, where he teaches courses in American, Soviet, and comparative politics.

Kozak, David C. (B.A., Gannon University; M.A., Kent State University; Ph.D., University of Pittsburgh). David Kozak was formerly Associate Professor of Political Science, U.S. Air Force Academy; Adjunct Professor in the Graduate School of Public Affairs, the University of Colorado; and 1981-82 American Political Science Association Congressional Fellow on the staffs of Congressman Andy Jacobs (D., Ind.) and Senator J. J. Exon (D., Neb.). He is a professor in the Department of Public Policy at the National War College, National Defense University, where he teaches courses in American government, politics, and public policy making. He is co-editor of and contributor to *Sourcebook on Congress* and author of *Contexts of Congressional Decision Behavior* (forthcoming).

Contents

Foreword xiii

Preface xv

1 Introduction: The Presidency in the American Political System   1

1.1 The Origins of the Presidency   1
Gregor Reinhard

Illustration 1a: Article II, U.S. Constitution   14

1.2 Presidential Powers   15
Louis Fisher

Illustration 1b: The Presidential Job Description: The Subpresidencies   46
Thomas Cronin

1.3 The President and the Control of Nuclear Weapons   47
Frank Klotz, Jr.

1.4 Presidents View Their Office   58

a. Theodore Roosevelt, The Stewardship Doctrine   58

b. William Howard Taft, A Restricted View of the Office   59

2 Presidents: How They Get to the White House   61

2.1 The Brittle Mandate   62
Everett C. Ladd

2.2 Reform of the Party System and the Conduct of the Presidency   83
Nelson W. Polsby

Illustration 2a: The Constitution on the Electoral College and Presidential Elections   94

Illustration 2b: The Hunt Commission, Report of the Commission on Presidential Nomination   98

Illustration 2c: An Excerpt from Federal Election Campaign Laws   101

3 Organizing the Presidency: The Administrative Presidency — 105

3.1 Growth and Development of the President's Office — 105
Harold Relyea

Illustration 3a: Introduction to the Brownlow Report — 144

3.2 The Institutional Presidency: A View from the White House — 149
Edwin Meese III

Illustration 3b: The Executive Office of the President — 157

Illustration 3c: The White House Staff — 162

Illustration 3d: OMB Enrolled Bill Memo — 164

Illustration 3e: NSC Structure — 169

Illustration 3f: NSC Decision Process — 176

3.3 Presidents and Their Foreign Policy Advisors — 183
David N. Farnsworth

3.4 Presidential Leadership and the CIA — 192
James W. McKenney

3.5 Decision Settings in the White House Presidency — 200
David C. Kozak

3.6 Perspectives on the Vice Presidency — 208
Marie D. Natoli

4 Presidential Policy Relationships I: Press, Polls, and Public Opinion — 213

4.1 The Presidency and the Press — 213
George E. Reedy

4.2 Presidential Popularity from Truman to Johnson — 221
John E. Mueller

Illustration 4a: Presidential Popularity and Approval Polls — 249

5 Presidential Policy Relationships II: Congress and "The Inevitable Struggle" — 255

5.1 Legislative Leadership — 256
Richard M. Pious

Illustration 5a: An Example of a Veto Message — 282

5.2 Presidential Leadership Skills 284
George C. Edwards III

Illustration 5b: The Supreme Court and the Legislative Veto: Excerpts from the Chadha Case 305

5.3 Presidential Effectiveness in Congressional Foreign Policymaking: A Reconsideration 311
Ralph G. Carter

6 Presidential Policy Relationships III: The Bureaucracy 327

6.1 White House-Departmental Relations 327
Thomas Cronin

Illustration 6a: The Federal Executive Establishment 359

6.2 Two Models of Legitimacy 362
Nelson W. Polsby

6.3 Politics, Policy, and Bureaucracy at the Top 363
James W. Fesler

7 Presidential Leadership and the Policy Process 379

7.1 The Power to Persuade 379
Richard E. Neustadt

Illustration 7a: Neustadt Presidential Power 389

7.2 Taking the "X" out of MX or Finding a Home for the Missile 390
Kenneth N. Ciboski

7.3 The Presidency and Domestic Policy: The Civil Rights Act of 1964 411
Robert D. Loevy

7.4 The President and Foreign Policy 420
James Keagle

7.5 The President and the Budget 430
Robert W. Hartman

7.6 Evaluating the Presidents of the United States 437
Arthur B. Murphy

8 The Modern Presidency 449

8.1 Constants, Cycles, Trends, and Persona in Presidential Governance: Carter's Troubles Reviewed 449
Bert A. Rockman

8.2 The Pulse of Politics 474
James David Barber

Illustration 8a: A Presidential Executive Order 483

Illustration 8b: Presidential Daily Schedule 484

Illustration 8c: A President's Correspondence with a Member of Congress 487

Illustration 8d: A Memo to the President 490

Illustration 8e: A Memo from the President 492

Illustration 8f: Minutes of a Cabinet Meeting 493

Illustration 8g: Memorandum: Remarks to the Cabinet 497

Illustration 8h: Minutes of an NSC Meeting 498

Illustration 8i: President's Presidential Press Plan 509

Illustration 8j: Recommend Presidential Telephone Call 511

Illustration 8k: Excerpts from Weekly Compilation of Presidential Documents 512

9 Differing Perspectives on the Presidency 515

Perspectives on the Individual

9.1 Presidential Character and How to Foresee It 515
James David Barber

9.2 It Can Happen Here 523
George E. Reedy

9.3 Job Specs for the Oval Office 528
Hedley Donovan

Perspectives on Structure

9.4 The Presidency and the Crisis of Public Management, A Panel of the National Academy of Public Administration 537

9.5 The Multiple Advocacy Prescription for Presidential Decisionmaking: An Explication and Analysis 542
David C. Kozak

Perspectives on the System

9.6 The Reform Agenda 563
William Lammers

Illustration 9a: Classification of Presidential Reforms
by Level and Focus   567
Norman Thomas

9.7 Reassessing the Imperial Presidency   568
Louis W. Koenig

9.8 To Form a Government   577
Lloyd N. Cutler

9.9 Conclusion: The Presidency in the 1980s   588
Richard M. Pious

Foreword

The American presidency. That noble office that Washington assumed with reluctance and then proceeded to dignify with restraint in the use of its power and with vision in terms of national unity. That lofty pinnacle of political power that, to the great good fortune of the American people, has been occupied (with few exceptions) by men worthy of the traditions set by the good general. That office whose occupant can, if he chooses, set the tone and direction of our political life and articulate the hopes and aspirations of the American people. That office whose occupant in today's world has at his fingertips the awesome power of nuclear weapons, and whose leadership role carries with it the destinies of much of what we call the Free World. Or so we have come to believe.

This is a book about all of that, a book of many sources describing the job of that person who is at the same time our head of state and the head of our government, with all that entails. In good times and bad, the occupant of that office, alone with the vice-president elected by all the American people, has a fundamental impact on our political life and the view Americans have of their government. But it is in times of national crisis, whether at home or abroad, that the president assumes larger proportions of leadership. Only he can claim to speak for all the people. His use of what Theodore Roosevelt called the "bully pulpit" can determine whether the country rallies round or risks aimless drift in party bickering. His capacity to inspire a sense of unity and to speak for that unity will massively influence the attitude of foreign adversaries or domestic doomsayers.

So it has been often in our history. So it was with the presidency's early incumbents—Jefferson, Madison, Jackson. So it might have been, to the nation's betterment, had Lincoln not been felled by an assassin's bullet. Theodore Roosevelt's gregarious optimism set much of the tone for the feisty spirit and achievements of the first decade of this century. Harding and Coolidge set quite a different tone in their time. Perhaps no president so effectively used the power of the office in crises as did Franklin Roosevelt, in his assault on the nation's crisis of confidence in the depression and in his skillful use of power to prepare the nation for the war he was convinced was coming. Harry Truman, in turn, demonstrated what aggressive leadership, bolstered by trust in able cabinet secretaries, can do in his responses to the origins of the cold war and to aggression in Korea. Kennedy carried the nation with him in a dramatic display of collegial crisis management in the Cuban missile crisis, when television for the first time displayed its utility as a tool in influencing the public's view of a crisis. And by the time of the Iranian hostage crisis, Jimmy Carter was to learn how effectively that medium could affect a president's capacity to deal with a crisis.

The modern presidency is surrounded by what since the late 1940s has become an established bureaucracy of crisis management—the National Security Advisor and his supporting staff, a kind of meeting ground between the political administration and the

---

Editors' note: Ambassador Laingen is currently vice-president of National Defense University. A career Foreign Service officer, he was propelled into the national limelight while serving as the ranking diplomat in Iran during the embassy takeover and hostage crisis.

professionals of government. Presidential use of that bureaucracy—as well as its interaction with the vastly larger bureaucracies of State, Defense, and CIA—has varied in the postwar period. But fundamentally it is the president himself, his style, and his personality that will determine how a crisis of national proportions will be handled. Nowhere, of course, was that more evident than in the Iranian hostage crisis, a crisis that ultimately, in Carter's words, amounted to "one of the most intricate financial and political problems ever faced by any nation." History has yet to judge whether that president's handling of that particular crisis best served the United States, but certainly there can be no better example of how a president's personal role influences the way a crisis is seen by the public and affects its evolution.

This book of readings and documents, ranging widely over both the powers and limitations of the presidency, is a milestone contribution to the library of analyses of that office and to public understanding of its role in times of both crisis and calm. Its breadth of coverage is testimony in itself to what the presidency is—an office rich in its historic evolution, fascinating in its human dimensions, and unparalleled, at least in modern times, in its command of the world stage and the influence it can have both at home and abroad. Through its pages run evidence as well of the checks and balances that characterize the American federal system overall, reminding one of Jefferson's counsel: "Every government degenerates when entrusted to the rulers of the people alone. The people themselves, therefore, are its only safe depositories." The president who forgets that counsel will soon be reminded of his lapse—and be reminded in the process of the obligation that rests on him to ensure that that degeneration of trust does not occur.

Ambassador L. Bruce Laingen

Preface

Political scientists who teach the presidency as a single course or as part of a course in American politics often observe that the topic lends itself poorly to systematic analysis—that it is extremely difficult for teachers and students alike to get "handle-holds," as we have heard it expressed, on the subject matter of the president and the presidency.

In presenting this collection of original essays, reprints, and documents emphasizing the policy process, we do not lay claim to any major "systematic" breakthroughs in the study of the presidency. We think, however, that the collection will help the student distinguish between myth and reality. Most Americans grow up with the image that the president is powerful, strong, a superhuman in politics—that levers are pulled and the machinery responds to what the president wants done for the good of the commonweal.

On the other end, of course, is Congress, which appears unruly and formidable to any President. President John Kennedy remarked that it is much different to be one of 435 in the United States House of Representatives and one of 100 in the United States Senate: the president faces 535 legislators, and they are collectively a formidable power. The committee and subcommittee reforms of the 1970s in the Congress have compounded the president's "problem" with a greater diffusion of power away from leadership centers.

The various departments of the government also develop an identity of their own and may respond to their constituencies in ways that diverge from the president's agenda for the nation. Add to this the separation of powers, checks and balances, and the pluralistic milieu in which the president must operate, and one can understand President Lyndon Johnson when he said the only power he has is nuclear, and he cannot use that—this in response to the notion that people think the president has all the power he needs and then some.

Other factors affecting presidential power are the rise of single-issue interest groups that are bent against political compromise, and the use of television and public opinion polls. The latter two devices put the president in instant touch with the people, but the dilemma is that the people are thus more likely to hold the chief executive responsible for the nation's problems. As the president responds to perceived public opinion, it becomes increasingly difficult to engage in consistent and persistent policies. The consequences for the future of the democratic polity could be far-reaching. An example is United States foreign policy toward the Soviet Union. In the summer of 1983, the press reverberated with news stories speculating that President Reagan wanted to appear to change U.S. policy toward the Soviet Union in consonance with anticipated public opinion leading to the 1984 election.

For students of the presidency, the question is whether or not the expectations and responsibilities exceed the authority and the resources of the office. For the president, the question might be pragmatic or political: What is to be done with public opinion results that challenge the president's political perspective? The struggle for a balance between the demands on the presidency and the democratic constraints on that office is likely to continue. Desanctifying the office could bring us a step closer to reality.

Somehow this thing must be made human again. Somehow we must learn to govern our people from an office that is secular and not from a court that is sanctified. If our destruction comes, it will be because we placed our faith—our unquestioning faith—in institutions that were only brick and wood and in men who were only flesh and blood and this seems to be the condition of the last half of the twentieth century.[1]

We have assembled a collection of manuscripts and documents that emphasize some of the usual themes in a study of the presidency and also fill some gaps in the literature. These include the presidency in the American political system, how presidents get to the White House, and what they confront after they get there. Our choices emphasize the relationship of the president and Congress, the president and the bureaucracy, the president and the press, and presidential leadership in the policy process. We conclude with discussions of perspectives on the presidency, particularly as these relate to the "imperial presidency" thesis that developed after the Watergate crisis and to proposals for reform and the future of the presidency.

Almost one-third of the manuscripts appear in print for the first time, as do a number of the illustrations. We have included an array of excerpts and articles by leading scholars from academic books and journals. Space limitations do not permit us to include more manuscripts on presidential elections, the presidency and the judiciary, and the presidency and executive privilege and impeachment.

Archivists at the Hoover, Roosevelt, Truman, Eisenhower, Johnson, and Ford presidential libraries exerted great effort to locate material that reflected the activity of these presidents in office. In particular, we extend thanks to John Wickman of the Eisenhower Library for his advice and encouragement.

Roger Davidson and Louis Fisher of the Congressional Research Service, a division of the Library of Congress, were especially helpful in providing documents and manuscripts.

Thanks also are due Ron Warncke, Nelson-Hall Publishers, for assistance in publishing the work; to Sam Patterson, editorial advisor, Nelson-Hall, for his encouragement; and to James McKenney, chairperson, Department of Political Science, Wichita State University, for providing secretarial and student assistance on the project.

We also thank our wives, Barbara Ciboski and Maryanne Kozak, for their patience, support, and helpful comments. We thank Maryanne Kozak for editing the original essays and editorial comments.

The division of labor in this undertaking went as follows: Ciboski gathered documents from presidential libraries while Kozak collected documents in Washington, D.C. Both commissioned original essays and both made selections from existing literature during a week in Wichita in June of 1983. Kozak wrote all editorial introductions to chapters and readings. Ciboski wrote this introduction.

We dedicate this publication to Professor Nelson W. Polsby, whose published works, thinking, and presentations at our respective institutions have stimulated our thinking about American politics. The way we and many of our colleagues throughout the discipline approach, teach, and think about American government, politics, and policymaking has been affected strongly and positively by his many thoughtful contributions.

---

1. George E. Reedy, *The Twilight of the Presidency*, (New York: World Pub. Co., 1970), 197.

Introduction: The Presidency in the American Political System

The president and the supporting institutions that comprise the presidency are important forces in American policymaking. Although not necessarily intended to be so by the architects of the Constitution, the presidency is the center of contemporary American government. Most important policy initiatives are coordinated from the White House, and the president—as our first citizen—is the hub of our national political life.

In a general way, the major contributions of the presidency to policymaking are leadership and a comprehensive perspective. In contrast, the role of Congress is lawmaking and representation, with a subdivision of labor between House and Senate. The House provides policy expertise and the Senate affords high debate on national priorities. The main contributions of the courts are interpreting the laws and refereeing group struggles arising out of litigation. As many presidents have acknowledged, the presidency is above all else a place of leadership—a pulpit—from which the country can be inspired, encouraged, warned, and uplifted. The unique contribution of the presidency lies in its potential for consolidated and concentrated perspectives in policymaking. In the midst of our constitutional order of fragmented political authority with separation and division of powers and checks and balances, the presidency is the one truly centripetal force—the one place in the system where things can be brought together.

The readings in this chapter examine the origins and scope of presidential power, its contexts, and its uses.

The Origins of the Presidency

Gregor Reinhard

As is the case with the study of any institution, an understanding of the U.S. presidency requires an appreciation for both the origins of the office and the intentions of those who devised it. The contemporary presidency is strongly affected by the political thought, culture, and experiences of colonial and revolutionary America.

Upon winning independence from Great Britain, the founding fathers devised a government known as the Articles of Confederation. Reflecting the revolutionary mistrust of strong government and arbitrary exercises of executive authority, a feature of the Articles was the lack of a central chief executive. After more than a decade of experience, it became obvious that the weak government of the Articles was ill-suited for the task of nation-building. Political notables of the day gathered in Philadelphia in 1787 to revise the Articles. Their task was to devise a government that would be stronger than the Articles but would not pose a threat to individual liberties. They fashioned a new government on the basis of a number of compromises. The office of president was one of those compromises.

The following original essay examines the development of the presidency at the Philadelphia Convention. As we approach the bicentennial of the American Constitution, it is important that all Americans reflect on the underlying values and intentions of the founding framers. Important questions to ask are: (1) Has the revolutionary spirit of freedom from tyranny continued to color the American system? (2) How well served are we by the government of 1787? and (3) Are there alternative arrangements that might be preferable? We shall return to this final question in our concluding chapter.

The written Constitution of the United States provides only the barest outline of the powers and responsibilities of the president of the United States. The framers of the Constitution wisely refused to attempt to spell out in great detail the precise extent and limits of presidential power. It is this intentional vagueness and even ambiguity in the Constitution which gives to that document its flexibility and to the American constitutional system its capacity for dynamic growth. Still, the elasticity of the Constitution has limits, and constitutional provisions remain the foundation of the modern presidency.

Virtually every major crisis in American politics has involved issues of constitutional interpretation. Certainly this was true in the cases of Vietnam and Watergate when the "imperial presidency" came under strong and often telling criticism.[1] This is appropriate since in our system the policies and processes of government must be grounded in law and particularly in that fundamental law which is the Constitution. In such periods, debate on the scope and nature of presidential power often focuses on constitutional origins, on the views and intentions of the framers and others of their time who helped create the foundations of American government.

The fifty-five delegates to the Constitutional Convention who assembled in Philadelphia in the spring and summer of 1787 were an extraordinarily intelligent, literate, and thoughtful group of men. They came from a highly homogenous society, though divergent political and economic interests between states and regions provided the basis for their political disputes. They had been selected by their state governments, generally from among the most prominent of their citizens. Most were well educated and representative of the more wealthy and privileged class in America. The delegates were above all men of substantial political experience. They had served variously in the colonial legislatures, in the Continental Congress or the Congress under the Articles of Confederation, or in the state governments. Most had had a part in the American War of Independence in military or civil office. They were members of a small group of public men who were acquainted with one another personally or by reputation.

At the onset, it is important to understand that the Constitution was shaped by both principles and politics. The delegates' ideas of executive power reflected the political theory and practice of their day. Most of the delegates were born Englishmen, heirs to a long tradition of responsible government and civil rights. The more academically minded had read deeply in the rich heritage of western political thought, from the classical writers of Greece and Rome, through the Christian theorists of the medieval period, to the modern ideas of Machiavelli, Hobbes, Locke, Montesquieu, Hume, and Adam Smith. Most were religious men who believed in a higher law stemming from God and from which human law must derive its authority. They were thus convinced constitutionalists in the sense of the conviction that the powers of government ought to be defined and limited to those which promoted the common good of the community. In the course of the preceding century the belief in a higher law had become wedded to the social contract theory of the origin of the state, as expounded by such writers as Hobbes and Locke. Both concepts were given institutional expression in that uniquely American contribution, the popularly ratified and written Constitution.

To argue that the framers were men of principle is by no means inconsistent with the view that they were also consummate, practical politicians. They were particularly skilled in the legislative process, in the resolution of conflict through negotiation and compromise. Their proceedings were held in secret, with most debate conducted in the free-wheeling committee of the whole. When discussion led to apparent stalemate, they made use of committees that worked out the essential compromises on such issues as representation, slavery, and the election of the president. This made final agreement possible. Three such committees were crucial in the formation of the constitutional presidency: the five-member Committee on Detail, the eleven-member Committee on Postponed Matters, and the final five-member Committee on Style.

Throughout the Convention the delegates displayed an acute sensitivity to the political feasibility of their constitutional design. In particular they successfully anticipated the opposition that was to arise in the ratification struggles that followed. They were, as John Roche has said, "first and foremost superb democratic politicians committed to working within the democratic framework within a universe of public approval."[2] William Patterson captured this spirit of the convention when he declared: "I come here not to speak my own sentiments, but the sentiments of those who sent me. Our object is not such a government as may be best in itself, but such a one as our Constituents have authorized us to prepare and as they will approve."[3]

Each generation and philosophic school has been inclined to interpret the framers and their works through different lenses. Today we find a welter of different interpretations: historical, economic, behavioral, democratic, oligarchic, aristocratic, and so on.[4] Often the debates that follow upon conflicting interpretations shed more heat than light, for unfortunately the evidence from the framers' own lives and works lends support to diverse conclusions. The intentions of the framers are indeed pertinent to our current understanding of the Constitution. But human motivation is complex, and the deeper one investigates, the more murky questions of intent are likely to become. The reasons for this become clearer if you recognize that the Constitution and, for that matter, laws generally are not the product of some single Solomon-like law giver but the result of a political process. Often statements of intent are deliberately vague as legislators seek to build a coalition in support of their proposals. It is not uncommon for those holding conflicting interests to join in such a coalition, each believing that ultimately their own priorities will be served. Furthermore the framers, like other democratic legislators, possessed diverse goals and intentions. Considerable agreement on the general nature of the problems confronting them was evident. However, while agreement on problems and the need for remedial action may exist, it does not follow that legislators will have clear, specific goals and priorities. Wisely, the framers left much of the Constitution open for further interpretation and elaboration, in effect delegating to the future the task of establishing the precise meaning of its provisions.

The attitudes that helped to shape the founding fathers' view of the presidency included a deep distrust of unchecked and irresponsive executive power. The repeated injuries and usurpations attributed to George III in the Declaration of Independence were, in the colonial perspective, part of a long train of abuses that had developed over a hundred years or more. The colonists' struggle with royal authority had focused especially on the political conflicts between colonial governors, who were representatives of the crown, and the colonial assemblies. Over the years these assemblies won important concessions and in some cases established considerable influence over executives, especially through their extensive control over finance. Generally, the colonists had claimed the right to limit executive power and to be governed by their popular assemblies after the manner of Parliament. Actually, in pursuit of the rights of Englishmen as they perceived them, the colonial leaders often pressed claims and won concessions beyond what was common in the English practice of the times.

The colonial period, as Professor Corwin has pointed out, "ended with the belief prevalent that 'the executive magistry' was the natural enemy, the legislative assembly the natural friend of liberty."[5] Most of the early state constitutions and our first national constitution, the Articles of Confederation and Perpetual Union, displayed a deep distrust of executive authority. The early state constitutions, with few exceptions, reduced the gubernatorial office to a legislative dependency. "The executive powers of government," read the Virginia Constitution of 1776, are to be exercised "according to the laws of this commonwealth" and the governor "shall not, under any pretence, exercise any power of prerogative by virtue of any law, statute or custom of England."[6] Likewise, the Articles of Confederation provided for no real executive at all. A congress made up of delegates selected annually "in such a manner as the legislature of each state shall direct" represented the "sovereign states" and exercised very little real power over them. The Congress could legislate in a wide range of areas but lacked the capacity to enforce its laws, depending almost entirely upon the willingness of the state governments to requisition taxes, raise an army or navy, or otherwise implement its will.

Legislative supremacy in the states also, in the view of the founding fathers, tended toward legislative omnipotence that ignored all constitutional limits. As Madison was later to remark in Federalist No. 48:

> The founders of our republics . . . seem never for a moment to have turned their eyes from the overgrown and all-grasping prerogative of an hereditary magistrate, supported and fortified by an hereditary branch of the legislative authority. They seem never to have recollected the danger from legislative usurpations, which, by assembling all power in the same hands, must lead to the same tyranny as is threatened by executive usurpations.[7]

Neither state nor national governments seemed able to cope with the problems of the deteriorating economy, declining international confidence, social unrest, and political turmoil that confronted the American people in the aftermath of the Revolution. Indeed, these governments themselves were perceived by the framers as important causes of what many saw as the impending collapse of the nation. Nonpayment of the national debt, the debasement of currency, excessively liberal bankruptcy laws, and the increasing barriers thrown up to interstate commerce were all due to policies adopted by the state governments as the national government stood helplessly by.

Thus the framers came to realize the need for a more powerful national government, but they also assumed that power unless adequately checked would be abused. The chief device that they found for preventing abuse of power was the principle of separation of powers as elaborated by such political theorists as John Locke and particularly Baron Montesquieu who, in his *Spirit of the Laws* (1748), had argued that the English constitutional system had achieved political liberty because of a functional separation of powers. "When the legislative and executive powers are limited in the same person or in the same body of magistrates, there can be no liberty."[8] No concept found greater support among the delegates to the Constitutional Convention than that of separation of powers, though their creation provides more for a separation of institutions and a blending of powers and functions than the scheme proposed by Montesquieu. Indeed, the final result resembles the more ancient conception of a mixed constitution originally elaborated by Aristotle, which involved the balancing and blending of the socio-economic and political characteristics of aristocracy, democracy, and oligarchy in a middle-class polity.

By 1783, most delegates agreed on the

need for a national government consisting of a "legislative, judiciary, and executive." But what were to be the powers and responsibilities of the executive, and how were these to be restrained and limited? There was general agreement that the executive should ensure national compliance with law. Beyond this there was considerable uncertainty, and the precise dimensions of the constitutional presidency had to be hammered out through debate and negotiation during the long months the convention remained in session.

The delegates were familiar with the executive powers exercised by state and colonial governors and above all with those possessed by the British monarch. The delegates anticipated their opposition and took pains to distinguish between the president and a king. Yet, Professor Corwin's observation seems cogent: "The presidency was designed in great measure to reproduce the monarchy of George III with the corruption left out and also of course the hereditary features."[9] The framers could also draw on the models of those state constitutions, notably New York and Massachusetts, which had established a strong separate executive. The New York State Constitution of 1777 in particular contains many provisions that closely parallel those adopted in Article II.

Support for a strong executive was to be found in the writings of the political theorists with which the framers were familiar. Of particular importance was the idea of executive prerogative as developed by John Locke and Sir William Blackstone. For Locke's prerogative included the "power to act according to discretion for the public good without the prescription of law and sometimes even against it."[10] Sir William Blackstone, whose *Commentaries on the Laws of England* was known to most of the delegates to the convention as the standard reference on the British Constitution and the common law, emphasized that the "prerogative" is not to be understood as an absolute power limited by law. "In the exercise of Lawful prerogative," Blackstone wrote, "the king is and ought to be absolute." The prerogative power is justified by the need to act in defense of the public interest in situations in which existing laws provide no guidelines or, because they were drafted for different circumstances, actually impede the pursuit of the public interest. "One of the principal bulwarks of civil liberty" in the British Constitution, according to Blackstone, was the limitation of the king's prerogative "by bands so certain and notorious that it is impossible that he should ever exceed them without the consent of the people . . . or a violation of . . . [the Constitution]."[11]

II

Art. II as it emerged from the constitutional convention begins, "The executive power shall be vested in a President of the United States." The president is made commander-in-chief of the army and navy. He is given power to require the opinion in writing of the principal officers of each of the executive departments, and to grant reprieves and pardons in federal cases (except in cases of impeachment). He may make treaties by and with the advice and consent of the Senate and may appoint, subject to senatorial confirmation, ambassadors and other public ministers, judges of the Supreme Court, and all other officers of the United States in cases where their selection is not otherwise provided for. [Congress, however, may vest by law the appointment of inferior officers in the president alone, in the courts of law, or in the heads of departments.] He receives foreign ambassadors and ministers, and commissions all military officers. He is directed to give the Congress information on the state of the Union and may recommend measures to them. He may on extraordinary occasions convene either or both houses and adjourn them when they disagree on the time for adjournment. He may veto bills passed by Congress, and his veto stands unless there is repassage by a two-thirds majority in both chambers. Finally, the president is given the responsibility for taking care that the laws be faithfully executed.

To reach agreement on these provisions required a lengthy period of debate, negotiation, conflict, and compromise conducted in secret behind closed doors during the hot and humid Philadelphia summer. It should not be imagined that each of the framers began with a fully formed conception of the office he wished to establish. Instead, ideas were exchanged, positions once taken were later abandoned, and the conception of the presidency developed and grew out of this extended dialogue.

The agenda of the Convention was set by the Virginia Plan introduced by Governor Randolph which had been drafted by the pre-convention caucus of the delegates from Virginia, especially by James Madison. The plan called for the replacement of the government under the Articles of Confederation with a national government "consisting of a supreme legislative, judiciary and executive."[12] The legislature would be divided into two houses, one directly elected, the other chosen indirectly. The executive was to be selected by the national legislature for a single term initially defined as seven years.

These and other provisions of the Virginia Plan suggested an executive essentially subordinate to the legislature. If they had been accepted, as they very nearly were, American government might have evolved more in the direction of the British parliamentary model. However, Madison and many other delegates were uncertain in their views.[13]

Almost at once a different position was taken by James Wilson of Pennsylvania, who argued for a single executive independent of the legislature and vested with powers to veto legislation. This plan was designed, he said, to give "most energy, dispatch and responsibility to the office."[14] Most importantly, Wilson called for popular election with a relatively short term of office but with unlimited re-eligibility.

The battle was drawn between the nationalists who desired a strong, independent executive and those who desired a weaker executive dependent on the legislature. The latter view was well represented by Roger Sherman of Connecticut. Madison noted:

> Mr. Sherman said he considered the Executive magistracy as nothing more than an institution for carrying the will of the legislature into effect, and that the person or persons ought to be appointed by and accountable to the legislature only, which was the depository of the supreme will of the Society. They were the best judges of the business which ought to be done by the Executive department and consequently of the number necessary from time to time for doing it. He wished that the number might not be fixed but that the legislature should be at liberty to appoint one or more as experience might dictate.[15]

The issue of a single or plural executive was soon solved in favor of the former alternative despite the view of Randolph, who contended that "unity in the Executive" would be the "foetus of monarchy."[16] The attempt to restrain the executive by requiring him to work through a council—a practice common to English, colonial, and state governments—was hotly debated and only abandoned toward the end of the Convention.

Both the Virginia and the New Jersey Plans accepted the ideas of executive separation from the legislature, executive control over military operations, and executive appointment of federal officers including judges, indicating that broad consensus had been reached on these principles. Shortly after the introduction of the New Jersey Plan on June 18, 1787, Alexander Hamilton delivered his famous convention speech which lasted for almost six hours. Although persistently outvoted in the convention by the other New York delegates [voting was by state according to a unit rule], Hamilton was certainly influential. His work in the Convention, in the ratification struggle that followed, and as secretary of the Treasury in Washington's cabinet made him one of the chief architects of the American constitutional system. Indeed, Professor Edward Corwin, the preeminent constitutional scholar of the twentieth century, found that "the modern theory of presidential power" was "the contribution primarily of Alexander Hamilton."[17]

Hamilton's speech is controversial. In it he expressed admiration for the British form of limited monarchy which, he believed, provided best for "public strength and individual security" and for an extreme centralized form of government. He would not propose monarchy for this country as republican commitments were too strong. The problem was that "it seems to be admitted that no good [executive] . . . could be established on republican principles. . . . Was not this giving up the merits of the question: for can there be good government without a good executive?" he asked. The British monarchy was one in which the interests of the monarch were so interwoven with those of the nation as a whole and his personal powers and privileges so great that he was placed above the danger of being corrupted from abroad. At the same time, he was sufficiently independent and sufficiently controlled to provide for effective and constitutional government. One of the weaknesses of republics was a tendency toward foreign manipulation and corruption. Domestically, there was always likely to be a conflict between those with wealth and power and the unprosperous many. Government in the hands of either class was likely to lead to tyranny. Government should be in the hands of both, with a popularly elected assembly (lower house) whose members would serve for three years, and a senate whose members would be chosen by electors and who would serve for an indefinite term during good behavior (the counterpart of the British House of Lords). The check on both chambers was an "Executive Magistrate" who was to be selected by electors chosen by the people and who would serve on good behavior for life. He was to possess an absolute veto on all legislation, and act as "the executor of all laws passed" and "the director of war when authorized or begun." He would have the power to make treaties with "the advice and approbation of the Senate," and to "have the sole appointment power of the heads of the departments of Finance, War and Foreign Affairs." He would have the capacity to nominate all other officers including ambassadors, subject to the veto of the Senate. He was to possess the pardoning power, except in the case of treason where senatorial approval would be required. Removal of the chief executive was to be for "mal-and corrupt practice," all impeachments being triable by a court composed of the chief justices of the respective states.[18]

Hamilton clearly believed that the executive should possess policy-making authority at least in foreign affairs, defense, and finance, and not simply be confined to the execution of legislative acts. It may also be that he had in mind some form of ministerial government, after the British model. However, the delegates, including Hamilton, rejected almost unanimously the possession by legislators of other offices, a key element of parliamentary government. While his enthusiasm for a life-term president, virtually an elected monarch, was obviously politically unfeasible and was given no real consideration by the Convention, other elements of his position were later incorporated into the consitutional design. His argument for executive independence also doubtlessly contributed to erosion of support for the principle of legislative selection.

No question was as hotly debated at the convention as that of the method of selecting the president. Wilson's initial enthusiasm for direct election was soon abandoned by him in favor of selection by electors chosen by the people. This proposal was rejected by a substantial margin by the Committee of the Whole. Altogether no fewer than eight methods for selecting a president were suggested to the Convention. Both the Virginia Plan and the New Jersey or Patterson Plan, which represented the views of the small states (and New York), proposed that Congress should elect the executive, who would be eligible for only a single term. The delegates on several occasions voted to endorse this scheme. Direct election was supported by Wilson, whose position as chairman of the Committee of Detail gave him ample opportunity to incorporate his ideas of the office into the draft reports submitted to the convention. Gouverneur Morris of Pennsylvania, later chairman of the Committee of Style which polished and to some degree revised the final draft of the Constitution, was likewise an advocate of a strong executive and favored direct election. Opponents, like George Mason of Virginia, who was to join the Anti-Federalists in opposing ratification of the Constitution, claimed that "it would be as unnatural to refer the choice of a proper character for chief magistrate to the people, as it would to refer a trial of colors to a blind man."[19]

All generally agreed on the need for executive independence, but the weak-executive faction argued that a longer term, without eligibility for reelection, would suffice for an executive chosen by the legislature. Wilson and Morris made renewed appeals for a popularly elected executive with a shorter term but eligibility for reelection. However, as late as July 17 the Committee of the Whole voted unanimously for choice by the legislature, a seven-year term, and ineligibility for reelection.[20] Wilson's argument for popular election gained little support among the delegates, some of whom opposed the idea in principle. More seemed to doubt its political feasibility. The smaller states had forced a compromise on the representation issue.[21] They would certainly not accept a method of executive selection that might lead to dominance of the executive by the larger states. Other practical problems existed, especially relating to regional differences between North and South. Yet sentiment for a strong, independent executive was growing. When it became apparent that some delegates favored legislative election with reeligibility, Madison rose to oppose the parliamentary scheme he had originally suggested. Such reeligibility, he thought, would threaten the principle of separation of powers which he believed to be essential to the preservation of liberty. "The executive could not be independent of the Legislure [sic], if dependent on the pleasure of that branch for re-appointment . . . a dependence of the Executive on the Legislature, would render it the Executor as well as the maker of laws."

> Mr. Madison was not apprehensive of being thought to favor any step towards monarchy. The real object with him was to prevent its introduction. Experience had proved a tendency in our governments to throw all power into the Legislative vortex. The Executives of the States are in general little more than Cyphers; the legislatures omnipotent. If no effectual check be devised for restraining the instability and encroachment of the latter, a revolution of some kind or other would be inevitable.[22]

Gouverneur Morris joined Madison in persuasively arguing the case for an independent executive. It has, he remarked "been a maxim in political science that Republican Government is not adopted to a large extent of country, because the energy of the Executive Magistracy can not reach the extreme part of it. We must either renounce the blessing of the Union, or provide an Executive with sufficient vigor to provide every part of it." One great object of the Executive is to control the Legislature whose members can be expected to continually "seek to aggrandize and perpetuate themselves." It is necessary that the executive "be the guardian of the people, even of the lower classes, ags. Legislative tyranny, against the Great and the wealthy who in the course of things will necessarily compose the Legislative body."[23]

The executive, in Morris' view, must be granted both a great deal of power and independence if he were to defend himself against legislative encroachment and act with energy and dispatch. Madison, reversing his earlier position, now agreed. "It is essential . . . that the appointment of the Executive should either be drawn from some source or held by some tenure, that will give him a free agency with regard to the Legislature." Appointment by the legislature, even with ineligibility, might "establish an improper connection between the two departments."[24] Morris went further: "Of all possible modes of appointment that by the Legislature is the worst."[25] As to ineligibility, he thought this unwise and even dangerous to the very constitutional scheme it was meant to secure. Forced retirement of a popular executive would not only remove political incentives for good performance while in office but also raise the possibility that he might seek to retain power through unconstitutional means.

Morris saw no alternative for making the executive independent of the legislature except office for life or popular selection with reeligibility, in which case a two-year term was suggested. For a time he even favored making the chief executive unimpeachable, though he soon changed his mind.

"He was not sensible of the necessity of impeachment, if the Executive was to continue for any time in office. Our Executive was not like a Magistrate having a life interest, much less like one having an hereditary interest in his office. . . . The Executive ought to be impeachable for treachery, corruption or incapacity. . . . This Magistrate is not the King, but the prime-minister. The people are the King."[26]

Madison also now found appointment of the executive by "the people at large" to be the "fittest method." "It would be as likely as any that could be devised to produce an Executive Magistrate of Distinguished Character." However, because of political obstacles, the substitution of electors for direct popular election "seemed on the whole to be liable to the fewest objections."[27]

Despite growing support for the scheme for selection of the chief executive by electors chosen by the state legislatures, debate deadlocked on the question of the appointment of electors. This, despite a last minute suggestion by James Wilson that electors be taken by lot from the national legislature.

On July 26, after two months of sporadic debate, the Committee of the Whole again endorsed the original proposal of legislative selection for a seven-year term without eligibility for reelection. There the matter rested till August 24 when Gouverneur Morris again urged popular election in a motion that was defeated by a single state's vote. He then proposed selection by electors chosen by the people with a resulting four to four tie, several states being divided and one absent. Sentiment had clearly gravitated away from the parliamentary model, though not necessarily toward direct popular election. Differences in state population, suffrage requirements, and the question of how to count slaves complicated the search for agreement.

It was at this point on August 31 that the issue was turned over to an eleven member Committee on Postponed Matters consisting of one member from each state delegation. The results of the committee's deliberation were reported to the Convention on September 4 and subsequently adopted with only minor changes. The president was to hold office for four years with reeligibility. Selection was to be by an electoral college composed of electors equal in number to the senators and representatives for each state. Electors would be chosen in such manner as the state legislature would determine. In case no majority was obtained in the electoral vote, legislative selection was provided for. The original committee report proposed that the Senate would elect the president in the event of electoral deadlock. However, Wilson and others considered the Senate already too strong and this plan as displaying "a dangerous tendency toward aristocracy" that struck directly against the principle of executive independence and personal presidential responsibility.[28] It was subsequently suggested that in cases where no majority of electors could be obtained, the selection of a president would be decided by the House of Representatives voting by states.

This method of presidential selection is controversial. It is well established that the clear expectations of the delegates to the Convention were that George Washington would be the first president and that the mechanics of selection would only subsequently become important. Doubtless the compromise on executive selection was, as Professor John Roche would have it, "a masterpiece of political improvisation."

> To a body of working politicians the merits of the ... proposal were obvious: everybody got a piece of cake. (Or to put it more academically, each viewpoint could leave the Convention and argue to its constituents that it had really won the day.) First the state legislatures had the right to determine the mode of selection of the electors; second the small states received a bonus in the Electoral College in the form of a guaranteed minimum of three votes while the big states got acceptance of the principle of proportioned power; third, if the state legislatures agreed (as six did in the first presidential election), the people could be involved directly in the choice of electors; and finally, if no candidate received a majority of the College, the right of decision passed to the National Legislature with each state exercising equal strength.[29]

Roche finds the electoral college to be "a Rube Goldberg mechanism, . . . [a] jury rigged improvisation with little in its favor as an institution." Other scholars disagree and see in the electoral college system the logical conclusion of a long and thoughtful process of deliberation which implies an image of the presidency quite different from that of modern times. Most of the framers clearly did not intend to create a popular democracy but a mixed regime incorporating aristocratic (merit), oligarchic (wealth), and democratic (popular) principles.[30] In this view the president was never intended to be chosen by the people directly, though the people might or might not choose his electors. The immediate choice was to be made, as Hamilton pointed out in Federalist No. 68, "by men most capable of analyzing the qualities adapted to the station." Such electors, it was anticipated, would generally be drawn from the more distinguished and influential members of the community and would, Hamilton said, "be most likely to possess the information and discernment requisite to such complicated investigation."[31] Deliberating separately and in secret, the electoral colleges of the various states were to nominate for the presidency the person deemed best qualified for the office.

> The Founders sought to devise a system that would prevent electoral contests that turned on the "popular arts," meaning issue arousal and the emphasis on those aspects of character that played to popular positions for an attractive or interesting leader. Such contests, the framers believed, would undermine the intended role for the president and introduce the danger of unnecessary electoral divisions. The direction of their solution was to base the choice of the president not on monetary campaign appeals, but on the candidate's reputation as determined largely by previous public service. Their electoral system was designed to divert the ambition of aspirants for making issue appeals and channel it in the direction of establishing a distinguished record.[32]

Be that as it may, the framers did not anticipate nor would they have approved of the development of national political parties or the role such parties would play in presidential selection. Yet their scheme did guarantee that the American presidency would evolve in a way quite differently than if the parliamentary model had been adopted.

Earlier, toward the end of July, the Convention had referred the resolutions on executive powers to a five-member Committee of Detail chaired by James Wilson, the leader of the strong executive group. Madison's original idea had been that the executive would possess a general authority to execute laws enacted by the national legislature. It had subsequently been decided that the executive should be able to veto legislation and make appointments, though not originally of judges. The committee had before it the Randolph Plan as discussed and amended, Patterson's resolutions, and a plan submitted early in the convention by Charles Pinckney of South Carolina, at twenty-nine the youngest delegate to the Convention. At no time had Pinckney's plan been a subject of discussion by the Committee of the Whole, whose members may have regarded this individual submission of its youngest member as presumptuous. Pinckney had borrowed copiously in his draft from the strong executive model to be found in New York State's constitution.[33] Wilson's report, subsequently approved with only minor changes by the convention, incorporated ideas drawn from Pinckney's plan, the New York constitution, and the deliberations of the Convention. This report was later accepted with comparatively minor changes.[34]

"The Executive Power of the United States shall be vested in a single person. His title shall be The President of the United States." Previously the chief executive had been variously designated, usually as governor. "He shall from time to time give information of the State of the Nation; he may recommend matters for their [the Congress's] consideration, and he may convene them on extraordinary occasions." These provisions as incorporated in the final Constitution had their counterparts in the New York State system. Though little debated in the Convention, they provided important constitutional support for legislative leadership by the president. The president was, of course, to "take care to the best of his ability that the laws" be faithfully executed and was entitled to grant reprieves and pardons except in cases of impeachment. He was to "commission all the officers in all cases of the United States and shall appoint officers in all cases not otherwise provided for." The appointment power was to become one of the president's most important tools for controlling the executive branch and carrying out his constitutional responsibilities. As Wilson had earlier pointed out, "A principle reason for unity in the Executive was that officers might be appointed by a single responsible person."[35]

The convention was initially disposed to assign the appointment of ambassadors and federal judges to the Senate, and this was the recommendation of the Committee on Detail. Opposition to this proposal resulted in the matter being referred to the Committee on Postponed Matters. This committee approved a system whereby the president was to nominate all officers, including ambassadors and judges, subject to the approval of a majority of the Senate. The capacity to appoint and receive ambassadors and ministers became one of the seeds from which the conception of presidential primacy in foreign affairs developed. So important have the appointment of members of the Supreme Court and the federal judiciary become that some recent presidents have regarded such appointments as their proudest and most enduring achievement.

The report of the Committee on Detail further recommended that the president be commander-in-chief of the armed forces while the Congress was to have the power to "make war." Even then there were questions about assigning the war powers to a deliberative body that might prove incapable of acting swiftly enough in time of crisis. Some were for vesting full power in the president but others, like Elbridge Gerry of Massachusetts, believed this concept unrepublican and too similar to monarchy. Gerry and Madison then moved to have "declare" substituted for "make," "leaving to the Executive the power to repel sudden attacks." Rufus King of Massachusetts thought the phrase "make war" might be understood to mean "to conduct war." This was in his view clearly an executive function, an argument that seemed convincing to other members. The change was subsequently approved by a vote of seven to two.

Thus, the two vital provisions of the strong executive faction won acceptance by the convention. The president was to be selected by a source independent of the legislature, and he was to possess substantial enumerated powers derived directly from the Constitution and ultimately from the people.

Finally, from the pen of Gouverneur Morris, that indefatigable champion of strong executive power, came a subtle change in wording that provokes conflicting interpretations to this day. Morris, as chairman of the Committee of Style, had the opportunity to polish and revise the final language in which the Constitution was cast. By his own admission, he used this opportunity to bring its provisions closer to his own notions.

Based on the committee's report, the present opening clause of the Constitution reads: "The executive power shall be vested in a President of the United States of America." On the other hand, the corresponding provision of Article I specifies, "All legislative powers herein granted shall be vested in a Congress." This suggests that the "executive power" may extend beyond those expressly granted by the Constitution or derived from congressional enactment. In other words, the president may possess a wide range of implied powers, perhaps extending to the prerogatives described by John Locke or Blackstone as inherent in the executive office.

III

Criticism of the presidency during the ratification period followed predictable lines. Many agreed with Patrick Henry that the office "squints toward monarchy." Specific challenges focused on the method of election, the term of office, the nature and powers of the presidency, and other points previously debated in the Convention.[36]

The most notable defense of the Constitution was mounted in the *Federalist Papers*, a series of newspaper articles written by Alexander Hamilton, James Madison, and John Jay to influence the critical New York ratification convention. The task of supporting the presidency fell almost entirely to Hamilton. In a series of ten essays, Federalist Nos. 67 through 77, Hamilton put aside his previous doubts and presented a brilliant and persuasive analysis of Article II.

Hamilton believed in the necessity of strong presidential leadership. He had come to the conclusion that this could be developed within the framework of the broad definition of the office contained within Article II. His eloquent argument in Federalist No. 70 recalls the earlier doubts he had expressed at the Convention concerning the compatibility of a strong executive and republican principles.

There is an idea, which is not without its advocates, that a vigorous executive is inconsistent with the genius of republican government. The enlightened well-wishers to this species of government must at least hope that the supposition is destitute of foundation; since they can never admit its truth, without at the same time admitting the condemnation of their own principles.

Energy in the executive is a leading character in the definition of good government. It is essential to the protection of the community against foreign attacks; it is not less essential to the steady administration of the laws, to the protection of property against those irregular and high handed combinations which sometimes interrupt the ordinary course of justice, to the security of liberty against the enterprises and assaults of ambition, of faction, and of anarchy.[37]

What does Hamilton mean by "energy" in the executive? At a minimum he means "vigor and expedition." The ingredients that constitute energy in the executive, Hamilton tells us, "are first unity, secondly duration, thirdly an adequate provision for its support," and "fourthly, competent powers."[38]

That unity is conducive to energy will not, Hamilton thought, be disputed. "Decision, activity, secrecy, and dispatch" are requisites of effective executive decision-making and are more likely to be found in one man than in a collective body that may be more suitable for "deliberation and wisdom."

Hamilton was mainly concerned with "competent powers" as ingredients of executive energy. Yet he does not mention the first sentence of Article II and confines himself to an exposition of the powers enumerated in the Constitution. The "executive power vested in the President" is nowhere otherwise defined. This omission by Hamilton seems to have been intended as part of his effort to distance the presidency from the British monarchy. Sometime later Hamilton, writing as Pacificus in defense of the foreign policy of the Washington administration, adopted the position that Article II is a "general grant" of power suggesting a view of inherent executive authority that recalls Locke's "prerogative." However, Pacificus makes it clear that: "The executive power of the nation is vested in the President; subject only to the exception and qualification, which are expressed in the instrument which are to be interpreted in conformity with other parts of the Constitution and with the Principles of free government."[39]

Thus it was that Hamilton, often considered as a supporter of presidential aggrandizement, reveals himself a convinced constitutionalist who recognized the need to balance power with accountability. This needs to be sharply recalled in light of the awesome power of the modern presidency.

Notes

1. Cf. Arthur Schlesinger, Jr., *The Imperial Presidency* (New York: Popular Library, 1973).

2. John P. Roche, "The Founding Fathers: A Reform Caucus in Action," *American Political Science Review* 55 (Dec. 1961): 799.

3. Max Farrand, *Records of the Federal Convention*, vol. 3 (New Haven: Yale University Press, 1911), 250.

4. Cf. Martin Diamond, "Democracy and the Federalist: A Reconsideration of the Framers Intent," *American Political Science Review* 53 (March 1959): 52–68. Paul Eidelsberg, *The Philosophy of the American Constitution* (New York: Free Press, 1968).

5. Edward S. Corwin, *The President: Office and Powers 1787–1957* (New York: New York University Press, 1958), 5–6.

6. Cited in Charles C. Thatch, *The Creation of the Presidency* (Baltimore, Md.: Johns Hopkins Press, 1923), 29.

7. Jacob E. Cooke, ed., *The Federalist* (Middletown, Vt.: Wesleyan University Press, 1961), 333.

8. Charles de Secondate, Baron de Montesquieu, "The Spirit of the Laws," in *Great Books of the Western World*, 38 (Chicago: Encyclopedia Britannica), 70.

9. Corwin, *The President*, 14.

10. John Locke, "Concerning Civil Government, Second Essay," in *Great Books of the Western World*, 35, 62.

11. Sir William Blackstone, *Commentaries on the Laws of England*, Thomas M. Cooley, ed. (Chicago: Callaghan and Co., 1884), 147.

12. Max Farrand, *Records of the Federal Convention* (New Haven, Conn.: Yale Union Press, 1911), 20-21.

13. As late as April 16, 1787 Madison had written to Washington, "I have scarcely ventured as yet to form my own opinion either of the manner in which [the executive] ought to be constituted or of the authorities with which it ought to be cloathed." Madison to Washington, April 16, 1787; *Writings of James Madison*, Gaillard Hunt, ed. (New York: G.P. Putnam's Sons, 1903), vol. 2, 348.

14. Farrand, *Records*, vol. 1, 65.

15. Ibid.

16. Ibid., 66.

17. Cited in Richard Loss, "Alexander Hamilton and the Modern Presidency: Continuity or Discontinuity," *Presidential Studies Quarterly* 12 (Winter, 1982): 6. Loss concludes that the modern theory of the presidency cannot be properly anchored in Hamilton's thought.

18. Farrand, *Records*, vol. 1, 292.

19. Ibid., vol. 2, 31.

20. Ibid., 134. It should be remembered that voting was by states according to the unit rule.

21. The Great Compromise provided for equal representation in the Senate, satisfying the interests of the smaller states. For purposes of determining population, three-fifths of slaves were to be included, thus accommodating the interests of the South and those northern delegates who anticipated (incorrectly) that southern population growth would be more rapid than northern population growth.

22. Farrand, *Records*, vol. 2, 34-35.

23. Ibid., 52-54.

24. Ibid., 56.

25. Ibid., 103.

26. Ibid., 69.

27. Ibid., 57.

28. Ibid., 522-99.

29. Roche, "The Founding Fathers," 810.

30. Eidelberg, *American Constitution*, 169.

31. Hamilton, *Federalist No. 68*, Cooke, ed., 458.

32. James W. Caesar, *Presidential Selection* (Princeton, N.J.: Princeton University Press, 1979), 29.

33. Gouverneur Morris had assisted in the drafting of the New York State Constitution of 1777.

34. Farrand, *Records*, vol. 2, 171–72.

35. Ibid., vol. 1, 119.

36. Cf. Jonathan Elliott, ed., *The Debates in the Several State Conventions on the Adoption of the Federal Constitution*, 2nd ed., 5 vols. (Philadelphia, 1861), and Cecelia M. Kenyon, ed., *The Antifederalists* (New York: Bobbs-Merrill, 1966).

37. Hamilton, *Federalist No. 70*, Cooke, ed., 471.

38. Ibid., 472.

39. Alexander Hamilton and James Madison, *The Letters of Pacificus and Helvidius on the Neutrality of 1793* (Delmar, N.Y.: Scholars Facsimiles and Reprints, 1976), 10.

Illustration 1a: Article II, U.S. Constitution

When studying the U.S. presidency, one should start with Article II of the Constitution. As can be seen, only the most basic outline of power was granted by the Constitution. It is important to be aware that in addition to this basic authority, the power of the presidency has grown immensely as a result of statutes and customs, the growth of government, America's emergence as a world power, and activist presidents. In addition to the constitutional responsibilities of chief executive, head of state, chief diplomat, and commander-in-chief, the modern president, as the late Clinton Rossiter emphasized, wears extraconstitutional hats such as "keeper of the peace" and "leader of the free world."

Article II

Section 1.
The executive Power shall be vested in a President of the United States of America. He shall hold his Office during the Term of four Years, and, together with the Vice President, chosen for the same Term, be elected, as follows:

Section 2.
The President shall be Commander in Chief of the Army and Navy of the United States, and of the Militia of the several States, when called into the actual Service of the United States; he may require the Opinion, in writing, of the principal Officer in each of the executive Departments, upon any Subject relating to the Duties of their respective Offices, and he shall have Power to grant Reprieves and Pardons for Offences against the United States, except in Cases of Impeachment.

He shall have Power, by and with the Advice and Consent of the Senate, to make Treaties, provided two thirds of the Senators present concur; and he shall nominate, and by and with the Advice and Consent of the Senate, shall appoint Ambassadors, other public Ministers and Consuls, Judges of the supreme Court, and all other Officers of the United States, whose Appointments are not herein otherwise provided for, and which shall be established by Law; but the Congress may by Law vest the Appointment of such inferior Officers, as they think proper in the President alone, in the Courts of Law, or in the Heads of Departments.

The President shall have Power to fill up all Vacancies that may happen during the Recess of the Senate, by granting Commissions which shall expire at the end of their next Session.

Section 3.
He shall from time to time give to the Congress Information of the State of the Union, and recommend to their Consideration such Measures as he shall judge necessary and expedient; he may, on extraordinary Occasions, convene both Houses, or either of them, and in Case of Disagreement between them, with Respect to the Time of Adjournment, he may adjourn them to such Time as he shall think proper; he shall receive Ambassadors and other public Ministers; he shall take Care that Laws be faithfully executed, and shall Commission all the Officers of the United States.

Section 4.
The President, Vice President and all civil Officers of the United States, shall be removed from Office on Impeachment for, and Conviction of, Treason, Bribery, or other high Crimes and Misdemeanors.

Presidential Powers   1.2

Louis Fisher

Although only briefly outlined in Illustration 1a, the powers of the presidency—especially in the modern era—are enormous. The following essay (originally a background paper prepared under the auspices of the Congressional Research Service, Library of Congress) by a leading public law scholar gives an excellent overview of the important policy roles conferred upon the modern presidency by the Constitution, Supreme Court decisions, statutes, and customs. Fisher concludes with a review of contemporary scholarly perspectives on presidential powers.

I. Introduction

Even after its brief history of two centuries, the American presidency bears some resemblance to a geological formation. At the very bottom, forming a thin layer, are the powers expressly conferred by the Constitution. Superimposed upon that foundation, and creating many strata, are other powers deposited over time. They find their source in statutory delegations, implied powers, judicial interpretations, custom, executive initiative, and congressional acquiescence.

This growth of presidential power . . . has generated opposition from many scholars and legislators. To them the Constitution should be interpreted strictly and literally, rather than being bent and compromised to accommodate shifting political needs. They fear that the doctrine of "adaptation by usage" will erode the constitutional structure and undermine fundamental principles.

While there is legitimate concern about the circumvention of constitutional restrictions whenever they present an inconvenience, the time has long since passed (if it ever existed) when we can confine each branch of the national government to powers expressly stated in the Constitution. More valid is the question: does the evolution of presidential power threaten the general framework and values of government intended by the framers?

An artificial test, widely used, divides presidential activity into two rival schools of thought: the "strong" executive model of Teddy Roosevelt versus the "weak" executive model of William Howard Taft. By lifting certain passages from their writings, and examining them out of context, it is possible to construct two philosophies of presidential power that seem to be polar opposites. Roosevelt claimed that the president had a right and duty to do "anything that the needs of the Nation demanded, unless such action was forbidden by the Constitution or by the laws." Taft argued that the president "can exercise no power which cannot be fairly and reasonably traced to some specific grant of power or justly implied and included within such express grant as proper and necessary to its exercise. Such specific grant must be either in the Federal Constitution or in an act of Congress passed in pursuance thereof."[1]

Read narrowly, it appears that Roosevelt believed that the president could do anything not explicitly forbidden by the Constitution or by law, while Taft held that the president could not act unless specifically authorized by the Constitution or by law. This simplification is contradicted by the performances of Roosevelt and Taft in office and the more generous conception of presidential power found elsewhere in Taft's study and his later opinions as chief justice of the Supreme Court. Even in the passage quoted above it is evident that Taft recognized the need for powers that could be "justly implied within such express grant as proper and necessary to its exercise." Other passages in the study demonstrate that Taft conferred upon the presi-

---

From the Congressional Research Service, Library of Congress.

dent not only implied powers but inferable powers, emergency powers, powers created by custom, and powers incident to specific constitutional authority.

The development of implied powers does not subvert the framers' intent. They knew that it was unrealistic to devise watertight compartments to separate the three branches of government. The experiences of the Continental Congress, from 1774 to 1787, convinced them of the need for a separate executive to impart efficiency and accountability to government. The exact line between executive and legislature, however, could not be drawn with any sense of precision.

Prior to the Philadelphia Convention, Madison confided to Edmund Randolph that he had not decided on either the manner in which the executive should be constituted or "of the authorities with which it ought to be clothed."[2] After the Convention he admitted to Jefferson that the boundaries between executive, legislative, and judicial power, "though in general so strongly marked in themselves, consist in many instances of mere shades of difference."[3] Federalist No. 37 contains a similar observation by Madison. Just as naturalists had difficulty in defining the exact line between vegetable life and the animal world, so was it an even greater task to draw the boundary between the departments of government or "even the privileges and powers of the different legislative branches. Questions daily occur in the course of practice, which prove the obscurity which reigns in these subjects, and which puzzle the greatest adepts in political science."

Executive-legislative struggles over the past decade have popularized Justice Brandeis' comment that the doctrine of the separation of powers was adopted in 1787 "not to promote efficiency but to preclude the exercise of arbitrary power."[4] While it is true that the Constitution contains numerous checks and balances intended to restrain arbitrary action, this elaborate system was constructed for the purpose of making government more effective than the discredited Articles of Confederation. The Continental Congress had experimented with committees, boards, and single executives in an effort to discover some means of providing administrative efficiency. Creation of a separate executive in 1787 was one way to foster unity, dispatch, and responsibility.[5]

II. Executive Power

Article II of the Constitution begins: "The executive Power shall be vested in a President of the United States of America." Scholars hold fundamentally different opinions about the meaning of this clause. Some regard it as a mere conferral of a title: President of the United States. Others believe that it grants to the president powers that are not specifically enumerated in the Constitution.

The latter interpretation was forcefully advocated by Alexander Hamilton in his Pacificus essays in 1793. He argued that President Washington had authority to issue a neutrality proclamation on the basis of the general grant of authority found in the executive-power clause. It was untenable, he said, to confine the president to powers expressly stated. The president had access to the "comprehensive grant" of power in the general clause, except for express restrictions or limitations placed in the Constitution. Hamilton identified four restrictions: the Senate's participation in the appointment of officers, the Senate's participation in the making of treaties, and Congress' power to declare war and to grant letters of marque and reprisal. All other executive powers, he reasoned, were lodged solely in the president. Madison attempted to rebut this line of argument (writing under the pseudonym Helvidius) by charging that Hamilton had improperly lifted the notion of a royal prerogative from English history. By and large, however, the Hamiltonian position has prevailed.[6]

Hamilton's essays triggered a debate on the sources of constitutional power. Are they only enumerated or also implied? If we admit powers by implication can we retain the meaning of "constitutionalism" as limited government? Who decides on the limits once we depart from the express language of the Constitution?

All three branches have recognized that it is impracticable to confine government to powers expressly stated. The necessity for implied powers was settled in 1789 during debate on the Bill of Rights. Members of the

First Congress suggested that the Tenth Amendment be so worded that all powers not "expressly delegated" to the federal government be reserved to the states. That would have resuscitated the philosophy and language of the Articles of Confederation, under which the states retained their sovereignty and independence. Madison objected to the proposal, insisting that it was impossible to limit a government to the exercise of express powers. There "must necessarily be admitted powers by implication, unless the Constitution descended to recount every minutiae." "Expressly" was eliminated and the Tenth Amendment came to read: "The powers not delegated to the United States by the Constitution, nor prohibited by it to the States, are reserved to the States respectively, or to the people."[7]

In 1803, in *Marbury* v. *Mason*, the Supreme Court claimed for itself the power to strike down unconstitutional legislation, even though the Constitution does not specifically provide for judicial review. Chief Justice Marshall argued that it "is a proposition too plain to be contested, that the constitution controls any legislative act repugnant to it; or that the legislature may alter the constitution by an ordinary act." Either the Constitution was a superior law or it could be altered whenever the legislature decides. If superior, a legislative act contrary to the Constitution could not be law. Marshall had no doubt as to where the responsibility lay: "It is emphatically the province and duty of the judicial department to say what the law is."[8]

Having acquired the power of judicial review in this manner, the Court proceeded in other cases to recognize implied powers for the legislative and executive branches. In 1819 the Court faced the question whether Congress had authority to establish a United States Bank. Chief Justice Marshall, again delivering the opinion for the Court, said that there was nothing in the language of the Constitution to require that "everything granted shall be expressly and minutely described." The Constitution represented a general structure of government, not a detailed instruction manual. The Court upheld the bank.[9] In other decisions, to be discussed later, the Court acknowledged implied powers for the president.

Executive Prerogative

Implied powers are used to carry out a constitutional function. Quite different is the notion of an "executive prerogative," which temporarily suspends the Constitution while the President responds to an emergency. The theory supporting such actions can be traced back to John Locke, who anticipated situations where the executive power must act "according to discretion for the public good, without the prescription of the law and sometimes even against it." Thomas Jefferson, after leaving the office of president, stated that while the observance of the written law is a high duty of a public official, it is not the highest. The laws of self-preservation and national security claimed a higher priority: "To lose our country by a scrupulous adherence to written law, would be to lose the law itself, with life, liberty, property and all those who are enjoying them with us; thus absurdly sacrificing the end to the means." Jefferson said it was the duty of the executive to act outside the law when necessity demanded it, to explain his actions, and ask the legislature for acquittance.[10]

That procedure was followed by President Lincoln during his extraordinary Civil War actions. With open military rebellion in the South when he took office, and with Congress in recess in April 1861, he issued proclamations calling forth the state militia, suspending the writ of habeas corpus, and placing a blockade on the rebellious states. When Congress returned he explained that his actions, "whether strictly legal or not, were ventured upon under what appeared to be a popular demand and a public necessity, trusting then, as now, that Congress would readily ratify them." Congress proceeded to pass an act "approving, legalizing, and making valid all the acts, proclamations, and orders of the president, etc., as if they had been issued and done under the previous express authority and direction of the Congress of the United States."[11]

The claim of an inherent presidential power to protect the nation from domestic economic emergencies was rebuffed in 1952 when the Supreme Court struck down President Truman's seizure of the steel mills. Although the Court was badly splintered, with each of the six justices for the majority writing separate opinions, at least in this case the president could not act legally in the absence of specific statutory or constitutional grants of power.[12]

Executive-Ministerial Distinction

Historically the federal courts have recognized two types of administrative duties: those that require judgment and discretion (called "executive") and those that do not ("ministerial"). That distinction was made in the celebrated case of *Marbury* v. *Madison*. President John Adams had nominated a number of men to serve in the judiciary. The Senate gave its advice and consent; commissions for the offices were signed by President Adams; even the seal of the United States had been affixed to the commissions to attest their validity. But after a change in administrations the new secretary of State, James Madison, refused to deliver some of the commissions. Could the Supreme Court compel him to act?

In 1789 Congress had authorized the Supreme Court to issue writs of mandamus, but in *Marbury* the Court decided that this grant of authority had improperly augmented the original jurisdiction of the Supreme Court. The jurisdiction fixed by the Constitution could not, said the Court, be changed by statute. Prior to reaching that decision, however, the Court distinguished between two types of duties for the secretary of State. One duty (as a public ministerial officer of the United States) extended to the United States or to its citizens, the second (as agent of the president) to the president alone. For ministerial actions someone could be compelled by *mandamus* to carry out a duty. The secretary of State, as an officer of the United States, had to obey the laws: "He acts, in this respect, as has been very properly stated at the bar, under the authority of law, and not by the instructions of the president. It is a ministerial act which the law enjoins on a particular officer for a particular purpose."[13]

The federal courts applied the ministerial-executive distinction during the impoundment disputes of the Nixon administration. One case involved the farm disaster loan program of the Department of Agriculture. After heavy rainfall in parts of Minnesota had caused extensive crop damage in 1972, Secretary of Agriculture Butz declared 15 counties eligible for Federal assistance. The administration told farmers in those areas that applications would be received through June 30, 1973. They were further advised to file after the harvest (late November and early December) to ensure that all eligible losses would be included in their applications. A heavy work schedule in the local offices delayed appointments still further until early in the year. Then, on December 22, 1972, as part of the administration's effort to curb federal spending and change budget priorities, Secretary Butz terminated the disaster loan program.

A federal judge in Minnesota ruled that there were two types of secretarial actions: discretionary (declaring an area entitled to assistance) and ministerial (processing applications after a designation had been made). Since the secretary had made his declaration it was incumbent upon his department to accept loan applications and process them.[14]

III. Administrative Duties

During the decade prior to the Philadelphia Convention, the Continental Congress attempted to handle administrative duties in addition to its legislative responsibilities. Every experiment—through committees, boards or single executives—was found wanting. One of the major incentives for a separate executive branch was the desire to instill a measure of effectiveness and reliability to government. George Washington, early in the War of Independence against England, explained to the Continental Congress that executive officers would "not only conduce to Order, Dispatch, and Discipline, but that is a Measure of Economy. The Delay, the Waste, and unpunishable Neglect of Duty arising from these Offices being in commission in several Hands, evidently shew that the Public Expense must be finally enhanced." Thomas Jefferson, while the Philadelphia Convention was in session, commented on the administrative advantages of [a] separate executive. Congress, he said, had shown a propensity to wait until the "last extremities" before executing any of its powers: "Nothing is so embarrassing nor so mischievous in a great assembly as the details of execution."[15]

Among the administrative duties discussed in this section are the president's power to remove executive officials, his power to nominate, the reorganization powers delegated to him by Congress, and the president's authority to withhold certain kinds of information from Congress (executive privilege).

Removal Power

The Constitution does not grant to the president an express power to remove administrators from their offices. The existence of that power was vigorously debated at the First Congress. Some members claimed that since the Senate participated in the appointment of officers, it deserved equal participation in their removal. Others believed that removals could be made only by the constitutional process of impeachment, or solely at the behest of the president as an incident to the executive power. Still others argued that Congress, through its power to create an office, could attach to it any condition it decided appropriate for tenure and removal.[16]

During debate in 1789, concerning creation of a Department of Foreign Affairs, James Madison adhered to the principle of presidential responsibility. He recommended that the Secretary of Foreign Affairs should be "removable by the President." After the first day of debate the House, by a "considerable majority," declared that the removal power lay with the president. Over the next few weeks it shifted back and forth on the question, uncertain whether to recognize the president's power by declaration or implication. Declaration would suggest that Congress had delegated the power to the president. If handled by implication, this would indicate that the power belonged to the president by way of constitutional interpretation. The House gravitated in the direction of the latter, striking the language "to be removable by the President" and providing that the chief clerk (second-in-command in the Foreign Affairs Department) would take charge of all records whenever the secretary "shall be removed from office" by the president. After several close votes on the Senate side, with some tie votes broken by Vice President Adams, the House position prevailed. Congress passed legislation to adopt the same approach for the departments of Foreign Affairs, War, and Treasury. The subordinate officers would have charge and custody of all records whenever the secretary "shall be removed from office by the President of the United States."[17]

Throughout the nineteenth century and the first two decades of the twentieth, the courts explored the basis and scope of the president's removal power. Though the decisions were sprinkled with some dissents and a number of qualifications, there was generally broad agreement that the president possessed the power to remove officials, particularly when the Senate acquiesced and Congress did not use "plain language" to curb the power.[18] The major case, *Myers* v. *United States* (1926), resulted from President Wilson's removal of a postmaster in contravention of a statute enacted in 1876. Chief Justice Taft, writing for a 6-3 majority, claimed that the president's power of removal was unrestricted, even in the face of statutory limitations. From the debate in 1789 he concluded that Congress had recognized that the power rested solely in the President.[19]

Taft's opinion provoked not only three dissents—from Justices Holmes, McReynolds, and Brandeis—but a blistering critique from Edward S. Corwin, whose monograph, *The President's Removal Power Under the Constitution*, appeared in 1972. Corwin conceded that when an executive officer is appointed by the president, with the advice and consent of the Senate, the removal power belonged to the president alone. What he found intolerable was the more sweeping proposition that *all* executive officers are removable at the discretion of the president. Corwin believed that a balance had to be struck between the president's removal power and Congress' power under the "necessary and proper" clause to create an office and determine the tenure of an officer. Decisive for Corwin was the nature of the office involved.[20]

That very issue arose in *Humphrey's Executor* v. *United States* (1935), which limited the reach of the Myers holding. William E. Humphrey, nominated by President Hoover to the Federal Trade Commission in 1931, had been confirmed by the Senate. President Roosevelt removed him in 1933 for purely policy reasons, explaining to Humphrey that "I do not feel that your mind and my mind go along together on either the policies or the administering of the Federal Trade Commission." The basis for this removal conflicted with the statutory criteria. The FTC Act provided that any commissioner may be removed by the president for "inefficiency, neglect of duty, or malfeasance in office." The Supreme Court described the FTC as charged with the enforcement of "no policy except the policy of the law. Its duties are neither political nor executive, but predominantly quasi-judicial and quasi-legislative." A unanimous Court held that the removal was invalid.[21]

Still, the decision left many questions unanswered. "Quasi" did not meet the standard of legal precision, nor did the uncertain status of the FTC fit within the existing three branches of government. Also, Congress had not specified a method of removal for officials of all regulatory agencies. No limitation existed on the removal power for the Federal Communications Commission, the Federal Power Commission, or the Securities and Exchange Commission. Could the president dismiss the members of those commissions at pleasure or did the "nature" of their work insulate them from presidential control? In his closing paragraph in the Humphrey case, Justice Sutherland admitted that there existed a "field of doubt" between *Myers* and *Humphrey*: "We leave such cases as may fall within it for future consideration and determination as they may arise."

This grey area of the law returned to the courts. Within a few years after *Humphrey* a federal court faced the ouster of Arthur E. Morgan, chairman of the Board of Directors of the Tennessee Valley Authority. President Roosevelt removed him after a dispute between Morgan and his fellow directors threatened to paralyze the agency. A district court admitted that Roosevelt's action was not specifically based on statutory consideration, but neither did the TVA Act clearly express an intent by Congress to limit the executive power over removals. An appellate court sustained that opinion, adding that TVA was predominantly an administrative arm of the executive branch and therefore distinguishable from the regulatory commission involved in the Humphrey case.[22]

More akin to *Humphrey* is President Eisenhower's removal of a member of the War Claims Commission. The enabling statute, anticipating a short-lived agency, made no provision for removal. Eisenhower proceeded to remove someone from the commission on the ground that the act should be administered "with personnel of my own selection." The Court of Claims dismissed the plaintiff's suit but the Supreme Court, in *Wiener* v. *United States* (1958), unanimously reversed that decision. The Court ruled that the president had no power under the Constitution or the statute to remove a member from the War Claims Commission. The agency's task, said the Court, had an "intrinsic judicial character." In fact, Congress had explicitly rejected a legislative option that would have placed responsibility with the administration.[23]

The removal power twice became a legal issue during the Nixon administration. In 1973 Congress passed legislation to require the advice and consent of the Senate for the director and deputy director of the Office of Management and Budget. The effect of the legislation would have been to abolish the offices and establish them later subject to Senate confirmation. The administration contended that the Constitution prohibited not only direct attempts but also sophisticated attempts to interfere with the president's removal power. President Nixon vetoed the bill on the ground that it would require the "forced removal by an unconstitutional procedure."[24] After failing to override the veto, Congress passed legislation to require confirmation of future OMB directors and deputy directors.[25]

The other removal issue in the Nixon administration concerned the "Saturday Night Massacre," which sent Archibald Cox (Special Prosecutor in the Office of Watergate), Attorney General Elliot Richardson, and Deputy Attorney General William Ruckelshaus out of the government. Cox was dismissed from his post after pursuing too vigorously certain presidential documents and tapes. As an official in the executive branch, normally he would have been subject to presidential removal, but President Nixon relinquished that power when the Justice Department conferred special autonomy on the Special Prosecutor. The department's order gave him the "greatest degree of independence that is consistent with the Attorney General's statutory accountability.... The Attorney General will not countermand or interfere with the Special Prosecutor's decisions or actions." The order added that the Special Prosecutor would not be removed from his duties "except for extraordinary improprieties on his part."[26]

The administration made no claim that Cox had been removed for "extraordinary improprieties." A suit brought in a district court claimed that Cox had been removed illegally. The Court denied that the controversy was moot, even though Cox had returned to Harvard University and a new Special Prosecutor [had been] sworn in. There remained the possibility that the new Special Prosecutor might be dismissed "if he presses too hard." The Court held that Cox had been illegally discharged from office.[27]

Nomination

The Constitution provides that the president "shall nominate, and by and with the Advice and Consent of the Senate, shall appoint Ambassadors, other public Ministers and Consuls, Judges of the supreme Court, and all other Officers of the United States, whose Appointments are not herein otherwise provided for, and which shall be established by Law: but the Congress may by Law vest the Appointment of such inferior Officers, as they think proper in the President alone, in the Courts of Law, or in the Heads of Departments." Officially the power over appointments is divided into two basic steps: nomination by the president and confirmation by the Senate. In practice, however, the process parts markedly from the constitutional scheme.

In *Marbury* v. *Madison* (1803), Chief Justice Marshall described the nomination process as the "sole act of the president, and is completely voluntary." An attorney general's opinion, consistent with that judgment, declared that it would be "inadmissible" for a mode of selection to deprive the president of his exercise of judgment and will. To require the president to appoint a person judged by an outside group (such as examiners for the Civil Service) as the fittest was no different "in constitutional principle from an enactment that he shall appoint John Doe to that office."[28] In order to preserve the president's prerogative, it is customary to provide him with some choice as to the nominee, e.g., selecting from a list of three eligibles for each vacancy.

This exclusive right to nominate has been curbed by a number of developments. In creating an office, Congress may stipulate the qualifications of appointees: citizenship, residency in a particular state or district, specific professional attainments, occupation experience, test or examinations, requirements of age, selection on a nonpartisan basis, and other criteria. And while Alexander Hamilton asserted in Federalist No. 66 that there could be "no exertion of *choice* on the part of the Senate . . . they can only ratify or reject the choice of President," that is by no means the practice. Senators from the same party as the president often "nominate" to the White House candidates for judge, U. S. attorney, marshal to serve from their state. The president is then placed in the position of giving or withholding his "advice and consent." If the president and his advisers object to a senator's recommendation, they can offer suggestions and hope for a more acceptable name.

To provide some independence from the Senate, President Eisenhower and his successors entered into an alliance with the American Bar Association. A special ABA committee was formed to determine the professional qualifications of judicial candidates. Acting only on names submitted by the attorney general, the committee informs the chairman of the Senate Judiciary Committee whether a candidate is "qualified," "well qualified," "exceptionally well qualified," or "not qualified." In 1977 President Carter established thirteen panels responsible for recommending nominees to the U.S. courts of appeals. His constitutional authority is protected by having the panels recommend five candidates for each vacancy.[29]

Statutory qualifications for appointees, together with Senate initiative in submitting names for consideration, restrict the latitude of a president. Some legislative actions, however, exceed the constitutional boundaries. The most recent example concerned the establishment of the Federal Election Commission. Congress, pursuant to statute, appointed four members to the commission. All six voting members (including two nominated by the president) required confirmation by the majority of *both* houses. In 1976 the Supreme Court struck down this provision. While the "necessary and proper" clause of the Constitution empowers Congress to create the commission, the language cannot be read so expansively [as] to permit Congress to appoint its members. That is especially the case when a commission created by Congress is designed to discharge more than legislative functions.[30]

The courts have also placed limits on what a president may do with the appointment power. In 1973 President Nixon tried to unilaterally dismantle the Office of Economic Opportunity. Instead of nominating a director of OEO, who would be subject to the Senate's advice and consent, he designated Howard J. Phillips as acting director to preside over the dismemberment. A federal court declared the appointment invalid because it neither followed the statute (which required Senate participation) nor was it made during Senate recess, as permitted under the Constitution.[31]

The Senate's role in providing advice and consent on nominations has been uneven throughout its history. According to the initial understanding, the Senate would share with the president a coequal status on appointments. President Washington, in an early communication to the Senate, stated that just as he had "a right to nominate without assigning his reasons, so has the Senate a right to dissent without giving theirs." Madison, in the First Congress, noted that senators were joined with the president on the appointment power because they were, "from their nature, better acquainted with the character of the candidates than an individual."[32] During its first session the Senate did not hesitate to reject a presidential nomination it considered unacceptable.

The Senate has been most vigorous when reviewing nominations to the Supreme Court, rejecting approximately one out of five. In recent years, especially after the controversy created by the rejection of two Nixon nominees (Haynsworth and Carswell), the Senate has been studying the criteria that should be applied. One study concluded that lawyers with broad experience in their discipline, including political experience, are regarded as best suited to handle the responsibilities thrust upon members of the Court. Senators, for their part, have a right to consider not merely a nominee's political and constitutional philosophy but also other appointments by the president and the balance of views on the Court.[33]

More circumspect and deferential has been the Senate's behavior toward cabinet officers and other departmental positions. Broad support exists for the doctrine that the president is entitled to a cabinet of his own choice, but the Senate is reexamining this attitude. Complete deference to the president would make a nullity of the Senate's constitutional duty. Departmental heads and their assistants are not merely staff support for the president. They are called upon to administer programs that Congress has enacted into law. Still, the criteria needed for cabinet positions—expertise, experience, etc.—remain undecided.[34]

For ambassadorial appointments the Senate has been pushing for higher standards of professionalism. The Foreign Relations Authorization Act of 1975 provides that it is the sense of Congress that the position of U.S. ambassador to a foreign country "should be accorded to men and women possessing clearly demonstrated competence to perform ambassadorial duties." No individual should be accorded the position of ambassador "primarily because of financial contributions to political campaigns." The following year Congress agreed to the general proposition that a greater number of ambassadorial positions should be occupied by career Foreign Service personnel.[35]

Senate studies in 1976 and 1977 concluded that neither the White House nor the Senate had demonstrated a sustained commitment to high-quality appointments to regulatory agencies. Senate scrutiny is becoming more intense. In 1973, for the first time in decades, the Senate rejected a nominee to a regulatory agency by a recorded floor vote. Senators concluded that Robert H. Morris, nominated to the Federal Power Commission, was too closely associated with the industry he would have to regulate. Since that time the Senate has refused to confirm other nominees to regulatory agencies. Some Senate committees are devoting greater attention to the background and financial statements submitted by nominees, their depth of knowledge, policy commitments, and regulatory philosophy.[36]

Reorganization Power

Largely in an effort to produce administrative economies, Congress has granted to the president authority to reorganize executive agencies and bureaus. President Hoover received authority in 1932 to make partial layoffs, reduce compensation for public officials, and consolidate executive agencies in order to effect savings. The latter authority was subject to the disapproval of either house within 60 days (a one-house "legislative veto"). Hoover subsequently issued executive orders to regroup and consolidate a total of 58 agencies but the House of Representatives disapproved all of the orders, preferring to leave reorganization changes to the new president, Franklin D. Roosevelt.[37]

On the basis of recommendations by the Committee on Administrative Management (the Brownlow Committee), President Roosevelt proposed in 1937 that Congress establish general principles by which the president could reorganize the executive branch on a continuing basis. He wanted the authority subject to disapproval by a joint resolution of Congress, which would have to be presented to him for his signature. Yet if he exercised his veto power, legislators were doubtful that they could muster the necessary two-thirds majority in each house to override him. In effect they would have delegated authority by majority vote but could regain control only by a two-thirds majority. Partly because of that misgiving, Congress did not enact the reorganization bill in 1938.[38] Also, members interpreted the proposal (especially in light of Roosevelt's plan to "pack" the Supreme Court with additional justices) as part of a broad campaign of executive usurpation.[39]

The next year some members proposed that reorganization plans be subject to disapproval by a concurrent resolution, which requires passage by each house but is not presented to the president. This raised the question of whether a concurrent resolution would be "legislative in effect," for the Constitution provides that "Every Order, Resolution, or Vote to which the Concurrence of the Senate and House of Representatives may be necessary (except on a question of Adjournment) shall be presented to the President." This presentation clause has not been strictly adhered to. For example, Congress adopted constitutional amendments by passing resolutions and referred them not to the president but directly to the states for ratification. That procedure was upheld by the Supreme Court in 1798.[40]

From an early date Congress also developed the practice of passing simple resolutions (adopted by either house) and concurrent resolutions (by both houses) for internal, housekeeping matters. Since they were not regarded as "legislative in effect" there was no need to present them to the president. A Senate report in 1897 concluded that "legislative in effect" depended on the substance, not the mere form, of a resolution. If it contained matter "legislative in its character and effect, it must be presented to the President."[41]

During the 1939 debate on the reorganization bill, Congressman Cox argued that the concurrent resolution feature was not legislative in effect. Rather, it represented a condition attached to reorganization authority delegated to the president. If he disagreed with the condition he could exercise his veto power. Otherwise, the signing of the bill would indicate a willingness to abide by the condition. The House Select Committee on Government Organization defended the concurrent resolution procedure by pointing to a recent Supreme Court decision which upheld a delegation of authority to the secretary of agriculture. That authority depended upon the votes of farmers during a referendum. To the committee it seemed absurd "to believe that the effectiveness of action legislative in character may be conditional upon a vote of farmers but may not be conditioned on a vote of the two legislative bodies of the Congress."[42]

As enacted in 1939 the Reorganization Act

authorized the president to submit plans for executive reorganization. The plans would take effect after 60 days unless Congress, within that time, disapproved them by concurrent resolution. Renewal of the authority in 1949 permitted disapproval by a single house. Presidents, whatever their constitutional reservations concerning the legislative veto, acquiesced in this type of conditional legislation. They realized that Congress would not delegate such authority without attaching strings to it.[43]

The president's authority to reorganize the executive branch, after lapsing in 1973, was revived in 1977 at the request of President Carter. Congressman Jack Brooks, chairman of the House Government Operations Committee, challenged the constitutionality of the one-house veto feature. He wanted Congress to vote affirmatively on a reorganization plan instead of letting it become law after 60 days without legislative action. While Congressman Brooks was unsuccessful in passing his version (with an affirmative vote), the Reorganization Act of 1977 includes a number of new restrictions and conditions. It prohibits the abolition of enforcement functions or statutory programs. No more than three reorganization plans may be pending before Congress at one time. The act also provides that for 30 days after a plan has been submitted to Congress, but before a resolution of disapproval is reported from committee, the president may amend or modify his plan. This will permit the president to respond to weaknesses that are brought to light by the congressional process.[44]

Executive Privilege

The Constitution does not explicitly grant to the president a power to withhold information from Congress. Under certain conditions, however, papers and documents are withheld on constitutional grounds. President Washington, for example, declined to give the House of Representatives papers relating to the Hay Treaty because the treaty-making power belongs exclusively to the president and the Senate.[45] President Polk, who once refused to give the House of Representatives information on confidential funds, reminded the legislators that Congress had delegated to the president the authority to decide the extent to which such funds should be made public.[46] In those cases, and others, presidents withheld information either on the ground of specific constitutional provisions or authority delegated by law.

The claim to a general executive privilege, constitutionally-based, is of more recent origin. Not until 1974 did the Supreme Court specifically recognize a constitutional source for executive privilege. It decided that the president's interest in withholding information for the purpose of maintaining confidentiality in executive deliberations is implied in the Constitution: "To the extent this interest relates to the effective discharge of a President's powers, it is constitutionally based."[47] But does the president's privilege automatically override the needs of Congress for information? Does it override the needs of the judiciary?

Only the latter question was at issue in the 1974 decision. President Nixon claimed that the president, not the courts, should determine the scope of executive privilege. Even when information is needed for a criminal prosecution the "public interest in a conviction, important though it is, must yield to the public interest in preserving the confidentiality of the President's office."[48] The Supreme Court unanimously rejected that proposition. In ordering President Nixon to produce certain Watergate tape recordings and documents, relating to his conversations with aides, the Court held that an absolute, unqualified executive privilege would prevent the judiciary from carrying out its duties under the Constitution. The adversary nature of the American judicial system requires access to information in order to establish guilt or innocence. "The ends of criminal justice," said the Court, "would be defeated if judgments were to be founded on a partial or speculative presentation of the facts." The integrity of the judicial system depended on the compulsory process of producing evidence needed by the prosecution or defense.[49]

Several questions are left unresolved: access by *Congress* to information in the executive branch, and the application of executive privilege when *civil* litigation is at issue. In the

1974 case the president's general privilege of confidentiality in communications did not outweigh the needs of criminal justice. In 1977 the Supreme Court (dividing 7-2) narrowed the presumptive confidentiality of presidential communications by upholding a statute that gave custody of Mr. Nixon's public papers and tapes to Congress and the head of the General Services Administration.[50]

In *Nixon* (1974) the Court suggested that the president's "need to protect military, diplomatic or sensitive national security secrets" may be even more privileged than executive confidentiality in communications.[51] Previous decisions had shown great deference to the president's need to protect information concerning foreign policy and national security, even when information is needed for a civil trial.[52] But the courts have not been able to treat such issues consistently as a "political question" to be resolved solely by the president and Congress.

In 1971, in the Pentagon Papers case, the courts refused to enjoin two newspapers from publishing Defense Department documents that had been leaked to the press. Here the administration's effort to control information collided with freedom of the press under the First Amendment.[53] The following year a federal court required an author (previously employed by the Central Intelligence Agency) to submit to the agency a manuscript prepared for publication. The court order gave the CIA an opportunity to excise any passage that contained undisclosed classified information. The decision was based on a number of grounds: the fact that the employee had relinquished some of his First Amendment rights by entering into a secrecy agreement with [the] CIA; statutory provisions authorized the CIA to protect confidential information (delegated power); and the president possessed constitutional responsibilities in foreign affairs and national security to prevent disclosure of classified materials (executive privilege).[54]

IV. Legislative Powers

The Constitution recognizes but one legislative power for the president: the veto power. He shall also "from time to time give to the Congress Information on the State of the Union, and recommend to their consideration such Measures as he shall judge necessary and expedient." In addition, the president acquired the power to withhold (impound) funds that Congress had appropriated—in effect exercising a type of "item veto" not granted by the Constitution. Other legislative powers have their source in the need for Congress to delegate a substantial portion of its responsibilities to the president. Presidents and executive officials also wield important powers through executive orders, proclamations, issuance of rules and regulations, and other instruments of administrative legislation.

Veto

Every bill which passes the House of Representatives and the Senate shall, before it becomes law, be presented to the president. If he approves, he signs it. If he disapproves, he returns it with his objections to the house from which it originated. A vetoed bill becomes law when each house, by a two-thirds majority, votes to override the president.

The purpose of the veto has been debated ever since the administration of Andrew Jackson. An original objective of the veto, as Alexander Hamilton noted in Federalist No. 73, is to protect the executive from legislative encroachments. There is also general agreement that the president may veto bills which he regards as unconstitutional. But vetoes for *policy* purposes (bills struck down because the president thinks they are unwise in substance) have generated periodic objections from members of Congress and scholars.[55]

Despite this controversy, a broad conception of the veto power has prevailed. That view is supported by statements from some of the leading framers. James Madison, at the Philadelphia Convention, said the veto is available "to restrain the Legislative from encroaching on the other co-ordinate Departments, or on the rights of the people at large; or from passing laws unwise in their principle, or incorrect in their form."[56] Hamilton, in Federalist No. 73, defended the veto as necessary not only to protect the president but to furnish "an additional security against the enaction of improper laws. It establishes a salutary check upon the legislative body, calculated to guard the community against the effects of faction, precipitancy, or of any impulse unfriendly to the public good, which may happen to influence a majority of that body." The veto, Hamilton said, protects the community from the passage of "bad laws, through haste, inadvertence, or design."[57]

Some of the ambiguities about the veto power have been clarified by court decisions. It is uncertain from the language of the Constitution whether an override requires two-thirds of the total membership of each house or merely two-thirds of a quorum (two-thirds of a majority of its members). The Supreme Court decided in 1919 that two-thirds of a quorum is sufficient. It is also unclear from the Constitution whether the president may sign a bill after Congress has recessed. The Court, in 1899, held that he could. The president may even sign a bill after a final adjournment, as decided by a 1932 ruling.[58]

Legal controversies have resulted from the president's "pocket veto." The Constitution provides that any bill not returned by the president "within ten Days (Sundays excepted)" shall become law "unless the Congress by their Adjournment prevent its Return, in which Case it shall not be a Law." President Madison exercised the first pocket veto, in 1812.

The meaning of this provision of the Constitution became the subject of judicial scrutiny in the Pocket Veto case of 1929. A bill had been presented to President Coolidge less than ten days prior to an end-of-the-session adjournment, which lasted from July to December. The Supreme Court unanimously upheld the pocket veto, concluding that the adjournment had indeed prevented the president from returning the bill.[59] A different situation was at issue in *Wright* v. *United States* (1938). In this case only the Senate recessed—for three days—and the secretary of the Senate was authorized during the recess to receive (and did receive) messages from the president. The Court stressed that the veto procedure served two fundamental purposes: (1) to give the president an opportunity to consider a bill presented to him, and (2) to give Congress an opportunity to consider his objections and override them. Both objectives required protection. Through such reasoning the Court struck down this use of the pocket veto.[60]

The issue was reopened in 1970 when President Nixon exercised the pocket veto against the Family Practice of Medicine Bill. Both houses of Congress had adjourned on December 22 for the Christmas holidays. The Senate returned December 28 and the House the following day. Not counting December 27 (a Sunday) the Senate was absent for four days, the House for five. The Senate had designated its secretary to receive messages from the president. Unlike the 1929 decision, this case applied to a short adjournment during a session rather than a lengthy adjournment at the end of a session. Relying heavily on that distinction, a district court in 1973 held that the Christmas adjournment had not prevented Nixon from returning the bill to Congress. The following year an appellate court suggested that pocket vetoes during *any* intrasession adjournment, no matter how long, were invalid. Circuit Judge Tamm stated that an intrasession adjournment of Congress "does not prevent the president from returning a bill which he disapproves so long as appropriate arrangements are made for the receipt of presidential messages during the adjournment."[61]

Since the interval between the first and second sessions of a Congress can be less than an intrasession adjournment, it would be logical to prohibit *inter*session pocket vetoes as well. That was the position eventually announced by the Ford administration. President Ford decided that he would use the return veto rather than the pocket veto during intrasession and intersession recesses and adjournments of Congress (other than the adjournment at the end of a Congress), provided that the house of Congress to which the bill is returned specifically authorizes an officer or other agent to receive return vetoes during that period.[62]

Impoundment

Impoundment—the withholdings of funds appropriated by Congress—has become a familiar term only in recent decades. But the practice itself is an old one. President Jefferson, for example, regularly returned an unused portion of a contingency fund to the Treasury.[63] In 1803 he withheld $50,000 for gunboats because the Louisiana Purchase made it unnecessary to immediately spend the funds, which were later used to construct a different type of gunboat.[64] These early cases all involved routine withholdings of funds; members of Congress regarded such administrative actions as reasonable and in no way an infringement on the legislative powers of Congress.

Controversial impoundments developed for the most part after World War II, at first involving defense funds (an area in which the president could invoke his commander-in-chief powers) but gradually moving into the domestic area under Presidents Johnson and Nixon. After the 1972 elections, with the return of President Nixon to office, the intensity of impoundment escalated to the point of canceling entire programs or drastically curtailing them (such as cutting the clean-water program in half). Federal courts handed down dozens of decisions, almost all of them against the practices of the Nixon administration. Only one case reached the Supreme Court: the impoundment of funds for the clean-water program. The Court, in 1975, decided unanimously that the legislative history did not support the administration's policy to withhold the funds.[65] The decision was out of statutory construction, not constitutional power.

The Impoundment Control Act of 1974 (Title X of P.L. 93-344) provides new procedures. If the president decides to withhold funds he must report either one of two actions to Congress: a *deferral* (delaying the use of the funds) or a *rescission* (terminating the funds). Either house of Congress may disapprove a deferral at any time. For rescissions, both houses of Congress must complete action in approving the president's request within 45 days of continuous session. Otherwise, the funds must be made available for obligation. In other words, in the case of deferrals the burden is on one house to overturn the president's decision. For rescissions the burden is on the president to obtain the support of both houses within a specified period of time.[66]

Delegation

Traditional political theory holds that power delegated by the people to an agent cannot be further delegated (*delegata potestas non potest delegari*). Read literally, that would prohibit Congress from delegating its powers to the president or to his assistants. In practice, however, Congress and the courts have long recognized that a strict application of that theory would make government unworkable.[67]

An early test case was the Judiciary Act of 1789, which authorized the courts to make and establish rules for the conduct of their business. Plaintiffs objected that the rulemaking power, vested in Congress, could not be delegated to others. But in *Wayman* v. *Southard* (1825) Chief Justice Marshall turned aside such arguments as impracticable. It is permissible for Congress to supply guidelines for national policy while leaving to other departments of government the responsibility for "filling up the details."[68] The same pragmatic interpretation of the delegation doctrine appears in other decisions. The courts repeatedly warn that it would be a breach of the Constitution for Congress to transfer its legislative power to the president, yet in the same decisions the courts regularly uphold the delegation in question.[69]

Delegation to the president has been struck down only on two occasions. Both decisions, in 1935, involved the National Industrial Recovery Act, which placed upon industrial and trade associations the responsibility for drawing up codes to minimize competition, raise prices, and restrict production. If the president regarded the codes as unacceptable he was authorized to prescribe codes and enforce them as law. Private companies contested the legislation as an invalid delegation, claiming that congressional guidelines were inadequate. The Supreme Court agreed. In one of the cases, *Schechter*, Justice Cardozo exclaimed that "This is delegation running riot."[70]

Subsequent delegations of power to [the] president have been successfully defended in the courts. The composition of the Supreme Court changed after 1935, Congress took more care in drafting legislation, and even when the bills were vague in content, and lacking in specific standards or guidelines, the courts upheld the delegation as constitutional. Such legislation is saved not because of the specificity of its language but because Congress supplies standards of due process to guide administrative officials: giving notice, holding hearings, allowing for public participation, providing for judicial review, etc. In the 1940 *Sunshine Anthracite* case, the Supreme Court said that delegation by Congress "has long been recognized as necessary in order that the exertion of legislative power does not become a futility . . . the burdens of minutiae would be apt to clog the administration of the law and deprive the agency of that flexibility and dispatch which are its salient virtues."[71]

Congress has many valid reasons for delegating power to the president, departmental officials, and regulatory agencies. To place excessive detail in a statute can impair the administrative flexibility needed to execute the legislative policy. Neither Congress nor the agencies always know, at the time an act is passed, the precise guidelines to be included. Congress may prefer to draft legislation in general terms and depend on administrators, through their rulemaking power, to establish more explicit standards for agency action.[72] One difficulty with general grants of power is that the standards adopted by the agency may be framed largely in response to private interests focused upon the rulemakers.[73] Also, delegation may represent an attempt by Congress to evade political responsibility—an effort to transfer critical questions to another body rather than resolving them first through legislative means.[74]

The issue of excessive delegation was raised in 1970 when Congress passed the Economic Stabilization Act. It authorized the president to "issue such orders and regulations as he may deem appropriate to stabilize prices, rents, wages, and salaries at levels not less than those prevailing on May 25, 1970." The statute lacked specific standards, procedural safeguards, and opportunity for judicial review of decisions made by administrators of the statute. And yet all of the courts called upon to review the act upheld this broad grant of authority. In one of the principal decisions, Circuit Judge Leventhal noted that some of the congressional guidelines had been included in the committee reports and the legislative history: "Whether legislative purposes are to be obtained from committee reports, or are set forth in a separate section of the text of the law, is largely a matter of drafting style."[75]

This suggests that congressional control may be exercised either through statutory language or nonstatutory devices. Generally that is the case, but the two techniques are fundamentally different: agencies are bound by statute; they are not necessarily bound by language and directives found elsewhere. That point was underscored by an incident in 1975. The conference report on the defense appropriations bill directed the Navy to produce, as its air combat fighter, a derivative of the plane selected by the Air Force.[76] Instead, the Navy picked an aircraft that was not a derivative. A contractor, who had bid with the expectation that the Navy would follow the understanding in the conference report, lodged a formal protest with the General Accounting Office. The contractor wanted the Navy's decision declared null and void. The comptroller general ruled that nonstatutory directives had legal force only when some ambiguity in the language of the public law required recourse to the legislative history. Otherwise, agencies follow nonstatutory controls for practical, not legal, reasons. Agencies may ignore nonstatutory controls, said the comptroller general, but only "at the peril of strained relations with the Congress." To be legally binding the directive on the Navy aircraft had to appear in the public law.[77]

The courts adopt a different standard when delegation concerns external affairs. In 1936, one year after the Supreme Court struck down the delegation of power to the president under the National Industrial Recovery Act, the Court sustained a statute that authorized the president to prohibit the shipment of arms or munitions to any country in South America whenever he decided the materials would promote domestic violence. In this landmark decision, *United States* v. *Curtiss-Wright*, the Court argued that legislation in the international field must often accord to the president "a degree of discretion and freedom from statutory restriction which would not be admissible were domestic affairs alone involved."[78]

Although the *Curtiss-Wright* case has been subjected to criticism in the scholarly literature, it is still invoked to justify Presidential actions in external matters. In 1965, for example, the Supreme Court upheld a statute that authorized the secretary of State to refuse to validate the passports of U.S. citizens for travel to Cuba. Making reference to the *Curtiss-Wright* decision, the Court argued that the changeable nature of international relations made it necessary for Congress to "paint with a brush broader than that it customarily wields in domestic areas." In 1975 the U.S. Court of Customs and Patent Appeals relied in part on *Curtiss-Wright* to sustain a 10 percent surcharge that President Nixon had placed on imported goods.[79] But in 1974 a circuit court rejected Justice Sutherland's dicta in the *Curtiss-Wright* case that the president possessed extra constitutional foreign affairs powers (powers that passed directly to the colonies upon America's break with England). The court held that the president's foreign affairs power is implied in the language of Article II of the Constitution.[80]

Administrative Legislation

The need to interpret statutory grants of power and to supplement them by issuing rules and regulations is one source of legislative power for the executive branch. Said the Supreme Court in 1974: "The power of an administrative agency to administer a congressionally created and funded program necessarily requires the formulation of policy and the making of rules to fill any gap left, implicitly or explicitly, by Congress."[81] But while administrative regulations are entitled to respect, "the authority to prescribe rules and regulations is not the power to make laws, for no such power can be delegated by the Congress."[82] Nor are agencies free to ignore or depart from the policies and procedures that they have promulgated.[83]

The 94th Congress showed intense interest in the rules and regulations issued by executive agencies. Many members of Congress believed that administrators were promulgating hundreds of regulations, sometimes with criminal sanctions, that Congress never intended. Legislators introduced bills to address this problem. On September 21, 1976, the House of Representatives recorded a vote of 265-135 for the Administrative Rulemaking Reform Act. Although far greater than a majority, the vote fell short of the two-thirds needed under suspension of the rules. The purpose of the legislation is to permit Congress to review—and reject—agency regulations. Practical, as well as constitutional, arguments were presented by both sides. Should Congress attempt to review the thousands of regulations issued each year? Does it have the staff, the expertise, and the time? Is it constitutional for Congress to act through one-house or two-house vetoes? If Congress believes that agencies are departing from legislative intent, would it be better to draft statutes in more explicit fashion and pass remedial legislation to handle specific controversies over regulation?[84]

Two special instruments of legislative power for the president are proclamations and executive orders. A proclamation is often of a declaratory nature, such as announcing Law Day or another issue of general interest. Some proclamations, however, have substantive impact. Recent examples include Proclamation 4074, issued by President Nixon in 1971 as the "New Economic Policy." In part it involved a 10 percent surcharge placed on articles imported into the United States. Although no statute specifically authorized the imposition of a surcharge, the proclamation was upheld in the courts.[85] Proclamation 4341 by President Ford, which contemplated a $3 a barrel license fee on imported oil (amounting to several billions of dollars in additional costs to the consumers), was also upheld.[86]

In a recent dispute over an executive order, the comptroller general announced in 1969 that the "Philadelphia Plan" of the Nixon administration conflicted with the Civil Rights Act of 1964. The Plan required contractors to set specific goals for hiring members of minority groups as a condition for working on federally assisted projects. To the comptroller general this represented preferential treatment on the basis of race, color, or national origin, which was prohibited by the 1964 Act. However, the Department of Justice maintained that the Plan did not violate the act. Federal courts later upheld the legality of the Plan as well as the executive order that placed the Plan in operation.[87]

Also controversial was an executive order issued by President Nixon in 1971, expanding the power and field of inquiry of the Subversive

Activities Control Board. Senator Sam J. Ervin, Jr. introduced a resolution declaring that the president had no power "to alter by Executive order the content or effect of legislation enacted by Congress." The Senate adopted his amendment to prohibit the use of appropriated funds to implement the order, but the House did not support the restriction. In 1972 Congress adopted a compromise agreement expressly prohibiting the SACB from using appropriated funds to carry out the president's order. The following year the administration did not even request funds for SACB and the agency passed out of existence.[88]

V. International Affairs

The Constitution does not give to either Congress or to the president the predominant role in international affairs. Many of the crucial powers, in fact, are assigned to Congress: the power to regulate commerce with foreign nations, to declare war, to raise and support a military establishment, and to make all laws "which shall be necessary and proper for carrying into Execution the foregoing Powers." The Senate shares with the president the power to make treaties and to appoint diplomatic officers. The powers reserved to the president are comparatively limited: he shall be commander-in-chief and shall receive ambassadors and other public ministers. But through precedents, court decisions, statutory delegations, and congressional acquiescence, the president's powers over international affairs placed him in a dominant position. Over the past decade Congress has attempted to recapture its powers and responsibilities under the Constitution.

Treaties and Executive Agreements

During the initial deliberations at the Philadelphia Convention, the delegates considered entrusting to the Senate the major role in foreign affairs. Originally the Senate alone would have had power to make treaties and appoint ambassadors. Opposition soon surfaced and by early September the Convention decided that the president should make treaties "by and with the advice and consent of the Senate" and nominate "and by and with the advice and consent of the Senate shall appoint ambassadors." Treaties require a two-thirds support in the Senate.[89]

The process of drafting and negotiating a treaty is widely regarded as a "presidential monopoly."[90] However, that conclusion is not supported by the debates at Philadelphia, the early precedents under the First Congress, or the practices and understandings developed thereafter. The Constitution does not divide treatymaking into two distinct stages: negotiation by the president and consent by the Senate. The president "makes" treaties, by and with the advice and consent of the Senate. When President Washington first communicated to the Senate, regarding the appropriate procedure for treaties, he suggested that oral communications with the Senate "seem indispensably necessary; because in these a variety of matters are contained, all of which not only require consideration, but some of them may undergo much discussion; to do which by written communications would be tedious without being satisfactory." This suggests an active role for the Senate, not a simple "yes" or "no" to a president's submission.[91]

Because of Washington's frustrating experience with the Senate regarding an Indian treaty, he abandoned the idea of oral communications on treaties. That episode should not be misconstrued to suggest that, in future actions, the Senate was barred from any role in the negotiation stages. Washington continued to seek the Senate's advice, but through written communications rather than by personal appearances. Far from being a presidential monopoly, the process of making treaties has often been shared with the Senate in order to secure legislative understanding and support. One of the gravest miscalculations, with regrettable consequences, was the decision by Woodrow Wilson to exclude the Senate from the negotiation of the Versailles Treaty.[92]

The impact of World War II—followed by bilateral and multilateral defense treaties, vaguely worded congressional resolutions, and an increased reliance by the president on executive agreements—shifted the balance of power toward the president. Congress, particularly over the past decade, has been trying to restore its former position of influence.

Special attention has been paid to executive agreements.

Executive agreements, during the early years of the Republic, were carried out under statutory authority. Treaties, also, became a source of authority for executive agreements. The State Department has estimated that more than 95 percent of executive agreements (probably as high as 97 or 98 percent) are pursuant to congressional approval or implementation of treaties or legislation.[93]

Although executive agreements had been published in the U.S. statutes prior to 1950, and in *Treaties and Other International Agreements* after that, a number of important agreements were not reported to Congress at all. Congress, after it became aware of these secret agreements, passed the Case Act in 1972 (P.L. 92-403), which requires the secretary of State to transmit to Congress within 60 days of its signing any international agreement, other than a treaty, to which the United States is a party. If the president decides that publication of an agreement would be prejudicial to the national security, he may transmit it to the Senate Committee on Foreign Relations and the House Committee on International Relations under an injunction of secrecy removable only by the president.

Several senators have complained that the Nixon administration evaded the Case Act by entering into executive agreements, particularly with South Vietnam, without reporting them to Congress.[94] A study published by the General Accounting Office in 1976 disclosed that a number of agreements (called "arrangements" by the executive branch) had never been submitted to Congress or even to the Office of Treaty Affairs in the State Department.[95] Congress amended the Case Act in 1977 by providing that any department or agency that enters into any international agreement "shall transmit to the Department of State the text of such agreement not later than twenty days after such agreement has been signed."[96]

Members of the executive and legislative branches disagree on the scope of independent authority available to the president to conclude executive agreements. In addition to agreements made pursuant to treaties and to statutory authority, executive officials argue that the president may enter into certain agreements based on his constitutional authority (sole executive agreements). It appears that in most cases the Senate would participate in the negotiation process. It has been executive branch policy that appropriate congressional leaders and committees are to be advised of the intention to negotiate significant new international agreements, to be consulted concerning such agreements, and kept informed of developments affecting them, including especially whether any legislation is considered necessary or desirable for the implementation of the new treaty or agreement.[97]

But it has been the contention of executive officials that the president need not, in certain cases, consult with the Senate during the negotiation stage or even submit the international agreement, upon its completion, to the Senate for its advice and consent. According to the State Department's *Foreign Affairs Manual*, four constitutional sources of foreign affairs authority exist for the president: (1) his authority as chief executive to represent the nation in foreign affairs; (2) his authority to receive ambassadors and other public ministers; (3) his authority as commander-in-chief; and (4) his authority to take care that the laws be faithfully executed.[98]

Because of this claim of constitutional authority to enter into executive agreements, the Ford administration opposed the effort of Congress to subject agreements to some type of legislative veto (disapproval by both houses or by one house). A bill passed by the Senate in 1974 provided that executive agreements would go into effect unless Congress, within 60 days, passed a concurrent resolution of disapproval. This procedure would permit the two houses of Congress to "veto" an executive agreement without any participation by the president. Legislation has also been introduced to allow for disapproval by Senate resolution.[99] Another bill introduced on the House side would have permitted Congress to disapprove executive commitments at any time during a 60-day waiting period by passing a concurrent resolution. This bill is aimed at national commitments regarding the introduction, basing or deployment of armed forces in foreign territory, as well as any military training, equipment, financial or material resources provided to a foreign country.[100]

The courts have attempted to circumscribe the use of executive agreements so that they do not trench upon the powers of Congress or the rights of citizens. President Roosevelt's recognition of the Soviet government in 1933, followed by an executive agreement (the "Litvinov Assignment") that assigned to the United States all Russian claims against American nationals, led to two Supreme Court decisions. Each case recognized the executive agreement as a valid international compact. The question largely involved the respective rights of the federal government against those of the states. Left unresolved was the issue of whether an executive agreement could infringe such Fifth Amendment freedoms as the right to just compensation for private property taken for public use and the right not to be deprived of life, liberty or property, without due process of law.[101]

The balance between the president's power to enter into executive agreements, and the rights secured to individuals under the Constitution, is addressed in *Seery* v. *United States* (1955). During World War II a woman's home in Austria was used as a U.S. officers' club. Extensive damage was done to her home; practically all of her personal property disappeared. As a naturalized U.S. citizen she claimed a right to just compensation for the "taking." The American government offered several arguments to deny her claim, including an executive agreement entered into with Austria in 1947 that provided a lump-sum payment to Austria for all obligations incurred by U.S. forces during the period in which her home was occupied. The U.S. Court of Claims concluded that "there can be no doubt that an executive agreement, not being a transaction which is even mentioned in the Constitution, cannot impair Constitutional right."[102] Two years later the Supreme Court struck down an executive agreement that permitted U.S. military courts martial rather than trial by jury (a Sixth Amendment right). The Court held that executive agreements could not confer power "free from the restraints of the Constitution."[103]

Congressional powers were at stake in the 1953 *Capps* decision. The Administration had entered into an executive agreement that contravened an existing commerical statute with Canada. An appellate court declared that the "power to regulate foreign commerce is vested in Congress, not in the executive or the courts.... The executive may not by-pass congressional limitations regulating such commerce by entering into an agreement with the foreign country that the regulation be exercised by that country through its control over exports."[104] But when Congress has not specifically covered an area of foreign commerce, by statute, executive agreements may be upheld.[105]

The War Power

The Constitution contains a built-in tension between the president's power as commander-in-chief and the power of Congress to declare war. The limits and boundaries of those powers, and the relationship between them, have never been defined with any precision. Nor are they likely to be. As Justice Jackson noted in the Steel Seizure case of 1952, the commander-in-chief clause implied "something more than an empty title. But just what authority goes with the name has plagued presidential advisers who would not waive or narrow it by nonassertion yet cannot say where it begins or ends."[106]

There is little disagreement on one point: the president's responsibility to protect the nation from sudden attack. This authority, while not expressly stated in the Constitution, is implied in the debates at the Philadelphia Convention. When a delegate proposed that Congress be empowered to "make war," Pinckney objected that legislative proceedings "were too slow." He anticipated that Congress would meet but once a year. Madison and Gerry moved to insert "declare" for "make," thereby "leaving to the executive the power to repel sudden attacks." Their motion carried.[107]

Ever since that time there has been conflict between the war-making power of the president and the war-declaring power of Congress. Many of our military activities are carried out without a formal declaration of war. The Supreme Court has recognized the existence of limited, partial, or "imperfect" wars that are conducted without a declaration from Congress. Legislators may either declare a general war or authorize and finance a partial war.[108] American presidents have used military force hundreds of times, but only on five occasions has Congress declared war: the War of 1812, the Mexican War, the Spanish-American War, and the two World Wars. And only in the War of 1812 did Congress actually debate the merits of entering into hostilities. On all other occasions it merely recognized, after executive initiatives, that war did in fact exist.

Congressional control has been further weakened by the elastic notion of "defensive war." The responsibility for "repelling sudden attacks" on the U.S. mainland has been broadened by executive interpretation to include threats to our troops positioned around the world. Life-and-property actions of the president, used in the past for brief military interventions in foreign countries, have the potential for engaging the country in deeper conflicts. President Nixon sent troops into Cambodia in 1970, and supported the South Vietnamese invasion of Laos in 1971, on the justification that it would protect American lives. The doctrine of "hot pursuit," as used in Korea in 1950, offers another opportunity for the president and his military commanders to expand hostilities without congressional action or approval.[109]

During the late 1960s the Senate, especially through hearings and staff studies, openly challenged the president's dominance in foreign affairs and national security. In 1969 it passed the National Commitments Resolution, defining a national commitment as the use of U.S. armed forces on foreign territory, or a promise to assist a foreign country, government, or people by the use of armed forces or financial resources of the United States, either immediately or upon the happening of certain events. The Senate declared that a national commitment by the United States results "only from affirmative action taken by the executive and legislative branches of the U.S. Government by means of a treaty, statute, or concurrent resolution of both Houses of Congress specifically providing for such commitment."[110]

As a sense-of-the-Senate resolution, it is not legally binding on the president. However, statutory restrictions were later incorporated in the War Powers Resolution of 1973. The legislative history of that measure reflects the belief of the House of Representatives that Congress should not attempt to define or codify presidential war powers. The Senate, in contrast, attempted to spell out the conditions under which presidents could take unilateral action. Armed force under the Senate bill would be used in three situations: (1) to repel an armed attack upon the United States, its territories, and possessions; to take necessary and appropriate retaliatory actions in the event of such an attack; and to forestall the direct and imminent threat of such an attack; (2) to repel an armed attack against U.S. armed forces located outside the United States, its territories, and possessions, and to forestall the direct and imminent threat of such an attack; and (3) to rescue endangered U.S. citizens and nationals located in foreign countries or on the high seas. The first situation, except for the final clause, fits in well with the understanding developed at the Philadelphia Convention. The next two conditions reflect the changes that have occurred in the concept of defensive war and life-and-property actions.

The War Powers Resolution (P.L. 93-148) borrows elements from the House and Senate bills but does not define the initiatives a president may take. Section 2(c) appears to restrict the president's exercise of commander-in-chief powers to three situations: a declaration of war, specific statutory authorization, or a national emergency created by attack upon the United States, its territories or possessions, or its armed forces. However, the conference report explains that the sections on consultation, reporting, and congressional action—the heart of the War Powers Resolution—are not dependent on the language of Section 2(c). That subsection is divorced from the procedural controls that follow.[111] Consequently, a president may use his own judgment as to when and where to introduce U.S. armed forces into hostilities.

The War Powers Resolution contains three main provisions: consultation with Congress, submitting reports to Congress, and a procedure that allows Congress to terminate military action. The purpose of the Resolution, according to Section 2(a), is "to insure that the collective judgment" of both branches will apply to the introduction of U.S. forces into hostilities. Yet an examination of other sections, as well as interpretations from the executive branch, demonstrate that collective judgment is not ensured.

The president shall consult with Congress "in every possible instance." That language obviously leaves considerable discretion on the part of the president as to the form and timing of consultation. Shall members of Congress be merely briefed or does consultation mean more of a coequal role? The legislative history indicates the latter.[112] Yet President Ford's rescue in 1975 of the *Mayaguez* vessel, and its crew, was accompanied by only minimal consultation with Congress. Congressman Clement Zablocki, principal author of the House-passed War Powers Resolution, called the administration's record of consultation inadequate. Senator Jacob Javits, a leading sponsor of the War Powers Resolution, also criticized the administration's record of consultation during recapture of the vessel. The House Committee on International Relations could not obtain information from administration officials who were at the center of the decision-making process.[113]

Under the War Powers Resolution, any military action initiated by the president must terminate within 60 days after he reports to Congress unless Congress (1) declares war or enacts a specific authorization, (2) extends by law the 60-day period, or (3) is physically unable to meet as a result of an armed attack upon the United States. The president may extend the period for an additional 30 days if he determines that force is needed to protect and remove U.S. forces. Congress has two forms of control. One is through inaction: a decision to let the 60- to 90-day period lapse without congressional authorization of further action. Also, Congress may pass a concurrent resolution at any time to direct the president to remove forces engaged in hostilities.

This procedure has yet to be tested. Once the president sends troops into battle he might invoke what he regards as constitutional authority to repel sudden attacks and protect his troops. It may not be possible for Congress to curb such activity by passing a concurrent resolution to disengage or by deciding to let the 90-day period expire without legislative support. Monroe Leigh, legal adviser to the State Department during the Ford administration, told a House committee in 1975 that if the president has the power to put men into combat, that power cannot be taken away by concurrent resolution because the power is constitutional in nature.[114]

The Ford administration interpreted in very broad terms the president's power to use military force. In addition to the president's responsibility to protect American territory and American armed forces, the administration identified six other situations in which the president has constitutional authority to introduce armed forces into hostilities: to rescue American citizens abroad, to rescue foreign nationals where such action directly facilitates the rescue of U.S. citizens abroad, to protect U.S. embassies and legations, to suppress civil insurrection, to implement and administer the terms of an armistice or ceasefire designed to terminate hostilities involving the United States, and to carry out the terms of security commitments contained in treaties. The administration statement added: "We do not, however, believe that any such list can be a complete one."[115]

Previous to the War Powers Resolution, administration officials and federal judges accepted the theory that Congress can indirectly assent to a war by appropriating the necessary funds. This proposition was challenged on the ground that Congress legislates through authorization bills, not appropriation bills. According to this view, Congress can declare its policy only directly and explicitly in an authorization measure. Some of the judges who initially accepted the equivalence between defense appropriations and congressional support later reversed their position. As Circuit Judge Wyzanski noted in 1973:

> The court cannot be unmindful of what every schoolboy knows: that in voting to appropriate money or to draft men a Congressman is not necessarily approving of the continuation of a war no matter how specifically the appropriation or draft act refers to that war. A Congressman wholly opposed to the war's commencement and continuation might vote for the

military appropriations and for the draft measures because he was unwilling to abandon without support men already fighting. An honorable, decent, compassionate act of aiding those already in peril is not proof of consent to the actions that placed and continued them in that dangerous posture. We should not construe votes cast in pity and piety as though they were votes freely given to express consent.[116]

This dispute has been clarified by the War Powers Resolution. Section 8(a) states that the authority of the president to introduce U.S. armed forces into hostilities, or into situations where hostilities are likely, shall not be inferred "from any provision of law (whether or not in effect before the date of the enactment of this joint resolution), including any provision contained in any appropriation Act, unless such provision specifically authorizes the introduction of United States Armed Forces into hostilities or into such situations and states that it is intended to constitute specific statutory authorization within the meaning of this joint resolution."

Two features of the War Powers Resolution have been the subject of proposed amendments. One relates to the restrictions that the Resolution places on the president's dispatch of *armed servicemen* into hostilities. What of civilian combatants (paramilitary operations)? An effort by Senator Eagleton to include such operations within the coverage of the War Powers Resolution was defeated in 1973. Two years later he introduced legislation to make the provisions of the Resolution apply to covert civilian combatants.[117]

A second amendment concerns the failure of the resolution to recognize the president's authority to rescue endangered civilians. Recognition has its risks, since presidents have resorted to various kinds of force under the umbrella justification of "saving American lives," but a refusal to recognize the authority carries risks of its own. Congress is then called upon to act in an emergency situation, as a coequal partner, in operations required to protect American lives. That dilemma faced Congress, in 1975, when President Ford asked Congress to clarify statutory restrictions on the use of force in Southeast Asia to permit him to evacuate American citizens and foreign nationals. Before Congress could complete action on the "clarifying authority," Ford carried out the evacuations.[118]

Following that action by President Ford, and his rescue of the *Mayaguez* crew, Senator Eagleton introduced legislation to explicitly recognize the president's right to protect American lives. He stipulated various conditions: the citizens to be rescued would have to be involuntarily held with the express or tacit consent of the foreign government; there would have to be a direct and imminent threat to their lives; the foreign government either could not or would not protect the individuals; and the evacuations would have to take place as expeditiously as possible and with a minimum of force.[119]

Delegated Emergency Power

Over the past decade, as a result of detailed studies by Congress, legislators have become increasingly aware of the magnitude of emergency authority delegated to the president. Originally these powers were delegated in response to a pressing wartime need. Long after the war was over, however, the powers could be brought to life whenever the president declared the existence of a national emergency. Moreover, applications of emergency power lost their former association with military needs. President Roosevelt proclaimed a national emergency in 1933 at the time of the banking crisis, while President Nixon invoked emergency powers in 1970 and 1971 with regard to a postal strike and to balance of payments and international financial problems.

A special committee created by the Senate to study the scope of emergency authority discovered that presidential proclamations could activate some 470 provisions of federal law. Under those statutory grants of power the president could seize property, organize and control the means of production, institute martial law, control all transportation and communication, restrict travel, and exercise other important authorities.[120]

The National Emergencies Act of 1976 terminates the legislative authorities triggered by a presidential declaration of a national emergency. The general thrust is to terminate all powers and authorities two years from the date the act became law (September 14, 1976). Under the provisions of the act, Congress reserves to itself the power to terminate future national emergencies by passing a concurrent resolution. Not later than six months after a national emergency is declared by a president, and not later than the end of each six-month period thereafter that the emergency continues, each house of Congress shall meet to consider a vote on a concurrent resolution to terminate the emergency.[121]

The National Emergencies Act exempted certain provisions of law, including Section 5(b) of the Trading With the Enemy Act. As originally enacted in 1917 (40 Stat. 411), the legislation defined "enemy" as a nation "with which the United States is at war" (including corporations and individuals within that nation). The "beginning of war" required Congress to declare war or declare the existence of a state of war. Under such circumstances the president had authority over trade restrictions, communications, insurance, coin exports, and other economic controls.

As a result of amendments to the Trading With the Enemy Act and presidential proclamations, Section 5(b) became available for actions far removed from "trading with the enemy." Legislation in 1933 approved emergency banking actions that had been taken by President Roosevelt. The legislation also revised the language of 1917 to read "During time of war or during any other period of national emergency declared by the president" (48 Stat. 1). This change, of course, severed the connection between enemy and war.

The House of Representatives passed legislation in 1977 designed to limit the use of the Trading With the Enemy Act to time of war as declared by Congress. A second set of powers, more restricted than those available during time of war, would be made available to the president whenever he declared a national emergency in time of peace. Those powers would be subject to the procedural restrictions of the National Emergencies Act (including an opportunity for Congress to terminate the emergency by passing a concurrent resolution). As passed by the House, the legislation "grandfathers in" the authorities contained in Section 5(b). They would continue in force provided the president determines each year that they are needed for the national interest.[122]

"The Two Presidencies"

The difference in the nature of domestic and international responsibilities has created what Aaron Wildavsky calls the "two presidencies." Since World War II, he notes, presidents have had "much greater success in controlling the nation's defense and foreign policies than in dominating its domestic policies." After studying presidential proposals submitted to Congress from 1948 to 1964, he concluded that the president had prevailed about 70 percent of the time for defense and foreign policy, compared with 40 percent for the domestic section.[123]

Evaluating Wildavsky's thesis about eight years later, Donald Peppers agreed that presidential power in foreign affairs is greater than at home, and yet the intervening years of Lyndon Johnson and Richard Nixon had in many ways narrowed the gap between foreign and domestic. The distinction is not as clear-cut. Whereas Wildavsky acknowledged that presidential power in foreign policy derived from the immediacy of the cold war, the war in Vietnam and negotiations with Soviet Russia and Communist China had relaxed some of the cold war tensions. Also, congressional reassertion through such statutes as the War Powers Resolution of 1973 challenged some of the formal powers available to the president when Wildavsky wrote. Court decisions and other legislative actions—regarding executive agreements, freedom of information, the U.S. Intelligence Community, etc.—reduced the president's control of "secret" information, while a new mood of skepticism encouraged closer scrutiny of executive proposals in national-security matters. Weapons systems, such as the ABM (antiballistic missile) system, were contested in Congress with unprecedented vigor. Furthermore, "foreign policy" issues were having a demonstrably greater impact on the domestic economy: energy policy, the monetary system, grain sales to Russia, technology, and inflation and unemployment. New studies on bureaucratic politics cast doubt on the president's ability to maintain effective control over the agencies responsible for foreign affairs and national security.[124]

The overlap between foreign and domestic is evident in the dispute over wiretapping and electronic surveillance by executive officials without a warrant. The Fourth Amendment requires that a judicial warrant be obtained, upon probable cause, prior to a search and seizure, but various administrations claimed an inherent right to wiretap without a warrant when necessary for the defense of the nation.

The Supreme Court's decision in *United States v. United States District Court* (also called *Keith*) concerned wiretaps on domestic organizations suspected of attacking and subverting the existing structure of government. The Nixon administration ordered the wiretaps pursuant to the doctrine of inherent presidential powers. A unanimous decision by the Court in 1972 held that Fourth Amendment freedoms could not be guaranteed if domestic security surveillances were conducted solely at the discretion of the executive branch. Judicial warrants were necessary to maintain a neutral, independent magistrate to act as referee between the interests of individuals and the objectives of the administration.[125] But one week later the Court, divided 5-4, refused to decide whether the *army's* surveillance of domestic activities constituted a chilling effect on First Amendment freedoms. It suggested that Congress was the proper body to monitor such executive actions.[126]

Eventually a hybrid case presented itself to the federal courts: a domestic organization whose activities affected foreign relations. The Jewish Defense League (JDL), originally founded to protect Jews in New York neighborhoods, broadened its interests to include the treatment of Soviet Jews and Soviet emigration policies. Tactics of the group included peaceful picketing of the Soviet mission at the United Nations, vandalizing Soviet offices in New York and Washington, and bombing Soviet airline offices in New York City. To the Nixon administration the JDL, although a domestic organization, threatened the president's conduct of foreign relations. The Justice Department began wiretapping the JDL's New York office without a warrant.

In 1975 an appellate court held that the wiretap on the JDL violated the Fourth Amendment. A majority decided that warrants were necessary, at least in cases where a domestic organization acted neither as an agent nor collaborator of a foreign power. The court also denied that the executive branch possessed unique expertise in foreign affairs. Administration procedures placed upon the attorney general the responsibility for approving warrantless wiretaps. The court, after noting that there had been eight attorneys general in the past ten years (from Robert Kennedy through Edward Levi), as well as several acting attorneys general, remarked:

> We cannot blindly accept the argument that the Attorney General, who is chosen for his abilities as a lawyer rather than his acumen as a diplomat, is more likely than a federal judge to have the analytical ability or sensitivity to foreign affairs necessary to evaluate such recommendations.... We simply do not believe that any margin of expertise possessed by the Attorney General can compensate for the neutral and detached attitude that a judge would bring to his decision.[127]

As to the danger of "security leaks" when sharing information with the judiciary, the court said that the Supreme Court rejected such an argument in *Keith*, in the domestic security context, "and we find that it is no more persuasive in the foreign security context."[128]

VI. Contemporary Views on Presidential Power

It would be unrealistic to limit the "power" of the American presidency to the functions conferred by the Constitution, statutes, and custom. Broadly conceived, power means the ability to secure policy objectives—a process that depends on personal characteristics, historical circumstances, organizational factors, and countervailing forces at work within the political system. This section discusses some of the more recent studies that have added new dimensions to our understanding of presidential power.

With the exception of Edward S. Corwin's classic work on *The President* (four editions, the most recent in 1957) and a comprehensive study by Joseph E. Kallenbach, entitled *The American Chief Executive* (1966), recent literature on the presidency has devoted little attention to the formal powers of office. As one review of the literature noted, political scientists congratulated themselves for transcending the "formalistic" study of governmental institutions and constitutional or legal powers. They preferred to focus on techniques of persuasion, leadership, and the impact of personality and character, claiming that those elements described more realistically the dynamics of presidential power.[129]

Richard Neustadt's work on *Presidential Power*, first published in 1960, made a deep impression on the literature. In the preface he described his interest as "personal power and its politics: what it is, how to get it, how to keep it, how to use it." The book represents a manual designed for results. He did not attempt to study the presidency "as an organization, or as legal powers, or as precedents, or as procedures."[130]

Implicit is the assumption that an increase in presidential power will be beneficial to the nation. To Neustadt there is one central question: "What can *this* man accomplish to improve the prospect that he will have influence when he wants it? Strategically, the question is not how he masters Congress in a peculiar instance, but what he does to boost his chance for mastery in any instance, looking toward tomorrow from today."[131] Without reference to any moral guideposts or constitutional restrictions, Neustadt championed such neutral values as power, vigor, persuasion, energy, influence, expertise, and viability.[132]

One problem with Neustadt's analysis is that his emphasis is solely on influence and effectiveness, not on content or consequences. As a recent study observed, the passage of the Tonkin Gulf Resolution in 1964, with only two members of Congress opposed, would show President Johnson to be an "effective wielder of influence, but the fact that this influence led ultimately to a disastrous policy in Vietnam is irrelevant. Johnson would rate highly on Neustadt's scale in so far as this policy was concerned." The study also noted that the Nixon impoundments, in terms of results and influence, "would appear to be remarkably successful."[133]

Neustadt recognized that power could be abused, but the hope of the future clearly lay in a strong presidency:

> In a relative but real sense one can say of a president what Eisenhower's first Secretary of Defense once said of General Motors: what is good for the country is good for the president, and *vice versa*. There is no guarantee, of course, that every president will keep an eye on what is "good" for him; his sense of power and of purpose and the source of his self-confidence may turn his head away. If so, his "contributions" could be lethargy not energy, or policy that moves against, not with, the grain of history.[134]

Later in his book Neustadt warned that abuses are more likely to come from those who lack political experience and professional expertise:

> Any human judgment is worth fearing nowadays, but save for this the expert is a boon. His expertise assures a contribution to the system and it naturally commits him to proceed within the system. The system, after all, is what he knows. The danger lies in men who do not know it.[135]

This latter reference to the political amateur was aimed directly at the presidency of Dwight D. Eisenhower. Within a few years, however, the confidence of political scientists in an essentially benevolent president was severely shaken. The reputation of the presidency suffered under two later presidents who "knew the system well": Lyndon B. Johnson and Richard M. Nixon. Both men had extensive experience in party politics and Congress. Both had served as vice-president. Both were driven from office, one by removing his name from nomination for a second term, the other by resignation. In these cases failures came from political misjudgments, inability to rein in presidential powers voluntarily, a desire to push power and influence to the limit, and miscalculations as to what the system could tolerate.

The most recent edition of *Presidential Power*, published in 1976, includes an afterword on John F. Kennedy (prepared in 1968) and an introductory section on "Reflections on Johnson and Nixon." Neustadt did not alter the original text. Of Kennedy he is, on the whole, laudatory. In the section on Johnson and Nixon he writes: "in my view the power of a president today derives from roughly the same sources as a generation ago, is comparably limited, similarly frustrating, more changeable than ever, yet as central to our system as before, a far cry still from congressional government."[136] But whereas the 1960 edition warned against inexpert performance, now Neustadt was to concede, after the record of Johnson and Nixon, that "failures so spectacular cast doubt upon the adequacy of the warning!"[137] Borrowing in part from the studies on presidential character by James David Barber, Neustadt concludes that in addition to experience there is need for a special temperament in office. Essential to that temperament is "enjoyment of the job, and on it, and an ease in it, together with enjoyment of one's self." The second guide for Neustadt is the search for signs, independent of what happens during the campaign, that might cast light on a candidate's fitness for the job.[138]

Neustadt drew lessons from Barber, but with qualifications. The Barber classification of presidential character rests on two baselines: activity-passivity (how much energy does someone invest in the presidency?) and positive-negative (does the president enjoy the use of power?). Those baselines produce four types of presidential character: active-positive, active-negative, passive-positive, and passive-negative. All four types, to Barber, are represented in the first four administrations. George Washington was a passive-negative, John Adams an active-negative, and James Madison a passive-positive.[139] In the case of modern presidents, Barber ranks Franklin D. Roosevelt, Harry Truman, and John F. Kennedy as active-positives, Dwight D. Eisenhower as a passive-negative, and Lyndon B. Johnson and Richard M. Nixon as active-negatives. Barber counseled the American electorate to choose active-positives and shun active-negatives.

To Neustadt, it is difficult to predict how someone will behave in office on the basis of past performance. After Johnson and Nixon departed from the presidency they might be typed as active-negatives, but those traits were not so readily apparent before they entered the White House. Their political careers did not leave indisputable tell-tale signs of an active-negative. Writes Neustadt:

> The simple lesson, then, is to beware the insecure. But how are we to know them? Senate leader Johnson, job fitting like a glove, seemed wholly in command both of himself and of its resources. So he did again, remarkably, in the transition after Kennedy's assassination, to say nothing of his own campaign for election and the dazzling early months of his new term. New York lawyer Nixon, California left behind, was generally reported to have broadened, mellowed, calmed, and shed the tension of his gubernatorial campaign. And the president-elect who asked Americans to "lower our voice," while placing on his staff a Rockefeller Republican along with a Kennedy Democrat—Henry Kissinger and Daniel Patrick Moynihan, both from Harvard to boot—seemed more of the same.[140]

The resignation of President Nixon, accompanied by the disclosure of details surrounding the "Watergate affair," have been interpreted by some as validating Barber's "prediction" of Nixon as an active-negative and his propensity for disaster. Barber himself, in the 1977 edition of *Presidential Character*, claims that his theory correctly anticipated Nixon's downfall. With regard to the reelection of Nixon of 1972, Barber states that the American people had "every opportunity to know what they were getting. They elected Nixon despite the most abundant evidence ever available regarding the character of any presidential candidate"[141] "The clearest continuity," wrote Barber, "was Nixon's active-negative character."[142] "Like Presidents Wilson, Hoover, and Lyndon Johnson before him, something in his character attracted him to the path of grim perseverance, to the long, hard, lacerating march to a tragic denouement."[143]

But when one turns back to the 1972 edition, Nixon's direction was not at all so clear. Barber did not know at that time whether Nixon would follow his active-negative impulse or emulate the active-positive model of Harry Truman:

> Two heroes he has often expressed admiration for are Wilson and Churchill, both men who marked the world and then were rejected by their people. Their rhetorical styles and dra-

matic lives appeal to the theatrical in Nixon. But conceivably he could come to find an example in another man of independence, unheroic Harry Truman, who drew upon inner strengths he hardly knew to move beyond toughness to achievement.[144]

Alexander George, in a detailed analysis, expresses doubt that Barber's theory foretold the behavior of Nixon: "The question remains, however, whether this was the kind of catastrophe Barber predicted; additionally, whether and to what extent the events in question can be explained in terms of Nixon's character; and, if so, whether in terms of Barber's theory of character, some modification of it, or some other personality theory."[145] Also, George argues that performance in office reflects not merely psychological drives but political principles as well. Thus, President Hoover can be regarded as "rigid" in character because of his opposition to large federal spending as an antidote for the Great Depression. On the other hand, he may have found the idea "peculiarly antithetical to his political philosophy."[146] What is interpreted as rigid according to one theory can be seen alternatively as adhering faithfully to principles. Similarly, Erwin Hargrove objects to Barber's placement of Eisenhower as a passive-negative:

> Eisenhower actually seems very close to an active-positive. His personality was much freer of kinks than that of Truman; one can find in him no lack of self-esteem and very few, if any, instances of ego-defensive behavior. Ike was certainly not as active and energetic a political leader as the active-positive presidents described by Barber, but this may have been due to Eisenhower's conception of the office, a role requiring restraint, rather than in basic personality. Barber frankly admits that Eisenhower is the most difficult of presidents to classify, but we are left with his feet dangling over several boxes in the typology.[147]

In 1970 Thomas Cronin challenged the "textbook presidency"—his term for the "inflated and unrealistic interpretations of presidential competence and beneficence." His review of standard texts over a period of fifteen years revealed that the writers had created an idealized model of the presidency to fit their own liberal, New Deal outlook on government.[148] The result, Cronin wrote five years later, was a "halo for the chief" and a "cult of the presidency."[149]

The conduct of the war in Vietnam, followed by the scandals of Watergate and other developments that revealed an ominous quality to the presidency, produced a new note of sobriety and balance in the textbooks. Academics who had advocated a strong executive during the early years of the 1960s now found a need for reevaluation. A better understanding exists not only of the restrictions placed upon the presidency but the limitations that operate on government as a whole.

But scholarly support for a strong presidency, although couched in more modest terms, still exists. In an article published in 1977, John Hart studies the writings of three prominent students of the presidency (Arthur M. Schlesinger, Jr., Theodore Sorensen, and Louis Koenig) to determine how they have altered their views over the past decade. All three apologized somewhat for their earlier endorsements of presidential power. Sorensen, for example, looking back upon his views in the Kennedy White House, had this to say in 1975:

> I thought I knew a fair amount about the uses of presidential power. I didn't know half as much as I thought I did. I knew a fair amount about one president. I knew something about the presidency. But John F. Kennedy's two immediate successors operated the same levers of government so differently than he did . . . that it gradually became clear to me that many of my generalizations about the good that would flow from every aggrandizement of that office were more hope than reality.[150]

But all three writers look upon the Johnson-Nixon years as basically an aberration in the history of presidential power. Congress and the courts, they say, failed in their performance as checks on executive action. The public, also, became overly deferential toward the office. The three writers revised their views, but not to the extent of rejecting the strong presidency model. As Hart notes, "The view of most of the revisionists is simply that ways must be devised to prevent another Nixon or Johnson misusing the office—an office which might be occupied at some future date by another New Deal president."[151]

Notes

1. *The Works of Theodore Roosevelt*, XX, 347; William Howard Taft, *Our Chief Magistrate and His Powers* (1916), 138-140.
2. *Writings of James Madison* (Hunt, ed.), II, 339-340.
3. Ibid., V, 26.
4. Myers v. United States, 272 U.S. 52, 293 (1926).
5. See Jay Caesar Guggenheimer, "The Development of the Executive Departments, 1775-1789," in *Essays in the Constitutional History of the United States*, ed. J. Franklin Jameson (1889); Charles C. Thach, Jr., "The Creation of the Presidency, 1775-1789, A Study in Constitutional History," Johns Hopkins University Studies in Historical and Political Science, Series XL, No. 4 (1922), reprinted in 1969 as a Johns Hopkins paperback; Jennings B. Sanders, *Evolution of Executive Departments of the Continental Congress, 1774-1789* (1935); and Louis Fisher, *President and Congress: Power and Policy* (1972), 1-27, 241-270.
6. *The Works of Alexander Hamilton* (Lodge, ed.), IV, 432-444; *Writings of James Madison* (Hunt, ed.), VI, 138-188.
7. Annals of Congress, I (Aug. 18, 1789), 761.
8. 5 U.S. (1 Cr.), 137.
9. McCulloch v. Maryland, 17 U.S. (4 Wheat.) 315 (1819).
10. John Locke, *Second Treatise on Civil Government*, Ch. XIV; *Writings of Thomas Jefferson* (Washington, ed.), v, 542-545.
11. James D. Richardson, ed., *Messages and Papers of the Presidents*, VII, 3225. See James R. Hurtgen, "The Case for Presidential Prerogative," 7 Toledo Law Review 59 (1975). Regarding the exercise of emergency powers in Western democracies, see Clinton Rossiter, *Constitutional Dictatorship* (1963). Further discussion of presidential powers during a condition of national emergency may be found later in this multilith under section V, subsection "Delegated Emergency Power."
12. See Edward S. Corwin, "The Steel Seizure Case: A Judicial Brick Without Straw," 53 Columbia Law Review 53 (1953) and John P. Roche, "Executive Power and Domestic Emergency: The Quest for Prerogative," 5 West. Pol. Q. 592 (1952).
13. 5 U.S. (1 Cr.) 137, 157, 162. For other cases on the executive-ministerial distinction see Kendall v. United States, 37 U.S. (12 Pet.) 524, 610-613 (1838); Decatur v. Paulding, 39 U.S. (14 Pet.) 497, 516 (1840); Reeside v. Walker, 52 U.S. (11 How.) 272, 290 (1850); United States v. Price, 116 U.S. 43 (1885); and United States v. Louisville, 169 U.S. 249 (1898).

14. Berends v. Butz, 357 F.Supp. 143 (D. Minn. 1973).
15. *The Writings of Washington* (Fitzpatrick, ed.), III, 350; *The Papers of Thomas Jefferson* (Boyd, ed.), XI, 679.
16. This account is drawn from the debates of the First Congress. For secondary sources see James Hart, *The American Presidency in Action* (1948), 155-248; Edward S. Corwin, *The President* (1957), 85-95, 375-380; and Charles C. Thach, Jr., *The Creation of the Presidency* (1969 paper ed.), 140-165.
17. 1 Stat. 29, 50, 67. The House debate appears in the Annals of Congress, I, 363-615 (May 19 to July 1, 1789).
18. Shurtleff v. United States, 189 U.S. 311, 316 (1903). See also United States v. Guthrie, 58 U.S. (17 How.) 284 (1854); Parsons v. United States, 167 U.S. 324 (1897); and Wallace v. United States, 257 U.S. 541 (1922).
19. 272 U.S. 52 (1926).
20. Edward S. Corwin, *The President's Removal Power Under the Constitution* (1927), reproduced with little change as "Tenure of Office and the Removal Power Under the Constitution," 27 Columbia Law Review 353 (1927).
21. Humphrey's Executor v. United States, 295 U.S. 602 (1935). The Myers and Humphrey cases analyzed by William J. Donovan and Ralstone R. Irvine, "The President's Power to Remove Members of Administrative Agencies," 21 Cornell Law Quarterly 215 (1936).
22. Morgan v. Tennessee Valley Authority, 28 F.Supp. 732 (E.D. Tenn. 1939), aff'd, 115 F.2d 990 (6th Cir. 1940), cert. denied, 312 U.S. 701 (1941). Arthur Larson, "Has the President an Inherent Power of Removal of his Non-Executive Appointees?" 16 Tennessee Law Review 259 (1940), did not agree that TVA was predominantly an executive agency.
23. 357 U.S. 349 (1958).
24. *Public Papers of the Presidents*, 1973, at 539.
25. P.L. 93-250, 88 Stat. 11 (1974).
26. 38 Fed. Reg. 14688 (1973).
27. Nader v. Bork, 366 F.Supp. 104 (D.D.C. 1973).
28. U.S. (1 Cr.) 137, 155; 13 Op. Att'y Gen. 516 (1871).
29. Nicholas de B. Katzenbach, "The Roles of Executive and Legislative Branches in Judicial Appointments," New York Law Journal, Nov. 3, 1971, reprinted at 117 Cong. Rec. 40117-40119 (1971). Carter: Wkly. Comp. Pres. Doc., XIII 214-215, 810-811 (Feb. 14 and May 24, 1977). See Harold W. Chase, *Federal Judges: The Appointing Process* (1972).
30. Buckley v. Valeo, 424 U.S. 1, 134-143 (1976).
31. Williams v. Phillips, 360 F.Supp. 1363 (D.D.C. 1973). The D.C. Court of Appeals denied Phillips' motion for a stay, pending appeal, because he failed to show sufficient likelihood of success on the merits; Williams v. Phillips, 484 F.2d 669 (D.C. Cir. 1973). See Lois Reznick, "Temporary Appointment Power of the President," 41 University of Chicago Law Review 146 (1973). Congress may name members of national advisory commis-

sions by so specifying in statutes creating such bodies, but the key factor in this practice is that such entities are purely advisory.

32. *Writings of Washington* (Fitzpatrick, ed.), XXX, 374. Madison, *Annals of Congress*, I (May 19, 1789), 380.

33. Senate Committee on the Judiciary, "Advice and Consent on Supreme Court Nominations," 94th Cong., 2nd Sess. (Comm. Print 1976); 121 Cong. Rec. S20602 (daily ed. Nov. 20, 1975) and 117 Cong. Rec. S17788-17793 (daily ed. Nov. 8, 1971).

34. See the debates on the nomination of James Lynn and Carla Hills to be secretary of Housing and Urban Development; 119 Cong. Rec. 2783-2795 (1973); and 121 Cong. Rec. S3049-3056 (daily ed. March 5, 1975).

35. P.L. 94-141, 89 Stat. 757, sec. 104 (1975); P.L. 94-350, 90 Stat. 829, sec. 120 (1976); and H. Rept. No. 1302, 94th Cong., 2nd Sess. 37 (1976).

36. Senate studies: "Appointments to the Regulatory Agencies," printed for the use of the Senate Committee on Commerce, 94th Cong., 2nd Sess. (Comm. Print April 1976); and the Senate Committee on Government Operations, study on "Federal Regulations: The Regulatory Appointments Process" (Volume I), 95th Cong., 1st Sess. (Comm. Print Jan. 1977). 1973 action: 119 Cong. Rec. 19492-19508. See also 122 Cong. Rec. S3882 (daily ed. March 22, 1976).

37. 47 Stat. 399-415 (1932); 76 Cong. Rec. 2103-2126 (1933).

38. 83 Cong. Rec. 4487 (1938). See Donald G. Morgan, *Congress and the Constitution* (1966), 184-203.

39. Richard Polenberg, *Reorganizing Roosevelt's Government* (1966).

40. Hollingsworth v. Virginia, 3 Dall. 378.

41. S. Rept. No. 1335, 54th Cong., 2nd Sess. 8 (1897).

42. H. Rept. No. 120, 76th Cong., 1st Sess. 6 (1939). See Currin v. Wallace, 306 U.S. 1 (1939).

43. See Robert W. Ginnane, "The Control of Federal Administration by Congressional Resolutions and Committees," 66 Harvard Law Review 569 (1953); Cornelius P. Cotter and J. Malcolm Smith, "Administrative Accountability to Congress: The Concurrent Resolution," 9 West. Pol. Q. 955 (1956); and Clark F. Norton, "Congressional Review, Deferral and Disapproval of Executive Actions: A Summary and an Inventory of Statutory Authority," (Congressional Research Service multilith 76-88 G, April 30, 1976).

44. P.L. 95-17, 91 Stat. 29 (1977). See H. Rept. No. 105, 95th Cong., 1st. Sess. (1977).

45. Richardson, ed., *Messages and Papers of the Presidents*, I (March 30, 1976), 187.

46. Id. at V, 2284 (April 209, 1846). For CRS studies see Marjorie Ann Browne, "Executive Privilege—A Brief Survey; (71-238 F, July 23, 1971); Mary Louise Ramsey, "Executive Privilege: Withholding Information from the Congress—Selected Issue and Judicial Decisions" (75-127A, April 3, 1975); and Richard Ehlke, "The Proposed Congressional Right to Information Act and Executive Privilege: A Constitutional Analysis" (76-11A, Jan. 19, 1976).

47. United States v. Nixon, 418 U.S. 683, 711 (1974).

48. Wkly. Comp. Pres. Doc., IX, 968-969 (Aug. 7, 1973).

49. United States v. Nixon, 418 U.S. 683, 709 (1974). President Nixon also lost two court tests: In re Subpoena to Nixon, 360 F.Supp. 1 (D.D.C. 1973) and Nixon v. Sirica, 487 F.2d 700 (D.C. Cir. 1973).

50. Nixon v. Administrator of General Services, 45 U.S.L.W. 4917 (June 28, 1977).

51. United States v. Nixon, 418 U.S. 683, 706.

52. United States v. Reynolds, 345 U.S. 1 (1952). See also C. & S. Air Lines v. Waterman Corp., 333 U.S. 103, 111 (1948).

53. New York Times Co. v. United States, 403 U.S. 713 (1971).

54. United States v. Marchetti, 466 F.2d 1309 (4th Cir. 1972), cert. denied, 409 U.S. 1063 (1972). For further developments on the authority of the CIA to censor confidential information, prior to publication, see Knopf v. Colby, 509 F.2d 1362 (4th Cir. 1975), cert. denied, 421 U.S. 992 (1975).

55. E.g., see the views of Prof. Charles L. Black, Jr., reprinted at 122 Cong. Rec. E390-392 (daily ed. Feb. 3, 1976); id. at E454-455 (Feb. 4, 1976); and id. at E501-502 (Feb. 5, 1976).

56. Farrand, ed., *Records of the Federal Convention*, I, 139.

57. For general studies see Edward Campbell Mason, *The Veto Power* (1890); Carleton Jackson, *Presidential Vetoes* (1967); and Jong R. Lee, "Presidential Vetoes from Washington to Nixon," 37 J. Pol. 522 (1975).

58. Missouri Pac. Ry. Co. v. Kansas, 248 U.S. 277 (1919); La Abra Silver Mining Co. v. United States, 175 U.S. 423 (1899); and Edwards v. United States, 286 U.S. 482 (1932).

59. The Pocket Veto Case, 279 U.S. 644 (1929).

60. 302 U.S. 583.

61. Kennedy v. Sampson, 511 F.2d 430, 437 (D.C. Cir. 1974). See also Kennedy v. Sampson, 364 F.Supp. 1075 (D.D.C. 1973) and "Constitutionality of the President's 'Pocket Veto' Power," hearing before the Senate Committee on the Judiciary, 92nd Cong., 1st Sess. (1971).

62. 122 Cong. Rec. S5912 (daily ed. April 26, 1976). See Edward M. Kennedy, "Congress, the President, and the Pocket Veto," 63 Virginia Law Review 355 (1977).

63. Richardson, *Messages and Papers of the Presidents*, I, 325, 354, 366, 383-385, 405, 421, 447.

64. Ibid., 348, 360.

65. Train v. City of New York, 420 U.S. 35 (1975). For background on impoundment see Louis Fisher, *Presidential Spending Power* (1979), 147-201.

66. See Allen Schick, "The Impoundment Control Act of 1974: Legislative History and Implementation," Congressional Research Service multilith 76-45 S (Feb. 27, 1976) and Louis Fisher, "Congressional Budget Reform: The First Two Years," 14 Harv. J. Legis. 413 (1977).

67. See Patrick W. Duff and Horace E. Whiteside, "Delegata Potestas Non Potest Delegari: A Maxim of American Constitutional Law," 14 Cornell Law Quarterly 168 (1929); and Horst P. Ehmke, " 'Delegata Potestas Non Potest Delegari,' A Maxim of American Constitutional Law," 47 Cornell Law Quarterly 50 (1961).

68. 10 Wheat. 1 (1825).

69. E.g., Field v. Clark, 143 U.S. 649, 692 (1891) and Hampton & Co. v. United States, 276 U.S. 394, 406 (1928).

70. Panama Refining Co., v. Ryan, 293 U.S. 388 (1935); Schechter Corp. v. United States, 295 U.S. 495, 553 (1935).

71. Sunshine Coal Co. v. United States, 310 U.S. 381, 398 (1940). See also Opp Cotton Mills v. Administrator, 312 U.S. 126, 145 (1941); Louis Fisher, *President and Congress* (1972), 55-84; and Louis L. Jaffe, *Judicial Control of Administrative Action* (1965), ch. 2.

72. Kenneth Culp Davis, *Discretionary Justice* (1969).

73. J. Skelly Wright, "Beyond Discretionary Justice," 81 Yale Law Journal 575 (1972).

74. Sotirious A. Barber, *The Constitution and the Delegation of Congressional Power* (1975).

75. Amalgamated Meat Cutters & Butcher Work v. Connally, 337 F.Supp. 737, 750 (D.D.C. 1971); Stanley H. Friedelbaum, "The 1971 Wage-Freeze: Unchallenged Presidential Power," Supreme Court Review, 1974, at 33-80.

76. H. Rept. No. 1363, 93rd Cong., 2nd Sess. 27 (1974).

77. General Accounting Office, "LTV Aerospace Corp.," B-183851 (Oct. 1, 1975), at 21-22.

78. 299 U.S. 304, 320.

79. Zemel v. Rusk, 381 U.S. 1, 17 (1965) and United States v. Yoshida Intern., Inc., 526 F.2d 560, 582 (U.S. Ct. Cust. & Pat. App. 1975). For criticism of Curtiss-Wright see David M. Levitan, "The Foreign Relations Power: An Analysis of Mr. Justice Sutherland's Theory," 55 Yale Law Journal 467 (1946); and Charles A. Lofgren, "United States v. Curtiss-Wright Export Corporation: An Historical Reassessment," 83 Yale Law Journal 1 (1973).

80. United States v. Butenko, 494 F.2d 593, 602-603 (3rd Cir. 1974), cert. denied, 419 U.S. 881 (1974). The court referred favorably to a critique of Curtiss-Wright of Professor Lofgren (cited in footnote above).

81. Morton v. Ruiz, 415 U.S. 199, 231 (1974).

82. Lincoln Electric Co. v. Commissioner of Int. Rev. 190 F.2d 326, 330 (6th Cir. 1951). See also American Broadcasting Co. v. United States, 110 F.Supp. 374, 384 (S.D. N.Y. 1953), aff'd, 347 U.S. 284 (1954).

83. Vitarelli v. Seaton, 359 U.S. 535 (1959); Note, "Violations by Agencies of Their Own Regulations," 87 Harvard Law Review 629 (1974). See Arthur S. Miller, *Presidential Power* (1977), 62-104.

84. 122 Cong. Rec. H10666-10719 (daily ed. Sept. 21, 1976); "Congressional Review of Administrative Rulemaking," hearings before the House Committee on the Judiciary, 84th Cong., 1st Sess. (1975). See Harold H. Bruff and Ernest Gellhorn, "Congressional Control of Administrative Regulation: A Study of Legislative Vetoes," 90 Harvard Law Review 1369 (1977).

85. Proclamation 4074, 36 Fed. Reg. 15724 (1971), terminated by Proclamation 4098, 36 Fed. Reg. 24201 (1971). Upheld by United States v. Yoshida Intern., Inc., 526 F.2d 560 (Ct. Cust. & Pat. App. 1975). See David Pollard and David A. Boillot, "The Import Surcharge of 1971: A Case Study of Executive Power in Foreign Commerce," 7 Vand. J. Transnat'l L. 137 (1973).

86. Proclamation 4341, 36 Fed. Reg. 3965 (1975). Upheld by FEA v. Algonquin Sng. Inc., 426 U.S. 548 (1976).

87. 49 Comp. Gen. 59 (1969). Contractors Ass'n of Eastern Pa. v. Secretary of Labor, 442 F.2d 159 (3d Cir. 1971), cert. denied, 404 U.S. 854 (1971). See Robert P. Schuwerk, "The Philadelphia Plan: A Study in the Dynamics of Executive Power," 39 University of Chicago Law Review 723 (1972). General studies: Robert B. Cash, "Presidential Power: Use and Enforcement of Executive Orders," 39 Notre Dame Lawyer 44 (1963); William D. Neighbors, "Presidential Legislation by Executive Order," 37 University of Colorado Law Review 105 (1964); William Hebe, "Executive Orders and the Development of Presidential Power," 17 Villanova Law Review 688 (1972); and Grover Williams and Walter Albano, "Executive Orders: A Brief History of Their Use and the President's Power to Issue Them," Congressional Research Service multilith 77-105A (March 25, 1977).

88. Executive order 11605, 36 Fed. Reg. 12831 (1971). Ervin resolution; S. Res. 163, 92nd Cong., 1st Sess. (1971). For action on his amendment see 117 Cong. Rec. 25898-25902 (1971). Prohibition in 1972: 86 Stat. 1131, 1134. See "President Nixon's Executive Order 11605 Relating to the Subversive Activities Control Board," hearing before the Senate Committee on the Judiciary, 92nd Cong., 1st Sess. (1971).

89. Farrand, ed., *Records of the Federal Convention*, II, 155, 169, 183, 297, 392-393, 495.

90. The Constitution of the United States of America: Analysis and Interpretations, S. Doc. No. 92-82, at 481 (1973); Edward S. Corwin, *The President*, 211-212 (1957 ed.); and United States v. Curtiss-Wright, 299 U.S. 304, 319 (1936).

91. *Writings of Washington* (Fitzpatrick, ed.), xxx, 373, 378. See also Ellen Collier, " 'Consent of the Senate' in the Treaty-Making Process," Congressional Research Service multilith 69-220 F (Oct. 8, 1969).

92. See Forrest R. Black, "The United States Senate and the Treaty Power," 4 Rocky Mt. Law Review 1 (1931); and Richard E. Webb, "Treatymaking and the President's Obligation to Seek the Advice and Consent of the Senate With Special Reference to the Vietnam Peace Negotiations," 31 Ohio State Law Journal 490 (1970).

93. "Transmittal of Executive Agreements to Congress," hearings before the Senate Committee on Foreign Relations, 92nd Cong., 1st Sess. 59 (1971).

94. E.g., Senator James Abourezk said that the "administration has admitted to both Senator Case and myself that there are some agreements they do not submit at all under the Case Act"; "Early Warning System in

Sinai," hearings before the Senate Committee on Foreign Relations, 94th Cong., 1st Sess. 6 (1975).

95. General Accounting Office, "U.S. Agreements With the Republic of Korea," ID-76-20 (Feb. 20, 1976).

96. P.L. 95-45, 91 Stat. 224, sec. 5.

97. 11 FAM [Foreign Affairs Manual] 723.1(e) (Oct. 25, 1974).

98. Ibid., 721.2(b)(3).

99. Senate bill in 1974: S. Rept. No. 93-1286; 120 Cong. Rec. S19867 (daily ed. Nov. 21, 1974). Disapproval by Senate resolution: S. 1251, 94th Cong., 1st Sess.; 121 Cong. Rec. S4467 (daily ed. March 20, 1975).

100. 121 Cong. Rec. H1451-1452 (daily ed. March 6, 1975).

101. United States v. Belmont, 301 U.S. 324 (1937); United States v. Pink, 315 U.S. 203 (1942). See Note, "United States v. Pink—A Reappraisal," 48 Columbia Law Review 890 (1948).

102. 127 F.Supp. 601, 606 (Ct. cl. 1955). See Arthur E. Sutherland, Jr., "The Flag, the Constitution, and International Agreements," 68 Harvard Law Review 1374 (1955).

103. Reid v. Covert, 354 U.S. 1, 16 (1957).

104. United States v. Guy W. Capps, Inc. 204 F.2d 655, 658, 660 (4th Cir. 1953), aff'd on other grounds, 348 U.S. 296 (1955). See Arthur E. Sutherland, "The Bricker Amendment, Executive Agreements, and Imported Potatoes," 67 Harvard Law Review 281 (1953).

105. Consumers Union of U.S., Inc. v. Kissinger, 506 F.2d 136 (D.C. Cir. 1974), cert. denied, 421 U.S. 1004 (1975). For CRS multiliths see Marjorie Ann Browne, "Executive Agreements: A Survey of Legal and Political Controversies Concerning Their Use in United States Practice" (75-45A, Feb. 13, 1975).

106. Youngstown Co. v. Sawyer, 343 U.S. 579, 641 (1952).

107. Farrand, ed., *Records of the Federal Convention*, II, 318-319.

108. Bas v. Tingy, 4 U.S. (4 Dall.) 37, 40 (1800) and Talbot v. Seeman, 1 Cr. 1, 8 (1801).

109. Louis Fisher, *President and Congress* (1972), 175-200.

110. 115 Cong. Rec. 17214-17246 (1969).

111. H. Rept. No. 547, 93rd Cong., 1st Sess. 8 (1973). See Senator Thomas F. Eagleton, *War and Presidential Power: A Chronicle of Congressional Surrender* (1974), 202-203.

112. For the view that consultation means more than simply being informed, see H. Rept. No. 287, 93rd Cong., 1st Sess. 6-7 (1973).

113. Zablocki: "War Powers: A Test of Compliance," hearings before the House Committee on International Relations, 94th Cong., 1st Sess. VI, 62-62, 81-82, 100 (1975); Javits: 121 Cong. Rec. S10339 (daily ed., June 11, 1975). See the hearings by the House Committee on International Relations, "Seizure of the Mayaguez," 94th Cong., Part 2 at 137, 147-152, and Part 3 at 259-270 (1975).

114. "War Powers: A Test of Compliance," hearings before the House Committee on International Relations, 94th Cong., 1st Sess. 91 (1975).

115. Ibid., 90-91.

116. Mitchell v. Laird, 488 F.2d 611, 615 (D.C. Cir. 1973).

117. 121 Cong. Rec. S22254 (daily ed., Dec. 16, 1975).

118. The House, capping three weeks of intense effort, voted down the conference report that contained the clarifying authority. 121 Cong. Rec. H3540-3551 (daily ed., May 1, 1975).

119. S. 1790, 94th Cong., 1st Sess. (1975); 121 Cong. Rec. S8825-8828 (daily ed., May 21, 1975). Similar legislation was introduced by Congresswoman Gladys Noon Spellman, 121 Cong. Rec. E2969 (daily ed., June 9, 1975).

120. S. Rept. No. 549, 93rd Cong., 1st Sess. (1973).

121. P.L. 94-412, 90 Stat. 1255 (1976). See "The National Emergencies Act (Public Law 94-412), Source Book: Legislative History, Texts, and Other Documents," Senate Committee on Government Operations and Senate Special Committee on National Emergencies and Delegated Emergency Powers, 94th Cong., 2nd Sess. (Comm. Print, Nov. 1976). Also: J. Malcolm Smith and Cornelius P. Cotter, *Powers of the President During Crises* (1960).

122. H. Rept. No. 459, 95th Cong., 1st Sess. (1977); and 123 Cong. Rec. H6868-6872 (daily ed., July 12, 1977). See "Trading With the Enemy: Legislative and Executive Documents Concerning Regulation of International Transactions in Time of Declared National Emergency," prepared by the House Committee on International Relations, 94th Cong., 2nd Sess. (Comm. Print, Nov. 1976). The Senate passed this legislation, with amendments, on October 11, 1977: 123 Cong. Rec. S16912. See S. Rept. No. 466, 95th Cong., 1st Sess. (1977).

123. Aaron Wildavsky, "The Two Presidencies," Trans-Action (Dec. 1966), reprinted on pages 448-461 of *Perspectives on the Presidency*, ed. Aaron Wildavsky (1975).

124. Donald A. Peppers, "'The Two Presidencies': Eight Years Later," reprinted on pages 462-471 of *Perspectives on the Presidency*, ed. Aaron Wildavsky (1975).

125. United States v. United States District Court, 407 U.S. 297, 308 (1972).

126. Laird v. Tatum, 408 U.S. 1, 15 (1972).

127. Zweibon v. Mitchell, 516 F.2d 594, 644 (D.C. Cir. 1975), footnote omitted.

128. Ibid., 647. See Note, "The Fourth Amendment and Judicial Review of Foreign Intelligence Wiretapping: Zweibon v. Mitchell," 45 G.W. L. Rev. 55 (1976).

129. Richard M. Pious, "Is Presidential Power 'Poison'?" 89 Pol. Sci. Q. 627 (1974).

130. Richard E. Neustadt, *Presidential Power: The Politics of Leadership* (1960 ed.), VII.

131. Ibid., 2. Emphasis in original.

132. Ibid., 185, 192.

133. John Hart, "Presidential Power Revisited," 25 Political Studies 48, 56 (1977).

134. Presidential Power, 185.

135. Ibid., 193.

136. Richard E. Neustadt, *Presidential Power* (1976 ed.), 2.

137. Ibid., 3.

138. Ibid., 33.

139. James David Barber, *The Presidential Character: Predicting Performance in the White House* (1972), 11-14.

140. Neustadt, *Presidential Power* (1976 ed.), 32.

141. Barber, *Presidential Character* (1977 ed.), 459.

142. Ibid., 461.

143. Ibid., 475.

144. Barber, *Presidential Character* (1972 ed.), 442.

145. Alexander L. George, "Assessing Presidential Character," 26 World Politics 234, 239 (1974).

146. Ibid., 258.

147. Erwin C. Hargrove, "Presidential Personality and Revisionist Views of the Presidency," 17 Am. J. Pol. Sci. 819, 832 (1973). Other views on Barber's theory appear at 71 Am. Pol. Sci. Rev. 182-225, 597-599 (1977).

148. Thomas E. Cronin, "The Textbook Presidency and Political Science," paper delivered at the 1970 convention of the American Political Science Association, reprinted at 116 Cong. Rec. 34914-34928 (1970).

149. Thomas E. Cronin, *The State of the Presidency* (1975), 24-51.

150. John Hart, "Presidential Power Revisited," 25 Political Studies (1977), 48, 50, quoting from Theodore C. Sorensen, *Watchmen in the Night: Presidential Accountability After Watergate,* xvi (1972).

151. Ibid., 50.

Illustration 1b: The Presidential Job Description: The Subpresidencies
Thomas Cronin

The following is a most helpful table compiled by leading presidential scholar Thomas Cronin. It details analytical definitions of presidential responsibilities including a general description and distinctions of presidential contributions in three different realms of public policy. The important lesson to be learned is that presidential roles and power vary by policy domain.

The Presidential Job Description
The Subpresidencies

Types of Activity	Foreign Policy and National Security (A)	Aggregate Economics (B)	Domestic Policy and Programs (C)
Crisis Management	Wartime leadership; missile crisis, 1962	Coping with recessions	Confronting coal strikes of 1978
Symbolic and Morale-building Leadership	Presidential state visit to Middle East or to China	Boosting confidence in the dollar	Visiting disaster victims and morale building among government workers
Priority Setting and Program Design	Balancing pro-Israel policies with need for Arab oil	Choosing means of dealing with inflation	Designing a new welfare program
Recruitment Leadership (advisers, administrators, judges, ambassadors, etc.)	Selection of Secretary of Defense, U.N. Ambassador	Selection of Secretary of Treasury, Federal Reserve Board Governors	Nomination of federal judges
Legislative and Political Coalition Building	Selling Panama or SALT treaties to Senate for approval	Lobbying for energy-legislation package	Winning public support for transportation deregulation
Program Implementation and Evaluation	Encouraging negotiations between Israel and Egypt	Implementing tax cuts or fuel rationing	Improving quality health care, welfare retraining programs
Oversight of Government Routines and Establishment of an Early-Warning System for Future Problem Areas	Overseeing U.S. bases abroad; ensuring that foreign-aid programs work effectively	Overseeing the IRS or the Small Business Administration	Overseeing National Science Foundation or Environmental Protection Agency

From *The State of the Presidency* 2d ed. (p. 155) by Thomas E. Cronin, 1980, Boston: Little, Brown and Co. Copyright 1980 by Little, Brown and Co. Reprinted by permission.

The President and the Control of Nuclear Weapons

Frank Klotz, Jr.

A new and very important responsibility of the modern presidency is control of nuclear weapons. The technology of modern weaponry, combined with constitutional authority as commander-in-chief, have conferred upon presidents strategic and even tactical command authority with regard to the use of military force. The following essay addresses this awesome component of the presidential job description.

> *The control of nuclear weapons is one of the most solemn responsibilities of the president of the United States—the man who is president can never get away from that responsibility and can never forget it.*
>
> — **President Lyndon Baines Johnson**[1]

Since the late 1940s, nuclear weapons have been a major, perhaps even the most important, factor in American military strategy and power. For nearly four decades, the United States has developed and maintained a formidable arsenal of nuclear weaponry, ranging from intercontinental and sea-launched ballistic missiles to relatively small "tactical" weapons.

The power to unleash this awesome force is vested in a single individual. Only the president can authorize the use of nuclear weapons. This is, as President Lyndon Johnson stated on several occasions, the most solemn and grave responsibility the president bears.

This article examines the constitutional and historical basis of the president's exclusive authority to order the use of nuclear weapons. It then describes changes in the nature and requirements of presidential control over strategic nuclear weapons that have occurred since 1945. Finally, it considers the likely evolution of the concepts and means of presidential control in the years ahead.

The Constitutional and Historical Basis of Presidential Control

The fundamental basis of the president's authority with respect to military operations of any kind—including the possible use of nuclear weapons—is the Constitution. Article II, Section 2, states that

> The President shall be Commander-in-Chief of the Army and Navy of the United States, and of the Militia of the several States when called into the actual service of the United States.

Yet, beyond this categorical assertion, the Constitution itself does little to define precisely what the commander-in-chief is supposed to do or just how he is expected to do it. Nevertheless, the president has traditionally been assumed to have extensive powers to control military operations. Various learned commentaries on the power of the commander-in-chief have consistently held that the president may constitutionally do whatever any military commander does in accordance with the usual practice of carrying on war.[2]

Moreover, this power has not been subject to question in the courts or the legislature. While the Supreme Court has considered the

---

This article, written for academic purposes by a U.S. Air Force officer, does not necessarily reflect the views of the U.S. Department of Defense.

propriety of various acts justified in terms of the commander-in-chief clause, it has never challenged the president's authority to give orders to the military regarding operations against a recognized enemy.[3] Indeed, in several cases the Supreme Court specifically noted that the command of forces and the conduct of operations was a power and duty that belonged to the president and the president alone.[4]

Finally, presidents themselves have on occasion claimed an all-inclusive (and exclusive) authority over the military. For example, in 1817 President James Monroe reminded an obstreperous General Andrew Jackson:

> Whatever may be said of the right of a commander of a district and a division to command within his district and division, applies with full force to the president as commander-in-chief of the army. In that character, he is present everywhere, and no officer can, in my judgment, rightfully disobey his order.[5]

The actual, as opposed to permissible, degree of presidential involvement in the direction of military operations, however, varied considerably before the advent of the nuclear age. Each president performed his role as commander-in-chief according to his own personality and administrative style, his trust in the judgment of his subordinates, and the particular circumstances surrounding the conflict at hand. Some presidents—like Madison and Wilson—had very little to do with purely military matters, preferring instead to delegate the responsibilities for the conduct of war to the military departments and services. Others—such as Polk, Lincoln, and Roosevelt—played central and even dominant roles in the formulation of grand strategy.[6] Yet only rarely did presidents exploit their proximity to the battlefield or their access to communications in attempts to control the movements of forces in the field or at sea. Rather, prior to the nuclear age, the wartime commanders-in-chief tended to involve themselves only in setting the general objectives to be pursued by American military forces in an armed conflict. Operational details were generally left to civilian and military subordinates.

The president's experience with nuclear weapons has run counter to this tradition. From the very beginning, the atomic bomb was treated unlike any other weapon in the American arsenal. For example, President Roosevelt personally participated in every major decision concerning the new device during its development by the Manhattan Project. This practice led those officials who were associated with the bomb during the Second World War to assume that the president would make the final decisions concerning its actual use if and when it became available.[7] Roosevelt's successor, President Truman, had little personal impact on the plans and preparations to drop the atomic bombs on Japan. Nevertheless, he was apprised of all major developments and consulted on operational details, such as the target list and the schedule for the atomic bombing missions. More important, after the second atomic attack (on Nagasaki) he specifically made any further use of atomic bombs contingent upon his personal approval.[8]

Based on Roosevelt's and Truman's actions during the Second World War, most American officials *assumed* that only the president could authorize the employment of the atomic bomb. For example, in January 1946, Air Force Major General Hoyt S. Vandenberg predicted that in any future conflict

> the times of attack and targets for atomic bombs will be determined at a very high level—*probably by the president*—and the Strategic Air Force Commander will be charged with the responsibility of carrying out the operations.... [A]ctual operational instructions as to time and place will doubtless come from Washington.[9]

This assumption was reinforced by the passage of the Atomic Energy Act of 1946. This law accorded the president the authority to control the production and disposition of fissionable material and atomic weapons. The president was to decide the number of atomic weapons to be produced by the Atomic Energy Commission each year. He was also empowered to direct the AEC to transfer fissionable materials to the armed forces and to authorize the military to manufacture its own atomic bombs. Finally, the president was recognized as the final arbiter in disputes arising between the civilian Atomic Energy Commission and the military services.[10]

The Atomic Energy Act, in fact, represented an extraordinary grant of authority to the president. As Senator Millikin noted during hearings preceding passage of the law, Congress had traditionally determined the size and structure of the military establishment—such as the number of battleships to be built—under its constitutional powers to "raise and support armies" and "provide and maintain a navy."[11] That the legislators were willing to grant the president this particular role with respect to atomic weapons suggests that they somehow considered them to be altogether different from other categories of weapons and that they were willing to allow the president to continue to exercise many of the extraordinary powers he had wielded in connection with atomic energy during the Second World War.

Still, the actual authority to order the use of nuclear weapons was *never* made explicit during the first three years after Hiroshima and Nagasaki. In retrospect it seems odd that a matter this important was left undefined. Yet, during the first two years following Hiroshima and Nagasaki, there was little reason to question either the validity or the sufficiency of a tacit assumption that the president alone would decide if and when to employ the bomb. In the first place, war was not considered likely. The Soviet Union was the only nation that could pose a serious military threat to U.S. interests, and, although relations with the Soviets had shown increasing signs of strain throughout this period, most American officials had concluded that the Soviets would seek at all costs to avoid war for the immediate future.[12] For want of any danger of its imminent use, the arrangements for operational control of the atomic bomb simply were not an issue. Furthermore, in the event war did occur in 1946 or early 1947, the American military was planning to use the bomb in much the same way it had been used in the Second World War, that is, as the culminating act of a conflict characterized primarily by major conventional ground, naval, and air campaigns.[13] Under these circumstances, the respective roles of the commander-in-chief and the military in atomic operations could be worked out during the early stages of the conflict. Finally, under the provisions of the Atomic Energy Act, the entire atomic weapons stockpile was in the custody of the Atomic Energy Commission. As long as the nation's atomic bombs were stored under the control of the civilian commission, the armed services could not use the bomb until the president had at least directed the AEC to transfer weapons to them.

However, by the end of 1947 and throughout 1948, two different developments brought the atomic bomb to the forefront of American foreign and military policy and, in the process, forced civilian and military officials to consider virtually every facet of the nascent American atomic strategy, including the unwritten assumptions concerning the president's authority to order the bomb's use. First, during early 1947, the armed services—which had at first downplayed the military significance of the bomb—began to view the new device as an increasingly important element of national power and an indispensable, even potentially decisive, weapon of war. By 1948, the Joint Chiefs of Staff was basing its short-term, or emergency, plan for a possible war with the Soviet Union on the assumption that the United States would initiate a sustained atomic bombing offensive immediately after the start of major hostilities. The outbreak of war would, according to the JCS war plans, call for an early decision to employ the bomb.[14] Simple prudence dictated that the authority to make such a decision be defined well ahead of time so that the military would know what to expect and what actions they were allowed to take in crisis situations.

Second, during 1948, the military made a concerted effort to win Truman's support for the transfer of custody of atomic weapons from the civilian Atomic Energy Commission to the military establishment. This effort was motivated, in part, by the perceived need to use atomic weapons at the early stages of any major war.[15] Though Truman personally had doubts about the JCS emergency war plans and he vetoed the military's bid for custody, both developments raised questions about the ultimate authority to order the use of atomic weapons. Some officials—including the president's own military chief of staff and the secretary of the army—apparently felt that this authority did not necessarily have to reside in the person of the president.[16]

Against this background, the National Security Council explicitly addressed the authority to order the use of nuclear weapons in the summer of 1948. In doing so, the NSC unequivocally concluded that: "The decision as to the employment of atomic weapons in the event of war is to be made by the Chief Executive when he considers such decision to be required."[17] What had previously been assumed was thus made explicit: only the president could order the use of nuclear weapons.

The ultimate manifestations of the president's new formal role were barely perceptible in 1948. Those officials who were responsible for drafting and approving the NSC report could have had no more than an inkling of the strategic environment characterized by thermonuclear weapons, intercontinental ballistic missiles, instantaneous global communications, and a doctrine of deterrence based on the prospect of mutual annihilation. The principle of exclusive presidential control over the use of nuclear weapons was to remain unchanged. Yet, as the strategic environment—as well as the president's perceived role within that environment—grew more complex, the concepts associated with the maintenance and possible exercise of presidential control underwent significant changes.

The Changing Concepts of Presidential Control

The Truman Administration

Between 1948 and 1952, presidential control was assured by the division of responsibility for atomic operations between the Atomic Energy Commission and the military. President Truman recognized that civilian custody of atomic weapons precluded the military from using them without his expressed approval. Partly for this reason, he refused to accede to the military's bid for routine custody of the atomic stockpile. However, Truman's staunch opposition to military custody was ultimately undermined by three developments. First, the ability of the relatively small AEC to carry out the custody function was increasingly taxed. The military had, in fact, already assumed considerable responsibility and expertise in that function and could claim that it was fully qualified technically to assume custody.[18] At the same time, the continued emphasis on an early atomic offensive in the American emergency war plans implied that the military should be prepared to conduct atomic strikes with very little notice. The storage of weapons at a few stateside locations by a civilian organization worked against this perceived requirement. Finally, a number of incremental steps had already been taken in the direction of military custody during the first year of the Korean War. First, non-nuclear components were transferred to military custody for storage in Europe and the Pacific.[19] Then a small number of complete bombs were handed over to the air force on April 1951 when it appeared that the Chinese might launch a major offensive against United Nations forces.[20] Thus, in 1952, Truman agreed that the military could assume custody for a portion of the atomic stockpile to insure "operational flexibility and military readiness for use."[21]

From 1952 onwards, the military gained control over a steadily increasing portion of a steadily growing stockpile. When U.S. strategic offensive and defensive nuclear forces were put on 15-minute alert in case of a Soviet nuclear attack, and atomic weapons were integrated into tactical operations during the 1950s, custody by the delivery unit became a necessity. By the early 1960s almost all operational atomic weapons were under military custody.[22] As was noted earlier, AEC custody over the entire stockpile had insured that the bomb would not be used without presidential approval. The transfer of an increasing portion of the stockpile to the military signaled the end of this system of control.

As custody of nuclear weapons passed from the AEC to the armed forces, control over the use of nuclear weapons came to depend entirely upon the principle of military subordination to the authority of the commander-in-chief. The Truman administration had little time to grapple with the practical implications of this change. The task of developing new concepts and procedures for maintaining presidential control under the conditions of military custody correspondingly fell to the Eisenhower administration.

The Eisenhower Administration

During the 1950s, the nature and requirements of presidential control were largely determined by the so-called "massive retaliation doctrine." The doctrine itself was accepted and championed by President Eisenhower, who viewed it as a means of achieving American national security objectives with minimum disruption of the American economy. It implied that the American response to an attack on the United States or a major ally would be an immediate, all-out nuclear counterattack on the aggressor.[23] The President privately gave every indication that he would not shrink from authorizing the use of nuclear weapons in the event of war. For example, in a conversation with Admiral Radford and Army Chief of Staff Maxwell Taylor in May 1956, Eisenhower stated that it was "fatuous" to think the U.S. and the Soviet Union could ever engage in a major conflict without using the bomb. Consequently, the U.S. should develop its military plans on the assumption that atomic weapons would be employed by both sides. "Massive retaliation," in his words, was "likely to be the key to survival."[24]

After both the United States and the Soviet Union had deployed the immensely powerful hydrogen bomb, Eisenhower downplayed the "warfighting" aspects of nuclear weapons and stressed instead the importance of perfecting the American strategic deterrent.[25] If, however, deterrence failed, Eisenhower claimed it was clear in his mind that the United States would attack "cities and government concentrations."[26] At an NSC meeting in October 1960, he observed that the United States was so committed to nuclear weapons that the only practical course of action would be to start using them at the beginning of any major conflict, and if the Russians were directly involved, mount an all-out strike against the Soviet Union.[27]

The Eisenhower administration's concept of strategic nuclear warfare had important implications for the president's role in actually exercising control over the use of nuclear weapons. It suggested that the president would have to perform two functions in the event of war. First, since he was the only individual who could order the use of nuclear weapons, he would have to decide whether the circumstances warranted American retaliation. Just what those circumstances might be was never specified during the 1950s, despite the emphasis placed on massive retaliation in American foreign and defense policy. However, one can infer from Eisenhower's private remarks that a direct attack on the United States, or a major attack involving the Soviet Union against an American ally, were conditions the President personally felt would justify American nuclear retaliation.

The second aspect of the president's role in exercising control over nuclear weapons was to order the strategic forces to conduct nuclear strikes in accordance with their emergency war plan. The president had a very similar role with respect to nuclear operations during the late 1940s and early 1950s. There was, however, one crucial difference. During the late 1940s, an American atomic offensive would have lasted several days, maybe even weeks. The president could presumably have ordered the U.S. Air Force to initiate the emergency war plan and then terminate it after only a few strikes had been made and comparatively little damage had been inflicted. Under the assumptions of the massive retaliation doctrine, a presidential decision to use strategic nuclear weapons was essentially an all-or-nothing affair. There was only one "option" in the war plan. According to congressional testimony, the Strategic Air Command (SAC) intended to mount its preplanned attacks as quickly as possible in order to destroy enemy nuclear capabilities on the ground and thereby limit damage to American strategic forces and cities. Additionally, SAC did not plan to hold weapons in reserve for follow-up attacks.[28] Thus, there would be no reason (and probably no opportunity) for the president to attempt to control nuclear operations after he sent out the initial "go-code."

The doctrine of massive retaliation and the president's role in the event of nuclear war were relatively straightforward. There were, however, complicating factors. For the first half of the 1950s, the process of determining whether retaliation was necessary and sending out the go-code could have been pursued at whatever pace the president preferred. As long as the president and the American strategic nuclear forces were not in any imminent danger, the United States response to major enemy provocation could, in theory at least, have been delayed for a considerable period of time. However, this assumption changed dramatically during the course of the Eisenhower administration. The emergence of a Soviet capability to attack the United States with nuclear weapons suggested that the president might have to make a decision to retaliate very rapidly. Moreover, special procedures had to be adopted to allow the strategic bomber forces to escape from their bases upon first warning of an enemy attack, yet still remain under the control of the president.

The key innovation for protecting the bomber forces and maintaining presidential control was a set of operational procedures known as "positive control," or, more popularly, "fail safe." Under the positive control system, the SAC commander was authorized to launch his bombers in the event he received warning of an attack from the various radar networks operated by the North American Air Defense Command (NORAD). The order to launch was not, however, equivalent to an order to use the nuclear weapons on board the aircraft. Once airborne, the bombers would fly to a designated point and then return to base *unless* they received coded voice instructions to proceed on to their targets. According to General Thomas Power, former SAC Commander:

> The "go-code" can be given only upon direct orders of the president, and it must be authenticated by officers at each of several levels of command and by more than one member of the bomber crew. Coordinated action by several crew members is also required to arm nuclear weapons after the "go-code" has been received and authenticated.... [If] a bomber should not receive the attack order or if there is any doubt whatever regarding proper authentication, that bomber would turn back after reaching the "Positive Control" point.[29]

In other words, the system was designed to maintain presidential control over the weapons on board the aircraft by insuring that the bombers would not attack their targets unless they received explicit orders to do so. The positive control concept still assumed that the president would have to make a very quick decision concerning retaliation if warning of attack proved to be accurate. The potential costs of delay were severe. As Eisenhower wrote to Winston Churchill in 1955:

> I think it is possible that the very life of a nation, perhaps even of Western civilization, could, for example, come to depend on instantaneous reaction to news of an approaching air fleet; victory or defeat could hang upon minutes and seconds used decisively at top speed or tragically wasted in indecision.[30]

To this end, the Eisenhower administration streamlined the chain of command between the president and the JCS combatant commands, including the Strategic Air Command. During the 1958 reorganization of the Department of Defense, the JCS lost all vestiges of their formal command authority.[31] This had the effect of placing the president (and his secretary of defense) in more direct control of military operations of all kinds. In a related move, faster and more reliable communications systems were developed by the military for the strategic nuclear forces.

By the end of the Eisenhower era, the positive control concept constituted only a partial solution to the problem of maintaining and exercising presidential control over strategic nuclear weapons. In October 1959, the first American intercontinental ballistic missiles were placed on a fifteen-minute alert at Vandenberg Air Force Base. A year later the first *Polaris* submarine went on patrol armed with sixteen sea-launched ballistic missiles.[32] These new, fast-reacting strategic weapons gave rise to fundamentally new problems of control that had to be addressed. At the same time, many observers were expressing doubt about the massive retaliation doctrine in terms of its credibility as a deterrent threat and its rationality as a wartime strategy. Noted strategists, soldiers, and politicians called for the adoption of a strategic nuclear doctrine that would permit the president greater flexibility in the employment of nuclear weapons. These issues were at the top of the next administration's national security agenda.

The Kennedy Administration

During the early 1960s, the Kennedy administration placed considerable emphasis on the maintenance of presidential control over nuclear weapons. This concern was motivated in part by a general desire on the part of administration officials to exercise more direct control over military operations of all kinds. Kennedy, in contrast to Eisenhower, was an activist president. He intended to be "in the thick of things," including military activities.[33] Kennedy's natural inclination to be involved in all aspects of his office was reinforced by his early experiences in the Bay of Pigs fiasco. According to two close aides, Kennedy was embittered by what he regarded as poor advice from the JCS on the military aspects of the CIA operation. As a result, the White House assumed more responsibility for making national security decisions.[34] Thus, for example, during the Cuban missile crisis, Kennedy followed closely the movement of Soviet ships approaching Cuba as depicted on the maps in the White House situation room. In addition, he personally made several decisions regarding the operation of the quarantine, including the decision to move the quarantine line closer to Cuba than the navy preferred.[35] In both instances, Kennedy had chosen to exert a far more immediate and detailed influence over military operations than was traditionally expected or displayed by the commander-in-chief.

In addition to a general desire to exercise highly centralized and detailed control over executive branch activities, including military operations of all kinds, the Kennedy administration's intense interest in the maintenance of presidential control over the use of strategic nuclear weapons can also be attributed to a concern about the possibility of accidental war. During the late 1950s and early 1960s, there was considerable discussion in the American strategic literature about ways in which the inadvertent or unauthorized use of nuclear weapons by either the United States or the Soviet Union could result in an all-out nuclear exchange. The speculative literature on accidental war obviously made an impression on Kennedy administration officials. For example, in his March 1961 message to Congress on the defense budget, the president noted:

> Our defense posture must be designed to reduce the danger of irrational or unpremeditated general war.... We must make certain that our retaliatory power does not rest on decisions made in ambiguous circumstances, or permit a catastrophic mistake.[36]

The Kennedy administration adopted two approaches to reducing the risks of accidental war. The first was to reduce the vulnerability of U.S. strategic nuclear forces so that the president would not be tempted to order their use upon first warning of enemy nuclear attack. Specifically, the administration decided as early as March 1961 to step up deployment of more survivable silo-based and sea-based strategic missiles.[37]

The administration's second approach to reducing the risk of accidental war was to take additional measures to preclude the use of nuclear weapons unless such use was specifically authorized by the president. This effort involved two aspects. The first was to ensure that the president, as well as his communications links to the strategic forces, would survive and operate effectively under the conditions likely to exist during nuclear war. To increase the president's chances of surviving and remaining in control during a nuclear war, the administration established mobile emergency command posts for use by the president on board ships and aircraft.[38] At the same time, air force and navy programs to enhance the survivability and capabilities of the command control and communications systems associated with their strategic nuclear forces were encouraged.[39]

Additionally, with support from the White House, the Department of Defense established several different procedures to reduce the risk of accidental or unauthorized nuclear detonation resulting from human error or aberration. For example, under the so-called two-man rule, all tasks involved in the use of nuclear weapons were to be structured in such a way as to require separate actions on the part of two or more persons for their completion. Moreover, each individual involved in these tasks was to be trained to detect unauthorized or incorrect actions on the part of the others involved.[40] The Defense Department also inaugurated a program in 1962 to insure that emotionally unreliable or psychotic individuals were not assigned to or maintained in positions involving access to nuclear weapons or their controls.⁴¹ Finally, in July 1962, Kennedy reportedly asked Congress to increase the Atomic Energy Commission budget by $23.3 million in order to install "electronic locks" for American tactical nuclear weapons.⁴² The ultimate purpose of each of these nuclear weapon safety programs was to guarantee the inviolability of presidential control over nuclear weapons. Separately and in combination they served to reduce the chances that any one individual or group of individuals could deliberately or inadvertently cause the use of nuclear weapons without explicit approval from the president. As a result, the remote possibility of unauthorized or accidental use was rendered even more remote.

Perhaps the most significant factor behind the Kennedy administration's emphasis on presidential control was the adoption of a new doctrine regarding the manner in which strategic nuclear weapons might be employed in the event of nuclear war. In a speech in February, Secretary of Defense McNamara described for the first time in public the so-called controlled response doctrine that had been adopted by the Administration.

> Our forces can be used in several different ways. We may have to retaliate with a single massive attack. Or, we may be able to use our retaliatory forces to limit damage done to ourselves, and our allies, by knocking out the enemy's bases before he has had time to launch his second salvos.... Our new policy gives us the flexibility to choose among several operational plans, but does not require that we make any advance commitment with respect to doctrine or targets. We shall be committed only to a system that gives us the ability to use our forces in a controlled and deliberate way.⁴³

In other words, instead of having only one option to choose in the event of nuclear war as implied by the massive retaliation doctrine, the president would now have a few options from which to choose.

This change in U.S. strategic doctrine had important implications for the maintenance and exercise of presidential control over the use of nuclear weapons. It suggested that the president would have to perform a qualitatively different, more complex role in the event of nuclear war. Specifically, the president would have to decide not only whether the United States should retaliate, but also which particular option should be executed if retaliation were deemed appropriate. Since the nature of the American response was supposed to be determined in part by the nature of the provocation, the president would also be required to assess the nature and intention of the enemy attack and to calculate the probable outcome and effect of the options available. In other words, the president's decision would not be nearly so automatic under the controlled response doctrine as it was under the massive retaliation doctrine. Rather, it would require a higher degree of judgment under extremely difficult conditions.

Moreover, it also required a more extensive and enduring degree of control over the operations of the strategic nuclear forces. Under the massive retaliation doctrine, once the president was committed to nuclear war and his general order to attack had been sent, the president had no further need to exercise control over the strategic forces. However, the controlled response doctrine suggested that presidential control would have to be maintained through a series of nuclear exchanges with an adversary. In practical terms, this required steps be taken to insure that the president and his communication links with the American strategic nuclear forces could survive a nuclear attack on the United States. For this reason, as well as the desire to reduce the risks of accidental war, the Kennedy administration pushed the development of alternate command posts for the president and for less vulnerable communications from Washington to the strategic forces.

The Nixon Administration to the Present

The Kennedy administration put in place the basic concepts of presidential control over strategic weapons that continue to operate today. Successive administrations have, for the most part, merely extended and amplified the developments started in the early 1960s. They have done so in two important ways.

First, the president has been provided the means to exercise more direct control over military operations of all kinds. In 1962, Secretary of Defense McNamara had created the National and Worldwide Military Command

Systems to provide a single "command and control system" to support the so-called national command authorities, which include the president.[44] In response to the notable failures of the military command system during the late 1960s and the early 1970s (e.g., the North Korean seizure of the *Pueblo* in January 1968) and the criticism that ensued, the Nixon administration revised the charter of the Worldwide Military Command and Control System to provide for direct communication between the president and the secretary of defense, and the commanders of any military forces engaged in crisis or strategic nuclear operations.[45] The Defense Department and the military services correspondingly placed greater emphasis on fielding faster, more reliable communications systems, especially taking advantage of the relatively new satellite communications technology. At least one president was not averse to using the capabilities to monitor military operations afforded by rapid, worldwide communication. During the *Mayaguez* crisis in May 1975, President Gerald Ford personally approved the details of the rescue operations and closely watched their implementation.[46]

Second, since 1962, successive administrations have steadily increased the number of options available to the president in the event of nuclear war. For example, in 1974, Secretary of Defense James Schlesinger announced publicly that a change had taken place "in the strategies of the United States with regard to the hypothetical employment of central strategic forces."[47] The purpose of the announced change was to provide the president more options than provided by changes made in the strategic doctrine during the Kennedy-Johnson period. Schlesinger described the change as giving the president the option of "limiting strikes down to a few weapons."[48]

The momentum of these changes continued well into the Carter Administration. For example, in August 1980, Secretary of Defense Harold Brown noted:

> Implementing our strategy requires us to make some changes in our operational planning, such as gradually increasing the scope, variety, and flexibility of options open to us should the Soviets choose aggression. Some of this has already been done since 1977. More need to be done.[49]

The emphasis on targeting flexibility and more limited nuclear options had important implications for the concept of presidential control. The president's role in controlling the implementation of limited nuclear options is conceptually more difficult than the task of responding to massive attacks with massive options. The president would in effect have to make a series of very detailed decisions regarding the operations of strategic nuclear forces—such as the kind of targets to be attacked, the number of weapons involved, timing, and so on. The image conjured up by this role is that of Lyndon Johnson attempting to control the scope and pace of the American bombing campaign against North Vietnam from the White House Situation Room. (Indeed, the objectives of the two roles are conceptually very similar: to achieve American political-military objectives without resorting to total war.) Put another way, the incorporation of limited nuclear options into the American military plans has in a sense transformed the president into a theater commander, with strategic nuclear weapons as the forces under his command and the world as his theater of operations.

As for providing the president with the capabilities necessary to perform this role, successive administrations have described command, control, and communications as the single most important factor.[50] In order to direct the execution of limited nuclear options, the president would require systems that were survivable and capable of providing a fairly detailed assessment of the character of an enemy attack, transmitting perhaps several different messages over an extended period of time, retargeting surviving forces to carry out follow-on options (some of which might be formulated on an *ad hoc* basis), and reporting back the effect of those options. Thus, for the past several years, both the air force and the navy have been engaged in efforts to improve the survivability of the communications links to their strategic nuclear forces. The Defense Department has also pursued development of an advanced airborne command post to provide the president a greater capability to control nuclear operations from a mobile (and thus more survivable) command post, improved satellite communications systems, and a less vulnerable system for communicating with nuclear submarines.

The Future

At the risk of falling prey to the dangers that typically confront those who presume to speculate about the future, it might be useful to consider the likely course of the evolution of the concept and means of presidential control in the years ahead. First, it seems unlikely that the president will relinquish his exclusive authority to order the use of nuclear weapons by delegating that authority to subordinate officials. Ever since the Roosevelt administration, presidents have jealously guarded their prerogatives with respect to nuclear weapons and have taken various measures to insure that they retain ultimate control over their possible use. In light of this precedent, the political obstacles to changing this policy would be considerable, even if there seemed to be compelling military reasons for doing so.

Since the president is likely to insist on retaining exclusive control over strategic nuclear weapons, efforts will continue to be made to ensure that he can exercise that authority in the manner suggested by the prevailing strategic doctrine. The exploitation of advanced communications technology will probably continue to be the dominant approach to providing the president with the capabilities he is expected to require in controlling strategic nuclear operations. Given the possible development of enemy counters to such developments—such as anti-satellite weapons—the process of technological refinement will most likely continue unabated.

In many respects, the evolution toward an increasingly detailed role for the president in controlling nuclear operations would seem to have reached its practical limit. The current nuclear weapons doctrine already suggests that the president should be able to control nuclear operations down to implementation of preplanned options involving perhaps only a handful of weapons. Moreover, Secretary of Defense Schlesinger suggested in 1975 that the president might also require a capability to fashion options on an *ad hoc* basis in the midst of a crisis.[51] It is difficult to imagine how the president could be expected to exercise a control over nuclear weapons any more detailed than would be provided by a "real-time" retargeting capability responsive to presidential direction.

Finally, the principle of exclusive presidential control may well be extended in some form to additional weapons systems. A recent trend in weapons technology has been the development of increasingly accurate and powerful non-nuclear weapons. As a result, the distinction between "conventional" and "nuclear," or "strategic" and "tactical," weapons is becoming blurred. In the near future, it may well be possible to employ non-nuclear weapons in roles previously assigned to nuclear forces. Since the employment of new weapons in such roles may have all the political and military implications of the employment of strategic nuclear weapons—including the possibility of strategic nuclear retaliation—the president may choose to assume personal control over the decisions concerning their use. The end result may be an even further extension of the degree of control the commander-in-chief is expected to exercise over the operations of American military forces.

Notes

1. U.S., President, *Public Papers of the Presidents of the United States, Lyndon B. Johnson, 1963-1964* Washington, D.C.: U.S. Government Printing Office), ii, 890.

2. For example, Clarence A. Berdahl, *War Powers of the Executive in the United States* (Urbana: University of Illinois Studies in the Social Sciences, 1920), chap. vii; and Louis Henkin, *Foreign Affairs and the Constitution* (Mineola, N.Y.: Foundation Press, 1972), 50-53.

3. Cases involving the powers claimed under the commander-in-chief clause are discussed in Clinton Rossiter, *The Supreme Court and the Commander-in-Chief,* rev. ed. (Ithaca, N.Y.: Cornell University Press, 1976).

4. Especially, Fleming, *et al.*, v. Page, 9 Howard (U.S.) 646 (1850) and *Ex parte* Milligan, 4 Wallace (U.S.) 139 (1866).

5. Monroe to Jackson, Oct. 5, 1817, in John S. Bassett, ed., *Correspondence of Andrew Jackson* (Washington, D.C.: Carnegie Institute, 1927), ii, 330.

6. The best single account of the actions of the "wartime commanders-in-chief" is Ernest R. May, ed., *The Ultimate Decision: The President as Commander-in-Chief* (New York: George Braziller, 1960).

7. See, for example, Leslie R. Groves, *Now It Can Be Told: The Story of the Manhattan Project* (New York, Harper and Bros., 1962), 271. Groves headed the Manhattan Project.

8. Groves to Marshall, Aug. 10, 1945 (with handwritten notations by General Marshall), Top Secret Manhattan Project File, Records of the Manhattan Engineering District, Record Group 77, National Archives, Washington, D. C.

9. Vandenberg to Lieutenant General Ira Eaker, Jan. 2, 1946, "Subject: The Establishment of a Strategic Striking Force," File No. 145.86-90 (45-46), Simpson Historical Research Center, Maxwell Air Force Base, Alabama. Emphasis added.

10. The Atomic Energy Act of 1946, Public Law 79-585 (60 Stat. 755), sec. 2 and 6.

11. U.S., Congress, Senate, Special Committee on Atomic Energy, *Atomic Energy Act of 1946*, Hearings, 79th Cong., 2nd Sess. (1946), i, 82, and ii, 126.

12. See, for example, U.S., Department of State, *Foreign Relations of the United States, 1946* (Washington, D.C.: U.S. Government Printing Office, 1972), i, 1165-66, 1170-71.

13. JCS 1477/5, Jan. 12, 1946, "Statement of the Effect of Atomic Weapons on National Security and Military Organization," 471.6 (8-15-45), sec. 1, Records of the Joint Chiefs of Staff, Record Group 218, National Archives, Washington, D.C. (hereinafter referred to as JCS Records).

14. See the early and final drafts of the JCS war plans in JCS Records, 381 (USSR) 3-2-46).

15. Brereton to Lilienthal, Nov. 12, 1947, 471.6 (8-15-46), sec. 8, JCS Records.

16. Leahy to JCS, JCS 1854/1, March 29, 1948, 471.6 (8-15-45), sec. 9, JCS Records; Royall to the NSC, May 19, 1948, reproduced in the U.S., Department of State, *Foreign Relations of the United States, 1948*, vol. 1 (Washington, D.C.: U.S. Government Printing Office, 1976) i, 572.

17. NSC-30, Sept. 10, 1948, "United States Policy on Atomic Warfare," reproduced in ibid., 624-28.

18. Richard G. Hewlett and Francis Duncan, *A History of the Atomic Energy Commission*, vol. 2: *Atomic Shield, 1947/1952* (University Park: Pennsylvania State University Press), 537.

19. Lay to Dean, June 14, 1950, Atomic Weapons—Non-nuclear components folder, NSC Atomic file, President's Secretary's Files, Harry S. Truman Library, Independence, Missouri.

20. Hewlett and Duncan, *Atomic Shield*, 538-39. Marshall to Truman, April 9, 1951, with encl. Bradley to Marshall, April 5, 1951, Joint Chiefs of Staff folder, General file, President's Secretary's Files, Truman Library.

21. Lay to the Secretary of State, et al., July 3, 1952, Atomic Weapons—Agreed Concepts folder, NSC Atomic file, President's Secretary's Files, Truman Library, and Lay, Memorandum for the President, Sept. 10, 1952, ibid.

22. Colonel C. B. Stewart, "The Air Force Nuclear Weapon Safety Program," *Proceedings of the American Nuclear Society, Trinity Section* (Oct. 1963), 361.

23. NSC-162/2, Oct. 30, 1953, "Basic National Security Policy," reproduced in Senator Mike Gravel, ed., *The Pentagon Papers* (Boston, Mass.: Beacon Press, 1971), i, 412-29.

24. Goodpaster, Memorandum of Conference with the President, May 24, 1956, May 1956 Goodpaster folder, DDE Diary Series, Ann Whitman File, Dwight D. Eisenhower Library, Abilene, Kansas.

25. This attitude is noted in, for example, Goodpaster, Memorandum of Conference with the President (Nov. 5, 1959), Nov. 6, 1959, Staff Notes Nov. 1959 (3) folder, ibid.

26. Goodpaster, Memorandum of Conference with the President (Nov. 21, 1959), Jan. 2, 1960, Staff Notes Nov. 1959 (2) folder, ibid.

27. George B. Kistiakowsky, *A Scientist at the White House: The Private Diary of President Eisenhower's Special Assistant for Science and Technology* (Cambridge, Mass.: Harvard University Press, 1976), 400.

28. U.S., Congress, Committee on Armed Services, *Study of Air Power*, Hearings, 84th Cong., 2nd Sess., (1956), 171.

29. General Thomas S. Power, *Design for Survival* (New York: Coward-McCann, 1964), 155-56.

30. Eisenhower to Churchill, Jan. 25, 1955, DDE Diary Series, Ann Whitman File, Eisenhower Library.

31. U.S., President, *Public Papers of the Presidents of the United States, Dwight D. Eisenhower, 1958* (Washington, D.C.: U.S. Government Printing Office, 1959), 280-81; Public Law 85-577 (72 Stat. 514).

32. U.S., Strategic Air Command, Office of the Historian, *Development of the Strategic Air Command, 1946-1976*, March 1976, pp. 79-80; U.S., Department of the Navy, *FBM Facts: Polaris, Poseidon, Trident* (Washington, D.C.: U.S. Government Printing Office, 1978), 4-11.

33. Quoted in Joseph Kraft, "Kennedy's Working Staff," *Harper's Magazine*, 225 (Dec. 1962), 35.

34. Theodore C. Sorensen, *Kennedy* (New York: Harper and Row, 1965), p. 305; Arthur Schlesinger, *A Thousand Days: John F. Kennedy in the White House* (Boston, Mass.: Houghton Mifflin, 1965), 290, 296-97.

35. Sorensen, *Kennedy*, 708, 710; Graham T. Allison, *Essence of Decision: Explaining the Cuban Missile Crisis* (Boston, Mass.: Little Brown, 1971), 127-130.

36. U.S., President, *Public Papers of the President of the United States, John F. Kennedy, 1961* (Washington, D.C.: U.S. Government Printing Office, 1962), 232.

37. Ibid., 233-36.

38. Major General John B. Bestic, "NMCS Affords U.S. Full Control of Flexible Response," *Data*, 12 (Jan. 1967), 29.

39. U.S., President, *Public Papers, 1961*, 235-36.

40. U.S., Department of Defense, DOD Directive 5210.41, Dec. 8, 1962, "Criteria and Standards for Safeguarding Atomic Weapons."

41. U.S., Department of Defense, DOD Directive 5210.42, Dec. 8, 1962, "Reliability of Personnel Assigned to Duties Involving Nuclear Weapons and Nuclear Weapons Systems."

42. *New York Times*, July 6, 1962, 1, 6.

43. Quoted in William W. Kaufmann, *The Mc-*

Namara Strategy (New York: Harper and Row, 1964), 75.

44. U.S., Congress, House, Committee on Armed Services, *Hearings on Military Posture and H.R. 2440,* 88th Cong., 1st Sess. (1963), 488.

45. U.S., Department of Defense, DOD Directive 5100.30, Dec. 2, 1971, "World-wide Military Command and Control System."

46. Richard G. Head, Frisco Short, and Robert C. McFarland, *Crisis Resolution: Presidential Decision Making in the Mayaguez and Korean Confrontations* (Boulder, Colo.: Westview Press, 1978), 106 ff.

47. U.S., Department of Defense, Office of Public Affairs, "Remarks by Secretary of Defense James R. Schlesinger," Overseas Writers Association, Jan. 10, 1974.

48. U.S., Congress, Senate, Committee on Foreign Relations, *U.S.-U.S.S.R. Strategic Policies,* Hearings, 93rd Cong., 2nd Sess. (1975), 9.

49. Secretary of Defense Harold Brown, "Remarks at Naval War College," Aug. 20, 1980, reprinted in U.S., Department of the Air Force (SAFAA), *Selected Statements,* Sept. 1, 1980.

50. See, for example, James Schlesinger's testimony in U.S., Congress, Senate, Committee on Foreign Relations, *U.S.-U.S.S.R. Strategic Policies,* 24.

51. U.S., Congress, Senate, Committee on Foreign Relations, *Briefing on Counterforce Attacks,* Hearings, 93rd Cong., 2nd Sess. (1975), 37.

Presidents View Their Office 1.4

Debate about the proper roles and powers of the president is as old as the republic itself. The debate is best focused on the statements of presidents themselves concerning how the duties of the office should be approached and exercised. The following classic essays by two former presidents illustrate different conceptions of presidential roles. Theodore Roosevelt advocates a more activist presidency, while William Howard Taft counsels for a more restricted view. In reading these we should keep in mind the advantages and disadvantages of each approach. Questions for consideration are: (1) What are the pros and cons of each conception? (2) Do modern conditions permit presidents to take a literal restricted role?

1.4a   The Stewardship Doctrine

Theodore Roosevelt

The most important factor in getting the right spirit in my administration, next to the insistence upon courage, honesty, and a genuine democracy of desire to serve the plain people, was my insistence upon the theory that the executive power was limited only by specific restrictions and prohibitions appearing in the Constitution or imposed by the Congress under its constitutional powers. My view was that every executive officer, and above all every executive officer in high position, was a steward of the people bound actively and affirmatively to do all he could for the people, and not to content himself with the negative merit of keeping his talents undamaged in a napkin. I declined to adopt the view that what was imperatively necessary for the nation could not be done by the president unless he could find some specific authorization to do it. My belief was that it was not only his right but his duty to do anything that the needs of the nation demanded unless such action was forbidden by the Constitution or by the laws. Under this interpretation of executive power I did and caused to be done many things not previously done by the president and the heads of the departments. I did not usurp power, but I did greatly broaden the use of executive power. In other words, I acted for the public welfare, I acted for the common well-being of all our people, whenever and in whatever manner was necessary, unless prevented by direct constitutional or legislative prohibition. I did not care a rap for the mere form and show of power; I cared immensely for the use that could be made of the substance.

An Autobiography (p. 357) by Theodore Roosevelt, 1924, New York: Charles Scribner's Sons. Copyright 1913 by Charles Scribner's Sons. Reprinted by permission.

1.4b A Restricted View of the Office

William Howard Taft

While it is important to mark out the exclusive field of jurisdiction of each branch of the government, legislative, executive and judicial, it should be said that in the proper working of the government there must be co-operation of all branches, and without a willingness of each branch to perform its function, there will follow a hopeless obstruction to the progress of the whole government. Neither branch can compel the other to affirmative action, and each branch can greatly hinder the other in the attainment of the object of its activities and the exercise of its discretion.

. . . The true view of the executive function is, as I conceive it, that the president can exercise no power which cannot be fairly and reasonably traced to some specific grant of power or justly implied and included within such express grant as proper and necessary to its exercise. Such specific grant must be either in the federal constitution or in an act of Congress passed in pursuance thereof. There is no undefined residuum of power which he can exercise because it seems to him to be in the public interest, and there is nothing in the Neagle case and its definition of a law of the United States, or in other precedents, warranting such an inference. The grants of executive power are necessarily in general terms in order not to embarrass the executive within the field of action plainly marked for him, but his jurisdiction must be justified and vindicated by affirmative constitutional or statutory provision, or it does not exist. There have not been wanting, however, eminent men in high public office holding a different view and who have insisted upon the necessity for an undefined residuum of executive power in the public interest. They have not been confined to the present generation.

. . . I may add that Mr. Roosevelt, by way of illustrating his meaning as to the differing usefulness of presidents, divides the presidents into two classes, and designates them as "Lincoln presidents" and "Buchanan presidents." In order more fully to illustrate his division of presidents on their merits, he places himself in the Lincoln class of presidents, and me in the Buchanan class. The identification of Mr. Roosevelt with Mr. Lincoln might otherwise have escaped notice, because there are many differences between the two, presumably superficial, which would give the impartial student of history a different impression. It suggests a story which a friend of mine told of his little daughter Mary. As he came walking home after a business day, she ran out from the house to greet him, all aglow with the importance of what she wished to tell him. She said, "Papa, I am the best scholar in the class." The father's heart throbbed with pleasure as he inquired, "Why, Mary, you surprise me. When did the teacher tell you? This afternoon?" "Oh, no," Mary's reply was, "the teacher didn't tell me—I just noticed it myself."

My judgment is that the view of Mr. Garfield and Mr. Roosevelt, ascribing an undefined residuum of power to the president is an unsafe doctrine and that it might lead under emergencies to results of an arbitrary character, doing irremediable injustice to private right. The mainspring of such a view is that the executive is charged with responsibility for the welfare of all the people in a general way, that he is to play the part of a Universal Providence and set all things right, and that anything that in his judgment will help the people he ought to do, unless he is expressly forbidden not to do it. The wide field of action that this would give to the executive one can hardly limit.

Out Chief Magistrate and His Powers (pp. 138-40) by William Howard Taft, 1925, New York: Columbia University Press. Copyright 1916 by Columbia University Press. Reprinted by permission.

Presidents: How They Get to the White House

2

Presidential elections are high-theater melodramas, conducted under myriad federal and state rules and regulations. Actually, the "road to the White House" involves two separate contests—the quest for the nomination and the campaign for the general election—and each can be subdivided further into substages. Figure 2.1 displays those various substages. It should be emphasized that each has its own dynamics and characteristics.

The strategies candidates use to get nominated are quite different from those used to get elected. In fact, candidate strengths and strategies successful in nominating politics may be liabilities in general election campaign politics, and vice versa.

Figure 2.1

Stages of the Road to the White House

Quest for the Nomination

- preliminaries—the "invisible primaries"
- the hunt for delegates
  — early primaries and caucuses
  — middle primaries
  — late primaries
- preconvention interlude
- the conventions

The Campaign for the General Election

- early days (Labor Day to late September)
- adjustment phase (late September to mid-October)
- time's up (late October to election day)

The game of presidential recruitment has been altered drastically in the last twenty-five years. The most obvious development has been the decline of political parties at both the organizational level and the level of the voting behavior of citizens. Other major developments are the increase in media coverage, the growth of campaign industries (and therefore the growth of campaign costs), and public financing. Frequently, amidst the campaign hoopla, we lose sight of the fact that the electoral gauntlet has a significant impact on how the eventual winner exercises power. In other words, how presidential aspirants seek power will strongly influence the perspective from which presidential power is wielded.

Essays in this chapter focus on how the selection process affects presidential power. With inevitable and multiple proposals for reform of the presidential selection process (a national primary, change or abolishment of the electoral college, party renewal), students should be prepared to discuss the proposed modifications in terms of consequences for the functioning of the presidency and the making of public policy.

2.1 The Brittle Mandate

Everett Carll Ladd

The 1980 election reflects major trends in presidential elections that have been unfolding since 1958-1960. In this important analysis of 1980 and the prospects it holds for the Reagan administration, Everett Carll Ladd illuminates these trends and speculates about their impact on the exercise of presidential power. His conclusions concerning the volatility of American politics provide important insights into presidential politics far beyond the 1980 and 1984 elections.

In the wake of the 1980 presidential balloting, an important debate has sprung up over what the election results actually mean and what their long-term consequences are likely to be. On the one side are those who argue that a marked ideological change has occurred in the United States in recent years—the populace has "swung to the right"—and that Ronald Reagan and the Republicans are building what is likely to be a lasting new majority on the more conservative public mood. On the other side are proponents of the view that the election was simply the rejection of an ineffective president who had to confront some intractable problems, and that at most the GOP won "an opportunity" to show that it could govern successfully.

This is not the first time in modern politics, of course, that some observers have detected the emergence of a coherent new majority. In the Eisenhower years, many concluded that the growing post-World War II prosperity, manifested in the burgeoning new suburbs, was prompting a long-term shift to the Republicans.[1] Then, between 1968 and 1973, a number of students of American politics again thought they saw the emergence of a new Republican majority. The social-issue conservatism of many of the groups—including blue-collar workers, Catholics, and white Southerners—that had long been mainstays of the Democratic majority seemed to be the critical development.[2] In between these three (including that of 1980-81) "emerging Re-

---

"The Brittle Mandate" by Everett Carll Ladd, Spring 1981, *Political Science Quarterly*. Copyright 1981 by The Academy of Political Science. Reprinted by permission.

publican majority" interpretations, there were two "decimation of the Republican minority" interpretations, following the 1964 Goldwater defeat, and again following Watergate. Something there is about journalism and social-science commentary that yearns for the decisiveness of a realignment.

The view that a new electoral majority has emerged, based on a decisive ideological change, appeals of course to those who desire a new popular majority to demand new programs and policies.[3] And in the same way, interpretations that minimize the 1980 election and paint its results as transitory, appeal to those who do not want to see sweeping partisan and ideological change. It is hardly surprising that many liberals and Democrats have argued since November 4 that the 1980 Republican victories resulted simply from the searching of a frustrated electorate for something new. Americans did not confer a broad new charter; rather, they simply said, "It is time for a change." In this view, Reagan and the Republicans will be unsuccessful in coping with the complex problems, foreign and domestic, that beset the United States, and voters will likely turn again as decisively in 1984 to the out-of-power Democrats as in 1980 they backed the out-of-power Republicans.[4]

This argument over the meaning of the 1980 election, then, is over the nature of the "mandate" that the voters conferred. Is it solid or brittle? This argument is important—indeed, the nature of the mandate seems to be the most important question of interpretation of the 1980 election—but the self-serving and ideological cast that has been given it is not very productive.

For some time now, political scientists have been engaging in their own version of the argument—one that they have couched in terms of whether a "realignment" or a "dealignment" is occurring. A realignment, of course, involves the movement of large numbers of voters across party lines, establishing a new majority coalition or at least the radical transformation of the makeup of the old party coalitions. In a dealignment, voters move away from parties altogether; loyalties to the parties, and to the parties' candidates and programs, weaken, and more and more of the electorate become "up for grabs" each election.[5]

By now it is wholly evident that the dealignment interpretation of contemporary American electoral politics is correct. Ideological and partisan preference apart, there is an impressive body of theory and data which support the argument that the present era in American electoral politics is one of dealignment and party decay, which specify the sources of this development, and which identify its implications for American political life. The progress of dealignment gives its distinctive cast to the 1980 presidential election. And the 1980 mandate is brittle, not because some liberals and Democrats want it thus, but because it cannot be otherwise with a dealigned electorate.

Dealignment and the 1980 Election

For some time now, a pronounced growth has been evident in the proportion of Americans who think of themselves as independents, rather than as adherents of one of the political parties. Gallup surveys in the early 1950s, for example, showed the proportion of self-described independents in the range of 19 to 20 percent; by the 1970s, however, the proportion had climbed into the 30 to 35 percent range.[6] The 1980 General Social Survey conducted by the National Opinion Research Center (NORC) of the University of Chicago found 38 percent of the public identifying as independents, and a poll taken by Market Opinion Research for the Republican National Committee in September 1980 placed independents at 40 percent—compared with 37 percent Democrats and 24 percent Republicans. Among younger Americans in professional jobs, and among those who have attended college, independents are now an absolute majority. According to Gallup polls in late 1980, for example, 50 percent of college graduates under thirty years of age are independents, as are 50 percent of men and women under thirty who hold professional occupations. This substantial growth in the number of self-described independents has been paralleled by large increases in actions that indicate independent political behavior—

that is, crossing party lines and ticket-splitting election contests.[7]

Even more revealing of the rapid progress of electoral dealignment are data showing that the majority of Americans, including those who continue to think of themselves as Democrats or Republicans, no longer either rank the parties highly or believe that it makes a substantial difference which party wins. "Do you think there are important differences in what the Democratic or Republican parties stand for?" the CBS News/*New York Times* poll asked its respondents in August 1980. Only 40 percent replied in the affirmative; and the proportion was not much higher—43 and 47 percent, respectively—among Democratic and Republican identifiers.[8] In July 1980, only 28 percent of the public gave the Democratic party a "highly favorable" rating in a survey conducted by the Gallup organization, down from 35 percent in 1970 and 42 percent in 1967. The Republicans' support also fell comparably: just 17 percent gave the GOP a highly favorable rating in the summer of 1980, as compared with 25 percent in 1970 and 34 percent in 1967.[9]

One of the most dramatic illustrations of the weakening of ties to the parties comes from a survey conducted by the University of Connecticut's Institute for Social Inquiry near the height of the presidential campaign, in September 1980. Respondents were asked, "Which party, the Republicans or the Democrats, does the better job [handling a specified set of problems] or don't you think there is much difference?" Depending on the problem area, between 52 and 70 percent indicated that they really did not see much of a difference. On some of the questions there was a pro-Democratic margin, on others a pro-Republican edge, but these differences were incidental to the main finding: large majorities simply did not think one party was better than the other. Only 29 percent perceived a partisan difference of consequence on the matter of handling inflation, 33 percent on reducing unemployment, and a somewhat higher but still minoritarian 47 percent on the handling of foreign affairs. Connecticut Republicans were somewhat more inclined to see a party difference and to favor their own party than were Democrats, but even here it was the size of the proportion that did not believe there was much of a difference that was most striking. With the Democrats in control of the presidency and both houses of Congress, while the country was in the midst of double-digit inflation, and with the Republican presidential candidate stressing this economic issue, 43 percent of the Connecticut Republicans said they did not see much of a partisan difference on the question of controlling inflation.

Dissatisfaction with the Presidential Nominees

Criticism of both the Republican and the Democratic standard-bearers was widespread in 1980. John Anderson's campaign grew out of a fairly general unease with the Carter-Reagan choice. The favorability ratings that Carter and Reagan received in October 1980 were the lowest for any pair of major-party candidates for president going back to 1952, when Gallup first employed this measure. Ronald Reagan's 23 percent "highly favorable" was just 2 points higher than George McGovern's record low of 21 percent in 1972, while Carter's 30 percent compared unfavorably with his own rating of 41 percent in 1976 and with Lyndon Johnson's 49 percent in 1964.[10]

Some argue, of course, that the low rankings Carter and Reagan received in 1980 simply indicate that both major parties produced weak nominees that year. But as Carter adviser and pollster Patrick Caddell has pointed out, it was not just Jimmy Carter and Ronald Reagan who received popular approval rankings well below what presidential candidates in times past routinely enjoyed. No candidate for the presidential nominations in either party won broad approval.[11] In its test of candidate popularity, CBS News/*New York Times* asked, "Do you have a favorable or not favorable opinion about [various candidates for president and vice-president], or don't you know enough about him to have an opinion?" In mid-October 1980, when the proportion expressing a favorable opinion of Reagan was 41 percent among likely voters, and that of

Table 2.1.1

Question: "Which party, the Republicans or the Democrats, does a better job [on the specific problem] or don't you think there is much difference?"*

	Republicans	Democrats	Not much Difference		Don't Know
Controlling Inflation	23%	6%	63%	(70%)†	7%
Foreign Affairs	33	14	41	(53%)	12
"for people like you"	11	21	61	(68%)	7
Planning Connecticut	16	33	32	(52%)	20
Reducing unemployment	14	19	59	(67%)	8

Source: These data are taken from Connecticut Poll no. 9, conducted by the Institute for Social Inquiry, University of Connecticut, 11-16 September 1980.
* Figures may not add up to 100 due to rounding.
† The figures in this column are the total percentage of the respondents who either thought there was not much difference or did not know.

Carter was 44 percent, George Bush was favorably assessed by 41 percent, Walter Mondale by 45 percent, and John Anderson by just 30 percent of the probable electorate.[12]

As party ties have grown weaker and the public's confidence in the parties has diminished, contenders for the presidency have been denied a measure of party-derived backing that has helped bolster them in times past. Neither Reagan nor Carter was able to count on a very large measure of approval by the rank and file of their fellow partisans on party loyalty alone.

Throughout his presidency, Jimmy Carter received unusually low scores from the public when asked whether they approved "the way [he] is handling his job as president." Even more striking is the depths to which Carter's backing dropped among Democrats. Thus, his lowest approval rating among Democrats came in the summer of 1979, according to Gallup polls, when just 34 percent of Democrats endorsed his conduct of the presidency. This was the lowest proportion endorsing a president of their own party since Gallup began using this measure during the second term of Franklin Roosevelt. Harry Truman's lowest approval among Democrats was 42 percent; Lyndon Johnson's 48 percent, John Kennedy's 71 percent, and Franklin Roosevelt's 79 percent; Richard Nixon never received, even at the depths of Watergate, the approval of less than 51 percent of Republicans, Gerald Ford not less than 60 percent, and Dwight Eisenhower not under 80 percent.[13] Party identification is increasingly nominal; it confers little automatic approbation of a president among the rank and file in his party. The 1980 election was held at a time when virtually all of the candidate and leadership rankings were at their all-time lows.

Certainly the trend toward negativism in public assessments of presidential candidates, evident over the 1970s, accelerated in 1980. "Are you satisfied in choosing among Carter, Reagan, and Anderson this fall, or do you want other choices?" the CBS News/*New York Times* poll asked respondents in mid-September of 1980. Only 50 percent of all respondents said they were satisfied, and the proportion expressing satisfaction was just 58 percent among those who planned to vote for Carter and 57 percent of those for Reagan.[14] "Did you decide on your candidate mainly because you liked him, or because you didn't like the others?" the CBS News/*New York Times* poll asked respondents just after the November election. Among those who had voted, just 50 percent said they picked their candidate primarily because they liked him: 50 percent among Carter voters and 51 percent among Reagan supporters.[15] A postelection poll by the Roper organization found only 21 percent of those who voted for Carter and 43 percent of those who backed Reagan saying that they had "a good deal of enthusiasm" for their man.[16] The loss of confidence in the parties and the weakening of the party ties have necessary adjuncts in the loss of confidence in and approval of the parties' nominees.

Volatility

Given the weakness of the public's attachment to the parties and candidates in 1980, it is hardly surprising that the electorate was so unstable throughout the campaign. "Volatility" was the watchword throughout much of the campaign, and though overused it was an apt description.

Obviously, the only real landslide was the one Ronald Reagan won on November 4. But the polls show that there were a number of other "landslides" in voter sentiment, the first of which came in the fall of 1979 and was won by Democratic contender Edward Kennedy. As Jimmy Carter's support plummeted in the wake of his "malaise" speech in August, and as more and more Democratic leaders began looking to an active Kennedy candidacy, the senator's public support soared. As the data in table 2.1.2 attest, among Democratic identifiers Kennedy achieved a margin of roughly two-to-one in trial heats with Carter in September and October 1979; and he had solid margins over both Reagan and Ford within the general public.

After Kennedy formally declared his candidacy in November 1979, however, he stumbled badly. A variety of different factors—including renewed criticism of his role in the tragedy at Chappaquiddick Island, scrutiny of his stands on various issues, poor personal campaign performance, and the nation's rallying behind the president after the seizure of American embassy employees in Iran—presumably came together to erode Kennedy's position and to usher in the Carter "landslide." In February 1980, the incumbent president was the choice of Democrats for the party's 1980 nomination by a margin of roughly two-to-one, and he was backed by decisive margins of the public at large over Reagan, Ford, and Bush, as well as other Republican hopefuls.

In the spring and early summer of 1980, however, Carter's public standing once again declined precipitously. He was under attack by a reinvigorated Kennedy campaign; the hostage situation continued without observable progress, much less a resolution; and the economy deteriorated. Polls conducted after the Republican convention in Detroit, which saw Reagan nominated in relative harmony, showed the makings of a third landslide—this one "won" by Reagan. The Republican nominee was preferred by roughly a two-to-one majority of voting-age Americans.

Following his nomination in August and in the early stumbles of the Reagan campaign following the convention, Jimmy Carter came back strongly, according to every major national poll. Two national surveys conducted by CBS News/*New York Times* in September actually showed Carter leading Reagan, with the lead at 5 percentage points in the poll of September 19-21.

That there would be some variations in candidate standings over the year preceding the 1980 election is hardly surprising. The early judgments—for example, that of October 1979 with Kennedy ahead—were obviously highly tentative and hypothetical. And the polls conducted between the two national conventions necessarily overstated the president's electoral weakness. Still, the magnitude of the shifts reflected by these various "landslides" and comebacks are unprecedentedly large. The potential for volatility that party dealignment creates was amply realized over the 1980 campaign.

The Decision Postponed

The weakness of voters' ties to the parties and to the candidates in 1980 was also apparent in both the high measure of uncertainty about how to vote and the unusually late decision by many voters. The NBC News/Associated Press (AP) polls asked respondents during the last three months of the campaign

Table 2.1.2

The Several "Landslides" of 1980 Campaign

Candidate Trial Heats

Nomination Choice	Intraparty Trials				Interparty Trials			
	Kennedy	Carter	Kennedy	Reagan	Carter	Reagan	Carter	Ford
7-10 September 1979			65	35			60	40
28 September–1 November 1979	69	31						
12-15 October 1979	67	33	59	41			55	45
2-5 November 1979	64	36						
16-19 November 1979	60	40	57	43				

	Kennedy	Carter	Carter	Reagan	Carter	Ford	Carter	Bush
4-6 January 1980	42	58	65	35	61	39		
1-4 February 1980	34	66	66	34	57	43		62	38
29 February-2 March 1980	29	71						

			Reagan	Carter	Carter	Anderson
18-21 July 1980			55		27	19

			Carter	Reagan	Reagan	Anderson
10-14 September 1980			44		40	16
19-21 September 1980			47		42	11

Source: The September-November 1979 data are from surveys by the Gallup organization: the January-February 1980 data are also from Gallup polls. The July 1980 data come from an ABC News/Harris Survey; while the September 1980 data are from a poll conducted by CBS News/New York Times.

whether "you [have] made up your mind for whom you will vote in the presidential election in November, or are you not planning to vote?" Of the likely voters, 52 percent said in early August that they had not yet made up their mind for whom to vote. And the last time NBC News/AP asked this question, in late October, the proportion undecided remained a very high 25 percent. More independents and Democrats than Republicans had not made up their mind how to vote.

The proportion of the electorate undecided in the last week or two of the campaign was the highest it has been in the last three decades, the period for which comparable survey data are available, and almost certainly the highest in American history. In 1952, only 11 percent of the voters polled said they made up their mind how to vote within the last two weeks before election day; in 1956, it was just 9 percent. The proportion was at 13 percent in 1972, but it jumped to 24 percent in 1976.[17] In 1980 the proportion deciding late was higher still. The election day poll of CBS News/*New York Times*, which had the lowest estimate, found 25 percent of all voters making up their minds during the "last week" of the campaign; according to the ABC election day poll, the proportion deciding within the "last week" before the November 4 balloting was 28 percent. The postelection poll of the Roper organization showed 34 percent deciding sometime during the two weeks preceding the election. According to the election poll of the Gallup organization, an extraordinary 37 percent made up their minds sometime during the last week of the campaign, with 10 percent saying they decided on election day itself!

With so many people so weakly tied to the presidential candidates in 1980 and with so many undecided how to vote late in the campaign, the potential for a large, late-breaking move to one candidate or another was especially great. And there was reason to expect, therefore, that the Carter-Reagan debate, coming one week before the election, would be very influential.

Table 2.1.3

Question: "Have you made up your mind for whom you will vote in the presidential election in November or are you not planning to vote?

	Made Up Mind	Have Not Made Up Mind
5-7 August 1980	48%	52%
15-16 August 1980	59	41
September 1980	62	38
8-10 October 1980	69	31
22-24 October 1980	75	25
By Party:		
Republicans	81	19
Independents	68	32
Democrats	72	28

Source: Surveys by NBC News/Associated Press, latest that of 22-24 October 1980.

Although no systematic study of the effects of the debate is available, some preliminary analysis does indicate that the debate in fact had a major impact.[18] For example, a study in Connecticut based on surveys conducted immediately prior to and immediately following the debate suggests strongly that the debate served to change significantly voters' perceptions of Reagan and their overall judgments about the nature of the presidential contest. The Republican came to be seen as more credible and presidential. The proportion of Connecticut voters describing Reagan as "forceful," as compared to "rash," increased substantially from the predebate to the postdebate poll. Similarly, the proportion believing the Republican candidate to be inclined to speak "carelessly, without having considered the consequences," dropped sharply in the postdebate survey. A large plurality of Connecticut voters before the debate said they thought that Carter would win the November election; in the postdebate poll, however, a clear plurality believed that Reagan would be elected president.[19]

Whatever the precise importance of the Carter-Reagan debate in shaping the outcome of the election, there seems little doubt that the volatility of the electorate, which had been evident at earlier stages in the campaign, continued over the final week, with a decisive late-break to Reagan taking place. All of the principal national polls conducted from October 29 to November 1, including those done for the major-party candidates, showed the contest to be very close—although all had Reagan ahead, by margins between 1 and 5 percentage points over Carter. If Ronald Reagan in fact had a solid lead at this time and the polls were underestimating his margin, perhaps because of the phenomenon of "closet Reaganism," then one must accept the somewhat ironic explanation that even Reagan's own polls were unable to detect "closet Reaganism."[20]

What is much more likely is that every poll was underestimating Reagan's final popular vote margin in the October 29-November 1 period—the last time most of the polling organizations were in the field before the vote—because *Reagan increased his margin substantially between November 1 and November 4*. The daily tracking polls of Patrick Caddell for the Democrats and Richard Wirthlin for the Republicans support this conclusion. Caddell estimated Reagan's margin over Carter at 5 percentage points on the Sunday before the election and at 11 points on Monday; Wirthlin's daily polls showed a comparably sharp move to the Republican candidate over the last few days.

The Disappearance of Stable Alignments

In a *realignment*, some old divisions within the electorate weaken, of course, but new ones appear in their place. In a *dealignment*, however, the old lines of cleavage erode without any new ones of a persisting sort arising in their stead. A dealigning electorate becomes increasingly less anchored by group loyalties and attachments to the parties.

For some time it has been possible to see an erosion of historic group attachments, but the 1980 presidential election extended this feature of the dealignment process. Many of the differences in the vote of various social groups that were so much a part of the New Deal configuration were scarcely evident in the 1980 voting. Consider, for example, the presidential choices of the various white ethnic groups. According to the large election-day survey conducted by ABC News, Jimmy Carter received the support of 32 percent of those of German ancestry, 31 percent of the English and Scots, 39 percent of the Irish, 32 percent of the Scandinavians, and 38 percent of the Italians.[21] Historically, of course, persons of Irish and Italian ancestry were vastly more Democratic than those of British stock. In 1980, only blacks and Hispanics, of all the principal ethnic collectivities in the United States, showed any substantial electoral distinctiveness: Hispanics were 18 percentage points more for Carter than for Reagan, while blacks gave Carter a huge 69 percentage point margin.

Throughout U.S. history, Protestants have been far more Republican than have Catholics. The Protestant-Catholic divide, a product of various salient ethnic and cultural differences, has encompassed some of the sharpest and most persisting electoral divisions that American politics has produced.[22] Over the last two decades, however, there has been a pronounced secular erosion of Protestant and Catholic voting differences (figure 2.1.1). In 1960, with John Kennedy on the ticket as only the second Roman Catholic to be nominated for president by a major party (and the first to win the presidency), Roman Catholics were 28 percentage points less Republican than the entire electorate, while Protestants were 12 percent more Republican. By this measure, Protestants and Catholics in the 1960 presidential contest were 40 percentage points apart in their presidential support. In 1964, Protestants were 6 percent more Republican than the national estimate, while Catholics were 15 percent less Republican, for an intergroup difference of 21 percentage points. Since 1964, there has been a steady decline of these differences, and in 1980 Protestants were just 3 percent more Republican than the country as a whole, and Catholics just 3 percent less so. This interreligious group vote difference of just 6 percentage points is decisively the smallest in U.S. history.[23]

Regionalism

Just as the New Deal alignment had a clear ethnic and religious cast, so was there a large regional component, with the South solidly Democratic as it had been since the Civil War. The ending of this distinctive attachment of white Southerners to the Democrats was accomplished in stages over the 1940s, 1950s, and 1960s.[24] By 1976, even with a native of the deep South the Democrats' presidential nominee, there was only a very limited restoration of Southern attachments to the national Democratic party. While Jimmy Carter received the electoral votes of every state of the old Confederacy except for Virginia, he was unable to win majority support from white Southerners. Only a large black vote permitted Carter to carry his region.

In 1980, there was simply no trace of the historic attachment of the white South to the Democratic party. The South Atlantic and South Central states split their presidential votes very similarly to New England and the Middle Atlantic States—their historic regional rival (table 2.1.4).

The West generally, and the Mountain States in particular, were more Republican than the country as a whole in the 1980 presidential voting. This might suggest the birth of a new east-west regionalism, in place of the old one which was north-south. In fact, though, closer examination of the polling data indicates that the east-west split in 1980 was a function of the contrasting ethnic makeup of these sections, rather than of the emergence of new regional loyalties. For example, the 1980 presidential vote of *whites only* by region—the Northeast and the Southeast have much larger black (and heavily Democratic) populations than does the West—establishes the 1980 election as the flattest in American history from a purely regional standpoint. Carter was backed by 34 percent of whites in the Northeast, by 36 percent of whites in the North Central states, 37 percent in the South, and 32 percent in the West. Among white voters, Ronald Reagan's best region was actually the South, not his native West.

Group Divisions without Memory

In this setting where groups are moving away from their historic ties to the parties, there are of course still divisions in the electorate—it is not a case of every group voting alike—but the new divisions tend to be election-specific. They are dictated by the particular appeals of a given campaign. In the absence of stable party ties, there is little "memory." This year's striking division may not be seen at all in the next election. Perhaps the most interesting group split in the 1980 voting that is new and not likely to persist is that on sex lines. Men and women usually vote alike, but they did not do so on November 4. According to the election day poll of CBS News, male voters gave Reagan a 17 percentage point margin over Carter (54 percent to 37 percent) while women split essentially even (46 percent for Reagan, 45 percent for Carter).

In an election distinguished by weak party ties and a high measure of voter indecision, Reagan's position and that of the GOP platform on the Equal Rights Amendment apparently cost the Republicans some support among women. It is also likely that the perception of Reagan as "tougher" than Carter,

Figure 2.1.1

Deviation of Protestants and Catholics from the National Percentage of the Vote for the Republican Presidential Candidate, 1960 to 1980

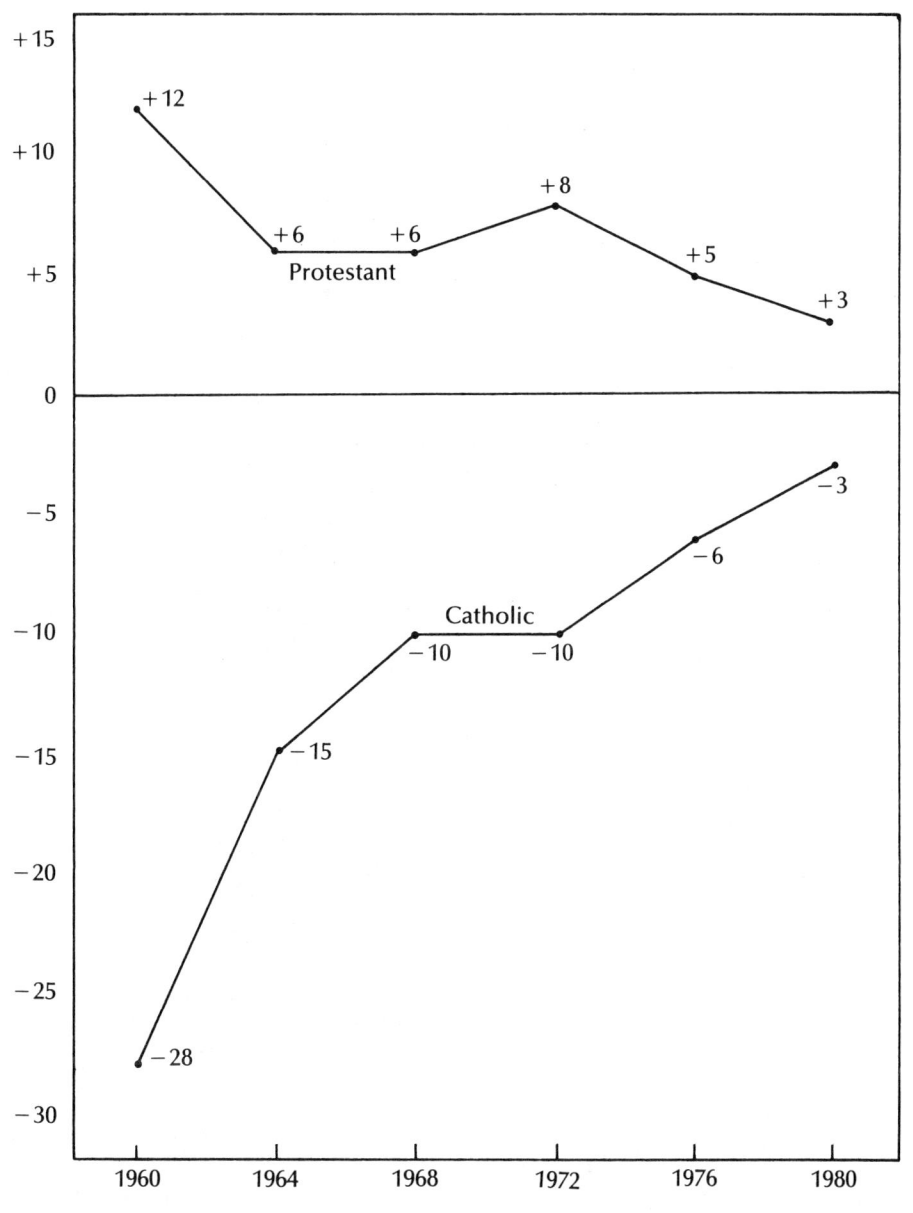

Source: Postelection surveys by the Gallup organization, latest that of 7-10 November 1980.

Table 2.1.4

Democratic and Republican Percentage of Popular Vote in the 1980 Presidential Election

	Democratic	Republican
New England	41%	45%
Middle Atlantic	44	49
East North Central	42	51
West North Central	40	53
South Atlantic	45	50
East South Central	49	50
West South Central	42	56
Mountain	30	62
Pacific	38	53

Source: Congressional Quarterly Weekly, *8 November 1980, 3338-45.*

perhaps even more "rash," in foreign affairs cut into his vote; women have regularly shown themselves to be more worried than men about the prospects of war. Women were much less inclined than men to agree with the proposition, posed in the CBS News election day poll, that "We should be more forceful in dealing with the Soviet Union even if it increases the risk of war." And whereas Reagan won the votes of 64 percent of women who thought the United States should be more forceful in dealing with the Soviet Union, he was backed by only 29 percent of those who opposed such an American assertiveness (table 2.1.6).

Interestingly, the difference between men and women in the 1980 presidential voting was limited largely to the college-trained and professional segments of the population. Men and women high-school graduates voted much the same in 1980, just as they had done in the past. But according to the CBS election-day poll, Reagan carried male college graduates by an extraordinary two-to-one margin, 58 percent to 29 percent, while he actually trailed the president narrowly, 41 to 44 percent, among female college graduates. Seemingly this male-female split, not based on clear and persisting group interests but rather substantially symbolic, was confined to those segments of the population where there is the greatest sensitivity to the symbolic dimension of politics.

The Born-Again Vote

What was expected to be an important new division in the 1980 presidential balloting—that separating Evangelical, or born-again, Christians from other Christians—did not materialize. Born-again white Protestants, and all other white Protestants, voted essentially the same in the 1980 presidential election. Indeed, according to these CBS data, Jimmy Carter actually received a slightly higher proportion of the born-again Protes-

Table 2.1.5

*1980 Presidential Vote by Region of Whites, White Protestants, and White Catholics**

	Anderson	Carter	Reagan	Other
All White Voters				
Northeast	13%	34%	51%	2%
North Central	9	36	53	2
South	5	34	60	1
West	11	32	54	4
White Protestant				
Northeast	11	24	64	1
North Central	7	30	61	1
South	3	31	65	1
West	8	28	61	2
White Catholic				
Northeast	11	41	46	3
North Central	9	43	45	3
South	5	37	58	1
West	10	35	52	3

Source: 1980 ABC election day poll.
* Figures may not add up to 100 due to rounding.

Table 2.1.6

*1980 Presidential Vote, by Various Social Groups**

	Carter	Reagan	Anderson	Carter 1980% minus Carter 1976%†
Women	45	46	7	−5
Men	37	54	7	−13
High-school-educated women	45	48	5	NA
High-school-educated men	45	52	2	NA

Table 2.1.6 (continued)

*1980 Presidential Vote, by Various Social Groups**

	Carter	Reagan	Anderson	Carter 1980% minus Carter 1976%†
College-educated women	44	41	13	NA
College-educated men	29	58	11	NA
Women, favor Equal Rights Amendment	54	32	11	NA
Women, oppose Equal Rights Amendment	29	66	4	NA
Women, agree U.S. should be more forceful dealing with USSR	30	64	6	NA
Women, disagree U.S. should be more forceful dealing with USSR	59	29	9	NA
Catholics	40	51	7	−14
Jews	45	39	14	−19
Protestants	37	56	6	−7
White Protestants	31	62	6	NA
Born-again white Protestants	35	61	3	NA
All other white Protestants	30	60	8	NA
Born-again white Catholics	35	58	6	NA
All other white Catholics	39	51	8	NA
Family finances—everyone				
Better off than a year ago	53	37	8	−23
Same	46	46	7	−5
Worse off than a year ago	25	64	8	−52
Family finances—blue-collar worker				
Better off than a year ago	73	22	2	NA
Same	55	39	6	NA
Worse off than a year ago	30	62	5	NA
Blacks	82	14	3	0
Hispanics	54	36	7	−21
Whites	36	55	8	−11
Family income				
Less than $10,000	50	41	6	−8
$10,000-14,999	47	42	8	−8
$15,000-24,999	38	53	7	−10

Table 2.1.6 (continued)

1980 Presidential Vote, by Various Social Groups*

	Carter	Reagan	Anderson	Carter 1980% minus Carter 1976%†
$25,000-50,000	32	58	8	−4
Over $50,000	25	65	8	NA
Professional or managerial	33	56	9	−8
Clerical, sales, or other white-collar	42	48	8	−4
Blue-collar workers	46	47	5	−9
Agriculture	29	66	3	NA
Looking for work	55	35	7	−10
Education				
High school or less	46	48	4	−11
Some college	35	55	8	−16
College graduate	35	51	11	−10
Labor union household	47	44	7	−12
No member of household in union	35	55	8	−8
18-21 years old	44	43	11	−4
22-29 years old	43	43	11	−8
30-44 years old	37	54	7	−12
45-59 years old	39	55	6	−8
60 years old or older	40	54	4	−7
Democrats	66	26	6	−11
Independents	30	54	12	−13
Republicans	11	84	4	+2
Liberals	57	27	11	−13
Moderates	42	48	8	−9
Conservatives	23	71	4	−6

Source: 1980 Election-day surveys by CBS News/New York Times; the comparison with 1976 is with the 1976 CBS News/New York Times election-day survey and (for selected variables) with the 1976 election-day survey by NBC News.

* Figures may not add to 100 either due to rounding or to fractional support for a candidate other than the three listed.

† The right hand column in this table compares Carter's 1980 vote within each group with his 1976 vote. Thus, the "minus 14" for Catholics means that Jimmy Carter's 40 percent support among Catholics in 1980 was 14 percentage points less than what he received from Catholics four years earlier.

tant vote than of the vote of other Protestants—even though spokesmen for various evangelical groups had criticized the president's positions and indicated a clear preference for Reagan's stands.

If born-again white Protestants were in fact more conservative than other white Protestants, they might well have voted more heavily for the conservative Republican nominee. But, in fact, as a group the born-agains are not ideologically distinct. On such issues as whether unemployment or inflation should be emphasized, cutting taxes, and U.S. foreign policy vis-à-vis the Soviet Union, born-again white Protestants and other white Protestants took identical stands in 1980.[25] And even on various social and cultural issues, according to two large surveys conducted by the Gallup organization in August 1980, Evangelical and non-Evangelical Christians hold very similar views. A few questions such as prayer in public schools, Gallup found, do indeed leave evangelicals and nonevangelicals sharply at odds. But there are no general ideological differences between these groups. Born-again Christians simply are not more conservative than other Christians, and they did not vote differently in 1980.[26]

Class Differences

The salience of class in American electoral politics has declined since the New Deal. In recent years the split between those of higher status and lower status has been further blurred by the rise of new issues that do not evoke the traditional class alignments. In the New Deal setting, higher-status Americans were fairly consistently and clearly more conservative than those in lower socioeconomic positions. Over the last two decades, however, precisely the opposite relationship has been found on many social and cultural questions, with those in the upper socioeconomic positions, especially those of college training, consistently and often sharply more in favor of liberal social change than the lower socioeconomic, noncollege populace.[27]

Given this recent experience, it surely is not surprising that the 1980 presidential election, pitting a moderate Democrat whose custody of the White House coincided with high inflation, high unemployment, and diminished economic growth against a Republican who assiduously sought out the middle ground during the campaign even though he had long worn the conservative mantle, did not evidence sharp class differences of any kind. Reagan apparently won a slight plurality among blue-collar workers, although he did better, as Republicans usually do, among people in professional and managerial occupations. Reagan's support within the various education strata was remarkably even—45 percent of those with less than a high-school education backed him, compared with 52 percent of high-school graduates, 52 percent of those with some college, and 50 percent of college graduates.[28] Low-income Americans were much more supportive of Carter than those in middle and upper incomes, but even here there was hardly any real polarization. Jimmy Carter had only a 9 point margin over Ronald Reagan among persons with annual family incomes of under $10,000—50 to 41 percent, with 6 percent for Anderson (table 2.1.6).

Frustration with high inflation is apparent all across the social spectrum, but it has been especially strong among the Democrats' traditional constituents, the less affluent.[29] And working-class Americans, fully as much as those in the upper-middle class, now believe that it is the workings of contemporary government, more than the actions of business and labor, that has brought about the inflationary surge. The electoral impact of the extraordinary shift in class perceptions of government and the Democrats' handling of it—together with the general weakening of group ties to the parties—was felt in 1980 as the Democrats suffered their greatest losses among Americans who thought they were in trouble economically.

"Compared to a year ago," the CBS News election day poll asked respondents, "is your financial situation better today, worse today, or about the same?" Among those who thought they were better off, Carter outpolled Reagan by 53 to 37 percent (table 2.1.6). On the other hand, among that third of the electorate who believed their economic position had declined, Reagan led Carter by a massive 64 to 25 percent. Reagan split the traditionally Democratic working-class vote with Carter, but most strikingly he did best among blue-collar workers who thought their economic position was deteriorating. Of the workers who believed they were better off than a year earlier 73 percent voted for Carter, compared with just 30 percent of those who considered themselves worse off. In 1980, not much could be seen of the Democrats' historic status as the party of the economically dispossessed.

In this year of electoral dealignment, an ever larger slice of the electorate is "up for grabs" each presidential contest. Part of this process, necessarily, entails the erosion of the partisan attachments of the various social, economic, religious, ethnic, and regional groups in the population without—as would be the case if realignment were in process—the emergence of persisting new group alignments. In any given election, of course, a candidate may well appeal to certain groups and offend others, producing large splits; electoral dealignment does not mean that there cannot be large group differences in voting. It does mean that *the stable and persisting group ties*, which in times have been an integral part of the fabric of the party system, are being removed.

Sources of Electoral Dealignment

Discussions of the progress of the electoral dealignment typically emphasize two broad sources—which may be called the *sociological* and the *political-institutional*. The sociological explanation properly notes that an affluent, leisured, highly educated public no longer perceives the need for political parties as intermediary institutions in the processes of representative democracy to the degree that less-educated and less-secure publics in times past have looked to the parties. The political-institutional explanation stresses the simultaneous deterioration of political-party organizations—producing a situation where the increasingly enfeebled and inefficacious party bodies hardly give voters reason to back them strongly—and the assumption by other institutions such as the national communications media and the welfare state of functions that the parties once performed.

These factors are surely important. There is another important precipitant of dealignment, though, that has received little attention. Large segments of the American public have become so ambivalent and undecided about the proper course of public policy that they are unable to give a clear endorsement to the stands of the parties. The parties offer contrasting approaches—arguably as distinct as at any time in American politics—but the people do not endorse their answers.

An examination of the platforms adopted by the Democratic and Republican parties in 1980 reveals sharp and consistent partisan differences across all of the principal policy areas. Although the Republicans and Democrats are not divided nearly so fundamentally as were, for example, the Gaullists, the Communists, and the Radical Socialists in Fourth Republic France, they are as much at odds as one could expect in the case of two large, diverse, middle-class parties in a country that has a remarkably unified ideological inheritance and history.

In their 1980 platform, the Democrats showed far more enthusiasm for the state and much more confidence in the capacities of governmental intervention than did the Republicans. Their greater governmental liberalism was matched by greater support for extensions of social liberalism. The Democrats opposed a constitutional amendment, for example, to overturn the 1973 Supreme Court decision allowing abortions, and they backed the use of Medicaid funds for abortions—whereas the 1980 Republican platform endorsed a constitutional amendment banning abortions. The Democrats passionately committed themselves to the Equal Rights Amendment, while the Republicans refused to endorse the ERA's ratification. On foreign affairs the Democrats talked much more about the need for a successful American accommodation to the aspirations of the nations of the Third World, the GOP more of the need for firmness and military strength.[30]

Popular Ambivalence

But if the political parties are thus committed to coherent and sharply contrasting positions, the voters themselves are in the middle, at once attracted to and put off by central features of each party's appeals. This public ambivalence is clearly evident on the basic question of the role of government and its appropriate interventions in American economic life. By the early 1970s, survey data make clear, Americans of all classes and most social positions had come to accept two basic propositions: first, that there is no alternative to a major role by government in regulating the economy, providing social services, and assuring economic progress; and second, that these generally desired interventions by the state frequently cause problems.

The broad support of Americans in all social strata for the "service state" is shown clearly by data from the General Social Surveys, conducted annually since 1973 by the National Opinion Research Center of the University of Chicago. NORC has asked respondents whether they think government spending in various sectors is too high, too low, or about right. The NORC data show that support for government service was at, or near, record levels in 1980 in virtually all of the specified program areas. Large majorities of Americans in 1980 believed that current spending was either too low or about right on environmental matters, health, the problems of big cities, controlling crime, combatting drug addiction, education, defense, meeting the needs of blacks, and the space program; only "foreign aid" and "welfare" found majorities of the public maintaining that current spending was too high (table 2.1.7).

Various other measures employed by survey organizations make clear that the NORC findings are a faithful rendering of public sentiment: Americans want government to do a lot in many different areas. But at the same time, confidence in government performance and in political leaders has dropped sharply. Various surveys show that large majorities of the public blame government for super inflation. The sense is widespread across the United States that the state is clumsy, inefficient, and wasteful.[31]

It is not at all clear, then, which of the two partisan approaches to government finds the greater favor with the American people. The conventional wisdom in 1980 held that Americans were notably disenchanted with government—and thus much closer to the Republican position. In some areas that clearly was so. But at the same time, people had not stopped looking to government for solutions and assistance. The popular sense of government as a "problem" clearly squares with established Republican doctrine and thus contributes positively to the fortunes of the GOP. Americans of all classes, however, now expect high levels of service and performance by government—and this commitment squares with traditional Democratic doctrine and is of electoral benefit to the Democratic party. Overall, the American people have become inordinately ambivalent with regard to the state.

Had Americans turned decisively against government and adopted a generally conservative response on matters involving public spending for social programs, the 1980 presidential election might well have evidenced a realignment ushering in long-term Republican ascendancy. This has not occurred because the public's antigovernment mood remains balanced by its progovernment mood. Ambivalent about the contemporary state, Americans in 1980 were ambivalent about the parties and their contrasting approaches.

This response extends to a broad range of questions involving social and cultural change. Should women assume new roles? Should individual preference and choice take precedence over older moral strictures against premarital sex, divorce, abortion, and the like? Should such old middle-class values as hard work and frugality give way to greater emphasis on personal fulfillment and expression? Should civil liberties and civil rights be extended and enlarged? On these questions, it is simply not true that Americans have been moving to the right. In many ways the opposite is the case.[32] There can be no doubt that overall the American people in 1980 were more supportive of social and cultural "liberalism" than they were in the 1960s—and much more so than they were in the 1950s before America's "great cultural revolution" began.

At the same time, various surveys show that there is general concern with the overall rate and amount of social change, and with the kind of society it is producing, and that various groups are especially resentful of developments in specific areas. The result of this mixing together of general support for contemporary social changes and substantial unease about them has been a high measure of popular uncertainty and frustration.[33]

Questions on foreign policy and defense also reveal a high measure of uncertainty and contradictory inclinations within much of the public. Thus, Americans think national defenses should be strengthened; by overwhelming margins they support more defense spending. They believe U.S. foreign policy has been too weak and vacillating in recent years, and the negative assessment of Carter's handling of foreign affairs generally, and of the hostage situation in particular, almost certainly contributed significantly to his defeat.[34] Nonetheless, the public clearly does not want too much "firmness" in U.S. foreign policy. Thus, surveys show that large majorities of Americans basically approved Carter's "patience" on the hostage issue and believed that preserving the lives of the hostages outweighed "preserving U.S. honor."[35] A widespread perception of Reagan as potentially "rash" in foreign affairs seemingly held back his campaign more than any other stand he was perceived taking.

Table 2.1.7

Public Opinion on Public Spending, 1980

Majorities say we are spending

Too little on		Too little or about the right amount on		Too much on	
Halting crime	(72%)	Halting Crime	(94%)	Foreign aid	(74%)
Drug addiction	(65%)	Drug addiction	(92%)	Welfare	(59%)
Defense	(60%)	Health	(92%)		
Health	(57%)	Education	(89%)		
Education	(55%)	Defense	(88%)		
The environment	(51%)	The environment	(84%)		
		Big cities	(76%)		
		Blacks	(74%)		
		Space exploration	(57%)		

Question: "We are faced with many problems in this country, none of which can be solved easily or inexpensively. I'm going to name some of these problems, and for each one I'd like you to tell me whether you think we're spending too much, too little, or about the right amount on [the item]?

(A) Space exploration program
(B) Improving and protecting the environment
(C) Improving and protecting the nation's health
(D) Solving the problems of the big cities
(E) Halting the rising crime rate
(F) Dealing with drug addiction
(G) Improving the nation's education system
(H) Improving the conditions of blacks
(I) The military, armaments, and defense
(J) Foreign aid
(K) Welfare."

From 1980 General Social Survey, The National Opinion Research Center, The University of Chicago. Reprinted by permission.

Carter strategists considered it the Republican's prime weak spot. While voters considered Carter's foreign policy generally deficient, by a large majority they supported the president over the Republican nominee as the candidate "best able to keep us out of war."[36]

Thus in all of the principal policy areas, Americans were of mixed minds in 1980. Such ambivalence and frustration is readily translated into an inclination to turn the "ins" out, but it hardly sustains a stable new majority.

The Brittle Mandate

Writing a decade ago, Samuel Lubell argued that the Republican coalition showed little prospect of becoming majoritarian and that there did not "seem to be much chance of reestablishing the New Deal coalition of its old form."[37] He saw party loyalties becoming ever more lightly held and the parties fading into the background before what he called "total elections"—in which presidents use their power in economic and foreign affairs in the attempt to orchestrate electoral results. When things go wrong, in this setting, the president is blamed massively and is banished from office. Thus the United States had arrived, Lubell argued, at an age of plebiscitary presidencies. These developments, contributing to an inability to establish any long-range resolution of conflicts dividing the country, produce "a new alignment of two incomplete, narrow-based coalitions polarized against each other," with the bulk of the populace dealigned and responding afresh every four years to the presidential "referendum."[38] Unfortunately, it now appears that Lubell was prescient in his 1971 argument, although few observers then appreciated this.

Much of the discussion following the 1980 presidential election has focused on the meaning of the "mandate." Is there a pronounced, persisting conservative swing in the populace, likely to sustain a coherent Republican majority for decades into the future? The answer seems clearly that the 1980 election manifested no mandate in this sense. Electoral dealignment was not interrupted in the 1980 balloting; it proceeded apace.

As they take office, Republican leaders are far from unaware of the limited nature of the mandate that the voters conferred upon them November 4. Such is the fluid and volatile character of the contemporary electorate that, although it voted decisively for the Republicans in 1980 "for a change," it could shift just as decisively against the party four years hence if its search for more effective leadership is not satisfied.

A president is elected, and the Americans pile high on him both expectations and problems. We subject him and his administration to an intense scrutiny by news media which cannot fail to reveal inadequacies and which become part of the staple of political commentary. Without strong party ties in the electorate and effective party machinery within government to support him, the president finds it hard to sustain a coherent course of action. His difficulty is compounded by the electorate's uncertain and ambivalent mood on many pressing questions. All this explains in part the fact that no president since Eisenhower has completed a second full term.

Voters want the Reagan administration to advance such general objectives as reducing inflation, increasing economic growth, and strengthening the U.S. position in foreign affairs. On this there can be no doubt about the clarity of the public voice. The test of a mandate comes, however, when one moves from general goals to the concrete measures needed to achieve them. And here the fact that a very large proportion of the electorate has been cut loose from relatively stable ties to the parties and party programs and has been left to float free, compounds the fragility of the mandate a modern president actually enjoys. The continuing referendum on his performance chronicled in the public-opinion polls can almost instantly turn against him.

In one sense the election of 1980 was decisive, but central to that decisiveness is something that cannot leave either of the major parties notably optimistic. For what was indicated most clearly is a new order where each presidential election is disconnected from the partisan past, a highly volatile referendum of the public record of the previous four years.

Notes

1. For statements of this Republican realignment position in the 1950s, see Louis Harris, *Is There a Republican Majority?* (New York: Harper & Brothers, 1954); Edward Banfield, "The Changing Political Environment of City Planning" (Paper delivered to the Annual Meeting of the American Political Science Association, Chicago, Ill., September 1956); Frederick Lewis Allen, "The Big Change in Suburbia," *Harper's*, July 1954, 50; and William Whyte, *The Organized Man* (New York: Simon and Schuster, 1959), esp. 295-305.

2. The best statement of this view was by Kevin Phillips, *The Emerging Republican Majority* (New Rochelle, N.Y.: Arlington House, 1969). See, too, idem., "How Nixon Will Win," *New York Times Magazine*, 6 August, 1972, 8-9, 34-38; and idem., "The Future of American Politics," *National Review*, 22 December 1972, 1396-98.

3. Both Richard Scammon and Ben Wattenberg, and Norman Podhoretz, for example, who have argued the case for seeing the 1980 election as a major ideological and partisan shift, acknowledge that they want to see the shift occur. See Richard M. Scammon and Ben J. Wattenberg, "Is It the End of an Era?" *Public Opinion* 3 (October-November 1980): 2-12; and Norman Podhoretz, " American Majority," *Commentary* 71 (January 1981): 19-28.

4. Democratic National Committee Chairman John White advanced this interpretation in a December 1980 interview. "As a nation we are now going through one of those very frustrating periods in our political life in which we must try this, and if it doesn't work we try that, and if that doesn't work we try something else. Americans may grumble but they are a people who will try different things. I am sorry that they tried the Republicans in 1980, but I am totally confident that the search for new answers will continue, since what the Republicans have proposed simply will not work. I think we are going through, for probably the rest of the century, a very unsettling political process in the United States.... This surely does not mean that our country has become more conservative, any more than the 1976 [Democratic] win meant that the country was more liberal!" (Interview with John White, conducted by the author for *Fortune* magazine, 3 December 1980).

5. I have reviewed this argument at length in another publication: Ladd, *Transformation of the American Party System: Political Coalitions from the New Deal to the 1970s*, 2d ed., rev. (New York: W. W. Norton and Co., 1978). One of the most cogent arguments of the "dealignment" thesis has been provided by Walter Dean Burnham. See his *Critical Elections and the Mainsprings of American Politics* (New York: W. W. Norton and Co., 1970).

6 The Gallup question is phrased, "In politics, as of today, do you consider yourself a Republican, a Democrat, or an Independent?" The entire collection of Gallup Polls, comprising more than 1,000 separate surveys reaching back into the 1930s, is contained within the archive of the Roper Center for Public Opinion Research, Storrs, Conn., and the distributions cited here are derived from scores of individual surveys within this collection.

7. Walter DeVries and Lance Tarrance noted that "throughout American history, most voters were straight-ticket voters, and until World War II more than 80 percent were still so classified. Through the 1950s, the statistic remained around 60-70 percent" (*The Ticket-Splitter: A New Force in American Politics* [Grand Rapids, Mich.: William B. Eerdmans Publishing Company, 1972], 22). In the late 1960s, however, there was a big increase in the amount of ticket-splitting, and since then the rate has remained fairly stable, at an unprecedentedly high level. In 1980, Gallup again asked: "For the various political offices, did you vote for all the candidates of one party, that is, a straight ticket, or did you vote for candidates of different parties?" Of the respondents, 62 percent were identified as ticket-splitters, compared with just 38 percent voting a straight ticket. This Gallup Poll was taken between 7 November and 10 November 1980.

8. Survey conducted by CBS News/*New York Times*, 2-7, August 1980.

9. These data are from a Gallup Poll release of 13 July 1980.

10. Gallup uses this time to compute its favorability scores: "You will notice that the 10 boxes on this card go from the highest position of plus five—for someone or something you have a FAVORABLE opinion of—all the way down to the lowest position of minus five—for someone or something you have a very UNFAVORABLE opinion of. How far up or down the scale would you rate the following [candidates' names]?" The favorability score that Gallup has regularly released is the percentage of the public giving the candidate a "highly favorable" rating of +4 or +5. The 1980 ratings cited in the text are from Gallup Poll no. 163, conducted 10-12 October 1980.

11. Interview with Patrick Caddell and Richard Wirthlin, conducted by the editors of *Public Opinion* magazine, 3 December 1980. Portions of this interview were published in *Public Opinion* 3 (December-January 1981): 2-12.

12. These data are from a survey by CBS News/*New York Times*, 16-20 October 1980.

13. These data, derived from Gallup Polls reaching back to 1936, have been summarized in *Public Opinion* 2 (October-November 1979): 21.

14. Survey by CBS News/*New York Times*, 10-14 September 1980.

15. Survey by CBS News/*New York Times*, 7-12 November 1980.

16. The question was: "Did you vote for [your candidate] with a good deal of enthusiasm, or with a feeling that you were making the right choice but with no real enthusiasm, or without even being sure you were picking the best man in the race?" This poll by the Roper organization was conducted 8-15 November 1980.

17. The data for each presidential year from 1952 through 1976 are taken from the election surveys of the Center for Political Studies (CPS) of the University of Michigan. The CPS question was framed the same way in each instance: "How long before the election did you decide that you were going to vote the way that you

did?" The two late-decision categories offered in this structured question were "decided within two weeks of the election" and "on election day." The 1980 Michigan data were not available when this article was written.

18. A number of national survey organizations asked respondents who they thought did the best job in the debate and whether the debate had changed their minds. The CBS News/*New York Times* poll conducted 30 October-1 November posed the question: "Which candidate do you think did the best job—or won the debate—Carter or Reagan?" In this instance, as in most of the other survey inquiries, a plurality was shown believing Reagan did the better job, but the margin was modest: 44 percent thought Reagan did the better job, 36 percent gave victory to Carter, 14 percent thought the debate was a draw, and 6 percent had no opinion.

19. The question was asked: "Regardless of who you *want* to win in November, who do you think will win?" Before the debate, 30 percent said Reagan, 43 percent Carter, and 26 percent "don't know"; after the debate, 40 percent said Reagan, 34 percent Carter, and 26 percent "don't know." These data come from surveys conducted by the Connecticut Poll, a unit of the University of Connecticut's Institute for Social Inquiry. Two independent surveys were conducted, one during October 25-27, the other October 29-31. Additional data on these survey findings have been published in *Public Opinion* 3 (December-January 1981): 34-35.

20. See Everett Carll Ladd and G. Donald Ferree, Jr., "Were the Pollsters Really Wrong?" *Public Opinion* 3 (December-January 1981): 13-20, for a discussion of the performance of the various national polls in the 1980 presidential election. It might be noted here that some confusion has arisen about whether the findings of polls of Cambridge Survey Research (Caddell) done for the Democrats, and those of Decisionmaking Information (Wirthlin) conducted for the Republicans, contradict one another with regard to the question of a late decisive swing to the Republicans. In fact, the findings of these two candidate polls are basically consistent. The confusion in press treatment was created in part because Caddell released his data identifying the polls with the day the field work was done, while Wirthlin released his data in three-day "rolling averages." That is, the Wirthlin figure for November 3 actually encompasses three polls—conducted on November 1, 2, and 3. Combining three days' polls, and weighing them, serve to produce averages that even out the considerably greater day-to-day voter movement and contribute to a seeming discrepancy with the Caddell findings.

21. ABC News election day poll, 4 November 1980. The raw data files are available to researchers through the Roper Center for Public Opinion Research, as are data from most of the other polls cited in this article.

22. For data on the Protestant-Catholic electoral differences historically, see Everett Carll Ladd, *American Political Parties: Social Change and Political Response* (New York: W. W. Norton and Co., 1979), 291-94; and idem., *Transformations of the American Party System*, esp. 46-57, 116-24, 271-74. Richard Jensen, *The Winning of the Midwest* (Chicago, Ill.: University of Chicago Press, 1971), 58-88, provides some revealing data on the extent of religious differences in voting in various midwestern counties in the late nineteenth century.

23. If one looks only at *white* Protestants and Catholics *outside* the South, one sees a comparably large shrinkage of group differences.

24. For a full discussion of the ending of the attachment of Southern whites to the Democratic party, see chapter 3, "First Rendings: The Case of the South," in *Transformations of the American Party System*, Ladd, 129-77.

25. These data are from the CBS News election day poll, 4 November 1980.

26. The findings of the Gallup organization on the views of Evangelical and non-Evangelical Christians are reported in the Gallup Poll release of 8 September 1980.

27. I have discussed these findings at great length in other publications. See, for example, Ladd, "Liberalism Upside Down: The Inversion of the New Deal Order," *Political Science Quarterly* 91 (Winter 1977-78): 557-600; idem., "Pursuing the New Class: Social Theory and Survey Data," in *The New Class*, ed. Barry Bruce Briggs (New Brunswick, N. J.: Transaction Books, 1979); and idem., "The New Divisions in U.S. Politics," *Fortune*, 26 March 1979, 88-96.

28. These data are from the ABC election day poll, 4 November 1980.

29. For further treatment of this, see Everett Carll Ladd, "What the Voters Really Want," *Fortune*, 18 December 1978, 40-48.

30. For further comparison of the 1980 Democratic and Republican platforms, see Everett Carll Ladd, "More than a Dime's Worth of Difference," *Commonsense* 3 (Summer 1980): 51-58.

31. For an extended analysis of popular ambivalence, see Everett Carll Ladd, *Where Have All the Voters Gone?* (New York: W. W. Norton and Co., 1978): idem,"The New Divisions in U.S. Politics"; idem., "What the Voters Really Want"; Everett Carll Ladd and Seymour Martin Lipset, "Public Opinion and Public Policy: Trends and the Likely Climate for the 1980's, in *The United States in the World of the 1980's*, eds. Peter Duignan and Alvin Rabushka (Stanford, Calif.: Hoover Institution Press, 1980); and Ladd and Lipset, "Anatomy of a Decade," *Public Opinion* 3 (December-January 1981): 2-9.

32. For a close examination of survey data supporting this argument see Ladd and Lipset, "Public Opinion and Public Policy."

33. For further data on the uncertain and mixed assessments of Americans on governmental interventions and on social cultural change, see the "Opinion Round-Up" sections of *Public Opinion* 3 (December-January 1981): 19-42; and ibid. (June-July 1980): 21-40.

34. According to surveys conducted by NBC News/Associated Press, large majorities of Americans throughout 1980 believed Carter's handling of foreign affairs was at best "only fair," and in September 1980, 78 percent gave the president this negative rating. The same NBC News/AP surveys showed a majority of Americans disapproving Carter's handling of the hostage situation after April 1980; in late October, 60 percent disapproved, while only 40 percent expressed approval.

35. For supporting data see the ABC News/Harris Survey, release of 29 December 1980.

36. Surveys by the Gallup organization conducted for

Reform of the Party System and the Conduct of the Presidency

Nelson W. Polsby

A concomitant of the party decomposition and dealignment at the voting level emphasized in the preceding essay is party decline at the organizational level. Due to the proliferation of presidential primaries, national conventions have become ratifying rather than nominating forums. The result is that political parties have partially lost and partially abdicated their role in candidate recruitment. More and more, pollsters, campaign operatives and the media have become the new presidential selection elite, replacing party stalwarts. The effect has been to reduce the potential for both peer review of prospective candidates and party cooperation in presidential-congressional relations. Polsby's thoughtful essay raises these points, with particular attention to how the presidency has suffered in the modern era of party reform.

In this paper, I propose to explore whether there is a discernible relationship between what happens in the U.S. party system and what happens in the conduct of the presidency. It is an analysis that draws heavily upon the contemporary history of the United States, and on that account alone may encounter disagreement from participants and observers who see things differently. Indeed, some measure not only of disagreement but disagreeableness seems hard to avoid in an area of study where any sort of contribution may easily be mistaken for ammunition in ongoing political controversy. But as much as it would simplify our lives if it were so, whether a causal connection is weak or strong, whether an ascertainable fact is true or false, does not depend on anyone's political sympathies. And so there is room for the sort of discourse in which political scientists sometimes engage, even on an issue like the consequences of party reform.

An ill-tempered quotation from a political activist sets the stage nicely:

> It has become fashionable among a certain group of pundits and political scientists to blame the reforms undertaken by the Democratic party after its 1968 convention for all manner of political ills—declining voter participation, the proliferation of single-issue groups, weak presidential leadership, poor congressional performance, and, above all, the decay of the political party. So great has been the hostility to these reforms, to the reformers who perpetrated them and to the proliferation of presidential nominating primaries that followed in their wake, that one expects any day now to see a book published that blames these reforms, not only for our political ills, but for cancer, heart disease, and falling arches.[1]

It goes beyond my current intentions to explore all the causal connections that this off-handed display of partisan pique seeks to dismiss but it does seem to me perfectly permissible to ask:

"Reform of the Party System and the Conduct of the Presidency" by Nelson W. Polsby from *Problems and Prospects of Presidential Leadership in the Nineteen Eighties* (pp. 103-21) Ed. by James S. Young, 1983, Lanham, Maryland: University Press of America. Copyright 1983 by University Press of America. Reprinted by permission.

1. Did party reforms change the probable outcomes of the three presidential elections since they were enacted?
2. Did party reforms have any direct effects on the conduct of the presidency beyond that?

I believe answers to both questions can be given in the affirmative, but think the grounds for belief in both cases are certainly not so obvious as to command immediate and unanimous assent. Indeed even after these grounds are more thoroughly explored reasonable observers may find ample bases for disagreement about the conclusions. Let us nevertheless see what the case for the affirmative looks like.

In three out of the last four presidential elections, the minority party has won.[2] The first of these, 1968, can be straightforwardly described as an occasion in which certain short-run forces having to do with the extraordinary saliency of the Vietnam War among Democratic élites caused the majority party to tear itself apart in public. This can be shown, among other ways, by the extremely low public opinion ratings of the 1968 Democratic nominee after the convention that nominated him. Conventions normally boost the ratings of their nominees.[3]

At that Democratic convention, other forces were set in motion which, it is now frequently argued, have in some degree institutionalized the handicap which hindered the Democratic nominee of 1968, and aided the Republicans in each of the subsequent presidential elections, two out of three of which resulted in victories for the Republican minority.

It is necessary to invoke a rather complicated chain of causal connections in order to maintain this argument. With apologies to Rube Goldberg, here is at least one account of how the process is supposed to have worked:

1. The 1968 Democratic convention mandated a reform commission on the selection of delegates for subsequent conventions.
2. This commission, named for its chairmen, George McGovern and Donald Fraser, issued a series of guidelines, which for various reasons became compulsory party legislation.
3. A series of lawsuits established the right of national parties, and their chosen instruments, to place requirements upon state parties with respect to the identities of state party delegates to national party conventions.
4. State party leaders, faced with complex requirements and the threat of exclusion of their state delegations from national party conventions, drastically changed delegation selection procedures.
5. Primary elections thus became the main instrument for delegate selection. The results of primaries were regarded as sure to pass muster in accordance with national guideline enforcement machinery, and hence assure seating at the national convention.
6. Delegate selection by this method, however, introduces certain distortions into the procedures which, though permissible under the guidelines, nevertheless drastically altered the incentive structure under which the nomination process was conducted.
7. This in turn has led to nominations of candidates unable to command widespread support, and thus has thrown at least two presidential elections—in 1972 and 1980—to the more ideologically cohesive but numerically smaller minority party.

Not all the steps in this argument are matters of much controversy. Nobody doubts that the McGovern Commission came into being, that it issued guidelines, that its recommendations were incorporated as Democratic party legislation, and that the legality of the centralization of the Democratic party—and consequently also of the Republicans—was secured by recourse to the courts.[4]

Starting at the fourth point in the argument, and increasingly as the argument progresses, objections of various sorts, and the needs for elucidation and further explanation crop up. These demand some attention.

It has, for example, been denied that the undoubted proliferation of primaries in the delegate selection process were inspired by McGovern-Fraser Commission reforms. Two former staff members of the Commission have generated a short list of other possible motives for switching to primary elections.[5] These include a desire on the part of state party leaders to attract the coverage of the national television networks for the purposes of drawing attention to state or regional problems. In addition, there is the simple financial attraction of having a primary, since "The candidates, their campaigns, and the press who cover them are known to spend a great deal of money in crucial primary states."[6]

These authors also mention several states—Texas, North Carolina, Georgia—in which primary elections were instituted because it was believed that such elections were going to be helpful to the favorite son presidential candidacies of Lloyd Bentsen, Terry Sanford and Jimmy Carter, respectively. They do not describe how or why these primaries were superior to the methods of delegate selection they replaced, from the standpoint of these candidates. In Georgia, for example, prior to the reforms "the entire national convention delegation was chosen by the state party chairman, in consultation with the Democratic governor."[7] It is easy to envisage such a system being even more advantageous to a favorite son than a primary. The other reasons given make sense as possible excuses for switching to primary elections at any time; what they do not explain is why all these reasons so suddenly occurred to so many state party leaders all at once, and only after the guidelines had come into being, unless it was because the compulsion of newly instituted guidelines may have suddenly stimulated an interest in publicizing state problems, or in raising money for the tourist industry. Thus the observation of the Winograd Commission of the Democratic party that "many states . . . felt that a primary offered the most protection against a challenge at the next convention"[8] does not seem so far-fetched after all. As former McGovern-Fraser Commissioner Austin Ranney said:

> Most of the fourteen states which adopted presidential primaries after 1968 did so as a direct response to the McGovern-Fraser rules. Some decided that primaries were the best way to provide genuine "full, meaningful and timely participation." Others decided that the best way to keep the new national delegate-selection rules from upsetting their accustomed and preferred ways of doing state and local party business would be to establish a presidential primary and

thereby split off presidential nomination matters from all other party affairs. And still others calculated that the new rules made caucuses and conventions much more vulnerable than a primary to being captured by small but dedicated bands of ideologues.[9]

At a decade's remove in time, and with the matter increasingly disputed by political adversaries rather than as a purely academic bone of contention, it may be exceedingly difficult to recover enough of the historical record to nail this point down conclusively. The matter of motivations is at best conjectural, not least on account of the probable existence of mixtures of motives among many actors, and the consequent overdetermination of the result. It is certainly worth a try, however, to ventilate even if we cannot conclusively settle this issue. There is no disputing, at any rate, that primary elections did proliferate as a means of delegate selection between 1968 and 1972. They have continued to do so. 17 such elections in 1968, 23 in 1972, 30 in 1976, 34 in 1980.

The claim that primaries as a method for selecting delegates introduces certain kinds of distortion into the process rests on two bases. One has to do with the sorts of participants who dominate primary electorates. The other has to do with the formal properties of choice in primary elections as they are run in the United States, in which outcomes are produced by aggregating the first—and only the first—preferences of voters who spread their selections over a broad field of contenders.

Because primary elections have long been a feature of American state politics, a line of argument that has some claim to venerability in political science establishes the first point. As V. O. Key, Jr., one of the ablest of those who have studied the matter, says, "The American political tradition caps decisions made by popular vote with a resplendent halo of legitimacy."[10] Yet the chapter of Key's book of which this is the first sentence is titled: *Participation in Primaries: The Illusion of Popular Rule*.

Key establishes that in the large number of state primaries which he examined, in several states and over a number of different elections, "the effective primary constituency" is often "a caricature of the entire party following."[11]

Key's major findings—that state primary electorates were unrepresentative of the state electorate, and that candidates frequently needed to mobilize only very small numbers of voters to win—are confirmed for more recent national primary elections, notably by work of Austin Ranney, James I. Lengle, and the Democratic party's own Winograd Commission.[12] Table 2.2.1 gives Winograd Commission findings comparing Democratic primary electorates with Democratic voters in the 1976 election for 13 states.

Consistently, and not only in the instant case, those voters lower down on the socioeconomic scale are disproportionately missing from primary electorates.

The second sort of distortion which primary elections promote is harder to describe. It is nevertheless as well founded in the literature of political science as the first, and rests on the seemingly intractable fact that once the number of alternatives available to an electorate gets above two, and so long as only the first choices of voters are counted, there is a lively possibility that the plurality winner of such an election will not be a true majority choice.[13] Two strategic imperatives are thus created: one suggests that it is in the interests of party leaders to restrict and channel choices by primary electorates so that majority sentiment in the general election can be mobilized. The other is that it is in the interests of candidates to put themselves forward into the lottery in large numbers, thus reducing the number of voters necessary for any candidate among them to attract in order to win. The interests of candidates are squarely counterpoised against those of party leaders: party leaders desire the assembly of coalitions, candidates the mobilization of factions.[14]

Key says:

> The small size of the blocs of voters necessary to win nominations has a most significant consequence for the nature of the party.... The direct communion of potential candidates with small groups of voters places enormous difficulties in the way of those party leaders disposed to work beyond the primaries to the general election and to put forward the most appealing slate. Individual politicians with a grasp on a small bloc of voters which can be turned into a primary victory are difficult to discipline or to bargain with. The support of even a weak personal organization, the loyalties and admiration of an ethnic group, a wide acquaintance within a religious group, simple notoriety achieved in a variety of ways, an alliance with an influential newspaper—these and a variety of other elements may create power within the narrow circle of people who share control in the politics of the direct primary.[15]

The risk in the general election is that dissatisfied party voters will bolt the party choice. This may happen if they feel deprived of their first choice by a sequence of primary wins by some other candidate or candidates, and/or deprived of their second or even third choice or of any satisfactory choice by the institutionalized lack of a genuine party deliberative process that weighs the expression of second choice opinion, or that juxtaposes pairs of alternatives *seriatim*, or that takes strongly negative feelings of party—or general election—voters into account. In 1972 and again in 1980 something like 30 percent of voters describing themselves as Democrats evidently deserted the presidential candidate of their party and voted Republican.[16]

The great bulk of the deserters in both years described themselves as dissatisfied with the candidate of their own party, not as ideologically attracted by the Republican candidate.[17] The point is worth underscoring because all three winners—in 1972, 1976, and 1980—have described themselves and been described by their supporters as vested with extraordinary electoral mandates. All behaved as though they thought they had such mandates. None did.[18]

II

The first major proposition of this paper was that the party reforms facilitated the defection of Democratic voters in disgust to the Republican party—twice in numbers sufficient to elect a Republican president—because they have gravely damaged the capacity of the Democratic party to organize a nomination process that can compose the diversity and the differences among party leaders and

Table 2.2.1

Comparison of Democratic Primary Electorate and Democratic General Electorate, 1976

(Percentage of Voters)

State	Less Than High School Education		Black		Over Age 65		College Degree or Beyond		Income Over $20,000/yr.	
	Primary	General	Primary	General	Primary	General	Primary	General	Primary	General
California	11	27	12	15	9	19	34	17	35	23
Florida	13	30	8	14	23	28	28	17	26	16
Illinois	19	34	15	16	8	17	23	6	25	21
Indiana	21	40	10	11	7	24	13	6	17	11
Mass.	12	19	2	3	10	18	36	22	24	24
Michigan	20	30	11	22	11	17	20	10	16	17
New Hamp.	11	18	—	—	6	13	38	18	15	14
New Jersey	12	41	17	26	9	16	35	14	37	19
New York	15	31	15	20	15	14	32	19	32	16
Ohio	15	32	11	17	7	19	25	10	23	17
Oregon	19	18	n.a.	n.a.	23	13	23	20	15	23
Pennsylvania	17	32	8	15	9	15	23	15	20	9
Wisconsin	18	25	3	7	13	19	22	15	n.a.	n.a.

Source: Democratic Party, Commission on Presidential Nomination and Party Structure, "Openness, Participation and Party Building: Reforms for a Stronger Democratic Party," Washington, D.C., Jan. 25, 1978, 11-13.

Note: n.a. signifies data are not available.

presidential hopefuls. The evidence is highly plausible, though for the most part indirect. Alternative explanations such as the idea that Democrats defect because they are closet Republicans founder on all sorts of difficulties: the fact that heavy majorities reject Republican positions on most political issues, that Democrats retain the nominal loyalties of more voters than Republicans, that Democratic voters outnumber Republicans for all other offices.[19]

The second proposition is even harder to establish by means of straightforward argument. Yet there are features of American government since 1972 which do lend themselves to the conclusion that party reform has had an impact on the conduct of the presidency beyond electing the candidate of the minority party in 1972 and 1980 and a factional rather than a consensus choice of the majority party in 1976.

Presumably this argument must rest primarily on the conduct of the Carter presidency, since the Nixon and Reagan presidencies can be set aside as directly attributable to the derangement of electoral results by virtue of the derangement of the nomination process. As more than a few observers have had occasion to remark, the Carter presidency did have a number of curious features.

The most significant of these no doubt was Mr. Carter's seeming inability to get along with Congress. Outside observers were entitled to view this inability with some amazement. After all, President Carter was a middle-of-the-road Democrat, and during his presidency the Congress was controlled—overwhelmingly controlled—by the Democratic party.[20] The last previous time an overwhelmingly Democratic Congress coincided with a Democratic president, after the 1964 landslide election, a bumper crop of new and innovative programs had resulted.[21]

Times had changed on Capitol Hill since the enactment of the Great Society however. Friends of President Carter were quick to point out that important changes had overtaken Congress in the intervening decade and a half, making the task of a president—any president—far more difficult. Congress had democratized its rules, for example, had endured a period of fierce antagonism with President Nixon, had created an enormous staff bureaucracy in part to wage war on the executive branch, and had undergone drastic turn-over in membership so that a majority of members could not hark back to the good old days of presidential-congressional cooperation.

In the old days, it was said, (the examples frequently coming from the Kennedy era of 1961-63) a president could strike a bargain with the congressional leadership, and the leadership could deliver the Congress. Committee chairmen ruled their roosts, and this meant that once a committee chairman committed himself to cooperation with the president, the president's task of assembling a majority in Congress was greatly simplified. By the time of the Carter presidency (1977-1980) the argument goes, committee chairmen had lost their power to the chairmen of subcommittees, and subcommittee chairmanships were dispersed among the multitudes. Instead of cultivating an alliance with twenty senior congressmen, presidential legislative liaison had to court 120 subcommittee chairmen, a much more complicated task.[22]

There is a grain of truth in this argument, but no more than a grain. The "good old days" existed only during the brief span of the 89th Congress. And the bad new days of the Carter era were structurally far more favorable to a middle-of-the-road Democratic president than anything Presidents Truman or Kennedy ever saw. Congressional reform devolved power not only downward to subcommittee chairmen but also upward to the House Democratic leadership. Mistakes, ineptitude and presidential neglect of Congress played a far more significant role in creating the Carter administration legislative record than Carter administration apologists admit. The litany of presidential mistakes toward Congress was nearly endless: an inability to settle upon legislative priorities, a reluctance to bring Congress into the process of formulating proposals before they arrived, fully blown, on Capitol Hill, a disinclination to interact or bargain directly with congressmen and a tendency to appeal to a mythical entity known as "the people" presumably over the heads of congressmen, themselves elected public officials, the vast majority of whom had run well ahead of Jimmy Carter in their home districts.[23]

President Carter's legislative liaison was in

the hands of a person totally inexperienced and unknown on Capitol Hill, but this was only the beginning of the problem. The Carter administration could—and eventually did—hire people more experienced in the ways of Congress to join the liaison staff. But for a time many of these people were housed in the White House's East Wing, physically and symbolically removed from the center of presidential power, and only Frank Moore, their chief, had direct access to the president. The Carter administration ignored the advice of friendly predecessors to establish regular beats for liaison personnel based on the bloc structure of Congress and instead at the beginning established issue specialties for them. This meant that different liaison people would deal with the same Congressman on different issues, and no regular relationship, no orchestration of give and take over the long haul, could easily be established. Worse, presidential liaison people, allegedly issue specialists, were never tied into the policy formation process in the White House and so were denied both flexibility and credibility in dealing with Congress.[24]

Despite repeated efforts from congressional leaders to bridge the gap between Capitol and White House, neither President Carter nor his closest aides who actually participated in policy-making made informal acquaintances in Congress. It became common coin on the Hill that Mr. Carter had conceptualized Congress as indistinguishable from the Georgia legislature.[25] Democrats from all parts of the political spectrum—but most notably those from his own part of the spectrum—began to collect and disburse, like children with bubble-gum cards, a fund of Jimmy Carter stories illustrating his utter lack of interest in listening to congressional advice, his stubbornness, his parochial insularity. He evidently had no back-channels to Capitol Hill and wanted none, no congressional cronies, no unofficial sources of information, indeed virtually no friends.

The political resources of such a president were bound to be easily depleted, even among those, undoubtedly a great number, who wished him no particular ill. Given heavy Democratic majorities, the speaker and the Senate majority leader could rally majorities in behalf of a president who could not or would not help himself, but not easily and not often. For since the rise of large congressional staffs, congressmen no longer need to take the word of the executive branch on any controverted point if they choose not to. The congressional party can now, if it chooses to do so, chart its own course with respect to policy fully in possession of adequate intellectual fortification. The capacity to do so, however, operates at least in part independently of the inclination to do so. The development of staff capacity was a congressional response to the presidency of President Nixon. The use of this capacity when the presidency was in Democratic hands was a response to the presidential style of Jimmy Carter.

In order to get a sense of the internal dynamics of the Carter Congresses in relation to the presidency some historical background is helpful. Essentially, throughout most of the last fifty years, the internal struggle of central importance to Congress has been between liberal Democrats on one hand, and a conservative coalition, encompassing conservative Southern Democrats and Republicans on the other. Franklin Roosevelt's abortive attempt to purge Congress of conservative Democrats was an early recognition of the capacity of the conservative coalition to hamper the political plans of liberal Democratic presidents.[26] The strength of these two grand coalitions has ebbed and flowed over the years, changing tidally with the results of biennial elections.[27] Both sides have taken what advantages they could from internal rules of Congress pertaining especially in the Senate to freedom of debate, in the House to control over the agenda and in both houses to seniority in committee assignments. And both have interacted strategically with the president—the conservative group mobilizing their strength, when they needed to, around threats of vetoes by conservative presidents, and the liberal group around the pressure of liberal presidents' programs. The great resources in the hands of the conservative coalition over most of the fifty years have been the seniority of their leaders, and their tactical skill and tenacity. The great resources of the liberal group were two: numbers, and the claims on the Democratic side of party loyalty.

By 1960, the liberals had the numbers in

the Senate, but in the House of Representatives the picture was quite different. The election of 1958 was a Democratic landslide year, sending 283 Democrats to the House. Yet, as Representative Clem Miller, a liberal Democrat from Northern California, pointed out: "The combination of Southern Democrats and Northern Republicans can always squeak out a majority when they want to, and they want to on a great number of significant issues.... Actually, the Democratic party as non-Southerners define it is a minority in the House."

"There are 160 Northern Democrats and roughly 99 Southern Democrats," Miller figured. "This includes Texas, but does not include the border states ... which generally cancel each other out. Maryland votes against us, West Virginia with us, Missouri cancels itself out, half liberal, half Southern, and Kentucky, ambivalent, sometimes with us and sometimes against us.... Begin with a base of 160 Northern Democratic votes. Add to it fifty percent of the (roughly 30) border state Democrats. We are always 15 to 30 votes shy."[28]

So long as the conservative Democrats from the South have a lively option of coalescing on the floor with a mostly united Republican party, efforts to organize the Democratic party in the House by requiring greater party loyalty of such a large minority are bound to come to grief. From 1958 to 1978, however, the strength of this minority within the Democratic party in the House eroded so as to permit effective action in the Democratic caucus. Meanwhile, liberal Democrats became better organized and better able to mobilize their big battalions as needed.

A slightly different way of doing Clem Miller's arithmetic yields the 20-year comparisons visible in table 2.2.2.

Over a 20-year period it was mostly conservative Southern Democrats who lost their seats to Republicans. Outside the South, Democrats, mostly liberal, replaced Republicans. So over the 20-year span the House became more liberal overall, and this trend was accentuated within the Democratic caucus.

And, indeed, the Democratic caucus was the engine of change within the House this last decade. Prodded by its organized liberals, the Democratic Study Group, the caucus established a subcommittee bill of rights, took power from committee chairmen, deposed chairmen in historic breaches of seniority, put the speaker in charge of committee assignments in general and of assignments to the Rules Committee in particular.[29]

Some of these changes clearly decentralized power; but some took powers previously dispersed to committees and their chairmen and vested them in the House Democratic leadership, and especially the speaker. And it was an organ of centralized party leadership, the caucus, that did it.

These observations must be kept in mind in evaluating the claim that Congress is less tractable than heretofore to leadership from a Democratic president. The twenty-year record of the institution suggests, rather, enormous gains in the numbers of regular Democratic seats, and a sizeable potential for favorable results for any Democratic president willing to work with the leadership in establishing legislative priorities and strategies. A proliferation of subcommittees means, after all, that leadership is needed in scheduling the orderly consideration of what would otherwise soon become an indigestible log-jam of proposals. And with his exclusive right to make appointments to the Rules Committee, the speaker gained the influence he needed to coordinate traffic headed for the House floor. This influence was denied all Speaker O'Neill's predecessors, reaching back to the revolt against Joseph Cannon at the turn of the century.[30]

So it will not do to argue that the undeniably significant changes in the way Congress does business were at the root of difficulties that President Carter had in mobilizing congressional support for his proposals. Congressional change was not a cause of President Carter's problems with Congress, and more generally in governing. Quite to the contrary, if anything, a hard look at Congress deepens the puzzle of Carter's difficulties. By any reasonable gauge, relations with Congress ought to have been bright, not a dark spot in President Carter's record. And so, far from being an explanation, Congress and its difficulties with the Carter administration themselves need explaining.

Why did Mr. Carter maintain such unsatisfactory relations with Congress? One explanation, which no doubt gained popularity from the way White House sources reinforced it, was that Mr. Carter believed he owed Congress nothing and could just as effectively as dealing with Congress directly reach out over the heads of Congress and gain the support of the people for his programs.[31] It is easy to see how such delusions might arise: a by-product of the reform of presidential nominations has been the removal of members of Congress from the process.[32] The gaining of the nomination is now an exercise in mass persuasion; not so long ago it was far more an exercise in élite persuasion. Not until he was far into his term of office did Mr. Carter give any indication that he understood that for a Democrat to govern successfully required the mobilization not merely of the fac-

Table 2.2.2

Coalitions in the House
(1960 and 1980)

	86th Congress 1959-60 Elected 1958	96th Congress 1979-80 Elected 1978
Democrats	280[a]	281
Republicans	152	154
Southern[b] seats	106	108
Conservative Democrats	66	47
Mainstream[c] Democrats	33[d]	31
Republicans	7	30
Non-Southern Seats		
Democrats	181	203
Republicans	145	124
Democratic Caucus Non-South plus		
Mainstream South	214	234
Conservative South	66	47
Conservative Coalition Republicans plus Conservative Southern Democrats	218	201

a. Three vacancies by the end of the Congress.
b. Southern seats are seats from 11 states of the old confederacy.
c. Mainstream Southern Democrats are those whose CQ Party support exceeds their party opposition scores by at least 2-1. Sources: 1960 CQ Almanac (Washington, D.C.: Congressional Quarterly, 1960), 140-141; Congressional Quarterly Weekly Report, Jan. 10, 1981, pp. 82-83.
d. Includes Speaker Rayburn.

tion that nominated him but also of the grand coalition that elects and reelects Democrats.

In the pattern of his cabinet appointments an observer could read President Carter's determination to neglect the broad Democratic coalition.[33] Interest groups traditionally tied to the party—most conspicuously labor unions and ethnic groups—were ignored. In office President Carter dedicated himself to highminded administrative goals: efficiency, uniformity, reduction of waste, zero-base budgeting, comprehensive reform, and finding once and for all solutions to problems.[34] Moreover, he maintained these theoretical commitments to general and far-reaching purposes while separating himself from the piecemeal accommodations of bureaucrats and the narrowly focused desires of interest groups. This poses a fundamental problem. How is it that President Carter found it possible to gratify this theoretical preference in the harsh arena of national politics?

The most satisfactory answer to this, and to all the other puzzles of the Carter presidency I have named, is that Mr. Carter learned the wrong lessons from his long and difficult struggle to achieve the presidential nomination. These lessons he took with him into the White House and they exercised a profound and lasting influence upon the way he sought to govern.

III

This seems to me a bare outline of the sort of argument that would have to be made in support of the proposition that the party reforms of 1968-72 succeeded so well that they influenced the conduct of the presidency. There is surely nothing inevitable about the way in which the Carter presidency took shape. Nevertheless, as the nomination machinery has evolved, it has been possible for candidates to emerge and be elected president without coming to terms with the need to build a broad party coalition. Nothing in the processes that screen and winnow candidates compels attentiveness to the field of forces that exists once a newly elected president is faced with the need to govern. He may never learn how to govern, or he may learn too late.

Notes

1. Curtis B. Gans, "How the White House Is Won," *Washington Post Book World* (Aug. 12, 1979), 10.

2. Compare, for example, the disparities between party identifications as monitored by public opinion surveys and presidential vote:

	Dem. % of Party ID	Dem. % of Pres. Vote	Rep. % of Party ID	Rep. % of Pres. Vote
1968	55	43	33	43
1972	51	38	34	61
1976	52	50	33	48
1980	52	41	33	51

Source: Center for Political Studies, University of Michigan, (Independent leaners included with the party toward which they lean).

3. In August of 1968, just before the Democratic convention, Humphrey got 29% of the vote in a Gallup trial heat with Ricahrd Nixon and George Wallace; in early September, he got 31%. On average, candidates jump about 8 points after they are nominated. See *Gallup Opinion Index* Report 183, Dec. 1980.

4. For accounts of the reform process, see Byron Shafer, *The Party Reformed: Reform Politics in the Democratic Party 1968-1972* (Ph.D. dissertation, University of California, Berkeley, 1979); and William J. Crotty, *Decision for the Democrats* (Baltimore: Johns Hopkins, 1978). The court cases are Cousins v. Wigoda, 419 US 477 (1975), and Democratic Party v. LaFollette, 49 US. Law Week 4178 (1981).

5. Kenneth A. Bode and Carol F. Casey, "Party Reform: Revisionism Revised" in Robert A. Goldwin (ed.), *Political Parties in the Eighties* (Washington: AEI, 1980), 3-19.

6. Ibid., 17.

7. Ibid., 10.

8. Report of the Commission on Presidential Nomination and Party Structure (Morley A. Winograd, Chairman), *Openness, Participation, and Party Building: Reforms for a Stronger Democratic Party* (Washington: Democratic National Committee, Jan. 1947), 25.

9. Austin Ranney, *The Federalization of Presidential Primaries* (Washington, D.C.: AEI, 1978), 2-3.

10. V. O. Key, Jr., *American State Politics* (New York: Knopf, 1956), 133.

11. Ibid., 152.

12. Ranney, op cit., and Ranney, *Curing the Mischiefs of Faction* (Berkeley: University of California, 1975); James I. Lengle, *Representation and Presidential Primaries: The Democratic Party in the Post-Reform Era* (Ph.D. dissertation, University of California, Berkeley, 1978); Report of the Commission on Presidential Nomination and Party Structure, op cit.

13. See Kenneth Arrow, *Social Choice and Individual Values* (New York: Wiley, 1963).

14. For more on this problem see Nelson W. Polsby, "Coalition and Faction in American Politics: An Insti-

tutional View," by Seymour Martin Lipset (ed.), *Emerging Coalitions in American Politics* (San Francisco, Calif.: Institute for Contemporary Studies, 1978), 103-123.

15. Key, op cit., 144-145.

16.
Defection Levels for Democrats
1952-1980

Year	To Rep. Cand.	To 3rd Party	Total
1980	26%	4%	30%
1976	18		18
1972	33		33
1968	12	14	26
1964	13		13
1960	16		16
1956	15		15
1952	23		23

Post-1968 mean: 27% Democratic defection
1952-1968 mean: 18.6% Democratic defection
Source: The Gallup Opinion Index Report No. 183, Dec. 1980, 6-7.

17. See Everett Carll Ladd, "The Brittle Mandate: Electoral Dealignment and the 1980 Presidential Election," *Political Science Quarterly* 96 (Spring, 1981), 1-25. Also, Adam Clymer, "Displeasure with Carter Turned Many to Reagan," *New York Times*, Nov. 9, 1980; and *Public Opinion* (Dec./Jan. 1981), 43.

18. See Nelson W. Polsby, "Interest Groups and the Presidency: Trends in Political Intermediation in America," in Walter Dean Burnham and Martha Wagner Weinberg (eds.), *American Politics and Public Policy* (Cambridge, Mass.: MIT Press, 1978), 41-52.

19. Ladd, op cit.; Arthur Miller, "What Mandate? What Realignment?" *Washington Post Outlook* (June 28, 1981); Louis Harris, "No Mandate for a Switch on Social Questions Seen," *Washington Post* (Dec. 4, 1980); George Skelton, "Conservative Mandate for Reagan Contains Limits," *Los Angeles Times* (Nov. 20, 1980); *Public Opinion* (Dec./Jan. 1981), 24-25.

20. The 95th Congress (1977-78) began with 292 Democrats and 143 Republicans (67% Democratic). The 96th Congress (1979-80) had 276 Democrats and 159 Republicans (63.4% Democratic).

21. Convenient overviews are contained in the *Congressional Quarterly Almanac* 21 (1965), 65-112, and ibid., 22 (1966), 69-130.

22. See e.g., Lance Morrow, "A Cry for Leadership," *Time* (Aug. 6, 1979), 24-28.

23. In 1976 President Carter ran ahead of just 22 winning Democrats in the House and behind 270. John F. Bibby, Thomas E. Mann, Norman Ornstein, *Vital Statistics on Congress, 1980* (Washington, D.C.: AEI, 1980), 20.

24. Eric L. Davis, "Legislative Liaison in the Carter Administration," *Political Science Quarterly* 94 (Summer, 1979), 287-301. For a compendium of complaints about Carter's handling of Congress, see Betty Glad, *Jimmy Carter: In Search of the Great White House* (New York: Norton, 1980), 417-27; Haynes Johnson, *In the Absence of Power* (New York: Viking, 1980), 154-168 and passim; Dom Bonafede, "Carter's Relationship with Congress—Making a Mountain Out of a 'Moorehill'" *National Journal* (March 26, 1977), 456-463 and "The Tough Job of Normalizing Relations with Capitol Hill," *National Journal* (Jan. 13, 1979), 54-57.

25. See Haynes Johnson, op cit., 22, 43.

26. J. B. Shannon, "Presidential Politics in the South, 1938—I," *Journal of Politics* 1 (May, 1939), 146-170. "Presidential Politics in the South 1938—II," *Journal of Politics* 1 (Aug. 1939), 278-300.

27. See John F. Manley, "The Conservative Coalition in Congress," in Robert L. Peabody and Nelson W. Polsby (eds.), *New Perspectives on the House of Representatives* (Chicago: Rand McNally, 1977), 97-117; James Patterson, *Congressional Conservatism and the New Deal* (Lexington: University of Kentucky Press, 1967); David W. Brady and Charles S. Bullock III, "Coalition Politics in the House of Representatives," in Lawrence C. Dodd and Bruce I. Oppenheimer, *Congress Reconsidered* 2nd edition (Washington, D.C.: C.Q. Press, 1981), 186-203; Mack C. Shelley II, "The Conservative Coalition and the President, 1953-1978," a paper delivered at the Southern Political Science Association Annual Meeting, Gatlinburg, Tennessee, Nov.1979.

28. Clem Miller, Member of the House: *Letters of a Congressman*, John W. Baker, ed. (New York: Scribners, 1962), 123-124.

29. On Congressional reforms during the 1970s, see Norman J. Ornstein and David W. Rhode, "Shifting Forces, Changing Rules and Political Outcomes: The Impact of Congressional Change on Four House Committees," in Peabody and Polsby, op cit., 186-269; Lawrence C. Dodd, "Congress and the Quest for Power," in Lawrence C. Dodd and Bruce I. Oppenheimer (eds.), *Congress Reconsidered*, 1st edition (New York: Praeger, 1977), 269-307; and Roger H. Davidson and Walter J. Oleszek, *Congress Against Itself* (Bloomington: Indiana University Press, 1977).

30. For a list of the powers lost by Cannon in the year 1909-10 and not regained in the intervening years, see *Guide to the Congress of the United States* (Washington, D.C.: Congressional Quarterly, 1971), 42-43, 134-135 and 603.

31. Glad, op cit., 420, and Johnson, op cit., 22.

32. For figures on the precipitous decline in the direct participation of members of Congress in the nomination process, see "Report of the Commission on Presidential Nomination and Party Structure," op cit., 18.

33. See Nelson W. Polsby, "Presidential Cabinet Making: Lessons for the Political System," *Political Science Quarterly* 93 (Spring, 1978), 15-25.

34. A discerning article which finds these themes in President Carter's 1976 campaign speeches is Jack Knott and Aaron Wildavsky, "Jimmy Carter's Theory of Governing," *The Wilson Quarterly* 1 (Winter, 1977), 49-67.

Illustration 2a: The Constitution on the Electoral College and Presidential Elections

The following are excerpts from the Constitution and amendments pertaining to presidential selection or removal. Article II establishes the electoral college—an American innovation whereby citizens vote as states not as individuals—and the impeachment and removal process. Amendment XII refines the electoral college so that presidents and vice-presidents will be of the same party. Amendment XX abbreviated lame-duck governments. Amendment XXII restricts presidents to two full terms. Amendment XXIII enfranchises voters in the District of Columbia. Amendment XXIII outlawed the poll tax. Amendment XXV provides for an appointed vice-president in case of a vacancy in the vice-presidency. It also details procedures for dealing with presidential inability. Amendment XXVI secured voting rights for eighteen-year-olds.

Article II

Each State shall appoint, in such Manner as the Legislature thereof may direct, a Number of Electors, equal to the whole Number of Senators and Representatives to which the State may be entitled in Congress: but no Senator or Representative, or Person holding an Office of Trust or Profit under the United States, shall be appointed an Elector.

The Electors shall meet in their respective States, and vote by Ballot for two Persons, of whom one at least shall not be an Inhabitant of the same State with themselves. And they shall make a List of all the Persons voted for, and of the Number of Votes for each; which List they shall sign and certify, and transmit sealed to the Seat of the Government of the United States, directed to the President of the Senate. The President of the Senate shall, in the Presence of the Senate and House of Representatives, open all the Certificates, and the Votes shall then be counted. The Person having the greatest Number of Votes shall be the President, if such Number be a Majority of the whole Number of Electors appointed; and if there be more than one who have such Majority, and have an equal Number of Votes, then the House of Representatives shall immediately chuse by Ballot one of them for President; and if no Person have a Majority, then from the five highest on the List the said House shall in like Manner chuse the President. But in chusing the President, the Votes shall be taken by States, the Representation from each State having one Vote; A quorum for this Purpose shall consist of a Member or Members from two thirds of the States, and a Majority of all the States shall be necessary to a Choice. In every Case, after the Choice of the President, the Person having the greatest Number of Votes of the Electors shall be the Vice President. But if there should remain two or more who have equal Votes, the Senate shall chuse from them by Ballot the Vice President.

The Congress may determine the Time of chusing the Electors, and the Day on which they shall give their Votes; which Day shall be the same throughout the United States.

No Person except a natural born Citizen, or a Citizen of the United States, at the time of the Adoption of this Constitution, shall be eligible to the Office of President; neither shall any Person be eligible to that Office who shall not have attained to the Age of thirty five Years, and been fourteen Years a Resident within the United States.

In Case of the Removal of the President from Office, or of his Death, Resignation, or Inability to discharge the Powers and Duties of the said Office, the Same shall devolve on the Vice President, and the Congress may by Law provide for the Case of Removal, Death, Resignation or Inability, both of the President and Vice President, declaring what Officer shall then act as President, and such Officer shall act accordingly, until the Disability be removed, or a President shall be elected.

The President shall, at stated Times, receive for his Services, a Compensation, which shall neither be encreased nor diminished during the Period for which he shall have been elected, and he shall not receive within that Period any other Emolument from the United States, or any of them.

Before he enter on the Execution of his Office, he shall take the following Oath or Affirmation:—"I do solemnly swear (or affirm) that I will faithfully execute the Office of President of the United States, and will to the best of my Ability, preserve, protect and defend the Constitution of the United States."

[Amendment XII]

The Electors shall meet in their respective states, and vote by ballot for President and Vice-President, one of whom, at least, shall not be an inhabitant of the same state with themselves; they shall name in their ballots the person voted for as President, and in distinct ballots the person voted for as Vice-President, and they shall make distinct lists of all persons voted for as President, and of all persons voted for as Vice-President, and of the number of votes for each, which lists they shall sign and certify, and transmit sealed to the seat of the government of the United States, directed to the President of the Senate;—The President of the Senate shall, in the presence of the Senate and House of Representatives, open all the certificates and the votes shall then be counted;—The person having the greatest number of votes for President, shall be the President, if such number be a majority of the whole number of Electors appointed; and if no person have such majority, then from the persons having the highest numbers not exceeding three on the list of those voted for as President, the House of Representatives shall choose immediately, by ballot, the President. But in choosing the President, the votes shall be taken by states, the representation from each state having one vote; a quorum for this purpose shall consist of a member or members from two-thirds of the states, and a majority of all the states shall be necessary to a choice. And if the House of Representatives shall not choose a President whenever the right of choice shall devolve upon them, before the fourth day of March next following, then the Vice-President shall act as President, as in the case of the death or other constitutional disability of the President.—The person having the greatest number of votes as Vice-President, shall be the Vice-President, if such number be a majority of the whole number of Electors appointed, and if no person have a majority, then from the two highest numbers on the list, the Senate shall choose the Vice-President; a quorum for the purpose shall consist of two-thirds of the whole number of Senators, and a majority of the whole number shall be necessary to a choice. But no person constitutionally ineligible to the office of President shall be eligible to that of Vice-President of the United States.

[Amendment XX]

Section 1.
The terms of the President and Vice President shall end at noon on the 20th day of January, and the terms of Senators and Representatives at noon on the 3d day of January, of the years in which such terms would have ended if this article had not been ratified; and the terms of their successors shall then begin.

Section 2.
The Congress shall assemble at least once a day in every year, and such meeting shall begin at noon on the 3d day of January, unless they shall by law appoint a different day.

Section 3.
If, at the time fixed for the beginning of the term of the President, the President elect shall have died, the Vice President elect shall become President. If a President shall not have been chosen before the time fixed for the beginning of his term, or if the President elect shall have failed to qualify, then the Vice

President elect shall act as President until a President shall have qualified; and the Congress may by law provide for the case wherein neither a President elect nor a Vice President elect shall have qualified, declaring who shall then act as President, or the manner in which one who is to act shall be selected, and such person shall act accordingly until a President or Vice President shall have qualified.

Section 4.

The Congress may by law provide for the case of the death of any of the persons from whom the House of Representatives may choose a President whenever the right of choice shall have devolved upon them, and for the case of the death of any of the persons from whom the Senate may choose a Vice President whenever the right of choice shall have devolved upon them.

Section 5.

Sections 1 and 2 shall take effect on the 15th day of October following the ratification of this article.

[Amendment XXII]

Section 1.

No person shall be elected to the office of the President more than twice, and no person who has held the office of President, or acted as President, for more than two years of a term to which some other person was elected President shall be elected to the office of the President more than once. But this Article shall not apply to any person holding the office of President when the Article was proposed by the Congress, and shall not prevent any person who may be holding the office of President, or acting as President, during the term within which this Article becomes operative from holding the office of President or acting as President during the remainder of such term.

Section 2.

This article shall be inoperative unless it shall have been ratified as an amendment to the Constitution by the legislatures of three-fourths of the several States within seven years from the date of its submission to the States by the Congress.

[Amendment XXIII]

Section 1.

The District constituting the seat of Government of the United States shall appoint in such manner as the Congress shall direct:

A number of electors of President and Vice President equal to the whole number of Senators and Representatives in Congress to which the District would be entitled if it were a State, but in no event more than the least populous State; they shall be in addition to those appointed by the States, but they shall be considered, for the purposes of the election of President and Vice President, to be electors appointed by a State; and they shall meet in the District and perform such duties as provided by the twelfth article of amendment.

Section 2.

The Congress shall have power to enforce this article by appropriate legislation.

[Amendment XXIV]

Section 1.

The right of citizens of the United States to vote in any primary or other election for President or Vice President, for electors for President or Vice President, or for Senator or Representative in Congress, shall not be denied or abridged by the United States or any state by reason of failure to pay any poll tax or other tax.

Section 2.

The Congress shall have the power to enforce this article by appropriate legislation.

[Amendment XXV]

Section 1.

In case of the removal of the President from office or his death or resignation, the Vice President shall become President.

Section 2.

Whenever there is a vacancy in the office of the Vice President, the President shall nominate a Vice President who shall take the office upon confirmation by a majority vote of both houses of Congress.

Section 3.

Whenever the President transmits to the President pro tempore of the Senate and the Speaker of the House of Representatives his written declaration that he is unable to discharge the powers and duties of his office, and until he transmits to them a written declaration to the contrary, such powers and duties shall be discharged by the Vice President as Acting President.

Section 4.

Whenever the Vice President and a majority of either the principal officers of the executive departments or of such other body as Congress may by law provide, transmit to the President pro tempore of the Senate and the Speaker of the House of Representatives their written declaration that the President is unable to discharge the powers and duties of his office, the Vice President shall immediately assume the powers and duties of the office as Acting President.

Thereafter, when the President transmits to the President pro tempore of the Senate and the Speaker of the House of Representatives his written declaration that no inability exists, he shall resume the powers and duties of his office unless the Vice President and a majority of either the principal officers of the executive department or of such other body as Congress may by law provide, transmit within four days to the President pro tempore of the Senate and the Speaker of the House of Representatives their written declaration that the President is unable to discharge the powers and duties of his office. Thereupon Congress shall decide the issue, assembling within 48 hours for that purpose if not in session. If the Congress, within 21 days after receipt of the latter written declaration, or, if Congress is not in session, within 21 days after Congress is required to assemble, determines by two-thirds vote of both houses that the President is unable to discharge the powers and duties of his office, the Vice President shall continue to discharge the same as Acting President; otherwise, the President shall resume the powers and duties of his office.

[Amendment XXVI]

Section 1.

The right of citizens of the United States, who are 18 years of age or older, to vote shall not be denied or abridged by the United States or any state on account of age.

Section 2.

The Congress shall have the power to enforce this article by appropriate legislation.

Illustration 2b: The Hunt Commission, Report of the Commission on Presidential Nomination

In the aftermath of the 1968 Democratic convention, the Democrats substantially altered their convention rules and delegate selection procedures with the adoption of the report of the McGovern-Fraser Commission. Since state law had to be changed, the Republicans were also caught up in the movement for more primaries, more participation, and less party control. Since 1972, the Democrats have tried to modify and soften McGovern-Fraser with three subsequent study commissions: Mikulski (1975), Winograd (1979), and Hunt (1982). Each of these sought to rectify problems with McGovern-Fraser rule changes and to re-establish a role for party regulars. The following excerpts from the summary of recommendations by the Hunt Commission reveal these efforts to "finetune," both to overcome defects and to restore a semblance of party control. In assessing the desirability of these changes, students should think of the pros and cons of party control of candidate selection vis-à-vis a more open system.

Summary of Recommendations

The major recommendations of the Commission can be summarized as follows:

1. Bring elected and party officials more effectively into the nomination process. In addition to the 10 percent "add-on" provided for in the 1980 rules, approximately 550 slots would be allocated to the states for the inclusion of party and elected officials as unpledged delegates. Some of these would be named by the House and Senate Democratic Caucuses—up to 3/5 of their respective numbers—and the balance named by the state parties, giving priority of consideration to governors and large-city mayors. Unpledged delegate slots would also be reserved for each state's chair and vice chair.

2. Shorten the primary/caucus season. The Commission proposes that the early March-early June "window" established in the 1980 rules be retained. Limited exemptions would be given for New Hampshire and Iowa, but neither these nor any other exempted states would be allowed to hold a primary more than one week in advance of the second Tuesday in March or a caucus more than 15 days in advance of that date. Had this rule been in effect in 1980, the season would have begun five weeks later.

3. Reaffirm the party's commitments to affirmative action and equal division. Goals and targets under these programs would apply to every state's entire delegation. The state parties' responsibility to help lower-income delegates find assistance would be established more clearly.

4. Return a measure of decisionmaking discretion to the national convention. Mechanisms such as candidate right of approval, designed to insure that delegates pledged to a candidate are bona fide supporters, would remain in the rules. But the addition of an increment of unpledged delegates, and the loosening of the "binding" rule (11H) as it applies to *all* delegates, would restore to the convention flexibility and an ability to respond to changed circumstances.

5. Give the states additional options under fair reflection guidelines. States could choose to operate under proportional representation as contained in the 1980 rules. Alternatively, they could award a "bonus"

delegate in each district to the winner in that district, or could choose to elect district-level delegates directly on the ballot.

6. Retain the ban on primaries in which non-Democrats can vote contained in the 1980 rules and upheld by the Supreme Court in the *Democratic Party* v. *LaFollette* decision (1981). Strengthen the rule against the imposition of fees and other undue restrictions on participation.

These rules changes reflect the Commission's determination to preserve the gains made in recent years in broadening participation and maintaining a fair and open process. They also reflect a determination to write rules consistent with our overall goals of party renewal. This is the common thread running through the proposals we have made: *building the party*. We propose to reduce the party's fragmentation and to increase the legitimacy of the nomination process by shortening the season and reducing the disproportionate impact of single early states. We strongly feel that the integrity of our nomination process should be protected, both against crossover voting and "raiding" and against any undue restrictions on participation. We propose to make our convention more representative, both by maintaining a strong affirmative action program and by giving a greater role to those elected and party officials who speak for broad constituencies within the party. Our proposals would restore a measure of decision-making flexibility and discretion to the national convention and strengthen the processes of peer review that are crucial to picking the strongest candidate. Finally, the Commission's recommendations would place a premium on coalition-building within the party prior to nomination and would promote a stronger party tie among our elected officials, changes that would make for more effective campaigning and would increase our capacity to govern.

Thus, while the Commission is proposing no wholesale departures from the rules-writing efforts of the past, we have not merely "tinkered." We are making significant proposals that bear on fundamental party goals. Our aim has been to help make the Democratic party a strong and vital organization, a broadly representative party, and a link uniting the elements of government for concerted action. While rules and procedures cannot achieve this alone, we make our recommendations in the firm belief that they can contribute measurably to the renewal of the Democratic party at this critical historical time.

Further Concerns: Primaries and Timing

The rules changes proposed by the Commission are a realistic response to many of our party's needs. In the course of our deliberations, however, we have been convinced of the seriousness of some additional problems which rules changes have only a limited capacity to influence but to which our party's national and state leaders should give serious attention as they plan for 1984. The Technical Advisory Committee and Commission staff have prepared analyses in two critical areas—the proliferation of primaries, and trends in the timing of delegate selection events within the March-June "window" period.

(1) Primaries were held in 33 states, D.C., and Puerto Rico in 1980. Four of these (Idaho, Vermont, Michigan, and Texas) were "beauty contest" primaries, not used to choose or allocate delegates. The delegate slots allocated by the remaining 31 contests accounted for some 71 percent of the votes at the convention. In 1968, by contrast, 17 states held binding primaries which allocated 42 percent of the votes at the convention.

Our Commission, like the Winograd Commission before it, has noted this trend with concern. We acknowledge the positive contributions primaries make to the delegate selection process: they can involve large numbers of people, test grass-roots sentiment, and provide a series of forums for the exposure of candidates and the development of issues. But primaries have critical shortcomings. Their proliferation has made for more protracted, more expensive, more divisive, and more media-dominated campaigns. They have threatened to eclipse the organized party. While caucuses may involve fewer people than primaries, the *quality* of participation—and the contribution to party-building—are much higher. Data from Iowa suggest, for example, that a large percentage of those who turn out for the first-stage caucuses work actively for the ticket in the Fall. Primaries often do little to draw people into party structures. In fact, they devalue party caucuses and conventions by removing decision-making power from them.

Critics of current trends generally do not see primaries as undesirable *per se*; the problem is rather an unbalanced *mix* of primary and caucus systems and the undue *weight* primary results have in determining the nomination outcome. What might the party do to encourage a better balance? The Commission has considered a range of possible measures: a "freeze" whereby states would be permitted to move from primaries to caucuses but not the reverse; a limit on the percentage of a state's delegates who could be selected in a primary or allocated by primary result (thus requiring a second allocation system for the remainder of the delegates); the awarding of delegate bonuses to caucus states. Most such measures are complex and are potentially coercive, and in the end the Commission chose not to employ them. But that does not mean we take the problem lightly. We note with some satisfaction that the proliferation of primaries leveled off between 1976 and 1980; current indications are that there will be no more binding primaries in 1984 than there were in 1980 and perhaps some fewer. It is our conviction that it should be the policy of the national party to use whatever incentives and persuasive power it has at its disposal to encourage more states to shift from primaries to caucuses so that a better overall balance might result. We urge the Democratic National Committee to undertake an immediate review of the steps required to implement this policy.

(2) A second matter worthy of sustained attention is the trend toward the "front-loading" of delegate selection events within the window period. In 1972, for example, only 17 percent of the delegates in primary states had been elected and/or bound to a primary candidate by mid-April; in 1976 the comparable percentage was 33 percent and in 1980, 44 percent. Such trends threaten the pacing and the responsiveness of the process in several respects. They give even greater influence to a few "pace-setting" early states. They threaten to "lock up" the nomination prematurely, foreshortening the period during which candidacies may be developed and issues may emerge. They make the party and its convention less able to respond to a changing political environment. And they devalue states whose primaries and caucuses come late, reducing the prospects of a meaningful showdown between major candidates at the end of the window period.

Some of the Commission's recommendations have some potential for alleviating the front-loading problem. Allowing states to depart from strict proportional representation as a basis for delegate allocation holds out the promise of a greater impact to large, closely contested states—and thus could relieve some of the pressure they have felt to move their events forward. And the presence of a sizable number of unpledged delegates will make it more difficult to "lock up" the nomination early, thus giving greater importance to the later states. But, as with the question of the proliferation of primaries, the Commission has declined to enact more complex or coercive measures. These might have included a "freeze" whereby states could move their events later but not earlier; allowing the direct election of delegates or other modifications of proportional representation only for states that scheduled their primaries or caucuses after a certain date; or awarding delegate bonuses to states that come late in the process. Again, our decision to refrain from these more intrusive measures does not signal a lack of concern. On the contrary: we urge our national and state party leadership to keep the front-loading problem uppermost in their minds as they schedule primaries and caucuses for 1984 and to do all within their power to maintain an even spread of events throughout the entire delegate season. Otherwise, the fairness and responsiveness of the process could be placed in jeopardy.

Illustration 2c: An Excerpt from Federal Election Campaign Laws

In addition to state law and party rules, presidential campaigns, with the advent of public financing of conventions and campaigns, are regulated by the Internal Revenue Code. The following is the section of that law providing for matching funds for primary contestants.

§9031. Short title

This chapter may be cited as the "Presidential Primary Matching Payment Account Act."

§9032. Definitions

For the purposes of this chapter—

(1) The term "authorized committee" means, with respect to the candidates of a political party for President and Vice President of the United States, any political committee which is authorized in writing by such candidates to incur expenses to further the election of such candidates. Such authorization shall be addressed to the chairman of such political committee, and a copy of such authorization shall be filed by such candidates with the Commission. Any withdrawal of any authorization shall also be in writing and shall be addressed and filed in the same manner as the authorization.

(2) The term "candidate" means an individual who seeks nomination for election to be President of the United States. For purposes of this paragraph, an individual shall be considered to seek nomination for election if he—
  (A) takes the action necessary under the law of a State to qualify himself for nomination for election,
  (B) receives contributions or incurs qualified campaign expenses, or
  (C) gives his consent for any other person to receive contributions or to incur qualified campaign expenses on his behalf.

The term "candidate" shall not include any individual who is not actively conducting campaigns in more than one State in connection with seeking nomination for election to be President of the United States.

(3) The term "Commission" means the Federal Election Commission established by section 437c(a)(1) of title 2.

(4) Except as provided by section 9034(a), the term "contribution"—
  (A) means a gift, subscription, loan, advance, or deposit of money, or anything of value, the payment of which was made on or after the beginning of the calendar year immediately preceding the calendar year of the presidential election with respect to which such gift, subscription, loan, advance, or deposit of money, or anything of value, is made, for the purpose of influencing the result of a primary election.
  (B) means a contract, promise, or agreement, whether or not legally enforceable, to make a contribution for any such purpose.
  (C) means funds received by a political committee which are transferred to that committee from another committee, and
  (D) means the payment by any person other than a candidate, or his authorized committee, of compensation for the personal services of another person

which are rendered to the candidate or committee without charge, but
(E) does not include—
  (i) except as provided in subparagraph (D), the value of personal services rendered to or for the benefit of a candidate by an individual who receives no compensation for rendering such service to or for the benefit of the candidate, or
  (ii) payments under section 9037.
(5) The term "matching payment account" means the Presidential Primary Matching Payment Account established under section 9037(a).
(6) The term "matching payment period" means the period beginning with the beginning of the calendar year in which a general election for the office of President of the United States will be held and ending on the date on which the national convention of the party whose nomination a candidate seeks nominates its candidate for the office of President of the United States, or, in the case of a party which does not make such nomination by national convention, ending on the earlier of—
(A) the date such party nominates its candidate for the office of President of the United States, or
(B) the last day of the last national convention held by a major party during such calendar year.
(7) The term "primary election" means an election, including a runoff election or a nominating convention or caucus held by a political party, for the selection of delegates to a national nominating convention of a political party, or for the expression of a preference for the nomination of persons for election to the office of President of the United States.
(8) The term "political committee" means any individual, committee, association, or organization (whether or not incorporated) which accepts contributions or incurs qualified campaign expenses for the purpose of influencing, or attempting to influence, the nomination of any person for election to the office of President of the United States.
(9) The term "qualified campaign expense" means a purchase, payment, distribution, loan, advance, deposit, or gift of money or of anything of value—
(A) incurred by a candidate, or by his authorized committee, in connection with his campaign for nomination for election, and
(B) neither the incurring nor payment of which constitutes a violation of any law of the United States or of the State in which the expense is incurred or paid.
For purposes of this paragraph, an expense is incurred by a candidate or by an authorized committee if it is incurred by a person specifically authorized in writing by the candidate or committee, as the case may be, to incur such expense on behalf of the candidate or the committee.
(10) The term "State" means each State of the United States and the District of Columbia.

§9033. Eligibility for payments

(a) *Conditions.* To be eligible to receive payments under section 9037, a candidate shall, in writing—
(1) agree to obtain and furnish to the Commission any evidence it may request of qualified campaign expenses,
(2) agree to keep and furnish to the Commission any records, books, and other information it may request, and
(3) agree to an audit and examination by the Commission under section 9038 and to pay any amounts required to be paid under such section.

Illustration 2c

(b) *Expense limitation; declaration of intent; minimum contributions.* To be eligible to receive payments under section 9037, a candidate shall certify to the Commission that—
(1) the candidate and his authorized committees will not incur qualified campaign expenses in excess of the limitations on such expenses under section 9035,
(2) the candidate is seeking nomination by a political party for election to the office of President of the United States,
(3) the candidate has received matching contributions which in the aggregate, exceed $5,000 in contributions from residents of each of at least 20 States, and
(4) the aggregate of contributions certified with respect to any person under paragraph (3) does not exceed $250.

Organizing the Presidency: The Administrative Presidency | 3

In understanding the executive function of government, it is best to think in terms of "the presidency," and not just "the president," for the office of the modern president now includes a huge staff network. The "institutionalized presidency" is comprised of the White House staff (counselors, press aids, advisors) and the Executive Office of the President, or presidential support agencies (e.g., NSC, OMB, Council of Economic Advisors). This formal advisory system is augmented informally with both insiders and outsiders.

This chapter surveys the institutionalized presidency: its structure, growth, procedures, and impacts. It also examines the relationships that develop between presidents and top advisors, including the vice-president. In surveying the operations of the White House, students should be attuned to questions that have been raised concerning both the growth and values of White House government. For some observers, the excessive growth of White House and executive office staff assists presidents in better performing their constitutional functions. For others, large White House staffs have led to a palace guard syndrome that isolates presidents.

Growth and Development of the President's Office 3.1

Harold Relyea[1]

The following essay, written as part of a report to Congress by the Congressional Research Service (CRS) of the Library of Congress, details the origins and growth of the president's office.

Since the beginning of World War II, successive American chief executives have utilized the services of a retinue of assistants, regarded by some as "the invisible presidency" and characterized by others in a more colorful manner as "the palace guard."[2] Such auxiliaries function as advisers, giving counsel on such matters as the president may designate; policy aides, coordinating programs, carrying out liaison with other institutions of government, performing political duties, or coordinating the managerial actions of other officials; or support staff, providing clerical

From the Congressional Research Service, Library of Congress.

assistance or operating and maintaining the executive mansion. These individuals usually are institutionally located in the White House Office, the cabinet, or the Executive Office agencies. The historical pattern of presidential staffing—involving these structures—has generally been (1) initial cabinet supremacy as an entity assisting the president which, (2) by the time of the Jackson administration, was supplanted by informal groups of counsel composed of politically significant individuals from within the government and outside of it. The cabinet's importance continued to decline, particularly during the regimes of strong and independent executives such as Lincoln, Cleveland, Roosevelt I, Wilson, and Roosevelt II, followed by (3) experimental administrative and managerial extensions of the presidency—the Council of National Defense, the Executive Council, and the National Emergency Council—further undermining the cabinet's advisory and policy-execution role. When these experimental efforts were subsumed, by the Executive Office of the President, the cabinet stood in a functionally subservient relationship to a panoply of presidential staff agencies containing a myriad number of advisers, policy aides, and support personnel. In accordance with statutory procedures (53 Stat. 561), President Franklin D. Roosevelt transmitted a reorganization plan (53 Stat. 1423) to Congress on April 25, 1939, formally establishing the Executive Office and outlining its components. By joint resolution (53 Stat. 813), Congress provided that this and a second plan would be effective on July 1, 1939. Following this action, the president issued a directive (E.O. 8248, 4 F.R. 3864) on September 8 organizing the Executive Office.

The creation of the E.O.P. not only greatly expanded formal staff assistance for the chief executive, but provided a framework to receive and cultivate special function units of government which, in the course of advising the president, would have greater access to and direct duties from the Oval Office. Both the fluid framework and the additional staff agencies enhanced presidential power, multiplying the eyes, ears, voice, thinking capacity, and analytical skills of the chief executive.

Constitutional Origins

In terms of the development of the Republic, the idea of providing the president with formal counselors and aides first arose in the Constitutional Convention and was championed in various forms by those who opposed a strong executive. The purpose of creating advisory councils was to impose consultation upon presidential decisionmaking. Although Charles Pinckney was the initial promoter of such bodies,[3] George Mason advanced the notion with regard to appointments[4] and Roger Sherman urged such a panel to curb the arbitrariness of a single executive.[5] Gouverneur Morris subsequently recommended a Council of State—composed of the chief justice and the heads of the departments of foreign affairs, commerce and finance, domestic affairs, war and marine—to which the president could submit any matter for discussion or otherwise require written opinions of any of the members.[6] Eventually, of course, such a council concept was vacated and Morris's idea for allowing the chief executive to require the written views of the principal departmental officers was retained (Article II, Section 2, paragraph 1).[7] From this provision would evolve the president's cabinet.

That there were those who sought advisers and assistants for the president for purposes other than restraining his power is clearly evidenced by Alexander Hamilton, the primary advocate of a strong executive, who, writing Federalist Paper No. 72, accurately predicted:

> The administration of government, in its largest sense, comprehends all the operations of the body politic, whether legislative, executive, or judiciary; but in its most usual and perhaps in its most precise signification, it is limited to executive details, and falls peculiarly within the province of the executive department. The actual conduct of foreign negotiations, the preparatory plans of finance, the application and disbursement of the public moneys in conformity to the general appropriations of the legislature, the arrangement of the army and navy, the direction of the operations of war—these, and other matters of a like nature, constitute what

seems to be most properly understood by the administration of government. The persons, therefore, to whose immediate management these different matters are committed, ought to be considered as the assistants or deputies of the chief magistrate, and on this account, they ought to derive their offices from his appointment, at least from his nomination, and ought to be subject to his superintendence.[8]

George Washington, president of the Constitutional Convention and the first chief executive, held the same view, regarding departmental secretaries as assistants to the president.[9] Reflecting upon the translation of his belief into action, one authority offers this summary of Washington's behavior in office:

Contacts between the president and his department heads were close and unremitting. In the official correspondence there remain hundreds of written communications and records of oral consultation. Washington invited Jefferson, Hamilton, and others to have breakfast with him to discuss matters which often he had transmitted to them on the previous day. He went to his secretaries' offices to consult them. He was accustomed to send a file to any one of his secretaries with the request that he come to the president's house on the following day at ten o'clock, or eleven o'clock, with a written or oral opinion. In due course of time these meetings with the heads of the departments grew into the cabinet.[10]

The Beginnings

Taking his oath of office on April 30, 1789, George Washington began the task of administering a government without an established executive organization. While John Jay temporarily continued as Secretary of Foreign Affairs, the old Treasury Board maintained its operations until Alexander Hamilton became secretary of the Treasury on September 11. Henry Knox continued as secretary of war, officially assuming his new duties the day after Hamilton took office. On September 26, Edmund Randolph was appointed attorney general, but there would be no Department of Justice until 1870.[11] Samuel Osgood was reappointed postmaster general and John Adams served as vice-president. The new secretary of state, Thomas Jefferson, would not return from France to join the administration until March 22, 1790. The government, seated in New York City, would not move to the District of Columbia until 1800.

Although Washington proposed that he receive no salary as chief executive and only be reimbursed for his expenses, as had been the case when he commanded the armies during the Revolution, Congress, nevertheless, fixed (1 Stat. 72, Chapt. 19) the president's compensation at $25,000 per year. The new chief executive was assisted by a secretary, his nephew, Lawrence Lewis, who was paid by Washington from personal funds.[12] Awaiting important actions of the legislature, the president reviewed the debts and assets he was inheriting from the Confederation. Only a quarter of the membership assembled on March 4, 1789, when Congress first convened and the absence of a quorum prevented the House from beginning its meetings until April 1. The Senate was similarly delayed until April 6. Soon the departments were created and Washington had the task of organizing and staffing them.

The Cabinet

Shortly after assuming office, President Washington, on various occasions, consulted with individual members of his administration. He also began implementing the constitutional provisions whereby he could require written reports from the departmental secretaries. It was also his view that he could solicit advice from quarters outside of the government and thus he became a letter writer of uncommon industry. Soon the written word was supplemented with collective oral deliberations.

It was also Washington's theory that advice should be competitive. He seldom took one man's word unquestioningly, but checked it against other sources, especially those that were apt to be critical. Adhering to the letter of the Constitution, he very early in his administration requested written opinions from all his department heads on decisions he was weighing. He skillfully exploited the opportunity of the cabinet, which he created in 1793, for the cross fire of debate. The separation of powers notwithstanding, he liked to check the favorite opinions of his executive subordinates against the judgement of the most distinguished members of Congress and the judiciary. Congressman James Madison was a favorite adviser on numerous matters of Anglo-American diplomacy, on executive appointments and on the president's reply to the formal addresses of the two houses of Congress. One of the busiest presidential consultants was the chief justice of the United States, John Jay. The chief justice's opinions were tapped on many a foreign policy matter, on troublous questions of constitutional law, and on the political aspects of a projected presidential tour of the New England states. When pulling together passages for an impending address to Congress, Washington requested from Jay, on a characteristically sweeping invitation, "ideas . . . not confined to matters judicial, but extended to all other topics which have occurred, or may not occur to you, as fit subjects for general or private communications."[13]

In time the advisers who came to best serve the president were the departmental secretaries. In 1789 Washington had found, by first-hand experience, that he could not directly consult with Congress. On August 22 and 24, accompanied by Secretary of War Knox, the chief executive had come onto the Senate floor to discuss an Indian treaty. It quickly became apparent, however, that the senators did not want to enter into any debate with either the president or with each other while he was present. By parliamentary maneuvering, consideration of the treaty was postponed for two days. Washington, angered, quickly left the chamber.[14] No chief executive would ever again come before Congress for purposes of direct dialogue or inquiry.[15]

The possibility of obtaining advice from the judiciary was precluded four years later.

> The Supreme Court decided, just after it was formed, that it would not advise the other branches of government on the legality of actions under their considerations. The issue came before the Court in 1793 when President Washington, through Secretary of State Jefferson, asked the Court if it would be willing to pass judgment upon a number of perplexing questions concerning this country's relations with Great Britain and France. The Court informed the president that both the principle of separation of powers and its own role as a court of last resort precluded its helping him.[16]

Under Washington, the cabinet was often called together on less than twenty-four hours' notice and frequently those attending were instructed to provide a written opinion on the matter to be discussed. Occasionally the entire membership would not be present.[17] On some occasions when Washington was away from the seat of government, he authorized the cabinet to deliberate and take collective action on some matters in his absence.[18] Frequently, however, the group was of divided opinion with Jefferson and Randolph usually comprising the minority. "Washington did not debate a case with his advisers, but listened to their arguments or read their written opinions and then decided the issue."[19]

When John Adams assumed the presidency in 1797, he retained Washington's cabinet as it was then constituted, holding his first deliberations with the collectivity two days after the inauguration.[20] During his absences from the seat of government—Adams was gone 385 days in four years—the chief executive apparently was willing to allow his cabinet to deliberate but "expected the department heads to communicate regularly with him on their respective affairs, and promised not to be away from his summer home in Quincy more than one day at a time."[21] However, because Adams failed on various occasions to settle departmental business before his departures and exhibited less decisive leadership than Washington, the cabinet did develop "a tendency toward independent collective action." During 1798, the secretary of war, in an attempt to protect himself against Adams' wrath, sought cabinet opinions supporting his official acts taken during the president's absence.[22] In spite of such behavior, Adams maintained the cabinet as his principal body of advisers until his term ended in 1801.

Twelve years' experience under the Federalists, therefore, served to establish the practice and habit of consultation between the president and the heads of departments collectively, but without any implication that the president was either bound to consult or to accept the advice that he received. The powers of the executive branch remained in the office of the president. So far as the conduct of administration in its narrower sense is concerned, the cabinet as a collective agency remained unimportant since departmental business continued to be transacted between the president and the head of each department separately. Neither under the cabinet nor within the office of the chief executive did any agencies of overhead management appear; the business of government was carried on directly and immediately through the lines of the departmental organizations. The duty to consult was one exercised at the discretion of the president.[23]

Staff Development

The Jeffersonians arrived to replace the Federalists; soon the Jacksonians would have their moment of control over the White House. And as the regimes arrived and departed, the incumbents of the presidential office continued to suffer the consequences of a paucity of personal staff.

> Monroe was bothered by the petty responsibilities of attending to the presidential household but tried in vain to secure release from them. As he was about to leave the White House, he sent Congress, "a few remarks . . . founded on my own experience, in this office." Beyond a certain limit, he wrote, no one can go, and if inferior details are forced upon the attention of the president he loses time to devote to matters of higher importance. The higher duties of his office, said Monroe, "are sufficient to employ the whole mind, and unceasing labors, of any individual. . . ." Among these duties he cited the message to Congress, the replies to calls for information, personal contact with members of Congress, and the "supervision and control of the several departments so as to preserve efficiency in each, and order and consistency in the general movement of the government." He suggested the desirability of aid to the president, perhaps the first statement of this need. Congress gave him no aides, and the broad stream of detail flowed steadily on.
>
> John Quincy Adams, too, was in need of help. He had no disposition to protect himself, however he might suffer from intrusion. The number of idle visitors, total strangers, increased until they became an almost daily annoyance. The president was becoming an object of attention like the exhibits in the Patent Office.[24]

Following Washington's example, the successive chief executives struggled to meet the demands of their office with the aid of a single personal secretary, usually a relative, compensated from their own private funds. President Monroe, for example, at different times retained his brother, Joseph, and two sons-in-law in this capacity; John Quincy Adams, who had served his father as private secretary, employed his son John.[25] Detailing clerks from the departments was unknown at this time and, undoubtedly, would have been anathema to Congress.

With the incumbency of Andrew Jackson, presidential staffing arrangements took a new turn when allowance was made for a departmental clerk to be assigned, de facto, to the White House.

> Major Andrew Jackson Donelson, Mrs. Jackson's nephew, held a clerkship in the General Land Office but served as Jackson's private secretary during most of his administration, being succeeded by Andrew Jackson, Jr. Tyler's private secretary was his son John. Both Polk and Buchanan employed nephews. The White House also possessed a "porter" who, from Polk's diary, would seem to have been occupied in bringing letters to the president, and vainly trying to keep visitors out of his office. In 1833, a clerk had been provided by Congress (4 Stat. 663, Chapt. 19) to sign land patents on behalf of the president. Clerks could be borrowed for long copying jobs, such as making fair copies in duplicate of the president's annual messages, but were not on loan for normal routine. Taylor wrote personal letters in his own hand, and the replies to a multitude of inquiries and invitations were written for him by Colonel William Bliss, his son-in-law.[26]

At long last, Congress appropriated (11 Stat. 228, Chapt. 108, sec. 2) funds to the chief executive in 1857 for an "official household." Now the president was authorized to appoint a private secretary at $2,500 per year, a steward to supervise the executive mansion at $1,200 annually, and a messenger who would receive a $900 salary. A contingency fund was also established in the amount of $750.

Both the number of presidential staff members and their salaries continued to grow as the nation moved toward the dawn of the new century. By 1900, the secretary to the chief executive was receiving $5,000 and thirty additional White House aides were authorized (31 Stat. 97) on a total budget of $48,540. In 1913, the secretary's salary was fixed at $7,500 (37 Stat. 913); thirteen years later it was increased (44 Stat. 305) to $10,000. Congress was persuaded in 1929 to authorize (45 Stat. 1230) an increase in the president's top personnel, adding two more secretaries and an administrative assistant. Until the arrival of the New Deal, White House aides, with very rare exception, had no direct political or partisan role; they were managers of files, appointments, and correspondence. Privy to the president's thinking and decisions, their advice on policy and direct involvement in government operations was sought only in the case of a very few exceptional personalities. For most chief executives, the cabinet served as the primary institution of advice and counsel until world war and a perilous economic emergency prompted resort to new experimental administrative and managerial extensions of the presidency.

Cabinet Development

In the aftermath of the Federalist regimes, the importance of the cabinet as an advisory council began to wane. The first blow was dealt by the "mischief of factions." To win the nation's highest office, presidential aspirants cultivated the support of various interests to form an effective political coalition. The successful candidate had to reward these allies by appointing an individual representative of, or otherwise agreeable to, their point of view. As a consequence of such obligations, chief executives were often confronted with cabinets containing individuals not personally well known to them, persons they did not completely trust, and people of only symbolic value.

Coupled with this development was another tendency which militated against the continued value of the cabinet as an institution of presidential counsel. Chief executives demonstrated an increasing willingness to resort to advisers outside of the executive branch both as a consequence of the development of political parties and as a necessary supplement to situations where the views of departmental secretaries were not regarded as reliable. Thus, legislators, party chieftains, and private citizens were consulted in lieu of cabinet officials.

Succeeding the Federalists, Jefferson reportedly maintained a harmonious and beneficial relationship with his departmental secretaries.[27]

> Madison's cabinet was a failure from the outset. Due to Senate opposition, . . . he was unable to place Gallatin in the State Department and had Robert Smith imposed upon him in this important office at a crucial time. He was unable to hold a cabinet together. He had two secretaries of state, four secretaries of the Treasury, four secretaries of war, three attorneys general, and four secretaries of the navy. He succeeded in picking, or having thrust upon him, four who were incompetent (Smith, Campbell, Hamilton, and Eustis), and two who were insubordinate (Armstrong and Granger). The dissension between Gallatin and Smith increased so as to cause a watchful Jefferson much misgiving. "I hope that the position of both gentlemen may be made so easy as to give no cause for either to withdraw." To this end he recommended written instead of oral opinions to the president: "It is better calculated . . . to prevent collision and irritation, and to cure it, or at least suppress its effects when it has already taken place." The cabinet, like the presidency, suffered a severe decline during these eight years.[28]

Calm, stability, and experience returned to the cabinet during the administration of James Monroe. During the eight-year existence of this regime, the incumbent president would be served by single enduring individuals at State, Treasury, and War; from this council would emerge the next chief executive, John Quincy Adams.[29]

But as the years passed, the more powerful and independent presidents sought new avenues of counsel, among the first of them being Andrew Jackson. The seventh chief executive cultivated a clique of personal advisers who came to be known as the "Kitchen Cabinet" and generally displaced their legitimate namesake.[30]

> Jackson's little band of gifted men had few characteristics of a cabinet. They had no regular time or place of meeting; indeed, it is doubtful if they ever gathered in plenary session. They never all worked simultaneously on the same policy problem. Their membership changed rather frequently. Historians estimate that close to a dozen men were identified with the Kitchen Cabinet at one time or another in Jackson's administration. Probably the Kitchen Cabinet's strongest underlying characteristic was the closeness of all its members to Jackson. But that circumstance was as much a factor of disunity as of unity. Such Kitchen Cabinet stalwarts as Kendall, Blair, Van Buren, Duff Green, John H. Eaton and Isaac Hill, were split on key policies and their differences were exacerbated because each had ready access to Jackson and good prospects of swaying his decisions. The principal instances of peaceful collaboration transpired when several members—but by no means all—took on a common assignment, such as drafting a speech or an editorial, and lobbying Congress.[31]

Similar informal advisory collectives would arise on occasion during later administrations, reflecting in each instance the languishing of the traditional cabinet as a source of presidential counsel. John Tyler had his "Virginia Schoolmasters;" Grover Cleveland maintained a "Fishing Cabinet;" Teddy Roosevelt sported the "Tennis Cabinet;" Warren Harding encouraged a "Poker Cabinet;" Herbert Hoover instituted a "Medicine Ball Cabinet," and Franklin Roosevelt utilized a "Brains Trust."[32]

Some chief executives avoided their cabinet when making certain important decisions or otherwise disparaged its advice. According to former President Taft, "Mr. Lincoln is said to have remarked that in the cabinet after discussion and intimation of opinions, there was only one vote—and that unanimous—it was the vote of the president."[33] Similarly, Ulysses Grant related the following confession regarding his veto of a currency bill in 1874:

> When the cabinet met, my message was written. I did not intend asking the advice of the cabinet, as I knew a majority would oppose the veto. I never allowed the cabinet to interfere when my mind was made up, and on this question it was inflexibly made up.[34]

And Grover Cleveland's biographer offered the same type of observation on cabinet deliberations when he commented:

> There were no set speeches, and no votes were taken, the president's theory being that in a cabinet there are many voices, but one vote. Each member was free to express his views; but when the illumination of frank comment and informal discussion was over, it was the president who must make the decision.[35]

Woodrow Wilson rarely met with his cabinet and sought another avenue of institutional counsel in the Council of National Defense. President Coolidge supposedly held fifteen-minute deliberations with his cabinet and the Hoover panel of departmental secretaries has been described as "the most august body of 'yes men' ever assembled in the United States history."[36]

Ultimately, the utility of the cabinet in providing assistance to the chief executive declined because the impersonal factors bearing upon the determination of its membership—politics, geography, aptitude—militated against a relationship of confidence and trust with the president. While the cabinet institution has persisted, it exists today largely as an historical vestige; much of its traditional role has been assumed by the White House staff and the Executive Office agencies, but this transition did not occur before a few experimental efforts at emergency counsel were attempted.

Emergency Experiments

Ultimately, it was world war which prompted the chief executive to seek administrative and managerial extensions of the presidency. American observation of large-scale foreign hostilities and defense during the latter half of the 19th century demonstrated a need to certain strategists for a coordination mechanism for both defense preparedness and wartime mobilization.

> As far back as 1910 the idea of a Council of National Defense had begun to take root in the minds of men who perceived how helpless the country would be in the event of war, for lack of forethought and planning, and General Leonard Wood and other army men were emphasizing the need even before that of a more extensive military system. As long ago as 1902, General Crozier, as chief of the Ordnance Bureau, had urged the wisdom of a great enlargement of the artillery arm. Had the advice of the officers been taken and had the government set about to plan for the expansion of the peacetime forces into an army of the size that was contemplated in Europe even before the revelations of the World War, the correlaries of such a course would have led to a large degree of industrial preparedness, though, as we now know, almost grotesquely inadequate. It really required a year's observation of the war in Europe for an understanding of the fact that modern wars are fought, not by armies, but by nations, and that the whole moral, spiritual, and physical energy of the nation must be summoned to the struggle.[37]

This, then, was the mission envisioned by some in the creation of such a council, and the opinion expressed here was that of Grosvenor B. Clarkson, the man who was the Council's most vigorous and challenged director. In recounting the evolution of the panel, Clarkson has written:

> It is important to note that the legislative roots of the Council of National Defense idea go back as far as 1910. In that year, in response to a resolution of the House of Representatives, the general staff of the army submitted to the House a confidential report on the military situation which included a recommendation for the creation of a Council of National Defense, "in order to stabilize the military policy of the United States." Even then there seemed to be an understanding in the army that there must be a body to unite the military and civil forces.

> Immediately after this report was received, Richmond Pearson Hobson, of the House Committee on Military Affairs, introduced a bill providing for a Council of National Defense to consist of the secretaries of War and Navy, two technical officers each from the army and the navy, and six members of Congress. This early idea that the Council should primarily unite the military arms of the government with the Congress persisted right down to 1917. Mr. Hobson brought his bill up again in the Sixty-Second Congress in 1912, but it never reached a final vote. The matter was considered important enough even to be included in the Democratic national platform in 1912 which had a clause expressing approval of such a body. The proposal was unavailingly renewed in the Sixty-Third Congress, and the matter was discussed in the newspapers and magazines in 1913 and 1914.[38]

The principal promoters and lobbyists for the Council were Dr. Hollis Godfrey, president of the Drexel Institute of Philadelphia, and Dr. Henry E. Crampton, an eminent scientist. In testimony before the Senate Committee on Expenditures in the War Department, Dr. Godfrey recounted on October 20, 1919, how he had met with Sir Henry Campbell-Bannerman and Winston Churchill in 1906 and discussed efforts then underway to create a "council of imperial defense" in Great Britain. After ten years of observing attempts to establish a similar body within the federal government, Godfrey began a campaign in May, 1916, to make such a panel a reality. He met with General Wood and Secretary of War Lindley Garrison, securing their support for the concept. A consultation with former Secretary of War Elihu Root came next, with Root advising that no existing unit of government was suited for the coordination task. The former secretary of war then outlined the fundamental principles which would be necessary in legislation creating such a council.

The basic bill was then submitted to Rep. Rollin B. Sanford (R.-N.Y.) and Sen. John W. Weeks (R.-Mass.). President Wilson's unofficial aide and confidant, Col. Edward House, approved of the effort, enlisted administration support for the measure, and assisted in marshalling votes for it. At the direction of Secretary of War Newton D. Baker the language establishing the panel was inserted in the Army Appropriation Act, becoming a small section of the bill which was signed into law on August 29, 1916 (39 Stat. 619 at 640).[39]

In announcing the formation of the Council of National Defense, President Wilson said:

The Council's chief functions are:

1. The coordination of all forms of transportation and the development of means of transportation to meet the military, industrial, and commercial needs of the nation.
2. The extension of the industrial mobilization work of the committee on Industrial Preparedness of the Naval Consulting Board. Complete information as to our present manufacturing and producing facilities adaptable to many-sided uses of modern warfare will be procured, analyzed, and made use of.

One of the objectives of the Council will be to inform American manufacturers as to the part they can and must play in a national emergency. It is empowered to establish at once and maintain through subordinate bodies of specially qualified persons and auxiliary organizations composed of men of the best creative and administrative capacity, capable of mobilizing to the utmost the resources of the country.[40]

Council of National Defense Organization

Established with an appropriation of $200,000, the Council first met on September 18, 1916, in the offices of Secretary of War Baker, the panel's first chairman.[41] The Council was assisted by a director, who initially was Walter S. Gifford, and a secretary, who was Grosvenor Clarkson. These administrative officials also assisted an advisory unit to the Council with staff services and direction.

In the nature of things the advisory commission of the Council of National Defense became the real executive branch of the Council. The Council proper was made up of the secretary of War, who was elected chairman, the secretary of the Navy, the secretary of the interior, the secretary of agriculture, the secretary of commerce, and the secretary of labor. It is true that the Council early distinctly affirmed that the duties of the advisory commission were advisory and that the power of decision lay with the Council, thus conforming to the letter of the law; but the initiative lay with the members of the commission and the Council inevitably came to accept its advice, and it was then charged with the execution of the things decided upon. Counsel and action united usually have their way under any executive.[42]

While there were a number of individuals engaged in the work of the Council, not all of them were directly compensated from its budget: some were unpaid volunteers and others received salaries as employees of different government agencies. At the end of June, 1917, for example, there were 408 individuals serving the Council but of these, only 168 were carried on its payroll.[43] Table 3.1.1 provides a general indication of Council staffing expenses.

In addition to a multiplicity of emergency subunits organized at the federal level under the umbrella-like authority of the Council, state councils of national defense were also created.[45]

Generally throughout the East, state defense councils had no legal powers; their work was chiefly advisory and educational. They stimulated among the people a greater understanding of war aims and co-operation in the government's policies and program, provided comforts and conveniences for soldiers in camp, looked out for their dependents at home, and sought to promote the welfare of citizens amid the unfamiliar conditions imposed by the war. Throughout much of the West, however, it was

Table 3.1.1

Council of National Defense Expenses[44]

Period	Staff Total	Salary Expenditure	Total Council Expenditure
06/30/17	168	$ 44,188	$127,126
11/30/18	295	355,700	----
12/31/18	183	220,420	----
06/30/19	139	184,960	398,219
06/30/20	22	109,608	125,089

a different story. Many western states gave their councils wide discretionary powers which permitted them to do everything not inconsistent with state or federal law, a limitation that proved quite flexible under the rubric of promulgating and carrying out "such measures as may be necessary to meet the exigencies of all situations occasioned by the war." Hence, idle persons could be compelled to work, and such persons could be classified and assigned according to occupations suffering from a shortage of labor. Councils so endowed were able to regulate not only industrial and agricultural relations but educational and religious affairs as well, and to suppress whatever in their estimation appeared unpatriotic or subversive. Such councils were, in some instances, a wartime version or revival of the vigilantes of pioneer days, and they carried out their functions in about the same rough-and-ready manner.[46]

While various federal-level subunits conducted much of the research, investigation, and administration necessary for wartime operations, the Council of National Defense held the ultimate authority and responsibility for these actions. It not only met as a unit apart from the cabinet, but specific directives were issued and enforced in its name.[47] As chairman of the Council, Secretary Baker "decreed that military supplies should have the right of way over all other goods on the nation's railroads.[48] Similarly, he took another action with regard to regulating the price of bituminous coal.[49] We are informed by one historian discussing the Wilson administration that "the Council of National Defense and Shipping Board came under heavy hostile fire for suspending the law requiring competitive bidding in the letting of war contracts."[50] In brief, the Council operated as an arm of the president during the period of the First World War. It stood as a mechanism for creating a number of emergency management units during the wartime crisis.

> It represented, in the first place, an abandonment of the idea of bringing into existence a body composed of representatives of Congress and the executive and having as its prime purpose the correlation of the activities of those two branches in the formulation of a comprehensive war preparedness and prosecution programme. The Council as established was wholly an organ of the administrative branch of the government, and its function was exclusively that of acting as an aid to the executive in taking steps for the protection of the public interests. In the second place, it departed from the earlier proposal in the greater emphasis that was given to the work of the civil departments of the government and the need for organizing the general industrial resources of the country for war purposes.[51]

There was apparently no unwillingness on the part of the members of the Council to come before Congress even though the questioning was probably very intense at certain times during the war years. It does not appear that the members of the Council came before the committees in any capacity other than their cabinet officer-departmental secretary roles.[52]

By the close of hostilities in Europe, the Council had practically ceased operations. The War Industries Board had assumed many of its responsibilities which were still in need of administration.[53] By 1921 the Council went into dormancy and for the period from 1922 to 1940, its only staff was a custodian of records.

Finding the nation once again threatened with armed conflict, President Franklin D. Roosevelt decided the Council of National Defense was worth reviving and announced plans to do so during a press conference of May 28, 1940.[54] Of primary interest to the chief executive was the Council's advisory commission which Roosevelt wanted to activate to mobilize public opinion and organize certain defense functions.

At the first official meeting of the resurrected Council, two days after the press announcement, "Roosevelt made it clear that the Council would meet and act only at meetings of the cabinet, and that the advisory commission would deal with the Council only through the president or William H. McReynolds [an administrative assistant to the president named chief administrative officer of the Council]".[55] F.D.R. utilized the advisory commission briefly to effect defense preparedness and then discarded it for a new unit within the Executive Office of the President which had recently come into existence. The Council was portrayed as the principal unit of the "National Defense Program" in the *United States Government Organization Manual(s)* of the war years. It was not located within the Executive Office of the President or accorded the status of an independent agency. Such organizational niceties were superfluous in view of the Council's operational status. Through the institutional revival and subsequent funding of the Council, the president, according to the federal budget appendix for 1942, obtained an estimated 1,345 new positions at a cost of $3,675,995 in FY 1941 and increased this staff allotment to 2,353 individuals on a $6,651,410 budget for FY 1942. Ultimately its functions were included in legislation creating the National Security Council (61 Stat. 496), which was established in 1947 and is now located within the Executive Office. Authority for the Council still exists but the unit is officially regarded as "inactive."

New Deal Experience

When Roosevelt reactivated the Council of National Defense, it was not his first experiment with such a coordinative and managerial forum. The Council was revived in 1940; the Executive Office of the President had been instituted the previous year. However, it was very early in the New Deal effort that F.D.R. felt the need for a special presidential unit to orchestrate a multiplicity of programs and do so with some degree of expertise on the part of presidential staff.

"Organizationally, in dealing with the depression, it was Roosevelt's general policy to assign new, emergency functions to newly created agencies, rather than to already existing departments."[56] The president had a variety of reasons for pursuing this course: he thought the departments were burdened with duties which preoccupied them in meeting the current crisis; he believed a new agency with a single task in attacking an exigency would be dedicated and persistent in its mission; he felt what such new agencies with emergency duties as might be created to deal with the depression could, when the crisis passed, be easily eradicated without disturbing the regular executive branch departments; he thought talented and expert personnel might be attracted to the specialized new emergency units; and there was also a desire on the part of the president to avoid the established civil service channels in staffing for the emergency period and to utilize political appointees.[57] With the exception of the last consideration, all of these concerns would mold the concept of the Executive Office of the President.

Executive Council

The first attempt at establishing an effective coordinating forum resulted in a temporary Executive Council, chartered by a presidential directive (E.O. 6202A) of July 11, 1933, issued pursuant to the authority of the Federal Emergency Relief Act (48 Stat. 22) and the National Industrial Recovery Act (48 Stat. 195). The unit's twenty-four members—inclusive of the entire cabinet, the director of the Bureau of the Budget, and the heads of the various economic recovery agencies—met at the White House on Tuesday afternoons. Roosevelt, himself, presided over the sessions and was assisted by the Council's executive secretary, Frank C. Walker, who performed "such duties as may be prescribed him by the president" and was the only professional staff assistant on the panel. Walker's role was purely administrative and limited to the activities of the Council: when the chief executive was absent from Council sessions, the senior cabinet officer was to preside. After a few months, the panel "proved too cumbersome for effective discussion."[58]

> Actually, the Executive Council functioned more or less as an enlarged cabinet, with Roosevelt conducting the Council meetings in much the same way as he did those of the regular cabinet. Although he may have originally intended that the Executive Council would serve as a broad coordinating agency, it did not function effectively in that way. The Council was not provided with a staff, nor did it have any normal power to coordinate the work of the departments and agencies other than that exercised by Roosevelt himself. The only coordinating function served by the Council was that of enabling the heads of the regular departments to meet once a week with the heads of the new emergency agencies and the president to exchange ideas and information on problems that were interdepartmental in scope.
>
> In itself, this was undoubtedly of considerable value in the early days of the New Deal, but neither the Council nor the Executive Secretary served in an important way to make decisions of a coordinative nature for the president. Such decisions were made by Roosevelt himself, with the Executive Council serving only as a source of information and advice. [Frank C.] Walker's most valuable role continued to be that of an informal "trouble shooter" who served the president behind-the-scenes in trying to iron out difficulties and smooth ruffled feelings, rather than in his formal role as executive secretary of the Executive Council. Except insofar as it may have been valuable as a device for exchanging information and for enabling the heads of the departments and agencies to get to know each other better, the Council did not serve as an effective mechanism for coordination.[59]

National Emergency Council

Recognizing the deficiencies of the Executive Council, the president established another coordinating organization with a more limited membership. Relying upon the same statutory authority utilized for chartering the Executive Council, together with the provision of the Agricultural Adjustment Act (48 Stat. 31), Roosevelt issued a new directive (E.O. 6433A) on November 17, 1933 setting up the National Emergency Council.

> In establishing the National Emergency Council Roosevelt had some significant political motives as well. The creation of the Council, with its attendant publicity, dramatized to the public that efforts were being made to improve the emergency programs. It was designed to serve as something of a "shot in the arm" to both those in the administration carrying out the emergency programs and to the general public in encouraging increased support of the New Deal's efforts.[60]

Composed of the secretaries of Interior (or Administrator of Public Works), Agriculture, Commerce, and Labor, the administrators of Agricultural Adjustment and Federal Emergency Relief, the chairman of the Home Owners Loan Corporation, the governor of the Farm Credit Administration, a representative from the Consumer's Council, and an executive director, the Council had directors "in each of the states to establish closer coordination in the operations of the different federal agencies working within the state, and also to coordinate federal activities within those being undertaken by the states themselves in such fields as relief and public works."[61]

In addition, the Council was assigned the task of serving as a centralized agency to disseminate information and to provide guidance to the people of the country about how to make use of the various recovery and relief agencies. By making a single field organization under the National Emergency Council responsible for reporting and disseminating information, rather than allowing each agency to continue to do these things for itself, Roosevelt stated that he was trying to "wipe out all needless and costly duplication of personnel" and "make for a more effective administration." In performing these functions, the Council did a competent job which contributed to the overall effectiveness of the emergency programs. In the area of providing coordination between the heads of the various agencies in Washington, however, the Council proved rather early not to be a particularly valuable device. The Council itself was undoubtedly too large to act effectively as a coordinative agency, and the executive director was not given sufficient authority by Roosevelt to act for him in making final decisions. Along with problems of major importance, many petty difficulties were raised at the meetings, and a lot of time was undoubtedly wasted by the busy men who attended.[62]

Like the Executive Council, the National Emergency Council met every Tuesday but at two-week intervals. The agenda was set by the executive director in consultation with the president. The member agencies submitted progress reports to inform other participants and reduce misunderstandings and conflicts in administration. With the president presiding, disputes might be settled at his decision. While Donald Richberg was first to hold the position of executive director with the Council, his tenure was brief and Frank C. Walker assumed these duties, leaving the collapsed Executive Council and being compensated from general executive funds.

Recognizing the limitations of the National Emergency Council for coordinating the activities and administration of New Deal programs in the area of relief and unemployment, the president, on June 30, 1934, directed (E.O. 6770) the establishment of an industrial emergency committee as a subunit of the Council. This panel functioned until the autumn of that year when Roosevelt, through an order (E.O. 6889A) of October 31, 1934, consolidated the Executive Council, the National Emergency Council, and the industrial emergency committee. By late 1935 and early 1936 the reconstituted National Emergency Council was itself in steady decline with very few meetings occurring. On September 16, 1937, Roosevelt abolished (E.O. 7709A) the panel. The administrative staff of the Council, added at the time of its being reconstituted, continued to serve the president until the Executive Office of the President was established and many of these personnel were absorbed by this new presidential staff entity. An examination of relevant Federal budget appendices indicates that in 1934 the Council had a staff of 88 individuals on a budget of $194,634 with 106 people projected for 1935 at a cost of $232,350. By 1936, in addition to 246 permanent and detailed staff in Washington, the Council counted 185 field personnel. The following year saw 191 Council employees at the seat of government and 198 in the field at a cost of $347,180 and $511,300, respectively ($858,480 total). Projections for 1938 were 124 national staffers and 121 field personnel on a payroll of about $600,000.

On his experience with the National Emergency Council, Roosevelt said:

> The whole NEC was a wonderful essay in democracy. It was exactly like a New England town meeting. It gave everybody a chance to blow off. I learned many things there—many things that those who were reporting never suspected that I learned and some that they wouldn't have liked me to know anything about. They also learned a lot about each other. At the beginning it was a wonderful device for keeping up the morale of the whole team, as long as instant relief and recovery were the sole goals.
>
> But like a New England town meeting, it was too big to do much actual work. It had to split up into committees and subcommittees until in the end I couldn't take it anymore because I found myself making stump speeches to the Council instead of listening to its members. The time came when I could get most out of it by just talking to [NEC executive director] Frank Walker alone, especially after the organization of the whole relief set up in the spring of '35.[63]

What these mechanisms reflect are (1) an attempt to coordinate existing federal policies through a sounding board of department and agency heads, (2) a desire to foster a special staff to assist the president in such coordination efforts but not to grant such personnel a direct role in deliberations and (3) an experimentation with a noncabinet structure situated between the chief executive's office and other units of government, whether executive departments and agencies or subnational entities, with a flexibility for sustaining presidentially created specialized subunits. While these innovations are apparent to some extent in each of these panels, they would manifest themselves in maturity with the establishment of the Executive Office of the President.

The "Circus"

The last of Roosevelt's coordinative schemes for depression programs was created to administer the Emergency Relief Appropriation Act (49 Stat. 115). While it served its purpose, the effect was also one of graphically portraying the bizarre structural arrangements a president might be forced to resort to in the absence of some more flexible organization of his own shaping. Popularly dubbed the "five-ring-circus," here is how one observer described the operation:

> First, a new unit was established in the National Emergency Council called the Division of Applications and Information, under the supervision of Frank Walker, who had been recalled to his old job as executive director for that very purpose. All applications for projects were to come to Frank Walker and be examined and reviewed by him with the aid and assistance of all governmental departments and agencies. Then Walker was to transmit the application to another new outfit.
>
> Second, the Advisory Committee on Allotments was set up to receive the applications after they had been processed by Walker. This committee had Harold Ickes, secretary of the interior and public works administrator, as its chairman. It had twenty-three members, including Franklin D. Roosevelt. There were two other members of the cabinet besides Ickes: Henry Wallace of agriculture and Frances Perkins of labor. The others were the executive director of the National Emergency Council, Frank Walker; the administrator of the Works Progress Administration, which up to that time had not existed but was created in the same executive order, and which turned out to be Harry Hopkins; the director of the budget; the director of procurement in *propria persona*; the chief of engineers of the Army; the commissioner of reclamation; the director of soil conservation; the chief of the Forest Service; the director of emergency conservation work (CCC); the chief of the Public Roads Bureau; the resettlement administrator; the rural electrification administrator; the emergency relief administrator, which put Harry Hopkins in twice for good luck; the director of the Housing Division of the National Emergency Council, the vice-chairman of the National Resources Board; and five nongovernmental members representing the Business Advisory Council of the Department of Commerce, organized labor, farm organizations, the American Bankers Association, and the United States Conference of Mayors.
>
> This Advisory Committee on Allotments was supposed to make recommendations to the president on the allotment of funds for the projects passed on to the committee by Frank Walker and the Division of Applications.
>
> Third, he set up the Works Progress Administration, which was to be responsible for the co-ordinated execution of the work relief program as a whole and was to move as many persons as possible from the relief rolls to work projects or private employment in the shortest possible time. The federal emergency relief administrator, under the terms of the order, was to serve as head of the Works Progress Administration. This meant Harry Hopkins.
>
> Fourth, the secretary of the Treasury was required to set up disbursing and accounting facilities and maintain a system of accounts which would enable the president to exercise direct executive control over the funds and to provide current accounting information for all the agencies concerned.
>
> Fifth, the control of the allotment of funds for administrative expenses of all of the agencies was turned over to the director of the budget.
>
> This was the five-ring-circus. This was what shocked the experts. The applications were to

go to Frank Walker. If he approved them, a huge committee presided over by Ickes would pass them to the president. When the president personally approved them, they would go to Harry Hopkins to be executed, with Morgenthau keeping the accounts and with Danny Bell doling out a nickel here and a dime there for administrative expenses. It confused nearly everybody and in particular the practitioners of orderly administration. But the confusion the experts then suffered was greatly to be compounded later on.

The thing worked.[64]

Undoubtedly the "five-ring-circus" worked largely because of the personal political skill and energy of F.D.R. and the devotion of those within the "circus" to him. Nonetheless, the experience had a certain amount of impact in terms of the evolution of the Executive Office of the President. As one expert has commented:

> First, it demonstrated the growing dependence of the president on official staff other than cabinet members (whose departmental duties were already sufficient to occupy them fully) working exceedingly close to the president's own sphere of daily operation. Ideally speaking they executed the president's will without possessing direct authority of their own; but it was difficult to say where the line was to be drawn.

This problem would be amplified with the establishment of the White House Office within the Executive Office of the President. From this presidential preserve a growing panoply of aides have sought to exert the chief executive's will upon the bureaucracy, cloaking their activities in the mantle of executive privilege. Returning to the comments of the expert, he concludes:

> Secondly, the system recognized that lump sum appropriations could underline, as few other things had done, the weaknesses of the executive with respect to the management and control of expenditures. Congress had made the appropriation in this form because it seemed to be willing, at least for the moment, to recognize the fact that it could not administer and control so complex an operation as federal relief. But there was some question at first as to whether or not the executive could do so either, given the inadequate machinery in his possession. Roosevelt's system, regardless of its weaknesses, was an attempt to deal with the problems.
>
> Finally, and in part as a result of questions raised by the recognition of the above problem, the system called the attention of the president to those who had been suggesting that the emergency agencies had to be absorbed into the existing executive framework, regardless of the length of time they were supposed to exist. Whatever offense this may have been to those who viewed emergency measures as temporary accretions to be dropped as soon as conditions permitted, some form of absorption could meet a very practical question by placing agencies within the purview of budget and accounting procedures already in existence. Despite the problems inherent in the fiscal machinery as it stood, a continued development of governments within governments could only lead to a dangerous chaos over which the president would have no control whatsoever.[65]

Probably the most fundamental impact of these various experiments upon program coordination was realized in a new view of government reorganization on the part of the president. Embarking upon his second term as chief executive, F.D.R. was shifting away from the traditional position of structural revision for purposes of economy and efficiency and began to regard the matter in terms of improving over-all top management within the executive branch. At a press conference shortly after the November, 1936, election, Roosevelt confided that his opponents had failed to perceive the chief weakness of the New Deal. Queried on this undetected flaw, the president responded with a single word: "Administration."[66] But in making this revelation, Roosevelt had plans well underway to correct the acknowledged shortcoming.

Intellectual Posture of E.O.P.

Prior to Roosevelt's own concern with the subject, previous executive reorganization investigations had largely ignored presidential staffing arrangements.[67] In 1920, Charles E.

McGuire suggested in the development of his own unique reorganization scheme that the function of coordinating independent regulatory commission policy be located in the president's office.[68] In March of the next year, amidst efforts to establish a national budget through the enactment of the Budget and Accounting Act of 1921, the Institute for Government Research proposed the establishment of a Bureau of General Administration which would be a subordinate service directly assisting the president. The recommendation was the only one bearing upon presidential staffing and was but a small portion of a larger study of executive branch reorganization prepared by the Institute.[69] The proponent of the idea, Institute Director William F. Willoughby, was a well-known planner of government organization and administration. His familiarity with the complexities of a burgeoning federal government dated from World War I experience where he undoubtedly gained significant knowledge of the role of the Council of National Defense and related presidential staffing problems.[70] After the passage of the Budget and Accounting Act (42 Stat. 20), Willoughby transformed his proposed Bureau of General Administration into the operating Bureau of the Budget and in 1923 advocated the transfer of BOB from the Treasury Department to the president's office.[71] These scant references appear to be the only published accounts of interest in the presidential staffing function prior to Roosevelt's undertaking.

Administrative Management

The central concept of the Roosevelt reorganization effort—"administrative management"—was an idea developed by a new group of public administration experts befriended by the New Deal in its grappling with emergency program administration. With the passage of the National Industrial Recovery Act (48 Stat. 195) in 1933, the president asked Gen. Hugh Johnson to administer the industrial aspect of the law and delegated responsibility for the public works title to Interior Secretary Harold Ickes.

The public works aspect of national recovery posed problems which were in some respects different from those envisioned by its original proponents. To be sure, it could stimulate the economy through government spending, as the economists thought it would. And for those concerned with the social and psychological effects of relief and "dole" it provided useful, respectable work for citizens seeking livelihoods rather than charity. But above and beyond these functions was the fact that the "works" were "things," presumably useful and purposeful whether or not the economy was spurred and people put to work. Roads had to go where people wanted to go, just as bridges had to cross rivers with some intelligible utility. Schoolhouses and post offices had to be built with a view to their functioning long after immediate emergencies were over.

As requests poured into Washington for a road here, a schoolhouse there, a bridge somewhere else, it became clear that the complex of motives could produce chaos and waste if left undirected. A rationality would have to be provided to give logic to the relationship of needs to one another, to balance the relief function of public works against local and general economic needs, as well as against the functions of the works themselves. There was no point sacrificing future needs for the satisfaction of immediate demands. What was required was planning, yet it would not be easy to find plans that would please economists, local governments, and congressional politicians, let alone the engineers who have to execute them.[72]

To assist him in developing the planning and execution of this public works effort, Secretary Ickes recruited Louis Brownlow, director of the Public Administration Clearing House in Chicago, as a consultant. Asked to recommend persons who might assist in planning the public works program, Brownlow selected Frederick Delano, the president's uncle and familiar to Ickes as head of the Chicago Regional Planning Association, Charles Merriam, an academic who had long been a personal friend of the secretary's, and Wesley C. Mitchell, who was a new acquaintance to Ickes. Both Merriam and Mitchell had played key roles on President Hoover's Research

Committee on Social Trends. The work of this panel, though thoroughly neglected by the chief executive and Congress, was the first major attempt at governmental planning.

> Brownlow's choice of such interested and knowledgeable men for the job would not in itself have been sufficient had he not also been aware of the particular problems posed by Ickes' habits of administration. Ickes knew Merriam and Delano. Merriam, like Ickes, had been one of the early members of the Progressive party, although Ickes' Republicanism was of a steadier sort. Ickes trusted Merriam and Brownlow. For a congenitally suspicious man, this was an advantage of the highest order. Merriam and Brownlow together operated to manipulate Ickes into more useful administrative attitudes than his personality sometimes permitted; but most important of all, Ickes' respect for Merriam gave the latter an independence in the Ickes' camp which few others would have been allowed.[73]

In November of 1933, the group undertook studies on broad aspects of national planning. Given free rein by Ickes, Delano began probing physical public works planning; Mitchell examined economic planning; and Merriam's project on governmental and political planning became known as "a plan for a plan." In 1934 Merriam prepared an essay entitled "A Plan for Planning" which accompanied the final report of the National Planning Board which was about to become the National Resources Committee, "a change which signified, among other things, the President's increasing interest in its work."[74]

> During the spring and summer of 1935 as committee meetings in the White House brought Merriam and the president into constant contact, Roosevelt began to express curiosity about Merriam's view of a broader concept of planning and its relation to the presidency. He asked Merriam to prepare a memorandum on the subject. The memorandum, written by Merriam in consultation with Brownlow, opened with the statement: "One of the greatest assets of America is that of executive skills, sometimes developed in industry, sometimes in education and engineering, sometimes in the domain of government. The city manager, the large-scale industrial executive, the national executive officer, are examples of leadership which have justly attracted attention everywhere." In that memorandum the basic statement of planning as a guide to governmental and political policy, distinguished from problems of personnel and budget—indeed well above them—was set forth.[75]

In his autobiography, Louis Brownlow set forth this October, 1935, memorandum by Merriam, and—except for the opening paragraph which appears in the above quotation—it is reproduced here in full:

> From the point of view of national planning of natural and human resources, it is evident that management is of fundamental importance. Management and administration are national resources incalculable in importance, highly developed in various sections of our national activities. Our resources have meaning and effect in proportion to the skill with which they are managed by those responsible for their administration. In particular it is clear that it is important to canvass with the greatest care the arrangements by and through which the planning function and agency can best fit into and be more effective in our national organization. The National Resources Committee is conceived as a general staff to the executive and in order to be most useful must be adjusted with the greatest pains to the other technical functions and agencies of the going concern known as administration.
>
> The organization, development, and position of the American executive is one of the great contributions of American genius; and the continuance and development of this agency is one of the brightest prospects of modern democracy. It is important, however, that the executive office be developed on the side of management and administrative supervision as well as on the political side if its full possibilities are to be realized in our national affairs.
>
> The political relations of the executive are organized in the political parties and its officials, in the party caucus in the Congress and the various congressional leaders, and in the cabi-

net, reflecting representative political leadership. These relations seem likely to go forward with relatively little change, and in any case require special and separate consideration.

The technical services, however, present a different problem in view of the rapid increase of functions, the development of specialized ability, the increasing number of industrial and scientific contacts, the necessity for continuity in administration, and a form of overall administrative supervision or management. Steps have already been taken on the personnel side in the establishment of the merit system and the civil service commission; on the fiscal side through the establishment of the budget director and the comptroller general; and in the coordination of longtime planning policies through the National Resources Committee.

It would be possible to make a thorough study of this whole problem as it develops in American public life—a study directed toward the institutional arrangements, general understandings and practices which would most effectively aid the executive in the double task of management plus political leadership and direction.

Should the National Resources Committee request the Public Administration Committee of the Social Science Research Council to make a study of management in federal administration? (Reporting December, 1936?) Such a study might involve, roughly, an examination of the trends, emerging problems and possible rearrangement of such national services as are directed primarily toward what may be called management in the larger sense of the term. The research would go back some distance—perhaps to the Civil War period when the work of government began to expand rapidly—reviewing the development of functions and mechanisms and the problems arising in their growth and interrelationship.

The committee suggested above is already engaged in the task of contemporary observation of the Works Progress Administration on its administrative side, and it might be persuaded to broaden the scope of its inquiry, if requested to do so by the National Resources Committee—with the understanding that the report was to be made in November or December of 1936, in order that it might have a nonpolitical setting and effect.

This Committee has as its chairman Louis Brownlow, who has long experience in Washington (D.C. Commissioner under Wilson), has had wide journalistic experience and is now director of the Public Administration Clearing House. The services of technicians such as Lewis Meriam, Arthur Macmahon, Lindsay Rogers, Leonard White, Colonel Henry M. Waite, and others with wide knowledge and experience would undoubtedly be available for such a study. In addition, the judgment of a number of men with wide experience in management, political and industrial, might be solicited and utilized in such a manner as to give great public weight to the findings and recommendations of the Committee.[76]

Administrative management stood apart from the traditional views of executive reorganization: efficiency and economy of operation were to give way to centralized executive control over programs, resource allocation, and decision making. Merriam begged the "rearrangement of . . . national services" to conform with these ideas of "management in the larger sense of the term." Roosevelt shied away from passing the project on to the Social Science Research Council because that forum was associated with the Rockefeller family name. Instead, he sought his own committee, instructed by the president. The result was the President's Committee on Administrative Management, announced on March 22, 1936, and consisting of Merriam, Brownlow, and Luther Gulick. Its task, as revealed in the president's letter to Congress, would be to make "a careful study of the organization of the executive branch of the government . . . with the primary purpose of considering the problem of administrative management." The chief executive went on to stress that "many new agencies have been created during the emergency, some of which will, with the recovery, be dropped or greatly curtailed, while others, in order to meet the newly realized needs of the nation, will have to be fitted into the permanent organization of the executive branch."[77] Little concern with efficiency and economy through government reorganization was evident in the president's letter. Instead, the emphasis was upon structuring the chief executive's authority for effectively executing his constitutional responsibilities. The House and Senate were urged to appoint committees to work with the president's panel, largely because Roosevelt knew that efforts to this end were already underway in Congress. There subsequently appeared a Joint Committee on Government Organization; a Senate Select Committee to Investigate the Executive Agencies of the Government, and a Senate Select Committee on Government Organization, all of which scrutinized executive branch reorganization with a view to efficiency and economy of operation.

The President's Committee

Roosevelt embraced the concept of administrative management which Merriam had developed. The president organized a panel to expand upon the idea; gave it a membership which would sympathetically develop this view; and charged it to be responsive to the chief executive's favor for the administrative management idea.

> By choosing to commit himself at the beginning, in effect, to the conclusions of his Committee on Administrative Management, Roosevelt both drew more sharply than ever the line between politics and political science and obscured it. For he was admitting that he could not commit himself as a politician to objective conclusions before he had an opportunity to examine them and test his agreement with them, at the same time that he was admitting the need of the advice of the community of social scientists for purposes of running his government. The refusal to commit himself in advance to unknown conclusions marked a difference, crucial in the extreme, between the conclusions of the politician and those of the social scientists. But the recognition of and selection of the community of social science as the center of the best advice was a request to that community that, in the interest of politics, it enter the arena of government but divested, temporarily of course, of its traditional commitment to objectivity. For some, as we shall see, this proved to be a request which would have been rejected—had they understood it at the beginning.[78]

To facilitate the Committee's endeavors, the president asked Brownlow, chairman of the panel, to prepare a memorandum outlining the content and order of the group's final report. On November 5, 1936, Brownlow prepared the following format:

The report should declare:

That managerial direction and control of all departments and agencies of the executive branch of the government should be centered in the president;

That while he now has popular responsibility for this direction and control he is not equipped with adequate legal authority or administrative machinery to enable him to exercise it; and

That certain changes in law and administrative practice are required to restore the executive to that position of power balanced with compensating responsibility which is the clear purpose and intent of our constitutional system.

The report should recommend:

That the staff or institutional agencies be made directly responsible to the president; that the president establish a White House secretariat which will include not only such functions as have been exercised in the past, but which under an executive secretary will establish the direct lines of communication with all the staff agencies except the Budget (which should report directly to the president);

That to facilitate coordinated over-all management and to improve internal agency administration a single responsible administrator be placed at the head of all administrative agencies, staff and line, which are not headed by boards or commissions;

That while no recommendation may be made at this time for the segregation of administrative duties from the quasi-judicial duties of the regulatory agencies now in existence, the danger of the development of an irresponsible fourth branch of the government be recognized and that consideration be given in all future regulatory legislation to the devolution of such work upon the regular departments of government as already often has been done;

That the president be given continuing power, subject to a congressional veto of the type provided in the Economy Act of 1933 to regroup, rearrange, consolidate, and reorganize the departments, agencies, and bureaus; and that to facilitate his work in this respect there be developed in the Bureau of the Budget the research function already provided for by law.

That in the presence of an emergency the temporary creation of emergency agencies to handle new types of activities is not only justified but necessary; that as the emergency situation lessens the new activities be fitted into the permanent establishment by order of the President (subject to the same type of congressional veto suggested above);

That to effectuate these recommendations which are to be elaborated in detail, it is necessary to establish direct lines of relationship which will enable the president to control effectively the fiscal machinery of the government, to extend the merit system to all branches of the executive excluding only policy making positions, to command the research and intellectual resources of an adequately equipped planning agency, to require the coordination of statistical and reporting services and to establish a coordinated scheme for the clearance of legislative recommendations or reports proper to the sphere of the executive as well as to provide clearance and control for the issue of executive orders and administrative rules and regulations which require presidential authority or approval;

That effective congressional control of the executive cannot be exercised by detailed and uncoordinated legislative action whether by general law or limitations attached to particular budgetary items of appropriation bills or by the type of control exercised by the comptroller general who is the agent of Congress but who in fact is irresponsible to either the executive or legislative branch; but that congressional control of the executive will be advantaged by a concentration of administrative responsibility upon the president in accordance with the Constitution, and will be made fully effective only by the creation by Congress of its own agent to review and audit the conduct of the executive branch and to report to Congress through committees especially set up by the two houses of Congress to receive and digest the results of such a review and audit.[79]

Nine days later the memo was placed on the president's desk. Roosevelt's objections were two: more than one executive secretary was necessary just to protect the functionary from press criticism that this was an "assistant president"; also, he was disappointed that no firm plan was offered on coordinating the activities of the independent regulatory commissions.[80] A month later, with both points altered to F.D.R.'s wishes, the outline had the president's approval.

The Committee proposed to strengthen the president in five ways. First, furnish six executive assistants to lighten the intolerable personal burden upon him. Second, reinvigorate the civil service by expanding the merit system and raising government salaries, and by replacing the ineffectual Civil Service Commission with an energetic administrator. Third, improve fiscal management by encouraging budget-planning, by restoring control of accounts to the executive, and by providing Congress with an independent audit of all transactions. Fourth, establish the National Resources Planning Board as a permanent central planning agency to coordinate government programs. Fifth, reorganize the government by creating two new cabinet posts and by bringing every executive agency, including the independent regulatory commissions, under one of the twelve major departments.[81]

Although a research staff was assembled and projects were developed by assisting scholars, the Committee's final report was prepared by Brownlow, Merriam, and Gulick with little direct use of these commissioned materials.[82] The document was written and delivered to the White House in wraps of secrecy. Released to Congress on January 12, 1937, with an accompanying presidential statement, the report soon became lost in high politics. On the afternoon of January 11, Roosevelt presented the Committee's views to the Democratic congressional leadership. Those assembled greeted the radical recommendations with an air of gloom reflective of the rainy Sunday. Some were shocked, viewing the suggestions as disruptive of congressional political relationships with the executive branch agencies and departments, or a power play by the president, or both.[83]

Other factors soon complicated Roosevelt's hopes for the executive branch reorganization scheme. Three weeks after submitting the Committee for Administrative Management report to Congress, the president announced his desire to reform the federal judiciary, especially the Supreme Court. Not only did this proposal feed fears of presidential power but Congress became preoccupied with it to the extent of ignoring the reorganization program. Initially at least two personalities figured prominently in the reorganization. Sen. Joseph Robinson (D.-Ariz.), an influential New Deal supporter, the Senate majority leader and chairman of the Senate Select Committee on Government Organization, died suddenly on July 14. Sen. Harry Byrd, Sr. (D.-Va.), chairman of the Senate Select Committee to Investigate the Executive Agencies of the Government, became increasingly disenchanted with New Deal politics generally and the reorganization proposals in particular.[84]

> Opposition to the reorganization plan was quickened by the recommendations of the Brookings Institution. As an organization specializing in the appraisal of government administration, Brookings had been employed by both the Senate and House Committees in the spring of 1936. Despite good intentions and certain precautions, its study overlapped that of the president's Committee in crucial areas. As the realization grew that conflicting findings might result, sporadic efforts were made to avert an open break. Finally, frustrated by the fruitless negotiations and prodded by its Congressional sponsors, Brookings released a report that sharply challenged Brownlow's recommendations and provided a store of ammunition for Senator Byrd and other critics. Roosevelt's position—that of merely endorsing what "experts" had proposed—was badly undermined by his opponents' ability to summon their own, contradictory, "expert" opinion.[85]

And what had the Committee on Administrative Management suggested with regard to immediate presidential staffing and staff agencies? The modest proposal did not envision an Executive Office of the President or auxiliary staff agencies in 1937. All that was sought was an enlargement of the number of presidential assistants. In part, the report said:

> In this broad program of administrative reorganization, the White House itself is involved. The president needs help. His immediate staff assistance is entirely inadequate. He should be given a small number of executive assistants who would be his direct aides in dealing with the managerial agencies and administrative departments of the government. These assistants, probably not exceeding six in number, would be in addition to the present secretaries, who deal with the public, with the Congress, and with the press and radio. These aides would have no power to make decisions or issue instructions in their own right. They would not be interposed between the president and the heads of his departments. They would not be assistant presidents in any sense. Their function would be, when any matter was presented to the president for action affecting any part of the administrative work of the government, to assist him in obtaining quickly and without delay all pertinent information possessed by any of the executive departments so as to guide him in making his responsible decisions; and then when decisions have been made, to assist him in seeing to it that every administrative department and agency affected is promptly informed. Their effectiveness in assisting the president will, we think, be directly proportional to their ability to discharge their functions with restraint. They would remain in the background, issue no orders, make no decisions, emit no public statements. Men for these positions should be carefully chosen by the president from within and without the government. They should be men in whom the president has personal confidence and whose character and attitude is such that they would not attempt to exercise power on their own account. They should be possessed of high competence, great physical vigor, and a passion for anonymity. They should be installed in the White House itself, directly accessible to the president. In the selection of these aides, the president should be free to call on departments from time to time

for the assignment of persons who, after a tour of duty as his aides, might be restored to their old positions.[86]

While this particular recommendation did not attract fervent opposition in Congress, the forces of resistance carried sway and Roosevelt's hopes for executive branch reforms died in the 75th Congress.

Resurrected Executive Office

Although efforts at implementing the Committee on Administrative Management's recommendations and adoption of a reorganization authority bill lay in ruin in the spring of 1938, the buoyant chief executive had not deserted the cause. Both popular and congressional support for the president accelerated with his submission of a $3 billion recovery and relief program to combat the recession and with his request that Congress study the concentration of economic power in the United States. Proposed in April, both measures passed by large majorities.

By July Roosevelt was meeting with Brownlow, Merriam and Gulick. The Committee would not be officially reassembled; instead, the president sought out the Democratic congressional leadership to confront them with a new reorganization proposal. Some who had deserted F.D.R. on legislation that spring were under critical attack from their constituents by summer. Loyalists among the congressional Democrats wanted to make the vote on reorganization a test of fidelity to the administration. In late June the president had announced his intentions of purging the party of conservatives but no ultimatum was attached to the reorganizational proposal.

> The Reorganization bill introduced in 1939 stood in sharp contrast to the measure defeated by the House the previous year. It was extremely mild, omitting nearly every controversial feature of its predecessor. It was drawn up by legislative leaders who paid little heed to the recommendations of the Brownlow Committee. It sparked no storm of controversy; public fear was absent and pressure groups were quiescent. And although the Republicans picked up eighty seats in the House and seven in the Senate in November 1938, the Reorganization bill of 1939 passed with little difficulty.[87]

Legislative strategy was set in early December, 1938, by Roosevelt, Gulick, Merriam, and Senator James Byrnes (D.-S.C.), the chairman of the Select Committee on Government Organization and manager of the reorganization legislation after Sen. Robinson's death (Brownlow was convalescing from a heart attack at this time). Provisions regarding civil service administration, accounting, and reorganization of various bureaus were eliminated from the new proposal and authority for Congress to overrule a presidential reorganization plan by a majority vote was added. Byrnes asked that the bill be initiated in the House where debate could be limited and the Senate would be free to pursue other business of the moment. Rep. Lindsay Warren (D.-N.C.), who had some timidity regarding acceptance of the proposal, drafted the revised bill without consulting members of the president's Committee. The resulting measure (H.R. 4425) empowered the president to propose plans of reorganization, subject to a veto by a majority of both houses of Congress, and to also appoint six administrative assistants. Language for modernizing the civil service, renovating government accounting procedures, and creating new departments included in the 1937 proposal was eliminated.

After three days of debate, the House adopted the bill on March 8, 1939. Twelve days later the Senate began considering the proposal. Following two days of sparring over amendments, the Senate adopted the bill. A quick conference cleared the proposal for Roosevelt's signature on April 3 (53 Stat. 651).

Although administrative experts had little to do with drafting the act, they were largely responsible for its implementation. On March 20 Roosevelt asked Brownlow, Merriam, and Gulick to "come right down" to Washington when the bill passed so that reorganization plans could be presented at least sixty days before Congress adjourned. Gulick thought that the president should bring forth an extensive and sweeping program, but Brownlow hoped Roosevelt would not be "too optimistic about what can be done" in the short time available. On March 31 Brownlow's group drew up a timetable for reorganization: the first step would be to consolidate agencies into existing departments and into a new Social Security Administration and Public Works Administration; then, interdepartmental agency transfers and intradepartmental changes could be made.[88]

After consulting with Budget Director Harold D. Smith, the group presented two reorganization proposals to the president on April 23. Plan I (53 Stat. 1423) submitted to Congress on April 25, contained the model of the Executive Office of the President. While this and the interdepartmental changes plan were acceptable to the legislature, their effective dates were troublesome in terms of accommodating fiscal calendar necessities. By joint resolution (53 Stat. 813), Congress provided that both plans would be effective on July 1, 1939. Following this action, the president issued a directive (E.O. 8248) on September 8 organizing the Executive Office entities.

In the view of its architect who drafted the initial reorganization plan—Louis Brownlow—the most innovative aspect of the scheme was the creation of the Executive Office.

> Part I created the Executive Office of the President. It was then apparent, and subsequent events have proved, that was the major revolutionary feature of the whole business. A great many students of administration have expressed the opinion that the establishment of the Executive Office, the effective coordination of the tremendously wide-spread federal machinery, enabled the United States to win World War II and meet the consequent problems with which the nation had to deal.
>
> The Executive Office as it was conceived and organized under Plan I in the summer of 1939 was indeed a little thing compared to its present size. It expanded under President Roosevelt during the years; it continued to expand and was further regularized by statute, by appropriation acts, and by more reorganization plans under President Truman. Under President Eisenhower, it has had a tremendous expansion not only in the number of its personnel but in the scope of its reorganization.[89]

The initial reorganization directive for the Executive Office (E.O. 8248) established the following units within this domain: The White House Office, the Bureau of the Budget, the National Resources Planning Board, the Liaison Office for Personnel Management, the Office of Government Reports, and, "in the event of a national emergency, such office for emergency management as the president shall determine." The Office for Emergency Management was created by an administrative order on May 25, 1940 and its functions were specified in a presidential directive (E.O. 8629) of January 7, 1941, and in an administrative order issued on the same date—these actions taking place as prospects grew for the United States being drawn into war.

> Most, but not all, of the agencies concerned with the defense program became a part of O.E.M. The organization of the government in crisis proceeded upon the theory that the regular departments and agencies should dispose of crisis matters insofar as they were capable. Otherwise, the matters should be handled by new agencies created especially for the crisis. The new agencies might be a part of the Executive Office of the President or they might be independent of it. The allocation of the new agencies was determined by the belief of Mr. Roosevelt that direct operating duties should be brought into the Executive Office under either of two circumstances. First, when the attitude of an existing agency toward defense problems is hostile and a change in personnel of the agency cannot otherwise be justified. Second, when the activity is peculiarly related to the crisis and is of such importance that it must be brought under the president's control.
>
> The president . . . concluded that many defense agencies should be a part of the Executive Office of the President. He could not attend to each agency personally, and, consequently, established the Office for Emergency Management, in the Executive Office of the President, to aid him in the coordination and direction of the defense agencies.[90]

O.E.M. served as the umbrella parent unit for a number of subordinate emergency management bodies. Eventually its functions were assumed by the Office of War Mobilization created by a presidential directive (E.O. 9347) of May 27, 1943. This unit was transferred at the president's order (E.O. 9488) in October, 1944, to the statutorily established (58 Stat. 785) Office of War Mobilization and Reconstruction.[91]

Agencies appeared and disappeared within the Executive Office in the aftermath of the World War. Steadily, however, lasting units and a growing staff materialized. Commenting upon the physical growth of the E.O.P. in his 1958 autobiography, Louis Brownlow said: "I am quite sure that Franklin D. Roosevelt, when he sent up Plan I, had not in his wildest dreams conceived of such an expansion."[92]

Hoover Commission Evaluation

A decade before Brownlow's comment, the Executive Office underwent an initial evaluation. Segments of its organization and functions had been scrutinized at different times but the first total review was made in a February, 1949, report of the Commission on Organization of the Executive Branch of the Government, chaired by former President Herbert C. Hoover. Popularly known as the First Hoover Commission (there was a Second Hoover Commission, 1953-1955), the panel evaluated the E.O.P. in its study of the general management of the executive branch, reflecting an awareness of the administrative management concept of the Brownlow Committee as well as a concern with economy and efficiency.

After considering the current working arrangements of the Executive Office and the problems of presidential staff assistance, the Hoover Commission offered the following recommendations:[93]

1. addition of an Office of Personnel to the E.O.P. with a director who would also serve as chairman of the Civil Service Commission;
2. addition of a staff secretary or chief of staff to the White House Office with responsibilities for overall staff management and issue awareness;
3. expansion of both the budgetary and program management functions of the Bureau of the Budget;
4. avoiding a grant of statutory authority vesting authority over the operating departments in any staff members of staff agency of the Executive Office;
5. avoiding a statutory prevention of the president from reorganizing the E.O.P. or transferring functions and personnel from one part of it to another segment;
6. appointment of the head of each presidential staff agency without Senate confirmation (with the exception of the Civil Service Commission-related position);
7. replacement of the Council of Economic Advisers with a single-headed Office of the Economic Adviser;
8. allocations of sufficient funds to the president to employ consultants or personal advisers on special matters from time to time;
9. allocation of sufficient funds to allow the president to secure a staff secretary, in addition to the existing principal secretaries, to assist him by clearing information on the major problems on which staff work is being done within the president's office, or by cabinet or interdepartmental committees; and
10. addition of an Office of General Services to assist the president in the direction and supervision of the operations of the executive branch with regard to services provided to all the departments.

With two exceptions, none of these recommendations have been realized. Presidents Eisenhower, Nixon, and Ford appointed a formal chief of staff comparable to the staff secretary suggested by the Hoover Commission. These were not statutorily designated positions or specially created outside of the standard staffing patterns available to the president at the time.

President Nixon also utilized "ungraded positions" normally reserved for the employment of custodial and wage-board personnel serving the housekeeping function at the executive residence, to employ both consultants and regular E.O.P. staff.[94] For the most part, however, the recommendations of the Hoover panel regarding the E.O.P. went unheeded.

Carter Reorganization

When Jimmy Carter became chief executive in 1977, he began action on a number of executive branch reorganization innovations to which he had pledged himself during the campaign of the previous year. He sought, and obtained, renewal of the president's authority to reorganize the government by the submission of formal plans to Congress (91 Stat. 29); he offered a proposal creating a Department of Energy which was also given congressional sanction (91 Stat. 565); and he initiated the first thorough study of the activities and operations of the Executive Office of the President since the Hoover Commission evaluation. By March 14, 1977, a task force on E.O.P. reorganization and reconstitution was underway and by late June had placed its recommendations on the president's desk. After due consideration, the chief executive transmitted Reorganization Plan No. 1. to Congress on July 15. Hearings on the proposal were held late in the same month before the Senate Committee on Governmental Affairs and in early August before the House Committee on Government Operations.[95] After certain amendments and modifications were obtained from the White House, both houses of Congress accepted the E.O.P. plan in October.

While the promise of major changes in the executive office was seemingly great at the time of President Carter's announcement of a reorganization of his staff agencies, reality was disappointing. No underlying theory or explanation for the alterations in the E.O.P. structure was forthcoming and the possibility of effecting economy was questionable. Among other modifications, the plan abolished the Economic Opportunity Council, the Domestic Council, the Office of Telecommunications Policy, and the Office of Drug Abuse Policy; simultaneously, the proposal created a Domestic Policy Staff and a Central Administrative Unit (later renamed the Office of Administration). There was, however, a certain amount of confusion regarding these restructurings. The Economic Opportunity Council was merely a paper entity, had no staff, and never met after it was transferred to the Executive Office in 1967. It was unclear if the Domestic Policy Staff was a subunit of the White House Office or a standing unit within the E.O.P. And though arguments were made that staff reductions had occurred within the White House Office and the Office of Management and Budget, the majority of these personnel were merely transferred to the Office of Administration or outside the E.O.P. In brief, there appeared to be little staff reduction and slight budget curtailment within the E.O.P. as a consequence of this reorganization.

Utilization of the E.O.P.

As an extension of the managerial presidency, the E.O.P. since its inception, has reflected a corps of permanent administrative assistants and a collection of temporary units designed to aid the chief executive in meeting a momentary crisis. Commenting on the political aspect of the Executive Office, former presidential aide Theodore Sorensen has quipped: "Some White Houses use the E.O.P. as a farm league, some use it as a source of experts and implementers, and some use it as Elba."[96]

Among the more permanent constructs are the White House Office and the budget office (initially the Bureau of the Budget and now the Office of Management and Budget), both of which were among the initial E.O.P. structures. The Council of Economic Advisers, established in 1946, and the National Security Council, created in 1947 and added to the E.O.P. two years later, also appear to hold permanent status. Created by the legislative branch to assist the president in specialized policy matters, these two panels have been of varying utility to succeeding chief executives due to conditions of managerial style: a tendency on the part of most presidents since Franklin Roosevelt has been toward nonreliance upon formal advisory institutions. Thus, while the chairman of the C.E.A. and the Assistant to the President for National Security Affairs may be close presidential advisers, the formal institutions to which they are attached have not been particularly influential sources of counsel to the Chief Executive.

A number of temporary units within the E.O.P. have been memorable as instruments for meeting crisis and exigencies. Franklin Roosevelt utilized the Office for Emergency Management to create a variety of civilian war agencies during World War II. President Truman created a number of E.O.P. entities to convert the domestic economy to a peacetime status as well as to manage American assistance to European nations recovering from the ravages of war. With the onset of the cold war President Eisenhower coordinated civil defense preparedness through E.O.P. structures. Presidents Kennedy and Johnson promoted scientific endeavors through E.O.P. councils and advisory bodies while the Office of Economic Opportunity coordinated the "war on poverty" inaugurated by these administrations. New E.O.P. entities of the Nixon and Ford years reflected presidential concern with economic problems and energy crises, both of which threatened the welfare and well-being of the nation.

Apart from these considerations, no other observable trends are immediately apparent with regard to the composition of the Executive Office of the President. Generally, the E.O.P. is a sector subject to the chief executive's almost exclusive organizational whim. Yet, entities created within this domain are the objects of the most serious consideration for they constitute essential instruments of assistance for the managerial presidency. Until such time as prevailing views of the chief executive being the primary manager of the administrative forces of government are abandoned or radically altered, the composition of the Executive Office will undoubtedly fluctuate with the addition of an occasional new unit of permanent durability as well as various fleeting entities born of crisis management.[97]

Special Staffing Considerations

The record is not clear regarding the beginning of staff assistance for the First Lady. Undoubtedly, the chief executive's wife initially realized such service through the occasional utilization of a White House stenographer or clerk. It is known that during the regime of the nation's twenty-eighth president, Mrs. Edith Bolling Galt Wilson had found a close personal aide in Miss Edith Benham (later Mrs. James Helm) who was the social secretary for the executive mansion. The position of White House social secretary would not become formalized until the establishment of the White House Office in 1939. Mrs. Grace Coolidge also had a close working relationship with the social secretaries of her husband's tenure: Miss Laura Harlan and Miss Mary (Polly) Randolph, the latter also assisting Mrs. Lou Henry Hoover. However, the position of secretary to the wife of the president did not literally appear prior to 1948 when Reathel M. Odum was unofficially credited with the role in the *United States Government Manual*. The *Official Register of the United States* for 1948 officially listed her as the White House Office Social Secretary. By 1953, the *Official Register* indicated Mary Jean McCaffree was acting secretary to the wife of the president and the following year officially credited her in this position without the "acting" status. The salary of the secretary to the First Lady was $7,040 during these years. The immediate personal staff available to the First Lady today probably numbers approximately a dozen individuals who handle scheduling, correspondence, press, and personal matters of an official nature. These employees are compensated from funds appropriated to the president for White House Office personnel.

Since the creation of the office, the vice-president, as an executive branch official, has also been plagued by staffing problems (as presiding officer of the Senate, the vice-president is provided with personnel for the execution and performance of legislative branch responsibilities). Because the vice-president only lately has been given specific and continuing duties, it has been difficult for incumbents occupying the position to make a convincing case regarding their personnel needs. In recent times, vice-presidents have found it necessary to borrow staff on detail from the departments and agencies. However, in order to provide the office a more distinctive identification and to alleviate past personnel problems, a new "Special Assistance to the President" account was established with the federal budget for fiscal year 1971. These funds may be drawn upon for expenses necessary to enable the vice-president to provide certain assistance to the chief executive in connection with specifically assigned functions. During the past five years, the vice-president has maintained an executive branch staff of approximately 24 individuals. Since 1972, the *United States Government Organization Manual* has described functions of the Office of the Vice-President and has listed the principal assistants of the vice-president.

Contemporary Presidential Staffing

The contemporary chief executive utilizes the services of a variety of assistants, their diversity and number perhaps being best reflected in the following consideration regarding presidential advisers:

> Each president receives advice in the way he finds most congenial. Big meetings. Small meetings. No meetings. Long reports. Short memos. Each picks his own advice systems. He convenes conferences, commissions, task forces, and committees. He turns to cabinet members, cronies, family, and staff. Each picks his own immediate subordinates, relying on lawyers and businessmen, generals and diplomats, scholars, union leaders, and party leaders. He seeks advice that is agreeable and advice that is representative. From blacks, westerners, Catholics, bankers. He seeks assistants who are loyal yet independent, free thinkers yet team players.[98]

The cabinet continues to be available to every chief executive as a primary assistance institution. During the past few decades, a certain amount of support staff has been created for the president through the auxiliaries of cabinet committees. Established to focus concentrated attention on pressing policy matters of concern to two or more departments, these temporary panels are usually launched at the direction of the president, chaired by a cabinet member (sometimes the vice-president), and obtain personnel and operating resources through details and donations from the affected departments. President Johnson established the Cabinet Committee on the Environment and a Cabinet Task Force on Oil Import Control. President Nixon created similar such bodies to examine price stability and school desegregation. In an unusual development, Congress authorized (83 Stat. 838) a Cabinet Committee on Opportunities for Spanish-Speaking People in 1969, giving it a five-year mandate, a separate staff of approximately thirty employees, and an independent appropriation which reached the million dollar mark one year. Thus, on a temporary basis, the chief executive can look to cabinet-level advisory panels for both counsel and policy aides.

The president's principal source of assistants, however, continues to be the White House Office staff and the personnel of selected Executive Office agencies. These aides are the creation of the Brownlow Commission, envisioned as having "no power to make decisions or issue instructions in their own right" and "possessed of high competence, great vigor, and a passion for anonymity."[99] Commenting on the suggestion of establishing executive assistants, a later analysis of the Commission's report noted:

> These men were to act as anonymous servants exercising no initiative independently of the president's wishes. No authority was delegated to them. Their function was to extend the president's power to listen wherever useful information could be gathered and to see whatever needed to be seen to provide the information required for decisions. In order to give them the utmost responsibility, to presidential will, as well as ultimate flexibility, their functions were not to be defined except as the president saw fit to define them. As such they would not constitute either an additional institution or certainly not an independent one, but rather an extension of the presidency itself.[100]

In spite of these high hopes, White House

assistants to succeeding presidents, since 1939, have become highly conspicuous, multiple in number, possessed of great power, and virtually unaccountable to anyone but the chief executive for their actions. The number of presidential advisers and policy aides within the White House office and the larger executive office has exhibited generally steady growth, regardless of national or international events, changes of administration, or differing management styles of chief executives. (See manpower table 3.1.2.)

While presidents apparently, without authorization, had engaged in the detailing of departmental employees to the White House for temporary service, thus stimulating congressional wrath in 1878 (see 20 Stat. 183), the chief executive was granted such discretion in 1905 (33 Stat. 642) and retains this power today (3 U.S.C. 107). Such staff transfers constitute another avenue for obtaining experts to assist the president. The extent to which the practice has been utilized is depicted in table 3.1.3.

Managerial authority and program responsibility has been given over to presidential assistants because other coordinating and administrative guidance institutions, such as the cabinet, have proven to be unsuitable for these functions. In this regard, one expert has commented:

> Whether manifested by a benign lack of interest or by purposeful competition, departmentalism operated to reduce the potentialities of the cabinet as a coordinating mechanism. Yet in view of the extent to which executive decisionmaking must now be conducted across departmental boundaries, it does not seem too much to say that the chief executive's primary managerial task is precisely this one of coordination. From the seminal recommendations of the President's Committee on Administrative Management in 1939 to the present day, the president's need for assistance in this area has been widely recognized. This, indeed, is the raison d'etre for the phenomenal proliferation of those staff organs with interdepartmental planning, operating, and advisory functions which now comprise the Executive Office of the President. The expansion of this Office—of, for instance, the Budget Bureau, the National Security Council, the Office of Defense Mobilization, the Council of Economic Advisers, the White House Office—must be considered in part as an inevitable response to the new dimensions of governmental activity, but also in part as an adverse reflection on the ability of the cabinet in coping with the difficult problems of coordination involved.[101]

Thus, it is the White House Office and the Executive Office satellites which have come to better serve the president as coordinators of executive functions. And as managers of the government, as well, they have come to play policy roles, refining policy suggestions and sometimes even the access of other policymakers to the chief executive. But, as Theodore Sorensen has noted, such a role carries with it certain dangers.

> A White House adviser may see a departmental problem in a wider context than a secretary, but he also has less contact with actual operations and pressures, with Congress and interested groups. If his own staff grows too large, his office may become only another department, another level of clearances and concurrencies instead of a personal instrument of the president. If his confidential relationship with the president causes either one to be too uncritical of the other's judgment, errors may go uncorrected. If he develops . . . a confidence in his own competence which outruns the fact, his contribution may be more mischievous than useful. If, on the other hand, he defers too readily to the authority of the renowned experts and cabinet powers, then the president is denied the skeptical, critical service his staff should be providing.[102]

Of course, as presidential assistants move toward the possibility of the equivalent of departmental authority, whether such power be measured in fiscal or political influence terms, the wrath of official department heads can, and often is, incurred. As Sorensen has noted:

> No doubt at times our roles were resented. Secretary Hodges, apparently disgruntled by his inability to see the president more often, arranged to have placed on the cabinet agenda for June 15, 1961, an item entitled "A candid dis-

Table 3.1.2.

Growth of Presidential Staff

Year	White House Office Budgeted Positions	White House Office Actual Manpower[a]	Executive Office Actual Manpower[a]
1939	37	753 [b]	894 [c]
1940	55	912 [d]	1,098
1941	55	2,673 [e]	2,814
1942	40.5	857 [f]	958
1943	39.5	51	738
1944	47.5	58	707
1945	48.6	66	849
1946	51.5	216	1,066
1947	210	219	1,055
1948	288	209	1,205
1949	241	243	1,240
1950	238	313	1,507
1951	254	246	1,326
1952	261	248	1,296
1953	279	247	1,183
1954	246	262	1,078
1955	260	366	1,221
1956	271	372	1,228
1957	268	399	1,255
1958	270	395	2,605
1959	275	406	2,735
1960	268	416	2,755
1961	270	439	1,586
1962	273	338	1,492
1963	270	376	1,572
1964	270	328	1,470
1965	255	292	3,310
1966	255	270	4,050
1967	250	271	4,747
1968	250	261	4,964
1969	250	337	4,116
1970	250	491	4,806
1971	533	583	4,812
1972	540	583	5,722
1973	510	524	3,878
1974	505	560	2,868
1975	553	525	1,801
1976	500	534	1,796

a. Statistics supplied by U.S. Civil Service Commission, Bureau of Personnel Management Information Systems. All citations are end of calendar year totals as of December 31.
b. Statistic for Office of the President and includes employees paid from funds provided by the Emergency Relief Appropriations Acts. The White House Office was not operational until late in 1939. Citation is given as 224 regular staff and 529 E.R.A staff.
c. Citation includes employees paid from funds provided by the Emergency Relief Appropriations Acts.
d. Ibid.; citation is given as 562 regular staff and 350 E.R.A. staff.
e. Ibid.; citation is given as 2,672 regular staff and 1 E.R.A. staff.
f. Termination of E.R.A. funding; citation is given as 857 regular staff.

Table 3.1.3

Detailees on White House Office Staff, 1919-1976

Year	Detailees[a]	Budgeted Positions[b]
1939	112	37
1940	114	55
1941	118	55
1942	137	40.5
1943	148	39.5
1944	144	47.5
1945	167	48.6
1946	161	51.5
1947	19 [c]	210
1948	17 (estimate)	288
1949	17 (estimate)	241
1950 through 1969 unavailable from public records		
1970	273 [d]	250
1971	15 [e]	533
1972	12	540
1973	22	510
1974	34	505
1975	27	553
1976	27	500

a. Figures for 1939 through 1949 taken from Senate Appropriations Committee hearing on Independent Offices Appropriations Bill for 1949, p. 9. Figures for 1970 through 1976 taken from Senate and House Appropriation Committees' hearings for those years.
b. Figures taken from U.S. Budget Appendix.
c. In 1947 the president transferred to White House Office rolls the greater portion of employees that had in prior years been detailed to the White House Office from other agencies.
d. In 1970, there were 576 persons on the White House Office staff (208 were paid from appropriations for salaries for the White House Office staff, 95 were paid from appropriations from Special Projects, and 273 (detailees) were paid by their agencies.
e. In 1971, the president transferred to White House Office rolls the greater portion of employees that had in prior years been detailed to the White House Office from other agencies, and most of those who were permanently working in the White House Office but were paid out of Special Projects appropriations.

cussion with the president on relationships with the White House staff." Upon discovering this in the meeting, I passed the president a note asking "Shall I leave?"—but the president ignored both the note and the agenda.[103]

Such disputes within the executive "family" can be viewed as merely matters of paternal favor. When these encroachments of power become enmeshed in executive relationships with other branches of government, then a constitutional crisis may be in the offing.

A short time ago, in testimony before a subcommittee of the House Committee on Government Operations, former White House press secretary George Reedy made the following observation on the increasing authority of the White House staff and the significance of this development both in terms of information flow and accountability.

> At one time the White House staff was a relatively small group of people. They consisted of personal advisers to the president, and here you have the whole question of executive privilege which has been exercised, in my judgment, in an extremely legitimate form. I do not think that you should be able to pry loose from a president what he does not want to be pried loose. But, even if you should be allowed to do it, there is simply no way of getting at it. I do not care what law you write, or what you put through the Congress, or how many safeguards you set up, there is another branch of the government, and to really try to pry loose from the president his thoughts, and his personal advice, I think, would even come close to participating [sic] a constitutional crisis. But, because the authority lies within the White House, rather this ability lies within the White House, of exercising executive privilege, what has happened with the proliferation of White House staff members is that you are to the point where you are gradually getting a shift of the operating agencies into the White House itself.[104]

What may be approaching is a government controlled by executive decisionmakers, untouchable by either Congress or perhaps even the departmental bureaucracy. The most controversial example of such an elite policymaker in recent times was Dr. Henry Kissinger and his National Security Council staff which usurped the field of American diplomatic affairs during the initial years of the first Nixon administration. Not only did Kissinger and his retinue undermine the State Department and the career foreign service, but Congress could not compel him or any member of his staff to provide an account of any aspect of their activities.[105] Commenting on the situation, Senate Foreign Relation Committee Chairman J. William Fulbright remarked: "Mr. Kissinger and his entire staff have taken the position of executive privilege."[106]

And the matter was really no different with regard to domestic policy. In the course of delivering a speech in San Jose, California, in May, 1971, Senator Ernest F. Hollings remarked:

> It used to be that if I had a problem with food stamps, I went to see the secretary of agriculture, whose department had jurisdiction over that program. Not any more. Now, if I want to learn the policy, I must go the White House and consult John Price.
> If I want the latest on textiles, I won't get it from the secretary of commerce, who has the authority and responsibility. No, I am forced to go to the White House and see Mr. Peter Flanigan. I shouldn't feel too badly. Secretary Stans has to do the same thing.[107]

At the time of these comments, Price was a special assistant to the president; Peter Flanigan was an assistant to the president and later became executive director of the Council on International Economic Policy within the executive office. Maurice Stans was, of course, the incumbent Secretary of Commerce.

During the Nixon regime, officials in the executive agencies became distraught over the power of the White House staff and their usurpation of line department functions. A top Commerce Department bureaucrat typically complained that "the business community pays no attention to this department; if you have a policy problem, you go see Peter Flanigan—and he is available."

"Peter Flanigan," the official said with a sigh, "is to the Department of Commerce what Henry Kissinger is to the Department of State."[108]

The problem posed is not merely one of obtaining information from the executive, but, more importantly, a matter of accountability. And, as will be seen shortly, the occasions when a member of the White House staff has testified before a congressional committee have been quite minimal. In brief, the president's immediate assistants reflect a propensity for seeking an exclusive prerogative in terms of information, decisionmaking, and policy priorities. Such a trend has been increasingly evident with the passage of the various recent administrations, embracing not only White House personnel but segments of the executive office as well.

Exercising Privilege

The concept of executive privilege is currently one of various understandings. To some, it constitutes an attempt by the chief executive to thwart efforts by the other branches of the federal government to obtain information either of a documentary or testimonial nature. The legal community tends to regard the practice as a formal power of the president which is implied by the Constitution and lately has been recognized by the Supreme Court.[109] For others, any executive branch refusal to supply requested information to Congress or the courts constitutes an assertion of executive privilege. And certainly those sources, whether White House records or presidential assistants, closest to the chief executive would seemingly be subject to the closest protection.

It is beyond the scope of this discussion to determine the propriety of executive privilege claims. The judiciary has given credence to the practice and at least three different, though not necessarily mutually exclusive, justifications for presidential refusals to disclose information presently exist: (1) that Congress or one of its houses has no authority to make such a demand because its inquiry does not relate to any function constitutionally vested in the legislative branch; (2) that the separation of powers doctrine allows the executive branch to withhold information even though it would be useful to Congress in the execution of a constitutional function; or (3) that the executive branch may refuse to provide information to Congress when the law of evidence justifies exclusive retention of the material in question.

The first assertion of executive privilege occurred in 1792 when President Washington was confronted with a demand from the House for the original letters and instructions of the executive to General Arthur St. Clair, commander of an ill-fated expedition exploring portions of northwestern Ohio. In March 1792, the House created a special committee to investigate the St. Clair debacle, empowering the panel "to call for such persons, papers, and records, as may be necessary to assist their inquiries."[110] Upon receiving the committee's request for documents pertaining to the mission and operations of the expedition, Secretary of War Knox conferred with President Washington. This led to two discussions of the property of the executive branch providing information to Congress. On March 31, 1792, at a cabinet meeting attended by Secretary of State Thomas Jefferson, Secretary of the Treasury Alexander Hamilton, Attorney General Edmund Randolph, and Knox, the president, according to the notes kept by Jefferson,

> had called us to consult, merely because it was the first example, and he wished that so far as it should become a precedent, it should be rightly conducted. He neither acknowledged nor denied, nor even doubted the propriety of what the House was doing, for he had not thought upon it, nor was acquainted with subjects of this kind: he could readily conceive there might be papers of so secret a nature, as that they ought not to be given-up. We were not prepared, and wished time to think and inquire.[111]

The Cabinet met again on April 2, with Jefferson noting:

> We all had considered, and were of one mind, first, that the House was in inquest, and therefore might institute inquiries. Second, that it might call for papers generally. Third, that the executive ought to communicate such papers as the public good would permit, and ought to refuse those, the disclosure of which would injure the public: consequently were to exercise a discretion. Fourth, that neither the committee nor House had a right to call on the head of a department, who and whose papers were under the president alone; but that the committee should instruct their chairman to move the House to address the president. . . . Note; Hamilton agreed with us in all these points, except as to the power of the House to call on heads of departments.
>
> He observed that as to his department, the act constituting it had made it subject to Congress in some points, but he thought himself not so far subject, as to be obliged to produce all the papers they might call for. They might demand secrets of a very mischievous nature. (Here I thought he began to fear they would

go on to examining how far their own members and other persons in the government had been dabbling in stocks, banks & c., and that he probably would choose in this case to deny their power; and, in short, he endeavored to place himself subject to the House, when the executive should propose what he did not like, and subject to the executive, when the House should propose anything disagreeable.) I observed here a difference between the British Parliament and our Congress; that the former was a legislature, an inquest, and a council . . . for the king. The latter was, by the construction, a legislature and an inquest, but not a council. Finally agreed, to speak separately to the members of the committee, and bring them by persuasion into the right channel. It was agreed in this case, that *there was not a paper which might not be properly produced*; that copies only should be sent, with an assurance, that if they should desire it, a clerk should attend with the originals to be verified by themselves. [emphasis added].[112]

Thus agreed, Secretary Knox transmitted the requested papers, but was not given an opportunity to testify before the special investigating committee.[113] The theoretical basis for the doctrine of executive privilege, though expressed, had yet to be asserted in practice.

The occasion for implementing the theory arose in 1796 when the House again requested documents in the possession of the executive. And, as in the instance of the St. Clair investigation, the matter prompting the demand was one of high emotion.

So many controversies with England growing out of the Revolutionary War still remained unsettled that in 1796 President Washington sent Chief Justice Jay to London to negotiate a treaty. The anti-administration forces, bitterly disappointed at Washington's proclamation of neutrality instead of a declaration of war against England in order to aid France, wanted no such treaty. When, in due time, Jay returned with a treaty containing extraordinary benefits for Federalist interests and not one item favorable to anyone south of the Potomac, the rage against it was, as Washington said, "like that against a mad dog."[114]

Obligated to appropriate funds in order that the requirements of the treaty might be carried out, the House sought the instructions to Jay for negotiating the agreement, together with the correspondence and documents relative to it as well. In refusing to transmit the requested papers, Washington first stated the constitutional nature of his action, saying:

> I trust that no part of my conduct has ever indicated a disposition to withhold any information which the Constitution has enjoined upon the president as a duty to give, or which could be required of him by either house of Congress as a right; and with truth I affirm that it has been, as it will continue to be while I have the honor to preside in the government, my constant endeavor to harmonize with the other branches thereof so far as the trust delegated to me by the people of the United States and my sense of the obligation it imposes to "preserve, protect, and defend the Constitution" will permit.[115]

At the close of his letter, the president, with regard to the role of the House, added a pragmatic reason for his refusal of their request and again stated the constitutional basis for his action.

> As, therefore, it is perfectly clear to my understanding that the assent of the House of Representatives is not necessary to the validity of a treaty; as the treaty with Great Britain exhibits in itself all the objects requiring legislative provision, and on these the papers called for can throw no light, and as it is essential to the due administration of the government that the boundaries fixed by the Constitution between the different departments should be preserved, a just regard to the Constitution and to the duty of my office, under all the circumstances of this case, forbids a compliance with your request.[116]

The information was thus denied and withheld.

It is impossible in our day to understand the heat generated by the prolonged controversy over Jay's treaty. The fate of the government seemed to be hanging in the balance. The Senate ceased its sittings. [Senator Rufus] King bluntly declared that unless the House appropriated the required funds the Senate would regard all legislation at an end and the union dissolved. Finally, the House, exercising the recognized constitutional freedom of judgment appropriated the needed funds and another constitutional crisis had passed.[117]

While this incident was the first instance of a document denied to Congress by the executive, it was apparently not until 1877 that an executive branch witness refused to provide information by testimony before a congressional committee. Asked to provide details on the circumstances surrounding the removal of Chester A. Arthur as collector of the port of New York and the appointment of Theodore Roosevelt to that position, Secretary of the Treasury John Sherman, in a letter to Chairman Roscoe Conkling (R.-N.Y.) of the Senate Commerce Committee, argued:[118]

> To answer in an official way the questions put to me would not only compel me to violate that trust and confidence repose in me by the president, necessary for the transaction of the business of this department, but to disclose papers of a confidential character filed in the department and require me to enter into the discussion of questions totally immaterial to the nominations submitted to the Senate. I do not think it within the just limits of the intercourse of the Senate with executive officers to answer in writing, or even verbally, all the questions submitted by you, nor have I ever known such an instance.
>
> The president has the power to nominate to the Senate a proper person for collector of the port of New York, whether that office be already vacant or not, and it is within the power of the Senate to either confirm or reject.
>
> These are independent powers. No law requires the president to give the reasons for his nominations, and it does not appear that in this case the Senate even has directed this inquiry. The tenure-of-office act required of the president the reasons of a suspension made during the recess of the Senate, but this provision, after a very brief period, was repealed. To answer your questions would compel me to state to a committee of the Senate the reasons of an appointment by the president, to disclose confidential communications between the president and the secretary, and to enter into an arrangement and accusation of the officers superseded. In the free exercise of independent powers it is the common practice, as we both know, for members of the Senate to have full conference with the heads of executive departments on all matters in which the concurrent action of the president and the Senate is required, and therefore it will give me pleasure to confer with the committee, or any member of it, on the subject of the fitness of the appointment of Mr. Roosevelt to the office of collector of the port of New York.[119]

Thus, while the president's reasons for selecting his nominee and communications between the chief executive and the secretary of the Treasury on matters pertaining to the nominee were thought to be privileged, the secretary was not unwilling to testify on the qualifications and suitability of the nominee. The events were such that Secretary Sherman had no opportunity to testify. Conkling kept Hayes' nominations for the New York Custom House confined to the Commerce Committee and they were unreported at the time when the special session expired. With the next regular session, fifteen of the New York delegation's seventeen Republican members of the House petitioned the president urging the retention of Chester A. Arthur, whom Roosevelt was supposed to replace, and Alonzo B. Cornell. Hayes subsequently returned his three nominations for the Custom House. The Commerce Committee reported favorably on one and unfavorably on the other two, Roosevelt being in the latter category. After a stormy Senate debate, the nominees receiving the adverse report were defeated. Arthur remained in his position but was cast out a year later when Hayes appointed new officials to the Custom House while the Senate was out of session. Roosevelt died shortly after his nomination was lost. His son, who was destined to later become President, became an ardent civil service reformer and attacked the spoils system which had cost his father his collector's position. In 1883 Chester Arthur would be the president signing, and the first chief executive to administer, the Pendleton Act which set the course for the institution of a competitive and nonpartisan civil service.[120]

In contemporary times, the mantle of executive privilege usually falls on politically sensitive or politically coveted information. Nowhere is such information more prevalent than in the White House Office and the satellite presidential agencies of the Executive Office. As originally conceived, the immediate assistants of the president, in the words of the Brownlow Committee report, "would have no power to make decisions or issue instructions in their own right . . . would not be interposed between the president and the heads of his departments . . . would remain in the background, issue no orders, make no decisions, emit no public statements . . . would not attempt to exercise power on their account" and would be possessed of "a passion for anonymity." In the words of the chief executive's own directive (E.O. 8248) organizing the Executive Office, his personal assistants would "have no authority over anyone in any department or agency, including the Executive Office of the President, other than the personnel assigned to their immediate office." As has already been seen in the history of the evolution of the president's staff, this ideal situation did not remain for long; the White House assistants easily, rapidly, and obviously assumed political power. Soon the lines of responsibility became tangled, reaching a pinnacle of enmeshed authority during the Nixon administration. Principal presidential assistants working within the White House Office were granted dual roles with Executive Office entities: Henry Kissinger directed the National Security Council staff and Peter Flanigan assumed control of the personnel of the Council on International Economic Policy. An Executive Office agency head, Office of Management and Budget Director Roy Ash, was afforded a White House Office position to provide him closer proximity to the president. And even a department head, Treasury Secretary George Shultz, enjoyed a White House position in addition to his traditional responsibilities. Whatever their other duties and roles, each of these individuals, as White House personnel, held a high degree of potential immunity from accounting for their activities before congressional committees. The shadow of executive privilege beclouded normal accountability arrangements.

During the almost two score years of the existence of the White House Office, there have been only about a half dozen occasions when presidential assistants within this enclave have appeared before congressional committees and then only to testify about their personal actions and not their official duties. Only recently did this tradition change when a member of the Carter Administration's White House staff assisted in a presentation of the new regime's financial needs in appropriations hearings. Such presidential aides as have so testified before congressional committees are as follows:

Jonathan Daniels, administrative assistant to the president, who appeared before the Senate Agriculture and Forestry Committee on February 28, March 7, and March 8, 1944, to discuss his involvement in the personnel policy of the Rural Electrification Administration;[121]

Wallace H. Graham, physician to the president, who appeared before the Senate Appropriations Committee on January 13, 1948 to discuss information to which he might have been privy with regard to the commodities market;[122]

Harry H. Vaughan, military aide to the president, appeared before the Senate Committee on Expenditures in Executive Departments on August 30 and 31, 1949 to discuss his personal involvement in certain government procurement contracts;[123]

Donald S. Dawson, administrative assistant to the president, appeared before the Senate Banking and Currency Committee on May 10 and 11, 1951 to discuss allegations he had attempted to "dominate" the Reconstruction Finance Corporation and influence appointments to that body;[124]

Sherman Adams, assistant to the president, appeared before the House Interstate and Foreign Commerce Committee on June 17,

1958 to discuss his involvement with certain lobbyists;[125]

Peter Flanigan, assistant to the president, appeared before the Senate Judiciary Committee on April 20, 1972 during the course of hearings on the confirmation of Richard Kleindienst as attorney general to discuss his involvement in apparent lobbying activities by the International Telephone and Telegraph Company;[162]

Richard M. Harden, special assistant to the president, who appeared before the Senate Appropriations Subcommittee on Treasury, Postal Service and General Government on March 9, 1977, to discuss funds for the White House Office; he again appeared before the House Appropriations Subcommittee on Treasury, Postal Service and General Government appropriations on March 15, 1977, to discuss these same matters.[127]

Such a record of White House staff appearances before congressional committee would seem to reflect a distinct unwillingness of the president to allow any personal assistant to be questioned by the legislative branch on any matter other than an individual's misconduct or misuse of his or her official position. No chief executive is about to allow discussions with aides or advice from assistants to be aired in congressional hearings. While Congress generally has been willing to respect the sanctity of these communications, conflicts over the accountability of such presidential auxiliaries occur when they exert any degree of program supervision or policy administration. Thus, unless a president is willing to accommodate congressional oversight requirements that executive branch managers account for their actions, no White House Office personnel should be placed in a position of program responsibility or policy control. To date, however, no reconciliation of this issue has been established by the president and Congress.

Overview

The history of presidential staffing arrangements indicates that the earliest chief executives suffered severe limitations with regard to available assistants to advise them or serve as policy aides. Largely as a matter of necessity, the cabinet emerged to meet this need for auxiliaries in the faithful execution of the laws. However, due to considerations of executive independence, partisanship, ideology, geography, and political power, the cabinet declined as a useful instrument of presidential counsel or assistance. During the nineteenth century, presidents could seek advisers wherever they desired but continued to lack any institutional arrangements for maintaining a body of effective assistants. With the arrival of the twentieth century, Theodore Roosevelt obtained authority to detail departmental staff to the White House; Woodrow Wilson expanded his immediate personnel through the Council of National Defense; Herbert Hoover saw the addition of three more high level assistants to the Oval Office; and Franklin Roosevelt toyed with a variety of councils and auxiliary panels before the institution of the Executive Office revolutionized presidential staffing arrangements. However, the expansion of the number of personal assistants available to the chief executive has raised a variety of questions concerning their number, duties, and accountability to Congress.

Notes

1. Mr. Relyea is a specialist in American national government of the Congressional Research Service.

2. These descriptions are drawn directly from Louis W. Koening, *The Invisible Presidency* (New York and Toronto: Rinehart and Company, 1960) and Dan Rather and Gary Paul Gates, *The Palace Guard* (New York: Harper and Row, 1974).

3. See Max Farrand, ed., *The Records of the Federal Convention of 1787* (New Haven, Conn.: Yale University Press, 1927), Vol. 1, 23; Vol. II, 135; Vol III, 606.

4. See ibid., Vol. II, 537-543.

5. See ibid., Vol. I, 97.

6. See ibid., Vol. II, 342-344.

7. See Richard F. Fenno, Jr., *The President's Cabinet* (New York: Random House, Vintage Books, 1959), 12-13; also see generally Henry Barrett Learned, *The President's Cabinet* (New Haven, Conn.: Yale University Press, 1912), 66-95.

8. See Benjamin Fletcher Wright, ed., *The Federalist* (Cambridge, Mass.: The Belknap Press of Harvard University Press, 1966), 462-463.

9. Leonard D. White, *The Federalists* (New York: Macmillan, 1948), 27; for examples of the assistance provided to the president, see 27n, 32-36.

10. Ibid., 32.

11. The early humble status of the attorney general is discussed in Albert George Langeluttig, *The Department of Justice of the United States* (Baltimore, Md.: Johns Hopkins Press), 6-18.

12. Edward H. Hobbs, *Behind the President* (Washington, D.C.: Public Affairs Press, 1954), 86.

13. Koenig, op. cit., 13.

14. See Stephen Horn, *Cabinet and Congress* (New York: Columbia University Press, 1960), 16-18.

15. In 1974, President Ford made an unprecedented appearance before a subcommittee of the House Committee on the Judiciary to discuss the pardoning of President Nixon. See U.S. Congress. House Committee on the Judiciary, Subcommittee on Criminal Justice, Pardon on Richard M. Nixon and Related Matters, hearing, 93d Congress, 2d session, September 24, October 1, and 17, 1974.

16. Robert Scigliano, *The Supreme Court and the Presidency* (New York: The Free Press, 1971), 62-63; the response of the Court was in the form of a letter and not an actual opinion.

17. White, op. cit., 40.

18. Ibid., 39-41.

19. Ibid., 41.

20. Ibid., 42.

21. Ibid., 42-43.

22. Ibid., 43.

23. Ibid., 48-49.

24. Leonard D. White, *The Jeffersonians* (New York: Macmillan, 1951), 72.

25. Ibid., 74.

26. Leonard D. White, *The Jacksonians* (New York: Macmillan, 1954), 83; of note in terms of congressional influence over presidential staff is the requirement that the land patent clerk assigned to the White House was subject to Senate confirmation of appointment to such position.

27. White, *The Jeffersonians*, op. cit., 79.

28. Ibid., 80-81.

29. Ibid., 81.

30. See Arthur M. Schlesinger, Jr., *The Age of Jackson* (Boston: Little, Brown, 1953), 67-74.

31. Koenig, op. cit., 40.

32. Ibid., 40-43.

33. Taft, *Our Chief Magistrate and His Powers,* op. cit., 35.

34. John Russell Young, *Around the World with General Grant* (New York: American News Company, 1879), Vol. II, 154.

35. Robert McElroy, *Grover Cleveland: The Man and the Statesman* (New York: Harper and Brothers, 1923), Vol. I, 115.

36. Koenig, *The Invisible Presidency*, 17.

37. Grosvenor B. Clarkson, *Industrial America in the World War* (Boston and New York: Houghton Mifflin, 1923), 11-12.

38. Ibid., 17-18.

39. Background information on the events leading to the creation of the Council may be found in Clarkson, op. cit., 15-17 and John Dos Passos. *Mr. Wilson's War* (New York: Doubleday, 1962), 220-223.

40. Clarkson, op. cit., 22.

41. Daniel R. Beaver, *Newton D. Baker and the American War Effort, 1917-1919* (Lincoln: University of Nebraska Press, 1966), 53.

42. Clarkson, op. cit., 22-23.

43. See U.S. Council of National Defense, *First Annual Report* (Washington, D.C.: U.S. Government Printing Office, 1917), 128.

44. Statistics compiled from: ibid., p. 128; U.S. Council of National Defense, *Third Annual Report* (Washington, D.C.: U.S. Government Printing Office, 1919), 19, 147; U.S. Council of National Defense *Fourth Annual Report* (Washington, D.C.: U.S. Government Printing Office, 1920), 14, 94.

45. For a compilation of federal level subunits of the Council, see U.S. Council of National Defense, Division of Statistics, *Director of Auxiliary War Organizations* (Washington, D.C.: Council of National Defense, 1917).

46. Seward W. Livermore, *Politics is Adjourned* (Middletown, Conn.: Wesleyan University Press, 1966), 42-**43**.

47. For the record of Council meetings see Franklin H. Martin, *Digest of Proceedings of the Council of National Defense During the World War* (Washington, D.C.: U.S. Government Printing Office, 1934).

48. Beaver, op. cit., 61.

49. Ibid., 65.

50. Livermore, op. cit., 39.

51. William Franklin Willoughby, *Government Organization In War Time and After* (New York: D. Appleton and Company, 1919), 12.

52. See, for example, U.S. Congress, House Committee on Appropriations, Council of National Defense hearings, 65th Congress, 1st session.

53. See Robert D. Cuff, *The War Industries Board* (Baltimore, Md.: Johns Hopkins University Press, 1973).

54. See *The Public Papers and Addresses of Franklin D. Roosevelt: 1940 Volume, The Call to Battle Stations* (New York: Macmillan, 1941), 241-250.

55. A. J. Wann, *The President as Chief Administrator* (Washington, D.C.: Public Affairs Press, 1968), 129.

56. Ibid., 26.

57. Ibid., 26-27.

58. Lester G. Seligman and Elmer E. Cornwell, Jr., eds., *New Deal Mosaic* (Eugene: University of Oregon Press, 1965), XV.

59. Wann, op. cit., 51.

60. Ibid., 52-53.

61. Ibid., 56.

62. Ibid., note 58.

63. Louis Brownlow, *A Passion for Anonymity: The Autobiography of Louis Brownlow, Second Half* (Chicago: University of Chicago Press, 1958), 321. Copyright 1958 by the University of Chicago. Reprinted by permission.

64. Ibid., 323-324.

65. Barry Karl, *Executive Reorganization and Reform in the New Deal* (Chicago, Ill.: University of Chicago Press, 1979), 197-198. Copyright 1963 by Barry Dean Karl. Reprinted by permission.

66. Ibid.; also see Brownlow, op. cit., 392.

67. Hobbs, op. cit., p. 15; also see Edward H. Hobbs, *Executive Reorganization in the National Government* (University: University of Mississippi, Bureau of Public Administration, 1953).

68. See Charles E. McGuire, "A Program of Administrative Reform at Washington," *Harvard Graduates Magazine*, June 1920, 473-581.

69. Institute for Government Research, *The Reorganization of the Administrative Branch of the National Government* (Washington, D.C.: Institute for Government Research, 1921), 78-79.

70. See William Franklin Willoughby, *Government Organization in War Time and After* (New York: D. Appleton and Company, 1919).

71. W. F. Willoughby, *The Organization of the Administrative Branch of the National Government* (Baltimore, Md.: Johns Hopkins University Press, 1923), 59.

72. Karl, op. cit., 200-201.

73. Ibid., 202.

74. Ibid.

75. Ibid., 203.

76. Brownlow, op. cit., 327-328.

77. *The Public Papers and Addresses of Franklin D. Roosevelt: 1936 Volume, The People Approve* (New York: Random House, 1938), 144-146.

78. Karl, op. cit., 207.

79. Brownlow, op. cit., 376-377.

80. Richard Polenberg, *Reorganizing Roosevelt's Government* (Cambridge, Mass.: Harvard University Press, 1966), 20-21.

81. Ibid., 21.

82. See Brownlow, op. cit., 383; Karl, op. cit., 222; Polenberg, op. cit., 17.

83. See Brownlow, op. cit., 385-391.

84. See Polenberg, op. cit., 31-35.

85. Ibid., 35-36.

86. President's Committee on Administrative Management, *Reorganization of the Executive Departments*, 75th Congress, 1st session, Senate Document no. 8, 19.

87. Polenberg, op. cit., 184.

88. Ibid., 187.

89. Brownlow, op. cit., 416.

90. Louis W. Koenig, *The Presidency and the Crisis* (New York: King's Crown Press, 1944), 82.

91. See Herman M. Somers, *Presidential Agency* (Cambridge, Mass.: Harvard University Press, 1950).

92. Brownlow, op. cit., 417.

93. Commission on the Organization of the Executive Branch, *General Management of the Executive Branch* (Washington, D.C.: U.S. Government Printing Office, 1949), 13-28.

94. See U.S. Congress, House Committee on Post Office and Civil Service, *A Report on the Growth of the Executive Office of the President, 1955-1973* (Washington, D.C.: U.S. Government Printing Office, 1972), 6-8. (At head of title: 92d Congress, 2d session. Committee Print No. 19).

95. See U.S. Congress, Senate Committee on Governmental Affairs, *Reorganization Plan No. 1 of 1977*, hearings, 95th Congress, 1st Session; U.S. Congress, House Committee on Government Operations, *Reorganization Plan No. 1 of 1977 (Executive Office of the President)*, hearings, 95th Congress, 1st session.

96. Theodore C. Sorensen, *Watchmen in the Night* (Cambridge, Mass.: M.I.T. Press, 1975), 100.

97. A list of E.O.P. agencies and authority for same is appended to this report.

98. Stephen Hess, *Organizing the Presidency* (Washington, D.C.: The Brookings Institution, 1976), 3.

99. President's Committee on Administrative Management, op. cit., 5.

100. Karl, op. cit., 241.

101. Fenno, op. cit., 141-142.

102. Theodore C. Sorensen, *Decision-Making in the White House* (New York: Columbia University Press, 1963), 71-72.

103. Theodore C. Sorensen, *Kennedy* (New York: Harper and Row, 1965), 259.

104. U.S. Congress, House Committee on Government Operations, *U.S. Government Information Policies and Practices—Administration and Operation of the Freedom of Information Act*, hearings, 92d Congress, 2d session, 1013.

105. See I. M. Destler, "Can One Man Do?" *Foreign Policy*, No. 5, Winter, 1971-72, pp. 28-40; John P. Leacacos, "Kissinger's Aparat." *Foreign Policy*, No. 5, Winter, 1971-72, 3-27; George Sherman, "A Sickness At State," *Washington Evening Star*, March 7, 1972, A-1, A-4.

106. U.S. Congress, Senate Committee on Foreign Relations, *War Powers Legislation*, hearings, 92nd Congress, 1st session, 453.

107. Dom Bonafede, "Ehrlichman Acts As Policy Broker in Nixon's Formalized Domestic Council," *National Journal*, v. 3, June 12, 1971, 1240.

108. *New York Times*, March 20, 1972.

109. See *United States v. Nixon*, 418 U.S. 683 (1974); and *Nixon v. Administrator of General Services*, 433 U.S. 425 (1977).

110. Horn, op. cit., 22-25.

111. Andrew A. Lipscomb, ed., *The Writings of Thomas Jefferson* (Washington, D.C.: Thomas Jefferson Memorial Association, 1903), Vol. I, 303.

112. Ibid., 303-305.

113. Horn, op. cit., 28-29.

114. Wilfred E. Binkley, *President and Congress* (New York: Alfred A. Knopf, 1947), 42-43.

115. James D. Richardson, ed., *A Compilation of the Messages and Papers of the Presidents 1789-1897*. (Washington, D.C.: U.S. Government Printing Office, 1896), Vol. I, 194.

116. Ibid., 196.

117. Binkley, op. cit., 44.

118. Conkling's letter of questions appears in the Congressional Record, v. 17, March 22, 1886, 2618; on the general circumstances prompting this inquiry see Binkley, op. cit., 155-158.

119. *Congressional Record*, vol. 17, March 12, 1886, 2332.

120. H. J. Eckenrode, *Rutherford B. Hayes* (New York: Dodd, Meade, 1930), 272-275.

121. U.S. Congress, Senate Committee on Agriculture and Forestry, *Administration of the Rural Electrification Act*, hearings, 78th Congress, 2d session, 611ff, 695ff, 721ff.

122. U.S. Congress, Senate Committee on Appropriations, *Speculation in Commodity Markets*, hearings, 80th Congress, 2d session, 49ff.

123. U.S. Congress, Senate Committee on Expenditures in the Executive Departments, *Influence in Government Procurement*, hearings, 81st Congress, 1st session, 495ff, 563ff.

124. U.S.Congress, Senate Committee on Banking and Currency, *Study of Reconstruction Finance Corporation*, hearings, 82d Congress, 1st session, 1708ff, 1795ff.

125. U.S. Congress, House Committee on Interstate and Foreign Commerce, *Investigation of Regulatory Commissions and Agencies*, hearings, 85th Congress, 2d session, 3712ff.

126. U.S. Congress, Senate Committee on the Judiciary, *Nominations of Richard G. Kleindienst and Louis Patrick Gray III*, hearings, 92nd Congress, 2d session, 1585ff.

127. U.S. Congress, Senate Committee on Appropriations, *Treasury, Postal Service, and General Government Appropriations: Fiscal Year 1978*, hearings, 95th Congress, 1st session, 1021ff; House Committee on Appropriations, *Treasury, Postal Service, and General Government Appropriations for Fiscal Year 1978*, hearings, 95th Congress, 1st session, 77ff.

Illustration 3a: Introduction to the Brownlow Report

The original impetus for the development of the Executive Office of the President (EOP) and the White House staff was the Committee on Administrative Management, in what has come to be known as the Brownlow Report (1937). This report, which concluded "the president needs help," urged that a staff assistance network for presidents be organized according to the dictums of classical and orthodox administrative management. The subsequent development of the White House staff and the EOP have been based on this report.

The government of the United States is the largest and most difficult task undertaken by the American people, and at the same time the most important and the noblest. Our government does more for more men, women, and children than any other institution; it employs more persons in its work than any other employer. It covers a wider range of aims and activities than any other enterprise; it sustains the frame of our national and our community life, our economic system, our individual rights and liberties. Moreover, it is a government of, by, and for the people—a democracy that has survived for a century and a half and flourished among competing forms of government of many different types and colors, old and new.

From time to time the decay, destruction, and death of democracy has been gloomily predicted by false prophets who mocked at us, but our American system has matched its massive strength successfully against all the forces of destruction through parts of three centuries.

Our American government rests on the truth that the general interest is superior to and has priority over any special or private interest, and that final decision in matters of common interest to the nation should be made by free choice of the people of the nation, expressed in such manner as they shall from time to time provide, and enforced by such agencies as they may from time to time set up. Our goal is the constant raising of the level of the happiness and dignity of human life, the steady sharing of the gains of our nation, whether material or spiritual, among those who make the nation what it is.

We are too practical a people to be satisfied by merely looking forward to glittering goals or with mere plans, talk, and pledges. By democracy we mean getting things done that we, the American people, want done in the general interest. Without results we know that democracy means nothing and ceases to be alive in the minds and hearts of men. With us the people's will is not merely an empty phrase; it denotes a grave and stern determination in the major affairs of our nation—a determination which we propose to make good as promptly and firmly as may be necessary and appropriate—a determination which does not intend to be baffled in its basic plans and purposes by any cluttering or confusion in the machinery for doing what it has been deliberately decided to do.

After the people's judgment has been expressed in due form, after the representatives of the nation have made the necessary laws, we intend that these decisions shall be promptly, effectively, and economically put into action.

The American Executive

The need for action in realizing democracy was as great in 1789 as it is today. It was thus not by accident but by deliberate design that the founding fathers set the American executive in the Constitution on a solid foundation. Sad experience under the Articles of Confederation, with an almost headless government and committee management, had brought the American Republic to the edge of ruin. Our forefathers had broken away from hereditary government and pinned their faith on democratic rule, but they had not found a way to equip the new democracy for action. Consequently, there was grim purpose in resolutely providing for a presidency which was to be a national office. The president is indeed the one and only national officer representative of the entire nation. There was hesitation on the part of some timid souls in providing the president with an election independent of the Congress; with a longer term than most governors of that day; with the duty of informing the Congress as to the state of the Union and of recommending to its consideration "such Measures as he shall judge necessary and expedient"; with a two-thirds veto; with a wide power of appointment; and with military and diplomatic authority. But this reluctance was overcome in the face of need and a democratic executive established.

Equipped with these broad constitutional powers, reinforced by statute, by custom, by general consent, the American executive must be regarded as one of the very greatest contributions made by our nation to the development of modern democracy—a unique institution the value of which is as evident in times of stress and strain as in periods of quiet.

As an instrument for carrying out the judgment and will of the people of a nation, the American executive occupies an enviable position among the executives of the states of the world, combining as it does the elements of popular control and the means for vigorous action and leadership—uniting stability and flexibility. The American executive as an institution stands across the path of those who mistakenly assert that democracy must fail because it can neither decide promptly nor act vigorously.

Our presidency unites at least three important functions. From one point of view the president is a political leader—leader of a party, leader of the Congress, leader of a people. From another point of view he is head of the nation in the ceremonial sense of the term, the symbol of our American national solidarity. From still another point of view the president is the chief executive and administrator within the federal system and service.

In many types of government these duties are divided or only in part combined, but in the United States they have always been united in one and the same person whose duty it is to perform all of these tasks.

Your Committee on Administrative Management has been asked to investigate and report particularly upon the last function; namely, that of administrative management—the organization for the performance of the duties imposed upon the president in exercising the executive power vested in him by the Constitution of the United States.

Improving the Machinery of Government

Throughout our history we have paused now and then to see how well the spirit and purpose of our nation is working out in the machinery of everyday government with a view to making such modifications and improvements as prudence and the spirit of progress might suggest. Our government was the first to set up in its formal Constitution a method of amendment, and the spirit of America has been from the beginning of our history the spirit of progressive changes to meet conditions shifting perhaps more rapidly here than elsewhere in the world.

Since the Civil War, as the tasks and responsibilities of our government have grown with the growth of the nation in sweep and power, some notable attempts have been made to keep our administrative system abreast of the new times. The assassination of President Garfield by a disappointed office seeker aroused the nation against the spoils system and led to the enactment of the civil-service law of 1883. We have struggled to make the principle of this law effective for half a century. The confusion in fiscal management led to the establishment of the Bureau of the Budget and the budgetary system in 1921. We still strive to realize the goal set for the nation at that time. And, indeed, many other important forward steps have been taken.

Now we face again the problem of governmental readjustment, in part as the result of the activities of the nation during the desperate years of the industrial depression, in part because of the very growth of the nation, and in part because of the vexing social problems of our times. There is room for vast increase in our national productivity and there is much bitter wrong to set right in neglected ways of human life. There is need for improvement of our governmental machinery to meet new conditions and to make us ready for the problems just ahead.

Facing one of the most troubled periods in all the troubled history of mankind, we wish to set our affairs in the very best possible order to make the best use of all of our national resources and to make good our democratic claims. If America fails, the hopes and dreams of democracy over all the world go down. We shall not fail in our task and our responsibility, but we cannot live upon our laurels alone.

We seek modern types of management in national government best fitted for the stern situations we are bound to meet, both at home and elsewhere. As to ways and means of improvement, there are naturally sincere differences of judgment and opinion, but only a treasonable design could oppose careful attention to the best and soundest practices of government available for the American nation in the conduct of its heavy responsibilities.

The Foundations of Governmental Efficiency

The efficiency of government rests upon two factors: the consent of the governed and good management. In a democracy consent may be achieved readily, though not without some effort, as it is the cornerstone of the constitution. Efficient management in a democracy is a factor of peculiar significance.

Administrative efficiency is not merely a matter of paper clips, time clocks, and standardized economies of motion. These are but minor gadgets. Real efficiency goes much deeper down. It must be built into the structure of a government just as it is built into a piece of machinery.

Fortunately the foundations of effective management in public affairs, no less than in private, are well known. They have emerged universally wherever men have worked together for some common purpose, whether through the state, the church, the private association, or the commercial enterprise. They have been written into constitutions, charters, and articles of incorporation, and exist as habits of work in the daily life of all organized peoples. Stated in simple terms these canons of efficiency require the establishment of a responsible and effective chief executive as the center of energy, direction, and administrative management; the systematic organization of all activities in the hands of a qualified personnel under the direction of the chief executive; and to aid him in this, the establishment of appropriate managerial and staff agencies. There must also be provision for planning, a complete fiscal system, and means for holding the executive accountable for his program.

Taken together, these principles, drawn from the experience of mankind in carrying on large scale enterprises, may be considered as the first requirement of good management. They comprehend the subject matter of administrative management as it is dealt with in this report. Administrative management concerns itself in a democracy with the executive and his duties, with managerial and staff aides, with organization, with personnel, and with the fiscal system because these are the indispensable means of making good the popular will in a people's government.

Modernizing Our Governmental Management

In the light of these canons of efficiency, what must be said of the government of the United States today? Speaking in the broadest terms at this point, and in detail later on, we find in the American government at the present time that the effectiveness of the chief executive is limited and restricted, in spite of the clear intent of the Constitution to the contrary; that the work of the executive branch is badly organized; that the managerial agencies are weak and out of date; that the public service does not include its share of men and women of outstanding capacity and charac-

Illustration 3a

ter; and that the fiscal and auditing systems are inadequate. These weaknesses are found at the center of our government and involve the office of the chief executive itself.

While in general principle our organization of the presidency challenges the admiration of the world, yet in equipment for administrative management our executive office is not fully abreast of the trend of our American times, either in business or in government. Where, for example, can there be found an executive in any way comparable upon whom so much petty work is thrown? Or who is forced to see so many persons on unrelated matters and to make so many decisions on the basis of what may be, because of the very press of work, incomplete information? How is it humanly possible to know fully the affairs and problems of over 100 separate major agencies, to say nothing of being responsible for their general direction and coordination?

These facts have been known for many years and are so well appreciated that it is not necessary for us to prove again that the president's administrative equipment is far less developed than his responsibilities, and that a major task before the American government is to remedy this dangerous situation. What we need is not a new principle, but a modernizing of our managerial equipment.

This is not a difficult problem in itself. In fact, we have already dealt with it successfully in state governments, in city governments, and in large-scale private industry. Gov. Frank O. Lowden in Illinois, Gov. Alfred E. Smith in New York, Gov. Harry F. Byrd in Virginia, and Gov. William Tudor Gardiner in Maine, among others, have all shown how similar problems can be dealt with in large governmental units. The federal government is more extensive and more complicated, but the principles of reorganization are the same. On the basis of this experience and our examination of the executive branch we conclude that the following steps should now be taken:

1. To deal with the greatly increased duties of executive management falling upon the president the White House staff should be expanded.
2. The managerial agencies of the government, particularly those dealing with the budget, efficiency research, personnel, and planning, should be greatly strengthened and developed as arms of the chief executive.
3. The merit system should be extended upward, outward, and downward to cover all non-policy-determining posts, and the civil service system should be reorganized and opportunities established for a career system attractive to the best talent of the nation.
4. The whole executive branch of the government should be overhauled and the present 100 agencies reorganized under a few large departments in which every executive activity would find its place.
5. The fiscal system should be extensively revised in the light of the best governmental and private practice, particularly with reference to financial records, audit, and accountability of the executive to the Congress.

These recommendations are explained and discussed in the following sections of this report.

The Purpose of Reorganization

In proceeding to the reorganization of the government it is important to keep prominently before us the ends of reorganization. Too close a view of machinery must not cut off from sight the true purpose of efficient management. Economy is not the only objective, though reorganization is the first step to savings; the elimination of duplication and contradictory policies is not the only objective, though this will follow; a simple and symmetrical organization is not the only objective, though the new organization will be simple and symmetrical; higher salaries and better jobs are not the only objectives, though these are necessary; better business methods and fiscal controls are not the only objectives, though these too are demanded. There is but one grand purpose, namely, to make democracy work today in our national government; that is, to make our government an up-to-date, efficient, and effective instrument for carrying out the will of the nation. It is for this purpose that the government needs thoroughly modern tools of management.

As a people we congratulate ourselves justly on our skill as managers—in the home, on the farm, in business big and little—and we properly expect that management in government shall be of the best American model. We do not always get these results, and we must modestly say "we count not ourselves to have attained", but there is a steady purpose in America to press forward until the practices of our governmental administration are as high as the purpose and standards of our people. We know that bad management may spoil good purposes, and that without good management democracy itself cannot achieve its highest goals.

The Institutional Presidency: A View from the White House

Edwin Meese III

Each administration develops a distinctive internal policy process. In the following article, a prominent counsellor to the president details the apparatus used by the Reagan administration for the formulation and implementation of domestic policy. The Reagan administration's comparable structure for foreign and security policy is presented in Illustration 3e.

Stop and ask any professor for a list of the great presidents. Odds are he will answer the question with names like Washington, Jefferson, Jackson, Lincoln, the two Roosevelts, and Wilson. The near-great category is likely to include men like James Polk, Grover Cleveland, Harry Truman—leaders who put the stamp of their own personality on the office and the nation—men who swashbuckled their way through great events, who delighted in battle, despised the status quo, and never shied away from use of the personal pronoun. Men, in short, who centralized authority, and personified change.

Interestingly enough, only a handful of these presidents had any institutional presidency to implement their orders (a cynic would say that most of them had no White House bureaucracy to fragment their consensus or frustrate their larger-than-life ambitions).

Throughout the history of the modern presidency, its occupants have achieved their greatest successes largely on their own. Cabinets or staffs did not win Harry Truman his upset victory in 1948—nor sustain Eisenhower's popularity through eight years—nor rally the nation behind President Kennedy during the Cuban Missile crisis—nor echo Lyndon Johnson's promise of civil rights for every citizen, regardless of race—nor produce Richard Nixon's historic outreach to Peking—nor achieve the dramatic drop in inflation credited to President Ford—nor produce the Camp David Accords under President Carter. Neither did they persuade Congress to adopt under President Reagan the most sweeping tax and spending cuts in U.S. history—or undertake a series of bold initiatives aimed at reversing a half century of centralization of authority and wealth in Washington, D.C.

This is no accident. It was Emerson who said that an institution is the lengthened shadow of a single man. You do not have to be either a transcendentalist or an advocate of the "Great-Man" school of history to agree that for most Americans, the institutional presidency remains a shadow government, better suited to making policy than shaping politics.

Woodrow Wilson once said that being president required "the constitution of an athlete, the patience of a mother, the endurance of an early Christian." These days, not even that exhausts the catalogue of skills we demand from our leaders. Therein lies the paradox of the modern presidency—and also the singular challenge confronting the institutional office. For never before have we expected more from our chief executives. Never before has the office been more highly personalized, or its occupant a more ubiquitous presence in our daily lives. At the same time, never before have presidents been forced to contend with more forces that drown out their own voices, or stunt their own growth in office. A cabinet, staff and vice-president can help a president convey his message, as well as manage the bureaucracy. But they can-

---

This paper is Mr. Meese's condensation of his keynote address at the 14th Annual Leadership Conference of the Center for the Study of the Presidency, November 5, 1982. "The Institutional Presidency: 'A View from the White House" by Edwin Meese, Spring 1983, *Presidential Studies Quarterly*, 13, pp. 191-97. Copyright 1983 by the Center for the Study of the Presidency. Reprinted by permission.

not take the place of one individual large enough and forceful enough to dominate the nation's attention. And even at their best, they cannot perform for themselves the chief presidential function of these times, which President Truman defined with eloquent simplicity.

First and foremost, he said, a president must be a leader, and "a leader is a man who has the ability to get other people to do what they don't want to do, and like it." Another time, he said that being president of the United States was like "riding a tiger, you either stay on or get swallowed." And it is unlikely that any staff or organizational set-up can decide alone which presidents stay on the tiger and which ones get swallowed.

So what, then, is leadership? And how does it flourish within the institutional context? First of all, leadership is an evolving thing, changing with time, responding to events. A century ago, fresh from Andrew Johnson's impeachment and the scandals of the Grant era, Wilson wrote a book called *Congressional Government*. Not surprisingly, he concluded, presidential prestige had suffered. The pendulum had shifted Congress' way. "Our latter-day presidents," he wrote, "live by proxy; they are the executive in theory, but the secretaries are the executive in fact." Yet by the time Wilson himself held the presidential office, it had been revolutionized by Theodore Roosevelt, and all of a sudden he was far less eager to pursue his theory of the presidency as a sort of American prime minister. Veering away from what he had once taught in the classroom, Wilson instead railed away at his congressional critics—"A little group of willful men" he called them—and he painted a highly personal picture of America and her place in the world emerging from war.

The men who framed our Constitution made no provision for the institutional presidency. They assigned him no cabinet and no advisory staff. They did assign him the almost impossible task of being two very different things at one and the same time: First, a head of state—above the fray, an almost regal symbol of national unity. And second, they expected him also to be a political leader, advocate of necessarily contentious programs that might produce many things, but would almost certainly fracture national unity and with it, much of his consensus for governing. In Wilson's case, he managed to close the gap largely by the force of words.

Forty years later, Dwight Eisenhower epitomized another school of presidential leadership. A man who preferred to work his will through subordinates, he was the product of a military background and a hero who attained many of his exploits by persuading other men to do what he wanted. Unlike Wilson, Ike often used words deliberately to confuse rather than inspire. For instance, when the issue of whether or not the United States would go to war over the offshore Chinese islands of Quemoy and Matsu arose, Eisenhower assured Jim Hagerty, his press secretary, that he knew exactly how to handle it. He would simply obfuscate his way through the whole thing.

"Well . . . I must confess I cannot answer that question in advance," said the president. "The only thing I know about war are two things: The most unpredictable factor in war is human nature in its day-to-day manifestation, but the only unchanging factor in war is human nature. And the next thing is that war is going to astonish you in the way it occurred, and in the way it is carried out. So for a man to predict, particularly if he has the responsibility for making the decision, to predict what he is going to use, how he is going to do it, would I think exhibit his ignorance of war; that is what I believe. So I think you just have to wait; and that is the kind of prayerful decision that may some day face a president."

Now when the press and certain sophisticated elements of the political community heard talk like that, they took it at face value. They concluded that Ike was better at golf than presidential leadership. What they failed to see was what Professor Fred Greenstein in his recent book on the Eisenhower presidency calls "hidden-hand leadership"—an almost Machiavellian strain that worked best behind the scenes, that accepted incremental progress as the most one could reasonably hope to achieve from the governing process, and that looked upon governnment's main priority as the avoidance of crises, rather than the heroic response to them once they occurred. For Eisenhower, the institutional presidency was extremely important. He relied on subordinates, for example, to gradually reduce the room for maneuver open to Senator Joseph McCarthy. He created the first real cabinet secretariat in the U.S. history, gave his vice-president a significant role in domestic and foreign affairs, and pursued the practice of delegating authority first picked up while in military uniform. Again, this was shrewd. Not only did it help preserve Eisenhower's non-political appeal, it also held up lightning rods like Chief of Staff Sherman Adams and Secretary of State John Foster Dulles to whom criticism could be deflected.

On President Reagan's desk in Washington sits a small brass plaque with the motto: "There's no limit to what one man can accomplish, as long as he's willing to let someone else have the credit." To a striking degree, Eisenhower's presidency was a reflection of that sentiment. Eisenhower abhorred the use of the first person personal pronoun.

Eisenhower succeeded at least in part because he was able to mold the institutional presidency to his own unique set of personal leadership gifts. Other occupants of the office have achieved equal success with radically different methods. Teddy Roosevelt added the West Wing on the White House, almost as a symbolic addition to the president's own role in American life. Part St. Vitus and part St. Paul, T. R. agitated a war with Colombia in order to gain his cherished path between the seas. But he also mediated a war between Russia and Japan, did perpetual battle with Congress and much of his own party, and launched the conservation and regulatory movements in defiance of those who believed in a strict laissez-faire approach to government. Who among us recalls the name of his vice-president, or the pedigree of his cabinet and personal staff? The fact is, that T. R. might actually have been hampered by an institutional presidency. He might have been forced to expend some of his pulsing energy in day-to-day management, rather than historic initiatives and political theatrics.

For entirely different reasons, Calvin Coolidge neither wanted nor needed an institutional presidency. One of his greatest achievements in five and a half years in office, he boasted near the end of his term, "has been minding my own business." His successor, Herbert Hoover, was the first chief executive to have more than one secretary—and a telephone on his desk. He was also the first to abolish the daily public reception of citizens who wanted to shake the presidential hand—and allow direct quotation by the press. Before the depression cut short his plans for sweeping administrative changes, Hoover hoped to overhaul the entire structure of government. And there was a kind of historical justice when he later gave his name to two presidential commissions that achieved hundreds of organizational reforms and saved billions of dollars in the process of pruning the executive branch of government.

Of course, the modern institutional presidency was largely the creation of Franklin Roosevelt. It was in 1939 that the Executive Office of the President was formally proclaimed, along with the Bureau of the Budget and six administrative assistants with "a passion for anonymity" in place of Hoover's three secretaries. But unlike Hoover, FDR had little interest in boxes on an organizational chart. On purpose, he sought to maximize conflict among his advisors. The competition not only made him more than ever the central figure of the administration—it also bred a kind of creative tension that looked like chaos to outsiders. Members of the Roosevelt cabinet were engaged in endless wars for turf and presidential proximity. Harold Ickes and his Interior Department fought Henry Wallace and the Agriculture Department for the Forestry Service. Cordell Hull did battle with Henry Morgenthau over postwar economic policy toward defeated Germany. World War II alone spawned 156 agencies, many of them duplicative and some useless.

The President himself sat benignly at the top of the pyramid, enjoying the ruckus and reserving to himself center stage. Through it all, no one ever doubted who was in command. And who among us, whatever he thinks of such a style of operations, can question Roosevelt's dominant place in the twentieth century, or his fundamental greatness as a leader of men?

Harry Truman was tidier than his predecessor. Nonetheless, despite his reservations, with Congressional initiative the institutional presidency picked up new appendages, like the National Security Council and the Council of Economic Advisers.

The White House staff remained small and congenial. Truman himself attended only two meetings of the NSC between its creation in 1947 and the start of the Korean War. He relied heavily on his staff for information vital to the decision-making process. The cabinet still predominated over the White House staff in Truman's time—something which Eisenhower was eager to continue. But this did not mean that he shied away from institutional innovation under his own roof. To improve relations with Congress, for instance, he created the first congressional liaison office. He made Sherman Adams the most powerful chief of staff in modern times, and elevated Jim Hagerty to a position of influence enjoyed by few other press secretaries before or since.

By contrast to the highly politicized atmosphere of the Roosevelt and Truman White Houses, Eisenhower's exuded a button-down professionalism. As Ike used to say, "Only two kinds of problems ever reach my desk—those marked 'urgent' and those marked 'important'—and I spend so much time on the 'urgent' I never get to the 'important.'" Eisenhower was criticized for supposed over-reliance on "government by committee." But then, a few more committees might have prevented the Bay of Pigs or Watergate.

John F. Kennedy dismantled much of Eisenhower's machinery, along with the formalistic approach to policy-making favored by his predecessor. In its place, he instituted a highly personal style, with aides outside the formal command structure performing much of the administration's work. Informality predominated, and ambiguity was tolerated as a price of "creative decision-making." The cabinet met as a body only infrequently, and in place of the NSC, the president placed emphasis on ad hoc groups during the Berlin crisis in 1961 and the Cuban Missile crisis a year later. Kennedy raised the press conference to an art form. That was not the only instance where presidential persuasion was enhanced by staffing changes. Speechwriting, for instance, came to be regarded as part and parcel of policy-making and this was reflected in the Kennedy organizational arrangement. Most of all, like FDR before him, Kennedy reached out into academic circles for bright young people with fresh ideas as well as enthusiasm. Under him, Harvard was said to have been the fourth branch of government.

President Johnson had an equally personal but still very different approach to government. From his days in the Senate, he had learned to rely heavily on his own ability to garner information from other participants in the governing process. As one observer of the Johnson presidency has written, "Men were his books; his knowledge of them became instruments of control. He even took notes of handshakes." This was the practical approach, the appeal of men who could "get things done." Relying on written memos rather than personal contacts, Johnson insisted that all internal communications flow through him. Staffers who attempted to carve out independent bases of support did not last long. At the same time, LBJ's increased commitment to what he called the Great Society led to the development of a domestic policy staff that was far more formalized in its frenetic pursuit of domestic tranquility than anything seen previously.

President Nixon built upon this start by making John Ehrlichman head of a new Domestic Council, while reserving primarily political and housekeeping chores for his chief of staff, H. R. Haldeman. Nixon also came up with the concept of a super cabinet—the reorganization of seven existing cabinet departments into four new ones: Human Resources, Natural Resources, Community Development, and Economic Affairs. The idea did not survive, but the Council on Environmental Quality, created in 1969, was an outgrowth of the nation's newfound interest in cleaner air and water; so was the Environmental Protection Agency.

But it was in the field of foreign policy where the Nixon presidency contributed most to the modern structure of government. Again, personal preference dictated public policy, as Nixon's long-time distrust of the State Department merged with the unique gifts of his National Security Adviser, Henry Kissinger. The result was a vastly enlarged NSC, with over 100 professional staff members, a kind of miniature State Department within the White House itself.

By the time Nixon left office, Harry Truman's White House staff of 13 had swelled to over 550. And cabinet officers were complaining that they were shut out of key decisions.

One thing that had not changed very much was the role of the vice-president. A lot of water has flowed under the constitutional bridge since a Broadway show called "Of Thee I Sing" immortalized a hapless vice-president named Alexander Throttlebottom, who conducted tours of the Capitol because he had nothing else to do. Back then, Mrs. Warren Harding killed a proposed national residence for the vice-president because, as she put it, a Washington hotel was plenty good enough for "those Coolidges."

One of the best things done by both the Ford and Carter White Houses was their upgrading of the vice-presidency. Nelson Rockefeller and Walter Mondale had meaningful roles carved out for them in domestic and foreign policy. Mondale occupied an office in the same West Wing as the president, and the presidential and vice-presidential staffs were coordinated as never before. Before that, the Ford presidency undid some of the centralization that went on in the Nixon White House, de-emphasizing the chief of staff and placing renewed emphasis on department and agency heads.

Jimmy Carter arrived in Washington hopeful of reinvigorating the cabinet, and downgrading his own personal circle of advisers. "There will never be an instance while I am in office," he announced early on, "where the members of the White House staff dominate or act in a superior position to the members of the Cabinet." And during the first six months of his term, President Carter actually did spend more time with his cabinet than with the White House staff. Yet a strong inner circle of Georgian advisers gradually assumed authority. Protective of their chief, they moved from personnel and patronage decisions to foreign policy. Credit for victories on the Panama Canal treaties and a Middle East peace were claimed by the White House staff. Responsibility for defeats on energy and the economy was laid at the doors of cabinet officers. The Domestic Council reasserted its own role, especially after the dramatic cabinet shakeup in the summer of 1979.

After 31 months, President Carter named Hamilton Jordan chief of staff. The cabinet was repopulated, and staffers like Jordan, Jody Powell, and Stuart Eizenstat and Gerald Rafshoon became staples of presidential policy-making and promotion.

Much has changed since 1939. Eight presidents since FDR have grappled with an office grown infinitely more complex than anything known by T. R. or Wilson. So the institution takes on a life of its own. Some things, however, have remained constant. One is the effort, often frustrated, to turn the cabinet into a fully functioning arm of government. The second is how to make the White House staff a natural ally of the cabinet. And the third is how to develop the vice-presidency into something more than a constitutional fifth wheel, and its occupant into something besides an attender of state funerals and a breaker of tie votes in the Senate.

It has been President Reagan's purpose, largely based upon his own experiences as governor of California, both to revitalize the cabinet and establish a working procedure comfortable for him. As one who enjoys having issues, on which there are divisions of opinions, debated in his presence, it was only logical for him to reinstitute the cabinet concept and make it a vital part of his governing style. Believing that a strong White House staff and an effective cabinet are not mutually exclusive concepts, he set out to change the way in which the cabinet had been utilized. And talk of the cabinet leads to other functions of the institutionalized presidency.

The vice-president, for example, functions as a very important member of the cabinet. He chairs its meetings in those rare times when the president is not available. Moreover, the fact that President Reagan had given Vice-

President Bush the most authority of any vice-president in history was of immense help in smoothly maintaining executive branch activities after the president was shot and hospitalized in the spring of 1981.

It was only natural for the vice-president,

Table 3.2.1

The Reagan Cabinet Councils

President Reagan has instituted the following presidential cabinet councils. These are in addition to the National Security Council established by statute.

Cabinet Council on Economic Affairs

- Secretary of the Treasury, chairman *pro tempore*
- Secretary of State
- Secretary of Commerce
- Secretary of Labor
- Secretary of Transportation
- Director, Office of Management and Budget
- U.S. Trade Representative
- Chairman, Council of Economic Advisers

(*Ex officio* members—The vice-president, counsellor to the president, White House chief of staff, assistant to the president for policy development.)

Cabinet Council on Natural Resources and Environment

- Secretary of the Interior, chairman *pro tempore*
- Attorney General
- Secretary of Agriculture
- Secretary of Transportation
- Secretary of Housing and Urban Development
- Secretary of Energy
- Chairman, Council of Environmental Quality
- Chairman, Council of Economic Advisers

(*Ex officio* members—The vice-president, counsellor to the president, chief of staff, assistant to the president for policy development.)

Cabinet Council on Human Resources

- Secretary of Health and Human Services, chairman *pro tempore*
- Attorney General
- Secretary of Agriculture
- Secretary of Labor
- Secretary of Housing and Urban Development
- Secretary of Education

(*Ex officio* members—The vice-president, counselor to the president, chief of staff, assistant to the president for policy development.)

Cabinet Council on Food and Agriculture

- Secretary of Agriculture, Chairman *pro tempore*
- Secretary of State
- Secretary of the Interior
- Secretary of Commerce
- Secretary of Transportation
- U.S. Trade Representative

(*Ex officio* members—The vice-president, counsellor to the president, chief of staff, assistant to the president for policy development.)

who is a part of every major decision and a participant in every policy making meeting, to assume that responsibility. As a member himself of the cabinet he has also taken on specific substantive assignments, from regulatory reform to the South Florida task force

---

Table 3.2.1 (continued)

The Reagan Cabinet Councils

President Reagan has instituted the following presidential cabinet councils. These are in addition to the National Security Council established by statute.

Cabinet Council on Legal Policy	Cabinet Council on Commerce and Trade
• Attorney General, chairman *pro tempore*	• Secretary of Commerce, chairman *pro tempore*
• Secretary of State	• Secretary of State
• Secretary of the Treasury	• Secretary of the Treasury
• Secretary of the Interior	• Attorney General
• Secretary of Commerce	• Secretary of Agriculture
• Secretary of Labor	• Secretary of Labor
• Secretary of Health and Human Services	• Secretary of Transportation
• Secretary of Housing and Urban Development	• Secretary of Energy
• Secretary of Transportation	• U.S. Trade Representative
• Director of Office of Management and Budget	• Chairman, Council of Economic Advisers
• White House Counsel	(*Ex officio* members—The vice-president, counsellor to the president, chief of staff, assistant to the president for policy development.)
• Chairman of the Administrative Conference of the U.S.	
(*Ex officio* members—The vice-president, counsellor to the president, chief of staff, assistant to the president for policy development.)	

Cabinet Council for Management and Administration

- Counsellor to the President, chairman *pro tempore*
- Secretary of the Treasury
- Secretary of Defense
- Secretary of Commerce
- Secretary of Health and Human Services
- Secretary of Transportation
- Secretary of Energy
- Director of Office of Mangement and Budget
- Administration of General Services Administration
- Director of the Office of Personnel Mangement

(*Ex officio* members—The vice-president, chief of staff, assistant to the president for policy development.)

designed to stop the flow of narcotics into this country.

All this was a part of the president's cabinet concept; just as he had used a lieutenant governor to good advantage, he thought it necessary for the vice-president to be an integral part of his administration. The next priority was to adapt the cabinet itself to his needs and the current needs of the country. And to do that he recognized that you don't have to have every cabinet member at every cabinet meeting. For instance, the secretary of agriculture or labor need not participate in defense planning or urban policy formulation. And so the president developed a concept of cabinet councils, grouped around specific subject areas, such as economic affairs, commerce and trade, food and agriculture, human resources, and natural resources and environment. There is also a cabinet council on legal policy, and another on management and administration, addressing items of general management that cut across the whole executive branch.

Interestingly, this structure has solved the dilemma facing previous presidents who wished to utilize department heads as other principal immediate subordinates in the executive branch, yet ran afoul of the need to convene the cabinet as a body, rather than parcel out its expertise among different policy areas. Looking back over the first year and a half of cabinet operations, one finds nearly 200 major policy issues were considered by these cabinet councils and then as pros and cons were developed, the cabinet council met with the president as its chairman for a fuller debate prior to a final presidential decision.

The value of such a system, augmented by senior members of the White House staff who occupy the back benches in the cabinet room, lies in the cohesion developed between the White House and the heads of the various cabinet departments, and in a structure of decision-making that retains both flexibility and inclusiveness. When the president does make his decision, cabinet and staff alike know what that decision is. They also know, each of them having had their chance at input, that they are now accountable for carrying out that particular decision.

Over two years now we have proved that the cabinet concept of government does work when adapted to the personal and administrative preferences of a particular president. And I think history will record that one of the major structural contributions made by President Reagan to the institutional presidency is this restoration of the cabinet as a vital part of the decision-making machinery and the governmental structure of the executive branch.

The presidency remains a personalized institution. But we also know that absolutely critical to the way in which it operates are the vice-president, the White House staff, and the cabinet. This is especially true as the office they support becomes more and more identified with technical and social forces beyond the mastery of any one person's leadership skills, no matter how great.

Having quoted Woodrow Wilson, a scholar who became a politician, I would like to close with the words of Teddy Roosevelt, a politician who never stopped being a scholar. They are addressed not only to students of the presidency, but to a generation which so soon will inherit all of the problems and potential that each president makes his own for such a short time. Roosevelt said, "It is far better to dare mighty things, to win glorious triumphs, even though checkered with failure, than to take rank with those poor spirits who neither enjoy much nor suffer much. Because they live in the great twilight that knows not victory nor defeat." Over the years our nation has been fortunate to have presidents who have dared. We have had presidents who have triumphed. Occasionally, we have seen presidents grapple with failure. But through victory and through defeat, the presidency as an institution remains unique.

Whatever form its organization may take, the most important responsibility that falls to those of us charged with serving in the institutional presidency is to make sure that this high office is and continues to be one of which all Americans can be proud. That is the ultimate yardstick by which our chief executives can be measured and "greatness" apportioned.

Illustration 3b: The Executive Office of the President

The EOP is comprised of four types of organizations: (1) those that provide advice and information for decisionmaking (i.e., the Council of Economic Advisors), (2) those that facilitate presidential control and policy integration (i.e., NSC, OMB), (3) those that indicate presidential policy priorities and commitments (i.e., Office of the U.S. Trade Representative), and (4) those that symbolize national commitments (i.e., previously the Office of Economic Opportunity and presently the Council on Environmental Quality). The following is an overview of all of the major organizations in the EOP.

Under authority of the Reorganization Act of 1939 (53 Stat. 561; 5 U.S.C. 133-133r, 133t note), various agencies were transferred to the Executive Office of the President by the President's Reorganization Plans I and II of 1939, effective July 1, 1939. Executive Order 8248 of September 8, 1939, established the divisions of the Executive Office and defined their functions. Subsequently, presidents have used executive orders, reorganization plans, and legislative initiatives to reorganize the Executive Office to make its composition compatible with the goals of their administrations.

The White House Office serves the president in the performance of the many detailed activities incident to his immediate office.

The staff of the president facilitates and maintains communication with the Congress, the individual members of the Congress, the heads of executive agencies, the press and other information media, and the general public.

The various assistants to the president are personal aides and assist the president in such matters as he may direct.

The Office of Management and Budget was established in the Executive Office of the President pursuant to Reorganization Plan 2 of 1970 (5 U.S.C. App.), effective July 1, 1970.

By Executive Order 11541 of July 1, 1970 (31 U.S.C. 16 note), all functions transferred to the president of the United States by part I of Reorganization Plan 2 of 1970 were delegated to the director of the Office of Management and Budget. Such functions are to be carried out by the director under the direction of the president. Reorganization Plan No. 1 of 1977 (91 Stat. 1633; 5 U.S.C. App.) and executive orders issued pursuant to that plan amended further the functions of the Office. The Office's functions include the following:

To assist the president in his program to develop and maintain effective government by reviewing the organizational structure and management procedures of the executive branch to ensure that they are capable of producing the intended results;

To assist in developing efficient coordinating mechanisms to implement government activities and to expand interagency cooperation;

To assist the president in the preparation of the budget and the formulation of the fiscal program of the government;

To supervise and control the administration of the budget;

To assist the president by clearing and coordinating departmental advice on proposed legislation and by making recommendations as to presidential action on legislative enactments, in accordance with past practice;

To assist in the development of regulatory reform proposals and in programs for paperwork reduction, especially reporting burdens of the public;

To assist in the consideration and clearance and, where necessary, in the preparation of proposed executive orders and proclamations;

To plan and develop information systems to provide the president with program performance data;

To plan, conduct, and promote evalua-

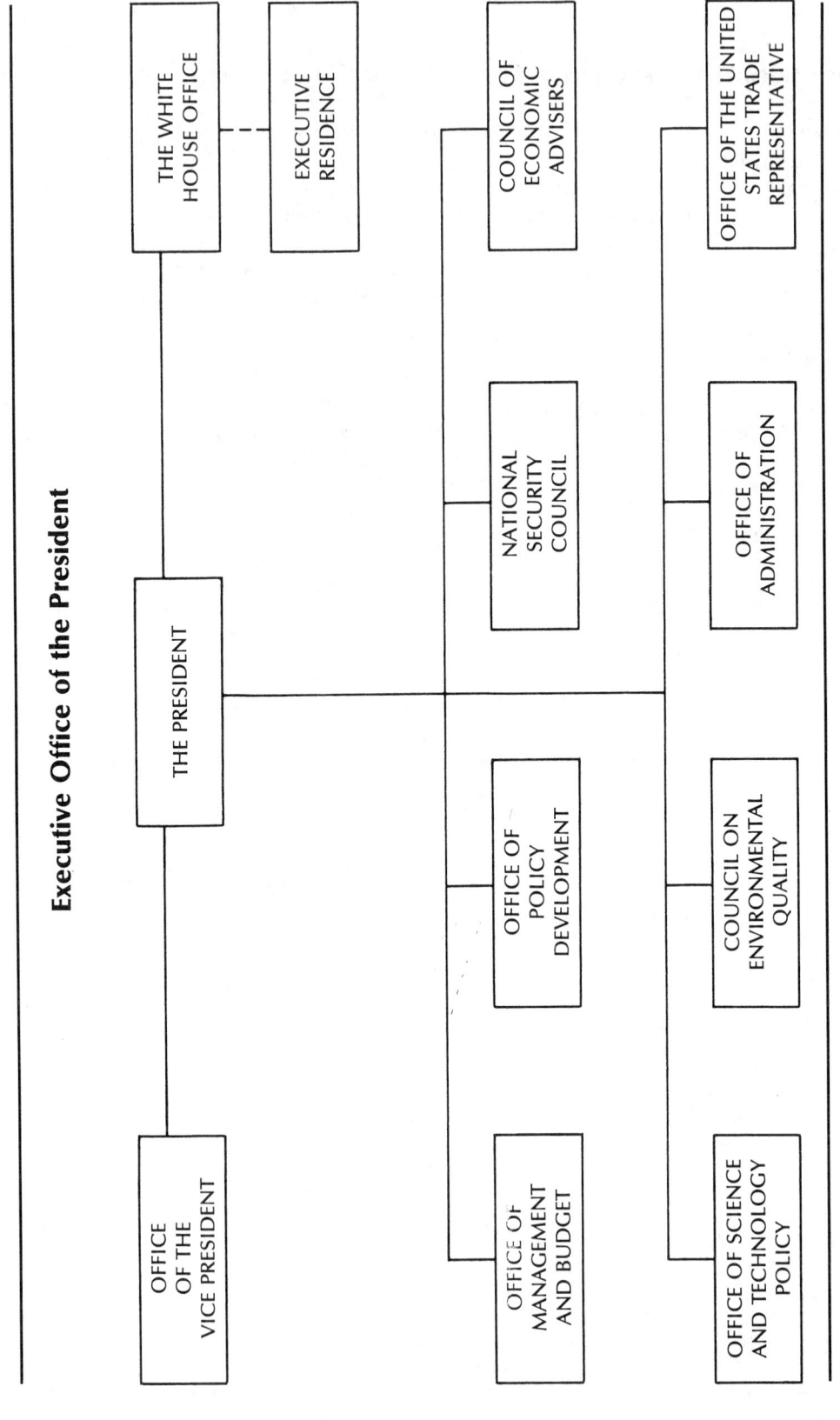

tion efforts to assist the president in the assessment of program objectives, performance, and efficiency;

To keep the president informed of the progress of activities by agencies of the government with respect to work proposed, work actually initiated, and work completed, together with the relative timing of work between the several agencies of the government all to the end that the work programs of the several agencies of the executive branch of the government may be coordinated and that the moneys appropriated by the Congress may be expended in the most economical manner with the least possible overlapping and duplication of effort.

The Office of Federal Procurement Policy Act (88 Stat. 796; 41 U.S.C. 401) established the Office of Federal Procurement Policy (OFPP) within the Office of Management and Budget to improve the economy, efficiency, and effectiveness of the procurement processes by providing overall direction of procurement policies, regulations, procedures, and forms. The establishment of the OFPP implemented the first recommendation made by the Commission on Government Procurement (COGP) in its report to Congress in December 1972. The OFPP authority applies to procurement by executive agencies and recipients of federal grants or assistance of: property, other than real property in being; services, including research and development; and construction, alteration, repair, or maintenance of real property.

The Council of Economic Advisers was established in the Executive Office of the President by the Employment Act of 1946 (60 Stat. 24; 15 U.S.C. 1023). It now functions under that statute and Reorganization Plan 9 of 1953, effective August 1, 1953.

The Council consists of three members appointed by the president by and with the advice and consent of the Senate. One of the members is designated by the president as chairman.

The Council analyzes the national economy and its various segments; advises the president on economic developments; appraises the economic programs and policies of the federal government; recommends to the president policies for economic growth and stability; and assists in the preparation of the economic reports of the president to the Congress.

The National Security Council was established by the National Security Act of 1947 (61 Stat. 496; 50 U.S.C. 402), amended by the National Security Act Amendments of 1949 (63 Stat. 579; 50 U.S.C. 401 et seq.). By the Reorganization Plan of 1949, the Council was placed in the Executive Office of the President.

The National Security Council is chaired by the president. Its statutory members are the vice-president and the secretaries of state and defense. The chairman of the Joint Chiefs of Staff is the statutory military adviser to the Council and the director of Central Intelligence is its intelligence adviser.

The statutory function of the Council is to advise the president with respect to the integration of domestic, foreign, and military policies relating to national security.

The Office of Policy Development (OPD), formerly the Domestic Policy Staff, was redesignated as such in 1981 to replace the Domestic Policy Staff, which was established in the Executive Office of the President by Reorganization Plan No. 1 of 1977, effective March 26, 1978, pursuant to Executive Order 12045 of March 27, 1978.

The Office of Policy Development assists the president in the formulation, coordination, and implementation of economic and domestic policy. In addition, OPD serves as the policy staff for the president's cabinet councils.

The Office of Policy Development is responsible to the assistant to the president for policy development. The Office operates under a director.

The Office of the United States Trade Representative was created, as the Office of the Special Representative for Trade Negotiations, by Executive Order 11075 of January 15, 1963. Congress, as part of the Trade Act of 1974 (88 Stat. 1999; 19 U.S.C. 2171), established the office as an agency of the Executive

Office of the President charged with administering the trade agreements program under the Tariff Act of 1930 (19 U.S.C. 1351), the Trade Expansion Act of 1962 (19 U.S.C. 1801), and the Trade Act of 1974 (19 U.S.C. 2171). Other powers and responsibilities for coordinating trade policy were assigned to the Office by the Trade Act of 1974 and by the president in Executive Order 11846 of March 27, 1975, as amended.

Reorganization Plan No. 3 of 1979 (44 FR 69273), implemented by Executive Order 12188 of January 4, 1980, charged the Office with responsibility for setting and administering overall trade policy. It also provides that the United States Trade Representative shall be chief representative of the United States for all activities of the General Agreement on Tariffs and Trade; for discussions, meetings, and negotiations in the Organization for Economic Cooperation and Development when such activities deal primarily with trade and commodity issues; for negotiations in the United Nations Conference on Trade and Development and other multilateral institutions when such negotiations deal primarily with trade and commodity issues; for other bilateral and multilateral negotiations when trade, including East-West trade, or commodities is the primary issue; for negotiations under sections 704 and 734 of the Tariff Act of 1930 and for negotiations concerning direct investment incentives and disincentives and bilateral investment issues concerning barriers to investment.

The Office is headed by the United States trade representative, a cabinet-level official with the rank of ambassador, who is directly responsible to the president. There are two deputy United States trade representatives, who also hold the rank of ambassador, one located in Washington and one in Geneva. The office is supported by a small professional staff.

The United States trade representative chairs the cabinet-level Trade Policy Committee. Established by, and under the chairmanship of, the Office of United States Trade Representative are three other interagency committees: the Trade Policy Review Group, the Trade Negotiations Committee, and the Trade Policy Staff Committee.

The trade representative serves as an *ex officio* member of the boards of directors of the Export-Import Bank and the Overseas Private Investment Corporation, and serves on the National Advisory Council for International Monetary and Financial Policy.

The United States trade representative is responsible for the direction of all trade negotiations of the United States and for the formulation of trade policy for the United States.

The Office of Science and Technology Policy was established within the Executive Office of the President by the National Science and Technology Policy, Organization, and Priorities Act of 1976 (90 Stat. 463; 42 U.S.C. 6611), approved May 11, 1976.

The Office serves as a source of scientific, engineering, and technological analysis and judgment for the president with respect to major policies, plans, and programs of the federal government. In carrying out this mission, the act provides that the Office shall advise the president of scientific and technological considerations involved in areas of national concern, including the economy, national security, health, foreign relations, and the environment; evaluate the scale, quality, and effectiveness of the federal effort in science and technology; provide advice and assistance to the president, the Office of Management and Budget, and federal agencies throughout the federal budget development process; and assist the president in providing leadership and coordination of the research and development programs in the federal government.

The Office of Administration, headed by the director, provides administrative support services to all units within the Executive Office of the President, except those services which are in direct support of the president. The services provided by the Office of Administration include information, personnel, and financial management; data processing; library services; records maintenance; and general office operations, such as non-presidential mail, messenger, print-

Illustration 3b

ing, procurement, and supply services.

Article II, section I, of the Constitution provides that the president "shall hold his Office during the Term of four Years * * * together with the Vice President * * *." In addition to his role as president of the Senate, the vice-president is empowered to succeed to the presidency, pursuant to Article II and the 20th and 25th amendments to the Constitution.

The executive functions of the vice-president include participation in all cabinet meetings, and, by statute, membership in the National Security Council, and the Board of Regents of the Smithsonian Institution.

Illustration 3c: The White House Staff

The White House staff is more than a collection of offices, and the people who occupy them are more than bureaucratic functionaries. By virtue of their proximity to power and access to and influence with the president, White House staffers become power politicians and celebrities in their own right. Although some have since

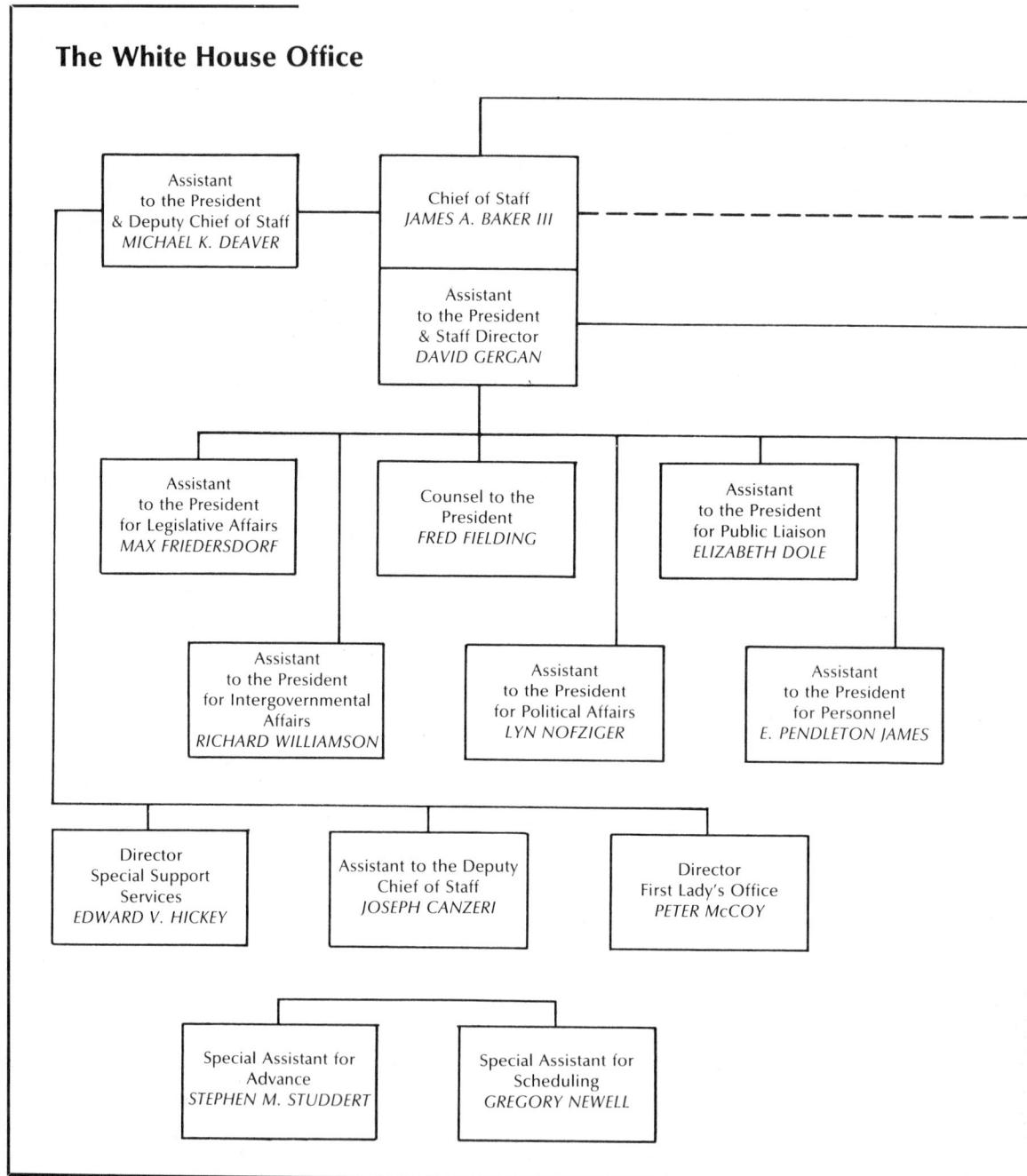

Illustration 3c

left the White House (for example, Mr. Allen has been replaced by Judge Clark), the following list of top Reagan aides at the beginning of the administration reads like a who's who of Washington—especially the troika of Baker, Deaver, and Meese.

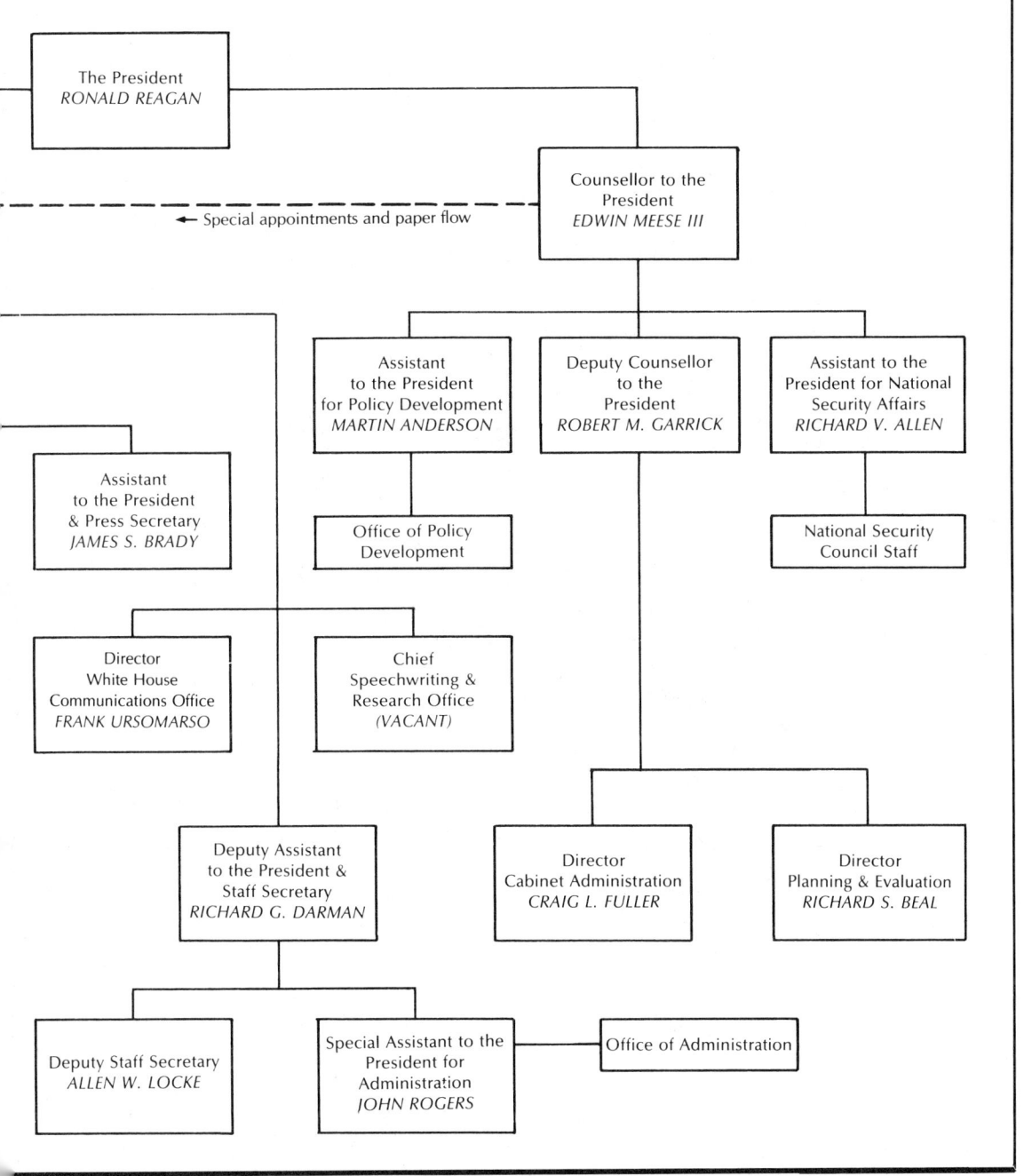

Illustration 3d: OMB Enrolled Bill Memo

One of the functions of OMB is to provide advice to presidents with regard to possible vetoes of enrolled bills (i.e., bills that have already cleared both houses of Congress in identical form). The following enrolled bill memo illustrates the format and system used by OMB.

EXECUTIVE OFFICE OF THE PRESIDENT
OFFICE OF MANAGEMENT AND BUDGET
WASHINGTON, D.C. 20503

DEC 24 1975

MEMORANDUM FOR THE PRESIDENT

Subject: Enrolled Bill S. 2327 - Real Estate Settlement Procedures Act Amendments of 1975
Sponsor - Sen. Morgan (D) North Carolina and 6 others

Last Day for Action

January 2, 1976 - Friday. HUD requests delay in approval until last day.

Purpose

Amends the Real Estate Settlement Procedures Act of 1974 (RESPA), P.L. 93-533, to: revise provisions concerning advance disclosure of settlement costs, repeal the requirement for disclosure of the previous selling price of certain property, and make certain clarifying and technical changes. Repeals section 121(c) of the Truth in Lending Act which requires a full statement of closing costs in connection with consumer and home mortgage lending.

Agency Recommendations

Office of Management and Budget	Approval
Department of Housing and Urban Development	Approval
Federal Home Loan Bank Board	Approval
Federal Trade Commission	Approval
Department of Agriculture	Approval
Federal Deposit Insurance Corporation	No objection
Department of the Treasury	No objection
Federal Reserve Board	No objection (informal)
Veterans Administration	Defers to others
Department of Justice	Defers to others
Office of Consumer Affairs, Department of Health, Education, and Welfare	Disapproval

Illustration 3d

Discussion

The main purpose of RESPA, enacted last year, was to correct abusive practices in the real estate settlement process, primarily through increased disclosure of charges and previous selling prices. RESPA applies to all settlement transactions involving a "federally related mortgage loan," a term so broadly defined that it covers almost all residential real estate mortgage loans involving properties for occupancy by 1 to 4 families.

The provisions of RESPA became effective as of June 20, 1975. The House and Senate Committee reports on S. 2327 indicate that since then, the Congress has received a large volume of complaints about the Act from consumers, mortgage lenders, real estate agents, and other interested parties. The complainants object to the high cost, delay, and red tape involved in complying with some of the provisions of RESPA. S. 2327 seeks to alleviate these problems.

Major provisions of S. 2327

The enrolled bill would make changes of major significance in RESPA's disclosure requirements with respect to settlement costs.

Information booklets, advance disclosure, and uniform statement--Currently, section 5 of RESPA requires the Department of Housing and Urban Development (HUD) to prepare, and lenders to distribute to homebuyers, special information booklets explaining the nature and cost of settlement services. Section 6 generally requires lenders, at least 12 days before closing, to provide the borrower, seller, or any related Federal agency an itemized disclosure of each settlement charge. This information must be included in the uniform settlement statement which is required under section 4 to be prescribed by HUD itemizing all charges imposed on the borrower and seller in settlement transactions.

S. 2327 would repeal section 6 of RESPA. Instead of the 12-day advance disclosure provision in that section, the enrolled bill would require lenders to include with the information booklet provided under section 5 a good faith estimate of the amount or range of charges for specific settlement services which the borrower is likely to incur. In addition, the settlement agent would be required to make the uniform settlement form provided for under section 4 available to the borrower at or before settlement and to disclose, upon the borrower's request, any information he may have with respect to items on the form during the day immediately preceding settlement.

3

With respect to these sections, the enrolled bill would also:

-- authorize the Secretary of HUD, by regulation, to permit deletion from the uniform settlement form of items which are not applicable in particular localities.

-- permit the Secretary to waive the requirement that the form be available at or before settlement in localities where this practice is not customary or in situations where the requirement is impractical.

-- authorize the borrower to waive his right to have the form available at or before settlement.

-- delete the requirement that the form include all information and data required under the Truth in Lending Act.

-- make clear that a lender is required to provide the informational booklet and settlement cost estimates only upon receipt or preparation of a written application.

-- permit the Secretary to suspend any provision of sections 4 and 5 of RESPA for up to 180 days from the date of enactment of S. 2327.

HUD states that the 12-day advance disclosure notice requirement of section 6 has been RESPA's most troublesome provision, that it has caused a considerable increase in administrative costs to lenders, and that it has contributed to delays in mortgage loan closings. HUD believes repeal of the provision, coupled with the requirement that the lender provide the borrower at the time of loan application with a good faith estimate of likely settlement costs, would alleviate administrative burdens and provide the prospective homebuyer with early and meaningful information regarding settlement costs.

The Federal Home Loan Bank Board (FHLBB) is concerned over the removal of Truth in Lending disclosures from the uniform settlement form, but generally concurs with HUD as to the salutary effect of the provisions of S. 2327 described above.

Previous selling prices--Section 7 of RESPA now requires lenders making mortgage loans on existing property at least one year old to confirm that the seller has informed the buyer of the name and address of the present owner and the present owner's purchase date; and if the seller has owned the property for less than two years and has not used it as a residence, the purchase price the seller paid and a list and costs of any improvements made to the property. Criminal penalties are imposed for failure to comply.

S. 2327 would repeal this section of RESPA.

HUD notes that serious difficulties have also arisen in connection with section 7, whose primary purpose was to protect purchasers of existing properties from real estate speculators who acquire such properties, make cosmetic repairs, and then resell them at inflated prices. The Department states that in most cases the only information that must be disclosed is the name and address of the owner and the date of his acquisition of the property, and that such disclosure is of almost no value to the buyer and should not be part of a criminal statute. HUD concludes that, although the Administration had proposed a replacement for the present section, repeal is acceptable.

The Federal Trade Commission (FTC) opposes the repeal of section 7 (Commissioner Nye dissenting). FTC believes that "by requiring disclosure of the seller's investment in the property, this section protects persons purchasing housing from real estate speculators...."

Other provisions of S. 2327

Other RESPA amendments contained in the enrolled bill include:

-- repeal of section 121(c) of the Truth in Lending Act which requires a full statement of closing costs in connection with consumer and home mortgage loans.

-- exemption from RESPA's coverage of temporary financing (such as construction loans), second liens, most mortgages given by individual sellers, and loans made by State agencies or instrumentalities.

-- clarification that cooperative brokerage and referral arrangements between real estate agents and brokers relating to sales commissions are exempt from RESPA's prohibition of kickbacks and unearned fees, and authority for HUD to exempt other payments or classes of payments from this prohibition.

-- an increase in the maximum permissible amount in escrow accounts for taxes, insurance, and other similar charges from one-twelfth to one-sixth of the estimated taxes and insurance payable in the ensuing twelve months.

-- specific authority for the Secretary to interpret all provisions of RESPA and to grant reasonable exemptions for classes of transations.

HUD states that these provisions would be helpful to the effective administration and operation of RESPA and that most were made in response to Administration recommendations.

Recommendations

HUD believes the enrolled bill would provide a sound resolution of the problems which have arisen since RESPA took effect. As explained further in its attached views letter, the Department requests delay in signing, and notification of the signing date, to permit necessary implementation actions.

The Office of Consumer Affairs (OCA) does not recommend favorable action on this bill. OCA believes that "...the outright repeal of Sections 6 & 7 go too far and that disclosure of the 'range of (settlement) charges' at application and the charges 'known' by the settlement lawyer on the business day prior to settlement do not sufficiently promote competition in lowering settlement charges or provide sufficient peace of mind regarding the absence of speculation or the funds needed at settlement. In effect, the enrolled bill is still a repeal of the concept of prior disclosure to the buyer of real estate where reform of the concept was the preferred choice."

* * * * *

On balance, we agree with HUD's assessment of S. 2327, and recommend that you sign the bill.

James M. Frey
Assistant Director for
Legislative Reference

Enclosures

Courtesy Gerald R. Ford Library.

Illustration 3e: NSC Structure

The following statement by the president establishes the Reagan NSC structure. An outline of the Reagan administration domestic policy process is contained in article 3.2, "The Institutional Presidency," of this collection.

THE WHITE HOUSE

Office of the Press Secretary

1786

FOR IMMEDIATE RELEASE					JANUARY 12, 1982

STATEMENT BY THE PRESIDENT

NATIONAL SECURITY COUNCIL STRUCTURE

I. National Security Council

   The National Security Council (NSC) shall be the principal forum for consideration of national security policy issues requiring Presidential decision.

   The functions and responsibilities of the NSC shall be as set forth in the National Security Act of 1947, as amended.

   The NSC shall meet regularly. Those heads of Departments and Agencies who are not regular members shall participate as appropriate, when matters affecting their Departments or Agencies are considered.

   The Assistant to the President for National Security Affairs, in consultation with the regular members of the NSC, shall be responsible for developing, coordinating and implementing national security policy as approved by me. He shall determine and publish the agenda of NSC meetings. He shall ensure that the necessary papers are prepared and -- except in unusual circumstances -- distributed in advance to Council members. He shall staff and administer the National Security Council.

   Decision documents shall be prepared by the Assistant to the President for National Security Affairs, and disseminated by him after approval by the President.

II. NSC Responsibilities of the Secretary of State

   The Secretary of State is my principal foreign policy advisor. As such, he is responsible for the formulation of foreign policy and for the execution of approved policy.

   I have assigned to the Secretary of State authority and responsibility, to the extent permitted by law, for the overall direction, coordination, and supervision of the interdepartmental activities incident to foreign policy formulation, and the activities of Executive Departments and Agencies of the United States overseas. Such activities do not include those of United States military forces operating in the field under the command of a United States area military commander, and such other military activities as I elect, as Commander-in-Chief, to conduct exclusively through military or other channels. Activities that are internal to the execution and administration of the approved programs of a single Department or Agency and which are not of such nature as to affect significantly the overall US overseas program in a country or region are not considered to be activities covered within the meaning of this Directive.

The Secretary of State is responsible for preparation of those papers addressing matters affecting the foreign policy and foreign relations of the United States for consideration by the NSC.

III. NSC Responsibilities of the Secretary of Defense

The Secretary of Defense is my principal defense policy advisor. As such, he is responsible for the formulation of general defense policy, policy related to all matters of direct and primary concern to the Department of Defense, and for the execution of approved policy. The Joint Chiefs of Staff are the principal military advisors to me, the Secretary of Defense, and the NSC.

I have assigned to the Secretary of Defense authority and responsibility, to the extent permitted by law, for the overall direction, coordination, and supervision of the interdepartmental activities incident to defense policy formulation.

The Secretary of Defense is responsible for preparation of those papers addressing matters affecting the defense policy of the United States for consideration by the NSC.

IV. NSC Responsibilities of the Director of Central Intelligence

The Director of Central Intelligence is my principal advisor on intelligence matters. As such, he is responsible for the formulation of intelligence activities, policy, and proposals, as set forth in relevant Executive Orders. I have assigned to the Director of Central Intelligence authority and responsibility, to the extent permitted by law and Executive Order, for the overall direction, coordination, and supervision of the interdepartmental activities incident to intelligence matters.

The Director of Central Intelligence is responsible for the preparation of those papers addressing matters affecting the intelligence activities, policy, and proposals of the United States for consideration by the NSC.

V. Interagency Groups

To assist the NSC at large and its individual members in fulfilling their responsibilities, interagency groups are established as described herein. The focus of these interagency

Illustration 3e

groups is to establish policy objectives, develop policy options, make appropriate recommendations, consider the implications of agency programs for foreign policy or overall national security policy, and undertake such other activities as may be assigned by the NSC.

    A.   The Senior Interagency Group -- Foreign Policy (SIG-FP)

To advise and assist the NSC in exercising its authority and discharging its responsibility for foreign policy and foreign affairs matters, the SIG-FP is established. The SIG-FP shall be composed of the Director of Central Intelligence; the Assistant to the President for National Security Affairs; the Deputy Secretary of State (Chairman); the Deputy Secretary of Defense or Under Secretary of Defense for Policy; and the Chairman, Joint Chiefs of Staff. Representatives of other Departments and Agencies with responsibility for specific matters to be considered will attend on invitation by the Chairman.

When meeting to consider arms control matters, the Group will be augmented by the Director, Arms Control and Disarmament Agency.

The SIG-FP will:

    1.   Ensure that important foreign policy issues requiring interagency attention receive full, prompt, and systematic consideration;

    2.   Deal with interdepartmental matters raised by any member or referred to it by subordinate interagency groups, or, if such matters require higher-level consideration, report them to the Secretary of State for decision or referral to the NSC;

    3.   Assure a proper selectivity of the foreign policy/foreign affairs areas and issues to which the United States applies its efforts;

    4.   Monitor the execution of approved policies and decisions; and

    5.   Evaluate the adequacy and effectiveness of interdepartmental overseas programs and activities.

A permanent secretariat, composed of personnel of the State Department augmented as necessary by personnel provided in response to the Chairman's request by the Departments and Agencies represented on the SIG-FP, shall be established.

4

B. The Senior Interagency Group -- Defense Policy (SIG-DP)

To advise and assist the NSC in exercising its authority and discharging its responsibility for defense policy and defense matters, the SIG-DP is established. The SIG-DP shall consist of the Director of Central Intelligence; the Assistant to the President for National Security Affairs; the Deputy or an Under Secretary of State; the Deputy Secretary of Defense (Chairman); and the Chairman, Joint Chiefs of Staff. Representatives of other Departments and Agencies with responsibility for specific matters to be considered will attend on invitation by the Chairman.

The SIG-DP will:

1. Ensure that important defense policy issues requiring interagency attention receive full, prompt, and systematic consideration;

2. Deal with interdepartmental matters raised by any member or referred to it by subordinate interagency groups, or if such matters require higher-level consideration, report them to the Secretary of Defense for decision or referral to the NSC; and

3. Monitor the execution of approved policies and decisions.

A permanent secretariat, composed of personnel of the Department of Defense augmented as necessary by personnel provided in response to the Chairman's request by the Departments and Agencies represented on the SIG-DP, shall be established.

C. The Senior Interagency Group -- Intelligence (SIG-I)

To advise and assist the NSC in exercising its authority and discharging its responsibility for intelligence policy and intelligence matters, the SIG-I is established. The SIG-I shall consist of Director of Central Intelligence (Chairman); the Assistant to the President for National Security Affairs; the Deputy Secretary of State; the Deputy Secretary of Defense; and the Chairman, Joint Chiefs of Staff. Representatives of other Departments and Agencies will attend on invitation by the Chairman when such Departments and agencies have a direct interest in intelligence activities under consideration.

Illustration 3e

    When meeting to consider sensitive intelligence collection activities referred by the Director of Central Intelligence, the membership of the Group shall be augmented, as necessary, by the head of each organization within the Intelligence Community directly involved in the activity in question. When meeting to consider counterintelligence activities, the Group shall be augmented by the Director, Federal Bureau of Investigation and the Director, National Security Agency.

    The SIG-I will:

    (1) Establish requirements and priorities for national foreign intelligence;

    (2) Review such National Foreign Intelligence Program and budget proposals and other matters as are referred to it by the Director of Central Intelligence;

    (3) Review proposals for sensitive foreign intelligence collection operations referred by the Director of Central Intelligence;

    (4) Develop standards and doctrine for the counterintelligence activities of the United States; resolve interagency differences concerning the implementation of counterintelligence policy; and develop and monitor guidelines, consistent with applicable law and Executive orders, for the maintenance of central counterintelligence records;

    (5) Consider and approve any counterintelligence activity referred to the Group by the head of any organization in the Intelligence Community;

    (6) Submit to the NSC an overall annual assessment of the relative threat to United States interests from intelligence and security services of foreign powers and from international terrorist activities; including an assessment of the effectiveness of the United States counterintelligence activities;

    (7) Conduct an annual review of ongoing sensitive national foreign intelligence collection operations and sensitive counterintelligence activities and report thereon to the NSC; and

    (8) Carry out such additional coordination review and approval of intelligence activities as the President may direct.

A permanent secretariat, composed of personnel of the Central Intelligence Agency augmented as necessary by personnel provided in response to the Chairman's request by the Departments and Agencies represented on the SIG-I, shall be established.

D. Regional and Functional Interagency Groups

To assist the SIG-FP, Interagency Groups (IGS) shall be established by the Secretary of State for each geographic region corresponding to the jurisdiction of the geographic bureaus in the Department of State, for Political-Military Affairs, and for International Economic Affairs. Each IG shall be comprised of the Director of Central Intelligence; the Assistant to the President for National Security Affairs; the Chairman, Joint Chiefs of Staff; the appropriate Assistant Secretary of State (Chairman); and a designated representative of the Secretary of Defense. Representatives of other Departments and Agencies with responsibility for specific matters to be considered will attend on invitation by the Chairman. The IG for International Economic Affairs will, in addition to the above membership, include representatives of the Secretary of Treasury, the Secretary of Commerce, and the U.S. Trade Representative.

IGs for arms control matters will, in addition to the above membership, include a representative of the Director, Arms Control and Disarmament Agency. Arms control IGs will be chaired by the representative of the Secretary of State or the representative of the Director, Arms Control and Disarmament Agency in accordance with guidelines to be provided by the SIG-FP.

To assist the SIG-DP, IGs shall be established by the Secretary of Defense corresponding to the functional areas within the Department of Defense. Each IG shall be comprised of the appropriate Under or Assistant Secretary of Defense (Chairman); a representative of the Secretary of State; the Director of Central Intelligence; the Assistant to the President for National Security Affairs; and the Chairman, Joint Chiefs of Staff. Representatives of other Departments and Agencies will attend on invitation by the Chairman.

Under and Assistant Secretaries, in their capacities as Chairmen of the IGs, will assure the adequacy of United States policy in the areas of their responsibility and of the plans, programs, resources, and performance for implementing that policy. They will be responsible for the conduct of interagency policy studies within the areas of their responsibility for consideration by the SIG.

The Regional IGs also shall prepare contingency plans pertaining to potential crises in their respective areas of responsibility. Contingency planning will be conducted in coordination with the Chairman of the Political-Military IG, with the exception of the military response option for employment of forces in potential crises, which will remain within the purview of the Department of Defense and will be developed by the Joint Chiefs of Staff.

To deal with specific contingencies, the IGs will establish full-time working groups, which will provide support to the crisis management operations of the NSC. These groups will reflect the institutional membership of the parent body, together with such additional members as may be required to respond to the contingency with the full weight of available expertise.

To assist the SIG-I, IGs shall be established by the Director of Central Intelligence. The IG for Counterintelligence shall consist of representatives of the Secretary of State; Secretary of Defense; the Director of Central Intelligence; the Director, Federal Bureau of Investigation; the Assistant to the President for National Security Affairs; Chairman, Joint Chiefs of Staff; the Director, National Security Agency; and a representative of the head of any other Intelligence Community organization directly involved in the activities under discussion. The IG for Counterintelligence will be under the chairmanship of the representative of the Director of Central Intelligence or the Director, Federal Bureau of Investigation in accordance with guidelines to be provided by the SIG-I.

The operational responsibility or authority of a Secretary or other Agency head over personnel from the Department or Agency concerned serving on IGs -- including the authority to give necessary guidance to the representatives in the performance of IG duties -- is not limited by this Directive.

Illustration 3f: NSC Decision Process

The following is an example of the NSC decision process in the Carter administration. The presidential review memorandum commissions a study. The presidential directive announces a presidential decision and directs implementation.

THE WHITE HOUSE

WASHINGTON

September 30, 1977

Presidential Review Memorandum/NSC-32

TO: The Vice President
             The Secretary of State
             The Secretary of Defense

             ALSO: The Director, Office of Management and Budget
                   The Director, Arms Control and Disarmament
                      Agency
                   The Chairman, Joint Chiefs of Staff
                   The Director of Central Intelligence
                   The Administrator, General Services Administration

SUBJECT: Civil Defense   (U)

The President has directed that the Policy Review Committee undertake a review of issues related to civil defense in the United States and the Soviet Union. The purpose of this study is to analyze the strategic implications of civil defense programs in the United States and the Soviet Union, and to determine what changes, if any, should be made in current U.S. policies related to civil defense questions. For the purpose of this study, the term "civil defense" will be assumed to include all activities related to the protection from attack of population, industry, and political leadership below the level of the national command authority.

The study, to be prepared for the Policy Review Committee, chaired by DOD, is to be conducted by a working group chaired by the NSC staff (with Sam Huntington designated as chairman). This study should be completed for PRC review by February 15, 1978.

This review should include an analysis of the following issues:

    -- The nature and capabilities of current U.S. and Soviet civil defense programs.

Declassified/Released on 6/23/80
By the National Security Council
under provisions of E.O. 12065
by CHRISTINE DODSON

UNCLASSIFIED

-- Doctrines, policies and objectives of U.S. and Soviet civil defense programs.

-- The strategic usefulness of current and potential U.S. and Soviet civil defense programs.

-- Alternative U.S. policy responses to Soviet civil defense and alternative policies for U.S. civil defense.

Attached are more detailed Terms of Reference for this study.

Zbigniew Brzezinski

UNCLASSIFIED

Declassified/~~Released~~ on 6/23/80
By the National Security Council
under provisions of E.O. 12065
by CHRISTINE DODSON

UNCLASSIFIED

PRM/NSC-32

Civil Defense

TERMS OF REFERENCE

I. PURPOSE

The purpose of this study is to analyze the strategic implications of civil defense in the United States and the Soviet Union and to determine what changes, if any, should be made in current U.S. policies related to civil defense questions.

II. DEFINITION OF CIVIL DEFENSE

In common usage, the term "civil defense," as applied to U.S. programs, usually refers only to the protection of population -- although at times the protection of local political leadership and industry is also included. In contrast, when applied to Soviet programs, the term civil defense encompasses programs for the protection of population, political leadership, and industry. To avoid any ambiguity, for the purposes of this study, the term civil defense will be assumed to encompass protection from attack of population, industry, and political, governmental, and economic leadership below the level of the national command authority.

III. STUDY OUTLINE

A. Nature and Capabilities of Current Civil Defense Programs. This part of the study will be a factual summary description of: (1) the nature, extent, and major elements of current US and Soviet civil defense programs including organization, command and control, training, material and fiscal support, and (2) the capabilities and effectiveness of these programs during, immediately after, and for up to six months after an attack. This effort should draw on, among other sources, the NSSM 244 study, the recently completed study on a possible US-Soviet civil defense working group, and the soon to be completed intelligence community study of the Soviet civil defense program.

UNCLASSIFIED

Declassified/Released on 6/23/80
By the National Security Council
under provisions of E.O. 12065
by CHRISTINE DODSON

UNCLASSIFIED

B. *Civil Defense Doctrine, Policy, and Objectives.* This portion of the study should analyze the stated objectives of US and Soviet civil defense programs and the purposes which they actually do serve. The rationale for civil defense capabilities should be put in the context of the distinctive military and political structures and national purposes of each state. For the Soviet Union this will involve analysis of their programs in light of the shift from strategic nuclear inferiority to strategic nuclear parity, the developing threat from the PRC, U.S. theater nuclear capabilities in Europe, and the impact on them of the ABM treaty. For the U.S. this will involve analysis of the role of civil defense in light of the shift from strategic nuclear superiority to strategic nuclear parity, the low level of US air defense, the impact of the ABM treaty and lower US sensitivity to proliferating nuclear attack threats, i.e., other nuclear powers unfriendly to the U.S.

C. *Strategic Usefulness of Civil Defense.* This portion of the study will assess the strategic usefulness of civil defense for both the U.S. and the Soviet Union under conditions of strategic nuclear parity. It will examine a broad range of attack scenarios designed to explore and reveal the ability of current and alternative U.S. and Soviet civil defense programs to limit the other's strategic attack capabilities as well as attacks by other powers including those with far more limited nuclear attack capabilities.

D. *Implications for U.S. Policy.* Drawing on the analysis of the other sections, this portion of the study will identify alternative US policy responses (for example, changes in U.S. targeting and nuclear weapons employment policies) to current and likely future Soviet civil defense programs and their policies and strategies for using these programs. It will also identify alternative policies for US civil defense programs to deal with a variety of attack scenarios. The costs, benefits, and organizational implications of these alternative policies should be identified, and appropriate issues defined for NSC and Presidential decision.

UNCLASSIFIED

Declassified/Reviewed on 6/23/80
By the National Security Council
under provisions of E.O. 12065
by CHRISTINE DODSON

THE WHITE HOUSE

WASHINGTON

September 29, 1978

Presidential Directive/NSC-41

TO: The Vice President
         The Secretary of State
         The Secretary of Defense

     ALSO: The Chairman, Joint Chiefs of Staff
             The Director of Central Intelligence
             The Administrator, General Services
                Administration

SUBJECT: U.S. Civil Defense Policy (U)

I have reviewed the recommendations of the Policy Review Committee meeting on PRM-32. Based on them, I direct that the U.S. Civil Defense program seek to:

-- Enhance deterrence and stability in conjunction with our strategic offensive and other strategic defensive forces. Civil defense, as an element of the strategic balance, should assist in maintaining perceptions of that balance favorable to the U.S.

-- Reduce the possibility that the U.S. could be coerced in time of crisis.

-- Provide some increase in the number of surviving population and for greater continuity of government, should deterrence and escalation control fail, in order to provide an improved basis for dealing with the crisis and carrying out eventual national recovery.

This policy does not suggest any change in continuing U.S. reliance on strategic offensive nuclear forces as the preponderant factor in maintaining deterrence. U.S. civil defense programs will take advantage of the mobility of the population stemming from wide ownership of private automobiles, the extensive highway systems, and the large number of

Declassified/Released on 23 JUNE 1980
By the National Security Council
under provisions of E.O. 12065
by CHRISTINE DODSON

UNCLASSIFIED

non-urban potential housing facilities to achieve crisis relocation of the urban population. Civil defense programs should also help deal with natural disasters and other national emergencies.

Jimmy Carter

UNCLASSIFIED

Declassified/Released on 6/23/80
By the National Security Council
under provisions of E.O. 12065
by CHRISTINE DODSON

NATIONAL SECURITY COUNCIL
WASHINGTON, D.C. 20506

NSC - 6095

UNCLASSIFIED

October 12, 1978

MEMORANDUM FOR:

    The Vice President
    The Secretary of State
    The Secretary of Defense

    ALSO: The Chairman, Joint Chiefs of Staff
             The Director of Central Intelligence
             The Administrator, General Services
                Administration

SUBJECT: Omittance of Director, ACDA on
            Addressee List of PD/NSC-41

The Director, ACDA, was inadvertently omitted from the addressee list of PD/NSC-41. Please change your records as necessary.

Christine Dodson
Staff Secretary

cc: Director, Arms Control and
    Disarmament Agency

Declassified/Released on 23 JUNE 1980
By the National Security Council
under provisions of E.O. 12065
by CHRISTINE DODSON

UNCLASSIFIED

Presidents and Their Foreign Policy Advisors 3.3

David N. Farnsworth

The National Security Council (NSC) is an excellent case study of the impetus for, and the development and problems of, the institutionalized presidency. In the following original essay, Farnsworth makes an historical survey of the relationships between modern presidents and their foreign policy advisors, both the special assistant who heads the NSC and the secretary of state. His examination of these relationships illuminates the forces that drive burgeoning White House government and presents the advantages and disadvantages of this development.

Since the early 1960s, the most publicized area of conflict in foreign policy decision-making has been the struggle between the president's national security advisor and the secretary of state. (Bundy 1982-83, p. 94; Gelb 1980) They compete for the president's ear to establish which of them will be the stronger policy advocate. Although the media have tended to concentrate on the personalities involved, the competition is broader than this and includes the bureaucracies each has behind him—the national security staff and the State Department's foreign service. (Rockman 1981, p. 911)

Within the twenty-odd year time frame since the early 1960s, the flow of influence each advisor and bureaucracy has had with the president has gone from one advisor or group of advisors to the other. The high points of influence for the national security advisor have been during McGeorge Bundy's (1961-1965) and Henry Kissinger's (1969-1975) tenures. The greatest influence for the secretary of state came during the latter years of Dean Rusk's (1961-1969) tenure in office and the period when Henry Kissinger (1973-1977) was secretary of state. While the flow of influence has shifted from time to time, the overall trend has been toward greater influence for the national security advisor and his staff. This has resulted in centralization of control over foreign policy in the White House to the detriment of the State Department and the secretary. (Destler 1980; Allison and Szanton 1976)

Before the development of this conflict, the traditional question concerning executive foreign policy-making was whether the president wished to be his own secretary of state or to use his secretary as his advisor and frontline foreign policy spokesman. An alternate advocate was not available.

The shift to the current situation of conflict grew out of the National Security Act of 1947, which established the National Security Council and a national security advisor.[1] The act was in effect for nearly fourteen years, however, before a strong national security advisor emerged during the Kennedy administration. While Truman and Eisenhower used the National Security Council and organized the national security staff differently, neither used his advisor in such a way as to undercut the influence of the secretary of state.

The origins of the National Security Act came out of the experiences the United States had during World War II. When the United States entered the war in 1941, the executive branch was ill-prepared for planning the conduct of the war. There was no intelligence-gathering agency outside the armed services; we had no presidential advisory group that could carry out the role of the British wartime cabinet; and the branches of the armed services had no structure through which they could jointly plan the war effort. "[The National Security Council's] roots lay in the British Committee of Imperial Defense, a Cabinet agency for coordinating national security matters. . . ." (Falk 1964, p. 403) But during the war the United States lacked such an arrangement.

President Roosevelt had not used his secretary of state, Cordell Hull (1933-1944), as a policy advisor before the war, and the war brought about little change in their relationship. In matters of foreign policy, Roosevelt was his own secretary. His emissaries and advisors were Sumner Welles, James Byrnes, and Harry Hopkins, not Secretary Hull. Regarding military matters, Roosevelt relied on his Army Chief of Staff, George Marshall, and Chief of Naval Operations, Ernest King. (Maechling 1976, p. 6) In addition, usually without consultation with the State Department, Roosevelt maintained close contact with Churchill on the conduct of the war—contact that predated United States entry into the war by two years. (Hoxie 1982, p. 108) Roosevelt enjoyed the bureaucratic conflict between those in competition for his support over policy options. His style tended to encourage conflict and thus force the final decision up to him. (George 1980, p. 149)

This ad hoc system of decision-making had little institutional framework and functioned solely at the discretion and on the authority of the president. Agencies established during the war did include the beginnings of institutions that were developed further in the National Security Act, however. The Office of Strategic Services (OSS) was the embryo of a central intelligence gathering agency, and the State-War-Navy Coordinating Committee (SWNCC) provided an organizational contact for the secretaries of those three executive departments. This latter group was, in a sense, the predecessor of the National Security Council. (Hoxie 1982, p. 108)

This loose structure of organization to handle national security matters caused concern, especially on the part of Secretary of the Navy James Forrestal, as to how future presidents would deal with an international crisis, if not another major war. While the analogy was inappropriate to the U.S. political system, the hope was to find for the United States an equivalent of the British wartime cabinet, and thus consolidate and institutionalize the president's power to handle emergencies. (Hammond 1960, p. 901; Maechling 1976, p. 2) At Forrestal's request a study was made of this problem, and the result was the Eberstadt Report in 1945.[2] This report in turn resulted in the National Security Act passed by the Republican-controlled Eightieth Congress in 1947. (Hammond 1960, p. 899; Destler 1977, p. 147) The act not only established the National Security Council and its staff, it also created the Central Intelligence Agency and the Joint Chiefs of Staff (with the Air Force as a separate branch). By 1947 the Cold War was developing rapidly and the need for national security organization seemed imminent. (Campbell 1971, pp. 26-28) The act was an attempt to institutionalize the presidential advisory system by including within the National Security Council those advisors that Congress felt should be heard before decisions concerning national security were made.

Under Truman, the first president to implement the National Security Act, the introduction of the National Security Council and a national security staff produced little change in the foreign policy decision-making process. The two secretaries of state who served under Truman after the act was passed, George Marshall (1947-1949) and Dean Acheson (1949-1953), were consistently used by Truman as close advisors, policy advocates, policy spokesmen, and chief negotiators. This was a period in which the president was decisive and the secretary and the State Department were dominant. (Bundy 1982-83, p. 95; Destler 1977, pp. 151-152) Throughout his administration, Truman was protective of what he regarded as presidential prerogatives. To use the National Security Council for decision-making would have, in Truman's view, weakened those prerogatives. (Rockman 1981, pp. 911-912; Falk 1964, p. 412)

The significant foreign policy decisions during the Truman era—the Truman Doctrine, the creation of NATO, the Marshall Plan, and the conduct of the war in Korea—were made outside the National Security Council and its staff. Even the important National Security Council paper NSC-68 was a product of a joint State-Defense study group, not the National Security Council. (Hoxie 1982, p. 109; Destler 1977, p. 151) Both of the men who served as national security advisors under Truman, Sidney Souers (1947-1950) and James Lay (1950-1953), were relatively unknown and certainly were not public figures. The national security staff was small, and the advisor's role was limited to coordination of the staff and the meetings of the National Security Council. (Bundy 1982-83, p. 96; Hoxie 1982, p. 109)

In these early years, the National Security Council consisted of the president, the vice-president (after 1949), the secretaries of state and defense, and the chairman of the National Security Resources Board. The chairman of the Joint Chiefs of Staff and the director of the CIA served as advisors to the council. The council was not a source of policy advocacy. Before the beginning of the Korean War in June 1950, Truman often did not preside over National Security Council meetings. His explanation for his absence was that he felt his presence would restrict the discussion, but, in fact, he did not wish to imply that the council was authoritative. (Hammond 1960, p. 901) After the Korean War began, Truman called National Security Council meetings more frequently and usually presided over them. This increased use of the National Security Council did not undercut the secretary of state's influence with the president, however. (Destler 1977, p. 148; Hoxie 1982, p. 109; Falk 1964, pp. 407, 414)

Eisenhower shared with Truman the view that the secretary of state should be the president's principal policy advisor and advocate. Throughout the six and a half years John Foster Dulles (1953-1959) was secretary, he maintained his position as presidential advisor and policy spokesman. He was a well-known public figure and, to the point of being the brunt of political jokes, was often out of the country acting as negotiator and chief diplomat for U.S. foreign policy. The three men who served Eisenhower as national security advisors, Robert Cutler, Dillon Anderson, and Gordon Gray, were known only to the attentive students of the presidency. As was the case with their predecessors under Truman, their tasks were limited to coordination within the National Security Council and staff. (Destler 1977, p. 152)

During the 1952 presidential campaign, Eisenhower had criticized Truman's use of the National Security Council on the grounds that it had not been organized or used effectively. (Falk 1964, p. 418) As president, Eisenhower expanded the organizational structure of the Council by setting up the Operations Coordinating Board and the Planning Board. He also enlarged the staff. (Hoxie 1982, p. 410) The National Security Council met regularly, usually with Eisenhower presiding, except during the periods of his three serious illnesses. The council did not handle day-to-day policy or crises, however, but rather developed policy papers and long-range policy objectives. (Bundy 1982-83, p. 99) It was a well-organized system, but it produced no new thrusts of policy nor did it engage in policy advocacy. Eisenhower and Dulles were in charge of foreign policy-making. (Falk 1964, p. 425; Hammond 1960, p. 905)

The dramatic shift in the role of the national security advisor began with the Kennedy administration. (Campbell 1971, p. 91) McGeorge Bundy, Kennedy's only national security advisor, became both a policy coordinator (the traditional role of advisors) and a policy advocate. The Eisenhower structure—the Operations Coordinating Board and the Planning Board—was dismantled, as well as the policy restrictions on the National Security Council and its staff. (Falk 1964, p. 429)

Kennedy preferred Bundy's counsel as a policy advocate to that of his secretary of state, Dean Rusk, and the State Department. Kennedy often used ad hoc advisory groups for foreign policy and national security issues instead of the established structure of the State Department. This occasionally left the National Security Council out of the process as well. William Bundy asserts, however, that his brother usually gave his advice to the president in the presence of other senior advisors, including the secretaries of state and defense. (Bundy 1982-83, p. 100) "Under President Eisenhower, the NSC was a form of super-department placed atop the traditional structure of executive departments and agencies to solve the problems that individual departments were unable to handle. Under Kennedy, the NSC became only one of several means by which problems may be solved." (Falk 1964, p. 429)

The result of Kennedy's consultative practices was that the State Department and Dean Rusk became nearly as isolated from the president during the Kennedy years as had Cordell Hull during the Roosevelt presidency. Rusk was included among the various senior advisors Kennedy consulted, however, whereas Hull was rarely consulted. This shift in the relationship of the national security advisor and the secretary of state to the president could be explained as a temporary aberration peculiar to the Kennedy years, if it were not for the continuation, with variations, of the advisor's dominance during the presidencies after Kennedy's.

Bundy remained as national security advisor for over two years after Kennedy's death. When he was replaced by Walt Rostow (1966-1969) in 1966, President Johnson reduced the emphasis on the office in two ways. The title was shortened to "special assistant to the president" and after the war in Vietnam became a preoccupation of the presidency, Rostow devoted much of his time to the war as well. Rostow was a hawk relative to the conduct of the war, and his policy advocacy to Johnson was mainly in that vein.

The de facto removal of the national security advisor from other areas of foreign policy allowed for the revival of the secretary of state and the State Department. The neglect and isolation Rusk and his department had experienced under Kennedy ended, at least outside the realm of policy in Vietnam. In that realm of policy, Rostow and the Defense Department prevailed as presidential advisors. Policies in the Middle East and Western Europe were left to Rusk and the State Department. Though Rusk had been treated as only one of several senior advisors earlier, as had been the situation during the Cuban Missile Crisis, some of the status of his office now was restored. While the partial restoration of the status of the State Department and the secretary was welcome to those who supported a traditional advisory system for the president, this came about through the preoccupation of the president and his national security advisor with the Vietnam War, not necessarily as a result of a conscious shift in presidential policy.

The apogee in the influence of the national security advisor occurred during the Nixon administration. (Destler 1980-81, p. 575) When Henry Kissinger became national security advisor in 1969, the office had already had two advisors, Bundy and Rostow, who had been both policy coordinators and policy advocates. Kissinger added to these roles that of policy negotiator. Kissinger conducted in secret the negotiations that led to Nixon's visit to China in February 1972. Also, Kissinger personally served as the U.S. negotiator in Paris for the agreement that resulted in the U.S. withdrawal from Vietnam. In general, the policy of detente, with all the policy development this required, was a product of Kissinger acting in a partnership with Nixon. Never had a national security advisor so obviously been the president's emissary and frontline representative.

Nixon undoubtedly intended, when he appointed Kissinger, that this sort of relationship would develop. (Destler 1980-81, p. 580) Nixon wanted central and personal control over foreign policy and, by doing so, to avoid bureaucratic conflict outside the White House. This also would significantly reduce the amount of bargaining necessary when a large bureaucracy, such as the State Department, is involved in policy-making. (George 1972, p. 753)

While this centralized control of foreign policy effectively left the secretary of state and the State Department out of many of the major decisions during Nixon's first term in office, the influence of the National Security Council was a different matter. Kissinger roughly doubled the size of the national security staff and set up a number of committees, all of which Kissinger chaired; these committees further centralized control of foreign policy in the White House. (Hoxie 1982, p. 110) The result was an inundation of studies from the national security staff and the new committees, all under Kissinger's control. Foreign policy advice was essentially under the control of one man, Kissinger, to the exclusion of other advisory sources. (Destler 1977, p. 154; Hoxie 1982, p. 110) The impact of Watergate further placed control in Kissinger's hands. With Nixon occupied with Watergate, Kissinger was in control of foreign policy to even a greater extent than in the pre-1973 era of the Nixon administration. (Bundy 1982-83, pp. 101-102)

Throughout Kissinger's rise to control of

U.S. foreign policy, Secretary of State William Rogers (1969-1973) saw his duties reduced to those of chief administrative officer of the State Department. Rogers and his department played little more than a day-to-day routine role in policy-making. (Destler 1980-81, p. 581)

In September 1973, after more than four and a half years in office, Rogers resigned. When Nixon appointed Kissinger secretary, it perhaps seemed to Kissinger that his new appointment had the quality of being a demotion when the influence of the national security advisor, as developed by Kissinger, was compared to that of the secretary of state. The possibility of a strong advisor challenging Kissinger in his new position was forestalled when Kissinger retained the title of national security advisor as well as gaining that of secretary of state. Brent Scowcroft, who had been Kissinger's assistant, carried out the coordination duties of advisor, but Kissinger lost none of his influence as policy advocate and negotiator. After more than two years of this arrangement, Kissinger, apparently feeling secure as secretary, resigned as national security advisor, and the president appointed Scowcroft instead. After this appointment, Scowcroft continued to limit his activities to policy coordination much in the tradition of the advisors under Truman and Eisenhower. Throughout, however, there apparently was good coordination between Kissinger and Scowcroft. (Bundy 1982-83, p. 102)

Nixon resigned less than a year after Kissinger became secretary, but the close relationship between Kissinger and the new president, Gerald Ford, altered little from what it had been between Kissinger and Nixon. Ford did not display the same intense interest in foreign policy initiatives that Nixon had. This, in addition to Ford's support, allowed Kissinger to continue as principal U.S. foreign policy maker and negotiator. Kissinger's shuttle diplomacy in the Middle East was the focal point of his overseas activities.

The Carter administration presented an example of confusion over who was responsible for foreign policy rather than one advisor or another being dominant. Cyrus Vance (1977-1980), Carter's secretary of state, was for the most part the president's foreign policy advisor and conducted negotiations. Carter's national security advisor, Zbigniew Brzezinski (1977-1981), was more than simply a coordinator of the national security staff, however. He was, in addition, a second policy advocate. (Gelb 1980; Destler 1980-81, pp. 575, 582, 584) Brzezinski enjoyed considerable public visibility and, to add to the confusion, Carter elevated the position of national security advisor to cabinet rank. Although Brzezinski was given cabinet rank, the move was largely symbolic in that it did not carry with it an expansion of his position as advisor.

When Carter took office, he pledged to restore the State Department and the secretary to control of foreign policy. This was a promise usually made by post-World War II presidents but often not carried out. The six committees of the National Security Council established during Kissinger's tenure as advisor were reduced to two by Carter. Carter's actions seemed to be contradictory. Carter appeared to strengthen the national security advisor by giving him cabinet rank and then seemed to reduce his influence by cutting back on the organizational structure of the National Security Council.

There were various media stories concerning conflict between the secretary and the advisor during the Carter years. Vance appeared to be ahead in the competition until the attempt in April 1980 to rescue the hostages held in Teheran. The operation was planned by the president and the national security staff with little or no involvement by the secretary or the State Department. (Sullivan 1980, pp. 175-186) Vance opposed the operation and he resigned shortly after the abortive mission was attempted.

The rationale for limiting the planning of the rescue mission to the White House was the need for secrecy and the possibility of leaks if more people were involved in the planning. Whatever the president's intentions, the final result was a secretary who felt he had been left out of a major policy decision, a decision strongly influenced by the national security advisor. Vance was replaced with Edmund Muskie (1980-1981). Muskie, as had Vance, fought hard for his department position as advisor, but the confusion of roles continued. (Gelb 1980)

The Carter administration produced some dramatic developments in foreign policy—the Panama Canal treaties, the Camp David agreements, an emphasis on human rights, SALT II, and improved relations with China—but the problem for Carter was policy process, not substance of policy. (Bundy 1982-83, p. 104)

The Reagan administration also went through some confusion concerning foreign policy advisors, especially in its early months. Richard Allen (1981-1982), the new national security advisor, and Alexander Haig (1981-1982), Reagan's first secretary of state, never came to a major policy confrontation. Nevertheless, Haig, perhaps looking back on the experiences of past secretaries, fought hard to protect what he considered to be the prerogative of his office, a defense that ultimately brought him into disfavor with the president. Allen never established himself in his position as advisor and resigned following charges of questionable ethics in office. The challenge over policy development for Haig came not from Allen, but from Secretary of Defense Casper Weinberger, especially over policy in the Middle East. Such clashes between the secretaries of defense and state are not unusual, however. Kissinger, while secretary, had had similar problems with then Secretary of Defense James Schlesinger. Haig, as a result of presidential pressure, was forced to resign only a short while after Allen left office. Because Allen and Haig left so early in the Reagan presidency, neither man was able to establish a strong working relationship with the president.

Allen was replaced with William Clark (1981-   ). Clark had been serving as deputy secretary of state under Haig. Clark proved, at least during his first year in office, to be essentially a policy coordinator. If he served as a policy advocate, he did so without becoming a public figure as had Kissinger and Brzezinski. (Bundy 1982-83, p. 105) The new secretary of state, George Shultz (1982-   ), assumed what can best be described as the traditional role. He traveled abroad as the president's emissary, and Clark stayed in the White House. Shultz's style was quiet and outwardly more professional than had been Haig's. Shultz appeared to assume a relationship with the president that fit into the mode for a secretary such as Acheson and Dulles had had with their respective presidents. (Destler 1983, pp. 277-278)

Since the Kennedy administration, the person who traveled abroad as the president's emissary was only one outward indication of who had the favor of the president. Another indicator, reflecting the degree to which the media picked up on the personalities involved, was the number of times the national security advisor was mentioned in the *New York Times Index*. (Destler 1980-81, p. 582) An advisor who received only a few references a year usually was known as limiting his activities to policy coordination; an advisor who traveled and was a policy advocate would receive dozens of citations. Another indicator was which person, the advisor or the secretary, appeared on such television programs as "Face the Nation" or "Meet the Press" to explain or defend U.S. foreign policy. (Gelb 1980) Certainly an important test was which person conducted top-level negotiations for the United States. Any of these activities by the national security advisor was an indication that the advisor was operating beyond the scope of policy and organizational coordination in the White House. The overall observation, however, as to what role either the advisor or secretary played depended on the approval of the president. No postwar president simply allowed the two to struggle until one proved more influential in his own right. The outcome in conflicts between advisor and secretary is determined by the president. (Destler 1980-81, pp. 575-577)

The emphasis thus far has been on the competition between the national security advisor and the secretary of state. During those periods when the national security advisor is the dominant advisor to the president, his national security staff shares his influence. The advisor has direct control over this relatively small bureaucracy and makes appointments to it. Thus, the staff shares the advisor's fate. However, during those times when the secretary seems to be secure in his position as foreign policy advisor to the president, it does not follow that the bureaucracy of the State Department exerts a similar influence.

The State Department has suffered various

periods of low morale since World War II. The morale of the department to a great extent depends on how influential the foreign service feels itself to be. Under at least two secretaries, Dulles and Kissinger, both of whom have been described as strong secretaries, the foreign service felt it did not share the secretary's influence.

Under Dulles, morale in the foreign service perhaps was at its lowest point in the postwar period. In part, this is attributable to the integration of the foreign service, the foreign service reserve, and the civil service personnel into a single service following the Wriston Report in 1954. This disruptive organizational change came at a time when morale already was low due to the attacks on the foreign service by Senator Joseph McCarthy.

Although McCarthy's attacks were not limited to the State Department, his charges of subversion in government had its greatest impact there, charges that originated with his search for those within the department responsible for "losing China." The result of McCarthyism was the resignation of a number of experienced foreign service officers who were China specialists. Other officers saved their careers only by transferring to other areas of speciality.

Dulles did little to protect the officers under attack and even cooperated with those attacking the foreign service by bringing Scott McLeod into the department as security officer. McLeod continued the pattern of wreaking havoc with careers and morale inside the department. (Campbell 1971, pp. 116-119)

Thus, at a time when the secretary had the full confidence of the president and was clearly the administration's spokesman and policy advocate, the State Department bureaucracy felt the secretary neither protected them nor included them in policy development. Dulles was close to being a one-man operation. (Silberman 1979, p. 5; Rockman 1981, p. 918)

Kissinger, as secretary, was not as isolated from the State Department as was Dulles, although he had the reputation of consulting with only the top three or four people in the department, individuals he had appointed. He did not appear to trust lower levels in the department, as a result. (Rockman 1981, p. 918; Silberman 1979, p. 888)

The secretary of state essentially has two potential roles. One is presidential advisor and the second is chief administrator of the department. Secretaries, as has been demonstrated, do not necessarily perform both roles equally well. Dulles, to a great extent, ignored his administrative role, but secretaries who are not used by the president as advisors are left with only their administrative role.

This raises the question as to whether a secretary who is a good representative of the department's bureaucratic interests can also be an effective advisor to the president. While the secretary's advisory role does not inevitably conflict with his departmental representative role, the roles can potentially be in conflict. This is especially the case if the secretary assumes the same position as the foreign service is often seen as assuming—that of critic and source of arguments as to why something cannot or should not be done.

Kennedy is reputed, in a moment of annoyance with the State Department, to have asked of Charles Bohlen, "What is wrong with that goddamned department of yours, Chip?" Bohlen is said to have replied, "You are." (Schlesinger 1965, p. 405) Kennedy was upset over two characteristics of the foreign service. The first was its resistance to change in policy. As mentioned, the foreign service often is put in the position of telling a president why his innovations in policy are inappropriate. The second reason is the length of time the State Department bureaucracy takes to develop a statement of policy that has been requested by the president. (Silberman 1979; Rockman, 1981, p. 915; Destler 1980-81, p. 579) It is quicker and easier for the president to obtain answers elsewhere, such as from the much smaller bureaucracy of the national security staff.

Presidents other than Kennedy also have reflected this attitude about the State Department. "Nixon, it seems, distrusted State even more than the domestic bureaucracies. Truman, Eisenhower, Kennedy and Johnson all, at one point or another, expressed the same exasperation with the State Department and sought to circumvent its institutional hostility." (Silberman 1979, p. 885)

Presidents interested in policy change thus find it convenient to avoid the foreign service, and the easiest manner in which to do this is to use the national security staff. If the State Department delivers messages not wanted, then that bureaucracy is avoided. (Maechling, 1976, pp.11-12) The State Department bureaucracy may be avoided for a second reason as well. The State Department has the reputation of framing foreign policy poorly in terms of domestic impact. The president is, of course, sensitive to the domestic impact of his foreign policy decisions, and the national security staff is seen as being more cognizant of such considerations than is the State Department. The national security staff thus is the one the president turns to. In addition, the State Department tends to frame policy recommendations in long-range goals and emphasizes quiet diplomacy. The National Security Council and staff are more apt to give more immediate policy advice and are less apt to advocate quiet diplomacy in the recommendations they make to the president. (Gelb 1980)

These factors alone do not explain fully the preference of some presidents for their national security staff and advisor. An additional explanation rests with the demise of the cabinet as an advisory group. Before World War II, cabinet members, collectively, were an advisory group to the president and, individually, each was the administrative head of his department. Their administrative responsibilities grew as the size and programs of the departments expanded. The administrative role of cabinet members developed until it became dominant over the cabinet member's role as advisor to the president. The secretary of state, as a cabinet member, has also been a victim, along with the rest of the cabinet, of the demise of the cabinet's advisory function. The cabinet as an advisory group shows no signs of revival. (Rockman 1981, p. 914)

The national security advisor and his staff enjoy a locational advantage in competition with the secretary and the State Department. Since the advisor and his staff are physically located in the executive office, they have the advantage of proximity to the president. These advisors thus have better access to the president and the opportunity of day-to-day contact. The secretary and the State Department bureaucracy are available to the president essentially only at his initiative. (Destler 1980-81, pp. 575, 584; Rockman 1981, pp. 912, 921; Hoxie 1982, p. 111)

A related factor to proximity is what has been described as the sense of "them" and "us." (Rockman 1981, p. 916) "Them" are those outside the White House who are obstacles to the president's policy choices, such as is often the case with the State Department through the sorts of messages it sends to the White House. "Us" are those whom the president trusts and who support him. The national security staff is often the "us."

Also related to the president's view of friends and foes is the conflict between career and noncareer advisors and policy-makers. The foreign service, of course, is made up primarily of career people. They have a long-term commitment to their positions and to the bureaucracy of which they are a part. The career bureaucracy tends to feel that noncareer people do not share this commitment. The noncareer people are seen as serving temporarily, probably at the discretion of the president, and as likely to return to their law firms, corporations, or universities when the president leaves office. The career people can wait them out and hope that the short-termers do not do much harm in the meantime. (Rockman 1981, p. 921)

Although there are some political appointees in the State Department, they are mainly in the top-level positions. On the other hand, the national security staff, which may have some career people on loan to it, is made up mainly of noncareer people. No advisor since 1961 has been a professional diplomat. (Destler 1980, pp. 84-85) Four of the last seven national security advisors have had an academic background (Bundy, Rostow, Kissinger, and Brzezinski). In addition, Kissinger, as well as other advisors from academe, drew heavily on the academic community for his staff. (Rockman 1981, p. 918) Since the noncareer people are seen as more interested in policy change than are professionals, a degree of conflict between the two bureaucracies seems inevitable. This, in turn, would likely make the proposals of the national security staff more attractive in the eyes of the president.

The element of secrecy is yet another factor in this relationship. As mentioned, during the planning of the hostage rescue mission, secrecy was essential if the operation was to have any chance of success. This became the justification for confining the planning to the national security staff to the exclusion of the State Department. If the national security staff is viewed by the president as generally having tighter security than the larger bureaucracy of the State Department, then the State Department will be seen more than ever as "them."

Conflict over national security and foreign policy-making is not, of course, limited to the two bureaucracies that have been the center of this discussion. Another competing bureaucracy of major importance is certainly the Defense Department. It, too, competes for the president's ear and at times has been a strong policy advocate, especially during the war in Vietnam. Which bureaucracies are involved depends on the policy question, but the most frequent conflict since the Kennedy years has been between the National Security Council, its staff and the national security advisor on the one hand, and the State Department and the secretary on the other. Overall, the advisors and bureaucracy in the White House have benefited most in this conflict of bureaucracies.

The opportunities for conflict among the various bureaucracies are many. Conflict is a normal part of the policy-making process and probably inevitable. (George 1972, p. 756) The important factor, however, is how this conflict is managed, and that ultimately depends on the president. If policy is a product of conflicts between bureaucracies or the result of one bureaucracy gaining dominance over others, the president must control the scope and intensity of the conflict. If the president wishes as many viewpoints as possible presented to him, he may actively encourage conflict and thus receive multiple advocacy from various bureaucracies. If, however, the president wishes to limit the conflict, he may choose one bureaucracy in preference to others. When such a choice was made by presidents since the early 1960s, the preference usually has been the national security advisor and his staff.

Notes

1. Throughout this study this office will be referred to as "national security advisor." The office has undergone several name changes, however. Under Truman, the position was called simply "executive secretary." Eisenhower changed the name to "special assistant for national security affairs." When Johnson appointed Walt Rostow to the post, he shortened the title to "special assistant." Nixon in 1969 began the use of the title of "president's assistant for national security affairs," which has remained to the present (1983).

2. U.S. Senate, Committee on Naval Affairs, *Unification of the War and Navy Departments and Postwar Organization for National Security*, Report to Hon. James Forrestal, secretary of the navy, by Ferdinand Eberstadt, 70th Congress, 1st Session, 1945.

References

Aberbach, Joel D., and Bert A. Rockman. 1976. Clashing beliefs within the executive branch: the Nixon administration bureaucracy. *American Political Science Review* 70: 456-468.

Allison, Graham, and Peter Szanton. 1976. *Remaking foreign policy*. New York: Basic Books.

Bundy, William P. 1982-83. The national security process: plus ca change . . . ? *International Security* 7: 94-109.

Campbell, John Franklin. 1971. *The foreign affairs fudge factory*. New York: Basic Books.

Destler, I. M. 1980-81. National security management: What presidents have wrought. *Political Science Quarterly* 95: 573-588.

_____. 1980. A job that doesn't work. *Foreign Policy* 38: 80-88.

_____. 1977. National security advice to U.S. presidents: Some lessons from thirty years. *World Politics* 29: 143-176.

_____. 1972. *Presidents, bureaucrats and foreign policy: The politics of organizational reform*. Princeton, N.J.: Princeton University Press.

Falk, Stanley L. 1964. The National Security Council under Truman, Eisenhower, and Kennedy. *Political Science Quarterly* 79: 403-434.

Gelb, Leslie H. 1980. Muskie and Brzezinski: The struggle over foreign policy. *New York Times Magazine*, 20 July 1980, pp. 26-40.

George, Alexander L. 1980. *Presidential decisionmaking in foreign policy: The effective use of information and advice*. Boulder, Colo.: Westview Press.

_____. 1972. The case for multiple advocacy in making foreign policy. *American Political Science Review* 66: 751-785.

Hammond, Paul Y. 1960. The National Security Council as a device for interdepartmental coordination: an interpretation and appraisal. *American Political Science Review* 52: 1-23.

Maechling, Charles, Jr. 1976. Foreign policymakers: The weakest link? *Virginia Quarterly Review* 52: 1-23.

Neustadt, Richard E. 1980. *Presidential power: The politics of leadership from FDR to Carter.* New York: John Wiley.

Rockman, Bert A. 1981. America's departments of state: Irregular and regular syndromes of policy making. *American Political Science Review* 75: 911-927.

Schlesinger, Arthur M., Jr. 1965. *A thousand days.* Boston: Houghton Mifflin.

Silberman, Laurence H. 1979. Toward presidential control of the state department. *Foreign Affairs* 57: 872-893.

Smith, Hedrick. 1981. A scaled-down version of security adviser's task. *New York Times,* 4 March 1981, p. A2.

Sullivan, William H. 1980. Dateline Iran: The road not taken. *Foreign Policy* 40: 175-186.

Presidential Leadership and the CIA 3.4

James W. McKenney

An important consideration when examining the institutionalized presidency is the role of the presidency in the direction, control, and coordination of intelligence collection and operations. Organizationally, the Central Intelligence Agency is part of the executive office and responsibility for it falls to the president and the NSC. The following original essay examines the relationship between modern presidents and their intelligence advisors.

An examination of the Central Intelligence Agency clearly reveals that its organizational mission and structure are in large part a function of the leadership or lack of leadership exercised by the president as the chief intelligence consumer. Besides his role as the primary consumer of intelligence collected and produced by the CIA, at least three other presidential roles have emerged during the evolution of the agency: first, the president's role as the chief initiator of covert operations; second, the president's role as the executive controller of the agency; and, finally, the president's role as defender of the CIA's power. Each of these succeeding roles has emerged during the evolution of the agency, and its founders did not necessarily anticipate that these several relationships would develop between the president and the CIA.

The CIA as a Bureaucratic Organization

Prior to World War II, the United States did not have a large intelligence bureaucracy and found it necessary to create one, the Office of Strategic Service, or OSS, during the struggle against the Axis powers.

The OSS was broken up shortly after the end of World War II. This, despite the objections of its organizers, who felt that an intelligence institution was critically important to the foreign policy process.

The CIA emerged as a bureaucratic organization shortly after World War II with the passage of the National Security Act in 1947. Initially, the CIA's chief function was to collect, coordinate, and analyze all the intelligence to be utilized by the president. However, its mission quickly changed within the environment of the east-west conflict when several policy makers felt the need to respond to the covert abilities of the Soviet intelligence apparatus. Although he later disavowed any intention to create an organization with the power to carry out covert activities and conduct paramilitary operations, President Truman approved a revision of the CIA's charter. This occurred at the urging of various high placed officials, including James Forrestal, secretary of the navy, and George Kennan, director for policy planning in the State Department, who felt there was a need for such an organization. Kennan presented the rationale for its creation in his memoirs:

> In 1948 and 1949, several government officials, including myself, were concerned with the problem of how to frustrate Communist efforts at penetration and subversion of governmental systems of Western Europe and other continents. We concluded that the United States had a need for some sort of facilities through which, from time to time, it could conduct operations in the international field that it would not be proper for any regular departments or agencies to take responsibility or for which the regular agencies of governing were too cumbersome. In other words, an agency for secret operations.[1]

This capability was created shortly thereafter when National Security Directive 10/2 provided for the establishment of a branch to undertake secret political and paramilitary operations. This branch was designated the Office of Policy Coordination (OPC). The creation of OPC was to have significant influence on the CIA, for it subordinated intelligence collection and analysis to covert operations and created the conditions for the bureaucratic conflict that continues even today.

The first three men appointed director of Central Intelligence played relatively minor parts in the development of the CIA, but in 1950 General Walter Bedell Smith became the fourth man to hold the director's position. His direction was to provide the basic form and structure of the CIA for the next twenty years. Drawing heavily on the recommendation of the Dulles-Jackson-Correa report, which advocated significant reorganization of the intelligence structure, General Smith set out to establish administrative control over the CIA. To help him accomplish this, he persuaded two of the report's authors, William Jackson and Allen Dulles, to join the agency. Jackson became the deputy director of Central Intelligence, while Dulles became deputy director of plans.

Smith's first attempt at reform was to give greater importance to the research and analysis aspect of intelligence by establishing a board of National Intelligence Estimates. He sought to bring together the very best analytical minds from the military, academia, and business to operate in an ivory tower situation where they would not be caught up in the responsibilities of day-to-day intelligence analysis but would be able to produce long term intelligence predictions and estimates.

His next task was to bring covert operations under his control. To accomplish this, he insisted that if he were to have the support and maintenance responsibility for this branch, then he would also have to have the authority to direct its activities. Whereas previous directives from the secretary of defense and the secretary of state came directly to the Office of Policy Coordination, they should now come to Smith, who would then pass them along. This objective was secured when he met no serious objections from the two officials.

Finally, General Smith set out to combine the two clandestine elements into one branch. He brought together the OSO (espionage) and the OPC (paramilitary operations) under the control of the Directorate for Plans. By 1952, when General Smith left the CIA and moved over to the State Department, the structure of the CIA had been established. But the forced unification of the espionage and paramilitary elements would not succeed in reducing tensions between the two groups.

At Smith's departure, the CIA was a sprawling bureaucracy much larger than the modest organization envisioned by President Truman in 1947. It was a loose confederation made up of three groups—the researchers and analysts, the clandestine operators, and the paramilitary types. Each group viewed the mission of the agency differently. Their relations were comparable to a marriage of convenience with all of them brought together to satisfy their individual interests and thereafter forced to live together, albeit unwillingly. While the analysts profited from the glamorous images of the clandestine branches, the covert operators were given the organizational cover they needed to carry out their undercover activities. Despite this, the various viewpoints would often come into conflict with one another and produce the protracted bureaucratic warfare that detracted from the

Table 3.4.1

Presidents and Their Directors of Central Intelligence

Harry S. Truman	Rear Admiral Sidney W. Souers, U.S.N.R. January 23, 1946
	Lt. General Hoyt S. Vandenberg, U.S.A. June 10, 1946
	Rear Admiral Roscoe H. Hillenkoelter, U.S.N. May 1, 1947
	General Walter Bedell Smith, U.S.A. October 7, 1950
Dwight D. Eisenhower	Allen Dulles February 26, 1953
John F. Kennedy	John A. McCone November 19, 1961
Lyndon B. Johnson	Vice Admiral William F. Raborn April 28, 1965
	Richard Helms June 30, 1966
Richard M. Nixon	James R. Schlesinger February 2, 1973
	William E. Colby September 4, 1973
Gerald R. Ford	George Bush January 30, 1976
James E. Carter	Admiral Stansfield Turner March 9, 1977
Ronald Reagan	William J. Casey January 28, 1981

organizational mission and darkened the public image of the CIA.

The need for wartime intelligence during the Korean conflict resulted in a rapid expansion of the CIA's personnel and budget. By the close of 1953, the agency had 10,000 employees, of whom almost 6,000 were in covert operations.[2] Today, the agency has a budget in excess of 1.5 billion and more than 16,000 employees. Policy statements by the Reagan administration indicates that both the size of its budget and its number of personnel will continue to increase significantly during the 1980s.[3]

The President as an Intelligence Consumer

The ultimate success of an intelligence organization rests in its ability to get its product to the intelligence consumer, which for the CIA is the president of the United States. It is not enough to simply collect, evaluate, and analyze data. The CIA must be able to sell that intelligence to the president. Often that is a formidable task, for the CIA is only one of several equal intelligence agencies within the U.S. government. To sell its product, the intelligence directorate of the agency must compete with other organizations such as the Defense Intelligence Agency (DIA), the National Security Agency (NSA), and the Bureau of Intelligence, Department of State (INR).

The president may be provided with either "raw" intelligence or "finished" intelligence. Raw intelligence is the unevaluated information that is received from the field without the originator being able to determine either its accuracy or its reliability. Finished intelligence is data that have been evaluated for both accuracy and credibility based on source and their collection method. The data are collated with other available data to evaluate their validity and content and to determine their impact on U.S. interests, operations, and objectives. It is the task of the analytical branch to produce finished intelligence which is fed up through the line of command to the president where it can be used in making policy or operational decision.

Hypothetically, all intelligence must go through the analyst for evaluation. In practice, it often does not work that way. Some presidents have preferred raw intelligence over finished intelligence, especially when they trust their abilities to analyze the information more than they trust the analyst. For several reasons, this was particularly true of John Kennedy. One reason was his skepticism arising out of the Bay of Pigs failure, when he believed that he had not been given sufficient correct information to allow him to decide whether or not to proceed with the operation. His belief was not shaken despite the fact that the intelligence he received was furnished by the operations branch and was not subjected to evaluation by the intelligence directorate. The entire agency received the blame for what Kennedy perceived as an intelligence failure.

Another reason was Kennedy's belief that, as president, he had a broader view of the total policy issue and could, therefore, make more reasoned judgments than the middle-level analyst. Finally, Kennedy's voracious reading habits caused him to demand the raw intelligence which he could use to make his own judgments.

Kennedy's preference for raw intelligence resulted in the analytical branch being bypassed. To meet this challenge to its prerogatives, the intelligence directorate began sending analysts into the field to evaluate and develop intelligence before sending it on to the president. Knowing that the point of origination affected Kennedy's willingness to give greater attention to its intelligence reports, analyses were often prepared in Washington and then sent to Saigon for retransmission with a Vietnam dateline. This was sure to get a more receptive response from the president than if it had been passed up through ordinary channels.

Lyndon Johnson reflected the typical frustration that presidents have with the tone of the intelligence that analysts bring to them. He saw the analytical branch as unduly pessimistic and not attuned to the policies that he was wed to. In his words, "Policymaking is like milking a fat cow. You can see the milk coming, you press some more and the milk bubbles and flows and just as the bucket is full, the cow whips the bucket with its tail and all is spilled. That's what the CIA does to policymaking."[4] In part because of the pessimistic nature of his reports on the Vietnam War, John McCone found himself outside the president's circle of intimate advisers. This loss of access was crucial to the agency if it was to successfully compete with the other intelligence agencies and have some idea of the president's policy concerns. These concerns must be known if the analytical branch is able to collect the necessary data. To avoid this loss of access, the agency has often shaped its analysis to give an optimistic view of presidential policy despite serious reservations that individual analysts may have.

Presidents frequently complain about the lack of long-term intelligence studies but cannot find the time to read them when they are produced. Typically, presidents prefer daily current intelligence reports—no more than 5 to 6 pages long—and only complain about the lack of in-depth analysis after an event, like the fall of the shah of Iran, occurs.

The President as the Chief for Covert Operations

One of the prevailing struggles within the CIA has occurred between the covert operators and the intelligence analysts. This split has resulted from the two branches' basic disagreement about the mission of the agency. The crux of the argument is whether the CIA should primarily concern itself with the collection, evaluation, and production of intelligence, or whether it should function first as a secret operational arm of the presidency. Despite frequent protestations by CIA officials to the contrary, the operational position has usually prevailed. This is reflected in the size of the two branches' respective budgets and staff.

Covert action as practiced by the Central Intelligence Agency has been defined as "clandestine activity designed to influence foreign governments, events, organizations or persons in support of U.S. foreign policy conducted in such a way that the involvement of the U.S. government is not apparent." Covert actions fall within three broad categories: espionage, counter-intelligence, and paramilitary operations.

Beginning with the Eisenhower administration, presidents were persuaded that the CIA could remove regimes whose policies or ideologies were distasteful to the United States without involving any official intervention by the Americans. This initial perception helped to give the CIA the status to become an integral part in the policymaking process. However, later, these same covert operations would embarrass several presidents and damage U.S. foreign policy.

Eisenhower was embarrassed when the Soviets shot down Gary Power's U-2 spy flight just two weeks before the 1960 Paris summit meetings, which were then postponed by Khrushchev until the next U.S. administration. The next president, Kennedy, was humiliated when he took responsibility for the operation to overthrow Fidel Castro at the Bay of Pigs. The agency's efforts to place high-level agents in the USSR during the Carter administration resulted in the recruitment of an *agent provocateur*, who later implicated a number of Jewish dissidents in a spy ring. This proved to be very embarrassing to President Carter who had to come forward and state publicly that the Jewish dissidents were not CIA spies.

Despite these recurring embarrassments, presidents continue to consider covert operations as a routine instrument of foreign policy. William Casey, DCI for Ronald Reagan, commented on this view when he noted that "Very few people concluded that the U.S. could deprive itself of the ability to move quietly to react to or to influence the policies of other countries."[5]

The degree of presidential involvement in covert operations varies. John Kennedy was deeply involved in the planning and review that preceded the Bay of Pigs. He presided at all the sessions of the planning group. When it appeared that the *New York Times* would publish an article blowing the operations' cover, he personally called the *Times* publisher and asked him to delay the article until after the operation was underway. Prior to 1974 and the passage of the Hughes-Ryan Amendment, presidential involvement did not proceed very far beyond the initial discussions that trigger an operation.[6] This was done deliberately, as presidents sought to place some distance between themselves and the clandestine activity so as to allow them to plausibly deny any U.S. involvement if the operation were exposed. A covert operation often began with a broad, ambiguous discussion about a particular foreign policy problem that the president wished to deal with. Presidential approval for an operation was given orally so that it was possible to deny involvement later if necessary. Richard Helms recalls Richard Nixon as saying, "One in ten chance, perhaps, but save Chile! . . . Not concerned risks involved."[7] Helms took this as a "blank check" to do anything necessary to keep Allende from coming to power.[8] It does not appear that presidents review the agency's plan on a step-by-step basis after the broad authorization is granted for an operation.

After 1974, presidents were required under the Hughes-Ryan Act to approve covert actions as important to the national security and to report to several congressional oversight committees. This, to some degree, frustrated the presidents' ability for plausible denial.

The President as the Executive Controller of the CIA

The structure and leadership of the CIA may be described as most closely approaching a "self-directing bureaucracy" rather than a "constituency agency." The difference between the two bureaucracies is that the former is dominated by its career officials, who set its policies and establish its administrative practices, unlike the latter which is tied to a clientele group or groups that shape its policies outside the bureaucracy. The Central Intelligence Agency is an example of a self-directing bureaucracy.

The control of a self-directing bureaucracy is difficult because it comes from within and usually takes the form of a formal or informal code of professional ethics based on the organization's members' own expectations of behavior or job performance. Outside control is frequently weak or simply not attempted because the bureaucracy is able to lay claim to a special expertise that the government or public is willing to accept or defer to. The CIA has claimed that its involvement in national security affairs requires that it be able to prevent infiltration by hostile foreign groups. To prevent infiltration, the agency has emphasized secrecy and compartmentation that keep the various parts of the intelligence agency separate. Thus, if one aspect of the intelligence operation is compromised it will be less harmful if only a few people have any knowledge about it. The justification for secrecy is that it is directed against the outsider who might seek to block or limit agency operations. However, it has also proven to be a useful bureaucratic technique to protect or enhance special interests in internal bureaucratic struggles and to resist oversight by external agencies or groups.

In its formative years, the CIA was able to use this special claim to resist or minimize external control. However, public revelations of various improper activities, including domestic espionage, during the early 1970s provoked an intense debate over the CIA and produced a call for greater control of the agency. Critics charged that the agency was governed by ambiguous commands and subject to inadequate controls. John McCone, a former DCI, responded to the agency's critics.

> The president himself exercises control in a number of ways: through personal contact with his director, through the Office of Management and Budget and a subcommittee of the National Security Council that oversees covert activities, and also through a civilian advisory board that meets frequently, reviews the community's operations and reports to the president.[9]

Although these presidential controls do exist, it is not clear how often they have been applied or how effective they would be even if the president chose to implement them. However, it is clear that the president's orientation toward the DCI is critical to control of the agency because of the extraordinary powers possessed by that individual.

In the environment of the cold war, the National Security Act was amended in 1949 to give the DCI some significant powers. These powers made the DCI responsible for protecting the agency's sources and methods from disclosure even from Congress, exempted the director from having to reveal the agency's size and budget, and authorized him to spend funds for secret operations on his own personal voucher.

Beside these powers, it is important to recognize that the behavior and attitudes of the individuals appointed by the president to be DCI may have as much effect on bureaucratic patterns and structure as do formal directives and organizational charts. The DCI can shape the structure of the organization by restricting or expanding it scope, by how he relates to intelligence consumers, by whom he chooses to make up the key administrative staff, and by demonstrating special affection for one mission as compared to another.

One is provoked to speculate what might have been the agency's future if President Eisenhower had accepted General Smith's recommendation to appoint Lyman Kirkpatrick as DCI rather than Allen Dulles. Kirkpatrick's administrative and managerial bent was in marked contrast to the clandestine preferences of Dulles. One of the first things that Dulles did when he became DCI was to abolish the position of deputy director for administration. He considered it dangerous and therefore undesirable that any administrator acquire more information about the organization than he should have. He took this action despite the fact that he hated bureaucratic infighting. Eisenhower recognized that Dulles was a poor administrator, but he refused to try to change him although he was frequently pressed to appoint a deputy director to coordinate agency programs, budgets, and analytic findings.

Dulles' clear affection for the clandestine side of the organization resulted in the unequivocal dominance of the agency by the covert operators. By 1957, Eisenhower's Board of Consultants on Foreign Intelligence Activities would warn that the CIA Directorate for Plans "is operating for the most part on an autonomous and free-wheeling basis in highly critical areas." Despite this warning and others, Eisenhower largely chose to evade the responsibility for establishing effective political controls over the CIA.

The President as Protector of CIA Power

Although there were various congressional critics of the CIA prior to 1970, legislative efforts to oversee the CIA were limited. Congressional intelligence committees were dominated by senior legislators who generally acted more to protect the agency than to control it and who frequently took the position that they would rather not know about agency activities. These oversight committees met only infrequently and generally reflected a congressional reluctance to exercise its oversight powers. However, with the Watergate scandal and its accompanying disclosures of CIA improprieties, Congress became more and more interested in controlling the "rogue elephant" that Senator Frank Church described the CIA as being. Even in these troubled times, the agency was able to rely upon the president to protect it against those critics who would question its rationale and tactics.

Presidents have fulfilled this defensive role almost from the founding of the agency. The president has served as a poweful third party able to intervene whenever the CIA has been questioned or attacked by external individuals or groups. In the early 1950s, the agency found itself the target of Senator Joseph McCarthy, who saw the CIA as a nest of communists. Upon the request of the DCI, Eisenhower gave fulsome praise to the agency and let it be known that he would not let its employees respond to McCarthy's subpoenas. By these and other actions, the president protected the agency from having to participate in the congressional hearings.

Another protective technique was developed during the Eisenhower administration to shield the agency. The president established the Doolittle Commission to investigate the covert activity of the agency. The purported purpose of the commission was to determine if a need for reform existed, but in reality the commission was constituted to forestall efforts by Congress to put together a similar committee. As with successive presidential commissions, its members were close to the president and were generally sympathetic to the agency and its mission. Although the commission report questioned the purpose and value of covert operations, its conclusions were generally positive and justified the agency's use of any and all means in its continuing struggle against the aggressive forces of communism.

Later presidents would also appoint "damage control" committees to protect the CIA from the charges of its critics. Lyndon Johnson appointed the Katzenbach committee after it was revealed that the agency had been deeply involved in the National Student Association through paid informers and secret foundation grants. While investigating CIA involvement in educational and voluntary associations, the Katzenbach committee was successful in preventing the disclosure of other questionable activities. President Ford appointed the Rockefeller commission as the executive's response to hearings being conducted by the Senate Select Committee on Intelligence. Its conclusions would stress the need for a competent professional intelligence service to respond to threats of the Communist intelligence bloc, while diminishing CIA infractions, with one or two exceptions, as minor. The Rockefeller commission demonstrated once again that presidential intelligence commissions serve primarily to deflect criticism of the agency or to neutralize its critics by pointing out past accomplishments and by reiterating the necessity for an agency that can respond to the continuing Communist threat.

President Reagan typified this deflection and neutralization strategy at the time he signed the 1982 Intelligence Identities Protection Act. Initially, the president spoke of "those heroes, the men and women who are locked in a dangerous, sometimes deadly conflict with the forces of totalitarianism."[10] Later, he would justify the CIA's continued use of secrecy while announcing the formation of a new Intelligence Oversight Board and Foreign Intelligence Advisory Board to assist him "in ensuring that the rule of law is maintained in areas which must remain secret and out of the normal realm of public scrutiny."[11]

Presidents have also protected the agency in several other ways. They have questioned the credibility and motivations of critics of the agency. They have questioned the propriety of congressional oversight by imputing dangerous leaks of intelligence and operational information to members of the oversight committees. Finally, presidents may protect the agency simply by removing the DCI, thereby implying that the means for controlling the CIA already exist and can be implemented simply by appointing a new director. It is important to note that presidential efforts to protect the CIA have been most successful in periods when the cold war heated up and have been less successful in periods of relaxed tensions.

President Jimmy Carter broke this protective pattern somewhat when he came into office pledging to control the rogue elephant. This pledge took the form of initial support for a revised CIA charter that would define with reasonable precision the parameters for covert operations, including the setting of constraints on what the agency is permitted to do. Carter's enthusiasm for stricter controls on the CIA noticeably diminished after the Iranian hostage incident and the Soviet invasion of Afghanistan. As one observer noted, "presidential attitudes toward controlling the CIA change when it becomes their agency."[12]

Some Consequences of Presidential Leadership

Like other bureaucracies in the federal government, the CIA has attempted to respond to presidential leadership in such a way as to promote its organizational objectives and to assure a minimum of presidential interference in its bureaucratic functioning. Although the personalities and operating styles of individual presidents cannot be ignored, it is notable that the several presidential roles have had important consequences for the agency's structure and mission.

At least four of these consequences are noted, although there may be others of equal importance.

1. The president's inability or reluctance to limit competition among the various intelligence organizations has diminished the CIA's role as the primary producer of intelligence for foreign policy decisionmaking. The ultimate result of this continuing competition may be significant intelligence failures when agency analysts produce reports supportive of administration policy rather than simply providing objective intelligence.
2. The president's preference for the covert directorate of the agency has given it the paramount position with the CIA hierarchy. This position has been exploited by the covert operators during the bureaucratic struggles within the organization.
3. The president's desire to maintain a suitable distance from the covert operations of the agency has weakened the ability of the executive to control the CIA. The high level of autonomy enjoyed by the CIA bureaucracy is a function of this distance and the president's willingness to delegate his responsibility for control to his director of Central Intelligence.
4. The contradiction between the president's responsibility for controlling the agency and his perceived need to defend its powers

has created a situation of ambiguity within the CIA itself as to what its proper mission ought to be and to what lengths it ought to go to fulfill that mission.

Notes

1. George F. Kennan, *Memoirs, 1950-1963* (Boston: Little Brown, 1972), 202.
2. Ray S. Cline, *The CIA Under Reagan, Bush and Casey* (Washington, D.C.: Aeropolis Books, 1981), 137.
3. Philip Taubman, "Casey and His C.I.A. on the Rebound," *New York Times Magazine* (Jan. 16, 1983), 62.
4. James Follows, "Putting the Wisdom Back Into Intelligence," *Washington Monthly* (June 1973), 12.
5. Taubman, op. cit., 60-61.
6. The Hughes-Ryan Amendment required that the CIA report on its covert operations to eight legislative committees, four in the Senate and four in the House.
7. Emanuel Adler, "Executive Command and Control in Foreign Policy: The C.I.A.'s Covert Activities," *Orbis* (Fall 1979), 691.
8. Seymour M. Hersh, "The Price of Power: Kissinger, Nixon, and Chile," *Atlantic Monthly* (Dec. 1982), 41.
9. John McCone, "Why We Need the CIA," *T.V. Guide*, v. 24, no. 2 (Jan. 10, 1976), 9.
10. Ronald Reagan, "Remarks on Signing the Intelligence Identities Protection Act of 1982," in John Stack, *Policy Choices: Critical Issues in American Foreign Policy* (Guilford, Conn.: Dushkin Pub., 1983), 115.
11. Ibid., 116.
12. Harry Howe Ransom, "Strategic Intelligence and Intermestic Politics," in Charles W. Kegley, Jr., and Eugene R. Wittkopf, eds., *Perspectives on American Foreign Policy* (New York: St. Martin's Press, 1983), 314.

Decision Settings in the White House 3.5

David C. Kozak

The following article examines presidential decision-making by inventorying the various concepts that political scientists use to study the White House decision process. Disparate concepts are used to illustrate both the various components of presidential decision-making and the different decision settings that arise within the White House.

How do policymakers reach decisions? How do they make up their minds? What is the flow of policy? Where are the decision points, and who exercises influence at them? What variables come into play? These are important—perhaps the most crucial—questions to be raised in political analysis.

With regard to the presidency, answers to these questions have been difficult to obtain. While studies of Congress, the Supreme Court, and, more recently, the bureaucracy have shed some light on the decision process, studies of presidential policymaking have not been as fruitful. As Hugh Heclo concluded in an inventory of scholarly literature on the presidency,

> Beneath the extensive veneer of presidential literature, there are immense gaps and deficiencies.... Too much attention is paid to presidential powers, personality, and crisis decisions; there is too little reliable, empirical analysis of how presidential institutions and staff have actually functioned within and across different administrations. Little effort has been made to draw lessons of operational relevance for future administrations dealing with similar problems. (1977, pp. 5-6)

There are three major reasons why studies of the inner workings of the presidency are difficult to accomplish. First, there are relatively few decisionmakers (there have been only forty presidencies), and changing conditions and different contexts make comparisons somewhat difficult. Second, unlike the Congress, courts, and bureaucracy, there is not a definite decision point. Finally, the presidency is harder to study because of the relative difficulties of obtaining access to the decisionmakers.

The purpose of this essay is not to take

issue with Heclo. More studies of presidential decisionmaking are needed. Few rich theoretical approaches have been developed and employed in a methodical way. The purpose of this essay is to survey what we know about the components of the presidential decision process. In doing so, two conclusions are made. First, we have some very helpful analytical perspectives for studying selected aspects of the White House decision process, although we have failed to integrate them. Second, in integrating these various trends, we have the rudiments of an emerging framework for studying presidential decisionmaking, a framework that emphasizes the variability of the process in different issue settings.

Components of Presidential Decisionmaking

A survey of the literature on the presidency reveals at least eight different concepts or components of presidential decisionmaking that have been stressed by various authors. They are (1) type of decision (or decision setting), (2) decision constraints, (3) decision structure, (4) role of the president, (5) role of White House staff, (6) role of the advisory system, (7) presidential policy tools, and (8) model of the decision process. Each highlights different but important aspects of the decision process.

Type of Decision

A sophisticated notion of the policy process is that there are different kinds of policies and that they get handled differently. Theodore Lowi, Randall Ripley, and Grace Franklin make the distinction between distributive, regulatory and redistributive policies, arguing that patterns of influence and decisionmaking vary for each type (Lowi, 1964; Ripley and Franklin, 1980). With specific reference to the presidency, Louis Koenig, in his text *The Chief Executive*, identifies different decision settings or "varieties of decision." In his words:

> Actually, the President makes all kinds of decisions: routine or programmed decisions (which focus upon tasks rather than problems); adaptive decisions (the adjustment of existing policy to new circumstances); and innovative decisions (major departures from established policy). (1968, p. 345)

For students of presidential decisionmaking, the important contribution here is to alert us to the fact that all presidents encounter different types of decisions.

Decisionmaking Constraints

Students of policymaking argue that the key concept for studying policy formation is "constraint." Policy is not made under optimal "the sky's the limit" conditions, with a free hand and a blank check. Certain forces and factors are at work that reduce the decision latitude of policymakers by ruling out certain options and militating in favor of the selection of others. With regard to the presidency, former presidential advisor Theodore Sorenson in *Decision Making in the White House* (1963) identifies five of the constraining forces and factors he feels were influential during the Kennedy administration. They are: (1) the limits of political permissibility; (2) the limits of available resources; (3) the limits of available time; (4) the limits of previous commitments; and (5) the limits of available information. Knowledge of these is important for appreciating that presidents are not completely free to choose when making decisions.

Decision Structure and Style

An important focus in the study of decisionmaking is the structure for making decisions. The concept of structure points to the flow of information, patterns of access, and sources of input in the decision process. The structure or executive style of presidential decisionmaking recently has been studied by Richard T. Johnson (1975). He identifies three different "dominant" styles of presidential decisionmaking: formalistic, competitive, and collegial. According to Johnson, each is associated with particular administrations. Single presidencies are best described in terms of one of these models.

The formalistic approach involves a "chain of command" structure, a neat hierarchy of assigned responsibilities whereby all information and advice is "funneled up" to the president or key aides with assigned responsibility. It is the approach that most characterized the Eisenhower and Nixon structures.

The competitive approach is most associated with President Franklin D. Roosevelt. It entails assigning overlapping responsibility to different agencies or aides in the hope of getting the widest spectrum of information and advice and the best performance as the result of the interplay of competition.

The collegial approach, exemplified in President John Kennedy's handling of the Cuban Missile Crisis, is the use of group deliberation for the purpose of brainstorming for the president a range of options and recommended courses of action.

Johnson details the strengths and weaknesses of the three approaches. His summary is presented in table 3.5.1.

The Role of the President

The role of the president is a crucial factor in the decision process. Specifically, as many case studies show, decisions in the presidency vary by the degree of presidential involvement, interest, and latitude (see DiClerico, 1979, pp. 228-52). In some instances, presidents are involved and interested, while in others they aren't. In some cases presidents have wide latitude and numerous options. In others they are severely circumscribed in what they can do. Focusing on the role of the president—or any top executive in an organization—sheds light on when and the conditions under which a decision is made.

The Role of the White House Staff

As is the case with the role of the president, the role of the White House staff is an important consideration in the study of presidential decisionmaking. On some decisions, staff is extremely influential if not determinative, as presidents delegate decisions to staff or defer to staff study. On other decisions, staff is only one of many inputs, and, although they assist the president in defining a problem and structuring a solution, they are only one of many sources of input and the actual choice rests with the president.

The Role of Other Advisory System Components

A major variable in the decision process is the component of the presidential advisory network most involved and influential in a given decision. Cronin and Greenberg (1969) present an extensive overview of the different components of the presidential advisory system. Table 3.5.2 is a listing of all of the actors thought by Cronin and Greenberg and others to be major forces in the presidential advisory system, depicted in concentric circles of proximity to the president. Table 3.5.3 differentiates advisory system components by their location (inside or outside the executive branch) and their formality (official or unofficial). The study of the advisory system has led to an appreciation for how presidential decisions are shaped and influenced.

Presidential Policy Tools

The policy options that presidents have to choose from have been reviewed by William Lammers in his discussion of presidential policy roles (1976, pp. 133-42). To him, the major policy roles and tools are (1) ratifying the decisions of others, (2) altering bargaining outcomes, (3) mobilizing policy support and (4) taking *fait accompli* action. His list shows the range of presidential action on any given issue.

Conceptual Models of the Decision Process

Policy-studies scholars have employed conceptual models of policymaking in an effort to give an explanation of how policy in a given area or case was developed. Models serve as summary statements on how a decision was made and what factor best accounts for it. Graham Allison's work has been very influential and helpful here. He argues that presidential decisions can be explained by one of three models: (1) rational actor, (2) organizational process, and (3) bureaucratic politics.

The rational actor model views the decision process as a deliberate and conscious attempt by individual policymakers to arrive at the best possible solution to a given problem. Decisions are viewed as rational choices made after a careful search for information and on the

Table 3.5.1
Comparison Between Three Management Systems

	Benefits	Costs
Formalistic Approach	Orderly decision process enforces more thorough analysis	The hierarchy which screens information may also distort it
	Conserves the decisionmaker's time and attention for the "big" decisions	Tendency of the screening process to wash out or distort political pressures and public sentiments
	Emphasizes "the optimal"	Tendency to respond slowly or inappropriately in crisis
Competitive Approach	Places the decisionmaker in the mainstream of the information network	Places large demands on decisionmaker's time and attention
	Tends to generate solutions that are politically feasible and bureaucratically "do-able"	Exposes decisionmaker to partial or biased information
	Generates creative ideas, partially as a result of the "stimulus" of competition, but also because this unstructured kind of information network is more open to ideas from the outside	Decision process may overly sacrifice "optimality" for "do-ability"
		Tendency to aggravate staff competition with the risk that aides may pursue their own interests at the expense of the decisionmaker
		Wear and tear on aides fosters attrition and high turnover
Collegial Approach	Seeks to achieve both "optimality" and "do-ability"	Places substantial demands on the decisionmakers's time and attention
	Involves the decisionmaker in the information network but somewhat eases the demands upon him by stressing teamwork over competition	Requires unusual interpersonal skills in dealing with subordinates, mediating differences, and maintaining teamwork among colleagues
		Risk that "teamwork" will degenerate into a closed system of mutual support

From "Presidential Style" by Richard T. Johnson in *Perspectives on the Presidency* (p. 297) Ed. by Aaron Wildavsky, 1975, Boston: Little, Brown and Company. Copyright 1975 by Richard T. Johnson. Reprinted by permission.

Table 3.5.2

The Presidential Advisory Network — Circles of Influence

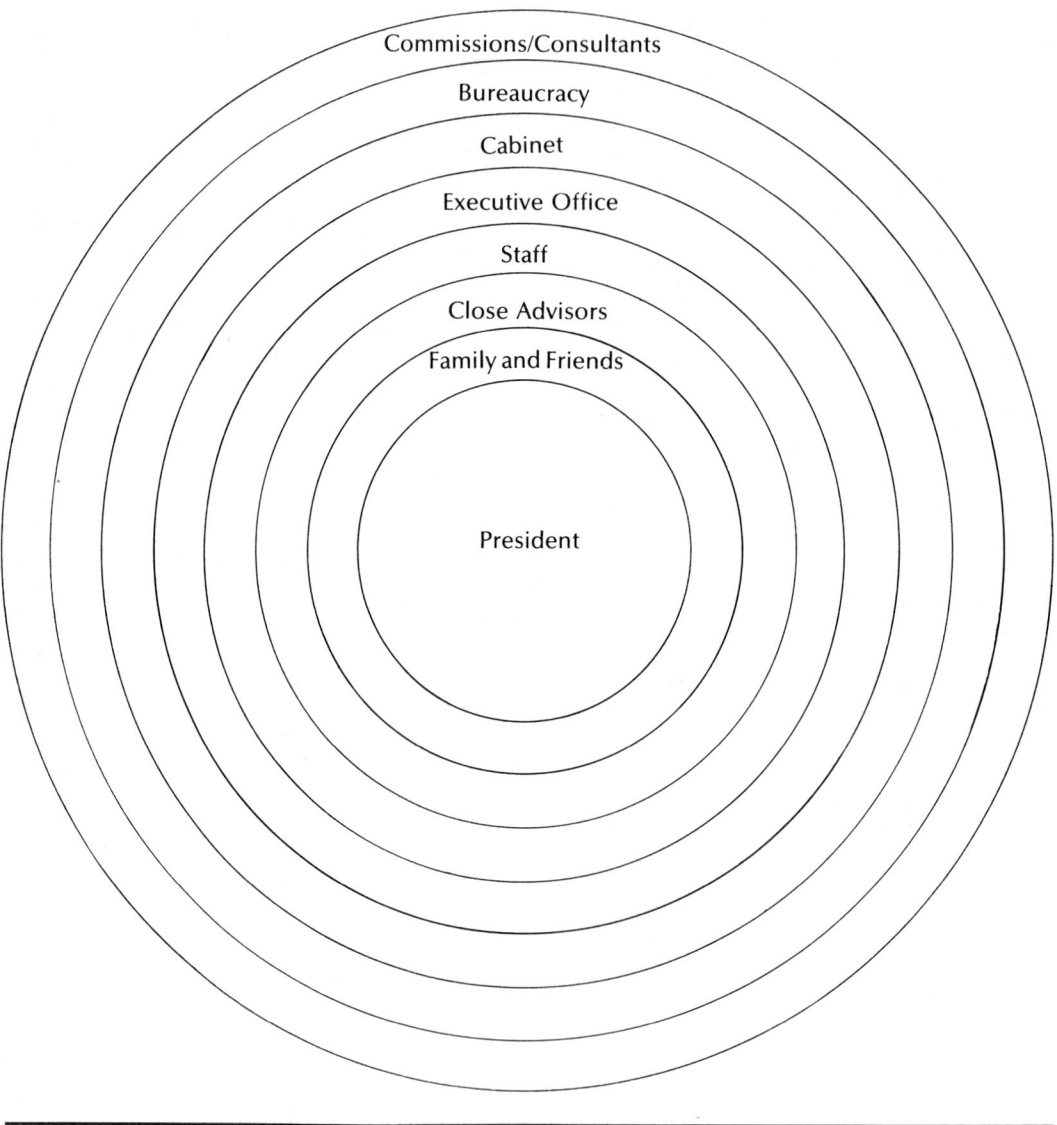

Table 3.5.3

The Presidential Advisory System: A Classification

	Formal (official)	Informal (unofficial)
Inside	White House Office Executive Office Cabinet Vice President Departments/Agencies	Favorites
Outside	Party Leaders Commissions Consultants	Kitchen Cabinet Friends/Cronies Congressmen Reading Media

basis of a listing, study, and consideration of policy options.

The organizational process and bureaucratic politics models stress the arational (but not necessarily irrational) aspects of the decision process. The organizational process model stresses the nonhierarchical nature of government. Large organizations such as government are depicted as confederacies rather than hierarchies. Policy is determined mainly by standard operating procedures and the other internal processes (such as uncertainty avoidance, conflict resolution, and problem-oriented search) of large organizations.

The bureaucratic politics approach views government as a political arena of bureaucratic competition. Different organizations and actors representing different interests vie and maneuver for various stakes and prizes, power, position, budgets, missions, roles, and prestige. Policy reflects the outcome or result of the interaction and bargaining among the competitors.

Others, most notably James David Barber, emphasize a human dimensions or personality model. They call attention to the role of the decisionmaker's operational code and definition of the situation in the decision process.

The importance of these models is that, through analytical explanation, they illuminate the various factors influential in and determinative of particular decision cases.

Synthesis

The foregoing analysis makes it clear that the different concepts are not mutually exclusive. It is not a case of one being more helpful or important than the others. Each illuminates important forces and factors in the presidential decision process. Moreover, individual presidencies cannot be typed easily with these concepts. Presidents do not always do business in the same way. They are not guided nor governed by the same forces on each and every issue. Rather, it seems that each presidency involves different kinds of decision processes varying by issue contexts. The different concepts are associated and configured distinctively in the different issue settings that are found in all administrations.

Table 3.5.4 presents suppositional relationships of the different components of presidential decisionmaking. Various published case studies (DiClerico, 1979, pp. 228-52; Cronin, 1980, ch. 9; Head et al., 1978; Thompson, 1983) and some general impressions argue that each of the three decision settings identified by Koenig is associated with a distinctive configuration of constraints, decision structures, presidential and staff and advisory systems roles, policy tools, and explanatory models. It also seems clear that these patterns are to be found in all administrations. For example, although Eisenhower primarily used a formalistic style for decisionmaking, there were instances where he also used collegial and competitive approaches. Moreover, the kinds of issues associated with each approach are likely to be handled with the same process when faced in other administrations, although, to be sure, the substance of the decisions may vary.

Conclusions

Of course, the suppositions presented in table 3.5.4 need to be explored and verified by subsequent studies. However, by using such an approach, we can (1) provide direction to case studies with benchmark concepts; (2) integrate the major conclusions drawn concerning discreet cases; and (3) familiarize students of White House decision processes with both the similarities and differences in those processes across both administrations and issues.

For those who are oriented to the future functioning of the presidency, a major implication of this scheme is that presidential personality and character are the most salient decisionmaking factors in crisis situations. Thus, if one is concerned about how crises might be handled, one ought to be very attentive to the president's character and operating style, scrutinizing perspective candidates in terms of how they would conduct government during times of emergency. Better than any other factor, personality gives us an indication of how presidents will react to and handle themselves in high-stakes situations.

References

Allison, Graham T. *Essence of Decision*. Boston, Mass.: Little, Brown, 1971.

Cronin, Thomas E. *The State of the Presidency*, 2nd ed. Boston, Mass.: Little, Brown, 1980.

Cronin, Thomas E., and Sanford D. Greenberg eds. *The Presidential Advisory System*. New York: Harper and Row, 1969.

DiClerico, Robert E. *The American President*. New York: Prentice-Hall, 1979.

Head, Richard G., et al. *Crisis Resolution: Presidential Decision Making in the Mayaguez and Korean Confrontations*. Boulder, Colo.: Westview, 1978.

Heclo, Hugh. *Studying the Presidency*. A Report to the Ford Foundation, 1977.

Johnson, Richard T. "Presidential Style." In *Perspectives on the Presidency*, ed. by Aaron Wildavsky. Boston, Mass.: Little, Brown, 1975. pp. 262-300.

Koenig, Louis W. *The Chief Executive*, rev. ed. New York: Harcourt, Brace, 1968.

Lammers, William W. *Presidential Politics: Patterns and Prospects*. New York: Harper and Row, 1976.

Lowi, Theodore J. "American Business, Public Policy, Case Studies, and Political Theory." *World Politics* 16 (1964), 677-715.

Ripley, Randall B., and Grace A. Franklin. *Congress, the Bureaucracy, and Public Policy*, rev. ed. Homewood, Ill.: Dorsey, 1980.

Sorenson, Theodore C. *Decisionmaking in the White House*. New York: Columbia University Press, 1963.

Thompson, Roy L. "Barber's Typology of Presidential Character: A Critical Evaluation" and "Research Problem Statement," University of Southern California, Sacramento Public Affairs Center, 1983.

Table 3.5.4

**Decision Settings in the White House:
Variations in Components of Decisionmaking across Different Decision Arenas**

Type of Decision	Operative Constraints	Decision Structure	Role of the President	Role of White House Staff	Salient Advisory System Component	Presidential Policy Tool	Model of the Decision Process
Routine (programmed)	previous commitments, available resources	formalistic	low	high	bureaucracy and cabinet	ratifying decisions hammered out by others	organizational process
Adaptive	political permissibility	competitive	medium	medium	executive office; White House staff	altering bargaining outcomes	bureaucratic politics
Innovative/ major crisis	time, information (and all others to a lesser extent)	collegial	high	low	kitchen cabinet; inner circles	choosing a course of action; mobilizing policy support; taking *fait accompli* action	rational decision-maker; human dimensions, character and personality

Perspectives on the Vice-Presidency 3.6

Marie D. Natoli

The office of vice-president is also part of the executive office of the president. The relationship between a president and vice-president is strongly colored by their personalities and by their agreement on the vice-president's responsibilities. The following article details the different perspectives on the vice-presidency found among modern presidents, with an emphasis on the changing nature and growing responsibilities of recent vice-presidents.

"Whatever the president wants is what I want," Spiro Agnew had reportedly claimed. "I envisage this as the principal role of the vice-presidency—to implement the policies of the chief executive."[1] Hubert Humphrey was a bit more descriptive:

> It's like being naked in the middle of a blizzard, with no one to even offer you a match to help you keep warm—that's the vice-presidency. You are trapped, vulnerable and alone, and it does not matter who happens to be president.[2]

"A cow's fifth teat," said Harry Truman.[3] And although he referred to the vice-presidency as a way of getting rid of competitors, Truman's own vice-president, Alben Barkley, seemed to adapt well to the uncertainties of the office. He was much more optimistic that the office was considerably more than "a fifth wheel on the machinery of government," as John Adams, the first incumbent of the Vice Presidency, had proclaimed.[4] Adams had also referred to the office as "Your Superfluous Highness."[5]

John Nance Garner, who had served as vice-president under Franklin D. Roosevelt for two terms and been ignored, advised Lyndon Johnson to decline the offer of the vice-presidency because it "isn't worth a pitcher of warm spit."[6] Johnson himself, as senator and majority leader, had often said he would never accept the vice-presidency; the second officer, he said, does nothing in the legislature, and he was not about to trade a vote for a gavel.[7]

But Johnson did accept it, and once he did he found himself more frustrated than he had ever imagined possible.[8] However Johnson had astutely grasped the nature of the office as one almost entirely at the disposal of the president.[9] A vice-president, he would later emphasize, must be above all loyal to his president.[10] As he reflected in his memoirs, he was the kind of vice-president he would want—loyal and self-effacing.[11] Johnson seemed to over-generalize, however, in his remark in April, 1961 when he said: "I think that the office of the vice-president is really the same under any administration."[12] Johnson might have been on more solid ground had his statement indicated that the vice-presidency is the same under any administration in the sense that it is always dependent upon the characteristics of a particular presidential administration. As Richard Nixon pointed out, "it is rather difficult to summarize the duties of the vice-president, because, of course, those duties vary with everyone who holds the office."[13]

Johnson's experience in the vice-presidency seems to have blended with his personal nature to result in a very determined view of his expectations in a vice-president, and these expectations are reflected in the view of the office expressed by the man who was his choice as a running mate in 1964. Just several days prior to being selected by Johnson, Hubert Humphrey revealed his astute understanding of what a vice-president must be: "He must have a quality of fidelity, a willingness literally to give himself, to be what the president wants him to be, a loyal, faithful friend and servant."[14]

President Dwight D. Eisenhower was undoubtedly responsible for the turning point

---

"Perspectives on the Vice-Presidency" by Marie D. Natoli, Fall 1982, *Presidential Studies Quarterly, 12,* pp. 598-602. Copyright 1982 by the Center for the Study of the Presidency. Reprinted by permission.

in the development of the vice-presidency. "I personally believe," he said, "the vice-president of the United States should never be a nonentity. I believe he should be used. I believe he should have a very useful job."[15] And Eisenhower met with Nixon prior to the 1952 campaign to discuss what was expected to be a more active role for the vice-president.[16]

Eisenhower's vice-president seemed to fluctuate in his view of the office. "A hollow shell," Nixon had once said of the second office,[17] although he reportedly preferred the vice-presidency to the legislature.[18] As vice-president, Nixon felt the incumbent of the second office must be "given vast responsibility."[19]

> Because of the burden of the presidency, particularly with foreign policy problems becoming more acute than they had been previously, are so great . . . the vice-president can and should be used more even than he has been in either the Kennedy or the Eisenhower administration.[20]

Emphasizing the need for and anticipating that future presidents would make greater use of their vice-presidents, Nixon noted the most critical duties of the office.

> First, his participation in the deliberations of the National Security Council, his participation in the deliberations of the cabinet; and then the increasingly greater use of the vice-president as a trouble-shooter and as a representative of the president in the field of foreign policy.[21]

While Nixon's views did not fully coincide with the assignment of tasks to his own vice-president, other expressions of his view of the office emphasize the trouble-shooter function. The vice-president, he said, "should sustain presidential policy"[22]; he should "clearly represent views of the president and be [someone] the president could trust to carry out very important assignments."[23] And as president, Nixon said of the vice-president, "He is dealing with expressing established policy to opinion leaders throughout the country."[24]

Vice-president George Bush's two most recent predecessors, Nelson Rockefeller and Walter Mondale, both succinctly grasped the essence of the office. Despite the peculiar circumstances under which he had come to the vice-presidency, despite his own personal prestige—which in a sense exceeded that of the president who had appointed him—Nelson Rockefeller knew what his future as vice-president would be. Commenting that he had known every vice-president since Henry Wallace, Rockefeller noted that "they were all frustrated, every one of them."[25] At another point, he said, "I don't expect anything. This, I think, is my greatest strength."[26]

And Walter Mondale—who had prepared himself for the office by talking with Nelson Rockefeller and Hubert Humphrey—immediately saw his job as that of the president's "advisor on crucial, broad issues affecting government; to be the bearer of bad news. . . . My future in public life really depends upon the success of the Carter presidency."[27] Just one month prior to his statement, the newly inaugurated Vice-President Mondale symbolically underscored another key understanding of his relationship to the president, and he talked about this in a February television interview. "When he walked in that parade . . . I told the president, 'I don't want to upstage you, I think I'll ride—I wouldn't want to take this away from you'".[28] Mondale's understanding of the linkage between the president and his administration and the success of the vice-president was significant.

Despite political pundits' jokes, the vice-presidency has come a long way during the period of the "modern presidency." The growth of the presidency itself has undoubtedly contributed to the necessity of an increased role for his successor. And a succession of events have likewise continued to focus attention upon the likelihood that a vice-president may be called upon to lead the nation. Franklin Roosevelt's death, just three months after the beginning of his fourth term, left his new vice-president, Harry Truman, with the seemingly inhuman task of filling the shoes of a president who had been larger than life, who had unhesitatingly guided the United States through twelve incredible years of depression and war, and who had done little to prepare his vice-presidents for the possibility of taking over. The Truman succession would mark the beginning of a new vice-president—at least insofar as all future presidents would be conscious of their responsibility to prepare for the smooth transfer of power and leadership, should the need arise. Other events would continue this trend towards an increased awareness of the office of the vice-presidency.

The very active Nixon vice-presidency of the 1950s resulted from the Eisenhower conception and coincided with the three Eisenhower bouts with physical disabilities. As a result the new image of the vice-presidency was well on its way. Increasingly, individuals of stature would be attracted to it as candidates.

No sensitive person old enough to recall the hours of anxiety throughout the nation and beyond which followed the assassination of President John F. Kennedy in Dallas that fateful November 22, 1963 day can fail to appreciate the reassuring aspects of having a vice-president available and ready to assume the reins of government. The Kennedy assassination might justifiably be ranked as the cataclysmic event which would definitively underscore the importance of the office; the death of the youngest elected president in the history of the Republic loudly proclaimed the mortality of all of us. "The King is dead; long live the King!" would bear greater significance as Lyndon Johnson, the man nobody had chosen for the presidency, masterfully assumed the stewardship of the country he inherited. With the Kennedy assassination came, too, the renewed interest in providing a mechanism for filling vacancies in the vice-presidency, and thus the relatively swift drafting and ratification of the 25th Amendment. Never again would the country be without a crowned prince, as it had been for practically the duration of the first Truman administration following FDR's death in office.

Events of the 1970s had a profound impact on the vice-presidential office. First there was the hasty selection of Senator Thomas Eagleton by presidential candidate George McGovern and the resulting "Eagleton Affair" in which the Missouri senator's controversial health record would force his resignation from the 1972 Democratic ticket. Then there was the resignation of Vice-President Spiro Agnew following charges of misconduct during his tenure as Baltimore County executive several years previous. This was followed by the floodgates of Watergate which engulfed the nation and ended in the resignation of President Richard Nixon, who had two years earlier won reelection by a landslide. Nixon was succeeded by Gerald Ford, the man Nixon himself nominated to replace Spiro Agnew in the vice-presidency. Finally, there were the protracted Congressional hearings over Ford's own nominee for the vice-presidency, Nelson Rockefeller. All of this would have a cumulative effect on the attention paid to the vice-presidency. Politicians and average citizens alike would be hard-pressed to forget that one in five presidents have come to that office via the vice-presidency.

The development of the vice-president's role as administration spokesman came during the incumbency of Hubert Humphrey, who so clearly understood that the essence of the vice-presidency constituted loyalty to the president. Humphrey was the man LBJ would assign the distasteful and, as the campaign of 1968 indicated, politically damning task of defending an unpopular war policy he had had little role in shaping. The spokesman role was furthered during the incumbency of Spiro Agnew, the man who fulfilled his campaign promise to become a household word. Agnew became "Nixon's Nixon" in his attack upon so many internal "enemies." This assignment marked off a new unofficial task that would often have profound political reverberations. Serving as administration spokesman would be an assignment of mixed blessings.

That vice-presidents often find themselves "naked in a blizzard" despite their own expertise and constituencies is a point no better made than through looking at the Rockefeller vice-presidency. Clearly, the office had come a long way, attracting the likes of Lyndon Johnson, Hubert Humphrey, and Nelson Rockefeller. And the peculiar circumstances of the Rockefeller incumbency might have suggested that he would have had a freer hand in carving out a role for himself under the presidency of Gerald Ford.

One of the most prestigious and influential men to serve in the second office, Nelson

Rockefeller had an extensive interest and background in foreign affairs. He found himself serving under the presidency of a man who admitted he held little expertise in that area. Although the figure of Secretary of State Henry Kissinger loomed large in foreign affairs, the personal relations between Kissinger and Rockefeller were friendly, harmonious, and cooperative. At the outset of his incumbency, Rockefeller seemed not apt to suffer the same fate of many of his predecessors, i.e., spending a good deal of time making good will tours and raising funds for the party. In his initial functioning as vice-president, Rockefeller was astute enough to maintain a low profile deferring to the higher office of the presidency. This is essentially the position any vice-president who hopes to survive must maintain.

Unlike many of his predecessors, Rockefeller did not need to waste time focusing attention on his image and personality; he was probably the most well-known figure both nationally and internationally in the history of the vice-presidency. Already a household word and holding many constituencies of his own, Rockefeller needed to spend little time convincing the president of his abilities or usefulness. Indeed, the president himself seemed awed by the Rockefeller power and talent. In short, the Rockefeller vice-presidency was in many ways unique. But ultimately, however, the promise held by Nelson Rockefeller's incumbency in the second office never fully materialized. The victim of the political considerations of the 1976 campaign, Rockefeller, too, was expendable. When push comes to shove, the interests of the president always prevail.

Hubert Humphrey's insights on the presidential-vice-presidential relationship were well-stated:

> In most instances you will find a president seldom ever remembered when he called on a vice-president. There is a love-hate relationship. There is a faith and doubt relationship. A comradeship and an adversary—if not an adversary, at least a competitor. It's just in the nature of it. It's a marriage, as Lyndon Johnson pointed out to me, but it's one in which both the husband and wife are constantly looking at each other, and saying, "What is he/she up to?" And in this sense, male chauvinism is supreme.[30]

Walter Mondale, Humphrey's protege of many years, seemed to understand the nature of this relationship. He enjoyed the more active role Jimmy Carter had promised from the outset. But this increased role was reflective of the basic nature of the vice-presidency: entirely subject to the wishes of the president. Mondale was viable because he was not visible. And this is what the vice-presidency is all about, as George Bush has discovered.

George Bush's early incumbency witnessed the continuation of at least the symbolic change brought by the Carter-Mondale White House. The vice-president's office remains in the White House, exactly where Mondale's was. And his early assignments—first heading the task force to investigate governmental regulations and later one to deal with the growing tragedy of the Atlanta murders—continued the historical precedent that presidents initially promise an active role for their vice-president and visibly underscore this promise by assignments early in the course of the administration. What follows, of course, is subject to all of the traditional variables. Vice-president Bush's assignment—charge of the administration's "crisis management" team—although of considerable importance may be viewed in retrospect as one of the steps to curtail the personal ambitions of Secretary of State Alexander M. Haig, Jr.

Vice-President Bush quickly discerned the essence of the second office and has served accordingly. Bush has consistently defended the president and has spoken forcefully in support of administration policies. Candidly referring to his role, Bush has stated, "I have taken a very low profile. Because I think that the way you become an effective vice-president—have something substantive to do—is to have the confidence of the president. And if you are always out there in the newspapers or in some news conference and talking about your close relationship with the president—well, it just won't work." Bush forsees himself as having the same potential room for activity as did Mondale, "if I don't blow it. Because the president is giving me every opportunity."[31] Thus, the essence of the contemporary vice-presidency: subject to the presidential direction, needed and viable, but not too visible.

Notes

1. As quoted by Rowland Evans and Robert D. Novak, *Nixon in the White House* (New York: Random House, 1971), 310.

2. As quoted by Dale Vinyard, *The Presidency* (New York: Scribner's, 1971), 29-30; see also *Time*, November 14, 1969, 19.

3. Joseph Ernest Kallenbach, *The American Chief Executive* (New York: Harper and Row, 1966), 232-3.

4. Speech File 63M143, Box XXII, 1952, The Papers of Alben W. Barkley, University of Kentucky Library, Lexington, Kentucky.

5. Ibid.

6. Kallenbach, 232-3. See also Sidney Hyman, *The American President* (New York: Harper, 1954), 315-16; Michale Dorman, *The Second Man* (New York: Delacorte Press, 1968), 193; Harry S. Truman, *Year of Decisions* (New York: Doubleday, 1955), 196.

7. Vice President Statements, Container 3, Folder 7/10/60, "Meet the Press," The Papers of Lyndon B. Johnson, The Lyndon B. Johnson Library, Austin, Texas. See also "A Conversation with the Vice President," Vice President Statements, Box 43. Interview, ABC News 3/26/63. Lyndon B. Johnson Library, Austin, Texas; Whitney M. Young, Jr., Oral History Interview, Lyndon B. Johnson Library, Austin, Texas, 1-11 for a review of Johnson's views of the historical role of the office.

8. *Economist* 213:1423, December 26, 1964, "Apprentice President."

9. "A Conversation with the Vice President."

10. *Economist* 213:1423, December 26, 1964, "Apprentice President."

11. Ohio State University Speech, Vice President Statements, Container 3. Folder: 9/29/60, Lyndon B. Johnson Papers, Lyndon B. Johnson Library, Austin, Texas. See also *Economist* 213:1423, December 26, 1964, "Apprentice President;" Lyndon B. Johnson, *The Vantage Point* (New York: Holt, Rinehart, Winston, 1971), 2; Kenneth P. O'Donnell, Telephone Interview, Boston, Massachusetts, February 1974.

12. Vice President Statements, "Today" Show, April 20, 1961, Lyndon B. Johnson Papers, Lyndon B. Johnson Library, Austin, Texas.

13. As quoted by Birch Bayh, *One Heartbeat Away* (New York: Bobbs-Merrill, 1968), 87.

14. Albert Eisele, *Almost to the Presidency* (Minnesota: The Piper Company, 1972), 226.

15. President's Press Conference, 5/31/55. Box 10 (SF) Fox, Folder: Vice President. President's Press Conference 5/31/55, Dwight D. Eisenhower Papers, Dwight D. Eisenhower Library. Abilene, Kansas. See also Dorman, 209.

16. Dorman, 209.

17. Joseph Albright, *What Makes Spiro Run* (New York: Dodd, Mead, 1972), 227.

18. Dorman, 224.

19. *U.S. News* 48: 98-106, May 16, 1969, "Nixon's Own Story of Seven Years in the Vice Presidency."

20. Bayh, 87.

21. Ibid.

22. Evans and Novak, 168. This is a view with which Vice-President Agnew concurred; see *U.S. News* 66:32-4 March 17, 1969, "A New Kind of Vice President?"

23. Bayh, 87.

24. *Time*, July 2, 1973, 17.

25. *New York Daily News*, August 3, 1975.

26. *Time*, January 20, 1975.

27. MacNeil/Lehrer Report, "Walter Mondale," February 22, 1977.

28. Ibid.

29. For a fuller discussion of the development of the vice-presidency, see Natoli, Marie D., The Vice Presidency Since World War II," unpublished doctoral dissertation, Tufts University, 1975.

30. Hubert H. Humphrey, Interview, March, 1974.

31. *Christian Science Monitor*, March 3, 1981.

Presidential Policy Relationships I: Press, Polls, and Public Opinion

4

The presidency, of course, does not formulate policy in a vacuum. Presidents are constrained by and forced to work with a host of other actors and forces. In this chapter we will consider the most basic of policy relationships: the presidency and the press and public opinion.

Throughout American history, relationships between presidents and press have been somewhat adversarial—especially in this modern period. But, as all students of the presidency are quick to point out, presidential-press relations are a two-way street, for politically adroit presidents have tried, and many times have succeeded, in manipulating the press to the president's political advantage.

One fact that emerges quite clearly in the post-1960 American political environment is the fickleness of American public opinion. Since 1960, the electorate has evinced wide mood swings, delivering victories of landslide proportion to both liberals and conservatives. So uncertain and unpredictable has the political climate been that a prominent foreign observer—Anthony King—has concluded that current American politics is comprised of "coalitions made of sand." For presidential politics, the manifestation of this volatility has been pronounced shifts in public support for and approval of incumbent presidents, frequently placing presidents in the predicament of what presidential scholar Paul C. Light calls "the no-win" or "winless" presidency. Presidents have enormous difficulty both gauging and pleasing public opinion.

The Presidency and the Press 4.1

George E. Reedy

This article—written by a professional journalist, professor of journalism, and former presidential press secretary—addresses the nuances, give and take, and problems of presidential-press relations.

Of the few social institutions which tend to keep a president in touch with reality, the most effective—and the most resented by the chief beneficiary—is the press. It is the only force to enter the White House from the outside world with a direct impact upon the man in the Oval Room which cannot be softened by intermediary interpreters or deflected by sympathetic attendants.

The Twilight of the Presidency (pp. 99-118) by George E. Reedy, 1970, New York and Cleveland: The World Book Publishing Co. Copyright 1970 by George E. Reedy. Reprinted by permission.

This state of affairs does not arise out of any special integrity on the part of the press which, after all, is an institution manned by human beings subject to the same forces that govern human conduct generally. Neither does it spring from any unusual defenses or counterforces working against manipulation on the part of the president. It is simply a matter of the press function, which is to inform the public of the president's actions. No matter how sympathetically that function is performed, a foolish act will appear foolish, an unpopular act will arouse antagonism, and an act in conflict with previous actions will appear contradictory.

The significant impact of the press upon the president lies not in its critical reflections but in its capacity to tell him what he is doing as seen through other eyes. This is a service which, though little appreciated, is indispensable, as it will rarely, if ever, be performed by any other medium. Virtually all other communications that reach him will be shaped either directly or indirectly by people who wish either to conciliate or antagonize the chief executive. In either case, the contents of the message and the manner in which it is phrased will be governed as much by the sender's judgment of how best to produce a desired effect upon the recipient as by the substantive matters with which the sender deals.

Many newspapers stories and a much higher number of columns are written solely for their impact upon the president. Newspapermen are not exempt from the universal urge to shape history—or even to curry favor with an important element in their livelihood. But the newspaper itself is addressed to the public. If it is to survive, it must, on a daily basis, offer a reasonable presentation of events within certain bounds of accuracy and perspective. It cannot dedicate itself solely to the edification of one man, no matter how important that man may be. And while it can rearrange facts or interpret them in the best or worst possible light, its ability to *change* facts is severely limited as long as any degree of competition remains.

Presidents have considerable leverage with which to manipulate part of the press and all try to do so with varying degrees of success. The principal source of the leverage is the unusual position of the president as one of the very few figures in public life who has in his exclusive possession a type of news virtually indispensable to the social and economic security of any reporter assigned to cover the White House full time. This category of newsworthy material consists of the president himself— his thoughts, his relationship with his friends and employees, his routine habits, his personal likes and dislikes, his intimate moments with his family and his associates. The fact that these things constitute "news" of a front-page variety gives the president a trading power with individual newsmen of such magnitude that it must be seen at close quarters to be credited.

There is no other official of the government who can make a top headline story merely by releasing a routine list of his daily activities. There is no other official of the government who can be certain of universal newspaper play by merely releasing a picture of a quiet dinner with boyhood friends. There is no other official who can attract public attention merely by granting an interview consisting of reflections, no matter how banal or mundane, on social trends in fields where he has no expertise and in which his concepts are totally irrelevant to his function as a public servant.

It is not too hard for any other high official of the government "to make news." But, with the exception of notorious scandal, he can do so only through activities which bear a direct relationship to his official function. A secretary of state can command headlines by denouncing the Soviet Union, but no one really cares about his views on dogs. A secretary of labor can inspire widespread interest by commenting on a nationwide strike, but only in his hometown is any newspaper likely to print a picture of him playing with his grandson. An attorney general will receive respectful attention when he delivers an opinion on crime in the streets, but no reporter will be credited with an exclusive for revealing that he prefers Scotch to bourbon. As the interest of correspondents in government officials extends primarily to their *public* acts, it is not possible for those officials to monopolize the release of their activities. Consequently, the press can approach such officials on the basis of a total independence which cannot be sustained by those who cover the president. It is not at all unusual for newspapers to assign correspondents to cover cabinet agencies who are personally at odds with the heads of the agencies, but any responsible editor will have long second thoughts before assigning to the White House a man or a woman who has personally incurred presidential wrath or even the dislike of secretaries in the press office. Sometimes, long second thoughts will result in the assignment of the offending reporter anyway. But such occasions are rare.

The temptations inherent in this situation to "trade out"—to swap golden nuggets for "good" stories—are so overwhelming that few, if any, presidents of the modern era have been able to resist. It is taken for granted in the Washington press corps that there are certain "favorite" reporters who have "an in with the old man," as it is impossible for this state of affairs to be concealed for any great period of time. The press corps, in the early days of any administration, watches nervously for the first signs of a story that begins "the president is known to feel" or "the president has told close associates." There is a constant jockeying for a position which will permit the correspondent to deliver to his paper a set of exclusive photographs of the president and the First Lady walking in the White House garden (pictures taken by the official White House photographer). And the competition among the television networks for exclusive film reaches heights of savagery.

Any president would be well advised to resist the opportunities that are held forth so temptingly. Many presidents have been so advised. But it is not yet recorded that the advice has been accepted. The rewards of "trading out" are immediate and apparent. The penalties, which follow inexorably, are far down the road—so far down, in fact, that when they are exacted, it is difficult to trace back their origins. Every president who has played favorites has suffered in the long run. It is doubtful whether any of them will ever accept the truth of that statement. To understand it, it is necessary to back up for a moment and analyze the problem of presidential press relations.

A president's press problems are really quite simple. He does not have to make any extraordinary effort to attract attention. All channels of public communication are open to him any hour of the day or night. Every word that he utters will, sooner or later, find its way into print. If he does not like the paraphrases used by writing reporters, he can always take to the airwaves and the electronic media will deliver his exact language, with his own intonations, into every American home. He can keep newspapermen at his side twenty-four hours a day, if he so chooses, and he can depend upon their listening to his every argument. There is no other human being on the face of the globe who has any comparable facilities for projecting every thought, every nuance, that is in his mind.

Theodore Roosevelt considered the White House "a bully pulpit" and more than fifty years later an assistant wrote the phrase into a speech by Lyndon B. Johnson. It is likely that, left to his own devices, Johnson would have thought in terms of a magnificent stage—and the transition from pulpit to stage is one of the more significant trends in modern history.

A pulpit is a platform for persuasion and exhortation. A stage is a setting for a presentation which may or may not carry a message. It can be an instrument for education and leadership or an attention-getting device for entertainment.

As a stage, the White House has no equal in the electronic age. It is equipped with props that cannot be matched by Hollywood, Broadway, and Madison Avenue combined. It is staffed by technicians capable of solving the most difficult electronics problems in the wink of an eye. And above all, it has the faculty of commanding the instant and total attention of television networks that dominate the largest audience in all history.

In no other field is the power of a president so immediately apparent as in his relationship with the television networks. His slightest wish is treated as an imperial ukase, and no press secretary ever has to ask for time on the air. He need indicate only that the president will be available.

During the Johnson administration the networks went so far as to staff a highly expensive TV room in the White House with warm cameras manned throughout the working day. This gave the president the potential of appearing live on nationwide networks at a few minutes' notice, and the fact that he used the facility only rarely did not deter television executives from meeting high weekly bills for its operation.

Presented with instrumentalities like this, the average public-relations man planning an industrial or political campaign would, with justification, consider himself in seventh heaven. He would regard as absolutely ludicrous an assertion that he had a "press problem" (although he might be tempted to leave this impression with his client). And he would be absolutely correct. The reality is that a president has no press problems (except for a few minor administrative technicalities), but he does have political problems, all of which are reflected in their most acute form by the press.

Why, then, do presidents spend so much time discussing with their confidants—and sometimes with the public—their "press problems"? Why, then, have the relationships between presidents and the press over the years traveled such a rocky road? The answer involves some complicated and subtle points which no one comprehends completely but which are worthy of study not just in terms of the press but in terms of the presidency itself.

There is a deep-seated human tendency to confuse unhappy news with unhappy events and to assume that if the news can be altered, so can the events. This tendency is particularly accentuated among monarchs. As previously noted Peter the Great strangled the courier who brought him the tidings of the defeat at Narva. John F. Kennedy (or at least someone on his staff) cancelled the White House subscription to the *New York Herald Tribune*. The two acts were closely related and differed only in the degree of retaliation available to the two men.

At stake is a twentieth-century form of the word magic of primitive society. There is a widespread tendency to assume that the qualities that words represent can somehow be transferred to objects, regardless of their content. Thus, the advertising man holds, as an article of faith, that any stale idea will become "exciting" if the word "exciting" is drummed into the human consciousness a sufficient number of times by the electronic media. And similarly, it is assumed that a man somehow becomes "dedicated" and "forward looking" if he can just persuade people to associate the two adjectives with his name in print.

The techniques of word magic are unquestionably successful when they are applied to commodities which are necessities of life and which do not differ essentially from competing commodities, such as soap. Whether they apply in a more sophisticated environment is questionable. And whether they can override objective facts is something that has yet to be demonstrated. A president deals in objective facts. If the nation is at war, he must draft young men to risk their lives in battle. If the nation embarks on great projects, he must tax the people in order to finance the federal activities. When he makes the promises that all political leaders make in moments of euphoria, he arouses expectations that will not be quieted except through fulfillment.

It is only in George Orwell's world that war can be labeled peace; brutality labeled justice; economic misery labeled prosperity. Within the White House itself, of course, it is possible to apply much of the Orwellian formula with a high degree of success. No assistant or secretary has ever yet won an argument with a president—and very few have tried. It is entirely possible within the walls of 1600 Pennsylvania Avenue to create a universe that is utterly to the liking of the principal occupant. He will not go so far as to alter all facts. But he can be certain that the facts will be brought to him in the most sympathetic of forms and with the harshest blows softened. Within this atmosphere, the only grating note comes from the newspapers and the electronic media which are produced on the outside and which are not subject to rewriting. The *Congressional Record* and the White House record can be "corrected"—but not, at least at present, the record of the Fourth Estate.

Unfortunately for the mental peace of presidents, events cannot be altered significantly by control over the printed word—at least not for any extended period of time. While the White House does not have at its command instrumentalities for manipulating the press, they are effective only in regard to adjectives, not to the hard, substantive news that is the ultimate shaper of public opinion. Furthermore, the more successful the manipulation, the less useful becomes that part of the press which has been manipulated.

This situation arises out of the principal communications problem that faces every president—maintaining believability. The very factors that give the chief executive his tremendous advantage in the field of public relations also give him his greatest problem. It is simply that he is covered around the clock, with every word taken down and filed somewhere. Consequently, he is under the compulsion—if he is to be believed—of making his actions fit his words. Both his words and his actions make an extremely deep impression. He can lose the confidence of the people very quickly when the two do not coincide.

In this respect, a president is subjected to rules and to tests which do not apply to other types of political leaders. A senator can announce his ringing support of law and order in the streets of our cities without any fear of embarrassment over the future trend of crime statistics. But a president who makes the same statement must follow it up with action against muggers, thieves, and rapists and if the crime statistics do not go down, he is in trouble. A governor of a state can take a firm stand on cleaning up air pollution, and if the atmosphere remains foul he can explain to his constituents that the cause is the noisome discharge of sulphur-laden smoke from across the state line and there is nothing he can do about it. But a president who assumes a similar stance can never convince the American people that the problem is beyond his control.

In assessing a president, there is a deeply ingrained public assumption that his choices are determined by what he wants to do and what he does not want to do and he is, quite rightly, not accorded the benefit of the doubt when reality fails to measure up to his predictions. This is a very harsh test indeed, but there is a simple answer—presidents need not open their mouths until they have thought their way through the problem and devised workable solutions for which they need not apologize. It would be a great day for the country if this were to become the rule, but that is one day which will never arrive.

Idle words are a luxury in which no president can indulge. Of course, every presidential inauguration has been preceded by a campaign in which the promises are, at the very least, extravagant. Fortunately, the beginning of a term is marked by a public willingness to give the new president every opportunity, and if he uses this "honeymoon period" to establish his credibility, he can look forward to a relatively secure eight-year tenure in office.

The classic story of the gap between promise and performance goes back to the political grand master Franklin D. Roosevelt. In the 1932 campaign he promised the American people that he would cut governmental spending and balance the budget—a foolish promise which was forgotten almost immediately after the New Dealers entered Washington, frantic in their desire to deliver some relief to the depression-stricken populace. A torrent of spending measures spewed out of the Capitol in the famous "100 Days" of FDR. Republicans, as soon as they recovered from their shock over the magnitude of their defeat, launched a campaign to remind Mr. Roosevelt publicly of his promises to cut spending. The principal promise had been made in a speech in Pittsburgh, and after a few days of particularly vehement GOP attack, Mr. Roosevelt called in his adviser Judge Samuel Rosenman and asked him to study the speech and produce an explanation. Mr. Rosenman returned in a matter of hours and said: "Mr. President, there is only one way to explain this speech. Deny that you ever made it!"

Fortunately, Mr. Roosevelt was still in the "honeymoon" period and the problems confronting the American people were so great that no one really cared about budget cutting. He was never again, however, granted such leeway and he quickly learned to match words with action and to forgo statements, or at least make them so fuzzy that they were incomprehensible, when he clearly lacked the resources to back his promises. As has been stated many times in this book, Mr. Roosevelt was a remarkable man who learned even from his own mistakes. This is one trait that few of his predecessors or his successors emulated.

Furthermore, the influence of a president is so great that people very soon identify those who are known as his "spokesmen." He eventually finds thoughts and programs attributed to him solely because they appeared in the columns of "pet" newspapermen. When those newspapermen move to his defense in print, their explanations of his actions are suspect and discounted in the opinion of presidential observers.

It is actually dangerous for a newspaperman to have a close personal friendship with a political leader. Such unfortunates find themselves identified as "sycophants" regardless of how scrupulous they are in handling their contacts. One of the outstanding examples is the columnist William S. White, a man of massive integrity, whose fortunes declined under the Lyndon Johnson administration simply because of a friendship with the president which dated back more than thirty-five years. White, whose politics were far more conservative than those of the president, found that he could not write as forcefully as he wished on many subjects without embarrassing the White House because his words were interpreted as emanating from the Oval Room. His circulation actually picked up when Johnson left the White House because people started to read him for what *he* was saying rather than for what they thought the *president* was saying, and he had a natural audience for his point of view.

Even more important is the fact that since manipulation of the press involves favoritism to some newsmen it inevitably creates antagonism among others. There is an old political rule which is generally stated: "Every time a man does a favor he makes nineteen enemies and one ingrate." Obviously, favors cannot be done for every member of the press or they would become meaningless. For every newspaperman who is placed in an advantageous position, several others must be placed in a disadvantageous position. Every president who plays the game inevitably winds up with more enemies than friends.

Basically, however, the long-standing antagonism between presidents and the press has deeper roots than the childish games that the White House usually plays with the Washington press corps. It is more validly traced to the fundamental dichotomy of interest that exists between newspapermen and politicians. No amount of manipulation can ever produce newspapers that are satisfactory to political leaders, or politicians who are satisfactory to newspapermen (unless George Orwell's nightmare, in which politicians had the capacity not only to produce newspapers but to rewrite the newspapers of the past, comes to fruition). A few words are necessary on this point.

Politicians, as a class, are dedicated to changing the world. With very few exceptions, they have in their minds some bright and shining ideal which is so obviously superior to what exists that it seems to be reality, with the actual world around them merely some kind of an aberration. Newspapermen, on the other hand, are held, to some degree, to the facts. They can play with adjectives; they can arrange the facts in any order that suits their convenience; they can give their prejudices full sway. But it is still their principal mission to present the world as it is. The two points of view are fundamentally incompatible.

Since the politician is oriented toward changing the world, he is constantly in a search for help. He divides the people with whom he must deal into friend or foe—those who have a "constructive" attitude and those who are purely "aginners." To have any force and effect as a political leader, he must be a partisan. And no partisan ever seized and maintained a position of power on the basis of self-examination and inner doubts. An Adlai Stevenson could arouse the respect and admiration of millions of people, but, like Hamlet who never became king, he never became president and it is doubtful that there is any conceivable set of circumstances under which he would ever have achieved the prize.

It is an article of faith with most politicians that any newspaper item even remotely touching upon the government was written through partisan inspiration, not just because it happened. The concept that there are professional standards which determine news leads and news placement is alien to their view of society.

In justice, it must be recognized that a large proportion of political stories originate with a choice morsel leaked to the press for a partisan purpose. The Washington reporter who does not play Democrats off against Republicans and vice versa is simply ignoring a fundamental tool of his trade and is not destined for success. An occasional plug in return for a hot item is considered within the bounds of ethical conduct.

But the politician's view of the press is not limited to recognition of this obvious aspect of the game. He refuses to concede that there are events which will find their way into newspapers without any partisan help whatsoever. Moreover, he is incapable of crediting newsmen with the ability to make simple deductions unassisted by people with an ax to grind.

An illustrative incident which stays vividly in my mind took place in the late 1940s when I was a reporter for the United Press. The Democrats had just recaptured Congress after two years of Republican domination and the interregnum had produced some interesting shifts in the Democratic hierarchy. Among other things, the inexorable workings of the seniority system had placed Representative William L. Dawson of Illinois in the top spot on the House Executive Expenditures Committee. Since Mr. Dawson was the first Negro to be in this position since Reconstruction, this was news by any standard, particularly as the committee had broad investigative powers. Furthermore, there were a number of Southern members in the group.

A poll of the committee was practically a reflex action. My first call was to a Southern congressman. My question was simply whether there would be any trouble. The response was a snarl: "When did [some name unknown to me] reach you?" I was completely taken aback—even more so when I discovered that the congressman, with whom I had reasonably cordial relations, was referring to a smalltown lawyer who was building an opposition political machine in his district. He accepted my statement that I had never heard of his foe but remained unshaken in his conviction that someone had "told" me there would be trouble or I would not have phoned him. His conviction was reinforced later in the day when he was called with the identical query by members of other wire services and newspapers. This, to him, was proof of conspiracy, not simply evidence that professional newsmen were reacting to a professional standard of judgment. (It should be added that the committee poll disclosed no opposition to Mr. Dawson and the stories that were written merely stated that he would become chairman.)

There are very few politicians who do not cherish privately the notion that there should be some regulation of the news. To most of them, "freedom of the press" is a gigantic put-on, a clever ploy which has enabled publishers as an economic group in our society to conduct themselves with a degree of arrogance and disregard of the public interest that is denied to other groups. The "ploy" has succeeded to an extent where it cannot be challenged publicly and therefore must be accorded formal deference. But the deference is purely formal and rarely expressed with heartfelt enthusiasm.

If censorship ever comes to the United States, it will explode out of the frustrations of a political leader convinced that the public good is being thwarted by self-serving reporters distorting the news. It will be the culmination of the natural political instinct to extend to the press the same standards he applies to the rest of society—does this help or hurt a worthy cause? The crusader is much more likely to sound the death knell of free expression than the cynic.

The great game of politics is a highly personal pursuit in which official activity and social amenities are inextricably intermingled. A politician really does not expect a fellow human being to sell his soul for a handshake or a free barbecue. But he is always hurt and bewildered when the recipient of the shake or the beef responds in a mood that he interprets as antagonistic. This attitude is extended not only to other politicians but to businessmen, professionals, clergymen, and the press. It is impossible for newspapermen—even those who are psychologically disposed to walk in the footsteps of the world's oldest profession—to respond on every occasion with what the political leader regards as an appropriately grateful reciprocity. Therefore, in the politician's mind newspapermen are invariably guilty of "ingratitude." Furthermore, politicians look to members of the press to be "constructive," to help them put across worthwhile programs for the betterment of humanity. It should be added, in all justice, that this is strikingly similar to the attitude of civic leaders, who always begin any crusade for municipal betterment by calling upon the editor of the local newspaper and asking him to "get behind" it.

The concept of a "constructive reporter" is a contradiction in terms. A newspaperman who selects his stories on the basis of "the national interest" is actually doing the national interest a disservice. He has no business making such decisions. The closest he can come to it and still remain true to his trade is to report what others conceive to be "in the national interest." This is a point which no successful politician can grasp.

Frequently, newspapers themselves fail to grasp the point. The classic case is the downplaying by the *New York Times* of the projected invasion of the Bay of Pigs in Cuba. Here was an instance where those who decided to temper the news were thoroughly convinced that they were acting "in the national interest" because if they featured the story, the invasion would have been called off. They did not feature the story, the invasion did take place, the result was a debacle because of inadequate planning, and American prestige dipped to a new low.

This, of course, will not serve in the slightest to convince political leaders of the future that newspapers should place reporting of the news ahead of what they consider to be "the national interest." It is impossible for them to think otherwise. The political leader who rises to the top moves through a world which is sharply delineated between those who are helping him; those who are opposing him; and those who are uncommitted but can be swung in any direction. His success has been based upon the manipulation of these three groups to achieve what he regards as fulfillment of the national interest—and such manipulation is, in most instances, entirely legitimate. The whole political process would break down and democratic government would be impossible without the existence of men skilled in this art. To persuade them that the press should be an exception would be pushing their credulity beyond human limits.

Furthermore, the politician is a human being subject to the normal tendency to overgeneralize from his own experiences. He knows that some members of the press can be manipulated. Therefore, he assumes that those who resist his blandishments have simply been reached first by a competitor. He is consciously encouraged in this belief by the newspapermen who "play ball" with him.

The importance of a "source" can be measured not only by its news value but by the degree of its exclusivity. To maintain his position in his industry, a reporter must display professional competence in judging and presenting the news. But to advance, he must also demonstrate a capacity to obtain information unavailable to others—or at least available only on a restricted or delayed basis. There are both positive and negative paths that can be followed in achieving this capacity, and the artful journalist is capable of following both courses.

The positive path is to persuade important newsmakers that they can have confidence in the manner in which the reporter will handle a story. The newsman presents himself as one who will not divulge off-the-record material; who will not embarrass his informant by identifying his source; who will not twist the facts to present an event in an unfavorable light. This approach is vital to a successful reporting career and is not to be disdained.

The negative path is consciously to feed the paranoia that characterizes virtually every politician to some degree. A few words of sympathy over the unfair treatment by the "Eastern press" (or the liberal press or the conservative press) is an effective method of slamming doors against competitors. An important leader who can be persuaded that his journalistic "friend" is the lone holdout against a "press conspiracy" can serve as a meal ticket for many years.

Since the press as a whole cannot be "won over" by tactics which political leaders regard as legitimate, it is inevitable that newspapermen eventually become the "enemy." In addition, they also become the personification of all the frustrating forces that make the life of a president so difficult. Therefore, over a period of time, it is certain that the political leader will vent his spleen against the press, never realizing that what he is really doing is venting his spleen against the whole intractable environment that surrounds him. It is a very easy matter to find legitimate grounds for criticizing the press. It is a less easy matter to realize that all these grounds apply to the world generally.

Every president has his collection of inaccuracies in press coverage and is willing to regale his listeners by recounting them for hours. Seen in perspective, these inaccuracies are usually trivial and reflect merely the fact that reporters are human beings who are bound to make errors under the constant pressure of reporting world-shaking events almost as soon as they happen. An objective evaluation would be that the degree of accuracy with which the news is reported is astounding when it is contrasted with the conditions under which it is gathered. But a politician smarting under the lash of public criticism is not very likely to be objective.

Every president has his horror stories of press arrogance. But press arrogance is merely a reflection of public arrogance. Almost every American feels qualified to give the president advice on the most complicated and subtle questions of economics, law, and international relations. It would be surprising if newspapermen were exempt from this universal temptation.

Every president can recite valid examples of press bias and is entitled legitimately to some sympathy for the manner in which he is treated by opposition newspapers. But the assumption that bias is a journalistic characteristic rather than a condition of humanity is a distorted view of the universe. When a man enters politics, he undertakes to deal with *all* human characteristics and it is not an acceptable alibi to cite some of them as overwhelming. If press bias were an absolute bar to political success, this nation would never have had an Abraham Lincoln, and Franklin D. Roosevelt and Harry S Truman would have been denied second terms.

In reality, the problem of a president in dealing with the press is precisely the same as his problem in dealing with the public at large. But no president can find it within his ego to concede that he has failed in any degree with the public. It is far more satisfying to blame his failures on the press because his problems then can be attributed to a conspiracy. He can blame the "Eastern press," the "Republican press," or the "liberal press." He then does not stand indicted within his own consciousness (the most terrible court of all) as having failed. He was merely the victim of vindictiveness on the part of a selfish group and his failure can be attributed to the meanness of others rather than to his own inadequacies.

In the mythical world of philosopher-kings, the press policies of the White House would be very simple indeed. They would consist solely and simply of according all media equal access to whatever information was available. The philosopher-king would realize that the press is merely a part of the public, even though it is charged with some special functions in the nation's economy. Unfortunately, we do not live in the world of philosopher-kings and it is unlikely that we ever will.

Presidential Popularity from Truman to Johnson   4.2

John E. Mueller

In this piece, Mueller offers an assessment of presidential popularity. His conclusions shed light on some of the constraining influences at work in the modern presidency, especially the inevitable loss of popular support for all recent presidents. In reading this article, students should pay close attention to the empirical nature of the analysis, one of the few such available or feasible with regard to

War, Presidents and Public Opinion by John E. Mueller, 1973, New York: John Wiley & Sons. Copyright 1973 by John E. Mueller. Reprinted by permission.

the presidency. They should also reflect on what these conclusions reveal about the incentive system present in the modern presidency. Should presidents avoid protracted wars? Should they emphasize prosperity and economic health above all else? Are there incentives for short military forays? These are some of the fascinating questions raised by Mueller's research.

I think (my grandchildren) will be proud of two things. What I did for the Negro and seeing it through in Vietnam for all of Asia. The Negro cost me 15 points in the polls and Vietnam cost me 20.

Lyndon B. Johnson[1]

With tenacious regularity since 1945 the Gallup poll has posed to its cross-section samples of the American public the following query: "Do you approve or disapprove of the way (the incumbent) is handling his job as president?" The responses to this curious question form an index known as "presidential popularity." According to Richard Neustadt, the index is "widely taken to approximate reality" in Washington and reports about its behavior are "very widely read" there including, the quotation above would suggest, the highest circles (1960:205n).

Plotted over time as in figure 4.2.1, the index forms probably the longest continuous trend line in polling history. This chapter will analyze the behavior of this line, focusing on the period from the beginning of the Truman administration in 1945 to the end of the Johnson administration in January 1969 during which time the popularity question was asked some three hundred times.[2] Occasional commentary on the popularity of Presidents Roosevelt and Nixon will also be included.

Efforts will be made to associate four variables with a president's popularity. These include a measure of the length of time the incumbent has been in office as well as variables that attempt to estimate the influence on his rating of major international events, economic slump, and war.

To assess the independent impact of each of these variables as they interact in association with presidential popularity, multiple regression analysis is used as the basic analytic technique. Although rather sparingly applied in political science, the approach has a large literature and a long history in other fields, especially economics where it is frequently applied to the analysis of time trends and other phenomena.[3]

1 The Dependent Variable: The Presidential Popularity Question

The presidential popularity question taps a general impression about the way the incumbent seems to be handling his job at the present moment. As Neustadt notes, the response, like the question, is "unfocused," unrelated to specific issues or electoral outcomes (1960:95). The respondent is asked to "approve" or "disapprove" and if he has "no opinion," he must volunteer that response himself. He has infrequently been asked *why* he feels that way—and many respondents when asked are able only vaguely to rationalize their position.[4] And only at times has he been asked to register how strongly he approves or disapproves.

A disapproving response might be considered a nonconstructive vote of no confidence: the respondent registers his discontent, but he does not need to state *whom* he would prefer in the presidency. Thus the index is likely to be a very imperfect indicator of electoral success or failure for a president seeking reelection. While approvers are doubtless more likely than disapprovers to endorse his reelection, on considering the opposition some approvers may be attracted into voting against the incumbent just as some disapprovers may be led grudgingly to vote for him.

There is also a more technical reason why the popularity index has little direct relevance to the electoral result: Gallup does not ask the question during a president's reelection campaign. Thus for the months between early summer and late fall in 1948, 1956, and 1964 no Gallup data on presidential popularity exist.[5]

Whatever peculiarities there are in this question, they are at least constant. Unlike many questions asked by the polling organizations, wording has not varied from time to time by whim or fashion. The stimulus has therefore been essentially fixed; only the response has varied.

And the variation has been considerable. Harry Truman was our most popular president in this period—for a few weeks in 1945 when more than 85 percent of the public expressed their approval—and our least popular—from early 1951 until March 1952 when less than 30 percent were usually found to be favorably inclined. Others presidents have stayed within these limits with Lyndon Johnson most nearly approaching the Truman extremes. President Eisenhower's popularity was never higher than 79 percent, but it never dropped below 49 percent either; the consistently high level of support that he was able to maintain especially throughout his first term is, in comparison with other presidents of the period, quite remarkable and is given special attention in Section 6 below. President Kennedy also maintained a rather high level of popularity but was in noticeable decline at the time of his death.

The proportion of respondents selecting the "no opinion" option (represented as the space between the lines in figure 4.2.1) averaging 14 percent, remained strikingly constant throughout the period.[6] This is a little surprising, since it might be expected that when opinion moves, say, from approval to disapproval of a president, the change would be revealed first in a decrease in the support figure with an increase in the no opinion percentage, followed in a later survey by an increase in the disapproval column with a decrease in the no opinion portion. There are a few occasions in which the no opinion percentage seems to rise and fall in this manner, one occurring in the early weeks of the Korean War, but by and large it seems that, if movements into the no opinion column do occur, they are compensated for by movements out of it.

This means therefore that the trend in approval is largely a mirror image of the trend in disapproval; the correlation between the two for the Truman-Johnson period is −.979. And, most conveniently, this almost means that the president's popularity at a given moment can be rendered by a single number: the percentage approving his handling of the job. The no opinion percentage is almost always close to 14 percent, and the percentage disapproving is, of course, the remainder.

There is, however, one small wrinkle. The no opinion percentage does get a bit out of hand on three highly understandable occasions—the early weeks of the Kennedy, Eisenhower, and Nixon administrations as substantial numbers of respondents felt inclined to withhold judgment of these new men (see figure 4.2.1). This inordinate withholding of opinion declined in the first weeks to more "normal" levels with the result that either *both* the level of approval *and* disapproval tended to increase thus for a while showing a *positive* correlation, or else the approval rating remained constant while the disapproval rating rose.

Since one of the propositions to be tested in this study proposes that there exists a general downward trend in each president's popularity, this initial rating situation causes something of a problem. If the approved score is taken as the dependent variable, there will be a slight bias against this proposition; if the disapproval score is used as the dependent variable, there will be a similar bias in favor of the proposition. It seems preferable to load things against the proposition; hence, for the purposes of this study *the dependent variable is the percentage approving the way the incumbent is handling his job as president.*[7] The average approval rating for the Truman-Johnson period is 58 percent.

The size of the no opinion response at the beginning of the Nixon administration is truly remarkable. Since the man had been prominent on the national political scene for two decades, one might expect the public to feel they knew him pretty well by the time he attained the presidency; yet far more withheld

Figure 4.2.1
Trends in presidential popularity, 1941 to 1971.

The area below the bottom line represents the approving percentage, the area above the top line represents the disapproving percentage, and the white area represents the no opinion percentage.

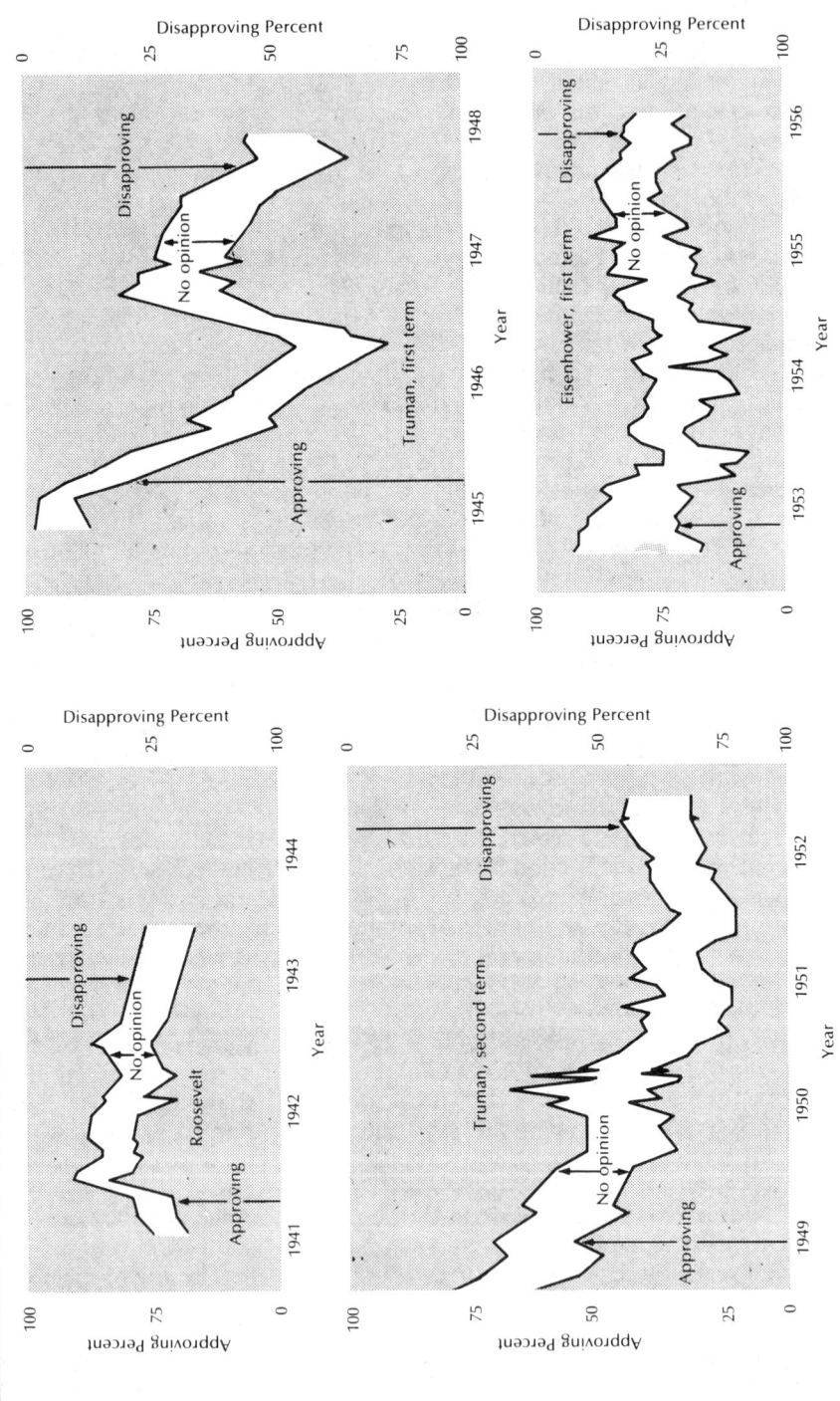

224

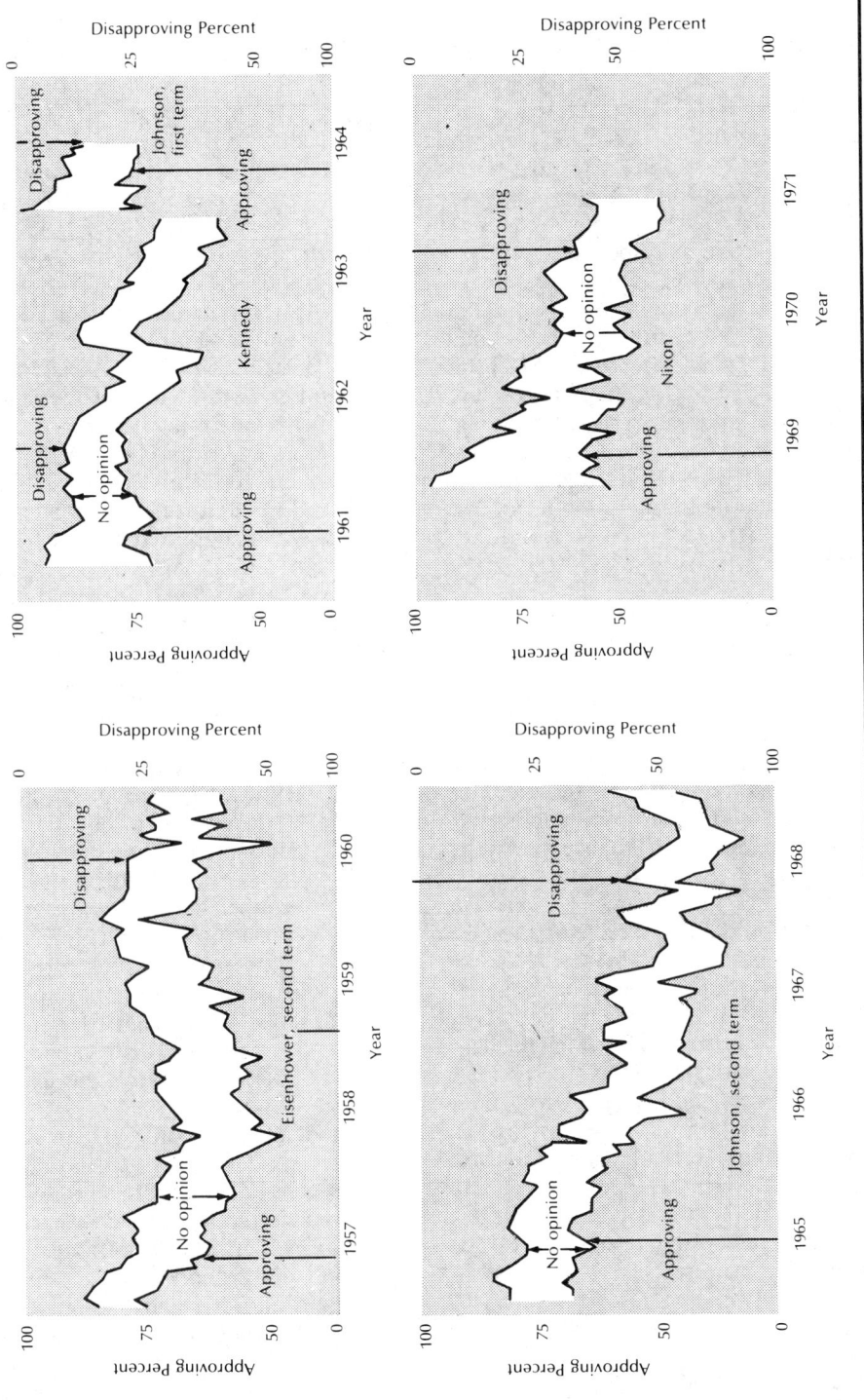

opinion on him than had for any other president, including the political neophyte, Eisenhower. Apparently, familiarity does not necessarily breed understanding.

As shown in figure 4.2.1, initial popularity ratings for other terms do not show the same degree of uncertainty. Presidents Truman and Johnson entered the presidency under highly traumatic circumstances, and the public was strongly inclined to express its confidence in them: the no opinion response is relatively low and disapproval registers at a bare whisper. The other initial ratings are for second terms when, of course, the incumbent would be well known. Presidents Truman and Johnson began their second terms at almost precisely the same level of popularity, although President Johnson had done far better in the preceding reelection contest, suggesting perhaps that Senator Goldwater's candidacy contributed as much to that triumph as did President Johnson's efforts.

2 The Independent Variables

If one stares at presidential popularity trend lines long enough, one begins to imagine one is seeing things. If the things imagined seem also to be mentioned in the literature about the way presidential popularity should or does behave, one begins to take the visions seriously and to move to test them.

In this manner were formulated four basic "independent" variables—predictor variables of presidential popularity. They are (1) a "coalition of minorities" variable that suggests the overall trend in a president's popularity will be downward; (2) a "rally round the flag" variable which anticipates that international crises and similar phenomena will give a president a short-term boost in popularity; (3) an "economic slump" variable that associates recessions with decreased popularity; and (4) a "war" variable that predicts a decrease in popularity under the conditions of the Korean and Vietnam wars.

2.1 The Coalition-of-Minorities Variable

In a somewhat different context Anthony Downs (1957:55-60) has suggested the possibility that an administration, even if it always acts with majority support on each issue, can gradually alienate enough minorities to be defeated. This could occur when the minority on each issue feels so intensely about its loss that it is unable to be placated by administration support on other policies that it favors. A clever opposition, under appropriate circumstances, could therefore form a coalition of these intense minorities until it had enough votes to overthrow the incumbent.

Transposed to presidential popularity, this concept would predict that a president's popularity would show an overall downward trend as he is forced on a variety of issues to act and thus to create intense, unforgiving opponents of former supporters. It is quite easy to point to cases where this may have occurred. President Kennedy's rather dramatic efforts to force back a steel price rise in 1962, while supported by most Americans, tended to alienate many in the business community (see Erskine 1964:341 and 338). Administration enforcement of the Supreme Court's original school desegregation order tended to create intense opposition among white Southerners even though the presidential moves had passive majority support in most of the country (Fenton 1960:146).

Realistically, the concept can be extended somewhat. From time to time there arise bitter dilemmas in which the president must act and in which he will tend to alienate *both* sides no matter what he does, a phenomenon related to what Aaron Wildavsky (1968) has called a "minus sum" game. President Truman's seizure of the steel mills in 1952 made neither labor nor management (nor the Supreme Court, for that matter) happy. For the mayor of New York, situations like this seem to arise weekly.

There are other, only vaguely related, reasons to expect an overall decline in popularity. One would be disillusionment. In the process of being elected, the president invariably says or implies that he will do more than he can do, and disaffection of once bemused supporters is all but inevitable. A most notable example would be the case of those who supported President Johnson in 1964 because he seemed opposed to escalation in Vietnam. Furthermore initial popularity ratings are puffed up by a variety of weak followers. These might include leering opposition partisans looking for the first excuse to join the aggrieved, excitable types who soon become bored by the humdrum of postelection existence, and bandwagon riders whose fair weather support dissolves with the first sprinkle.[8] As Burns Roper (1969) notes, "In a sense, presidential elections are quadrennial myth builders which every four years make voters believe some man is better than he is. The president takes office with most of the nation on his side, but this artificial 'unity' soon begins to evaporate."

For these reasons the coalition-of-minorities variable, as it is dubbed here, predicts decline. "Love," said Machiavelli, "is held by a chain of obligation which, men being selfish, is broken whenever it serves their purpose."[9]

The variable itself is measured simply by the length of time, in years, since the incumbent was inaugurated (for first terms) or reelected (for second terms). It varies then from zero to about four and should be negatively correlated with popularity: the longer the man has been in office, the lower his popularity. It is. The simple correlation for the Truman-Johnson period is $-.48$. The decline is assumed to start over again for second terms because the president is expected to have spent the campaign rebuilding his popular coalition by soothing the disaffected, redeluding the disillusioned, and putting on a show for the bored. If he is unable to do this, he will not be reelected, something which has not happened in the postwar era, although twice presidents have declined to make the effort.

Actually, what one would expect then is a decline until the reelection campaign period when popularity should rise again.[10] As noted in Section 1, however, Gallup does not ask his question during reelection periods, so the upturn effect cannot be assessed.

The analysis will assume a *linear* decline in popularity. That is, a president's popularity is assumed to decline at an even rate for all four years of his term: if a decline of 6 percentage points per year is indicated, he will be down 6 points at the end of his first year, 12 at the end of the second, 18 at the end of the third, and 24 after four years.

There is nothing, however, in the justification for the coalition-of-minorities variable which demands that the decline must occur with such tedious regularity. At least two variants of this basic theme are entirely sensible. One, which might be called the "honeymoon" variant, would argue that the decline would be *exponential*—slow in the first year as the public gives the president a chance to show his true colors and then faster in each successive year as greater and greater portions of the public decide that they prefer different shades. If the decline is a squared function, for example, a president who lost 2 percentage points in the first year (and most of that would occur toward the end of the year), would lose 6 points more in the second year, 10 in the third, and 14 in the fourth.

The second variant would employ a *logarithmic* transformation and would postulate a slowing rate of decline as was found to be the case for war support in chapter 3. Thus in one version using natural logarithms, a president who lost 6 percentage points between his first and third months in office would take until his seventh month to lose another 6, until the end of his second year to lose another 6, and at least until the end of his term to lose another 6.

Intuitively the justification for the coalitions-of-minorities variable would tend to find the logarithmic variant more palatable than the honeymoon variant. Initial popularity ratings, it was noted, are undoubtedly inflated with many very weak supporters who are easily and very quickly turned off. After their conversion to the disaffected camp the president is left with relatively hard core supporters whom he will find more difficult to alienate. Thus decline might be expected to occur disproportionally in the early part of his term.

Happily for intuition, if not necessarily for truth and wisdom, the honeymoon variant does rather poorly when tested: the regression fit is worse, and the behavior of the predictor variables becomes more incoherent. While the logarithmic variant sometimes shows some improvement over the linear version, the improvement is usually quite minor, hence the rather general reliance here on the linear version which has the advantage of simplicity and ease of communication.

2.2 The Rally-Round-the-Flag Variable

This variable seeks to bring into the analysis a phenomenon often noted by students of the presidency and of public opinion: certain intense international events generate a rally-round-the-flag effect which tends to give a boost to the president's popularity rating. As Kenneth Waltz (1967:272) has observed, "In the face of such an event, the people rally behind their chief executive." Tom Wicker (1967): "Simply being president through a great crisis or a big event . . . draws Americans together in his support." Richard Neustadt (1960:100) notes "the correspondence between popularity and happenings"; Burns Roper (1969) finds "approval has usually risen during international crises"; and Nelson Polsby (1964:25) observes: "invariably, the popular response to a president during international crisis is favorable, regardless of the wisdom of the policies he pursues." A rather clearcut example can be seen in the data in figure 4.2.1 where President Roosevelt's popularity is found to soar after the Japanese attack on Pearl Harbor in late 1941.

The difficulty with this concept is in operationalizing it. There is a terrible temptation to find a bump on a popularity plot and then to scurry to historical records to find an international "rally point" to associate with them. This process all but guarantees that the variable will prove significant.

The strategy adopted here to identify rally points was somewhat different, and hopefully more objective. A definition of what a rally point should look like was created largely on a priori grounds, and then a search of historical records was made to find events that fit the definition. Most of the points so identified *are* associated with bumps on the plot—that, after all, was how the concept was thought of in the first place—but quite a few are not, and the bumps associated with some are considerably more obvious than others.

In general, a rally point must be associated with an event which (1) is international and (2) involves the United States and particularly the president directly; and it must be (3) specific, dramatic, and sharply focused.

It must be international because only developments confronting the nation as a whole are likely to generate a rally-round-the-flag effect. Major domestic events—riots, scandals, strikes—are at least as likely to exacerbate internal divisions as they are to soothe them.

To qualify as a rally point, an international event is required to involve the United States and the president directly because major conflicts between other powers are likely to engender split loyalties and are less likely to seem relevant to the average American.

Finally, the event must be specific, dramatic, and sharply focused to assure public attention and interest. As part of this, important events that transpire gradually, no matter how important, are excluded from consideration because their impact on public attitudes is likely to be diffused. Thus sudden changes in the bombing levels in Vietnam are expected to create a reaction, but the gradual increase of American troops is not.

Errors in this process could occur by including events whose importance is only obvious in retrospect or by ignoring events like the Geneva summit of 1955 that may seem minor in historical perspective but were held significant at the time. For this reason more reliance has been put on indexes of newspaper content than on broad, historical accounts of the period.[11] In general, if there has been a bias in selecting rally points, it has been in the direction of excluding borderline cases. This was done in profound respect for the extent of the lack of public interest and knowledge on most items of international affairs. For example, the 1954 crisis over Quemoy and Matsu, seen by some to have had relevance to presidential popularity, is excluded partly because fully 45 percent of the population stated after the event that it had neither heard nor read anything about the islands.[12]

At that, some 34 rally points for the Truman-Johnson period were designated. They are listed in table 4.2.1. In general, they can be said to fall into six categories. First, there are the four instances of sudden American military intervention: Korea, Lebanon, the Bay of Pigs, and the Dominican Republic. A second closely related category encompasses major military developments in ongoing wars: in Korea, the Inchon landing and the Chinese intervention; in Vietnam, the Tonkin Bay episode, the beginning of the bombing of North

Vietnam, the major extension of this bombing, and the Tet offensive. Third are the major diplomatic developments of the period: crises over Cuban missiles, the U-2 and atomic testing, the enunciation of the "Truman doctrine" with its offer of aid to Greece and Turkey, the beginning of and major changes in the peace talks in Korea and Vietnam, and the several crises in Berlin. Fourth are the two dramatic technological developments: Sputnik and the

Table 4.2.1

Rally Points for the Truman-Johnson Period

April	1945	Death of FDR, Truman takes office
August	1945	Potsdam Conference, Japan surrenders
March	1947	Truman Doctrine announced
Spring-Summer	1948	Beginning of Berlin blockade (reelection campaign, no polls)
November	1948	Truman reelection
September	1949	Truman announces Soviet A-bomb test
June	1950	Korean invasion
September	1950	Inchon landing
November	1950	China enters Korean War
July	1951	Korean peace negotiations begin
January	1953	Eisenhower inauguration
July	1953	Final resumption of Korean talks, truce signed
July	1955	Geneva conference of the Big Four
November	1956	Eisenhower reelected
October	1957	Sputnik I launched
July	1958	United States troops sent to Lebanon
September	1959	Talks with Khrushchev at Camp David
May	1960	U-2 incident, Paris summit
January	1961	Kennedy inauguration
April	1961	Bay of Pigs invasion
June	1961	Vienna meeting with Khrushchev
August	1961	Berlin wall erected, USSR resumes testing
October	1961	Berlin crisis, tank confrontation
October	1962	Cuban missile crisis
November	1963	Kennedy assassination, Johnson takes office
August	1964	Bay of Tonkin episode (reelection campaign, no polls)
November	1964	Johnson reelected
February	1965	Retaliatory bombing of North Vietnam begun
April	1965	United States troops sent to Dominican Republic
June	1966	Extension of bombing to north of Hanoi (oil dumps)
June	1967	Glassboro summit
January	1968	Tet offensive
April	1968	North Vietnam agrees to beginning of Vietnam talks after partial bombing halt
October	1968	Full bomb halt, talks to get substantive

announcement of the first Soviet atomic test. The fifth category includes the meetings between the president and the head of the Soviet Union at Potsdam in 1945, Geneva in 1955, Camp David in 1959, Paris in 1960, Vienna in 1961, and Glassboro in 1967. Although these events are rarely spectacular they, like crises, do generate a let's-get-behind-the-president effect. Because they are far less dramatic—even if sometimes more important—presidential conferences with other powers (for example, the British at Nassau) are excluded as are meetings with the Soviet Union at the foreign minister level.

Sixth and finally, as an analytic convenience the start of each presidential term is rather arbitrarily designated as a rally point. Presidents Truman and Johnson came in under circumstances that can justifiably be classified under the rally-round-the-flag rubric, although the crisis was a domestic one. The other points all involve elections or reelections that, perhaps, might also be viewed as a somewhat unifying and cathartic experience.

These, then, are the events chosen to be associated with the rally-round-the-flag variable. No listing will satisfy everyone's perspective about what has or has not been important to Americans in this twenty-four-year period. However, in the analysis the variable has proved to be a rather hardy one. Experimentation with it suggests that the addition or subtraction of a few rally points is likely to make little difference.

The rally-round-the-flag variable is measured by the length of time, in years, since the last rally point. It varies then from zero to a theoretical maximum of about four or an empirical one of 1.9. Like the coalition-of-minorities variable, it should be negatively correlated with popularity: the longer it has been since the last rally-round-the-flag event, the lower the popularity of the incumbent. It is. The simple correlation for the Truman-Johnson period was $-.16$. Some experiments with curvilinear transformations of the variable were attempted but, since improvement was marginal at best, the variable has been left in linear form.

Each rally point is given the same weighting in the analysis. One effort to soften this rather crude policy was made. The rally points were separated into two groups: "good" rally points (for example, the Cuban missile crisis) in which the lasting effect on opinion was likely to be favorable to the president, and "bad" ones (for example the U-2 crisis, the Bay of Pigs) in which the initial favorable surge could be expected to be rather transitory. Two separate rally-round-the-flag variables were then created with the anticipation that they would generate somewhat different regression coefficients. The differences however were small and inconsistent. The public seems to react to "good" and "bad" international events in about the same way. Thus, to this limited extent, the equal weighting of rally points seems justified.

Writing shortly after the Glasssboro summit, Tom Wicker (1967) observed, "the reality behind Johnson's improved position in the polls is that his latest short-term gain is no more likely to reverse the long-term trend than any of the others did." This expresses quite well for a specific case the relationship between the coalition-of-minorities variable and the rally-round-the-flag variable assumed to be general in this study. In tandem the concepts underlying these variables predict that the president's popularity will continually decline over time and that international crises and similar events will explain short-term bumps and wiggles in this otherwise inexorable descent.[13]

2.3 The Economic-Slump Variable

There is a goodly amount of evidence, and an ever goodlier amount of speculation, suggesting a relationship between economic conditions and electoral behavior.[14] The extension of such thinking to presidential popularity is both natural and precedented. Neustadt, for example, concludes that the recession in 1958 caused a drop in President Eisenhower's popularity.[15]

The economic indicator used here will be the unemployment rate. This statistic recommends itself because it is available for the entire period and is reported on a monthly basis.[16] It is used as a general indicator of economic health or malaise and is not taken simply as a comment about the unemployed. Presumably the unemployed—especially the newly unemployed—are likely to be inclined toward disapproval of the president who presides over their unhappy state but, with a maximum unemployment rate of 7 or 8 percent during the period, there simply are too few unemployed greatly to affect the president's rating; furthermore, public opinion polls tend to underrepresent somewhat the poor and the unemployed, since people in those categories are harder to find and are more likely to be uncooperative respondents.

In dealing with the relation between unemployment and popularity, one is immediately presented with a grossly unpleasant fact: there is a positive correlation—+.39 to be exact—between the two. That is, the higher the unemployment rate, the higher the popularity.

Fortunately the variable can be made to suggest sensible results, but only after it has been modified a bit. Three alterations are required.

First, notice that unemployment reached some of its highest points during the recessions under the Eisenhower administration. The problem here, to be examined more fully in Section 6 below, is that Eisenhower was a *generally* popular president. Thus even though his popularity seemed to dip during the recessions—the correlation between unemployment and popularity during the Eisenhower years was a reassuring −.68—high unemployment comes to be associated with a relatively popular president. This problem can be handled rather easily within regression analysis by assigning to each of the presidential administrations a "dummy" or "binary" variable, the care and feeding of which will be discussed more fully in Section 3 below (Suits 1957; Draper and Smith 1966:134-41).

Second, observe that if the simple unemployment rate is used, a gross injustice is done to President Kennedy. Specifically, unemployment was very high at his inauguration; but to expect the public to blame *him* for the high rate at that point is absurd, since he won the election in 1960 in part because of discontent over the economic policies of the Republicans. Therefore, a more sensible approach is to assume that the individual respondent, in allowing economic perceptions to influence his approval or disapproval of the president, essentially does so by comparing how things are *now* with how they were when the incumbent began his present term of office. If conditions are worse, he is inclined to disapprove the president's handling of his job, if things are better, he is inclined to approve.

The economic variable, therefore, becomes the unemployment rate at the time the incumbent's term began subtracted from the rate at the time of the poll.[17] It is positive when things are worse and negative when things are better and should be negatively correlated with popularity.

But it isn't. Both the correlation coefficient and the regression coefficient, even when the effects of the other variables are taken into account, remain positive. This seems to be largely because *both* unemployment and the popularity of the incumbent president were in general decline between 1961 and 1968. The correlation for the period is .77.

Therefore, the third alteration administered to the economic variable was to set it equal to zero whenever the unemployment rate was lower at the time of the survey than it had been at the start of the incumbent's present term. The first two alterations merely took account of certain peculiarities in conception in the data, but this one is substantive and is executed as the only way the data can be made to come out "right." In essence, it suggests that *an economy in slump harms a president's popularity, but an economy that is improving does not seem to help his rating*. Bust is bad for him but boom is not particularly good. There is punishment but never reward.

Perhaps this can be seen in a comparison of the 1960 and the 1968 campaigns. In 1960, as Harvey Segal (1968) notes, "What was important was the vague but pervasive feeling of dissatisfaction with the performance of the economy, the pain that made the public receptive to JFK's appeals." In 1968, representing administrations that had presided over an unprecedented period of boom, Vice-President Humphrey seemed never able to turn this fact to his advantage.

It is important to notice that in practice this variable, which will be called the "economic slump" variable because of its inability to credit boom, takes on a nonzero value only during the Eisenhower administration and during the unemployment rise of 1949 to 1950. In symbolic form the variable's peculiarities can be expressed in the following (the units are the percentage of unemployed).

$$E = U_t - U_{t_0} \quad \text{if} \quad U_t - U_{t_0} > 0$$
$$= 0 \quad \text{if} \quad U_t - U_{t_0} \leq 0$$

where U_t = unemployment rate at the time of the survey
and U_{t_0} = unemployment rate at the beginning of the incumbent's present term.

2.4 The War Variable

It is widely held that the unpopular, puzzling, indecisive wars in Korea and Vietnam severely hurt the popularity of Presidents Truman and Johnson (Waltz 1967:273 ff, 288; Neustadt 1960:97-99; Wicker 1967; B. Roper 1969). As stated in the quotation that heads this chapter, President Johnson himself apportioned 20 percentage points of his drop in popularity to the Vietnam War.

This notion seems highly plausible. The popularity of Presidents Truman and Johnson was in steady decline as the wars progressed, with record lows occurring during each president's last year in office at points when the wars seemed most hopeless and meaningless. The wars unquestionably contributed in a major way to their decisions not to seek third terms and then, when they had stepped aside, the wars proved to be major liabilities for their party's candidates in the next elections (Campbell et al. 1960:50-51). Overall, the correlation between presidential popularity and the presence of war is $-.67$.

There are problems with this analysis, however. The coalition-of-minorities concept argues that decline is a natural phenomenon and, indeed, a glance at the plot of presidential popularity clearly shows Truman and Johnson in decline *before* the wars started. Furthermore, both men experienced noticeable decline (in Johnson's case, only in the disapproval rating) during their *first* terms when they had no war to contend with. The real question is then: Did the war somehow add to the decline of popularity beyond that which might be expected to occur on other grounds?

An answer can be approached through multiple regression analysis, although there are some special problems. After allowing for a general pattern of decline under the coalition-of-minorities variable, the additional impact of a variable chosen to represent war can be assessed. It is also possible in this manner to compare the two wars to see if their association with presidential popularity differed.

The presence of war is incorporated in the analysis simply by a dummy variable that takes on a value of one when a war is on and remains zero otherwise. The beginning of the Vietnam War was taken to be June 1965 with the beginnings of the major United States troop involvement. At that point it became an American war for the public; before that, ignorance of the war was considerable: as late as mid-1964 twenty-five percent of the public admitted that it had never heard of the fighting in Vietnam.

Other war measures of a more sophisticated nature were experimented with. They increase in magnitude as the war progresses and thus should be negatively associated with popularity. One of these is the length of time since the war began. Another, closely related, but one that develops at a different pace, is the total American casualties (or the logarithm of this figure) suffered in the war at the time of the survey.

These latter measures, however, are almost identical to the coalition-of-minorities variable for the two relevant presidential terms and, hence, are all but useless in the analysis, since their independent impacts cannot be sorted out. The simple dummy variable suffers this defect in lesser measure (although the correlations still come in at around the .90 level), and thus, despite its crudities, has been used. The multicollinearity problem is discussed more fully in Section 4.

Although the Korean War continued into President Eisenhower's administration, he is not "blamed" for the war in the analysis since, of course, he was elected partly because of discontent over the war. Accordingly, the war variable is set at zero for this period.

2.5 Other Variables

The analysis of presidential popularity will apply in various permutations only the four variables discussed above—a rather austere representation of a presumably complex process. As will be seen, it is quite possible to get a sound fit with these four variables, but at various stages in the investigation—which involved the examination of hundreds of regression equations—a search was made for other variables that could profitably be added to the predictor set.

International developments are reasonably well incorporated into the analysis with a specific variable included for war and another for major crisislike activities. Domestically, however, there is only the half-time variable for economic slump and the important but very inspecific coalition-of-minorities variable.

Accordingly, it would be valuable to generate some sort of domestic equivalent to the rally-round-the-flag variable to assess more precisely how major domestic events affect presidential popularity. Operationally, however, this is a difficult task. First, while it is a justifiable assertion that international crises will redound in the short term to a president's benefit, it is by no means clear how a domestic crisis, whether riot, strike, or scandal, should affect his popularity. Furthermore major domestic concerns vary quite widely not only in intensity and duration but also in nature over time. Labor relations, which rarely made big news in the mid-1960s, were of profound concern in the middle and late 1940s as a multitude of major strikes threatened to cripple the nation and the adventures of John L. Lewis and the Taft-Hartley bill dominated the headlines. In the 1950s, however, labor broke into the news only with an occasional steel or auto strike or with the labor racketeering scandals in the last years of the decade. On the other hand, race relations, extremely important in the 1960s made, except for the Little Rock crisis of 1957 and an occasional election-time outburst, little claim to public attention before that time. From the late 1940s into the mid-1950s sundry spy and Communist hunts were of concern, but the issue fairly well fizzled after that. Other issues had even briefer or more erratic days in the sun: the food shortage of 1947, the MacArthur hearing of 1951, and various space flights. Similarly, personal crises for the presidents such as heart attacks and major surgery for Presidents Eisenhower and Johnson and the attempted assassination of President Truman could not readily be fashioned into a predictor variable. In any event, these events seem to have far more impact on the stock market than on popularity ratings.

Scandal is a recurring feature of public awareness and thus is more promising as a potential variable in the analysis. Besides the scandals associated with alleged spies and Communists in the government during the McCarthy era and those associated with labor in the late 1950s, Americans, with greatly varying degrees of pain, have suffered through the five-percenter scandal of 1949 to 1950; charges of corruption in the RFC in 1951, in the Justice Department in 1952, and in the FHA in 1954; and scandals over Sherman Adams in 1958, over television quiz shows in 1959, over industry "payola" in the late 1950s, over Billie Sol Estes in 1962, and over Bobby Baker in 1963. While scandal is never worked into the regression analysis, some preliminary suggestions as to its relevance to a "moral crisis" phenomenon which may, in turn, affect presidential popularity are developed in Section 6 below.

Some thought was given to including a "lame duck" variable when it was observed that the popularity of Presidents Truman and Johnson rose noticeably after they decided not to seek third terms (see figure 4.2.1). The trouble is, however, that President Eisenhower was a lame duck for his entire second term, and it was found easier to ignore the whole idea than to decide what to do about this uncomfortable fact.

One domestic variable which did show some very minor promise was a dummy variable that takes the value of one during a major strike. The variable was zero almost everywhere except in parts of President Truman's first term. After that time major strikes were rather unusual and, when they did occur, usually lasted for such a short time that there was barely time to have a public opinion survey conducted to test their effects. Despite these peculiarities, the variable did show statistical significance, although only after the Korean War dummy had been incorporated in the equation to allow for a major peculiarity of President Truman's *second* term. Substantively the variable suggests a popularity drop of less than 3 percentage points when a major strike is on and, as such a minor contributor, it is not included in the discussion below. Its small success, however, may suggest that further experimentation with the effects of specific domestic events could prove profitable.

3 Results Without the War Variable

In *summary* the expected behavior of presidential popularity is as follows. It is anticipated (1) that each president will experience in each term a general decline of popularity; (2) that this decline will be interrupted from time to time with temporary upsurges associated with international crises and similar events; (3) that the decline will be accelerated in direct relation to increases in unemployment rates over those prevailing when the president began his term, but that *improvement* in unemployment rates will not affect his popularity one way or the other; and (4) that the president will experience an additional loss of popularity if a war is on.

In this section the relation of the first three variables to presidential popularity in the Truman-Johnson period will be assessed. In the next section the war variable will be added to the analysis.

The association between the first three variables and presidential popularity is given in its baldest form in eq. 1 in table 4.2.2. The equation explains a respectable, if not sensational, 23 percent of the variance (the R^2 figure). The coalition-of-minorities variable shows, in conformity with the speculation above, a significant negative relationship. The equation suggests that, in general, a president's popularity rating starts at about 70 percent and declines at a rate of some 6 percentage points per year.

However, while the coefficients for the rally-round-the-flag and economic-slump variables are in the expected direction, they are not significant either in a statistical or a substantive sense. The trouble with the economic-slump variable was anticipated in the discussion about it in Section 2: the economic decline occurred during the relatively popular reign of President Eisenhower; although the slump seems to have hurt his popularity, even with the decline he remained popular compared to other presidents; hence, what is needed is a variable to take into account this peculiar "Eisenhower effect." To a much smaller extent the same things can be said to affect the rally-round-the-flag variable: the variable reaches somewhat higher values than usual during President Eisenhower's highly popular first term when, as can be seen from table 4.2.2, little happened internationally.

To account for this phenomenon, eq. 2 mixes into the analysis a dummy variable for each of the presidents. This formulation insists that all presidents must decline (or increase) in popularity at the same rate but, unlike eq. 1, it allows each president to begin at his own particular level. Thus peculiar effects of personality, style, and party and of differences in the conditions under which the president came into office can be taken into account.[18]

The addition improves things considerably. The fit is much better (the R^2 is .64) and the rally-round-the-flag and economic-slump variables attain respectable magnitudes in the right direction. The equation suggests that the presidents have declined at an overall rate of more than 5 percentage points per year, but that each has done so at his own particular level. President Truman's decline is measured from a starting point of about 55 percent (the intercept figure—what remains when the dummy variables for the Eisenhower, Kennedy, and Johnson administrations are all zero). President Eisenhower declines from a much higher level, about 79 percent (the intercept plus the Eisenhower value: 55.10 + 24.03), President Kennedy also from 79 percent, and President Johnson from 66 percent.

The importance of these dummy variables clearly demonstrates that *any analysis of presidential popularity cannot rely entirely on the variables discussed in Section 2, but must also incorporate parameters designed to allow for the special character of each administration*. To an extent this is unfortunate. The beauty of eq. 1 is that it affords a prediction of a president's

Table 4.2.2

Regression Results Including Administration Effects, Truman to Johnson

	Equations			
	(1)	(2)	(3)	(4)
Intercept	69.91	55.10	68.15	72.01
Independent variables				
Coalition of minorities (in years)	−6.32 (0.69)	−5.43 (0.48)		
Rally round the flag (in years)	−0.35 (1.92)	−2.06 (1.35)	−1.85 (1.06)	−2.62 (1.07)
Economic slump (in percent unemployed)	−0.17 (0.95)	−3.16 (0.75)	−5.30 (0.60)	−5.95 (0.59)
Dummy variables for administrations				
Eisenhower		24.03 (1.43)	0.50 (2.28)	
Kennedy		23.69 (1.83)	11.34 (2.95)	
Johnson		11.43 (1.52)	5.41 (2.36)	
Coalition-of-minorities variable for administrations (in years)				
Truman			−11.45 (0.84)	−12.72 (0.49)
Eisenhower			0.83 (0.57)	−0.03 (0.46)
Kennedy			−5.96 (1.36)	−1.84 (0.81)
Johnson			−9.52 (0.62)	−8.81 (0.49)
Standard error of estimate	13.05	8.93	6.83	7.05
R^2	.23	.64	.79	.78

Each equation in tables 4.2.2 and 4.2.3 is displayed vertically. The dependent variable, the percentage approving the way the president is handling his job, has a mean of 57.9 and a standard deviation of 14.8. The number of cases is 299. The figures in parentheses are the standard errors for the respective partial regression coefficients. To be regarded statistically significant, a regression coefficient should be, conventionally, at least twice its standard error. All equations in this chapter are significant (F test) at well beyond the .01 level. All equations exhibit a statistically significant amount of positive serial correlation (see Section 5).

popular rating simply by measuring how long he has been in office, how long it has been since the rally point, and how many people are unemployed. Such predictions, however, would be intolerably inaccurate because the fit of the equation is rather poor. Instead one must include the administration variables, the magnitudes of which cannot be known until the president's term is over. So much for beauty.

Because of this phenomenon, it is not possible to incorporate President Nixon's popularity into the analysis until he completes a term. Nevertheless, it seems clear from the incomplete data in figure 4.2.1 that the coalition of minorities decline is very much present. Because of the extraordinarily large no-opinion percentage he inspired in his early months in office, the decline is shown more clearly in the disapproval percentages than in those in the support column. A decline can also be seen in the Roosevelt figures.

In eq. 3, administration effects are incorporated in a different manner, greatly improving fit (the R^2 is .79). In this formulation each president is allowed to begin at his own level of popularity as in eq. 2, but in addition each may decline (or increase) at his own rate: for each administration there is a different coefficient for the coalition-of-minorities variable. Three of the four values so generated are strongly significant while the magnitudes of the administration dummies drop greatly. When the administration dummies are dropped entirely from consideration, as in eq. 4, the regression coefficients remain quite firm, and the fit of the equation is scarcely weakened. Clearly, *the important differences between administrations do not lie so much in different overall levels of popularity but, instead, in the widely differing rates at which the coalition-of-minorities variable takes effect.*

The popular decline of Presidents Truman and Johnson has been almost precipitous. President Truman's rating fell off at some 11 to 13 percentage points per year while President Johnson's declined at a rate of 8 or 9 points a year. President Kennedy was noticeably more successful at holding on to his supporters. Then there is the Eisenhower phenomenon: in spite of all the rationalizations for the coalitions-of-minorities concept tediously arrayed in Section 2, President Eisenhower's rating uncooperatively refuses to decline at all.

It was stated in Section 1 that some minor bias in these results is introduced by an embellished rate of "no opinion" in the first weeks of the Kennedy and first Eisenhower terms. As this rate declined, there was a tendency for the presidents' approval *and* disapproval rates to rise. To see if this peculiarity had any major impact, eqs. 3 and 4 were recalculated by using the percentage disapproving as the dependent variable. This manipulation caused no fundamental difference, although President Eisenhower's rating behaved a little less outrageously. In the version comparable to eq. 3, his "unpopularity" rating barely rises, and in the eq. 4 version it climbs at a rate of nine-tenths of a point per year, the latter coefficient barely being statistically significant. President Kennedy's "unpopularity" rating rises 7 percentage points a year in the eq. 3 version and 3 points a year in the eq. 4 version, both coefficients significant. This rate, however, is still much less steep than the Truman and Johnson rates.

In eq. 3, presidents who served two terms were required to begin each term at the same level and their rate of decline or increase also had to be the same in each term. Liberation from these restrictions is gained by the rather cluttered eq. 5 of table 4.2.3 which affords a term-by-term comparison. That is, eq. 5 is the same as eq. 3 except that each *term* is treated separately rather than each *administration*. As can be seen, President Eisenhower managed a statistically significant *increase* of popularity of some 2.5 percentage points per year in his first term. His second term ratings showed a more human, but very minor and statistically nonsignificant decline.[19] When the percent *disapproving* is made the dependent variable, the results remain the same.

Nor do important differences emerge in this phenomenon when the economic slump variable, which functions mainly during the Eisenhower years, is dropped from the equation.

No matter how the data are looked at then the conclusion remains the same, *President Eisenhower's ability to maintain his popularity, especially during his first term, is striking and un-*

paralleled. An examination of some of the possible reasons for this phenomenon is conducted in Section 6 below.

The rally-round-the-flag and the economic-slump variables emerge alive and well in eqs. 3, 4, and 5 (and 6). Both are statistically significant, but their substantive importance varies as one moves from an administration-by-administration formulation of the coalition-of-minorities variable (eqs. 3 and 4) to the term-by-term formulation in table 4.2.3. Specifically, the rally-round-the-flag variable gets stronger while the economic-slump variable weakens.

Table 4.2.3

Regression Results Including Term Effects and the War Variables, Truman to Johnson

	Equations	
	(5)	(6)
Intercept	72.00	72.38
Independent variables		
Rally round the flag (in years)	−4.87(1.03)	−6.17(1.03)
Economic slump (in percent unemployed)	−2.67(0.64)	−3.72(0.64)
Dummy variables for terms		
Truman, second	−15.25(3.65)	−12.42(3.53)
Eisenhower, first	−3.77(3.11)	−2.41(2.98)
Eisenhower, second	−5.30(3.03)	−4.35(2.90)
Kennedy	7.53(3.25)	7.18(3.10)
Johnson, first	4.40(4.07)	4.02(3.89)
Johnson, second	−1.28(3.02)	−1.06(3.21)
Coalition-of-minorities variable for terms (in years)		
Truman, first	−9.21(1.39)	−8.92(1.33)
Truman, second	−7.98(0.99)	−2.82(1.35)
Eisenhower, first	2.45(0.85)	2.58(0.81)
Eisenhower, second	−0.07(0.64)	0.22(0.62)
Kennedy	−5.12(1.20)	−4.75(1.15)
Johnson, first	1.24(8.81)	2.53(8.43)
Johnson, second	−8.10(0.65)	−8.13(0.79)
Dummy variables for wars		
Korea		−18.20(3.39)
Vietnam		0.01(2.77)
Standard error of estimate	6.00	5.73
R^2	.84	.86

The rally-round-the-flag variable is very much a parasite—it is designed to explain bumps and wiggles on a pattern measured mainly by the coalition-of-minorites variable. Consequently, the rally-round-the-flag varibale does very poorly on its own and only begins to shine when the overall trends become well determined by the rest of the equation. In the end, *the rally-round-the-flag variable suggests a popularity decline of about 5 or 6 percentage points for every year since the last rally point*—about the same magnitude as the coalition-of-minorities variable in its general state as in eqs. 1 and 2.

The declining fortunes of the economic-slump variable suggest that the variable in eqs. 3 and 4 was partly covering for the differences between the two Eisenhower terms: the first term was associated with increasing popularity and a smaller recession, the second with somewhat declining popularity and a larger recession. With the Eisenhower terms more thoroughly differentiated in eq. 5, the variable is reduced to a more purely economic function. The magnitude of the coefficient of the *economic-slump variable* in this equation *suggests a decline of popularity of about 3 percentage points for every percentage point rise in the unemployment rate over the level holding when the president began his present term.* Since the unemployment rate has varied in the postwar period only from about 3 to 7 percent, the substantive impact of the economic-slump variable on presidential popularity is somewhat limited.

The evidence for a "second term effect" is minimal.[20] President Eisenhower began his second term at a very slightly lower level than his first and was not able to maintain his popularity as well in the second term. But President Truman, while he began his second term at a much lower level than his first, declined at a *slower* rate in the second term.

4 Results with a War Variable Added

Because of the multicollinearity problem as discussed in Section 2.4, the variable designed to tap the impact on presidential popularity of the wars in Korea and Vietnam was applied with no great confidence that it would prove to have an independent, added effect when the coalition of minorities had already been incorporated into the equation. As is obvious from a perusal of figure 4.2.1, Presidents Truman and Johnson were in popular decline during their warless first terms.[21] Furthermore each was in clear decline in the first part of his second term before the wars started, and it is not at all clear that this trend altered when the wars began.

The equations suggest otherwise, however. When a war dummy (a variable that took on a value of one if either war happened to be on at the time of the survey and that was zero otherwise) was appended to the equations already discussed, it emerged significant and suggested that the presence of war depressed the popularity of Presidents Truman and Johnson by several percentage points.

The next step, obviously, was to set up a separate dummy variable for each war. This brought forth the incredible result documented in eq. 6: *the Korean War had a large, significant, independent negative impact on President Truman's popularity of some 18 percentage points, but the Vietnam War had no independent impact on President Johnson's popularity at all.*

When confronted with a result like this, one's first impulse is to do something to make it go away. This impulse was fully indulged. Variables were transformed and transmuted, sections of the analysis were reformed or removed, potentially biasing data were sectioned out.[22] But nothing worked. The relationship persisted. In fact, under some manipulations the relationship became *stronger*.

One's second impulse is to explain the phenomenon away as a statistical freak. Because of the high correlations that the war variables had with the term dummies and with the coalition-of-minorities variables for the Truman and Johnson second terms, it is clear that the multiple regression procedure is being strained. What one would expect under these circumstances is to see the pairs of correlated variables wiping each other out (as, indeed, happened when the nondummy war variables mentioned in section 2.4, such as the casualty figures, were applied). There is some evidence of this in eq. 6 as the coalition-of-minorites variable for Truman's second term is reduced to a level that seems unrealistically low; it remains, however, statistically significant.

Nevertheless, the *same* considerable difficulties are posed for *both* dummy variables and, under those circumstances, the equation suggests the best guess as to what is going on: Korea had an *added* impact on Truman's decline, Vietnam did not have one on Johnson's decline. It probably would be unwise to make book on the precise 18 percentage point difference because some of its strength is doubtless stolen from the Truman coalition-of-minorities variable; and one may be able to trace special Vietnam effects in a more microscopic analysis of Johnson's popularity[23]; but, at least at this level, it seems that something of the sort indicated is going on in the data. Furthermore, as noted above, the war variable that did not distinguish between the wars also was found to have a significant effect, and its correlation with other independent variables was fairly low—in the .50 to .60 range.

One's third impulse, then, is to attempt to explain the result. One speculates.

The wars in Korea and Vietnam differed from each other in many respects of course, but it seems unlikely that these differences can be used in any simple manner to explain the curious regression finding. This is the case because public response to the wars themselves was quite similar.

Therefore, it is probably a sounder approach in seeking to explain the regression finding to look specifically at popular attitudes toward *the president's relation to war*, rather than to perceptions of the war itself. A comment by Richard Neustadt (1960:97) seems strikingly relevant in this respect. "Truman," he observes, "seems to have run afoul of the twin notions that a wartime Chief Executive ought to be 'above politics' and that he ought to help the generals 'win.'"

President Johnson seems to have run considerably less afoul. In seeking to keep the war "above politics," he assiduously cultivated bipartisan support for the war and repeatedly sought to demonstrate that the war effort was simply an extension of the policies and actions of previous presidents. He was especially successful at generating public expressions of approval from the most popular Republican of them all: General Eisenhower. Vocal opposition to the war in Vietnam came either from groups largely unassociated with either party or from members of the president's own party. Then, when the latter opposition began to move from expressions of misgivings at congressional hearings to explicit challenges in the primaries, President Johnson removed himself from the battle precisely, he said, to keep the war "above politics." And, while there were occasional complaints from the Right during Vietnam that President Johnson had adopted a "no win" policy there, they were continually being undercut by public statements from General William Westmoreland—a man highly respected by the Right—insisting that he was receiving all the support he needed from the president and was getting it as fast as he needed it.

If these observations are sound, the single event that best differentiates the impact of the Korean and Vietnam wars on presidential popularity was President Truman's dismissal of General Douglas MacArthur. That move was a major factor in the politicization of the war as Republicans took the General's side and echoed his complaints that it was the president's meddling in policy that was keeping the war from being won (Spanier 1960; Neustadt 1960; Higgins 1960).

That the public was strongly inclined to support General MacArthur in the dispute seems apparent from the data in table 4.2.4.[24] The first two polls, conducted as the general was making his triumphal, "old soldiers never die" return to the United States, suggest more than twice as many people supported the general as supported the president on this measure. As Neustadt suggests (1960:97), emotion on the issue faded during the Senate hearings on the issue which lasted until June, and this seems to have benefited President Truman's position. The Truman point of view received its greatest support in late June and early July as peace talks were begun. As the talks began to prove unproductive, however, public opinion began to revert to its previous support of General MacArthur until, by the first days of 1952 (when the polling agencies grew bored with the issue), the MacArthur position was as strongly approved and Pres-

Table. 4.2.4

Public Attitudes on the Truman-MacArthur Controversy, 1951

Date Survey Sent to Field	Do you approve or disapprove of President Truman's action in removing General MacArthur? (AIPO)			Do you think President Truman was right or wrong in dismissing General MacArthur? (NORC)		
	Approve	Disapprove	DK	Right	Wrong	DK
	(In Percent)			(In Percent)		
April 14	25	66	9			
April 18				28	58	14
May 17	29	56	15			
May 24				34	49	17
June 14	29	55	17			
June 29				39	48	13
August 27				32	54	14
October 2				28	59	13
November 22				27	61	12
December 28				29	60	11

Source. RC.

ident Truman's position was as strongly rejected as ever.[25]

The differing impact of the wars on presidential popularity, therefore, seems to result from the fact that Korea became "Truman's war" while Vietnam never really became "Johnson's war" in the same sense.

One other item of speculation should be mentioned. Domestically, the war in Vietnam was accompanied by a profoundly important crisis as America confronted its long-ignored racial dilemma head on. There seems to have been nothing comparable during the Korean War. The clamor associated with McCarthyism comes to mind but many analysts feel that, however important to politicians, intellectuals, and journalists, McCarthyism was of less than major concern to public opinion.[26] Furthermore its dramatic climax, the Army-McCarthy hearings, took place months after the Korean War had ended and more than a year after President Truman left office.

It may be, then, that the discontent associated with the racial crisis was enough by itself to cause much of President Johnson's popular decline and that the unhappiness over the Vietnam War could make little additional inroad. In the Truman case, there was no profound independent domestic source of discontent: his second term coalition-of-minorities decline is usually found, as in eq. 5, to have been less than his first term decline and when, as in eq. 6, a variable has already accounted for the war effect, his decline is quite moderate. Hence, in a sense there was "room" for the war to have an independent impact.

It would be wise in concluding this section to emphasize what has and what has not been said. It has *not* been argued that the war in Vietnam had nothing to do with President Johnson's decline in popularity, and thus the analysis cannot really be used to refute the president's own estimation of the impact of Vietnam as indicated in the quotation that heads this chapter. However, it is argued that whatever impact the war had was tapped by the other variables in the equation, especially in the coalition-of-minorities variable, which is specifically designed to account for general overall decline. When the same sort of analysis is applied in the Korean period, it is found that a variable associated with the Korean War emerges as strong and significant even after other variables have been taken into account. Therefore, the regression analysis shows that, while the Korean War does seem to have had an *independent, additional* impact on President Truman's decline in popularity, the Vietnam War shows no such relation to President Johnson's decline.[27]

5 The Residuals

Equations 5 and 6 can be applied to each data point in the presidential popularity series and, with the appropriate quantities inserted for the independent variables in each case, they will generate a series of "predicted" data points that can then be compared to the actual series. An analysis of the difference between the actual and predicted data points, the residuals, finds that the equations predict worst in President Truman's first term. If that term is dropped from consideration, the equation explains 90 percent of the variance in the remaining set of data. The President's extremely high initial ratings are not well predicted, suggesting that the equation does not adequately account for the trauma of President Roosevelt's death, combined as it was with the ending of World War II and with important peace conferences. It was almost as if Americans were afraid to disapprove of President Truman.

From these spectacular highs, President Truman plunged to great lows during the labor turmoil of 1946 as is shown in figure 4.2.1. These ratings are also badly specified by the equation. The Truman popularity rose in early 1947, as the labor situation eased, and then declined for the rest of the term. Thus, although President Truman's first term, like the other non-Eisenhower terms, shows an overall decline of popularity, that decline was considerably more erratic than the others. The dummy variable for strikes, discussed briefly in Section 2.5, improved matters only slightly.

Beyond this, the residuals are reasonably well behaved. There are small but noticeable effects from the lame-duck phenomenon at the end of the Truman and Johnson administrations and from the "no opinion" peculiarity of the initial weeks of the Eisenhower and Kennedy administrations. And here and there are data points whose magnitudes have somehow managed to escape specification by the variables in the regression equation. One can, of course, generate a unique explanation for each of these, but this procedure clutters the analysis more than it is worth. Besides, the laws of sampling insist that Gallup must have made *some* mistakes.

As noted in table 4.2.2, serial correlation has by no means been eliminated in the regression equations.[28] Allowing the coalition-of-minorities variable to be specified for each administration improved things considerably, but much is left to be desired.

6 The Eisenhower Phenomenon

Much was made in Section 2.1 of the coalition-of-minorities variable with its stern prediction that a president's popularity would decline inexorably over his four-year term. This emphasis was not entirely unjustified, since the variable generally proved to be a hardy and tenacious predictor for the postwar Democratic administrations. In addition, judged from figure 4.2.1, a decline of popularity was also experienced by Nixon and probably by Roosevelt.

The variable fails for the Eisenhower administration, however, especially for the general's first term. The analysis suggests then that if a president wants to leave office a popular man, he should either (1) be Dwight David Eisenhower, or (2) resign the day after inauguration.

The Eisenhower phenomenon, noted but left dangling without explanation or rationalization in Section 3, deserves special examination. Why didn't President Eisenhower decline in popularity like everybody else? Since Nixon's popularity declined noticeably, the phenomenon is not simply a Republican one. A number of suggestions can be made.

1. First, credit must be given to President

Eisenhower's *personal appeal*: he was extremely likeable—a quality very beneficial in a popularity contest and one lacked in abundance by, say, Lyndon Johnson. Part of this, but only part, may be because of the admiration he engendered in the public because of his war record—even before he entered politics he was consistently at or near the top of Gallup's "most admired men" lists. But this could only give him a certain initial favorable inertia. Americans are fully capable of becoming disillusioned with, or at least bored with, former heroes. President Eisenhower kept them from doing so, and it took more than memories of his old record to accomplish this. As Fillmore Sanford (1951:198) has commented, "The American people, in reacting to a national leader, put great emphasis on his personal warmth"—a quality projected to an unusual degree by President Eisenhower. As part of this, he was able to project an image of integrity and sincerity that many found to be enormously attractive (see Converse and Dupeux 1966).

2. Early in his first term, President Eisenhower was able to present to the public one sensational achievement: he *ended the Korean War*—or, at any rate, presided over its end. This accomplishment was seen by the public as he left office to be a great one[29] and was used with profit by the Republicans in a presidential campaign a full fifteen years after it happened. From the standpoint of public opinion it may well have been the most favorable achievement turned in by any postwar president. As such, it may have tended to overwhelm the negative impact of anything else the president did, at least for the first years of his administration. Some credit for this is given in the regression analysis, since the signing of the truce is counted as a rally point, but this may be a totally inadequate recognition.

There is another aspect of President Eisenhower's first term that may not be sufficiently accounted for in the rally-round-the-flag variable: the euphoria of the "spirit of Geneva" period toward the end of this term when the president's popularity should have been at its lowest ebb.

3. President Eisenhower's *amateur status* may also have worked to his benefit, at least for a while. He entered office an unknown political quantity. Under these circumstances, the public may be more willing to grant the benefit of a doubt, to extend the "honeymoon" period, than it would for a president who is a political professional. It is also easier under these circumstances for the president to appear "above the battle," an image fostered in a number of ways, and thus to be blamed only belatedly and indirectly for political mishaps, thereby softening their impact.

4. President Eisenhower may have been curiously benefited by the fact that, especially on the domestic front, *he didn't do anything*. As Irving Kristol (1968:16) argues, "when a conservative administration does take office, it pursues no coherent program but merely takes satisfaction in not doing the things that the liberals may be clamoring for. This, in effect, is what happened during the two terms of President Eisenhower. . . ." Indeed, analysts of the Eisenhower Administration often argue that its contribution lies in what it *didn't* do. The times called for consolidation, they argue, and President Eisenhower's achievement was that he neither innovated nor repealed, but was content to preside over a period of placidity in which he tacitly gave Republican respectability to major Democratic innovations of earlier years: the programs of the New Deal domestically, and the policies of the Truman Doctrine internationally (see Rossiter 1960:161-78).

In the justification for the coalition-of-minorities variable, as discussed in Section 2.2, such behavior could have a peculiar result. It was assumed, in part, that the president would enact programs which, while approved by the majority, would alienate intense minorities that would gradually cumulate to his disadvantage. But, suppose the president doesn't do anything. Those who want no change are happy while, if things are sufficiently ambiguous, those who support change have not really been denied by an explicit decision and can still patiently wait and hope. At some point, of course, those who want change begin to see that they are never going to get their desire and may become alienated, but this will be a delayed process. Also, if the demands for change are intense enough, delay can be harmful to a president's popularity—

as Herbert Hoover found. Perhaps this happened to President Eisenhower when he confronted the recession of his second term: "Eisenhower, once so satisfying as a 'man above the struggle,' apparently collided during 1958 with yearnings for a president who made his presence felt"(Neustadt 1960:97). But in moderate, placid times, a conservative policy may dissipate some of the power of the coalition-of-minorities phenomenon. If polls were available, one might find that President Warren Harding maintained his popularity as strikingly as President Eisenhower.

5. Although it might be difficult to sort out cause and effect, it is worth noting that President Eisenhower's first term (and most of his second) coincided with a *period of national goodness*. In a brilliant article Meg Greenfield (1961) has observed that "moral crises" as appraised and bemoaned by intellectuals seem to follow a cyclic pattern: we go through a period in which the popular journals are filled with articles telling us how bad we are after which there is a period of respite.

Miss Greenfield's main indicator of these ethical cycles is exquisite: the number of items under the heading, "US: Moral Conditions," in the *Readers' Guide to Periodical Literature*. The pattern, elaborated and duly pedantified, is given in table 4.2.5. As she points out, our first moral crisis in the postwar period arose in the early 1950s and was associated with "'five percenters,' deep freezes, mink coats, the Kefauver hearings, and a series of basketball fixes," while "the symbols of our present [1961] decline are Charles Van Doren, payola, cheating in school, and the decision of Francis Gary Powers not to kill himself." We never recovered as thoroughly from that crisis as we did from the earlier one for, as the crisis showed signs of waning, new elements—Billie Sol Estes, Bobby Baker, President Kennedy's assassination, campus revolts, the hippies, and the city riots—proved once again that we have a "sick society." Our moral crises are regenerated every 8 years and seem largely to coincide with the end of presidential administrations.[30]

Of course, objective indicators of public morality have not been careening in this manner. Even the most alarmist of crime wave enthusiasts would never argue that crime rates

Table 4.2.5

The Greenfield Index

Number of Items under the Heading, "US: Moral Conditions" in the Readers' Guide to Periodical Literature, 1945 to 1968, by year

1945	1	1958	0
1946	0	1959	9
1947	8	1960	32
1948	1	1961	23
1949	1	1962	10
1950	3	1963	11
1951	35	1964	5
1952	17	1965	6
1953	1	1966	7
1954	4	1967	18
1955	2	1968	10
1956	0	1969	14
1957	7	1970	25

fluctuate in such a wild pattern (see Wilson 1966). Church attendance, measured by Gallup since the mid-1950s, shows only the smallest of changes (GOI 31; Lipset 1959). And careful sociological studies of American sexual practices found little sign of revolution during the period.[31]

Much of the fluctuation in the Greenfield index is, no doubt, due to journalistic fad. A sensational fraud, scandal, or disruption causes theologians, journalists, and other intellectuals to sociologize: society is sick. Others pick up the idea, and it blossoms into a full moral crisis. In a year or two the theme no longer sells magazines and the space is filled with other profundities, for example, the generation gap. Fraud, scandal, and disruption continue, but the moral crisis eases.

But—and this is a logical and empirical leap of some magnitude—to the extent that these patterns reflect and influence public attitudes, they may be relevant to presidential popularity. The early Eisenhower years are notable for their absence of moral anguish, and they differ from other between-crisis periods in an important respect: not only were we not demonstrably bad, we were positively good for we were undergoing a religious revival. Miss Greenfield looked at the items under the heading, "US: Religious Institutions." She finds only six items in the 1951 to 1953 period, but 25 in the 1953 to 1955 period, while "in the 1955-57 volume, at the height of our virtue . . . the religious listings reached thirty-four with twenty-eight 'see alsos.'"

If we were so good ourselves, how could we possibly find fault in our leader?

7 Further Research

A regression equation has been generated, based on only four rather simple variables, that fits quite well the erratic behavior over twenty-four years of the presidential popularity index. There is, however, much room for improvement and refinement.

Little has been done to separate out from the coalition-of-minorities variable the specific and divergent influences of domestic events on presidential popularity. One variable is designed to account in a general way for changes in the economy, some limited analysis is made of the relevance of major strikes, and comments are interjected about the role of scandal and "moral crisis." But domestic life is considerably more complicated than this, and more precise indicators can be sought.

It would also be of value to get better estimates of the impact of different *kinds* of international events on presidential popularity—although, as already suggested, such analysis may find that all dramatic international events affect popularity in much the same way no matter how they may differ in historical significance. It may prove valuable to attempt to see how spectacular and cumulative international events and shifts in governmental policy—to use the distinction made by Deutsch and Merritt (1965)—differ in impact.

The analysis strongly suggests that presidential style, as well as the ideological and political nature of the administration and the times, can make a sizeable difference in popularity ratings. A more precise assessment of these relationships along the lines developed by James Barber (1968) would be most desirable.

By the end of the analysis, the economic variable, though significant, proved to be of less than major importance. Experiments with other economic variables, such as price indexes and personal income figures, might prove valuable (see Goodhart and Bhansali 1970 and Kramer 1971). Furthermore, the only lag applied was one in which the respondent, it was supposed, compared the current state of the economy with the one that prevailed when the incumbent President was elected. Other lags such as a moving-six-month comparison, might prove more sensitive.

A major defect in the equations, as noted, was the high degree of serial correlation that remained. Various lagging procedures could be used in an effort to reduce this.

It would be interesting to extend the analysis to other bodies of data. Although the popularity question was posed with far less regularity during the Roosevelt administration (and was largely dropped during World War II) and although there are problems with varying question wording, students of President Roosevelt's popularity ratings emerge with findings that fit well with those of this study. Wesley C. Clark (1943:41, 28, 35) has found some relation between a measure of Roosevelt's popularity and the state of the economy in the 1937 to 1940 period. He also notes a general "downward slant" in the rating over time and finds a rise of popularity during international crises. And V. O. Key (1952:596) has observed that during 1940 "the popularity of Roosevelt rose and fell with European crises" (see also B. Roper 1969 and E. Roper 1957: chaps. 2 and 3).

The popularity ratings of governors and senators in states with active statewide polls can also be analyzed as can data on national leaders from countries such as Britain, Canada, and France. In their investigation of British data, Goodhart and Bhansali (1970) have applied economic variables and ones similar to the coalition-of-minorities variable to good effect (see also Durant 1965). Extensive data from France on the popularity of General De Gaulle have been published (GOI 33), and a study by Howard Rosenthal (1967) has investigated regional aspects of the general's popularity.

The analysis in this chapter deals entirely with general popular approval of the president. Unexamined are the ways population groups differ in their approach to the president. The next chapter considers the reaction of the partisan groups—Democrats, Republicans, and Independents—to the presidential popularity question.

8 Summary

Presidential popularity is investigated in this chapter, and multiple regression analysis is applied to the behavior of the responses to the Gallup poll's presidential popularity question in the twenty-four-year period from the beginning of the Truman administration to the end of the Johnson administration. Predictor variables include a measure of the length of time the incumbent has been in office as well as variables that attempt to assess the influence on his rating of major international events, economic slump, and war. Despite the austerity of this representation of a presumably complex process, the fit of the resulting equation is very good: it explains 86 percent of the variance in presidential popularity.

This degree of fit can only be attained, however, by allowing the special character of each presidential administration to be expressed in the equation. Thus it does not seem possible to predict a given president's popularity well simply by taking into account such general phenomena as the state of the economy or of international affairs.

The first variable, dubbed the coalition-of-minorities variable, found, as expected, the popularity of most presidents to be in decline during each term. The important differences between administrations do not lie so much in different overall levels of popularity but, instead, in the widely differing rates at which this coalition-of-minorities variable takes effect. Specifically, the popular decline of Presidents Truman and Johnson was quite steep, but President Kennedy seems to have maintained his popularity somewhat better. President Eisenhower's popularity declined only slightly during his second term and not at all during his first term.

In considering this Eisenhower phenomenon, a combination of several causes may be relevant: the president's personal appeal, his ending of the Korean War, his amateur status, his domestic conservatism at a time when a policy of this kind was acceptable, and his fortune in coming to office at a time of national goodness.

The second variable, the rally-round-the-flag variable, predicts short-term boosts in a president's popularity whenever an international crisis or a similar event occurs. The variable proves to be a sturdy one and suggests a popular decline of about 5 or 6 percentage points for every year since the last "rally point."

Economic effects are estimated in the third variable. The variable can only be made to function if it is assumed that an economy in slump harms a president's popularity, but that an economy in boom does not help his rating. A decline of popularity of about 3 percentage points is suggested for every percentage point rise in the unemployment rate over the level holding when the president began his present term.

The fourth variable attempts to take into account the influence of war on presidential popularity. It is found that the Korean War had a large, significant independent negative impact on President Truman's popularity of 18 percentage points, but that the Vietnam War had no independent impact on President Johnson's popularity. It is suggested that this difference may result from the relationship between the presidents and the wars: President Truman was less able than President Johnson to keep the war "above" partisan politics, and he seemed to the public to be interfering and restraining its generals. The absence in the Truman case of a domestic crisis comparable to the racial turmoil of the Johnson era may also be relevant.

Notes

1. Quoted, Wise (1968:131).
2. The presidential popularity data for most of the Johnson administration and for all of the Nixon administration have been taken from the *Gallup Opinion Index*. The Roosevelt data appeared in Cantril and Strunk (1951:756). All other data have come from the Roper Center.
3. For a discussion, see Ezekiel and Fox (1959); Draper and Smith (1966); Christ (1966).
4. See, for example, the breakdowns in GOI 10, p. 4.
5. One other technicality is worth mentioning. There is a slight underrepresentation of data points in Truman's first years. By 1950, except for the election-year phenomenon already noted, the Gallup organization was asking the question on virtually every survey conducted—some dozen or 16 per year. Before that time the question was posed on the average only about half as frequently. Neither of these technical problems, however, is likely to bias the results in any important way, especially since so much of the analysis allows each administration a fair amount of distinctiveness.
6. The standard deviation for the no opinion response for the Truman-Johnson period is 2.97. By contrast, the comparable statistic is 14.8 for the approve response and 14.5 for the disapprove response.
7. Some argue that percentages should not be used in their pure state as variables but, instead, should be transformed into logits $\{Y^* = \log_e [Y/(1-Y)]\}$. The transformation was tried in the analysis, but it made little difference. Therefore, the more easily communicated percentage version has been kept. In any event, the dependent variable rarely takes extreme values. It rises to 80 percent only three or four times and never dips below 23 percent.
8. For the bandwagon effect among nonvoters, see Campbell et al. (1960:110-15).
9. *The Prince*, chap. XVII.
10. Such an effect is found in British data by Goodhart and Bhansali (1970).
11. Especially valuable was Nordheim and Wilcox (1967). Other sources often consulted included the *New York Times Index* and the Chronology section of the *World Almanac*.
12. National Opinion Research Center polls 370 (March 1955) and 371 (May 1955).
13. Burns Roper (1969) observes that a high point of President Kennedy's popularity occurred after the Bay of Pigs invasion and concludes this fact says something special about that crisis event. But this phenomenon is due to *two* effects: the rally-round-the-flag effect *and* the fact that the events occurred very early in Kennedy's administration when the value for the coalition-of-minorities variable was yet very low.
14. See Campbell et al. (1960: chap. 14); Key (1952: chap. 20 and references); Kramer (1971); Segal (1968); Rees et al. (1962).
15. (1960:97ff.) See also the discussion in Section 7 below.
16. Data were gathered from Moore (1961:122) and, for more recent data, issues of the *Monthly Labor Review*.
17. One additional wrinkle, which is intuitively comfortable but makes little difference in the actual results, was to do something about the unemployment rates at the start of the first terms of Presidents Truman and Eisenhower when unemployment was "artificially" depressed because of ongoing wars. Presumably the public would be understanding about the immediate postwar rise in unemployment. Therefore, for these two terms the initial unemployment level was taken to be the level that held 6 months after the war ended, while the economic variable for the few months of the war and the 6-month period was set equal to zero.
18. The dummy variables formalize the sort of discussion found in Neustadt (1960:98). They account for what a singer might call *tessitura*.
19. If the term dummies are dropped from the equation to attain a version comparable to eq. 4, the Eisenhower phenomenon holds true except that his first-term increase drops to 1.98 (still significant) and his second-term decrease is a slightly steeper -0.38 (still not significant).
20. The concept is mentioned, without enthusiasm, by Neustadt (1960:205-6n). See also B. Roper (1969).
21. Regression statistics relating to President Johnson's first term are very unreliable, as the size of the standard errors suggests, because the popularity question was posed so few times during this brief period. As is clear from figure 4.2.1, his "disapprove" rating ascended steeply while his approval rating held level. Regression equations comparable to eqs. 5 and 6 using disapproval as a dependent variable suggest an almost statistically significant growth in disapproval at the rate of 13 or 14 percentage points per year for this term.
22. For example, the 1949 data were removed from consideration thereby making it appear that the Korean War started only six months into Truman's second term as the Vietnam War had been taken to start six months into Johnson's.
23. A preliminary report on some efforts to do this: Stone and Brody (1970).
24. See also the data in Belknap and Campbell (1951-52). Notice especially the strong party polarization on the issue. A sample of citizens listed in *Who's Who* were asked Gallup's question in May 1951 and were found to be far more in favor of the president's position than the general public: 51 percent approved Truman's action and 46 disapproved. The British public was found at the same time to support the president by a 55-19 margin with 26 percent undecided. AIPOr, May 16, 1951 and May 20, 1951.
25. It is interesting, incidentally, to compare how the public responded to the slightly different questions posed by the two polling agencies in surveys conducted essentially at the same time. Americans appear noticeably more willing to say they "disapprove" actions by their president than to say he did "wrong."
26. Stouffer (1955: especially chap. 3); Campbell et al. (1960:50-51): Polsby (1960); E. Roper (1957:250-51).

27. There is evidence to suggest that World War II, a more popular (and much larger) war than either Korea or Vietnam, may have worked to the distinct *benefit* of President Roosevelt. In its postelection poll in 1944, NORC asked Roosevelt supporters if they would have voted for Dewey "if the war had been over." Enough answered in the affirmative to suggest that Dewey might well have won in a warless atmosphere (SRCc). E. Roper (1957: 53-54) reports similar data from a 1943 survey.

28. The Durbin-Watson statistic, which ideally should register at about 2.00, reached at best only about .70 for eq. 6.

29. In December 1960, the public was asked what it believed was Eisenhower's greatest accomplishment. The ending of the Korean War was mentioned by 11 percent and a related comment, "he kept us out of war," was suggested by an additional 32 percent. No other specific accomplishment was mentioned by more than 5 percent; only 3 percent mentioned anything having to do with the domestic scene (RC). See also Neustadt (1960:98).

30. It may, or then again may not, be worth noting that presidential elections in which the incumbent party was removed (1952, 1960, and 1968) occurred during moral crises, but the elections in which the president was retained (1948, 1956, and 1964) all took place during times of relative goodness. This relationship, however, is undoubtedly much too beautiful to be true.

31. See *The Public Interest*, Spring 1968, pp. 93-95.

References

Barber, James D., *1968*. "Classifying and Predicting Styles" 24 *Journal of Social Issues* 51-80 (No. 3, July).

Belknap, George and Angus Campbell, *1951-1952*. "Political Party Identification and Attitudes Toward Foreign Policy" 15 *Public Opinion Quarterly* 601-23 (Winter).

Campbell, Angus, Philip E. Converse, Warren E. Miller, and Donald E. Stokes, *1960*. *The American Voter* (New York: Wiley).

Cantril, Hadley and Mildred Strunk, *1951*. *Public Opinion 1935-1946* (Princeton, N.J.: Princeton University Press).

Christ, Carl F., *1966*. *Econometric Models and Methods* (New York: Wiley).

Clark, Wesley C., *1943*. "Economic Aspects of a President's Popularity," Ph.D. Dissertation, University of Pennsylvania.

Converse, Philip E. and George Dupeux, *1966*. "DeGaulle and Eisenhower: The Public Image of the Victorious General" in Angus Campbell et al., *Elections and the Political Order* (New York: Wiley), pp. 292-345.

Deutsch, Karl W. and Richard C. Merritt, *1965*. "Effects of Events on National and International Images," in Herbert C. Kelman (ed.), *International Behavior* (New York: Holt), pp. 132-87.

Downs, Anthony, *1957*. *An Economic Theory of Democracy* (New York: Harper and Row).

Draper, N. R. and H. Smith, *1966*. *Applied Regression Analysis* (New York: Wiley).

Durant, Henry, *1965*. "Indirect Influences on Voting Behavior" 1 *Polls* 7-11 (Spring).

Erskine, Hazel, *1964*. "The Polls: Kennedy as President" 28 *Public Opinion Quarterly* 334-38 (Summer).

Ezekiel, Mordecai and Karl A. Fox, *1959*. *Methods of Correlation and Regression Analysis* (New York: Wiley).

Fenton, John M., *1960*. *In Your Opinion* (Boston: Little, Brown).

Gallup Opinion Index (GOI) (originally titled *Gallup Political Index*) 1965-

Goodhart, C. A. E. and R. J. Bhansali, *1970*. "Political Economy" 18 *Political Studies* 43-106 (March).

Greenfield, Meg, *1961*. "The Great American Morality Play," *The Reporter*, June 8, pp. 13-18.

Higgins, Trumbull, *1960*. *Korea and the Fall of MacArthur* (New York: Oxford).

Key, V. O., Jr., *1952*. *Politics, Parties, and Pressure Groups* (New York: Crowell, 3rd ed.).

Kramer, Gerald H., *1971*. "Short-Term Fluctuations in U.S. Voting Behavior, 1896-1964," *American Political Science Review* 131-43 (March).

Kristol, Irving, *1968*. "The Old Politics, the New Politics, and the *New*, New Politics," *New York Times Magazine*, November 24.

Lipset, Seymour Martin, *1959*. "What Religious Revival?" *Columbia University Forum*, 17-21 (Winter).

Moore, Geoffrey H. (ed.), *1961*. *Business Cycle Indicators*, Vol. II (Princeton: Princeton University Press).

Neustadt, Richard E., *1960*. *Presidential Power: The Politics of Leadership* (New York: Wiley).

Nordheim, Eric V. and Pamela B. Wilcox, *1967*. "Major Events of the Nuclear Age: A Chronology to Assist in the Analysis of American Public Opinion," Oak Ridge National Laboratory, Oak Ridge, Tennessee, August.

Polsby, Nelson W., *1960*. "Toward an Explanation of McCarthyism" 8 *Political Studies* 250-71 (October).

Polsby, Nelson W., *1964*. *Congress and the Presidency* (Englewood Cliffs, N.J.: Prentice-Hall).

Rees, Albert, Herbert Kaufman, Samuel J. Eldersveld, and Frank Freidel, *1962*. "The Effect of Economic Conditions on Congressional Elections 1946-1958" 44 *Review of Economics and Statistics* 458-65 (November).

Roper, Burns, *1969*. "The Public Looks at Presidents," *The Public Pulse*, January.

Roper, Elmo, *1957*. *You and Your Leaders* (New York: Morrow).

Rosenthal, Howard, *1967*. "The Popularity of Charles De Gaulle" 31 *Public Opinion Quarterly* 381-98 (Fall).

Rossiter, Clinton, *1960*. *The American Presidency* (New York: Harcourt, Brace).

Sanford, Fillmore H., *1951*. "Public Orientation to Roosevelt" **15** *Public Opinion Quarterly* 189-216 (Summer).

Segal, Harvey H., *1968*. "The Pain Threshold of Economics in an Election Year," *New York Times*, July 15.

Spanier, John W., *1960*. *The Truman-MacArthur Controversy and the Korean War* (Cambridge, Mass.: Belknap).

Stouffer, Samuel, *1955*. *Communism, Conformity, and Civil Liberties* (Garden City, N.Y.: Doubleday).

Suits, Daniel B., *1957*. "Use of Dummy Variables in Regression Equations" **52** *American Statistical Association Journal* 548-51 (December).

Waltz, Kenneth N., *1967*. "Electoral Punishment and Foreign Policy Crises" in James N. Rosenau (ed.), *Domestic Sources of Foreign Policy* (New York: Free Press).

Wicker, Tom, *1967*. "In the Nation: Peace, It's Wonderful," *New York Times*, July 4, p. 18.

Wildavsky, Aaron, *1968*. "The Empty-head Blues: Black Rebellion and White Reaction" *Public Interests* 3-16 (Spring).

Wilson, James Q., *1966*. "Crime in the Streets," *The Public Interest* 26-35 (Fall).

Wise, David, *1968*. "The Twilight of a President," *New York Times Magazine*, November 3, p. 27 ff.

Illustration 4a: Presidential Popularity and Approval Polls

Presidential popularity polls of public support and approval of the type cited in the preceding article by Mueller have an impact on the presidency. Presidents read, heed, anticipate, use, and game them. Support and approval ratings affect presidential relations with the press, Congress, and other power-brokers. The following is an illustration of the Gallup Poll of presidential popularity.

President Reagan began his third year in office with the lowest approval rating recorded during his tenure. An average of three surveys conducted throughout January shows only 37 percent approving of Reagan's job performance, while 54 percent disapproved, and nine percent are uncommitted.

In the Gallup Poll's mid-December audit the President's popularity stood at 41 percent approval, with 50 percent disapproving. During 1982, Reagan's performance rating averaged 44 percent approval. Only eight percentage points separate his high for the year (49 percent, in early January) and his low of 41 percent, in December.

Comparison with other recent elected presidents after their second year in office shows Reagan's 44 percent average approval to be only marginally below the 47 percent average approval score accorded Jimmy Carter in 1978, but far lower than Richard Nixon's 57 percent in 1970, John Kennedy's 72 percent in 1962, and Dwight Eisenhower's 65 percent in 1954. Equally interesting is that three of the four—Carter, Nixon, and Kennedy—declined in popularity during their third year in office.

Table 4a.1 compares Reagan's average popularity during his first two years and his elected predecessor's during their first three years.

Table 4a.1

Presidential Performance Ratings
(Average approval rating for year)

	First year	Second year	Third year
Ronald Reagan	58%	44%	?
Jimmy Carter	62	47	38
Richard Nixon	61	57	50
John Kennedy	75	72	64
Dwight Eisenhower	69	65	71

Gallup Report No. 210 (pp. 16-17, 24-25), March 1983. Reprinted by permission of the Gallup Poll.

Decline Recorded in Most Key Population Groups

Comparison of the January findings with the mid-December survey shows decreases in Reagan's popularity in almost all major population groups. With the exception of Republicans, 68 percent of whom give the President a favorable job rating, Reagan's January approval score does not top 50 percent in any group, including persons from households in which the chief wage earner is employed in business or the professions and persons from families with $20,000 or more yearly income.

Reagan's 68 percent approval among Republicans is slightly better than the 57 percent positive rating Democrats accorded Jimmy Carter at a similar point in his tenure. However, Nixon, Kennedy, and Eisenhower each had the approval of over 80 percent of their own party members at comparable periods.

Little Inter-Party Support

The polarization of President Reagan's political support is illustrated by the fact that only 19 percent of Democrats and 39 percent of Independents approved of his job performance in January. These figures are well below the approval ratings of nonparty members recorded for any of Reagan's four elected predecessors at this time in their tenure, as shown in table 4a.2.

Although President Reagan's overall job performance rating has declined to its lowest point since he took office, an early January survey shows approval of his handling of foreign policy issues has slipped relatively little since the previous (October) measurements.

In this single January survey, the president's overall approval rating was 37 percent. However, on handling relations with the So-

Table 4a.2

Presidential Performance Ratings
(Percent approving)

	National	Republicans	Democrats	Independents
Reagan* (Jan. 1983)	37%	68%	19%	39%
Carter** (Jan. 1979)	47	29	57	47
Nixon (Jan. 1971)	56	83	38	57
Kennedy (Feb. 1963)	70	47	85	66
Eisenhower (Feb. 1955)	72	90	61	79

* Three-survey average
** Two-survey average

viet Union, Reagan received a 41 percent approval rating, nearly matching the 40 percent approval reported in October.

On foreign policy, 36 percent approved of the president's performance, close to the 38 percent recorded earlier. On handling national defense, 44 percent expressed approval, only moderately less positive than the 47 percent approval recorded in the fall.

Fares Worse on Economic Issues

Offsetting the public support given the president on foreign policy issues has been growing public disapproval of his handling of domestic economic issues. Last fall, 36 percent approved of Reagan's handling of economic conditions; in the latest survey 29 percent approved.

On the issue of unemployment, the public's assessment of the president's performance is least favorable (19 percent approval), although virtually no change has occurred in this figure since the earlier survey.

Even on an issue for which the Reagan Administration can claim considerable credit—reducing inflation—public opinion remains more negative than positive. In the latest survey, 36 percent approved of Reagan's handling of inflation, compared to 41 percent approval in the October survey. (This drop in approval came despite the fact that the Consumer Price Index shows the rate of inflation in 1982 to have increased only 3.9 percent compared to 8.9 percent in 1981 and 12.4 percent in 1980.)

"Gender Gap"

Since he took office, President Reagan has been plagued by a "gender gap"—he receives markedly lower assessments of his policies and performance in office from women voters than from men. This sex differential cuts across all social and economic boundaries and is found in every region of the nation.

A special Gallup analysis of more than 4,500 interviews conducted in January permits a detailed examination of Reagan's gender gap for the first time.

In these January surveys, 37 percent of adult Americans said they approved of the way President Reagan is handling the duties of his office, while 54 percent disapproved and 9 percent were uncommitted. During this period 40 percent of men but only 33 percent of women had a favorable opinion of Reagan's job performance—a significant 7-percentage-point difference.

This discrepancy by sex is found—to a greater or lesser degree—in each of the 41 national surveys Gallup has conducted since Reagan took office. A summary is shown in table 4a.3.

Table 4a.3

Reagan Performance Ratings
(Percent approving)

	Both sexes	Men	Women	Difference
1983 (3 surveys)	37%	40%	33%	7 points
1982 (19 surveys)	44	48	40	8
1981 (19 surveys)	58	62	53	9
Average to date	50	54	45	9

Table 4a.4

Presidential Performance Ratings
(Average percent approving)

	Both sexes	Men	Women	Difference
Reagan	50%	54%	45%	9 points
Carter	47	46	47	1
Ford	46	45	46	1
Nixon	49	50	47	3
Johnson	55	56	54	2
Kennedy	70	70	70	–
Eisenhower	64	63	65	2

In a single January survey, the gender gap extended to men's and women's assessment of President Reagan's handling of the economy (33 percent of men approved, but only 26 percent of women did), inflation (43 percent approval from men, 30 percent from women), unemployment (21 percent and 18 percent), and, especially, to Reagan's defense program (53 percent of men and 36 percent of women approved).

These differences by sex are not found in the public's assessments of Reagan's predecessors. As shown in table 4a.4, the greatest previous disparity was during Richard Nixon's presidency, when 50 percent of men and 47 percent of women approved of his job performance.

Underlying Causes

President Reagan's gender gap actually began *before* the 1980 presidential election, in which men voted for Reagan to a greater extent than did women. The reasons underlying this discrepancy are generally considered to center on the peace issue—with women more likely than men to feel Reagan might get the U.S. into war—and on women's consistently more liberal stance on many social issues. Women, for instance, have been more opposed than men to the death penalty and to relaxing environmental standards and more supportive of stricter gun-control legislation. Women have also tended more than men to perceive the Reagan Administration's economic programs as treating minorities, the elderly, and low-income groups unfairly.

These political differences between men and women take on special significance because of changes in the composition of the voting public. According to the U.S. Census, in each election a progressively larger percentage of the electorate is female. The Census studies show that for the first time in history equal proportions of men and women reported voting in the 1980 election. As a consequence, women now represent a majority of the voting public. If the trend persists, they will constitute an increasing majority.

Sex Differences Cross Regional, Social Lines

Not only are women less supportive than men of the Reagan Administration on the national level, but the gender gap is found in every major population subgroup as well.

Among groups which have included the Administration's staunchest supporters: 42

Table 4a.5

Reagan Popularity
(Three-survey average)

Question: Do you approve or disapprove of the way Ronald Reagan is handling his job as president?

	January 1983		
	Approve	*Disapprove*	*No opinion*
National	37%	54%	9%
Sex			
Male	40	53	7
Female	33	56	11
Race			
White	40	51	9
Non-white	13	76	11
Education			
College	46	49	5
High school	36	55	9
Grade school	20	64	16
Region			
East	34	58	8
Midwest	38	52	10
South	36	53	11
West	38	53	9
Age			
18 - 29 years	41	50	9
30 - 49 years	36	56	8
50 & older	34	56	10
Income			
$20,000 & over	44	49	7
Less than $20,000	31	58	11
Politics			
Republican	68	24	8
Democrat	19	74	7
Independent	39	50	11
Religion			
Protestant	38	52	10
Catholic	37	55	8

Table 4a.5

Reagan Popularity (continued)
(Three-survey average)

Occupation			
Professional & business	48	46	6
Clerical & sales	34	58	8
Manual workers	33	57	10
Non-labor force	31	58	11
City Size			
1,000,000 & over	29	62	9
500,000 - 999,999	38	55	7
50,000 - 499,999	34	57	9
2,500 - 49,999	42	49	9
Under 2,500, rural	40	50	10
Labor Union			
Labor union families	30	62	8
Non-labor union families	38	52	10

percent of college-educated women compared to 49 percent of college-educated men approved of Reagan's conduct in office. Among Republicans, a 12-percentage-point gap between the sexes exists, with 74 percent of men but only 62 percent of women approving of the president. In households in which the chief wage-earner is employed in business or the professions, 52 percent of men and 45 percent of women approved.

The principle also embraces population groups which have been least supportive of President Reagan. Among blue-collar occupational groups, for example, 35 percent of men and 30 percent of women gave the president a favorable rating. Also 16 percent of black men but only six percent of black women approved of Reagan's job performance. The gender gap is found in each of the four major geographic regions, with the greatest disparity in the far western states.

Presidential Policy Relationships II: Congress and "The Inevitable Struggle"

5

This chapter focuses on the interaction between the executive and the legislature. Congress and presidents must work together and coordinate in the making of U.S. public policy. The relationship between these actors has been described as "an invitation to struggle" and "separate institutions sharing power." In accordance with the "checks and balances" feature of the Constitution, the two branches are made rivals by intrusions of each into the business of the other. Further exacerbating this rivalry is the fact that each is organized and structured in different ways, with distinctive constituencies, time frames, and policy roles. Presidencies are more hierarchical and reference national coalitions. They are driven by four-year time frames and are preoccupied with policy design and implementation. Congresses are less hierarchical and serve geographical constituencies. They are driven by two- or six-year time frames and are preoccupied with policy formulation and legitimation. Because of these differences, Congress and the President are frequently at loggerheads.

The decade of the 1970s was an extremely conflictual one for executive-congressional relations. Congress and the president competed intensely. Congress passed the National Commitments Resolution restricting the use of presidential "executive agreements" that might involve potential use of U.S. forces and requiring that such agreements be ratified by the Senate in the manner of a treaty. This was just the first of many similar congressional assertions. Congress passed the War Powers Act, in an override of President Nixon's veto, stipulating the length and conditions of presidential deployment of U.S. military forces without a declaration of war. Congress required presidents to submit their nominees for director of OMB to the Senate for approval through the advise and consent process. Congress established a new budget process, restricting presidential impoundments and consolidating congressional budget authority. Finally, Congress intervened in international hotspots, cutting off funds for U.S. involvement in Angola and Southeast Asia and embargoing U.S. arms aid to Turkey during the crisis in Cyprus.

Yet, the relationship between president and Congress is not always this acrimonious. During times of crisis, during honeymoon periods after presidential elections—especially landslide ones—and during what are called majoritarian alignments (in which one party controls both branches), cooperation between the president and Congress is generally good and the president is influential. However, during periods of divided party control, when there are perceived threats to congressional prerogatives, relationships between president and Congress will be quite conflictual. In reading the following essays, students should give consideration to the strengths and weaknesses traded off in both cooperative and conflictual arrangements. Another question to be addressed is: Has the congressional assertiveness of the 1970s given way to a more cooperative or dormant Congress? If so, why?

Legislative Leadership   5.1

Richard M. Pious

An interesting facet of presidential-congressional relations is the expectation from many quarters, including many members of Congress, that presidents will lead Congress in the formulation and development of public policy. The following essay gives an overview of presidential leadership of Congress, with an emphasis on the modes and methods of presidential influence.

Presidents must lead Congress. They need Senate consent to their nominations and treaties, and congressional assent to their legislative proposals, reorganization plans, and certain administrative actions. They want Congress to appropriate the funds they recommend in their executive budgets. But presidents rarely succeed as legislative leaders. Lyndon Johnson could talk of "my Congress" after winning passage of much Great Society legislation, but most presidents echo Theodore Roosevelt, who pleaded, "Oh, if I could be President and Congress too for just ten minutes," and his cousin Franklin, who remarked "I suppose, if the truth were told, he is not the only President that has had that idea."[1]

The Constitution permits the president to propose measures to Congress that he thinks expedient, address or otherwise communicate to it on the state of the Union, call it into special session or adjourn it if the two chambers fail to agree on a date, and use the suspensory or pocket veto. Congress is assigned seventeen enumerated powers, the "necessary and proper" power, and the right to override the suspensory veto. It uses its constitutional authority to teach one president after another that it is a coordinate rather than subordinate branch of government.

Each president asks for a marriage with Congress, but after an initial honeymoon period each winds up filing for divorce. "It is much easier in many ways for me," John Kennedy admitted, "when Congress is not in town."[2] Much of Eisenhower's Modern Republicanism, Kennedy's New Frontier, and Nixon's New American Revolution wound up the casualty of the war between the branches. Lyndon Johnson had his tax program delayed, reorganization plans stalled, and nomination for chief justice defeated by a legislature he supposedly dominated. After just two months of Carter's presidency, the majority leader of the Senate, Robert Byrd, told a news conference, "I wrote to the President that there's a great sense of frustration, the feeling on the part of members that they had not been consulted, brought into decisions before they were made."[3] By the fall the Senate had gutted the energy program, withdrawn the tax rebate bill, and stalled a package of political reforms. In an end-of-year television interview with several network correspondents, Carter admitted that as a novice in the ways of Washington he had a lot to learn about Congress, but that legislative leaders had taught him several hard lessons about consultation and compromise.

Congress insists on being treated as a partner. Party and committee leaders balk at pre-

---

The American Presidency (pp. 176-210) by Richard M. Pious, 1979, New York: Basic Books, Inc., Publishers. Copyright 1979 by Basic Books, Inc. Reprinted by permission.

rogative government and react when presidents ride roughshod, take them for granted, or refuse to bargain with them. The opposition speaks of cooperation in the national interest but awaits any situation ripe for a partisan ambush. Always there are the complicated parliamentary procedures which a new administration must master in order to move its proposals along.

But Congress will accept strong presidential leadership because it simply is not very good at developing or passing comprehensive programs when left to its own devices. The so-called veto-proof Democratic Congress elected in 1974 fought President Ford to a standstill, but could not pass a coherent energy package, failed to reform the banking system, and did not pass proposals for structural economic reform. The president is best situated to propose comprehensive programs, articulate a conception of the national interest, and educate the public to the dimensions of national problems. A president who is weak as a leader does not, by his failure to lead Congress, create conditions for legislative policymaking: there is no "see-saw" effect. When the president cannot lead Congress the result is scattered innovation, incremental rather than comprehensive programming, or deadlock between the branches. Crisis then forces the president to assert prerogative powers, with all the resulting problems this may cause him. However hard it may seem, the president must make the effort to lead Congress, even though what Lord Chesterton once said of "sexual congress" applies equally well to his job: "The pleasure is temporary, the position is ludicrous, and the expense is damnable."

The Presidential Program

When a president sends a bill to Congress he usually asks for broad authority for his executives, for responsibility expressed in terms of goals rather than specific methods, and for any delegation of legislative power to be given to the president, who then subdelegates to subordinate officials, ensuring a "chain of command" from the White House to the departments.[4] Officials are to be given power to "legislate" the details of the law by issuing regulations. Bills generally provide for indefinite or long-term authorizations. In crises Congress often passes laws with these broad provisions, and even in normal times some bills may delegate authority in this way, as examination of some of the Great Society laws indicates. But most of the time Congress will modify presidential proposals. It will provide only narrow statutory authority for officials, include detailed descriptions of authorized activities, and include specific limitations and prohibitions on agency activities. Congress often rewrites and revises the statutory bases of agencies, placing administrative procedures and standards into the law, as well as agency regulations and directives as Congress itself interprets them. It delegates authority directly to subcabinet officials, some at the career level, limiting presidential authority to set policy for the agency. It may require detailed reporting to committees or the full chamber prior to action by officials, and certain administrative actions may even require committee or chamber approval from one or both houses of Congress prior to implementation. Often agencies are authorized to act for only one or two years. Authority may be delegated to agencies not controlled by the president, such as public corporations, regulatory commissions and boards, or autonomous units within departments that function as quasi-judicial commissions.

Presidents do not control distributive or "pork-barrel" measures. Congress usually rewrites various formulae governing grant distributions, because cleavages form on regional (e.g., sunbelt versus snowbelt) or county (e.g., urban versus rural) lines. Presidents do better in shepherding welfare legislation through the legislature. Their proposals involving fiscal policy, including appropriations and tax measures, are usually reworked substantially by Congress, and their priorities are often given short shrift. Defense and national security bills provide a mixed picture: presidents have least influence in the distributions (e.g., military bases, procurement contracts); they are often defeated in amounts they request for foreign aid; and they must compromise when they attempt to reorganize the defense establishment. But they do obtain congressional resolutions backing them in crises, such as the Formosa, Middle East, Berlin, Cuban, and Gulf of Tonkin resolutions. They have won in the past authorizations and appropriations to conduct undeclared wars in Korea and Indochina. More recently Congress has placed restrictions on the conduct of presidential warmaking, created a veto over arms sales and nuclear reactor sales abroad, prevented aid to an American-backed faction in the civil war in Angola, and placed some restrictions on Pentagon contracting and budgeting. No longer can a president count automatically on congressional backing for his diplomatic or military initiatives.

Presidents seem to have good records as legislative leaders, if one simply looks at the percentage of measures they support that Congress eventually passes—a figure that ranges from 50 percent to 90 percent. But the president often simply goes on record in support of department or legislative initiatives about which he cares little. Congress passes a far smaller proportion of the president's own program—generally between 25 percent and 35 percent when a Republican president faces a Democratic Congress, and between 40 percent to 60 percent when a Democratic president enjoys partisan majorities in both houses. Yet in only four years between 1961 and 1977 have over half the presidential programs been passed into law. Some measures that are passed actually represent defeats for the president: titles of his bills may remain after their content has been changed, with revisions destined to weaken his influence over policymaking. At times the program a president submits will have already been modified in anticipation of the reactions of Congress, so even if it is passed intact, it may still incorporate a "congressional" rather than a "presidential" position. Or a president may support or even introduce a bill that he does not care about, as part of an arrangement with a member of Congress whose cooperation on another issue he needs. It isn't often that a president wins passage of a bill he really wants in exactly the form he wants it.

Party Leaders

No president controls his legislative party. Its leaders, the Speaker of the House, the House leader and whips, and the Senate leader and whips, are not his lieutenants, for he neither chooses them nor do they serve at his pleasure. The legislative party chooses its leaders, and the president does not intervene because such intervention would violate the separation of powers and alienate the loser and his faction, and because most contests are already sewn up by a favorite.[5] The Speaker of the House is usually elected after more than twenty years' service in Congress, through an established succession from whip to leader to Speaker.[6] "When I'm talking about my party," Speaker "Tip" O'Neill observed, "I'm talking about the House," for it is to the legislative party that loyalties of the leaders run. In the Senate, party leaders may be elected as early as their first term, but they are also loyal to the chamber; in the words of Majority Leader Robert Byrd, "The role of the Senate is not to be a rubber stamp for any president."[7]

But sometimes a president may dominate the legislative party, and for brief periods the leaders subordinate themselves to White House domination. Usually friction between leaders and the president ends the brief foray into party government. Jefferson founded his party and personally led it: Speaker of the House Nathaniel Macon and chairman of the Ways and Means Committee John Randolph were his personal selections. Committees were packed with administration supporters, and Jefferson presided over a party caucus to set policy. Even so, the president could not maintain control of the party, which split along regional lines on several domestic issues and failed to back his foreign policy by repealing the neutrality laws. In 1806 Randolph split with him over an administration proposal for a secret fund to bribe the Spanish and French courts in order to acquire Florida, and Jefferson had trouble with a succession of other congressional leaders.

Woodrow Wilson, considered a strong party leader, fared even worse with the congressional leaders. At the beginning of his presidency, 114 freshmen Democrats looked to him for leadership, and Speaker Champ Clark and Ways and Means Chairman Oscar Underwood hoped to work closely with the president. Most of the committee chairmen came from the progressive wing of the party as a result of assignments Democrats had made when they won control of the house in 1911. Wilson might have been able to use the House caucus much as Jefferson had done, since in 1909 the Democrats adopted a rule that provided that members must back any position that won a two-thirds vote in the caucus. In the Senate Wilson's choice for majority leader, John Kern, replaced Thomas Martin, and the new leader appointed a Steering Committee dominated by progressives, which in turn reorganized committee assignments to give Wilson's allies key positions.[8] Given these initial circumstances, Wilson functioned for some time as an effective leader, with successes on the tariff, the Federal Reserve System, the Federal Trade Commission, a Department of Labor, workmen's compensation, and an income tax. But Senate Majority Leader Claude Kitchin opposed Wilson's foreign policies, and even voted against the declaration of war. On several major bills Wilson used Democrats on the Rules Committee to undercut Speaker Clark and his majority leader.[9] Wilson made a routine practice of using committee leaders to manage legislation, which weakened the position of party leaders and the usefulness of the caucus. Although he had begun his presidency as an advocate of party government, Wilson could not work well with his leaders, and actually promoted the centrifugal tendencies in Congress.

The Speaker of the House

Presidents want to work closely with the Speaker, especially if they are of the same party. But presidents also know that the Speaker is a potential rival to dominate policymaking. That this danger is not hypothetical is illustrated by the strong Speaker system that developed between 1880 and 1910. Rules changes gave the Speaker power to appoint members to committees, to appoint and chair the Rules Committee (giving him control of the legislative calendar and procedures for debate), to appoint committee chairmen, and to preside over his party caucus. The majority leader chaired the Appropriations Committee and the majority whip the Judiciary Committee, and the patronage they could bestow was used to ensure that the Speaker would dominate the party caucus. In the 1890s adherence to caucus decisions became an expected norm, and party discipline on roll call votes increased.

Some journalists and political scientists, observing these developments, predicted that the Speaker would soon become a "prime minister" running the government under a figurehead president. The Speaker and his committee chairmen would form a "ministry" that, through laws and appropriations, would direct the departments. The figurehead president would invite the Speaker and his "ministry" to sit with department secretaries in a "supercabinet" arrangement, with the Speaker presiding. Policy would be set by Congress and routine administration left to the secretaries. The president would remain ceremonial head of state, but the real contest for power would center around control of the House, for the party with the majority would elect the Speaker. Voters, in choosing members of Congress, would in effect be indicating their choice for a Speaker who would run the government through the "supercabinet."

For several reasons such a system never evolved. The majority party in the House sometimes dealt with a president from the opposition, and it would have been absurd to expect Cleveland or McKinley or Taft to invite a Speaker from the other party to control their administrations. The Senate also experienced centralization of power. In the 1890s the Republican Senate caucus permitted the majority leader to set the legislative agenda and make committee assignments. Party voting increased, and the Republican majority was dominated by men representing the great financial empires of the nation (William Allison, Nelson Aldrich, Mark Hannah, James McMillan, and Orville Platt), and these men were not about to relinquish the great constitutional prerogatives of their chamber in appointments and foreign affairs to a "super-ministry" dominated by the Speaker of the House. The president could play off the Senate against the House on issues involving taxes, tariffs, currency and foreign policy. The House itself chafed under the Speaker's rule and eventually ended the system. In 1910 a coalition of Democrats and insurgent Republicans stripped Speaker Joe Cannon of the power to appoint and chair the Rules Committee, set calendars, and control floor debate. In 1911, when Democrats took control of the House, they took from the Speaker the power to appoint committee chairs, and soon both parties established special "committees on committees" to make these assignments. The majority leader lost the chairmanship of Ways and Means in 1921, and henceforth party and committee positions were left separated. No Speaker in modern times can accumulate enough power in the chamber to become a "prime minister," and no president is so weak that he would permit such a development.

Although power remains decentralized in Congress, some strengthening of party leadership occurred in the 1970s. The Democratic caucus began to hold a meeting every month, provided fifty members requested it, and in 1972 the caucus ordered Democrats on the House Foreign Affairs Committee to legislate an end of American combat in Indochina, in an attempt to force a confrontation with the Nixon administration. In 1973 the caucus debated Watergate, war powers, and budget bills; in 1974 it developed positions on energy and tax legislation; and in 1975 it voted to end assistance to South Vietnam. The caucus also gained some authority over the selection of committee chairmen. In 1973 it provided for secret voting for election of chairmen, and in 1975 it gave the function of making nominations to the Steering and Policy Committee of the caucus. When this committee recommended that two chairmen be deposed, the caucus went one better and deposed three. In 1977 it also ousted the chairman of an appropriations subcommittee. Henceforth no committee leaders could be assured of their positions if they defied express instructions of the caucus on a significant issue.

This centralization of party leadership might be useful to a Democratic president if he could persuade the caucus of the merits of his program. As Carter assumed office in 1977, however, the trend to strengthen party leaders seemed to increase his problems. Instead of following the White House line, leaders became even more responsive to sentiment within the chamber, and the caucus often took its own initiatives to pressure the administration to advance its scheduling of new measures. Committee leaders managed to retain independence from both caucus and president on most issues, while Carter was unable to dominate the caucus and make it an instrument of party leadership.

The Speaker presides over the House, assigns bills to committees, schedules floor debates, and, if a Democrat, chooses the Democratic members of the Rules Committee. Since the House does not provide the president with a special calendar for executive proposals, the president must seek the cooperation of the Speaker on his terms. When the president does work closely with the Speaker, he finds that his program is facilitated. Speaker O'Neill's efforts on behalf of the Carter energy program are illustrative. The Speaker created an ad hoc energy committee to consider the program once the regular standing committees had completed their work. He used party leaders and his allies on the Rules Committee to make compromises among various party factions. He set deadlines, and the energy bill sailed through the House in less than one hundred days, in substantially the form that the president could accept. In another example, when Democrats were about to rebuff the president and restore funds he had cut from the B-1 bomber program, the Speaker made a speech urging Democrats who were thinking of defecting to "stay with the President of the United States, who is the leader of our party." Alluding to criticisms of the president, the Speaker continued, "I know there are those who believe that they haven't been treated right by this administration. I know there are those who say, 'I haven't been able to get a job in my district. I haven't been able to get a dam.' Cast that aside. This is a national issue."[10] The Speaker managed to hold over two-thirds of his party in line and carried the day for the president.

Senate Democrats have never centralized power formally in the manner of their colleagues in the House, but in 1975 they provided for a secret vote for election of committee chairmen, and their caucus began to discuss issues. But since 1934 there has been no rule binding members to support the caucus position, and even when such rules existed in 1903-13 and 1933 they were never applied. Republicans also maintain a decentralized system. In neither party are committee chairs ousted from their positions for disagreements with a president of their party. Senate leaders confine themselves to scheduling, arranging floor debate, and persuading members to support the party consensus on floor votes. When a president has a hard time working with the leader, as Carter does, he may be abruptly "notified" that his major welfare reform and tax proposals and his Panama Canal treaty will be delayed for several months until the administration can round up more support.

The president consults with party leaders about the content and timing of his proposals. They sense the mood of the chamber and advise the president when to move ahead and when to lay back, when to make a dramatic gesture and when to adopt a low profile. They can advise the president on his choice of a sponsor for the bill and on his choice of a person to manage it in committee and on the floor. Party leaders also help choose members of the "conference committee" that reconciles the versions passed by the two chambers—the final stage of the legislative process when the president wants supporters revising the measure. Neither the president nor the party leaders control Congress, but working together they can develop a strategy that offers the White House some chance of success.

Party Voting

Although the president cannot enforce party discipline, party voting in the chamber is usually high. Such cohesion cannot be ascribed to efforts the president or his party leaders make, nor to the limited authority of the caucuses. The president provides no "gravitational attraction" that induces members of his party to support his position on domestic issues. Kennedy did not change Democratic patterns in 1961, and Nixon did not change Republican patterns in 1969.[11] But the president may have some influence in foreign affairs and national security matters. Republican support for foreign aid programs rose sharply when Eisenhower was in office, and similar gains were recorded when Kennedy was president on the Democratic side.[12] Congressional party leaders have little influence and caucuses almost none.[13] If the president and an administrative agency disagree on a bill, legislators are likely to support the agency position, especially on authorizations and appropriations.[14] Party cohesion is high primarily because members of the same party draw on similar kinds of voter coalitions and make similar appeals to the electorate. Different factions in the party that come from different regions or appeal to diverse constituencies have an incentive to logroll and compromise rather than defect to the opposition. These deals are facilitated by party leaders and the White House. Democrats especially encourage their leaders to arrange compromises to benefit each of the various factions in its turn, and this style of leadership results in high party voting.[15]

On important issues approximately 70 percent of the key roll call votes will put a majority of one party against a majority of the other. But even on these votes there will be defections: one study concluded that between 1949 and 1969 on only 13 percent of the votes did as much as 90 percent of the Democrats vote together, and on only 31 percent of the votes did 90 percent of the Republicans vote together.[16] Democrats win three out of four party votes, since they are almost always the majority in both houses. But when southerners defect and join with Republicans to form a conservative coalition on distributive or social welfare issues, a Democratic president may be defeated. The conservative coalition appeared on approximately one-quarter of the roll call votes between 1961 and 1976, winning as little as 35 percent of them in 1965 and as much as 83 percent of the votes in 1971.[17] The president relies on party leaders to try to forestall the emergence of such a coalition, or else he will be defeated on his urban-oriented welfare measures.[18] Republicans may split along conservative-liberal lines, or may fragment on a regional basis so that Republican presidents may lose enough votes to doom their program from the start. A conservative president may not be able to piece together a coalition if enough southern Democrats remain with their party. A Democratic president who can compromise with liberal Republicans may create a bipartisan majority sufficient to pass major parts of his program.

Coalition Building

The president must persuade and bargain with legislators to build working majorities in each chamber. Some presidents, like Franklin Roosevelt, are fierce partisans who work with the opposition only in crises. Others, like Eisenhower, prefer a bipartisan approach. Kennedy and Johnson combined partisan leadership with overtures to the Republicans when necessary. Kennedy rarely succeeded, but Johnson, working closely with Republican Senate Minority Leader Everett Dirksen, won passage of the Civil Rights Act of 1964, the Voting Rights Act of 1965, and foreign aid, minimum wage, and rent subsidy legislation.[19] Johnson made sure that credit was shared with Dirksen, so that "a hero's niche could be carved out for Senator Dirksen, not me."[20] Nixon and Ford tried to create a bipartisan conservative coalition. William Safire recalls that at a meeting of senior White House aides Nixon reminded them that "some Democrats support us better than some Republicans do."[21] The conservative coalition achieved some of its greatest successes in the Nixon and Ford presidencies.

Influencing the Committees

The key to success with Congress is influencing what happens in the committees. A sympathetic majority can speed consideration of presidential proposals, arrange for "friendly" hearings, and "mark up" the bill to reflect White House priorities. Its members can lead the floor debate and work with party leaders to create a coalition for passage. A hostile committee can pigeonhole the bill by refusing to report it to the chamber, delay hearings, or revise the measure so thoroughly that it no longer is a presidential bill. When a committee bottles up a measure it is almost impossible for the president to win its release. House procedures permit the discharge of bills from committees; but between 1910 and 1971, while thousands of bills were delayed, there were only 835 discharge petitions circulated and only 24 gained floor consideration. Only two of those measures ever became law. A hostile committee majority may also speed consideration of measures when the president prefers to wait.

Usually administration bills are revised thoroughly in the "markup" sessions, so that the committee version is reported to the chamber for consideration. The president must negotiate with committee and subcommittee leaders, who are not lieutenants of the president, do not necessarily represent the sentiment of rank-and-file members of the legislative party, and need not pay attention to the caucus under most circumstances. Committee leaders are specialists who identify with particular programs and are intimately familiar with the details of the laws they write. Most will support agencies in conflicts with the president. They have close ties with the bureaucracy and with the interest and clientele groups that government agencies serve. They come for the most part from safe districts and therefore are insulated from electoral pressure. They have the most seniority in Congress (uninterrupted service in the chamber) and the most committee seniority (uninterrupted service on the committee). Almost all of them become chairmen (or ranking minority members) through operation of the rule of seniority, which gives the position to the member of the party with the most seniority on the committee. The almost automatic operation of the seniority rule prevents the president from assembling his own team of loyalists whom he can install as committee leaders. Unlike Jefferson or Wilson, presidents now must take committee leaders and rosters as they find them.[22]

Once committee leaders were all-powerful, especially after the decline of the strong-Speaker system and weakening of caucuses. The autocratic chairman of the House Rules Committee, Charles Campbell, once told his colleagues, "You can go to hell; it makes no difference what a majority of you decide, if it meets with my disapproval, it shall not be done. I am the committee!"[23] But in the past few years a quiet revolution has taken place: chairmen must now obtain approval of majorities for everything from scheduling hearings to making subcommittee appointments; the subcommittees in turn have gained a "bill of rights" that gives them some autonomy from the full committees. Legislative power has been diffused, to encompass most senators and over one hundred representatives who chair such subcommittees. No longer can a president simply win over a committee chairman; he must now win over a majority. But an obstructive chairman is no longer an insurmountable obstacle: when Carter attempted to win House approval of his proposals for new reorganization authority, he faced opposition from the chairman of the Government Operations Committee in the House. Taking advantage of the new committee procedures, the president was able to build a majority coalition on the committee and win favorable action on his proposal.

Liaison and Lobbying

To build his coalitions the president must communicate with legislative leaders and rank-and-file members. Lyndon Johnson told his cabinet after the 1964 elections, "I want to be especially sure that each of you selects a top man to serve as your legislative liaison. Next to the cabinet officer himself, I consider this the most important position in the department."[24] Prior to the Second World War presidents were assisted by cabinet and subcabinet officials, especially those with prior congressional service. Wilson relied on his attorney general and also instituted the "Common Council Club," a group of thirty subcabinet officials (including Assistant Secretary of the Navy Franklin Roosevelt) to round up support on Capitol Hill for administration measures. Franklin Roosevelt used his postmaster general, and the position of assistant secretary of commerce was filled by an official in charge of White House lobbying efforts.

During the Second World War the War Department performed liaison for the administration, with over 200 officers assigned to its Legislation and Liaison Division. Several White House aides and the BOB's Legislative Reference Division also lobbied in Congress. After the war the Department of Defense created an assistant secretary for congressional liaison, the Department of State named an assistant secretary for congressional relations, and between 1949 and 1963 the other departments followed suit, assigning over five hundred officials to these units.

Departmental liaison offices were supervised by a White House unit. Truman assigned the lobbying function to two aides, and Eisenhower created the first formal office, headed by Jerry Parsons and Bryce Harlow, both of whom had operated within the original War Department office. Kennedy kept the unit and named Lawrence O'Brien to head it; Johnson retained O'Brien, and occasionally attended staff meetings to regale department liaison officers with anecdotes and to give them advice based on his long experience as a party leader in the Senate.[25] Bryce Harlow returned to serve under Nixon, and after he left, William Timmons served both Nixon and Ford. The Office of Congressional Relations (OCR) was enlarged and divided into a "Senate Staff," "House Staff," a group to service requests by legislators to the departments, and a group that circulated a "reporter" of committee and chamber schedules for hearings, markups, floor debates, and votes. Frank Moore headed Carter's operation, but the president also relied on Vice-President Mondale to develop strategy and contact key congressional leaders.

In every administration, OCR staff members have backgrounds as legislators, legislative aides, lobbyists, or public relations experts. Some move from departmental liaison offices to the White House. They rely on expertise to present the president's case. As Ralph Huitt, a political scientist who was a department lobbyist in the Johnson administration pointed out,

> The most effective tool . . . is knowledge, expertise, a command of the business at hand. The member wants to do his job well and succeed as a congressman. The person who can help him do that, who knows how to solve a problem—especially if he can offer a "little language," i.e. a well drafted provision that can go into a bill—never has trouble getting access and a thoughtful hearing.[26]

Administration lobbyists work closely with interest groups. In support of Johnson's 1965 aid to education bill, U.S. Commissioner of Education Francis Keppel won support from Catholic lay organizations, Jack Valenti at the White House maintained communication with the Vatican apostolic delegate, Lee White worked with Jewish groups, Henry Hall Wilson rounded up southern support, and Douglass Cater drummed up support from the National Education Association.[27] Campaigning to raise the debt ceiling, the Nixon administration mobilized defense contractors, who called conservative Republicans and urged them to support the measure on national security grounds. When Kennedy submitted a school construction bill, White House aides worked to get Democratic votes, and construction company lobbyists were dispatched to work on the Republicans. White House aides work with the American Bar Association on bills providing legal services, with the American Medical Association when issues involve medical care, and with other professional organizations as the need arises.[28]

The administration will work with local and state party leaders, public officials, and interest groups who might hold the key to how legislators will vote.[29] During the fight to pass a federal aid to education measure, a legislator offered a parochial school amendment that Kennedy opposed. The White House contacted his local party leader, who then phoned the Roman Catholic congressman and urged him to withdraw the amendment, asking "Who sent you there, me or the Bishop? And who's going to keep you there, me or the Bishop?"[30] In 1977 Vice-President Mondale appealed to Democratic state party leaders to support Carter's ill-fated tax rebate proposal at a luncheon for the Democratic State Chairmen's Association—efforts that could not salvage the proposal. Just three days after the Kennedy assassination Lyndon Johnson invited the governors to the White House for a discussion of his legislative program, and convinced many of them to support his tax and civil rights proposals. The governors in turn used their influence on congressional delegations.[31] The Nixon administration lobbied with governors and mayors of both parties to gain support for its revenue-sharing proposals, and they pressured a reluctant committee chairman, Wilbur Mills, to speed consideration of the measure.

The president will "stroke" important legislators. The master of the art, Lyndon Johnson, noted that "there is but one way for a President to deal with Congress, and that is continuously, incessantly, and without interruption," adding that "if it's really going to work, the relationship between the President and Congress has got to be almost incestuous."[32] The president meets with members of Congress for breakfast and luncheons, strolls with them in the White House Rose Garden, and may on exceptional occasions invite them to spend the weekend with him at Camp David or another retreat. Eisenhower invited the entire Congress to a series of luncheons and met regularly with Democratic leaders Rayburn and Johnson over drinks. Kennedy hosted cocktail parties, and Lawrence O'Brien invited members to brunches. Johnson held buffet dinners followed by briefings from cabinet members, and he would brief about one hundred members of his party the evening before a major new bill would be sent up. The president may offer certain key legislators unlimited access; Eisenhower gave Majority Leader Robert Taft the go-ahead to phone or visit at any time at the senator's convenience.

These techniques rarely change votes. At best they keep the president and his opponents on speaking terms, and let members who support the administration know that their help is appreciated. Eisenhower's luncheons were held amidst his feuds with the Republican right wing, and Taft was a fierce opponent of the president on many issues. Even Lyndon Johnson's "treatment," which involved bringing lawmakers into the White House for doses of flattery, bullying, and every possible psychological ploy, did not prevent Congress from obstructing much of his domestic program after 1966.

The institutionalization of legislative liaison provides an object lesson for anyone who would equate a large White House staff with effective use of presidential power. An aide needs immediate access to the president and the authority to speak for him, deal for him, and act in his name. Bryce Harlow has observed that "for real effectiveness a White House congressional man must be known on Capitol Hill as a confidant of the president; he must be in the know, he must have the stature to obtain immediate contact with the President, directly or indirectly, when emergency requires."[33] Aides like Harlow or O'Brien recount the times they have spoken in the name of the president during sensitive negotiations with congressional leaders, and how impressed these leaders were with the degree of access the liaison officers enjoyed. But the president can give such access and authority to only a few aides, for otherwise he would be under seige. No matter how large the office, only a few staff members have the stature and access to the president necessary to impress legislative leaders. Low-ranking aides can neither deal for the president nor bring him accurate information, for Lyndon Johnson notes that "the key to accurate head counts is personal knowledge or trust, and the ability to probe beneath the surface to see what individuals are really thinking and feeling"[34] Unless a liaison officer is close to the president, he will be unable to communicate presidential views to legislators, and they in turn will not confide their intentions to a low-ranking aide.

The liaison staff argues that to be effective it must serve as "counsel" to the president on legislative strategy. It therefore may attempt to influence the content of program proposals as well as advise on strategy and tactics. But if it claims a program "won't fly" in Congress, it may interfere with the interests of the OMB, the Domestic Policy Staff, the Council of Economic Advisors, and other White House aides, councils, or offices. The OCR is often involved in bureaucratic infighting and may contribute to conflict within the inner circle. When presidential bills are delayed, gutted, amended, or defeated, the OCR takes the heat, and other White House units are likely to argue that its performance (rather than the content of the measure) was responsible for the outcome.

No Office of Congressional Relations, however run, can substitute for intimate and sustained presidential involvement in the legislative process. The incumbent must know the mood in each chamber, and demonstrate some mastery of legislative strategy and tactics. He must know the details of the process that involves his bill—budgetary, fiscal, reorganization, nomination, treaty—or other measure. By mastering the details, he impresses his supporters with his personal commitment and his opponents with his ability. His legislative program will languish if he does not pay attention to it. Theodore Roosevelt, Woodrow Wilson, and Franklin Roosevelt had no formal liaison offices, yet each, by personally involving himself, won major victories.

Transactions

The presidential power to persuade legislators rests on more than expertise, lobbying, or "stroking." A president may offer tangible quid pro quos to win votes for his measures. As one congressman described how the Eisenhower administration sought to win passage of the Landrum-Griffin act regulating labor union activities, "If a man goes along, he gets money for his campaign; if he doesn't go along, he gets nothing. It's that simple."[35] Former White House assistant Doris Kearns reports that during the Johnson administration, Senate Minority Leader Everett Dirksen "would blatantly and without hesitation send long memos to the White House detailing his requests for that week: a judgeship in the fifth district, a post office in Peoria, a presidential speech in Springfield, a tax exemption for peanuts."[36] Such favors are useful for low-visibility (yet crucial) actions such as voting for a measure in committee or on votes prior to final passage of bills. Legislators can vote one way on final passage, shielding themselves from constituent reprisals, while at the same time helping the president move his program along prior to that vote.

The president can offer patronage. Most of the approximately five hundred federal district judges are nominated by arrangements with state and local party organizations through the custom of "senatorial courtesy," in effect making the president a "clerk" for members of the Senate from his party. The ninety-four U.S. attorneys and the marshalls are also chosen by party leaders. Some nominees for specialized and appellate federal courts are sponsored by members of the House and Senate Judiciary Committees.

The White House fills executive branch positions in consultation with members of Congress, who may sponsor aides or committee staff members for positions. Former legislators defeated in the elections may also be offered positions with the administration. The president may trade his appointment power for passage of a program. To win the support of Republican Senator Arthur Vandenburg for the Marshall Plan aiding Europe after the Second World War, Truman promised congressional Republicans that they could staff the program. They in turn pressed Truman to name corporate executives, rather than state department careerists, to run the program. Vandenburg himself nominated the director of the program.[37] Lyndon Johnson cleared nominations of black officials with southern senators; they opposed his choices but appreciated his courtesy in giving them advance notice.[38] Carter named several protégés of House Speaker O'Neill to high positions, including the Speaker's choice to run the General Services Administration, with its pork-barrel distributions.

Members of Congress may support the administration in return for assistance in expediting contracts or grants that will benefit their states or districts. But presidents share power over distributions with committee leaders, and legislation may limit the extent to which the White House can affect the awarding of grants. Some transactions backfire: Rep. Edith Green was outraged by what she considered to be a heavy-handed attempt to "buy" her support for an administration measure combating juvenile delinquency (through the award of a large grant to her district) and turned against the White House. Because she was a committee leader with jurisdiction over the subject, the result was a measure that incorporated her views rather than the White House proposals.[39]

Often presidents make transactions as part of a general strategy. Kennedy cultivated the southern wing of his party: he refrained from issuing an executive order ending racial discrimination in federally assisted housing for two years, and the order he finally signed included only a small fraction of future construction; he kept open unneeded military facilities in the South and made sure defense contracts were disproportionately placed there; he approved a manned space center for Texas; he proposed formulae for grant programs channeling funds to rural areas; he offered a farm program with high price supports for southern crops. In return for the accommodation of southern interests, Kennedy won support from legislators for his economic, military, and foreign assistance programs.

The president must know when to bargain and when to draw the line. Like Wilson or Franklin Roosevelt, he may pass the word that all patronage and distributions will be given near the end of the congressional session once loyalty to the administration has been demonstrated. Lyndon Johnson rewarded legislators who generally supported his program rather than dealing with individuals on each issue in a quid pro quo arrangement. Johnson recalled that with few exceptions, favors were "generally delivered by the White House staff after the fact, and on the basis of a pattern of voting, not by the President personally in exchange for a specific vote."[40] But at times a specific deal is absolutely necessary: Franklin Roosevelt saved his measure extending the draft just prior to American entry into the Second World War with a transaction that provided passage by one vote in the House. Carter preferred not to engage in payoffs, but after the defection of 101 Democrats in the House on his consumer protection bill, a meeting of 26 whips was arranged with the president, and he agreed to facilitate their requests for appointments, grants, and contracts.[41]

Sometimes presidential favors lead to tensions in the chamber. If partisan opponents are rewarded, the president weakens his position with his own party. Transactions merely whet the appetite of lawmakers, and as Johnson explained, "I could not trade patronage for votes in any direct exchange. If word spread that I was trading, everyone would want to trade and all other efforts at persuasion would automatically fail."[42] But a president who announces a "no deal" policy will find himself in trouble: President Carter decided to cut out funding for 19 water-development projects in his fiscal year 1978 budget. He announced that he would review the economic feasibility of another 320 such projects. Both the Senate and the House reacted by voting to require the president to spend any previously appropriated funds for these projects. After the firestorm of protest against the interference in the pork-barrel arrangements, the president backed down, releasing from his review 307 of the projects and restoring to funding 3 of the 19 he had dropped. Still later he restored most of the projects. Carter had damaged his relationship with Congress in a futile attempt to control these distributions, a setback that took him months to repair.

Hardball Tactics

Successful party leaders such as Speaker Sam Rayburn would advise new members "to get along, go along" but they would never ask a member to put his career in jeopardy or violate his conscience on a vote. A corollary of the Rayburn rule was developed by Lawrence O'Brien, who eschewed the hard sell for a softer approach. O'Brien later observed, "I never expected any member to commit political suicide in order to help the president, no matter how noble our cause. I expected politicians to be concerned with their own interests; I only hoped to convince them that our interests were often the same."[43] But at times presidents use rough tactics. Kennedy once lost a crucial Senate vote when West Virginia's Randolph voted against the administration measure. Kennedy ordered the Bureau of the Budget to drop a project that the senator had sponsored. But as White House aide Theodore Sorensen recounted, conservative senators supported Randolph by channeling new projects to his state through other pieces of legislation.[44] Johnson retaliated against Senate criticism of his war policies by cutting off projects in his critics' states, but this only hurt him in the Senate. During both the Haynesworth and Carswell nomination struggles, Nixon threatened senators who planned to vote against his choices for justices of the Supreme Court with opposition in their next primaries, a cutoff of national campaign funds, elimination of public works and grants, and an end to their access to the White House. Some senators were even threatened with an Internal Revenue Service audit of their tax returns. Both nominations were defeated.[45] Larry Pressler, a Republican congressman from South Dakota, charged during Ford's presidency that "a political threat was made to me by a White House lobbyist last week concerning my vote on the natural gas deregulation issue."[46] Two Maine Republicans, William Cohen and David Emery, charged that White House aides told them that if they did not vote to sustain a Ford veto, a former Maine governor would not be reappointed as chairman of the National Transportation Board. They didn't, he wasn't, and they leaked the threat to the press, which prompted Ford, after the public outcry, to send his liaison officials over to the Capitol to make a public apology to the representatives.[47] When the director of the Office of Management and Budget, Bert Lance, was being investigated by the Senate for alleged improprieties as a banker in Georgia, Carter's Press Secretary Jody Powell encouraged publication of a charge that Republican senator Charles Percy had been involved in a violation of the law in financing his 1972 reelection campaign. When Powell's "plant" of the rumor was made known, Carter had him apologize and admit that his action was "inappropriate, regrettable, and dumb."[48] Within a fortnight Lance had resigned, as the Senate continued its investigation into his affairs. In the post-Watergate climate, rough tactics were counterproductive, since there was more political profit to be made by revealing the pressure and standing up to it than there was in knuckling under to it and remaining silent. Neither Ford nor Carter had much success in using "dirty tricks" in their legislative campaigns.

National Agenda Politics

If the president calculates that his attempts at persuasion, negotiation, coalition building, and lobbying will fail, he may move from the "closed" arena of legislative politics to an enlarged arena of the attentive and mass publics.[49] By gaining support for his program in the constituencies of the legislators, he hopes to pressure them to vote for his program. As Lyndon Johnson put it,

> When traditional methods fail, a president must be willing to bypass the Congress and take the issue to the people. By instinct and experience, I preferred to work from within, knowing that good legislation is the product not of public rhetoric but of private negotiations and compromise. But sometimes a president has to put Congress' feet to the fire.[50]

The president "goes public" out of weakness, for if he had the votes he would pass the measure first and go to the public only for the bill-signing ceremonies. But public appeals are one of the few credible threats a president can make. Eisenhower threatened the party leaders who stalled his measures in 1953 that if they did so the next year he would take his case to the people. Only then did his bills begin to move through Congress.[51] Lyndon Johnson had to make an appeal to the people to obtain passage of his Civil Rights Act of 1964, Voting Rights Act of 1965, and Housing Act of 1968. Both Ford and Carter attempted to rally the public behind their energy programs.

The White House may attempt to make its proposals part of the "national agenda," consisting of matters that the public is interested in and that may influence voting behavior in subsequent presidential and congressional elections. (But only a handful of his bills will ever receive sustained public attention; for most of this a strategy cannot be employed.)

A presidential decision to "go public" galvanizes the White House pollsters, speechwriters, and media experts into action. The president must "package" his legislation prior to presenting it to Congress; decisions about substance may be influenced by media advisors. The president needs a theme for a national agenda proposal. Lyndon Johnson called his grab bag of community action, public works, and job training programs a "War on Poverty" because, as he put it, "I wanted to rally the nation, to sound a call to arms."[52] Other presidents have declared "wars" against crime, drugs, or disease. Some presidents present their initiatives in the context of the cold war. Kennedy sold the nation on high expenditures for space exploration by insisting that Americans had to beat the Russians in a manned lunar landing. In the Eisenhower administration, federal aid to education was billed as a way to surpass Soviet scientific achievements, and the program of highway construction was named the Interstate Highway Defense System, since it supposedly had some military value.

The president may package liberal programs in conservative wrappings. Revenue sharing was billed by the Nixon administration as a return to "states rights" and "grass-roots control" of programs. Job training and public works employment measures are promoted to get the "able-bodied" off welfare rolls and onto tax rolls, even though studies have shown that most welfare recipients are not presently employable. The Demonstration Cities proposal of the Great Society was hastily renamed Model Cities after rioting in urban areas gave a bad odor to the original title. The Nixon administration proposal for welfare reform was called the Family Assistance Plan to gain public support. Ford's energy program was called Operation Independence as a means to harness national pride to price decontrol measures.

The president may lose control of the definition of an issue. Truman's program of national health insurance was dubbed socialized medicine by the American Medical Association; after a multimillion dollar public relations campaign, public opinion turned against the plan and Congress never passed it. Also, the president cannot always control the timing of a national agenda issue. In 1961 Kennedy shelved plans to introduce civil rights legislation in Congress in order to gain southern congressional support for his economic and military programs. Black leaders took their followers to the streets in nonviolent demonstrations, and by 1963 the violent response to their activities had made civil rights the major domestic issue. Extensive media coverage was instrumental in placing public opinion on the side of the demonstrators. Kennedy and Johnson then introduced bills that eventually became the Civil Rights Act of 1964. Johnson had no intention of introducing more legislation, preferring a brief cooling-off period, but civil rights leaders again took to the streets, and the violence committed against them by law-enforcement officials in Selma, Alabama, again focused public attention on their cause. The administration then introduced a voting rights bill, which became law in 1965.

The president uses the same media politics techniques that helped him win the nomination and election to make an issue part of the national agenda and to control the debate. He can leave Washington and "work the country," making speeches at rallies and before local parties. White House staff members have worked in campaigns and are eager to replicate their election victory in a new campaign. Such efforts are institutionalized: in the Ford administration the Office of Public Liaison organized conferences between administration leaders and interest groups; the Office of Communications handled television and radio exposure; the Editorial Office coordinated most communications and speeches. Carter's efforts included an assistant to the president for political affairs (Hamilton Jordan), an assistant to the president for intergovernmental affairs (Jack Watson), an assistant to the president for public liaison (Margaret Costanza), a press secretary (Jody Powell), a media advisor (Gerald Rafshoon), a special assistant to the president for appointments (Tim Kraft) in charge of "advance" scheduling and transportation, and a director of White House projects (Gregory Schneiders) who arranged the "town meetings" and other media extravaganzas. In addition, Carter made extensive use of Vice-President Mondale and received advice from his pollsters and media advisors. While the names of these offices change from one administration to the next, the services they provide to the president remain the same.

The president presents national agenda issues in his state of the Union address, his annual budget message, and his economic message. He also may appear on television prior to submitting major programs to Congress, making a "need speech" to the public. He defines the issues, characterizes the program, presents a thematic title, and anticipates criticisms.[53] The White House television studio has a "warm" color camera ready to project the presidential image at a moment's notice. Each studio camera is equipped with a TelePrompTer two-way mirror, so the president can look straight at the camera while following his script. The White House requests air time from the three network news directors, who constitute themselves as an informal committee to consider the request. Each network, however, makes its own decision. Occasionally a network will deny a request or move it to a different time slot and show the speech on videotape.[54] Presidents argue that they have the right to preempt network schedules because what they say is inherently newsworthy, and the networks have an obligation to the public to broadcast their speeches. But the networks have maintained that theirs is a public trust, not a presidential one, and that the final decision on programming must be theirs to make. Although few requests are denied, the network committee may bargain with the White House over the time slot and the length of the speech.

The president has an advantage over his political opponents when he goes public. Between 1969 and 1975, Democratic congressional leaders requested air time eleven times, and were turned down on eight occasions. No group, under the law and the rulings of the Federal Communications Commission, has an automatic "right of reply" to a presidential speech. The FCC's "fairness doctrine" requires that the networks present other viewpoints, but it permits them to determine who represents responsible persons for opposing views, and allows them to determine the format in which these views are presented. At times congressional leaders or the national chairman of the opposition party has received free time to reply to a presidential address, but on other occasions they have been refused prime time and the matter has gone to the courts or to the FCC.[55]

The president always gets a larger audience share than his opposition: Ford's state of the Union address in 1975 was seen by 75 million viewers, whereas three broadcasts on separate evenings of the reply by Democratic congressional leaders drew a total audience of only 47 million. But the president can hardly resort to television for most of his program. His popularity will decline if he preempts prime time too often, and he will suffer from over-exposure. Carter's 1978 Panama Canal "need" speech drew only 48 million viewers, while a movie playing at the same time on CBS drew 35 million.[56] If a presidential appearance generates a temporary surge of public support, congressional leaders may delay consideration of the measure until the media effects wear off. Neither Ford nor Carter could time their use of television to coincide effectively with congressional consideration of their energy programs, and after brief flings with national agenda politics, both returned to the "closed politics" methods of bargaining and compromise.[57]

The president may use news conferences to build support for his programs. Originated by Wilson, conferences were held twice weekly by his Republican successors, dropped entirely by Hoover in the midst of the Depression, then revived by Roosevelt on a biweekly basis. Since then, the frequency has dropped: Truman held almost one a week, Eisenhower two a month, Johnson one a month, Nixon once every two months. In the post-Watergate atmosphere presidents have tried to become more accessible to the media: Ford held a conference approximately once a month, and Carter attempted to meet a schedule of one every two weeks.

The conferences may be keyed to pending legislation. Eisenhower often pressed Congress to take specific actions to move his program along.[58] Staff aides may "plant" a question with a reporter so that the president can comment on congressional committee actions. He may use the conference to signal willingness to compromise, or instead to rally the public to his line. Presidential statements made early in the day may then be circulated by party leaders on the floor to rally administration supporters in close votes. Eisenhower used this tactic to fight cuts in his foreign aid program in 1953, although it had little impact on the voting.[59] The president may even use a news conference to disassociate himself from proposals of his own departments. In 1957 Eisenhower was asked if he favored a provision of the civil rights measure that had been drafted by the Justice Department; his equivocation signaled to Congress that it could amend the measure. Asked in another conference if he supported the spending totals in his budget submitted to Congress, Eisenhower invited Congress to make additional cuts, thus signaling that he would not stand behind the requests of his cabinet secretaries.[60]

Held at the president's pleasure, the news conference enables him to project his strength when he is popular. He will postpone conferences when he is in trouble. He is under no obligation to respond to questions. Presidents generally follow the ground rules set by Franklin Roosevelt, who told reporters at his first conference, "There will be a great many questions, of course, that I won't answer . . . questions which for various reasons I do not want to discuss, or am not ready to

---

President Ford Dramatizes the Issue

. . . I asked the Congress in January to enact this urgent ten-year program for energy independence within 80 days. . . . Now what did the Congress do in February about energy? Congress did nothing. . . . [tears page off calendar] What did the Congress do in March? [tears page] What did the Congress do in April about energy? Congress did nothing. . . . [tears page]

So, what has the Congress done in May about energy? [tears page] Congress did nothing and went home for a 10 day recess. . . . The Congress cannot drift, dawdle, and debate forever with America's future.

I need your help to energize this Congress into comprehensive action. I will continue to press for my January program, which is still the only total energy program there is. I cannot sit here idly while nothing is done. We must get on with the job right now.

President Ford, May 27, 1975 radio and television address.

discuss, or I simply do not know anything about."[61]

Presidents make remarks at conferences that sometimes do more harm than good. Truman called poll taxes, imposed by several states to discourage blacks from voting, a "states rights" issue with which the federal government should not interfere; later, after consulting with his political advisors, he reversed himself.[62] Eisenhower, after inviting Congress to cut his budget, later issued a strong defense of his original requests. Lyndon Johnson was so afraid of making slips that he refused to permit conferences to be televised for almost a year. After his foreign policies were challenged by reporters, he began to call conferences on weekends, often at his ranch in Texas, so that few foreign affairs specialists or reporters would be present, and so that reporters filing stories would be unable to verify details or obtain comments from congressional opponents of the war.[63] In the midst of a war, the president may find his news conference useless for purposes of pressuring Congress on legislation.

The president may cultivate editors, syndicated columnists, and network executives. Kennedy's press secretary, Pierre Salinger, describes such treatment of columnists:

> A request from one of them to see the president personally was usually honored, and the White House staff members on the policy level like Ted Sorensen and McGeorge Bundy made sure that they had the administration's views on prevailing problems.[64]

The president may go over the head of a reporter or bureau chief to the editor or publisher in order to push the administration position on pending legislation, the tactics favored by Kennedy and Johnson. Or he may use "hardball" tactics favored by Nixon: dispatching his vice-president to make an issue of "media bias"; threatening to influence applications by television stations for license renewals before the FCC; having the IRS audit tax returns of reporters; and using White House plumbers to wiretap members of the press.[65]

Most presidents use the carrot more than the stick. Lyndon Johnson gave reporters a version of "the treatment," and as White House correspondent Hugh Sidey described it:

> His idea of great flattery to a correspondent was to take the man under his arm, wine him and dine him and entertain him, treat him to a few innocuous secrets, and then suggest a story line. If it came out as Johnson wanted it to, he invited the fellow back for more intimate moments.[66]

For their favorites, presidents grant exclusive interviews and off-the-record briefings. Kennedy was famous for his "rocking chair" interviews. Johnson participated in a television interview with three network correspondents that was then edited under White House supervision. Nixon telephoned columnists to thank them for defending administration policies.[67] Lyndon Johnson gave publishers advance notice of his intention to develop an antipoverty program so that magazine articles and books about poverty appeared just about the time the program was sent to Congress. Then the president appealed to newspaper editors to mold public opinion through editorials. "Let them know," he told a group of editors and publishers, "that everybody is not eating three meals a day the way they are, that there are conditions in this country that are insupportable, and except for the grace of God they could find themselves in the same spot."[68]

But the president's opponents may use the media effectively. Many former White House political, public relations, editorial, and legislative liaison aides set up shops as lobbyists in the private sector once they leave government service. They know the techniques the White House will use to control the national agenda and can try to develop their own counters on behalf of their clients. Washington "superlawyers" are retained by interest groups to oppose legislation that the administration favors. The investigative media may have its own priorities: documentaries and news articles about malnutrition and hunger in America permitted senators to focus public attention on the inadequacies of the food-stamp program and allowed Congress to expand the program beyond the limits set by the Nixon administration.

The White House may use cabinet secretaries and lower-ranking officials to publicize its programs. During his second term Franklin Roosevelt had 203 officials make radio addresses extolling the accomplishments of the New Deal. Other presidents have dispatched officials around the country to fight for a controversial measure. If the president uses White House speechwriters to monitor addresses given by his secretaries, the press and his opponents may charge that he is "muzzling" the cabinet. But if he gives his secretaries free reign to speak on the issues, they may promote departmental priorities at the expense of his own. Truman fired Secretary of Commerce Henry Wallace for his public campaign to force the president into a reconsideration of his foreign policies. Ford fired James Schlesinger as secretary of defense when he attempted to make a national agenda issue of alleged Soviet arms buildups in strategic and conventional weaponry just at the time Congress was considering the Pentagon's procurement requests. Carter's secretary of agriculture, Robert Berglund, took the side of the farmers and urged them to continue their "strike" until Congress passed measures to raise farm income—measures that the president did not support. The White House often must counter national agenda efforts made by its own departments. A constant flood of news releases, messages to Congress, letters to committee leaders, memoranda to cabinet officials, remarks at political functions, and meetings with interest groups—all serve as correctives to present the administration "line" and undercut secretaries who have staked out their own positions.

A president stands a better chance of success with national agenda politics when he takes his initiatives early in his term, or if his popularity increases due to a successful venture in foreign affairs. Every president begins his term with high ratings during the "honeymoon" period. Each, with the exception of Eisenhower, experienced a long-term decline in his approval rating, with a slight "rebound" effect near the end of his term.[69] The decline-rebound effect gives the "approval rating" as measured by public opinion polls a parabolic curve that appears natural and inevitable. Declines may often be sharp and can be traced in part to specific events, such as recession or scandal: recent examples include Watergate, Ford's pardon of Nixon, and Carter's problems with the Bert Lance affair. Presidential popularity may not be much of a resource for most presidents: Truman conducted much of his first and almost all of his second term with low ratings; Lyndon Johnson was unpopular after he escalated the war in Vietnam; and during Nixon's second term and Ford's caretaker term public approval ratings for presidents reached new postwar lows. Carter had not yet completed his first year in office when his ratings tumbled as a result of the Lance affair, and many polls found low levels of confidence in the executive branch that almost matched levels during the Ford administration (see figure 5.1.1).

Sometimes the making of a national agenda issue may be the unmaking of a president. Truman's agricultural program, the Brannan Plan, became a national agenda issue but proved unpopular with urban voters when they learned that its implementation would mean higher food prices. Nixon's attempt to curtail several Great Society education programs failed after education lobbies rallied grass-roots constituencies and even turned many Republican county parties off the plan. A Ford proposal to decontrol domestic oil prices ran into stiff opposition from motorists who opposed higher prices at the gasoline pumps. Support for Carter's energy program tumbled soon after his nationwide television address in 1977.

To dramatize an issue a president may call one or both houses of Congress into special session.[70] He presents a program, often just before an election, and puts the opposition party on the defensive by forcing it to go on record in support of or opposition to his measure. Truman used this tactic brilliantly by calling a session to force Republicans controlling Congress to vote against his Fair Deal measures. The sessions he called were "failures" in the sense that little legislation passed, but Truman then campaigned against a "do-nothing" Congress and was elected to the presidency in 1948, so in a political sense these sessions were a great success. No president since has used this tactic.

When the president raises a national agenda issue his opponents may counter with the charge that he is expanding the powers of

Figure 5.1.1

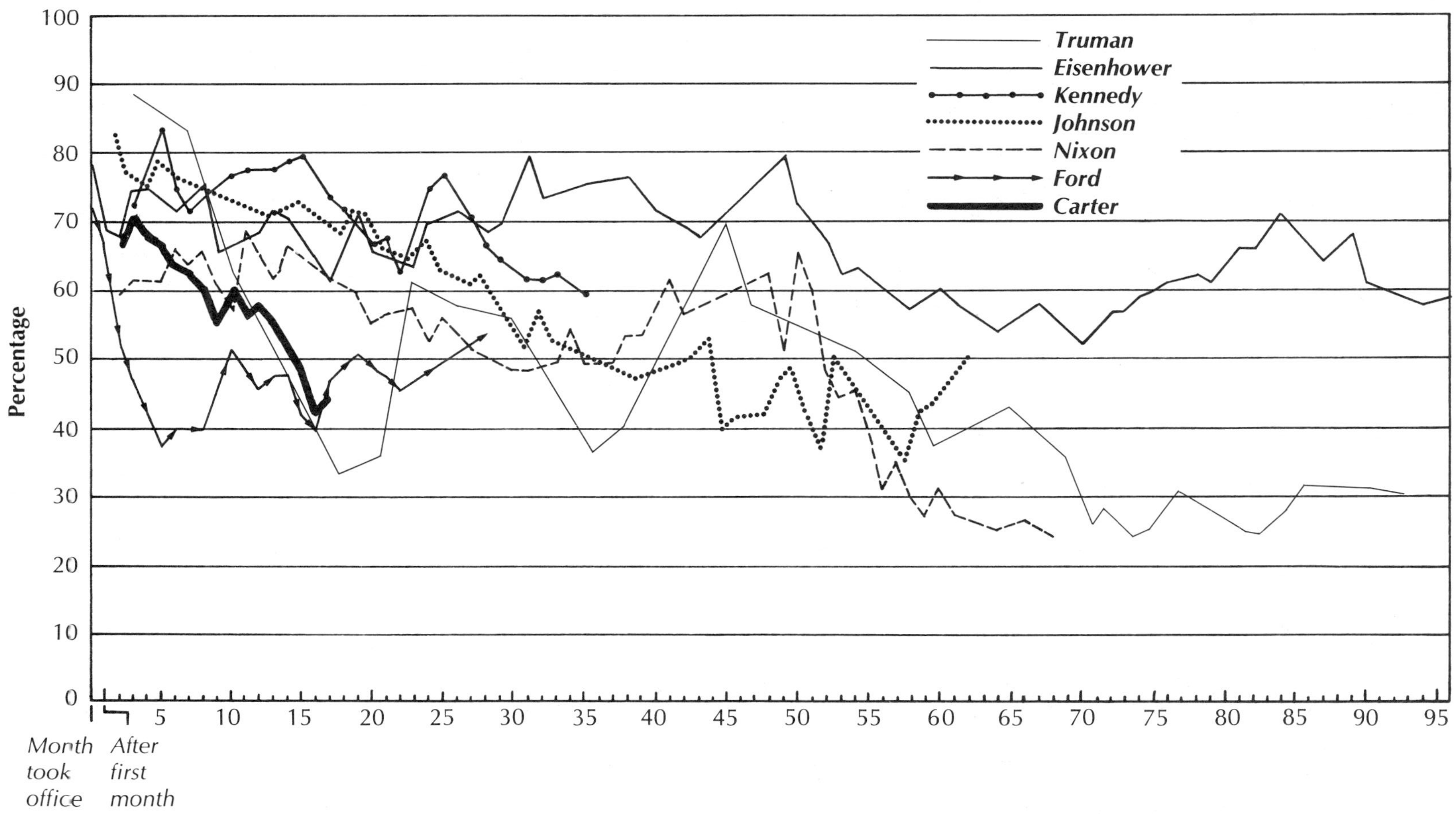

Truman
Eisenhower
Kennedy
Johnson
Nixon
Ford
Carter
Percentage
100
90
80
70
60
50
40
30
20
10
0
5
10
15
20
25
30
35
40
45
50
55
60
65
70
75
80
85
90
95
Month took office
After first month

the office beyond the constitutional limits. An appeal to the people always raises the danger of a *plebiscitary* presidency, and opponents of a measure may claim that they are preventing an "imperial presidency" from riding roughshod over the separation of powers. Woodrow Wilson was defeated in his attempt to win Senate consent to the Treaty of Versailles partly on these grounds, and it was not by chance that the "reservations" to the treaty introduced by its opponents in the Senate dealt specifically with the powers of the president to conduct foreign affairs or engage in hostilities with other nations. Franklin Roosevelt's bill to add additional members to the Supreme Court (one for each sitting justice over the age of sixty-five) was attacked by opponents who charged that he was attempting to "pack" the court and undermine its part in the checks and balances system. Many New Dealers broke with Roosevelt on this issue, and not only did he lose the measure, but his defeat marked a turning point for the New Deal; thereafter Congress passed only a small fraction of his domestic program, and control of the legislature passed to a coalition of Republicans and anti-Roosevelt Democrats.[71]

National agenda politics may be a useful tactic, but it has its drawbacks and is not always successful. It may be pointed out that Great Society laws were passed by Congress even though Lyndon Johnson was awkward and unsure of himself in dealing with the media, while the far slicker and glamorous Kennedy White House had a lesser success with Congress. It only states the obvious to point out that a president who has mastered legislative strategy and tactics, who has a "feel" for Congress and good rapport with its leaders, and who is blessed with large party margins in both chambers, is likely to have more legislative success than a president who relies on national agenda politics to make up for his weaknesses as a legislative tactician and party leader.

The Veto Powers

The president may always attempt to influence Congress by substituting prerogative government and the veto power for efforts at persuasion. He may use the veto to induce an antiadministration coalition to negotiate with him, or to frustrate the opposition party if it controls Congress. The veto is employed in the following situations:

1. When the president believes a measure is unconstitutional. Some presidents have vetoed bills that they thought infringed on their prerogatives.
2. To discourage "riders," which are nongermane amendments tacked on to popular measures such as appropriations bills. The president may call the congressional bluff and veto the bill rather than accept the rider. (The Legislative Reorganization Act of 1970 provides that riders are subject to a point of order, which then requires a two-thirds vote to attach it to the bill, thus eliminating the rider for most measures.)
3. To modify a bill through bargaining. On some occasions, the president vetoes a bill, and Congress then passes a version that he can sign.
4. To defeat a measure passed by Congress, often in order to define differences between the parties for forthcoming elections.

Political scientists have attempted to specify the conditions under which the veto is likely to be exercised. One study by Jong R. Lee, tracing the use of the veto from Washington through Nixon, found that Democratic presidents are more likely to wield the veto than Republicans, and that presidents with prior service in Congress are least likely to veto bills.[72] But for recent years these results are misleading. Democrats such as Kennedy and Johnson vetoed fewer measures than Republicans Eisenhower, Nixon, and Ford. And Ford, who had spent most of his political career in the House of Representatives, had no hesitation in using the veto to frustrate the will of Congress. He vetoed a foreign aid authorization in 1976 because he believed it infringed on his constitutional prerogatives, a housing bill in 1975 to force Congress to send him a more palatable version, a tax measure with rates he did not approve, and a series of appropriations bills to make the level of federal spending an issue in the presidential campaign of 1976. As Lee points out, the important factor underlying the stastistical correlations is partisanship: in periods of split government, the veto is likely to be used more than it will be when one party controls both the White House and the Congress. Carter, for example, vetoed very few measures—though he used the veto threat frequently.

After a bill is passed by both houses, the enrolled copy, signed by the president of the Senate and the Speaker of the House, is processed and sent to the White House within ten days. If the president approves the bill, he signs it into law within ten days of its presentation to him. If he wishes he may hold a public signing ceremony. Johnson signed the 1965 education measure at a one-room schoolhouse in Texas, the voting rights measure in a room at the Capitol next to the chamber where Lincoln had signed the Emancipation Proclamation, and a new immigration law at the Statue of Liberty. But if the president opposes the bill, he may exercise one of these options:

1. He may withhold his signature for ten days, and the bill becomes law. He may issue a statement outlining his objections and indicating his reasons. He may take this action if a bill he favors has a rider attached, or if he opposes a measure but thinks it would be overridden by a large margin, or if he thinks a veto would damage him politically.
2. He can permit the bill to become law without his signature, but indicates that he will not enforce a section that he believes to be unconstitutional. He then forces his opponents to take him to court, which tests the constitutionality of the measure. He may, alternatively, enforce a section of the law in a way not intended by the majority that passed the measure.
3. He may take actions in the ten-day period after the bill is passed that limit the effect of the measure. Theodore Roosevelt established much of the National Forest System by executive order in the ten-day period, prior to signing a bill (which he wanted) that had a provision (of which he strongly disapproved) restricting the use of federal lands.
4. He may veto the measure within ten days of its presentation to him, sending it back to its chamber of origin with a message indicating his reasons. He may use this message to suggest changes Congress might make that would enable him to sign a revised version. (An incoming president succeeding to the office may sign bills presented to his predecessor within the ten-day period).

If, during the ten-day period, Congress adjourns, the president may still sign the measure into law. But if he chooses not to sign it, the Constitutional provisions regarding the *pocket veto* take effect. The president need not return the bill to either chamber, need not provide reasons for the pocket veto, or send a message to Congress. Most important, the legislature cannot override a pocket veto and enact the measure into law. Congress must pass a new measure in its next session, even one identical to the version pocket-vetoed, and present it to the president after it reconvenes from adjournment.[73]

The prerogative to pocket veto has been misused by several presidents, who prefer it to the regular veto because it cannot be overridden. They have killed measures when Congress adjourned or recessed for short vacations prior to the end of the legislative session. Both Nixon and Ford used the pocket veto during interim adjournments—Nixon to kill a health bill and Ford to kill vocational rehabilitation, farm labor, and wildlife refuge measures. Congress responded by recessing rather than adjourning for vacations, and by designating officers in each chamber to receive suspensory veto messages from the president, thus attempting to retain the ordinary veto and prevent the president from exercising the pocket veto. The Senate majority leader, as a further precaution, would wait until the Senate returned from short vacations before sending down bills to the president for his consideration. In August 1974, a U.S. Court of Appeals decision barred the president's use of the pocket veto during congressional recesses, provided an officer was appointed by the chamber to receive a suspensory veto message.[74] In 1976 Attorney General Edward Levi announced a new Ford administration policy; pocket vetoes would be used only for the period after the final adjournment of Congress at the end of its second session, and not during the vacation adjournments or for the period between the sessions of Congress.[75] Courts and Congress had combined to limit the misuse of prerogative government.

The Constitution provides that the suspensory and pocket veto provisions apply to "every order, resolution, or vote to which the concurrence of the Senate or House of Representatives may be necessary." But Congress has construed this presidential check on its actions narrowly. The president cannot veto constitutional amendments proposed by both Houses of Congress, nor must he sign them.[76] Although he may veto joint resolutions of Congress with the force of law, he does not veto concurrent resolutions of both chambers, or simple resolutions passed by a single chamber. (In theory such resolutions do not have binding force, but in practice Congress has used them either to institute or to prohibit activities involving reorganization, war powers, and the budget process.) The president cannot veto measures of the House or Senate that deal with internal organization, such as election of officers, assignments of members to committees, or establishment of rules. He may veto laws passed by Congress that deal with legislative reorganization, but under the principle of comity he gives his approval.

The veto power is employed as part of an action-forcing process involving review of enrolled bills. After presentation of every measure passed by Congress, the president has ten days to decide whether to sign the bill or exercise other options. White House aides, advisory councils, the OMB, the departments, legislative leaders, and lobbyists all offer advice to the president. The classic conflict is usually between a cabinet member who wants the president to sign a bill and the OMB or members of the staff who urge a veto. When the OMB urges the president to sign, he will almost always do so: between 1953 and 1960 Eisenhower approved 99 percent of the bills recommended by the Bureau of the Budget, and figures were also high in later administrations.[77] When the OMB recommends a veto, the picture is mixed. Eisenhower followed the BOB recommendation three-quarters of the time, while Johnson signed twenty-seven of sixty-two bills the Bureau wanted him to veto.[78] Nixon and Ford often faced situations in which the OMB urged a veto and other agencies and advisors urged them to sign—often the president sided with the departments and went against the OMB recommendation.[79]

The president and his advisors make the decisions on the key bills, but for the thousand or so other measures that reach his desk each year, the president must rely on staff work. In the 1930s the Bureau of the Budget began to submit "briefs" on bills that flooded the White House at the end of the session that were subject to the pocket veto. Gradually the Bureau assumed responsibility of preparing memoranda for bills during the session, and worked up drafts of messages approving or disapproving minor bills. By 1960 the Bureau was given responsibility to comment on all enrolled legislation within five days of its presentation to the White House.[80] In the 1970s the OMB maintained its role for low-level measures, but faced competition from the Domestic Council and other White House agencies in advising the president on more important bills. In determining whether to sign or veto measures, presidents obtain advice from every unit of the institutionalized presidency rather than simply from the OMB and its Legislative Reference Division.

The president uses the OMB, the Domestic Staff, and the other units of his office to intervene with a veto threat early in the legislative process, when committees are marking up administration measures. Timely warnings by the White House may induce committees to compromise with White House representatives. The negotiations involve calculations on the part of all participants about the likelihood that the president will actually employ the veto; it is said that Franklin Roosevelt occasionally asked his aides to find him "something I can veto" just to impress on Congress that he had the power to frustrate members' bills. The actual use of the veto is often not a demonstration of presidential strength, but an indication that White House influence in Congress has eroded and the system of bargaining and accommodation has broken down.

The veto is always a credible weapon. The president must obtain the votes of only one-third of a *quorum* of a single chamber to defeat an override attempt.[81] Only about 4 percent of presidential vetoes have been overridden. But sometimes presidents lose on those issues that matter to them the most. Andrew Johnson's vetoes of civil rights, reconstruction, and tenure of office acts were overridden by a Congress determined to control postwar policies. Truman's vetoes of the Taft-Hartley labor law, McCarran immigration law, and internal security measures were overridden by a conservative coalition and constituted severe defeats for the Fair Deal president. Nixon's vetoes of curbs on presidential war-making were overridden. Ford's vetoes of education and health measures were overturned, and Congress twice voted to end military aid to Turkey over his veto in a significant rebuff to his conduct of foreign policy.

Conflict between the branches leads to proposals for constitutional amendments to strengthen or weaken the veto power. After Andrew Jackson frustrated the Whig economic program, the Whigs proposed to abolish the veto by constitutional amendment. After Tyler vetoed a bank bill, the Whigs proposed an amendment that would permit a majority in each house to override, in effect nullifying the veto. Following the impeachment and acquittal of Andrew Johnson, "presidentialists" suggested strengthening the veto in order to restore the prestige of the office. President Hayes, beset by "riders" attached to appropriations measures, recommended a constitutional amendment that would give him an item veto on appropriations, and between 1877 and 1888 several such amendments were introduced in Congress but never passed. Eisenhower also proposed an item veto in his 1959 budget message. But the item veto would strike at the heart of the system of transactions and payoffs that form the core of the legislative process. If the president could strike out specific provisions of laws or appropriations, no one in Congress could be sure that deals made with party or committee leaders would bring him benefits—especially if the president were not party to the arrangements. Committees would lose influence in the distributive process, and their leaders would lose power in the chamber. If the president exercised his item veto to strike out particular projects, members might think he was doing so for the benefit of some party or committee leader, and there would be charges of bad faith and double-cross in the chamber. What makes good sense to the president on fiscal grounds runs counter to the logic and politics of Congress. It is unlikely that proposals to strengthen the veto power will be adopted.

The Reform Agenda

There are two schools of thought about making the president a more effective legislative leader: one suggests that a responsible party system be instituted; the other emphasizes modifications of the legislative process to speed consideration of the presidential program. Some reforms of the legislative process have been instituted. Although there is still no "executive calendar" in each chamber, reforms make it likely that some version of administrative bills can be brought to a vote in each chamber.

In the House, the problem for the president for many years involved the power of the Rules Committee. At one time an arm of the Speaker, the committee became autonomous after the 1911 reforms. After the Second World War it was dominated by conservatives who could kill measures reported to it by standing committees by refusing to grant a "rule" for floor debate. In 1960, after Kennedy was nominated by the Democrats, Congress reconvened at his urging to consider the Democratic convention program, including aid to education, extension of the minimum wage, and medicare. The Rules Committee blocked consideration of some of these measures, so Kennedy's election strategy of forcing Republicans to vote on these bills was frustrated. Once president, Kennedy encouraged Democratic liberals and party leaders in Congress to enlarge the committee to add members that would end conservative domination. By working closely with Speaker Rayburn, the administration won a vote adding three new members, which had the effect of unblocking the New Frontier legislative pro-

Table 5.1.1

Presidential Vetoes

President	Total Vetoes	Overridden
Washington	2	—
Adams	—	—
Jefferson	—	—
Madison	7	—
Monroe	1	—
Adams	—	—
Jackson	12	—
Van Buren	—	—
Harrison	—	—
Tyler	10	1
Polk	3	—
Taylor	—	—
Fillmore	—	—
Pierce	9	5
Buchanan	7	—
Lincoln	6	—
Johnson	29	15
Grant	93	4
Hayes	13	1
Garfield	—	—
Arthur	12	1
Cleveland	413	2
Harrison	44	1
Cleveland	170	5
McKinley	42	—
Roosevelt	82	1
Taft	39	1
Wilson	44	6
Harding	6	—
Coolidge	50	4
Hoover	37	3
Roosevelt	635	9
Truman	250	12
Eisenhower	181	2
Kennedy	21	—
Johnson	30	—
Nixon	43	6
Ford	66	12
Carter (through 9/1/78)	3	—

Source: Presidential Vetoes: 1789-1961 (Washington, D.C., U..S. Government Printing Office, 1961) iv.; Congressional Quarterly Almanac, 1976, 28.

gram. In 1975 the Democratic caucus gave Democratic Speakers the right to nominate members to the committee, in effect converting it into an arm of the leadership. The president, if a Democrat, can work with the Speaker to obtain the rule he wants for debate on his measures, which is the next best thing to obtaining an executive calendar.

In the Senate the problem for the president has been the filibuster. The tradition of unlimited debate may tie up the chamber for days or weeks. It was used to protect regional interests, especially southern concerns about race, and enabled the South to delay or kill civil rights legislation for decades. But it has also been used by liberals: in 1962 against the COMSAT bill for a corporation to develop space communications, and in 1977 against the Carter energy program. The filibuster is a formidable weapon, but debate may be ended under rule 22, instituted in 1917, which provides that a cloture motion may be passed. Until 1975 passage required two-thirds of the members present; since that time three-fifths of the entire Senate, sixty members, has been required.[82] The vice-president presides over the Senate and may make parliamentary rulings that favor the administration. In recent years presidents have defeated filibusters on many important issues, including the COMSAT bill of 1962, the Civil Rights Act of 1964, the Voting Rights Act of 1965, the Civil Rights Act of 1968, and the U.S.-Soviet Arms Agreement of 1972. After being defeated in 1977 by a filibuster of a measure to provide for public financing of Senate election campaigns, the Carter administration determined to weaken the filibuster still further. Vice-President Mondale made certain parliamentary rulings that led to a cloture vote. The irony was that cloture having been achieved, the Senate could then proceed to pass an energy bill that represented a substantial setback for the administration. But the principle had been won and the signal given that the administration was determined to continue the assault on the filibuster as a weapon to prevent consideration of the White House program.

The major procedural changes currently in progress involve strengthening of the checks and balances system through passage of various measures that provide for an ordered confrontation between the two branches.[83] Congress has created various action-forcing processes that require the president to submit a program and that set a deadline for various kinds of congressional responses. . . . They fit into the constitutional and political logic of the American system. The administration must present a program, work closely with party and committee leaders, and obtain majority support in the chambers. The processes created provide for an exchange of information and viewpoints as a prelude to bargaining and completion of transactions. They do not threaten the power of legislators in the distributive process. They require that actions be taken in specified time periods, ending the deadlock or inconclusive results that may plague an administration. They minimize the president's inclination and ability to act unilaterally through instituting prerogative government. Most important, operation of these processes does not require changes in the electoral process or a restructuring of the existing decentralized party system. The autonomy of Congress is maintained and strengthened, and with it the probability that the legislature can function effectively as a coordinate branch of government.

Notes

1. Franklin Roosevelt, *Public Papers and Addresses of Franklin Roosevelt* (New York: Random House, 1936), 5:215.

2. Theodore Sorensen, *Kennedy* (New York: Harper and Row, 1965), 352.

3. *New York Times*, March 12, 1977.

4. On the broad delegations of authority by Congress to the executive, see Louis Fisher, *President and Congress* (New York: The Free Press, 1972), Chapter 3, "Delegation of Power"; also Theodore Lowi, *The End of Liberalism* (New York: W.W. Norton, 1969), Chapter 8, "Interest Group Liberalism and Poverty."

5. Robert Peabody, *Leadership in Congress* (Boston: Little, Brown, 1976), 493; for a general treatment, see Randall Ripley, *Party Leaders in the House of Representatives* (Washington, D.C.: The Brookings Institution, 1967).

6. Peabody, *Leadership in Congress*, 477; in situations in which the Speaker is from the opposition party the president obviously does not consider him a lieutenant.

7. *New York Times*, March 27, 1977.

8. For a discussion of these events see Joseph Clark, *Congress: The Sapless Branch* (New York: Harper and Row, 1964), Chapter 7, "Prologue to Reform."

9. See the argument of Stephen Balch, "Do Strong Presidents Really Want Strong Legislative Parties?", *Presidential Studies Quarterly 7*, no. 4 (Fall 1977): 231-237.

10. *New York Times*, October 21, 1977.

11. Aage Clausen, *How Congressmen Decide* (New York: St. Martin's Press, 1975), 196; John Kingdon, *Congressmen's Voting Decisions* (New York: Harper and Row, 1973), 169-170; but on Nixon's ability to win Republican support for some domestic measures they opposed when Democratic presidents first introduced them, see Demetrios Caraley, "Congressional Politics and Urban Aid," *Political Science Quarterly* 91, no. 1 (Spring 1976): 26.

12. Mark Kesselman, "A Note: Presidential Leadership of Congress on Foreign Policy," *Midwest Journal of Political Science* 5, no. 3 (August 1961): 284-289; Mark Kesselman, "Presidential Leadership in Congress on Foreign Policy," *Midwest Journal of Political Science* 9, no. 4 (November 1965): 401-406.

13. Kingdon, *Congressmen's Voting Decisions*, 17-21; see also John Schwarz and Earl Shaw, *The United States Congress in Comparative Perspective* (Hinsdale, Ill.: The Dryden Press, 1976), 171.

14. Kingdon, *Congressmen's Voting Decisions*, 179.

15. David Mayhew, *Party Loyalty Among Congressmen* (Cambridge: Harvard University Press, 1966), 148-168; Demetrios Caraley notes that support for urban programs depends primarily on party affiliation, since the average rural Democrat in Congress had urban support scores twice as high as those of the average urban Republican, and even southern Democrats in the House scored higher than all but eastern Republicans, which seems to support Mayhew's argument; cf. Demetrios Caraley, "The Carter Congress and Urban Voting," in *American Politics and Public Policy*, ed. Walter Dean Burnham and Martha Wagner Weinberg (Cambridge: MIT Press, 1978).

16. Schwarz and Shaw, *Congress in Comparative Perspective*, 120.

17. *Congressional Quarterly Almanac*, 32, 1976, 1008.

18. Demetrios Caraley, "Congressional Politics and Urban Aid," *Political Science Quarterly* 91, no. 1 (Spring 1976): 19-47.

19. Charles Jones, *Minority Party Leadership* (Boston: Little, Brown, 1970), 79.

20. Lyndon Johnson, *The Vantage Point* (New York: Holt, Rinehart and Winston, 1971), 159.

21. William Safire, *Before the Fall* (Garden City, N.Y.: Doubleday, 1975), 685.

22. Schwarz and Shaw, *Congress in Comparative Perspective*, 48-49; see also Norman Ornstein, Robert Peabody, and David Rohde, "The Changing Senate," *Congress Reconsidered*, ed. Lawrence Dodd and Bruce Oppenheimer (New York: Praeger, 1977).

23. Richard Bolling, *House Out of Order* (New York: E. P. Dutton, 1966), 39.

24. Abraham Holtzman, *Legislative Liaison* (Indianapolis: Bobbs-Merrill, 1973), 1.

25. Lawrence F. O'Brien, Jr., "The Invisible Bridge," (Harvard College senior thesis, 1967); also G. Russell Pipe, "Congressional Liaison: The Executive Branch Consolidates its Relations with Congress," *Public Administration Review* 26, no. 1 (March 1966): 14-24.

26. Ralph Huitt, "White House Channels to the Hill," in *Congress Against the President*, ed., Harvey C. Mansfield (New York: Praeger, 1976), 83.

27. Holtzman, *Legislative Liaison*, 251, 254.

28. See Richard Pious, "Congress, the Organized Bar, and the Legal Services Program," *Wisconsin Law Review*, 1972, no. 2, 418-447.

29. On mobilization at the grassroots level, see Morton Grodzins, *The American System* (Chicago: Rand McNally, 1966), especially Chapter 9, "The Mobilization of Public-Private Influence."

30. *Time*, September 1, 1961, 14.

31. Johnson, *The Vantage Point*, 28.

32. Doris Kearns, *Lyndon Johnson and the American Dream* (New York: Harper and Row, 1976), 226.

33. "Text of Bryce Harlow Keynote Address at Nashville Symposium" in *Center House Bulletin* 4, no. 1 (Winter 1974).

34. Johnson, *The Vantage Point*, Chapter 9, "Bite the Bullet."

35. Charles Clapp, *The Congressmen* (Washington, D.C.: The Brookings Institution, 1963), 182.

36. Doris Kearns, *Lyndon Johnson and the American Dream*, 182.

37. Richard Neustadt, *Presidential Power* (New York: John Wiley, 1961), 52-53.

38. Kearns, *Lyndon Johnson and the American Dream*, 185.

39. John E. Moore, "Controlling Delinquency," in *Congress and Urban Problems*, ed. Frederic Cleaveland (Washington, D.C.: The Brookings Institution, 1969), 145-146.

40. Johnson, *The Vantage Point*, 458.

41. *New York Times*, February 15, 1978.

42. Johnson, *The Vantage Point*, 457.

43. Lawrence O'Brien, *No Final Victories* (Garden City, N.Y.: Doubleday, 1974), 118.

44. Sorensen, *Kennedy*, 344.

45. Robert Sickels, *Presidential Transactions* (Englewood Cliffs, N.J.: Prentice-Hall, 1974), 117.

46. *New York Times*, March 10, 1976.

47. *New York Times*, March 10, 1976.

48. *New York Times*, September 15, 1977.

49. A discussion of the strategy of widening arenas is contained in E.E. Schattschneider, *The Semi-Sovereign People* (New York: Holt, Rinehart and Winston, 1960).

50. Johnson, *The Vantage Point*, 450.

51. Robert Donovan, *Eisenhower: The Inside Story* (New York: Harper and Brothers, 1956), 230.

52. Johnson, *The Vantage Point*, 74.

53. Most presidential addresses are not keyed to pending measures. The ninety-five speeches Hoover made were devoted to restoring confidence, and Roosevelt made radio "fireside chats" that summed up the accomplishments of his administration, since half were given when Congress was out of session. See Edward W. Chester, *Radio, Television and American Politics* (New York: Sheed and Ward, 1969), 33.

54. Eisenhower was refused time on NBC and CBS in 1958 during the Quemoy crisis. In 1961, Kennedy was given a 10:00 p.m. (EST) time slot rather than the 6:00 p.m. time he requested during disturbances over racial integration at the University of Mississippi. In 1967 ABC and CBS did not televise one of Johnson's speeches on Vietnam. In 1975, CBS and NBC refused Ford's request for air time to discuss his tax reform measures, claiming that the speech was political and would subject them to demands for equal time from the opposition. In 1977 Carter's energy speech was broadcast by CBS only after a special White House appeal.

55. Newton Minow et al., *Presidential Television* (New York: Basic Books, 1974), 126-159.

56. *New York Times*, February 14, 1978.

57. In May 1977, Carter's aides proposed a television blitz for his energy program, which would have included endorsements by Hollywood stars and various media events. Instead, the president chose a low-key strategy while his proposals went smoothly through the House and only "went public" with one major address while the bills were in the Senate. On the Carter media options, see *New York Times*, May 19, 1977.

58. Elmer Cornwell, *Presidential Leadership of Public Opinion* (Bloomington: University of Indiana Press, 1965), 180-181.

59. Donovan, *Eisenhower: The Inside Story*, 150.

60. Neustadt, *Presidential Power*, 65-67.

61. Transcript of remarks of President Franklin D. Roosevelt, May 8, 1933.

62. Alonzo Hamby, *Beyond the New Deal* (New York: Columbia University Press, 1973), 74.

63. Gerald Benjamin, "Nixon and the Press in Perspective" (unpublished), 15.

64. Pierre Salinger, *With Kennedy* (Garden City, N.Y.: Doubleday, 1966), 120.

65. For a general discussion see William Porter, *Assault on the Media* (Ann Arbor: University of Michigan Press, 1976); on surveillance of reporters, see David Wise, *The American Police State* (New York: Random House, 1976), 3-31.

66. Hugh Sidey, *A Very Personal Presidency* (New York: Atheneum, 1968), 88.

67. Arthur Krock, *The Consent of the Governed* (Boston: Little, Brown, 1971), 228-242; William Safire, *Before the Fall* (Garden City, N.Y.: Doubleday, 1975), 49-50.

68. Johnson, *The Vantage Point*, 80.

69. Presidents begin with very high ratings: (Truman) 77, (Eisenhower) 69, (Kennedy) 76, (Johnson) 76, (Nixon) 61, (Ford) 47, (Carter) 62 were the averages from Gallup Polls for the first year; cf. *Gallup Opinion Index* No. 152 (March 1978), 4. On the parabolic curve, see James Stimson, "Public Support for American Presidents: A Cyclical Model," *Public Opinion Quarterly* 40, no. 1 (Spring 1976): 1-22. Other studies have shown a high correlation between presidential popularity and foreign affairs measures, and a low—even negative—correlation between popularity and success in passing domestic legislation; cf. George Edwards III, "Presidential Influence in the House: Presidential Prestige as a Source of Presidential Power," *The American Political Science Review*, 70, no. 1 (March 1976): 101-113; on the kinds of foreign crises that raise or lower presidential popularity, see Jong R. Lee, "Foreign Policy Events and Presidential Popularity," *Presidential Studies Quarterly* 7, no. 4 (Fall 1977): 252-256.

70. Through the Lincoln administration, special sessions were called only nine times. Taft called one special session in 1909, Wilson in 1913 and in 1917, Harding in 1921, Hoover in 1929, and Roosevelt in 1933. These sessions were called because Congress did not normally meet until December following the inauguration of the president, and the special sessions enabled the administration to present Congress with a program in the spring of its first year in office. The adoption of the Twentieth Amendment provided that Congress would convene just prior to the inauguration of the new president, ending the need for special sessions in the first year. Since then the only sessions have been called by Harry Truman in 1947 and 1948.

71. See James Patterson, *Congressional Conservatism and the New Deal* (Lexington: University of Kentucky Press, 1967).

72. Jong R. Lee, "Presidential Vetoes from Washington to Nixon," *Journal of Politics*, 37, no. 2 (May 1975): 526-540.

73. The Pocket Veto Case, 279 U.S. 653.

74. Kennedy v. Sampson, 511 Federal Reporter, 2nd Series 430 (1974).

75. *New York Times*, April 14, 1976.

76. Hollingsworth v. Virginia, 3 Dallas 378 (1798).

77. Stephen Wayne, *The Legislative Presidency* (New York: Harper and Row, 1978), 76.

78. Ibid., 81.

79. Ibid., 86-87.

80. Clement Vose, "The Memorandum Pocket Veto," *Journal of Politics* 26, no. 2 (May 1964): 397-405.

81. North Pacific Railway Co. v. Kansas, 248 U.S. 276 (1919).

82. Between 1917 and 1976, there were 127 votes for cloture, of which 38 were successful. In recent years there have been several mini-filibusters led by one or two senators to dramatize a point, with no real chance of success; far fewer major filibusters have occurred.

83. For a similar discussion, see Pendleton Herring, *Presidential Leadership* (New York: Farrar and Rinehart, 1940), especially Chapter 6, "The Limits of Presidential Responsibility."

Illustration 5a: An Example of a Veto Message

As emphasized in the preceding essay, the veto is perhaps the most awesome of presidential powers in dealing with Congress. The possibility of a veto guarantees that the president will be a force in legislative policymaking, as proponents of legislation anticipate and check out what the administration's reaction will be. The veto gives the president an edge in policymaking. A veto can be overridden only with a two-thirds vote in both houses. Thus, if the president can muster a modest one-third plus one vote in one house, the veto sticks. Each presidential veto is accompanied with a veto message detailing the reasons for the veto. An example of such a recent message is provided below.

THE WHITE HOUSE

Office of the Press Secretary

For Immediate Release   June 18, 1983

TO THE SENATE OF THE UNITED STATES:

I am returning, without my approval, S. 973, "an Act to make technical amendments to the Indian Self-Determination and Education Assistance Act and other Acts." I have no objection to these technical amendments.

However, section 5 of the bill, added by an amendment on the Senate floor, would allow a particular school to transfer to taxable investors tax benefits attributable to a building that it refurbished with Federal funds. Without this legislation, the proposed transaction would result in the school being required to repay the Federal funds used to refurbish the building.

Recently there has been a great deal of concern about the sale of tax benefits by tax-exempt entities through leasing transactions. Leasing transactions similar to the one contemplated by this legislation present tremendous potential for abuse and could result in billions of dollars of revenue loss to the Federal Government. The transaction that this legislation would condone would permit a school that has already received tax deductible contributions and Federal grant money to sell certain tax benefits to outside investors. This case is particularly offensive in that the tax benefits being sold are attributable to property that was paid for with Federal grant money. In addition to receiving money for selling tax benefits, the school, as a tax-exempt entity, would be able to invest the proceeds of the sale and receive the income from such investment tax-free.

The propriety of leasing transactions involving the sale by tax-exempt organizations of tax benefits needs to be scrutinized very carefully. Where the tax benefits being sold are attributable to expenditures of Federal funds, the transaction becomes totally unjustifiable. We cannot condone the sale by a tax-exempt entity of tax benefits produced through the use of Federal funds.

As I have noted, the Indian-related amendments contained in this bill are not objectionable. Accordingly, I urge the Congress to reenact sections 1-4 of S. 973 without delay.

RONALD REAGAN

THE WHITE HOUSE,
June 17, 1983.

# # # # # #

Presidential Leadership Skills 5.2

George C. Edwards III

The most important factor affecting presidential relations with Congress is the personality and bargaining skills of the president. The following chapter from a major study of presidential influence in Congress gives an overview of the personal aspects of presidential-congressional interaction.

[In this chapter] we will investigate the more personal and manipulatable potential sources of presidential influence in Congress, to which we assign the general label "presidential legislative skills." These skills range from direct appeals for support to the bestowal of amenities.

Not only is the range of potential presidential legislative skills great, but so is the range of situations in which they may be needed. The words of one presidential aide illustrate this complexity:

> Senator A might come with us if Senator B, an admired friend, could be persuaded to talk to him. Senator C wanted a major project out of Chairman D's committee: maybe D, a supporter of our bill, would release it in exchange for C's commitment. Senator E might be reached through people in his home state. If Senator F could not vote with us on final passage, could he vote with us on key amendments? Could G take a trip? Would the President call Senator H?[1]

We have several goals. . . . First, we want to categorize and describe the degree of legislative skills exercised by recent presidents. Second, we want to analyze these skills to see if they could logically serve as broad sources of influence in Congress. . . .

This chapter focuses on presidential involvement in the legislative process, bargaining, professional reputation, and arm-twisting. . . .

Presidential Influence in Congress (pp. 116-31, 139-44) by George C. Edwards III, 1980, San Francisco: W. H. Freeman and Company. Copyright 1980 by George C. Edwards III. Reprinted by permission.

Presidential Involvement in the Legislative Process

According to Lyndon Johnson, "There is only one way for a President to deal with the Congress, and that is continuously, incessantly, and without interruption."[2] He believed that "merely placing a program before Congress is not enough. Without constant attention from the administration most legislation moves through the congressional process at the speed of a glacier." Thus, one of a president's most important jobs is to keep Congress concentrated on his legislative program.[3] "The thing that counts," Johnson remarked, "is getting those bills through."[4] Following his own advice, Johnson got to know members of Congress well and developed a legislative system that involved activities from drafting bills to pushing them through Congress. We shall focus on Johnson's involvement with Congress first because of its intensity before considering the involvement of other presidents.

Lyndon Johnson

Intimate Knowledge. The foundation of Johnson's involvement was intimate knowledge of Congress, knowledge that came from beyond even his own vast experience.[5] At least in the Eighty-ninth Congress (1965-1966), his favorite reading was the *Congressional Record*. A White House messenger picked up the newest issue at the Government Printing Office every morning, and an aide then read it before dawn, clipping each page on which a member of Congress praised or criticized Johnson and summarizing and marking up other important parts for Johnson's breakfast reading. When he read criticism, Johnson often asked his chief legislative aide, Lawrence O'Brien, to find out the cause of the problem.[6]

Before retiring at night, Johnson read detailed memos from his staff on their legislative contacts of the day, special problems that arose, and noteworthy conversations, all of which he absorbed rapidly and thoroughly.[7] When Congress was in session, he received continuous status reports. The White House staff had a standing order to put through calls from O'Brien to Johnson at any hour. O'Brien's office phone was directly connected to the phone on the president's desk. Johnson also developed a system (rarely used) whereby any memo with a red tag would be brought to his attention immediately.[8] "No detail of the legislative program was too minute to involve him." While Kennedy gave congressional affairs the time that O'Brien requested, Congress was for Johnson "a twenty-four-hour-a-day obsession."[9]

Johnson was disturbed if his staff was not on top of every detail of government, particularly legislation, and he expected them to work as hard as he did. He arranged for all of them to have radios in their offices so they could catch the news, and he even had a hot line put into Joseph Califano's bathroom so that Califano would not miss presidential calls.[10]

Johnson also kept in touch with Congress by spending time with its members. He liked to spend free time with them and was more approachable than Kennedy—more "one of the boys." Thus, early in his tenure, he might be found lunching with some senators in a Capitol hideaway, dining with the Texas delegation, or spending an evening with the House Rules Committee.[11]

All of this time and effort spent on congressional relations helped Johnson to maintain an intimate knowledge of Congress and its personnel, which he felt was essential in order to get his legislation passed. He sometimes viewed Congress as a sensitive animal. If pushed gently, it would go his way. If pushed too hard, it would balk. Thus, he had to be constantly aware of how much pressure Congress would take and what its mood was.[12]

This detailed knowledge helped Johnson to know which people should or could be approached and how to approach them. He felt that knowing members of Congress was important so that he could interpret their reactions, their "tone, nuance, and spirit," to presidential requests for support. He also found it useful to know who faced a tough election and who had higher ambitions, who had power and who was gaining and losing it, what the rules and habits of committees were, what skeletons were in whose closets, what issues were critical to whom and why, and what organizational needs leaders had.[13]

Before calling members of Congress who opposed legislation that he supported, Johnson would study detailed staff memos on the bill in question that indicated the reason for the members' opposition, what was necessary to change their minds, and their vulnerabilities. He also knew the politics of their states and of many of their districts. He knew he could not just call and compliment them and expect their votes. He needed to know them and to have a sympathetic understanding of their situations.[14]

Doris Kearns argues that Johnson's achievements in civil rights were made possible by his intimate knowledge of Southerners in Congress, upon which he could base his efforts to influence or manipulate. When he spoke with them privately, his accent deepened, his manner suggested that although he understood and even shared their attitudes toward blacks, he was president and had to answer to the entire nation. Employing teasing humor that implied intimacy, he decreased the intensity of their opposition.[15]

On the 1968 income tax surcharge, Johnson had members asked not only how they would vote but also what criteria would determine whether they would vote for or against the bill (for example, their state delegation's vote breakdown or the closeness of the vote). On the basis of their answers, they were categorized in one of five ways: "with us," "probably with us," "uncommitted," "probably against," and "against." He and his aides then concentrated on the uncommitteds and those probably against the tax, with the approach to each member tailored to meet his or her needs.[16]

Timing. Johnson also felt that sending his bills to Congress at the right moment was important, and he based his timing on the facts he learned and the moods he sensed. The right moment to him depended on momentum, the availability of sponsors in the right place at the right time, and the opportunities for neutralizing the opposition. The timing of legislation was also viewed as important in overcoming Congress's tendency to bog down. In 1965 he decided to push for Medicare and aid to education before pushing for housing and home rule for the District of Columbia on the basis of his estimates of the time needed for each to be considered in Congress and his estimates of which bills would provoke debate and controversy.[17]

He sent bills one by one rather than in a clump, which he felt would lead to automatic opposition. Also, he sent them when the agendas of the receiving committees were clear so that they could be considered right away, without time for opposition to develop and when the members most intensely concerned about the bills would be most likely to support them. Nor did he allow premature disclosure of the details of his bills, which would allow the opposition to coalesce.[18]

Consultation. Johnson consulted with Congress at all stages of the legislative process, from what problems and issues his task forces should consider to the drafting of bills. He appointed members to secret task forces, thus implicating them in the resulting proposals. Sometimes legislators were intimately involved in the drafting of programs because Johnson felt that they would then give the programs more support.[19]

Before sending a bill to Congress, Johnson made special efforts to clear it in advance with key representatives and interest groups. He would not approve draft bills until the relevant department head had proved that he or she had consulted with Congress and had gauged the level of support for the legislation. Lining up support in advance helped a bill to move quickly and aided in strategic planning.[20]

To Johnson, legislative drafting was a "political art." He sought congressional advice on a bill's prospects and had his aides make their own estimates. These analyses gave him a sense of his likely supporters and opponents and an opportunity to redraft a bill so that it would be assigned to a more favorable committee. This was not always possible, but his staff tried through secret consultations with the official parliamentarian and discussions with himself. Along with these efforts, he sought congressional judgments on tactical decisions, such as whether a bill should be single purpose or omnibus in form, how it should be packaged, and when it should be sent.[21]

Advance Notice. The evening before transmitting a bill to Congress, Johnson would hold a White House briefing with congressional leaders, during which cabinet members and the White House staff reviewed and explained the bill and answered questions. He felt that the risk of leaks was worth the good will gained from the leaders.[22] Once, when aide Joseph Califano wanted to brief the press ahead of time about the upcoming and complex Model Cities program, Johnson refused permission until Congress had been told first.[23]

Johnson found that giving important senators advance notice was useful in clearing controversial appointments. Thus, he called Senator John McClelland of Arkansas concerning the appointment of Carl Rowan to head the United States Information Agency, and he invited Senator Russell Long of Louisiana to the White House concerning the appointment of Andrew Brimmer to the Federal Reserve Board. Both appointees were black, and Johnson's show of respect and deference helped clear the path for their confirmations.[24]

Preemption of Problems. Officials in both the Kennedy and Johnson administrations criticized Kennedy for coming too late to many of his problems in Congress, waiting for problems to develop and then intervening at the height of crises, after positions had hardened. Johnson, more intimately involved with Congress and more knowledgeable about it, anticipated problems and, as shown above, acted to preempt them.[25]

Use of the Cabinet. Before Vietnam dominated his time, Johnson made pending legislation a major item of every cabinet meeting. Each department secretary reported on the progress of legislation in his area, and the president used charts on the status of bills to put cabinet members on the spot and urge them to exert more effort. He also emphasized to the cabinet the importance of congressional liaison and liaison officials, and he gave its members responsibility for team efforts in congressional relations. He wanted to be able to use the secretary of agriculture on an education bill if he had friends on the Hill who could help.[26] Johnson also insisted that the appropriate executive branch officials be ready with strong testimony when congressional hearings began.[27]

On the weekends each department official gave status reports for each bill assigned to him or her. On Monday all legislative officers met with the White House staff. These meetings were frequently attended by ranking executive officers, who sometimes gave briefings on national problems. Johnson attended these meetings about once every six weeks, boosting morale. Occasionally legislative officers were allowed to bring a staff member to make a special report, a special treat to the staff member if the president was present. Agency legislative officers also had access, direct or indirect, through the White House staff to the president, giving them more respect in Congress.[28]

Demands on the President. Johnson paid great attention to detail, controlling legislative strategy and organizing support for his legislation.[29] This put great demands on his time and energy. He alone knew the full implications of the many decisions that had to be made concerning congressional relations, and he alone was in contact with all the groups and subgroups in Congress and the administration. His personality and interests were complementary to his legislative activity, but because of the escalation of the war in Vietnam, he was not able to maintain this commitment to legislation.[30]

Other Presidents

The involvement of other recent presidents in the legislative process pales in comparison with Johnson's, at least at its peak. Other presidents lacked Johnson's compulsion for detail, his consuming interest in the legislative process and the passage of legislation, and his deep respect for and understanding of Congress, which led him to seek useful information, anticipate problems, devote his energies to Congress, and work closely with its members.

This is not to argue that efforts similar to Johnson's were not made. According to Lawrence O'Brien, President Kennedy believed that he would have to take an "active, aggressive role with Congress" if his programs were to pass, and the White House engaged in vigorous advocacy from the outset of his administration. Soon after the election, O'Brien met with three leading Democratic members of the House and they reviewed every member in regard to the prospects of supporting Kennedy. Occasionally, leading members of Congress were also consulted on legislation in advance.[31] Kennedy aide Arthur Schlesinger felt that Kennedy spent more time working with Congress than people realized.[32]

Nevertheless, Johnson's actions were on another plane. One political scientist reports that at first Kennedy felt that once he made proposals, it was up to Congress to decide details without him continuously intervening. (Having learned from experience, he changed this view during his first year in office.)[33] President Johnson felt that Kennedy had less interest than he did in dealing with Congress and that Kennedy often appeared to look upon congressional liaison with contempt.[34]

According to columnists Evans and Novak, President Nixon knew little of the workings of Congress and cared less.[35] His top aide, H.R. Haldeman, was quoted by other journalists as saying, "I don't think Congress is supposed to work with the White House."[36] The 1970 Senate vote on the confirmation of G. Harrold Carswell as Supreme Court justice is an example of problems that arise when the White House lacks intimate knowledge of

Congress. The White House mistakenly thought that Senator Margaret Chase Smith would vote yes and told other senators this. However, she had not made up her mind, was angered by the White House's actions, and eventually cast a crucial no vote. The president's staff wasted its time trying to influence Senator William Fulbright, who had already decided to oppose Carswell. Similarly, the White House focused on the vote to recommit the nomination to committee while the opposition focused on the final vote, which turned out to be the wiser action. Meanwhile, the White House was wasting further efforts searching for a paired vote for Senator Carl Mundt, a Nixon supporter who was in the hospital, totally incapacitated. No one was going to waste a no vote unnecessarily, and the Senate was unlikely to believe that Mundt could decide how to vote, given his state of health. Finally, the White House was clearly off on both the final vote count and its confidence that almost anyone would be confirmed following the rejection of Haynsworth.[37]

President Dwight Eisenhower also had problems due to inadequate involvement in Congress. Senator William Knowland, the Senate Republican leader, was irritated when he read in the newspapers about the Eisenhower Doctrine on the Middle East before he was told about it by the president: by proposing a school construction bill in 1955 without consulting educators and members of Congress who favored federal aid to education, Eisenhower angered those whose support he needed to pass the bill; members of the cabinet provided conflicting testimony to Congress on submerged lands and reciprocal trade because of the president's failure to coordinate the testimony; and the president failed to consult the Republican Senate Foreign Relations Committee chairperson, Alexander Wiley, on a strategy regarding the Bricker amendment.[38]

Next to Johnson, Gerald Ford was probably the most intimately involved in Congress of the recent presidents. He worked hard at his congressional relations, had a detailed knowledge of Congress and its members, and was sensitive to their needs and desires. He spent time with them and gave them access, and he frequently participated in "head count" sessions.[39]

Working with Congressional Leaders

Johnson's consultation with Congress did not end with the introduction of a bill or nomination. When Congress was in session, he met with the Democratic leaders at Tuesday breakfasts. Here he spoke frankly and traced the course of each bill on a huge chart.[40] He often called leaders on the Hill[41] and . . . worked closely with Republicans like Senator Dirksen as well. Naturally, he worked with the leaders on more than just the short-run attainment of votes.[42]

Johnson's staff also worked closely with Democratic leaders. They attended strategy sessions in the leaders' Capitol offices and were present at the president's weekly meetings. At these meetings strategy, tactics, and the substance of legislation was discussed; the participants felt that the meetings were valuable. The congressional leadership and the White House formed an effective team, not only in planning but also in operations such as head counts.[43]

Kennedy also had Tuesday breakfasts with the Democratic leadership, but Theodore Sorenson, one of the president's closest aides, reports that these meetings merely maintained morale and kept channels of communication with Congress open; little was learned.[44] It does not appear as though Kennedy sought to "guide" the leaders as Johnson was to do, but he did receive solid support from them, and they worked closely with the White House.

Nixon met with congressional leaders of both parties before many of his major national addresses, but these speeches usually dealt with foreign policy and required little, if any, direct legislative support. Moreover, the meetings tended to be *pro forma* and did not entail consultation.[46] Following one of these sessions in mid-1972, House Minority Whip Leslie Arends said he had yet to sit in conference with Nixon and have him ask, "What should we do?"[47]

Nixon's scheduled meetings with congressional leaders were not very useful. He only had two sessions with Republican leaders per month during his second term, with less frequent bipartisan meetings.[48] Although the president was in frequent contact with Senate Minority Leader Everett Dirksen, their relationship lacked the rapport, confidence, and easy access that characterized the senator's relationship with Johnson.[49] The president's meetings with Majority Leader Mike Mansfield were unproductive, and Mansfield could or would do little for him.[50]

Eisenhower held many bipartisan meetings with congressional floor and committee leaders on foreign policy and defense issues, especially during his second term, and he sought cooperation across the center aisles in Congress. Sometimes these leaders met as a group, and at other times the president saw individuals. Aside from foreign aid and his defense reorganization proposal, most of these meetings did not deal with issues calling for immediate legislation but with crises such as Vietnam, Germany, Lebanon, or the Suez Canal. In these meetings he often sought congressional views and did not just inform the leaders of his decisions.[51]

Eisenhower got along well with Democratic leaders Lyndon Johnson and Sam Rayburn and had many sessions with them.[52] Nevertheless, he did not feel broader bipartisan meetings would be useful in domestic policy areas.[53] From the beginning he regularly saw Republican floor leaders and Republican committee leaders and was open to requests from congressional leaders for meetings. The meetings appear to have been informal with a free exchange of views, and the president did not pressure the legislators, thereby avoiding the risk of a breakdown in relations. He did, however, give his views on issues of importance to him.[54] From 1956 to the end of Eisenhower's tenure, all Republican senators were invited to hear reports on these meetings, and House Minority Leader Charles Halleck reported on them to all House Republicans in 1959 and 1960.[55]

How should we evaluate these meetings with congressional leaders, meetings that Eisenhower felt were his most effective mechanism for coordinating relations with Congress? Even he admitted that the meetings "were sometimes tiresome,"[56] and one can readily imagine this to be true, with, for example, Senate Republican leader William Knowland spending hours advocating to the president.[57] House Republican leader Joseph Martin termed them generally "empty affairs" that accomplished little.[58] Inspiration and not the development of strategy or the application of pressure seems to have been the main goal, and the results appear to have been mixed at best.[59] Perhaps by being so low-keyed and by relying so heavily on institutionalized means such as leadership meetings for carrying out relations with Congress, Eisenhower lost opportunities to influence its members.

Personal Appeals and Access

A special aspect of presidential involvement in the legislative process is the personal appeal for votes and giving members of Congress access to the president. According to Richard Neustadt, "when the chips are down, there is no substitute for the President's own footwork, his personal negotiation, his direct appeal, his voice and no other's on the telephone."[60] This view is seconded by Johnson aide Harry McPherson, who "had an almost mystical faith in Presidential intervention."[61] The distinguished correspondent Neil McNeil, writing of Kennedy's personal lobbying, adds that "direct lobbying by the President with individual Representatives had a profound effect on how they voted."[62]

One reason that phone calls from the president are often effective is human nature. Lyndon Johnson understood that representatives were human beings who liked to feel important and that they were impressed when he called.[63] He knew that, in the words of aide Jack Valenti, "most congressmen can go through a lifetime without ever having talked to the President over the phone in a conversation not initiated by the congressmen."[64] (President Kennedy once remarked that he didn't recall Truman, Eisenhower, or any of their staff ever talking to him about legislation during his fourteen years in Congress.)[65]

Calls from the president must be relatively rare to maintain their usefulness. If the president calls too often, his calls will have less impact. Moreover, members might begin to expect calls, for which the president has limited time, or they may resent high-level pressure being applied on them. On the other hand, they may exploit a call and say that they are uncertain about an issue in order to extract a favor from the president. In addition, the president does not want to commit his prestige to a bill by personal lobbying and then lose. Also, his staff's credibility when speaking for him will decrease the more he speaks for himself.[66]

Johnson became intensely involved only after the long winnowing process of lining up votes was almost done and his calls were needed to win on an important issue, a situation that arose only a few times a year.[67] Other presidents have followed similar patterns.[68] When Johnson did call about a vote, he, like other presidents, focused on key members of Congress, whose votes served as cues for other members,[69] and other members who were uncommitted or weakly committed in either direction. He learned the latter by studying the head counts prepared by the White House staff, which provided detailed information on each member's position.[70]

When Johnson decided to intervene, his actions were intensive. One White House aide has said that the president never let Senate Republican leader Everett Dirksen alone for thirty minutes during Senate consideration of the 1964 Civil Rights Act.[71] On the 1965 Voting Rights Act he even had one senator's mistress contacted.[72] That same year several education bills were in the House Education and Labor Committee, and its mercurial chairperson, Adam Clayton Powell, was nowhere to be found. Johnson had aide Jack Valenti scour Washington to find Powell and then bawled out Powell for holding up legislation; Powell returned to work the next day (without anger). On the 1963 foreign aid bill, his calling in key representatives for private chats was described by one aide as "endless talking, ceaseless importuning, torrential laying on of the facts, [and] it went on for several days."[73]

Johnson's persistence in searching for votes was extraordinary. He had a dogged reluctance to accept no and went to great lengths to gain a yes or bring a supporter to the floor. His actions on the 1963 foreign aid bill illustrate this last point. He called Congress back into session near Christmas but delayed the vote until his supporters were all back to cast their ayes. House Majority Leader Carl Albert was found fishing in Canada by a Mountie pushing his horse upstream. Representative J. J. Picket, newly elected in a special election in Texas, could not be certified until December 24, seven days after his election. So Johnson had the governor and the secretary of state of Texas swear Picket in at 12 midnight, and he arrived in Washington at 3:30 a.m., in time for the vote taken that day. The president also had the Georgia State Patrol track down Representative Elijah Forrester, who was driving home for the holidays, and bring him back to Washington by helicopter. Historian Eric Goldman attributes Johnson's victory on the final vote to his recall of favorable votes.[74]

The president personally rounded up votes on a number of other issues, including the poverty program, food stamps, farm bills, a federal pay increase, rent supplements, and the vote to discharge the District of Columbia home rule bill from the District of Columbia Committee.[75] On the latter issue a discharge petition was also needed to release the bill from the House Rules Committee and get it on the floor for a vote. The petition required 218 signatures, and Johnson had a list of twenty-two representatives who should have signed but had not. He called each one and "persuaded, cajoled, and pleaded" with them to sign, speaking movingly of the inequity of denying the city democratic government; he got the required signatures.[76]

On the 1964 tax cut, Johnson, after intensive personal lobbying within the Senate Finance Committee to reverse a vote on one of Senator Dirksen's amendments, sent word that he wanted no amendments on the Senate floor. Meanwhile, Senator Hubert Humphrey (soon to be vice president) was urging a change in the bill. Nevertheless, after a call from the White House, he voted against his own amendment.[77]

Johnson's telephone technique varied from person to person. He might begin, "What's this I read about your opposing my bill?" or "What do you think of this bill?" or "Say, Congressman, I haven't seen you around in a while, just wondering how you've been?"[78] His style always reflected a personal, reasonable approach: "Man to man. Phone to ear. Come let us reason together. This is Lyndon Johnson talking. Now, we don't have to be at each other's throat, do we? Your country needs your help and so do I."[79] The approach would vary with the party and ideology of the member of Congress. He was a master of role manipulation. On a tax question he might emphasize budget balancing with Republicans and personal loyalty with Democrats. On a rat extermination bill, he argued politics with Republicans, morality with moderates, and economics with conservatives.[80] He felt that members of Congress needed to feel like people of principle. Therefore, he sought to say whatever called up the best in each person. Emotional patriotism played a role here, since it was easier for a member to say yes to the "country's good" than to a politician in the White House.[81]

If the president could not obtain a favorable vote, he might ask, in effect, for an abstention. For example, he once called some Southern Democrats and asked them to stay away from a committee markup session on foreign aid,[82] knowing that if they attended they would vote against his program.

President Eisenhower's personal efforts at gathering votes are not as well understood as President Johnson's. On the one hand, we hear that he was accessible and a good listener who spent many hours listening to members of Congress in the hope of getting them to support his policies. Moreover, he sometimes "argued himself hoarse," especially on foreign aid, employing the rhetoric of self-interest, the economy, or national security, according to his needs. Much of this arguing, according to aide Bryce Harlow, was off-the-record.[83] Eisenhower himself wrote in his memoirs that he had to change congressional votes and ceaselessly explain, persuade, cajole, and cultivate the understanding and confidence of members of Congress through countless meetings and phone calls. He felt that his personal involvement in vote gathering was successful more often than not, and there is evidence that on several issues he was successful in switching a few votes.[84]

On the other hand, we learn that Eisenhower rarely made calls himself, not liking to use the telephone for public business. His order that calls to him from members of Congress be put through as soon as was convenient does not seem to have pleased even his own party members in Congress. His staff reviewed requests to see him, and a member of the congressional liaison staff sat in on any meetings with the president that were requested by a member.[85] House Republican leader Joseph Martin complained that the rank and file in Congress "found it extremely difficult, if not impossible, to see the President, and hard enough to get an appointment with his top assistants." Eisenhower, he said, worked too much through subordinates in dealing with Congress, and members resented this. They liked to hear from the president personally and felt that they were entitled to such communication.[86]

Eisenhower was not anxious to jump into the political fray. One of his aides later said Eisenhower did not understand that he had to fight for his programs and that he showed a lack of drive and leadership on the Hill. For instance, he was particularly interested in the 1954 trade bill. However, it was not enthusiastically supported by the conservative Republican congressional leaders and was held up in the House Ways and Means Committee without hearings or action. Nevertheless, the president refused to prod the committee.[87]

There is no lack of commentators to point out that President Kennedy felt personal contacts with Congress were important and that he spent considerable time with members, much of it off-the-record, and did not deny access to anyone in Congress who insisted on seeing him. Yet it appears that his staff tried to conserve his efforts in personal relations and his involvement in details, knowing that he was impatient with such activities, that he felt uncomfortable with many members of Congress (who had previously outranked him), and that he had limited time for and interest in domestic legislation. He was less likely than Johnson to call legislators and ask for their votes.[88]

When Kennedy did personally seek support, he sometimes had unexpected success. On one occasion Kennedy, during a walk in the White House gardens, convinced House Armed Services Committee chairperson Carl Vinson to cut language forcing him to spend money on the RS-70 bomber, which the president opposed.[89] In 1963 he found to his surprise in a talk with House Republican leader Charles Halleck that the latter supported his civil rights bill. After their talk, Halleck helped get the bill out of the House Judiciary Committee.[90] His willingness to talk to certain conservative members of Congress may have helped to gain their votes for liberal legislation that they had previously opposed.[91]

President Nixon reportedly did not feel that he should have to lobby for his programs. He saw himself more as an administrator and executive decision maker and not as a power broker pushing to get his bills through Congress. He usually called only members of Congress whom he knew and then mainly for small talk. Moreover, his interchange with Congress became more formal and less frequent, and he became less accessible to nonfriends and rank and file members. Calls to the president from members of Congress were carefully screened, and 90 percent never got through to Nixon. Nixon was briefed if he needed to call back. Occasionally the White House asked a department or agency to call a legislator concerning some specific legislation. The president rarely made such requests himself.[92]

While every president has to have his calls screened, the Nixon administration seemed to overuse the policy, or at least Capitol Hill thought so. There was also a widespread feeling among members of Congress from both parties that Nixon would not be informed of their calls or letters, and there were doubts about whether he could be spoken to at all.[93] During the Senate debate on Nixon's nomination of G. Harrold Carswell to the Supreme Court, Republican Senator Charles Mathias asked to interview the nominee. His request received no response until right before the vote, when he was told that he could see Carswell in a motel room after midnight. By then it was too late.[94]

Gerald Ford was much less hesitant to use the phone to ask for votes than his predecessor, and he kept notes of his calls for follow-up action by his staff.[95] Once in 1975 he took three Republican representatives on a trip on Air Force One and lectured each on how strongly he felt about the House sustaining his veto of a jobs bill. On the trip back he called member after member from the presidential plane. In all, eighteen members switched their votes from the vote on the bill's passage, and the president's veto was sustained.[96] Ford was personally involved in his legislative battles and was willing to call, see, and keep in contact with many members of Congress.[97]

Failure of Personal Appeals

Despite the prestige of their office, their invocations of national interest, and their persuasiveness, presidents have often failed in their personal appeals. President Eisenhower liked to depend heavily on charm and reason, but in 1953 he tried to persuade Republican chairperson Daniel Reed of the House Ways and Means Committee to support the continuance of the excess profits tax and to oppose a tax cut. "I used every possible reason, argument, and device, and every kind of personal and indirect contact," he wrote, "to bring Chairman Reed to my way of thinking." But he failed.[98]

At the same time, Eisenhower frequently failed to bring around Republican Styles Bridges, the chairperson of the Senate Foreign Relations Committee (ranking minority member after 1954). He had similar disappointments in his personal appeals to members of Congress concerning the St. Lawrence Seaway, the nomination of Chip Bohlen as ambassador to the Soviet Union, the 1953 immigration bill, his Defense Department reorganization bill, and foreign policy in general.[99] As he noted in his memoirs, while his exhortations seemed to be effective at the time, they were often forgotten later as other pressures, such as the next congressional election, were brought to bear.[100]

Eisenhower, Kennedy, and Johnson all failed, despite considerable personal effort, to convince Representative Otto Passman, chairperson of the House Appropriations Committee's Subcommittee on Foreign Aid, to support foreign aid.[101] To beat Passman, Johnson finally had to stack the subcommittee with members who would vote against the chairperson.

Johnson, renowned for his persuasiveness,

nevertheless failed on many issues, ranging from civil rights and education to Medicare and the Panama uprising. "No matter how many times I told Congress to do something," he wrote, "I could never force it to act."[102] If Eisenhower and Johnson often failed in their efforts at persuasion, we should not be surprised that other presidents did also.[103]

Bargaining

The authors of *Who Runs Congress?*, which was commissioned by Ralph Nader, argue that the president can buy votes in Congress with a pen at a bill-signing ceremony, by attending a local school dedication, with a government favor, or with confidential information.[104] Conversely, Kennedy-Johnson legislative liaison chief Lawrence O'Brien said near the end of his government service, "This suggestion that you trade the bridge or the dam or some project for a vote, . . . it's just not the case."[105] Similarly, William Timmons, O'Brien's counterpart in the Nixon administration, maintains that there were no blatant trades for votes in his experience.[106] Which view is correct? Are trades—that is, bargains—made, and are these bargains as easy to strike and as fundamental to presidential influence in Congress as the Nader researchers seem to believe?

Examples of Bargains

There is considerable evidence that bargaining does take place, as the examples below illustrate. John Kennedy was trying to make a case to Senator Robert Kerr for an investment credit tax bill that was bottled up in the Senate Finance Committee, of which Kerr was an influential member. Kerr responded by asking why the administration opposed his Arkansas River project and by demanding a trade. Kennedy smiled and replied, "You know, Bob, I never really understood that Arkansas River bill before today." Kerr got his project as well as several other benefits. In return, he provided Kennedy with important support and managed the president's high-priority Trade Expansion Act in the Senate.[107]

President Johnson wanted a tax cut in 1964, while Senate Finance Committee chairperson Harry Byrd wanted a decrease in spending. Byrd promised to get a tax cut out of his committee if the president pared the 1965 budget below $100 billion. Both men got what they wanted. To get Senator Russell Long to sponsor the tax cut, Johnson agreed to several tax provisions that Long desired.[108] That same year he directly offered Democrats everything from personal notes and photos to projects and judgeships to aid passage of the Civil Rights Act, and he gave Republican leaders an important role in the act's language to gain their support for ending the Senate's filibuster.[109] He reluctantly acceded to the demands of the North Carolina congressional delegation that in return for their support of the War on Poverty legislation, Adam Yarmolinsky, a leading figure in the development of the bill, would not be associated with the Office of Economic Opportunity. Johnson also increased the Farmers' Home Administration loan authorization and rural water supply and waste disposal system grants to gain support from Southern Democrats on the House Agriculture Committee.[110]

The next year, concerned about Senate amendments to the Medicare bill, Johnson began talking to individual senators. He made a campaign appearance for one and offered the possibility of "other things," too. To another senator Johnson mused out loud, "It seems that your state may not be getting its fair share of conservation projects here of late." Johnson got what he wanted. He also persuaded the House leadership to give Education and Labor Committee chairperson Adam Clayton Powell more committee expense funds so that Powell would get to work on the education bill.[111]

Johnson at times was quite overt in his trading. He once called Representative Porter Hardy of Virginia to seek his vote and said, in effect, "You may need me some time, and I'll remember this if you'll do it." (Hardy had decided to vote for Johnson's bill but pretended to be doing the president a favor. He later called on Johnson to return the favor and Johnson did).[112] He regularly traded favors with Senate Republican leader Everett Dirksen, such as when he supported the Kaskaskia River navigation project in return for Dirksen's support on excise taxes. According to Johnson biographer Doris Kearns, their "brazen exchange of memos" occupies a file six inches thick in the LBJ library. When Dirksen was sick, a messenger brought his week's requests on jobs, tariff rulings, Illinois projects, complaints, and so on, to the White House.[113]

In 1971 Representative Chet Holifield, the chairperson of the House Government Operations Committee, opposed President Nixon's proposal to consolidate several cabinet departments into four new departments—until he went on a jet ride with President Nixon. Subsequently the president came out in support of the breeder reactor Holifield wanted for his district. North American Rockwell, a contractor for the reactor, was also in his district. On his part, the representative found new virtues in the president's reorganization plan.[114]

Just before the Senate voted on the appointment of Judge Clement Haynsworth to the Supreme Court, the White House announced through the office of Senator William Jennings Randolph the awarding of a $3 million grant for urban renewal in Randolph's state of West Virginia. Representative Ken Hechler, in whose district the grant was to be used, was not mentioned; Hechler was Randolph's potential primary opponent, and Randolph had been the center of lobbying efforts on the confirmation vote. The senator voted for Haynsworth.[115]

Representative F. Edward Hebert, chairperson of the House Armed Services Committee, told Defense Secretary Elliot Richardson in 1973 that he would not introduce a multi-billion-dollar military spending bill if Richardson did not appoint a board of regents (including an Hebert constituent) for the new military medical school (which the secretary opposed). Hebert eventually went to President Nixon and told him the same thing. Then the board was appointed and the spending bill was introduced.[116] Nixon also forced the Department of Health, Education and Welfare to make concessions on school desegregation to Senator John Stennis of Mississippi, chairperson of the Senate Armed Services Committee, in return for the senator's support of the ABM (antiballistic missile).[117]

President Ford was involved in bargaining, also. In 1975 Representative Donald Mitchell of New York switched his vote on an emergency jobs bill, voting to sustain President Ford's veto. Three weeks later the Air Force reversed its decision to close the Rome Air Development Center in his district.[118]

Presidents also sometimes facilitate bargaining between groups in Congress—or force them to bargain to achieve their own goals. President Kennedy included a wide range of educational programs in his 1963 omnibus education bill to encourage education groups to work for each other's programs. The bill also carried as hostage the renewal of aid to federally impacted areas, a program strongly supported by school officials all across the country.[119] In 1964 President Johnson conceived the idea of trading the food stamps program for his farm bill. Thus, he called members supporting each and told them to support each other's bills.[120] Both Kennedy's and Johnson's strategies worked.

Sometimes the bargaining becomes quite involved and a bit abused. During Kennedy's tenure, Representative Mike Kirwan of Ohio wanted to build an aquarium in Washington, D.C. Senator Wayne Morse made a speech in his home state of Oregon criticizing the idea. Irritated by this, Kirwan used his position as a subcommittee chairperson on the House Appropriations Committee to cut out a major public works project in Oregon. Morse then appealed to the president, who supported the aquarium in return for Kirwan's support of the Oregon project. (Kennedy held a one-person bill signing ceremony in the White House for the aquarium bill.)[121]

Limits of Bargaining

Hindering direct and open deals is the scarcity of resources to deal with and the desire of members of Congress for these resources. If many direct bargains are struck, word will rapidly spread, everyone will want to trade, and persuasive efforts will fail. Thus, most of the bargains that are reached are implicit.[122] The lack of respectability surrounding bargaining also encourages implicitness. This, however, has drawbacks. The terms of an implicit bargain are likely to be less clear than those of an explicit one, increasing the likelihood for misunderstanding and subsequent ill will when the member of Congress wishes to reap his or her reward for supporting the president.[123]

The president cannot bargain with Congress as a whole because it is too large and decentralized for one bargain to satisfy everyone. Also, the president's time is limited, as are his resources—only so many appointive jobs are available and the federal budget is limited. Moreover, funding for public works projects is in the hands of Congress.[124]

Fortunately for the president, bargaining with everyone in Congress is not necessary. Except on vetoes and treaties, he only needs a simple majority of those voting. A large part of Congress can be "written off" on any given vote. Moreover, we have already seen that the president generally starts with a substantial core of party support and then adds to this number those of the other party who agree with his views on ideological or policy grounds. Others may support him on the basis of goodwill that he has generated through his services or because of public support for him or his policies. Thus, the president only needs to bargain if all these groups do not provide a majority for crucial votes, and he need only bargain with enough people to provide him with that majority. As Vice President Lyndon Johnson said in 1963, "Not many votes are converted in the corridors."[125]

Since resources are scarce, the president will usually try to use them for bargaining with powerful members of Congress, such as committee chairpersons or those whose votes are crucial on an issue, as the above examples of bargaining illustrate. However, there is no guarantee that a tendered bargain will be accepted. The members may not desire what the president offers, or they may be able to obtain what they want on their own. This is, of course, particularly true of the most powerful members, whose support the president needs most.

Sometimes members of Congress do not want to trade at all. This may be due to either constraints such as constituency opinion or personal views. In 1961 Representative Jim Delaney cast the vote responsible for holding the federal aid-to-education bill in the House Rules Committee. He wanted to include aid to parochial schools, which Kennedy opposed. The president desperately needed his vote, but Delaney was not interested in bargaining on other subjects. As legislative liaison chief Lawrence O'Brien exclaimed, "He didn't want a thing. I wish he had."[126]

At other times the president is unwilling to bargain. In 1961 Representative D. B. Saund of California was angered by President Kennedy's closing of a veteran's hospital in his district, and in retaliation he opposed an important provision of the president's foreign aid bill. Nevertheless, Kennedy refused to reopen the inadequate and unsafe hospital in return for Saund's support on foreign aid (his opposition was ultimately successful.)[127]

At yet other times the president is simply unable to bargain. A representative told one high White House official that he would vote to sustain an important presidential veto "if, and only if, we could get a CAB route into his town." The official responded, "Congressman, that is impossible. We can't touch regulatory agencies." Thus, the member voted against the president.[128]

Richard Neustadt argues in *Presidential Power* that the president must bargain even with those who agree with him in order to insure their support because most people in government have interests of their own beyond the realm of policy objectives.[129] Yet . . . the limitations on bargaining mentioned above indicate that Neustadts's view needs to be revised. The president does not have to bargain with everyone to receive his or her support, and he cannot bargain with very many members of Congress at any one time.

However, we have also seen that some bargains are struck. It is important to distinguish between a president's usual supporters and opponents. All bargains are not equal. Rewarding one's opponents for short-term support is much costlier than rewarding supporters, since the former action may not only alienate supporters who did not receive benefits but also give opponents greater strength in the future. Rewarding supporters, on the other hand, may make them more effective in advancing the president's policies, thus multiplying the positive effect of bargains. Thus, people who recommend that presidents rely upon bargaining, such as Neustadt, should specify with whom bargains should be made and what their long-run consequences are.

Much of what the president offers in bargaining is ultimately in the hands of the bureaucracy or other members of Congress. Consequently, he must often bargain within the executive branch or within Congress before he can bargain with a particular member of Congress whose vote he needs. This uses the president's time, energy, and bargaining resources. In addition, once credit is built up between a department (which has done a favor) and a member of Congress, it may be drawn upon by the department without the president's approval.

According to the *Congressional Quarterly*, most of the pressure for bargaining actually comes from the Hill. When the White House calls and asks for support, representatives and senators frequently raise a question regarding some request that they have made.[130] In the words of an Eisenhower aide, "Every time we make a special appeal to a Congressman to change his position, he eventually comes back with a request for a favor ranging in importance from one of the President's packages of matches to a judgeship or cabinet appointment for a 'worthy constituent.'"[131]

Another frustrated presidential aide spoke of his experience with one representative as follows:

> Every time you wanted a vote from him he wanted something for the walnut growers in his district or something else. Finally, I sat him down and said, "Look, I can't bargain for every vote. Why don't you draw up a shopping list of things that would be really helpful to you and we'll do our best to help. In turn, how about giving us a little more support?"[132]

We have already seen other examples of members of Congress responding to White House requests for support with a request of their own. Sometimes members of Congress try to initiate bargains as well. Senator Carl Curtis of Nebraska wanted to cut his staff in 1975 and told Commerce Secretary Rogers Morton that he would aid President Ford in his fight with Congress over energy legislation if the Commerce Department hired one of his aides.[133]

More general bargains also take place. In the words of Nixon's chief congressional aide, William Timmons, "I think they [members of Congress] knew that we would try our best to help them on all kinds of requests if they supported the President, and we did. It kind of goes without saying." His successor, Max Friedersdorf, added his assurance that people who want things want to be in the position of supporting the president. This implicit trading on "accounts" is more common than explicit bargaining.[134]

The Kennedy, Johnson, and Nixon administrations kept a record of presidential support given by each member of Congress. The Ford administration kept a less formal tally. Each president checked the record before granting requests.[135] Although the White House generally tries to be helpful to everyone, it is likely to be most helpful to those members providing the most support.[136]

In interviews with members of the congressional liaison staffs in the Kennedy, Johnson, Nixon, and Ford administrations, Joe Pika found near unanimity on the view that the relationships between the White House and members of Congress were reciprocal: Voting support by members was exchanged for administrative responsiveness to their requests for assistance.[137] The White House tried to get members of Congress in its debt by providing favors and sympathetic hearings. Many members, in turn, tried to create favorable impressions in the White House of their support for the president, sometimes writing to the president and reminding him of their votes.[138]

For the White House, a member of Congress indebted to the president is easier to approach and ask for a vote. For the member, previous support increases the chances of a request being honored. Thus, office holders at both ends of Pennsylvania Avenue want to be in the other's favor. The degree of debt determines the strategy used in presidential request for support. While services and favors increase the president's chances of obtaining support, they are not usually exchanged for votes directly. They are strategic and not tactical weapons.[139]

This point is illustrated in the following statement by Lawrence O'Brien, discussing various White House services for Congress:

[There is] no single element of [them] that is overridingly important, but [in] the over-all activity . . . in putting the package together over a period of years [we] can only hope the member up there has the view that the White House is interested in him and his problems . . . and therefore when we have our problems—we will get favorable reaction at least from the sense of giving us a hearing, seriously considering our viewpoint, if he feels that we in turn understand his problem.

....

Arm-Twisting

One special variant of presidential involvement in seeking support from Congress is arm-twisting. This term has no precise definition. We may define arm-twisting as the use of coercive techniques like pressure and threats to gain support from members of Congress.

Lawrence O'Brien once claimed that "arm twisting . . . does not exist."[141] In discussing President Johnson's treatment of Congress, former aide Jack Valenti argued that a president really cannot twist the arms of powerful, influential members lest they become "sullen, intractable and vengeful." Thus, a president must be more sophisticated.[142] In his memoirs Johnson comments on arm-twisting, arguing that he could not rely on threats. "It is daydreaming," he wrote, "to assume that any experienced Congressman would ignore his basic instincts or his constituents' deepest concerns in quaking fear of the White House. My best hope was to make him a good, solid, convincing case for the administration's position."[143] O'Brien supports this view in his comments that the Johnson White House was not going to ask anyone to commit political suicide. Rather, it had to rely on the soft sell, looking to develop long-run influence.[144]

One Southern Democrat agreed with this in his description of Johnson's efforts to influence him. "What he really twists," the representative said, "is your heart. He says he's got to have your help, and the tears are practically coming out of the telephone receiver."[145] Barefoot Sanders, chief of the Office of Congressional Relations at the end of Johnson's presidency, said that his office generally tried to be helpful to everyone and took no revenge on opponents.[146]

Nevertheless, Johnson's behavior was not always so gentle. One aide recalls his systematic use of "sheer force—embarrassing, bullying, and threatening." If these tactics failed, he used reprisals to make the members more amenable to his desires in the future. During the debate on Medicare, Johnson told one senator that he understood the senator's problems, but worse ones would occur if he did not see the light.[147]

Johnson often had Senate Republican leader Everett Dirksen sit at the head table at state dinners as a reward for the senator's support of Johnson's Vietnam policy and other policies. Conversely, after their opposition to the war was clear, Senate Foreign Relations Committee chairperson William Fulbright frequently was not invited to state dinners, and Senate Majority Leader Mike Mansfield was seated at a side table. Johnson also exhorted, "The next time [Senator] Frank Church [who opposed his policies in Vietnam] wants a dam, let him build it," and reviewed the Army Corps of Engineers budget to hurt those who opposed him. His aides also could be "pretty insistent."[148]

One interesting bit of Johnsonian highhandedness occurred when he was trying to get Senate Finance Committee chairperson Harry Byrd to hold hearings on Johnson's Medicare bill. Unknown to Byrd, television cameras awaited him after a meeting between the president and congressional leaders. As the president and the senator faced the cameras, Johnson was able to extract publicly a promise from Byrd for quick hearings.

President Eisenhower relied very little on arm-twisting. It was contrary to his style of leadership, which developed over the four decades of his successful military career. He said of himself, "I am not the desk-pounding type that likes to stick out his jaw and look like he is bossing the show." He preferred to persuade members of Congress into giving him their support rather than scare them with "noisy, strong-armed tactics." It was his belief as well as his inclination that persuasion would be more successful with Republicans, who had grown accustomed to opposing the president through the Roosevelt-Truman years and who might be alienated by pressure. He also believed members would stick by him more if they were persuaded as to the correctness of their actions. Thus, his leadership style emphasized persuasion, conciliation, education, and patience.[150] He courted rather than challenged Congress.

Several months after leaving office, Eisenhower was asked if he ever "turned the screw on Congress to get something done . . . saying you'll withhold an appointment or something like that." He responded, "No, never. . . I never thought that any of these appointments should be used for bringing pressure on the Congress." In the opinion of one of his aides, this reluctance to pressure Congress contributed to the floundering of his legislative program and a blurring of his party's image.[151]

About the closest Eisenhower came to arm-twisting were occasional threats to withhold campaign support from unresponsive Republicans and telling Republican leaders in 1957 that if members of Congress failed to support his national security proposals, "I would not be able to understand them should they ever request my help in the future." His postmaster general, Arthur Summerfield, sometimes threatened to cut off patronage to Republicans who broke party ranks.[152]

In a January 1954 cabinet meeting, Vice President Nixon suggested that administration officials accept or reject speaking engagements in Republican congressional districts and states depending upon the support that those members of Congress had given to the administration's programs. But the president said that Republicans in Congress should know that this policy *might* be implemented, hoping that the administration would, never have to resort to such a course later.[153]

Senator Joseph McCarthy regularly attacked the president and at one point even publicly apologized for supporting him in 1952. Yet Eisenhower levied no sanctions against him beyond ignoring him. (On the Senate's censure vote on the senator, most of the Republican leadership in the Senate voted for McCarthy.)[154] At an April 1953 cabinet meeting, Eisenhower said that anyone who wanted to support the Bricker amendment (which he strongly opposed) could do so. In 1958 Senator Andrew Schoeppel, chairperson of the Republican Senatorial Campaign Committee, announced that candidates could ignore reciprocal trade and foreign aid (two of the issues closest to Eisenhower's heart) if they found it convenient during the campaign.[155]

On his desk the president had a small block of wood bearing the inscription "Gentle in manner, strong in deed." This reflects the fact that he was temperamentally unable to impose sanctions to enforce discipline on recalcitrant Republicans. He also refused to criticize Republicans publicly because he felt to do so would do more harm than good. At a news conference he once said that he did not think it was the function of a president to punish anyone for not voting right. These words were undoubtedly not lost upon Congress. Even on issues about which he was deeply concerned, such as mutual security legislation, and on which he received little support from Republican leaders, he did not try to punish them.[156]

Lawrence O'Brien, who headed the White House Office of Congressional Relations under both Kennedy and Johnson, has contrasted the former's "more restrained approach" with the latter's "hard-sell, arm-twisting style of operation."[157] Generally, the Kennedy White House employed a positive rather than a negative approach to congressional relations.[158] Nevertheless, there are examples of arm-twisting in the Kennedy years. In the midst of the 1962 fight over raising the ceiling on the national debt, then representative Gerald Ford, among others, accused the Kennedy administration of threatening to cancel military contracts in his Michigan district if he did not support the bill. At other times during the Kennedy era, there were threats to cancel National Guard and reserve armories.[159]

After he lost the Senate vote on Medicare in 1962 by a vote of 52 to 48, Kennedy had Senator Jennings Randolph of West Virginia (who voted against the bill) notified that his controversial $11 million grant, which the president had promised to support before the vote, was being dropped from the budget. Other Kennedy opponents had federal buildings for their constituencies dropped from the budget. Kennedy once excluded a local representative from the platform on a California trip because of his consistent desertion on foreign aid votes.[160]

In the 1961 battle over expanding the House Rules Committee, the president's supporters in the House threatened freshmen with poor committee assignments (his opponents did the same), and Secretary of Interior Stewart Udall called four Republicans and suggested that their projects might have problems with the pro-Kennedy forces if they voted against expansion of the committee.[161]

Thus, although Kennedy rarely asked a member of Congress for a specific vote, his aides did at times apply pressure. Even when members of Congress complained that their constituents were opposed to an item high on the president's priority list, they were sometimes told that they had "to take the heat."[162]

The Nixon administration also employed arm-twisting. During the legislative fight over the ABM in 1969, which Nixon favored, heavy pressure was applied. Senator James Pearson of Kansas, a Republican, was opposed to the ABM. At a crucial point in the debate, he was told by a Kansas plane manufacturer that an army general had informed him that Pentagon contracts might not be forthcoming to Kansas if the ABM failed in the Senate. The senator was also told by the Department of Agriculture that the rural job development bill that he and the department had backed would not now receive the latter's support. Besides threatening him with the loss of benefits, the White House did not tell him that it was moving a regional federal office from Denver to Kansas City, thus denying him the opportunity to take credit for the move.[163]

In that same year there was a major fight, which the president eventually lost, over the confirmation of Clement Haynsworth to the Supreme Court. During the consideration of the nomination, the White House attempted to generate mail supporting Haynsworth to senators and threatened Republicans with strong primary opponents, cutoffs or slowdowns of public works funds, withdrawing personal and monetary campaign support, reviews of income tax returns, the loss of agricultural subsidies, and the loss of access to the White House. When G. Harrold Carswell was nominated to fill the same seat, the White House relied on polite inquiries and quiet persuasion until the end of the fight, when it once again began its high-pressure campaign. Two Democratic senators (Howard Cannon and Quentin Burdick) were told that they would face weak Republican opposition in their re-election campaigns that year if they supported the president and that Nixon and Vice President Agnew would personally campaign against them if they voted against confirmation. (Following Cannon's vote against Carswell, the White House did make special efforts, in vain, to defeat him in the fall election.) The White House also released to *Newsweek* a list of all the people that it had called in Pennsylvania and asked to support the president in order to pressure Senator Richard Schweiker;[164] thus, Schweiker was placed in the position of publicly opposing these people if he voted against confirmation.

Despite the fact that the Nixon administration sometimes applied heavy pressure on Congress,[165] the president did not apply it himself. Nixon could not bring himself to ask for a vote and would frequently end meetings with representatives with "I know you're going to do what you have to do and that's fine. Whatever you do is OK with me." He hated face-to-face confrontations and did not demand or plead for votes, even on a matter as important to him as the Carswell nomination. The hard sell came from the White House staff.[166]

Congress was not immune to White House arm-twisting when Gerald Ford, a "man of Congress," occupied the presidency, either. Again, this came from the staff rather than the president. In 1975, White House aide Douglas Bennett threatened to block an appointment in which two Republican representatives from Maine were interested if they failed to support President Ford on a veto override attempt. The following year Representative Larry Pressler of South Dakota complained of a threat from one of President Ford's lobbyists that he would have "political trouble" in his district if he failed to support the president on a natural gas deregulation bill. He was also warned after the vote that he could be cut off from White House favors.[167] Other complaints of arm-twisting by White House aide Vernon Loen came from Senator James Abourezk, who was threatened with, "We're going to get you in '78," and Representative Berkley Bedell, a religious freshmen, who was told by a White House aide, "I don't have to have any _____ from a freshman."[168]

At the beginning of this section we heard disclaimers about both the existence and effectiveness of arm-twisting. We have since seen that presidents have occasionally used high-pressure tactics on members of Congress, often unsuccessfully. None of the four Republicans threatened with the loss of public works projects in their districts voted for Kennedy in the 1961 House Rules Committee fight,[169] and Nixon's staff's actions in the Haynsworth and Carswell episodes either were ineffective or backfired.[170]

Members of Congress do not like arm-twisting. As one prominent student of Congress put it, "The rule here is to forgive and remember."[171] Given the limited success and the possibility of backfiring, it is not surprising that arm-twisting is generally relied upon only as a last resort and then only on particularly important votes.[172]

Notes

1. Harry McPherson, *A Political Education* (Boston: Little, Brown, 1972), 192.

2. Doris Kearns, *Lyndon Johnson and the American Dream* (New York: Harper & Row, 1976), 226.

3. Lyndon B. Johnson, *The Vantage Point: Perspectives on the Presidency 1963-1969* (New York: Popular Library, 1971), 448.

4. Eric F. Goldman, *The Tragedy of Lyndon Johnson* (New York: Dell, 1974), 68.

5. Joseph A. Califano, Jr., *A Presidential Nation* (New York: Norton, 1975), 217. The author suggests this attention to detail was in part due to Johnson's natural skepticism.

6. Lawrence F. O'Brien, *No Final Victories* (Garden City, N.Y.: Doubleday, 1974), 194; George Christian, *The President Steps Down: A Personal Memoir of the Transfer of Power* (New York: Macmillan, 1970), 6. See also Goldman, *Tragedy of Lyndon Johnson*, 72.

7. Kearns, *Lyndon Johnson*, 233; Stephen J. Wayne, *The Legislative Presidency* (New York: Harper & Row, 1978), 151.

8. O'Brien, *No Final Victories*, 172; Wayne, *Legislative Presidency*, 148.

9. O'Brien, *No Final Victories*, 171-172. See also Johnson, *Vantage Point*, 159-211; Goldman, *Tragedy of Lyndon Johnson*, 340-341; Wayne, *Legislative Presidency*, 151; Kearns, *Lyndon Johnson*, 233; Califano, *Presidential Nation*, 215; Jack Valenti, *A Very Human President* (New York: Norton, 1975), 189.

10. O'Brien, *No Final Victories*, 184.

11. Goldman, *Tragedy of Lyndon Johnson*, 71; Jack Bell, *The Johnson Treatment* (New York: Harper & Row, 1965), 178.

12. Johnson, *Vantage Point*, 451. See also Goldman, *Tragedy of Lyndon Johnson*, 70.

13. Kearns, *Lyndon Johnson*, 186, 225; Johnson, *Vantage Point*, 447; Goldman, *Tragedy of Lyndon Johnson*, 70; "Carter Seeks More Effective Use of Departmental Lobbyists' Skills," *Congressional Quarterly Weekly Report*, March 4, 1978, 581; Joseph A. Pika, "White House Office of Congressional Relations: A Longitudinal Analysis," paper presented at the annual meeting of the Midwest Political Science Association, Chicago, April 1978, 13. See also Rowland Evans and Robert Novak, *Nixon in the White House: The Frustration of Power* (New York: Vintage, 1972), 109, for Bryce Harlow's argument for this need for intimate knowledge.

14. Kearns, *Lyndon Johnson*, 236; Wayne, *Legislative Presidency*, 151; Goldman, *Tragedy of Lyndon Johnson*, 73-74; Valenti, *Very Human President*, 304.

15. Kearns, *Lyndon Johnson*, 185.

16. Johnson, *Vantage Point*, 457. For another example, see Wayne, *Legislative Presidency*, 147.

17. Goldman, *Tragedy of Lyndon Johnson*, 70, 227; Kearns, *Lyndon Johnson*, 226, 337.

18. Goldman, *Tragedy of Lyndon Johnson*, 308.

19. Kearns, *Lyndon Johnson*, 222; Johnson, *Vantage Point*, 446; Goldman, *Tragedy of Lyndon Johnson*, 382; Neil MacNeil, *Dirksen: Portrait of a Public Man* (New York: World, 1970), 252-254.

20. Johnson, *Vantage Point*, 209-210, 447; Goldman, *Tragedy of Lyndon Johnson*, 74; Kearns, *Lyndon Johnson*, 223; Alan L. Otten, "By Courting Congress Assiduously Johnson Furthers His Program," *Wall Street Journal*, April 9, 1965, 1.

21. Kearns, *Lyndon Johnson*, 222-223.

22. Ibid., 222-224.

23. Califano, *Presidential Nation*, 222. See also Johnson, *Vantage Point*, 447-448, 456, on briefing Congress ahead of time.

24. Kearns, *Lyndon Johnson*, 184-186.

25. Tom Wicker, "The Johnson Way with Congress," *New York Times Magazine*, March 8, 1964, 103.

26. O'Brien, *No Final Victories*, 183-184; Wayne, *Legislative Presidency*, 150; Kearns, *Lyndon Johnson*, 233-234; "Carter Seeks More Effective Use," 581; "Larry O'Brien Discusses White House Contacts with Capitol Hill," in *The Presidency*, ed. Aaron Wildavsky (Boston: Little, Brown, 1969), 480.

27. For example, see Johnson, *Vantage Point*, 448.

28. Ralph K. Huitt, "White House Channels to the Hill," in *Congress against the President*, ed. Harvey C. Mansfield, Sr. (New York: Praeger, 1975), 75; "Carter Seeks More Effective Use," 581, 586.

29. Goldman, *Tragedy of Lyndon Johnson*, 81-82.

30. Kearns, *Lyndon Johnson*, 225.

31. O'Brien, *No Final Victories*, 111-112; MacNeil, *Dirksen*, 225; Neil MacNeil, *Forge of Democracy* (New York: McKay, 1963), 258. See Donald C. Lord, "JFK and Civil Rights," *Presidential Studies Quarterly* 8 (Spring 1978): 151-163; for a very positive view of Kennedy's legislative skills regarding his civil rights bill.

32. Arthur M. Schlesinger, Jr., *A Thousand Days: John F. Kennedy in the White House* (New York: Houghton Mifflin, 1965), 711.

33. Randall B. Ripley, *Majority Party Leadership in Congress* (Boston: Little, Brown, 1969), 37.

34. Valenti, *Very Human President*, 304.

35. Evans and Novak, *Nixon in the White House*, 106.

36. Dan Rather and Gary P. Gates, *The Palace Guard* (New York: Warner, 1975), 279.

37. Evans and Novak, *Nixon in the White House*, 168; Richard Harris, *Decision* (New York: Dutton, 1971), 29, 32, 176-177, 179, 185-186, 189-190, 197-199. See 100, 129-132, 139, for other examples of the Nixon White House's lack of knowledge of Congress on this issue. For another example, see William Safire, *Before the Fall: An Inside View of the Pre-Watergate White House* (New York: Doubleday, 1975), 487-490.

38. Sherman Adams, *Firsthand Report* (New York: Popular Library, 1962), 296; James L. Sundquist, *Politics and Policy: The Eisenhower, Kennedy, and Johnson Years* (Washington, D.C.: Brookings Institution, 1968), 161-162; Gary W. Reichard, *The Reaffirmation of Republicanism: Eisenhower and the Eighty-third Congress* (Knoxville: University of Tennessee Press, 1975), 225; Malcolm E. Jewell, *Senatorial Politics and Foreign Policy* (Lexington: University of Kentucky Press, 1962), 117-118; Ripley, *Majority Party Leadership*, 121.

39. "Carter Seeks More Effective Use," 586; "House GOP: Its Survival May Be at Stake," *Congressional Quarterly Weekly Report*, June 26, 1976, 1634.

40. Johnson, *Vantage Point*, 456; Kearns, *Lyndon Johnson*, 233; Wayne, *Legislative Presidency*, 151.

41. For example, see Bell, *Johnson Treatment*, 40.

42. For example, see Johnson, *Vantage Point*, 214.

43. Wayne, *Legislative Presidency*, 152-153; John F. Manley, "White House Lobbying and the Problem of Presidential Power," paper presented at the annual meeting of the American Political Science Association, Washington, D.C., September 1977, 27-28.

44. Theodore C. Sorensen, *Kennedy* (New York: Bantam, 1966), 398.

45. Abraham Holtzman, *Legislative Liaison: Executive Leadership in Congress* (Chicago: Rand McNally, 1970), 223-229, 249; Benjamin Bradlee, *Conversations with Kennedy* (New York: Norton, 1975), 65; O'Brien, *No Final Victories*, 111-113, 117-119, 127, 134.

46. Safire, *Before the Fall*, 375-376, 422, 676. Sometimes his staff briefed congressional leaders. See, for example, 172-173.

47. Emmet J. Hughes, *The Living Presidency* (Baltimore: Penguin, 1974), 258.

48. Stephen J. Wayne, personal communication, January 9, 1979.

49. MacNeil, *Dirksen*, 343-344, 346, 358.

50. Evans and Novak, *Nixon in the White House*, 107.

51. Adams, *Firsthand Report*, 284, 288, 359-360, 372; Dwight D. Eisenhower, *Waging Peace: 1956-1961* (Garden City, N.Y.: Doubleday, 1965), 44-46, 246-249, 252, 271-272; Jewell, *Senatorial Politics*, 128, 156, 158; Robert J. Donovan, *Eisenhower: The Inside Story* (New York: Harper & Row, 1956), 226-227, 311.

52. Wayne, *Legislative Presidency*, 145; Donovan, *Eisenhower*, 312.

53. See, for example, Eisenhower, *Waging Peace*, 642. See also Merlo J. Pusey, *Eisenhower the President* (New York: Macmillan, 1956), 206. For an exception, see Richard E. Neustadt, "Presidency and Legislation: Planning the President's Program," in *The Presidency*, ed. Aaron Wildavsky (Boston: Little, Brown), 571.

54. Reichard, *Reaffirmation of Republicanism*, 219, 290-291; William S. White, *The Taft Story* (New York: Harper & Row, 1954), 213; Wayne, *Legislative Presidency*, 144-145; Pusey, *Eisenhower the President*, 206-207; Adams, *Firsthand Report*, 214-215.

55. Jewell, *Senatorial Politics*, 92; MacNeil, *Dirksen*, 168; "The Congress: The Gut Fighter," *Time*, June 8, 1959, 18.

56. Dwight D. Eisenhower, *Mandate for Change, 1953-1956* (New York: Signet, 1963), 245, 365; Donovan, *Eisenhower*, 235.

57. Emmet J. Hughes, *The Ordeal of Power: A Political Memoir of the Eisenhower Years* (New York: Atheneum, 1975), 123; "The Gut Fighter," 15, 18.

58. Joe Martin, *My First Fifty Years in Politics* (New York: McGraw-Hill, 1960), 13. Nevertheless, Martin drew upon his personal goodwill with Republicans to help the president (230). See also Neustadt, "Presidency and Legislation," 596.

59. See Eisenhower, *Mandate for Change*, 349; Eisenhower, *Waging Peace*, 146, 151-152; Reichard, *Reaffirmation of Republicanism*, 91-92, 197-199, 220-221; Neustadt, "Presidency and Legislation," 569-570; Adams, *Firsthand Report*, 372, 379-380; Donovan, *Eisenhower*, 232; Jewell, *Senatorial Politics*, 95-96, 158.

60. Neustadt, "Presidency and Legislation," 596.

61. McPherson, *Political Education*, 192.

62. MacNeil, *Forge of Democracy*, 265. See also Stephen Horn, *Unused Power: The Work of the Senate Committee on Appropriations* (Washington, D.C.: Brookings Institution, 1970), 195.

63. Goldman, *Tragedy of Lyndon Johnson*, 71; Bell, *Johnson Treatment*, 37; "Turning Screws: Winning Votes in Congress," *Congressional Quarterly Weekly Report*, April 24, 1976, 954.

64. Valenti, *Very Human President*, 178.

65. O'Brien, *No Final Victories*, 111.

66. Otten, "By Courting Congress," 1; Wayne, *Legislative Presidency*, 151; Horn, *Unused Power*, 195; John W. Kingdon, *Congressmen's Voting Decisions* (New York: Harper & Row, 1973), 184, 187; McPherson, *Political Education*, 192; Jewell, *Senatorial Politics*, 160-161; Holtzman, *Legislative Liaison*, 247.

67. Kearns, *Lyndon Johnson*, 235; William Chapman, "LBJ's Way: Tears, Not Arm-Twists," *Washington Post*, October 17, 1965, E-1.

68. Pusey, *Eisenhower the President*, 212; Horn, *Unused Power*, 195; "White House Report: Ford's Lobbyists Expect Democrats to Revise Tactics," *National Journal*, June 21, 1975, 926.

69. Johnson, *Vantage Point*, 459; Wayne, *Legislative Presidency*, 151; Kearns, *Lyndon Johnson*, 236; "Ford's Lobbyists," 926.

70. Kearns, *Lyndon Johnson*, 234-236.

71. Sundquist, *Politics and Policy*, 268.

72. Califano, *Presidential Nation*, 215.

73. Valenti, *Very Human President*, 187, 192-193. See also 302-303 for Johnson discussing his toughness.

74. Goldman, *Tragedy of Lyndon Johnson*, 35-38, 75.

75. Sundquist, *Politics and Policy*, 146; Bell, *Johnson Treatment*, 187, 189; Chapman, "LBJ's Way," 1.

76. O'Brien, *No Final Victories*, 175.

77. Goldman, *Tragedy of Lyndon Johnson*, 77-78. See also MacNeil, *Dirksen*, 228; Bell, *Johnson Treatment*, 93-94.

78. Johnson, *Vantage Point*, 459.

79. Valenti, *Very Human President*, 194.

80. Bell, *Johnson Treatment*, 93-94, 181; Johnson, *Vantage Point*, 85.

81. Goldman, Tragedy of Lyndon Johnson, 72-73, 75-76.

82. Horn, *Unused Power*, 200.

83. Wayne, *Legislative Presidency*, 144-145; Hughes, *Ordeal of Power*, 125; Adams, *Firsthand Report*, 369, 373; Holtzman, *Legislative Liaison*, 246; Eisenhower, *Waging Peace*, 642; Reichard, *Reaffirmation of Republicanism*, 71, 77, 170.

84. Eisenhower, *Mandate for Change*, 347, 364; Reichard, *Reaffirmation of Republicanism*, 67-68, 151-152, 169-171. See also Donovan, *Eisenhower*, 84-86, 284, 313, for his urging the cabinet to cooperate with Congress and his discussing ways to improve relations with it.

85. Wayne, *Legislative Presidency*, 145; Reichard, *Reaffirmation of Republicanism*, 221.

86. Martin, *My First Fifty Years*, 226-227; Reichard, *Reaffirmation of Republicanism*, 92, 224. Martin did not think Eisenhower's aides were skillful in solving this problem.

87. Wayne, *Legislative Presidency*, 144; Ripley, *Majority Party Leadership*, 126-127.

88. Sorensen, *Kennedy*, 386, 391-392, 399-400; O'Brien, *No Final Victories*, 113-114; MacNeil, *Forge of Democracy*, 256-257, 264-265; McPherson, *Political Education*, 192-193; Wayne, *Legislative Presidency*, 151. Even in the extremely close and important fight over expanding the House Rules Committee in 1961, he hardly made personal contact at all (partly to maintain the symbol of presidential non-involvement in internal congressional affairs). See also O'Brien, *No Final Victories*, 109.

89. Sorensen, *Kennedy*, 389; O'Brien, *No Final Victories*, 119-120.

90. O'Brien, *No Final Victories*, 147-148.

91. MacNeil, *Forge of Democracy*, 26, 266.

92. "Ford's Lobbyists," 925; Wayne, *Legislative Presidency*, 160-161. Nixon reports that he made several calls to members of Congress and had meetings with others on the ABM issue in 1969 but then stopped because he felt he was squandering his prestige; Richard M. Nixon, *RN: The Memoirs of Richard Nixon* (New York: Grosset and Dunlap, 1978), 417.

93. Wayne, *Legislative Presidency*, 161.

94. Evans and Novak, *Nixon in the White House*, 168. Administration officials conceded after the vote that they were not anxious for wavering senators to see Carswell.

95. Wayne, *Legislative Presidency*, 161.

96. "Ford's Lobbyists," 923; "The Veto Sticks," *Time*, June 16, 1975, 12.

97. "Ford's Lobbyists," 923; "House GOP," 1634.

98. Eisenhower, *Mandate for Change*, 254-255. See also Reichard, *Reaffirmation of Republicanism*, 104; Donovan, *Eisenhower*, 60.

99. Horn, *Unused Power*, 196; Reichard, *Reaffirmation of Republicanism*, 169; Martin, *My First Fifty Years*, 234; Jewell, *Senatorial Politics*, 163; Eisenhower, *Mandate for Change*, 267, 273; Eisenhower, *Waging Peace*, 162.

100. Eisenhower, *Mandate for Change*, 365.

101. MacNeil, *Dirksen*, 171-172; O'Brien, *No Final Victories*, 122-123; Adams, *Firsthand Report*, 370; Bell, *Johnson Treatment*, 176, 178.

102. Johnson, *Vantage Point*, 40. See also Bell, *Johnson Treatment*, 103-105; MacNeil, *Dirksen*, 287; O'Brien, *No Final Victories*, 188; Otten, "By Courting Congress," 1.

103. For example, see Harris, *Decision*, 183; Tom Wicker, *JFK and LBJ: The Influence of Personality upon Politics* (Baltimore: Penguin, 1968), 79-80; MacNeil, *Forge of Democracy*, 264.

104. Mark J. Green, James M. Fallows, and David R. Zwick, *Who Runs Congress?* (New York: Bantam, 1972), 95-97.

105. "Larry O'Brien Discusses," 481.

106. "Turning Screws," 952.

107. McPherson, *Political Education*, 197; Russell D. Renka, "Legislative Leadership and Marginal Vote-Gaining Strategies in the Kennedy and Johnson Presidencies," paper presented at the annual meeting of the Southwestern Political Science Association, Houston, April 1978, 26-27.

108. Valenti, *Very Human President*, 196-197; Renka, "Legislative Leaderhip," 37. Hubert Humphrey reports that Johnson extracted the same promise from

Byrd after a late-night session at the White House, during which he employed the charms of Mrs. Johnson, liquor, and his famous "treatment" to persuade the senator; Hubert H. Humphrey, *The Education of a Public Man: My Life and Politics* (Garden City, N.Y.: Doubleday, 1976), 290-293.

109. Kearns, *Lyndon Johnson*, 191-192; Renka, "Legislative Leadership," 38.

110. Sundquist, *Politics and Policy*, 149; Bell, *Johnson Treatment*, 98-99; Rowland Evans and Robert Novak, *Lyndon B. Johnson: The Exercise of Power* (New York: Signet, 1966), 455; Renka, "Legislative Leadership," 40-41.

111. Goldman, *Tragedy of Lyndon Johnson*, 348-349, 357-358.

112. "Turning Screws," 954. For a view of the opposite technique of making necessary choices appear as discretionary favors, see Kearns, *Lyndon Johnson*, 186.

113. Kearns, *Lyndon Johnson*, 182-183; Valenti, *Very Human President*, 182-183; Renka, "Legislative Leadership," 28-30. Johnson's bargaining is also discussed in Goldman, *Tragedy of Lyndon Johnson*, 74-75.

114. Green, Fallows, and Zwick, *Who Runs Congress?*, 97.

115. Harris, *Decision*, 147-148.

116. *Weekend*, National Broadcasting Company, televised February 5, 1977; "Turning Screws," 949.

117. Evans and Novak, *Nixon in the White House*, 152-153.

118. "Turning Screws," 948, 953. See also Wayne, *Legislative Presidency*, 160.

119. Sundquist, *Politics and Policy*, 206, 210.

120. Bell, *Johnson Treatment*, 189.

121. O'Brien, *No Final Victories*, 123-124.

122. Johnson, *Vantage Point*, 457; Kearns, *Lyndon Johnson*, 236; "Turning Screws," 947, 949.

123. Stanley Kelly, Jr., "Patronage and Presidential Legislative Leadership," in *Presidency*, Wildavsky, 273.

124. O'Brien, *No Final Victories*, 121.

125. Schlesinger, *Thousand Days*, 970.

126. Sorensen, *Kennedy*, 404-405; O'Brien, *No Final Victories*, 129-130, 136-137.

127. O'Brien, *No Final Victories*, 122.

128. Wayne, *Legislative Presidency*, 160. However, some congressional liaison officers suggest that delivery on congressional requests is less important than members of Congress perceiving that the White House tried its best. See Pika, "White House Office of Congressional Relations," 16.

129. Richard E. Neustadt, *Presidential Power* (New York: Mentor, 1964), 54-61.

130. "Turning Screws," 947, 949, 954.

131. Reichard, *Reaffirmation of Republicanism*, 173.

132. Pika, "White House Office of Congressional Relations," 15.

133. "Turning Screws," 951.

134. Ibid., 952-953. Also see Holtzman, *Legislative Liaison*, 252; Johnson, *Vantage Point*, 457-458; Kearns, *Lyndon Johnson*, 236-237; Pika, "White House Office of Congressional Relations," 15.

135. Pika, "White House Office of Congressional Relations," 16.

136. Wayne, *Legislative Presidency*, 154-155.

137. Pika, "White House Office of Congressional Relations," 6.

138. Manley, "White House Lobbying," 12-13, 15-16.

139. Ibid., 13.

140. "Larry O'Brien Discusses," 485.

141. "Larry O'Brien Discusses," 480.

142. Valenti, *Very Human President*, 188-189.

143. Johnson, *Vantage Point*, 458. See also Wayne, *Legislative Presidency*, 155.

144. O'Brien, *No Final Victories*, 120; MacNeil, *Forge of Democracy*, 267.

145. Chapman, "LBJ's Way," E-1.

146. Wayne, *Legislative Presidency*, 154-155.

147. Goldman, *Tragedy of Lyndon Johnson*, 74-75, 348.

148. McNeil, *Dirksen*, 275; John A. Ferejohn, *Pork Barrel Politics: Rivers and Harbors Legislation, 1947-1968* (Stanford, Calif.: Stanford University Press, 1974), 72; Pika, "White House Office of Congressional Relations," 17; Manley, "White House Lobbying," 31. See also Bell, *Johnson Treatment*, 159, 165; Sundquist, *Politics and Policy*, 266, for another example of Johnson's toughness.

149. Johnson, *Vantage Point*, 216-217; Goldman *Tragedy of Lyndon Johnson*, 344-345; O'Brien, *No Final Victories*, 189-190.

150. Sundquist, *Politics and Policy*, 173, 421; Eisenhower, *Mandate for Change*, 243-244; Hughes, *Ordeal of Power*, 124-125, 347; Wayne, *Legislative Presidency*, 144; Ripley, *Majority Party Leadership*, 124.

151. Hughes, *Ordeal of Power*, 334-335.

152. Eisenhower, *Waging Peace*, 145-146, 642; Eisenhower, *Mandate for Change*, 366; Adams, *Firsthand Report*, 374; Reichard, *Reaffirmation of Republicanism*, 226; MacNeil, *Forge of Democracy*, 255.

153. Donovan, *Eisenhower*, 229.

154. Hughes, *Ordeal of Power*, 132.

155. Donovan, *Eisenhower*, 234; Childs, *Eisenhower: Captive Hero*, 282.

156. Hughes, *Ordeal of Power*, 124, 132-133; Adams, *Firsthand Report*, 36, 373-374; Donovan, *Eisenhower*, 224; Ripley, *Majority Party Leadership*, 121, 124; Larson, *Eisenhower*, 25.

157. O'Brien, *No Final Victories*, 171.

158. Holtzman, *Legislative Liaison*, 252.

159. "Turning Screws," 950.

160. Sorensen, *Kennedy*, 384-385, 392; MacNeil, *Forge of Democracy*, 251-252.

161. Wicker, *JFK and LBJ*, 34, 76-77.

162. O'Brien, *No Final Victories*, 114, Holtzman, *Legislative Liaison*, 239, 252.

163. Evans and Novak, *Nixon in the White House*, 113-114; Congressional Quarterly, *Guide to Current American Government: Fall 1969* (Washington, D.C.: Congressional Quarterly, 1969), 99-104.

164. Harris, *Decision*, 99, 176, 184, 191, 205-206.

165. For another example, see Green, Fallows, and Zwick, *Who Runs Congress?*, 99.

166. Wayne, *Legislative Presidency*, 160; Evans and Novak, *Nixon in the White House*, 107-108. See also H. R. Haldeman, *The Ends of Power* (New York: Times Books, 1978), 71, on Nixon's lack of ability in arm-twisting.

167. "Turning Screws," 947-948.

168. Jack Anderson and Les Whitten, "Ford Lobbyist Losing Friends on Hill." *Washington Post*, May 8, 1975, G-13.

169. Wicker, *JFK and LBJ*, 77.

170. Harris, *Decision*, 99, 192.

171. Huitt, "White House Channels," 83.

172. Holtzman, *Legislative Liaison*, 252. See also Kingdon, *Congressmen's Voting Decisions*, 156-157, 186-187; Pika, "White House Office of Congressional Relations," 16-17.

Illustration 5b: The Supreme Court and the Legislative Veto: Excerpts from the Chadha Case

The federal courts—especially the U.S. Supreme Court—play an important function in the U.S. policy process. One very important contribution is to serve as referee in disputes arising between the president and Congress. Nowhere is the contemporary exercise of this umpiring function better illustrated than in a 1983 ruling by the Court in the legislative veto case whereby the procedure was declared unconstitutional. The legislative veto is a recent (1932) congressional policy tool. Under a number of different statutes, Congress makes a broad delegation of power to the executive branch. This discretionary power is exercised by executive departments and agencies with the requirement that the decision be submitted to Congress for review. Congress has the opportunity to disapprove or "veto" administrative decisions with a majority vote in one or both houses, depending on how the legislation is written. The following excerpts from Chief Justice Burger's opinion for the Court and Justice White's dissent illustrate the umpiring role of the Court as well as differences in opinion concerning the proper relationship between the president and Congress.

Chief Justice Burger, for the Majority

The bicameral requirement of Art. I, §§1, 7 was of scarcely less concern to the framers than was the presidential veto and indeed the two concepts are interdependent. By providing that no law could take effect without the concurrence of the prescribed majority of the members of both houses, the framers re-emphasized their belief, already remarked upon in connection with the presentment clauses, that legislation should not be enacted unless it has been carefully and fully considered by the nation's elected officials. In the Constitutional Convention debates on the need for a bicameral legislature, James Wilson, later to become a justice of this Court, commented:

> Despotism comes on mankind in different shapes. Sometimes in an Executive, sometimes in a military, one. Is there danger of a Legislative despotism? Theory & practice both proclaim it. If the Legislative authority be not restrained, there can be neither liberty nor stability; and it can only be restrained by dividing it within itself, into distinct and independent branches. In a single house there is no check, but the inadequate one, of the virtue & good sense of those who compose it. 1 M. Farrand, *supra*, at 254.

Hamilton argued that a Congress comprised of a single house was antithetical to the very purposes of the Constitution. Were the nation to adopt a Constitution providing for only one legislative organ, he warned:

> ... we shall finally accumulate, in a single body, all the most important prerogatives of sovereignty, and thus entail upon our posterity one of the most execrable forms of government that human infatuation ever contrived. Thus we should create in reality that very tyranny which the adversaries of the new Constitution either are, or affect to be, solicitous to avert. The Federalist No. 22, *supra*, at 135.

This view was rooted in a general skepticism regarding the fallibility of human nature later commented on by Joseph Story:

Public bodies, like private persons, are occasionally under the dominion of strong passions and excitements; impatient, irritable, and impetuous. . . . If [a legislature] feels no check but its own will, it rarely has the firmness to insist upon holding a question long enough under its own view, to see and mark it in all its bearings and relations to society. 1 J. Story, *supra*, at 383–384.

These observations are consistent with what many of the framers expressed, none more cogently than Hamilton in pointing up the need to divide and disperse power in order to protect liberty:

In republican government, the legislative authority necessarily predominates. The remedy for this inconveniency is to divide the legislature into different branches; and to render them, by different modes of election and different principles of action, as little connected with each other as the nature of their common functions and their common dependence on the society will admit. The Federalist No. 51, *supra*, at 324.

See also The Federalist No. 62.

However familiar, it is useful to recall that apart from their fear that special interests could be favored at the expense of public needs, the framers were also concerned, although not of one mind, over the apprehensions of the smaller states. Those states feared a commonality of interest among the larger states would work to their disadvantage; representatives of the larger states, on the other hand, were skeptical of a legislature that could pass laws favoring a minority of the people. See 1 M. Farrand, *supra*, 176–177, 484–491. It need hardly be repeated here that the Great Compromise, under which one house was viewed as representing the people and the other the states, allayed the fears of both the large and small states.[1]

We see therefore that the framers were acutely conscious that the bicameral requirement and the presentment clauses would serve essential constitutional functions. The president's participation in the legislative process was to protect the executive branch from Congress and to protect the whole people from improvident laws. The division of the Congress into two distinctive bodies assures that the legislative power would be exercised only after opportunity for full study and debate in separate settings. The president's unilateral veto power, in turn, was limited by the power of two thirds of both Houses of Congress to overrule a veto thereby precluding final arbitrary action of one person. See 1 M. Farrand, *supra*, at 99–104. It emerges clearly that the prescription for legislative action in Art. I, §§1, 7 represents the framers' decision that the legislative power of the federal government be exercised in accord with a single, finely wrought and exhaustively considered, procedure.

IV

The Constitution sought to divide the delegated powers of the new federal government into three defined categories, legislative, executive and judicial, to assure, as nearly as possible, that each branch of government would confine itself to its assigned responsibility. The hydraulic pressure inherent within each of the separate branches to exceed the outer limits of its power, even to accomplish desirable objectives, must be resisted.

Although not "hermetically" sealed from one another, *Buckley* v. *Valeo, supra,* 424 U. S., at 121, the powers delegated to the three branches are functionally identifiable. When any branch acts, it is presumptively exercising the power the Constitution has delegated to it. See *Hampton & Co.* v. *United States,* 276 U. S. 394, 406 (1928). When the Executive acts, it presumptively acts in an executive or administrative capacity as defined in Art. II. And when, as here, one House of Congress purports to act, it is presumptively acting within its assigned sphere.

Beginning with this presumption, we must nevertheless establish that the challenged action under §244(c)(2) is of the kind to which the procedural requirements of Art. I, §7 apply. Not every action taken by either House is subject to the bicameralism and presentment requirements of Art. I. See *post,* at 35. Whether actions taken by either House are, in law and fact, an exercise of legislative power depends not on their form but upon "whether they contain matter which is properly to be regarded as legislative in its character and effect." S. Rep. No. 1335, 54th Cong., 2d Sess., 8 (1897).

Justice White, dissenting

Today the Court not only invalidates §244(c)(2) of the Immigration and Nationality Act, but also sounds the death knell for nearly 200 other statutory provisions in which Congress has reserved a "legislative veto." For this reason, the Court's decision is of surpassing importance. And it is for this reason that the Court would have been well-advised to decide the case, if possible, on the narrower grounds of separation of powers, leaving for full consideration the constitutionality of other congressional review statutes operating on such varied matters as war powers and agency rulemaking, some of which concern the independent regulatory agencies.

The prominence of the legislative veto mechanism in our contemporary political system and its importance to Congress can hardly be overstated. It has become a central means by which Congress secures the accountability of executive and independent agencies. Without the legislative veto, Congress is faced with a Hobson's choice: either to refrain from delegating the necessary authority, leaving itself with a hopeless task of writing laws with the requisite specificity to cover endless special circumstances across the entire policy landscape, or in the alternative, to abdicate its lawmaking function to the executive branch and independent agencies. To choose the former leaves major national problems unresolved; to opt for the latter risks unaccountable policymaking by those not elected to fill that role. Accordingly, over the past five decades, the legislative veto has been placed in nearly 200 statutes. The device is known in every field of governmental concern: reorganization, budgets, foreign affairs, war powers, and regulation of trade, safety, energy, the environment and the economy.

I

The legislative veto developed initially in response to the problems of reorganizing the sprawling government structure created in response to the Depression. The Reorganization Acts established the chief model for the legislative veto. When President Hoover requested authority to reorganize the government in 1929, he coupled his request that the "Congress be willing to delegate its authority over the problem (subject to defined principles) to the executive" with a proposal for legislative review. He proposed that the executive "should act upon approval of a joint committee of Congress or with the reservation of power of revision by Congress within some limited period adequate for its consideration." Pub. Papers 432 (1929). Congress followed President Hoover's suggestion and authorized reorganization subject to legislative review. Act of June 30, 1932, ch. 314, §407, 47 Stat. 382, 414. Although the reorganization authority reenacted in 1933 did not contain a legislative veto provision, the provision returned during the Roosevelt Administration and has since been renewed numerous times. Over the years, the provision was used extensively. Presidents submitted 115 reorganization plans to Congress of which 23 were disapproved by Congress pursuant to legislative veto provisions. See Brief of U. S. Senate on Reargument, App. A.

Shortly after adoption of the Reorganization Act of 1939, 54 Stat. 561, Congress and the president applied the legislative veto procedure to resolve the delegation problem for national security and foreign affairs. World War II occasioned the need to transfer greater authority to the president in these areas. The legislative veto offered the means by which Congress could confer additional authority while preserving its own constitutional role. During World War II, Congress enacted over thirty statutes conferring powers on the executive with legislative veto provisions. President Roosevelt accepted the veto as the necessary price for obtaining exceptional authority.

Over the quarter century following World War II, presidents continued to accept legislative vetoes by one or both Houses as constitutional, while regularly denouncing provisions by which congressional committees reviewed executive activity. The legislative veto balanced delegations of statutory authority in new areas of governmental involvement: the space program, international agreements on nuclear energy, tariff arrangements, and adjustment of federal pay rates.

During the 1970s the legislative veto was important in resolving a series of major constitutional disputes between the president and Congress over claims of the president to broad impoundment, war, and national emergency powers. The key provision of the War Powers Resolution, 50 U. S. C. §1544(c), authorizes the termination by concurrent resolution of the use of armed forces in hostilities. A similar measure resolved the problem posed by presidential claims of inherent power to impound appropriations. Congressional Budget and Impoundment Control Act of 1974, 31 U. S. C. §1403. In conference, a compromise was achieved under which permanent impoundments, termed "rescissions," would require approval through enactment of legislation. In contrast, temporary impoundments, or "deferrals," would become effective unless disapproved by one House. This compromise provided the President with flexibility, while preserving ultimate congressional control over the budget. Although the War Powers Resolution was enacted over President Nixon's veto, the Impoundment Control Act was enacted with the president's approval. These statutes were followed by others resolving similar problems: the National Emergencies Act, §202, 90 Stat. 1255, 50 U. S. C. §1622 (1976), resolving the longstanding problems with unchecked executive emergency power; the Arms Export Control Act, §211, 90 Stat. 729, 22 U. S. C. §2776(b)(1976), resolving the problem of foreign arms sales; and the Nuclear Non-Proliferation Act of 1978, §§303, 304(a), 306, 307, 401, 92 Stat. 120, 130, 134, 137, 139, 144–145, 42 U. S. C. §§2160(f), 2155(b), 2157(b), 2158, 2153(d) (Supp. IV. 1980), resolving the problem of exports of nuclear technology.

In the energy field, the legislative veto served to balance broad delegations in legislation emerging from the energy crisis of the 1970s. In the education field, it was found that fragmented and narrow grant programs "inevitably lead to executive-legislative confrontations" because they inaptly limited the Commissioner of Education's authority.

S. Rep. No. 763, 93d Cong., 2d Sess. 69 (1974). The response was to grant the Commissioner of Education rulemaking authority, subject to a legislative veto. In the trade regulation area, the veto preserved congressional authority over the Federal Trade Commission's broad mandate to make rules to prevent businesses from engaging in "unfair or deceptive acts or practices in commerce."

Even this brief review suffices to demonstrate that the legislative veto is more than "efficient, convenient, and useful." *Ante*, at 23. It is an important if not indispensable political invention that allows the president and Congress to resolve major constitutional and policy differences, assures the accountability of independent regulatory agencies, and preserves Congress' control over lawmaking. Perhaps there are other means of accommodation and accountability, but the increasing reliance of Congress upon the legislative veto suggests that the alternatives to which Congress must now turn are not entirely satisfactory.

The history of the legislative veto also makes clear that it has not been a sword with which Congress has struck out to aggrandize itself at the expense of the other branches—the concerns of Madison and Hamilton. Rather, the veto has been a means of defense, a reservation of ultimate authority necessary if Congress is to fulfill its designated role under Article I as the nation's lawmaker. While the president has often objected to particular legislative vetoes, generally those left in the hands of congressional committees, the executive has more often agreed to legislative review as the price for a broad delegation of authority. To be sure, the president may have preferred unrestricted power, but that could be precisely why Congress thought it essential to retain a check on the exercise of delegated authority.

II

For all these reasons, the apparent sweep of the Court's decision today is regrettable. The Court's Article I analysis appears to invalidate all legislative vetoes irrespective of form or subject. Because the legislative veto is commonly found as a check upon rulemaking by administrative agencies and upon broad-based policy decisions of the executive branch, it is particularly unfortunate that the Court reaches its decision in a case involving the exercise of a veto over deportation decisions regarding particular individuals. Courts should always be wary of striking statutes as unconstitutional; to strike an entire class of statutes based on consideration of a somewhat atypical and more-readily indictable exemplar of the class is irresponsible. It was for cases such as this one that Justice Brandeis wrote:

> The Court has frequently called attention to the "great gravity and delicacy" of its function in passing upon the validity of an act of Congress.... The Court will not "formulate a rule of constitutional law broader than is required by the precise facts to which it is to be applied." Liverpool, N. Y. & P. S. S. Co. v. Emigration Commissioners, supra. Ashwander v. Tennessee Valley Authority, 297 U. S. 288, 347 (1936) (concurring opinion).

Unfortunately, today's holding is not so limited.

If the legislative veto were as plainly unconstitutional as the Court strives to suggest, its broad ruling today would be more comprehensible. But, the constitutionality of the legislative veto is anything but clearcut. The issue divides scholars, courts, attorneys general, and the two other branches of the national government. If the veto devices so flagrantly disregarded the requirements of Article I as the Court today suggests, I find it incomprehensible that Congress, whose members are bound by oath to uphold the Constitution, would have placed these mechanisms in nearly 200 separate laws over a period of fifty years.

The reality of the situation is that the constitutional question posed today is one of immense difficulty over which the executive and legislative branches—as well as scholars and judges—have understandably disagreed. That disagreement stems from the silence of the Constitution on the precise question: The Constitution does not directly authorize or prohibit the legislative veto. Thus, our task should be to determine whether the legislative veto is consistent with the purposes of Art. I and the principles of separation of powers which are reflected in that article and throughout the Constitution. We should not find the lack of a specific constitutional authorization for the legislative veto surprising, and I would not infer disapproval of the mechanism from its absence. From the summer of 1787 to the present the government of the United States has become an endeavor far beyond the contemplation of the framers. Only within the last half century has the complexity and size of the federal government's responsibilities grown so greatly that the Congress must rely on the legislative veto as the most effective if not the only means to insure their role as the nation's lawmakers. But the wisdom of the framers was to anticipate that the nation would grow and new problems of governance would require different solutions. Accordingly, our federal government was intentionally chartered with the flexibility to respond to contemporary needs without losing sight of fundamental democratic principles. This was the spirit in which Justice Jackson penned his influential concurrence in the *Steel Seizure Case:*

> The actual art of governing under our Constitution does not and cannot conform to judicial definitions of the power of any of its branches based on isolated clauses or even single Articles torn from context. While the Constitution diffuses power the better to secure liberty, it also contemplates that practice will integrate the dispersed powers into a workable government. Youngstown Sheet & Tube Co. v. Sawyer, 343 U. S. 579, 635(1952).

This is the perspective from which we should approach the novel constitutional questions presented by the legislative veto. In my view, neither Article I of the Constitution nor the doctrine of separation of powers is violated by this mechanism by which our elected representatives preserve their voice in the governance of the nation.

III

The Court holds that the disapproval of a suspension of deportation by the resolution of one House of Congress is an exercise of legislative power without compliance with the prerequisites for lawmaking set forth in Art. I of the Constitution. Specifically, the Court maintains that the provisions of §244(c)(2) are inconsistent with the requirement of bicameral approval, implicit in Art. I, §1, and the requirement that all bills and resolutions that require the concurrence of both Houses be presented to the president, Art. I, §7, cl. 2 and 3.

I do not dispute the Court's truismatic exposition of these clauses. There is no question that a bill does not become a law until it is approved by both the House and the Senate, and presented to the president. Similarly, I would not hesitate to strike an action of Congress in the form of a concurrent resolution which constituted an exercise of original lawmaking authority. I agree with the Court that the president's qualified veto power is a critical element in the distribution of powers under the Constitution, widely endorsed among the framers, and intended to serve the president as a defense against legislative encroachment and to check the "passing of bad laws through haste, inadvertence, or design." The Federalist No. 73, at 458 (A. Hamilton). The records of the Convention reveal that it is the first purpose which figured most prominently but I acknowledge the vitality of the second. *Id.*, at 443. I also agree that the bicameral approval required by Art. I, §§1, 7 "was of scarcely less concern to the framers than was the presidential veto," *ante*, at 28, and that the need to divide and disperse legislative power figures significantly in our scheme of government. All of this, the third part of the Court's opinion, is entirely unexceptionable.

It does not, however, answer the constitutional question before us. The power to exercise a legislative veto is not the power to write new law without bicameral approval or presidential consideration. The veto must be authorized by statute and may only negative what an executive department or independent agency has proposed. On its face, the legislative veto no more allows one House of Congress to make law than does the presidential veto confer such power upon the president. Accordingly, the Court properly recognizes that it "must establish that the challenged action under §244(c)(2) is of the kind to which the procedural requirements of Art. I, §7 apply" and admits that "not every action taken by either House is subject to the bicameralism and presentation requirements of Art. I." *Ante*, at 31.

---

1. The Great Compromise was considered so important by the framers that they inserted a special provision to ensure that it could not be altered, even by constitutional amendment except with the consent of the states affected. See U. S. Const. Art. V.

Presidential Effectiveness in Congressional Foreign Policymaking: A Reconsideration

Ralph G. Carter

In 1966 a seminal essay, "The Two Presidencies," was written by Aaron Wildavsky, a leading student of the policy process. He argued that an understanding of presidential power requires an appreciation for the distinctive political dynamics of different policy domains. This essay is a classic because it posits the sophisticated notion that to understand presidential power one must make a distinction between foreign and domestic policymaking. To Wildavsky, in the domestic realm presidents are just one of many competitors, as members of Congress become advocates on behalf of mobilized constituents and interest groups. Not so with regard to foreign policy, Wildavsky argues. There, presidents have more free reign and are more likely to get their way. Members of Congress are more likely to defer to the president and less likely to be motivated to make their impact felt because of the relative absence of interest groups and constituency pressures.

A commonly heard criticism of social science pertains to the lack of additive research, whereby knowledge is furthered through the formulating, testing, and refining of stated propositions. The following original essay offers an exception to that normally valid criticism. In an assessment of Wildavsky's "The Two Presidencies" theory, Ralph Carter raises some important qualifications to that theory by illustrating the contexts and conditions of presidential effectiveness in foreign policymaking.

A common vision of the presidency has existed since the mid-1960s. As primarily elaborated by Aaron Wildavsky, this vision of presidential leadership has two major components.[1] There seem to be "two presidencies." In dealing with domestic policy issues, Congress is the dominant actor and the president has to fight tooth-and-nail to get his policy preferences enacted. However, for foreign and defense issues, the president is the dominant force in government policy-making. His heightened legitimacy combined with institutional advantages allow him to act forcefully in foreign and defense policy, confident that Congress will almost surely back him up.

Although Wildavsky's ideas on presidential foreign policy are largely accepted as part of the discipline's conventional wisdom, some scholars continue to examine the president's power relative to Congress in foreign policy. Wildavsky's study covered the years 1948-1964, and Lance LeLoup and Steven Shull have updated it.[2] Using similar measures for the 1965-1975 period, they found that the president still generates more congressional support for his foreign policy initiatives than for his domestic ones. However, they say the difference between these support scores has diminished over time.

A more critical view has been presented by Donald Peppers, who in 1975 said Wildavsky's thesis was no longer valid.[3] He said the president's influence over foreign policy had diminished due to changing circumstances such as the blurring of the distinction between domestic and foreign policy, the growth of nondefense-oriented foreign policy issues, and the shattering of the cold war consensus by the Vietnam War. Four years later, Lee Sigelman was even more challenging.[4] He said Wildavsky's original analysis was flawed since it relied on "presidential boxscores" as a data source. Since these boxscores include many trivial, noncontroversial foreign policy requests by the president, his foreign policy support score was unduly inflated. Sigelman examined congressional support for major, controversial presidential requests in both foreign and domestic policy and found no major differences. From 1957-1972, presidents received approximately one percent more congressional support for foreign, rather than for domestic, policy issues. From 1973-1978, presidents received approximately three percent more support on foreign policy issues than on domestic ones. Sigelman further found little opposition party support for the president on either type of controversial issue.[5]

The present work corroborates Sigelman's findings. The vision of a nearly-omnipotent presidency in foreign policy is marked by two fallacies. As Sigelman briefly notes, most who see an imperial presidency in foreign policy-making rely on the highly unusual cold war period to make their point. This period, from 1947 until the latter 1960s, did present the *image* of a strong presidency in foreign policy. However, the cold war has not been the only period in the nation's history and its events should be kept in proper perspective.

Until the Civil War, Congress dominated the presidency in the making of foreign policy. While the war brought on a brief period of executive dominance, after the war Congress reacted against the inroads made by Lincoln, and the resulting congressional dominance lasted until the turn of the century.[6] From 1900 to 1939, Congress and the executive vied for power. While presidents often got their way, Congress occasionally restricted their freedom of action. In 1905 Congress forced the executive branch to recognize Japan's control of Korea.[7] Six years later, the Senate so weakened a series of arbitration treaties that President Taft refused to sign the resolution of ratification.[8] In 1920, the Senate rejected the Treaty of Versailles.[9] Finally, Congress passed the Neutrality Acts of 1935-1937 which severely restricted President Roosevelt's options in dealing with belligerent states.[10]

The Second World War thrust the presidency back onto center stage, and from 1940 until the mid-1960s the president seemed to be the focus of American foreign policy-making. Congress, on the other hand, was seen as a junior partner in the foreign policy process.[11] During this time, James Robinson said,

"Congress's influence in foreign policy is primarily and increasingly one of legitimating and amending policies initiated by the executive to deal with problems usually identified by the executive."[12] He further said that congressional initiatives in the foreign policy field, when forthcoming at all, tend to relate to less important concerns.[13] Such alleged congressional inattention to foreign policy was made possible by the cold war consensus. The consensus decreed that communism should be contained, and that the president should be supported as long as his policies helped to contain the worldwide expansion of communism.[14] Consequently, the cold war consensus provided few incentives for members of Congress to act on foreign policy matters.[15]

The existence of the cold war consensus masks a fact many observers seem to have forgotten. During this period in which presidents were considered to be very successful in getting their foreign policy objectives enacted by Congress, the task of shepherding their requests through Congress was never easy. For example, a 1946 British loan designed to forestall any further weakening of the British economy was debated for seven months before Congress finally passed it on a close vote.[16] The next year's debate on emergency military aid for Greece and Turkey dragged on for two months before Congress appropriated the funds.[17] Finally, the debate on the Marshall Plan continued for three months before it was rescued by a dramatic external event, the Communist coup in Czechoslovakia in February 1948.[18]

The decade of the 1950s was no different. Congressional critics castigated the Eisenhower administration for asking for what they saw as a declaration of preventive war in the Formosa Resolution.[19] Throughout the 1950s and during the 1960s, foreign aid requests were routinely cut and seldom increased by Congress.[20] Presidents may have gotten a number of their requests fulfilled by Congress, but these victories were orchestrated by a great deal of hard work.

The failure of the American military involvement in Vietnam destroyed the cold war consensus and provided members of Congress with incentives to act on foreign policy issues.[21] In the mid-1960s a series of events cast doubt on the docility of Congress in the making of foreign policy. In 1966 the Senate Foreign Relations Committee criticized the administration's optimism concerning the progress of the Vietnam War and questioned U.S. policy toward Communist China. At the same time, Senators Mansfield and McCarthy urged a closer examination of CIA activities. The next year the Foreign Relations Committee held far-reaching hearings of the American role in the world, and the lowest foreign aid bill in history was passed. In 1969, the National Commitments Resolution passed the Senate, and the Symington subcommittee to study U.S. commitments overseas was created.[22]

As the new decade began, the executive's "dominance" over Congress weakened further. In 1970 the Senate repealed the Tonkin Gulf Resolution and passed the Cooper-Church amendment which prohibited the use of funds to support U.S. troops in Cambodia. In 1971 Congress refused for the first time in the program's history to pass a foreign aid bill. Moreover, the Senate conducted bruising hearings regarding administration policies toward Vietnam, Laos, and NATO. The Executive Agreements Act passed the following year, and the House Foreign Affairs Committee failed by one vote to report out a resolution endorsing an American withdrawal from Indochina by October 1, 1972. In 1973 the War Powers Resolution passed despite a presidential veto, and President Nixon was forced by Congress to go along with an August 15, 1973 deadline for the cessation of all American combat activity in Indochina.[23]

There has been little agreement on how to evaluate the apparent rise in congressional foreign policy-making. Some analysts view recent actions by Congress as aberrations to the norm and say that Congress is still content to leave foreign policy-making to the executive.[24] Others feel the current assertive pattern should not lead observers to believe Congress is ready to challenge the executive branch across-the-board.[25]

Other congressional observers disagree, saying the new assertiveness in Congress should lead to new expectations.[26] Some feel Congress will try to do more but that institutional limitations will plague their efforts.[27] Others say new institutional developments such as the 1974 Budget Act, the enhanced use of the legislative veto, and an increased informational base will help Congress maintain its assertiveness.[28] Finally, some analysts see these changes as a "violent reinstitution of congressional dominance that seems likely to endure for some time."[29]

This scholarly debate sheds much heat but unfortunately little light. Most of these analysts seem to have missed the more basic point. The cold war period was not an example of a usual, normal, or "traditional" congressional role in the making of foreign policy. When examined against the content of prior periods, the assumption that the cold war period can be used as a standard to measure either congressional or presidential effectiveness in foreign policy-making is mistaken. Consequently, much attention is devoted to *nonissues* such as whether or not the president can regain his "lost" position in foreign policy-making.

The impact of the above point is heightened when one considers the second major weakness of most of these studies. Most studies of foreign policy-making assume that the cold war period produced an assertive presidency and a passive Congress. Moe and Teel suggest that such an assumption is unwarranted. They argue that the congressional role in foreign policy has never been insignificant; it has simply been less visible than that of the executive.[30] Their assertion deserves close analysis since it challenges the basic assumption underlying much of the foreign policy research undertaken during the postwar period.

To check the validity of Moe and Teel's assertion, a model is developed to explain congressional foreign policy-making. This stimulus-response model utilizes five independent variables. These variables include the procedural issue area involved, party leader preferences, committee leader preferences, domestic pressures, and the level of presidential involvement. The resulting congressional foreign policy behavior is the dependent variable.

The model is tested by means of a comparative case study. Such an approach provides the analyst with a number of advantages. Comparative case studies provide the large amount of information needed to study phenomena of considerable complexity like congressional-presidential interactions. Such studies are also well-suited to testing new theoretical concepts and relationships to see if they are worth studying in further detail.[31] Another advantage found in such studies is their ability to uncover explanatory mechanisms behind correlations and also to help to determine the impacts of different variables, particularly when there are interaction effects among the variables.[32]

Nonetheless, a comparative case study is only as sound as the case selection process it utilizes. A skewed sample of cases can provide misleading or worthless conclusions. To avoid skewed samples, cases should be carefully selected to represent the different instances of the undertaking in question and should provide as much variance as possible in the dependent variable.[33]

In studying congressional foreign policymaking, a mechanism is needed to ensure that all types of relevant cases are represented. Rosenau's procedural issue area format meets that need since his reliance on dichotomies presents the analyst with four mutually exclusive and exhaustive categories of cases.[34] Cases with intangible ends and means are status cases. Those with tangible ends and means are nonhuman resource cases. Cases with intangible ends and tangible means deal with human resources. Those with tangible ends but intangible means are territorial cases.

The above prescription also requires a method of categorizing the dependent variable. Congressional foreign policy behavior can be categorized relative to what the administration desires. A trichotomy is used which represents a passive-active continuum. The first type of congressional foreign policy behavior is compliance with the administration's position. Here the congressional output is passive, since the administration gets what it wants. However, one must recognize that the process which results in a compliant behavior may not be passive at all. The second type represents resistant behaviors. These congressional outputs represent some modification of, or resistance to, the administration's position. In each of these two categorizations, the administration initiates the events leading to the congressional response. The administration acts and Congress reacts. The third value of the dependent variable represents a break in this pattern. Independent behaviors comprise the most active end of the continuum in which the issue is brought up for congressional action by Congress itself. Robinson notes the importance of the initiation of action by saying Congress has initiated less and less of its own foreign policy activity while the executive branch has initiated more and more. The initiator of the decision-making process is more likely to get what he wants, since he defines both the problem and the proposed alternative solutions.[35]

Overall, one set of cases is required which varies as evenly as possible across the postwar period, the four issue areas, and the three dependent variable measures. The set of cases selected for study here are listed below.[36]

1. The Japanese Peace Treaty, 1952
2. The Spanish Bases Agreement, 1953
3. The Guatemalan Intervention, 1954
4. The Formosa Resolution, 1955
5. The Mutual Security Act, 1957
6. The Bay of Pigs Intervention, 1961
7. The Nuclear Test Ban Treaty, 1963
8. The Advance Latin American Aid Authorization, 1967
9. The ABM Authorization, 1969
10. The Defense Appropriations Bill, 1969
11. The Executive Agreements Act, 1972
12. The War Powers Resolution, 1973
13. The Rejection of the Sugar Act, 1974
14. The Turkish Military Aid Cutoff, 1974
15. The Panama Canal Treaties, 1978

Table 5.3.1 demonstrates how these cases are distributed across these three dimensions.

This set of cases falls evenly across time with five cases from the 1950s, five from the 1960s, and five from the 1970s. Regarding issue areas, there are four status cases, two human resource cases, four territorial cases, and five nonhuman resource cases. The dependent variable is represented by five compliant behaviors, four resistant behaviors, and six independent behaviors. Consequently, these cases are evenly distributed over time, fall 11.7 percent short of the ideal distribution across issue areas, and are 6.7 percent short of the ideal distribution across the values of the dependent variable.[37] Averaging these percentages shows the cases fall short of the ideal distribution on all three combined criteria by only 6.1 percent.[38] Such a set of cases has distinct analytical advantages over a set like Robinson's, which consists of those congressional foreign policy cases others found interesting enough to study.[39]

In examining these cases, Robinson's findings can be rechecked. Table 5.3.2 displays the cases across the dimensions Robinson found important and lists the congressional output.

Table 5.3.1

Time Period, Issue Area, and Congressional Foreign Policy Behavior by Case

Cases	Time			Issue Area				Congressional Foreign Policy Behavior		
	1950s	1960s	1970s	S	HR	T	NHR	C	R	I
Japanese Peace	x			x				x		
Spanish Bases	x						x			x
Guatemalan Intervention	x					x		x		
Formosa Resolution	x					x		x		
Mutual Security Act	x				x				x	
Bay of Pigs		x				x				x
Nuclear Test Ban		x		x				x		
Latin American Aid		x			x					x
ABM Authorization		x					x	x		
Defense Appropriation		x					x		x	
Executive Agreements			x	x						x
War Powers			x	x						x
Sugar Act			x				x		x	
Turkish Aid			x				x			x
Panama Canal Treaties			x			x			x	
Totals	5	5	5	4	2	4	5	5	4	6

Issue Area: S = Status, HR = Human Resources, T = Territorial, NHR = Nonhuman Resources
Congressional Foreign Policy Behavior: C = Compliance, R = Resistance, I = Independence

Table 5.3.2
Congressional Involvement in Foreign and Defense Policy Decisions

Case	Congressional Involvement (High, Low, None)	Initiator (Congress or Executive)	Predominant Influence (Congress or Executive)	Legislation or Resolution	Violence At Stake	Decision Time (Long or Short)	Congressional Foreign Policy Behavior
Japanese Peace, 1952	High	Exec	Exec	Yes	No	Long	Compliant
Spanish Bases, 1953	High	Cong	Cong	Yes	No	Long	Independent
Guatamalan Inter., 1954	Low	Exec	Exec	Yes	Yes	Short	Compliant
Formosa Res., 1955	High	Exec	Exec	Yes	Yes	Long	Compliant
Mutual Security, 1957	High	Exec	Exec	Yes	No	Long	Resistant
Bay of Pigs, 1961	Low	Exec	Exec	No	Yes	Short	Independent
Nuclear Test Ban, 1963	Low	Exec	Exec	Yes	No	Long	Compliant
Latin American Aid, 1967	High	Exec	Cong	Yes	No	Short	Independent
ABM Authorization, 1969	High	Exec	Exec	Yes	No	Long	Compliant
Defense Appro., 1969	High	Exec	Cong	Yes	No	Long	Resistant
Executive Agreements, 1972	High	Cong	Cong	Yes	No	Long	Independent
War Powers, 1973	High	Cong	Cong	Yes	No	Long	Independent
Sugar Act, 1974	High	Exec	Cong	No	No	Long	Resistant
Turkish Aid, 1974	High	Cong	Cong	Yes	Yes	Short	Independent
Panama Canal, 1978	High	Exec	Exec	Yes	No	Long	Resistant

Table 5.3.2 shows mixed results for the general patterns Robinson found. Robinson's findings on the predominant influence dimension are confirmed. When the executive has predominant influence, he gets exactly what he wants over half of the time and part of what he wants a quarter of the time. When Congress has predominant influence, Congress gets part of what it wants in over a quarter of the instances and all it wants over two-thirds of the time. Robinson's finding, that cases involving violence favor the president, holds up as well. In the only two cases involving violence in which the president did not get what he wanted from Congress, the congressional initiatives came after the violence had ended. In nonviolent cases, Robinson's point about a more active congressional role is confirmed. In nonviolent cases, the president got exactly what he wanted a quarter of the time, part of what he wanted about one-third of the time, and none of what he wanted about one-third of the time.

Nonetheless, two other patterns isolated by Robinson are open to serious question. His contention that the initiator of an issue tends to get his way seems to hold more for Congress than for the president. When Congress initiated action, congressional desires were largely fulfilled. On the other hand, when the president initiated the issue, he got exactly what he wanted less than half of the time, some of what he wanted about one-third of the time, and almost two-fifths of the time Congress usurped the issue. Second, Robinson's contention that crises help the president is also questionable. When time was short, the president got what he wanted one-quarter of the time and Congress got what it wanted three-quarters of the time.

Beyond checking Robinson's conclusions, other patterns of influence are isolated. The conventional wisdom—that when the president pushes hard, Congress gives him what he wants in foreign policy—holds in only three of eleven cases: the Guatemalan intervention, Formosa Resolution, and the Nuclear Test Ban Treaty. In each case, party leader preferences, committee leader preferences, and domestic pressures were positive to the president's position. Five such cases resulted in independent congressional behaviors. In the Spanish bases, Bay of Pigs, and War Powers cases, strong presidential stands were overridden by negative party leader preferences, committee leader preferences, and domestic pressures. The result in each case was a congressional initiative contrary to the president's desires. In the Latin American aid case, Johnson's request for an advance authorization was opposed by party and committee leaders and was rejected in favor of a much weaker substitute bill by Senator Fulbright. In the Turkish military aid case, Ford's appeal to drop the military aid cutoff, which was endorsed by party leaders, was successfully opposed by committee leaders backed up by strongly negative domestic pressures.

In the three remaining cases in which presidents pushed hard, they got congressional outputs only after their drafts had been altered to meet congressional desires. Due to negative party leader preferences, committee leader preferences, and domestic pressures, a total of $5.6 billion was cut from the Defense Appropriations Bill of 1969. In late 1977 and early 1978, endorsements of the Panama Canal treaties by party leaders and members of the Senate Foreign Relations Committee were offset by opposition from the Armed Services Committee, the Judiciary Subcommittee on Separation of Powers, and the perception that constituents were strongly opposed to them. In order to secure the ratification of the treaties, the text of the Neutrality Treaty was changed by the Foreign Relations Committee even though such changes were opposed by the State Department. Moreover, the bipartisan leadership changed the DeConcini condition without consulting President Carter, who had previously endorsed it. Finally, in 1957, Eisenhower could not get the Mutual Security Act he wanted even though he had the support of the party leadership, the foreign affairs committees, and the public. The act was gutted on the House floor by members of the House Appropriations Subcommittee on Foreign Operations, who opposed the idea of multi-year continuing appropriations.

An examination of contextual factors reveals additional insights into the likelihood of presidential effectiveness. Not surprisingly, of the eight cases in which members of Congress categorized their overall relationship with the executive branch as poor, seven resulted in outputs undesired by the president.[40] The lone exception to this trend was the Japanese Peace Treaty of 1952. Since both he and Secretary of State Acheson were very unpopular with Congress, President Truman turned the executive branch's negotiation and ratification duties over to John Foster Dulles. By placing a noncontroversial Republican in charge, Truman went a long way toward assuring the successful ratification of the treaty.

Contextual factors played strong roles in two other cases. In 1961, the spectacular failure of the Bay of Pigs invasion produced the strongly negative preferences of party and committee leaders as well as the strongly negative domestic pressures mentioned earlier. The result was a series of humiliating congressional hearings in which executive branch members were taken-to-task for their roles in the ill-fated affair. Prior events also played an important role in the Panama Canal treaties case. The long lead time from the announcement of the impending treaties until their Senate debate allowed groups such as the Emergency Coalition to Save the Panama Canal and the Committee to Save the Panama Canal to dominate the news, creating an image of public dissatisfaction which was hard for senators

Table 5.3.3

Variable Potencies by the Case and Issue Area

Issue Area	Case	Variable Potencies			
		1	2	3	4
Status	Japanese Peace Treaty	CLP	PLP	DP	PI
	Nuclear Test Pan Treaty	PI	DP	CLP&PLP	
	Executive Agreements Act	CLP	PLP	DP	PI
	War Powers Resolution	DP	CLP	PLP	PI
Human Resources	Mutual Security Act	*	CLP	PLP	DP&PI
	Latin American Aid	CLP	PLP	PI	DP
Territorial	Guatemalan Intervention	DP	PI	PLP&CLP	
	Formosa Resoution	PI	DP	PLP&CLP	
	Bay of Pigs Intervention	DP	CLP	PLP	PI
	Panal Canal Treaties	DP	PLP	PI	CLP
Nonhuman Resources	Spanish Bases Agreement	CLP	DP	PLP	PI
	ABM Authorization	CLP	DP	PLP	PI
	Defense Appropriations	DP	CLP	PLP	PI
	Sugar Act	DP	CLP&PLP	PI	
	Turkish Aid Cutoff	DP	CLP	PLP	PI

* = House floor movement
CLP = Committee Leaders' Preferences
PLP = Party Leaders' Preferences
DP = Domestic Pressures
PI = Presidential Involvement

to ignore. Perceived domestic pressures made changes in the treaty drafts imperative in order to assure senatorial approval.

Finally, not only do presidents appear less influential with Congress than many have imagined, but presidential effectiveness also appears to vary across the different issue areas. After grouping the cases by issue area, table 5.3.3 indicates the relative potencies of the four other independent variables in explaining the resulting congressional foreign policy behavior.

The variables are ordered so that those listed under "1" are the most influential in explaining the dependent variable, while those under "4" are the least influential.

The patterns in relative potencies are more starkly illustrated in table 5.3.4.

To derive the values found in table 5.3.4, the numbers assigned to each variable for each case in table 5.3.3 can be averaged both for each issue area and over all the cases. These averaged rankings indicate *only* that, for the set of cases under consideration, variables with lower averages are more potent in explaining the resulting foreign policy behavior of Congress than are variables with higher averages. Thus, these averages represent an ordinal scale in which increasing averages indicate decreasing variable potencies.

Two major findings are demonstrated in table 5.3.4. First, across all fifteen cases, the level of presidential involvement is the *least* important variable in explaining congressional foreign policy behavior. Presidential involvement seems less important to the final output than do domestic pressures or the preferences of either committee or party leaders. However, this overall ordinal ranking masks some significant variation across the issue areas. A strong presidential push seems to be most effective in territorial cases, less effective in status cases, and least effective in human and nonhuman resources cases.

Conclusions

The literature throughout much of the postwar period paints the picture of a dominant president on foreign policy issues. This vision seems misguided on two counts. First, the cold war period is an historical anomaly. Presidential foreign policy dominance during peacetime is a deviant pattern, not a typical one, from which to measure presidential effectiveness in lobbying Congress. Second, and

Table 5.3.4

Average Rank Orders of Variable Potencies by Issue Area

Issue Area	Variables			
	DP	CLP	PLP	PI
Status	2.25	1.75	2.50	3.25
Human Resources	4.00	1.50	2.50	3.50
Territorial	1.25	3.00	2.75	2.50
Nonhuman Resources	1.40	1.60	2.80	3.80
Overall	1.93	2.00	2.47	3.27

DP = Domestic Pressures
CLP = Committee Leaders' Preferences
PLP = Party Leaders' Preferences
PI = Presidential Involvement

more fundamentally, the postwar period does not conclusively demonstrate presidential dominance. Presidents did not get as much from Congress as many analysts assume, and presidential victories were the result of *hard-fought* campaigns by the executive branch and its congressional allies. No one can deny that presidents *may* dominate the generation of alternatives prior to a decision, the implementation of a foreign policy decision, or those areas where, by law, they can act alone. However, when the president has to share decision-making authority with Congress, he becomes one of many important players in a much larger game. In such circumstances, presidential dominance cannot be assumed. Two distinct "presidencies," one for foreign policy and one for domestic policy, cannot be demonstrated.

Presidential failures to produce congressional foreign policy victories, as in domestic policy, are due to the president's inability to build a coalition of other important players. To succeed in Congress, presidents need the support of important domestic groups, committee leaders, and party leaders, because the influence wielded by these actors may often exceed that available to the president. The failure to get their support may be due to an inability to the see the political pressures facing these other power centers. Successful presidents are those who, perceiving how other important groups view their foreign policy requests, either shape their requests to fit congressional needs or find ways to bring congressional needs in line with their own policy preferences.

Recent presidents have tended to prefer the latter course. They have tried to utilize their access to both foreign policy expertise and the news media to create and lead supportive public opinion designed to bring Congress around. However, given the diplomatic, military, and intelligence failures associated with post-Vietnam and post-Watergate foreign policy, persuading reluctant domestic actors, committee leaders, and party leaders can be a monumental task. Even a landslide win at the polls may not provide enough leverage, as President Reagan has learned. If Congress truly represents the will of the people, and assuming democratic control of government is a primary value in this society, perhaps presidents should consider the former course more often. When faced with widespread opposition in Congress, presidents should be more willing to consider shaping their policies around public pressures. In the contemporary period, the American public does not seem to be as ignorant and unconcerned about foreign policy issues as they were assumed to be prior to World War II. If knowledge leads to power, one can easily presume that the representatives of a more knowledgeable public may become foreign policy players who are too powerful to be led like sheep by the chief executive. In the future, the branch shaping foreign policy most could be the branch with the best ideas, and not the one with the most information.

Appendix

The Japanese Peace Treaty of 1952 was a multilateral agreement between the United States, Japan, and ten other nations which ended the Pacific phase of World War II. Dealing with status issues, the treaty was negotiated and signed against the backdrop of the Korean War. The treaty required the Japanese to renounce their title to most lands not a part of the home islands, specified the general conditions under which occupying troops could remain in Japan, and set procedures for Japanese reparations. The Senate complied with the administration's draft of the treaty by a 66-10 vote.

The Spanish Bases Agreement of 1953 allowed the establishment of American military bases in Spain in return for economic and military aid. This nonhuman resource case represented an independent behavior since heavy, sustained congressional pressure on the Truman administration led to the agreement. President Truman was adamantly opposed to any dealings with the Spanish dictator, General Franco, but he finally succumbed to the four-year-old congressional push for Spanish bases.

The Guatemalan Intervention of 1954 was a CIA-sponsored coup. In this territorial case, client forces of the CIA toppled the popularly elected government of President Jacobo Arbenz Guzman and replaced it with a military regime led by Col. Carlos Castillo Armas. Two broad factors led to United States sponsorship of the coup. Arbenz had given the local communist party legal status, and he had instituted a series of social programs which required either direct or indirect financing by the American-based United Fruit Company. The congressional response to the coup was a two-part compliant behavior. First, Congress overwhelmingly passed a concurrent resolution which condemned communist activities in the Western Hemisphere. Second, the Subcommittee on Latin America of the House Select Committee on Communist Aggression held hearings in late 1954 which served to "document" the severity of the communist threat which had existed in Guatamala prior to the coup.

Again dealing with territorial issues, the Formosa Resolution of 1955 was requested by President Eisenhower to respond to Communist Chinese artillery attacks directed at Nationalistic Chinese positions on offshore islands. The resolution, a classic "blank check," authorized Eisenhower to do anything he felt necessary, for as long as he felt necessary, to defend Formosa (Taiwan) and the Pescadores Islands from attack. Congress complied with the administration's desires by approving the resolution, without amendment, in only four days.

The Mutual Security Act of 1957 was the foreign aid authorization bill for that year. In this human resource case, the Eisenhower administration tried to limit congressional controls on foreign aid by asking for both multi-year, continuing authorizations and the limited use of Treasury funds for foreign aid. The congressional response was a resistant behavior. Congress cut the administration's funding request by $500 million and disallowed the use of both continuing authorizations and Treasury funds.

The Bay of Pigs Intervention in 1961 was another CIA-sponsored coup attempt. In this territorial case, a force of 1500 Cuban exiles made an amphibious landing in Cuba, was pinned down on the beaches by Castro's air and ground forces, and was forced to surrender within two days. The congressional response was an independent behavior. Closed hearings of the House Foreign Affairs and Senate Foreign Relations Committees were held to determine why the operation was attempted and, more importantly, why it failed. Once the hearings ended, key senators assailed the Kennedy administration for going ahead with the invasion, roasted the CIA for its ineptitude, and questioned the performance of the Joint Chiefs of Staff. Senatorial confidence in the decision-making apparatus of the new Kennedy administration was shaken, and the administration's tarnished foreign policy image was not fully erased until after the Cuban Missile Crisis of 1962.

The Nuclear Test Ban Treaty of 1963 was an accord signed by United States, British and Soviet representatives. In this status case, the treaty's purpose was to prohibit the testing of nuclear devices underwater, in the atmosphere, or in outer space. The treaty represented a dramatic turnabout for the Soviets, since they had rejected the same proposal the year before. After strenuous lobbying by President Kennedy, the Senate complied with his desires by approving the treaty by an 80-19 vote.

The Advance Latin American Aid Authorization case of 1967 was an attempt by President Johnson to improve American relations with Latin American nations. Johnson wanted Congress to authorize a $1.5 billion economic aid package for these nations prior to his trip to the Latin American summit conference in Punta del Este, Uruguay. The aid package, which provided only tentative targets to guide a following appropriations bill, would strengthen Johnson's role at the summit conference. While the house easily passed the measure, the Senate refused. Further, the Senate substituted a new version by Senator Fulbright to give only "due consideration" to any agreements Johnson might make at the meeting. This independent behavior resulted from Senate fears that, like the Tonkin Gulf Resolution, any advance authorization could result in administrative policies undesired by Congress. Senators viewed this case in status terms, a case involving congressional versus executive rights.

The ABM Authorization of 1969 was a hotly contested nonhuman resources battle over whether to authorize funds for the Safeguard antiballistic missile system. While the measure passed the House with little fanfare, the Senate was evenly divided over the need for such a system. After an amendment to delete Safeguard's authorization failed on a dramatic 50-50 roll call vote, the Senate went on to authorize the system. Although both the political pressure and debate were intense, the final congressional output was a compliant behavior.

The Defense Appropriations Bill of 1969 represented President Nixon's modifications of the Johnson administration's last defense budget. In this nonhuman resource case, members of both congressional chambers wanted to punish the military for waste, mismanagement, and cost-overruns in the procurement process. Others wanted the defense budget reduced to fight inflation, while others were trying to free more funds for social welfare programs. The congressional response was to cut $5.6 billion from Nixon's defense requests. This resistant behavior represented the largest military budget cut in sixteen years.

The Executive Agreements Act of 1972 was an independent congressional behavior. Alarmed at both the growing reliance on executive agreements by the executive branch and how little members of Congress knew about those accords, Senator Case introduced a measure which said the secretary of state must inform Congress of the text of any executive agreement within sixty days of its execution. Viewing the matter in status terms, the Senate passed the bill unanimously, the House passed it by voice vote, and President Nixon allowed it to become law.

Another independent behavior was found in the 1973 War Powers Resolution. This status case followed the Cambodian incursion of 1970 when many members of Congress became concerned with the lack of restraints on the president's war powers. While a number of war powers bills were introduced over the next several years, not until 1973 did Senate and House members agree to the same version of such a bill. The resolution said that in the absence of a declaration of war, any time a president committed American combat forces to areas of real or imminent conflict he had to notify Congress within forty-eight hours. Congress then had a period of up to sixty days in which to either approve or disapprove the operation. This congressional decision was to be made in the form of a veto-proof concurrent resolution. If Congress disapproved, the president had to remove the troops. The president could request a thirty-day extension in order to withdraw the troops safely, but Congress could refuse to grant it. Both chambers passed the resolution by large margins, Nixon vetoed it, and Congress overrode his veto.

In 1974, Congress refused to extend the Sugar Act authorizing the American sugar program. The forty-year-old program had allocated both subsidies and a protected share of the domestic market to domestic sugar producers while setting import quotas for foreign sugar supplies. The rapid rise in sugar prices in 1973 and 1974 mobilized both residential sugar consumers and large industrial sugar users to work against the administration's call for an extension of the program. Although the House Agriculture Committee reported out the bill by a 30-5 vote, the bill was rejected on the House floor by a 175-209 recorded vote. The Senate failed to act on the measure, a congressional resistant behavior was the output, and this nonhuman resources case resulted in the expiration of the American sugar program on December 31, 1974.

The Turkish Military Aid Cutoff in 1974 was another nonhuman resources case; yet it produced an independent behavior. Many members of Congress were outraged in 1974 when Turkey, using American-supplied "defensive" arms, invaded the island of Cyprus, seized 50 percent of the island, and refused to leave. Hosue members attached an amendment to the emergency appropriations bill which cut off Turkish military aid. The Senate did likewise, and President Ford vetoed the appropriations bill. Unable to override the veto, Congress reattached the cutoff amendment to the appropriations bill and sent it to Ford once again. For the second time, Ford vetoed the measure. The House again failed to override the veto, but their second attempt fell only two votes short of the necessary two-thirds majority. Undeterred, Congress reattached the cutoff amendment to the appropriations bill. Upon the urging of the House Minority Leader John Rhodes, Ford conceded defeat and accepted the military aid cutoff.

The final case concerns the twisted tale of the Panama Canal Treaties, a territorial matter sponsored by the Carter administration. The Neutrality Treaty declared the Canal would be neutral in the future, and after 1999, only Panama could operate the Canal or put military bases in the Canal Zone. The Panama Canal Treaty provided for the transfer of control of the Canal and Canal Zone from the United States to Panama on January 1, 2000. The treaty established a Panama Canal Commission, composed of both Americans and Panamanians, to run the Canal until 2000, and it also specified the range of revenues Panama could receive from Canal tolls during that time.

Due to perceived domestic opposition to the treaties, senators were eager to make changes in them. Despite State Department opposition, the Neutrality Treaty was amended to include the "Statement of Understanding" signed by Presidents Carter and Torrijos late in 1977. In addressing discrepancies between the United States and Panamanian interpretations of the treaty, the agreement said Panama would allow American warships to go to the head of the line, if necessary, and both nations had the right to defend the Canal's neutrality. However, that right did not allow the United States to intervene in the domestic affairs of Panama.

Another concession on the part of the administration was the condition insisted upon by Senator DeConcini. His condition, approved by President Carter, stated that both the United States and Panama had the unilateral right to use whatever actions necessary to reopen the Canal should it be closed or its operation impaired in the future. The condition specifically included the use of force "in Panama" if necessary. With these two changes the Senate approved the treaty by a 68-32 vote, one vote more than the necessary two-thirds majority.

The Senate then considered the Panama Canal Treaty. Realizing the turmoil caused in Panama by the DeConcini condition, the Senate bipartisan leadership proposed a new reservation to the treaty. The reservation, on which Carter was not consulted, noted any American action taken pursuant to the DeConcini condition would be directed solely at keeping the Canal open. The reservation implied no American right to intervene in Panamanian affairs. Once this reservation passed, the treaty was approved. Like the prior treaty, the vote was 68-32. The congressional output was a resistant behavior. Although Carter got the treaties passed, they had been changed in the Senate to make them more palatable to both the American and Panamanian peoples.

Author's note: I wish to thank David Farnsworth, who read an earlier version of this work and made valuable suggestions.

Notes

1. Aaron Wildavsky, "The Two Presidencies," *TRANS-action*, 4 (December 1966), 7-14.

2. Lance T. LeLoup and Steven A. Shull, "Congress Versus the Executive: The 'Two Presidencies' Revisited" (Paper presented at the annual meeting of the Southwestern Political Science Association, Houston, Texas 1978).

3. Donald A Peppers, "The 'Two Presidencies': Eight Years Later" in *Perspectives on the Presidency*, ed. Aaron Wildavsky (Boston, Mass.: Little, Brown, 1975).

4. Lee Sigelman, "A Reassessment of the Two Presidencies Thesis," *Journal of Politics*, 41 (November 1979), 1195-1205.

5. A recent study of Frederick Paul Lee; "The Two Presidencies: Political Elite Perspectives Through Time, 1976-1980," *Presidential Studies Quarterly*, 12 (Winter 1983), 26-36, claims Wildavsky's thesis is still true. Unfortunately, an erroneous methodological assumption invalidates his findings. By equating aggregated trust scores for *individual members of Congress* with the concept of trust in *Congress as an institution*, Lee engages in the individualistic fallacy. Political elites could place more trust in the president than in their *individual* representatives in Congress while still preferring the *collective* wisdom of 535 individuals to that of one man. Congressional foreign policy resurgence after the Vietnam War rode to such a rallying cry. For a better presentation of the inappropriateness of equating feelings for individual members of Congress with feelings for Congress as a whole, see Richard F. Fenno, "If, As Ralph Nader Says, Congress Is 'The Broken Branch,' How Come We Love Our Congressmen So Much," in *Congress In Change*, ed. Norman Ornstein (New York: Praeger, 1975).

6. Stan Taylor, "Congressional Resurgence" in *Problems of American Foreign Policy*, ed. Martin Hickman (Beverly Hills, Calif.: Glencoe Press, 1975), 109.

7. Thomas Bailey, *A Diplomatic History of the American People*, ninth ed. (Englewood Cliffs, N.J.: Prentice-Hall, 1974), 519-520.

8. Ibid., 541.

9. Ibid., 662.

10. Ibid., 701-703; John Donovan, "Congressional Isolationists and the Roosevelt Foreign Policy" in *Essays on the History of American Foreing Relations*, ed. Lawrence Gelfand (New York: Holt, Rinehart, and Winston, 1972), 345-346.

11. Roger Hilsman, *The Politics of Policy Making in Defense and Foreign Affairs* (New York, Harper and Row, 1971), 67-68; Samuel Huntington, *The Common Defense* (New York, Columbia University Press, 1961), 127; Warner Schilling, "The American Foreign Policy Making Process" in *The Politics of U.S. Foreign Policy Making*, ed. Douglas Fox (Pacific Palisades, Cal., Goodyear, 1971), 38-39; John Spanier and Eric Uslaner, *How American Foreign Policy Is Made* (New York: Holt, Rinehart, and Winston, 1974), 54.

12. James Robinson, *Congress and Foreign Policy-Making* (Homewood, Ill.: Dorsey, 1962), v.

13. Ibid., 14-15.

14. Frans Bax, "The Legislative-Executive Relationship in Foreign Policy: New Relationship or New Competition," *Orbis*, 20 (Winter 1977), 887-888, 891.

15. John Manley, "The Rise of Congress in Foreign Policy-Making," *The Annals*, 397 (September 1971), 65.

16. Bailey, op.cit., 792-793.

17. Ibid., 798.

18. Ibid., 800-801.

19. *Congressional Quarterly Almanac* (Washington, D.C.: Congressional Quarterly Press, 1955), 277-280,

20. See the foreign aid sections of *Congressional Quarterly Almanacs*, 1950-1970.

21. John Lehman, *The Executive, Congress, and Foreign Policy* (New York, Praeger, 1974), 161-162; Manley, op.cit., 65-66.

22. Victor Johnson, *Congress and Foreign Policy: The House Foreign Affairs and Senate Foreign Relations Committees*. Unpublished Ph.D. dissertation, University of Wisconsin, 1975, 43-50.

23. Ibid.

24. Robert Sickels, *The Presidency: An Introduction* (Englewood Cliffs, N.J.: Prentice-Hall, 1980), 150-151; Phillipa Strum, *Presidential Power and American Democracy* (Santa Monica, Calif.: Goodyear, 1979), 43-48.

25. Richard Johnson, *The Administration of United States Foreign Policy* (Austin: University of Texas Press, 1971), 169; Bax. op.cit., 881-883.

26. William Keefe, *Congress and the American People* (Englewood Cliffs, N.J.: Prentice-Hall, 1980), 104; Larry Schwab, *Changing Patterns of Congressional Politics* (New York: D. Van Nostrand, 1980), 155.

27. Cecil Crabb and Pat Holt, *Invitation to Struggle: Congress, the President, and Foreign Policy* (Washington, D.C.: Congressional Quarterly Press, 1980), 33, 37.

28. Leroy Rieselbach,, "Change in the Congressional System" in *The Congressional System*, ed. Leroy Rieselbach (North Scituate, Mass.: Duxbury, 1979), 401.

29. Thomas Franck and Edward Weisband, *Foreign Policy By Congress* (New York, Oxford University Press, 1979), 6-8; Lehman, op.cit., vii.

30. Ronald Moe and Stevel Teel, "Congress as Policy Maker: A Necessary Reappraisal" in Fox, op.cit.

31. Harry Eckstein, "Case Study and Theory in Political Science," in *The Handbook of Political Science*, 7, ed. Fred Greenstein and Nelson Polsby (Reading, Mass.: Addison-Wesley, 1975), 85; Arend Lijphart, "Comparative Politics and the Comparative Method," *American Political Science Review*, 65 (September 1971), 685.

32. Robert Jervis, "Cumulation, Correlations, and Woozels," in *In Search of Global Patterns*, ed. James Rosenau (New York: Free Press, 1976), 184.

33. Alexander George, "Bridging the Gap Between Theory and Practice," in Rosenau, op.cit.

34. James Rosenau, "Pre-Theories and Theories of Foreign Policy," in *Approaches to Comparative and International Politics*, ed. R. Barry Farrell (Evanston, Ill.: Northwestern University Press, 1966).

35. Robinson, op.cit., v, 68-69.

36. For those unfamiliar with these cases, see the Appendix.

37. Theses percentages were produced by Tauber distributions which measure the difference between an actual distribution and the ideal one, with the results expressed in percentage points off of the ideal. It is computed by the formula:

$$T = \tfrac{1}{2}\Sigma\, P_i - P_j$$

Where P_i = percentage of the total distribution ideally found in each cell, and

P_j = percentage of the total distribution actually found in each cell.

I wish to thank Samuel Yeager of the Center for Urban

Studies, Wichita State University, for bringing this measure to my attention.

38. Attempts to improve the case distribution across either issue areas or the dependent variable measures caused maldistributions across the time dimension, resulting in higher percentages off the ideal distribution for the three combined criteria.

39. See Robinson, op.cit.

40. These seven cases are the Mutual Security Act of 1957, the advance Latin American aid authorization request of 1967, the Defense Appropriations Bill of 1969, the Executive Agreements Act of 1972, the War Powers Resolution of 1973, the rejection of the Sugar Act in 1974, and the cutoff of military aid to Turkey in 1974.

Presidential Policy Relationships III: The Bureaucracy

6

There are two major propositions that best explain presidential-bureaucratic relationships. The first is that, despite the fact that the president is the chief executive, his control over the bureaucracy (operating or line departments and agencies) is less than complete. Despite much managerial effort and for many different reasons, presidents lack chain of command and hierarchical control over the bureaucracy. All of the modern presidents have lamented an "unwieldy, unresponsive bureaucracy." From Franklin Roosevelt to Ronald Reagan, presidents have bemoaned and castigated intransigent bureaucrats who fail to heed their initiatives and direction.

A second proposition capturing this policy relationship is: the reason for tension between presidents and bureaucracy is best captured by the insightful dictum, "Where you stand depends upon where you sit." Presidents sit in the center of policy coordination, prioritizing and doing politics. Bureaucrats, with substantive expertise and organizational and programmatic loyalty, do policy for segmental constituencies and agency clientele. The two are destined to bump heads in the policy process.

White House-Departmental Relations 6.1

Thomas Cronin

The following essay examines the sources of tension between the White House and the federal bureaucracy. The author, a noted presidential scholar, based his analysis of the differences in perspectives and perceptions on extensive interviews with White House staffers and cabinet officers.

"Everybody Believes in Democracy until He Gets to the White House: An Examination of White House-Departmental Relations" by Thomas E. Cronin, 1970, *Law and Contemporary Problems, 35*, pp. 573-625. Copyright 1970, Duke University School of Law. Reprinted by permission.

On Directing the Federal Establishment from the White House

A president is expected to perform three overriding functions: to recast the nation's policy agenda in line with contemporary needs, to provide symbolic affirmation of the nation's basic values, and to galvanize the vast machinery of government to carry out his programs and those he has inherited. The slippage and gap between the first and third functions is the primary concern of this discussion. The annual unveiling of a president's legislative program now has much in common with Madison Avenue's broadsides advertising each year's "spectacular new line" of Detroit-made combustion engine automobiles: the perceptive citizenry is increasingly sensitive to performance standards of both.

And so it is that the recently arrived president, aspiring to "unite the nation" and "get the country moving again," expecting that he and his lieutenants will succeed where previous administrations faltered, customarily feels he must order first his own executive branch "household." Recent presidents often have gone out of their way to solicit the loyalty and support of senior civil servants. President Nixon, for example, immediately after his inauguration, personally traveled to each executive department and met with and addressed thousands of these senior officials. Presidents and their inner circle of aides continuously strive to secure greater internal managerial control over the executive departments. They even learn (after awhile) that one way to do this is to forge a unity on policy priorities among the general American public *outside* of the executive branch.

But, as Bailey has pointed out, the executive branch of the federal government is a many-splintered thing. The president is soon acquainted with the considerable difficulty of promoting unity in the face of the basic pluralism of the American political system. Presidents Kennedy, Johnson, and Nixon have each complained bitterly about the recalcitrance of the federal bureaucracy, and seemingly turned more and more to their personal White House staffs for help in gaining control of their own executive establishment. And the collective record of Kennedy, Johnson, and Nixon as chief executive, especially with respect to the achievement of their domestic policy goals, has raised considerable questioning and criticism. As Rexford Tugwell concluded:

> The truth is that Kennedy did not function as an executive. He had only the most meager contacts with the secretaries of the domestic departments, largely because he had no interest in their operations. This inability of a president—who must be political leader and chief legislator and who is sole custodian of the national security—to direct the domestic establishment has become almost total.[1]

Kennedy, after being in office two years, publicly complained that the nation's problems "are more difficult than I had imagined" and "there are greater limitations upon our ability to bring about a favorable result than I had imagined."

One Kennedy White House aide put the frustration more bluntly: "Everybody believes in democracy until he gets to the White House and then you begin to believe in dictatorship, because it's so hard to get things done. Every time you turn around, people just resist you, and even resist their own job." Again, the same John Kennedy who in many ways inspired the country was moved to quip about a relatively low priority project, the architectural remodeling of Lafayette Square across from the White House, "Let's stay with it. Hell, this may be the only thing I'll ever really get done." President Johnson also expressed disappointment over seemingly slow and uncooperative departmental responses. He attempted to "ride herd" on a multitude of programs by insisting on getting up-to-date figures on varied federal and international grant programs and routinely required departmental written reports. But he eventually resorted to vesting more and more authority for departmental coordination in the White House domestic policy aides and his Budget Bureau director. It was a no doubt disillusioned President Johnson, tired with continually battling the bureaucracy, who solemnly warned the incoming Nixon administration that they should spare no effort in selecting thoroughly loyal people to man key departmental positions. It is as though Johnson believed that a significant portion of the Great Society programs, for which he had fought so hard, had been sabotaged by indifferent federal officials. And, in the wake of the Great Society legislative victories, both Presidents Johnson and Nixon held that the scaffolding of the federal government and the federal system needed extensive revamping, if not major surgery. Said Nixon: "I have concluded that a sweeping reorganization of the executive branch is needed if the government is to keep up with the times and with the needs of the people."[2]

The thesis running implicitly if not explicitly through this paper is that White House staffs and executive department officials, upon whom contemporary presidents are exceptionally dependent, are more specialized, professionalized, and differentiated than has been generally acknowledged. Presidents find themselves continuously surrounded—some would say afflicted—by problems of complexity, diversity, and a seemingly endless series of jurisdictional and territorial disputes. Presidential staffs, cabinet members, and advisors are invariably associated with, if not captured by, professionally, politically, or personally skewed sets of policy preferences. No cabinet officer or White House advisor consistently and singularly acts for "Everyman" or "the public interest." Priority setting, budget cutting, and preferred procedural strategies necessarily promote selective interests at the expense of others. Hence, presidents are constantly, and rightfully, faced with conflicting claims; calibration and management of conflict is the core of presidential leadership. Those who would somehow reorganize the federal government so as to remove or elevate the American presidency away from bureaucratic or societal conflicts should be fully aware that they may at the same time be stripping the presidency of the strategic occasions for exercising essential leadership skills.

To the extent that White House staff and senior department officials maintain close communications and negotiations—or exchanges—we can speak of the existence of an executive branch exchange system. Both sides are needed to perform the functions of the executive branch; each wants certain types of help from the other, and each seeks to avoid overt antagonism toward the other. White House staff members can be viewed as performing important linkage roles in this exchange system, connecting a president with a vast network of administrative officials. Presidents and most of their staff grow well aware that cooperation from the permanent federal departments is earned rather than taken for granted. Loyalty and support as well as crucially needed expertise are eagerly sought, for a basic premise in the exchange system is that departmental officials, especially civil servants, play, or can play, a strategic role in administering federal government activities.

Some of the relationships within this exchange system can be briefly suggested here. Richard Neustadt has commented:

> Agencies need decisions, delegations, and support, along with bargaining arenas and a court of last resort, so organized as to assure that their advice is always heard and often taken. A president needs timely information, early warning, close surveillance, organized to yield him the controlling judgment, with his options open, his intent enforced. In practice these two sets of needs have proved quite incompatible; presidential organizations rarely serve one well without disservice to the other.[3]

And Bill Moyers adds:

> The job of the White House assistant is to help the president impress his priorities on the administration. This may throw him into a sharp adversary role between two cabinet members who are also competing with the president for their views of what the priorities should be.... Their [White House assistants] job is to make sure that decisions get implemented; it is not to manage the implementations. The follow-through aspect of it is very, very important. In recent years, the White House staff may have tended to become far too much of a managerial operation and less an overseer.[4]

The general White House view reflects a concern for teamwork, cohesiveness, interdepartmental coordination, follow-through on the president's program, and protection of the president's reputation. White House aides generally spend a sizable portion of their time engaged in intraexecutive branch alliance building. How best to communicate what the president wants done? How to give the departmental leaders a sense of involvement in presidential decisions? How politely but firmly to tell "them" of the president's dissatisfaction with department performance? How to motivate them to give added energy to get "our" programs moving? Should we promote an inside man into that new vacancy or bring in someone from the outside? How can we extricate this program operation from that nearly impossible group of people over there? A standard joke during the 1960s had White House staff members trying to figure out how to contract out to private enterprise or foundations the work that the State Department was assigned to perform. A standard exercise during the late 1960s, especially within the Nixon administration, was the design of programs that might shortcircuit the federal bureaucracy with the hope of getting federal monies and programs more swiftly into the hands of state and local officials. In short, the problem becomes how to employ the resources and sanctions of the presidency to make the machinery of government act in accord with the administration's overriding goals.

Senior departmental officials are no less involved in exchanges with the presidential staff. Some of them are temporary political appointees; most are career civil servants with a long legacy of dealing with the presidency, especially with the budget officials attached to the Executive Office of the President. Their concern is often a blend of wishing to satisfy and cooperate with the objectives of the current presidential team, but at the same time attending to departmental priorities and the always present need for maintaining departmental integrity. White House requests for the most part are honored; pressure and arrogant communications are resented. But the day-to-day concerns are reflected in the following types of questions: How can we get White House endorsement and increased budget approvals for this new department initiative? How can we get the White House to side with us in this jurisdictional matter? How can we make an end run around that unsympathetic and amateur White House aide and make sure the president hears about this new idea? When should we supply a potentially great news announcement to the White House and risk not being able to use it here to gain publicity for "our" cabinet officer and departmental programs? In short, how do we deal with the White House when necessary, or when it can help us, but otherwise preserve our autonomy?

Simple but previously neglected questions such as the following need to be asked: How much tension and strain exist between White House staff and departmental executives? Why do some White House staffers see considerable conflict whereas others view departmental relations as essentially harmonious? What variance exists over time or among the departments? What are the major sources of perceived conflicts? To what extent should and can conflict be resolved?

White House-Departmental Conflict: Presidential and Departmental Perspectives

The focus on conflict here deserves a note of explanation. In the strictest sense, conflict occurs when different people "seek to possess the same object, occupy the same space or the same exclusive position, play incompatible roles, maintain incompatible goals, or undertake mutually incompatible means for achieving their purposes."[5] Conflict, as well as its closely interrelated opposite, integration or harmony, is always more or less present in any large organization, and indeed in all human relations. If one looks for it, one will surely find it. One of the ironies of our government is that, although it exists to resolve conflict, *i.e.*, to pull together diverse class, regional, and ethnic interests and accentuate the common goals of prosperity, liberty, etc., it strives at the same time to make this nation safe for and supportive of certain types of conflict, *e.g.*, business competition in the marketplace, diversity in religion, and the clash of contending ideas and values. Within the federal executive branch there is more contention about the priorities and tempo of federal activity than there is about the basic ends or legitimacy of the government. In this sense, the executive branch exchange system operates much like a trading arena in which different participants hope that their preferences might prevail.

Conflict is not always an indicator of weakness or ill health of an organization. Critical adversary relationships may provide a much needed jolt toward system adaptation and renewal, and hence be a notable asset. Coser's suggestions are relevant:

> Conflict prevents the ossification of social systems by exerting pressures for innovation and creativity; it prevents habitual accommodations from freezing into rigid molds and hence progressively impoverishing the ability to react creatively to novel circumstances.[6]

Several former members of the executive branch have made a case that certain federal policies and practices have suffered not from too much conflict, but from too little. But assessing the utility or disutility of conflict requires an extremely sensitive appraisal of a large number of variables. The analysis here is limited to an exploration of participant perspectives on the existence and presumed sources of conflict in the White House–departmental exchange system.

It is hoped that studying the existence and nature of conflicts in the executive branch exchange system may add to our understanding about what makes the presidency work—or not work. Though contemporary presidents have been able to provide some semblance of integrating unity via their legislative messages and budgetary controls, presidents seem otherwise increasingly buried beneath their own institutional machinery. Conservatives and liberals alike join in faulting the executive branch as a bulwark against change and as largely unresponsive to contemporary needs. The phenomenal growth and differentiation of the executive establishment and the attributed independence of the permanent government (civil servants, foreign service and military officials, and so forth) from the presidential government (the president, his inner circle of White House counselors, and those politically appointed cabinet officials who can be thoroughly relied upon) make assessing the strength of the presidency quite complicated.

Let us examine the major competing schools of thought about functions and responsibilities belonging at the White House and those belonging within the departments. Just as there are those who want to strengthen Congress in all executive-legislative relations and thereby make Congress the "first branch of government," so also there are heated arguments about whether the cabinet and the departments need to be strengthened vis-à-vis the White House staff and the Executive Office of the President. While not doing justice to the richness of varied arguments, it is helpful to sum up the contending polar perspectives characterizing much of recent practice and prescription: the presidential perspective and the departmental. These are presented here as ideal type constructs and as such are not necessarily held by any one person or group. It is likely that admixtures of these perspectives will be found in instances of conflict and in proposals for reducing conflict.

The Presidential Perspective

This perspective, popular among most presidential advisors, university liberals (at least during the 1950s and 1960s), and probably a majority of the Washington press corps, holds that the presidency should be a strong and visible force in making sure that presidential policy objectives get effectively translated into desired policy performance. "This is the great office, the only truly national office in the whole system." The basic premise corresponds with Alexander Hamilton's point of view—that the requisite unity and drive for our political system would only come from a strong executive. Only the presidency should retain discretion over budget choices and over the way federal policies are administered. And only the presidency can provide the needed direction and orchestration of complex, functionally interdependent federal programs. Presidents and their staffs, if properly organized, can assure that the laws of the land not only will be administered faithfully, but also imaginatively. There is an explicit assumption that a strong presidency can make a major difference in the way government works and that this difference will be in the direction of a more constructive (desirable) set of policy outcomes.

Presidentialists invariably also argue that the presidency is not properly organized, staffed, or funded. The presidency needs not just "more help" but a major infusion of skills, talent, tools, and loyalty if it is to gain control over the permanent federal departments. Implicitly, if not explicitly, "More Power To The White House" is the slogan. Partly because so many previous presidents have bypassed existing departments and set up their own new independent agencies, and partly because of the sheer size and diversity of the executive establishment, the White House too often serves at the pleasure of the bureaucracy, rather than vice versa. McGeorge Bundy speaks for many believers of the presidential persuasion when he observes that the executive branch in many areas "more nearly resembles a collection of badly separated principalities than a single instrument of executive action."[7]

The presidential camp never completely trusts civil servants, and frequently mistrusts political appointees as well. Whatever of importance needs doing either ought to be done directly from the White House, or should be done with the expectation that the departmental people will temper or undermine the desired policy intentions. The goal of the presidentialists in its crudest form is "to presidentialize" the executive branch. Toward that end there are catalogues of reform proposals, a few of which can be mentioned as examples:

> The strong presidency will depend upon the chief executive's capacity to control and direct the vast bureaucracy of national administration. Ideally, the president should possess administrative powers comparable to those of business executives.... What the president needs most can be simply formulated: a power over personnel policy, planning, accounting, and the administration of the executive branch that approaches his power over the executive budget.[8]

Other variations on this theme call for better policy evaluation and program management staffs within the Executive Office. Presidentialists with narrow policy interests are always asking that the formulation and administration of their particular policy concerns be brought closer within the presidential orbit "much along the lines of the Council of Economic Advisers." Another suggestion would give the presidency some field agents or "expediters" (federal domestic program "czars") located in federal regional offices or large metropolitan areas to insure that presidential priorities are being properly effected at the grass roots level.

Departmental Perspective

This perspective holds that the success or failure of the federal government's efforts to manage federal programs rests almost entirely on the quality and competence of the executive departments. An assumption here is that all programs at the federal level possess considerable discretionary aspects. Those holding a departmental perspective say that for programs to be effectively administered, discretion and authority must (at least to a large extent) be vested in departmental and bureau leaders. The sentiment here is that the role of the White House, particularly in regard to the administration of domestic programs, should be a highly selective one, and one that is tremendously and rightfully dependent on career civil servants and professional departmental expertise. Certain department officials, for example, deplored the amount of White House involvement in AID grant clearances, HUD model city selections, and HEW desegregation proceedings. To be sure, even the most extreme departmentalist would agree that crisis situations and various types of national security matters necessarily should be subject to substantial presidential discretion.

The departmentalist view has varying support among professional civil servants, among some former cabinet officers, and even among some former White House staff assistants. Moreover, there are increasing numbers of skeptics who are persuaded that a larger and more "resourceful" presidency (or more "institutionalization" of the presidency) is not a realistic answer to the problem of managing a responsive federal government. There are even those who argue that it probably does not make much difference which of the various presidential candidates gets elected."You can elect your favorite presidential hopeful at the next election but the basic problems of government non-responsiveness will still be with us!"

Some advocates of the departmental perspective come to their position because of a recognition that the political facts of life just do not permit intensive or extensive presidential involvement in most matters of federal policy administration. The limits of the presidency are cited, such as in David Truman's appropriate cautions:

> [The president] cannot take a position on every major controversy over administrative policy, not merely because his time and energies are limited, but equally because of the positive requirements of his position. He cannot take sides in any dispute without giving offense in some quarters. He may intervene where the unity of his supporters will be threatened by inaction; he may even, by full use of the resources of his office, so dramatize his action as to augment the influence he commands. But he cannot "go to the country" too often, lest the tactic become familiar and his public jaded. Rather than force an administrative issue, he may choose to have his resources for a legislative effort.... [For effectiveness he] must preserve some of the detachment of a constitutional monarch.[9]

And while the president remains detached or "above" the day-to-day operations of the federal government, cabinet members and their staffs want both a relative independence and a vote of confidence with which to carry on their work. As one prerequisite, they insist that White House staff members should not have authority independent from the president to issue directives to cabinet and agency leaders. And when they need it, cabinet members and agency heads should have the right to direct access to the president. It follows too that presidents should get involved only in broad policy questions, not in the nuts and bolts concerns of program execution and application. White House people are viewed as "amateurs and terribly ill-informed nuisances" who are seen as "breathing down our necks."

The more the White House usurps functional responsibilities from their "proper" home in the departments, the more the White House may undermine the goal of competent departmental management of presidentially sponsored programs. A cabinet member who is made to look weak within his department will be treated with less respect by subordinates as well as by relevant congressional and client support groups. Department officials who must fight strenuously to maintain access and rapport with the White House have correspondingly less energy left over for their internal department management concerns. When the White House staff or other presidential advisors step in and temporarily take over certain departmental functions, the action may further diminish the capacity of the department to streamline or revitalize its capability for managing these functions in the future. Too frequent intervention from the White House creates morale problems within the departments. Resentment and hostility are likely to impede subsequent cooperation. Imaginative professional people will not long remain in their departmental posts if they are frequently underused or misused.

Departmentalists, charging that White House aides get rewarded for "meddling" in department affairs, note that on closer inspection it is frequently a disadvantageous strategy for everyone involved, excepting perhaps the White House aide who has to look "busy."

Amount of Conflict Perceived by White House Staffers

Conflicts in the executive branch system are widely acknowledged by most recent White House staff members. The forty-three aides interviewed for this study were asked whether they experienced major difficulties in working with the federal executive departments: "Can you give your view of this; is this really a problem?" As shown in table 6.1.1, approximately two-thirds answered that there were extensive and considerable troubles in dealing with the departments. Some talked of this as the single greatest problem in contemporary government. One man who had worked for both Presidents Kennedy and Johnson said that "it was an absolutely terrible problem.... There are major problems with cabinet members and civil servants alike. Even the great cabinet members like McNamara and Freeman were terrible in evading their share of many of our efforts." A senior Johnson administration counselor observed that

Table 6.1.1

White House Staff Perception of Conflict with Departments

Problem of tensions and conflict in these exchanges was:	Percentages N = 43
Considerable	65%
Moderate	25
Insignificant	10
Total	100

Source: Personal interviews with forty-three White House staff members serving between 1961 and 1970.

the "separation of governments is not so great between Congress and the president as between a president and those people like sub-cabinet and bureau officials, who become locked into their own special subsystems of self-interested policy concerns." Others talked about the increasing defiance of department people toward the White House:

> It's a terrible problem and it's getting worse, particularly with the State Department. The major problem is the lack of any identification [on their part] with the president's program priorities. At State they try to humor the president but hope he will not interfere in their complex matters and responsibilities. It is equally a problem with civil servants and cabinet types. It is amazing how soon the cabinet people get captured by the permanent staffs. Secretary [David] Kennedy [of Treasury] under Nixon, for example, was captured within days ... and Nixon's staff didn't even try to improve things. They just assumed there was a great problem. Personally, I think you can't expect too much from the bureaucracy. It is too much to expect that they will see things the president's way.

Some aides were more inclined to note that conflicts varied with different departments and with different cabinet members. For example: "Yes, there are certainly many problems, but it differs from area to area and from president to president. I think the amount of friction is related to the role of the White House staff and what they undertake and what presidents let them do." Another example of a more tempered assessment of the existence of conflict comes from a Congressional relations aide to the Kennedy-Johnson White House:

> Oh, yes—there are problems to an extent. There is deep suspicion around the whole government toward the new president when he comes into power.... But the fights you get in are different all around town.... We had some excellent men around town, and some bombs. The important thing for a president to do is to get good men and then decentralize the responsibility. Let the department people do their job and don't let your [White House] staff interfere too much.

Some White House staff who had less involvement with departments were the most likely to acknowledge little if any serious conflict.

On balance, a substantial majority of recent presidential staffers complain of considerable difficulty and conflict in their work with the federal executive departments.

What White House Staffers See as Sources of Conflict

Conflicts in the executive branch exchange system can be attributed to both subjective and objective factors. The difference in allegiance to the presidential or departmental perspectives illustrates a major subjective factor. Some other subjective factors include differing definitions of priorities and roles, personality clashes, and personal ambitions. Objective factors would include such things as sheer size of the federal effort (and the time and communications restrictions that stem from that size), restrictive budget limitations (presidents and cabinet heads find they have little control over ninety percent or more of "their" budgets), centrifugal pulls inherent in federalism and in the functionally independent departments, and various knowledge gaps (for example, "we don't have all the answers!"). Presidential staff members seem to be well aware of most of these sources, but seem to stress the subjective differences and the ill effects of the divorce between presidential and departmental perspectives.

Extended interviews with White House staff yield the persuasive impression that no one set of difficulties lies at the root of executive branch conflict. Their discussions often moved back and forth from noting causes to complaining about symptoms. But their multiple citations here (see table 6.1.2) are instructive both for their diversity and for unexpectedly candid criticism of the way the White House itself contributed to these difficulties.[10]

On White House "Sources" of Conflict. White House staffers suggest that their own definition of their roles, and the pressures they had to work under frequently exacerbate relations with cabinet and department officials. Presidents and their staffs arrive at the White House charged up to get things done, to produce results, to make good on the pledges of their campaign. The frenzy and simplification of problems and issues generated in the campaign, coupled with the postelection victory euphoria result in strategies of overextension and insensitivity:

Well, a Kennedy staff hallmark was to seize power from around town. In retrospect I think they often were insensitive to the channels of the existing government. They came in after the campaign with a pretentious "know it all" attitude and they hurt their case by this stance. For example, I think the White House staffers often called people low in the departments and deliberately undercut cabinet people too much in the early years. . . . In retrospect I don't think you can coordinate much from the White House. You just don't have the people and the numbers . . . [and] you can't evaluate all that much [not to mention managing it].

Staff insensitivity to cabinet and department executives occurs for a variety of reasons. Presidents often want to "put the heat on" some cabinet member or bureau chief, but prefer not to take the blame for being tough. Presidents understandably eschew the "bad guy" role; hence the bearing of unpleasant news befalls various staff assistants.

Discussions about the problem of staff insensitivity were often ambiguous. On the one hand, aides somewhat contemptuously talked of the need for more "care and feeding" of cabinet members (as though some of the cabinet were kept symbols for window dressing alone). But they would also insist that one just has to be aggressive and "hard-nosed" in order to get anything accomplished.

Some aides stressed that the always delicate distinction between *staff* or advisory roles at the White House, and operational administrative *line* responsibilities in the cabinet departments became overly blurred during the Kennedy and Johnson years. Too many of the staff tried to do more than they were supposed to be doing and gradually came "to give orders" rather than transmit requests. But as mentioned earlier, presidents frequently encouraged this development and some cabinet members respect decisive and competent White House aides, brusque though they may be. Impatient or disillusioned with some of their cabinet, Kennedy, Johnson and Nixon turned more and more to their White House staff for advice, coordination, and particularly for help in resolving jurisdictional disputes between executive agencies. One result, in the

Table 6.1.2

Presidency Staff Perspectives on the Sources of Conflict and Strain in White House-Executive Department Relationships

Types and Sources of Conflict	Percentages N = 41
White House "Sources":	
WH staff insensitivity toward department officials	51%
WH staff and president communications failures	44
WH staff usurpation of department roles and/or excessive interference in department affairs	37
WH "tried to do too much too quickly"	29
Departmental "Sources":	
Civil servant and bureaucratic parochialism	49
Cabinet "leadership" too weak or unimaginative	46
Departmental leaders captured by narrow special interests	46
Red tape, and inept staff work	37
Departments unable to work together	24
Complexity/Diversity Factors:	
Sheer size and complexity of federal efforts	37
Lack of time for the needed follow-through/ coordination/implementation	27
Substantive and ideological differences about policy choices within the federal system	27

Source: Personal interviews conducted by the author with forty-one presidential staff members who served at the White House during 1961-70. Respondents could give more than one reply.

words of one top Johnson aide, was that "after awhile he [Johnson] never even bothered to sit down with most of the cabinet members (domestic cabinet) even to discuss their major problems and program possibilities." Partly because of the war, and partly because he had grown used to leaning on his own staff so heavily, "Johnson became lazy and wound up using some of the staff as both line managers as well as staff and, I think in retrospect, *it frequently* didn't work out!"

Some of the most instructive commentary was devoted to the problem of intra-executive branch communications. Numerous aides mentioned that a "basic reason for conflict is the lack of communications." Fault in this regard is generally placed upon White House staff and sometimes on the president. Often it is not that cabinet and departmental officials fail to respond to White House policy directives, but rather that those directives are too hazy or inadequately communicated. Sometimes it is because presidents and their aides just have not made up their minds. Occasionally, different White House aides send out contradictory messages to the departments. For example, the domestic program and legislative development staff might be pressing a department or new program ideas while the budget director and his staff are warning department officials of the need to reduce their activities, especially their more costly programs. Often the president has not made his view known forcefully enough to overcome uncertainty and confusion. Presidents are handicapped in this sense because they often have multiple audiences in mind when preparing their remarks. The capacity of the departments to understand what the president means and to believe that he really means it should never be taken for granted.

One other problem discussed by close to a third of the White House aides (again, see table 6.1.2) was that their administration tried to do too much too fast. Even President Johnson was quoted to this effect in the last days of his presidential term. It was not that Great Society programs were ill-intentioned or misplaced, but rather that not enough planning had preceded implementation. One veteran budget counselor to presidents explained his view of the conflict this way:

> Too much was attempted under LBJ. We didn't ask ourselves enough questions about whether we could do these things. Expectations outran the capability to work things out. There were too many other demands or problems in the mid- and late 60s. Vietnam, inadequately trained manpower at all levels of government, and the structure of intergovernmental relations was inadequate. The space and missile programs had the backing of the people, but public support was terribly splintered over the War on Poverty, etc. . . . It was like a Tower of Babel with no one interested in the other people's programs.

If the departments are, in fact, occasionally "parochial" in their behavior, presidents and presidential staff can often be overly "political" in their behavior. For example, Nixon's vetoes of various health and education bills—for balancing his political budget—incurred the hostility of several HEW officials. Likewise President Kennedy's highly political decision to support federal subsidies for the construction of the Cross-Florida Barge Canal angered many budget and conservation counselors within his own administration. Likewise the typical executive office attitude toward the Agricultural Department—"Keep prices down and the farmers off our back!"—annoyed many department officials who held expansionary hopes for turning their department into a rural development and a major conservation agency. The point to be appreciated in several of these illustrations is that the political perspectives and substantive preferences of presidents and their staffs produce their share of executive branch conflicts.

On Departmental "Sources" of Conflict. There is an increasingly popular view that much of the conflict in the federal executive branch can be explained by the fact that the departments are "specialized, parochial, self-interested," while the president and his advisors have "a government-wide point of view." The extent to which this is the overriding explanation is easily overestimated. White House staff members (whom we would expect to be prime enthusiasts for this interpretation) fault the White House and its operations about as often as they fault the cabinet and the departments.

Approximately half of the White House aides mentioned a seeming inability of many government workers to adopt "the presidential perspective." This latter commodity, always ill-defined, seems capaciously to include "the public interest," responsiveness to the electorate, maturity of judgment, virtue, and wisdom. Whatever all this is, quite a number of the White House policy staff assistants are convinced that department people either do not understand it or just stubbornly resist it. "Mostly the bureaucrats are unresponsive, they view themselves as the professionals and see your [White House] impact as purely political. They don't fight you openly, but they don't cooperate if they can help it!"

Another way for White House aides to explain departmental sources of conflict is to question the competence or loyalty of the cabinet member. Cabinet members get faulted for being "too much of an individualist," "too aloof," "too stubborn," and sometimes for not being "a take charge type." In any event, the traditional complaint that cabinet members get captured by narrow special interests was a frequent response.

One of the most significant factors promoting conflict between the departments and the White House staffs is their different time perspectives. This same variable is also at play in White House-congressional relations. A president and his staff think in terms of two- and four-year time frames—at the most. They strive to fulfill campaign pledges, convention platforms, and earlier announced priorities as soon as possible, seeking always to build a respectable record for forthcoming election campaigns. The haste with which the White House rushed the announcements of the model cities and the teacher corps programs may well have damaged the chances for effective design and launching of these programs. Career civil servants, on the other hand, will be around after the elections regardless of outcomes and, more importantly, they are held accountable to the General Accounting Office, the Office of Management and Budget, or to congressional investigation committees for the way federal programs are administered (and for any mistakes that might be made). The work incentives for most careerists are stacked in the direction of doing a thorough, consistent, and even cautious job rather than any hurried dancing to the current tunes of the White House staff.

Conflict as a Result of Complexity

Nearly all of the White House aide commentary on executive branch conflict can be traced back to problems of government size and problem complexity. White House aides become arrogant and insensitive because they are often asked to do too much in too short a time. White House aides "breathe down the necks" of cabinet and department leaders because presidents become impatient and restless for results. Departments appear inert or unresponsive because they are having difficulty in pulling together diverse specialists to work on complex questions. Cabinet members give the impression of being "weak" (and sometimes are) because they must preside over huge holding companies of diverse, functionally specialized enterprises. White House aides are continuously disillusioned and disappointed by the lack of coordination both within and among departments; but the White House vision of coordination unrealistically presupposes that department people share an understanding of complex problems, and a sophisticated appreciation of the relatedness of one problem to another, of one agency to another. Communications problems exist because large numbers of people are involved in administering programs all over the country and are confronted by constantly changing and shifting circumstances. Legislative or executive intent, or the GAO and Civil Service Commission "rulebooks and regulations," even if they could be memorized, do not have all the answers for all seasons. Uncertainties, changing environment, and shifting priorities all make policy implementation harder (and pleasing the White House near impossible). One White House counselor to President Eisenhower summed up what he refers to as the pervasive fact of political life that continually affected the Eisenhower administration:

> The sheer size and intricacy of government conspire to taunt and to thwart all brisk pretensions to set sensationally new directions. The vast machinery of national leadership—the tens of thousands of levers and switches and gears—simply do not respond to the impatient jab of a finger or the angry pounding of a fist.[11]

There is, finally, the constantly faced dilemma of choosing between competing values. Ideological preferences enter here. That not many White House aides mention ideological factors as a source of conflict may imply that a relatively common political culture unites executive department officialdom with recent members of the presidential government. But there are differences of view, sometimes reflecting political party points of view, but more often reflecting differences about the role of the federal government in solving local or international problems. There is always the problem of making the critical distinction between what the federal government can do and what it cannot do. The occasional quest to push the governmental system to great levels of commitment and compassion gets generated in presidential elections and later by major presidential policy addresses (*e.g.*, the quest *to end* poverty, *to achieve* equality of opportunity, *to renew* our cities, *to help develop* Latin America, *to return power* to the people, and so forth). However, even the "best laid plans" of presidents or Congress often get rescinded because of the "bottlenecks" of problem complexity and jurisdictional interdependency. As White House aides well know, however, "you have to start somewhere"—despite manifest opposition and complexity.

Listening to White House aides' views of these conflicts heightens one's appreciation for the responsibilities of the chief executive. The president has to act, even in the face of uncertainties, complexity, and opposition; eventually the consequences of inaction may outweigh the results of an ill-fated action. The president can ask the right questions, can act as educator, can preside over appropriate compromises, and can do much to shape and sharpen new policy directions, but the constraints on directing an effective application of those policies to problems are enormous. As the general public expects more and more of the presidency, and as its responsibilities for performance become greater and greater, the president is often thrust in the middle of a disillusioning squeeze play.

A Differentiated White House Staff

Much has been written about the continuous growth and increasing importance of the White House staff. The popular verdict is that the White House staff is the "center of the action" within the executive branch, and that it, more than any other body of counselors, is now the prime mechanism for helping presidents shape and execute decisions. We are told that recent White House staffs have included favored assistants who have overshadowed the cabinet executives and challenged the importance of the "distinguished outsiders" to whom previous presidents may have turned. Senior presidential assistants often deny any superordinate status over the cabinet and claim they are there merely to help the president communicate with the departments.

To be sure, White House staff have been quite strategically important in policy formulation stages of federal policy. But their apparent "effectiveness" in this one sphere too often obscures an unimpressive record in policy direction or "follow-through." While White House staff may contribute to the distillation of a vast amount of incubating legislative proposals, congressional subcommittees along with departmental officials are often able to go about the work of steering and administering federal domestic programs with seeming immunity from White House influence.

Presidents, of course, use their staff differently from term to term, and from one season to the next. But several generalizations about the White House staff in the 1960s can be suggested. It is my estimate that the patterns of continuity and similarity of the way recent presidents (1960-1971) have organized and used their White House staffs far outweighed the differences. First, while the role of the White House staff has grown generally, its greatest increase in responsibility has been in information gathering and "policy distillation" activities: the culling of new ideas from task force and advisory group reports, the drafting of legislative messages, and the subsequent design of legislative strategies. As mentioned above, the execution or direction of far-flung federal enterprises have been less easily assumed by the White House (although there have been attempts). Second, the increased importance of the White House staff in policy making comes not so much at the expense of cabinet and departmental influence, as in proportion to the measurably expanding commitments of the federal government. Furthermore, just as current White House staff are significantly more important as a collectivity than most previous presidential staff, contemporary department leaders (excepting perhaps one or two) have vastly increased mandates, more administrative responsibilities, and larger staffs of their own than did their predecessors of some twenty or forty years ago. Finally, relatively few White House aides enjoy anything near the prominence of the more important members of the cabinet. Under recent presidents, only a small number of White House aides (ranging from six to a dozen) have had close and frequent access to the president. In practice, the large majority of White House aides deal much more frequently with sub-cabinet and cabinet secretariat staffs than directly with cabinet members. And White House aides have their largest influence on matters of small importance or in matters with which the president is indifferent.

The day of the "general purpose aide" with an entirely undefined portfolio seems a thing of the past for White House staff. To be sure, many of the White House jurisdictions are not rigidly prescribed, but those claiming to be generalists thrive not "at large," but in particular functional or substantive assignment areas, within, for example, public relations, foreign policy, or domestic program areas. It is easier than one might suspect to divide recent White House staff into five relatively distinct functional operations. (More could be defined, but a typology of five is sufficient for our purposes.) Overlapping assignments do exist and not a few White House aides claim they serve (or served) as bridges between factions within the staff. But with rare exceptions, presidential aides can be identified as members of one of the following staff units: (1) domestic policy and legislative program, (2) budget and economic policy, (3) national security and foreign policy, (4) congressional relations, and (5) administrative and public relations.[12]

As seen in table 6.1.3, perceptions of executive branch conflict vary quite measurably with the type of White House task assignment. The White House aides with more programmatic or policy oriented responsibilities are far more likely to observe "considerable conflict" with the departments than are the more political or public relations staff assistants to presidents. Is this just because they have more contact with the departments? Or is the nature of the work assignment responsible? Or is the type of man who is likely to be cast in one job at the White House basically different from the type of man he must deal with in the departments? A closer examination of this differentiated White House staff (at least as it existed from 1961-1970) may suggest some of the features about White House work and staff "operational codes" which both make life difficult within the White House and shape varying performances.

Domestic Policy and Legislative Program Staff.

Recent developments have had the effect of enhancing the need for a larger and more professional domestic policy and legislative program staff: the sheer growth of federal domestic programs, the fact that the initiative for setting the budget and formulating legislation has swung over to the president, and

Table 6.1.3

Varying Staff Perceptions of Conflict in Presidency—Executive Department Relations, with Staff Functions Held Constant

Presidency Staff Functional Groupings

Levels of Conflict	Domestic Policy & Legis. Prog. N = (12)	Budget/ Economic (6)	National Security/ Foreign (8)	Congress Relations (5) (Total N = 43)	Admin. Public Relations Staffs (12)
Considerable	100%	83%	75%	20%	25%
Moderate	0	17	12.5	80	50
Insignificant	0	0	12.5	0	25
	100%	100%	100%	100%	100%

Source: *Personal Interviews of White House Staff Members serving between 1961 and 1970.*

the vast increase in jurisdictional questions which are raised by multi-departmental programs such as model cities, mass transit, manpower training, early childhood education, and environmental protection. Another new dimension of White House staff domestic policy work has been the increased use and major reliance on presidential advisory networks outside of existing channels (*i.e.*, besides those within or connected with the executive departments).

Most of the Kennedy and Johnson domestic policy staff members were trained as lawyers (see table 6.1.4). Most also had previous and sometimes extensive Washington experience; the Kennedy aides came directly from the campaign and from Capitol Hill staff positions, the Johnson aides mainly came from within the executive departments. Many had both legislative and executive branch work experience. Presidents Kennedy and Johnson used their domestic policy staff to summarize and analyze departmental proposals, refine conflicting views (insofar as possible), and generally define issues or proposals that deserved presidential attention. The domestic policy staff have been particulary sensitive to the fact that they should help the

Table 6.1.4

Background Characteristics of Various White House Staff Groupings During the 1960s

Background Factors	Staff Groupings				
	Domestic Policy & Legis. Prog. N = (12)	Budget/ Economic (6)	Nat. Security, For. Affairs (8)	Congress. Relations (5)	Administrative Personal Staff (12)
				(Total N = 43)	
Lawyer	75%*	0%	0%	40%	17%
Economist	0	50	50	0	0
University Professor	8	50	38	0	0
Public Relations Journalist	0	0	0	0	58
Former Congressional Staffer	42	0	12	20	33
Former Executive Branch Employment	75	100	75	40	17
Political Activist	50	0	25	100	67

Source: *Personal Interviews*
  *Percentages to be read down the column.

president "make his decisions [based] on the full range of *his* considerations and constituencies, which no cabinet member shared." These staff usually see their works in terms of "getting things started," "getting bills to Capitol Hill," and later, once programs start getting enacted, "making things work."

The domestic aides, more frequently than any other group within the White House, usually fashion a distinctively adversary relationship with their counterparts in the domestic executive departments. Patrick Anderson captures some of the disquietude toward Johnson aide Califano:

> Serving as the chief expediter for an impatient and demanding president, Califano has made many enemies. Cabinet members seeking to carry an issue to the president are often told to "talk to Joe" and this breeds resentment. Part of Califano's job is to knock heads together, and this wins him no friends among those whose heads are knocked. Some cabinet members call him "Little Joe" behind his back, and they say it without smiling. Others who have crossed his path have called him a "hatchet man," and worse.[13]

These White House staff tend to be younger than the cabinet and senior civil servants with whom they conduct most of their business. Invariably, the White House lawyers explicitly view themselves as counsels to the president (who, of course, is "their" client). Often these lawyers interrogate or prod "their" departmental adversaries much in the spirit of the prosecuting attorney and, with the same tutored and dispassionate disregard for niceties, they soon earn the disapproval of many a departmental official. Priding themselves on possessing a superior capacity to think analytically, and the insight and foresight of that mysterious element called the "presidential perspective," White House domestic policy lawyers often view themselves as the necessary and indispensable catalysts who must stimulate and prod the departments into compliance with presidential intentions. Insensitive and arrogant as this appears, these aides are encouraged in this behavior by their perceptions of the constant need for speed, and by an often disillusioned and disbelieving president hardened by his inability to bend departmental bureaucracies in the direction of his policy priorities.

Budget and Economic Counselors

During the 1960s several members of the Council of Economic Advisers and of the Budget Bureau directorate functioned as full-fledged members of the White House staff. The previous distinctions between "Executive Office of the President" and "White House staff" became increasingly blurred as the White House domestic policy lawyers needed more sophisticated counsel on unemployment, tax policy, inflation control, and numerous related questions involved in "managing" the national economy. Concomitantly, budget directors and economists—assigned to the Executive Office—assumed a presidential perspective largely indistinguishable from that of senior White House policy aides.

Budget Bureau leadership in the past decade was recruited from among the economics profession or from respected "old hands" who successfully worked themselves up the career ladder within the Bureau. In theory at least, the president's domestic aides and political counselors serve the short term, immediate policy interests of *a president*, whereas the Budget Bureau serves the longer term perspective of *the presidency*, with particular responsibilities for program evaluation and budgeting analysis. By the mid-1960s both the Bureau of the Budget and the Council of Economic Advisers were involved in White House program formulation tasks as well as in quasi-operational activities such as inflation control or anti-poverty program activities. As these so-called Executive Office "staff" became increasingly involved in White House and cabinet-level operations, the distinctions between White House and "Executive Office of the President" *and* the distinctions between presidential *staff* and executive branch *management* became at best hazy, and often confusing.

The Bureau of the Budget—now the Office of Management and Budget—has long played a central role (although with differing success) as an intermediary between White House and the departments. The Bureau has been expected to raise tough questions about program promise and performance: "What will this program really do?"; "Why has this program taken so long to get off the ground?"; "Why does this cost so much?"; "Why haven't you been in closer collaboration with other departments on this part of that program?"; and so forth. Not surprisingly, and in no small part intentionally, these investigative questions and the budgetary examination processes themselves beget a more or less adversary relationship with the departments. Moreover, presidents and their senior White House staff assistants expect their budget and economic advisors to identify and bring to their attention department inconsistencies and specific program activities that run counter to the president's intentions.

Budget officials, even more than White House staff domestic policy aides, are now well accustomed to their often unfashionable role as the "abominable no-men" of the executive branch. Presidents frequently transmit some of their most unpleasant decisions for cabinet leaders *via* Budget Bureau leadership. One former director points out that conflict between the departments and the Budget Bureau is not only inevitable but, on balance, healthy. How else can you ferret out all the problems and possibilities? Said another Budget Bureau leader: "There is actually an inverse relationship between a cabinet member's effectiveness for the administration and his popularity with the Budget Bureau." That is to say, malleable and agreeable department people probably lack the capability for inventing and incubating needed new policy proposals and/or managerial strategies.

National Security and Foreign Policy Staff

It might seem that the president's national security staff would enjoy more harmonious relationships with "their" executive departments than is the case between the domestic policy staff and the domestic departments. Presumably the national security staff deals primarily with only two departments, State and Defense, in contrast to domestic policy aides who must deal with about ten departments plus numerous independent agencies. Moreover, it is generally held that the president is granted much greater leeway in determination of foreign policy than is the case in the various domestic policy spheres. But such a view is somewhat deceptive, for the Defense Department alone is really several departments rolled into one huge umbrella, employing at least three times as many *civilians* (not to mention military personnel) as the entire list of domestic departments (with the Post Office now excluded). In practice, the White House national security staff has responsibilities for at least seven or eight major departments and agencies, including Defense, State, Central Intelligence Agency, the Military (joint chiefs of staff), the United States Information Agency, the Agency for International Development, and frequently, when appropriate, for Treasury, Agriculture, and Commerce as well.

The hope that a strong secretary of state and a well organized State Department could act as the central coordinator for United States foreign policy has grown increasingly unrealistic. Contemporary presidents have generally held that United States national security policy is and must be presidential policy and, concomitantly, there has been a major shift in policy formulation and direction to the White House and away from the various departments.

All recent presidents have relied heavily on their national security staffs for keeping in close communication with the executive agencies making up the national security establishment.

White House Congressional Relations Staff

White House congressional relations aides differ from their fellow staff having substantive policy responsibilities in several ways. Their concern is less with policy formulation than it is with policy promotion. While the program and policy staff are busy trying to win support and cooperation for White House policy interests within the departments, congressional relations aides spend their time seeking political support from within congressional committees and among diverse factions on Capitol Hill. Not surprisingly, program and congressional liaison aides sometimes differ over the relative merits and feasibility of newly suggested program ideas. And at least under the recent Democratic administrations, the congressional relations aides have frequently mirrored the more conservative views of congressional chairmen in internal White House staff deliberations. Congressional relations aides only infrequently pay attention to policy implementation activities and on those occasions, more often than not, they argue the case as viewed on Capitol Hill to their White House colleagues.

Several factors help explain the congressional relations staff's more moderate estimates of contention between White House and departments. First, the White House congressional relations staff by vocation are far more geared to political accommodation and compromise than others on the White House staff. Consensus-building rather than policy incubation and program generation is their life style and preoccupation. They define their task as helping the president get his program passed by Congress. They consciously work for the reelections of the president (or his party) and the president's supporters within the Congress. To these ends they necessarily seek to minimize conflict and maximize cohesion. A reasonably unified executive branch is an added advantage for successful enactment of major legislation. Division and dissension within or among these departments will usually hurt a bill's chances for passage. Because they, more than any other staff at the White House, are conscious of the ingredients (*i.e.,* new proposals) that go into the making of the box scores of wins and losses that (albeit simplistically) characterize presidential-congressional relations, the legislative liaison aides favor "practical" proposals. While domestic and budget White House staff often remain disappointed by the dearth of new ideas or the hesitancy of the president to back a controversial proposal, the congressional relations officers are more easily satisfied by modest accomplishments and are also less inclined to encourage new or complicated legislative initiatives that might be difficult to pass—"we obviously don't want to be put in the position of having to sell programs that don't have a reasonable chance of passing."

Second, at least during the 1960s, the congressional relations officials had explicitly designated lieutenants in all major departments. For the most part these department officers were loyal partisans who owe allegiance almost equally to their cabinet members *and* to the White House congressional relations office, for the White House legislative liaison team had authority to remove or fire departmental legislative relations aides. These department contacts frequently had "graduated" to their posts from campaign or Capitol Hill staff work. In general, the White House staff enjoyed cordial and close (often with weekly meetings) relations with these "compatible" counterparts in the departments. In marked contrast with the White House domestic and budget aides it was quite rare for the White House congressional relations aides to have much if any contact with non-partisan civil servants or "bureaucrats." To some extent, their departmental lieutenants took the brunt of and absorbed department conflicts, thereby leaving the White House congressional relations aides relatively free to deal with senior congressional officials and preside over White House-congressional relations strategies.

Finally, the primary preoccupation of White House congressional relations aides is dealing with the leadership and committee chairmen in Congress. Since congressional aides are employed first and foremost to help forge viable coalitions of congressional support from bill to bill and from one legislative season to the next, their chief opposition consists of dissident members of their own party or influential opponents on the other side of the congressional aisle. Departmental concerns, especially departmental debates about alternative programs, are less appreciated and probably less well understood by congressional relations White House aides; these latter concerns necessarily take a back seat to their principal attention which is devoted to congressional and partisan strategy and tactics. In sum, then, both the fact that congressional relations aides have less actual contact with cabinet members and civil servants and the fact that they have distinctively different functional responsibilities account for less perceived conflict with departments.

Administrative and Public Relations Staff

As can be seen in table 6.1.3, the nonpolicy administrative and personal staff assistants to the president were the least disposed to see serious conflict between the White House and the departments. Strictly speaking, no one on the White House staff is far removed from policy matters, but in a relative sense, there is measurable variation in staff involvement in detailed substantive policy deliberations. We now have White House organizations with large staffs of communication specialists, campaign counselors, ceremony coordinators, and dozens of others who handle speechwriting, mail, T.V. and radio arrangements, travel arrangements, and so forth. One reason for their "happier" evaluation of departmental relations is that they are measurably less involved with the vast executive establishment. Their contact with the departments is either with the usually responsive Office of the Secretary or with their own carefully planted network of political aides.

It is not so much that many of these aides do not have some problems in their relations with department officials as it is that they have grown accustomed to accentuating the positive. That is, they are hired to secure maximum press and TV coverage for presidential accomplishments and, not surprisingly, to insure that the appealing rather than the appalling stories, the harmonious rather than the contentious character of a presidential administration are communicated to the American general public. Just as congressional relations aides experienced their conflicts more with certain members of Congress rather than departmental officials, so also many, if not most, of the administrative and public relations aides to presidents have their occupational difficulties with columnists, editors, and TV commentators outside the government rather than with department officials inside the government.

A Differentiated Cabinet

In the previous section it is suggested that the differentiated White House staff organization may be one of the contributing factors to the variance in staff perceptions of conflict with the departments. So also it is likely that diversity and dissimilarity of the executive departments may also contribute to a variance in White House staff perceptions of conflict. An essential premise here is that an understanding of White House-departmental relations must take into account the differences in the way cabinet and department roles are viewed from the White House.

Though the cabinet is not mentioned in the United States Constitution, presidents have appointed and consulted with their department heads ever since George Washington began the practice. President Washington actively solicited advice and counsel from his three department heads—State, Treasury, and War. In time he called these three together with his part-time attorney general (who continued a private practice on the side). Subsequently, cabinet meetings became tradition and almost all presidents used their cabinets as a political sounding board and as a convenient communications network. Over time, the cabinet changed greatly, especially affected by its growth from three to a dozen departmental members by 1967. While the notion of a cohesive presidential cabinet of collegial and interchangeable advisors persists with remarkable staying power, the cabinet as a collectivity has rarely been a policy making or program coordinating body. Indeed, the cabinet as a meaningful "collectivity" appears to be passing into oblivion (though not out of existence). And as Rossiter predicted more than twenty years ago, in its place there has grown up "a congeries of functional cabinets with reduced and appropriate membership."[14] The following discussion sketches several variables that undoubtedly affected White House assessments of and working relations with the cabinet departments under recent presidential administrations.

Any discussion of the cabinet, of course, should note that personality and individual levels of competence often affect the degree to which cordiality exists between White House and departments. Each cabinet usually has one or two cabinet members who excel in one way or another and become the dominant personalities in their cabinet.

Occasionally, too, there are times when the politics of the period and the functions of a department thrust particular cabinet members into prominence, and simultaneously into close collaborative relations with the White

House. Dean Acheson's unusually close and cordial ties with the Truman White House and Lyndon Johnson's highly respectful appreciation of Dean Rusk illustrate the cases of internationally tense periods in which diplomatic political strategy looms large. Secretary John Gardner (HEW 1965-68) enjoyed great prominence and relatively good relations with the Johnson White House during the middle 1960s around the time in which major educational and health legislation were being ratified and placed into operation. Soon thereafter, however, when the Vietnam war began overshadowing all else and consuming more and more of the president's time and potential budget increases, White House communications with HEW's Gardner began to resemble those of most other domestic cabinet members—less frequent and less supportive.

The rise in prominence or fashion of an issue relevant to a department's activities can occasionally also work to the detriment of White House-department relations. The "law and order" issue in the late 1960s occasioned cutting partisan attacks to be mounted against President Johnson's attorney general. Ramsey Clark resisted most temptations to act in any retaliatory or repressive manner. But, evidently, Clark's response was viewed as overly dispassionate and tolerant by his president. And the more recent case of former Secretary Walter Hickel and his varied efforts apparently illustrates the case of a cabinet member who decides to champion popular issues (environmental protection and youth) measurably further than the administration of which he is a part.

There are, of course, numerous other reasons why presidents and their staff may deliberately choose to have "cool" relations with a cabinet member. Sometimes this may be due to presidential lack of interest in a department's domain. Sometimes there is ill will existing between a strong president and a strong and quite stubborn cabinet member. Part of the problem undoubtedly arises because presidents just don't have time to spend with cabinet officers, not to mention the leaders of independent agencies and major bureau chiefs. The blunt fact of the contemporary period is that approximately two-thirds of presidential time has been spent on national security and foreign policy considerations.

An apparent pattern characterizes White House-cabinet relations over time. Just as there is a distinctive presidential "honeymoon" with the press and with partisan critics, so also White House-department ties usually are the closest and most cooperative during the first year of an administration. The first six months of the relationship is usually cordial, "healthy," and often bordering on the euphoric. The election victory is still being celebrated. A new team of "leaders" has arrived in Washington. New faces provide for extensive news copy. A new federal policy agenda is being recast. The newly staffed executive branch gives everyone an impression of bubbling over with new ideas, new possibilities, and imminent break-throughs. In contrast to the much publicized arrival of the cabinet members, White House staff receive less publicity at this time.

But as policy formulation is accentuated in the early years of a presidential term, program management and implementation receive increasing attention in the later period (especially if a president has been successful in passing a fair amount of new legislation by then). Critical domestic developments and international crises begin to monopolize the presidential schedule. Presidents gradually find that they have much less time for personally dealing with cabinet members than they had in the administration's early months. Cabinet members become less inclined to refer "too much" to the president, knowing full well that they may prematurely exhaust their personal political credit with him. Additionally, the president's program becomes somewhat fixed; priorities get set and budget ceilings produce some new rules of the game. Ambitious, expansionist cabinet officers become painfully familiar with various Executive Office staff refrains, usually to the effect that "There just isn't any more money available for programs of that magnitude," "Budget projections for the next two or three years just can't absorb that type of increment," and perhaps the harshest of all—"Yes, I agree that this is an excellent proposal, but excellent though it may be, it will just have to wait until the next term."

When, in the course of an administration, cabinet members grow bitter about the way they are treated and increasingly left out of White House affairs, they seldom make their opinions public. There are, of course, some exceptions and privately a good number of cabinet officers will talk about the problem. The case of Interior Secretary Walter Hickel is perhaps an extreme case; the fact that he had only two or three private meetings with his president during a two year period seems an unusually restrictive arrangement. Most recent cabinet officers have had more frequent relations with their White House superiors, but few of the domestic cabinet members have been wholly pleased by the quantity or quality of these meetings.

Conventional rankings of the departments are based on their longevity, annual expenditure outlays, or their personnel totals. Rankings according to these indicators can be seen in the first three columns of table 6.1.5. A preliminary appreciation of department diversity can be gained by even a casual comparison of these columns. For example, while the State Department is more than 175 years older than some of the newest departments, its expenditures rank as the lowest of any department. On the other hand, the Department of Health, Education and Welfare, although formally less than twenty years old, ranks second only to Defense in having more personnel and higher annual expenditures.

Some other ways of classifying the departments deserve note. One is suggested by Stewart Alsop's journalistic appraisal of real political "power and impact."[15] Alsop's 1967 ranking takes into account not only the conventional data mentioned above, but also the Washington, D.C., status considerations toward contemporary cabinet members and departmental activities. Upon closer inspection the Alsop listing varies only slightly from longevity or seniority rankings, with minor adjustments added to acknowledge the higher budget allocations of Defense and HEW as well as the personal Washington "celebrity" status of Robert S. McNamara and John W. Gardner (HEW).

The contemporary cabinet can also be differentiated into "inner" and "outer" departmental clusterings as illustrated in the fifth column of table 6.1.5. The inner cabinet, at least throughout the 1960s, was generally recognized as the primary presidential counseling as well as strategic information gathering departments. (A cabinet counselor is a source of information and advice, someone to whom a president can turn for appraisals and consultation on highly sensitive or critical problems.) The outer cabinet are the explicitly domestic policy departments (Justice excepted). By custom, if not by designation, these cabinet officers assume a relatively straight-forward advocate orientation that overshadows their counseling role. (An advocate is someone who argues for a cause, who supports, defends and on occasion pleads in behalf of some special concern.)

State, Defense, Treasury, and Justice, each for different reasons (discussed below), are the cabinet posts most consistently considered as part of the inner cabinet. The pattern in the past few presidential administrations suggests somewhat strongly that these counseling cabinet positions are vested with high priority responsibilities that almost naturally bring presidents and their top staff into close and continually collaborative relations with the occupants of these inner cabinet leadership posts. Sorensen wrote that it was the "nature of their responsibilities and the competence with which they did their jobs" that brought certain department executives particularly close to President Kennedy in this counseling manner. Speaking of the Eisenhower period, Emmet J. Hughes sees a convergence of raw strength of personality and leadership with the Defense, Treasury, and State cabinet posts. Sorensen cites six cabinet members as enjoying particularly close ties to John Kennedy, and one gathers that the general order of their importance and closeness to Kennedy amounted to this: Defense Secretary Robert McNamara, Attorney General Robert Kennedy, Secretary of State Dean Rusk, Treasury Secretary Douglas Dillon, and in varying ways Labor Secretary Arthur Goldberg and Vice-President Lyndon Johnson. And it is abundantly clear that Rusk and McNamara continued to hold superordinate status in the Lyndon Johnson cabinet vis-à-vis their cabinet colleagues. On balance, the period between 1961 and 1971 can be characterized by having had an "inner cabinet" group made up of the Defense, State, and Treasury secretaries along with the attorney general. Then, too, as will be discussed a little later, certain White House staff counselors were also included in an inner circle if not in the inner cabinet.

The inner cabinet grouping of this inner/outer breakdown suggested here corresponds

Table 6.1.5

Various Ways of Viewing the Executive Departments

Seniority	Expenditures[a]	Personnel[b]	A Journalist's Assessment of "Real Political Power & Impact"[c]
1 State	1 Defense	1 Defense	1 Defense
2 Treasury	2 HEW	2 HEW	2 State
3 War/Defense	3 Treasury	3 Agriculture	3 Treasury
4 Justice	4 Agriculture	4 Treasury	4 Justice
5 Interior	5 Labor	5 Interior	5 Interior
6 Agriculture	6 Transportation	6 Transportation	6 HEW
7 Commerce	7 HUD	7 State	7 Labor
8 Labor	8 Commerce	8 Justice	8 Agriculture
9 HEW	9 Justice	9 Commerce	9 Commerce
10 HUD	10 Interior	10 HUD	10 HUD
11 Transportation	11 State	11 Labor	11 Transportation

Inner & Outer Clusterings[d]	Super-Cabinet Plan A[e]	Super-Cabinet Plan B[f]	President Nixon's 1971 Proposals[g]
{ State, Defense, Treasury, Justice }	National Security, Economic Stability and Growth, Domestic Policy	Foreign Affairs, Economic Affairs, Natural Resources, Science and Technology, Social Services and Justice	{ State, Defense, Treasury, Justice }
{ Agriculture, Interior, Transportation, HEW, HUD, Labor, Commerce }			{ Human Resources, Natural Resources, Economic Development, Community Development }

[a] *Estimated budget outlays of the executive departments in 1971.*
[b] *Statistical Abstract, data for 1970.*
[c] *See S. Alsop, The Center 254 (1968).*
[d] *Generic clustering according to counseling/advocacy dimensions—see text discussion.*
[e] *The way some White House aides view aggregate departmental concerns, and the apparent priority of these concerns as viewed by recent presidents.*
[f] *An example of cabinet consolidation that is one of many plausible but politically unlikely reforms.*
[g] *Richard M. Nixon, State of the Union message to Congress, January 22, 1971.*

identically to George Washington's original foursome, to Stewart Alsop's journalistic appraisal, and also to Sorensen's account of the Kennedy administration. Moreover, the inner cabinet departments were the only ones immune to President Nixon's proposed overhaul of the executive branch; all others were nominated for abolition. My own classification of inner/outer derives from the examination of how White House aides viewed the departments. The status accorded these cabinet roles is, of course, subject to ebb and flow, for the status is rooted in performance and the fashions of the day as well as reputation. But, in general, White House staff during the 1960s acted far more deferentially toward these inner cabinet positions and the men who occupied them than toward outer cabinet officials.

With the exception of the State *Department*, as distinguished from the *Office of the Secretary* of State, the inner cabinet and the inner cabinet departments were almost always viewed as executive branch allies of the White House staff. An implicit operational code to this effect seemingly guided the manner in which most White House staff aides participated in executive branch activities during the 1960s. For this reason, these ties deserve further attention.

The State and Defense Departments have long been considered counseling and inner-cabinet departments. And the special closeness of Secretaries Rusk and McNamara with both Kennedy and Johnson is illustrative. One Johnson aide said it was his belief that President Johnson personally trusted only two of his cabinet—Rusk and McNamara (though it appears that the trust relationship between Johnson and McNamara diminished somewhat in 1967). Contemporary presidents view national security and foreign policy matters as life and death considerations; President Kennedy, for example, noted that while mistakes in domestic policy "can only defeat us [at the next election, mistakes in] foreign policy can kill us." The seemingly endless series of crises (Berlin, Cuba, Congo, Dominican Republic, Vietnam, and the Middle East, to name just a few) during the 1960s make it mandatory for recent presidents to maintain close relations with these two national security cabinet heads. Just as George Washington had met almost every day with his four "cabinet" members during the national security concern over the French crisis of 1793, so also John Kennedy and Lyndon Johnson were likely to meet at least weekly and be in daily telephone communication with their inner cabinet of national security advisors.

It needs to be added, however, that throughout the past decade there has been more than a little White House discontent with the operational lethargy of the State Department. We see here an anomaly in which the Secretary of State clearly was regarded as a member of the president's inner cabinet, but the Department of State was regarded as one of the most deficient and inadequate cabinet departments. More than twenty-five percent of the White House staff interviewed for this study cited the State Department as an excellent illustration of the problem of White House-department conflicts. White House staff scorned the narrowness and timidity of the encrusted and elitist foreign service officers and complained also of the custodial conservatism reflected in State Department working papers. Part of this problem may stem from the threats and philosophy of the Joseph McCarthy era which intimidated State Department careerists into holding only the puristic interpretations of the accepted policies of the day, thereby inhibiting their imaginative and inventive policy faculties. No doubt, though, part of the problem stems from the way recent secretaries, especially Secretary Rusk, defined their job. The demands on the secretary were such that the State Department and its management were not Rusk's personal top priority. John Leacacos has surmised that the priorities appeared to have been:

> First, the president and his immediate desires; second, the top operations of the current crisis; third, public opinion as reflected in the press, radio and TV and in the vast inflow of letters from the public; fourth, Congressional opinion; fifth, Rusk's need to be aware, at least, of everything that was going on in the world; and only sixth and last, the routine of the State Department itself.[16]

The fact that the Secretary of State so frequently serves as the president's representative abroad or his number one witness on foreign policy matters before the Congress undoubtedly is another reason so few Secretaries of State have had the time or energy available for managing the State Department's widely scattered staff. It needs to be added that more than sixty federal departments, agencies, and committees are involved some way in the administration of our foreign policy. Recent presidents increasingly have vested authority in their own White House-based NSC staff partly to compensate for State's uneven performance as a coordination arm for foreign policy matters and partly because presidents need instant analysis during international crisis periods. In this regard, McGeorge Bundy's White House national security staff was dubbed by the press as "Bundy's little State Department." In another step to centralize and coordinate basic foreign policy activities, Richard Nixon has instituted a White House-level Council of International Economic Policy with broad authorities. Nonetheless, the Secretary of State still enjoys a relative closeness to the incumbent president and even with the rise in importance of White House national security counselors the Secretary of State is likely to continue as a full-fledged member of future presidential inner cabinets.

The Justice Department, also a counseling department, is frequently identified with the "inner circle" of cabinet agencies and its chieftains usually associated with the inner cabinet. That both Kennedy and Nixon appointed their most trusted campaign managers to the attorney generalship is an indicator of the importance of this position as a presidential counseling location. The Justice Department traditionally serves as the president's attorney and lawyer. This special obligation results in continually close professional relations between White House domestic policy lawyers and Justice Department lawyers. Few people realize that the White House is constantly dependent on Justice Department lawyers for counsel on civil rights development, presidential veto procedures, tax prosecutions, anti-trust controversies, presidential pardons recommendations, regulatory agency oversight, and a continual overview of the congressional judiciary committees. That this particular exchange sees lawyer working with lawyer may well account for some of the generally higher levels of satisfaction characterizing White House-Justice Department transactions.

The Treasury Department continues to play an all-important role as an interpreter of the nation's leading financial interests and as key presidential advisor on both domestic and international fiscal and monetary policy considerations. At one time, of course, the Bureau of the Budget existed within Treasury. Now the budget staff and numerous economists, particularly within the Council of Economic Advisers, are attached to the White House itself, thereby somewhat diminishing the monopoly of economic counsel once available only from the Treasury. But Treasury is a department with major institutional authority, having considerable responsibility for income and corporate tax administration, currency control, public borrowing, and counseling the president with respect to questions of balance of gold, the federal debt and international trade, development, and monetary matters. By custom, if not by law, the Secretary of the Treasury sits in on deliberations of important national security controversies. Indeed, Treasury Secretary Douglas Dillon played a significant role in Kennedy's Cuban Missile Crisis policy determinations. There is here, as in the case of the Justice Department lawyers, a common professional linkage among economists and financial specialists at Treasury and their professional counterparts on the White House staff.

The inner circle of cabinet members are noticeably more interchangeable than the outer circle cabinet. Henry Stimson, for example, alternated from Taft's Secretary of War to Hoover's Secretary of State and then back once more as FDR's Secretary of the War Department. Dean Acheson was an FDR Under Secretary of the Treasury but later a Truman Secretary of State. C. Douglas Dillon reversed this pattern by being an Eisenhower Under Secretary of State and later a Kennedy Secretary of the Treasury. When Kennedy was trying to lure Robert McNamara to his new cabinet he offered McNamara his choice between Defense and Treasury. More recently, former Attorney General Nicholas Katzenbach went from Justice to an Under Secretaryship of State, and former Attorney General William Rogers is now the thirteenth Justice Department head to have served in another inner cabinet position. John Connally, once a Secretary of the Navy, became a Nixon Secretary of the Treasury. There have been occasional shifts between inner and outer cabinet (*e.g.*, Harriman—Commerce to State, and Richardson—State to HEW), but such examples are an exception to the general pattern. What this interchangeability means is hard to discern, but it suggests perhaps that presidents find it easier as well as more necessary to work with inner cabinet members and that inner cabinet members find it easier for their part to adopt a counseling style that allows them to identify more closely with the presidential "perspective" than is the case for outer cabinet members.

Quite related to the interchangeability of inner cabinet roles is the little-appreciated fact that, at least in recent years, White House staff aides recruited from within the executive branch have come mainly from among the inner-cabinet departments, often directly from service as assistants to cabinet members. And many of the recent White House staff who did not come from the executive branch had served (at one time or another) as departmental consultants to inner cabinet officials.

In recent years several members of the White House staff have performed cabinet-level counselor roles. Eisenhower, for example, explicitly designated Sherman Adams as a protocol member of his cabinet. Kennedy clearly looked upon Theodore Sorensen, McGeorge Bundy, and some of his economic advisors as co-equals if not more vital to his work than most of his cabinet members. Johnson and Nixon have likewise assigned many of their "staff" men to cabinet-type counseling responsibilities. Indeed, President Nixon, quite reasonably, has appropriated this term—cabinet counselor—for several of his personal staff, including Messrs. Burns, Moynihan, Harlow, and Finch. These counselors, whether in department posts or on the White House staff, are expected to rise above the narrowing frame of reference of the conventional advocate and, in Moynihan's view, "It is not enough [that they] know one subject, one department. The president's men must know them all, must understand how one thing relates to another, must find in the words the spirit that animates them." The people to whom presidents turn for White House overview presentations to congressmen and cabinet gatherings provide another indicator of inner "cabinet" status. When Kennedy wanted to have his cabinet briefed on his major priorities, he would typically ask Secretary of State Dean Rusk to review foreign affairs considerations, Chairman of the Council of Economic Advisers Walter Heller would review major questions about the economy, and Ted Sorensen might sum up and give a status report on the domestic legislative program. In like manner, when Lyndon Johnson would hold special "seminars" for large gatherings of congressmen and their staffs, he would invariably call upon the Secretaries of State and Defense to explain national security matters, and then ask his budget director and his chairman of the Council of Economic Advisers to comment upon economic, budgetary, and domestic program considerations. More recently, President Nixon would typically call upon his Secretary of State, his director of the Office of Management and Budget, and one of his chief White House domestic policy counselors to inform and instruct members of his assembled cabinet and sub-cabinet. These illustrations indicate that recent presidents often believe that members of their own Executive Office are better equipped to talk about and counsel "significant others" regarding the "president's" program rather than let most cabinet members attempt to do the same. Kallenbach's reasoning in this regard seems appropriate:

> [A]s the departments have grown and supervision of their operations has become more burdensome, the heads have less opportunity to concern themselves with questions of general policy outside their own spheres of interest. Another factor is the steady enlargement of the cabinet group itself. . . . This creates a condition which tends to induce the president to rely more heavily upon one or more individuals in the group for general advice, rather than upon all equally.[17]

What has generally happened in recent years is that the Secretaries of State and Defense still remain as prominent national security advisors though the National Security Assistant to the President has joined them as an inner-circle counselor. In domestic and economic matters Treasury secretaries and most attorney generals still play a major role in rendering advice and broad-ranging policy counsel, but they have been joined in the inner "cabinet" by the budget director, and variously prominent White House and staff economists and domestic policy coordinators. President Nixon's 1971 cabinet reform proposal is an apparent recognition of the problem of the outer cabinet's "distance" from the presidency. His proposals would abolish some of the outer cabinet departments and attempt to bring four newly packaged or consolidated "outer" departments into closer proximity if not full-fledged status with his inner cabinet. It is impossible to tell whether his recommendations will make any significant difference in this regard, although his motives for proposing this change are no doubt related to the seemingly estranged relationships between the outer departments and the White House.

The outer cabinet is the collection of cabinet posts and departments most often nominated as candidates for reform or abolition. These are the cabinet posts that experience the great cross pressures from clientele groups and congressional interests that often run counter to presidential interests or priorities. It is the outer cabinet departments that have the most intensive and competitive exchange with White House and Budget Bureau staff, and many an outer cabinet member has complained bitterly about the political pressures on and unmanageability of their departments.

Most of the White House domestic and budget policy aides interviewed for this study cited five departments as the ones with which they had the most difficult or truculent working relations—HEW, HUD, Labor, Commerce, and Interior. Invariably, the White House staff suspects that outer cabinet departmental executives often accentuate the concerns of their department and their department's more obvious clientele over the concerns that might be broadly ascribed to the president or the president's party.

Most of the reform proposals espoused by White House aides (two of which are noted as columns 6 and 7 in table 6.1.5), would reduce the number of cabinet posts in the hope of strengthening the president's ties with the outer cabinet and increasing the stature of the outer cabinet vis-à-vis the inner cabinet. The implicit (but by no means clear) assumption behind most of these reforms is that the fundamental conflict in the executive branch is not between the president and various cabinet members, but rather between special and general (or presidential) interests. Some of the outer cabinet departments could and perhaps will eventually be collapsed into a few broader purpose departments. Alternatives depicted in table 6.1.5 indicate that department reduction could conceivably be pushed to five or even three basic core departments (even more "revolutionary" than the Nixon proposals). As is usually the case, talk about the need to reform and the move in this direction (however gradual) has been preceded by an implicit or unconscious set of practices that have already recognized a distinctively differentiated cabinet. The way White House aides define their work and how presidents allocate their time and energy indicate that there currently exist three specialized "cabinet" concentrations—national security, aggregate economics, and domestic policy affairs. And at least during the 1960s it happened that these three areas were attended to in approximately this same order of importance or deference.

In the future it is likely that regardless of how organization charts are drawn, presidential use of the cabinet and White House staff will take into greater consideration the realities of the differentiated roles and activities of the federal departments. It is likely, too, that presidents will move in the direction of utilizing specialized "cabinets" for concentrated purposes of the federal government. This is to say, the generalized cabinet will more or less pass into oblivion as a national security "cabinet," an economics directorate, and a domestic policy "cabinet" continue to emerge, each of which will be presided over by some combination of presidential counselors, some based in redesigned executive departments and others located on the president's personal staff. Cabinet advocates will surely still exist, but it may be possible to have them operate from posts within rather than on top of the executive departments. (It may well turn out, of course, that these concentrated and realigned cabinets will find that their internal rivalries become so intense and so often tumultuous that new reform movements will then champion the goal of breaking up the super-cabinet framework.) On balance, the White House staff for the forseeable future is not likely to become much smaller or see its importance measurably diminished by these reorganizational developments, but a redesigned and consolidated outer cabinet might enable White House staff to abstain more often from the temptation of pulling administrative responsibilities into itself than has been the case in the last ten years.

Strengthening White House-Department Relations?

There is little difficulty in establishing the existence of considerable White House frustration with department "unresponsiveness" or parochialism and the existence of cabinet and department distress at the sometimes unnecessarily political and abrasive behavior of the White House staff. But it is much less easy to evaluate the varied prescriptions that are put forth as a means toward improving White House-department relations.

We have seen in preceding sections that there is no one single cause of White House-department conflicts; moreover there is no one simple solution. Indeed, it would seem reasonable that the appropriate reforms will vary not only with the type of problem but also according to staff functions at the White House and the differentiated departments involved. Most of the White House aides at least implicitly acknowledge that numerous remedial or regenerating efforts are needed within the White House as well as between the White House and departments.

Many former presidential aides began their discussion of reforms by pointing out the obvious: no two presidents are exactly alike; styles differ as well as policy preferences. Hence, "each president should organize his office more or less as he sees fit."

As seen in table 6.1.6, rather than uniformly calling for the presidential or "more power to the White House" perspective, these aides support what might be called an integration model just as much, and many of them support a department/cabinet approach as well. Almost eighty percent of the domestic and budget policy aides offered suggestions that would strengthen White House policy planning and management capabilities. Even those who complained about White House staff arrogance often concluded that presidents must have tough and aggressive staff help.

Although there is a good deal of overlap between those supporting the presidential and integrative perspectives, the integration approach was relatively more supported among the administrative and public relations assistants and among the national security policy aides than among the domestic and budget policy advisers. Integrative recommendations are seemingly based on the assumption that the White House is not likely to have much of an effect on federal program implementation unless it can win supportive cooperation from among the middle and higher echelons of the executive branch departments.

Some forty percent of the former White House staff aides noted that a strong presidency could only succeed in an executive branch which also was characterized by the existence of strong cabinet and departmental leadership. Many of these aides felt that Kennedy, and Johnson, and their senior staff had neglected the cabinet members and underestimated their importance in making the government work. One aide insisted that it was a major mistake to let the domestic cabinet departments become so divorced from the White House:

> One way to improve things is to have the president and the cabinet members, particularly in domestic areas, meet at least six or seven times a year and talk in great detail, and in highly substantive terms, about the major priorities of the administration. You have to have better communication. Basically you have to make the cabinet less insecure.

Other aides criticized certain of their colleagues for having taken over operational responsibilities of the regular agencies, adding that too often these aides neither expedited program implementation nor accomplished anything else except possibly enlarging their

Table 6.1.6

Presidency Staff Perspectives on the Question of Improving Cooperation and Reducing Conflict Between White House and the Executive Departments

Strategy Perspectives[b]	*Percentages*[a] $N = 43$
I. Presidential Perspective:	
— Stronger WH Management-Monitoring System	45%
— More Aggressive WH Sanctions and Controls over Executive Departments	41
— Stronger WH Policy Determinating Capability	33
II. Integrative Perspective:	
— Make It More of a "Two-Way Street"	45
— More Collaboration and Departmental Involvement in Policy Setting	40
— More WH Staff Sensitivity and Homework Re: Intra-Departmental Concern	36
III. Departmental—Cabinet Perspective:	
— Strengthen Cabinet Secretaries and Cabinet-President Linkage	26
— Delegate More to Departments—Less WH Interference and Primacy; More Trust and Better Communications	24

Source: Personal Interviews of White House Staff Members Who Served During 1961-1970 period.
[a]Percentages here reflect multiple responses.
[b]Aggregate responses to the three perspectives were as follows: 69 percent of the respondents recommended the presidential perspective, 69 percent recommended the integrative perspective, and 40 percent recommended the departmental/cabinet perspective.

own importance. Those aides who held sub-cabinet positions in one of the departments or agencies (either before or immediately after they worked on the White House staff) were significantly more sympathetic to the departmental/cabinet perspective than most of their White House colleagues who had not served "in the other fellow's shoes."

Conclusion

A democracy must serve as a forum or arena for the practical and just mediation of conflicts. If our elected chief executive and his lieutenants were not constantly surrounded, or "afflicted," by a wide diversity of conflicts, they would probably be avoiding their legitimate public responsibilities. The conflicts discussed in this paper are those that exist within the executive branch, but it seems fair to assume that executive branch conflicts in large part mirror the existing and potential conflicts of society at large and as such they deserve far more detailed scrutiny. In general, however, we can conclude with Lewis Coser that such conflicts as exist are multilateral rather than unilateral, multidimensional rather than unidimensional, and occasioned by mixed rather than single motives. This paper suggests, if anything, that the conflicts which abound in the executive branch admit no single source, nor are they generated by any one set of political actors or agents. Size, complexity, specialization, and differing policy preferences are but a few of the factors contributing to that richness of contention that often exists within the American executive establishment.

The intent of this paper has been to answer only the most simple and elementary of questions pertaining to conflict and cooperation within the executive branch. It is tempting to pontificate about "solutions" and "remedies" that might ameliorate these conflicts and "strengthen" White House-department relations. But such an exercise would be premature and diversionary from the much needed analysis that must precede sophisticated political engineering. For example, we know little about the impact of conflict on the way public policies are selected and applied, or the conditions under which conflict in the executive branch is useful or necessary or valuable rather than a liability. It might be feasible to devise some indicators or scales on which to measure the amount and intensity of conflict, and the degree to which it helps or hinders certain sets of actors or certain sets of preferences within given decisional arenas. The very definition of conflict deserves more attention: how to distinguish between *routine* and *critical* conflicts; is there a point at which creative or constructive conflict becomes debilitating to the institutions within which they have been fostered? What are the effects of varied types of conflicts on system stability, system renewal, and system innovation?

But having duly displayed the appropriately detached professional caution, let me at least stick a toe into the water, and indulge just a little in a few suggestions that emerge from this analysis. Some readers may find these suggestions to be mere common sense or unnecessarily overbearing. And to some extent so they are. I would only add that these suggestions are offered in the spirit of experimentation and tentativeness and urge that these too be tested.

Ted Sorensen has written that President John Kennedy was always more interested in policy than in the administration of policies. We can extend that observation to President Johnson and the White House staffs of both presidents as well. The way in which our elections and campaign systems are run makes it easy to accentuate discussions about policy issues rather than policy strategies, and this emphasis seemed overextended during the 1960s. At the beginning of a presidential term White House staffs are initially comprised of policy-generating and policy-distillating activists who attempt to make good on the sweeping proposals that were vaguely articulated in previous campaigns. The emphasis is on policy change and the development of brand new sets of policies rather than the adaptation or improvement of existing policy. It may well be that the initial investment in a staff gathered for the purpose of developing and selling new policies skews the White House counseling resources in such a way that the White House is less effective in managerial and implementation aspects of policy leadership. Since it appears that White House work emphases are somewhat subject to cycles of accentuated policy formulation or accentuated policy implementation, it may be that staffing patterns should similarly be subject to shifting composition. During the Kennedy-Johnson presidencies, however, the internal composition of the staff did not noticeably change. The domestic policy staff, for example, continued to be comprised of youthful Washington lawyers who were geared to putting together new programs for the next state of the Union. But during periods when program implementation and interdepartmental jurisdictional disputes become the overriding concerns of a presidential administration it may not be enough to rely solely upon this type of staff. And to overcome some of the operational deficiencies of major new programs such as those making up the core of the War on Poverty, Alliance for Progress, and Great Society it may not be enough to have White House lawyers and economists occasionally seek the advice of management consultants or appoint managerial project directors to secondary departmental posts.

Even if presidents reshuffle their executive branch departments, even if presidents could redesign the congressional committee structure to their own preference and banish lobbyists from the metropolitan Washington community—conflicts would still exist and flourish within the executive establishment. Therefore, no matter what other reforms are attempted, presidents and their senior-most advisors ought to give far more consideration to the need for skilled management mediators, who will not be afraid occasionally to widen the scope of conflict, who can selectively step in and divide up controversial pieces of the action. By custom if not by preparation, White House aides have increasingly been forced to serve as arbitrators among competing agencies, competing policies, and competing priorities. Indeed, the increasing prominence and importance of domestic, budget, and national security policy aides at the White House derive from their sitting as judges on the high court of executive branch jurisdictional claims. But ironically many of these people were recruited to the White House not because of their special talents in this area, but because of their help on the campaign trail or as an academic advisor to a presidential candidate or a president-elect in search of a legislative program. It is an understatement to suggest that the White House is in great need of decisive executive branch mediators who can, with the full confidence of the president, preside over the thorniest of complicated claims and counter-claims by competing cabinet members and know when worthy and important elements of a debate are being seriously neglected or misrepresented within these cabinet level negotiations. In the recent past presidents have used people who were already "on-board" to perform tasks for which they were ill-suited or unprepared.

Presidents and their White House staff should never assume that departmental executives will intuitively divine presidential intentions. White House staff themselves have sometimes not clearly understood their own and their own president's policy positions and often do not adequately communicate their policy positions when they do know their position. While it is true that department officials sometimes do not want to hear or understand what the White House is saying, just as often White House aides have misunderstood the degree to which their job is that of a communications agent. Ironically, those White House staffs who have had most experience in the field of communications are those assigned to deal with external groups and publics, such as the Congress, the press, and the general public, rather than the various components of the executive branch itself.

We have suggested in this paper the distinction between an inner and outer clustering of the cabinet. Inner cabinet members seem to enjoy closer and more collaborative ties with the White House; outer departments are more characterized by centrifugal pulls that dissipate close counseling relationships with the White House. But there are some implications of this dichotomy which are not entirely clear at first glance; the problem for the White House may not be to try to make the outer cabinet precisely like the inner cabinet, but to consider whether the inner cabinet might not benefit from some aspects of the way in which the White House relates to the outer cabinet. That is, the cordial and frequent contact between White House and Defense, Justice, Treasury, and the Secretary of State may actually camouflage substantive problems that should be contended, and issues that should be subject to the clashing of adversary viewpoints. United States policy in Vietnam, the Bay of Pigs episode, inadequate tax reform, and too casual a concern for civil liberties are general illustrations that come most readily to mind as byproducts of the inner cabinet in the 1960s. It may be that because White House relationships with the counseling departments seem so close, comfortable, and professional in comparison with White House relationships with the overt advocate departments, that the White House too readily accepts the judgments of these departments, overlooks potentially divisive issues, and neglects the creation of an effective system of multiple and critical advocacy for the substantive and operational aspects of these departments. Too often in the 1960s the debates and adversary proceedings came too late or were procedurally foreclosed with reference to inner cabinet policy choices. If this be so, then many of the more conventional structural reforms (including some of those which President Nixon proposed in his 1971 State of the Union address) misunderstand an important aspect of White House-department relationships. Efforts must be made to increase certain types of conflicts and advocacy proceedings to ferret out differences of views, to generate alternative policy choices (and their rationale), and to estimate the likely consequences of diverse policies.

Many of the White House staff with executive branch experience previously served within inner cabinet departments, and this may explain both their greater difficulties with the outer cabinet and their preference for reforms which would place presidential counselors, as opposed to advocates, in charge of realigned and consolidated outer cabinet departments. But an assumption by which these aides are guided is that the policies or products of the inner cabinet have somehow been more acceptable or wise than those of the outer departments. There may be a tendency here, mistakenly, to interpret closeness and loyalty to the presidency as equivalents of intelligent policy and competent administrative performance. In any event, presidents should be wary of receiving their counsel exclusively from inner cabinet and staff who maintain only a presidential perspective. I am among those who feel that people who protest that a president is drastically isolated are, more often than not, merely signifying that a president has rejected or ignored their pet preferences, but there is nonetheless often a tendency for presidents to indulge in only those views and opinions that sound like music to the ear, a situation that can of course lead to a state of alarming deficiency.

No one should dispute that our modern presidency is charged with enormous new obligations to act as an overseer of executive branch *responsiveness* and *integrity*. Who else can recruit talented department leadership? Who else can better motivate, educate, and inspire federal officials to higher levels of public commitment? And who else can both authoritatively mediate interdepartmental squabbles and wage vigilant pressure campaigns against those within the federal government who see themselves as the chief constituency of their own federal departments? All this and more is expected of the modern presidency and the expanded super staffs at the White House. But notions of government integrity and responsiveness are always slippery and should necessarily be subject to continuous definitional disputes. Responsiveness to whom? Is the presidentialists' perspective really free of special interests, or does this depend almost entirely on whether one happens to like the sitting president?

We come back, invariably, to a realization that presidents are limited in the degree to which they can eliminate executive branch conflicts, and alternatively try to strengthen White House-department ties. Presidents have been and will continue to be frustrated by the sluggishness of the federal executive branch's response to new priorities. And increasingly, presidents are disillusioned by the seeming incapacity to inspire and recharge the batteries of the sprawling federal government. But there are occasions, I think, when presidents and their staff are justifiably thwarted from any easy resolution of substantive and procedural conflicts. We must be careful to maintain a political climate in which uncomfortable questions can be asked of a president from within—or without—the White House. Sometimes an issue is of sufficient divisiveness that it is not then amenable to any majoritarian point of view, and displacement or avoidance of conflict may be the best approach. Moreover, certain types of conflict-resolution or coordination are essentially forms of coercion that might threaten the rightfully independent bases of influence and opposing viewpoints in Congress or society.

We might measurably contribute to the health of our presidency by examining and ultimately appreciating those conflicts that are avoidable or unavoidable, appropriate or inappropriate, and by trying to understand how these conflicts can limit as well as strengthen the presidency. Properly conceived and carried through, such analyses will undoubtedly help to limit and refine our expectations and assessments of democratic presidential leadership.

Notes

1. Tugwell, "The President and His Helpers: A Review Article," 82 *Pol. Sci. Q.* 253, 262, 265 (1967).

2. Nixon, State of the Union address, Jan. 22, 1971, in 117 *Cong. Rec.* H92, H94 (daily ed. Jan. 22, 1971).

3. Neustadt, "Politicians and Bureaucrats," in *The Congress and America's Future* 102, 113 (D. Truman ed. 1965).

4. Quoted in an interview by Sidey, "The White House Staff vs. the Cabinet," *The Washington Monthly*, Feb. 1969, at 4.

5. North, "Conflict—Political Aspects," in 3 *International Encyclopedia of the Social Sciences* 226 (D. Sills ed. 1968).

6. Coser, "Conflict—Social Aspects," in 3 *International Encyclopedia of the Social Sciences, supra* note 13, at 232, 235.

7. M. Bundy, *The Strength of Government* 37 (1968).

8. L. Koenig, *The Chief Executive* 417 (rev. ed. 1968).

9. D. Truman, *The Governmental Process* 407-8 (1951).

10. The staff perceptions of the sources of conflict shown in table 6.1.2 do not adequately reflect the intensity of the respondents' views. Although they blamed White House staff operations approximately as often as they faulted the departments, the author feels their criticisms of department officials and civil servants were more intense than their criticisms of their White House colleagues.

11. E. Hughes, *The Ordeal of Power* 59 (1963).

12. One of the more distinguishing characteristics of the expanding Nixon White House has been its newly-created Office of Communications for the Executive Branch—a public relations and image-making functional group that will no doubt continue to exist in the same or somewhat similar format under future presidents. *See* Bonafede, "Men Behind Nixon—Herbert G. Klein: Spokesman for the Administration," *Nat'l J.* 258-62 (Dec. 6, 1969).

13. P. Anderson, *The President's Men* 367 (1968).

14. Rossiter, "The Constitutional Significance of the Executive Office of the President," 43 *Am. Pol. Sci. Rev.* 1206, 1216 (1949).

15. *See* Alsop, *The Center* (1968), ch. 9.

16. Leacacos, *Fires in the In-Basket* 110 (1968).

17. J. Kallenbach, *The American Chief Executive* 439-40 (1966).

Illustration 6a: The Federal Executive Establishment

The federal bureaucratic establishment that the president as chief executive must confront is decentralized, dispersed, and deconcentrated. Although the major administrative departments and agencies report directly to the president, there are a number of commissions, boards, and panels that are semi-autonomous and thus somewhat independent of presidential control. The following illustration dramatizes both the hefty responsibilities presidents have with regard to the bureaucracy and their disunified administrative authority. (See following pages for chart.)

360 6/The Bureaucracy

Illustration 6a: The Federal Executive Establishment (continued).

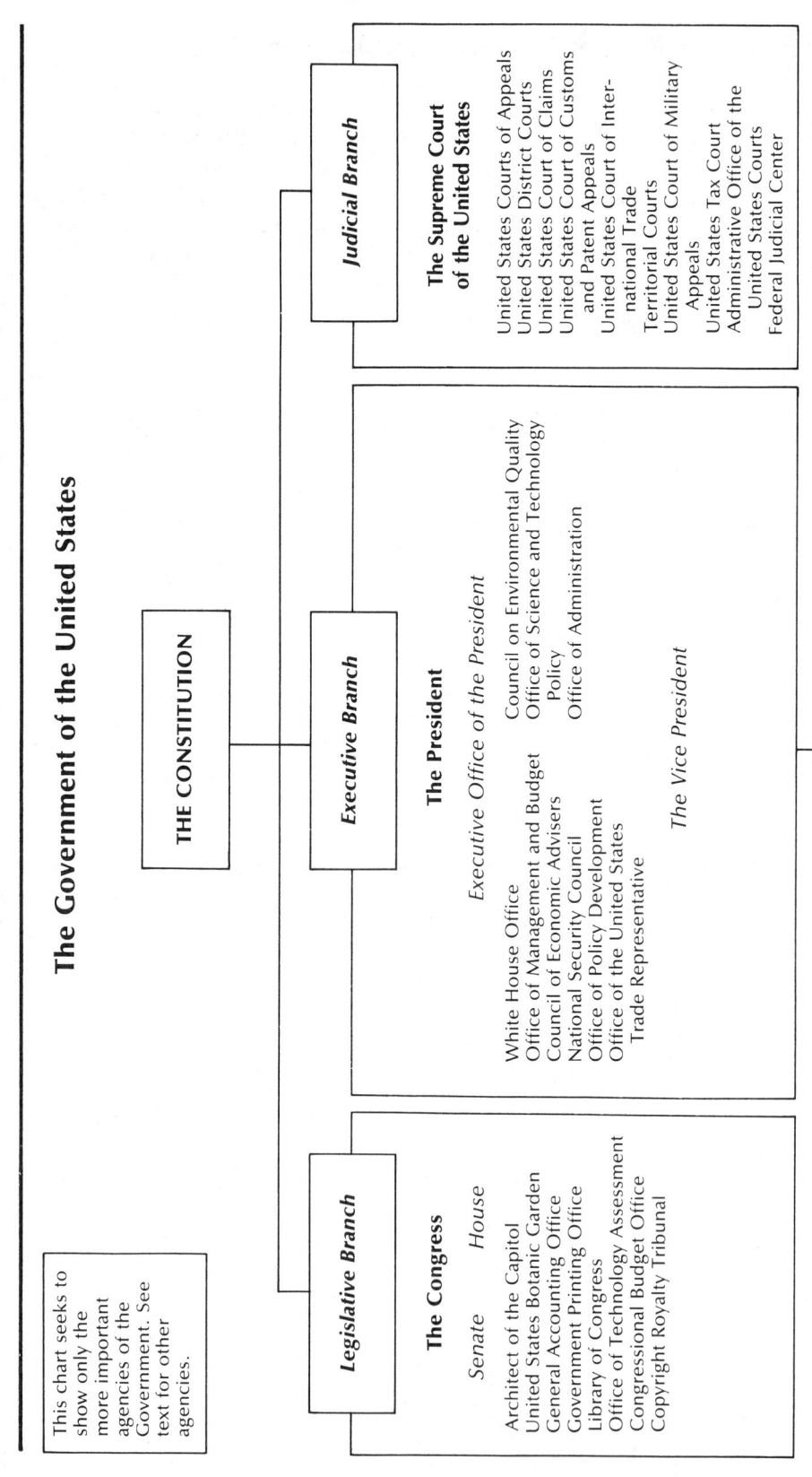

Illustration 6a

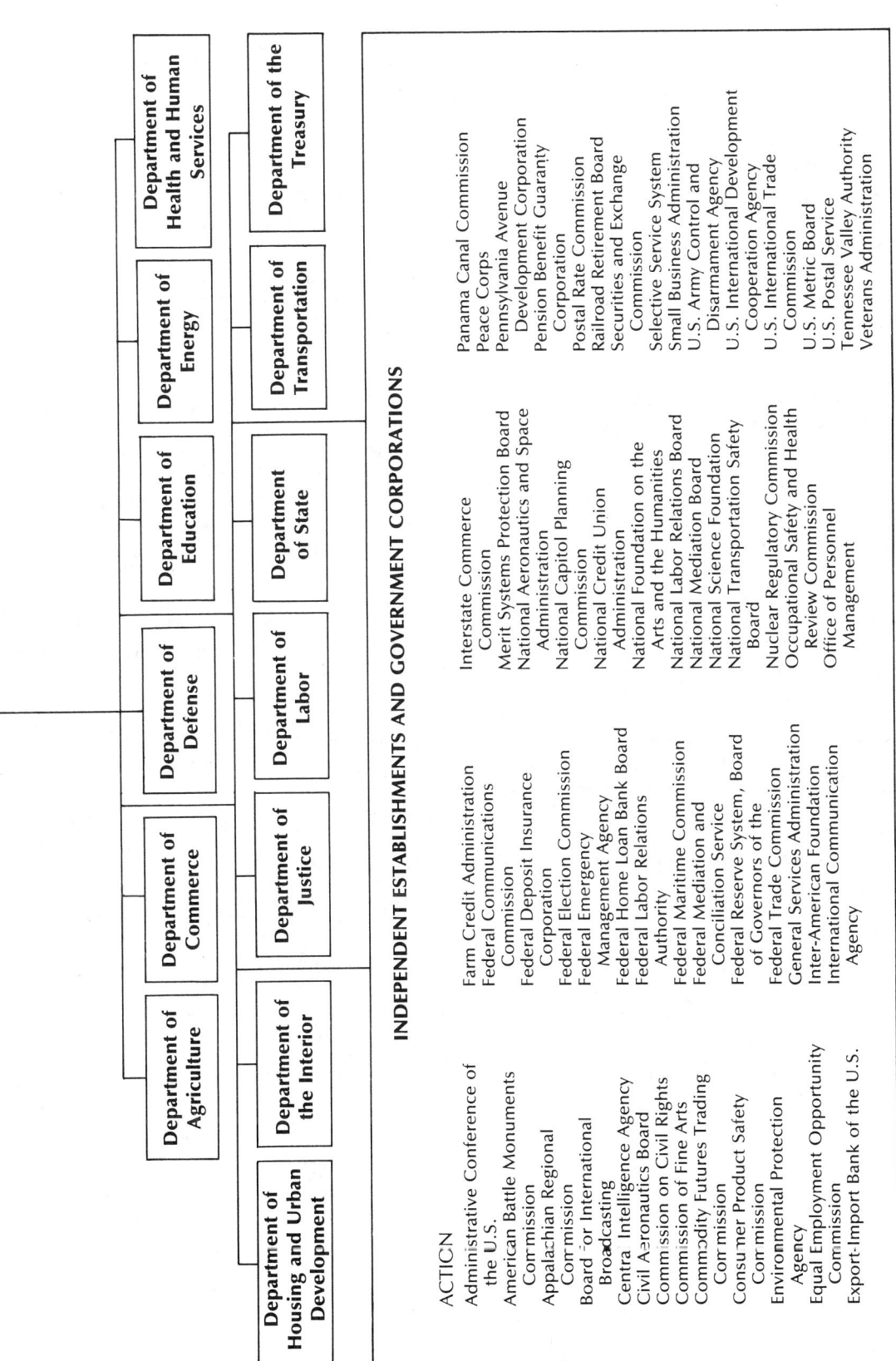

Two Models of Legitimacy

Nelson W. Polsby

How one views White House-departmental conflicts and attempts by presidents to control and dominate the bureaucracy depends upon the model of American policy one espouses. In the following excerpt from his important essay, Nelson Polsby illuminates two different models that lead to two very different assessments. Advocates of the presidential or mandate model will applaud presidential and White House control. Adherents of the federalist or pluralistic model will be more comfortable with a bureaucracy that responds to segmental and clientele interests.

I have suggested that there are currently two models available through which the claims of the executive branch to be properly vested with power can be validated. One model, the presidential model, sees the conferring of legitimacy in our political system as having the following four features. It is episodic, in that it relies heavily upon the results of the last presidential election, which for present purposes is treated as conferring a sweeping mandate. It is concentrated, in that only the winner of the last election receives the endorsement that is claimed to be at the root of the government's entitlement to act. It is direct, in that it is claimed that permission to act is conferred by voters not on the basis of their interest group or other affiliations but through their individual, atomized responses to a particular candidate and his presentation of self during the campaign. Finally, it reflects the present or the recent past, in that only the results of the most recent presidential election are taken into account in determining the right of an official to claim the acquiescence of citizens in public policy.

A view of legitimacy in our political system alternative to the presidential model is contained in what readers will recognize as a federalist model since it draws upon the thoughts of the earliest expositors of the logic underlying the original design of the U.S. Constitution. In this view, legitimacy is conferred not episodically, as in elections, but continuously. It is conferred both through elections and through continuous interaction among decision makers. Legitimacy is not concentrated, but dispersed, to elected officials, to appointed officials, to career bureaucrats. It is based not on election alone, but on organizational norms such as seniority, or selection by congressional caucus, or neutral competence or expertise. In the federalist view, legitimacy is conferred not just directly, but also indirectly; for example, by the workings of the congressional committee system. Finally, not the present alone, but the more distant past as well is invoked by the federalist model, which explicitly recognizes the legitimacy of law-making majorities of the earlier eras that produced programs that persist to this day and are embodied in the agencies of government.

"Presidential Cabinet Making: Lessons for the Political System" by Nelson W. Polsby, Spring 1978, *Political Science Quarterly*, pp. 24-25. Copyright 1978 by the Academy of Political Science. Reprinted by permission.

Politics, Policy, and Bureaucracy at the Top

James W. Fesler

In the path-breaking book *A Government of Strangers*, Hugh Heclo advocates a more sophisticated approach by presidential political appointees to the bureaucracy in an effort to make government work better. Specifically, Heclo advocates a theory "Z" of conditional cooperation whereby political appointees play the balancing act of furthering agency interests in exchange for internal agency support for top-level direction. The following recent statement by Fesler continues this focus on political appointees as lynchpins in the relationship between president and bureaucracy, advocating changes in current practice.

Abstract: Innovation reflecting presidential priorities stems in part from the interplay among political appointees and senior civil servants. Members within each set share distinctive capabilities and disabilities. The brief tenure of political appointees, along with the two-year interval between elections, imposes short time perspectives on political executives, in contrast to those of career executives. The large number of political appointees and their initial distrust of the bureaucracy reduce the contribution that careerists might make to the development and implementation of policies. This is a serious loss, given many political appointees' lack of governmental experience and weak preparation for managing or operating within large organizations. Most career executives are disposed to adapt to a new administration's policy initiatives; resistance is as likely among political executives when the president changes course. Centrifugal forces disperse policymaking into overly discrete, semiautonomous compartments. Centripetal forces draw policymaking to the White House staff, whose members are only occasionally qualified for such responsibility. Reducing the number of political appointees would permit more discriminating selection and lead to greater involvement of careerists. However, the careerist's preparation for a larger role needs improvement.

The exceptional nature of the American governmental system has attracted many interpreters, some grandly addressing the whole complexity, others focusing on particular sectors of the system. Our concern here is the sector in which the president, political executives, and career executives interact in the formulation of policy initiatives and in responding to policy decisions. The character of this sector is unique to the United States. In a major study of bureaucrats and politicians in seven Western democracies, the authors frequently interrupt their main course of cross-national generalization to acknowledge "American exceptionalism" and "the American aberration."[1]

Though our focus is on only one part of the whole system, that part is remarkably interactive with other elements of the system, most prominently Congress, interest groups, communications media, public opinion, and the courts. Even within this sector the dynamics of interactions among officials with different capabilities and time frames, and the dynamics energized by competing values—the free market and government intervention, politics and neutral competence, innovation, and continuity, for instance—are so complex as to have uncertain outcomes. It is not clear whether and when these dynamics work synergistically to effect forward movement, are so constructively conflictual as to assure prudence, or immobilize government when action is needed.

At the Top

The upper reaches of the executive branch are a curious mélange. They include roughly

---

"Politics, Policy, and Bureaucracy at the Top" by James W. Fesler, March 1938, *The Annals*, pp. 23-41. Copyright 1983 by The American Academy of Political and Social Science. Reprinted by permission.

9000 officials: about 100 in the White House and other parts of the Executive Office of the President; about 700 cabinet and subcabinet posts, commissionerships, and bureau chiefships filled by presidential appointment, usually with the advice and consent of the Senate; some 7000 members of the Senior Executive Service, of whom 700 are political appointees and 6300 are senior civil servants; and about 1200 scientists and other specialists without managerial responsibilities.[2] Altogether these top officials amount to four-tenths of one percent of total federal civilian employment.

Except immediately under the cabinet, no line can be drawn across the executive branch, or across a single department, above which all senior officials are political executives and below which all are civil-service careerists. By law, some bureau chiefs are presidential appointees confirmed by the Senate, some are noncareer appointees of a cabinet member, and some are career appointees. A further complexity is that some civil-service careerists accept appointment as political executives, though until recently they thereby lost civil-service status, including tenure.

The United States outdoes all other modern democracies in its provision for change when party control of the executive branch shifts. About 1600 higher positions are filled by political appointment. This contrasts with the approximately 100 top officials in Britain and 360 in France—though 85 percent of France's are drawn from the civil service—that a new administration is entitled to choose afresh. In a typical American department, the secretary, deputy and under secretaries, assistant and deputy assistant secretaries, administrators of large aggregates, chiefs of several bureaus, and regional directors are replaced by a new set of officials. In the Department of Commerce, 93 high political incumbents can be displaced; in the Department of Agriculture, 65.

For three decades the number of politically filled posts has increased. This occurred partly by interposition of new layers of political appointees and partly by multiplication of executives' staff assistants. But existing positions were also shifted from the career service to political appointment; examples are departments' assistant secretaries for administration and regional directors. If political executives are the principal means by which a president and a department head can grasp control of the bureaucracy and institute changes in policy and program, the United States has abundantly provided for it.

The President's Entourage

Nearest the president are the White House staff and the agencies housed in the Executive Office of the President, especially the mostly career-staffed Office of Management and Budget (OMB). Between them one might expect a happy melding of short-term political and long-term careerist points of view in service of the president's policy and management responsibilities.

The White House Staff

Every president needs near him a few intimate advisers who are politically astute and personally loyal. He turns to those with whom he has been closely associated in the campaigns for nomination and election and to friends in his home state. The problem that arises is twofold. One is that his closest advisers are often poorly qualified for the responsible governmental roles in which they are suddenly cast, roles that have become magnified by the centripetal pull of policy and short-term decision making to the White House and by the president's delegation of the tangle of domestic affairs to his aides as he increasingly becomes absorbed in foreign affairs.

The other form of the problem is extension downward in White House staffing of the same recruitment criteria, except for prior intimacy with the president: personal loyalty, campaign service, and congruence of substantive policy views, if any, with those voiced in the election campaign. In 1981, runs one report, "with few exceptions, the professionals on the policy development staff were active in Reagan's 1980 campaign for the presidency." Two of them, in their mid-twenties, had been campaign speech writers.[3] In the Carter administration, the then associate OMB director recalls, "OMB felt that the Domestic Policy Staff was too pervasive, too concerned with short-term political considerations and that some of its junior people were not too capable."[4]

Characterizations of the presidential assistants constituting the White House staff vary more in tone than in essentials. One, kinder than most, reads, "They tend to be young, highly intelligent, and unashamedly on the make. They take chances, they cut corners, and unlike most politicians they sometimes have a little spontaneity and irreverence left in them. This accounts for much of their charm and most of their problems."[5] The words are from Patrick Anderson's study of assistants serving presidents from Roosevelt to Johnson. Characterizations of assistants to Nixon, Ford, Carter, and Reagan have a darker cast.

Efforts to strengthen the president by furnishing him with a staff of several hundred creates more problems than it solves. The White House itself becomes a complex, layered bureaucracy that is difficult to manage. The number of aides with the ready access to the president that propinquity promotes reduces his opportunities for conferring with cabinet members and seeking counsel from knowledgeable persons outside the government. The number, energy, and policy-area assignments of lower-level aides draw business to the White House that might well be left to cabinet departments. Such aides' intrusiveness into departmental affairs often bypasses department heads, thus weakening the prestige of those on whom the president depends for departmental management. The policy-formation process is slowed and complicated by in-house clearance procedures and by substantive and personal controversies among aides.[6] The White House contribution, then, becomes not the comprehensive, long-range view of policy and honest brokering of conflicting departmental advocacy positions, but often a poorly coordinated battle for the president's mind among his own assistants.

The Office of Management and Budget

Established in 1921 and brought into the new Executive Office in 1939, the Bureau of the Budget was a major resource for management of much of the presidential-level policy-formation process. It was staffed with unusually able careerists and generally headed by a well-qualified presidential appointee. Its skeptical review of departments' budget requests gave it control, under the president's direction, over one of the two major presidential policy instruments: the budget and the State of the Union message. Additionally, its legislative clearance role enabled it to review all departments' legislative proposals and positions in support of or opposition to pending legislation, all with a view to advising whether they were in accord with the president's program. And its review of bills passed by Congress, including gathering of concerned departments' reactions, gave it a key role in advising the president whether to approve or veto the bills. Its administrative management staff had broad responsibility for improving the organization and efficiency of executive agencies.

After 1960, while its budgetary power did not decline, presidential aides largely superseded the bureau's policy-level role in legislative clearance and review of enrolled congressional bills. And its work on administrative management declined as the budgetary staff gained dominance, so much so that it could not monitor compliance with its own administrative directives.

Despite Nixon's change of its name, in 1970, to the Office of Management and Budget, and despite its sizable staff, now about 600, these tendencies have persisted and new tendencies have appeared. Appointees to director and deputy director positions are more often political men, closely associated with the president, lobbying with Congress, and soliciting public support of his policies. A layer of noncareer appointees has been inserted between the director and the civil servants on the staff. New presidents and their aides initially distrust the bureaucrats in OMB, so that its rich fund of knowledge about the executive branch, the fate of earlier presidential initiatives, and the policy-affecting potential of the budget process are rarely tapped in the crucial first year. Though OMB mounts specific administrative management undertakings for particular presidents—as in executive branch reorganization, regulatory review, and paperwork management—the management staff for longer-range responsibilities has been successively cut, most recently in mid-1982. Informed observers believe that OMB needs reinvigoration, greater high-level participation by senior careerists, and either strengthening of its nonbudgetary activities or transfer of them to a new staff agency.

Cabinet Members

The initial selection of members of the cabinet receives more personal attention by the president-elect than that of any other set of political executives, save his few top aides. Recent presidents have had such confidence in those they select as to assert an intention to institute cabinet government, meaning reliance on cabinet members for counsel and for the staffing and running of their departments.

Cabinet members are an abler lot than the conspicuous exceptions lead us to believe. Many have achieved distinction in their careers and, for good or ill, are members of the establishment. Eisenhower appointed nine millionaires and Reagan at least eight. Carter's 1977 cabinet included five members with Ph.D.s and five who were lawyers.[7] Most have had federal government experience. From 1953 to 1976, this was true of 55 percent of the initial appointees and of 85 percent of replacement appointees.[8] They often are generalists who have served in other cabinet posts, at the subcabinet level in the same or other departments, or as top presidential aides. Early exemplars of the pattern are George Marshall, Dean Acheson, Robert Lovett, Averell Harriman, and Douglas Dillon. Later ones are Elliot Richardson, James Schlesinger, Rufus Vance, Harold Brown, Joseph Califano, Alexander Haig, Caspar Weinberger, and George Schultz. Many are highly qualified, whether by public or private experience, for the processes of advocacy, negotiation, and compromise that are at the heart of governmental policy-making—lawyers more so, corporate executives and academics somewhat less so, the few ideologues not at all.

However able and experienced they are, the president's early promise of cabinet government soon evaporates. Why should this be so? A too easy explanation, favored by White House aides, is that cabinet members "marry the natives"; each, headquartered in his department, is captured by the bureaucracy and by the clientele groups in the department's immediate environment. Responsiveness to the president, and to his aides, lapses.

An explanation that receives too little attention is that each cabinet member, as department head, is obligated to see to the faithful execution of the laws that fall within his department's jurisdiction. In most of its statutes, Congress vests authority directly in departments and their heads, not in the president. A department head is bound to resist White House aides' urging that he neglect or distort any of his principal statutory responsibilities. Should he not resist, he will alienate his career executives and will have to answer to clientele groups, congressional committees, and the courts.

A political element helps to poison the well. Though the president may initially promise cabinet members free hands in filling their subcabinet and other executive posts, this commitment eventually yields to the White House staff's insistence on clearance of nominees and, often, appointment of candidates centrally identified and preferred.

A variety of factors set cabinet members and White House aides on a collision course. In addition to those mentioned, petty and not-so-petty behaviors play their part. Cabinet members' access to the president is denied, White House aides fail to return cabinet members' telephone calls, and deliberate slights of protocol signal that individual members are out of favor. President Carter's purge of his cabinet in 1979 focused on those who had incurred White House aides' displeasure.

Joseph Califano quotes from his exit interview with Carter: " 'Your performance as secretary has been outstanding,' the President said. 'You have put the department in better shape than it has ever been before. You've been the best Secretary of HEW. . . . The problem is the friction with the White House staff. The same qualities and drive and managerial ability that make you such a superb secretary create problems with the White House staff.' "[9] The secretary must have sensed an odd reversal of role, for in the Johnson White House, "serving as the chief expediter for an impatient and demanding president, Califano made many enemies," some among cabinet members. "Time and again . . . Califano fought to impose Johnson's interests over the narrower interests of the departments of government."[10]

Whether by their own or the president's choice, cabinet members' median term since World War II has been barely more than two years. Over one-fifth of the secretaries were in place for less than 11 months.[11] From 1953 through 1976, there were 5 presidents, but 12 secretaries of commerce, 11 secretaries of HEW, 10 attorneys general, 9 secretaries of labor and of the treasury, and 8 secretaries of defense.[12]

Brevity of tenure, perhaps because it is not anticipated, does not deflect cabinet members from according highest priority to the making and influencing of policy. This is no doubt appropriate, but there is a price to pay. Many give very low priority to departmental management, which is the key to assuring responsiveness and effectiveness of the bureaucracy. This is as true of able corporate executives as of their colleagues from other walks of life. Secretary of the Treasury Michael Blumenthal, formerly head of the Bendix Corporation, made the point: "You learn very quickly that you do not go down in history as a good or bad secretary in terms of how well you ran the place, whether you're a good administrator or not. You're perceived to be a good secretary in terms of whether the policies for which you are responsible are adjudged successful or not. . . . But that's not true in a company. In a company it's how well you run the place."[13]

Political Executives

Below cabinet members and other major agencies' heads are most of the 1600 political executives. A president intent on effecting change within the executive branch normally transmits his intentions through these appointees and, at least in theory, should be able to rely on them for vigorous translation of intentions into action. Yet the multiplicity, qualifications, and tenure of political executives probably hamper the effecting of change more than does any obduracy of the permanent bureaucracy.

Numbers

The large number of political appointments available guarantees that errors of choice will be made, and the earlier the more. In the 10-week post-election rush, self-nomination, others' recommendations, the old-boy network, the BOGSAT technique ("a bunch of guys sitting around a table"), and a variety of other means provide the large pool of candidates and the disorderly modes of selection.

The numbers also account for how deeply political appointments extend into the bowels of departmental administration. The proliferation of subcabinet posts, strictly defined, affords one clue. These positions—of under secretary, deputy under secretary, and assistant secretary—increased from 55 in 1950 to 84 in 1960, 113 in 1970, and 145 in 1978.[14] The secretary may have as many as 15 politically appointed assistants attached to his own office, and the subcabinet officials may average two such assistants apiece.[15] Below the subcabinet level are a number of political appointees with such titles as deputy assistant secretary, bureau chief, deputy bureau chief, and regional director.[16]

The large number of political executives and their penetration of departments, bureaus, and the field service distance able careerists from the centers of decision making. Their rich potential remains untapped, especially in the early period when the administration's and departments' major policy proposals are formulated.

Qualifications

By most standard criteria, especially educational level and subject-matter knowledge relevant to their particular program area re sponsibilities, political executives are a well-qualified elite. Three other criteria concern us here. These are partisan and policy compatibility with the president, governmental experience, and capacity to manage large organizations.

Political executives are less partisan than their designation suggests. From 1961 to 1978, members of the president's party averaged only 58 percent among the four administrations' sets of political appointees, with a range of 47 percent under Johnson to 65 percent under Nixon. Within cabinet departments, two-thirds of the political appointees, on average, belonged to the president's party, with State and Defense on the low side (44 and 47 percent) and Housing and Urban Development and Agriculture (89 and 86 percent) on the high side.[17]

Old images of party patronage have largely ceased to reflect reality. White House personnel staffs try to deflect partisan pressures by rewarding large financial contributors and taking care of defeated candidates for electoral office by minor, though sometimes major, ambassadorships; membership in multimember bodies—regulatory boards and commissions, presidential advisory commissions, and departmental advisory committees—and invitations to White House galas for foreign dignitaries.

The politics of policy, if not of party, plays a large role in recruitment. This politics takes two forms: loyalty to the president and his policies throughout his term, including the possibility of his changing course, and inflexible loyalty to particular policies, most of them compatible with the president's campaign rhetoric but selectively erosive during his term. The second kind of loyalty can turn antipresidential. Initial selection of subcabinet and subordinate executives depends heavily on nominations and recommendations from the economic and professional communities interested in particular programs. A number of those chosen are likely to be drawn from interest groups, single-cause movements, conservative or liberal think tanks, and congressional staff members who share the president's initial orientation. Many such are advocates, with agendas of their own. There is little assurance that such political appointees will flexibly respond to the president's initiatives for change rather than firmly adhere to their convictions, constituencies, political patrons. Yet they are arrayed in many layers between the good to be done, as the president perceives it, and those who can do it, the career executives in closest touch with implementation.

Advocates, it is true, have a strong impulse to innovate, whether to turn the clock forward or backward. But innovations can be good or bad, well timed or ill timed, contributors or embarrassments to a larger strategy of change. Advocacy-oriented political executives are not the president's men and women. They march to a different drummer.

Prior experience in the federal government is a criterion closely linked to political executives' performance. Looking back, former appointees confess that they were poorly prepared for the Washington setting of interest groups, congressional committees, the White House staff, the goldfish-bowl exposure to the media, the budget process, and the permanent bureaucracy. In 1970 over two-thirds of presidential and two-fifths of departmental political appointees had less than two years of federal governmental experience.[18] Another two-fifths of the departmentally appointed political officials had over 10 years of federal experience and, like the top civil servants, were better prepared. Hugh Heclo notes the anomaly, that "unlike the situation in most private organizations, in the U.S. executive branch those in the top positions of formal authority [that is, presidential appointees] are likely to be substantially less familiar with their working environment than both their civil service and political subordinates."[19]

Capability for the management of large organizations or for operating in them is a third criterion of executives' effectiveness. Few of the political executives who are lawyers or who are recruited from universities and research institutes, interest-group organizations, congressional staffs, and small business firms have had experience that prepares them for running a bureau of 5000 employees, let alone for operating in one of the cabinet departments, which range from 15,000 to one million employees. Sometimes, as Dean Acheson and George W. Ball have noted, even the head of a major corporation may have served only an ornamental function there and can do no more in government.[20]

Tenure

Independently of other attributes, the brief tenure of political executives suffices to explain the marginality of their impact. In the period of 1960 to 1972, over half of the under secretaries and assistant secretaries moved out within less than two years, including a fifth who left in less than one year.[21] How much time does a new political executive need to achieve effectiveness? Maurice Stans, former secretary of commerce, said, "A business executive needs at least two years to become effective in government, to understand the intricacies of his programs, and to make beneficial changes."[22]

Rapid turnover not only reduces individual effectiveness, it impairs three relationships that are at the heart of the administration's effectiveness. First, it complicates a department head's effort to establish teamwork among his principal subordinates, for they are ever changing. Second, rapid turnover near the top recurrently breaks up interdepartmental networks of political executives sharing concern with, and perhaps having divergent views on, particular policy and program areas extending across several departments. For these, especially, there need to be what Heclo terms "relationships of confidence and trust."[23] The chemistry involved in these interpersonal relations takes time to develop and is upset if new elements are constantly being introduced. Third, top civil servants' relations with political superiors that are here today and gone tomorrow cannot faithfully follow copybook maxims. Some careerists, if called on, will patiently tutor one after another political executive to speed his learning process. Others, particularly those in charge of bureaus and programs, will take protective measures to minimize the damage an ill-prepared and very temporary political executive can do.

Political executives share a number of attributes that limit their effectiveness as the president's agents of change. Their number is too large. Partisanship is too weak to make them a cohesive group. In its place is the politics of policy. For some this means a commitment to support the president and, so, to adapt flexibly to his changing policy agenda and priorities. But for many it means tenacious devotion to particular program areas and particular policies, whether or not they comport with the president's strategic emphases. Too few political executives have prior governmental experience; fewer know how to run a large organization well. Finally, political appointees' stay is short and their comings and goings erratic.

Career Executives

Recent presidents campaigned against the bureaucracy and complained during their terms of the unresponsiveness of the bureaucracy. Most political appointees enter office with a stereotypical view of bureaucrats. This inhibits their seeking a collaborative relation with those best informed on departmental programs and best prepared to warn inexperienced superiors of minefields in the surrounding terrain. The three elements of the president's and political executives' stance are an assumption that the bureaucracy is swollen, a doubt of careerists' competence, and an expectation of their unresponsiveness to the administration in power. The first is quickly disposed of. For three decades the number of federal civilian employees has been substantially stable, in contrast to increases in the nation's population, its employed labor force, and the range of governmental responsibilities.

Doubt of careerists' competence is ill founded. Elmer Staats, after a distinguished career in politically appointive posts, said on ending his term as the comptroller general of the United States that ever since World War II days, "I have worked with business people who have been in the government....And I have yet to find a single one of those business executives after their experience here who doesn't go out and have nothing but praise for the calibre and the hard work of the people in the government."[24] And Alan K. Campbell, an executive vice-president of ARA Services, Inc.—and earlier a Carter appointee—reports that "the quality of top managers I knew in the federal government . . . is every bit as high as we have at ARA; and on the whole, the people at ARA are paid from 1½ to 3 times more than their public sector counterparts."[25]

An expectation that the bureaucracy will be unresponsive to the administration in power is too simplistic to fit comfortably with the complexity of factors determining senior civil servants' behavior. Top careerists are remarkably diverse in ideological orientation and in party identification. On a scale of attitudes ranging from state intervention to free enterprise, Joel D. Aberbach and his colleagues found that their sample of such American careerists was "more heterogeneous than any of the European bureaucratic samples." The basic picture is a distribution of attitudes that is not only wide but substantially congruent with the distribution pattern in Congress.[26]

Party affiliations of careerists are weaker predictors of behavior. In social-service agencies in 1970, "even Republican administrators . . . were not wholly sympathetic to the social service retrenchments sought by the Nixon administration."[27] Sample surveys in 1970 and 1976 found that top careerists were 47 percent Democratic (38 percent in 1976), 36 percent independent (48 percent in 1976), and 17 percent Republican (16 percent in 1976). Using different tests of independents' leanings, the surveyors drew different conclusions. For 1970, Joel Aberbach and Bert Rockman held that "the belief that a Republican administration does not have natural political allies within the federal bureaucracy seems well-justified."[28] For 1976, Richard Cole and David Caputo believed that "independents and party identifiers combined assure either a Republican or a Democratic president substantial support at the senior career levels of the federal bureaucracy."[29]

Beyond ideologies and party affiliations, and often overriding them, is another attitudinal orientation. Most careerists perceive their role as one entailing the obligation to serve loyally the people's choice as president. Because senior careerists have served through several changes in administration, this is a well-internalized commitment. It is qualified, to be sure, by resistance to illegality, a resistance that served the nation well in the Watergate era.

This basic commitment, however, can be attenuated by another attitude toward role performance. Typically, senior civil servants identify with their agency and its responsibilities. Their finding fulfillment in achieving the purposes of statutes entrusted to them, instead of being passively neutral, generally strengthens the faithful execution of the laws. But it lures some into bureaucratic politics—protection of the agency's turf, development of a degree of autonomy, and mobilization of allies in Congress and clientele groups.

How responsive careerists are to presidential policy shifts is a complex product of ideologies, party affiliations, the civil-service doctrine of loyalty to the incumbent president, and devotion to particular programs and agencies. The relative weights of these factors vary with circumstances. The most negative reactions can be expected when the president orders termination of an agency or of well-established programs, reduction of funds, or slashing of staff. Yet when, by President Reagan's order, the Community Services Administration, an antipoverty agency, was dismantled in three months, the agency director reports, "The career service had demonstrated in a dramatic way the best of professional integrity in executing a difficult assignment most of them opposed." It shows, he adds, that "the mythology of an untrustworthy bureaucracy poised to undermine a policy with which it disagreed was simply not true."[30]

The Shared World of Political and Career Executives

Though political and career executives differ in important regards, the considerable degree of congruence of orientations permits expectation that they might harmoniously collaborate in their shared world. The recent institution of the Senior Executive Service is designed to facilitate such collaboration. Yet careerists' morale has fallen to perhaps its lowest point, and their career paths often poorly prepare them for engagement in the fashioning of broad policy.

Some Congruent Orientations

Political executives and top careerists have a good deal in common. Both groups are highly educated; more than half the members of each hold graduate or professional degrees. However, more of the senior civil servants, 40 percent, majored in technology and natural science; only 10 percent of political executives did so. Members of the two groups do not differ substantially in the proportions that see their role, or roles, as that of advocate, legalist, broker, trustee, facilitator, policymaker, or ombudsman. The civil servants, though, are twice as likely as political executives to have a technician-role focus, and half as likely to have a partisan-role focus. Their external activities disclose a common pattern: nearly two-thirds of each group have regular contacts with members of Congress; over 90 percent of each have regular contacts with representatives of clientele groups. Internally, not surprisingly, political executives have about twice as much contact with their department heads as do senior civil servants.[31] But, if not surprising, it indicates exclusion or filtering of counsel from members of the permanent government.

Top careerists share political executives' frustrations with bureaucratic obstacles to effective performance, particularly the pervasiveness of red tape and the constricting personnel system. At least two-thirds of those sampled in 1981 answered no when asked whether "the administrative support systems" provide a pool of qualified professional and managerial talent to hire from, make it easy to hire employees, or make it easy to fire or to apply lesser sanctions against poorly performing employees.[32]

Finally, the infiltration of political-executive ranks by career civil servants fosters congruence of outlook with those continuing in civil-service status. Former careerists filled 25 percent of assistant secretaryships in the 1933-61 period—an average for the three presidencies. In the mid-1970s they held nearly half of such posts, and in 1978, under Carter, 61 percent.[33] Below the assistant secretaries, Heclo reports, "one-third to one-half of the noncareer . . . posts . . . are usually filled by career civil servants."[34] In the period Heclo deals with, such cooptation by the incumbent administration required sacrifice of civil-service status and possible dismissal from government service by the next administration. This has changed.

The Senior Executive Service

The 1978 Civil Service Reform Act pooled most political executives and top career executives in a Senior Executive Service (SES). The service currently includes about 7000 executives, 90 percent of them careerists and 10 percent political appointees. This is a specified governmentwide ratio; within it an individual agency's political appointees may rise as high as 25 percent. Except for presidential appointees requiring senatorial confirmation, or requiring White House clearance, a department head freely chooses political appointees who meet his previously established qualification standards. In making career appointments to the SES, he must adhere to competitive merit principles.

The key feature is the new flexibility with which the department head can assign and reassign SES members, whether political or career, to particular positions. Only two restrictions apply. A careerist is protected against involuntary reassignment for the first 120 days after appointment of a new department head, or of a political executive with reassignment authority. And in about 45 percent of the positions, the department head can assign and reassign only careerists, not political appointees. These are posts reserved for civil servants "to ensure impartiality, or the public's confidence in the impartiality of the Government," as the statute phrases it.[35]

These necessary protections accounted for, the system is one in which the department head can assemble his large management team, mixing political and career executives as suits his purpose. Additionally, advised by performance-review boards, he can at any time remove from SES a career member rated "less than fully successful."

Morale

The Senior Executive Service had a troubled start.[36] Pay was a major problem. Though the Reform Act directs the president to establish SES pay levels, Congress later set a pay ceiling that in 1982 put 84 percent of SES members at the same pay, $6000 below the president's top pay level. The performance awards and substantial bonuses for abler SES careerists, provided in the act, were also later curtailed. The most basic problem was eased when, at the end of 1982, Congress authorized pay increases of up to 15 percent for some 32,000 senior government employees.

For nonpay reasons, too, the morale of SES career members fell to a lamentably low point. They tired of being flayed as bureaucrats by a succession of recent administrations. They believed that "the quality of political leadership in the agencies has been declining" in the last several years, so that "career staffs are being directed by persons who are simply not capable of providing the kind of leadership and guidance that the programs of agencies and the public deserve."[37] They were disturbed by political executives' short time frames. In 1981 over three-fifths of top careerists sampled said that rapid turnover of political appointees made long-term planning difficult, and that such appointees focus on short-term projects "nearly all the time" or "rather often."[38] And, rightly or wrongly, they reacted negatively to the reversal of programs by foxes in the chicken coop.

Whatever the causes, an alarming exodus of top careerists occurred. About 1600 career executives left the federal service between July 1979 and June 1981. In 1981 about 95 percent of the most experienced senior careerists, those eligible for voluntary retirement at ages 55 to 59, with 30 years' service, were deciding to leave, compared to about 18 percent in 1978.[39]

Career Paths

Two features of the careers of senior civil servants weaken their potential contribution to high-level policymaking and management. Most were initially recruited in their twenties and thirties as specialists—scientists, engineers, economists, and the like. What they know about public affairs and the management of large organizations must, therefore, be haphazardly acquired as they move forward in their careers. The second career feature is confinement of most of their experience to one agency. The two specializations, by discipline and by agency, reinforce each other. Top careerists, therefore, have depth of expertness but not the breadth of training and experience that in other countries produces generalist administrators. For the same reasons, many American senior civil servants develop a myopic loyalty to particular agencies and programs.

These disabilities are not necessarily compensated for by political executives. Many of them qualify for particular political positions because their professional specialties and private-sector activities closely relate to the programs they are to administer. Though this may make for some congruence of outlook with that of top careerists, it also imposes blinders that remove much of the world from their field of vision.

Policymaking Problems

Formation and effectuation of an administration's policies are plagued by two major problems. One is the counterpull of centrifugal and centripetal forces. The other is the prevalence of short time perspectives.

Centrifugal and Centripetal Forces

The multiplication of governmental responsibilities has generated a geometrical growth of interrelations among programs and among departments. Whether the focus is on reduction of poverty, environmental protection, or foreign policy, the range of relevant factors and of concerned departments casts a shadow of quaintness on classic organizational doctrines of compartmentalization of authority and responsibility. Everything seems to be connected with everything else. Yet centrifugal forces create narrowly oriented, substantially autonomous policy communities in the governmental system.

George P. Shultz and Kenneth W. Dam, before becoming the secretary and deputy secretary of state, wrote of the costs of such partitioning: "In a balkanized executive branch, policymaking is necessarily a piecemeal affair; policymakers are under the constraint that they are not permitted to view problems whole."[40] Many share their concern that "the trend of events is toward greater fragmentation" and inveigh against iron triangles—enduring alliances of bureau, relevant congressional committees, and special-interest groups concerned with the bureau's programs. Joseph Califano believes that "the severest threat to governing for all the people" comes from the pernicious fact that "we have institutionalized, in law and bureaucracy, single-interest organizations that can accede only in the narrow interest and are incapable of adjudicating in the national interest." "We must," he says, "have people and institutions . . . that will render national policy more than the sum of the atomistic interests. We must design bureaucratic structures that permit and encourage top government officials to assess special interests, rather than pander to them."[41]

How to counter these tendencies is a problem far from solution. The principal, though problematic, counterstrategy is the centripetal pull to the White House of matters that earlier might have been left for resolution within individual departments. Elliot Richardson, holder of four cabinet posts, writes that "the delegation of responsibilities and their interposition between the president and department or agency heads are symptoms, not causes. The fundamental problems are the growth of presidential tasks and the inescapable burdens of interrelatedness which lead inexorably to the enlargement of staff functions."[42] White House assistants, we have seen, are weakly prepared for the formulation of broad, long-range policies.

A hazard that attends the centripetal tendency is the swamping of deliberative policymaking at the top by strong pressures on the White House for quick decisions on myriad problems, which arise seriatim in no discernible pattern and are mistakenly thought to be discrete. Responses to sudden surprises can rarely be tested for compatibility with recent and pending actions or checked for consistency with long-range policy. Shultz and Dam attest to the phenomenon: "Most decisions in government . . . are made . . . in the day-to-day process of responding to crises of the moment. The danger is that this daily firefighting leaves the policymaker further and further from his goal. . . . Many of the failures of government in dealing with the economy can be traced to an attempt to solve minor problems piecemeal."[43]

Efforts are made, of course, to involve cabinet members in top-level policymaking. The Reagan administration, with six cabinet councils, was not the first to assemble cabinet members concerned with the same policy area in hopes of a coordinated approach to policy formation. But, as Richardson says, "Interdepartmental committees cannot do the job alone because their disagreements can all too easily end in deadlock. To prevent deadlocks some external authority is needed—and here is a role that invites reliance on the anonymous Presidential staff."[44] Furthermore, cabinet-level committees, including the Reagan cabinet councils, though they were staffed by White House aides, do not monopolize policymaking channels. In 1981 and 1982, major presidential policy decisions and proposals emerged without cabinet input.

Time Perspectives

George W. Ball, the under secretary of state under Kennedy, recalls, "When one tried to point out the long-range implications of a current problem or how it meshed or collided with other major national interests, Kennedy would often say, politely but impatiently, 'Let's not worry about five years from now, what do we do tomorrow?'"[45] This attitude pervades the White House staff, is less operative among cabinet members and their deputy and under secretaries, gets strongly reinforced among assistant secretaries and other political executives, and is the despair of career civil servants. Systemic factors, not personal quirkiness, account for its prevalence.

The president's major opportunity for formulating his major policies with an expectation of favorable congressional action falls in the period between the popular election and the end of his first six months in office. He can, or does, claim a mandate for change, his public-approval ratings quickly register 70 percent or so, Congress grants a honeymoon period, the president can usually focus on domestic rather than principally foreign policies, and his cabinet members are not yet alienated by the White House staff.

Most presidents seize the opportunity offered. They initiate more requests for legislation in the first than in any later year. If wise, they act early in that year, for, Paul C. Light reports, 72 percent of requests introduced in January to March of the first year are eventually enacted, but only 25 percent of third- and fourth-quarter requests are so successful.[46]

The period of greatest opportunity is also the period when the administration may be least capable of carefully fashioning a policy program. Legislative proposals advanced in the first three months are largely products of the campaign staff and pro tem transition advisers. Though the cabinet is completed in December, appointment of subcabinet and other political executives stretches through several months. The permanent bureaucracy is not fully available in the preinaugural period. After the inauguration the bureaucracy is not trusted. So the new administration deprives itself of data, expertness, sophisticated understanding of the Washington environment, and longer time perspectives, all of which could strengthen the policy-formation process.

Coming elections, congressional and presidential, soon cast their shadows. That, together with the president's increasing absorption an foreign affairs, explains why, as John Helmer writes, "for only one year, the first for a one-term president, can it be said that he has time and some political incentive to consider longer-term problems and to make decisions and commitments whose results may not be immediately apparent."[47] In the second year, seeking to minimize loss of his party's congressional seats, he and his aides prefer initiatives with quick impact. The presidential reelection campaign begins in the third year and becomes all-important in the fourth year. Furthermore, neither Congress nor foreign governments welcome major policy proposals for which negotiation must bridge the current and a possibly different successor administration.

The irony is that by the second half of the presidential term, the administration has become better equipped to formulate long-range policies. The White House usually has achieved a clearer structure and more orderly processes, though it may have increased friction with cabinet members. Half the initial political appointees have left their posts and replacements have been more prudently chosen, often by promotion or transfer of able and responsive political executives and by promotion of careerists.[48] Continuing political executives have acquired Washington experience, discovered that civil servants are colleagues, not enemies, and learned that the designing of policies needs to take account of their implementability.[49] Regrettably, these resources cannot be exploited in a period dominated by short time perspectives.

A Modest Proposal

Deficiencies in the making and implementing of policy at the top levels of the executive branch derive from many sources. Some of the most basic lie outside the scope of this article. Within our framework one thing is clear: exhorting officials to behave differently than they do is profitless unless incentives are created that will alter their behavior. That daunting task might be circumvented by changing the mix of top executives.

Reducing the number of political executives would permit greater care in their selection and would open opportunities for experienced careerists, with their longer time perspectives, to contribute to the design and implementation of programs that embody the administration's innovative policies. Surprisingly, this is strongly advocated by President Nixon's top political recruiter. Frederick Malek writes,

> The solution to problems of rigidity and resistance to change in government is *not* to increase the number of appointive positions at the top, as so many politicians are wont to do.... An optimum balance between the number of career and noncareer appointments ... should be struck in favor of fewer political appointees, not more. In many cases, the effectiveness of an agency would be improved and political appointments would be reduced by roughly 25 percent if line positions beneath the assistant secretary level were reserved for career officials.[50]

If his prescription were followed, top careerists would play a more significant role, one that is common in Europe and one that would bolster their morale and reduce the rate of prime-age resignations and retirements.

James L. Sundquist compared the policy-making capacity of the United States with that of five Western European countries that successfully developed and applied policies to influence the regional distribution of their populations—largely a matter of incentives for private investment in declining areas and disincentives for investment in regions growing too rapidly. By 1970 the United States had a clear national policy, in principle. It was embraced in both major parties' platforms, was frequently set forth by President Nixon, and was partially reflected in two congressional statutes. But, in contrast to European countries, "the institutional structure in the United States did not respond to the political directives."[51] Why not?

Among several reasons, Sundquist emphasizes the "gulf between the career bureaucracy, which was familiar with the data and had some degree of competence to analyze it, and the [White House] staff advisers who had responsibility for developing policy recommendations." In Europe a typical participant "was at the same time the long-time career civil servant and the respected policy adviser." In the United States, "many of the most competent and ambitious of the career officials—the kind that rise to the top in European civil services—find themselves excluded from the inner policy-making circles, or subordinated to younger, less experienced political appointees, and so depart. The capability of the career service is reduced, which leads to pressures for further politicization, in a vicious circle."[52]

If the quality of senior civil servants has been declining and if the policy-making process needs greater participation by careerists, we urgently need to repair the damage and strengthen careerists' capabilities for high-level responsibilities. Raising the level of positions to which able careerists can aspire will help. Beyond that, the top civil service needs strengthening of executive development programs. These are a mix of identifying the comers, moving them among a variety of broadening assignments, and providing sabbatical leave years in university graduate programs and shorter training periods at federal academies such as the Federal Executive Institute. Such leaves and training opportunities should come at the career point when a careerist's special professional discipline and narrow, single-agency experience are inadequate preparation for the work that lies ahead. This includes management of large organizations, negotiations with other agencies, the White House, Congress, and interest groups, shaping of legislative and presidential-directive drafts to assure successful implementation, and relating of policy ideas to one another and to the social fabric of America.

From 1953 on, says Sundquist, "no administration devoted any appreciable attention to training and developing a new generation of career managers, or even seemed to care."[53] The reason is a familiar one. This requires a long time perspective and yields no credit for an administration in its short life.

Notes

1. Joel D. Aberbach, Robert D. Putnam, and Bert A. Rockman, *Bureaucrats and Politicians in Western Democracies* (Cambridge, MA: Harvard University Press, 1981).

2. U.S. House Committee on Post Office and Civil Service, *United States Government Policy and Supporting Positions*, 96th Cong., 2nd sess., 18 November 1980 (Washington, DC: Government Printing Office, 1980); "The Pick of the Plums," *National Journal*, 12:I (29 Nov. 1980), Special Insert. The Senior Executive Service, with an authorized strength of 8500, is not fully staffed.

3. Dick Kirschten, "Reagan Sings of Cabinet Government, and Anderson Leads the Chorus," *National Journal*, 13:824-27, 827, 824 (9 May 1981). In 1982, Martin Anderson's resignation as director of the staff was accepted.

4. W. Bowman Cutter, quoted in Dick Kirschten, "Decision Making in the White House: How Well Does It Serve the President?" *National Journal*, 14:584-89, 588 (3 Apr. 1982).

5. Patrick Anderson, *The President's Men: White House Assistants of Franklin D. Roosevelt . . . Lyndon Johnson* (Garden City, NY: Doubleday, Anchor Books, 1969), 469. In the 1976 campaign, Anderson was a speech writer for Jimmy Carter; he declined appointment to the White House staff.

6. "The Carter decision loop covered well over a dozen separate offices within the White House; the process could take several weeks to complete, and it often generated considerable conflict." Paul C. Light, *The President's Agenda: Domestic Policy Choice from Kennedy to Carter* (Baltimore: Johns Hopkins University Press, 1982), 55.

7. Nelson Polsby, "Presidential Cabinet Making: Lessons for the Political System," *Political Science Quarterly*, 93:15-25 (Spring 1978); "Financial Reports Show that

10 Members of Cabinet Are Worth $1 Million or More," AP dispatch in *New York Times*, 26 Jan. 1981, A24. Our text's count excludes cabinet members without departmental portfolios.

8. James J. Best, "Presidential Cabinet Appointments: 1953-1976," *Presidential Studies Quarterly*, 11:62-66, 65 (Winter 1981).

9. Joseph A. Califano, Jr., *Governing America: An Insider's Report from the White House and the Cabinet* (New York: Simon & Schuster, 1981), 434-35.

10. Anderson, *The President's Men*, 443, 446.

11. G. Calvin Mackenzie, *The Politics of Presidential Appointments* (New York: Free Press, 1981), 7. The period covered was 1945-77; in 1979, President Carter replaced five cabinet members.

12. Best, "Presidential Cabinet Appointments," 63.

13. W. Michael Blumenthal, "Candid Reflections of a Businessman in Washington," *Fortune*, 99(2):36ff., 39 (Jan. 1979).

14. Thomas P. Murphy, Donald E. Neuchterlein, and Ronald J. Stupak, *Inside the Bureaucracy: The View from the Assistant Secretary's Desk* (Boulder, CO: Westview Press, 1978), 5-6.

15. Based on the Interior Department's management pattern, as charted in Hugh Heclo, *A Government of Strangers: Executive Politics in Washington* (Washington, DC: Brookings Institution, 1977), 58.

16. In 1977, political appointees in the Department of Health, Education and Welfare included 13 deputy assistant secretaries, 12 bureau chiefs, 10 deputy bureau chiefs, and 10 regional directors. James W. Fesler, *Public Administration: Theory and Practice* (Englewood Cliffs, NJ: Prentice-Hall, 1980), 135-36.

17. Calculated from tables in Roger G. Brown, "Party and Bureaucracy: From Kennedy to Reagan," *Political Science Quarterly*, 97:279-94, 283, 285 (Summer 1982). These and related data in the text partly reflect the promotion of civil servants to political-executive posts, especially in the last half of a president's term.

18. Heclo, *A Government of Strangers*, 101 (drawing on a study by Joel D. Aberbach). The year 1970 may seem unrepresentative, as the Nixon administration had followed almost a decade of Democratic administrations. However, experienced Eisenhower executives had aged no more than 10 years in the decade.

19. Ibid.

20. Both write acidly about Edward R. Stettinius, who had been vice-president of General Motors and chairman of the board of United States Steel. Between 1939 and 1945, he served as a defense production official, land-lease administrator, under secretary of state, and secretary of state. Dean Acheson, *Present at the Creation: My Years in the State Department* (New York: W. W. Norton, 1969), 88-91; and George W. Ball, *The Past Has Another Pattern: Memoirs* (New York: W. W. Norton, 1982), 29-30.

21. Arch Patton, "Government's Revolving Door," *Business Week*, Sept. 1973, 12-13.

22. Quoted, ibid., 12. The same estimate is made in Frederick V. Malek, *Washington's Hidden Tragedy* (New York: Macmillan, 1978), 49.

23. Heclo, *A Government of Strangers*, 158 and passim.

24. Transcript, *The MacNeil/Lehrer Report: Elmer Staats Interview*, 6 Mar. 1981, 6-7.

25. Alan K. Campbell, in a symposium, "The Public Service as Institution," *Public Administration Review*, 42:304-20, 315 (July-Aug. 1982).

26. Aberbach, Putnam, and Rockman, *Bureaucrats and Politicians*, 122, 124-25. On congruence with Congress, see Joel D. Aberbach and Bert A. Rockman, "The Overlapping Worlds of American Federal Executives and Congressmen," *British Journal of Political Science*, 7:38 (Jan. 1967), Table 6.

27. Joel D. Aberbach and Bert A. Rockman, "Clashing Beliefs Within the Executive Branch: The Nixon Administration Bureaucracy," *American Political Science Review*, 70:456-68, 467 (June 1976).

28. Ibid., 458.

29. Richard L. Cole and David A. Caputo, "Presidential Control of the Senior Civil Service: Assessing the Strategies of the Nixon Years," *American Political Science Review*, 73:399-413, 412 (June 1979).

30. Dwight Ink, "CSA Closedown—A Myth Challenged," *Bureaucrat*, 11:39-43, 39, 43 (Summer 1982).

31. Aberbach, Putnam, and Rockman, *Bureaucrats and Politicans*, 52, 94, 230-31, 234; Aberbach and Rockman, "The Overlapping Worlds," 28. On meagerness of bureau chiefs' contacts with department heads, see Herbert Kaufman, *The Administrative Behavior of Federal Bureau Chiefs* (Washington, DC: Brookings Institution, 1981), 59-62, 184-90.

32. Thomas D. Lynch and Gerald T. Gabris, "Obstacles to Effective Management," *Bureaucrat*, 10:8-14, 9-10 (Spring 1981).

33. Murphy, Nuechterlein, and Stupak, *Inside the Bureaucracy*, 7, 195.

34. Heclo, *A Government of Strangers*, 131.

35. *U.S. Code*, Title V, secs. 3395, 3132(b).

36. Panel on the Public Service, National Academy of Public Administration, *The Senior Executive Service: An Interim Report, October 1981* (Washington, DC: National Academy of Public Administration, 1981).

37. Ibid., 34-35.

38. Lynch and Gabris, "Obstacles to Effective Management," 9-10.

39. Annette Gaul, "Why Do Executives Leave the Federal Service?" *Management* (published by the U.S. Office of Personnel Management), 2:13-15 (Fall 1981); William J. Lanouette, "SES—From Civil Service Showpiece to Incipient Failure in Two Years," *National Journal*, 13:1296 (18 July 1981).

40. George P. Shultz and Kenneth W. Dam, *Economic Policy Beyond the Headlines* (New York: W. W. Norton, 1977), 173.

41. Califano, *Governing America*, 451, 452. "Government by advocacy" (Shultz and Dam's term) has invaded the White House itself. Charged with "public liaison" are

assistants and deputy assistants to the president for the elderly, youth, women, consumers, Hispanics, blacks, the Jewish community, and other groups.

42. Elliot Richardson, *The Creative Balance: Government, Politics, and the Individual in America's Third Century* (New York: Holt, Rinehart & Winston, 1976), 80.

43. Shultz and Dam, *Economic Policy*, 18.

44. Richardson, *The Creative Balance*, 73.

45. Ball, *The Past Has Another Pattern*, 167.

46. Light, *The President's Agenda*, 44-45. See 42 for comparison of the number of the first and later years' requests.

47. John Helmer, "The Presidential Office: Velvet Fist in an Iron Glove," in *The Illusion of Presidential Government*, eds. Hugh Heclo and Lester M. Salamon (Boulder, CO: Westview Press for the National Academy of Public Administration, 1981), 78-79.

48. This staffing strategy partly reflects reluctance of persons in the private sector to accept appointments in the terminal years or months of an administration.

49. However, negative factors are the fall in the president's public-approval ratings, the shift of his personal energies to foreign affairs, and, consequently, substantial delegation of domestic affairs to his aides.

50. Malek, *Washington's Hidden Tragedy*, 102-3.

51. James L. Sundquist, "A Comparison of Policy-Making Capacity in the United States and Five European Countries: The Case of Population Distribution," in *Population Policy Analysis,* eds. Michael E. Kraft and Mark Schneider (Lexington, MA: D. C. Heath, 1978), 67-80, 71.

52. Ibid., 73. The theme is more fully developed in James L. Sundquist, "Jimmy Carter as Public Administrator: An Appraisal at Mid-Term," *Public Administration Review*, 39:3-11, 6-8 (Jan.-Feb. 1979).

53. Sundquist, "Jimmy Carter as Public Administrator," 8.

Presidential Leadership and the Policy Process | 7

The preceding essays on presidential policy relationships make it obvious that within the U.S. system of fragmented powers and multiple centers of power, the potential exists for the president to be hemmed in by other political actors. From the standpoint of policymaking, the excessive constraining of the presidency might be undesirable if it impairs the executive functions of coordination and comprehensive overview.

To avoid excessive constraining and to be able to put their imprint on public policy, presidents must adroitly wield and add to presidential powers. The essays in this chapter focus on presidential leadership in general and on attempts by presidents to exercise influence in specific realms of public policy: strategic systems, civil rights, foreign policy, and the budget. A final concern addressed is the evaluation of presidential leadership, influence, and success. Throughout this chapter the main focus of students should be on the question: How much presidential power and leadership is both possible and desirable?

The Power to Persuade | 7.1

Richard E. Neustadt

Richard Neustadt's *Presidential Power* is perhaps the most influential book with regard to the presidency—influential in the conduct of the presidency itself. Originally published in 1960, Neustadt's statement so struck President Kennedy that he made the book required reading for White House staffers. Many practitioners and academicians turned practitioner have stated that *Presidential Power* is the rare book that offers useful advice to decisionmakers. Illustration 7a gives an outline of the Neustadt thesis. The following chapter on "the power to persuade" emphasizes the need for presidents and other decisionmakers to have an appreciation for power. As students study Neustadt's important statement, they should be aware of the debate concerning the ethics and values of his prescriptions. Some have concluded that Neustadt offers an amoral "the end justifies the means"

Presidential Power (pp. 33-57) by Richard E. Neustadt, 1960, New York: John Wiley & Sons. Copyright 1960 by John Wiley & Sons. Reprinted by permission.

approach reminiscent of Machiavelli. Others hold that Neustadt is no more amoral or immoral or morally insensitive than a roadmap.

The limits on command suggest the structure of our government. The constitutional convention of 1787 is supposed to have created a government of "separated powers." It did nothing of the sort. Rather, it created a government of separated institutions *sharing* powers.[1] "I am part of the legislative process," Eisenhower often said in 1959 as a reminder of his veto.[2] Congress, the dispenser of authority and funds, is no less part of the administrative process. Federalism adds another set of separated institutions. The Bill of Rights adds others. Many public purposes can only be achieved by voluntary acts of private institutions; the press, for one, in Douglass Cater's phrase, is a "fourth branch of government."[3] And with the coming of alliances abroad, the separate institutions of a London, or a Bonn, share in the making of American public policy.

What the Constitution separates our political parties do not combine. The parties are themselves composed of separated organizations sharing public authority. The authority consists of nominating powers. Our national parties are confederations of state and local party institutions, with a headquarters that represents the White House, more or less, if the party has a president in office. These confederacies manage presidential nominations. All other public offices depend upon electorates confined within the states.[4] All other nominations are controlled within the states. The president and congressmen who bear one party's label are divided by independence upon different sets of voters. The differences are sharpest at the stage of nomination. The White House has too small a share in nominating congressmen, and Congress has too little weight in nominating presidents for party to erase their constitutional separation. Party links are stronger than is frequently supposed, but nominating processes assure the separation.[5]

The separateness of institutions and the sharing of authority prescribe the terms on which a president persuades. When one man shares authority with another, but does not gain or lose his job upon the other's whim, his willingness to act upon the urging of the other turns on whether he conceives the action right for him. The essence of a president's persuasive task is to convince such men that what the White House wants of them is what they ought to do for their sake and on their authority.

Persuasive power, thus defined, amounts to more than charm or reasoned argument. These have their uses for a president, but these are not the whole of his resources. For the men he would induce to do what he wants done on their own responsibility will need or fear some acts by him on his responsibility. If they share his authority, he has some share in theirs. Presidential "powers" may be inconclusive when a president commands, but always remain relevant as he persuades. The status and authority inherent in his office reinforce his logic and his charm.

Status adds something to persuasiveness; authority adds still more. When Truman urged wage changes on his secretary of commerce while the latter was administering the steel mills, he and Secretary Sawyer were not just two men reasoning with one another. Had they been so, Sawyer probably would never have agreed to act. Truman's status gave him special claims to Sawyer's loyalty, or at least attention. In Walter Bagehot's charming phrase "no man can *argue* on his knees." Although there is no kneeling in this country, few men—and exceedingly few cabinet officers— are immune to the impulse to say "yes" to the president of the United States. It grows harder to say "no" when they are seated in his oval office at the White House, or in his study on the second floor, where almost tangibly he partakes of the aura of his physical surroundings. In Sawyer's case, moreover, the president possessed formal authority to intervene in many matters of concern to the secretary of commerce. These matters ranged from jurisdictional disputes among the defense agencies to legislation pending before Congress and, ultimately, to the tenure of the secretary, himself. There is nothing in the record to suggest that Truman voiced specific threats when they negotiated over wage increases. But given his *formal* powers and their relevance to Sawyer's other interests, it is safe to assume that Truman's very advocacy of wage action conveyed an implicit threat.

A president's authority and status give him great advantages in dealing with the men he would persuade. Each "power" is a vantage point for him in the degree that other men have use for his authority. From the veto to appointments, from publicity to budgeting, and so down a long list, the White House now controls the most encompassing array of vantage points in the American political system. With hardly an exception, the men who share in governing this country are aware that at some time, in some degree, the doing of *their* jobs, the furthering of *their* ambitions, may depend upon the president of the United States. Their need for presidential action, or their fear of it, is bound to be recurrent if not actually continuous. Their need or fear is his advantage.

A president's advantages are greater than mere listing of his "powers" might suggest. The men with whom he deals must deal with him until the last day of his term. Because they have continuing relationships with him, his future, while it lasts, supports his present influence. Even though there is no need or fear of him today, what he could do tomorrow may supply today's advantage. Continuing relationships may convert any "power," any aspect of his status, into vantage points in almost any case. When he induces other men to do what he wants done, a president can trade on their dependence now *and* later.

The president's advantages are checked by the advantages of others. Continuing relationships will pull in both directions. These are relationships of mutual dependence. A president depends upon the men he would persuade; he has to reckon with his need or fear of them. They too will possess status, or authority, or both, else they would be of little use to him. Their vantage points confront his own; their power tempers his.

Persuasion is a two-way street. Sawyer, it will be recalled, did not respond at once to Truman's plan for wage increases at the steel mills. On the contrary, the secretary hesitated and delayed and only acquiesced when he was satisfied that publicly he would not bear the onus of decision. Sawyer had some points of vantage all his own from which to resist presidential pressure. If he had to reckon with coercive implications in the president's "situations of strength," so had Truman to be mindful of the implications underlying Sawyer's place as a department head, as steel administrator, and as a cabinet spokesman for business. Loyalty is reciprocal. Having taken on a dirty job in the steel crisis, Sawyer had strong claims to loyal support. Besides, he had authority to do some things that the White House could ill afford. Emulating Wilson, he might have resigned in a huff (the removal power also works two ways). Or emulating Ellis Arnall, he might have declined to sign necessary orders. Or, he might have let it be known publicly that he deplored what he was told to do and protested its doing. By following any of these courses Sawyer almost surely would have strengthened the position of management, weakened the position of the White House, and embittered the union. But the whole purpose of a wage increase was to enhance White House persuasiveness in urging settlement upon union and companies alike. Although Sawyer's status and authority did not give him the power to prevent an increase outright, they gave him capability to undermine its purpose. If his authority over wage rates had been vested by a statute, not by revocable presidential order, his power of prevention might have been complete. So Harold Ickes demonstrated in the famous case of helium sales to Germany before the Second World War.[6]

The power to persuade is the power to bargain. Status and authority yield bargaining advantages. But in a government of "separated institutions sharing powers," they yield them to all sides. With the array of vantage points at his disposal, a president may be far more persuasive than his logic or his charm could make him. But outcomes are not guaranteed by his advantages. There remain the counter pressures those whom he would influence can bring to bear on him from vantage points at their disposal. Command has limited utility; persuasion becomes give-and-take. It is well that the White House holds the vantage points it does. In such a business any president may need them all—and more.

II

This view of power as akin to bargaining is one we commonly accept in the sphere of congressional relations. Every textbook states and every legislative session demonstrates that save in times like the extraordinary Hundred Days of 1933—times virtually ruled out by definition at mid-century—a president will often be unable to obtain congressional action on his terms or even to halt action he opposes. The reverse is equally accepted: Congress often is frustrated by the president. Their formal powers are so intertwined that neither will accomplish very much, for very long, without the acquiescence of the other. By the same token, though, what one demands the other can resist. The stage is set for that great game, much like collective bargaining, in which each seeks to profit from the other's needs and fears. It is a game played catch-as-catch-can, case by case. And everybody knows the game, observers and participants alike.

The concept of real power as a give-and-take is equally familiar when applied to presidential influence outside the formal structure of the federal government. The Little Rock affair may be extreme, but Eisenhower's dealings with the governor—and with the citizens—become a case in point. Less extreme but no less pertinent is the steel seizure case with respect to union leaders, and to workers, and to company executives as well. When he deals with such people a president draws bargaining advantage from his status or authority. By virtue of their public places or their private rights they have some capability to reply in kind.

In spheres of party politics the same thing follows, necessarily, from the confederal nature of our party organizations. Even in the case of national nominations a president's advantages are checked by those of others. In 1944 it is by no means clear that Roosevelt got his first choice as his running mate. In 1948 Truman, then the president, faced serious revolts against his nomination. In 1952 his intervention from the White House helped assure the choice of Adlai Stevenson, but it is far from clear that Truman could have done as much for any other candidate acceptable to him.[7] In 1956 when Eisenhower was president, the record leaves obscure just who backed Harold Stassen's effort to block Richard Nixon's renomination as vice-president. But evidently everything did not go quite as Eisenhower wanted, whatever his intentions may have been.[8] The outcomes in these instances bear all the marks of limits on command and of power checked by power that characterize congressional relations. Both in and out of politics these checks and limits seem to be quite widely understood.

Influence becomes still more a matter of give-and-take when presidents attempt to deal with allied governments. A classic illustration is the long unhappy wrangle over Suez policy in 1956. In dealing with the British and the French before their military intervention, Eisenhower had his share of bargaining advantages but no effective power of command. His allies had their share of counter pressures, and they finally tried the most extreme of all: action despite him. His pressure then was instrumental in reversing them. But had the British government been on safe ground *at home*, Eisenhower's wishes might have made as little difference after intervention as before. Behind the decorum of diplomacy—which was not very decorous in the Suez affair—relationships among allies are not unlike relationships among state delegations at a national convention. Power is persuasion and persuasion becomes bargaining. The concept is familiar to everyone who watches foreign policy.

In only one sphere is the concept unfamiliar: the sphere of executive relations. Perhaps because of civics textbooks and teaching in our schools, Americans instinctively resist the view that power in this sphere resembles power in all others. Even Washington reporters, White House aides, and congressmen are not immune to the illusion that administrative agencies comprise a single structure, "the" executive branch, where presidential word is law, or ought to be. Yet . . . when a president seeks something from executive officials his persuasiveness is subject to the same sorts of limitations as in the case of congressmen, or governors, or national committeemen, or private citizens, or foreign governments. There are no generic differences, no differences in kind and only sometimes in degree. The incidents preceding the dismissal of MacArthur and the incidents surrounding seizure of the steel mills make it plain that here as elsewhere influence derives from bargaining advantages; power is a give-and-take.

Like our governmental structure as whole, the executive establishment consists of separated institutions sharing powers. The president heads one of these; cabinet officers, agency administrators, and military commanders head others. Below the departmental level, virtually independent bureau chiefs head many more. Under mid-century conditions, federal operations spill across dividing lines on organization charts, almost every policy entangles many agencies; almost every program calls for interagency collaboration. Everything somehow involves the president. But operating agencies owe their existence least of all to one another—and only in some part to him. Each has a separate statutory base; each has its statutes to administer; each deals with a different set of subcommittees at the Capitol. Each has its own peculiar set of clients, friends, and enemies outside the formal government. Each has a different set of specialized careerists inside its own bailiwick. Our Constitution gives the president the "take-care" clause and the appointive power. Our statutes give him central budgeting and a degree of personnel control. All agency administrators are responsible to him. But they *also* are responsible to Congress, to their clients, to their staffs, and to themselves. In short, they have five masters. Only after all of those do they owe any loyalty to each other.

"The members of the Cabinet," Charles G. Dawes used to remark, "are a president's natural enemies." Dawes had been Harding's budget director, Coolidge's vice-president, and Hoover's ambassador to London; he also had been General Pershing's chief assistant for supply in the First World War. The words are highly colored, but Dawes knew whereof he spoke. The men who have to serve so many masters cannot help but be somewhat the "enemy" of any one of them. By the same token, any master wanting service is in some degree the "enemy" of such a servant. A president is likely to want loyal support but not to relish trouble on his doorstep. Yet the more his cabinet members cleave to him, the more they may need help from him in fending off the wrath of rival masters. Help, though, is synonymous with trouble. Many a cabinet officer, with loyalty ill-rewarded by his lights and help withheld, has come to view the White House as innately hostile to department heads. Dawes's dictum can be turned around.

A senior presidential aide remarked to me in Eisenhower's time: "If some of these cabinet members would just take time out to stop and ask themselves 'What would I want if I were president?', they wouldn't give him all the trouble he's been having." But even if they asked themselves the question, such officials often could not act upon the answer. Their personal attachment to the president is all too often overwhelmed by duty to their other masters.

Executive officials are not equally advantaged in their dealings with a president. Nor are the same officials equally advantaged all the time. Not every officeholder can resist like a MacArthur, or like Arnall, Sawyer, Wilson, in a rough descending order of effective counter pressure. The vantage points conferred upon officials by their own authority and status vary enormously. The variance is heightened by particulars of time and circumstance. In mid-October 1950, Truman, at a press conference, remarked of the man he had considered firing in August and would fire the next April for intolerable insubordination:

> Let me tell you something that will be good for your souls. It's a pity that you . . . can't understand the ideas of two intellectually honest men when they meet. General MacArthur . . . is a member of the government of the United States. He is loyal to that government. He is loyal to the president. He is loyal to the president in his foreign policy. . . . There is no disagreement between General MacArthur and myself.[9]

MacArthur's status in and out of government was never higher than when Truman spoke those words. The words, once spoken, added to the general's credibility thereafter when he sought to use the press in his campaign against the president. And what had happened between August and October? Near-victory had happened, together with that premature conference on *post*-war plans, the meeting at Wake Island.

If the bargaining advantages of a MacArthur fluctuate with changing circumstances, this is bound to be so with subordinates who have at their disposal fewer "powers," lesser status, to fall back on. And when officials have no "powers" in their own right, or depend upon the president for status, their counter pressure may be limited indeed. White House aides, who fit both categories, are among the most responsive men of all, and for good reason. As a director of the budget once remarked to me, "Thank God I'm here and not across the street. If the president doesn't call me, I've got plenty I can do right here and plenty coming up to me, by rights, to justify my calling him. But those poor fellows over there, if the boss doesn't call them, doesn't ask them to do something, what *can* they do but sit?" Authority and status so conditional are frail reliances in resisting a president's own wants. Within the White House precincts, lifted eyebrows may suffice to set an aide in motion; command, coercion, even charm aside. But even in the White House a president does not monopolize effective power. Even there persuasion is akin to bargaining. A former Roosevelt aide once wrote of cabinet officers:

> Half of a president's suggestions, which theoretically carry the weight of orders, can be safely forgotten by a cabinet member. And if the president asks about a suggestion a second time, he can be told that it is being investigated. If he asks a third time, a wise cabinet officer will give him at least part of what he suggests. But only occasionally, except about the most important matters, do presidents ever get around to asking three times.[10]

The rule applies to staff as well as to the cabinet, and certainly has been applied *by* staff in Truman's time and Eisenhower's.

Some aides will have more vantage points than a selective memory. Sherman Adams, for example, as *the* assistant to the president under Eisenhower, scarcely deserved the appelation "White House aide" in the meaning of the term before his time or as applied to other members of the Eisenhower entourage. Although Adams was by no means "chief of staff" in any sense so sweeping—or so simple—as press commentaries often took for granted, he apparently became no more dependent on the president than Eisenhower on him. "I need him," said the president when Adams turned out to have been remarkably imprudent in the Goldfine case, and delegated to him even the decision on his own departure.[11] This instance is extreme, but the tendency it illustrates is common enough. Any aide who demonstrates to others that he has the president's consistent confidence and a consistent part in presidential business will acquire so much business on his own account that he becomes in some sense independent of his chief. Nothing in the Constitution keeps a well-placed aide from converting status into power of his own, usable in some degree even against the president—an outcome not unknown in Truman's regime or, by all accounts, in Eisenhower's.

The more an officeholder's status and his "powers" stem from sources independent of the president, the stronger will be his potential pressure *on* the president. Department heads in general have more bargaining power than do most members of the White House staff; but bureau chiefs may have still more, and specialists at upper levels of established career services may have almost unlimited reserves of the enormous power which consists of sitting still. As Franklin Roosevelt once remarked:

> The Treasury is so large and far-flung and ingrained in its practices that I find it is almost impossible to get the action and results I want—even with Henry [Morgenthau] there. But the Treasury is not to be compared with the State Department. You should go through the experience of trying to get any changes in the thinking, policy, and action of the career diplomats and then you'd know what a real problem was. But the Treasury and the State Department put together are nothing compared with the Na-a-vy. The admirals are really something to cope with—and I should know. To change anything in the Na-a-vy is like punching a feather bed. You punch it with your right and

you punch it with your left until you are finally exhausted, and then you find the damn bed just as it was before you started punching.[12]

In the right circumstances, of course, a president can have his way with any of these people. Chapter 2 includes three instances where circumstances were "right" and a presidential order was promptly carried out. But one need only note the favorable factors giving those three orders their self-executing quality to recognize that as between a president and his "subordinates," no less than others on whom he depends, real power is reciprocal and varies markedly with organization, subject matter, personality, and situation. The mere fact that persuasion is directed at executive officials signifies no necessary easing of his way. Any new congressman of the administration's party, especially if narrowly elected, may turn out more amenable (though less useful) to the president than any seasoned bureau chief "downtown." *The probabilities of power do not derive from the literary theory of the Constitution.*

III

There is a widely held belief in the United States that were it not for folly or for knavery, a reasonable president would need no power other than the logic of his argument. No less a personage than Eisenhower has subscribed to that belief in many a campaign speech and press-conference remark. But faulty reasoning and bad intentions do not cause all quarrels with presidents. The best of reasoning and of intent cannot compose them all. For in the first place, what the president wants will rarely seem a trifle to the men he wants it from. And in the second place, they will be bound to judge it by the standard of their own responsibilities, not his. However logical his argument according to his lights, their judgment may not bring them to his view.

The men who share in governing this country frequently appear to act as though they were in business for themselves. So, in a real though not entire sense, they are and have to be. When Truman and MacArthur fell to quarreling, for example, the stakes were no less than the substance of American foreign policy, the risks of greater war or military stalemate, the prerogatives of presidents and field commanders, the pride of a pro-consul, and his place in history. Intertwined, inevitably, were other stakes, as well: political stakes for men and factions of both parties; power stakes for interest groups with which they were or wished to be affiliated. And every stake was raised by the apparent discontent in the American public mood. There is no reason to suppose that in such circumstances men of large but differing responsibilities will see all things through the same glasses. On the contrary, it is to be expected that their views of what ought to be done and what they then should do will vary with the differing perspectives their particular responsibilities evoke. Since their duties are not vested in a "team" or a "collegium" but in themselves, as individuals, one must expect that they will see things *for* themselves. Moreover, when they are responsible to many masters and when an event or policy turns loyalty against loyalty—a day-by-day occurrence in the nature of the case—one must assume that those who have the duties to perform will choose the terms of reconciliation. This is the essence of their personal responsibility. When their own duties pull in opposite directions, who else but they can choose what they will do?

When Truman dismissed MacArthur, the latter lost three posts: the American command in the Far East, the Allied command for the occupation of Japan, and the United Nations command in Korea. He also lost his status as the senior officer on active duty in the United States armed forces. So long as he held those positions and that status, though, he had a duty to his troops, to his profession, to himself (the last is hard for any man to disentangle from the rest). As a public figure and a focus for men's hopes he had a duty to constituents at home, and in Korea and Japan. He owed a duty also to those other constituents, the UN governments contributing to his field forces. As a patriot he had a duty to his country. As an accountable official and an expert guide he stood at the call of Congress. As a military officer he had, besides, a duty to the president, his constitutional commander,

Some of these duties may have manifested themselves in terms more tangible or more direct than others. But it would be nonsense to argue that the last *negated* all the rest, however much it might be claimed to override them. And it makes no more sense to think that anybody but MacArthur was effectively empowered to decide how he, himself, would reconcile the competing demands his duties made upon him.

Similar observations could be made about the rest of the executive officials encountered in Chapter 2. Price Director Arnall, it will be recalled, refused in advance to sign a major price increase for steel if Mobilization Director Wilson or the White House should concede one before management had settled with the union. When Arnall did this, he took his stand, in substance, on his oath of office. He would do what he had sworn to do in *his* best judgment, so long as he was there to do it. This posture may have been assumed for purposes of bargaining and might have been abandoned had his challenge been accepted by the president. But no one could be sure and no one, certainly, could question Arnall's right to make the judgment for himself. As head of an agency and as a politician, with a program to defend and a future to advance, *he* had to decide what he had to do on matters that, from his perspective, were exceedingly important. Neither in policy nor in personal terms, nor in terms of agency survival, were the issues of a sort to be considered secondary by an Arnall, however much they might have seemed so to a Wilson (or a Truman). Nor were the merits likely to appear the same to a price stabilizer and to men with broader duties. Reasonable men, it is so often said, *ought* to be able to agree on the requirements of given situations. But when the outlook varies with the placement of each man, and the response required in his place is for each to decide, their reasoning may lead to disagreement quite as well—and quite as reasonably. Vanity, or vice, may weaken reason, to be sure, but it is idle to assign these as the cause of Arnall's threat of MacArthur's defiance. Secretary Sawyer's hesitations, cited earlier, are in the same category. One need not denigrate such men to explain their conduct. For the responsibilities they felt, the "facts" they saw, simply were not the same as those of their superiors; yet they, not the superiors, had to decide what they would do.

Outside the executive branch the situation is the same, except that loyalty to the president may often matter *less*. There is no need to spell out the comparison with governors of Arkansas, steel company executives, trade union leaders, and the like. And when one comes to congressmen who can do nothing for themselves (or their constituents) save as they are elected, term by term, in districts and through party structures *differing* from those on which a president depends, the case is very clear. An able Eisenhower aide with long congressional experience remarked to me in 1958: "The people on the Hill don't do what they might *like* to do, they do what they think they *have* to do in their own interest as *they* see it...." This states the case precisely.

The essence of a president's persuasive task with congressmen and everybody else *is to induce them to believe that what he wants of them is what their own appraisal of their own responsibilities requires them to do in their interest, not his.* Because men may differ in their views on public policy, because differences in outlook stem from differences in duty—duty to one's office, one's constituents, oneself—that task is bound to be more like collective bargaining than like a reasoned argument among philosopher kings. Overtly or implicitly, hard bargaining has characterized all illustrations offered up to now. This is the reason why: persuasion deals in the coin of self-interest with men who have some freedom to reject what they find counterfeit.

Notes

1. The reader will want to keep in mind the distinction between two senses in which the word *power* is employed. When I have used the word (or its plural) to refer to formal constitutional, statutory, or customary authority, it is either qualified by the adjective "formal" or placed in quotation marks as "power(s)." Where I have used it in the sense of effective influence upon the conduct of others, it appears without quotation marks (and always in the singular). Where clarity and convenience permit, *authority* is substituted for "power" in the first sense and *influence* for power in the second sense.

2. See, for example, his press conference of July 22,

1959, as reported in the *New York Times* for July 23, 1959.

3. See Douglass Cater, *The Fourth Branch of Government*, Boston: Houghton-Mifflin, 1959.

4. With the exception of the vice-presidency, of course.

5. See David B. Truman's illuminating study of party relationships in the 81st Congress, *The Congressional Party*, New York: Wiley, 1959, especially chaps. 4, 6, and 8.

6. As Secretary of the Interior in 1939, Harold Ickes refused to approve the sale of helium to Germany despite the insistence of the State Department and the urging of President Roosevelt. Without the Secretary's approval, such sales were forbidden by statute. See *The Secret Diaries of Harold L. Ickes*, New York: Simon and Schuster, 1954, Vol. 2, especially 391-393, 396-399. See also Michael J. Reagan, "The Helium Controversy" in the forthcoming case book on civil-military relations prepared for the Twentieth Century Fund under the editorial direction of Harold Stein.

In this instance the statutory authority ran to the secretary as a matter of *his* discretion. A president is unlikely to fire cabinet officers for the conscientious exercise of such authority. If the president did so, their successors might well be embarrassed both publicly and at the Capitol were they to reverse decisions previously taken. As for a president's authority to set aside discretionary determination of this sort, it rests, if it exists at all, on shaky legal ground not likely to be trod save in the gravest situations.

7. Truman's *Memoirs* indicate that having tried and failed to make Stevenson an avowed candidate in the spring of 1952, the president decided to support the candidacy of vice-president Barkley. But Barkley withdrew early in the convention for lack of key northern support. Though Truman is silent on the matter, Barkley's active candidacy nearly was revived during the balloting, but the forces then aligning to revive it were led by opponents of Truman's Fair Deal, principally Southerners. As a practical matter, the president could not have lent his weight to *their* endeavors and could back no one but Stevenson to counter them. The latter's strength could not be shifted, then, to Harriman or Kefauver. Instead the other Northerners had to be withdrawn. Truman helped withdraw them. But he had no other option. See Memoirs by Harry S. Truman, Vol. 2, *Years of Trial and Hope*, Garden City: Doubleday, 1956, copr. 1956 Time Inc., 495-496.

8. The reference is to Stassen's public statement of July 23, 1956, calling for Nixon's replacement on the Republican ticket by Governor Herter of Massachusetts, the later secretary of state. Stassen's statement was issued after a conference with the president. Eisenhower's public statements on the vice-presidential nomination, both before and after Stassen's call, permit of alternative inferences: either that the president would have preferred another candidate, provided this could be arranged without a showing of White House dictation, or that he wanted Nixon on condition that the latter could show popular appeal. In the event, neither result was achieved. Eisenhower's own remarks lent strength to rapid party moves which smothered Stassen's effort. Nixon's nomination thus was guaranteed too quickly to appear the consequence of popular demand. For the public record on this matter see reported statements by Eisenhower, Nixon, Stassen, Herter, and Leonard Hall (the National Republican Chairman) in the *New York Times* for March 1, 8, 15, 16; April 27; July 15, 16, 25-31; August 3, 4, 17, 23, 1956. See also the account from private sources by Earl Mazo in *Richard Nixon: A Personal and Political Portrait*, New York: Harper, 1959, 158-187.

9. Stenographic transcript of presidential press conference, October 19, 1950, on file in the Truman Library at Independence, Missouri.

10. Jonathan Daniels, *Frontier on the Potomac*, New York: Macmillan, 1946, 31-32.

11. Transcript of presidential press conference, June 18, 1958, in *Public Papers of the Presidents: Dwight D. Eisenhower, 1958,* Washington: The National Archives, 1959, 479. In the summer of 1958, a congressional investigation into the affairs of a New England textile manufacturer, Bernard Goldfine, revealed that Sherman Adams had accepted various gifts and favors from him (the most notoriety attached to a vicuña coat). Adams also had made inquiries about the status of a Federal Communications Commission proceeding in which Goldfine was involved. In September 1958, Adams was allowed to resign. The episode was highly publicized and much discussed in that year's congressional campaigns.

12. As reported in Marriner S. Eccles, *Beckoning Frontiers*, New York: Knopf, 1951, 336.

13. In drawing together these observations on the Marshall Plan, I have relied on the record of personal participation by Joseph M. Jones, *The Fifteen Weeks*, New York: Viking, 1955, especially 89-256; on the recent study by Harry Bayard Price, *The Marshall Plan and Its Meaning*, Ithaca: Cornell University Press, 1955, especially 1-86; on the Truman *Memoirs*, Vol. 2, chaps. 7-9; on Arthur H. Vandenberg, Jr., editor, *The Private Papers of Senator Vandenberg*, Boston: Houghton Mifflin, 1952, especially 373ff.; and on notes of my own made at the time. This is an instance of policy development not covered, to my knowledge, by any of the university programs engaged in the production of case studies.

14. Secretary Marshall's speech, formally suggesting what became known as the Marshall Plan, was made at Harvard on June 5, 1947. On June 20 the President vetoed the Taft-Hartley Act; his veto was overridden three days later. On June 16 he vetoed the first of two tax reduction bills (HR 1) passed at the first session of the 80th Congress; the second of these (HR 3950), a replacement for the other, he also disapproved on July 18. In both instances his veto was narrowly sustained.

15. *Private Papers of Senator Vandenberg*, 378-379 and 446.

16. The initial reluctance of Secretary of the Treasury John Snyder to support large-scale spending overseas became a matter of public knowledge on June 25, 1947. At a press conference on that day he interpreted Marshall's Harvard speech as a call on Europeans to help themselves, by themselves. At another press conference

the same day, Marshall for his own part had indicated that the U.S. would consider helping programs on which Europeans agreed. The next day Truman held a press conference and was asked the inevitable question. He replied, "General Marshall and I are in complete agreement." When pressed further, Truman remarked sharply, "The secretary of the treasury and the secretary of state and the president are in complete agreement." Thus the president cut Snyder off, but had programming gathered less momentum overseas, no doubt he would have been heard from again as time passed and opportunity offered.

The foregoing quotations are from the stenographic transcript of the presidential press conference June 26, 1947, on file in the Truman Library at Independence, Missouri.

17. A remark made in December 1955, three years after he left office, but not unrepresentative of views he expressed, on occasion, while he was president.

18. This might also be taken as testimony to the political timidity of officials in the State Department and the Budget Bureau where that fear seems to have been strongest. However, conversations at the time with White House aides incline me to believe that there, too, interjection of the price issue was thought a gamble and a risk. For further comment see my "Congress and the Fair Deal: A Legislative Balance Sheet," *Public Policy*, Cambridge: Harvard University Press, 1954, Vol. 5, 362-364.

Illustration 7a: A Diagram of Neustadt's Presidential Power

General Propositions	Advice	Prescriptions
There are many competitors to the president's power.	To survive in our system of divided authority, a president must have the "power to persuade," which allows him to add to his clerk responsibilities (authority) and become a *leader with power* engendering "self-enforcing" decrees.	1. Appreciate power! —understand that there are limited stocks —be shrewd, cunning, skillful —tend to power stakes 2. Develop bargaining skills! 3. Guard professional reputation! 4. Secure and maintain public support and standing!
The president is potentially hemmed in.		
As the presidency functions so functions the nation.		
We expect much from the president but give him little.		
Command (authority) does not equal leadership.		
The presidency is no place for amateurs.		

7.2 Taking the "X" out of MX or Finding a Home for the Missile

Kenneth N. Ciboski

The controversy over U.S. efforts to develop and deploy the MX missile illustrates the prospects for and constraints on presidential power. The following original essay traces the MX case against the backdrop of presidential power.

Decisions affecting national security and national defense in the United States involve a number of participants. Such decisions are likely to involve the president, the Joint Chiefs of Staff, the Department of Defense, business corporations concerned about contracts, the Congress, the press and, as in the case of the MX (Missile Experimental) decision, religious groups, environmentalists, state and local politicians, and to some extent West European allies.

To understand the intricacies of the process leading to a decision on the MX program and how to deploy the missile, one needs to examine the part played by the participants. Specifically, as several recent works argue, one should look at the participants and try to determine how each sees the issue. Students of national security policy need to understand the domestic political processes that have a major impact on national security decisions for which presidents must ultimately be accountable in a democratic political system.[1]

The bureaucratic politics model has been employed to describe decision-making as it occurs in the executive branch. Studies by Allison and Halperin, for example, focus on that part of the process involving the bureaucracy and the president as he deals with the bureaucracy.[2] This study will focus instead on presidential-congressional relations in the MX decision, although other participants will not be ignored.

An important question is the nature of the constraints imposed by the participants on the president in the process leading to the MX decision. To what extent does the democratic political process provide a milieu that leads to constraints on presidential decision-making?

One study suggests that decision-making will always involve the clash of interests, which automatically lead to constraints in the exercise of power:

> The individuals involved in decisionmaking do not see the problem in the same way, nor do they have the same interests. Each participant, because of his background and his particular role in the government, has access to different information and has different concerns. Each sees a different *face* of the issue. What is a budget issue to one participant will be a foreign relations issue to a second or a Congressional relations issue to a third.[3]

Richard Neustadt in *Presidential Power: The Politics of Leadership* emphasizes that the power of the president is not automatic. The president's influence comes from three major sources: the bargaining advantages inherent in the job, the professional reputation of the president, and his public prestige. The president must work continually and guard carefully those areas that will promote his influence.[4]

Essentially, the bureaucratic politics model has several components. First is the notion that, for any single issue, there will be numerous individuals and organizations in the executive branch, with each possibly seeking different goals and objectives in the process leading to a national defense or foreign policy decision. The result is conflict over the issue.

The "maker" of government policy is not a single calculating decisionmaker, but rather a conglomerate of large organizations and political

---

The author had the privilege of being a student of Professor Louis Koenig in a 1981 National Endowment Summer Seminar on the presidency, and he thanks Professor Koenig for criticism of an early draft of the paper.

actors who differ substantially about what their government should do on any particular issue and who compete in attempting to affect both governmental decisions and the actions of their government.[5]

A government is not, in fact, a single individual with a single purpose and an ability to control completely his actions. Rather each government consists of numerous individuals, many of them working in large organizations. Constrained, to be sure, by the shared images of their society, these individuals nevertheless have very different interests, very different priorities, and are concerned with very different questions.[6]

A second proposition is that no individual or organization is omnipotent. This includes the president, who is one participant among many. The president might be the most powerful but, as some studies indicate, the president is one of many chiefs.[7]

A third proposition is that the final decision is not what is necessarily the "best" decision from the standpoint of the nonparticipant observer of a decision. Rather, the outcome is the result of bargaining, negotiating, conflict, and compromise among the participants. Confusion can reign and individuals or groups with unequal influence can characterize the process. Essentially, this process takes place because individuals want to advance the "best" interests of their groups, organizations, and what they think are the national interests of the country.

A fourth proposition is that differences can exist between the decision as it was intended to be implemented and the reality of implementation. The result is usually unintended, particularly from the standpoint of Congress. One scholar asserts—and the record would seem to support his conclusions—that certain kinds of policies relevant to this topic face implementation problems. These are new policies that have to be geared up from scratch, and the officials do not always know what to order the implementers to do. Decentralized policies are another category. So many people and resources are involved that it is difficult for all of them to know exactly what should be done and how it should be done. Controversial policies (and the MX is certainly controversial) also have implementation problems. Those who are to implement the policy might disagree with how the decision was made and why, and they might resist the goals of implementation. The more complex a policy, the more likely there will be problems of implementation. Too many goals contribute to complexity, which in turn makes it difficult for policymakers to provide the specifics of implementation or to oversee the implementation process. Executive follow-up and legislative oversight are haphazard and intermittent at best.[8]

Background on the MX (Missile Experimental)

Concepts like the MX missile have been contemplated and discussed since at least the 1960s. For the first time the air force, on October 25, 1974, successfully tested an intercontinental ballistic missile dropped from an airplane. The missile was dropped from a C-5A transport flying at 20,000 feet over the Pacific Ocean off the Southern California coast. The 78,000 pound missile was mounted on a carriage and was pulled by drogue parachutes out of the rear door of the huge transport. It was held upright by parachutes and fell to 8,000 feet before its engines were ignited. The engines burned for ten seconds, carrying the missile to 20,000 feet before they were turned off. It fell into the ocean.

A Pentagon spokesman announced that the test was a success. The missile was the largest object ever to be dropped from an airplane and fulfilled the objective of testing the stability of a plane when it drops such a heavy object. The test was part of a revolutionary concept being pursued by the air force, which was to develop a mobile intercontinental ballistic missile that could be launched from an airplane, from truck or railroad cars on the ground, or from underground silos.

The concept of the MX springs from a concern that the present generation of fixed land-based ICBM missiles in their underground silos might become vulnerable to the Soviet Union's larger missiles with warheads, known as MIRV (multiple independently-targeted re-entry vehicles). The concern has been with the Soviet blockbuster missile, the SS-18, which was not included in the SALT II agreement of June 1979. The United States Air Force test of the MX had been made as former Secretary of State Henry Kissinger arrived in Moscow for arms talks, and he was to attempt to convince the Soviet Union to agree to a halt in development of mobile intercontinental missiles. A Pentagon spokesman said the events were a coincidence. It should be recalled that the Soviet Union objected to United States efforts to get an agreement in 1972 that would ban mobile strategic missiles. That agreement did not prevent development of mobile missiles, and from autumn 1973 to autumn 1974, the Soviet Union periodically test-fired a mobile missile. As a result, the Pentagon took the position that the Soviet Union was ahead of the United States in development of mobile missiles. In mid-October 1974, the Soviet Union fired two tests in one week into the mid-Pacific, which confirmed this part of the Soviet missile development program.

Some arms control specialists have questioned the development of the mobile missile because they think it could complicate any future agreements on offensive strategic weapons. They argue that deployment of the MX can also encourage a first strike mentality in the Soviet leadership. Generally, critics view the weapon as destabilizing.

The difficulty is that the ordinary "national technical means" to verify arms agreements between the Soviet Union and the United States could not be applied to mobile missiles, which can be moved and concealed. The result is that each side would find it difficult to monitor the number of missiles deployed. The number of fixed land-based missiles can be established with a high degree of assurance by reconnaissance satellites photographing silo covers. For these reasons, the Ford administration was pressing the Soviet Union for a ban on deployment of any mobile missile. If a ban were not achieved, the administration made it clear that it would press ahead with development and deployment of mobile missiles.

At the time the air force made its first test of the MX concept, it faced a dilemma. The air force had taken great pains to demonstrate that land-based missiles cannot be destroyed in a surprise attack. At the same time, however, the air force did not want to lose its stake in the strategic missile field to the navy, and the air force advanced the argument that land-based ICBMs were becoming vulnerable. The navy has mobile missiles on nuclear submarines.

In October 1977, Secretary of Defense Harold Brown approved full-scale development funds for the new mobile MX missile system. The Defense Department was to ask Congress for $245 million in development for the fiscal year 1979. The Carter administration had not made a decision on development and deployment of the weapon, which would be the largest and most costly ever undertaken by the United States. The proposal was designed to replace the present Minuteman missile system and to have the new missile placed at launch points along a 10 to 12 mile tunnel. Estimates at that time were that the development would cost $35 billion to $40 billion. Defense Secretary Brown argued that the missile system could buoy U.S. defenses and make the nation's strategic arsenal much less vulnerable to attack in the 1980s.

In December 1977, however, President Jimmy Carter turned down the Pentagon's request for full-scale development funds for the MX missile amid growing debate within the administration about the future of the strategic weapons arsenal. At the time, the decision was viewed as a setback for Defense Secretary Brown and air force leaders who had urged its development. Administration and Pentagon sources indicated that Carter's decision was based on uncertainty within the administration about how new missiles should be deployed and what the potential impact of their deployment and development would be on relations with the USSR. There were also indications that the National Security Council had argued against full-scale development at that time.

After much debate in the Congress and within the administration, President Carter, following a meeting with the National Security Council, announced in June 1979 a decision to proceed with full-scale development of the MX missile. The decision left open the questions of where and how to deploy the missile. The public stance of the Carter administration became known in September 1979. On September 7, President Carter stated that he was concerned about the Soviet threat to current U.S. fixed-based missiles and announced plans for deploying 200 new missiles in a mobile position in western desert valleys. He said that deployment would be fully operational in 1989, and that the mobility of the system would enable the missiles to elude a Soviet assault on the system. Secretary of Defense Brown announced that the decision had the support of representatives from the states of Utah and Nevada where the missile would be deployed. The plan called for putting the missiles into a 4,600 shelter area. Each missile then would have 23 shelters among which it could be shuttled to keep the Soviet Union from knowing its location. By this time the missile was in full-scale engineering development, the last stage before deployment.

Thus the stage was set for controversy about the development and deployment of the missile. There appeared to be a consensus among interests on the need for a new missile system, but a great debate developed about how the missile should be deployed. Many interests had an impact on the decision President Ronald Reagan made in 1983 on how to proceed with deployment of the MX.

Defense Department

As noted, the Defense Department approved full-scale development funds for the new MX missile in October 1977. The Defense Department was to ask Congress for $245 million in development for the fiscal year in 1979. In December 1977, however, President Carter turned down the Pentagon's request. As noted also, President Carter reversed himself in June 1979, and then in September 1979 a decision was made on the development and deployment of the missile.

At the time the decision was made, the Carter administration was in the final stages of the Strategic Arms Limitations Treaty II (SALT II). President Carter was fond of referring to SALT II as the "centerpiece" of his foreign policy. Skeptics of the decisions were inclined to think that the administration needed support in Congress and among others in the public opposed to SALT II, and the thinking was that the Carter administration could garner more support, or at least pacify the opposition to some provisions of SALT II, by proceeding with the MX system. Some members of the Congress and Lieutenant General Daniel Graham (U.S. Army, retired) surmised that the Carter administration was buying time without being committed to the MX development and deployment. General Graham testified in January 1980 before the subcommittee on public lands of the Interior and Insular Affairs committee, U.S. House of Representatives:

> I do not think it too unreasonable to wonder, given the track record of the Carter administration, whether the deployment scheme selected by the administration is the one which they felt relatively sure would never be funded by the Senate of the United States or the Congress of the United States, and would never be deployed, because in fact the racetrack system is in many ways a military inanity.[9]

The reasons for the MX decision by the Carter administration seem less important than the consequences of the decision. In the heat of the 1980 presidential election campaign, Ronald Reagan indicated on several occasions that he questioned the Carter decision to base the MX missile in Nevada and Utah. Shortly after the Reagan administration took office, new Secretary of Defense Caspar W. Weinberger took steps that appeared to be leading to a reversal of the Carter administration decision.

On March 16, 1981, Weinberger named a panel of nongovernmental experts to study where the system ought to be based. The panel was to report July 1, 1981, when a decision was to have been made on where to place the MX or what to do with the whole system. The committee, known as the Townes committee because it was chaired by Dr. Charles Townes, Nobel prize-winning physicist from the University of California, Berkeley, was composed of lawyers, scientific experts, retired generals and admirals, and a former defense official in the Nixon administration, among others. The appointment of the Townes committee presented the appearance of objectivity by the secretary of defense and the Reagan administration. Also, the technique could legitimize the ultimate decision, and it tended to promote the notion that neither the secretary of defense nor others in the Reagan administration could be held solely responsible for the final decision.

Secretary Weinberger feared lawsuits by environmentalists and economists if the underground mode of deployment in Nevada and Utah were implemented. Shortly after taking office, Secretary Weinberger considered deploying the MX at sea, but the Pentagon dismissed his view, charging that he was not an expert.[10] The Townes panel included three naval experts, an indication that the sea concept had not been abandoned, but as a congressional source told the writer in the summer of 1981, "It is the air force's turn." The new defense secretary was also reported to have believed that the MX system proposed by Carter had an element of the Rube Goldberg unreal about it.[11] This remark was said to have been directed at the plans for lids on the missile holes so they could be opened to show the Soviets where the missiles were. Weinberger said, "Why open up the lid and let them see the missiles and then move them on?"

The Townes committee was to have reported by July 1, 1981, but a newspaper report of July 23 indicated that a decision would not be made by the administration until after the Labor Day congressional recess. The committee reported, but the contents of the report were not revealed. The committee might not have been unanimous in a decision on how to base the missile, or, possibly, it supported a position that would have opposed the air force. In an "executive summary" of the report released March 23, 1982, the panel found "no practical mode" of basing missiles on the ground that would guarantee survival of an enemy attack. It recommended putting the missiles on large airplanes that could patrol for several days at a time.[12] The air force opposed the airborne plan.

Air Force

The air force obtained President Carter's approval of a plan to shuttle 200 missiles between and among 4,600 shelters in Utah and Nevada in an effort to prevent the Soviet Union from locating them. The air force favored this plan over all other alternatives. However, indications are that other forces were at work in the Reagan administration to move toward a different decision. The executive summary of the Townes committee report supports this conclusion.

Because the Townes committee report or the executive summary were not revealed in the summer of 1981, press leaks about what Secretary Weinberger intended to do began to occur. The air force told White House and congressional officials that Secretary Weinberger had decided to recommend basing the MX nuclear missile aboard a fleet of aircraft. A Defense spokesman, however, indicated that no decision had been made.[13] Air force officials began meeting July 16, 1981 with officials on Capitol Hill and in the White House to express their concern. Indications are that the air force was attempting to generate opposition in order to dissuade Secretary Weinberger from recommending an airborne option, which they contended would be increasingly costly and less able than other alternatives to survive a Soviet attack. As the decisions on the MX and the selection of a new long-range bomber were delayed, Weinberger's ostensible preferences were mentioned more frequently. Weinberger was said to favor putting 200 intercontinental ballistic missiles on a new fleet of 100 C-5A aircraft. The United States has about 70 C-5 aircraft, which are giant cargo transport planes manufactured by the Lockheed Corporation. Production stopped in the mid-1970s. The air force secretary, Verne Orr, was critical of the airborne proposal.

Air Force officials indicated that the first fifteen airplanes would have to be deployed by 1986, but that the C-5A planes would only be used to transport the missiles until a new, more sophisticated airplane, known in air force circles as the "Big Bird," would be developed. The airplane, which could stay aloft from five to seven days and thus presumably survive a nuclear attack, was being developed by the Boeing Company. The air force contended that the system would result in a less accurate fleet of missiles, have a less dependable system for commanding them, and have a cost increase of $15 billion to $20 billion for construction of basing sites for the airplanes. Critics also argued that the runways could be destroyed while the airplanes were aloft.

Proponents such as Secretary Weinberger argued that the basing system, unlike one on land, could be expanded greatly, would cost less initially, and would have none of the political costs inherent in a decision to base the system on land. Advocates of a strong military, among them Republican senators Paul Laxalt of Nevada and Jake Garn of Utah, some of the president's strongest supporters, repeatedly expressed their opposition to the Nevada-Utah plan for basing the missile. Opposition also came from the Mormon church and from a coalition of cattlemen, Indians, environmentalists, miners, antiwar groups, and citizens' committees.

Previous Decision and Constraints on Decision-Making in the Reagan Administration

Previous decisions can have an impact on a new presidential administration if officials of any administration wish to make changes at variance with earlier decisions. The MX missile decision made by the Carter administration for deployment of the system in Utah and Nevada is no exception.

There were few indications that the MX concept could be scuttled easily. A consensus seemed to exist that something like the MX or a good alternative was needed. The issue confronting the Congress and the Reagan administration was the possibility that the Carter basing mode choice for the missile was not the most feasible or desirable.

Congress debated how best to base the new missile and the Reagan administration reviewed the MX program, but the air force and American industry mobilized to build the system approved by President Carter. Work proceeded on the development and deployment of the MX system in shelters in Nevada and Utah.

Major General Forrest S. McCartney, commander of the Ballistic Missile office in San Bernardino, California, headquarters of the MX project, stated in the spring of 1981 that the MX program as approved by the Carter administration had "significant momentum."[14] This momentum presented Congress and the Reagan administration with a special urgency.

Construction crews poured cement and erected steel girders on a strip at Vandenberg Air Force Base in California. They built a complex to be used for twenty test flights beginning in 1983. Hundreds of officials at the California headquarters for the MX project worked on the development of the missile and a multiple-shelter basing system in Nevada and Utah.

All financing for the MX project was being funneled through the Ballistic Missile office of the air force in San Bernardino. The office was housed in a windowless former warehouse at Norton Air Force Base. As of March 19, 1981, the office under the direction of General McCartney employed 567 military and civilian officials. The office, which reported to the air force system command, was broken down into thirty-six divisions responsible for such matters as propulsion, guidance and control, financial management, contract review, and safety. The office was responsible for overseeing design, engineering, and eventual production.

As of early March 1981 the missile office had awarded major contracts to more than thirty corporations. The biggest, totaling $588 million, went to Martin Marietta Aerospace in Denver for assembly and testing of the missile. Other major recipients included AVCO Systems Division of Wilmington, Massachusetts, $175 million for re-entry systems; the Aerojet Strategic Propulsion Company of Sacramento, California, $152 million for stage two development; GTE Sylvania, Waltham, Massachusetts, $325 million for command control and communications; Hercules Inc., of Magna, Utah, $175 million for stage three development; Rockwell International Autonetics, Anaheim, California, $389 million for guidance and control; Rockwell International Rocketdyne, Canoga Park, California, $382 million for stage four; and the Thickol Corporation of Brigham City, Utah, $162 million for stage one development. With the approval of production of the missile, these companies would receive the multibillion dollar contracts to produce their components. In 1982 Common Cause reported that for nineteen months ending July 30, 1982, members of the Congress had received from the political action committees (PAC) of a dozen missile contractors a total of $780,000. Many of the companies mentioned here were contributors, an indication of their enormous economic stakes in the MX.

More than $2 billion had been invested in the program by spring 1981 and more than $5 billion had been committed when the second MX commission, the Scowcroft commission, got around to making its recommendations in early 1983. The sizeable sum already committed to the program was given by the commission as one reason for its recommendations.

These considerations loomed large and urgently in early 1981 as Secretary of Defense Weinberger and President Reagan had to decide what to do with the MX program. In addition, they faced a growing body of scientific, political, and environmental opinion opposed to a land-based multiple-shelter system. To make matters worse, Secretary of State Alexander M. Haig, Jr., supported the underground plan in Nevada and Utah. His fear was that yielding to opponents of land-basing would undermine efforts to sustain the NATO support for basing medium-range missiles in Europe.[15]

Technical Considerations

The congressional Office of Technology and Assessment (OTA), in a congressional report released in March 1981, noted that the MX would be vulnerable to Soviet attack on the ground and also would cause great environmental and economic dislocations in Nevada and Utah. The report also mentioned the possibility of putting the missile on submarines.

On June 22, 1981, the Office of Technology and Assessment presented a briefing on MX missile basing to the Subcommittee on Public Lands and National Parks of the House Committee on Interior and Insular Affairs. The briefing purposely avoided larger issues, such as whether and why the missile itself is needed, and instead concentrated on a review of all the basing modes the assessment panel was able to identify. The OTA found that five basing modes offered reasonable prospects for feasibility and survivability. OTA also emphasized that each of the five modes had serious problems, risks, uncertainties, and other drawbacks. Particularly, the OTA report indicated that no basing mode could be advanced which would provide the likelihood that a substantial number of survivable missiles could be guaranteed before the end of this decade. OTA concluded that the "window of vulnerability" cannot be closed quickly.

According to OTA, five basing modes are probably feasible and offer reasonable prospects of survivability in the 1990s:

1. Multiple protective shelter (MPS) basing. This is essentially the system proposed by the Carter administration. It would preserve the land-based component of the strategic triad of land, sea, and air missiles. The major problem with the system is that if the Soviets deploy large numbers of warheads by 1990, the original 4,600 shelters would not be enough. This is what upset citizens of Utah and Nevada. They feared that the initial environmental impact of building 4,600 shelters with 200 missiles might be just the beginning of the program. OTA found that a prudent construction schedule might aim at somewhere between 8,000 and 9,000 shelters and the deployment of 350 missiles by 1990. And General David Jones, chairman of the Joint Chiefs of Staff, indicated that possibility. The cost would be more than $50 billion (1980 dollars) over the next nine years. There would be severe socioeconomic and physical impact on the deployment region. The system would offer survivability only if the United States could succeed at what the air force calls "preservation of location uncertainty" (PLU). But high confidence in PLU cannot be given until prototypes have been constructed and tested.

2. MPS basing defended by a low-altitude ABM system known as LoADS. This would make a significant number of shelters viable against a larger Soviet threat, but the technical risk associated with preservation of location uncertainty would increase and this could be catastrophic. Adding LoADS would also require that the United States withdraw from or get the ABM treaty amended.

3. Launch under attack. This would be the cheapest way to base the MX. With improved communications systems, the system might be reliable. The biggest problem would be that it would require national command authorities to be available instantly at all times, and they would have to be willing to make an effectively irreversible decision to launch U.S. nuclear missiles in a few minutes on the basis of information from remote sensors. Soviet ICBMs can arrive at U.S. targets within thirty minutes of launch, so some concern about not having time to evaluate the threat before making a decision or to detect and correct errors has been expressed with this basing mode.

4. Small submarines. OTA thought this mode would be the most survivable of available basing options, especially under conditions of partial deployment. The report indicated that the panel was not certain that the marginal difference—in accuracy, responsiveness, time-on-target control, and rapid retargeting when compared with the land-based missile—would have any military or strategic significance. The panel recognized that abandoning the notion of giving equal importance to land, sea, and air basing for strategic forces could create serious institutional problems, and that severe political and diplomatic impacts were probable. One advantage at the time of the report was that no known Soviet technology existed to determine the location of a ballistic missile submarine at sea. However, the possibility of an unexpected technological development in antisubmarine warfare could not be excluded. Another major drawback was the lack of appropriate shipyard capacity in the United States, which would probably delay initial deployment of MX-carrying submarines until 1990.

5. Air mobile. This mode would be highly survivable against a Soviet strike if it received and acted immediately on adequate warning. Since the aircraft could launch missiles only while airborne, take-off during a crisis situation might be destabilizing if the Soviets interpreted it as preparation for a U.S. first strike. If the Soviets were willing to attack the few hundred military and civilian airfields at which such a force could land after an attack, the MX missiles would have to be used or lost within five to eight hours.

The panel concluded that problems with other basing modes appeared more substantial.[16]

Parts of the MX system such as launching technology, the missile itself, and missile guidance would be affected differently by a Reagan administration decision to alter the basing. If a sea-based or air-based system were selected, the basing engineering and developmental work would have to be abandoned. The work involving the design of the 4,600 horizontal shelters, a 7,800-mile network of roads connecting them, and the development of a vehicle to transport the missiles from shelter to shelter would be useless.

A shift to basing the missile in a vertical silo (for example, revamping the present Minuteman missile silos for MX) would also preclude use of most of the basing work already completed. The Townes committee recommended to the Pentagon in summer 1981 that the program be cut in half, from 200 to 100 missiles, and that the missiles be placed in vertical silos rather than among horizontal shelters, presumably in Utah and Nevada.[17] In addition, the panel recommended the development of an air-launched MX system and advised that intensified research and development of an Anti-Ballistic Missile (ABM) system be undertaken.

State and Local Entities

MX coordinating offices were organized in Carson City, Nevada, and Salt Lake City, Utah, in order to cope with the myriad of dissent, problems, and possible impact of the MX development in the respective states. Each office had a staff that was concerned with studying the impact of the project and with developing a plan for getting money for schools, roads, housing, and the like if the project should be based in the respective states. The states were concerned that the federal government might not provide the needed funds. An anonymous source in summer 1981 told the writer that the air force was not very forthcoming in providing information about developments and plans for the Utah-Nevada area. The offices operated under a sunset clause: they were to close after they were no longer needed.

Groups for almost every interest—land, ranching, mining, water, energy, and the like—sprung into action to express their concern. In May 1981, the Mormon church came out in opposition to the MX basing in southern Utah. One poll indicated that more than 76 percent of those questioned by a Salt Lake City television station opposed MX for Utah. Only a few months earlier, there was almost an even split.[18] The Mormons issued their statement on May 5 and wired it to President Reagan and to Utah and Nevada congressional delegations. The statement noted that church pioneers had chosen Utah as a "base from which to carry the gospel of peace to the peoples of the earth," and they said that basing the system in their region would be a "denial of the very essence of that gospel." People also feared that the missiles based in their states would make them prime targets for nuclear attack by the Soviet Union.

Congressional Behavior and the MX Program

Congress has consistently authorized and appropriated funds requested for MX research and development, and it has rejected amendments to delete funding. The Appropriations and Armed Services committees of both the House and Senate have consistently supported the concept of the MX in authorizing and appropriating money for research and development.

Support has continued because most members of the Congress have thought that fixed-silo ICBMs in the United States would soon be vulnerable to Soviet attack and that the United States must do something to maintain a survivable ICBM force. Also, many agreed with the position that the United States should deploy a larger, more accurate missile with more warheads as a follow-up to existing ICBMs.

Some opposition emerged in the Congress to the MX missile. Two supporters, Paul Laxalt (R.-Nev.) and Jake Garn (R.-Utah), announced June 25, 1981, their opposition to placing the missile in underground shelters in their home states. Both Senator Laxalt, a close friend of Ronald Reagan, and Senator Garn, a strong advocate for improving the nation's defenses, represent constituencies that were strong supporters of Reagan in the 1980 presidential election.

As an alternative, the two senators urged that the ballistic missiles be based throughout the Middle West in silos that housed older Minuteman III missiles. The senators' objections coincided with the mounting constituency opposition in Utah and Nevada. The senators indicated they might be willing to have 100 of the 200 proposed missiles divided equally between their states and the remainder placed elsewhere. They argued, however, that the Carter plan should be scrapped because the missiles would eventually be vulnerable to Soviet attack. They also noted the great environmental impact, disrupting up to 10,000 square miles in the region.

Other opponents of the MX missile contended that the missile would not be survivable, that it would be too costly, that it promoted instability in the military balance between the United States and the Soviet Union, and that it would trigger more costly arms development in the future. Besides, opponents argued, it would be difficult for the Soviet Union to destroy more than 1,000 ICBMs scattered throughout the country.

Congressional support did not extend to the basing mode and the racetrack method proposed by President Carter. By a vote of 89-0 in November, 1979, the Senate passed an amendment by Senator Ted Stevens of Alaska to the fiscal year 1980 defense appropriation bill, which included the provision that none of the funds could be used in a way which would commit the United States to only one basing mode for the MX.[19] Senator Henry Bellmon (R.-Okla.) wondered if the basing mode presented by the Carter administration was not done deliberately to make the system so outrageous and expensive that Congress would reject the system and not allow it to be built.[20] Senator Henry Jackson (D.-Wash.) said the racetrack system presented problems both as to its survivability and in terms of cost.

Other aspects or questions about basing the missile surfaced. Representative Virginia Smith (R.-Neb.) proposed an amendment to the fiscal year 1979 Department of Defense supplemental authorization bill expressing the sense of the Congress that MX be deployed in the least productive land that is available and suitable. She wanted to be sure that the MX would not be placed on a possible deployment site in southwest Nebraska. The amendment was incorporated into law. In 1980, Senator John Tower (R.-Tex.), a formidable force on the Senate Armed Services Committee, stated that Texas would be glad to have some of the missiles, but he wanted them on the least productive land areas. The cost to acquire agriculturally productive land would run into billions of dollars.

Representative Jim Santini (D.-Nev.) estimated that his state would contain 70 percent of the MX shelters, and he expressed concern about the potential impact. On September 1, 1979, he offered an amendment to the fiscal year 1980 Department of Defense authorization bill to prevent more than 25 percent of the shelters from being located in any one state. The amendment was defeated.

In addition, the Committee on Interior and Insular Affairs of the U.S. House of Representatives conducted extensive hearings in Nevada and Utah and on Capitol Hill. Groups opposed to the MX underground shuttle system proposed by President Carter voiced their opposition in these hearings.

In 1979 the Carter administration provided evidence that it was not certain about how to base the MX. As noted, some concept of the MX appeared to have congressional support, but the major problem for both the Carter and Reagan administration was to find a basing mode that would be acceptable to the Congress and others with a vested interest in the program.

As the House voted 314-71 in May 1979 requiring Carter to build a version of the MX, the administration was touting a new deployment system for the missile. The proposal was to use a rail system among thirty or more armored launch sites in an underground trench. If radar detected a missile attack at the launch sites, the trains with missiles on them could be moved quickly. Another option was to build 400 smaller ones which could be deployed in existing silos. Another plan called for putting 480 on submarines. The House Armed Services Committee voted to require work on the multiple protective shelter plan (the underground shuttle plan) unless the secretary of defense certified that another version was superior or unless President Carter thought it jeopardized national security interests. At the same time the House rejected the first attempt by Ronald Dellums (D.-Cal.) to ban all development by a vote of 89-311.

On June 8, 1979, President Carter announced that the preferred plan would be to shuttle the missile underground. If the missile were carried by rail from launch site to launch site, the missile would have to rest horizontally or at about a 45 degree angle. Missiles on their side could be verified more easily. The conferees on a supplemental authorization bill of the armed services committees included in their report a requirement that if the administration chose any version of MX other than the vertical system, it would have to provide Congress with a complete justification. The vertical system would save an estimated $10 billion over the horizontal system, and it was thought by some members of Congress that President Carter was trying to drive up the costs so the program would be killed. On May 6, 1980, Defense Secretary Brown said that the administration was abandoning the oval-shaped track for a "linear" system that would save land, money, and manpower.

On August 1, 1980, a Senate-House conference report called the 4,600 shelter MX missile system "vital to the security of the United States." It ordered Secretary of Defense Brown to proceed immediately with full-scale development in time to have the system operational by the end of 1986.

Attempts were made by congressional opponents during 1980 to curtail or kill the program. Representative Paul Simon (D.-Ill.) offered an amendment to cut $500 million from development; Utah and Nevada House members remained unpersuaded about the basing mode; and Representative Patricia Schroeder (D.-Colo.) and others questioned spending money for a system that seemed to change frequently. Representative Melvin Price (D.-

Ill.), chairman of the House Armed Services Committee, charged that Simon was trying to kill the program and that the linear basing mode would be the Pentagon's final choice which, of course, was not to be the case.

Throughout 1981, the Congress reacted in response to the lack of a presidential and Department of Defense commitment to a basing plan. The House denied $26.5 million on request for construction of the Carter basing system and ordered the Pentagon not to spend $92 million appropriated earlier in fiscal 1981 until the president had selected a basing mode and an environmental impact statement had been completed. The Senate also deleted funds for the program, but it added $8 million for research to provide water in support of MX construction. Generally, the Congress approved funding for continuing development of the missile. However, all four defense measures that were before Congress by August 1, 1981, included provisions requiring congressional endorsement by concurrent resolution if President Reagan changed the MX basing technique recommended by President Carter.

A senior Pentagon official announced on July 27 that President Reagan would not make a decision on MX basing until the August congressional recess, even though the Townes committee report was to have been completed before that date. Some bills dealing with military construction included the provision barring expenditure of funds until sixty days after Reagan's decision. Other language, such as "deferring without prejudice," was used by committees in response to funding requests for the MX.

Rumors proliferated in August 1981 that President Reagan wanted the MX system to be airborne. Senator Tower warned that Congress would not approve the program, reminding that it had been rejected in 1979 as too unreliable, too costly, and not survivable. Besides Tower and other influential members of the congressional armed services committee, the air force opposed the air-mobile system. One rumor was that Reagan wanted to break from the Carter administration and that he might request 100 missiles instead of 200 in a shuttle plan underground.

On October 2, 1981, President Reagan announced that twenty to forty underground Titan II silos would be used for the MX while plans for other launching systems would be explored. Senator Tower criticized the proposed "interim" plan, saying it provided "more lucrative targets in already vulnerable fixed silos." The administration proposed to "superharden" the silos with cement and concrete so that they could stand up to 5,000 pounds pressure per square inch. Claiming the decision was made "within a small circle, without the coordination of the best military expertise," Tower announced he would hold hearings beginning October 5 to investigate extensively.[21] In contrast, Senator Howard Baker applauded the decision, as did Senators Garn and Laxalt. Both Tower and Representative William L. Dickinson (R.-Ala.), senior Republican on the House Armed Services Committee, warned President Reagan in person in August that the air-launched missile program would not be approved. Despite protests by influential members of Congress to the Reagan proposal, the view was expressed that the Carter proposal was dead. Senator Tower had made arguments to the president that if the decision were made to put the MX in Nevada and Utah and if the president stayed with his decision, the opposition would eventually acquiesce because of the enormous popularity of Ronald Reagan at the time.

The debate continued about President Reagan's concerns to "close the window of vulnerability" that he had talked about in the 1980 campaign. Supporters of multiple protective shelters did not think it would, and Senator Tower had always told reporters that the president was being educated on the MPS system and that he would eventually approve it.[22]

On a "Meet the Press" program October 4, Senator Tower blamed the decision on presidential advisers, but Senator Thomas Eagleton (D.-Mo.) had a different view. "If President Carter had recommended this [MX plan], Senator Tower would have called for his impeachment," he told the Senate on October 6.[23] On "Face the Nation," the same day as Tower appeared on "Meet the Press," Defense Secretary Weinberger said that, had he followed the generals and the admirals, he would have to tell why he was not under their subservience. Former Secretary of Defense Harold Brown said on "Issues and Answers" the same day that, if the silo were in a Soviet crater, it would topple and be worthless, but the silo would remain undamaged. Weinberger argued the system would "buy time" to develop a newer MX version, but the Senate Armed Services Committee members expressed the concern that, after being told so often that fixed silos were vulnerable, that is exactly what was being proposed.

Senator John Warner (R.-Va.), chairman of the subcommittee on strategic warfare of the Senate Armed Services Committee, held hearings for nine days on the president's proposal. The hearings opened with Defense Secretary Weinberger hearing Senator Tower say that the president's strategic modernization program was "undefined" and "subject to considerable debate and confusion within the executive branch."[24] Senator Carl Levin (D.-Mich.) charged the program was a "shambles." Weinberger tried to defend his position, but none of the Republicans came to his aid.

Following the hearings, the Congress continued to restrict the administration on what it could do with the MX program. A congressional conference committee diverted $76 million from development of the missile, expressly barring any use of funds for research on an airborne system. The committee adopted a procedure that would allow them to kill Reagan's alternative basing program by passing a concurrent resolution by November 18.

The House and the Senate adopted a conference report December 15, 1981, by overwhelming margins. The report provided the $1.913 billion requested for development of the MX. Senators William Cohen (R.-Maine) and Sam Nunn (D.-Ga.) had an amendment incorporated into the final measure that would allow $334 million of the $354 million requested to be used for existing silos that are not superhardened. This was intended to move the administration away from the notion of "superhardening" silos for deployment of the MX. Another provision ordered the administration to make a final basing decision by July 1, 1983, instead of by 1984 as planned. Other steps were taken in Congress in 1981 which required that, before funds could be spent for contracts on specific sites, the respective committees be given information on a plan identifying the silos to be used and the cost for modifying and operating them, a study of the cost and the survivability of such superhardened silos against Soviet attack, a notice that all environmental requirements had been met, and an audit of the use of previously appropriated MX design and planning funds. The primary reason for all these activities and for the Nunn-Cohen amendment was to discourage the administration's pursuing the "superhardened" silo alternative. Congressional backers of the MX feared that if the first few were deployed in the superhardened silos, the entire system might rely on this alternative.

In January 1982 the administration again changed the October 1981 plan. The 1981 plan called for deployment of 36 missiles to be based in Arkansas, Kansas, or Missouri in silos now occupied by nearly obsolete Titan intercontinental missiles. The administration then announced that at least forty MX missiles would be placed in existing Minuteman silos without any protection or hardening of the silos. In between these two proposals was a proposal to put the MX in superhardened Minuteman missile silos. An air force officer said at a news briefing that the first plan "looked attractive until you began to see the engineering problems involved."[25] The Congress would not accept the plan to harden Minuteman missile sites for deployment of the MX.

On March 23, 1982, the Senate Armed Services subcommittee on strategic weapons chaired by Senator John Warner (R.-Va.), which had conducted four weeks of hearings on the fiscal 1983 defense request, voted 9-0 to reject the interim basing plan that would deploy forty missiles in Minuteman silos without hardening of silos. The subcommittee approved $1.73 billion for continued development of the MX. Senator Warner said that the vulnerability of the missiles was the reason for the vote, and the subcommittee recommended that the administration choose by December 1982 a permanent basing mode instead of by July 1, 1983, as Congress had requested in 1981. Senator Tower endorsed the plan. These moves were taken because congressional supporters of the MX feared the entire program might be scuttled. Members of the Congress were not interested in supporting a program that made the missile vulnerable; administration witnesses before the Warner committee conceded that the forty missiles would be vulnerable but that they could deter Soviet aggressiveness because they are more powerful. The Senate did not accept the argument, even though Secretary Weinberger tried to demonstrate a "close correspondence" between the interim program and the Townes committee report of 1981 which had never been released in full. (The "executive summary" of the report was issued on March 23, 1982.)

In July 1982, the House took up the issue of the MX, and opponents argued that the United States could send the Soviet Union a message without the MX. Representative Samuel Stratton (D.-N.Y.) argued that, in the context of what the Soviets focused on, the MX was needed. To underscore their points, supporters urged House members to study the large scale models of the MX and the three front-line Soviet missiles located in the Speaker's lobby adjacent to the House floor. Stratton offered a substitute amendment that retained the full amount recommended by the Armed Services Committee but barred expenditure of the $259.9 million earmarked for basing until thirty legislative days after the president reported to Congress on the basing mode selected. This killed an amendment that would have removed $1.1 billion for production of the first nine missiles when the substitute amendment passed 212-209. A week later Paul Simon (D.-Ill.) and Bill Green (R.-N.Y.) were defeated on a voice vote in a try to delete funds earmarked for development of a way to base the first forty missiles. On August 18 a conference committee authorized $830 million for the first five production-line missiles and $158 million for support equipment.

The Senate Appropriations Committee came close on September 23, 1982, to rejecting or removing $550.7 million from the budget for the development of five completed missiles. It was leaning to supporting the procurement of components for nine MX missiles. Senator Stennis (D.-Miss.) asked for overnight consultation with the administration, and the following day the panel agreed to restore MX funding to the authorized levels.

In a major speech on November 22, 1982, the president said he favored putting 100 MX missiles close together in one place in a "dense pack." He also announced that henceforth the missile would be called the "Peacekeeper." One congressional Democrat dubbed the grouping system "dunce pack."

In the first round of House action on fiscal 1983 funds, the House Defense Appropriations Subcommittee barely supported (7-6) the funding of $4.3 billion for MX production and development. Subcommittee Chairperson Joseph P. Addabbo (D.-N.Y.) said he would renew the fight in the full committee and on the floor if necessary. He had won by a one-vote margin in 1981 in an effort to deny funds for the weapon, but a coalition of Republicans and Southern Democrats restored the $1.9 billion in the full Appropriations Committee by a 25-23 vote.

On December 2, 1982, the House Appropriations Committee voted 26-26, which sustained the effort against deleting funds. This was after Secretary of State Shultz and President Reagan made intercontinental telephone calls from Brazil to respective House members, and Secretary Weinberger did the same from Belgium where he was attending a NATO meeting. The closeness of the vote was attributed to opposition to dense pack. On December 7, 1982, the House voted 245-176 to delete from the defense appropriations bill $988 million to buy the first five production-line versions of the missile.

The president then went into action to have the Senate reverse the December 7 vote. In a December 10 news conference he urged the Senate to restore the funds, and he hinted that he might forget about dense pack if Congress proposed a more acceptable mode for basing the missile. On December 17, the Senate voted 56-42 to back an amendment to the continuing resolution that would guarantee congressional action on a basing mode by summer, 1983. The administration backed the amendment. The amendment, sponsored by Senator Henry Jackson (D.-Wash.), would guarantee congressional action within 45 days of the time the president submitted a report on dense pack and alternative basing methods. The March 1983 deadline was dropped.

Conferees then approved in late December the second continuing resolution denying $988 million requested by the administration to begin procurement of the MX missile. This marked the first time that Congress denied production funds for a strategic weapon sought by a president, and the vote came after the administration worked hard to retain the funds. It was interpreted as a rejection of dense pack. Even so, the body approved funding for research and development of the missile and its base, and it asked the president to report to Congress on his choice for a basing system after March 1, 1983. Flight tests also were prohibited until both Houses of Congress approved expenditures for the basing mode. The latter was undoubtedly included to keep the administration, the air force, and others from making tests they could tout as being highly successful in trying to gain support for the missile regardless of the basing mode used.

The year 1983 proved to be a better year for the survivability of the MX proposal. The major problem for the MX as the Ninety-eighth Congress began was to find a suitable hole in the ground as a home for the weapon.

A second commission on the MX was named by President Reagan on January 3 to advise him on the future of the missile. The commission reported April 11, 1983, and recommended that 100 MX missiles be deployed in existing missile silos while the Pentagon developed a new, smaller mobile single-warhead missile that would try to move the United States and the Soviet Union away from MIRVed missiles. The commission was headed by retired General Brent Scowcroft, former national security adviser in the Ford administration, and included four individuals who had been prominent in defense circles. On April 19, 1983, President Reagan endorsed the Scowcroft proposals.

During the week of April 18, both Senate and House Armed Services committees began hearings on the proposal. Some Senators and House members remained skeptical of the Scowcroft report. Senators Sam Nunn (D.-Ga.), William Cohen (R.-Maine), and Charles Percy (R.-Ill.), chair of the Senate Foreign Relations Committee, sent a letter to the president on April 29, asking him to commit himself fully to the Scowcroft report. Nine House members did the same on May 2. They were concerned that the administration might pursue only part of the recommendations—for example, deploy MX, forget about the single-warhead missile development, and fail to make new proposals on arms control with the Soviet Union. The president responded by pledging himself to the entire package of weapons development and arms control initiatives.

House and Senate appropriations committees then acted accordingly and during the week of May 9 approved the use of some fiscal 1983 funds to implement a new MX basing plan. The designated committees then voted to permit flight testing of the missile, and the full House voted on May 24 and the Senate on May 25 to approve flight testing and the beginning of engineering and design work on the emplacement of the missile in existing Minuteman missile silos. The victory for the president was decisive in both houses. Some of the moderate to liberal members of the Congress moved to support the president in key votes. Albert Gore, Jr. (D.-Tenn.) and Les Aspin (R.-Wis.) were among wavering House members who supported the MX. Several said they would include provisions in congressional action that would let the president know where they stood and what might be done if the administration reneged on any part of the Scowcroft proposals. They wanted to make sure there was not a prevailing bias against the testing of the proposed small mobile missile. They were suspicious that the air force was not enthusiastic about the new missile, and they feared that pressures might build to go beyond the 100 MX missiles proposed by the Scowcroft panel. There was discussion, for example, about limiting the MX deployment to no more than 35 before testing the small missile.

Senators Percy, Nunn, and Cohen supported the "build down" approach to arms control in which they would ask for the retirement of a larger number of existing weapons when a new one is developed. They negotiated with the White House, and the president said that progress was being made to include this in his arms talk proposals. Senator Cohen and others insisted that a good-faith effort had to be made by the administration, and this would have to be done before the Senate defense appropriations bill would be taken up in September. "What you have is not a consensus on MX. What you have is a consensus that a barter has been made," said Senator Cohen.[26] Following these actions the MX missile was tested in flight on June 17, and the test was reported successful. The word "Peacekeeper" appeared vertically on the missile in pictures in the newspapers announcing the test.

The Senate and the House then voted to approve the procurement of the first production-line models of the MX. The House voted 220-207 on July 20 to reject an amendment by Charles E. Bennett (D.-Fla.) that would have removed $2.6 billion earmarked for procurement of the first twenty-seven missiles. It accepted an amendment by Albert Gore, Jr. (D.-Tenn.) to reduce the number authorized to twenty-one, and it supported an amendment by Melvin Price (D.-Ill.) requiring that future MX procurement and deployment not outrun development of the small, single-warhead missile.

The Senate ended two weeks of stalling tactics by opponents and voted 58-41 on July 26 to authorize approval of $4.6 billion to build twenty-seven MX missiles. The Senate also refused in a 54-42 vote to block deployment of the MX.

Senator Gary Hart (D.-Colo.), the most widely publicized senatorial opponent of the MX, gave up his attempt at filibustering the MX program after the House vote. Hart's actions were thought to be highly motivated politically as he tried to distinguish himself from other Democrats who were hoping to win their party's nomination for president in 1984.

In the House, about one-third of the members who supported MX in May but became opponents in July are relatively senior members who hold leadership positions or aspire to them. Les Aspin (D.-Wis.), a supporter of MX, commented: "We've got more guys running for Speaker than we have running for president."[27]

The MX program appeared to be on its way, but it still faced the appropriations hurdle in September. The critical issue would be congressional perceptions of the administration's seriousness in seeking an early agreement with the Soviet Union in the Strategic Arms Reduction Talks (START). As Representative Gore stated, the House does not have to hold a majority in the appropriations bill. "The administration has to come through with more movement on arms control. They've got to deal effectively with the anti-arms control elements within the administration."[28] The Soviet reaction was predictable as it tried to encourage more opposition to the MX in the United States. On August 2, U.S.-Soviet strategic arms talks in Geneva were adjourned for nine weeks. The chief Soviet negotiator said the United States was "marking time" in the talks and that the decision to deploy the MX escalated the arms race and could not be used as a "lever" to get Soviet concessions.

Several House members also expressed the view that the 1982 elections had demonstrated that the voters thought too much was being spent on defense and that the Reagan administration was not making enough progress in arms control talks with the Soviet Union. Americans, they found when on break from Congress, were more concerned with personal economic issues and problems than they were with El Salvador, Soviet aggression, or other international problems.

Presidential Behavior and the MX

One can see how Congress put limits on presidential actions in the MX case. Certainly, the president has had history on his side. The Congress traditionally has been reluctant to deny a president a strategic weapons system, but why did President Reagan come so close to losing the MX on several occasions? Or, some might ask, why did he finally win congressional approval for test firing and for basing the MX missile? The president's problem has been to find a basing mode for the MX missile that was politically, economically, and strategically acceptable to members of the Congress and to the American people.

Before President Reagan announced his decision October 1981 to scrap Carter's Nevada and Utah plan for the MX missile, rumors held that the president was open to looking at alternatives to the Carter basing plan. On August 26, 1981, Defense Secretary Weinberger said he was prepared to make a specific proposal to the president about the MX missile. Other administration officials confirmed that the president was leaning toward a modified version of the land-based system developed by Carter. Ed Meese, the President's close personal aide, said that after Weinberger and the president met, the secretary did not state his recommendations to the president. A White House spokesman confirmed that, according to Meese, Reagan had essentially ruled out the track system for the MX. Meese reported that all options remained open, including deployment of the missiles among land, air and sea bases or ships. Some reports indicated the president might scrap the entire program.

As noted, the Office of Technology and Assessment report said there is no way to base the MX that is without flaws and serious risks—this after considering at least thirty basing plans. The problem was so difficult that Stephen Webbe of the *Christian Science Monitor* characterized it as one of the "severest strategic dilemmas ever faced by a U.S. commander in chief."[29] Public discussion of the issue added complex political dimensions as many groups and prominent individuals recommended conflicting alternatives.

When the president announced the first departure from the Carter plan, which was to put the MX in fixed silos that would be "superhardened," he faced opposition from members of his own party in the Congress and from individuals within the administration. Presidential aides reported that the president thought the hardened sites were the most "expedient." The president, it was said, made the decision very late with his closest advisers—Ed Meese, Mike Deaver, and Jim Baker—Richard Allen, the national security advisor, and Caspar Weinberger, secretary of defense. Secretary of State Alexander Haig, General David Jones, chairman of the Joint Chiefs of Staff, and William Casey, director of the CIA, were later informed of the decision.[30]

Perhaps those excluded would have opposed the president's plan. Haig and Jones were known opponents of the president's decision. General Jones testified before the Senate Armed Services Committee that he could not convince Weinberger and the president of his position on the shuttle system. General Lew Allen, air force chief of staff, with a doctorate in physics, favored the shuttle system. Former Defense Secretary James Schlesinger said the new proposal was advanced to satisfy every interest group and that it represented "political patchwork."

Secretary of Defense Caspar Weinberger was put in the awkward position of defending a system he had condemned at his confirmation hearings in January 1981. At those hearings, Weinberger said, "I would feel that simply putting it into existing silos would not answer two or three concerns that I have, namely, that these are well known and are not hardened sufficiently, nor could they be, to be of sufficient strategic value to count as an improvement of our forces."[31]

At Senate Armed Services Committee hearings in October and November 1981 Weinberger said the silos would be "superhardened" to 5,000 pounds per square inch. Weinberger plunged ahead to use Titan II silos, then was told to shift to Minuteman silos, then gave that up as technically not feasible, and then shifted to Minuteman silos without any protection. Senator Sam Nunn (D.-Ga.) thought Weinberger had not done his homework, and he thought it was puzzling that the information that persuaded the administration to reverse itself in 1982 had been available in 1981.

The president began to change his style of rhetoric when he announced the dense pack scheme. He did not talk about limited nuclear war as a possibility as he had in 1981. He described the MX as a counterweight to the Soviet missile system, as a replacement for existing but aging U.S. weapons, and as a means to get Moscow to accept mutual arms reduction. There was an absence of military detail as he announced he would call the MX the "Peacekeeper." The president reportedly told an aide, "If we don't get this thing, we might as well bring our negotiators home from Geneva."[32] General Edward Rowny, the president's chief negotiator in START talks with the Soviet Union, reportedly took the same position.

On January 3, 1983, the president named a panel of eleven defense experts to advise him on the future of the MX missile. This came after dissatisfaction was expressed in the Congress and by others over the dense pack proposal and after administration defeats on previous proposals. The announcement followed a pattern in the Reagan administration toward appointing presidential commissions to work on troublesome issues and problems and make recommendations. There were four commissions during the first thirty months of the Reagan administration—one on social security, two on the MX, and one on Latin America. Some critics even wondered when a bipartisan commission on bipartisan commissions would be established! The commissions, including those on MX, have been served by many individuals drawn from previous administrations. For the second MX commission, the president, as noted, appointed retired General Brent Scowcroft, national security advisor to President Ford, to chair the group. Prominent individuals associated with defense and other high level positions in previous administrations were also appointed.

Besides serving the purpose of making a decision more legitimate, the establishment of commissions could be interpreted as a failure in leadership, as a way to postpone a tough decision, as a way to "spread about" the responsibility for a decision, or as a means of compromise that might not bring a solution. The argument can be made that the politicians in the White House and in the Congress want someone else to take the risk of doing what everybody knows needs to be done. Commissions can be appointed because everyone knows the answer to the issue at hand but no one is willing to take political responsibility for it.

The problem in the case of MX that the two commissions or no one else seemed to address clearly is how to create a nuclear deterrent that will prevent Soviet nuclear intimidation or a successful first strike, and not how to base the missile. But the focus, as the Scowcroft committee admitted, was on the basing mode, and the decision was as much political as it was military. Scowcroft told a Senate committee hearing on April 18, 1983, that if politics had been put aside the decision would have been different. The decision, he said, included "political practicality elements." Former Secretary of Defense Harold Brown and Scowcroft both said they preferred putting the missile in some mobile mode. Scowcroft said that option was precluded by "the nature of the environment in which the decision was made." He acknowledged that the panel's recommendations were not an optimal solution and that the MX would be vulnerable to Soviet attack, but he said the missile was necessary to demonstrate U.S. national will and cohesion and to induce Moscow to arms agreement. He said the panel wanted the small missile, which was recommended, to be mobile and to succeed MX in the 1990s.[33]

After an extension of time the Scowcroft commission recommended April 11, 1983, that 100 missiles be deployed in existing silos while the Pentagon worked for development of a new, smaller mobile single-warhead missile. The commission admitted that the 100 missiles would be as vulnerable as the Minuteman missiles they would replace, and the notion of the MX as a more "survivable" missile was abandoned by the group. The only justifications for this position were the MX's great military potency and its counterweight potential to several hundred existing Soviet missiles, some more powerful than MX.

The major themes of the Scowcroft report were:

1. To work toward the goal of shifting from large, multiwarhead missiles like MX to the smaller, single-warhead missile, which was recommended.
2. To develop a small missile for deployment in the early 1990s. This was to begin immediately.
3. To focus arms control agreements on the number of missile warheads and not the number of missiles each country has.
4. To deploy 100 MX missiles in existing silos to encourage the Soviet Union to shift toward smaller missiles.

The commission appeared to seek support of moderate Democrats as well as some influential Republicans such as Senator Charles Percy, Illinois, who might be in re-election difficulties in 1984. The commission also wanted a technically feasible plan.

Members of the panel consulted widely on Capitol Hill with members of the Congress to find a package that the president could "sell" to the Congress and to the country. It was reported that the commission had extensive discussions with Representatives Les Aspin (D.-Wis.), a major Pentagon critic, and Albert Gore, Jr. (D.-Tenn.). Gore had pushed for single warheads in recent months and Aspin could provide the astute political analysis that the commission needed for the president's purposes—to get an acceptable MX basing system approved by Congress. Almost immediately, the Congress began hearings on the proposals. On May 3, in an effort to demonstrate good faith in adhering to the Scowcroft panel findings, the Pentagon announced the creation of a major program office to manage development of the small missile for which about $500 million would be earmarked in the fiscal 1984 budget. This was done to appease senators Nunn, Percy, and Cohen and nine House members after they sent letters on April 29 and May 2, respectively, asking for the president's and the administration's commitment to the report and inquiring as to what the president's arms control philosophy was now going to be. The president responded, expressing total commitment, including to those aspects of arms control approaches which concerned them most. The linkage of congressional support for the MX and the extraction of a commitment from the president to pursue the arms control policies wanted by some congressional members worked well politically. The validity of the arms control philosophy that was being promulgated might be questionable, but the most important matter was their vote in support of the MX and the "political cover" provided for others who might be wavering in their support of the MX and the president's position. The political antennae of some of the members had determined that Americans did not think the administration was making a strong enough effort to reach an arms agreement with the Soviet Union.

Before the May 25 vote in the House of Representatives, the president called many members of the Congress and had meetings with others in his office. More than sixty House members were invited to a White House dinner the night before the House vote to permit flight tests of the MX.[34] Most of the sixty were undoubtedly legislators who the president and his congressional liaison staff knew were not committed strongly to any position on MX. The president won important votes in the Congress on the MX in May and July, but as the discussion of congressional behavior has indicated, the president's troubles had not ended.

Conclusion

When President Reagan decided in late 1981 that he would abandon any form of the Carter plan for deploying the MX missile in an underground shuttle system preferred by the U.S. Air Force, some members of the Congress, and interests gearing themselves for great monetary rewards with deployment of the missile in Utah and Nevada, the president sought alternative deployment modes rather than canceling the project.

This study has detailed some of the interaction and reactions to the alternative proposals produced by the Reagan administration. When the plan was changed several times—from Carter's system to deployment in "superhardened" Titan II silos, to deployment in Minuteman silos, to dense pack—the president's proposals were questioned and rejected both by members of the Congress and some technical and military experts.

After attempts for two years—1981 and 1982—to find an alternative to the Carter plan, the president felt compelled to appoint still another commission to look into the remaining alternatives or into some combination of past proposals, which numbered more than thirty. The Reagan administration demonstrated that it could keep things going rather than get things started. It was the task of the second commission—the Scowcroft commission—to get things started. Thus, it was a problem of getting a proposed policy—one redesigned many times—implemented into public policy.

As the Scowcroft commission met, it undoubtedly was aware of the individuals and forces that had been responsible for rejecting Reagan's earlier proposals. They were also undoubtedly aware of the controversy that had raged over President Reagan's appointment of Kenneth Adelman to succeed Eugene Rostow as head of the Arms Control and Disarmament Agency, and they must not have missed the controversy that involved General Edward Rowny, the president's chief negotiator in START talks in Geneva.

Further, the president's tough rhetoric toward the Soviet Union in his first eighteen months in office and the difficulty in getting arms control discussions started—all of this, rightly or wrongly—contributed to the public image that the administration's arms control effort was limp. Members of the Congress also sensed a growing public negativism toward President Reagan's efforts on arms control and his call for a greater defense effort.

The problem for the commission was to find a solution that would win over key individuals in the Congress and bring about a more positive public attitude which would make it possible for members of the Congress to support the president. Members of the commission might have asked, "What can we substitute that will be acceptable to Congress, to the air force, to the public, and to others involved in the process?" Already noted is that the commission had no intention of setting the program aside after over $5 billion had been committed to the project by spring 1983. The commission needed to frame the right question if implementation of the proposed policy were to succeed. In a sense, the commission "became creators as well as implementers of policy."[35] The commission devised a political formula rationalized in military terms—"we need to demonstrate our resolve toward the Soviet Union and seek an arms control agreement, too." This appeared politically appealing to the Congress, and it was an approach its members would likely be able to sell constituents. The essential thrust of the formula—deploying 100 MX missiles into Minuteman III silos—had been rejected in the past. The missiles were thought to be too vulnerable, and this did not square with the president's assertions throughout the 1980 presidential campaign and later that the "window of vulnerability" needed to be closed. Also, as already noted, the recommendation is one which Defense Secretary Weinberger rejected in his confirmation hearings in January 1981.

The thrust of the policy began to cover different realities. The rationale no longer was to close the "window of vulnerability" but to decide what to do with a program that has gathered considerable momentum. Instead of the "window of vulnerability," the rationale was to "scale down the arms buildup" or move away from MIRVed missiles. The stated intention of the policy was to induce certain behaviors in the Soviet Union, but the realities of the 1983 proposal seemed to have more to do with winning over wavering members of the Congress to support of a program that had gathered considerable momentum. Perhaps that is why Representative Albert Gore, Jr. (D.-Tenn.) and others feared that only the MX would be given attention and complained about rumors that the Pentagon was not enthusiastic about the mobile single-warhead missile or that the air force itself might oppose the idea. The May and July 1983 discussions and votes in the Congress indicated that some members intend to make certain that the administration adhere to the commission's recommendations to the "letter" or else scuttle the remainder of the MX program. A "wait and see" attitude was behind Representative Gore's amendment to scale down from twenty-seven to twenty-one the initial number of MX missiles developed and procured. Even if Congress succeeds, the question would be whether or not the development of the small missile would have a significant impact on arms control goals, and the president might pay a high price politically if the opposition judges that he has not made a "good faith effort" in arms control negotiations with the Soviet Union.

The conclusion is that what began as a major policy concern—what to do about the "vulnerability" of the ICBM force in the United States—turned into a long-term discussion on how to base the MX missile. Ultimately, what won out was political symbolism—appeasement of domestic political opposition while at the same time appearing to take the best course in the national defense interests of the United States.

Chronology of Events
MX Missile Development, 1978-1983

Late 1978—Carter administration decides to insist that SALT II allow for development of the mobile version of the MX (Missile Experimental).

January 1979—$265 million is included as a supplemental appropriation request for accelerating development of the MX.

May 3, 1979—$190 million is included in supplemental appropriations bill to begin work on test models of the MX.

May 1979—House votes 314-71 to force President Carter to build a version of the MX; rejects 100-291 an amendment that would have reversed the presumption toward the MX Multiple Protective Shelter (MPS) system.

June 8, 1979—White House announces that MX missiles will be shuttled underground on an oval-shaped track among various shelters.

May 6, 1980—Defense Secretary Harold Brown announces abandonment of oval-shaped track for a "linear" system in order to save land, money, and manpower.

August 1, 1980—Senate-House Conference Committee reaches agreement on funding MX program with $1.6 billion.

Autumn 1980—Ronald Reagan raises questions during presidential campaign about deploying the missile in shuttle system located in Utah and Nevada.

Spring 1981—Defense Secretary Caspar Weinberger establishes Townes Commission to study the alternatives for basing the missile and to make a recommendation.

March 10, 1981—The Office of Technology and Assessment (OTA), a research arm of the Congress, issues a report saying that submarines would be better than the Carter shuttle plan for deploying the missile; says Soviet Union could build enough missiles to destroy launch sites under Carter plan.

October 2, 1981—President Reagan announces that he will put 20 to 40 MX missiles in "superhardened" Titan II silos; Senator John Tower (R.-Tex.) attacks the proposal and announces that he will hold Armed Services Committee hearings beginning October 5.

December 15, 1981—Senate and House adopt a conference report on defense spending including MX but accept provisions discouraging "superhardened" silo approach; July 1, 1983, is set as the deadline for the president to find an acceptable basing mode for the missile.

August 18, 1982—Senate-House Conference Committee authorizes $2.51 billion for MX development but refuses to allow expenditures for testing the missile and for basing the missile; subjects a portion of the president's request to thirty legislative days' prior notice on a suitable basing mode being recommended and approved by Congress.

November 22, 1982—President Reagan, in a major speech, urges congressional and public support of the MX program; announces that henceforth the MX will be called the "Peacekeeper" and proposes basing 100 MX missiles in a "dense pack" scheme in existing Minuteman silos.

Late December 1982—House-Senate Conference Committee denies $988 million requested to begin procurement of the MX missile; this marks the first time that funds for a strategic weapon sought by a president are denied.

January 3, 1983—President Reagan announces establishment of second commission, the Scowcroft commission, to study ways to base the MX missile; panel has until February 18 to report, but deadline is extended several times as panel members consult with key members of the Congress to find a "solution."

April 11, 1983—Scowcroft commission recommends that 100 missiles be deployed in existing Minuteman III silos without "superhardening," while the Pentagon develops a new smaller single-warhead mobile missile to be deployed in the 1990s; says plan will cost $3 billion less than "dense pack."

April 19, 1983—President Reagan endorses Scowcroft commission proposals.

May 3, 1983—Pentagon announces a new program office to manage development of the small missile proposed by the Scowcroft commission.

May 24 and 25, 1983—House on May 24 and Senate on May 25 approve flight testing of the MX and development work on the latest proposal for basing the missiles.

June 17, 1983—First flight test of the MX is reported successful; picture of the missile appears in newspapers with "Peacekeeper" spelled vertically down the side of the missile.

July 20, 1983—House votes to authorize procurement of 21 MX missiles.

July 26, 1983—The Senate votes to authorize approval of $4.6 billion to build 27 MX missiles and refuses, 57-42, to block deployment of the missile.

Notes

1. See Kenneth N. Ciboski, "The Bureaucratic Connection: Explaining the Skybolt Decision," in John E. Endicott and Roy W. Stafford, Jr., eds. *American Defense Policy,* 4th ed. (Baltimore, Md.: Johns Hopkins University Press, 1977), 374-88; Morton H. Halperin and Arnold Kanter, eds., *Readings in American Foreign Policy: A Bureaucratic Perspective* (Boston, Mass.: Little, Brown, 1973), and Morton H. Halperin with the assistance of Priscilla Clapp and Arnold Kanter, *Bureaucratic Politics and Foreign Policy* (Washington, D.C.: Brookings Institution, 1974).

2. See Graham T. Allison and Morton H. Halperin, "Bureaucratic Politics: A Paradigm and Some Policy Implications," *World Politics,* 24 (Spring 1972, Supplement), 40-79.

3. Halperin and Kanter, eds., *Readings in American Foreign Policy,* 6, their italics.

4. Richard E. Neustadt, *Presidential Power: The Politics of Leadership* (New York: John Wiley and Sons, 1960).

5. Allison and Halperin, "Bureaucratic Politics," 44.

6. Halperin with Clapp and Kanter, *Bureaucratic Politics and Foreign Policy,* 311-12.

7. Ciboski, "The Bureaucratic Connection."

8. George C. Edwards III, *Implementing Public Policy* (Washington, D.C.: Congressional Quarterly Press, 1980).

9. *The MX Missile System.* Oversight Hearings before the Subcommittee on Public Lands of the Committee on Interior and Insular Affairs, House of Representatives, Ninety-sixth Congress, U.S. Government Printing Office, 1981, 317-18.

10. *New York Times,* Mar. 17, 1981, B14.

11. Ibid., Mar. 18, 1981, A26.

12. *Congressional Quarterly Weekly Report,* Vol. 40, No. 13, March 27, 1982, 668.

13. *New York Times,* July 16, 1981, A18.

14. Ibid., Mar. 19, 1981, 1.

15. *Ibid.,* B10.

16. "Briefing on MX Missile Basing," delivered by Peter Sharfman, program manager, International Security and Commerce Office of Technology Assessment to the Subcommittee on Public Lands and National Parks of the House Committee on Interior and Insular Affairs, June 22, 1981.

17. *Wichita Eagle-Beacon,* July 17, 1981, 1.

18. Ibid., June 11, 1981, 16A.

19. *Congressional Record,* Nov. 9, 1979, S16369-S16370.

20. Ibid., S16371.

21. *Congressional Quarterly Weekly Report,* Vol. 39, No. 40, Oct. 3, 1981, 1890.

22. Ibid., No. 41, Oct. 10, 1981, 1987.

23. Ibid.

24. Ibid., No. 45, Nov. 7, 1981, 2166.

25. *New York Times,* Jan. 2, 1982, 1.

26. *Congressional Quarterly Weekly Report,* Vol. 41, No. 23, June 11, 1983, 1146.

27. Ibid., No. 29, July 23, 1983, 1483.

28. Ibid., 1485.

29. *Christian Science Monitor,* Sept. 29, 1981, 13.

30. Ibid., Oct. 5, 1981, 1.

31. *New York Times,* Feb. 23, 1982, A18.

32. *Congressional Quarterly Weekly Report,* Vol. 40, No. 48, Nov. 27, 1982, 2921.

33. *New York Times,* April 19, 1983, 1.

34. *Congressional Quarterly Weekly Report,* Vol. 41, No. 21, May 28, 1983, 1046.

35. This idea is suggested in Giandomenico Majone and Aaron Wildavsky, "Implementation as Evolution (1979)" in Jeffrey L. Pressman and Aaron Wildavsky, *Implementation,* 2d ed. (Berkeley: University of California Press, 1979), 190.

The Presidency and Domestic Policy: The Civil Rights Act of 1964

Robert D. Loevy

The following case study of the presidency and civil rights stresses the political constraints on and the political requirements of presidential power in the realm of civil rights policy.

An almost perfect illustration of the relative powerlessness of the United States president in domestic matters is the history of civil rights legislation prior to 1964. From the time of the withdrawal of Union troops from the southern United States in 1876 until the passage of the Civil Rights Act of 1957, Congress refused to pass any civil rights legislation whatsoever. The 1957 Act is considered an historic breakthrough because it was the first civil rights bill to get through Congress since Civil War Reconstruction, but the new law was so watered down to meet the criticisms of southern Democrats in the Senate that it had little or no effect on racial segregation in the United States. A 1960 Civil Rights Act, equally watered-down to meet southern requirements, was regarded as equally ineffectual.

On February 28, 1963, President John F. Kennedy sent Congress a strong message on the immediate need for civil rights legislation: "The Negro baby born in America today . . . has about one-half as much chance of completing high school as a white baby born in the same place on the same day—one-third as much chance of completing college—one-third as much chance of becoming a professional man—twice as much chance of becoming unemployed . . . a life expectancy which is seven years less—and the prospects of earning only half as much."[1]

This forthright statement was not backed up with a strong civil rights legislative proposal. President Kennedy limited his recommendations to minor improvements in voting rights laws (none of which were very effective in the South), technical assistance to school districts desegregating voluntarily, and an extension of the Civil Rights Commission, a government body which could study civil rights problems but had no power to remedy them.

Why were the president's words so strong and his proposed legislation so weak? "President Kennedy was never one to demand congressional action on need alone. His sense of timing told him he could not overcome the legislative roadblocks in the way of civil rights legislation, and defeat, no matter how gallant, had no appeal for him."[2] As had happened so often in American political history, a United States president was bowing to the reality that a strong civil rights bill, one that would really end racial segregation and racial oppression in the southern United States, was simply not politically achievable, no matter how much of his political will and his political strength a president might throw into the battle.

The Southern Civil Rights "Veto"

The obstacles to passing a civil rights bill were truly formidable in early 1963. In the House of Representatives, regular legislative committees such as the House Judiciary Committee do not report bills directly to the House floor for a vote. Because debate is limited in the House of Representatives, committee bills first go to the House Rules Committee, where the length of time the bill will be debated and the manner in which the bill will be debated is decided. Many bills that make it through the regular committees, however, often are not reported out of the Rules Committee at all, and usually when this happens the particular bill is dead for the remainder of that session of Congress.

In 1963 the chairman of the House Rules Committee was Howard Smith, a conservative southern Democrat from Virginia. Smith was ardently opposed to all civil rights legislation, and it was clear he would use his powers as chairman of the Rules Committee to delay any civil rights bill as long as possible. If Democratic President Kennedy wanted a tough civil rights bill, he would have to blast it past Democratic Rules Committee Chairman Smith.

Over in the Senate, the situation was even more difficult. The chairman of the Senate Judiciary Committee was James O. Eastland, a Democrat from Mississippi and, as one would expect, a staunch opponent of civil rights. Eastland had used his powers as Judiciary Committee chairman to kill more than one hundred proposed civil rights bills throughout the late 1950s and early 1960s. If Democrat Kennedy wanted a civil rights bill, he would have to find a way around Democrat Eastland and his Judiciary Committee.

The big obstacle to a civil rights bill in the Senate, however, was the filibuster. Senate rules provide for unlimited debate, which means that a group of senators can kill a bill by simply talking it to death. Over the years southern Democratic senators had clearly established the idea they would filibuster any strong civil rights proposal. In fact, the reason the 1957 and 1960 Civil Rights Acts were so weak was that southern filibusters had succeeded. Rather than wait-out a lengthy filibuster, liberal senators supporting civil rights had compromised on both bills to the point where the southern Democrats would stop talking and let the bill come to a vote and, eventually, final passage.

President Kennedy's real problem with civil rights, however, was the crucial role of the South in the Democratic party. In 1963, the Democratic party was made up of an uneasy coalition of conservative southern Democrats on the one hand and liberal northern and western Democrats on the other. The only way Kennedy could hope to get a major tax-cut bill and other economic programs through the Congress was to keep the southerners in the Democratic fold. Pushing hard for civil rights, however, would have antagonized the southern Democrats.

In addition, there was the political problem of keeping the support of southern Democratic voters in the upcoming 1964 presidential election. Kennedy had defeated Richard Nixon in 1960 in one of the closest presidential races in American history. The electoral votes of several southern states, particularly Texas, had been essential to Kennedy's victory. Kennedy was going to need that southern Democratic support again in the 1964 presidential race. Similar to all Democratic presidents, Kennedy knew that, as of 1963, no Democrat had ever been elected president of the United States without carrying a substantial portion of the South. To antagonize the South with a strong push for civil rights could well be presidential political suicide.

The president also was aware that a civil rights battle could harm his foreign policy proposals and weaken his position in international affairs. Overseas problems such as the Soviet construction of the Berlin Wall and the Cuban missile crisis could be handled more successfully if public opinion in the United States was united behind the chief executive. Kennedy was currently negotiating a nuclear test ban treaty with the Soviet Union that would require a two-thirds vote of ratification in the Senate. The president knew that "to provoke a bitter national controversy (over civil rights) without achieving any gain would divide the American people at a time when the international scene required maximum unity."[3] As had so often been the case in the past, Kennedy elected to press forward in the international field, where the Constitution gave him much greater freedom of movement, and go slow in the domestic field, where presidential options are much more limited.

Thus it was that, when dealing with civil rights, President Kennedy faced all the crippling constraints that hamper a president's ability to act on domestic policy. Clearly it would be better to forget about civil rights legislation and only do for black Americans those things which a president can do without congressional approval—appoint large numbers of blacks to important government jobs and order the Justice Department to help black and white integrationists arrested in civil rights demonstrations.

The Leadership Conference on Civil Rights

Shortly after President Kennedy's recommended civil rights bill was released to the press and public, the leaders of more than seventy civil rights organizations, operating under the name of the Leadership Conference on Civil Rights, met to discuss the Kennedy proposal. They were dismayed. "The consensus was clear; President Kennedy had yielded on civil rights legislation before the fighting had even begun. The proposed bill was hardly worth the fight. Such comfort as there was came from the hope that (if Kennedy were reelected in 1964) the second Kennedy administration would be different."[4]

Birmingham

As so often happens to American presidents, unexpected external events totally changed the picture and completely undid Kennedy's political strategy. In May of 1963, Martin Luther King and his Southern Christian Leadership Conference began a series of nonviolent demonstrations protesting the rigid segregation of public facilities in Birmingham, Alabama. The city police chief, T. Eugene (Bull) Connor, was an avowed segregationist and brought out police dogs, fire hoses, and, most shocking of all in every sense of the word, electric cattle prods ordinarily used to drive reluctant cattle from the holding pen into the slaughter house.

Newspaper photographs and evening television reports of the violence in Birmingham brought about an immediate change in national public opinion on civil rights, particularly in the North and the West. The nation had seen first hand the worst aspects of Southern white oppression of blacks. Demands for action began pouring into the White House and the Congress from across the country.

President Kennedy was well aware that it was Birmingham that had forced him to change his position on civil rights. At a White House strategy meeting with civil rights leaders, one of those present referred in a hostile way to Bull Connor. Kennedy responded that "Bull Connor has done more for civil rights than anyone in this room."[5] Thereafter the president was often heard to say, "The civil rights movement should thank God for Bull Connor. He's helped it as much as Abraham Lincoln."[6]

Suddenly John F. Kennedy and his White House advisers were flooded with advice on what form a new administration proposal for civil rights legislation should take. The leadership conference on civil rights sent message after message to the president detailing needed civil rights reforms. At the president's weekly breakfasts with the Democratic congressional leadership, Senate Democratic Whip Hubert Humphrey of Minnesota advised and urged the president to send up to Capitol Hill a really strong bill. Kennedy responded by having his brother Robert, the attorney general, draw up the most sweeping civil rights proposal that any president has ever presented to Congress.

The Kennedy Civil Rights Bill

The civil rights bill which President Kennedy sent to Congress in June of 1963 included a strong provision giving black Americans equal access to all public accommodations throughout the United States. It would make illegal the segregated restaurants, cocktail lounges, hotels, and motels which were the most visible forms of racial discrimination in the American South. It also provided for the cut-off of any U.S. government aid programs in the South that were administered in a racially discriminatory fashion.

Perhaps most important of all, the new Kennedy civil rights package gave the attorney general of the United States the power to sue southern state governments that operated segregated schools. This "power to sue" would free the individual black citizen in the South from having to publicly stand up and file a suit in the local court to desegregate the local school system. Such personal attempts to gain civil rights by southern blacks were too frequently met by covert white reprisals, the most violent and brutal of which were beating and lynching.

Because a northern Democrat, Emanuel Celler of New York, was chairman of the House Judiciary Committee, the Kennedy civil rights proposals received a very favorable hearing at the committee level in the House of Representatives. From the president's point of view, in fact, the hearings were too favorable. Liberal Democrats and Republicans on the Judiciary Committee combined to press for a fair employment practices section of the bill that would ban racial discrimination in the hiring of employees by private industry. There also was support for empowering the attorney general to intervene in all civil rights cases in the South rather than only in school desegregation cases. The president was forced to become directly involved. Calling civil rights leaders and the Democratic and Republican House leadership together for five days of high-pressure negotiations, the president emerged with a compromise. A Fair Employment Practices section would be added to the bill, but the power of the attorney general to intervene in civil rights cases in the South would remain limited.

The compromise civil rights bill was reported out of the House Judiciary Committee in late November of 1963. It immediately went to the House Rules Committee, where Chairman Howard Smith had announced his firm intention of bottling up the bill, forever if possible. As the nation's capital prepared itself for the inevitable Rules Committee fight, President Kennedy boarded Air Force One to fly to Dallas. It was to be the first step in his campaign for re-election. It was symptomatic of the problems of Democratic presidents that Kennedy was taking his re-election bid first to Texas, the key southern state that had to be kept in the Democratic party if the Democrats were to retain the White House in 1964.

"To Write It in the Books of Law"

The assassin's bullet that killed President Kennedy in Dallas changed many things, but nothing quite so much as the political situation concerning civil rights. Kennedy's successor, Vice-President Lyndon Johnson, was a Democrat from Texas. At first civil rights supporters believed this would doom the civil rights bill, but actually the reverse was the case. As a southerner, Lyndon Johnson was mainly concerned with winning political support in the North. Similar to Kennedy, he would have to run for re-election in 1964, and he had less than a year to convince skeptical northern and western liberals that a southerner was an acceptable leader for the national Democratic party.

Johnson seized on the civil rights bill as the perfect instrument for establishing his credentials with northern and western liberals. Five days after Kennedy's assassination, the new president told a joint session of the House and Senate: "We have talked long enough in this country about equal rights.... It is time now to write the next chapter—and to write it in the books of law."[7] Johnson then asked the Congress to adopt the civil rights bill in memory of his slain predecessor, John F. Kennedy.

If Kennedy's behavior on civil rights was a case study in a president trying to avoid a divisive domestic issue that could not be avoided, Johnson's behavior was a case study in what a president can do when he throws himself and the vast powers of his office totally into the fight. Johnson's first move was to call black leaders and civil rights leaders to well-publicized meetings in the oval office at the White House.

As Johnson himself told it: "I spoke with black groups and with individual leaders of the black community and told them that John Kennedy's dream of equality had not died with him. I assured them that I was going to press for the civil rights bill with every ounce of energy I possessed."[8]

Johnson spoke out in favor of the civil rights bill at every suitable occasion—press conferences, public speeches, messages to Congress, and so on. Knowing that civil rights advocates feared this civil rights bill would be compromised and watered down the way all the previous ones had, Johnson took the position that he and his administration would not compromise with the segregationist southern Democrats in any way. "So far as this administration is concerned," Johnson told a press conference, "its position is firm."⁹ There would be no room for bargaining. Johnson would win his spurs as a pro-civil rights president by getting the newly strengthened civil rights bill past the House Rules Committee, the House, the Senate Judiciary Committee, and the Senate filibuster. Furthermore, he would get the bill through substantially intact.

Unlike Kennedy, who had been something of an outsider when he was in the House and the Senate, Lyndon Johnson had been the Senate majority leader when he was elected vice-president in 1960. Johnson thus was a congressional insider, a man with a detailed knowledge of the way things work on Capitol Hill and with an abundance of contacts and friendships. President Kennedy's funeral was hardly ended when the telephones began ringing in the House of Representatives. Members of Congress in key positions began hearing first-hand from the president about how he wanted the civil rights bill moved out of the House Rules Committee and on to the House floor.

The Discharge Petition

On December 9, 1963, House Judiciary Chairman Emanuel Celler filed a petition to discharge the civil rights bill from the Rules Committee. If a majority of the members of the House signed the discharge petition, the civil rights bill would move directly from the Rules Committee to the House floor. Signatures were hard to obtain at first, mainly because senators and representatives believe in the committee system of reviewing legislation and are hesitant to ever bypass a committee or its chairman. By the time of the Christmas recess, the discharge petition still was more than fifty signatures short.

The situation changed immediately after the Christmas recess. Members of Congress had found strong support for the civil rights bill when they went home to their districts for the holidays. President Johnson's constant referrals to the civil rights bill were having a dramatic effect on home town public opinion. Voters suddenly had become aware of the bill and knew that the president wanted it moved quickly through the House and Senate. The number of signatures on the discharge petition began nearing a majority, and a sizable number of the signatures were from Lyndon Johnson's fellow Texans in the House of Representatives. Both the Democratic and the Republican leadership in the House joined the president in pressuring Chairman Smith to release the bill.

Finally the pressure became too great and Chairman Smith gave in, saying, "I know the facts of life around here."¹⁰ Rather than suffer the embarrassment of having a bill discharged from his committee without his consent, Smith allowed the bill to be reported out to the House floor.

Lyndon Johnson was never one to miss any opportunity to increase the public awareness of civil rights. The president repeatedly linked the civil rights bill to Abraham Lincoln and the fact that the nation had just celebrated (in July of 1963) the hundredth anniversary of the Emancipation Proclamation. In response to a reporter's question about the civil rights bill at a White House press conference, Johnson said: "I hope it is acted upon in the House before the members leave to attend Lincoln Day birthday meetings throughout the nation, because it would be a great tribute to President Lincoln to have that bill finally acted upon in the House before we go out to celebrate his birthday."¹¹

Throughout a ten-day debate on the House floor, President Johnson and his congressional allies beat back every attempt to weaken the civil rights bill by amending it. Johnson had pledged he would pass the Kennedy bill, and that was essentially what occurred. In fact, the only major amendment to the bill actually furthered the cause of civil rights. It outlawed discrimination on the basis of sex as well as race in all the major provisions of the bill. On a Monday night, February 10, 1964, the House passed the civil rights bill by a vote of 290 to 130 and sent it to the Senate.

No Rest with Lyndon

Ordinarily, the hard-working lobbyists for the Leadership Conference on Civil Rights might have expected to have a moment of rest once the civil rights bill had been passed by the House. There was no rest, however, with Lyndon Johnson running the show. Clarence Mitchell, Washington director of the National Association for the Advancement of Colored People, recalls that the bill had just passed the House when a message came to call the president. "What are you fellows doing about the Senate," the commander-in-chief had called to say, very much at his post. "We've got it through the House, and now we've got the big job of getting it through the Senate!"[12]

Bypassing the Senate Judiciary Committee

With President Johnson's support, the Democratic leadership in the Senate made short work of Senator Eastland and his Senate Judiciary Committee. Senate Democratic leader Mike Mansfield of Montana moved, on February 26, to place the civil rights bill directly on the Senate calendar, thereby bypassing the Judiciary Committee completely. Although this procedural move provoked a small filibuster of its own from the southern Democrats in the Senate (labeled by Senate insiders as a "mini-buster"), by March 30 the civil rights bill was on the floor of the Senate and the main event, an extended southern filibuster, was underway.

President Johnson had skillfully arranged for the Senate to pass every piece of legislation he considered critical before the civil rights filibuster began. Thus the Kennedy tax-cut bill and a wheat and cotton bill had both been moved out of the Senate before the civil rights bill arrived. "President Johnson had made it clear . . . that he would not care if the Senate did not do another thing for three months until the civil rights bill was enacted. This removed the filibusterers' greatest weapon—that they could hold out until other needed legislation required the Senate to put aside the civil rights bill."[13]

Johnson's strategy was to let the southerners talk and talk until it became clear to everyone that a small minority was frustrating the majority will in the Senate. As the debate droned on through the month of April and then into early May, the president kept the pressure on with a regular weekly statement that he wanted a bill, and he wanted a strong bill. One week the president was quoted as saying he was "committed" to the bill with "no wheels and no deals."[14] Another week he stated: "I believe at the proper time, after all members have had a chance to present their viewpoints both pro and con, the majority of the Senate will work its will and . . . we will pass the bill."[15] Late in April the president said: "We need a good civil rights bill, and the bill now pending in the Senate is a good bill. I hope it can be passed in a reasonable time."[16]

The Wallace Candidacy for President

Early in 1964, Alabama Governor George Wallace announced that he was a candidate for the Democratic nomination for president of the United States and that he would run on a platform of all-out opposition to the civil rights bill. Governor Wallace would be a formidable candidate running on the anti-civil rights issue. He had gained tremendous national publicity by personally "barring the school house door" at the University of Alabama in a futile attempt to prevent integration of the university by U.S. marshals. Although Wallace had been forced to stand aside and let the university be integrated, he had emerged from the fracas as a southern segregationist hero and as the national symbol of opposition to school integration and black civil rights.

The Wallace candidacy called for quick action on President Johnson's part, and such action was soon forthcoming. Unwilling to permit "open season" on his presidential administration by running against Wallace himself, Johnson set to work recruiting stand-in candidates to run against Wallace in three crucial Democratic presidential primaries—Wisconsin, Indiana, and Maryland.

The Wallace threat to the civil rights bill was serious. Everywhere he went Wallace stated that his presidential candidacy was a referendum on the civil rights bill then being filibustered in the Senate. If Wallace could win only one presidential primary outside the old South, President Johnson's chance of beating the filibuster would be seriously jeopardized. Johnson himself noted that the Wallace campaign "stiffened the southerners' will to keep on fighting the civil rights measure until the liberal ranks (in the Senate) began to crumble."[17]

After Governor Wallace polled 33.9 percent of the vote in the Wisconsin primary and did almost as well in Indiana, political analysts began writing that Wallace just might win the Democratic presidential contest in Maryland. Maryland had not seceded from the Union during the Civil War, but it was, after all, a former slave state and south of the Mason-Dixon line. If Wallace could get more than 30 percent of the vote in a northern state like Wisconsin, he could conceivably get 50 percent or more in a border state like Maryland.

Johnson pulled out all the stops in his support of his Maryland stand-in, U.S. Senator Daniel Brewster. A key White House aide, Clifton Carter of the Democratic National Committee, was dispatched to help Brewster in every way possible. Money for the Brewster campaign was raised and spent freely by the Democratic National Committee. Johnson even arranged for a top campaign publicist to come to Maryland and help Brewster with his campaign speeches and press releases.

Although the president never officially endorsed any of his stand-in candidates in the 1964 Democratic presidential primaries, Johnson skillfully scheduled a trip to western Maryland to study "Appalachian regional problems." The president saw to it that Brewster was at his side every minute he was in Maryland.[18]

Thanks to the president's all-out support, Brewster defeated Wallace in Maryland with more than 57 percent of the vote. A combination of black votes in Baltimore coupled with upper-income suburban white votes in the Maryland suburbs produced a clear-cut majority for civil rights. Wallace and his anti-civil rights campaign had been stopped in their tracks. The filibusterers' hope that Wallace would win Maryland and start a national groundswell of opposition to the civil rights bill quickly faded.

Is the president's position with regard to domestic policy so tenuous that he has to intervene in presidential primary elections in order to get what he wants out of Congress? In the case of the Civil Rights Act of 1964, it appears clear that such action was required. In this case, the president and his political allies proved equal to the challenge.

Cloture

Senate rules provided that extended debate (a filibuster) could be brought to a close by two-thirds vote of those present and voting. Such a vote is called a cloture vote. Although cloture votes had been attempted many times in the past on civil rights bills, none had ever succeeded. The main reason was that Senators from small states, mainly in the midwestern and western United States, viewed the filibuster as the only instrument by which small states could protect themselves from the large states. Even if they believed firmly in civil rights, midwestern and western senators, most of them Republicans, did not want to weaken the idea of the filibuster by voting for cloture.

It thus was clear from the beginning that a small group of Republican senators, mainly from small midwestern and western states, would be the key to getting a two-thirds vote for cloture. It was equally clear that the man who could persuade these small-state Republicans to vote for cloture was Everett McKinley Dirksen of Illinois, the Republican leader in the Senate. Dirksen had worked hard to gain the confidence of his fellow party members in the Senate, and it was believed that his support for the civil rights bill would bring along the necessary Republican votes to put the two-thirds cloture vote over the top.

President Johnson saw from the very first that Dirksen was the key to getting the civil rights bill out of the Senate. Shortly after President Kennedy's assassination, Johnson telephoned Dirksen and asked him to convey to his Republican colleagues in the Senate that the time had come to forget partisan politics and get the legislative machinery of the United States moving forward. As Johnson recalled the phone conversation: "There was a long pause on the other end of the line and I could hear him (Dirksen) breathing heavily. When he finally spoke, he expressed obvious disappointment that I would even raise the question of marshaling his party behind the president. 'Mr. President,' he said, 'you know I will.' "[19]

Turning Senator Dirksen's general statement of support for the president into support for a cloture vote on the civil rights bill was something else again. The strategy designed by Johnson was to give Dirksen the opportunity to be a "hero in history!" Johnson noted: "I gave to this fight everything I had in prestige, power, and commitment. At the same time, I deliberately tried to tone down my personal involvement in the daily struggle so that my colleagues on the Hill could take tactical responsibility—and credit so that a hero's niche could be carved out for Senator Dirksen, not me."[20]

The lion's share of the task of winning Everett Dirksen over to the civil rights bill fell to Hubert Humphrey, the Democratic whip in the Senate. Humphrey recalls a telephone call from Johnson just as the civil rights bill was arriving in the Senate. "Now you know that this bill can't pass unless you get Ev Dirksen," the President told Humphrey. "You and I are going to get him. You make up your mind now that you've got to spend time with Ev Dirksen. You've got to let him have a piece of the action. He's got to look good all the time."[21]

Early in May, Senator Dirksen invited Senator Humphrey to his office to begin negotiating amendments to the civil rights bill that would make the new legislation acceptable to Dirksen and his band of midwestern and western Republicans. Representatives from the Justice Department as well as other Democratic and Republican senators began attending these meetings. In some areas Dirksen's amendments actually strengthened the bill. As a general rule, however, Dirksen pressed to have the bill affect only those states and those business organizations where a "pattern or practice" of racial discrimination could be shown. Dirksen did not want the U.S. government interfering in isolated personal instances of discrimination, and his view eventually prevailed with the civil rights supporters. By mid-May Humphrey and Dirksen emerged from Dirksen's office with an amended bill that had both Dirksen's support and the approval of the Leadership Conference on Civil Rights.

In retrospect, everyone realized that the meetings in Dirksen's office to write amendments for the bill had, in effect, been the Senate committee meetings on the civil rights bill. The Senate had bypassed the regular channel, consideration by the Senate Judiciary Committee, but Everett Dirksen succeeded in seeing that the equivalent of the committee work took place in his office.

Once Dirksen and Humphrey had negotiated an amended bill, the outcome was inevitable. On June 10, 1964, for the first time in its history, the U.S. Senate voted cloture on a civil rights bill. Soon afterward the Senate adopted the Dirksen-Humphrey amendments, and then the final bill as amended. The House of Representatives quickly agreed to the Senate amendments, and on July 2, 1964, before an audience of more than one hundred senators, representatives, cabinet members, and civil rights leaders, President Lyndon Johnson signed the Civil Rights Act of 1964 into law.

Conclusions

The Civil Rights Act of 1964 clearly demonstrates the constraints on the president of the United States in the general area of domestic policy. Both President Kennedy and President Johnson had to deal with opposition in Congress, opposition within the Democratic party, and the political realities of their prospective campaigns for re-election.

It is important to note that, in the case of Congress, the two presidents were forced, almost every step of the way, to support extraordinary measures to get the civil rights bill passed. President Kennedy had to set up special negotiating sessions at the White House to get an acceptable compromise bill out of the House Judiciary Committee. President Johnson had to support a discharge petition to get the bill out of the House Rules Committee. The Judiciary Committee had to be bypassed in the Senate, and the ultimate extraordinary measure, a cloture vote, had to be used to end the filibuster in the Senate. The fact that such unusual and rarely used techniques were required to get the bill passed is a measure of the severe constraints facing any presidential effort to enact a civil rights bill.

Although the Civil Rights Act of 1964 illustrates the constraints on the president vis-à-vis domestic policy making, the act also illustrates what is required for the president to successfully achieve domestic changes. Clearly the crisis created by the white violence in Birmingham against black demonstrators was required for this legislation to get the push needed to move through Congress. This clear relationship between violent crisis and the president's ability to act raises a real question for American democracy, however. Can a governmental system long survive if a major crisis, often involving violence, is required every time conditions on the domestic front are going to change?

Above all, the Civil Rights Act of 1964 illustrates the effective powers the president has at his disposal once he commits himself to a particular course of action. Both Kennedy's and Johnson's use of television to dramatize the nature of the civil rights crisis to the American people was outstanding—and in both cases effective. Johnson also demonstrated how the president, making effective use of the telephone, can put the most intense kinds of personal pressure on members of Congress. Never underestimate the psychological impact, and the excitement and self-esteem, that comes from receiving a phone call from the principal resident of the White House.

The Civil Rights Act of 1964 also revealed that Congress really can change conditions in the United States if it truly wishes to do so. The act ended virtually immediately and completely all forms of public segregation in the nation, both North and South. The threat of cutting off U.S. funds to government programs and business concerns that discriminate against minorities has made "equal employment opportunity" and "affirmative action in hiring" fixed institutions in American life. The act empowered the attorney general of the United States to sue for the desegregation of schools, a program which has resulted in the use of school busing to achieve racial balance in the nation's schools. The act was the first national law to guarantee significant equal rights for women, and it set the precedent for using cloture to stop a filibuster on a civil rights bill—a precedent that was used in 1965 to pass a national law guaranteeing equal housing opportunity.

The Civil Rights Act of 1964 finally illustrates that there are times in a president's career when a domestic issue cannot be avoided, regardless of the final outcome. A politician who also happened to be a good poker player once told Lyndon Johnson that there comes a time in every president's career when he has to throw caution to the winds and bet his entire stack of chips. President Johnson studied the political tumult surrounding the civil rights bill and "decided to shove in all my stack on this vital measure."[22] The president gambled, and that time around he won—big!

Notes

1. *Congressional Quarterly Weekly Report*, Mar. 8, 1963, 303.
2. Unpublished manuscript on the role of the Leadership Conference on Civil Rights in the civil rights struggle of 1963-1964, Joseph Rauh, legal adviser to the Leadership Conference on Civil Rights, Washington, D.C., 1964, 1.
3. Theodore C. Sorensen, *Kennedy* (New York: Harper and Row, 1965), 476.
4. Rauh manuscript, 2.
5. Ibid., 5.
6. Sorensen, *Kennedy*, 489.
7. *Congressional Quarterly Weekly Report*, Nov. 29, 1963, 2089
8. Lyndon B. Johnson, *The Vantage Point* (New York: Popular Library, 1971), 29.
9. Ibid., 29.
10. Rauh manuscript, 15.
11. *Congressional Quarterly Weekly Report*, Feb. 7, 1964, 281.
12. Merle Miller, *Lyndon* (New York: G. P. Putnam's Sons, 1980), 367. See also Rauh manuscript, 19.
13. Rauh manuscript, 21.
14. *Congressional Quarterly Weekly Report*, Feb. 28, 1964, 385.
15. Ibid., April 17, 1964, 747.
16. Ibid., April 24, 1964, 789.
17. Johnson, *Vantage Point*, 159.
18. Personal interview with former U.S. Senator Daniel Brewster, Baltimore County, Aug. 1982.
19. Johnson, *Vantage Point*, 30.
20. Ibid., 159.
21. Miller, *Lyndon*, 368.
22. Johnson, *Vantage Point*, 37.

The President and Foreign Policy   7.4

James Keagle

Important variables for understanding the presidency and foreign policy are the role of presidential personality and the president's operational code and definition of the situation. The following essay focuses on President Eisenhower's brand of "hidden hand" leadership in the realm of foreign policy and national security affairs. The essay concludes with a comparison between the Eisenhower and Reagan approaches to foreign policy

American foreign policy is determined in part by the structure of the presidential foreign policymaking system as well as the personalities of the individuals who operate within that system. It is the president who occupies a position of preeminence within that system. In him lies the foremost capability to establish the structure, select the players, and determine many of the ground rules operative in the process—thereby influencing significantly the substance of foreign policy.

It is not a simple task, however, for journalists, news commentators and analysts, academicians, and others "outside" an administration to determine precisely a president's role and influence within the decisionmaking apparati. National security considerations, leadership strategies of a president, and lack of first-hand access to the policymaking process are among those factors which make it difficult to assess the inner workings of a presidency and the impact of a particular president.

As time passes, though, additional information becomes available. Government documents that have recorded debate and discussion among a president and his advisors about sensitive issues are declassified. Key actors in an administration often offer fresh insight into how it functioned.

Such is the case today with the Eisenhower presidency. Evidence in recently declassified government documents and testimony by former members of Eisenhower's staff in the form of oral histories and other interviews granted to scholarly researchers have led to a rising tide of Eisenhower revisionism. No longer is Eisenhower viewed purely as a passive president who spent the majority of his day practicing his putting on the lawns of the White House. No longer is Eisenhower's relationship with John Foster Dulles (and later, Christian Herter) viewed as one in which the president willingly abdicated his responsibility and authority for the tone and substance of American foreign policy to the secretary of state. Rather, at least one noted scholar depicts Eisenhower as an activist president who exercised "hidden-hand leadership" consistent with his clear strategy for the presidency.[2]

An accurate assessment of the Eisenhower administration acquires added significance and importance when one considers many of the similarities that scholars are suggesting exist between the Eisenhower and Reagan ways of conducting their respective presidencies. Following a brief examination of the structure Eisenhower established for conducting foreign policy and some of the key players involved, I will present a case study of the Eisenhower team at work. I will then examine Reagan's Central American strategy and outline many of the parallels that have been suggested between the Eisenhower and Reagan foreign policies. I will conclude by suggesting that it is far too early to deliver a verdict on Reagan's foreign policy.

Eisenhower, 1953-1960

Eisenhower chose to incorporate within his foreign policymaking machinery a mix of formal structure and mechanics and informal,

---

This article, written for academic purposes by a U.S. Air Force officer, does not necessarily reflect the views of the U.S. Department of Defense.

often unpublicized, proceedings. The relationships among the president, the State Department, and the National Security Council as well as those among Eisenhower, Dulles (and later, Herter) and Cutler (and later, Anderson and Gray) were crucial. Simply put, it was a system in which Eisenhower relied heavily on the expertise and experience of his Department of State for the making of policy. Individuals understood their roles and were content with them.

The system served Eisenhower well.

The Operations Coordinating Board (OCB) was the implementation machinery of the NSC. Together with the NSC and its Planning Board, these bodies were Eisenhower's organizational tools in the policy *planning* process. The NSC was designed to shape the general framework for policy, including plans for contingencies. "The OCB's job was to see that decisions did not go into files in the form of re-edited policy papers, but actually resulted in plans for carrying out the decided policies."[3] However, these agencies were not policy*makers*. Eisenhower, "in consultation with small groups of advisors,"[4] made the day-to-day concrete national security policy decisions. Rapidly unfolding events made it impossible to anticipate everything with plans. The planning process included the development of many contingency plans. Their possible use and effectiveness was constantly re-evaluated in response to Eisenhower's assessment, in consultation with his close advisors, of changing conditions. There were timetables, strategies, long-range objectives, plans, tactics, and flexibility.

Eisenhower also utilized other formal structures such as cabinet meetings and legislative leadership meetings. These fostered team spirit and loyalty and served as mediums for disseminating information. While there was quite often lively debate at these gatherings, they were primarily vehicles for developing consensus rather than determining policy.

It was in the less formal setting that Eisenhower reached key decisions. Informal, off-the-record meetings between Eisenhower and his closest advisors (John Foster Dulles, Christian Herter, Gordon Gray, Andrew Goodpaster, Milton Eisenhower, John Eisenhower, Thomas Gates, Allen Dulles) and meetings of a subgroup of the NSC (the special group, or 5412 committee) appear to be the arenas where foreign policy decisions were hammered out.

It is also true that Eisenhower delegated significant responsibilities and authorities to his trusted aides, staff, and cabinet members, particularly John Foster Dulles in the field of foreign policy (and Sherman Adams in domestic policy). Yet this did not mean that crucial decisions were not presidential ones. On the contrary, while Eisenhower recognized, respected, and made use of the expertise of many of his staff members, he maintained control of the decision-making process, albeit in an indirect way.

Eisenhower operated behind the scenes for two reasons. First, he preferred that his involvement in political bargaining remain invisible to the general public. Repeated public exposures in this manner would only serve to lessen the dignity of the office of the president. Second, he believed that government had become

> too big, too complex, and too pervasive in its influence on all of our lives for one individual to pretend to direct the details of its important and critical programming. Competent assistants are mandatory; without them the executive branch would bog down. To command the loyalties and dedication and best efforts of capable and outstanding individuals requires patience, understanding, a readiness to delegate, and an acceptance of responsibility for any honest errors—real or apparent—those associates and subordinates might make. Such loyalty from such people cannot be won by shifting the responsibility, whining, scolding or demagoguery. Principal subordinates must have confidence that they and their positions are widely respected and the chief must do his part in assuring that this is so.[5]

This notion of delegation of authority aided Eisenhower as he struggled to remain visibly aloof from confrontational politics. He collaborated with his close advisors, oftentimes allowing them to weather the heat and public outcry over unpopular policies.

Yet Eisenhower did not rely exclusively on his top aides either for information or the implementation of policy decisions. Neither his secretaries of state, special assistants for national security affairs, nor Sherman Adams ever served as omnipotent gatekeepers who restricted access and information to the president. While it may be a bit strong to suggest that, on the other hand, Eisenhower used his subordinates,[6] it is apparent that Eisenhower's conscious choice to work through his staff and behind the scenes, to deny to the press that he was familiar with the details of an issue and to use ambiguous language, and to emphasize the dignity of the presidency were all parts of his strategy of presidential leadership which Reagan may well be emulating today.

The Eisenhower Administration, Castro, and Cuba, 1959-1961

Eisenhower's foreign policy system served him well as he wrestled with the problems of the Cuban Revolution during the last two years of his administration. His formal and informal mechanisms kept him well informed of developments and prepared numerous policy options that he discarded or employed as he deemed necessary in reaching conclusions that precipitated U.S. policy changes.

Previous research[7] has pinpointed March, 1960, as a crucial decisionmaking period in U.S. policy toward Castro and Cuba that ultimately led to the abortive Bay of Pigs fiasco during the first few months of the Kennedy administration. While recent research[8] does not dispute this finding, it does strongly suggest that Eisenhower's decision to approve on March 17, 1960, a "Program of Covert Action Against the Castro Regime" was not isolated in time—a split-second decision on the part of the president influenced more by momentary emotions than by careful analysis. Nor did the program approved in March, 1960, remain static and beyond the president's control. Rather, U.S. policy toward Castro and Cuba was carefully thought out and prepared during the period 1959-1961. The president received a multitude of assessments, interpretations, predictions, and recommendations. He weighed the evidence and the constraints to American actions and inactions. His policy was deliberate, flexible, and timely.

Relying heavily on State Department and CIA intelligence reports, Eisenhower was initially uncertain about Castro's ideological orientation and the direction of the Cuban Revolution. One report stated that "little evidence exists" to substantiate the allegations that the 26th of July Movement was "penetrated and influenced by communism." Yet the report suggested continued political instability following a Castro victory,[9] and Eisenhower's own memoirs state that the CIA was advising him that Communists would participate in Castro's government. The threat Eisenhower perceived was neither severe nor immediate. He had time. Therefore he watched and waited.[10]

During the first six months of 1959, Eisenhower clearly did not like what he witnessed happening to the Cuban Revolution. While official policy remained defined as "strictly one of nonintervention in Cuban domestic affairs,"[11] Eisenhower's concern was mounting. Official reports lent credence to such mounting concern. The CIA reported to the State Department and the president that the situation in Cuba was deteriorating to the point that a counterrevolution was likely if Castro did not soon accept moderates in his government.[12]

Castro visited the United States in April, 1959. Eisenhower did not meet with him but Secretary of State Christian Herter and Vice-President Richard Nixon did. Their evaluations of Castro, which they reported to Eisenhower, yield some of the reasons why Eisenhower did not respond immediately to Castro's demand for a $30 billion United States aid program to Latin America. Herter described Castro's behavior as "contrived" and informed Eisenhower that Castro had not altered the essentially "radical" nature of his revolution.[13] Nixon's evaluation was that Castro felt he could always "put them [Communists] in their place." The naiveté about communism stained the prospects for U.S. policymakers, increasing the likelihood that the Cuban Revolution was headed toward Communist control regardless of Castro's personal ideological orientation.[14]

Yet neither the American press nor the Latin American community accepted this line of reasoning and condemned Castro. Therefore, Eisenhower proceeded publicly with caution, praising Cuban efforts to reduce tensions in the Caribbean[15] and expressing hope for an improvement in United States-Cuban relations in a diplomatic note delivered to the Cuban foreign minister.

U.S. policy changed dramatically during the second half of 1959. Crucial conclusions about the nature of Castro and the Cuban revolution that would inevitably lead to a "tougher" American policy were reached as early as November, 1959, at least four months prior to the fateful March 17, 1960, decision.[16]

As American journalists spoke of "darkening skies"[17] and the "growing Red tinge" in Cuba,[18] Foreign Minister Agramonte and four other responsible moderates resigned from the Cuban government. In late June, 1959, the chief of the Cuban Air Force, Diaz Lanz, resigned, fled to the United States, and declared that the Cuban government and armed forces had been penetrated by communism.

The administration began almost immediately to press this viewpoint to the Latin American community. The U.S. representative to the OAS, Dreier, barely veiled his inference in a statement before that body that communism had penetrated the Cuban revolution.[19] Latin American support was crucial, and Eisenhower publicly repeated his pledge that any U.S. response would be based upon a multilateral initiative by the OAS.[20] He attempted to lay the groundwork for such an initiative through the workings of Herter at a meeting of hemisphere foreign ministers in Chile in August 1959. A consensus was reached at that conference on certain principles of democracy and anticommunism—principles Eisenhower would use as a yardstick in attempting to measure the performance of Castro and gain that multilateral initiative for U.S. action.

Evidence of Cuban complicity in various events came pouring in. There were the attempted invasions of Nicaragua, the Dominican Republic, and Haiti during the spring and summer of 1959. There was President Urrutia's forced ouster from the Cuban government. There were the Communist takeovers of key Cuban labor and student organizations during the summer of 1959 and Che Guevara's travels to the Soviet bloc in September of the same year. There were increases in trials (notably, Huber Matos), executions, and anti-American attacks, and the rise in power of Communists within Castro's government (Raul Castro, Ché Guevara, Martinez). Eisenhower concluded that without U.S. action, the power struggle going on within the Cuban government, which was already tilting in favor of the Communist party, would lead to the tightening grip of Soviet communism in Cuba.[21]

Publicly, Ambassador to Cuba Philip Bonsal acted as the administration's front man, implicitly linking communism to Castro and the danger it posed to the Western Hemisphere.[22] When quizzed by the U.S. press about developments in Cuba, Eisenhower expressed puzzlement and bewilderment over Castro's behavior. He did not directly link Castro with communism and remained somewhat ambiguous, "I don't know exactly what the difficulty is."[23] Arguably, he was giving the Latin Americans room and time to form their own judgments. But his public statement less than one week later (November 4, 1959) did not cloak a tougher line of analysis, for he went out of his way to address the "seriousness of the Communist menace" in Cuba.[24]

Privately, Eisenhower worked behind the scenes with his advisors to decide on a course of action. Herter recommended a dramatic end to the policy of watchful waiting in a memo to the president dated November 5, 1959. The secretary's striking conclusion was that "the prolonged continuation of the Castro regime in Cuba in its present form would have serious adverse effects on the United States position in Latin America and corresponding advantages for international Communism." Castro had chosen a "course inimical to the United States," and there existed "no reasonable basis to found our policy on a hope that Castro will voluntarily adopt policies and attitudes consistent with minimum U.S. security requirements." Therefore, Herter recommended "building up . . . a coherent opposition . . . within Cuba and elsewhere" in order that the Castro regime could "be checked or replaced."[25]

Roy Richard Rubottom, assistant secretary of state for Latin American affairs, described the reasoning behind such a policy shift. By mid-1959, Castro was "so bitterly hostile to the US that the things he was actually carrying out at the time made it pretty clear that we were not going to be able to get along with him, and that these actions played into the hands of the Communists."[26]

Herter recommended a twelve-month timetable to develop a coherent opposition. At the same time, Eisenhower would have his team work publicly and privately to develop a mood in the United States and Latin America supportive of any moves against Castro. He apparently gave the green light for the development of programs and plans designed to "effect a change" in the Cuban government by either checking or replacing it.[27]

Part of the strategy included the development of programs to tighten the economic and diplomatic nooses around Castro, with the intended effect of increasing domestic and foreign opposition to Castro and forcing him to reconsider his position. Part of the strategy called for contingency plans to oust Castro should efforts to moderate him prove fruitless.

Although these programs were not formalized and approved by the NSC (March 14, 1960) and the president until March 17, 1960, the recently declassified record clearly demonstrates that the president concurred with this change in thrust in U.S. policy on November 9, 1959. In response to the president's go-ahead, the State Department and CIA worked closely with the special group of the NSC between November, 1959, and March, 1960, developing the details and specifics of this program.[28]

Viewed from this perspective, the March, 1960, decision was not a spur-of-the-moment decision launched in response to Castro's bitter personal attacks on President Eisenhower and Vice-President Nixon during February/March 1960. Nor was the decision an emotional response to Castro's charges of U.S. government responsibility for the explosion of the *LaCoubre* in March, 1960.

Public clues of this shift in policy were evident at the time it was taking place. CIA Deputy Director Cabell testified to a subcommittee of the Senate Judiciary Committee in November, 1959, that at a minimum Castro's tolerance and encouragement of Communists in his government was compatible with the Communist strategy for the Third World outlined in Moscow in February 1959 at the 21st Party Congress—"the infiltration of crypto-Communists or secret Communist party members into progressive movements."[29] CIA Director Allen Dulles directly linked such a strategy with developments in Cuba during a speech he delivered at Georgetown University on March 23, 1960. The themes of nationalism and liberation from the Colossus of the North were to be stressed by Latin American Communists, who were to minimize their references to relations with Moscow.

Eisenhower knew something had to be done, but he also realized the sensitivity of American intervention. During private meetings with his advisors in January 1960 he discussed the possibilities of blockade and quarantine in the context of labeling Castro a "wildman" and "madman."[30] Paramount in his decision to proceed against Castro were OAS support and a viable government-in-exile.

The program he approved in March had four points:

1. The creation of a responsible and unified Cuban opposition to the Castro regime located outside of Cuba.
2. The development of means for mass communication to the Cuban people as part of a powerful propaganda offensive.
3. The creation and development of a covert intelligence and action organization within Cuba which would be responsive to the orders and directions of the exile opposition.
4. The development of a paramilitary force outside of Cuba for future guerrilla action.[31]

Eisenhower also approved sabotage and economic sanctions.[32] From March 1960 on, his advisors implemented the program, suggesting and making changes as developments dictated. The president remained informed, and he was the final decision-making authority. But by summer of 1960, circumstances changed. Soviet involvement in Cuba had become plain, and Eisenhower no longer enjoyed the luxury of time.

Herter repeatedly informed the president on the status of possible OAS action against Cuba from March 1960 until January 1961.[33] Herter pushed the propaganda offensive against Castro throughout the summer of 1960, culminating with his presentation of the formal case against the Cuban government to the Inter-American Peace Committee and at the meeting of the foreign ministers of the American states between June and August 1960. The record clearly indicates Eisenhower was keenly disappointed that the aforementioned meeting did not produce a specific condemnation of Castro. Until the very last days of his administration he continued to work towards a multilateral OAS legitimization of any U.S. action.

Despite his continuing doubts about their efficacy, Eisenhower approved the implementation of economic sanctions against Cuba in early July after being swayed by the advice of Treasury Secretary Robert Anderson and National Security Advisor Gordon Gray.[34]

Finally, in July 1960, after evidence of Soviet bloc arms in Cuba became unequivocal and after Soviet leader Nikita Khrushchev threatened the use of ICBMs to defend Cuba from any U.S. attack and denounced the vitality of the Monroe Doctrine, Eisenhower added the Soviet connection in his attempts to convince the American people and Latin American community of the dangers posed to the Western Hemisphere by developments in Cuba.[35]

Eisenhower also took his case to Congress, emphasizing that any action would have to be carefully timed with evolving American, Cuban, Latin American, and world public opinion about Soviet involvement in the Cuban revolution.[36]

In response to the growing evidence of the strategic threat of a Soviet military presence in the Western Hemisphere, Eisenhower approved an expanded scope to the military option against Cuba on August 18, 1960. On that very same day he discussed the implementation of the key planning decisions approved in March 1960. Meeting with a small group of advisors following the regularly scheduled meeting of the NSC, Eisenhower apparently discussed a wide range of military options, including quarantine and blockade, as possible means to deal with the "large packages" arriving in Cuba.[37]

The record also reveals that the president kept in close contact with Herter while the secretary was at the gathering of the foreign ministers in San José in August 1960. Clearly, Herter was carrying out the president's instructions in attempting to gain specific condemnation of Cuba.[38]

With the Soviet threat looming increasingly ominously, Eisenhower elected to pick up the tempo against Castro after Herter returned from San José with only a lukewarm general condemnation of communism and external presences in the Western Hemisphere. Eisenhower pressed his case to the Latin American public and leaders, the American public, and the world, even utilizing the forum of the United Nations. The United States also shut down the Nicaro nickel plant in Cuba and prohibited the export of most American products to Cuba.[39]

All these actions fit neatly into Eisenhower's packaged strategy for dealing with Castro—to effect a change in government. But the evidence suggests that despite the administration's intense efforts through January 1961, no "government-in-exile" developed. Latin American leaders remained reluctant to support any employment of a U.S. sponsored military option against Castro—a last resort option in Eisenhower's strategy that was fast becoming an only remaining option—until such a coherent and unified Cuban opposition to Castro emerged. The last days of the Eisenhower administration were filled with a sense of urgency and strenuous efforts to establish that government-in-exile and produce that multilateral OAS support.[40] But neither happened by January 20, 1961, and for that reason the president refused to give the final go-ahead, even though his advisors were informing him that the narrow window of opportunity to employ the military option was rapidly closing.

Reagan and Foreign Policy

Structure and key personalities are essential determinants of Reagan's foreign policy substance and strategy. Initially, Reagan opted for a weak NSC, strong State Department system. Apparently Reagan desired a low-profile, NSC White House staff. This was consistent with his overall approach to cabinet government (cabinet councils, senior interdepartmental groups) and chairman-of-the-board style of leadership. Also, the president's own predilections and preferences were toward domestic issues. The similarities between Reagan's initial structure and Eisenhower's foreign policy machinery are striking. In both cases, however, criticisms of the structures mounted. In Eisenhower's case, the Jackson Committee investigated the extent to which the president was an uninvolved and uninformed chief executive as his secretaries conducted policy independent of him. As for the Reagan administration, many have criticized his weak, bureaucratically impotent NSC for leaving no formal actor to overcome the system's inherent inertia, to force other actors (particularly DOD) to cooperate, and to resolve disputes. The failure of the formal mechanisms—particularly the failure of the NSC to act as a policeman—has led to an informal policy process involving smaller, private meetings among the president, his secretaries, and the national security advisor; the emergence of other informal machineries such as the National Security Planning Group; memoranda to the president through the national security advisor; and the rising stature of Edwin Meese as the gatekeeper and ultimate arbitrator of disputes before they reach Reagan.

The similarities between players within the administrations are also striking. Deposed Secretary of State Alexander Haig clearly wanted to establish himself as the "vicar" of foreign policy so much so that he often would boycott meetings on international issues if the State Department did not chair the debate. Stated US News and World Report on June 15, 1981, "He [Haig] left little doubt that he desired to play the pre-eminent foreign policy role that John Foster Dulles had in the Eisenhower administration."[41]

The vice-president is also playing an active role in the conduct of foreign policy reminiscent of that played by Richard Nixon when he served as Eisenhower's vice president. George Bush's appointment as crisis manager and his trip in early 1983 to Western Europe to deal with problems associated with the scheduled deployment of Pershing II and ground-launched cruise missiles are indicative of the confidence Reagan has in his abilities.

Whether Haig was desirous of a coherent integrated foreign policy or merely expanding his prerogatives and power and State's turf remains uncertain. However, his forced resignation strongly suggests that his operating style—forcefully pressing his viewpoint to the president before ensuring that a consensus had emerged—did not fit well with Reagan's demand for team loyalty. Haig battled with everyone—locking horns with Meese, Deaver, and Baker for the right to occupy the president's doorstep; challenging David Stockman over budget cuts that affected foreign aid; contesting Agriculture Secretary Block's stance on the Soviet grain embargo; and frequently taking on Caspar Weinberger and/or Richard Allen, including the now famous, "I'm in charge" episode during the hours immediately following the Reagan assassination attempt.

Today, both Haig and National Security Advisor Allen are gone, having been replaced by George Schultz and William Clark. The formal structure though has remained relatively constant. Informal structures remain the dominant machinery for consensus-making (including breakfasts and lunches between Schultz, Weinberger, Clark, and Casey) and decision-making. Inherent bureaucratic tensions remain without a strong NSC to keep the peace. The president and his inner circle quartet (Meese, Baker, Deaver, and Clark) still focus their attentions on the domestic arena. Yet Shultz and Clark, perhaps partly due to their abilities to avoid controversy (by touching base with others and seeking a consensus position to take to Reagan) and their less abrasive personalities, have been able to establish their influence in the foreign policy process far more than their predecessors. Neither openly challenges the authority of the man who still has the last word on policy—

President Reagan. But crucial transformations have taken place nonetheless.

Reagan and Central America

Reagan's Central American policy started off reflecting the hard-line ideological positions of himself and Secretary Haig. This translated into a policy which placed events—particularly those related to revolutionary movements—in an East-West framework. The way to deal with such "revolutions" was to "draw the line" in our front yard. The administration perceived civil wars such as El Salvador's as penetrated by the Soviet Union and its stooge, Cuba. Haig revealed the extent to which the perspective of strategic confrontation between the USSR and the United States dominated the visions of American policymakers by suggesting that the Reagan administration was considering a blockade to cut off arms from Cuba as a policy option to deal with the Salvadoran rebels.

Partly as a reaction to Eagleburger's failure to "sell" to the Europeans the administration's White Paper on Soviet and Cuban intervention in Central America, partly as a result of Secretary Schultz's pragmatism, and partly as a result of growing dissatisfaction with his policies within Congress and among the Latin Americans, Reagan has softened his tactics. Economic as well as military assistance has emerged as part of the Reagan strategy. The administration also held secret talks with the Nicaraguan government in order to explore the possibility of evolving from a hostile relationship toward a more cooperative one.

Still, the administration continues to send out mixed signals: continuing its punitive policies toward Cuba; maintaining and hinting at the need to increase the number of its military advisors in El Salvador, completing its certification to Congress of El Salvador's progress in human rights, and proceeding with its covert efforts to destabilize the Nicaraguan government. In spite of such contradictions, the evidence of softer tactics suggests a flexibility in Reagan's policies that is often overlooked.

Schultz does not dominate the foreign policy process. Rather, he must struggle for influence with other powerful actors, including Defense Secretary Weinberger and national security advisor William Clark. Reagan, however, still has the last word on policy and often exercises that prerogative despite the public perception of a president who is both disinterested and ill-informed in foreign affairs.

Cabinet-style government demand active players competing for the chairman's ear, presenting divergent opinions but remaining loyal. Most important, there can be, and is, only one ultimate decisionmaker—the president.

Eisenhower/Reagan Parallels

Many of the labels attached to Eisenhower's style of leadership during his two terms in office also appear to characterize the Reagan presidency today. For example, Robert Divine comments that Ike's "lack of stamina and enthusiasm for the daily grind of diplomacy"[42] as well as his lack of knowledge about many foreign policy issues contributed to a complementary, team relationship between Eisenhower and Dulles. Divine also adds that Eisenhower preferred oral briefings from his inner circle to reading long memoranda.[43] Reagan's dozing at meetings, delegating to Bush and Schultz the conduct of diplomacy, and preferring oral briefs and one-page memos seem to be part of his working style.

David Capitanchik refers to Eisenhower's ability to appear as a dignified father-figure, yet remain a simple man of immense goodwill only slightly interested in politics as one of his greatest political assets. He adds, like Divine, that Eisenhower was impatient with the endless paperwork of the presidency and tried to get his staff to condense long documents into one-page summaries.[44]

Eisenhower delegated power broadly, and vast duties fell on the shoulders of Sherman Adams, assistant to the president. While neither Adams nor Counselor Edwin Meese ever attempt(ed) to act as domestic policymakers, both funnel(ed) issues to the president and unquestionably wield(ed) great power.

Eisenhower's cabinet occupied a position of unique prominence as a consultative body, much like Reagan's cabinet. Both presidents rely (relied) heavily on staff counsel and collective judgment.

Both men also disapprove(d) of "big government," yet neither surrender(ed) any of the powers of the president. Both saw the role of the White House staff as one of policy coordination and the oversight of policy planning and implementation rather than strictly policy-making.

Hyman and Sheatsley conclude that the pivot of Eisenhower's governance was his extraordinary appeal to the general public and those he met in face-to-face settings. He literally restored the dignity of the presidency.[45] His search for consensus and teamwork and his approach to delegation of power also suggest parallels to Reagan.

Perhaps Reagan's leadership hand is hidden just as deftly as Eisenhower's was, not to be unveiled through diligent scholarly research for years to come. Regardless, the similarities between Eisenhower's and Reagan's leadership suggest that perhaps it is a bit too early to conclude, based on contemporary analyses of Reagan's foreign policy structure and the key actors working within it, that Reagan is ill-informed about and disinterested in foreign affairs and that American foreign policy is aimless, adrift, and lacking direction from the president.

This speculation is not unfounded. Bert Rockman has written a persuasive analysis of the roles of the Department of State and the White House staff/National Security Council in the foreign policy making process of the United States. Rockman argues that many factors push the system toward a "growth of both coordinative institutions and of 'irregular' staffers in government."[46] Among the factors which Rockman cites are:

1. Overload, or the massive expansion of policy agendas, which necessitates institutionalized coordinative functions and structures that can filter and simplify the complexity of foreign affairs;
2. Institutional and organizational explanations: the analysis of the State Department being soft, oft-times slow, impressionistic, and politically judgmental is highly vulnerable and the kind of analysis any president would want to keep to himself; distance from the White House, a problem affecting all line departments, merely compounds the difficulties;
3. The political culture of Washington: emphasizing an "us" versus "them" mentality, Washingtonian culture highlights the relatively long and tenuous lifelines linking the president to his cabinet officers and the relatively short and controllable connections between the president and his Executive Office;
4. Foreign policy as crisis management: State Department bureaucrats, who tend to think incrementally and present the perception of advocating parochial interests, are often excluded from the process by the White House staff, which can operate in a think-tank environment readily adaptable to wide oscillations in foreign policy themes.[47]

For these reasons, Rockman visualizes a general tendency for presidents to build a policy-making apparatus close to them rather than to rely exclusively upon their cabinet.

What relevance does this trend toward foreign policy by "irregulars" have for an analysis of the Reagan presidency? In addition to the tendency developed above, the actual role of Reagan's White House staff may differ from the diminished capacity that has been publicly proclaimed. For example, Richard Allen played a largely advocacy and advisory role, despite his pronouncements that he would tailor his role after Eisenhower's "neutral competent" special assistant, Gordon Gray.[48] Such a model of the Reagan presidency operates under the premises that foreign policy is a high-priority item on the presidential agenda, that presidents ultimately determine foreign policy, that the foreign policy system has inexorably marched toward a system in which the national security assistant has vied with the secretary of state and other cabinet officers for influence, and that the secretary of state and the State Department operate at significant disadvantages in the competition.

The implication of such an analysis is that the Reagan model, which deemphasizes the public visibility of the national security advisor and the activities of the White House staff demands leadership and direction from either the president or a dominant "irregular," most probably William Clark. Only recently has the literature suggested that Clark might indeed occupy such a central position in the foreign policy making system, and/or that the president is more involved than he is given credit for.[49] Regardless, it is early, perhaps premature, to make a final judgment that Reagan's foreign policy is adrift and lacking central direction. Visibility does not necessarily equate with responsibility and authority. Nor is it a simple task to determine from visible channels of access and flow charts indicating delegations of authority how policy is made. The jury must remain out on the Reagan administration.

Eisenhower revisionists would have us believe that Ike's record—for which he deserves much of the credit—is clear and impressive. Peace, low inflation, restrained defense spending (in the context of Democratic charges of a "bomber gap" and later, a "missile gap"), a balanced budget, and reorientation of the mutual security program away from military and toward economic assistance to the developing world stand high among Eisenhower's accomplishments.[50]

While there exists a darker side of Ike's foreign policy—namely, the frequent covert use of the CIA in "knee-jerk" opposition to communism—the Eisenhower record remains enviable. Should Reagan, perhaps as immensely self-confident and successfully independent of his presidency as was Ike, choose to follow the Eisenhower path, he must follow it in substance as well as style. Only then will he approximate Ike's achievements.

Notes

1. Charles Kegley, Jr., ed., *American Foreign Policy* (New York: St. Martin's Press, 1982).

2. Fred I. Greenstein, *The Hidden-hand Presidency: Eisenhower as Leader* (New York: Basic Books, 1982).

3. Ibid., 124-132, 133.

4. Ibid, 133-134.

5. Eisenhower to Henry Luce, Dwight David Eisenhower Library (DDE), Abilene, Kansas, Aug. 8, 1960.

6. Richard Immerman, "Eisenhower and Dulles: Who Made the Decision?" *Political Psychology*, 1 no. 2 (Autumn 1979).

7. See particularly Ambrose, 1981; Taylor, Maxwell D., 1961; Church, Frank, 1975.

8. James Keagle, *Toward an Understanding of U.S.-Latin American Policy*, Ph.D. dissertation, Princeton, 1982.

9. Bureau of Intelligence and Research, Division of Research and Analysis for the American Republics, Report No. 7780, Aug. 15, 1958, DDE Library.

10. Dwight D. Eisenhower, *Waging Peace* (New York: Doubleday, 1965).

11. *Department of State Bulletin* (*DSB*), Feb. 2, 1959, 162-163.

12. Memo, Allen Dulles to Christian Herter, Feb. 4, 1959, DDE Library.

13. Memo, Herter to the President, April 23, 1959, DDE Library.

14. Memo, Richard Nixon to Eisenhower, Herter, Allen Dulles, and John Foster Dulles, April 25, 1959, papers of Mike Mansfield, University of Montana Library.

15. Dreier, Statement before the Council of the OAS, April 28, 1959.

16. Department of State Press Release No. 417, June 11, 1959, in *DSB*, June 29, 1959, 958-959.

17. *Newsweek*, June 18, 1959.

18. *US News and World Report*, June 28, 1959

19. Dreier, Statement to the OAS, July 10, 1959.

20. Eisenhower, statement at a news conference, July 15, 1959, in *Public Papers of the President* (*PP*), 1960, 522.

21. Keagle, op.cit., 78-79.

22. Bonsal, *DSB*, Nov. 16, 1959.

23. Eisenhower, Oct. 28, 1959, in *PP*, 1960, 751.

24. *PP*, 1960, 769-770.

25. Memo, Herter to Eisenhower, Nov. 5, 1959, in DDE Library.

26. Rubottom, John Foster Dulles Oral History Project, Mudd Library, Princeton, NJ., 70-74.

27. Memo, Goodpaster to Herter, Nov. 9, 1959, in DDE Library.

28. See Ambrose, 1981, and Church, 1975.

29. Cabell, US Senate Judiciary Committee, Subcommittee to Investigate the Administration of the Internal Security Act and other Internal Security Laws, Nov. 5, 1959; See Keagle, op.cit., 90-93.

30. Goodpaster, Memos of Conferences with the President, Jan. 23, 25, 1960; See Keagle, op.cit., 99-103.

31. See Ambrose, op.cit., 309, or Taylor, 1961, as sanitized and declassified on May 8, 1977.

32. Gordon Gray, in Church, op.cit., 114.

33. For example, see Memo, Herter to Eisenhower, March 17, 1960; April 23, 1960, DDE Library.

34. Keagle, op.cit., 132-136; Gray, Memo of Meet-

ing with the President, July 7, 1960, DDE Library.

35. Department of State Circular No. 174, July 28, 1960.

36. Legislative Leadership Minutes, Aug. 16, 1960, DDE Library.

37. Gray, Memo of Meeting with the President, Aug. 17, 1960.

38. Keagle, op.cit., 156-160; Herter and Goodpaster, phone conversations' memoranda, Aug. 29, 30, 1960, DDE Library.

39. Keagle, op.cit., 164-168.

40. Ibid., 169-197.

41. *US News and World Report*, June 15, 1981.

42. Robert Durne, *Eisenhower and the Cold War* (New York: Oxford University Press, 1981), 22.

43. Ibid., 24.

44. David Capitanchik, The Eisenhower Presidency and American Foreign Policy (New York: Humanities Press, 1969).

45. Herbert Hyman and Paul Sheatsley, "The Political Appeal of President Eisenhower," *Public Opinion Quarterly* 17 (1953-1954), 443-460.

46. Bert A. Rockman, "America's Departments of State," *American Political Science Review* (Dec. 1981), 912.

47. Ibid., 914-918.

48. Hedrick Smith, "A Scaled-down Version of the Security Advisor's Task," *New York Times*, March 4, 1981, A2.

49. *Newsweek*, Feb. 7, 1983.

50. Stephen E. Ambrose, *Ike's Spies: Eisenhower and the Espionage Establishment* (New York: Doubleday, 1981).

The President and the Budget 7.5

Robert W. Hartman

The policy process is currently dominated by concern over fiscal and macro economic issues. As of late, official Washington has been and will continue to be preoccupied with the size of the deficit, sources of revenue, defense vs. social spending, uncontrollable spending, entitlements vs. discretionary spending, and the like. The 1974 Congressional Budget Act provided Congress with a new budget process. Among other things, it created new budget committees in each house, a new process providing for omnibus budget resolutions and reconciliation procedures (whereby committee decisions could be overridden). The act was intended to strengthen Congress's hand in the development of the federal budget vis-à-vis the president. An unforeseen outcome of those reforms—reflecting what political scientists refer to as the law of unanticipated consequences—is President Reagan's employment of them to impose his priorities on Congress with the help of his allies in the Congress. The president's legislative successes on key votes became the centerpiece of the early days of his administration. The following excerpt gives an overview of President Reagan's role in the budget process.

The procedural developments in the 1981 budgetary process were a turning point. In January 1980, President Carter sent Congress his budget proposal, tailored to election-year politics. It dropped the austerity theme and tried to offend no important constituency. Perhaps because of the public's awareness that the second budget resolution for fiscal 1980 was phony in the sense that its assumptions were not likely to be realized, a sharp eye was cast on Carter's January proposal. The reaction was skepticism, and this contributed to plummeting financial markets early in 1980. Interest rates on three-month Treasury bills

"Congress and Budget-Making" by Robert W. Hartman, Fall 1982, *Political Science Quarterly, 97*, pp. 387-96. Copyright 1982 by the Academy of Political Science. Reprinted by permission.

rose from 12 to 15.5 percent between January and March. Bond and stock prices fell precipitously.

President Carter withdrew his budget seven weeks after it was submitted and began an extensive series of conferences with members of Congress on an acceptable alternative. The chairmen and members of the Budget Committees played a major role along with the leadership of Congress in these negotiations. After Carter submitted his revised budget in March, the Budget Committees took advantage of this enhanced role and supported a first concurrent resolution that included reconciliation instructions directing eight House and ten Senate authorizing committees to report legislation reducing outlays by over $6 billion in 1981. Tax committees were instructed to raise more than $4 billion in revenues. These actions were only a small part of those needed to balance the budget as promised in the resolution.[1] The committees were instructed to report legislation within a few weeks of the first resolution, which passed in June 1980.

The move to cut spending stalled in the middle of 1980. The recession coupled with an election led to a stalemate. The Senate passed a reconciliation bill in July, and the House passed its quite different bill in September. The conference committee, which numbered over one hundred, repeatedly deadlocked and did not pass the reconciliation act until early December after the long-delayed second budget resolution was voted.

The Omnibus Budget Reconciliation Act of 1980 was a disappointing piece of legislation. Since the reconciliation instructions included the first concurrent resolution specified savings targets for fiscal 1981 only, a number of committees "complied" by drafting changes in law that shifted expenditures from 1981 to future years. Other committees included legislation that actually raised spending in some programs in part to offset cuts made. A reduction in cost-of-living adjustments for federal civilian and military retirees that passed the Senate was dropped by the conference. In all, the Omnibus Budget Reconciliation Act provided $4.6 billion in outlay reductions and $3.6 billion in new taxes, for a total deficit-reduction package of about $8 billion, well under the action needed to balance the budget as originally intended.

Two additional innovations in the fiscal 1981 congressional budgetary process are worth noting. First, both houses of Congress made a start on multiyear budgeting. The budget resolutions incorporated budget targets for the out-years fiscal 1982 and 1983 as well as for the budget year 1981, but each house set different targets for future years. Second, for the first time, levels of federal credit activity were specified. This "credit budget" attempted to curb the total volume of both new direct loans and guaranteed loan commitments of federal agencies by requesting that appropriation limitations be extended to all federal credit activity. Such actions were intended to increase control since many federal credit activities are subject to weak limits imposed by authorizing legislation that sets the terms of loans by executive discretion, or even by market demand. As in the early years of the new budgetary process, however, these "credit limits" were revised during fiscal 1981 to conform to what was happening to federal credit, rather than the other way around.

The Reagan Revolution in the Budget Process

In many ways the stage had been set for President Reagan's entrance. Over time, the Budget Committees had increasingly extended their roles in and influence over budgeting outcomes. A major procedural breakthrough had been made in 1980 when reconciliation instructions were incorporated in the first concurrent resolution. Yet the Stockman-directed progress of President Reagan's budgetary legislation through the summer of 1981 is regarded by many as a revolution because of the size and scope of the changes made and the threat they pose to hallowed congressional procedures.

Within about seven weeks of taking office, President Reagan sent Congress a full-blown set of budget revisions for fiscal 1982 and beyond. The most controversial proposals were an increase in spending for national defense, a reduction in business and personal taxes, and a huge cut in federal nondefense spending. The administration, with the support of the Republican-controlled Senate Budget Committee, sought to carry out as much of the spending reduction program as possible in the form of reconciliation action. The Senate in late March—just a few days after the president's budget revisions were submitted—passed a resolution instructing its committees to make major budget cuts.

These instructions were incorporated in the Senate's first concurrent resolution, which passed in May. The House proceeded along a more conventional track. The budget committee reported a first concurrent resolution that included reconciliation instructions. This resolution, bearing the stamp of chairman James R. Jones, was challenged on the floor of the House by a substitute resolution cosponsored by Delbert L. Latta, the ranking Republican on the House Budget Committee, and Phil Gramm, a Democratic member of the committe and a leader of a group of conservative Democrats called "Boll Weevils." Gramm-Latta I, as the budget resolution became known, passed the House in late May, after an apparently effective presidential television plea for it. The Senate passed an equivalent resolution the next day.

Gramm-Latta was monumental in a number of respects. First, it contained instructions for budget reductions addressed to fifteen House committees and fourteen Senate committees. The instructions specified amounts to be saved for fiscal years 1982, 1983, and 1984. This multiyear focus was designed to avoid the temporary cosmetic cuts of the previous year's legislation and to complement the administration's multiyear tax-cutting plan. Second, the outlay reductions totaled $36 billion, $47 billion, and $56 billion for the three fiscal years, over eight percent of nondefense, noninterest outlays. These sums were several times larger than previous reconciliation actions. Third, the reconciliation savings were to be made in two types of authorizing legislation: entitlements and discretionary programs. For entitlement spending, a reconciliation directive to the authorizing committee is recognized as the only way to impose restraint since subsequent appropriations are perfunctory. But spending for other programs—for example, grants to states for education programs—can be limited either by proposing limits on annual appropriations or by the much stronger measure of directing the committee that authorized the program to lower the authorization ceiling over several years. The latter arrangement was a feature of Gramm-Latta and was not part of the Jones proposal that was defeated.

The congressional committees responded to the reconciliation instructions by submitting legislation affecting 250 different federal programs.[2] Arguing that some of the changes proposed in the House showed a "clear danger of Congressional backsliding and a return to spending as usual,"[3] the administration quickly fashioned an alternative reconciliation bill, called Gramm-Latta II; to replace the work of several committees. Gramm-Latta II, like its predecessor, narrowly passed the House, after gaining support from the Boll Weevils and a group of moderate Republicans called "Gypsy Moths" who demanded and received certain concessions from the administration. After an efficiently run conference, the president in August signed the Omnibus Budget Reconciliation Act of 1981, an inch-thick compendium of twenty separate titles covering a range from agriculture and forestry to health professions. The law changed entitlement program eligibility rules (for example, for food stamps), limited the amounts authorized in scores of programs for 1982-84, rewrote major parts of substantive law having little effect on the budget (for example, for radio and TV broadcasting), and probably did a few other things that have not been discovered yet.

This extraordinary law was debated on the floor of the House for two days. There were no hearings at all on some sections of the law. The possibility of amending the bill was strictly limited, and it was voted on in a single vote, not section by section.

The reconciliation act's companion legislation, the Economic Recovery Tax Act of 1981, was meanwhile wending its way through the Senate Finance Committee and the House Ways and Means Committee. The first concurrent resolution had set targets for tax cuts for 1982-84. A period of negotiation between the White House and the Democratic chairman of the Ways and Means Committee, Congressman Dan Rostenkowski, had produced no agreement, especially on the size and phasing-in of a personal income tax. Accordingly, the administration decided to attract enough Boll Weevil votes to its side to command a majority in the House by offering to include tax changes that would appeal to them. Rostenkowski countered with additional lures to keep the Boll Weevils in the fold. OMB Director Stockman characterized the resulting scramble as: "The hogs were really feeding. The greed level, the level of opportunism, just got out of control."[4] Despite this, the Economic Recovery Tax Act complied with the revenue reduction limits in the first concurrent resolution, although the act's tax cut for 1985, which was deepened by adding indexation of the individual income tax in that year, probably went beyond what the supporters of the concurrent resolution had envisioned.

Aftermath

Congress adjourned in August. The members heard from constituents about high interest rates, and they had time to think about what had transpired in the first half of the budget policy under President Reagan. Congress prides itself on being a deliberative body. The helter-skelter of enacting reconciliation and the tax bill was the opposite of a careful legislative process. The modus operandi of the Congress had for a long time been that the work is done by committees that share power. In 1981 the Senate had ceded full control to the Budget Committee, and in the House the committee proposals for reconciliation had been thrown out. The main function of Appropriations Committee members had been as watchdog on the Treasury. But the reconciliation process had given the play to the Budget Committees and the authorizing committees, leaving Appropriations a cipher. Members of Congress like to show their expertise and independence by sponsoring amendments and the like, but the whole legislative show in 1981 had boiled down to two votes for or against President Reagan's entire program. These concerns, as well as uneasiness about the economy, presaged trouble ahead.

The president's initial budget plan had contemplated program cuts to be made in areas not covered by reconciliation. So had the first concurrent resolution on the 1982 budget. The exact size of these cuts was a matter of confusion, in part because the president's cuts were measured from a baseline different from that used in reconciliation. Moreover, some of the members of Congress who had been lured into the administration's camp for the reconciliation thought they had been promised some relenting in the pursuit of further cuts.

Against this backdrop came the Reagan administration's fall offensive. A new package of budget cuts encompassing entitlement reductions, appropriations reductions, and even some "revenue enhancement" was announced by the administration on September 24—incidentally making it absolutely impossible to meet the deadlines set by the 1974 act. The program was not well received by Congress. The entitlement package was never even formally introduced and the tax enhancers were withdrawn. The administration decided, however, to make yet another fight over its proposed across-the-board (with some exceptions) reductions in appropriations.

When the fiscal year began on October 1, no appropriations bills had been signed into law.[5] As a result, the entire government was being funded under a continuing appropriation law. The first continuing appropriation resolution, signed into law on September 30, is a relatively short document setting limits on the commitment of funds for the first part of the year. Instead of specifying appropriations on a line-by-line basis as in ordinary appropriations laws, the resolution sets spending limits by mechanical rules. Thus the limit on spending for each program is as follows: If both houses have passed an appropriation for that program, it may operate at the lesser of the two appropriated amounts; if only one house has passed an appropriation, spending may continue at the lesser of the appropriated amount or the "current rate." The current rate generally means the rate of the previous fiscal year.[6] The first continuing appropriation set an expiration date of 20 November 1981, in the expectation that regular appropriations laws, which supersede continuing appropriations, would be on the books by that time.

As it turned out, very few appropriations—and none of the major ones—had been passed by Friday, November 20, because of the continuing controversy over the administration's fall-offensive cuts, and a second continuing appropriation was needed. The Congress agreed on such a bill at the final hour and sent it to President Reagan. Over the weekend of November 21-22, President Reagan decided to veto the continuing resolution and did so on Monday, November 23. As a result, federal offices throughout the country closed that day, nonessential workers were sent home, and President Reagan and members of Congress (who stayed on the job—their appropriation had passed) got together that same day on a compromise extension of the continuing resolution until December 15. On December 15, with few appropriations yet enacted, still another continuing appropriation was passed until 15 February 1982.

By the end of December 1981, most appropriations laws—though not the biggest nondefense one, for the Departments of Labor, Health and Human Services, and Education—had been signed into law. As indicated in table 7.5.1, the administration was forced to accept some increases over its fall proposals in the appropriations that passed. In defense and foreign aid, appropriations were below the administration's request; but the Agriculture, Interior, and combined Housing and Urban Development, Veterans Administration, and National Aeronautics and Space Administration appropriations exceeded the administration's request. While it is probably true that these appropriations would have been even higher if the administration had not waged a fall offensive, it is clear that President Reagan's total mastery over budgeting began to erode in the appropriations process. It is also evident that the patent disregard for the Appropriations Committees' prerogatives in the reconciliation process stiffened these committees' resistance to further cuts.

It is universally agreed that operating a large part of the government under continuing appropriations is a most unsatisfactory way of doing the public's business. First, because the continuing resolution is simply a set of general rules to limit spending, it tends to perpetuate spending patterns that conform to no one's preferences, and it can lead to unintended consequences. For example, if one house of Congress passes a low appropriation for a particular program, quite conceivably as a result of a vendetta by one member of the Appropriations Committee, that low appropriation governs the program no matter how high the other house sets it. On a regular appropriation, matters such as this as well as simple mistakes are taken care of in conference before a final bill is approved. Second, continuing appropriations lead to even greater managerial inefficiency than is customary in government activities. When an agency manager does not know what level of funds will be available for the whole fiscal year, the inevitable tendency is to be cautious in committing funds. Contracts are not let early in the year, to ensure that funds will be available later in the year. Then when the full appropriation is finally voted, there is frantic activity to commit funds before they expire. On some accounts, particularly those pertaining to salaries and expenses of employees, the tendency is to be optimistic: don't fire anybody until it is absolutely necessary. If the optimism proves to have been false when the full appropriation becomes law, the agency may have to fire too many people or furlough (put on unpaid leave) an entire staff. There is ample evidence that this kind of behavior was developing as fiscal 1982 unfolded.

The legislative history of the 1982 budget ended on a sour note. In November, in the midst of the dispute over the administration's reductions in appropriations and well after it had become evident that economic events had transformed the projected budget outcomes of the first concurrent resolution, both houses passed a second concurrent resolution. Instead of acknowledging the sharply changed economic circumstances and reaching some decision on appropriations still outstanding, the second concurrent resolution simply rubber-stamped the outdated first resolution. In effect, Congress decided to put over into calendar 1982 any further decisions on the budget.

Table 7.5.1

Status of Fiscal Year 1982 Appropriations, as of 15 March 1982 Budget Authority in Billions of Dollars

Title of appropriation	Date enacted	September administration request	House bill	Senate bill	Final action	Difference between final action and administration request
Agriculture and related agencies	12/23/81	22.3	22.7	22.9	22.6	+0.3
Defense Department	12/29/81	200.9	197.4	203.7	199.9	−1.0
District of Columbia	12/4/81	0.6	0.5	0.6	0.6	*
Energy and Water Development	12/4/81	12.1	13.2	12.8	12.5	+0.4
Foreign Aid	12/29/81	7.8	7.4	7.3	7.5	−0.3
HUD, Veterans, NASA	12/23/81	58.7	62.6	60.5	60.4	+1.7
Interior and related agencies	12/23/81	6.4	11.1	7.4	7.2	+0.8
Legislative Branch	10/1/81	1.4	1.1[a]	0.9[a]	1.3	−0.1
Military Construction	12/23/81	7.3	6.9	7.3	7.1	−0.2
Transportation and related agencies	12/23/81	9.8	11.1	10.4	10.1	+0.3
Subtotal		327.3	334.0	333.8	329.2	+1.9
Labor, HHS, Education	...	82.5	85.2	84.8[b]	...	...
State, Justice, Commerce, Judiciary	...	8.2	8.7	8.6[b]	...	...
Treasury, Postal Service, General Government	...	9.1	9.7	9.4[b]	...	...

Sources: Congressional Quarterly Weekly Report 40 (16 January 1982), 103; and Weekly Compilation of Presidential Documents 17, nos. 43-53 (26 October 1981-4 January 1982).
* Less than $100 million.
a. House bill excludes cost of Senate operation and vice versa.
b. Committee approved amount.

Prospects for Peaceful Reform

The six years that the new congressional budget has been in effect cover a rough period in the nation's economic history, encompassing a recovery from the worst recession since the 1930s, the onset of high and highly variable inflation and interest rates, and the beginning of a period of retrenchment in federal spending. The congressional budgetary process has emerged from this period with some scars, but with the solid achievement of having proved resilient to changing needs. Stimulating the economy called for accommodative Budget Committees, but as the economic and political trend moved toward spending restraint, the control mechanism was strengthened. When a president needed support in making a credible budget, the budgetary process provided an opportunity for joint action with the Congress, but it also provided room for a confrontation when the parties differed sharply. Such resilience could be interpreted as a lack of discipline, a process with no firm direction. But a more accurate lesson to be learned is that economic and political circumstances do change, and a flexible procedure is needed to allow changes in direction.

The budgetary history of the last few years raises two kinds of questions for the future. First, how will budget procedures affect the decisions to be made in the coming year? Second, what modifications in budgetary processes should be made in the longer term?

Stalemate and Its Alternatives, 1983

Congressional final action on President Reagan's 1983 budget is uncommonly difficult to forecast. The public and Congress seem to agree that the projected deficits—especially if adjusted to more realistic economic assumptions than those of the administration—are too high, but there is little evidence of a consensus on how to lower them. The major disagreements are over whether to raise revenues or lower outlays and which types of spending and taxing should bear the brunt of the burden. The prospects for a repeat performance by President Reagan in securing substantially complete acceptance of his budget seem remote. On the other hand, expecting Congress to fashion a budget entirely on its own is unrealistic. Any group in Congress that takes the lead on formulating a package—which would necessarily involve both higher taxes and major program cuts—would face the attendant political danger of being blamed (possibly by the president) for being the enemy of the elderly or the taxpayer, among others. It is hard to imagine that many congressmen would relish that role, and it is nearly inconceivable that the Democratic chairmen of the House Budget Committee and the Ways and Means Committee, who lost out to President Reagan in 1981, would voluntarily take that chance again.

Another possibility is that the president and Congress will agree to compromise. A bipartisan coalition in the Congress and the president would concur on a set of budgetary actions perceived as being built on the president's plan but with significant modifications. The agreed-upon package would almost certainly require a single vote since the individual parts of it could not pass in an election year; accordingly, such a package would probably take the form either of firm reconciliation instructions or even of specific legislation attached to some other bill, such as an impending act to raise the limit on the public debt. These shortcuts would further erode the conventional way of doing business in Congress; thus, opposition should be expected not only on substantive and partisan political grounds but also on procedural ones. This is a substantial number of hurdles to get over.

If an agreement is not reached, a stalemate is possible. Unlike other legislative action, a budgetary stalemate does not mean that nothing happens. In this case it would probably mean passing a first concurrent resolution on the budget that did not contain mandatory instructions to authorizing committees to come up with budget-saving legislation, and it might mean passing some appropriations that would greatly exceed the president's proposals, which would then be vetoed. Or the appropriations committees could fail to act at all. By October 1, a continuing resolution covering spending for most of the agencies and extending through the November election would be needed. Essentially, stalemate means that the difficult budget decisions of early 1982 would be pushed ahead to a post-election session of Congress, where a clearer consensus might emerge. This scenario appears to be fraught with great risks to the economy as uncertainty about the budget stretches out over months, and it greatly increases the possibility of a radical reaction to what will be perceived as an intractable budget mess. . . .

It is important to end this account with the reminder that, if there were a solution to the budgetary impasse that commanded strong popular support, the budgetary process in the Congress would not stand in its way. Even with presidential opposition, one can imagine the congressional leadership riding the crest of a popular wave to beat back whatever fragmentary congressional opposition to a popular outcome developed. The Congressional Budget and Impoundment Control Act is proof that Congress, acting alone, can undertake changes that roil customary legislative relationships. Only when an attempt is made to preempt traditional legislative procedures with legislation that does not enjoy wide popular support does the system seem to fail. Should stalemate ensue in 1982, the blame should rest more on the failure to reach a consensus than on a shortcoming of the budgetary process. Indeed, the only hope of a better outcome lies in the budgetary process forcing all parties to attempt to reach such an agreement.

Notes

1. Further savings were assumed to be made on appropriations. As a safeguard, the first resolution called for delaying the transmittal to the president of appropriations bills that exceeded the resolution targets until a second resolution had been approved.

2. One committee, the House Energy and Commerce Committee, could not agree on a response. Its chairman forwarded Democratic proposals to the House Budget Committee. It is not clear what sanctions can be taken against a committee that refuses to comply—other than the Budget Committee writing its own legislation.

3. Ronald Reagan, "The President's News Conference of June 16, 1981," *Weekly Compilation of Presidential Documents* 17 (22 June 1981), 632.

4. As quoted in William Greider, "The Education of David Stockman," *Atlantic Monthly*, Dec. 1981, 47-59.

5. The legislative branch appropriation was incorporated into the first continuing appropriation resolution.

6. Even so, "current rate" is an ambiguous term because "the" rate of the previous fiscal year may be quite different; rates for each quarter (which is generally the period over which the OMB apportions appropriations to agencies) and the final quarter of the fiscal year may not reflect what the Appropriations Committee intends as the limit for the next period.

Evaluating the Presidents of the United States 7.6

Arthur B. Murphy

Over the years there have been a number of polls that have surveyed academic opinion on presidential greatness and performance. Such evaluations and ratings provide interesting perspectives on presidential power. They give us as good an indication as we can get on how "history" judges presidents. The following original essay undertakes a comprehensive survey of these polls and attempts to relate what they tell us about presidents and the presidency.

Scholars are showing increasing interest in rating the accomplishments of American presidents. Two significant surveys were conducted in 1982. Forty-nine political scientists and historians were polled by the Chicago Tribune, and in January 1982 their list of the "ten best" and "ten worst" presidents was published. Later in the year, Dr. Robert K. Murray of Pennsylvania State University sent 155 questions on seventeen pages to 1,997 historians. A total of 953 American history PH.D.s responded in detail. The ranking of the presidents that resulted from the Murray survey will probably become rather widely accepted by the academic community and possibly by the more responsible news media as well. It is most impressive that such a large number of American history professors took valuable time for this endeavor. The largest number of scholars who participated in a related analysis was 571, in the Maranell/Dodder poll of 1970. When one considers the sheer volume of data Dr. Murray has available to him, 147,715 total responses (953 x 155), his analysis of why persons rank presidents the way they do should prove most valuable. His ranking of the presidents will also make an important contribution, partly because it confirms the ranking recent polls have assigned to modern presidents, and partly because it is consistent with other prestigious polls conducted in the last thirty-five years.

The actual presidential rank order arrived at by Dr. Murray's 953 historians is very similar to the ranking of the forty-nine scholars, many of them political scientists, who responded earlier in 1982 to the Chicago Tribune questionnaire. Both polls had the same names for the first eight "best presidents," with only relatively minor differences in order of listing. The Murray poll ranked F. Roosevelt second and Washington third. The Chicago Tribune poll placed Washington second and F. Roosevelt third. The Tribune poll ranked T. Roosevelt fourth and Jefferson fifth, whereas the Murray poll reversed that order. Both polls ranked Lincoln first, Wilson sixth, Jackson seventh, and Truman eighth. The Tribune poll ranked Eisenhower nine and Polk ten. The Murray poll placed Eisenhower eleven and Polk twelve, preferring J. Adams and L. Johnson for the ninth and tenth positions. Both polls had the same names for the bottom nine positions, both designating Harding as our "worst president," but differing slightly on how bad the other eight "poor presidents" were. The Tribune poll ranked Carter our tenth worst president causing Atlanta Mayor Andrew Young to condemn the scholars for "insensitive elitism," a charge he might also make against Dr. Murray's 953 historians, who considered Carter to be the twelfth worst president. The similarity of the two polls enhances their credibility.

An examination of the various presidential rankings that were published from 1948 through 1982 makes it clear that the similarities of the polls are more striking than the differences. (See table 7.6.1) Lincoln is considered to be our greatest president by all the scholars' polls, while Harding is consistently called our "worst president." Every poll ranks Washington and F. Roosevelt right behind Lincoln, although there is a difference of opinion as to which of these two undeniably great presidents should be ranked in second place. The fourth, fifth, and sixth positions are typically occupied by three of the following four presidents: Jefferson, Jackson, T. Roosevelt, and Wilson, although which one occupies which position depends on the particular poll you examine, and in one instance (Maranell Accomplishment Poll, 1970) Harry Truman moved temporarily from his normal eighth position to sixth place. The lists of the remaining top ten presidents are also similar. The more recent polls tend to replace Cleveland, a somewhat weak early "near great," with a more modern president. The polls are remarkably consistent in their designation of "below average" and "failure" presidents. Those involved in major scandals—Harding, Grant, and Nixon—are ranked near the bottom. The remaining ten worst presidents in the 1982 polls are virtually identical with those of earlier polls. Presidential scholars agree more than they disagree.

A good case can be made to ignore the early polls and accept the Murray poll as an accurate appraisal of presidential performance. Part of the case can be made by simply stating that things equal to the same thing are equal to each other. But the case is even stronger than that. We have never had a poll with such a wide participation of presidential scholars with undeniable credentials who were so conscientious about completing their assigned tasks. Although it could be argued that similar results would have been obtained from a smaller sample, it is best to use the

Table 7.6.1

Presidential Performance Evaluations

Schlesinger Poll 1948 (1)	Schlesinger Poll 1962 (2)	Maranell Accomplishment Poll 1970 (3)
		Accomplishments of Administrations
Great	*Great*	
1) Lincoln	1) Lincoln	1) Lincoln
2) Washington	2) Washington	2) F. Roosevelt
3) F. Roosevelt	3) F. Roosevelt	3) Washington
4) Wilson	4) Wilson	4) Jefferson
5) Jefferson	5) Jefferson	5) T. Roosevelt
6) Jackson		6) Truman
Near Great	*Near Great*	7) Wilson
7) T. Roosevelt	6) Jackson	8) Jackson
8) Cleveland	7) T. Roosevelt	9) L. Johnson
9) J. Adams	8) Polk	10) Polk
10) Polk	8) Truman	11) J. Adams
	9) J. Adams	12) Kennedy
Average	10) Cleveland	13) Monroe
11) J. Q. Adams		14) Cleveland
12) Monroe	*Average*	15) Madison
13) Hayes	11) Madison	16) Taft
14) Madison	12) J. Q. Adams	17) McKinley
15) VanBuren	13) Hayes	18) J. Q. Adams
16) Taft	14) McKinley	19) Hoover
17) Arthur	15) Taft	20) Eisenhower
18) McKinley	16) VanBuren	21) A. Johnson
19) A. Johnson	17) Monroe	22) VanBuren
20) Hoover	18) Hoover	23) Arthur
21) B. Harrison	19) B. Harrison	24) Hayes
	20) Arthur	25) Tyler
Below Average	20) Eisenhower	26) B. Harrison
22) Tyler	21) A. Johnson	27) Taylor
23) Coolidge		28) Buchanan
24) Fillmore	*Below Average*	29) Fillmore
25) Taylor	22) Taylor	30) Coolidge
26) Buchanan	23) Tyler	31) Pierce
27) Pierce	24) Fillmore	32) Grant
	25) Coolidge	33) Harding
Failure	26) Pierce	
28) Grant	27) Buchanan	
29) Harding		
	Failure	
	28) Grant	
	29) Harding	

Table 7.6.1 (continued)

Presidential Performance Evaluations

U.S. Historical Society Poll 1977 (4)	Chicago Tribune Poll 1982 (5)	Murray Poll 1982 (6)
Ten Greatest Presidents	*Ten Best Presidents*	*Presidential Rank*
1) Lincoln	1) Lincoln (best)	1) Lincoln
2) Washington	2) Washington	2) F. Roosevelt
3) F. Roosevelt	3) F. Roosevelt	3) Washington
4) Jefferson	4) T. Roosevelt	4) Jefferson
5) T. Roosevelt	5) Jefferson	5) T. Roosevelt
6) Wilson	6) Wilson	6) Wilson
7) Jackson	7) Jackson	7) Jackson
8) Truman	8) Truman	8) Truman
9) Polk	9) Eisenhower	9) J. Adams
10) J. Adams	10) Polk (10th best)	10) L. Johnson
		11) Eisenhower
	Ten Worst Presidents	12) Polk
	1) Harding (worst)	13) Kennedy
	2) Nixon	14) Madison
	3) Buchanan	15) Monroe
	4) Pierce	16) J. Q. Adams
	5) Grant	17) Cleveland
	6) Fillmore	18) McKinley
	7) A. Johnson	19) Taft
	8) Coolidge	20) VanBuren
	9) Tyler	21) Hoover
	10) Carter (10th worst)	22) Hayes
		23) Arthur
		24) Ford
		25) Carter
		26) B. Harrison
		27) Taylor
		28) Tyler
		29) Fillmore
		30) Coolidge
		31) Pierce
		32) A. Johnson
		33) Buchanan
		34) Nixon
		35) Grant
		36) Harding

No polls rate either W. Harrison or Garfield due to their short tenures of office.

Table 7.6.1 (continued)

Sources:
1–Arthur Schlesinger, Sr., "The U.S. Presidents," Life 65; 55 scholars polled.
2–Arthur Schlesinger, Sr., "Our Presidents: A Rating by 75 Scholars," New York Times Magazine (July 29, 1962), 12ff.
3–is a poll of 571 historians, the results published by Gary Maranell and Richard Dodder, "Political Orientation and Evaluation of Presidential Prestige," Social Science Quarterly, 51 (Sept. 1970). 418.
4–was first published by Robert E. DiClerico in his book The American President (Englewood Cliffs, N.J.: Prentice Hall, 1979) 332; 93 historians were polled.
5–is a survey of 49 leading scholars conducted by the Chicago Tribune. The analysis is in the US News and World Report (Jan. 25, 1982), 29.
6–is a survey conducted by Dr. Robert K. Murray, professor of history at Pennsylvania State University in which 953 historians completed a seventeen-page questionnaire containing 155 questions. Dr. Murray's study is to be published in Journal of American History, Dec. 1983; however, he furnished the author with the survey ratings Dec. 15, 1982.

poll based on the most recent scholarship. New books about our presidents are published every month, and new sources of information about the presidents are constantly being made available. That is why we can always expect several minor changes in ranking when new polls are released, and once in a great while there will be major changes. As more definitive books are published about the Ford and Carter presidencies, changes in ranking are possible. Of course the jury is still out on Ronald Reagan.

There is only one vivid example of a major change in a presidential performance rating in the 1982 polls, and this example strengthens the argument that the most recent scholarly analyses must be examined in order to have a viable poll. In the 1962 Schlesinger Poll, Dwight Eisenhower was tied with Chester Arthur for twentieth place. In the Maranell Accomplishment Poll of 1970, Eisenhower was also ranked number twenty, between Hoover and Andrew Johnson. In the 1982 Chicago Tribune Poll, Eisenhower jumped to ninth place, and the Murray Poll awarded him a similar high rank, eleventh place. The oversimplified explanation for this rating improvement is that Ike benefited by comparison with his successors, particularly Richard Nixon, and also from a realization that presidential power should not be overly used. However, a much more complete explanation is required in order to understand the viability and rationale of the 1982 ratings. Consequently, a short historical presentation seems to be appropriate.

During and prior to the Eisenhower presidency, many political scientists and historians argued persuasively that the only good presidents were "activist presidents." They cited Lincoln, Washington, F. Roosevelt, Jefferson, T. Roosevelt, Wilson, and Truman as examples. However, sometimes their arguments tended to exaggerate the point to the extreme. Clinton Rossiter claimed that the truly eminent presidents invariably subverted the constitution. Richard Neustadt argued that "power purifies." James MacGregor Burns agreed, and also supported the concept that "*only* the man at the top" has the vision to make the right decisions. (Although the best view may be from the top, every single presidential scholar can cite many instances when Congress or the Supreme Court was right and the president was wrong.) The worship of presidential power received wide support despite the warnings of many historians that power did not purify Harding and Grant, and that although some activist policies were productive, even some of our "great" and "near great" presidents harmed the country by their activism. Both T. Roosevelt and Wilson interfered dramatically, with disastrous results, in Latin America. America's tendency to follow dollars with troops hurt our relationships with our southern neighbors. Although the construction of the Panama Canal delighted us all, the accuracy of one observer's account, "We stole it fair and square," did not in the long run improve our relations with Latin America.

Despite the fact he had been elected to reduce government activity and government spending, Dwight Eisenhower was constantly pressured to return to the vigorous policies of the F.D.R./Truman era. Sometimes he did, but more often than not, either because of necessity, design, or luck, or a combination of these factors, he avoided some of the dysfunctions of overt presidential activism and embarked on a policy of consolidation of the social and foreign policy gains of the previous twenty years. His hidden-hand style of management enabled him to accomplish his goals to a reasonable degree. He ended the Korean war, balanced the budget, and did not rock the boat.

At the start of the Kennedy administration, activism was rejuvenated with the "Bay of Pigs" fiasco and John Kennedy's famous speech "Let every nation know ... that we will pay any price, bear any burden, meet any hardship, support any friend, oppose any foe to assure the survival and success of liberty." (President Kennedy could hardly predict that the legacy of the Kennedy/Johnson/Nixon activism would make it extremely difficult for Presidents Ford, Carter, and Reagan to take aggressive steps to support friends and oppose foes.) At the end of Kennedy's thirty-five months in office, his four major legislative proposals—civil rights, tax reduction, Medicare, and federal aid to education—were still without congressional approval, while the country had become more involved in the war in Vietnam. One week prior to his assassination, Kennedy's approval rating in a public opinion poll was down from 85 percent to 59 percent. However, Kennedy's supporters had a right to be proud of his initiation of a program to land a man on the moon, his successful resolution of the Cuban missile crisis, and the establishment of the Peace Corps. Moreover, he had made many proposals that eventually would become laws. (In this respect John Kennedy was like Teddy Roosevelt. Both talked a great deal and got people thinking.)

Although activism was only marginally successful in the Kennedy regime, it was reinstituted in the "Great Society" program under Lyndon Johnson. Kennedy's legislative proposals were approved, and the Congress established the Poverty Program. Lyndon Johnson's success with the legislative branch of the government was almost as spectacular as that of FDR. Johnson's activism was quite productive on the domestic front. However, despite the increase from 20,000 U.S. troops in Vietnam to over 400,000, Lyndon Johnson was unable to bring the war to a successful conclusion and announced he would not seek another presidential term. At this point the case for activism had suffered a severe blow, and the American people concluded we should be more cautious about future use of troops in foreign lands.

Many of the critics of Lyndon Johnson's Vietnam war policies emphasized that use of power was one thing, but abuse of power could not be tolerated, and continued abuse of power would certainly result in legislative and judicial actions to weaken the executive branch of government. It is too bad that Richard Nixon did not pay serious attention to this reasoning, which proved to be correct. In his first term President Nixon actively abused the power of his office by approving a series of illegal acts that eventually led to his resignation to avoid certain impeachment by the House and conviction by the Senate. The thirty-eight-member House of Representatives Judiciary Committee voted unanimously to recommend impeachment by the full House on Article I, *Obstruction of Justice*. The decision on another article of impeachment was even more significant. By a vote of twenty-eight to ten the Committee approved Article II, *Abuse of Power*. Abuse of power was the overriding issue of the Nixon difficulties. He was right when he said that "petty, indecent things" done by some of his friends, and some of his enemies as well, were not important. But, as Arthur Schlesinger, Jr., has told us, Richard Nixon never really understood that the sickness of his presidency was caused by the "expansion and abuse of presidential power itself." He was the only president in our history to resign. It is hardly coincidental that the Nixon administration produced the only vice-presidential resignation as well. The president hand-picked Spiro Agnew and praised him saying, "There can be a mystique about a man. You can look him in the eye and know he's got it. This guy has got it." Vice-President Agnew and his boss both resigned under threat of certain indictment and likely conviction on several criminal charges. Agnew also contributed to the abuse of power of the oval office.

The real tragedy of Richard Nixon was that he made the presidency so powerful that he inevitably weakened it for his successors. One positive result of this distressing experience is that we now have an excellent book, *The Imperial Presidency* by Arthur Schlesinger, Jr., to counterbalance some of the ideas in another excellent book, *Presidential Power* by Richard Neustadt. A further positive result is that now we can really see the contributions of Dwight Eisenhower, a man who kept the ship of state on an even keel and avoided undue involvement in foreign wars and domestic corruption.

The Murray Poll ranks Nixon number thirty four; only Grant and Harding have lower ratings. Some of Nixon's foreign policy accomplishments, particularly the revision of our relationship with China, give him some plus marks, but one historian calls him "the most corrupt president in our history." An important consequence of the Nixon presidency to the scholars of 1982 was a more even-handed treatment of the functions and dysfunctions of presidential power. Due weight to the achievements of both the activist presidents and those not so active was required. The principal beneficiary of this change in evaluation criteria was Dwight Eisenhower. The change in thinking came gradually, first as some of the problems of the Kennedy/Johnson activism became evident, and finally when Richard Nixon taught us once and for all that a glorification of presidential power is not always wise.

A perceptive treatment of the Eisenhower presidency is contained in a book printed in 1966, *Presidential Greatness* by Thomas A. Bailey, Professor of American History at Stanford University. Some partial quotes from this book will provide the essence of the summary analysis. "Eisenhower reigned too much and ruled too little." He was not "a truly distinguished leader who made things happen in the fields of education, civil rights, health insurance and other areas. Historians will almost certainly never give him as high a mark as the voters did." However, "he was an eminently respectable and respected President, remembered for his dignity, decency and dedication. The Schlesinger experts ... put him near the bottom of the Average group, just above bumbling Andrew Johnson. In my judgment he belongs *at least* several notches higher." The historians of 1982 agree with Professor Bailey's assessment made way back in 1966. The fact that Eisenhower "ruled too little" is less of a problem these days. Ike is now right up there with his activist contemporaries, Jack Kennedy and Lyndon Johnson, and probably coincidentally, Andrew Johnson has fallen in the ratings, now twenty-one positions below Eisenhower. The Murray scholars seem to have placed Eisenhower, Kennedy, and L. Johnson in the proper perspective. They were particularly wise to rank nine presidents above all three of them. The historian Henry Steele Commager was right when he characterized these three presidents "estimable men, but *not one* of world stature."

At this point a summary defense of the viability of the scholars' presidential performance evaluations is appropriate. (There are many scholars's polls that have not been dealt with in this analysis. Those omitted have similar characteristics to those shown in table 7.6.1 and were not considered simply because of lack of time and space.) The polls are viable because, first, they reflect the opinions of scholars who have been trained to be objective; second, those polled have all studied all of the presidents in some detail; third, the scholars have continually kept up to date on new literature pertaining to the presidency; and finally, the polling techniques and statistical analyses are invariably based on the latest most reliable methodology. Historians make up the bulk of the participants in the polls. They are most likely to be most familiar with the early presidents. However, bonafide scholars from the fields of political science, public administration, economics, and journalism have also participated. The consistency in the various rankings is remarkable when it is realized that no two polls use the same participants. A good example of the similarity of the polls is the comparison of the two 1982 polls as shown earlier in this paper. The poll results do not indicate major differences between the judgments of the political scientists and the historians. It is true that they could have arrived at similar conclusions for different reasons, and an analysis of whether that in fact was the case would provide a deeper understanding of presidential greatness. However, it is clear that the rankings themselves have significance. A discussion of some of the criticisms of the polls will be presented later, but for now it is important to conclude that the scholars' polls give us an excellent tool to use in the study of the presidency. By and large we can believe the polls.

It is possible now to proceed to use the Murray Poll rankings as a vehicle to better understand and evaluate various judgments that have been made from time to time about the presidency. Because the Murray Poll is a valid instrument, there are a number of uses we can put it to.

Many scholars have praised our first six presidents. James Bryce's classic *The American Commonwealth*, published in 1888, called these presidents "statesmen in the European sense of the word, men of education, of administrative experience, of a certain largeness of view and dignity of character." In contrast Bryce found the presidents from Jackson through Buchanan to be "intellectual pygmies." The Murray survey certainly supports the Bryce analysis. The Murray ranking of the first six presidents shows an average rank of 10.1, whereas the Jacksonian Era presidents have an average ranking of 23.3. In this instance our modern scholars support an early classic evaluation of presidential greatness.

In June of 1980 the American historian Henry Steele Commager published an article which stated in part, "In the last fifty years only one man of world stature, Franklin Delano Roosevelt, has occupied the presidency." Commager contrasted the Truman through Carter presidencies with "the wisdom and good fortune" of the American voters in the Washington through John Quincy Adams era, asking, "How can we explain the decline of the American presidency?" The Murray survey also supports the Commager assessment, giving Truman through Carter an average rank of 17.8, compared with the 10.1 average of the first presidents.

Bryce, Commager, and others have indicated that in their minds our greatest presidential era was our earliest era. Although the Murray scholars agree, as shown on the following table, it is clear that what Commager called the "decline" of the presidency since the days of Washington, John Adams, and Jefferson has had some peaks and valleys.

Many historians contend that "great times make great men." To some degree the Murray ranking of the *first* president in each of the various eras shown above (Washington, 3; Jackson, 7; Lincoln 1; T. Roosevelt, 5; and F. Roosevelt, 2) illustrates that there is some truth to this contention. These presidents are five of the top seven in the Murray survey. Scholars would concede, however, that at least some of the five great presidents above would have been great in other times, and that the counter argument that "great men make great times" also has some validity.

One criticism of the presidential polls is that they are biased in favor of the Democrats

Table 7.6.2

Presidential Era	Murray Rank	Rank Order
The Virginia Dynasty (Washington–J.Q. Adams)	10.1	1
The Super Power Era (F. Roosevelt–Carter)	15.8	2
The USA is a New World Power (T. Roosevelt–Hoover)	19.5	3
The Gilded Age (Lincoln–McKinley)	21.7	4
The Jacksonians (Jackson–Buchanan)	23.3	5

and against the Federalist/Whig/Republican parties. This claim does not appear to be justified in the case of the Murray poll, which jumped Eisenhower from twentieth to eleventh place and ranked Lincoln first, Washington third, and Theodore Roosevelt fifth. As shown previously, the lowest rated presidential era in the Murray survey was the Democratic era of the Jacksonians. It is true that the few Whig presidents in that era also were given low ratings, but it is not at all clear that this was due to anti-Whig bias. The Whig presidents were not widely perceived as "true Whigs" as were Henry Clay and Daniel Webster. John Tyler and Millard Fillmore both succeeded ex-generals—W. Harrison and Z. Taylor—who were "token Whigs" and died in office as a result of old age and infirmities. Tyler and Fillmore were not in the inner circle of the Whig party. Both made substantial cabinet changes in the Whig leadership-directed appointments of their predecessors. Both were rejected by the Whig conventions as presidential nominees, even after they had served as presidents. Both attempted to run for reelection under the label of another party, Tyler as a Democrat and Fillmore as a Know-Nothing. Their low ratings (Tyler, twenty-eight and Fillmore, twenty-nine) probably had little to do with the Whig party. In Tyler's case, if there were a bias at all, it could possibly have been an anti-Democrat bias, because he was widely perceived as sort of a latter-day Jeffersonian Democrat. (To a degree the low rating of the Republican Andrew Johnson is a similar situation. A. Johnson is sometimes thought of as "the last of the Jacksonian Democrats.") It is interesting that the worst three presidents who served consecutively (according to the Murray poll) were Fillmore, Pierce, and Buchanan, with an average rating of thirty-one. Fillmore, a semi-Whig, and two Democrats, Pierce and Buchanan, are "our worst three in a row." The Murray scholars did not show bias in favor of the Democrats in this instance. (It should be pointed out that other trios—A. Johnson, Grant, and Hayes, 29.6; Harding, Coolidge, and Hoover, 29; and Nixon, Ford, and Carter, 27.6—also received unfavorable ratings.)

The Murray scholars considered that the Whig W. H. Harrison's short tenure qualified him for the category "insufficient data for ranking," and Clinton Rossiter assigned Z. Taylor to the same category by virtue of his sixteen months in office. However, the Murray rank of twenty-seven is consistent with the significant literature on the Taylor presidency and also consistent with the other polls. Z. Taylor had the largest number of presidential removals of office holders in American history up to his time, a total of 540. (W. H. Harrison managed to make second place, with 458 removed in his one month's total time in office. Andrew Jackson's 252 removals started the trend of massive changes in the federal work force upon inauguration of a new president.) The relatively low ranking of the Whig presidents is not because of anti-Whig bias.

The scholars' rankings reflect the literature they read. There are only a limited number of important books on most of the minor presidents, and virtually every American history scholar has read all of them. The literature on the great presidents and the more controversial presidents is so massive that selective reading is necessary. However, it is not wise to assume that historians will fail to investigate the many-sidedness of our complex presidents. For one thing the scholars are always looking for new approaches to enhance publication possibilities, so nothing in the literature of the presidents is more constant than change. With all of this in mind, it is somewhat perplexing to deal with a charge such as pro-Democratic bias. It is particularly difficult to consider something as nebulous as the Federalist/Whig/Republican tradition. It is not clear that such a tradition now exists, or ever did exist. One might think that the phrase "that the government is best that governs least," which has been repeated by so many Republican presidents for so long a time, is part of the "Republican tradition." But as we know, the president who first spoke those words was ranked number four in the Murray poll, and he was a Democrat. Jefferson's words also were repeated by more modern Democratic presidents as well. The term "Republican tradition" is virtually indefinable; consequently, a bias against this "tradition" is virtually unmeasurable.

The Murray poll rates Washington,

J. Adams, and Jefferson as the best three consecutive presidents in American history, with an average rank of 5.3. The next best trio is F. Roosevelt, Truman, and Eisenhower, with an average rank of seven, followed by T. Roosevelt, Taft, and Wilson with an average rank of ten. It is interesting that these nine presidents include five members of the Federalist/Republican parties and four Democrats, which is an even-handed treatment that should be applauded. The Murray Poll is not pro-Democrat or pro-Republican, and that is just the way it should be.

One interesting use of the Murray Poll is to investigate the claim that any president over sixty-five at the time of inauguration may well be too old for the job. Prior to Ronald Reagan, our oldest president at inauguration was William Henry Harrison, who failed to wear a coat during the inauguration ceremony conducted on a cold day in March. He gave the longest inauguration address in history, went to bed with pneumonia, and died thirty-two days later. Our second oldest president was James Buchanan, who had a little over a month to go to reach his sixty-sixth birthday when he was inaugurated on March 4. He was overwhelmed by the trials and vicissitudes of office and gave his successor the impression that one term in the presidency was more than any man can stand. He wished President Lincoln the best of good luck, implying that he would need it. Buchanan was ranked thirty-three in the Murray survey. The third oldest president, Zachary Taylor, was age 64 years, 100 days on his inauguration day. He died after serving one year and 127 days as a result of becoming over-heated on a warm day in Washington, D.C. His age at death was 65 years, 277 days. The Murray Poll ranked him twenty-seventh.

All our other presidents were age sixty-two or younger at the time of inauguration. However, even our fourth oldest president, Dwight Eisenhower, had some health problems during his term of office, although he was only age 62 years, 98 days when he was inaugurated. Ike was hospitalized three times: in September 1955 for a heart attack, in June 1956 for an ileitis operation, and in November 1957 for a stroke. He survived, however, and was ranked eleventh by the Murray scholars.

The ages at inauguration of the five greatest presidents in the Murray Poll were as follows: Lincoln 52, F. D. Roosevelt 51, Washington 57, Jefferson 57, and T. Roosevelt 42. The average age of the "five greatest" was 51.8. The oldest was 57. Clearly our great presidents were young, and our "over 64" presidents were not so great.

It is true that life expectancy is increasing. However, based on past performance, we should not become too optimistic about the likely success of our oldest presidents. We must of course look at the record and rating of Ronald Reagan after his time in office ends. However, even if his record is good, we should be cautious about selecting a nominee over sixty-five. The tasks of the presidency are onerous and demanding, more suited to the young than the old. The total record bears this out, and if Reagan does well, he will be the exception, not the rule.

The relationship between presidential performance and academic background is a riddle that the Murray Poll may help us to solve. The presidential eras that had the most presidents with a college degree were the highest ranked eras in the Murray Poll, as shown in table 7.6.3.

During the twentieth century there were only two presidents without a college degree (Harding and Truman), so the political process has made some adjustment to the public need for educated leaders. It is also important to note that some of our presidents who did not graduate from college received high rankings from the Murray scholars (Lincoln 1; Washington, 3; Jackson, 7; and Truman, 8). However, the knowledge explosion in virtually all fields has been so dramatic in the last ten years that those recruiting for leadership positions in the United States invariably require recent graduate level education as a minimum prerequisite for all applicants. We see increasing evidence of a major "knowledge gap" between the older leaders of our public and corporate structure and the bright "young Turks" who have kept up with the latest developments. We also see new evidence of presidential failure to know about and exploit the rapid advances in many fields of learning and to comprehend the best ways to use the decision-making methods of the new techno-

Table 7.6.3

Presidential Era	Murray Rank	Number of Presidents WITHOUT a College Degree
Washington – J. Q. Adams	1	1
F. Roosevelt – Carter	2	1
T. Roosevelt – Hoover	3	1
Lincoln – McKinley	4	4
Jackson – Buchanan	5	5

logical era. Future presidents will need the experience and educational background to deal with the problems of the twenty-first century. Just as we now accept a college degree as a requirement for a viable presidential candidate, we will realize that recent graduate level education is a basic minimum requirement for the future. It is hoped that this public awareness will not come too late.

Two criticisms of the presidential polls more or less cancel each other out. On the one hand some critics ask, "What do they know about it anyway?" The answer, that a list of the poll participants reads like a "Who's Who" of the people who know the most about all the presidents, gives rise to the next criticism. "Will not young scholars be so overwhelmed by the fame of these experts that they will always agree with their ratings?" This latter criticism reveals a lack of knowledge about the new breed of scholars who are confident of their own abilities and are most unlikely to be intimidated. It is true that in cases of doubt they will tend to go along with the most recent creditable poll or check with colleagues who are recognized experts on the presidency in question. This simply makes good sense, but it is only a partial explanation of the similarities of the polls. Intellectual incest has its good and bad features.

The most important and logical criticism of the polls is the observation that subjective evaluations of multifaceted presidential administrations cannot be precisely accurate. In this connection, Robert DeClerico's opinion that achievement is in the eye of the beholder, whose background and experience inevitably influence the rater, is undoubtedly correct. At the outset we must note that background and experience *properly* influence the rater. That is why a scholars' poll should include respondents who are knowledgeable about the subject and have been educated to be objective, just as was done in the Murray survey. However, despite the careful selection of the Murray poll participants, there is little doubt that the scholars' answers to the 155 item Murray questionnaire will uncover some biases similar to those revealed in the Maranell/Dodder analysis of their own poll in 1970. (For example, it was found that liberal scholars valued flexibility and idealism in presidents, while conservative scholars did not.) The pollsters themselves are continually trying to determine why persons rank presidents the way they do. The evaluator constantly asks, "How do we know that the answers of a particular responder are not more valid than the total poll results?" I have wondered about that myself, and the way I analyzed it is shown in the next paragraph.

My judgments of the Washington through Carter presidencies agreed, or were one position removed from the Murray scholars, in twenty of the thirty-six ratings. In fourteen cases my ratings were two or three positions different than the Murray Poll, and in two instances I had differences of four positions. (My evaluation was completed before I saw the Murray Poll, so the eminence of the Murray scholars was not a factor in my ratings.) In my view, the Murray scholars ranked Madison, Fillmore, and Hoover higher than they should have, and gave Arthur, Cleveland, and Taft lower grades than they deserved. There are important scholars who agree with my judgments, but that is not to say that those who agree with my assessment of Madison will also agree with my assessment of Hoover. It is unlikely that the Madison scholars and Hoover scholars have all that much in common, even though both have studied all the presidents in some detail. Now it is possible to see the value of a combined rating system. The best possible results can be obtained when the considered judgments of many professionals in the field of the presidency are averaged out. It is necessary to recognize that there is an acceptable margin for error in any subjective rating system, and the Murray Poll falls well within that acceptable range. There is not one single Murray ranking that is so far out of line with the available scholarly writings that it cannot be supported with a reasonable amount of evidence. Individual scholars should be able to present the case for the Murray ratings and then give reasons for their own differences with the Murray conclusions.

Because we have been able defend the use of the Murray Poll it is now possible to summarize our findings:

The Murray Poll:

1. Provides a bench mark to assist scholars in making some tentative judgments about the presidents. The Murray ranking of Dwight Eisenhower in eleventh place, a jump from the rank of twenty in previous polls, is a significant contribution to the study of the presidency. Earlier scholars who viewed "activism" as the single most important measuring stick to use in evaluating presidents, should now realize that some less active presidents must also receive due consideration. The ability to avoid foreign wars and domestic corruption is an important talent.
2. Confirms the Bryce and Commager views that our first presidential era (Washington-J. Q. Adams) was our best presidential era. The Bryce description of the Jackson-Buchanan presidents as "intellectual pygmies" is supported, as is the Commager conclusion that our earliest presidents were better than the Truman-Carter presidents.
3. Does not support the idea that the Federalist/Whig/Republican presidents have been mistreated by the polls, confirming instead that there are good and bad presidents from both major political parties. A president's political party affiliation is a poor predictor of presidential success.
4. Rates those presidents who were inaugurated at age sixty-four or older as rather poor presidents. On the other hand, the average age of the Murray "five greatest presidents" was 51.8 years at inauguration. These figures, taken together with other factors, support the conclusion that it is best to be cautious about selecting presidential nominees over the age of sixty-five for such demanding duties.
5. Verifies other evidence that there is a public need for educated presidents. The lowest-ranked presidential eras had the most presidents without a college degree, and the highest-ranked eras had the least number of presidents without a college degree.

There will be many other uses made of the Murray Poll. It is a very valuable instrument.

As a final footnote, it should be understood that there are a number of important questions about the presidents concerning which the Murray Poll cannot help us at all. For example, how good are women presidents? How good are blacks, members of the Jewish faith, and other minorities? Because all of our presidents have been males, white, and all but one were Protestants, no poll of previous presidents will help us answer these questions.

The Modern Presidency 8

The work-setting of modern presidents (Franklin Roosevelt to the present) is enormously different from that of preceding administrations. Presidents are more visible and more covered by the media. They are busier, reflecting the complexity of modern government and what Thomas Cronin calls the "textbook" syndrome of visiting all of our problems on the doorstep of a presumed omnipotent policymaker. Presidents have larger staffs, more policy relationships, and more to think and worry about. Some have forcefully argued that modern presidents are more constrained.

A major feature of the modern presidency is that it has become a paper mill, governed by schedules, memos, minutes of meetings, and mail and other forms of correspondence.

This chapter features two thoughtful and insightful essays on the characteristics of the modern presidency and the implications for government. Also presented are a variety of presidential papers, obtained from presidential libraries of modern presidents, showing the working environment of the "paper mill" presidency.

8.1 Constants, Cycles, Trends, and Persona in Presidential Governance: Carter's Troubles Reviewed

Bert A. Rockman

Midway though the Carter presidency, during some of its most troubled times, a debate emerged concerning the causes and sources of Carter's problems. Some placed the blame squarely on the president himself, focusing on his lack of Washington experience, his amateurism in dealing with Congress, and his penchant for micromanagement. Others argued that recent developments in government, especially in the realm of presidential-congressional relations, made it difficult for any president to be successful. The following award-winning paper, written at the midpoint of the Carter presidency, addresses this debate, evaluating different interpretations and perspectives.

Paper delivered at the annual meeting of the American Political Science Association, 1980. Reprinted by permission.

This paper begins with the fact of President Carter's political troubles, but seeks to generalize from them a theory of presidential governance. Four factors are discussed as significantly affecting presidential capacities to govern. These can be thought of as being historically given constants, cyclical phenomena, recent trends, and presidential style and background. A fundamental thesis of this paper is that an excess of attention is paid to the last (and least) factor and too little to the first (and foremost) factor.

The very design of our government was meant to inhibit the exercise of power and, thus, presidents were not meant to be vigorous leaders. While the Madisonian design is the most essential constant of all, it is reinforced by a strongly antistatist, highly individualistic culture and by weak national political organization. Despite much romance about presidential leadership and success, the definition of leadership remains obscure while the evidence of success is rare.

Cyclical phenomena affecting the presidency as a source of governance have especially affected our two most recent presidents in ways that have weakened further their capacities to exercise authority.

Recent trends, especially the growth of knowledge and with it ironically the reduction of certainty, have widened the gap between the requirements of governance and the problems of obtaining political support sufficient to govern.

The Carter presidential style emphasizes analytic, rational solutions to discrete problems. This approach fails to resonate with predictable political ideologies or traditional partisan constituencies. Consequently, when viewed from that standpoint, the programs of the Carter administration appear to lack thematic consistency.

In the end, the conclusion here is that Carter's troubles, while surely personal, are also institutional. Having asked presidents to perform in ways that the system does not readily permit, political analysis has centered obsessively upon the tricks of the presidential trade at the expense of a theory of political authority and institutional design.

Jimmy Carter's troubles in the White House bring to mind reminiscences of the childhood saga of Humpty-Dumpty (who some saw as a good egg with only a thin shell of support built around him). For like the mythical Humpty-Dumpty, the presidency of Jimmy Carter has taken a great fall. Whether as in the Mother Goose rhyme all the president's men (ensconced at Camp David as of this writing) are unable to put Carter's presidency back together again is a matter of some immediate concern, especially to Carter. But of far more fundamental importance is the question of whether the modern presidency has become the metaphorical equivalent of Humpty-Dumpty—a fragile institution easily and irrevocably shattered.

It is certainly clear that Carter is in trouble and has been with minor perturbations throughout the life of his administration. It hardly need follow from this, of course, that the institution of the presidency is in trouble. Institutions, after all, are meant to withstand the weak, the willful, and even the paranoid—descriptors that have been variously applied to the last four occupants of the White House. I think, however, that the institution of the presidency is in serious trouble and that Carter's own difficulties cannot be easily divested from this. In the broadest sense, the origin of these troubles is located in the growing gap between our expectations of what government, let alone presidents, can do and what it (and therefore they) in fact can deliver. And this expectation, in turn, is rooted in the growth of governmental activities and of political awareness.

Somewhat more narrowly, these difficulties arise also from a failure to think in institutional terms rather than personal ones, a failure that is greatly reinforced by media emphasis upon personalities rather than institutions. In a constitutional order, institutions rather than leaders are of primary importance. Americans celebrate their political institutions, yet dwell endlessly on political personalities. One cannot have it both ways. Either institutions are important or leaders are. Either institutions are to be strong or leaders will have to be. The former frequently induces responsibility, the latter demagoguery. We have, perhaps, too eagerly acclaimed our institutions without carefully examining their contemporary capacities to govern. We readily proclaim presidents (or potential presidents) as inept at governing when a decent case can be made that they were never meant to do much governing.

I am mindful, if not deterred, by the fact that theories of the presidency qua institution are difficult to appraise because at their most majestic, they are fundamentally theories about political authority and of the American political system and yet, more crassly, they tend mainly to reflect the theorist's immediate partisan and policy preferences and his [or her] judgments of the incumbent. As one writer, discussing the "strong leader" theories of the presidency which abounded in the decade prior to Vietnam, remarked: "Constitutional theory followed the party flag."[1] This same writer, William Andrews, was remarkably prescient in noting that once the "strong leader" theories of the early sixties were eclipsed by the "skeptical" theories of the early seventies, the latter body of theory would "last no longer than the next stormy blast."[2] Unfortunately, as present concerns with "leadership" from the White House mount, it seems increasingly that the wrong lessons from each body of theory are those which have become today's conventional wisdom. Put another way, the institutional powers of the presidency as a source of political direction and authority have been weakened (more informally than otherwise), while increased stress has been placed upon the inspirational and entrepreneurial qualities of presidential leadership. Calling for strong presidents in a weakened center of authority strikes me as an improbable prescription to strengthen constitutionalism. Indeed, it strikes me as tempting constitutional crises.

If a theory of the presidency is inherently both a theory of the exercise of political authority and of the American political system, regardless of what less noble motives inspire it, then we need to first reflect upon the desired relationship between government and the citizenry, and the role of the polity in society. Second, we must consider how the package of institutional relationships developed from the American constitutional framework has predisposed us toward a theory (if implicit) about the relationship between government and citizens, and between polity and society. Thirdly, we must consider how far we have in reality moved from the constitutional theory in our expectations about these relationships.

I am aware that such suggestions seem like so much reinventing of the wheel and I would be inclined to withdraw them were it not for the fact that we so often seem to miss the obvious when we analyze our political institutions. The Madisonian system, we know, was meant to fractionate political authority, to deter the decisive control of any one faction over the government. Whereas Hamilton was skeptical of the citizenry, Madison's skepticism extended to "the rulers" as well as "the *ruled.*" The result is a system which, for better or worse, was not meant to provide a source of direction. The constitutional system devised by the framers, in spite of being a product of compromise, represents a coherent package of choices about the exercise of political authority and, by indirection, the role of government.

A government meant to do much could not sustain the architectural awkwardness of the Madisonian system; only a government meant to deny the directive force of political authority could. But however little government was meant to do in the absence of overwhelming consensus, we have come to expect much from it, where the "it" increasingly has become synonymous with the presidency. Whether this tendency has been promoted by modern intellectual currents as suggested by scholars such as Thomas Cronin, Nelson Polsby, and William Andrews,[3] or is the inevitable outgrowth of large-scale government, mass political awareness, and weak political organization, there is little doubt that notwithstanding the revisionist literature of the 1970s and the ill-fated presidencies of Lyndon Johnson and Richard Nixon which stimulated it, we remain presidency-centered in our expectations. In this presidency-centered atmosphere, presidents are inclined to assume that which is expected of them rather than that which has been constitutionally granted to them. What once seemed the necessary meal ticket to writing one's way into the presidential hall-of-fame seems lately to have become merely a necessity for reelection, perhaps even renomination. In a recent past for which one fears a growing excess of nostalgia, Presidents Johnson and Nixon, especially the latter, became symbols of an "imperial presidency." The apparent fatal defect of Jimmy Carter is that he hasn't as yet decided to rewrite the Constitution to his liking. Moreover, outside of the Mayaguez incident when Gerald Ford upended the recently enacted War Powers Act, he too could stand accused of excessively seemly behavior. But such defects are readily forgiven by the intelligentsia (if not the electorate) in Republican presidents since most of the intelligentsia, chastened by Nixon, figure that the less a Republican does in the White House the better.

Theories of the presidency seem hopelessly fickle, mainly because they are empirically rooted in so few cases and intertwined with criteria that elude sound operationalization. I make no claim to being immune from this. That is, to inducing from the specific observations of a given presidency a general framework for thinking about the presidency; indeed, to be even more grandiose here, a framework for thinking about the state of public authority in the American system. In fact, to inject an autobiographical note, this paper originated in my mind almost a year ago in an effort to understand the unusually lowly status accorded the presidency of Jimmy Carter by public opinion polls, political professionals, political scientists, and just about everyone outside of the immediate Carter entourage. Whatever my own beliefs about the Carter presidency, and they are ones that even Groucho Marx would have recognized these days as placing me in an exclusive club, a singular concern with a particular presidential administration is no cause for a paper, much less pretensions about a theory. While some readers undoubtedly will believe the cause remains obscure while the pretensions are all too clear, my thinking about Carter's troubles led me to see some patterns in broader social and institutional forces affecting the American presidency generally and some which I think influence Carter's own presidential style. In short, I began this merely as an intellectual exercise to try to understand what was happening to the Carter presidency by isolating factors in the political environment affecting presidential governance into those which are *constants,* those which are *cyclical,* and those which seem to me to be *trends.* My assumption is that these considerations, the non-manipulables, account for most of what we *need* to know to understand the contemporary paralysis of political authority in the United States. A fourth factor, however, the *persona* of presidential governance has, since the first edition of Richard Neustadt's *Presidential Power,* become the most frequently discussed element of presidential governance.[4] It is the element about which we most *want* to know, though I believe it is the element that explains least what we need to know about presidential governance. Yet, talk of Carter's political ineptitude, his lack of bargaining skill, his lack of inspirational vision, and the like is rampant, even if it merely constitutes a resort to the cliché of least resistance. For my own part, I do not claim (nor know) whether Carter is politically inept or not, in part because I do not know what the standard of aptitude happens to be other than what the intellectual consensus says it is. Nor do I claim (or know) whether Carter is possessed of bargaining skills because I don't know what these are outside of a desire to bargain on everything with everybody (if anyone can be found to consistently bargain with). In turn, a president perceived as an expert in political wheeling and dealing will do little for whatever vision a president is supposed to be inspiring his countrymen on behalf of. The last president who was notably acclaimed for his bargaining skills seemed to inspire in his countrymen a vision of the man who sold the used car to the used car dealer.

In brief, my argument is that by focusing so narrowly on Carter's political aptitude or lack thereof in assessing the state of his presidency, the marginalia has come to displace attentiveness to the far more powerful constraints on presidential power both rooted and evolving in our constitutional system, in our political culture, in our institutional capacities, in our social and political cleavages, and in the modern revolution in communications. I do not mean to dismiss the actors themselves, but their characteristics and their particular types of talents and backgrounds are, I think, largely secondary symptoms.

The arguments I am about to distill will not, I believe, strike the student of American politics as particularly novel. They are not necessarily meant to. Many, if not all, are old chestnuts combed over by numerous scholars. What I am intent upon doing here in a narrow sense is to present the constant, cyclical, and trendlike forces which, mediated by the Carter presidential style, help us to understand the lowly esteem of the incumbent president. In a larger sense, however, I am interested in delineating the forces that are leading to a growing and dangerous gap between the expectations that we are imposing upon presidents to deliver the goods and their inherent incapacity to do so.

The statistically inclined reader will note that both here and throughout other sections of this paper, I shall be putting forth explanatory factors that in statistical jargon are probably multicollinear. If we were able to measure them, in other words, many of the independent variables would be strongly correlated with one another. Even gathering sound operational measures on presidential performance is quite a demanding task.[5] Collecting consistent data beyond a single aspect of presidential performance over a lengthy historical period is exceedingly difficult, perhaps impossible. Yet, doing precisely this in a way that permits adjustment for variation in environmental and institutional conditions that are themselves intercorrelated is the anvil on which historically generalizable theories of the presidency must be shaped. I will not, however desirable, be pounding operational data on that anvil here. Instead, my far more modest objective for now is to set forth the conditions—in a systematic, if not as yet testable, way—that may help us to better understand Carter's troubles and, by that, to better understand a troubled institution.

Constants in Presidential Governance

The constants in presidential governance are the historical and institutional parameters affecting the struggle of presidents to build support and exercise authority. Obviously, the potential inherent in these historically derived constraints is more nearly fulfilled as both the scope of presidential ambition and the ambit of public expectation have widened. Indeed, some of the "constants", such as the constitutional rights of the media, have for most of our history lain relatively dormant, awaiting both a technical revolution in communications and the receptiveness of a mass-based public to the information produced by this technical revolution. But what I am about to describe are features that have been a fundamental part of the American political and social landscape even though their impact has been differentially contingent upon the size of the public agenda and, to a degree, technical development. I see five constants affecting presidential governance, though I am sure that their number as well as their categorical status is at least somewhat arguable. They are: the constitutional system of separated powers, the political culture, the political party system, the continuity of regional cleavages, and the First Amendment to the Constitution guaranteeing the press virtually unrestricted rights.

The Constitutional System

The Madisonian system is, of course, the cornerstone of the American polity. Perhaps its foremost characteristic, as Norman Thomas recently has noted in contrasting the Canadian system of parliamentary government with the American system of separated powers, is its weakness for putting together coherent public policy and its fondness for compelling institutional accountability. As Thomas writes: "If Canadian government is short on institutional controls compared with the United States, it has greater policy coordination capability."[6] Since one could well argue that there are greater centrifugal tendencies in Canadian society and in its system of federalism even than those which exist in the United States, this is no mean feat.[7]

Authority in no system is ever as clear-cut and settled as it seems on paper, but the Madisonian system makes a virtue of messiness. Clear and coherent direction—the quest of the policy planner—is sacrificed to a seemingly incomprehensible jumble of overlapping, ambiguous, and uncertain powers. In the absence of consensus, the system predisposes toward deadlock to a far greater degree than most. This, simultaneously, is the monumental virtue as well as the monumental defect of the American system. To achieve anything substantial, a substantial consensus must be created; without this, it is assumed that it is better to do nothing.

Under rare conditions crisis creates consensus, if not necessarily on desired policy at least on the need for direction and deference to presidential leadership. (Like physicians, presidents are infrequently sought out for their advice until crisis intervenes.) Wars of full mobilization are the most frequent of these catastrophic events in which the rules of the Madisonian system are relaxed. This form of crisis seems highly improbable in the future, but should it come to pass the half-life of presidential rallying will be frightfully brief. Threats of such wars or confrontations to use the contemporary euphemism can produce a crisis, but the foreign policy president is on a shorter leash these days as the power of the national bite has diminished.[8] And as foreign policy issues come to have more perceptible domestic economic consequences, the leash is apt to be drawn tighter.

What other circumstances provide presidents with a deferential consensus? It helps apparently to follow a president of another party who has had the misfortune to preside over the country during a worldwide economic catastrophe and then to come into office with lop-sided majorities in Congress willing to heed the new president's call to action. It helps also if the call to action is followed by a call to arms since the latter at least alleviates the depression. A second circumstance may occur when one comes to the White House on the heels of a tragic assassination in which the country may be rallied around the unfulfilled legacy of the deceased. And it helps greatly to have an election soon thereafter before one's luster wears away. It further helps to be blessed in this election with an opponent who sprays voter repellant on his tongue. Should enough congressional candidates of the opponent's party have a lemming-like impulse for the sea[9] and, thus, conveniently make way for another lop-sided congressional majority ready to vote in programs that have been ripening on their party's agenda, it is enough to make one's head dizzy with thoughts about the unusual talents of the White House occupant.

A major problem, as I noted earlier, in theorizing about the presidency is that we frequently generalize from the unique, or at least the rare. What is worse is that we seem to uphold the rare event as the norm. The Rooseveltian model presented by Richard Neustadt in the first edition of *Presidential Power* seemed more instructive as a model of presidential conduct when compared with only two other presidents than when three and a fraction presidents have been added to the second edition.[10] Indeed, the trend in Neustadt's emphasis seems to have moved across the editions of his book from the manipulative skills and abilities necessary to master Washington politics to those needed to master image-building in the national media.

As much as presidents might like, they cannot as a matter of course easily circumvent the convoluted system of governance designed by the framers. The system was meant to frustrate ambition, and it was designed for a government largely meant to be a passive reflector and adjuster of social interests. I do not know whether the system effectively protects our freedoms by the clash of interests which it promotes,[11] or whether it is merely an appendage to a more fundamental set of norms accepted by members of the "political class."[12] What seems clear to me (if few others) is that clear-cut presidential successes are a rarity, not a normal occurrence. In an earlier and more simple era, before we developed large expectations about what government was supposed to do for us and before we came to believe that inspiration should emanate from the White House as well as the pulpit, the Madisonian system at least seemed more consonant with our beliefs about political authority. Even then, the system has never been notable for resolving potentially divisive crises.[13]

The Political Culture

What the Madisonian system produced, our historical legacy and individualistic political culture have conspired to reinforce. A set of institutions designed to deter the unity of authority are reinforced by an individualistic political culture skeptical of authority. The skepticism toward power articulated by Madison in the institutional blueprints has been supplemented in the culture by a Jeffersonian skepticism toward the power-wielders. If the Madisonian system fragments political authority, the Jeffersonian aspects of the political culture effectively shorten the distance between political authority and the citizenry. The conservative vision of Hamilton—a strong center of authority with limited citizen participation—lies in ruins.

Dealing with the ramifications of our political culture is a large-scale and complex undertaking. Let me deal all too briefly here with three elements of the political culture that affect presidential governance. The first is the overwhelming emphasis upon the privatization of the economy. This Lockeian element of economic individualism (sustained even during the growth of large corporate enterprise) has resulted in (or been the result of) an economy that developed largely independently of direct state intervention. In either event, the consequence is an economy which, among the industrial economies of the world, is least penetrated by government. Whether as Anthony King suggests this is due to the ideas of the American political class,[14] or as David Vogel suggests due to the anti-statist attitudes of American businessmen (as, say, contrasted with their French counterparts),[15] or due to factors which fractionated the political basis for socialist parties to emerge is an exceedingly difficult matter to sort out. Nor do I claim that the low level of direct state penetration into the economy is necessarily a social bad. All that needs to be said on this matter is that presidents generally have few governmental tools with which to manage the economy. Those which they do possess are both exceedingly blunt instruments and often require congressional approval. In the past there were even fewer tools, but there were also fewer expectations about the rights of citizens to be protected from economic misfortune. These days, presidents fall as rapidly as the dollar upon whose fortunes they have little direct influence one way or the other. Of course, it is also easy to be doubtful about the prospect of state capitalism, even in the sensitive banking and investment sectors, providing a magic elixir with which to control economic performance. The power to decide falls short of the capacity to control. Moreover, there are limits to what the economic doctors know, and there are also frequent differences between prescriptive economic theory and political feasibility. In addition, whatever the gap between decision and performance may be, even control over the decisions may not rest exclusively in the hands of the government of the day.[16] Substantial bureaucratic and legal impediments inhibit direct control, and the usual amounts of inertia governing the behavior of public enterprise frequently makes it no less resistant than private enterprise to the preferred directions of the political heads of governments.[17] Still, if the political chieftains of all the industrial economies are more or less expected to provide command performances from the economy, none begins this task with so few tools as the American president.

A second, and perhaps related, element of the political culture is its populism. In the view of L. J. Sharpe,[18] the populistic element of the American political culture derives from the revolutionary tradition which promoted the belief that all authority flows from the people. When combined with the Madisonian system this is, as Sharpe notes, "not a theory of government likely to be sympathetic to the idea that government must have some autonomy."[19] Where European politicians are given to speaking in terms of broad programmatic commitments, class interests, social and political doctrines, and even the grandeur of the nation, American political rhetoric frequently sounds like a freshman essay in political analysis (from which undoubtedly real freshman essays spring), beginning with and ending with what "the people" want and what government has conspired to deny them.

Style is not without consequence for substance. Endlessly repeated, we come to believe that "the people" are good and government "bad." We come therefore to expect much but to obligate ourselves to little. If things go badly, it cannot be due to our appetites; the fault must lie with our government—its leaders, its politicians, its bureaucrats—who (the last of these perhaps excepted) seem all too willing to concede the right to govern or even to defend their institutional integrity.[20] As Carter struggles to lift himself out of the depths of public esteem, he might reflect with more than considerable irony upon one of his pet campaign lines of 1976 in which he chirped about the need for "a government as good and loving and honest as the American people themselves." Mass narcissism is dysfunctional for an effective constitutional democracy because it leads to social indiscipline and scapegoating. The populism, of course, is not new in the culture. What is new is the level of expectation about government. Presidents have always since the Jacksonian era been confronted with the mood of populism, but less was then centered in, or directed toward, Washington. The populist impulse is not wholly a presidential disadvantage of course. FDR mastered it by making people feel good when things were grim. Nixon seemed equally masterful at making people feel angry when things were good. The populist impulse is, however, an inherently unstable prop for the political support needed to sustain governance. Moreover, it eats away at institutional roots.

A third aspect of the culture of some significance to presidential leadership is the bias against political organization. This seems especially odd in a society which dotes on management skills and schemes. Organization in America though is business-related, not political. Undoubtedly, recent times have been bad for party organization. But much of what purported to exist as political organization wasn't really "political" organization anyway. The old-time "machines" at their peak were heavily dependent upon the entrepreneurship of leading personalities or the needs of sub-local leaders to be cut into whatever payoffs were made available.

What distinguishes American political organization from its European form is the issueless personalism that surrounds the former. Committed neither to broad programs nor to coherent outlook, American political organization has been an arena for the displacement of private entrepreneurship and ambition. In these days of political atomization, there is nostalgia for the return of strong party organizations on the grounds that they would induce stability, coherence, and discipline in our politics. But it is difficult to return to what was rarely there to begin with. Our politics has produced moments of discipline as Walter Dean Burnham has observed,[21] but rarely have those moments been programmatically coherent. The essence of European political organization has been to generate discipline on behalf of some measure of political coherence;[22] the essence of American political organization more typically has formed around the central attraction of the greased palm.

Indeed, when parties in America were at their organizational peak, corruption was rife and political purpose was minimal.[23] Out of such conditions, few nationally attractive political leaders could emerge and, thus, there has been an unusual reliance over the years upon amateurs as presidential candidates. Generals and military heros, for example, have been abundantly represented in the White House, while those recruited directly from the political machinery itself—Chester Arthur, Harry Truman, Warren Harding—have been remarkably few. Anti-organization politics have emerged in our culture because organization was a synonym for corruption rather than for political purpose. Its absence means that presidents are denied disciplined support. It is less clear what its presence meant. My suspicion, and for the moment it is only that, is that our new era of antiparty politics may not be as fundamentally different from other eras as it is often thought to be.

The Factionalized Party System

American political parties seem never to have progressed much past local and personal factions. What the constitution has fragmented and what the culture has reinforced, the party system has been unable to counter. American political parties, anemic as they are, have adapted to their environment rather than overcome it, and thus have rarely effectively met the challenge of becoming national parties. In the uneven contest between disintegrative localism and national coherence, the two major American parties have usually performed as though they were each a hundred parties with the dominant party in any given era being particularly incohesive.

Presidents, to be sure, always have had to confront national vs. local issues and Congress has always been the bastion of localism. Only when our party politics was thoroughly regionalized was it possible for the localism of Congress to coincide easily with party until eventually regional contradictions within the dominant party coalition became excessive. (For the Republicans these occurred between the industrial Northeast and the agrarian

West, and for the Democrats they occurred after the New Deal between North and South.) The growth in federal activity, of course, has dramatized the tension built into our system between local pressures and federal distributions, a phenomenon that has been discussed impressively by writers such as Beer and Anton.[24] The tension has never been expunged, nor at least much mitigated, by the appearance of national political parties. In fact, the proliferation of congressional caucuses organized around regional and local-functional interests is surely symptomatic of the frail grip of national politics upon our two parties.

The modern presidency at least has been viewed as the national center of an otherwise localized system. But the image is deficient because the tools for constructing a national politics are nonexistent. A national politics is sporadically and momentarily constructed by the increased influence of party activists (as opposed to public officeholders) at our national party convention, but their example suggests that all of the other forces at work within our polity resist its consummation. Moreover, the example of this form of national politics suggests that it is wholly at odds with the possibility, and the spirit, of governance.

In contemporary terms, the problem is defined as how it is we might arrest the decline of our political parties.[25] For myself, I do not see the slide as steep. It is true that our parties aren't, but it is less clear that they ever were. All of this is not to deny that partisan decomposition has not been occurring; it is merely to suggest that parties as instruments of governance have not loomed large in our national political arena. I do not know how we can put together something that never clearly was. To undo some of what has been done recently may help, but I doubt very much. To ask our presidents to be fierce partisans as a means of restoring (if that is in fact the right word) party as a tool of governance is, I think, a prescription that mistakes cause for effect.

"Retrospect," as Richard Neustadt warns us, "can induce romance."[26] Presidents recently departed, no matter what knaves or incompetents we thought they were while in office, gain luster as compensation for their departure. Similarly, professional preoccupations can induce romance. And to political scientists, political parties are as close to a professional preoccupation as any we have. By their absence, political parties make the heart grow fonder. Not only do we come to believe that the frequently corrupt party hacks of yesteryear were political professionals able to instill political coherence, but we also come to believe that the root cause of the paralysis of political authority and public distrust lies in the decline of parties as intermediaries in the political system. Thus, the cry goes out for a restoration of partisanship. I do not fully know the cause of our present public malaise, but I am disinclined to believe that party has all that much to do with it. In my state of Pennsylvania, for instance, one can find veritable bushel loads of partisanship in the legislature, frequent deadlock, and deservedly little public respect for party politics or the legislature.

I am sure I have lingered at too great length over parties, but we typically expect them in any political system to do more than they can as an instrument of governance.[27] The Madisonian system, among other things however, denies the capacity for parties to emerge as a continuous and predictable source of political support for presidential governance. That has been a constant in our system. Recent trends have weakened further the connective tissue between presidents and the congressional party. What I am less certain about is whether continued harping on the need for partisan vitality (though preachment will not make it so) without an equal emphasis upon strengthening the institutions of governance—for example a more integrated and autonomous civil service—provides any solution to the governability problem.[28] To be particularly unfashionable about it, the idea of parties über alles without other reforms induces a serious imbalance between politics and governance. Governance requires politics; but it also requires much more. Politics, on the other hand, need not imply governance at all.

Continuities in Regionalism

A nation as physically large as the United States was destined from its beginning to spawn regional cleavages. Diverse climates, resources, and development lead to regional interests. With rare exceptions, largely those generated by the New Deal alignment, our politics has been heavily split along regional lines, though the precise structure of these cleavages has been altered from time to time. The Canadian system, faced with even more serious regional divisions than the United States, squeezes regional divisiveness out of its parliamentary politics through a nationalized parliamentary party system. At the same time it devolves greater authority to its provinces than the American system has devolved to the states.

The cost of making national decisions in the face of serious regional splits is erosion of legitimacy, as the Canadian experience with official bilingualism suggests. Not strong enough for the Francophobes in Quebec, the policy of official bilingualism is too strong for the Anglos in the West. The cost of not making national decisions in the face of regional splits, however, is drift. Unlike the Canadian system, there is no significant way in which the American political system has been nationalized. Where the parliamentary parties in Ottawa enforce direction, the American system mirrors its localistic and regional interests. Of our political officials only the president can provide any semblance of articulating "national interests" over and above regional and local ones. But he cannot command the resolution of regional divisions. Regional interests can be compromised up to a point, as the experience with the connecting issues of slavery and political representation suggest or as present-day formulas for federal programs indicate. But truly difficult decisions, ones which clearly shift burdens and resources or diminish largesse, are not easily compromised or resolved, as our efforts to define a national energy policy imply and, as ultimately, the onset of civil war showed.

Presidents never have been immune from these divisions. Lincoln's choices were made for him if he wished to preserve the original Union. Those of his predecessors were not, and we now regard them as having been calamitous. In their way, however, they largely reflected the drift that preceded the onset of the Civil War—the fear that national decisions would provoke secession. We expect clarion calls to a national interest to emanate from the White House these days, but we have never provided the tools for a national politics. Our political system places far greater value on legitimation and consent than upon decisive action or effectiveness. Implicitly, the assumption underlying our "localized" institutions is that without legitimacy and consent there can be no effectiveness. Emphasis has been placed upon patching, accommodating, and the strong possibility of doing nothing when regional interests conflict, at least until the costs of doing nothing either generate the consensus necessary for policy or promote severe, perhaps ruinous, conflict. What we cannot do is expect presidents to overcome these divisions (unless the issues themselves are temporarily nonregionalized) and then complain about their lack of leadership when they have failed to surmount what is mostly insurmountable.

The First Amendment and the Press

In this paper, the expansive role of the media and its impact upon presidential governance pops up in more than one place, violating a cardinal rule of coding. The legal-constitutional rights of the press in the United States are distinct, nevertheless, from the technical and social trends which have affected the media and their coverage of politics. To a considerable degree, the First Amendment rights of the press in their impact upon presidential governance have mainly represented a potential which the advent of the electronics media (one of the few national institutions in our society) has helped to bring to fruition.

Viewed from a comparative perspective, the potential conflict between "state interests" and the media are weighted substantially toward the media in the United States. Relative to other constitutional polities, the press in the United States has had a long tradition of largely unfettered freedom to probe and inquire. Journalists are applauded here for matters in which they might routinely be taken to jail even in the country which inspired many of our constitutional rights. While politics in all of the industrial countries has become saturated with media coverage as a result of modern technological and social trends, only in the United States is the exercise of media coverage and, above all, the absence of restrictions against prior publication exalted as an absolute constitutional right.

Since the press in Europe is restricted by law from inquiring into everything that its own government considers privileged information, the elite press often turns to coverage and analysis of foreign affairs, reflective journalism, even political debate. In the United States the press inadvertently is an active participant in the governing process itself. Trial balloons float across the daily news. Disgruntled and sometimes even satisfied participants in the policy process are ready sources of leaks. As contrasted with other flourishing constitutional systems, the American press has a unique capacity, though not always used, to make all the governmental wash look like dirty linen.

The legal scope to inquire and publish given to the American press often, in fact, leads it to a search for the dirty linen and to a search for those moments when leaders are at their most unleader-like. Our press often has most typically operated to uncover rather than to reflect, and to seek out kaleidoscopic fragments of information rather than to puzzle over broader pictures. The right to go over everything and anything produces a buzz-saw of images. It is not, in my own view, a wholly unrelieved blessing, although I have no plans to lobby against the First Amendment. A press with the capacity that our's has is in an excellent position to counter the deceptions that all presidential administrations engage in. But the size of the deception, the importance of the gaffe, the relevance of the foible are all magnified by the enlarged capacity to uncover them. We know to be skeptical of the Wilsonian notion of open covenants openly arrived at because we know that bargaining and negotiating require small public deceptions—some room for leaders to finesse earlier commitments. A press with the legal guarantees of inquiry that ours has, however, has an intrinsic interest in showing us that the emperor has no clothes. Our politics and our government inhabit a veritable fishbowl—I am not always sure to the betterment of our governance.[30] . . .

In sum, the constants affecting presidential governance are those built in by design and by historical legacy. It is all familiar terrain and, perhaps because of that, too frequently ignored in our evaluations of presidential capabilities. Or because of it, we are told to search for the select few who can live with, yet overcome, the burdens our system (formally and informally) places upon leadership. The prescriptions for finding such persons are, however, notoriously vague.

Cycles in Presidential Governance

Despite the limitations placed upon presidential governing capacity by the "constants," there are historical ebbs and flows in presidential power. Some of these cyclical conditions have a longer historical base while others are the product of the era of the modern institutionalized presidency and systems of mass communications. The most obvious of these cyclical phenomena is the congressional activism-passivism cycle. A second is the management style of the presidency. A third is public yearning (perhaps merely following intellectual fashion) for, and disillusionment with, leadership. There may well be a fourth, as recently suggested by Paul Beck who claims that the instability of partisan alignments at the mass level and the decomposition of partisan cohesiveness at the elite level are bound together in cycles.[31] Although Beck's thesis is persuasively argued, I think a better case can be made that mass partisan decomposition is a trend since it is affecting other polities to a lesser degree as well.[32] And, I am also inclined to believe that while there is connective tissue between mass partisan decomposition and the decline of party coherence as a tool for governance, they are not as directly or clearly linked as Beck's very interesting arguments suggest. As Brady and Althoff note in this regard, an essential ingredient is political centralization, i.e., the institutional power of congressional leadership.[33] In any event, let us begin here with the congressional activism-passivism cycle.

Congressional Activism-Passivism

Never as passive as the pre-1970s lore would have it, Congress can never be as coherently active as governance requires. In a recent and thoughtful essay, Lawrence Dodd contends that the Madisonian system was constructed around the expectation of internally coherent political institutions which, in some measure, were competitive with one another.[34] For Congress to play its proper role in this system, strong leadership to maintain internal cohesion and direction was required. Thus, since the revolt against Speaker Cannon (the reforms in the House of 1910), the Congress has been unable to assume the role that, in Dodd's view, the framers intended for it.

Earlier surges of congressional dominance (after the Civil War) seem to have been marked by recessive views of the presidency and unassertive presidents, a state of affairs which may more fully accord with how the system in theory was to operate. Congress never has been dominated or "broken" by presidents. It has generally resisted the idea that presidents are to govern the country except in those rare moments when congressional and presidential wills have been concurrent. But there are periods when institutionally Congress has been more, and some when it has been less, inclined to self-consciously flex its institutional authority. The "down" parts of the cycle are rarely as down as presidents would wish, but the "up" parts are often higher than anyone would wish. For the "up" parts of the cycle inherently mean political disaggregation. At least that is the product of the reforms of 1910 and the popular election of senators.

President Ford lived through the tail end of an epidemic of congressional "reform" in the 1970s, most of it in reaction to the excesses of his two predecessors. In this respect, the postbellum congressional resurgence, a reaction in large part to the shadow cast by Lincoln, was similarly inspired by the encroachment of presidential power upon congressional prerogatives. If we compare Ford to the two other Republican presidents whom *Congressional Quarterly* has immortalized for future generations of data analysts, we can see by comparing their average congressional support scores that he did considerably worse than his recent Republican predecessors. By eliminating the first two congressional sessions of the Eisenhower administration in which there were Republican congressional majorities and the last two sessions under Nixon in which his personal decline was intricately tied in with the congressional resurgence itself, we see that the Eisenhower-Nixon mean support score is 69.8 percent. Ford, however, was able to achieve only a mean support score of 57.7 percent. The CQ scores, of course, do not tell us a lot of what we might want to know about presidential-congressional relations, but they are instructive. In spite of his lengthy tenure in Congress, Ford did appreciably worse than his Republican predecessors.

The first Democrat to be confronted with the full blast of the recent congressional resurgence is Jimmy Carter. He, like Ford, has failed to do as well with Congress as his Democratic predecessors, Presidents Kennedy and Johnson. For example, the average CQ support score for the Kennedy-Johnson years is 83.4. It is 81.0 (perhaps a more accurate reading) if one drops the last session of the 88th Congress which met the year after Kennedy's death and the first session of the 89th Congress produced by the Goldwater debacle. In the first two years of the Carter administration, the average has been 76.9, a slightly lesser gap than that between Ford and his Republican predecessors. If Carter the amateur is having his troubles, Ford the professional had even thornier ones.

One mode of explanation obviously is to look to the two most recent occupants of the White House in order to find something deficient with them. Another, more fruitful, mode of explanation is to shift attention away from the White House to Capitol Hill. Each president (Ford and Carter) has been caught in a period during which the congressional resurgence has been at high tide. The period of resurgence has brought to Congress some important tools for policy analysis. This has given to Congress the way, but not the will. The possibilities for the cohesion that Dodd believes the Constitution calls for now lie within the congressional grasp. But the political impetus to move the possible into the realm of the probable is absent. That impetus cannot readily originate from the White House, though efforts to mold the congressional party into a legion of obedient foot soldiers are apt to bring a riptide of congressional resentment and mounting presidential frustration. One can only hope that the strong tide of congressional resurgence will pull with it a tendency to arrest institutional disaggregation. It may well be that the prevailing parties cannot be a fundamental basis for this regrouping. The Democrats are unable to govern because they are too many; the Republicans because they are too few.[35] Moreover, the disarray of the Democrats frequently invites doctrinaire solidarity from the Republicans. This condition seems to have led one Republican member of the House to conclude: "The problem of energy is so serious we're almost approaching a condition of war. Carter is in such bad trouble with his own people, we almost have to return to bipartisanship on that issue."[36]

Congress is inherently parochial and, in this, reflects the bias of our political system. Its parochialness has resisted a strong dosage of partisanship over long periods of time. Only an institutionalized and powerful leadership has been able to impose that. Such leadership no longer exists in this century, but Congress itself is on the "up" part of its cycle. The policy analysis capacities which Congress now possesses could give it the capacity to act responsibly in relation to the White House. For its policy capabilities give it the opportunity both to challenge presidential interpretations and to arrive at a policy consensus. Although I recognize that comparison as well as retrospect invites romance, perhaps the German Bundestag and, especially, the Bundesrat give us a clearer sense of these possibilities. More fully than any parliamentary body, these chambers have bureaucratized politics, substituted the importance of consensus-building for the impulse to the parochial, elevated the substance of policy over a boundless process.[37] If Congress is to retain its strength, it may have to exercise it in ways that make it institutionally a coherent bargaining partner with the White House.

Styles in Managing the Presidency: Open and Closed Administrations

Observing styles of presidential management is a relatively recent obsession. Before FDR, after all, there was not an enormous amount to manage. There seems, from these observations, to be a regular oscillation between White House operations designed to centralize control over the activities of government and over the origination of policy, and those which have diffused these responsibilities outward. The latter style tends to dramatize the multiplicity of direction inherent in a complex government.

Bureaucratic politics exists everywhere, but its visibility is enhanced in American government by the fragmentation of authority, the absence of collective cabinet decision-making, and the entrepreneurial traditions of our press. There are typically as many, if not more, incentives for cabinet officials to pursue their own visions of proper policy or to defend their own turf than there are to coordinate with the White House. Even with the best of intentions, however, there is much going on well below the surface in many departments and agencies that can confront the White House with problems of consistency of agenda and policy.[38]

"Everybody believes in democracy until he gets to the White House," Thomas Cronin quotes a former White House assistant as saying.[39] I suspect that the proposition is ultimately true, but it might be amended in some cases to read that "everyone believes in democracy until they stay in the White House long enough." The Nixon administration, of course, surely represented the extreme case of presidential centralization or closure.[40] Only when his presidency was mortally wounded by Watergate did things get out of hand. But even here, the public imbroglio between George Schultz and William Simon over whose "cotton-picking hands" were in whose business seems to fade into inconsequence by contrast with George Humphrey's (Eisenhower's Treasury secretary) "hair curling" blast at his boss's budget plans.

The traumas of Vietnam and Watergate seem to have led us to fears of an "imperial" and sealed-off presidency.[41] After Nixon's departure, Ford was welcomed not for being extraordinary, but for being ordinary; not for being seized with purpose and vision, but for his mental stability. He promised, and mostly delivered, to delegate authority and keep an "open" and decentralized administration.[42]

Openness may not invite chaos, but it invites the appearance of it. As matters turned out, the last thing Ford needed was anything that added to the belief that he made three-point landings at airports without the aid of an aircraft. Carter's campaign was the first election to be held after presidential power became unfashionable once again. He became the apostle of openness. Cabinet government was to be the order of the day in a system in which the only thing cabinet members do collectively is occasionally to have their picture taken in the same room.[43] Further, following and even exaggerating the early characteristics of the Ford White House, the communications system in the Carter White House seemed to model its system of handling information along the lines of the Italian postal system.

Openness has good public relations value (and maybe is even believed in) until it appears to conflict with competence. Presidents with clear desk tops may be able to tolerate openness more easily than presidents who have set forth an extensive agenda for themselves. Inevitably, true openness which leads toward error correction conflicts with the appearance of competent, commanding leadership. Partly I suspect by temperament, but surely in the wake of the centralized Johnson and Nixon administrations, Carter's presidency was apt to begin on a note of internal democracy. The contradictions have been highly visible partly as a consequence of the magnitude of the Carter agenda. With Carter's competency now so deeply suspect, it will not be surprising to see the wagons pulled in a circle, the reduction of decisional autonomy outside of the White House, and the conversion of the White House into a bunker. Democracy, whatever its virtues for diversifying the advice rendered to presidents, finds little nourishment in a state of siege. We seem now to have moved to the "strong leader" phase of the cycle with its accompanying demands for greater White House control. Since Carter arrived at the White House on the "openness" theme, it will be interesting to see how this is reconciled with the new phase of the cycle that seems to be upon us. One unfortunate possibility, as suggested by his recent night visitations with unsuspecting families, will be to ignore the real diversity in Washington while showing his openness to the policy advisers at Joe's Bar and Grill.

Yearning for and Disillusionment with Leadership

While I have not operationalized this "mood" cycle, there nonetheless seem to be cycles of expectations about the presidency itself. These are best characterized as primarily expressions of opinion leadership. In most respects, these expectations seem to overlap the "style" cycle discussed above. Presidents who come in heeding a perceived call to do great things are apt to be White House centralizers. Those coming in during a period of disillusionment are apt to be "democratizers."

The disillusionment with leadership may merely fulfill a desire for tranquility and consensus politics in the aftermath of presidencies filled with larger than life egos and stranger than fiction stories. At other moments, particularly those of economic drift, yearnings for a politics of action and of mobilization seem to be more significant.

It was Jimmy Carter's fate to become president at a time when a low profile politics occasioned by a disillusionment with political leadership was prominent. It was, to a considerable degree of course, Carter's own meal ticket to the White House itself. Carter's frustrations with Congress and the country's frustrations with gasoline lines and inflation, however, seemed to change the mood from one of being reasonably satisfied merely with honesty to one of demanding forcefulness (or, in any case, results). From being good—the theme of Carter's campaign, lusts and all—Carter was suddenly asked to be God.

Carter, in the tradition of Democratic presidents, is an activist. But his vision, as James Fallows has recently pointed out, is not grand in the traditional sense.[45] Thus, he has had the opportunity to be frustrated frequently without being able to be stylish about it. The Democratic predecessor to whom Carter is frequently unfavorably compared, John Kennedy (Lyndon Johnson who, unlike Kennedy, actually accomplished a good bit in his first two years has generally become an unperson for purposes of comparisons such as these), was reputed to have style to go along with his frustration.[46] If one is going to be frustrated in the presidency, as most incumbents barring an invasion by the Martians are destined to be, then one quite clearly had better carry it off with style and panache. Frustration without style is apparently a politically terminal disease.

Trends in Presidential Governance

"Democracy," Samuel Huntington tells us, "could have a longer life if it had a more balanced existence."[47] Whatever the present equilibrium between the demand side of the governing equation and the capabilities side, it is fair to say that recent trends have weighted the scales more heavily on the demand and expectations side of the equation than on the governance side. They have, for the most part, merely magnified tendencies already deeply rooted in our political system and our political culture. Their net effect, I think, has weakened the capacity to govern; they have at least weakened presidential governance. (Because they are so intertwined, I will discuss them together here rather than categorize them under separate readings.)

Several of these trends are social or technological as such rather than specifically political. The growth of the electronics media, for example, has affected politics everywhere, but it has undoubtedly hastened the decomposition of a not very sturdy political party system. The growth in political awareness, itself hastened by the impact of television according to some accounts, has narrowed the deference shown to and thus the latitude for political authority.[48] Most of all, the growth of knowledge and the rise of issue specialists has denied us the joys of certainty which earlier could be brought to government. The old bromides fade in the face of the intricate connectedness of issues and the delicate trade-offs to be made among them. Hugh Heclo, in his superb analysis of this phenomenon, notes that in the old days the primary problem of government was to do what was right whereas now it is to know what is right.[49] The rise of the issue specialists and the growth of knowledge has accelerated the tension between the skepticism of the policy technocrats and the passions of the political activists. Again, as Heclo contends, these trends have induced a depoliticization of government at a time when political awareness and politicization, albeit not along traditional partisan lines, has peaked in the society. The gap between governance and politics could not be greater.

An additional trend is environmental, I believe; namely, the long term decline of the United States as a dominant world economic power (perhaps military as well). The emerging order of things means a world of limits, of managing scarcities (though hardly of poverty) in a society neither notably equipped for dealing with, or socialized into thinking of, such problems. The messiness of the political system itself predisposes toward distributing benefits, not forcing sacrifices.[50]

Returning to the more familiar terrain of Congress, parties, and interests, the trends have been notably disaggregative. Through this century, Congress (at least the House) has moved from strong institutional leadership to committee fiefdoms to the proliferation of subcommittee holdings. Huey Long's fabled dictum, "every man a king," now nearly holds in Congress. Except in name, our parties for a long time have been organizational shells. What is new is that voters seem to have concluded that they have less meaning for electoral choice than do the candidates themselves for any office in reach of a television antenna. The parties quite expectedly can no longer effectively aggregate interests. The rise in notoriety, and I assume influence, of single-purpose groups is directly but not exclusively related to the weakness of political party organization. The primary system especially offers large opportunities for those concentrated of purpose and mind to influence, if not always the selection, at least the anticipated reactions of candidates for elective office.

These, then, are the major trends affecting presidential governance. The growth of knowledge weakens certainty. It is difficult to find inspiration around uncertainty and complexity. And this trend is not, I think, unconnected to the fact that Jimmy Carter, policy technocrat extraordinaire and veteran of the

Trilateral Commission, is our president.[51] The Trilateral Commission was Carter's medium for breaking into the national issue networks. Making contacts with the Cook County apparatus is likely to still be important for Democratic presidential nominees, but making connections with the policy intellectuals may take at least chronological precedence in the plans of future presidential aspirants. Carter may be an outsider to the politicians on Capitol Hill, but I doubt that he is to the policy technocrats in the bureaucracy or, for that matter, to the growing legion of policy analysts on Capitol Hill.

Not only does complexity induce uncertainty, it also induces apparent inconsistency. Consistency and simplicity are the essence of leadership. Communicating simple ideas (often oversimple ones) is not so difficult. Instilling an appreciation for complexity, as anyone who has been in front of a university classroom knows, is a different matter. Further, the medium of television concentrates attention to image. It is the medium of the mass society and perhaps its stimulant as well. It leaves us with a kaleidoscope of images and a shortened time span. It covers politics but not government, people but not institutions, dramatic gestures but not policies, contests for elective office but not the meaning of elections. It is kind to drama, but unable to convey complexity. It should not be forgotten that television works it charms for an effective user more on behalf of his politics than his governance capacities. Not that the two are unrelated of course. But the case of Kennedy ought to be instructive. The medium was kinder to his politics than it was to his capacity to rally the country on behalf of any policy more complex than marching off to Armaggedon.

The meteoric growth in political distrust too is an unnerving trend for the prospect of governance. A byproduct of rapid social change and of political leaders undeserving of confidence, the decline of trust is perhaps a rational response but it is also a poisonous one. It has increased the demands on governance while undermining the capacity to govern. It is also, as Arthur Miller has indicated, a malaise without a single source,[52] and therefore one incapable of a single solution, or at least a clear-cut response. Indeed, underneath distrust, as Miller notes, lies polarization. In the words of a leading Democratic congressman, "We're in a time of malaise and skepticism. You could dig up George Washington and put him in the White House and he probably wouldn't be successful."[53]

Overarching these other changes is an important if underplayed trend, namely, the inevitable decline in the economic dominance of the United States in the world. The management of decline, the softening and planning of a more limited future, is perhaps an impossible task in any system. Slack resources, as organization theory tells us, are related to innovation.[54] But the slack is disappearing and the political system and the individualistic culture may be insufficiently resilient to make the adjustments. Representative assemblies, it is said, typically exaggerate the popular sentiments of the moment. Only organizational strength and buffering can permit a more generous time frame. Yet, there is little in the disarray of our parties and the impact of that disarray in Congress to encourage a larger view, though this in and of itself is not a new coalition. What is discomforting is that while the disaggregation in Congress is a source of paralysis, the old party messages are often a source of irrelevance. Perhaps we know too much to be skeptical of the old saws, but not enough to construct any vision larger than a policy scientist's sense of consistency. We cannot any longer think of one policy proposal without thinking about others needed to make it work. National health insurance, for example, necessitates cost containment legislation. It cannot be a single bill; it is instead a series of actions requiring carefully planned steps. To rally support on behalf of this limited, cost-efficiency vision of society—one that will become increasingly important as our economic might wanes—is not a hopeful task. But to rally support on behalf of unreconstructed visions of the New Deal is even more hopeless.[55] I know of not a single drop of evidence that would suggest, for example, that Ted Kennedy would be able to move Congress any farther than Carter has. The enthusiasms of some of his own partisans notwithstanding, it is difficult to imagine Kennedy commanding more support than Carter in

Congress, though it would be more ardent and consistent within his own party. It is easy enough, however, to imagine his impact on the opposition party.

As for our parties, whatever the worth or dogmatism of their messages, without the capacity to discipline each party can oppose more coherently than it can govern. The Democrats in Congress but especially on the outside have few natural ingredients making for unity.[56] Once the imperial feathers were ruffled, opposing Nixon in Washington was much like opposing the shah in Iran. It was a cause destined to create delusions of unity. It could not and did not last, and I doubt that the underlying reason lies with the occupant of the White House. For a party as inherently dissentient about fundamentals as the Democrats are will always have difficulties governing. As for the Republicans, their presidents seem forever destined to attempt to govern under conditions of divided government. For those with a desire to be active, frustrations will be numerous. They may almost come to feel like Democratic presidents when their "party" controls Congress!

Some recent reforms have played a role in weakening the parties and their organization structure, but none of them has been so destructive organizationally as one brought about by the progressives half a century ago—the primary election. Overall, the more recent reforms, I agree, have made a bad condition worse. But they did not make the condition bad in the first place. Our parties always have been weak, but at least for a period societal interests had been more clearly aggregated within the party system. Of even more importance, though, is that parties have rarely seemed so irrelevant to the governance problem as they are now. I may, of course, be guilty of misplacing cause and effect and overgeneralizing from the antipartisan politics of the Carter administration and its tendencies toward technocratic governance. But I think that the trends are deeper than this, and they counterpose unique dilemmas imposed by the changes in our environment from an unlimited to a limited future. The old issues which distinguish partisans are still there, of course, as general sentiments. It is the agendas themselves that seem to have changed. These agendas are unclearly related to the repertoire of prevailing partisan symbols. The clarion call to party fails to resonate because the issues on the new agenda, while by no means wholly independent of partisan ideologies, do give off fainter partisan signals. Halting the slide of the dollar, trying to put a stopper on inflation, managing government more efficiently, balancing budgets, limiting consumption, and so on are the price of economic consolidation and the stimulant for partisan dissolution.

I am aware that Carter's agenda may be idiosyncratic—an agenda of a non-mainstream, antipolitics president. But my suspicion, and it is only that, is that our future policy agendas, whomever the president will be, will not resonate sharply with traditional partisan ideologies. The ground underneath the parties has shifted some, but changes in the atmospheric conditions are even more significant, if less immediately discernible. In short, the tensions between our "hot" politics and the growing constraints attached to governance are apt to remain, probably increase. They will continue, I believe, with or without technocratically inclined presidents.

Persona in Presidential Governance

As between system and person, I admit to giving far greater attention to the former because I think it is intrinsically of far greater importance. Yet, the characteristics of presidents, their styles, their character, their backgrounds, their approach to the role all shape the office (or are perceived to do so) in important ways. Excess attention to these attributes often leads us to erroneously widen the ambit of presidential possibilities. Presidents are mostly frustrated, and that condition owes more to the environment they operate in than how they shape the environment themselves. The environment, of course, sets the stage but presidents individually still write much of the script.

I do not pretend to offer either an exhaustive or definitive analysis of Carter as man and president. Instead, I mean to highlight three attributes of background and style that help us to understand the nature of his presidency and, therefore, his troubles. The first is his conception of the presidential role as an agenda-setter and activist. The second is his reputed status as an amateur and outsider. The third is his style of approaching problems. Each of these attributes has now attained the status of lore, so embellishing them further is not my primary purpose. Rather, what I want to do is to clarify the meaning of these attributes and link them to criticisms made of the Carter presidency.

Carter: An Activist Presidency

Partly armed with the messages of Richard Neustadt, Machiavelli, and some youthful experience at playing poker, I have trotted out to my unsuspecting underclass students the idea that the more that presidents actively seek to do, the fewer proportionately their successes will be. This notion, I fear, has been more intuitive than data-based, more a reflection of received wisdom than of hard-nosed empirical analysis. Fortunately, a recent paper by Jeffrey Cohen dealing quantitatively with presidential legislative successes reveals intuition to have been correct and conventionality to have been wise after all.[57] To put it in Cohen's own words: "Activity affects success. The number of messages sent to Congress negatively relates to presidential legislative success. This means more active presidents are less successful."[58] Cohen's measures, like those from *Congressional Quarterly*, are unweighted. The quantity of proposals supported by presidents is not necessarily equivalent to their importance or novelty. And while some presidents such as Lyndon Johnson have had lengthy agendas, they have been composed for the most part of familiar issues. Johnson's agenda largely represented the culmination of the New Deal.

That the litany of Carter proposals has been lengthy there can be little doubt.[59] Much complaining was heard during the first year about the administration overloading congressional channels. A large number of significant proposals and initiatives across a broad policy landscape has been a particular hallmark of the Carter administration. In terms of the length (not the complexity) of his agenda, Carter fits the image, but not always the reality, of the activist Democratic president. The activism, it is claimed, has been without purpose and priority, without the sacrifice of some legislative tinsel for the advancement of central purpose. I don't know whether Kennedy's efforts in 1961-62 on behalf of the trade bill which opened the way for the Kennedy Round reductions of international tariffs is the suggested model or not, but much certainly ended up being sacrificed on its behalf. Among other things, Kennedy was one of the least active presidents of recent vintage on the legislative front.[60]

As I hope my earlier comments suggest, the process of legislative reduction is a difficult one when the purpose is not merely to point to legislative scorecards but to build coherence into policy. Jack Knott and Aaron Wildavsky have pointed accurately, I believe, to a central feature of the Carter style, namely his concern for coherence.[61] Carter's concern with coherence is not, they argue, that of an ideologue but that of a planner. Aside from the fact that enough complex problems have imposed themselves on the administration without its seeking them out, the synoptic tendencies of the policy technocrat lead to a concern with analytic interrelationships between proposals. But this concern for comprehensiveness does not engender what Fallows hoped would be the belief in the one thing—a political ideology—that would make sense of the "fifty things" which Carter apparently believed in.[62] The point is that Carter does not possess an ideology about politics; he possesses one about governance. He is impatient with what is not rationally arrived at. In his words: "It is sometimes discouraging for someone who is deeply involved in questions concerning the bureaucacy or management efficiency of government, better delivery of services, tax programs or inflation programs or energy, to see that the message that gets out to the country is not based on analysis . . . but on the most superficial part of it"[63]; and, "It always causes me concern to see substantial modifications made in the proposals that we have labored so hard to produce"[64]; and, "Bad analysis inevitably leads to bad policy."[65]

The length of the agenda and its complexity

may have brought Carter to ruin. As a Democratic congressman noted, Carter's loss of support was largely a function of success in tackling difficult issues, since each success lost him an important group of supporters.[66] Another congressman suggested that the agenda, in any event, was not wholly of Carter's making: "You look at the issues, you tell me what president had to face the kind of problems Jimmy Carter has: energy, inflation, SALT, government reform. Who has had all that dumped on him at once?"[67]

If it is any consolation to Carter, he can take a small amount of comfort in words written about the Kennedy administration, a truly cautious one, during its term: "The basic fault of the Kennedy Administration is that it suffers from delusions of managerial omnicompetence."[68] Except for rare moments of consensus, activism invites ridicule because our political system was not fundamentally meant to withstand it.

Carter: The Amateur Outsider

It is hardly novel by this time to argue what brought Carter to the White House as a political amateur is also at the source of his difficulties in governing. However lacking in novelty, the proposition has the virtue of considerable truth. But the system rather than the person should be the initial focus of analysis, for a political system in which political amateurs are elevated to the presidency (and a myriad of other offices) is by definition unable to institutionalize political support. An elite structure so easily penetrated possesses some significant virtues, however. It tends to promote an influx of new ideas, skepticism toward stale ideologies, and a channel for stimulating innovation and change. Regrettably, there are also significant liabilities attached to the outsider aspect of the presidential nominating process, namely that the candidate will lack a consistent and reasonably predictable base of political support.

The distinction between amateurs and professionals or outsiders and insiders is, however, much less clear in the American system than in European politics where the only politicians are those who make it through party ranks and where the heads of government usually have had experience as cabinet ministers and not uncommonly as civil servants. Lacking the institutional apparatus that conditions political recruitment and collectivizes responsibility, American politics is by definition amateurish and its politicians mostly amateurs. It is doubtful, for example, that one can find another world capital other than Washington whose politicians specifically and regularly denounce it. A political culture which emphasizes the withering away of the state is unlikely to inspire professionalism in running it.

Politics in the United States is a highly entrepreneurial, individualistic business which specializes in packaging names rather than political programs. It is not clear what, for instance, congressional experience has to teach potential candidates for the White House. As Cohen notes, congressional experience has no discernible impact upon presidential success with Congress.[69] Unlike cabinet ministers in a cabinet system, few congressmen have had direct experience running government. In this sense, virtually all of our presidents are amateurs. The contrasts with foreign leaders such as Schmidt and Giscard, professionals at both politics and governance, is conspicuous.

Along with Eisenhower, Carter is seen as amateur and outsider. But outside of what? More amateur than whom? These are relevant questions. There is, I think, a strong Capitol Hill bias in the charge and, curiously, a strong White House centralizing bias too. A "political professional" in the White House presumably would be good at nuzzling up to congressmen (there are so many to nuzzle up to these days!) and playing to their interests, while at the same time imposing "democratic centralism" on his administration. I don't necessarily want to dig up old sod again, but Gerald Ford, the creature of Congress, was a good bit worse at dealing with it than his amateur predecessor Dwight Eisenhower, even worse than Richard Nixon who was little loved on the Hill. And as for Lyndon Johnson, success, if glowing, was brief. Yet, if Eisenhower was not a professional politician, for whatever meaning that conveys in our system, he displayed pre-eminent skills in rising to the top of military command and, incidentally, while president probably in controlling military expenditures better than any president since. Who is to say that a president who leaves office with his popularity intact (there has been no other since regularized opinion surveys have been taken) has not been politically successful? Carter, as I suggested, may well be an outsider to Washington (so too is most of Congress!); but he is not an outsider to the ways of thinking employed by the burgeoning corps of policy technocrats inside and outside of Washington, nor is he amateurish in thinking about the technical analysis of policy, a matter on which nearly all other presidents have been.

Used as adjective rather than noun, Carter has been amateurish at times in his exercise of judgment. (Perhaps never so evident as now with the rise of Hamilton Jordon to chief-of-staff.) All presidents have been amateurish at times, many with far worse consequences than anything resulting from Carter's sudden shifting of the ground beneath the feet of those members of the House who had been pressed to support his fifty dollar per capita tax cut. Roosevelt's court-packing scheme and Johnson's purported merger of the Commerce and Labor Departments qualify as instances of misapprehending the character of political support. But what of big mistakes that follow from bad analysis? The failure to mobilize efforts toward an energy policy earlier? Vietnam? The post-Vienna macho of Kennedy ordering a national guard mobilization in 1961 for a nonexistent crisis in Berlin? The passage of a rash of Great Society legislation without developing careful cost estimates or administrative infra-structure for monitoring and defining criteria for effectiveness? When does ad hoc policy making become amateurishness in the arts of governance? Presidents in our system are inherently amateurs, as Kennedy implied in December of 1962 during his interview with the three network correspondents when he commented that it looked different from there (the Senate) than it does from here (the White House).If our system makes presidents amateurs more or less in the exercise of political influence, we do not need to choose amateurishness in the capacity of presidential candidates to think about policy in a way that befits its complexity.

Carter: A Bureaucrat Without a Bureau

As Robert Putnam has argued and as subsequent evidence has further demonstrated, politicians are ideologizers whereas bureaucrats are problem-solvers.[70] Political ideology accounts for consistency among politicians as a rule, though less in the United States than elsewhere, whereas among bureaucrats who are generally lacking a comprehensive ideology about politics, bureaucratic self-interest normally accounts for consistency.[71] Bureaus focus and define problems in ways compatible with their technologies, skills, and routines—what Morton Halperin calls their "essence."[72] This helps make the behavior of bureaus and, therefore, bureaucrats reasonably predictable. But once the problem-solver is detached from his bureaucratically defined problems and placed in the role of a generalist (as a president is), the substance of his "solutions" becomes, without the anchor of a familiar political ideology, largely unpredictable.

I think that this explains much about the Carter presidential style, his apparant oscillations and "indecisiveness," the surface contradictions, and, most especially, how he is perceived. In the imperious tones of one writer:

> President Carter is in fact a weak leader, and may have been permanently injured beyond the possibility for full recovery by all of the apparent zigzags in foreign and defense policy matters thus far.[73]

As one reads further, however, this characterization seems to emanate less from presidential capacities for policy analysis than it does from the author's own penchant for a familiar and consistently hawkish posture in foreign and defense policy. As he gasps:

> Mr. Carter will undertake even unilateral disarmament measures in the nuclear weapons category, blocking new weapons developments and slowing down or halting the procurement of more older weapons, if the SALT negotiations should fail—although he will be prepared to make almost any concession so that SALT negotiations do not fail. The reality is a weaker and weaker United States.[74]

The author's penchant for the word "weak" is a revealing one, not for what it suggests about qualities such as intellectual strength, the capacity to think through options, the flexibility to alter policies when they need altering, the willingness to allow some policy-making to devolve from the White House to the bureaucracy (a facet which the present Carter self-assessment unfortunately is closing off), but for what it says about the author's own consistency of assumption.

Carter stands accused domestically also of lacking boldness, vigorous leadership, and vision. The counterparts of the foreign policy hawks on the domestic front are the hawks of the left—those with equal consistency of assumption about the broad substance of desirable policy. Those looking for predictable cues on matters of substance will not find them readily, if at all, in Carter. The lack of predictability is not, however, random. It is not that he has no value system; it is rather that his values do not fall along lines of immediate political comprehension. Skepticism and analysis—commodities that supposedly scientists and academicians prize—are, I believe, at the core of what he values. Dogmas and intellectual analysis do not easily coexist, though the latter runs the risk of becoming dogma itself, as Aaron Wildavsky has noted.[75] Alone, a problem-solving orientation cannot produce the political support necessary for governance, however, and therein lies the tension between the spirit of politics and that of governance. Whatever the reality of Carter's politics, the die is so cast and the reputation so solidified that his capacity to govern may be beyond repair. The emergent, if all too conventional, wisdom emanating from Camp David is to reawaken from the campaign trail memories best forgotten. The triumph of electioneering over governing is at hand.

Imagery plays funny tricks with our capacity for intellectual discrimination. Among qualities, after all, which Richard Neustadt praises in President Kennedy were those of deliberately "reaching down for the details." When applied to Carter this frequently is seen as a penchant for the trivial. In Kennedy, Neustadt saw the virtue of "hard questioning of the alternatives, a drive to protect options from foreclosure by sheer urgency or by *ex parte* advocacy."[76] In the case of Carter, however, often indecisiveness and wishy-washiness appear as a description. In any event, what is in the eye of the beholder bears greatly upon interpretations of something as notoriously intangible and inherently judgmental as the conduct of office.

"Congress and the people," it is said, "will follow persuasive presidential leadership when it is linked with purpose."[77] If persuasive, I suppose that by definition it will be followed. But I know little that forces people to give up their illusions, their pet theories, and their need for scapegoats when the reality is multi-causal, as is inter alia the energy situation. Multi-causal reality does not coincide with a uni-causal politics. In the first place, complexity is difficult to explain. In the second place, while Congress has the tools to think about policy in sophisticated ways, its members do not show strong inclinations to educate. Congressmen, in the words of one House member, are reluctant to tell their constituents that "the golden age is over." Or, as stated by another, "Two hundred years of living in a cornucopia is over. I think the whole 'turn to Teddy' movement is yearning to ignore that fact, a yearning by Democrats and other Americans to go back to Camelot."[78] Quite frankly, I have no idea as to what purpose can be found to consistently rally the country. Politicians get to be president not by clarifying what they do or want, but by fuzzing it up; by selecting particular sets of symbols for particular segmented audiences so that most who are paying attention can hear what they want to believe. The myth of the Rooseveltian "fireside" chat lingers on, and, in death, so does the myth of Camelot. What after all was the central purpose of the Kennedy administration? Purposes are usually imposed, not sought out. The Great Depression and the call to arms brought purpose to the Roosevelt administrations. They were exciting times for those who write about leadership and dreadful times for those being led. Kennedy's death and an unfinished agenda brought purpose to the early days of "The Great Society." Purpose (though not of the kind we are most familiar with) I doubt is the key ingredient that is missing in the Carter administration. My suspicion is that what is missing most is a good label. Labels inspire. They suggest purpose. They also seduce. By contrast, the absence of a label implies drift or even the pursuit of crass political self-interest. I believe that I am not saying anything that is not well understood in advertising circles where indistinct products must be differentiated. Labels and our romance with them unfortunately produce more concern for image-building than for institutional capacities to govern.

Concluding Comments

To conclude, this paper originated as an attempt to explain (and generalize from) Jimmy Carter's political troubles. Carter's personal style, to which much attention has been given, mediates three sets of systemic factors which can be thought of as constants, cycles, and trends. Insofar as persona is concerned, Carter's style emphasizes an analytic (but not synthetic) approach to government. His style in the presidency and his concern with what government does has been managerial rather than ideological. Inconsistencies loom large because, on the whole, the style is a bureaucratic one of discrete problem-solving rather than one dominated by traditional political principal or partisan interest. Moreover, image precedes interpretation of his actions. Having no clear sense of what he was before he assumed the presidency, the more difficulty we have pigeon-holing him into a convenient political category. John F. Kennedy's much more cautious instincts (and perhaps policies as well) were called "pragmatic liberalism"; Carter's are called too conservative by his own partisans, too liberal by his partisan opponents, too vacillating by interested spectators.

To a degree, therefore, Carter's troubles derive from a presidential style that is unfamiliar to us, from a mode of thought that is highly complex and not readily susceptible to common labels. But this, I have argued, is the least of it. For the advance of modern communications and of widespread if superficial attentiveness, in concert with an individualistic political culture and inherent institutional incapacities, produces a politics of personalities rather than a politics of institutions and organizations means incessant politicking. Governance itself is eclipsed by politics.

In such a system, all presidents with designs on governing are bound to be frustrated. The constants, particularly the Madisonian framework, have historical relevance even though, because of the scope of government and the nature of our expectations, their impact has been most strongly felt in the era of the modern presidency. They do not yield easily before presidents, whatever their backgrounds or reputed skills.

On top of what affects all presidents, there are cyclical effects which can hem in presidential designs further. It was Jimmy Carter's fate (and in some respects his initial appeal) to step into the presidency at a point during which the constraining elements of these cycles were at high tide.

Finally, I have argued that the development of several trends add up to a growing gulf between the processes of governance and those of politics. Advanced decomposition of intermediate organizations has been accompanied by a surge of individualism among those in elective office, by a growing distrust of government, and by the immediacy and personalism of the communications media. At the same time, problems have grown more complex and so has the network of elites who deal with them. In the meantime, resources needed to buffer the immediate impact of resolving them have declined, a condition unrelieved by political bluster, while the problems attached to explaining what policy is or even ought to be have mounted. It is not easy to govern when answers are uncertain. That is the condition that Carter faces. And it is a condition not made easier by Carter's own (if declining) resistance to pushing what he perceives as nonrational solutions, or by his skepticism of political ideology, or by his lack of clear and familiar image.

When I began the writing of this paper, Jimmy Carter was at Camp David trying to salvage his administration. As I conclude it, the bloodletting has begun. What Carter has sought to salvage, he seems now more apt to wreck. The prescriptions are too familiar, and they wind up making public relations junkies of presidents. Be strong rather than judicious; be in command rather than allow diversity;

elevate image-building above policy; be forceful and bold rather than calm and careful; go back to the campaign for lessons inappropriate to the problems. The pattern is that the president will draw inward, occasionally relieved by the need to engage in a specious openness rather than a genuine one. The triumph of the political operatives is nearly complete.

Policy technocrats abound in Washington and in our universities and so do political technocrats. The former factor out political costs. The latter factor out policy and governance costs. Acquiring the reputation for being an effective political operator among the political technocrats, provides a tone and a context by which to judge presidential behavior. The political technocrats are singularly entranced by the day to day zigs and zags of Washington politics. Who has leverage over whom? Who failed to return whose call? Who scratched whose back? There is something to be said, of course, about finessing a system not meant to govern in order to squeeze something from it. But I know of no president within recent vintage, including Roosevelt after 1936, who consistently was able to gain congressional approval for a broad agenda. The political technocrats—and there is no shortage of them among political scientists—will pay most attention to who zigs and who zags and to the management of political reputation. Repute, in large part, will determine the context in which we think of presidents' political skills. Eisenhower, who retained his popularity, remains an amateur; Johnson and Nixon, who brought disaster upon themselves (and us), remain guileful, if spiteful, politicians. Carter will always be the engineer because whatever his successes, he lacks the attributes of a politician wise in the ways of Washington. He is no Russell Long or Robert Byrd, to be sure. To be equally sure, Russell Long or Robert Byrd will never be president. In the meantime, the search for "expert politicians" as future presidents continues without notable success.

Presidents, as Aaron Wildavsky reminds us, are likely to become increasingly unpopular while the presidency becomes increasingly important.[79] Thus far, it is fair to say that the first prediction is correct and perhaps correct precisely, as Wildavsky suggests, because we have assumed the importance of the presidency well beyond what may have been intended for it. Whether one agrees fully with Wildavsky's vigorous defense of the constitutional design or not, his analysis has the very large virtue of intellectual consistency. We have come to expect much from the office. We have even justified presidential unpopularity through the device of calling citizens rational when they assume a presidential cause to every event.[80] To educate a public and induce its representatives to diminish their constituents' expectations, as Wildavsky believes must happen,[81] may be an impossibility—especially, I think, if the diminution of expectations is to be done with any distributive equity. If that can be done, then the presidency will be restored for better or worse to a condition more nearly in accord with the arrangements of our system. If the culture and virtually all modern trends can be altered to accept a reduced governmental load, then the presidency, if not the country, will be healthier for it. In the likely event that this does not come to pass, we may need to give as much attention to reinventing the state and its institutions as to reinventing the car.

Notes

1. William G. Andrews, "The Presidency, Congress, and Constitutional Theory," in Norman C. Thomas (ed.), *The Presidency in Contemporary Context* (New York: Dodd, Mead, 1975), 29.

2. Ibid., 30.

3. For example, see Thomas E. Cronin, *The State of the Presidency* (Boston: Little, Brown, 1975), especially chap. 2, and his earlier, "The Textbook Presidency" (1970); Nelson W. Polsby, "Against Presidential Greatness," in Peter Woll, (ed.), *American Government: Readings and Cases*, 6th ed. (Boston: Little, Brown, 1978), 428-434; and Andrews, *The Presidency*, 11-33.

4. Richard E. Neustadt, *Presidential Power: The Politics of Leadership* (New York: Wiley, 1960). Future references to this volume are taken from Neustadt's post-Nixon revisions of his second edition. I want to take some care here to note that Neustadt begins with, and continually assumes, the importance of the Constitution in limiting presidential power. Only those who can squeeze every last drop of opportunity the office presumably affords merit the designation of "expert politician."

5. Two very useful analyses of a quantitative nature on one aspect of presidential performance, however, are George C. Edwards III, "Presidential Influence in the

House: Presidential Prestige as a Source of Presidential Power," *American Political Science Review*, 70 (March 1976): 101-113, and Jeffrey Elliott Cohen, "Passing the President's Program: Presidential-Congressional Relations, 1789-1974," a paper prepared for delivery at the 1979 Annual Meeting of the Midwest Political Science Association, Chicago, Ill., April 19-22.

6. Norman C. Thomas, "An Inquiry into Presidential and Parliamentary Government," a paper prepared for the Conference on Legislative Studies in Canada, 1979, Vancouver, British Columbia, Feb. 15-17. For a vintage comparison somewhat more sympathetic to presidential government, see Don K. Price, "The Parliamentary and Presidential Systems," *Public Administration Review*, 3 (Autumn 1943): 317-334.

7. Robert W. Jackman, "Political Parties, Voting, and National Integration: The Canadian Case," *Comparative Politics*, 4 (July 1972): 511-536.

8. Donald A. Peppers, "'The Two Presidencies': Eight Years Later," in Aaron Wildavsky (ed.), *Perspectives on the Presidency* (Boston: Little, Brown, 1975), 462-471.

9. For example, Robert Schoenberger has demonstrated that Goldwater loyalists were more vulnerable to defeat in the 1964 congressional contests than those who distanced themselves from their party's nominee. See Robert A. Schoenberger, "Campaign Strategy and Party Loyalty: The Electoral Relevance of Candidate Decision-Making in the 1964 Congressional Elections," *American Political Science Review*, 63 (June 1969): 515-520.

10. See Richard E. Neustadt, *Presidential Power: The Politics of Leadership with Reflections on Johnson and Nixon*, 2d ed. (New York: Wiley, 1976).

11. On this defense of the Madisonian system, see, for example, Aaron Wildavsky, "System is to Politics as Morality is to Man: A Sermon on the Presidency," in Wildavsky, *Perspectives on the Presidency*, 526-539.

12. As suggested by the arguments of Robert A. Dahl. See his *A Preface to Democratic Theory* (Chicago: University of Chicago Press, 1956).

13. See again the arguments of Robert Dahl on this point. Robert A. Dahl, *Democracy in America: Promise and Performance*, 3rd ed. (Chicago: Rand-McNally, 1976), especially 375-390.

14. Anthony King, "Ideas, Institutions, and Policies," Parts I-III, *British Journal of Political Science*, 3 (July-Oct. 1973): 291-313, 409-423.

15. David Vogel, "Why Businessmen Distrust Their State: The Political Consciousness of American Business Executives," *British Journal of Political Science*, 8 (Jan. 1978): 45-78.

16. For example, Cowart discovers that French monetary policy has been strangely impervious (given the tradition of state intervention) to shifts in economic conditions. For an excellent comparative analysis of the use of economic tools, see Andrew Cowart, "The Economic Policies of European Governments," Parts I (Monetary Policy) and II (Fiscal Policy), *British Journal of Political Science*, 8 (July-Oct. 1978): 285-311, 425-439.

17. As the TVA's defiance of the air pollution standards administered by the Environmental Protection Agency suggested a few years ago.

18. L. J. Sharpe, "American Democracy Reconsidered," Parts I, II, and Conclusions, *British Journal of Political Science*, 3 (Jan.-April 1973): 1-27, 129-167.

19. Ibid., 157.

20. As Richard Fenno has observed, members of Congress attempt to foster a close personal attachment between themselves and their constituents while denigrating the institution of Congress. See Richard F. Fenno, Jr., "If, As Ralph Nader Says, Congress Is 'The Broken Branch,' How Come We Love Our Congressmen So Much?" in Norman J. Ornstein (ed.), *Congress In Change: Evolution and Reform* (New York: Praeger, 1975), 277-287.

21. Walter Dean Burnham, *Critical Elections and the Mainsprings of American Politics* (New York: W. W. Norton, 1970). Much of the apparent discipline, however, is ascribed by Philip Converse to electoral corruption and other mundane considerations. See Philip E. Converse, "Change in the American Electorate," in Angus Campbell and Philip E. Converse (eds.), *The Human Meaning of Social Change* (New York: Russell Sage Foundation, 1972), 263-337.

22. The Italian Christian Democrats may be a notable exception here. They are a party united only by opposition to communism and support for the church. Personal factions and ideological heterogeneity are endemic to the party. But a more organized version of the Democratic party in the United States probably would not even be as coherent as the DC.

23. See, for example, Sharpe, "American Democracy Reconsidered" (163), who further comments that "The idea that corruption is warmer and more human and therefore more democratic is a strong one that has links with the American dislike of legal constraints in government." The major exceptions to the traditional organization of local fiefdoms have been in the upper Midwest (touched heavily by the Progressives) where strong political organizations formed around distinctive interests and programs of action.

24. See, for instance, Samuel H. Beer, "Political Overload and Federalism," *Polity*, 19 (Fall, 1977): 5-17, and Thomas J. Anton, "Federal Assistance Programs: The Politics of System Transformation," a paper delivered at the Urban Choice and State Power Conference, Center for International Studies, Cornell University, June 1-4, 1977.

25. For two recent, stimulating essays on this subject, see Austin Ranney, "The Political Parties: Reform and Decline," in Anthony King (ed.), *The New American Political System* (Washington: American Enterprise Institute, 1978), 213-248, and Charles O. Jones, "Can Our Parties Survive Our Politics?" A paper delivered at the Conference on the Role of the Legislature in Western Democracies, Selsdon Park, England, April 20-22, 1979.

26. Neustadt, 2d ed., 60.

27. For a classic essay on the limits of party as a governing instrument, see Richard Rose, "The Variability of Party Government: A Theoretical and Empirical Critique," *Political Studies*, 17 (Dec. 1969): 413-445.

28. See, for instance, James L. Sundquist, "Jimmy Carter as Public Administrator: An Appraisal at Mid-

Term," *Public Administration Review*, 39 (Jan.-Feb. 1979): 3-11.

29. As Neustadt suggests.

30. See, for instance, the findings of Arthur H. Miller, Edie N. Goldenberg, and Lutz Erbring, "Type-Set Politics: Impact of Newspapers on Public Confidence," *American Political Science Review*, 73 (March 1979): 67-84.

31. Paul Allen Beck, "The Electoral Cycle and Patterns of American Politics," *British Journal of Political Science*, 9 (April 1979): 129-156.

32. See, for instance, Ivor Crewe, Bo Särlvik, and James Alt, "Partisan Dealignment in Britain, 1964-74," *British Journal of Political Science*, 7 (April 1977): 129-190.

33. David W. Brady and Phillip Althoff, "Party Voting in the U.S. House of Representatives, 1890-1910: Elements of a Responsible Party System," *Journal of Politics*, 36 (Aug. 1974): 753-777.

34. Lawrence C. Dodd, "Cycles of Congressional Power," *Society*, 16 (Nov./Dec. 1978): 65-68.

35. Schneider and Schell discover fundamental differences, reflecting many of those at the rank and file level, between older and newer Democrats in the House of Representatives. The differences, however, are especially sharp between those of the newer Democrats who won formerly Republican seats and the main body of Democrats from traditionally Democratic constituencies. The former are more economically conservative and socially liberal than the "core" Democrats. If I understand the implications of this analysis correctly, the Democrats' disarray is indeed a function of their size. See William Schneider and Gregory Schell, "The New Democrats," *Public Opinion*, 1 (Nov./Dec. 1978): 7-13.

36. Mary Russell, "Congressmen Cite Growing Frustration on Hill and in Nation," *Washington Post*, June 4, 1979, A-4.

37. See, for instance, Nevil Johnson, *Government in the Federal Republic of Germany* (Oxford: Pergamon Press, 1973); Renate Mayntz and Fritz W. Scharpf, *Policy-Making in the German Federal Bureaucracy* (Amsterdam: Elsevier, 1975); Erhard Blankenburg and Hubert Treiber, "Bürokraten als Politiker, Parlamentarier als Bürokraten: Empirie des Entscheidungsprozesses und die Gewaltenteilung," *Die Verwaltung*, 5 (1972): 273-286; and Kenneth H. F. Dyson, *Party, State, and Bureaucracy in Western Germany* (Beverly Hills, Calif.: Sage Pub., 1977).

38. See, for example, Joel D. Aberbach and Bert A. Rockman, "Clashing Beliefs Within the Executive Branch: The Nixon Administration Bureaucracy," *American Political Science Review*, 70 (June 1976): 456-468.

39. Thomas E. Cronin, " 'Everybody Believes in Democracy Until He Gets to the White House . . .': An Examination of White House-Departmental Relations," in Wildavsky, *Perspectives on the Presidency*, 362-392.

40. See, for instance, Richard Nathan, *The Plot That Failed: Nixon and the Administrative Presidency* (New York: Wiley, 1975).

41. For example, Arthur Schlesinger, Jr., *The Imperial Presidency* (New York: Popular Library, 1973), and George Reedy, *The Twilight of the Presidency* (New York: World, 1970).

42. Juan Cameron, "The Management Problem in Ford's White House," *Fortune*, 92 (July 1975): 74-81.

43. Carter has convened his cabinet more frequently than any president since Eisenhower and also kept it intact for record length. See Terence Smith, "A Visit to Cabinet Meeting: Carter Sets the Pace and Tone," *New York Times*, May 22, 1979, A1, C17.

44. See, for instance, Martin A. Levin, "A Call For a Politics of Institutions, Not Men," *Society*, 16 (Nov./Dec. 1978): 49-56.

45. See James Fallows, "The Passionless Presidency: The Trouble with Jimmy Carter's Administration," Part 1, *Atlantic*, 243 (May 1979): 33-48.

46. For example, see Irving Kristol, "The Politics of 'Stylish Frustration,' " *New Leader* 46 (April 1, 1963): 9-11. The phrase was coined by James Reston.

47. Samuel P. Huntington, "The Democratic Distemper," in Nathan Glazer and Irving Kristol (eds.), *The American Commonwealth—1976* (New York: Basic Books, 1976), 38.

48. For example, Kernell, et. al., discover on the basis of a limited sample that measures of presidential support are inversely related to those characteristics of a population that are typically associated with awareness. Thus, they conclude that "the crisis of support is a compound of secular decline and current disapproval" and that this means that "the political system will come under increasingly heavy pressure to perform" (179). See Samuel Kernell, Peter W. Sperlich, and Aaron Wildavsky, "Public Support for Presidents," in Wildavsky, *Perspectives on the Presidency*, 148-181.

49. Hugh Heclo, "Issue Networks and the Executive Establishment," in King, *New American Political System*, 87-124.

50. Some writers have argued that the "democratic imperative" is mainly responsible for this condition rather than either the particular institutional arrangements or the structure of cleavage. See, for example, Samuel Brittan, "The Economic Contradictions of Democracy," *British Journal of Political Science*, 5 (April 1975): 153-175; Anthony King, "Overload: Problems of Governing in the 1970s," *Political Studies*, 23 (June-Sept. 1975): 284-296; and Richard Rose and B. Guy Peters, *Can Government Go Bankrupt?* (New York: Basic Books, 1978).

51. Polsby, for instance, notes a trend from political cabinet appointees and from clientele appointees to issue specialists and management and technical generalists. See Nelson W. Polsby, "Presidential Cabinet Making," *Political Science Quarterly*, 93 (Spring 1978): 15-26.

52. Arthur H. Miller, "Political Issues and Trust in Government: 1967-1970," *American Political Science Review*, 68 (Sept. 1974): 951-972.

53. Berl Schwartz, "Congressional Liberals Bored with Lack of Action," *Pittsburgh Press*, July 5, 1979, A-10.

54. For example, Richard Cyert and James G. March, *The Behavioral Theory of the Firm* (Englewood Cliffs, N.J.: Prentice-Hall, 1963).

55. See, for instance, Schneider and Schell, "The New Democrats."

56. For divisions among the Democratic electorate, see Everett Carll Ladd, Jr., *Where Have All the Voters Gone? The Fracturing of America's Political Parties* (New York: W. W. Norton, 1977), especially 26-49.

57. Cohen, "Passing the President's Program."

58. Ibid., 24.

59. As Cronin has noted, "Carter is an activist who wants to achieve countless comprehensive policy and process changes." (59). Thomas E. Cronin, "An Imperiled Presidency?" *Society*, 16 (Nov./Dec. 1978): 57-64.

60. Andrews, "The Presidency, Congress, and Constitutional Theory," in Thomas, *Presidency in Contemporary Context*, 24.

61. Jack Knott and Aaron Wildavsky, "Skepticism and Dogma in the White House: Jimmy Carter's Theory of Governing," in Aaron Wildavsky, *Speaking Truth to Power: The Art and Craft of Policy Analysis* (Boston: Little, Brown, 1979), ch. 10.

62. Fallows, "The Passionless Presidency," 42-43.

63. Peter Goldman, et al., "His Mood at Mid-Term," *Newsweek*, Aug. 28, 1978, 20.

64. Ibid., 21.

65. Terence Smith, "President Cautions Foreign Policy Foes: Says Overly Simple Interpretations Could Spur Dangerous Moves," *New York Times*, Feb. 23, 1979, A-1, A-6.

66. Russell, "Congressmen Cite Growing Frustration."

67. Ibid.

68. Kristol, "The Politics of 'Stylish Frustration,'" 10.

69. Cohen, "Passing the President's Program."

70. Robert D. Putnam, "Bureaucrats and Politicians: Contending Elites in the Policy Process," in William B. Gwyn and George C. Edwards III (eds.), *Perspectives on Public Policy-Making*, Tulane Studies in Political Science, Vol. 15, 179-202. For further evidence suggestive of this proposition see Bert A. Rockman, "The Roles of Bureaucrats and Politicians: Styles and Prescriptions," paper delivered at the Conference on Frontiers in Comparative Research on Bureaucratic and Political Elites, Netherlands Institute of Advanced Studies, Wassenaar, The Netherlands, Nov. 28-Dec. 2, 1977, and Joel D. Aberbach, Robert D. Putnam, and Bert A. Rockman, "The Structure of Elite Ideology: Reformism, Conservatism, and Models of Governance," 1979.

71. The generic distinctiveness between the ways in which bureaucrats and politicians think and the ways in which they define their roles is, however, much more blurred in the United States than elsewhere. In general, American bureaucrats are more, and American politicians less, ideological than their European peers. See especially Joel D. Aberbach and Bert A. Rockman, "The Overlapping Worlds of American Federal Executives and Congressmen," *British Journal of Political Science*, 7 (Jan. 1977): 23-47; Rockman, "The Roles of Bureaucrats and Politicians"; and Aberbach, et al., "The Structure of Elite Ideology."

72. l Morton Halperin, *Bureaucratic Politics and Foreign Policy* (Washington, D.C.: The Brookings Institution, 1974), especially 26-62.

73. Vincent Davis, "Carter Tries On the World for Size," *Society*, 16 (Nov./Dec. 1978), 41.

74. Ibid., 42.

75. Wildavsky, "The Political Economy of Efficiency," *Public Interest*, 8 (Summer 1967): 30-49.

76. Neustadt, rev. 2d ed., 271.

77. Cronin, "An Imperiled Presidency," 64.

78. Russell, "Congressmen Cite Growing Frustration."

79. Wildavsky, "The Past and Future Presidency," in Glazer and Kristol, *American Commonwealth*, 56-76.

80. See Richard A. Brody and Benjamin I. Page, "The Impact of Events on Presidential Popularity: The Johnson and Nixon Administrations," in Wildavsky, *Perspectives on the Presidency*, 136-148.

81. Wildavsky, "The Past and Future Presidency."

The Pulse of Politics 8.2

James David Barber

Individual presidencies are not discrete or separate historical occurrences. Presidencies do not function independently in an historical vacuum. The exercise of presidential power is strongly influenced by the events and political developments of preceding administrations. The following essay is a chapter from a book by noted presidential expert James David Barber in which he argues that the modern presidency is afflicted by a syncopative rhythm set in motion by the process of policy development.

The Pulse of Politics: Electing Presidents in the Media Age (pp. 13-22) by James David Barber, 1980, New York: W. W. Norton & Company, Inc. Copyright 1980 by W. W. Norton & Company, Inc. Reprinted by permission.

Seven times between 1900 and 1980 the cycle of elections dominated by themes of conflict, conscience, and conciliation beat through American presidential politics. Radically condensed, the sequence went like this:

Cycle I: 1900, 1904, 1908

1900 Conflict

The century opened with the battle election of 1900. Four years before, William McKinley had been chosen over William Jennings Bryan, in a great national sigh of relief that brought an end to a decade of economic hard times. Bryan the Democrat had offered a cure-all, "free silver," but McKinley, a calm, sweet-tempered fellow, personified the nation's need for harmony and peace. Prosperity followed his election. In time the public, spurred on by the newly burgeoning Yellow Press, began to lust for adventure. They got it in the Spanish-American War, which broke out in 1898 and provided the springboard for the century's most bellicose politician, Theodore Roosevelt. Roosevelt came roaring back from San Juan Hill to win the governorship of New York. In 1900 Republicans nominated him for vice-president to stand in for quiet McKinley in an all-out political war against Bryan; the two of them put aside their dignities and treated the nation to a hot partisan fight over foreign and domestic policy, racing around the country blasting each other from every available stump.

1904 Conscience

McKinley died the September after his inauguration and Roosevelt took over as president. He rapidly achieved immense popularity, a fascinating, self-dramatizing sparker of interest and attention. Roosevelt easily gained the presidential nomination in 1904 and the election itself turned into a Roosevelt landslide. Such excitement as emerged centered on moral questions: America's duty, in the name of civilization, to rescue victims of brutal regimes, the question of the legitimacy of giant trusts, the problem of civil rights for blacks in the South. The Democrats, in a chaotic convention, heard Bryan invoke God and high principle, and then turned to an unknown, Judge Alton B. Parker of New York, a farm-born nonpolitician valued for his clean and decent character, whose innocence had been repeatedly demonstrated by his reluctance to run for electoral office. Roosevelt, now standing on his presidential dignity, resolved to rise above the contest, avoiding the hustings as George Washington had. Only near the end of the campaign, when his conscience was challenged by a charge that he had been bought and blackmailed by rich contributors, did TR issue a harsh defense of his moral rectitude.

1908 Conciliation

Roosevelt, recognizing that reaction would set in after his era of action, announced that he would not run again in 1908. His measures had met increasing opposition; he responded by moderating his demands. Bryan did likewise, focusing his rhetoric more and more on the need for a time of peace, though he did not neglect to criticize the opposition. As the election season approached, the economy went shaky, with several temporary but frightening panics and increasing rates of unemployment. Roosevelt's choice as his successor could hardly have symbolized more clearly the nation's readiness for a time of conciliation: William Howard Taft, three hundred pounds of genial good cheer. Taft, with his slogan, "Smile, Smile, Smile," left his opponent—Bryan again—behind by a comfortable margin and eased into the White House.

Cycle II: 1912, 1916, 1920

1912 Conflict

Within two years, the Taftian consensus fell apart. The combative surge boiled up in both parties. Issues of interest—creditor vs. debtor, bosses vs. insurgents, East vs. West—cracked the temporarily smoothed surface of national politics. Taft broke with the Republican conservatives; Roosevelt came back from a hunting trip in Africa to break with Taft as *too* conservative and to battle against him for delegates. Bryan went down to defeat in his own state's convention. At a riotous Republican national convention in 1912, Roosevelt furiously marched his forces from the hall to form the Progressive (Bull Moose) party and took to the field to flail his old friend Taft. All over the country, political meetings broke up in fistfights and challenged votes. Even the Socialists fell apart, their moderates expelling their radicals. Bryan charged again in the Democratic convention, already split into wildly contending camps. The Democrats fought through forty-six convention ballots before the conservative faction finally won out, nominating a new face on the national scene, ex-professor Woodrow Wilson.

1916 Conscience

Wilson won. To the surprise of his backers and opponents, he turned out to be a progressive reformer, driving through Congress a substantial program of novel measures. He also turned out to be a remarkable rhetorician, and the public got to know him as a fervent moralist, given to justifying his every move on grounds of high principle. War broke out in Europe; the jingoes at home began to beat the drum for militant patriotism. Wilson stood firm against intervention—on grounds of principles he was absolutely sure were right. In 1916 he was easily renominated. The Republicans chose a clean outsider, Justice Charles Evans Hughes, who dutifully campaigned for "Americanism" while Wilson wrapped himself in the presidency. Questions of whom was more loyal to the country pervaded the campaign. Wilson won narrowly. Had Hughes won, the election would still stand as an example of the moral drama.

1920 Conciliation

There followed the horror of the Great War. Peace brought domestic strife—a wave of violent strikes, race riots, bombings, a Red scare, soaring inflation. An exhausted nation was ready for a rest. In 1920 the Republicans found just the man for that, harmonizing Warren G. Harding, with his call for a return to "normalcy." The Democrats, radically misreading the national mood, went for Ohio Governor James Cox, who lit out after Harding with a hard-fighting partisan campaign. Harding, the mellifluous conciliator, buried him in the heaviest landslide ever recorded.

Cycle III: 1924, 1928, 1932

1924 Conflict

The presidency killed Harding. His vice-president, Calvin Coolidge, took over, an odd president for the Jazz Age. By 1924, Harding and his harmony seemed nearly forgotten. A fighting election ensued—but one more strangely focused than any other. Silent Cal Coolidge said little, but he fought off several challengers by adroit, behind-the-scenes employment of the federal patronage. By convention time, he was securely in the saddle, though Senator Robert La Follette and his Progressives split off to wage a vigorous campaign, championing the interests of labor and the farmer. But the combative hit of the season was the Democratic convention; torn to shreds by factional fights, it took the Democrats three weeks of internecine combat and 103 ballots to light on a dull and ineffective Wall Street lawyer named John W. Davis. The party went into the election hopelessly split and debilitated. Coolidge's vice-presidential candidate, "Hell 'n' Maria" Dawes, blasted the Democrats while the president kept his silence—and the White House.

1928 Conscience

Coolidge finally decided not to run again in 1928, destined to be another season of moral concern. The Republicans turned to Herbert Hoover of Iowa, a clean-living Quaker untarnished by the political wars, who persistently shied away from any expression of presidential ambition until his first-ballot nomination. The Democrats nominated Governor Al Smith of New York in a convention as placid as the Republicans'. Then a storm of righteous indignation fell on Smith—that Catholic product of Tammany Hall who favored relaxing the liquor prohibition. The question of character leapt to the fore; Smith was painted as personifying everything alien to the American Eden. Hoover would not even mention his name. The voters chose the native son of pure principle and high ideals.

1932 Conciliation

Almost before he had settled into office, the bottom began to fall out from under Hoover's hopes for continued prosperity. By 1932 the American people, desperate for relief, were ready for any viable alternative. Hoover himself, with the full force of his wooden rhetoric, kept calling for confidence and optimism as the antidote to terror. The Democrats found their cure in Franklin D. Roosevelt, governor of New York, unknown to most Americans, depicted by those in the know as a mild-mannered gentleman of no particular conviction whose jaunty smile seemed to promise better times ahead—another Harding. Roosevelt's major appeal was that he was not Hoover. He floated in on a tide of votes in an election consumed with the quest for an end to trouble.

Cycle IV: 1936, 1940, 1944

1936 Conflict

The trouble did not go away. Roosevelt took action in a startling array of governmental experiments. By 1936, he had aroused allegiance and opposition unmatched in the twentieth century, polarizing the polity. The Republicans, encouraged by the crude polls of that time, thought they had a chance to whip him with Governor Alfred Landon of Kansas. The election was a battle royal. Roosevelt, the smiler of 1932, came across this time as a fighter, damning the "economic royalists," welcoming their hatred. The Republicans pulled out all the stops; some employers even threatened wage cuts if Roosevelt won. Demagogues of the left and right raved and ranted. Fighting Franklin Roosevelt took every state but Maine and Vermont.

1940 Conscience

In his second term, Roosevelt overreached himself. He tried to pack the Supreme Court, the American polity's church. The charges against him escalated from the partisan to the principled: he threatened the Constitution, they said, and he aimed to set up a dictatorship. The Republicans led off a crusade to preserve democracy, handing that flag to Wendell Willkie, son of the Indiana soil, a businessman like Hoover but even freer of the taint of political experience. Willkie's platform for 1940 was a creed, a faith, a reprise of the sacred American promise. Willkie had to be drafted—and so did Roosevelt, who held back until convention time. FDR campaigned as The President, consumed with the developing war in Europe, interrupting that high work for an occasional correction of Republican errors, calling on God to strengthen the patriotic cause. Despite the shock of his violation of George Washington's rule against a third term, he carried the day.

1944 Conciliation

One could say that Roosevelt won the election of 1944 on December 7, 1941, the day the Japanese attacked Pearl Harbor. For the second time in history, Americans went to the polls in the middle of a war. The universal purpose was to get to the end of it. Roosevelt, the confident continuer, reappeared with his old jaunty humor and comforting certainty intact, calling the nation together like a family around the dinner table, teasing his opposition for attacking his little dog, waving and smiling to the crowds as he drove through Manhattan in the rain. His challenger, New York Governor Thomas E. Dewey, echoed the conciliatory theme by calling for an end to New Deal bickering, but he seemed a bickerer himself as he flailed at the commander-in-chief's administrative imperfections. Once again, Roosevelt won by a safe margin.

Cycle V: 1948, 1952, 1956

1948 Conflict

Five months later, he was dead and Harry S. Truman was president. The year after that, the war was over, the Republicans captured both houses of Congress, as long-suppressed partisan passions revived. Dewey had a hard fight at the Republic convention of 1948, but won through to the nomination on the third ballot. His troubles were as nothing compared to Truman's. On the left, Roosevelt's former vice-president, Henry A. Wallace, formed a new Progressive party to fight for the presidency. On the right, the Dixiecrats split off to contend for Governor J. Strom Thurmond. A funereal convention nominated Truman—who proceeded, to nearly everyone's amazement, to battle the Republicans from one end of the country to the other, at last winning a shocking upset victory by the closest of margins.

1952 Conscience

Truman did his damnedest, but by 1952 it was time for a change. War broke out in Korea in 1950; the president was held responsible for failing to beat back the communists and end it. Charges of corruption in and around the White House gained credence, as did the suspicion that the Reds might have too many friends in the Truman administration. Perhaps as important, in an age of increasingly symbolic politics, Truman's image as a scrappy politician lacking in presidential dignity, a cusser, and a poker player, took hold. Truman saw the signs; he helped get Illinois Governor Adlai E. Stevenson to run—a man of evident high integrity, superbly literate propounder of the American conscience, who preached his sermons like a Puritan divine. The Republicans beat that move with General Dwight David Eisenhower, hero of World War II, son of Abilene, Kansas, reluctantly taking his first plunge into political controversy. Eisenhower conducted not a campaign, but a "crusade." Morals ruled the day and the Republican diatribe against "Communism, Korea, and Corruption" won it.

1956 Conciliation

Eisenhower went to Korea and the war there was settled. Back home the Red scare got going in earnest, complemented on the foreign front by the secretary of state's dire warnings. In the midst of prosperity came new anxieties: massive social shifts, escalating debt, newly demanding minorities. In 1955, the Soviets exploded a hydrogen bomb. Eisenhower, meanwhile, grinned and presided. Adlai Stevenson, renominated, added to the general anxiety by trying to get a fight going in 1956. Eisenhower, renominated, spoke of peace and harmony. The electorate responded: they liked Ike, their warmhearted friend in the White House.

Cycle VI: 1960, 1964, 1968

1960 Conflict

The appeal of placidity slowly waned in Eisenhower's second term; the appeal of adventure sparked again. Ike stepped aside in favor of his aggressive young vice-president, Richard M. Nixon, who fought his way to the Republican nomination in 1960 over the challenge of New York Governor Nelson Rockefeller. A young Democratic war hero, John F. Kennedy, muscled aside Senator Hubert Humphrey in the primaries and Senator Lyndon Johnson at the convention. A partisan battle ensued as the candidates lashed each other in a flat-out campaign, culminating in a novel confrontation: a series of "Great Debates" on television. Kennedy won by a whisker. The drama of that season was combat, in a new, cool mode.

1964 Conscience

Kennedy was gunned down in Dallas in 1963. President Lyndon B. Johnson went into the 1964 campaign as "Preacher Lyndon," dedicated to the martyred Kennedy's moral purposes: a peaceful resolution of the war in Vietnam and justice for blacks in America—a high-road campaign for grand principles. That year brought forward a new moral champion for the Republicans, who advertised his conscience as his primary qualification for the presidency. Senator Barry Goldwater of Arizona was hauled into the race by disgruntled conservatives, who undertook nothing less than a reorientation of American political philosophy. Goldwater railed against corruption, not in the name of clear programmatic alternatives, but in the name of civic virtue deductively defined. In the end he lost, but his moral concerns and the wildly deviant paths of policy they dictated dominated the national agenda.

1968 Conciliation

There followed, under Johnson the "dove" candidate of 1964, a hideous escalation of the war in Vietnam, setting off a period of political discord that made the anxieties of the 1950s look like a tea party. Those same years saw the boiling up of violent racial protest, as, in city after city, black ghetto residents and white police confronted each other in the streets. At last in April 1968, Johnson bowed out of contention for renomination. Martin Luther King, Jr., and Robert F. Kennedy were killed by assassins in the spring, chaotic violence seemed spreading everywhere, the country veering out of control. Candidates from one end of the political spectrum to the other called out for peace and quiet, a revival of national unity. The Democrats, meeting in the midst of a riot in Chicago, nominated their chief apostle of brotherhood, Hubert Humphrey. The Republicans turned to a new Nixon, calm and mellow, his lowered voice promising to bring us together again. Nixon won by an eyelash—the peacemaker, the conciliator, the bringer of harmony.

Cycle VII: 1972, 1976, 1980

1972 Conflict

It did not work out that way. Nixon spread the war—secretly. He got at his political enemies—secretly. By 1972, the first secret was out in the open and the second just beginning to emerge. Opponents to the war turned from demonstrations to hard-fought politics. But President Nixon would not meet in public challenge directly. Instead, in a carefully orchestrated image campaign, he presented himself as The President, negotiating with foreign powers, refusing to discuss the issues his opponents threw at him. Thus the story of politics as war had nowhere to go in 1972 but to the Democrats. There, in a long series of hot fights in the primaries, the contest of 1972 found its drama, as moralist Senator George S. McGovern carried his crusade to the nomination and then, in the summer, worked himself out of the election when he mishandled the resignation of his running mate, Senator Thomas Eagleton.

1976 Conscience

Nixon's secret war against his political enemies at last came to light in a slow process of uncovering, leading to his resignation from office in 1974. His vice-president, Gerald R. Ford, moved into the White House amidst high hopes for moral restoration—an honest man at last. But then Ford pardoned Nixon, raising the suspicion that he was not above a deal. Ford's demeanor helped allay that doubt; he went into the 1976 election season as a straight-shooting down-home American booster. The Democrats, after a long and wearing contest in the proliferating primaries, turned to an outsider from Plains, Georgia, running against the corruptions of the Capitol. Governor Jimmy Carter emerged, preaching the common American values of decency and compassion and honesty. A nation ready for moral revival voted him in.

1980 Conciliation

There were some highly praised foreign-policy moves but as the 1980 election approached, Carter's preacherly rhetoric began to wear thin with a public increasingly anxious over a deepening recession, galloping inflation, and an energy crisis. In the summer of 1979, the president took note of a "crisis of confidence" and the need to restore union. More than 100,000 citizens wrote in to praise his speech. Millions more turned out to see the visiting Pope, with his ecumenical message of love. The seizure of hostages in Iran and a Soviet invasion of Afghanistan rallied the nation to the president's side, while his critics fumed and fumbled. Whatever the outcome of the election, the emerging dominant theme was clear: worn with quarrels and demands for heroic sacrifice, the Americans seemed ready for a little relief, a little healing, a time of conciliation. There would be time enough for another hot policy battle in 1984.

The Power of the Pulse

That history happened. My reading of the extended accounts of these elections convinces me that this summary version does justice to the facts. On the record, the pulse of politics describes the major themes that dominated contest after contest. But description is not explanation. *Why* do these particular dimensions of modern politics keep returning to shape the nation's consciousness as we deliberate the presidential choice? Where does the force of it come from?

The pulse of politics is a mythic pulse. Political life shares in the national mythology, grows in the wider culture, draws its strength from the human passion for discovering, in our short span of life on this peripheral plant, the drama of human significance. Ours is a story-making civilization; we are a race of incorrigible narrators. The hunger to transform experience into meaning through story spurs the political imagination. We seem bound and determined to find in the mundane business of picking a chief executive a sage of the spirit.

That impulse marks us as human. But why do we concentrate so persistently on three themes: conflict, conscience, conciliation?

Part of the explanation may be that they resonate with the most deeply rooted and primitive human memories. No one knows how tale-telling got its start, long before life was reduced to writing. The conflict theme may trace all the way back to preliterate hunting stories, recounted by survivors returning to the fireside to report the frantic search and kill and escape—the origin of the "embroidered exploit,"one writer thinks. The conscience theme may echo the primordial "warning example": a mother, straining to "persuade her child from the fire," tells how another child, another time, ignored the commandment and suffered for it.[1] The conciliation theme may draw on the appeal of ancient acts of union: the young woman or man, driven by the incest taboo to seek a mate among foreigners, comes back with a tale of courtship and consummation, giving birth to an endless series of sweet stories of love. Reflections of these old sagas might be discerned in the psychological paradigm that dominates our age's thinking: the ego, instrument for coping with struggles of the external world; the superego, warning against harmful violations; the id, longing after the thrill and ease of sexual satisfaction. They are reflected again in the never-ending popularity of the war story, the morality play, the romantic comedy.

But there are also specifically American reasons for these emphases.

The American war story, from which the theme of politics as conflict derives its very language, reflects our peculiar experience. Here as elsewhere war has had its powerful appeal—cutting through the ambiguities and complexities and frustrations of life with simple, exciting, rejuvenating release of aggression. But war often came to other nations by the shock of invasion. In isolated America, the warmakers repeatedly confronted the special problem of arousing the martial spirit against distant enemies who had not yet attacked us. That arousal required propaganda—the substitution of drama for experience as a stimulus to action. Thus our history vibrates with *talk* about war, advertising its anticipated glories in rip-roaring tales of heroism. The war story echoes through the culture; no wonder political storytellers pick up on its thrilling, threatening theme.

Modern newspapering was born in combat; I will trace how that craft grew up with the political fight game and how it helped translate the fighting story from its primitive, axe-murder style to the gentler—but no less decisive—political combat of our time. There its drumbeat rattles to rouse us from the temptations of lassitude.

The politics of conscience bites deep in the American experience. From the Old Testament on, the tense drama of the making and breaking of the covenant between God and his people has electrified Western civilization. The American civilization was founded by godly people, determined to build a New Zion in the wilderness, a newly chosen people, set apart by the Almighty himself from the heathen Europeans to the East and the heathen Indians to the West. The Puritan God was no bemused observer of human folly, content to sit back and watch what his original act of creation had set in train. God was *in* history, the Calvinist god directing every flight of birds over Plymouth, every blast of lightning, the rise of every crop and plague, and the exact course of human events. America was a mission. The Declaration announces our "firm reliance on the protection of divine Providence." Thus America stepped into the family of nations claiming a kind of ordination. Lincoln confirmed it: we were a nation "under God." From then to now, our conscience has never been satisfied by government as a mere practical arrangement to secure our survival and see to the feeding of our animal appetites. If it was never perfectly clear whom God favored for president, it seemed self-evident that the question must be asked.

Our periodic revivals of the politics of conscience owe much to the preachers in the press. While reporters were covering the fights, editors and columnists ministered to our spiritual needs. That moral mission flourished most strikingly in magazine journalism. Magazine journalism on a national scale got underway in the nineteenth century, but it took off, in terms of mass circulation and political influence, in that era of moralistic reformism that culminated in Wilson's reign, the era of the moralizing "muckrakers." Editors got directly into presidential politics; one brought Wilson along, another fostered Hoover, behind the scenes as well as in the pages of their journals. The success of *Time* and the rise of the columnists lent force to the combination of reportage and moral commentary, recalling the power of the ancient parables, reinforcing the politics of conscience down to our day. Now as then, American politics focuses on the search for a good president to lead a good country.

The politics of conciliation has its own essential suspense: will Romeo and Juliet succeed in getting together despite the Montagues and Capulets? But again, the specifically American experience underscores the theme. We became a nation of nationalities, of strangers bearing conflicting heritages, scattered across a continent. Had we not found the path to union, there would have been no United States. Holding that vast and varied enterprise together became urgent American work, its necessity never more deeply burnt into the national consciousness than when union failed in the 1860s. Just as we are about to smash up the political saloon, someone has to have the sense to yell, "Don't shoot the piano player!" That calls for laughing off our oh-so-serious differences, for positive thinking, for the continual rediscovery of what we have in common. At least since Ben Franklin, Americans have stood apart from the world's stern aristocracies, dour dictatorships, and aching slumlands as a nation of incorrigible hopers and boosters. If we did not invent Santa Claus, we made him our own. Our politics is something we *play*, a great game, and a president is supposed to play that game with a smile on his face. That superficially light and vulgar story, the butt of ironists, is in fact the rock-bottom myth of our political existence.

The prime medium for illustrating the politics of conciliation in the modern era is broadcasting. The early nineteenth century had its "celebrations" mixing politics and entertainment, continued in the late nineteenth century in popular tent theater. But radio and then television reached out eventually to nearly every home, homogenizing the culture. Television burst into mass popularity just as the nation was discovering we liked Ike—and the peace and harmony he came to symbolize by 1956. Broadcasting aimed to please, wrapping politics in fun and games. Today it is our only truly national medium, conveying with unmatched reach and power its core message of conciliation.

In *every* presidential election season, these themes are reinforced. We could not possibly sort out from the many who present themselves the few who are serious without setting up a fight. Once the leading contenders merge, it is necessary to inquire into their qualifications—their characters—as potential replacements for George Washington. And then we need to sense whether this or that self-proclaimed hero can in fact draw together the nation's multifarious interests and energies for a unified march into the future. The slower, longer pulse of politics, by which we move from one dominant theme to the next, picks up momentum when, season after season, we confront the necessities of choice.

No wonder then that these myths grip the

American political mind. They trace back to deep and original challenges to the human condition. They grow from the bloody ground of this nation's experience. They give our major storytellers their channels to popularity. They make possible our quadrennial progress from many to one. Together, they compose the life force of the American political culture.

Note

1. Arthur Ransome, *A History of Story-Telling: Studies in the Development of Narrative* (New York: Frederick A. Stokes Co., N.D.), ch. 1.

Illustration 8a

Illustration 8a: A Presidential Executive Order

Executive orders are tangible policy outputs of the presidency. With them presidents make decisions and pronouncements pursuant to legislation.

IMMEDIATE RELEASE   MAY 23, 1947

EXECUTIVE ORDER
- - - -

REGULATIONS FOR CARRYING OUT THE
PROVISIONS OF THE ACT ENTITLED "AN
ACT TO PROVIDE FOR ASSISTANCE TO
GREECE AND TURKEY"

By virtue of the authority vested in me by the act of May 22, 1947, entitled "An Act to provide for assistance to Greece and Turkey", hereinafter referred to as the act, and as President of the United States, I hereby prescribe the following regulations for carrying out the provisions of the act:

1. Subject to such policies as the President may from time to time prescribe, the Secretary of State is hereby authorized, through such departments, agencies, and independent establishments of the Government as he may designate, to exercise any power or authority conferred upon the President by the act, including expenditure of funds made available for the purposes of the act.

2. The Chief of Mission to Greece or Turkey appointed by the President pursuant to section 8 of the act shall, under the guidance and instructions of the Secretary of State, direct United States activities within Greece or Turkey, as the case may be, in furnishing assistance under the act. The Secretary of State may delegate to the Chief of Mission such powers or authority conferred by this order as he may deem necessary and proper to the effective carrying out of the provisions of the act and of the basic agreement with the Government of Greece or Turkey, as the case may be, setting forth the general terms and conditions under which assistance is to be furnished.

3. The Secretary of State shall provide, and at his request other departments, agencies, independent establishments, and officers of the Government shall cooperate in providing to the extent considered feasible in keeping with their other established governmental responsibilities and to the extent that funds may be available therefor, such personnel, together with their compensation, allowances, and expenses, and such administrative supplies, facilities, and services as may be necessary and proper to the effective carrying out of the provisions of the act.

4. Subject to the provisions of paragraph 2 hereof, the powers and authority conferred upon the Secretary of State by this order shall be exercised by the Secretary or, subject to his direction and control, by such officers and agencies of the Department of State as he may designate, in the interest of effective administration and proper coordination of functions under the act.

5. The Secretary of State shall make appropriate arrangements with the Secretaries of War and the Navy, and the heads of other Government departments, agencies, and independent establishments concerned, in order to enable them to fulfill their responsibilities under the act.

HARRY S. TRUMAN

THE WHITE HOUSE,
May 22, 1947.

Courtesy Harry S Truman Library.

Illustration 8b: Presidential Daily Schedule

Presidents are extremely busy officeholders. This detailed example shows the variety of "dawn to dusk" presidential business.

```
              THE PRESIDENT'S APPOINTMENTS
                THURSDAY, JANUARY 21, 1954
```

8:00 am   The following had breakfast with the President:
              (Hon. Henry Cabot Lodge, Jr.)
              (Hon. Leonard Hall)   OFF THE RECORD
              (Hon. Sherman Adams)

8:55 am   (Hon. Leonard Hall, Chairman, Republican National Com.) OFF THE RECORD

9:00 am   National Security Council
              Hon. John Foster Dulles, Secretary of State
              Hon. Roger M. Kyes, Acting Secretary of Defense
              Hon. Harold E. Stassen, Director, Foreign Operations Adm.
              Hon. Arthur S. Flemming, Director, Office of Defense Mobilization
              Hon. George M. Humphrey, Secretary of the Treasury
              Hon. Herbert Brownell, Jr., The Attorney General
              Hon. Joseph M. Dodge, Jr, Director, Bureau of the Budget
              Hon. Henry Cabot Lodge, Jr., Ambassador to the United Nations
              Hon. Walter B. Smith, Under Secretary of State
              Hon. John Slezak, Acting Secretary of the Army
              Adm. Donald B. Duncan, for the Secretary of the Navy
              Hon. Harold E. Talbott, Secretary of the Air Force
              Adm. Arthur W. Radford, Chairman, Joint Chiefs of Staff
              Gen. Matthew B. Ridgway, Chief of Staff of the Army
              Gen. Nathan F. Twining, Chief of Staff of the Air Force
              Gen. Lemuel C. Shepherd, Jr., Commandant, U. S. Marine Corps
              Hon. Stanley N. Barnes, Assistant Attorney General
              Hon. Herbert Hoover, Jr., Department of State
              Hon. Allen W. Dulles, Director, Central Intelligence Agency
              Hon. Robert Cutler, Special Assistant to the President
              Hon. C. D. Jackson, Special Assistant to the President
              Hon. Bryce Harlow, Administrative Assistant to the President
              Hon. Sherman Adams, Assistant to the President
              Hon. Wilton B. Persons, Deputy Assistant to the President
              Hon. James S. Lay, Jr., Executive Secretary
              Hon. S. Everett Gleason, Deputy Executive Secretary

11:30 am   (Hon. Clarence Randall, Chairman, Commission on Foreign Economic
                 Policy)
              (Hon. Sherman Adams)   OFF THE RECORD
              (Hon. Gabriel Hauge)
                 (Half-hour, to discuss Randall's report)

12:00   (Hon. True D. Morse, Under Secretary of Agriculture) OFF THE RECORD
                 (Came in for a few minutes to brief the President before the
                  Members of the National Grange saw the President)

12:15 pm   The President received the Master of the National Grange, together
              with the Members of the Executive Committee and Staff.
                 (They asked for this so that they might tell the President of
                   their agreement with major portions of his farm message, and
                   to tell him of their apprehension concerning surpluses.)

Illustration 8b

THURSDAY, JANUARY 21, 1954   Page 2

12:15 pm   National Grange (Continued)
                    The following were present:
                         Herschel D. Newsom, Master, Washington, D. C.
                         Harry B. Caldwell, Greensboro, North Carolina; Exec. Com.
                         Henry P. Carstensen, Seattle, Washington; Exec. Com.
                         L. Roy Hawes, North Sudbury, Massachusetts; Exec. Com.
                         Ray Teagarden, LaCygne, Kansas, Exec. Com.
                         Fred Bailey, Consultant; Staff
                         Roy Battles, Assistant to the National Master; Staff
                         Lloyd C. Halvorson, Economist; Staff
                         Edward F. Holter; Staff

1:00 pm   (Dr. Milton Eisenhower had Luncheon with the President) OFF THE RECORD

2:00 pm   Dr. Milton Eisenhower
                Hon. Walter B. Smith, Under Secretary of State
                Hon. John M. Cabot, Assistant Secretary of State
                Hon. Samuel C. Waugh, Assistant Secretary of State
                Hon. George M. Humphrey, Secretary of the Treasury
                Hon. Sinclair Weeks, Secretary of Commerce
                Hon. Andrew N. Overby, Assistant Secretary of the Treasury
                Hon. Samuel W. Anderson, Assistant Secretary of Commerce
                Hon. Glen Edgerton, Export-Import Bank of Washington
                    (Discussed Latin-American affairs)

3:00 pm   Hon. William Rogers, Deputy Attorney General
                Senator John M. Butler, Maryland
                Senator J. Glenn Beall, Maryland
                Judge Simon Sobeloff, candidate for Solicitor Generalship

3:45 pm   Senator William F. Knowland, California
                Mrs. Carroll Kearns, National President of National Federation
                   of Republican Women
                Mrs. Jean Fuller, Third Vice President
                   (Came in at the request of Senator Knowland and invited
                      the President to attend the Convention next September
                      in San Francisco.)

4:15 pm   Mrs. Robert Murray, Oshkosh, Wisconsin
                   National Coordinator for Women for Bricker Amendment, Member
                   of Executive Committee of Wisconsin Republican Party, Vice
                   Chairman of Sixth District, Member of National Board of
                   Federation of Republican Women
                Mrs. Henry Stewart Jones, Marshfield, Wisconsin
                   Vice Chairman of Republican Party of Wisconsin, State
                   Chairman of campaign activities of Wisconsin Federation of
                   Republican Women, Member of National Board of Federation of
                   Republican Women
                Mrs. Lewis Borker, Chicago, Illinois
                   National Coordinator of Women for Bricker Amendment
                   First Vice President of Federation of Republican Women of
                   Illinois
                (Hon. Jack Martin)
                   (Came in to discuss Bricker Amendment)

THURSDAY, JANUARY 21, 1954

7:30 pm (The President gave a Stag Dinner at the White House for the following:)
Mr. Dillon Anderson, Lawyer – Houston
Mr. Sullivan Barnes, Chairman, Young Republican National Federation
Mr. Robert L. Biggers, President, Fargo Division, Chrysler Corporation
Dr. Milton S. Eisenhower, President, Pennsylvania State University
Hon. Marion B. Folsom, Under Secretary of the Treasury
Mr. Richard J. Gray, President, Building & Construction Trades Department, AF of L
Mr. Paul H. Helms, President, Helms Bakeries
Mr. John G. Jackson, Jr., Lawyer, New York
Vice Admiral C. Turner Joy, Supt., U. S. Naval Academy
Mr. Roy E. Larsen, President, Time, Inc.
Mr. Robert McLean, Publisher, Philadelphia Bulletin
Hon. Gerald Morgan, Administrative Assistant to the President
Mr. Robert Montgomery, TV Producer
Mr. William W. Prince, President, Union Stockyard & Transit Co. of Chicago
Hon. Clarence Randall, Chairman, Commission on Foreign Economic Policy
Mr. Merriman Smith, Correspondent, United Press
Mr. Roger W. Straus, Chairman of the Board, American Smelting and Refining Company

Illustration 8c: A President's Correspondence with a Member of Congress

Presidential correspondence is a medium through which presidents frequently exercise leadership and influence.

JOSEPH C. O'MAHONEY
WYOMING

COMMITTEES:
INTERIOR AND INSULAR AFFAIRS, CHAIRMAN
APPROPRIATIONS
JOINT COMMITTEE ON THE ECONOMIC REPORT, CHAIRMAN
SUBCOMMITTEES OF APPROPRIATIONS COMMITTEE:
INDEPENDENT OFFICES, CHAIRMAN
INTERIOR
ARMED SERVICES
AGRICULTURE
DISTRICT OF COLUMBIA

United States Senate
WASHINGTON, D. C.

June 27, 1950

Dear Mr. President:

    This is a hasty note to confirm in writing the message I shall presently telephone to Mr. Connelly for your information.

    The testimony which is being offered to the Appropriations Committee indicates that although for more than a year Central Intelligence has been reporting evidence of aggressive preparations in North Korea, no steps have been taken under the Mutual Defense Assistance Program to provide South Korea with any equipment capable of use in resisting an invasion from the north.

    The first appropriation to support the Mutual Defense Assistance Program was made in October 1949, but no agreement was made with South Korea until January 1950. As early as December 1949, and on several occasions since, the government of South Korea made request for the delivery of air fighters and other military equipment. None was delivered.

    Admiral Hillenkoeter, Head of Central Intelligence, presented the record of his reports, which were sent, according to his testimony, to the President, the National Security Council, the Secretary of State, the Secretary of Defense, and others. All of these reports, some of which he read to us, clearly showed preparations for attack. On June 20th, a specific report was submitted, the Admiral testified, warning that the preparations for invasion were in high tempo.

    This morning, Mr. Ohly of the State Department told the Committee that the only material shipped to South Korea was that which was intended primarily for internal security, not for resistance to an invasion from the north. General Lemnitzer testified that only a few hundred dollars worth of equipment of any kind has been sent under the Mutual Assistance Program. Except for the internal security equipment in South Korea is that which was left when our troops departed.

    You will see that the testimony which I have sketchily

The President - Page Two.

summarized will undoubtedly be used to support a charge that our policy was soft toward the Communists in Korea.

If I may make the suggestion, it seems to me that now is the time for the President to declare that it will be the policy of the United States government to veto the admission of Communist China to the Security Council of the United Nations.

Sincerely

Joseph C. O'Mahoney

The President
The White House

Illustration 8c

June 28, 1950

Dear Joe:

I certainly did appreciate your letter of the twenty-seventh.

You understand that our arming of Korea was only for internal security and to prevent raids across the Northern border, as I stated in the release which was made yesterday after consultation with a number of Congressional leaders.

I think we have now covered the situation to a point where we will either get results or we will have to go all-out to maintain our position.

I can't tell you how very much I appreciated your thoughtfulness in sending me the information contained in your letter.

Sincerely yours,

HARRY S. TRUMAN

Honorable Joseph C. O'Mahoney
United States Senate
Washington, D. C.

Courtesy Harry S Truman Library.

Illustration 8d: A Memo to the President

Information, advice and recommendations are usually forwarded to presidents via memoranda of which the following is a good example.

> THE WHITE HOUSE
> WASHINGTON
>
> ~~SECRET~~   January 27, 1965
>
> MEMORANDUM FOR THE PRESIDENT:
>
> Re: Basic Policy in Vietnam
>
> 1. Bob McNamara and I have asked for the meeting with you at 11:30 in order to have a very private discussion of the basic situation in Vietnam. In a way it is unfortunate that we are meeting the morning after a minor coup, because that is not the present point. All of us agree with Alexis Johnson that nothing should be done on that until we have particular recommendations from Saigon (though at that point we may well want to urge Taylor and Johnson to make the best of the matter and not try to undo it).
>
> 2. What we want to say to you is that both of us are now pretty well convinced that our current policy can lead only to disastrous defeat. What we are doing now, essentially, is to wait and hope for a stable government. Our December directives make it very plain that wider action against the Communists will not take place unless we can get such a government. In the last six weeks that effort has been unsuccessful, and Bob and I are persuaded that there is no real hope of success in this area unless and until our own policy and priorities change.
>
> 3. The underlying difficulties in Saigon arise from the spreading conviction there that the future is without hope for anti-Communists. More and more the good men are covering their flanks and avoiding executive responsibility for firm anti-Communist policy. Our best friends have been somewhat discouraged by our own inactivity in the face of major attacks on our own installations. The Vietnamese know just as well as we do that the Viet Cong are gaining in the countryside. Meanwhile, they see the enormous power of the United States withheld, and they get little sense of firm and active U. S. policy. They feel that we are unwilling to take serious risks. In one sense, all of this is outrageous, in the light of all that we have done and all that we are ready to do if they will only pull up their socks. But it is a fact -- or at least so McNamara and I now think.
>
> ~~SECRET~~

Illustration 8d

SECRET — 2 —

4. The uncertainty and lack of direction which pervades the Vietnamese authorities are also increasingly visible among our own people, even the most loyal and determined. Overtones of this sentiment appear in our cables from Saigon, and one can feel them also among our most loyal staff officers here in Washington. The basic directive says that we will not go further until there is a stable government, and no one has much hope that there is going to be a stable government while we sit still. The result is that we are pinned into a policy of first aid to squabbling politicos and passive reaction to events we do not try to control. Or so it seems.

5. Bob and I believe that the worst course of action is to continue in this essentially passive role which can only lead to eventual defeat and an invitation to get out in humiliating circumstances.

6. *We see two alternatives.* The *first* is to use our military power in the Far East and to force a change of Communist policy. The *second* is to deploy all our resources along a track of negotiation, aimed at salvaging what little can be preserved with no major addition to our present military risks. Bob and I tend to favor the first course, but we believe that both should be carefully studied and that alternative programs should be argued out before you.

7. Both of us understand the very grave questions presented by any decision of this sort. We both recognize that the ultimate responsibility is not ours. Both of us have fully supported your unwillingness, in earlier months, to move out of the middle course. We both agree that every effort should still be made to improve our operations on the ground and to prop up the authorities in South Vietnam as best we can. But we are both convinced that none of this is enough, and that the time has come for harder choices.

8. You should know that Dean Rusk does not agree with us. He does not quarrel with our assertion that things are going very badly and that the situation is unraveling. He does not assert that this deterioration can be stopped. What he does say is that the consequences of both escalation and withdrawal are so bad that we simply must find a way of making our present policy work. This would be good if it was possible. Bob and I do not think it is.

9. A topic of this magnitude can only be opened for initial discussion this morning, but McNamara and I have reached the point where our obligations to you simply do not permit us to administer our present directives in silence and let you think we see real hope in them.

McG. B.

SECRET

Illustration 8e: A Memo from the President

Presidents exercise direction and control of government via memoranda, as illustrated by the following.

PSF
Neutrality

THE WHITE HOUSE
WASHINGTON

PRIVATE

March 28, 1939.

MEMORANDUM FOR

    THE SECRETARY OF STATE
    THE UNDERSECRETARY OF STATE

You have doubtless read No. 202, March twenty-seventh, from Peck in Chungking referring to the cash and carry provisions of the Pittman bill. I think that before the bill gets too far it should be called to the attention of Senator Pittman that while the cash and carry plan works all right in the Atlantic, it works all wrong in the Pacific.

The more I think the problem through, the more I am convinced that the existing Neutrality Act should be repealed in toto without any substitute.

I do not mind if you pass this word to Senator Pittman and the leaders.

F. D. R.

Illustration 8f: Minutes of a Cabinet Meeting

Several of the recent presidents—notably Eisenhower, Ford, and Carter—made extensive use of the cabinet as a forum for exchanging views and information. The following minutes of an Eisenhower cabinet meeting illustrate this use of the cabinet.

~~CONFIDENTIAL~~

MINUTES OF CABINET MEETING

July 18, 1958
8:35 A. M. -- 10:08 A. M.

The following were present:

President Eisenhower

VP Nixon
Sec. Dulles
Sec. Anderson
Sec. McElroy
   and Deputy Sec. Quarles
Atty Gen Rogers
PMG Summerfield
Sec. Seaton
Sec. Benson
Sec. Weeks
Sec. Mitchell
Sec. Folsom

Director Stans
Deputy Director John Patterson
   (for Gov. Hoegh)
Dr. Saulnier

Gov. Adams
Gen. Persons
Mr. Robert Gray

Mr. Allen Dulles, CIA
Mr. Abbott Washburn, USIA
Mr. John A. McCone
Gen. Twining

Adm. Strauss
Gordon Gray
Mr. Larson
Dr. Killian, in part
Mr. Siciliano
Mr. Randall
Mr. Martin
Mr. Jack Anderson, in part
Mr. Hagerty, in part
Mrs. Wheaton
Gov. Pyle
Dr. Hauge
Gen. Goodpaster
Mr. Patterson
Mr. Minnich

<u>Mid East Situation</u> - Sec. Dulles first recounted a statement by Stalin in 1924 to the effect that the Communist road to victory over the West lies in nationalism among the peoples of Asia and Africa. He then noted three things inherently advantageous to the Communists, or disadvantages to the

~~CONFIDENTIAL~~

Cabinet Minutes, July 18, 1958 - page 2

Free World, as regards the Mid East: (1) the fact that the existence of Israel has served as a stimulant to Arab nationalism, especially since the Russians in 1955 switched from supporting Israel to direct aid to the Arabs; (2) the existence of anti-Western feeling which Russians can exploit but we cannot in view of the interests we and our allies have there; and (3) the effective demagoguery of Nasser is something the Russians encourage and exploit, whereas we in good conscience cannot do so.

Although the United States tried for a time to work with Nasser, said the Secretary, it became impossible to do so once Egypt accepted Russian arms in large quantity.

The Secretary called attention to the publication by us recently of approximately 125 specific acts by Syria to aid the rebels in Lebanon during the two months of what was originally a non-serious internal difference. This activity was considerably reduced following Hammarskjold's discussion with Nasser and the establishment of the UN observation team. Consequently, and since the team is very limited in size, it has not reported any evidence of further Syrian activity.

Sec. Dulles told how President Chamoun had some weeks ago sounded out what would be the US response to a request for assistance, and he was informed by us that aid would be forthcoming in any desperate situation. Prior to the Iraq coup it appeared that Chamoun would not have to request aid. The coup, however, frightened President Chamoun and Hussein as to their own positions and they called on the United States and the United Kingdom for assistance in sustaining their governments.

The President's decision to send aid, Mr. Dulles said, was not made under any illusion it would solve the problem; rather, it resulted from the awareness that failure to act would cause many other small nations to mistrust US policy and they would not be able to count on US assistance in time of crisis, hence they would be less willing to make a firm stand for freedom.

Mr. Dulles said that, although the United States went immediately to the Security Council to ask for a stronger UN force in Lebanon so that we might withdraw, the UN outcome is uncertain particularly because many nations have not accepted the fact of Syrian intrigue and look upon the Lebanon struggle as an internal one in which outside nations should not intervene. Mr. Dulles cited specific instances of intrigue originating in Cairo.

CONFIDENTIAL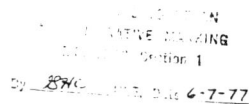

Cabinet Minutes, July 18, 1958 - page 3

In estimating the seriousness of the situation, Sec. Dulles said that one must estimate the relative power of the United States and Russia as a basis for estimating whether Russia would take steps likely to lead to war. He stated that our present estimate is that the United States is now in a very strong position, perhaps stronger than in years to come when Russia has operational missiles.

Regarding the Baghdad Pact, Sec. Dulles recalled that the United States had not favored Iraqi membership in the Pact, hence the United States had not joined in it. He believed that the strain placed upon the Iraqi Government by membership in the Pact may have considerably contributed to that government's downfall. He did not see much chance of retrieving the Iraqi situation since there appeared to be very few troops or people loyal to the old government.

Mr. Dulles then directed attention to oil resources, concerning which he believed there would be no problem so long as alternative resources are held in Iran, Kuwait and Saudi Arabia. Iraq would need oil revenues. He indicated also that none of the threats against pipelines crossing unfriendly area have been carried out. He stated that the Subcommittee on oil is keeping abreast of the situation.

In response to Secretaries Benson, Weeks and Anderson, Mr. Dulles noted that India stands opposed to our action whereas Pakistan supports it, that Secretary General Hammarskjold had been unable to persuade the Swedish Government to alter its policy to one of support for us, that the Baghdad Pact was not constituted in such a way that it could properly intervene to retrieve the Iraq situation. Mr. Anderson was most concerned with the rapidity of the coup and the absence of indications in advance of its happening. He also felt that other nations would be concerned with this and would be very worried as to their own future after US troops leave the area.

The President felt that our major effort must be one of getting our whole propaganda effort into a stronger position, which would require much money and a larger mutual security program. In the meantime, he believed Turkey and Iran must be strengthened, as also Lebanon and Jordan and perhaps also Libya, Tunis, and the Sudan. He repeated his emphasis on the need for money for the mutual security program so as to get on with the job of rehabilitating our position in the area.

CONFIDENTIAL

~~CONFIDENTIAL~~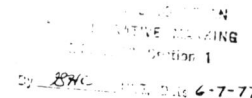

Cabinet Minutes, July 18, 1958 - page 4

Mr. Allen Dulles recalled that the CIA had pinpointed more than a year ago the movement against the Iraq Government and had warned last March about the precarious situation in Iraq, Jordan, and Lebanon, that the President had directed an intensive review be made but that it was almost impossible to predict the exact timing of any coup. He mentioned several happenings which had probably served to trigger the coup earlier than planned.

Economic Developments - Dr. Saulnier presented a set of charts showing the course of this recession month by month since the downturn began last July and as compared with the earlier cycles of 1953, 1948, 1937 and 1929. Typical of all the indices, industrial production had gone down from July through April but had turned upwards in May and June. Regarding manufacturers' inventories, he stated that signs of a pick-up are now beginning to appear after a long down trend. He expected to see a very fast rate of recovery when the inventory trend gets turned around and new orders by durable goods manufacturers start moving upwards more rapidly.

Dr. Saulnier spoke at length on the possible psychological impact of the economy on the Mid East situation but said that as yet he could find no signs of any impact. The President ironically compared this with the reverse situation last Fall when the public was deeply agitated with the advent of Sputnik while the Government attempted to keep feelings on an even keel. Now, the people show no awareness of the seriousness of the Mid East crisis which has been of such great concern to Government officials.

L. A. Minnich, Jr.

Copies to:
  Mrs. Whitman (2)
  Mr. Robert Gray
  Mr. Minnich

~~CONFIDENTIAL~~

Illustration 8g: Memorandum: Remarks to the Cabinet

Presidential remarks to the cabinet are intended to steer government. Their condensation in memo form become part of an administration's papers.

MEMORANDUM   November 23, 1963

SUBJECT: Remarks to the Cabinet -- 2:30 P.M. --
            The Cabinet Room, November 23, 1963

1. The President is dead.
   We must keep the business of this government moving.

2. None of us in this room can really express the sadness we all feel. Yet we have work to do. We must do it.

3. President Kennedy had confidence in you. He relied on you. I have confidence in you. I rely on you.

4. We, you and I, have the immediate task of letting the people know the nation will not falter, or hesitate -- but even in its grief, moves ahead with assurance.

   I need each of you to tell me what the problems are that press in on you. I want you to speak <u>frankly</u>, <u>candidly</u>.

5. The death of a leader is never an easy time for the people he leads. The death of a GREAT leader like President Kennedy magnifies the anxiety of a nation.

   With your help, the transition from President to President will go forward with dispatch -- and effectiveness -- as it must, as our responsibilities demand that it do.

6. I want you all to stay on. I need you.

Illustration 8h: Minutes of an NSC Meeting

Like cabinet meetings, NSC meetings are captured in memoranda of the minutes.

~~TOP SECRET~~

December 21, 1956

MEMORANDUM

SUBJECT: Discussion at the 307th Meeting
of the National Security Council,
Friday, December 21, 1956

Present at the 307th NSC meeting were the President of the United States, presiding; the Secretary of State; the Secretary of Defense; and the Director, Office of Defense Mobilization. Also present were the Secretary of the Treasury; the Attorney General; the Special Assistant to the President for Disarmament; the Director, Bureau of the Budget; the Chairman, Atomic Energy Commission; the Federal Civil Defense Administrator; the Director, U. S. Information Agency; the Under Secretary of State; the Deputy Secretary of Defense; Assistant Secretary of State Bowie; Assistant Secretaries of Defense Gray and McNeil; the Deputy Director, Bureau of the Budget; the Secretary of the Army; the Secretary of the Navy; the Secretary of the Air Force; the Chairman, Joint Chiefs of Staff; the Chief of Staff, U. S. Army; the Chief of Naval Operations; the Chief of Staff, U. S. Air Force; the Commandant, U. S. Marine Corps; the Director of Central Intelligence; the Deputy Assistant to the President; Special Assistant to the President Jackson; the White House Staff Secretary; the Executive Secretary, NSC; and the Deputy Executive Secretary, NSC. Also present, to assist in the presentation by the Department of Defense, were Colonel Carey Randall and Mr. Karl G. Harr, Jr..

There follows a summary of the discussion at the meeting and the main points taken.

U. S. MILITARY PROGRAM FOR FY 1958

The Special Assistant to the President informed the Council that the only item on the agenda for this meeting was a discussion of the U. S. military program for FY 1958. He then called upon Secretary Wilson, who in turn stated that Admiral Radford would make the initial statement with respect to this military program.

Admiral Radford said that he proposed to open the presentation with a brief review of the background of military thinking and estimates of the military situation as these two considerations bore on the Defense Department budget. He said he would start with the

DECLASSIFIED
Authority MR 78-99 #4
By bc Date 7/15/81

~~TOP SECRET~~

Illustration 8h

TOP SECRET

Joint Chiefs of Staff review initiated by an order of the Secretary of Defense in August 1953. The subsequent special study and review came up with certain important conclusions:

    (1) The primary national responsibility was to ensure the survival of the United States as a free nation with a viable free economy.

    (2) The principal threat to the United States was the long-range Soviet objective of destroying democracy and democratic institutions throughout the world.

    (3) The most critical military factors in defense against this Soviet threat were the air defense of the continental United States and maintenance of our retaliatory capabilities against the Soviet Union.

    (4) At the present time our military posture was seriously overextended.

    (5) In order to rectify this overextension, it would be necessary to curtail the deployment of U. S. forces overseas.

    (6) If such redeployment was carried out, the Joint Chiefs believed it to be essential that the national objectives of the United States short of a general war should be clearly stated so that our friends would be assured and our enemies made perfectly clear as to our intentions.

    (7) The Chiefs believed that the United States must significantly improve its intelligence effort.

Admiral Radford then stated that the foregoing conclusions had since that time constituted the broad basis of our military planning. In addition, however, in 1954 and in 1955 large-scale studies were undertaken with the objective of analyzing the effect on our military posture of the rapid development of technology. Examples of such studies were those of Mr. Robert Sprague and of the committee headed by Dr. Killian. The studies by Mr. Sprague and Dr. Killian's committee had made strong recommendations in favor of strengthening the continental defense of the United States. The Joint Chiefs of Staff, however, have reserved their opinion as to the ratio of resources to be devoted on the one hand to strengthening our continental defense and on the other to competing demands on these resources. They regarded this ratio as one requiring very delicate balancing.

TOP SECRET

TOP SECRET

By January 1956, continued Admiral Radford, it became evident that another full-scale review of our military program would be necessary. Such a re-examination was accordingly commenced by the Joint Chiefs of Staff on the orders of the Secretary of Defense. After the meeting of the Joint Chiefs of Staff in Puerto Rico, it was concluded that our basic military program remained generally valid, but that to maintain this program over the future years would certainly involve increasing costs because of such factors as missile development, development of continental defense measures, and the introduction of new weapons. Nevertheless, the Joint Chiefs estimated that our annual military expenditure up to 1960 could be held to a level of approximately $38 to $40 billion. Admiral Radford said that he personally had felt that this level was somewhat on the low side. The Chiefs also estimated that our military defense assistance program would require expenditures of approximately $3 billion a year, although under certain circumstances this amount could be increased by as much as $1 or $2 billion a year.

In this review, as in the earlier review of 1953, the Joint Chiefs reaffirmed their view as to the desirability of reducing our overseas commitments and deployments, although they pointed out that this would be next to impossible in the Far East and would be very difficult to accomplish without undermining NATO if the redeployment of U. S. forces occurred too rapidly. In any event, in this review the Joint Chiefs of Staff strongly recommended a full-scale review of our military aid programs.

The Joint Chiefs of Staff concluded in March and April of 1956 that, in spite of the fact that our own U. S. military posture was generally adequate, the military posture of the free world generally was deteriorating. Unless this deterioration were arrested, the results would put the United States in a very dangerous situation in the future. The Chiefs also stressed the need for vigorous political, economic and psychological courses of action, on grounds that we must assure the world that the United States was prepared to act in a timely fashion in the event of war in order to restore and bolster the morale of the free world.

Admiral Radford then noted that since this report of the spring of 1956, world events had moved quickly and not always in a direction which had been predicted. As examples he cited tension in the satellites and the crisis in the Middle East. These events have led the Joint Chiefs of Staff to recommend certain actions designed to achieve our national security objectives. After briefly referring to these measures, Admiral Radford said that in conclusion he wanted to emphasize once again that both now and in the future the costs of our military program would continue to rise. In his view it was not possible at one and the same time to maintain a fixed level of forces and a fixed budgetary level. It was

TOP SECRET

Illustration 8h

accordingly necessary for us to lower the level of our forces while at the same time assuring them increased effectiveness. He believed that this great problem could be solved if we kept ever in mind a basic objective and a basic fact. First, our objective of ensuring the survival of the United States and its free economy, and second, that the principal threat to the United States remained Russian-dominated world Communism.

At the conclusion of Admiral Radford's introductory remarks, Secretary Wilson said that General Taylor would outline the program of the Army for FY 1958. General Taylor stated that it was his proposal to present the kind of Army that could be attained at the end of FY 1958 within a budget of $9 billion. Such an Army would consist of 1,000,000 men in 17 reorganized divisions, etc., etc.. With the use of a chart, General Taylor discussed the five major categories of which this Army would consist--namely, overseas forces, strategic reserves, anti-aircraft defense forces for the United States, reserve forces, and forces for the support of our allies. These five categories, he pointed out, would be backed up by support forces deployed within the continental United States. Thereafter, General Taylor, with the assistance of a chart, briefly outlined the major Army unit forces deployment planned for FY 1958, after which he described in some detail the quality and qualifications of these forces. He added a warning that the Army could not afford to neglect so-called conventional arms and equipment.

In closing his report, General Taylor summed up assets and liabilities for the Army program as follows: With respect to assets, he indicated that the FY 1958 program would certainly enhance the combat effectiveness of the U. S. Army. A second asset would be the improved quality of our reserve forces. In the category of liabilities, General Taylor pointed out that the Army divisions would be reduced by two, and that the growing obsolescence factor was very serious. An additional liability was represented by the deterioration of our anti-aircraft capabilities for the air defense of the United States.

Upon the conclusion of General Taylor's presentation, Secretary Wilson called on Admiral Burke to describe the Navy Department program for FY 1958.

Admiral Burke remarked that the Navy had been working on this 1958 budget for a whole year past. The Navy Department proposed to request approximately $10.9 billion in new authorizations in its FY 1958 budget--a sum slightly less than that in the current Navy budget. Force levels for the Navy would be about the same as in FY 1957. Despite steady technological advances, Admiral Burke pointed out that the budget for research and development in the Navy had been reduced in favor of additional aircraft procurement and shipbuilding.

In the course of discussing the Navy's aircraft procurement program, Admiral Burke indicated that 1257 new aircraft would be ordered for the Navy in the course of FY 1958, a figure less than the figure for FY 1956 or FY 1957. Admiral Burke concluded his discussion of the Navy program by a detailed statement on the shipbuilding and conversion programs. This portion of his report was accompanied by a chart entitled "Combat Effective Ships, 1956, vs. Present Planned Strength" (over a period of five years).

At the conclusion of Admiral Burke's comments, Secretary Wilson asked General Pate if he wished to report on the Marine Corps program. General Pate replied that Admiral Burke had spoken for him, and that he had nothing to add. Secretary Wilson then called on General Twining to present the Air Force program for FY 1958.

General Twining spoke first from two charts. One was entitled "Comparison of Programs"; the second was entitled "New Obligating Authority and Service Obligations for FY 1957 and FY 1958". General Twining pointed out that the Air Force program called for a request on the Congress for $17.7 billion in new obligational authority. He indicated that this was about $3 billion less than the Air Force would have wished to ask for in order to meet its estimated requirements. In general, however, the Air Force proposed to cut its program to fit the cloth. For example, there would be a cut in procurement of B-52 aircraft from about 20 to 15 or 17 a month. The objective of the B-52 procurement program called ultimately for 11 wings of this type of aircraft.

At this point General Twining turned to a discussion of the combat structure of the Air Force. This indicated a reduction in program combat wings from a total of 137 to a total of 128. The reduction would occur in the categories of fighter aircraft and tactical bombers. General Twining believed that this cut could be justified by the expected increase in firing power. He also pointed out that each B-52 wing would contain over 40 aircraft instead of 32, as originally proposed. In addition, General Twining indicated that the intermediate-range ballistic missile would be put into the inventory of weapons in 1960. This would be followed shortly thereafter by the addition of the intercontinental ballistic missile to the inventory. General Twining concluded his remarks with the observation that the presently programmed Air Force for FY 1958 represented the very minimum force that the United States should have in order to protect the security of the United States and to carry out the missions assigned to the Air Force by NSC and JCS policies.

Secretary Wilson then called on Assistant Secretary of Defense Gray for a brief analysis of the MDA program. Secretary Gray made his report on the basis of a series of charts entitled "Status Report on Military Assistance Programs". Included in his remarks

Illustration 8h

TOP SECRET

was a statement of the five major purposes of our military assistance program. He pointed out that in FY 1958 there would be a request upon the Congress by way of new obligational authority in the amount of $2.45 billion. He predicted that expenditure for that fiscal year would probably amount to about $2.6 billion. Secretary Gray referred to the embarrassing carry-over from previous fiscal years, but pointed out that the carry-over for this year was the least in size in all recent years. The total investment to date, from FY 1950 through FY 1957, in the MDA programs amounted to $22.4 billion.

At the conclusion of Secretary Gray's report, the President turned to Secretary Brucker and asked him the following question: "Are you confident that the Army program previously described is the best Army program for the money?" Secretary Brucker replied in the affirmative, and said that the Army program for FY 1958 represented the best balanced program which could be gotten for the money. The one element, he said, which we wish to preserve is the combat edge, the razor edge. Secretary Brucker stated that he was opposed to simply dropping the personnel who could be saved in the proposed cutting of Army divisions from 19 to 17. He wanted this personnel to be enrolled in other extremely important Army units. Secretary Brucker also expressed anxiety over the cost of the upkeep of the Army plant, and emphasized the need for better housing for Army personnel in the near future.

In reply, the President stated his agreement that the Army is now producing better balanced forces than it had in the past; but what really concerned him, continued the President, was the correct balance between the proposed strength of our Army and the general economic strength and well-being of the country. This is the great decision which must be made, and the President said he judged that Secretary Brucker thought the proposed FY 1958 budget for the Army represented the best balance that we can devise. Secretary Brucker again replied that the program represented the best balance possible under the circumstance. He confessed that some of his people were unhappy over certain aspects of the proposed FY 1958 budget, but that he, Secretary Brucker, thought it was OK. The President said that, in short, Secretary Brucker believed that to go higher by way of budget for the Army would entail serious risk of inflation and damage to the nation's economy. Secretary Brucker agreed.

The President then turned to Secretary Thomas and asked him to address himself to the same questions with respect to the Navy that the President had just put to Secretary Brucker respecting the Army.

Secretary Thomas indicated that he would like to state briefly the philosophy behind the proposed FY 1958 budget for the Navy. In this connection he mentioned the President's statement

TOP SECRET

of last fall to the effect that while we must never put dollars above defense, we must at the same time have a strong and free economy. Secretary Thomas said that he stood firmly behind this philosophy, and added his belief that the proposed Navy budget represented the best balance that was possible. He added that he sincerely believed that this country had much more powerful military forces than many of the critics believe, and he paid warm tribute to the President and to the policies of the Administration.

Secretary Thomas then pointed out that the Navy had faced two very basic problems in the course of formulating its FY 1958 budget. The first of these stemmed from the Navy's worldwide commitments, as a result of which ships of the Navy had to be stationed all over the world. Secondly, the Navy was currently going through a transition greater than anything known in the past. The Navy was moving all at once from conventional to nuclear power and from conventional to nuclear weapons. The costs were obviously bound to be much greater. In conclusion, Secretary Thomas stated that in his opinion the proposed Navy budget was a very good and very acceptable program, even though, of course, it involved a calculated risk. Indeed, said Secretary Thomas, if he had had his own way he might have cut another billion or two from the Navy budget. But, he said to the President, the Navy was the most powerful Navy in the world, and that the proposed budget would keep the Navy in just that position.

The President then called on Secretary Quarles to answer the same questions. Secretary Quarles pointed out how carefully the Air Force budget had been worked over. He said that it represented the best balance which could be attained within the framework of the proposed 1958 budget. The program put first things first in terms of the missions of the Air Force. Though there were clearly to be fewer wings in the Air Force, the Air Force itself would actually be stronger. Nevertheless, Secretary Quarles warned that the Air Force program was marginal in certain respects. After the exercise at the National Security Council meeting of yesterday, Secretary Quarles said that he had come away with certain misgivings. (The reference by Secretary Quarles was to the report of the Net Evaluation Subcommittee of the NSC on the net capabilities of the USSR to damage the continental United States.) Secretary Quarles had wondered whether we were doing quite all we should do in the light of the terrible threat depicted in yesterday's report. Despite this, Secretary Quarles said, he did not question the proposed 1958 budget, and he assured the President that the Air Force would give the budget loyal support and make the best of it.

The President inquired of Secretary Quarles what he thought he could do right now to reduce the appalling threat depicted yesterday in the report of the Net Evaluation Subcommittee. Secretary Quarles said that so far as he could see, there was nothing that one

Illustration 8h

could do to reduce the threat markedly. Nevertheless, it might be wise to increase our air defense forces and to allocate larger funds to the building up of our own strategic striking force. Secretary Quarles said he was not actually recommending the above course of action, but found the problem troublesome.

The President stated firmly that the only area in which he disagreed with Secretary Quarles was that the President did not think that the suggested courses of action would markedly reduce the threat of the holocaust described yesterday. In short, if we do not now have enough military strength to deter the Soviet Union from nuclear attack, the President said he could not be sure that 20 times as much military strength would succeed in deterring the Soviets.

The President then said that he had one more question to address to General Twining. How many missiles can be carried in a B-52? General Twining replied that two of the largest missiles were within the capability of the B-52 to carry.

Secretary Wilson then inquired whether he might call on Assistant Secretary of Defense McNeil for an analysis of the overall figures for the Defense Department budget for FY 1958. With the assistance of charts, Secretary McNeil turned first to the new obligational authority, the direct obligations, and the estimated expenditures for FY 1958. He pointed out that the total new obligational authority sought in FY 1956 was $34.2 billion. In FY 1957 this amount had risen to $36.7 billion. The request for new obligational authority for FY 1958 would be $38.3 billion. Turning to expenditures, Secretary McNeil indicated that the total for FY 1956 had been $35.7 billion; for FY 1957, $36 billion; and the estimate for FY 1958 was $37.8 billion.

After further detailed analysis by Secretary McNeil, the President stated that he wanted to make sure that at some point or other in the future the country would at last be able to achieve a levelling-off period on these expenditures and not face continually mounting costs.

Secretary Dulles inquired whether the over-all figures given by Secretary McNeil included or excluded the figures earlier given by Secretary Gray covering the military assistance programs. When Secretary McNeil indicated that his figures did not include MDAP, Secretary Dulles emphasized that this fact should be made crystal clear when Congress was briefed on the FY 1958 budget.

At this point the President inquired whether there were any other questions, and directed his inquiry particularly to Secretary Humphrey. Secretary Humphrey replied that he thought it

TOP SECRET

unfortunate that everyone in the United States could not have heard this Council briefing. He believed that the results showed a marvelous coordination and teamwork. In fact, this was the "finest budget performance" since the Administration had come into power. The President replied facetiously that Secretary Humphrey had made his own speech for him. The President added that the proposed budget did represent some backing up in our hope that we could go along at an expenditure level of about $35 billion annually for the Defense Department program. Actually we were now pretty close to $40 billion, but the President confessed that he did not see how this latter amount could be reduced.

Secretary Wilson commented that other Executive departments' and agencies' expenditures had gone up by a comparatively larger ratio than had those of the Department of Defense. The President replied that this was no valid comparison. The other departments and agencies had done their best, just as had the Department of Defense. Secretary Wilson then added that he thought that by and large the FY 1958 Department of Defense budget was a good budget and that resources had been pretty well allocated among the Services. The preparation of the budget had been characterized by extraordinarily good teamwork.

Governor Stassen asked to be heard, and stated his agreement with the President that any small modification upward of the proposed budget would probably not greatly enhance our defensive capabilities against the Soviet Union. What we must really try hard to do was to open up the Soviet Union. The forthcoming year would provide the United States with the best opportunity to date to open up the Soviet Union. On the other hand, if we tried to drastically raise the levels of the U. S. defense budget, the Soviet Union might be led to conclude that war was inevitable and act accordingly.

The President stated that this reminded him that he wished to disagree with Admiral Radford's statement at the beginning of the discussion, that the likelihood of war was now increasing. On the contrary, in the President's opinion the USSR had taken a worse beating lately than at any time since 1945. Unless Admiral Radford meant that war might come from a miscalculation, he was therefore in disagreement with the point of view that the danger of war was increasing.

Admiral Radford replied that in part he had in mind the risk of miscalculation leading to war. He added that if the Soviets continue to have further troubles with their satellites, the United States would have to make up its mind what course of action to follow. The President said he was not impressed by this argument. He believed that the Soviets would be much more likely to worry about having to solidify themselves against satellite unrest. In present circumstances they were not likely to stick their necks out.

- 9 -

TOP SECRET

Secretary Dulles stated, apropos of this exchange of views, that in his opinion we had been witnessing a very drastic and very dramatic deterioration of the position of the Soviet Union in the course of the last two years. The men in the Kremlin do not now exert anything like the influence they exerted two years ago, either over the National Communist Parties outside the Soviet bloc or over the Soviet satellites themselves. Moreover, we can even discern in the Soviet Union itself a rising demand for greater freedom and a more liberal policy. All of this added up to a defeat and a setback for the Soviet rulers. In one sense, of course, this was a highly encouraging development for us. On the other hand, the setbacks of the last two years might call for a terrific effort by the Kremlin to achieve some kind of offsetting success. To achieve this the Soviets might therefore be willing to take risks which could be very dangerous to the free world, since they would be risks born of desperation.

The President said the only comment he had on this point was that there was no such thing as a success for any country involved in a major war today. Secretary Dulles expressed agreement, but pointed out the danger that the Soviets might be willing to run risks at the present time that they would have been unwilling to run two years ago. The President said that of course we must remain on the alert every single minute.

Secretary Wilson then suggested that, inasmuch as the budget cycle for FY 1959 would commence soon, it would be desirable to use the FY 1958 personnel strengths, force levels and dollar figures as the basis for planning for the FY 1959 military program and budget.

TOP SECRET

Modifications could subsequently be made with respect to this planning basis if circumstances so dictated. The President indicated approval of Secretary Wilson's suggestion. Secretary Wilson followed this suggestion with a question to the President as to whether he thought that the FY 1958 military program, as it had been presented in the morning's discussion, was generally satisfactory. The President replied that the Defense Department program for FY 1958 was acceptable to him.

At the conclusion of the meeting, the President warmly thanked those who had briefed him and the Council on the military program for FY 1958.

The National Security Council:

    a. Noted and discussed the U. S. military program for Fiscal Year 1958, as presented orally by the Secretary of Defense, the Chairman of the Joint Chiefs of Staff, the Service Secretaries and the Chiefs of Staff, and Assistant Secretaries of Defense Gray and McNeil.

    b. Agreed that the U. S. military program for Fiscal Year 1958 as presented was consistent with national security policy objectives.

    c. Noted that for initial planning purposes in Fiscal Year 1959, the Department of Defense will utilize as ceilings the over-all force levels contained in the approved Fiscal Year 1958 budget, and a planned ceiling of $39 billion for both new obligational authority and expenditures.

    NOTE: In approving the above actions the President stated that, except in the event of some unforeseen critical emergency of an international or economic character, he does not intend to request from the Congress during his term in office new obligational authority for the Department of Defense above $39 billion in any Fiscal Year.

    The actions in b and c above and the above statement by the President subsequently transmitted to the Secretary of Defense and the Director, Bureau of the Budget, for information and appropriate action.

S. Everett Gleason

S. Everett Gleason

TOP SECRET

Illustration 8i: President's Presidential Press Plan

The following press plan reveals the role that staff plays in structuring situations for presidents and outlining proposed courses of action.

THE WHITE HOUSE
WASHINGTON

April 10, 1975

MEETING WITH THE SPEAKER AND MINORITY LEADER RHODES
Thursday, April 10, 1975
3:45 – 4:15 p.m. (30 minutes)
The Oval Office

From: Max L. Friedersdorf

I. PURPOSE

　　To brief the leaders on the Vietnam situation and give them a preview of your speech tonight.

II. BACKGROUND, PARTICIPANTS AND PRESS PLAN

　A. Background:

　　1. The Speaker and John Rhodes returned at 3:00 p.m. yesterday from a trip to the Peoples Republic of China and were unable to attend the bipartisan leadership meeting.

　　2. During a press conference at Andrews Air Force Base, both leaders indicated they were out of touch with the situation and desired to meet as soon as possible with the President.

　　3. Both were non-commital on further military aid until they had the opportunity to speak to the President.

　　4. Reports indicate the leaders' trip was without major incident except for some tense discussions with Chinese leaders. Rhodes mentioned a particularly heated exchange about the Mid-East.

　B. Participants:　The President
　　　　　　　　　　The Speaker
　　　　　　　　　　Rep. John Rhodes
　　　　　　　　　　Jack Marsh (staff)
　　　　　　　　　　Max Friedersdorf (staff)

　C. Press Plan:

　　　Announce to the press only – Kennerly photographs

III. TALKING POINTS

　　1. I hope your trip was worthwhile and I would be interested in hearing about it when we have more time.

2. The situation in Vietnam is very serious. I would describe it as bleak but salvagable.

3. We have 6,000 Americans in South Vietnam and we are concerned about their safety and evacuation if that becomes necessary.

4. In addition, there are from 175,000 to 200,000 South Vietnamese who have worked for the United States, and they will be the first to go if the communists take over.

5. We are also concerned about the safety of Americans if an anti-American sentiment develops among the South Vietnamese. We are maximizing our efforts to get these Americans out and are developing contigency plans of a very sensitive nature.

6. We also have a moral responsibility to try and save those South Vietnamese people who have stood with us through thick and thin.

7. I intend to give a lot stronger speech tonight than when I originally planned to address the Congress on foreign policy.

8. I will describe the seriousness of the situation in Vietnam, together with my recommendations, but the speech will also include the Middle East, NATO, detente, the PRC and trade.

9. It will be a very frank speech and I will not recommend anything that is phony. My recommendations will be justified.

10. I believe we are at a very serious turning point in world affairs. We have achieved some excellent results in foreign policy over the past 25 years, and we have suffered some setbacks.

11. If we work together we can move to greater successes. This country has a great destiny to fulfill.

12. But, we cannot achieve our goals if we engage in finger-pointing and blaming one another.

13. I am hopeful you can support my recommendations to the Congress tonight, and continue to lend me the wisdom and strength of your experience and service to the Nation.

Courtesy Gerald R. Ford Library.

Illustration 8j

Illustration 8j: Recommend Presidential Telephone Call

The following staff recommendation to President Ford to call then California Governor Ronald Reagan also illustrates the role of staff assistance.

EXECUTIVE

10/14/76

THE WHITE HOUSE
WASHINGTON

RECOMMENDED PRESIDENTIAL TELEPHONE CALL

TO: Former Governor Ronald Reagan of California
214/748-5454 (until 11:30 AM)
713/654-1234 (after 4:30 PM)

DATE: As soon as possible

FROM: Richard B. Cheney (per Stu Spencer request)

PURPOSE: To inform Governor Reagan of a major effort to attack Carter and the important role he will play.

TALKING POINTS:
1. Next week we begin our major attack on Carter by advertising and advocates (Dole, Rockefeller, and Connally).
2. I understand you have a speech opportunity on the 25th in San Diego.
3. The PFC has asked Nofzieger to work with you and he has the materials on Carter to show you tonight.
4. Enjoyed seeing you in California last week.
5. Thank you for all your help.

Date Submitted:

October 14, 1976

ACTION: _____

RECEIVED
NOV 1976

Courtesy of Gerald R. Ford Library.

Illustration 8k: Excerpts from Weekly Compilation of Presidential Documents

For those who want to keep up with developments of the presidency, no better source exists than the *Weekly Compilation of Presidential Documents*, a public document available at most libraries. It contains all major presidential statements, speeches, announcements, and decisions. The following excerpts show the variety of materials found in this rich source.

Weekly Compilation of
Presidential Documents

Monday, July 18, 1983
Volume 19—Number 28
Pages 987–1006

Illustration 8k

Index of Contents

Addresses to the Nation

Economic and fair housing issues, radio address—987

Addresses and Remarks

Minority business enterprise development, remarks on signing Executive order—997
1983 State Teachers of the Year, White House luncheon—993

Announcements

Presidential Citizens Medal to Joe Delaney—997

Appointments and Nominations

African Development Foundation, member of the Board of Directors—1000
Board for International Food and Agricultural Development, Chairman and members—1002
Commerce Department, Assistant Secretary for Communications and Information—996
Education Department, Deputy Under Secretary for Intergovernmental and Interagency Affairs—996
Federal Council on the Aging, member—999
National Advisory Committee for Juvenile Justice and Delinquency Prevention, members—993
National Mediation Board, member—992
Pension Benefit Guaranty Corporation, members of Advisory Committee and Chairman—1000
President's Advisory Council on Private Sector Initiatives, members—991
President's Committee on the National Medal of Science, members—1003
U.S. Ambassador to Mozambique—990
White House staff, Deputy Assistant to the President and Director of the Office of Planning and Evaluation—990

Bill Signings

Minority business development bill, statement—996

Communications to Congress

Fair housing legislation, message—991
International Wheat Agreement, 1971, message to the Senate—990
U.S. Government's international science and technology activities, report transmittal—988

Executive Orders

Minority business enterprise development—998

Proclamations

National Atomic Veterans' Day, 1983—1002

Resignations and Retirements

Assistant to the President for Policy Development, exchange of letters—995
Deputy Press Secretary to the President, letter—1001

Statements by the President

Caribbean Basin Initiative, House action—1000
Economic recovery—1001
International Monetary Fund—999

Statements Other Than Presidential

Economic recovery, Principal Deputy Press Secretary—997

Supplementary Materials

Acts approved by the President—1006
Checklist of White House press releases—1005
Digest of other White House announcements—1003
Nominations submitted to the Senate—1005

[A Cumulative Index to Prior Issues appears at the end of this issue.]

WEEKLY COMPILATION OF

PRESIDENTIAL DOCUMENTS

Published every Monday by the Office of the Federal Register, National Archives and Records Service, General Services Administration, Washington, D.C. 20408, the *Weekly Compilation of Presidential Documents* contains statements, messages, and other Presidential materials released by the White House during the preceding week.

The *Weekly Compilation of Presidential Documents* is published pursuant to the authority contained in the Federal Register Act (49 Stat. 500, as amended; 44 U.S.C. Ch. 15), under regulations prescribed by the Administrative Committee of the Federal Register, approved by the President (37 FR 23607; 1 CFR Part 10).

Distribution is made only by the Superintendent of Documents, Government Printing Office, Washington, D.C. 20402. The *Weekly Compilation of Presidential Documents* will be furnished by mail to domestic subscribers for $55.00 per year ($96.00 for mailing first class) and to foreign subscribers for $68.75 per year, payable to the Superintendent of Documents, Government Printing Office, Washington, D.C. 20402. The charge for a single copy is $1.50 ($1.90 for foreign mailing).

There are no restrictions on the republication of material appearing in the *Weekly Compilation of Presidential Documents*.

Differing Perspectives on the Presidency: The Individual, Decision Structure, and the System

9

Readings in the preceding chapters lead to two related conclusions. First, our system of government—the Madisonian model of 1787—is predicated on a mistrust for governmental authority, especially executive power. Second, we paradoxically ask much of our presidents but give them little in the way of formal power to accomplish their tasks.

The problems that are implied by these conclusions have been addressed by several thoughtful essayists. Their thinking has taken place along three different dimensions. Some of the work focuses on presidents as individuals: their personality and character, mental health and balance, and qualifications and preparation for office. A second line of inquiry focuses on the decisionmaking structure, stressing alternative arrangements for the purpose of improving decisionmaking. The third category of perspectives looks at the system of political authority in America, specifically its capacity for coordinated and coherent government. Selections in this concluding chapter provide examples of all three. In considering changes to the system, structure, and recruitment, it is imperative that the values and criteria addressed by Richard M. Pious in the concluding essay be considered.

Perspectives on the Individual

Presidential Character and How to Foresee It 9.1

James David Barber

To fully understand the U.S. presidency, one must have a firm appreciation for the role played by individual personalities in the decision process. In reflective moments after leaving office, most past presidents and their high-level advisors—especially those who have served in more than one administration—highlight

The Presidential Character (pp. 3-14) by James David Barber, 1972, Englewood Cliffs: Prentice-Hall, Inc. Copyright 1972 by James David Barber. Reprinted by permission.

the critical role of personality. The following is an excerpt from James David Barber's *The Presidential Character*, an effort to provide a framework for analyzing and classifying the character component of presidential personality. The Barber scheme received attention in the 1970s after Barber had accurately predicted problems in the Nixon White House on the basis of his understanding of the Nixon character. As you read this framework, you should be aware of the strengths and weaknesses of his approach and should try to speculate about the most preferred personality and character traits for presidents.

When a citizen votes for a presidential candidate he makes, in effect, a prediction. He chooses from among the contenders the one he thinks (or feels, or guesses) would be the best president. He operates in a situation of immense uncertainty. If he has a long voting history, he can recall time and time again when he guessed wrong. He listens to the commentators, the politicians, and his friends, then adds it all up in some rough way to produce his prediction and his vote. Earlier in the game, his anticipations have been taken into account, either directly in the polls and primaries or indirectly in the minds of politicians who want to nominate someone he will like. But he must choose in the midst of a cloud of confusion, a rain of phony advertising, a storm of sermons, a hail of complex issues, a fog of charisma and boredom, and a thunder of accusation and defense. In the face of this chaos, a great many citizens fall back on the past, vote their old allegiances, and let it go at that. Nevertheless, the citizen's vote says that on balance he expects Mr. X would outshine Mr. Y in the presidency.

This book is meant to help citizens and those who advise them cut through the confusion and get at some clear criteria for choosing presidents. To understand what actual presidents do and what potential presidents might do, the first need is to see the man whole—not as some abstract embodiment of civic virtue, some scorecard of issue stands, or some reflection of a faction, but as a human being like the rest of us, a person trying to cope with a difficult environment. To that task he brings his own character, his own view of the world, his own political style. None of that is new for him. If we can see the pattern he has set for his political life we can, I contend, estimate much better his pattern as he confronts the stresses and chances of the presidency.

The presidency is a peculiar office. The founding fathers left it extraordinarily loose in definition, partly because they trusted George Washington to invent a tradition as he went along. It is an institution made a piece at a time by successive men in the White House. Jefferson reached out to Congress to put together the beginnings of political parties; Jackson's dramatic force extended electoral partisanship to its mass base; Lincoln vastly expanded the administrative reach of the office; Wilson and the Roosevelts showed its rhetorical possibilities—in fact every president's mind and demeanor has left its mark on a heritage still in lively development.

But the presidency is much more than an institution. It is a focus of feelings. In general, popular feelings about politics are low-key, shallow, casual. For example, the vast majority of Americans knows virtually nothing of what Congress is doing and cares less. The presidency is different. The presidency is the focus for the most intense and persistent emotions in the American polity. The president is a symbolic leader, the one figure who draws together the people's hopes and fears for the political future. On top of all his routine duties, he has to carry that off—or fail.

Our emotional attachment to presidents shows up when one dies in office. People were not just disappointed or worried when President Kennedy was killed; people wept at the loss of a man most had never even met. Kennedy was young and charismatic—but history shows that whenever a president dies in office, heroic Lincoln or debased Harding, McKinley or Garfield, the same wave of deep emotion sweeps across the country. On the other hand, the death of an ex-president brings forth no such intense emotional reaction.

The president is the first political figure children are aware of (later they add Congress, the Court, and others, as "helpers" of the president). With some exceptions among children in deprived circumstances, the president is seen as a "benevolent leader," one who nurtures, sustains, and inspires the citizenry. Presidents regularly show up among "most admired" contemporaries and forebears, and the president is the "best known" (in the sense of sheer name recognition) person in the country. At inauguration time, even presidents elected by close margins are supported by much larger majorities than the election returns show, for people rally round as he actually assumes office. There is a similar reaction when the people see their president threatened by crisis: if he takes action, there is a favorable spurt in the Gallup poll whether he succeeds or fails.

Obviously the president gets more attention in schoolbooks, press, and television than any other politician. He is one of very few who can make news by doing good things. *His* emotional state is a matter of continual public commentary, as is the manner in which his personal and official families conduct themselves. The media bring across the president not as some neutral administrator or corporate executive to be assessed by his production, but as a special being with mysterious dimensions.

We have no king. The sentiments English children—and adults—direct to the queen have no place to go in our system but to the president. Whatever his talents—Coolidge-type or Roosevelt-type—the president is the only available object for such national-religious-monarchical sentiments as Americans possess.

The president helps people make sense of politics. Congress is a tangle of committees, the bureaucracy is a maze of agencies. The president is one man trying to do a job—a picture much more understandable to the mass of people who find themselves in the same boat. Furthermore, he is the top man. He seeks to know what is going on and set it right. So when the economy goes sour, or war drags on, or domestic violence erupts, the president is available to take the blame. Then when things go right, it seems the president must have had a hand in it. Indeed, the flow of political life is marked off by presidents: the "Eisenhower Era," the "Kennedy Years."

What all this means is that the president's *main* responsibilities reach far beyond administering the executive branch or commanding the armed forces. The White House is first and foremost a place of public leadership. That inevitably brings to bear on the president intense moral, sentimental, and quasi-religious pressures which can, if he lets them, distort his own thinking and feeling. If there is such a thing as extraordinary sanity, it is needed nowhere so much as in the White House.

Who the president is at a given time can make a profound difference in the whole thrust and direction of national politics. Since we have only one president at a time, we can never prove this by comparison, but even the most superficial speculation confirms the commonsense view that the man himself weighs heavily among other historical factors. A Wilson re-elected in 1920, a Hoover in 1932, a John F. Kennedy in 1964 would, it seems very likely, have guided the body politic along rather different paths from those their actual successors chose. Or try to imagine a Theodore Roosevelt ensconced behind today's "bully pulpit" of a presidency, or Lyndon Johnson as president in the age of McKinley. Only someone mesmerized by the lures of historical inevitability can suppose that it would have made little or no difference to government policy had Alf Landon replaced FDR in 1936, had Dewey beaten Truman in 1948, or Adlai Stevenson reigned through the 1950s. Not only would these alternative presidents have advocated different policies—they would have approached the office from very different psychological angles. It stretches credibility to think that Eugene McCarthy would have run the institution the way Lyndon Johnson did.

The burden of this book is that the crucial differences can be anticipated by an understanding of a potential president's character, his world view, and his style. This kind of prediction is not easy; well-informed observers often have guessed wrong as they watched a man step toward the White House. One thinks of Woodrow Wilson, the scholar who would bring reason to politics; of Herbert Hoover, the Great Engineer who would organize chaos into progress; of Franklin D. Roosevelt, that champion of the balanced budget; of Harry Truman, whom the office would surely overwhelm; of Dwight D. Eisenhower, militant crusader; of John F. Kennedy, who would lead beyond moralisms to achievements; of Lyndon B. Johnson, the Southern conservative; and of Richard M. Nixon, conciliator. Spotting the errors is easy. Predicting with even approximate accuracy is going to require some sharp tools and close attention in their use. But the experiment is worth it because the question is critical and because it lends itself to correction by evidence.

My argument comes in layers.

First, a president's personality is an important shaper of his presidential behavior on nontrivial matters.

Second, presidential personality is patterned. His character, world view, and style fit together in a dynamic package understandable in psychological terms.

Third, a president's personality interacts with the power situation he faces and the national "climate of expectations" dominant at the time he serves. The tuning, the resonance—or lack of it—between these external factors and his personality sets in motion the dynamic of his presidency.

Fourth, the best way to predict a president's character, world view, and style is to see how they were put together in the first place: that happened in his early life, culminating in his first independent political success.

But the core of the argument (which organizes the structure of the book) is that presidential character—the basic stance a man takes toward his presidential experience—come in four varieties. The most important thing to know about a president or candidate is where he fits among these types, defined according to (a) how active he is and (b) whether or not he gives the impression he enjoys his political life.

Let me spell out these concepts briefly before getting down to cases.

Personality Shapes Performance

I am not about to argue that once you know a president's personality you know everything. But as the cases will demonstrate, the degree and quality of a president's emotional involvement in an issue are powerful influences on how he defines the issue itself, how much attention he pays to it, which facts and persons he sees as relevant to its resolution, and, finally, what principles and purposes he associates with the issue. Every story of presidential decision-making is really two stories: an outer one in which a rational man calculates and an inner one in which an emotional man feels. The two are forever connected. Any real president is one whole man and his deeds reflect his wholeness.

As for personality, it is a matter of tendencies. It is not that one president "has" some basic characteristic that another president does not "have." That old way of treating a trait as a possession, like a rock in a basket, ignores the universality of aggressiveness, compliancy, detachment, and other human drives. We all have all of them, but in different amounts and in different combinations.

The Pattern of Character, World View, and Style

The most visible part of the pattern is style. *Style is the president's habitual way of performing his three political roles: rhetoric, personal relations, and homework.* Not to be confused with "stylishness," charisma, or appearance, style is how the president goes about doing what the office requires him to to—to speak, directly or through media, to large audiences; to deal face to face with other politicians, individually and in small, relatively private groups; and to read, write, and calculate by himself in order to manage the endless flow of details that stream onto his desk. No president can escape doing at least some of each. But there are marked differences in stylistic emphasis from president to president. The *balance* among the three style elements varies; one president may put most of himself into rhetoric, another may stress close, informal dealing, while still another may devote his energies mainly to study and cogitation. Beyond the balance, we want to see each president's peculiar habits of style, his mode of coping with and adapting to these presidential demands. For example, I think both Calvin Coolidge and John F. Kennedy were primarily rhetoricians, but they went about it in contrasting ways.

A president's *world view consists of his primary, politically relevant beliefs, particularly his conceptions of social causality, human nature, and the central moral conflicts of the time*. This is how he sees the world and his lasting opinions about what he sees. Style is his way of acting; world view is his way of seeing. Like the rest of us, a president develops over a lifetime certain conceptions of reality—how things work in politics, what people are like, what the main purposes are. These assumptions or conceptions help him make sense of his world, give some semblance of order to the chaos of existence. Perhaps most important: a man's world view affects what he pays attention to, and a great deal of politics is about paying attention. The name of the game for many politicians is not so much "Do this, do that" as it is "Look here!"

"Character" comes from the Greek word for engraving; in one sense it is what life has marked into a man's being. As used here, *character is the way the president orients himself toward life*—not for the moment, but enduringly. Character is the person's stance as he confronts experience. And at the core of character, a man confronts himself. The president's fundamental self-esteem is his prime personal resource; to defend and advance that, he will sacrifice much else he values. Down there in the privacy of his heart, does he find himself superb, or ordinary, or debased, or in some intermediate range? No president has been utterly paralyzed by self-doubt and none has been utterly free of midnight self-mockery. In between, the real presidents move out on life from positions of relative strength or weakness. Equally important are the criteria by which they judge themselves. A president who rates himself by the standard of achievement, for instance, may be little affected by losses of affection.

Character, world view, and style are abstractions from the reality of the whole individual. In every case they form an integrated pattern: the man develops a combination which makes psychological sense for him, a dynamic arrangement of motives, beliefs, and habits in the service of his need for self-esteem.

The Power Situation and "Climate of Expectations"

Presidential character resonates with the political situation the president faces. It adapts him as he tries to adapt it. The support he has from the public and interest groups, the party balance in Congress, the thrust of Supreme Court opinion together set the basic power situation he must deal with. An activist president may run smack into a brick wall of resistance, then pull back and wait for a better moment. On the other hand, a president who sees himself as a quiet caretaker may not try to exploit even the most favorable power situation. So it is the relationship between president and the political configuration that makes the system tick.

Even before public opinion polls, the president's real or supposed popularity was a large factor in his performance. Besides the power mix in Washington, the president has to deal with a national climate of expectations, the predominant needs thrust up to him by the people. There are at least three recurrent themes around which these needs are focused.

People look to the president for *reassurance*, a feeling that things will be all right, that the president will take care of his people. The psychological request is for a surcease of anxiety. Obviously, modern life in America involves considerable doses of fear, tension, anxiety, worry; from time to time, the public mood calls for a rest, a time of peace, a breathing space, a "return to normalcy."

Another theme is the demand for a *sense of progress and action*. The president ought to do something to direct the nation's course—or at least be in there pitching for the people. The president is looked to as a take-charge man, a doer, a turner of the wheels, a producer of progress—even if that means some sacrifice of serenity.

A third type of climate of expectations is the public need for a sense of *legitimacy* from, and in, the presidency. The president should be a master politician who is above politics. He should have a right to his place and a rightful way of acting in it. The respectability—even religiosity—of the office has to be protected by a man who presents himself as defender of the faith. There is more to this than dignity, more than propriety. The president is expected to personify our betterness in an inspiring way, to express in what he does and is (not just in what he says) a moral idealism which, in much of the public mind, is the very opposite of "politics."

Over time the climate of expectations shifts and changes. Wars, depressions, and other national events contribute to that change, but there also is a rough cycle, from an emphasis on action (which begins to look too "political") to an emphasis on legitimacy (the moral uplift of which creates its own strains) to an emphasis on reassurance and rest (which comes to seem like drift) and back to action again. One need not be astrological about it. The point is that the climate of expectations at any given time is the political air the president has to breathe. Relating to this climate is a large part of his task.

Predicting Presidents

The best way to predict a president's character, world view, and style is to see how he constructed them in the first place. Especially in the early stages, life is experimental; consciously or not, a person tries out various ways of defining and maintaining and raising self-esteem. He looks to his environment for clues as to who he is and how well he is doing. These lessons of life slowly sink in: certain self-images and evaluations, certain ways of looking at the world, certain styles of action get confirmed by his experience and he gradually adopts them as his own. If we can see that process of development, we can understand the product. The features to note are those bearing on presidential performance.

Experimental development continues all the way to death; we will not blind ourselves to midlife changes, particularly in the full-scale prediction case, that of Richard Nixon. But it is often much easier to see the basic patterns in early life histories. Later on a whole host of distractions—especially the image-making all politicians learn to practice—clouds the picture.

In general, character has its *main* development in childhood, world view in adolescence, style in early adulthood. The stance toward life I call character grows out of the child's experiments in relating to parents, brothers and sisters, and peers at play and in school, as well as to his own body and the objects around it. Slowly the child defines an orientation toward experience; once established, that tends to last despite much subsequent contradiction. By adolescence, the child has been hearing and seeing how people make their worlds meaningful, and now he is moved to relate himself—his own meanings—to those around him. His focus of attention shifts toward the future; he senses that decisions about his fate are coming and he looks into the premises for those decisions. Thoughts about the way the world works and how one might work in it, about what people are like and how one might be like them or not, and about the values people share and how one might share in them too—these are typical concerns for the post-child, pre-adult mind of the adolescent.

These themes come together strongly in early adulthood, when the person moves from contemplation to responsible action and adopts a style. In most biographical accounts this period stands out in stark clarity—the time of emergence, the time the young man found himself. I call it his first independent political success. It was then he moved beyond the detailed guidance of his family; then his self-esteem was dramatically boosted; then he came forth as a person to be reckoned with by other people. The *way* he did that is profoundly important to him. Typically he grasps that style and hangs onto it. Much later, coming into the presidency, something in him remembers this earlier victory and reemphasizes the style that made it happen.

Character provides the main thrust and broad direction—but it does not *determine*, in any fixed sense, world view and style. The story of development does not end with the end of childhood. Thereafter, the culture one grows in and the ways that culture is translated by parents and peers shapes the meanings one makes of his character. The going world view gets learned and that learning helps channel character forces. Thus it will not necessarily be true that compulsive characters have reactionary beliefs, or that compliant characters believe in compromise. Similarly for style: historical accidents play a large part in furnishing special opportunities for action—and in blocking off alternatives. For example, however much anger a young man may feel, that anger will not be expressed in rhetoric unless and until his life situation provides a platform and an audience. Style thus has a stature and independence of its own. Those who would reduce all explanation to character neglect these highly significant later channelings. For beyond the root is the branch, above the foundation the superstructure, and starts do not prescribe finishes.

Four Types of Presidential Character

The five concepts—character, world view, style, power situation, and climate of expectations—run through the accounts of presidents in the chapters to follow, which cluster the presidents since Theodore Roosevelt into four types. This is the fundamental scheme of the study. It offers a way to move past the complexities to the main contrasts and comparisons.

The first baseline in defining presidential types is *activity-passivity*. How much energy does the man invest in his presidency? Lyndon Johnson went at his day like a human cyclone, coming to rest long after the sun went down. Calvin Coolidge often slept eleven hours a night and still needed a nap in the middle of the day. In between the presidents array themselves on the high or low side of the activity line.

The second baseline is *positive-negative affect* toward one's activity—that is, how he feels about what he does. Relatively speaking, does he seem to experience his political life as happy or sad, enjoyable or discouraging, positive or negative in its main effect. The feeling I am after here is not grim satisfaction in a job well done, not some philosophical conclusion. The idea is this: is he someone who, on the surfaces we can see, gives forth the feeling that he has *fun* in political life? Franklin Roosevelt's Secretary of War, Henry L. Stimson, wrote that the Roosevelts "not only understood the *use* of power, they knew the *enjoyment* of power, too.... Whether a man is burdened by power or enjoys power; whether he is trapped by responsibility or made free by it; whether he is moved by other people and outer forces or moves them—that is the essence of leadership."

The positive-negative baseline, then, is a general symptom of the fit between the man and his experience, a kind of register of *felt* satisfaction.

Why might we expect these two simple dimensions to outline the main character types? Because they stand for two central features of anyone's orientation toward life. In nearly every study of personality, some form of the active-passive contrast is critical; the general tendency to act or be acted upon is evident in such concepts as dominance-submission, extraversion-introversion, aggression-timidity, attack-defense, fight-flight, engagement-withdrawal, approach-avoidance. In everyday life we sense quickly the general energy output of the people we deal with. Similarly we catch on fairly quickly to the affect dimension—whether the person seems to be optimistic or pessimistic, hopeful or skeptical, happy or sad. The two baselines are clear and they are also independent of one another: all of us know people who are very active but seem discouraged, others who are quite passive but seem happy, and so forth. The activity baseline refers to what one does, the affect baseline to how one feels about what he does.

Both are crude clues to character. They are leads into four basic character patterns long familiar in psychological research. In summary form, these are the main configurations:

1. Active-positive: There is a congruence, a consistency, between much activity and the enjoyment of it, indicating relatively high self-esteem and relative success in relating to the environment. The man shows an orientation toward productiveness as a value and an ability to use his styles flexibly, adaptively, suiting the dance to the music. He sees himself as developing over time toward relatively well defined personal goals—growing toward his image of himself as he might yet be. There is an emphasis on rational mastery, on using the brain to move the feet. This may get him into trouble; he may fail to take account of the irrational in politics. Not everyone he deals with sees things his way and he may find it hard to understand why.

2. Active-negative: The contradiction here is between relatively intense effort and relatively low emotional reward for that effort. The activity has a compulsive quality, as if the man were trying to make up for something or to escape from anxiety into hard work. He seems ambitious, striving upward, power-seeking. His stance toward the environment is aggressive and he has a persistent problem in managing his aggressive feelings. His self-image is vague and discontinuous. Life is a hard struggle to achieve and hold power, hampered by the condemnations of a perfectionistic conscience. Active-negative types pour energy into the political system, but it is an energy distorted from within.

3. Passive-positive: This is the receptive, compliant, other-directed character whose life is a search for affection as a reward for being agreeable and cooperative rather than personally assertive. The contradiction is between low self-esteem (on grounds of being unlovable, unattractive) and a superficial optimism. A hopeful attitude helps dispel doubt and elicits encouragement from others. Passive-positive types help soften the harsh edges of politics. But their dependence and the fragility of their hopes and enjoyments make disappointment in politics likely.

4. Passive-negative: The factors are consistent—but how are we to account for the man's *political* role-taking? Why is someone who does little in politics and enjoys it less there at all? The answer lies in the passive-negative's character-rooted orientation toward doing dutiful service; this compensates for low self-esteem based on a sense of uselessness. Passive-negative types are in politics because they think they ought to be. They may be well adapted to certain nonpolitical roles, but they lack the experience and flexibility to perform effectively as political leaders. Their tendency is to withdraw, to escape from the conflict and uncertainty of politics by emphasizing vague principles (especially prohibitions) and procedural arrangements. They become guardians of the right and proper way, above the sordid politicking of lesser men.

Active-positive presidents want most to achieve results. Active-negatives aim to get and keep power. Passive-positives are after love. Passive-negatives emphasize their civic virtue. The relation of activity to enjoyment in a president thus tends to outline a cluster of characteristics, to set apart the adapted from the compulsive, compliant, and withdrawn types.

The first four presidents of the United States, conveniently, ran through this gamut of character types. (Remember, we are talking about tendencies, broad directions; no individual man exactly fits a category.) George Washington—clearly the most important president in the pantheon—established the fundamental legitimacy of an American government at a time when this was a matter in considerable question. Washington's dignity, judiciousness, his aloof air of reserve and dedication to duty fit the passive-negative or withdrawing type best. Washington did not seek innovation, he sought stability. He longed to retire to Mount Vernon, but fortunately was persuaded to stay on through a second term, in which, by rising above the political conflict between Hamilton and Jefferson and inspiring confidence in his own integrity, he gave the nation time to develop the organized means for peaceful change.

John Adams followed, a dour New England Puritan, much given to work and worry, an impatient and irascible man—an active-negative president, a compulsive type. Adams was far more partisan than Washington; the survival of the system through his presidency demonstrated that the nation could tolerate, for a time, domination by one of its nascent political parties. As president, an angry Adams brought the United States to the brink of war with France, and presided over the new nation's first experiment in political repression: the Alien and Sedition Acts, forbidding, among other things, unlawful combinations "with intent to oppose any measure or measures of the government of the United States," or "any false, scandalous, and malicious writing or writings against the United States, or the President of the United States, with intent to defame . . . or to bring them or either of them into contempt or disrepute."

Then came Jefferson. He too had his trouble and failures—in the design of national defense, for example. As for his presidential character (only one element in success or failure), Jefferson was clearly active-positive. A child of the Enlightenment, he applied his reason to organizing connections with Congress aimed at strengthening the more popular forces. A man of catholic interests and delightful humor, Jefferson combined a clear and open vision of what the country could be with a profound political sense, expressed in his famous phrase, "Every difference of opinion is not a difference of principle."

The fourth president was James Madison, "Little Jemmy," the constitutional philosopher thrown into the White House at a time of great international turmoil. Madison comes closest to the passive-positive, or compliant, type; he suffered from irresolution, tried to compromise his way out, and gave in too readily to the "warhawks" urging combat with Britain. The nation drifted into war, and Madison wound up ineptly commanding his collection of amateur generals in the streets of Washington. General Jackson's victory at New Orleans saved the Madison administration's historical reputation; but he left the presidency with the United States close to bankruptcy and secession.

These four presidents—like all presidents—were persons trying to cope with the roles they had won by using the equipment they had built over a lifetime. The president is not some shapeless organism in a flood of novelties, but a man with a memory in a system with a history. Like all of us, he draws on his past to shape his future. The pathetic hope that the White House will turn a Caligula into a Marcus Aurelius is as naive as the fear that ultimate power inevitably corrupts. The problem is to understand—and to state understandably—what in the personal past foreshadows the presidential future.

It Can Happen Here 9.2

George E. Reedy

In 1970 a book appeared that was most prescient in its analysis. George Reedy's *The Twilight of the Presidency* predicted major problems in the White House if trends toward presidential isolation continued. According to Reedy, presidents increasingly were surrounded by loyal yes-men who insulated them from reality, increasing the prospects for ill-informed and erroneous decisions. The following excerpt from this book speaks directly to problems concerning individual personalities. Here Reedy addresses the remote but important problem of possible personality disorders of future presidents.

A highly irrational personality, who under other circumstances might be medically certifiable for treatment, could take over the White House and the event never be known with any degree of assurance.

This statement is not based upon any pretensions to psychiatric knowledge, and any psychiatric words in this chapter are to be read in their popular sense. No effort will be made—or should be made—to indulge in amateur medical diagnosis. But I do have some experience with the reaction of human beings to irrational behavior, and it is clear to me that where presidents are concerned, the tolerance level for irrationality extends almost to the point of gibbering idiocy or delusions of identity.

To put it more simply, no one is going to act to interfere with the presidential exercise of authority unless the president drools in public or announces on television that he is

---

The Twilight of the Presidency (pp. 168-80) by George E. Reedy, 1970, New York and Cleveland: The World Book Publishing Co. Copyright 1970 by George E. Reedy. Reprinted by permission.

Alexander the Great. And even in these extreme cases, action would be taken hesitantly indeed.

This reluctance, of course, does not spring merely from awe of high office or fear of retaliation. At bottom, it is a reflection of the ultimate nature of the presidential office—an environment in which for all practical purposes the standards of normal conduct are set by the president himself. To those immediately around him, he is the one who determines what is rational and what is irrational, and the public reaction to whatever he does is not immediate unless it brings on catastrophe.

Added to this is the protective screen the White House draws around its principal occupant. He is surrounded by assistants who consider their number-one goal in life to be that of presenting their "chief" in the most favorable possible light. They have pipelines reaching into the vast federal bureaucracy comprising more than 2,500,000 people and they have the necessary levers to manipulate this machinery in order to achieve their goals—including the projection of a "positive" image. In any administration and under any circumstances, this bureaucracy may provide some sources for adverse stories in the press, but these stories come from an antiadministration "underground," usually left over from a preceding administration, which can never command quite the aura of credibility that surrounds even an unpopular president.

Finally, there is a widely accepted assumption (which is entirely valid) that a president lives under extraordinary pressures and must find extraordinary means of blowing off steam. A president will be forgiven for acts that would lead to the banishment from civilized society of almost any other human being—for blatant rudeness, for eccentric attire, for obsessive secrecy. Only a churl will "blow the whistle" on a man who is racked with the agony of facing daily apocalyptic decisions of life and death which are almost routine in the White House, and the churls rarely carry weight with large segments of the population. It is virtually certain that the personal attacks upon Franklin D. Roosevelt and his family by the conservative press were an asset from the standpoint of building popular sympathy. The American people thought that it just wasn't fair play.

Yet the fact remains that the problem of the unbalanced president is on the minds of every close observer of the political process. It is discussed in hushed tones—and the discussion becomes even more intense whenever a scientific or technological breakthrough produces some new and awe-inspiring weapon or some new method of eavesdropping upon the private life of another nation.

Although the implications are obvious, this is a matter that has been treated in literature almost entirely as a question of fiction. The best-known work is Fletcher Knebel's novel, *Night at Camp David*, which faced up to the issue squarely and explored the ramifications thoroughly. What Knebel discovered, and what every serious student of government has discovered, is that within the contemporary context there is no workable solution to the problem. In order to bring the book to an emotionally satisfying end, Knebel was forced to resort to the lame device of a presidential abdication in a moment of lucidity.

The issue, of course, does not arise out of the frothing-at-the-mouth or the "I am Napoleon" insanity which represents the popular stereotype of mental imbalance. Such manifestations are obviously incapacitating and easily handled under the recently enacted Twenty-fifth Amendment to the Constitution. The problem does arise out of the much more common phenomenon of erratic behavior which can still be presented to the world in a plausible form and which will not be recognized as irrational until disaster has resulted.

The framers of the Twenty-fifth Amendment stepped gingerly around this question. In private conversations, they admitted that it was their major motivation. On the record and for the legislative history, they contented themselves with devising language that applied only in the event of crippling or total disability.

A part of the language of the Twenty-fifth Amendment is worth quoting at this point:

> Whenever the Vice-President and a majority of either the principal officers of the Executive Departments or of such other body as Congress

may by law provide transmit to the President *pro tempore* of the Senate and the Speaker of the House of Representatives a written declaration that the President is unable to discharge the powers and duties of this office, the Vice-President shall immediately assume the powers and duties of the office as Acting President.

This language was followed by an outline of complicated procedures through which the president would resume his duties once the disability had ceased. But the very complications of the procedure for resumption indicate the inadequacy of the machinery. On great questions of political policy, complicated procedures are rarely workable. Legislative draftsmen resort to them only when they are confronted with a problem for which they really do not have a satisfactory solution. In effect, when the Twenty-fifth Amendment is reduced to its simplest terms, it states that the president shall take up his duties once again when he *thinks* he is no longer disabled, and nothing can stop him from doing so except the objections of the vice-president and a majority of the cabinet backed by a two-thirds vote from both houses of Congress—a rather difficult force to assemble.

On two, and possibly three, occasions in our history, this kind of machinery might have been valuable. The first involved the several weeks in which President Garfield vegetated in a comatose state that ended in death after he was shot in 1881. The second was the long period of almost total disability of President Woodrow Wilson after he suffered a stroke in 1919. In neither case did the vice-presidents assume any of the duties of the presidency, out of fear that they would be accused of usurping the powers of the office. To this day it is unclear who actually ran the United States during those periods, although it is generally assumed without proof that Mrs. Wilson exercised the presidential powers during the last year of her husband's term. The consequences were not catastrophic simply because humanity had not reached a stage of technological development in which men were capable of destroying life on this planet. But no one can study the last year of Wilson's administration without concluding that the seeds of serious trouble may have been planted during the time when a vital man at the helm of government could have been able to continue policies of international cooperation that might have forestalled World War II.

The third occasion was far less serious in scope. It was President Eisenhower's heart attack in 1955. No one but his doctors will ever be certain of the extent of the disability suffered by the president. It is unlikely that it was very great, as he was obviously a coherent, thinking man throughout the period. But by 1955, the atomic bomb was a major item in the arsenals of two great world powers and humanity had arrived at a point in technology where total destruction of life was at least a drawing-board possibility. The president's illness forced political leaders at least to face up to the possibility of total incapacity short of physiological death, and the Twenty-fifth Amendment was the result. It is interesting, however, to note that it took the Congress ten years to submit a constitutional amendment to the states. Even under these extreme circumstances, no one wanted to admit that a president might "lose his marbles."

In the background of the discussion was another fear. It was simply that any machinery which permitted any group of men to deprive a president of his powers for any reason whatsoever could open the doors to a *coup d'état* by an ambitious vice-president who could mobilize a majority of the members of the cabinet. The *coup d'état* has been unlikely in the United States because of the long traditions of democracy, but that is no reason to place temptation in front of ambitious men.

The real difficulty is that irrational behavior is not necessarily illogical behavior. In fact, the finest logicians that the average person meets in the course of a lifetime are likely to be people that any psychiatrist would promptly label as neurotic personalities. Plausibility is virtually the hallmark of the nut and the crank. The man who believes that the world is flat can usually outargue his fellow citizen who knows that the world is spherical. The anti-Semite who ascribes all the evils of history to a Jewish conspiracy can marshal many more convincing arguments in support of *his* thesis than can be countered by the more balanced human being who knows that the

Protocols of the Elders of Zion are sheer fantasy. And anyone who has ever made the mistake of arguing with a recently converted Marxist who has just traveled the road to Damascus has discovered that he simply cannot win. The "true believer"—neurotic or otherwise—always works harder than the "normal" person.

The problems of irrationality are complicated enough in ordinary everyday life. Most of us live in a world peopled by office troublemakers, guard-house lawyers, and neurotic relatives. Fortunately, most of them can cause only a minimum of trouble. But in the political world, the problem of the neurotic assumes proportions that are gigantic. Politics and neurosis are inextricably intermingled because the neurotic personality is usually more articulate and more logical in expressing stands on the great issues of the day. Politics probably would not exist at all without neurotic drives that compel men to exert leadership and extend their personalities to dominance over others. What keeps most political leaders from rushing headlong into catastrophe is the fact that their own neurotic drives must clash with the neurotic drives of others and in the conflict certain forms of social sanity are bound to emerge.

The presidential office, however, exists in an environment which is free of many of the restraints with which all other political leaders must contend. Face-to-face confrontations with opponents are rare and occur only at a time and place of the president's own choosing. He is obviously unlikely to select circumstances which are not to his advantage. When the president does confront his political enemies, he fires his salvos from a fortress—the White House. Here he is cushioned against all the hazards that must be faced by a politician in the field. The whole purpose of his physical environment is to cater to all his cravings—psychological as well as physical.

It is certain that whatever neurotic drives a president takes with him into the White House will be fostered and enhanced during his tenancy. He lives in a world that is the delight of the immature personality—a universe in which every temper tantrum is met by instant gratification of the desire which caused the tantrum. Nobody is going to say "no" to his little demands, and the "no's" that are said to the big demands come in the most diplomatic and tactful forms.

This is the condition which surrounds a man who has the power to order troops into battle; to decide the distribution of billions of dollars of the nation's wealth; and to use or withhold atomic weapons that can incinerate tens of millions of people in a matter of hours. The American system of government places in the hands of one man the responsibility for making decisions that require the utmost maturity and then surrounds him with an atmosphere that encourages the development of the most immature impulses.

The problem is compounded by the awareness of most people that their political leaders will be eccentric under any circumstances. Generally, Americans glory in the foibles of their presidents. Harry Truman's salty and sometimes explosive language was tut-tutted by prudish moralists, but for most Americans it established a bond of identification. Jack Kennedy's compulsive urge to play touch football delighted people who wished they could go through life like Peter Pan, without ever growing up. Lyndon Johnson's speed mania on the highways was a secret source of enjoyment to the millions of American males who would dearly love to roar down the roads subject to no check by highway patrolmen.

Neurotic behavior is merely eccentric behavior extended beyond the bounds within which it is merely amusing. Furthermore, who is to say what behavior is neurotic and what is merely eccentric? The entire history of psychiatry affords no workable guidepost in the field of political activity. Boiled down to essentials, neurotic behavior is manifested only by activity that does not conform to the standards and the structure of contemporary society, and what is "normal" in one age can be totally irrational in another. A fourteenth-century judge who believed that a man's guilt or innocence could be determined by forcing him to grasp a red-hot bar was evidencing rational behavior. He was expressing the considered wisdom of his age. But a twentieth-century judge who proposed such a test would be promptly locked in a padded cell. The juries who tried and executed witches in Salem,

Massachusetts, were in perfect conformity with the "normal" behavior of the seventeenth century. Anyone who suggested at the time that "witchcraft" was a figment of the imagination would have been treated as a fit candidate for the nearest lunatic asylum. Today, a trial for witchcraft would be at best a curiosity (possibly staged by a district attorney seeking to clear the statute books of some obsolete laws) and more likely evidence that a community had lost its senses.

The political community, furthermore, does not, and cannot, rely upon empirical evidence as a guide to truth. The fundamental material with which it deals consists of the hopes and fears of people. These hopes and fears always approximate some form of reality but the boundary lines are never clear. The danger is greater in the field of fear than it is in the field of hope because there are so many things in the world to fear that it is simple to interpret the whole universe in paranoiac terms. For example, there are Communist plots in just about every non-Communist nation in the world aimed at the overthrow of the existing government. To deny the existence of such plots is to commit an absurdity—to fly in the face of common sense. But the fact that there are Communist plots does not mean that all unorthodox activity or that all opposition to a government is based on Communist plots, or even that the Communist plots are of sufficient magnitude to present a real danger. Neurotic behavior can begin with a perfectly normal, sensible desire to preserve a government from those who would overthrow it. But who is there who can define the boundary between an illegitimate desire to overthrow a government and a legitimate desire to change it? Politicians, of course, must constantly make such assessments because it is essential to their activity that they correctly gauge the motivations of the opposition.

Since this is an age of tremendous faith in the validity of empirical science, the few proposals that have been made in this field assume that a board of psychiatrists could always be convened to pass upon the mental balance of a president. This idea is utterly impractical. In the first place, medical men are probably the least qualified of all professionals to pass judgment upon what political context is "normal" and what is "neurotic." They must spend far too much of their lives learning their highly complicated trade to absorb enough of the other intellectual disciplines. In the second place, however, what president who is in a coherent frame of mind would ever permit himself to submit to such a board? The question answers itself once we realize that coherence and plausibility are not incompatible with neurotic behavior.

We return, therefore, to the only possible test that can be applied to any political leader. This is the judgment of his peers on his *political* behavior. This, of course, does not address itself to psychiatric questions. But it would, of necessity, include psychiatric questions even though not considered under that name.

An unbalanced president invariably engages in activity which repels his political colleagues and spurs them to some form of negative action. Because of the semisacrosanct position of the president, this negative action cannot go so far as to remove him from office except under circumstances so extreme that the removal would be effected by revolution (or at least a *coup d'état*) if no legal machinery or impeachment were available. Consequently, people have a tendency to "put up" with irrational behavior on the part of a president. He can insult his closest friends, cut up his political allies and favor his political enemies, storm and rage over trifles. The worst that can happen to him is a muted grumbling and a steady erosion of confidence on the part of the people. Regardless of the grumbling and regardless of the erosion of confidence, the reins of power will stay in his hands. He will still have the authority to drop the atomic bomb on another nation even though in the privacy of Senate cloakrooms experienced men are whispering that "the president is nuts." And if anyone should raise the question in public and seek to initiate the constitutional process of impeachment or the processes of the Twenty-fifth Amendment, it would immediately become a political question, with strong suspicions on the part of the large segments of the public that a revolution is under way. Faced with this situation, responsible men would invariably conclude that it is wiser to put up with a president whose mental balance is suspect than to divide the country by a bitter debate over his removal.

Whatever the shortcomings of a parliamentary government, it does afford an answer to this problem. A prime minister can be removed from office by a vote of "no confidence" without any question ever being raised as to his mental or emotional capacity. As for the chief of state in a parliamentary system, his emotional stability is entirely irrelevant to the health of the government structure. He can give no orders, pass no judgments, control no funds. The only requirement is that his heart and his lungs function and that he be physically able to say the few words that are necessary when he meets the chief of another state or when he summons a new political leader to his official residence to direct him to form a new government. It is, of course, desirable that he be able to conduct himself with dignity, but even this is not absolutely essential. In a parliamentary form of government, the chief of state can be so surrounded by courtiers that any unpleasant idiosyncrasies will not be apparent.

It is obviously far too late for the United States to establish a parliamentary government on the lines of the British system. Systems of government are created only by a revolutionary act followed by a lengthy process of evolution. Therefore, men who are drawing up blueprints for governmental organization without revolution had best be certain that those blueprints fit the political realities of the nation.

Nevertheless, it is apparent that no satisfactory solution can ever be found to the potential problem of the mentally unstable president within the present framework. So long as a man stands without peers at a summit of power, he can be removed from office only by what amounts to a *coup d'état*. Complicated machinery for psychological testing or for medical declarations of incompetency will not be accepted by the American people—or for that matter any other people—without arousing strong suspicions. Anyone who has ever listened to conflicting psychiatric testimony in a criminal proceeding will never be willing to accept a technical verdict as to whether a man's psychic health is sufficient for him to exercise the instruments of power.

Somehow, there must be a conversion of the operating authority of the presidency to a managerial status—one in which a president can be challenged without impugning his sanity or his balance. The intuitive judgment of brother politicians, of course, is a vague standard which can never be defined with any precision. But ultimately, it represents the only method of solving a political problem and therefore it is the only direction in which there can be any hope.

Job Specs for the Oval Office — 9.3

Hedley Donovan

When reflecting on the role of personality in the presidency, we encounter a number of questions: Do we get the best people for the job? How can we insure that the best people are considered? What qualifications make for a good candidate and a good president? The following editorial from *Time* addresses these questions, attempts to provide some answers, and offers some proposals for change.

"Job Specs for the Oval Office" by Hedley Donovan, 13 December 1982, *Time*, pp. 20-22, 24, 29. Copyright 1982 by Time, Inc. Reprinted by permission.

The U.S. is halfway from the presidential election of 1980, which offered us the choice of Ronald Reagan or Jimmy Carter, to the election of 1984. With the midterm elections out of the way, and Ted Kennedy removing himself, the 1984 campaign is on. Various preliminaries have been visible for months, in the speaking schedules of the various Democratic possibles. If any Republican other than the incumbent entertains thoughts of 1984, he would be foolhardy to say so; the obligatory sentiment is that Reagan will run and be re-elected.

Still, many citizens of this populous Republic cannot help wondering if Reagan-Mondale, for instance, is the best we can come up with. This is not to deny the several estimable qualities of the president or the former vice-president. We could do worse; arguably we have, within the past 20 years; quite possibly we will again, within the next 20.

The question is: How did the machinery for identifying potential presidents, nominating candidates and choosing winners come to be so seriously out of sync with the modern requirements of the office? Compare the political leadership we are producing in this literate democratic society of some 230 million people with the leadership of the Thirteen Colonies in the late 18th century. For all its familiarity, the point is still a painful one. From 3 million people living on the edge of a wilderness: Washington, Jefferson, Hamilton, Madison, Franklin, the Adamses. (Would these men have survived the scrutiny of a Mike Wallace or Ben Bradlee? Probably so. The press was much more savage in those days.) But perhaps, out of all the mysterious historical chemistries that can produce a golden age—the Athens of Pericles, Renaissance Florence—the America of two centuries ago was a golden age for political thought and political leadership. Perhaps we should simply be grateful for the founders, not haunted by them.

If so, we could better be bothered by a comparison from our own time. The modern presidency begins with Franklin Roosevelt, and nine men have held the job. In the 28 years from 1933 to 1961, we had one great President, F.D.R., and two very good ones, Harry Truman and Dwight Eisenhower. None of the next six could be put in either of those categories. John Kennedy perhaps had a potential for greatness; the actual accomplishments of his presidency were meager. However, his short presidency and Gerald Ford's short presidency, for all the differences of style, were the best, or least unsuccessful, of the 1960s and 1970s. Lyndon Johnson's Great Society legislation was a noble achievement (though the programs went wildly out of control). But the L.B.J. presidency is forever blighted by the tragic failure in Viet Nam. Richard Nixon was our best president of foreign policy since Eisenhower, not just because he had the wit to employ Dr. Kissinger, but his presidency will never recover from Watergate. The returns are not yet in on Jimmy Carter's foreign policy. His economic policies were an unsuccessful muddle; it is not yet clear that Reagan's very different policies will work out better.

It is not an inspiring roll call. The gap between electability and the capacity to govern seems to be growing. No American under 40 has any adult experience of a reasonably successful and "normal" presidency. The country and the world have changed profoundly since the successful presidencies of the 1940s and 1950s. The job has surely grown more difficult and more important, even as the quality of the incumbents has fallen off. Since the mid-'60s, the U.S. has declined in relative military power, drastically. We have declined in political and economic muscle vis-à-vis our allies. We have lost some cohesiveness and social discipline within the U.S. We have lost, at least for the time being, the economic momentum that produced steadily higher living standards and steadily growing tax-funded entitlements. We are still, all in all, the strongest nation and society, but it is a very tough time to be president.

Yet our democracy cannot allow the failed presidencies of the 1960s and 1970s to foster the view that the job has become impossible. It hasn't. It isn't. If we can arrive at a better understanding of what the job requires today, and what it does not, we may arrive at ways of finding better candidates.

Lion or Prisoner?

The abiding paradox of the U.S. presidency is that it is the most powerful political office in the world—hedged about by a mighty host of contending powers: Congress, the bureaucracy, the press, business, the courts, lobbies, the great American electorate, and then all the other countries on earth, at last count 167. Ronald Reagan and Jimmy Carter could both be excused for feeling that checks and balances can be overdone.

Students of the modern presidency have tended to stress either its powers or its limitations. The living, changing amalgam of authority and constraints is perhaps too subtle to capture in any theoretical model. Bryce Harlow, a wise counselor to all the recent Republican presidents, saw the powers of the office as so great, even in the hands of the prudent Ike, as to leave Harlow in "almost fearful awe." The late Clinton Rossiter of Cornell took an equally sweeping view of the power, but rejoiced in it with a romantic fervor. He saw the president as "a kind of magnificent lion who can roam widely and do great deeds so long as he does not try to break loose from his broad reservation."

The heroic view of the presidency is powerfully fortified by modern U.S. journalism, with its insatiable demand for personalities, action, and movement, and its versatile technology. TV, in particular, gives new dimensions and intensities of exposure that are a priceless opportunity, and ever present danger, to a president. The heroic view of the presidency of course includes the possibility of failure on a grand scale.

Richard Neustadt of Harvard, in his classic *Presidential Power*, stressed the limitations. The most concise presidential summary of the "limited" view came from Truman, a strong president who didn't always get his way: "The principal power that the president has is to bring people in and try to persuade them to do what they ought to do without persuasion." Truman affected a view of the presidency as a kind of martyrdom and called the White House "a prison." In fact, he relished the job and, aside from his intense partisanship and flashes of pettiness, performed well at it. Lyndon Johnson, when the self-pity was running strong, could say, "Power? The only power I've got is nuclear—and I can't use that." This was silly, and Johnson's record didn't suggest he believed it.

Rossiter was closer to the truth, but the danger in the heroic view of the presidency is that it can lead to vastly inflated public expectations. Two generations of historians and their readers were prepared to be disappointed with anything less than a Roosevelt—Franklin or Theodore. The leading historian of the New Deal, Arthur Schlesinger Jr., saw F.D.R. in an exalted light and later found enough activist electricity around J.F.K. to want to work for him. Only during the Nixon administration did he begin to worry about the excesses of an "imperial presidency." James S. Young of the University of Virginia argues that there must be a "retrenching" of presidential power "to save the presidency for the things only it can do." The president can and should restrain public expectations of his office and distinguish between "threats to the republic and mere problems for the administration." Young and other advocates of a smaller presidency might have relished a comment in the White House the morning after a bad Carter primary in 1980: "I understand," confided one of the young Georgians, "that the leader of the Free World took quite a chewing out from his wife last night."

Even without war or depression, the times are sufficiently difficult to test presidents as severely as ever in our history. To be a "good" president in the 1980s may be even harder than to be a "great" president in the days of Antietam or Pearl Harbor.

Ideally . . .

So what are we looking for? Always, of course, enough of a good quality but not too much. With almost every presidential virtue, a little too much becomes a defect, even a danger. The president must be "a good politician" but not "too political." The president should be decent but not "too nice." Etc. To start at the easy end of the check list:

The Body

We prefer presidents to look like presidents. F.D.R. did (supremely so), also Ike, J.F.K., Reagan. Other recent incumbents, through no fault of their own, didn't.

A president needs tremendous physical stamina (though George Reedy, one of L.B.J.'s press secretaries, has noted that "no president ever died of overwork"). The 36-primary campaign, whatever else may be said of it, is a rigorous physical exam. We, at least, know that anybody who can get nominated and elected is in good shape.

The president ought to be an athlete (Ford, J.F.K., Ike) or at least an outdoorsman (Reagan), not just because it appeals to voters but because it helps make a rounded man, capable of relaxing. Carter, after that ruinous jogging photo, took up trout fishing in a big way. L.B.J. poured all his volcanic energies into politics; his was the youngest natural death (at 64) of any postwar president. Nixon is an essentially sedentary man. Truman's sports were walking, poker, and bourbon.

Character and Temperament

The presidential bedrock must be integrity, perceived and real. (Integrity includes an honorable private life.) There is an unavoidable tension between this necessity and the political necessities of maneuver, indirection, and calculated ambiguity. Of the two masterly political operators among the modern presidents, F.D.R. was frequently dancing along the ethical borderline, and L.B.J. was often well across it.

The president needs perseverance, and personal ambition within healthy limits. A fashionable cynicism is that anybody so ambitious that he would put up with what it takes to get nominated and elected is morally disqualified for the presidency. Neustadt puts it more sensibly: presidents need "drive but not drivenness." L.B.J., Nixon, and Carter were all driven. Henry Graff of Columbia notes that we like a presidential candidate to look "called," though it is hard to achieve this effect when you are trying to sell yourself on TV.

A president should be "fair" and look fair, magnanimous, willing to give trust, compassionate. No very high marks for any recent president. Reagan gives the impression of insensitivity to the poor. Liberal politicians for some reason can be highly compassionate about "the people" and insensitive to individuals.

The president needs presence, dignity, a certain touch of distance and even mystery; he is also expected to be "human." F.D.R. and Ike set a high standard. The aloofnesss of a De Gaulle would not sit well in the U.S. He needs courage, physical (just to go outdoors) and moral. He must be tough, even ruthless, but not find sick enjoyment in ruthlessness. He needs a deep self-confidence, stopping short of a grandiose sense of destiny.

He must be steady and stable, housing his exceptional combination of gifts within a personality approximately "normal." Among the modern presidents, the most nearly "normal" personalities are probably Truman, Ike, Ford, Reagan. "I am disgustingly sane," said Ford. It may be significant that Ford and Truman had not aspired to the presidency, and Ike began to think of it only in his late 50s, when he had already won world fame in a job about as big as president. Reagan had had two satisfying careers in the public eye, as actor and after-dinner free-enterprise speaker, before turning to politics.

Brains

Justice Holmes called Franklin Roosevelt "a second-class intellect but a first-class temperament." The president needs superior intelligence (at least a B from Holmes) but need not be brilliant, deep, or blindingly original. He needn't be an intellectual, and we have not been threatened with one lately.

The president must be a simplifier. Reagan is rightly criticized when he oversimplifies, which is often, but some of his simplifying is just right, not unlike good teaching or preaching.

In abstract intelligence it could be that L.B.J., Nixon, and Carter would rate highest among the modern presidents. All suffered from a lack of judgment and proportion, which does not show up in IQ tests.

A president needs a sense of history, including a feel for the situations where history does not apply. Jimmy Carter, despite his speed-reading studiousness and remarkable memory, was strangely deficient here. The present incumbent seems relatively innocent in the field. Truman and J.F.K. were well-steeped in history. From a sense of history (preferably not just American) flows an informed patriotism, a feel for the powers of an office unique in the world, the restraints upon it, and the tempo of a presidential term, including the special opportunities of the first twelve to 18 months and the special learning-curve problems of these same months.

A president must offer the country vision, and he must animate his administration with purposes larger than the enjoyment of office. A visible zest for the job is perfectly legal, even desirable. But the love of the job can contribute to a certain blurring of the national interest and the personal interest. F.D.R. doubtless convinced himself in 1940 that it was for the good of the nation and the world that he should be the first three-term president. It would be refreshing some time to hear a politician admit he wanted to be president simply because it is the top job in his business. (The motivation of J.F.K., Nixon, Carter.) But it is not an auspicious basis for a presidency. It suggests a lack of idealism and of a coherent political philosophy. Reagan and L.B.J., whatever their shortcomings, must be credited with a vision of using the presidency for the country. Walter Mondale puts it this way: "The candidate must know the mandate he wants from the people, and they must understand the mandate he is asking."

The president's political philosophy needs to be earned, hammered out in some detail, tested intellectually and in experience. It is good for the stability of the country that the American center, which is essentially where we want our presidents to be, is so spacious. But there are drawbacks in this vast and vague consensus; presidential candidates and presidents can evade the hard work of thinking out policy specifics and confronting the harsh choice between two good things.

As to the roots of a president's philosophy, a religious affiliation is necessary for a major-party candidate, but is religious conviction necessary in a president? Certified historians and political scientists shy from such an embarrassing "value judgment." But the voters know they would not want a nonbeliever president, and their instinct is correct. It has been settled that a Catholic can be president. The droll Bob Strauss goes about asking whether the country is grownup enough for "a Texas Jew."

The president must be a communicator. Reagan, by general agreement, is the best since F.D.R. Indeed, for a time in 1981, when he had Congress eating out of his hand, it seemed as though mastery of TV and one-on-one charm had become the very key to the presidency. Events and realities of 1982 suggest some limits on what a president can accomplish by communicating. TV is still a major resource for a president, more important in governing than in getting elected. Carter, Nixon, and L.B.J. all won elections (two of them landslides) without being compelling TV personalities. Nixon was excellent on radio. L.B.J. was an overwhelming persuader close in, a gripper of elbows, clutcher of lapels. We have not had high presidential eloquence since Ted Sorensen was writing for J.F.K., though Ford (speechwriter: Robert Hartmann) came close at times, and Reagan, a heavy contributor to his own speeches, can be forceful and moving. The arts of presidential communicating should also include a sense of when to keep quiet. No recent outstanding examples.

For his own sanity, a president needs a sense of humor. Reagan and J.F.K. get high marks. Ford so-so. Carter and Nixon each had a lively wit, on the biting side, but never developed an attractive way of showing it, just the right amount, in public. L.B.J. had little public humor and in private leaned heavily on the set-piece joke ("There was this colored boy once up in front of this judge in Panola County . . .").

The president needs to be an optimist. Ford: "You just can't sit back and say this is wrong, it is terrible, that is wrong . . . and I can't do anything about it." But the president should not be so optimistic that he cannot face unpleasant facts, and spot them early. Reagan doesn't seem to have much of a built-in early-warning system, and neither did Carter.

A president must be capable of thinking in contingencies: What if? Some of the biggest contingencies (What if the Soviet Union did A or B?) get steady attention at the White House. But many scarcely less important possibilities don't.

A president needs an ever fresh curiosity about this big and complicated country. He can help overcome his isolation by seeking and taking advice from a broad circle. But many otherwise courageous people will simply not talk candidly to a president. He may be a very courteous listener, as Carter was, and still be incapable of any real exchange with a very few intimates. Reagan is more open as a personality but not notably open to "new" facts.

We want the president to be flexible, pragmatic, capable of compromise—also firm, decisive, principled. Carter was hurt by zigzags. Reagan advisers are said to worry about their man being "Carterized" if he compromises too readily. Conversely, many Republican [members of] Congress worry about his being "mulish." This is a tough one to win. The president should be able to admit error to himself, once in a while out loud. Theoretically, the public confessions could become too frequent, but that is not a real-life danger.

A crucial executive ability, above all for the chief executive of the U.S., is perceptiveness about people. This will bear heavily on the quality of the president's appointments and his ability to mold his people into an effective administration. He must be shrewd enough to see when infighting is unavoidable, even useful, and when it is destructive. F.D.R., Truman, Ike, J.F.K. and for a time L.B.J. were good managers and motivators of people. Nixon's management methods brought us Watergate. Ford and Carter were weak as people managers. Reagan presided over some outlandish administrative arrangements last year, but the machinery is now running better. An awareness of gaps in his own knowledge and concerns should enter the president's criteria for his staff appointments. Self-knowledge without self-doubt is admittedly a lot to ask.

The president must manage more than people. The fearfully complex systems and institutions in his care need executive oversight and control. It is not enough to say a president "can hire managers"; as he delegates, he must know how to keep track of the delegated work; he must understand what his managers are managing.

A president needs a clear sense of priorities. Reagan has the ability to concentrate his energies and the country's attention. Detractors might say this was because he has less energy to deploy. Carter had prodigious energy and diffused it too widely. Presidents should have the knack for keeping three or four balls in the air, but not the urge to toss up ten.

Well, we have proposed no fewer than 31 attributes of presidential leadership. There could be longer or shorter lists, but they would all have this in common: no one of the cited qualities is by itself rare, and indeed we all know people who possess a number of them. The problem is to find somebody with all these qualities, or all but a very few, who is willing and able to seek a major-party nomination. Better yet, to find a dozen such people, so each party can choose from among first-class candidates before presenting the electorate the final decision.

The Résumé

Just to read the résumés of the modern presidents, you would have had a hard time predicting their effectiveness in office. The only fairly safe guess would be that one term as governor of Georgia is not ideal preparation. (This is a retroactive guess; in 1976, some 40 million voters, including the writer, didn't think the point mattered that much.)

Two of the modern presidents were two-term governors of our two most populous states: F.D.R. and Reagan. Many students of politics think the governor's job in a big complicated state is the closest thing there is, though nothing is very close to the presidency.

Truman has become a kind of democratic legend of the "common man" rising to lofty challenge. He came to the White House from out of the seamy politics of Kansas City and two terms as a "machine" senator.

When Ike was elected some of his critics were genuinely concerned about a "military mind" in the White House. Admirers who understood Ike's extraordinary kind of command success, at least as much political and diplomatic as military, may have expected a presidential greatness he did not quite achieve.

One might have expected less, or more, than we got from Kennedy and Ford. J.F.K. had spent 14 years on Capitol Hill, though he was not particularly diligent or influential there. Ford called himself "a child of the House," where he had spent 25 years, always in the minority; he served eight months as our first appointed vice-president.

Probably the best résumés of all were Lyndon Johnson's (federal bureaucrat, Navy, Congressman, senator, majority leader, three years as V.P.) and Nixon's (federal bureaucrat, Navy, Congressman, senator, eight years as V.P.).

Eight of the nine were college graduates, and the list of their institutions evokes the American dream. Harvard, Yale Law, and Michigan are there, and the senior service academies. But a fellow from Southwest Texas State Teachers can grow up to be president (and boast of the Ivy Leaguers working for him). So can a young man from Whittier, or from, perfect name, Eureka. Truman held no degree but had studied law at night school in Kansas City.

The academic performances are not very revealing. F.D.R. tended to the "gentleman's C." Nixon was No. 3 out of 25 in his class at Duke University Law School, Carter was 60 out of 820 at Annapolis, Ike an unostentatious 61 out of 164 at West Point.

Only three of the nine earned law degrees (F.D.R. and Ford as well as Nixon), a lower proportion than in the memberships of Congress (still about half lawyers). Apart from the lawyers, none of the nine held an advanced degree.

Lateral Entry

It will be interesting to see whether a Ph.D. can be elected again (Woodrow Wilson is the only one so far) before a woman or a black. Possibly a black female professor of economics who had become a university president (we could really use good economics) in 1996. Meanwhile, the U.S. is conferring about 400,000 advanced degrees a year, lawyers and doctors, M.A.s, M.B.A.s, Ph.D.s, etc. These people are a formidable talent pool.

This brings us to the perennial question: Isn't there some way to get good people from "outside" politics into politics—at the level where they might be considered for the presidency? The answer remains: probably not.

Wendell Willkie in 1940 was the last major-party nominee from totally outside politics.

In 1975 *Time* published an essay, "New Places to Look for Presidents." Out of reports from the *Time* news bureaus around the country, about 150 names made the working lists. Last month *Time* again asked its news bureaus for lists of people outside politics who might be presidential. The exercise yielded a national total of only 21 names. Among them: two former astronauts, Frank Borman, president of Eastern Airlines, and Neil Armstrong, oil-equipment executive; chairman Robert O. Anderson of Atlantic Richfield; Lee Iacocca of Chrysler; James Beré of Borg-Warner; Thomas Wyman of CBS; President Hanna Gray, University of Chicago; Marvin Goldberger, Caltech; Bartlett Giamatti of Yale; and, inevitably, Walter Cronkite.

TV is all over the place. The two former astronauts owe their high "name recognition" in good part to TV, and Borman helps keep his alive with TV commercials. Iacocca also gives himself heavy exposure as TV pitchman; it is an expressive face, an appealing tough-guy personality and, who knows, if he could pull Chrysler out of the hole, save American jobs . . . The president of CBS is an unknown face, but any heir apparent who can avoid being fired by Bill Paley has undeniable political talents.

"It's lists like this," says Jonathan Moore of Harvard, "that make you think the people inside politics aren't so bad after all." Nothing personal, he hastens to add, but the outside types tend to be "one-dimensional in experience."

How to give them another dimension? Most private institutions are proud when one of their people is offered a prestigious appointive job in Washington. Depending on the man's age and length of absence in Washington, the organization is glad to welcome him back, sometimes in a higher job than he left; and if that cannot be done, the individual will usually be snapped up elsewhere. There is no taint to cabinet or subcabinet experience under either party; it is highly marketable.

What is needed is for some courageous corporations, universities, foundations to give "electoral sabbaticals." A promising 40-year-old corporation V.P. or university dean could try for a nomination to Congress (or indeed the state legislature). If he wins, he is now in politics, and if he has the talents that would have made him an impressive figure in private life, at 55 say, he may at 55 be a governor, senator or cabinet officer with a shot at president. If he loses, he gets his old job back, and his organization learns not to be embarrassed that one of its people is an openly confessed Republican or Democrat. One of the reasons Congress and the state legislatures are so loaded with lawyers is that they can run and, win or lose, benefit from the publicity and contacts.

Why Not the Best?

More urgent than the "outside" talent question, however, is the inside talent question: Do the best people in politics get to the top?

As compared with the six presidents from Kennedy through Reagan, you can draw up a list of defeated candidates and defeated contenders for nomination that may well include some better presidential material than some of the presidents we actually got. On the Democratic side: Edmund Muskie, Hubert Humphrey, Scoop Jackson, Adlai Stevenson (still a factor in 1960). Republican: Nelson Rockefeller, William Scranton, Howard Baker, George Bush, John Connally.

For the Republicans, Bush and Baker are still available, for 1988 if not 1984, and perhaps Senator Robert Dole, steadily positioning himself toward the center, and Congressman Jack Kemp, steadily holding to the right. Also: Richard Thornburgh, governor of Pennsylvania: Robert Ray and William Milliken, retiring governors of Iowa and Michigan; and two attractive political alumni now in industry, former Congressman and Defense Secretary Donald Rumsfeld, chief executive officer of Searle, and William Ruckelshaus, former deputy attorney general, now senior vice president of Weyerhaeuser.

In the last poll of Democratic preferences before Kennedy withdrew, he had a huge lead: 43 percent to 13 percent for Mondale and 7 percent for Senator John Glenn. Senators Alan Cranston and Gary Hart of California and Colorado are cranking up to run; also former Governor Reubin Askew of Florida and Senator Fritz Hollings of South Carolina. Some impressive Democratic Governors: Robert Graham of Florida, just elected to a second term, and James Hunt of North Carolina and Richard Lamm of Colorado, now in their second terms. One suspects the veteran Indiana Congressman and former majority whip John Brademas, now president of New York University, has not forsworn politics for all time.

These are strong lists, for both parties. Many of these people will end up being "merely" vice presidential, but remember four of our nine modern presidents came from V.P.

Henry Graff points out that we have had no ex-mayor as president since Grover Cleveland. "Mayors deal with garbage and garbage rubs off." Hubert Humphrey (Minneapolis) came close, however, and Senator Richard Lugar (Indianapolis), one of the biggest Republican winners on Nov. 2, gets talked about.

Refining Expectations

Several changes would help the best of these people get serious consideration for the presidency:

• Shortening the marathon campaign for the nominations would reduce the numbing effect on the electorate, perhaps lead to higher voter turnout and, conceivably, more thoughtful voting. Shorter campaigns would be somewhat less expensive and might help the working officeholder get as much attention as the full-time presidential candidate. Senate Majority Leader Baker has complained of the difficulty of running against an "unemployed millionaire." In 1980 he was up against three of them: Reagan, Bush, Connally. Carter in 1976 was approximately a millionaire, and had been running full time for two years: all his rivals had demanding jobs.

• Speaking of money, the game is still heavily stacked toward those who have it, or whose policies (on the subject of unionism, insurance, Israel, oil, whatever) attract plentiful contributions. Once a candidate is rated as having a serious chance, the money tends to flow, but some first-class people never get sufficiently funded to be seen as "serious." Mainly because of the price of TV ads, it can cost millions to run for governor or senator in a populous state, a serious constriction on the size of the pool from which presidential possibilities are drawn. Republican Lew Lehrman spent about $7 million of his own money running this year for governor of New York. Democrat Mark Dayton spent about the same (but four times as much per voter) in his run for senator from Minnesota. Both lost, to be sure, and in Dayton's campaign in stolid Minnesota, the lavish spending may have hurt him. But adding up all 33 Senate races, we find 27 of the winners were the bigger spenders. Total spending on the 1982 congressional races exceeded $300 million. The cost of 1984, presidential and congressional, could hit $1 billion. This is not an excessive advertising budget for the most important act a democracy performs (Procter & Gamble spends $600 million a year on ads). The question is whether the money is fairly distributed, and whether contributors in effect can buy a politician's vote. But campaign financing is a very complicated thing to regulate. Freedom of speech is involved, also the law of unintended consequences: past "reforms" have often created whole new sets of problems.

• Perhaps the greatest stroke in behalf of better presidents would be for the incumbent president, starting with Ronald Reagan, to consider as one of his major responsibilities the identification and grooming of possible successors. (One of his close associates says he has never heard Reagan mention the subject.) A corporate C.E.O. would be considered shamefully derelict if he did as little about his successor as the president of the U.S. does. We do not want the president decreeing his successor, which he couldn't anyway, but he could do far more than most recent presidents have done to see that strong people are in the right places to get serious consideration. Ike gave fitful attention to the problem, and kept lists. He thought Robert Anderson, Texas businessman, his secretary of the Navy, and then of the Treasury, was best qualified to succeed him. But when Anderson was not interested, Ike seemed to lose interest. He was not a great Nixon fan, but would not move against his vice-president. Nixon as president came to think John Connally would be his best successor, toyed with the thought of moving Spiro Agnew to the Supreme Court (!) and making Connally his running mate in 1972. He could have commanded that, but backed off. Then, when Agnew had to quit in disgrace in 1973, Nixon was in enough trouble himself that he did not want to risk a congressional fight over the controversial Connally and chose the safe and well-liked Jerry Ford.

Not only in the choice for V.P., but in his major cabinet appointments, a president has the chance to put good people into the running for the future. Some can be from the "outside." The president needs to be big enough, of course, not to feel threatened or upstaged by strong people around him.

• There is more the sitting president can do. He can fight the idea that the presidency is unmanageable, for the sake of his own place in history, but also for the sake of the office and the appeal it could hold for others. There has been far too much lamentation about the president's helplessness vis-à-vis the bureaucracy. J.F.K. called the State Department "a foreign power." Presidents use the power of the permanent bureaucracy as an alibi for their own nonfeasance in the managerial role, and this encourages their cabinet officers to adopt the same attitude within their departments. When a candidate runs "against Washington," as Carter and Reagan did, this mind-set continues long after the candidate has himself become "Washington." Plenty of people will always seek the presidency, but we may be losing some principled people who have been persuaded by presidents that the job is hopeless.

• Finally, along with thinking of the presidency as manageable, we need to learn not to expect too much of the president. This is a difficult balance, but justly so, because we want an equally delicate balance within the mind and temperament of the president: just enough of this or that quality, but not too much.

We are a profoundly democratic people but deeply susceptible to heroes and leaders. TV can confer a celebrity that may be confused with leadership quality. TV also contributes, in these dragged-out campaigns, to the steady inflation of political promises. As the talking goes on and on, presidential candidates seem drawn to grander and grander claims of what they are going to do. You could cry or laugh or both on rereading some of the promises of Reagan, Carter, Nixon, Kennedy. The apparent necessity of talking such nonsense is one of the things that keep some good people out of politics. A presidential candidate who won on reasonably sober rhetoric might encourage good people for the future, and along the way save himself some trouble in office. For that to happen, the voters—the audience—would have to want it that way.

Thomas Cronin of Colorado College, one of the most perceptive of the new generation of presidential scholars, puts it well: "We must refine our expectations of the president and raise our expectations of ourselves."

Perspectives on Structure

9.4 The Presidency and the Crisis of Public Management, A Panel of the National Academy of Public Administration

In addition to being a decision arena dominated by the personality of an individual, the contemporary presidency is a public management system. The following overview of a study of the managerial presidency by the National Academy of Public Administration identifies some major administrative problems in the presidency and offers some specific proposals for their remedy. After reading the report, what do you feel are the biases underlying it? What would be some alternative biases concerning the organization and management of the presidency?

Two centuries ago, Americans were struggling to invent a new form of government, aware that history would regard their work as a vital test of whether or not a free people could govern themselves.

Since then the nation has survived many crises. Yet today, under vastly changed conditions, the challenge facing us in the 1980s harks back to that of the 1780s. It is not primarily our wealth, nor our power, nor our technical inventiveness that is in question: *It is our capacity to govern ourselves.* If we cannot so manage our public affairs as to bring unity out of diversity, we will be able to meet no other challenge in the decades to come.

Effective self-government cannot be manufactured in Washington; must less is it a process that can be run from the presidency. In our form of democracy, management of public affairs depends on all levels of government and all parts of society.

A Presidency for the 1980s. A Report on Presidential Management by a Panel of the National Academy of Public Administration, November 1980. Copyright 1980 by the National Academy of Public Administration. Reprinted by permission.

However, mismanagement in Washington can undermine all other efforts. This report focuses on the president's role in managing the federal government. To the framers of the Constitution, proper arrangement of the executive function was crucial to the success of their experiment in self-government. The presidency remains no less crucial today. *A more effective presidency can help strengthen the rest of our democracy.* That is the purpose and the message of this report.

The Crisis of Public Management

The cumulative effect of many trends and events is threatening America's capacity for self-government. A clear danger is bearing down on us: At the same time that the problems we face are becoming more complex and interwoven, the power to deal with them is becoming increasingly diffused.

Interrelated Problems

In earlier times it seemed possible to treat the issues on our national agenda as reasonably self-contained problems, and to deal with them one at a time on their own terms. Today the challenges seem neither clear nor unifying. They are interlocked with one another in confusing and divisive ways.

On the international front, the United States, while seeking to sustain an overall nuclear balance, has become both more competitive with and dependent on the rest of the world. Foreign power centers increasingly affect our domestic agenda and at times take advantage of the openness and due process of our democratic institutions. Yet we are reliant on many of these same foreign sources for vital raw materials, with oil being only the most obvious of our dependencies. The share of our national product that we export has doubled in the past 15 years; the import share has doubled in half that time.

In domestic affairs, most major issues transcend the scope of any single government agency, cut across federal-state-local relationships, and often blur the boundary between the public and private sectors. Americans have asked and expected the federal government to assume a greater role in many areas of national life, from the economy to the environment, from health care to energy supplies. This expectation has led to a proliferation in the instruments of policy and administration—an enormous growth in regulatory activity, in federal assistance to states and cities, in loan and loan guarantee programs, in special tax provisions, and in the creation of quasi-governmental organizations.

These increased demands have produced a fundamental shift over the past several decades in the nature of government management—a shift from direct to indirect means. Rather than delivering services itself, Washington has sought to achieve its objectives by sponsoring activities and pumping resources through individuals, states and cities, nonprofit organizations, the private sector, and foreign governments. During the last 25 years, activities performed directly by the federal government have declined as a share of the national budget. The number of full-time federal employees has remained stable at a little under 3 million persons, while the number indirectly employed through federally sponsored activities has grown to 8 million. The result has been a massive increase in the complexity and interdependence of the entire government system.

The Diffusion of Power

As problems have become more complex and interrelated, the power to deal with them has increasingly fragmented.

This dilemma is most obvious in world politics. Antagonism between the superpowers dominates the world scene at a time when social, economic, and political upheavals have led to a global fragmentation of power. Our resources for the continuing superpower confrontation are substantial. Yet our ability to influence events abroad has diminished as other centers of economic, political, and military power have grown. We must rely increasingly on our allies, yet all existing alliances—democratic and communist—have had to accommodate more independence from their members. The United Nations and other international agencies have made only limited headway. The posture of nonalignment has gained strength. Nuclear power has proliferated. Terrorism stalks all nations. Events abroad can and do have profound effects on our domestic life, yet our efforts to influence the course of those events can rarely be unilateral; almost always we must interact with other governments.

In recent years, Americans also have become more aware of the fragmentation of power on the domestic scene. There has been growing concern over such trends as:

- the progressive weakening of political parties;
- drawn-out nominating and campaign procedures that are often irrelevant to the realities of governing;
- the fragmentation of congressional leadership coupled with new aggressiveness and assertiveness by individual members of Congress;
- mounting costs and delays in the delivery of public services as the complexities of federalism increase;
- increased litigation on matters of public policy and detailed judicial involvement in program administration;
- a radical increase in the number, professionalism, and potency of special-interest groups;
- a declining faith of Americans in the fairness, integrity, and competence of their social institutions, particularly the institutions of government.

Several of these trends have been given impetus by worthwhile reforms, including the opening of the political process to more influences. Yet the undeniable cumulative effect of these trends has been a radical diffusion of power, a weakening of the forces for coherence and unity. Independence which is unrestrained by a sense of larger responsibility threatens our capacity for self-government. Without such responsibility there can be no real political accountability.

Just such a sense of responsibility and accountability has waned in recent years. Instead, confrontation has become more nearly the norm in our political life, accentuated by the attention of increasingly powerful news media. Rather than a tool of last resort, confrontation has become the point of departure on many issues of national importance. The result has been progressively lessened prospects for decisive action based on consensus or reconciliation of competing objectives.

The practical effect of these trends is an unprecedented need for coherence in responses at all levels of government and with the private sector, and with other countries.

Yet the diffusion of power militates against this very coherence. Our national government now has responsibilities that involve power centers over which it has little control. Our institutional tools and resources are ill-equipped to provide the needed unity. Traditional methods of organization, which separate international issues from domestic concerns, economic policy from national security policy, have hampered our ability to respond. We have yet to find a reliable means to bring a governmentwide perspective to interdepartmental and intergovernmental matters, within either the executive branch or the Congress—even though these are precisely the types of matters that dominate our agenda and create the crisis in public management.

Coping with the Dilemma

In dividing powers among the branches and levels of government, our Constitution deliberately was designed to require cooperative unified action; in that was seen to lie safety from arbitrary power. By this criterion, the system has worked well in the past.

We now have to face the reality that political power has become fragmented beyond what the founding fathers could have imagined. The cooperation so essential for coping with our national problems is not merely difficult, it has become nearly impossible.

There are three possible courses of action in dealing with this dilemma. One is to await events in the hope that the system contains some self-correcting mechanism that will in time remedy the situation. Another is to alter the Constitution so as to encourage unified action. The third is to undertake timely reforms to make our constitutional system more governable.

Neither of the first two courses is attractive. To await events is to drift toward a dangerous future, the possibility of a manifest political breakdown and a decline into arbitrary power. Although changing the Constitution may be unattractive, it is surely preferable to the consequences of inaction.

Various ideas for amending the Constitution have been advanced in recent years. Motivated by concern over the way that effective action is blocked by the division of powers, particularly the stalemate that too often exists between the president and the Congress, some highly responsible public officials have called for constitutional change. Yet achieving agreement sufficient for action on any of these proposals would be extraordinarily difficult; we may well have to be on the brink of a breakdown in government for such change to be possible. At the least, it would entail years of debate which might only contribute to the divisiveness in our society. And basic reforms, however well intentioned, often have unintended adverse consequences, including in this case the danger of removing the safeguard against arbitrary power.

The preference of this panel is for the third course: *To develop a strategy for change, within present constitutional boundaries, to improve the effectiveness of our national government in dealing with interrelated problems and diffused power.* To achieve this goal, change will be needed in many complex and difficult areas—in political parties, in our processes for nominating and electing officeholders, in the public's understanding of the need for change, in the attitudes and performance of the media, and in the Congress and the executive branch.

In the judgment of this panel, the place to begin is at the institution of the presidency. *We can begin to strengthen the forces of cohesion and integration in our political system by strengthening the capacity of the presidency for leadership.* It is to this need that our report is addressed.

In strengthening the capacity of the presidency, we do not propose to alter the balance of powers in the Constitution. Neither do we agree with those who have proclaimed that the president can become more effective only at the expense of Congress, or Congress more effective only at the expense of the presidency. The current problem is much less a power contest between the legislative and executive branches than a struggle between the forces for coherence and continuity *within each branch* and the more narrow, specialized forces that lead to fragmentation and irresponsibility in the total system.

Both presidential and congressional power can be enhanced if each improves its capacity for coordinated action. Indeed, the presidency would in all probability benefit if the Congress were more strongly united and disciplined, and thereby able to bargain as an entity with presidential officeholders and executive departments. In this report the focus is on the presidency, not Congress. But we are mindful that a more effectively organized and managed presidency would improve the capacity of Congress to fulfill its obligation of holding the executive accountable.

The world has become too complex, and power too widely shared, for anyone to believe that the nation and the government can be managed solely from the White House, that the president can solve every problem that arises. Yet the fact remains that the president and the vice-president are the only officeholders elected by the nation. The presidency is thus vital to the reconciling of regional and factional interests, to the collaboration that is necessary to manage our pluralism in the interest of national goals.

Toward a More Effective Presidency

Our deliberations over the past two years have led us to support the following principles as a foundation of recommendations to strengthen the presidency as an instrument of effective self-government.

1. Presidential management is primarily a matter of working with others to achieve national purposes. Presidents and the public should recognize that the president is politically accountable not for the day-to-day, detailed management of the executive branch, but rather for leading others to sensible, concerted action on the important matters facing the nation. Each president will adopt his own approach to this management task. Some will use a chief of staff; others will prefer a different arrangement. The exact structure is less important than the concept.

2. The dominant approach by the president in dealing with others should be a collaborative one. Both the Constitution and the nature of the current crisis in public management demonstrate that ours is a government of separated and shared powers. Presidents must normally strive to work in concert with others, especially the Congress.

3. To exercise effective political management, presidents need a reliable base of non-partisan, unbiased advice. The institutional staffs reporting to the president should have a highly professional ability to supply objective and factual information. This need is particularly stringent for those staffs responsible for policy development, administrative management and coordination, and budgeting.

4. The number, uncertainty, and interdependence of issues necessitate a systematic means for sorting and organizing matters coming before the president and for rejecting those which should not. Again, each president will have his own approach to this need, some preferring a regular flow of decision memoranda and others opting for a less formal arrangement of consultations. Whatever the method, a president should adopt and enforce an effective system to bring the necessary range of relevant information and conflicting opinion before him in a timely manner.

5. Because presidents manage primarily through other people, presidential appointments are of immense importance. Presidential appointments, both to the Executive Office of the President and to departments and agencies, should be made with the utmost care. A far higher level of managerial ability than has been customary will be required in the 1980s. Presidents are thus well advised to make effective use of career and noncareer personnel in the new Senior Executive Service.

6. The immediate staff of the president should be small. A large staff of personal assistants will reduce the president's ability to control those persons who speak directly in his name.

7. Except in extreme national emergency, broad operating responsibilities belong in the executive departments and agencies, not in the Executive Office of the President. Generally, statutory authority rests with departmental and agency officials. It is there that detailed knowledge exists, and it is there that legal accountability resides.

8. Limiting the operational responsibilities of the presidency requires a corresponding increase in the ability of the Executive Office to intervene selectively on matters of substance and to promote a central perspective. An effective Executive Office must be equipped to initiate, prod, convene, facilitate, educate, and follow-up on the processes of collaborative policy-making and administration—not as a blanket authority, but selectively and in a responsible and supportive manner.

9. The Executive Office should not mirror special interests represented elsewhere. There is often a short-term political advantage in adding units to the Executive Office which represent special interests. Unless this temptation is avoided, the presidency will be hampered in bringing a governmentwide, national perspective to problems and will tend to second-guess or duplicate the work of departments and agencies that possess operating responsibilities.

10. The Executive Office cannot promote steady courses of action on vital national issues unless it contains important elements of continuity and planning. Without these elements of continuity and planning, personnel dealing with daily issues are unlikely to benefit from the perspectives and knowledge of those with longer term frames of reference.

Goals and Rationale of This Report

Accepting these principles, we have examined the organization, processes, and capacities of the Executive Office of the President and have found them wanting. Despite the efforts and good intentions of many people concerned, serious gaps and inadequacies have come to exist in the Executive Office. *The presidency has acquired its own internal problems of governability.* The Office's internal structure and processes mirror, rather than help to resolve, the particularistic interests in our society. The Office's personnel reflect the larger discontinuities and fragmentation of our politics. Presidential decisions tend to become one more piece of adversarial politics, amplified by the media's interest in confrontation.

If the managerial capacity of the presidency is to be significantly improved, support for this effort will be required not only from the president and his close advisers, but also from the larger political establishment and citizens in general. For such support to be forthcoming, a common understanding is needed of the powers and constraints of the presidency and of the evolution and current state of the Executive Office. . . .

In preparing our recommendations we have recognized that no easy formula can remedy the problems we are addressing. Rather, we have proposed a range of practices and reforms designed to create a momentum in the right direction, arrangements that can work equally well under a variety of circumstances and in whatever legal manner a president may choose to perform the duties of his office. This is the second, also major, goal of our report.

9.5 The Multiple Advocacy Prescription for Presidential Decisionmaking: An Explication and Analysis

David C. Kozak

Presidential scholars are in general agreement that among the most fruitful contributions to the study of the presidency are Neustadt's notions of power, Barber's focus on character and his typology for understanding it, and Alexander George's prescription for multiple advocacy. This original essay explains and assesses the multiple advocacy proposal. Although this essay concludes that the scheme lacks practicality and is not always desirable, multiple advocacy's notions of open and collegial decision processes should be part of a president's operating style.

Perhaps the most striking aspect of presidential literature is its combination of empirical and normative concerns. The scheme of multiple advocacy, much in vogue with would-be reformers of the U.S. policy process, is an excellent example of this mesh of descriptive and prescriptive thought. Succinctly defined, multiple advocacy (hereafter noted simply as "MA") is a prescription for an open and systematic consideration of U.S. foreign policy options and alternatives. Its proponents make explicit assumptions about organizational and presidential behavior and on this basis proceed to prescribe a system for avoiding problems and pitfalls. The purpose of this investigation is to analyze the proposed MA network. It is the position of this author that given the dual character of MA—i.e., both empirical and normative components—an adequate analysis can be accomplished only through an investigation of the model's (1) logic, (2) empirical veracity, (3) feasibility, and (4) desirability. The details of this framework for the analysis, critique, and appraisal of a model of organizational theory that has descriptive and prescriptive aspects

---

The author would like to thank his former graduate school professors—Bert Rockman and Fred Thayer—for their thoughtful comments on earlier drafts of this paper.

will be spelled out later. Before performing the analysis, we will seek to explicate the empirical and normative propositions of MA. Thus, this paper will be developed as follows: Part I—Explication; Part II—Analysis.

I. Explication

In order to thoroughly identify and illuminate the major notions of MA, this explication will proceed in the following manner. First, the major tenets of MA, as garnered from major original prescriptions, will be listed. Second, MA will be placed in the context of communications theory research. Third, MA will be differentiated from other related schemes in an effort to further define its characteristics. Several concepts and distinctions of organization theory will be applied to MA in an effort to make more clear what MA involves in an organizational sense.

Origins and Sources of Multiple Advocacy

MA has its origins in several of the more prominent post-mortems of the decision-making process that established and maintained the policy of U.S. involvement in Southeast Asia. These works are David Halberstam's *The Best and the Brightest* and James C. Thompson's "How Could Vietnam Happen?: An Autopsy." Also influential are *The Pentagon Papers*. And, although they dealt with many topics other than Vietnam, George Reedy's *The Twilight of the Presidency* and Stephen Hess's *Organizing the Presidency* should also be noted. A strong, common theme of Halberstam, Thompson, and *The Pentagon Papers* is the indictment of what they perceive to be a closed decision-making arena. These works pinpoint the following flaws of foreign policy decision-making which they hold are responsible for a U.S. disaster in Indochina: (1) the incomplete consideration of all alternatives, (2) advice by a small, narrowly comprised group of characterized by ideological homogeneity, (3) the lack of adequate policy review and reevaluation, (4) excessive emphasis on consensus, (5) oversimplifications of the decision, (6) faulty, distorted, or incomplete information due to either organization complexity or bureaucratic particularism and parochialism, and (7) "vest-pocket" decision-making. Reedy adds that the presidency has become institutionalized in such a way in recent years that the president has come to be surrounded by "yes men" and sycophants. To him, this isolation is one of the causes of bad decisions. As a remedy, Hess calls for a more collegial presidency. It is against this backdrop of analyses that MA prescriptions were proposed.

The MA prescription is most notably put forth in two works: Irving L. Janis's *Victims of Groupthink* and Alexander L. George's "The Case for Multiple Advocacy in Foreign Policy." Both were published in 1972 during an intense period of reaction against the Vietnam War. Both concur with the above-mentioned analyses of decision-making malfunctions with regard to U.S. involvement in Indochina and with Reedy's assessment of "isolation." Both use MA as a way of opening up the decision process, of off-setting biased information, and of insuring that decision premises are re-examined periodically.

Janis is more comprehensive than George. He surveys various U.S. foreign policy fiascoes—the Bay of Pigs, the Korean Decision, Pearl Harbor, and escalation of the Vietnam War—and contrasts them with alleged policy successes—the Cuban Missile Crisis and the formation of the Marshall Plan. He then seeks to discover what the fiascoes have in common and what the successes have in common and how the two patterns differ. George, on the other hand, is more concerned with problems he feels might arise out of the type of organization that Henry Kissinger installed at the National Security Council (NSC). George fears that the Kissinger apparat may be a closed system and, thus, might lead to miscalculation and misconception.

Despite their differences in scope, Janis and George are very similar with regard to the general problems of decision-making that they respectively diagnose. To Janis, major malfunctions in decision-making occur as a result of the "groupthink" syndrome. According to Janis, groupthink is the process whereby a decision group, insecure with the stresses of decision-making that cannot be alleviated by standard operating procedures, engages in concurrence-seeking as a form of striving for mutual support (Janis, p. 202). Its symptoms are:

1. an illusion of invulnerability, shared by most or all the members, which creates excessive optimism and encourages taking extreme risks;
2. collective efforts to rationalize in order to discount warnings which might lead the members to reconsider their assumptions before they recommit themselves to their past policy decisions;
3. an unquestioned belief in the group's inherent morality, inclining the members to ignore the ethical or moral consequences of their decisions;
4. stereotyped views of enemy leaders as too evil to warrant genuine attempts to negotiate, or as too weak and stupid to counter whatever risky attempts are made to defeat their purposes;
5. direct pressure on any member who expresses strong arguments against any of the group's stereotypes, illusions, or commitments, making clear that this type of dissent is contrary to what is expected of all loyal members;
6. self-censorship of deviations from the apparent group consensus, reflecting each member's inclination to minimize to himself the importance of his doubts and counterarguments;
7. a shared illusion of unanimity concerning judgments conforming to the majority view (partly resulting from self-censorship of deviations, augmented by the false assumption that silence means consent);
8. the emergence of self-appointed mindguards—members who protect the group from adverse information that might shatter their shared complacency about the effectiveness and morality of their decisions. (Janis, pp. 197-98)

For George, malfunctions are likely:

1. When the president and his advisers agree too readily on the nature of the problem facing them and on a response to it.
2. When advisers and advocates take different positions and debate them before the president but their disagreements do not cover the full range of relevant hypotheses and alternative options.
3. When there is no advocate for an unpopular policy option.
4. When advisers to the president thrash out their own disagreements over policy without the president's knowledge and confront him with a unanimous recommendation.
5. When advisers agree privately among themselves that the president should face up to a difficult decision, but no one is willing to alert him to the need for doing so.
6. When the president, faced with an important problem to decide, is dependent upon a single channel of information.
7. When the key assumptions and premises of a plan have been evaluated only by the advocates of that option.
8. When the president asks advisers for their opinions on a preferred course of action but does not request a qualified group to examine more carefully the negative judgment offered by one or more advisers.
9. When the president is impressed by the consensus among his advisers on behalf of a particular policy but fails to ascertain how firm the consensus is, how it was achieved, and whether it is justified. (George, pp. 769-80)

The tie which binds their respective analyses is the notion that bad policy results from "closed" decision-making. For both, the likelihood that a malfunction will ensue is greatly increased in those situations when (1) policymakers are not aware of, or just do not seriously consider, all possible options, (2) there is too much emphasis on cohesion and consensus within the policy-making body, and (3) the leader reveals his preferences as decision alternatives are being explored by the group. Underlying these notions in both Janis and George seems to be the assumption that an incomplete consideration of alternatives, a premature consensus, and the toadyism engendered by the leader's announcement of his position will lead to a decision process far more shallow and less rigorous than what would naturally occur if these conditions were not present. In other words, by not fully coming to grips with all possible alternatives, decision-makers do not fully think through the implications of their decision. Or, to state in a positive manner, as a decision-maker considers a range of options and debates them, his thought processes will be more rigorous than if he did not consider the alternatives. By considering alternatives, he is forced to think through the implications and consequences of his decision. Presumably this reduces the probability that the eventual decision will be plagued by groupthink, mindsets, blinders, and negative externalities (i.e., unforeseen, unanticipated, and undesirable policy consequences).

Both Janis and George offer prescriptions for MA that propose to increase the number and variety of options presented to policymakers and, thus, to improve the rigor of the decision thought process. Basically, these prescriptions call for the president to establish a system of multiple, competing advisors. Janis's scheme is much less structured than George's. His prescriptions are directed to the leader (president). He calls for the leader to insure that all possible points of view are considered and that a premature consensus does not develop within the presidentially selected small decision group of advisors. His specific recommendations are:

1. The leader of a policy-forming group should assign the role of critical evaluator to each member, encouraging the group to give high priority to airing objections and doubts. This practice needs to be reinforced by the leader's acceptance of criticism of his own judgments in order to discourage the members from soft-pedaling their disagreements.
2. The leaders in an organization's hierarchy, when assigning a policy-planning mission to a group, should be impartial instead of stating preferences and expectations at the outset. This practice requires each leader to limit his briefings to unbiased statements about the scope of the problem and the limitations of available resources, without advocating specific proposals he would like to see adopted. This allows the conferees the opportunity to develop an atmosphere of open inquiry and to explore impartially a wide range of policy alternatives.
3. The organization should routinely follow the administrative practice of setting up several independent policy-planning and evaluation groups to work on the same policy question, each carrying out its deliberations under a different leader.
4. Throughout the period when the feasibility and effectiveness of policy alternatives are being surveyed, the policy-making group should from time to time divide into two or more subgroups to meet separately, under different chairmen, and then come together to hammer out their differences.
5. Each member of the policy-making group should discuss periodically the group's deliberations with trusted associates in his own unit of the organization and report back their reactions.
6. One or more outside experts or qualified colleagues within the organization who are not core members of the policy-making group should be invited to each meeting on a staggered basis and should be encouraged to challenge the views of the core members.
7. At every meeting devoted to evaluating policy alternatives, at least one member should be assigned the role of devil's advocate.
8. Whenever the policy issue involves relations with a rival nation or organization, a sizable bloc of time (perhaps an entire session) should be spent surveying all warning signals from the rivals and constructing alternative scenarios of the rivals' intentions.
9. After reaching a preliminary consensus about what seems to be the best policy alternative, the policy-making group should hold a "second chance" meeting at which every member is expected to express as vividly as he can all his residual doubts and then rethink the entire issue before making a definitive choice. (Janis, pp. 209-19)

George's prescriptions also go to the leader. However, unlike Janis, he assigns responsibility for assuring MA to the president's "Special Assistant for National Security Affairs," rather than directly to the president. To George, the special assistant (the equivalent of Kissinger at the White House during his pre-State Department days) will be the manager and monitor of the MA system. The special assistant's task is to insure that all possible points are considered and that all key actors are heard from. The special assistant will accomplish this by insuring that there is:

1. no major maldistribution among the various actors of the following resources:
   a) power, weight, influence
   b) competence relevant to the policy issues
   c) information relevant to the policy problem
   d) analytical resources
   e) bargaining and persuasion skills
2. presidential-level participation in organization policy-making. . . .
3. time for adequate debate and give-and-take. (George, p. 759)

It is imperative that the special assistant, in performing these functions, be completely non-partisan. In George's words,

> The special assistant will be able to perform the critical tasks associated with the custodian's role *only if he scrupulously refrains from becoming an advocate himself.* (George, p. 781, italics his)

The special assistant thus plays a crucially pivotal role in George's scheme. He is the one who will make MA work. As Cronin notes,

> This aide or set of aides would be charged with balancing advisory resources when necessary, strengthening weaker advocates, bringing in new advisers to argue for unpopular options, setting up new channels of information, and arranging for independent evaluations of options. (Cronin, 1975, p. 275)

In sum, both of our MA proponents address problems of decision-making stemming from an early curtailment of debate, a premature consensus, and the lack of information on possible policy options. Janis contributes heavily here by giving us a theory of "groupthink" syndrome that purports to explain why these problems occur. With groupthink, he argues that decision-makers, due to the pressure to decide and their doubt and anxiety about the correctness of the decision, have a strong tendency toward conformity. George concurs. Both authors offer prescriptions for opening up the policy process so that decision-makers can avoid the pitfalls of groupthink. Both would insure that there is an adequate number of advocates and that there is sufficient time for debate. Both desire an atmosphere of competition among advocates to insure that assumptions underlying the various proposed alternatives are challenged and subjected to the scrutiny of debate and deliberation. Janis prescribes that the president should make sure that multiple advocacy is part of his decision process. George goes further. He proposes that the job of multiple advocacy custodian be assigned to the president's special assistant. The special assistant will insure that advice and information is presented to the president under "guided" free market conditions.

Given the small differences that exist between George and Janis, and given the supplemental nature of their writings (Janis's ex-

Figure 9.5.1

Causal sequence of decision-making malfunction as implied by multiple advocacy.

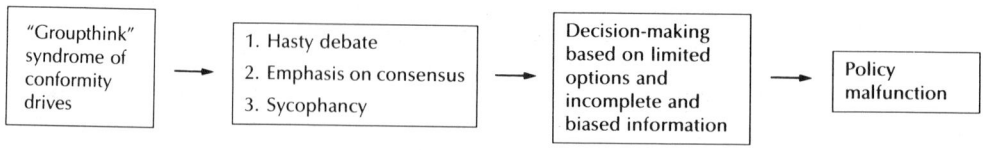

Figure 9.5.2

Causal sequence implied by multiple advocacy remedy.

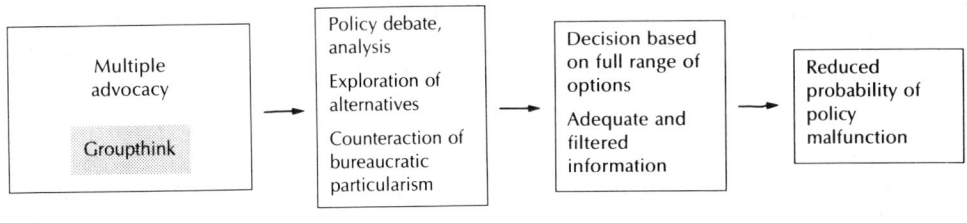

planatory theory, George's structure), and given that George relies heavily on Janis, we will continue throughout the remainder of this paper to cite them both as spokesmen for the multiple advocacy prescription. In the main, though, we will focus on George.

Empirical Propositions

Every proposal for structured reform, whether it concerns the presidency or some other institution, posits, either explicitly or implicitly, certain empirical propositions concerning the nature of reality. For a clear understanding of a proposal, these propositions should be formulated into hypotheses. By doing so, we (a) gain insight into the proponent's assumptions concerning the empirical order or "what is" and (b) put the proponent's propositions in a form suitable for testing. The formulation of hypotheses from the MA prospectus will be the task of this section of our explication. A critique and assessment of these propositions will follow in Part II of this paper.

MA posits a major causal scheme. It is depicted in figure 9.5.1. The groupthink syndrome (the drive for conformity) leads to hasty decisions, an emphasis within the group on consensus, and sycophancy (blind follow-ership). These in turn, lead to decision-making based on limited options and incomplete and biased information. The result is a policy malfunction. The MA prescription would provide the remedy sequence depicted in figure 9.5.2. A leader, by manipulating the sequence to insure that numerous points of view are put forth and that actors and agencies down the organization understand that it is legitimate to engage in debate, will be able to override or at least minimize the consequences of groupthink. Instead of groupthink, he will create a decision arena that gives full consideration to all alternatives. The result will be a policy less prone to malfunction. The possibility of policy malfunction in implementation (after a decision has already been made) will be reduced by the continuing debate in an MA forum concerning the decision's execution and administration.

Major hypotheses inherent in these schemes are:

1. The groupthink syndrome (drive for cohesion and consensus within the decision group) is naturally present in decision groups.
2. Groupthink is engendered by the pressures and apprehension of decision-making.

3. Groupthink leads to hasty debate, emphasis on consensus, and sycophancy.
4. Hasty debate, emphasis on consensus, and sycophancy lead to decision-making based on incomplete and biased information and on limited options.
5. A decision made under conditions of incomplete or biased information is likely to lead to policy malfunction.
6. A decision made without benefit of a complete range of options is likely to lead to policy malfunction.
7. The institutionalized search for policy alternatives avoids the consequences of the groupthink syndrome.
8. Institutionalized search for policy alternatives will lead to competitive policy debate and analysis.
9. The institutionalization of a search for policy alternatives will lead to an exploration of alternatives and a counteraction of bureaucratic particularism.
10. The exploration and debate of policy options will insure that a decision is based on the full range of options and on adequate information (at least more adequate than if debate had not occurred).
11. A decision based on a full range of options is less likely to involve policy malfunctions—i.e., the more complete the range of options, the better the decision.
12. A decision based on complete and unbiased information is less likely to result in policy malfunction—i.e., the more complete and unbiased the information, the better the decision.

The above hypotheses are implied by the schemes presented in figures 9.5.1 and 9.5.2. The two MA authors also make a number of other assumptions about organizational reality that are not so obvious in the figures but are implied in their narrative. For the convenience of our analysis, we will distinguish between those assumptions made concerning organizations and decision-making in general and those pertaining directly to the feasibility of implementing George's multiple advocacy structure. Other general hypotheses are:

13. "The more insulated a cohesive group of executives becomes, the greater are the chances that its policy decisions will be products of groupthink." (Janis, p. 197)
14. "The more accurately the leader of a cohesive policy-making group promotes his own preferred solution, the greater are the chances of a consensus based on groupthink, even when the leader does not want the members to be yes-men. . . ." (Janis, p. 197)
15. The more cohesive the decision group, the greater is the likelihood that it will succumb to groupthink.
16. The more diversified the group, the greater is the likelihood that a full range of options will be constructed—i.e., diversity is positively related to multiple advocacy. The more people represented from different backgrounds, the more competing positions put forth, since different actors desire to put forth their own preferred solution.
17. Many actors will generate more proposals than any one individual.
18. Structured advocacy will produce more proposals than an unstructured system.
19. Information is a crucial variable affecting policy output. The information on which policy-makers proceed strongly colors their decisions.
20. The information forwarded and filtered through the bureaucracy to decision-makers is an unstructured and unsystematic and noncompetitive communications network that will be biased and distorted by bureaucratic parochialism (i.e., the desire of agencies to gain power, prestige, mission embellishment, etc.).

Obviously implied in multiple advocacy is the assumption that it can be feasibly implemented. The following hypotheses are suggested by this assumption:

1. MA will be implemented—i.e., there is an incentive for a president to insure that MA becomes the decision-making mode.
2. The process of bureaucratic politics, if structured and directed, will provide multiple advocates. Bureaucratic competitors will function as a MA network. This will guarantee the formulation of numerous points of view.

3. Bureaucratic competition will lead to a *full* range of options.
4. Resources can be equalized among competitors.
5. The special advisor can and will remain neutral.
6. The president will pay attention to advocacy.
7. MA can be employed in most important decisions.

Normative Premises

Every reform package has normative biases. These biases may not be obvious. They may be, in fact, very difficult to detect. In any event, if a proposal is to be fully understood, its normative implications should be explicated. Usually, normative assumptions are present in several forms: prescriptions, evaluations, and "high level" value choices. The prescriptive component of the MA proposal is, obviously, the prescription for a managed and monitored system of competing, multiple advisors. Examples of evaluations are those statements in Janis and George that hold that closed systems are undesirable; debate, a consideration of all alternatives, is good; vest pocket decision-making is bad. Though these evaluations are held to be grounded in empirical truth, the lack of evidence requires our authors to make a "quantum leap" to draw these conclusions. As such, we will classify them as value judgments.

Identification of a "higher order" value premise in George and Janis is no easy task. They attempt to be scientific and thus do not intentionally promote a major value or norm except for the "managed" advocacy system. If one looks hard enough, however, a value preference for a "mechanistic," hierarchical perspective on organizations and its classical interpretation of hierarchy can be found in their writings. Throughout, Janis and George explicitly state that their major goal is "good" policy-making. Their desire is to prescribe a system that will reduce the probability of decision-making malfunctions. Though they never give us their precise definition of "good policy," presumably good policy is policy that does not end in a fiasco of negative externalities, sunken costs, inadequate planning, miscalculation, stereotypes, oversimplifications, or policy discontinuities. A reasonable inference from this emphasis on what constitutes a malfunction is that Janis and George subscribe to an hierarchically oriented interpretation of organizations. To them, decisions should be made by the leader who sits on top of the hierarchy. The decision-making apparatus should be designed to enhance the probability of the executive getting good advice and therefore making a "good," rational decision. Though Janis and George acknowledge the existence of an "organic" side to organizations (to borrow from Burns and Stalker) by noting that the organization is influenced by nonhierarchical considerations, informal groups, bargaining, etc., they show a preference for a "mechanistic," classical hierarchy. Those on top of the organization should shape the processes of the organization to serve their goals. Important decisions should be made formally through the hierarchy.

In sum, the major normative premise which underlies the prescription for MA is: The decision-making process should be manipulated so that it will serve the executive in making a "rational" decision.

Multiple Advocacy as a Communications Process

To fully understand the contribution of communications to organizations, it is necessary to specify the different kinds of communications. Though lists abound, an integration of various authors' inventories renders a sevenfold list of separate communications processes. They are: (1) upward, (2) downward, (3) lateral, (4) informal, (5) search, (6) public relations, and (7) feedback. Each performs a different function for the organization. Upward communications allow those up the hierarchy to receive the response of organization members. Downward communications are used primarily for control purposes, though control is not exclusively performed by downward communications. Lateral communications are primarily used for coordination. Informal or "grapevine" communications supplement the highly controlled, more formal upward and downward communications. Whereas formal communications supposedly follow definite lines of "accountability," informal communications are said to involve channels that are highly variable and unpredictable. Search involves intelligence gathering. With it, an organizational memory is developed and maintained. Public relations is used to build support in the environment. Feedback is used to get intelligence from the organization's clientele or constituency.

Within the vast literature of organization communications, problems concerning each of these different kinds of communications have been identified.

It should be noted that this literature is not uniform in specifying for whom or for what the identified problem is considered to be dysfunctional. In some works, certain communications problems are held to be dysfunctional for executives. In other writings the organization or the policy are seen as the eventual victims. In yet others the organization at large or the workers are considered victims. In any event, numerous proposals have been put forth for dealing with the various prob-

Figure 9.5.3

Multiple advocacy in context:
Communication types, problems, and proposed solutions.

Communication Type	Identified Problem	Proposed Solutions
Public Relations	deceit, fabrication, secrecy, manipulation	greater supervision
Lateral	redundancy, conflict of specialists, jurisdictional rivalries, suboptimization	more staff meetings, coordination
Informal	disruptive rumors, bad interpersonal relations	integration, cooptation, or dismissal of rumor mongers
Feedback	too much exit, not enough voice	(Hirchman) proper blend of exist and voice
Downward	selective compliance ambiguities over control	more control clearer directives less control
Search	inaccurate or incomplete intelligence, conceptual blinders, problems of prediction, remediality (search only when there is trouble)	*multiple advocacy
Upward	bad advice, filtered and distorted information, toadyism, insulation	*multiple advocacy

lems unique to different types of communications. Figure 9.5.3 lists the various types of communications, their respective problems, and some of the prescriptions that have been put forth for their amelioration. For our purposes, the usefulness of this figure lies in the fact that it places the MA network in the context of organizational communications literature. As is evident from this figure, *multiple advocacy is a proposed solution for problems which have been identified with regard to search and upward communications.* Just as staff meetings, for example, are offered as a solution for the problems of coordination that may result from excessive and undirected lateral communications, multiple advocacy is proposed as a remedy or "error correction mechanism" for problems of search, such as incomplete intelligence, conceptual blinders, remediality, etc. and problems of upward communications, such as distorted information and executive insulation.

Differentiation

Within recent years numerous prescriptions for better communications and better information within the presidency have been proposed. In explicating the major characteristics of multiple advocacy, it is necessary to demonstrate how MA is both similar to, and different from, these other schemes. The payoff for us, of course, is that by contrasting MA with like prescriptions, we gain a much better insight into the distinguishing features of MA.

At first glance, MA may be easily confused with proposals for collegial decision-making, "devil's advocate," "adversary proceedings," "Ex Com," "mutual partisan adjustment," the Kissinger apparat, and the "new administration." Though some similarities exist, MA is very different from each of these.

Collegial decision-making is decision by the group. Though both collegial decision-making and MA attempt to widen the decision arena and bring more points of view to bear on a given problem, multiple advocacy emphasizes an executive decision. While with collegiality the group itself will choose an option, under multiple advocacy the diversified group of multiple advocates presents the options and the executive decides.

The "devil's advocate" system calls for an advisor to assume the role of spokesman for an unpopular point of view. He then presses this point with decision-makers, hopefully forcing them to refine their thinking. The similarity here is that Janis's prescriptions call for a devil's advocate. The difference, however, is found in George's more elaborate scheme. George fears that a devil's advocate will not be an effective spokesman. To George, the advocate lacks the resources (and perhaps the commitment) necessary to make an effective case for his position. Thus, under George, it is hoped that the natural phenomenon of bureaucratic politics will provide the wide ranging points of view that would be presented under devil's advocate.

"Adversary proceedings" share multiple advocacy's assumption that a policy submitted to the rigors of debate, deliberation, and scrutiny in a market place of ideas will be a better policy. The notion here is that this exercise will cause the policy to be refined and perfected. Basically, the adversarial system requires that those representing different sides of a policy question sit down together (or with devil's advocates) and debate their respective positions. Hopefully, as a result of this exercise, all sides will understand the implication of their positions and will understand perhaps where their own vulnerability lies. This will give them an opportunity to perfect their position. The major difference between this and MA is that this scheme is for the benefit of the advocates. MA is for the benefit of the executive. A natural advocacy system provided by bureaucratic politics will present options to the president. Under George, primary interaction is to be between the president and the advocates. Under Janis, although the leader will interact in a decision group, the purpose of the adversary meeting is to enhance the rationality of the decision and not the position of the advocates.

As Allison (1971) points out, "Ex Comm" was a special, ad hoc group of advisors convened by President Kennedy during the Cuban Missile Crisis. The group was comprised mostly of the president's counselors and administration officials. The purpose of the group was to provide the president with a list of possible U.S. responses to the discovery of Soviet missiles in Cuba. Though this application addresses the same general problems addressed by multiple advocacy—incomplete options, incomplete information—and though it tries to bring a more rigorous thought process to presidential decision-making, there are two important differences. The first is that MA is a permanent ongoing system, while "Ex Com" was used only in crises. Second, MA has no set boundaries, in contrast to "Ex Com" where either you were or were not appointed to serve. As prescribed by George, the advocacy system is an open one. It is open to anyone with a point of view.

"Mutual partisan adjustment," according to Lindblom (1968), is a process whereby competitors accommodate and compromise. It is prescribed as a way of settling differences. The similarity is that both prescriptions assume a competitive, segmented policy arena. The major difference is that multiple advocacy holds that good policy results from competition, not compromise. In MA, the leader, not the process, should synthesize competing points of view.

"Participatory decision-making," as defined by Pateman and others, would have those most affected by a policy or most involved in the implementation of a policy assigned major responsibility in policy-making. There is a major difference between this and multiple advocacy. The latter reserves decision-making for the leader. Furthermore, decision-making by agencies with a major administrative responsibility or "interest" in a possible policy is one of those potential problems intended to be counteracted by MA.

The "Kissinger apparat" at NSC presents a most striking contrast with MA. As Leacocos (1971-72) notes, the apparat is an attempt to neutralize the parochial impact of bureaucrats on foreign policy-making that Kissinger finds so troublesome. According to Kissinger (1966), bureaucratic politics can have a pernicious impact on policy-making. Following Neustadt (1964), bureaucracy is seen as a threat to presidential power. To offset it, information for presidential policy-making is tightly controlled by the NSC advisor. He prepares a list of options and contingency plans for the president. Under George's proposal, in striking contrast, bureaucratic politics is a potentially positive force. The NSC advisor is a relay point for policy information—not an originator.

"New administration" is a most encompassing rubric. For some it means a new relevance and pragmatism for the academic field of public administration. For some it refers to innovations in contemporary organizations. For others, it means revolutionary, nonhierarchical prescriptions for organizational problems. And for yet others, it means all of these. From the writings of those most associated with "new administration"—Bennis, Thayer, Frederickson—a common core emerges. Basically, at a minimum, new administration puts a premium on "open systems," the acceptance and use of "conflict" in problem-solving, policy "interaction" without formal authority. It is obvious from the above explication of MA that MA does indeed incorporate some of the characteristics of what has come to be known as "new administration." MA attempts to have an "open communications system" of advocates. It does attempt to utilize organizational conflict and competition in an effort to preclude tunnel vision. It does not put a premium on consensus. By relying on the NSC, MA does employ a transorganizational mechanism. Wider participation is encouraged. The major difference is that MA utilizes a scheme of hierarchical authority. It exists for presidential use. It is not policy-making or infrastructure management by participants. MA is a control device employed to aid the executive.

The major conclusion to be drawn from this section is that multiple advocacy, by contrast with other prescriptions, is an executive-oriented, institutionalized form of competition among advocates, that uses, not neutralizes, bureaucratic politics. The president is presented, not with an option thrashed out by his advisors, but with a list of options, produced by the play of bureaucratic politics, from which he is to choose.

II. Analysis

In this section, MA will be critiqued in terms of its logic, veracity, feasibility, and desirability. The purpose of this section is to demonstrate that, given the empirical and normative aspects of a reform proposal such as MA, an adequate analysis must address all four of these considerations.

Logic

Every proposal should be assessed in terms of its logical coherence. "Logical coherence" requires that a proposal be examined for (1) its definitional completeness, (2) the compatibility of its premises, and (3) the relevance of the proposals to the problem identified. Consideration of these benchmarks of logic aids in our subsequent consideration of veracity, feasibility, and desirability.

In terms of *definitional adequacy*, MA leaves much to be desired. It is not a logically complete system. Many crucial aspects are not spelled out. For instance, neither George or Janis spell out precisely what they mean by "good" decision, the concept so central to MA. Also, nowhere in George's article are we told who the advocates will be. We know they are bureaucrats, but are they political appointees? "Mid-level" bureaucrats? Also, it is not spelled out what kind of information is to be transmitted. Is it policy options only? Or should there also be "political" and technical information? This is important because what kind of information is provided will determine what is thrashed out. Other examples of important gaps in multiple advocacy are the assumptions that: (1) the president will adopt it (What is the incentive?), (2) the special advisor will be able to coordinate all communications (How will he do this?), (3) issues are resolved at a single decision point (they often are not, Halperin and Kanter, p. 30), (4) presidents will pay attention to multiple advocacy (they might ignore it or act viscerally), (5) the scheme of competing multiple advisors and the debate it engenders will somehow override the natural tendency of agencies to skew and distort to their favor the information they process, filter, and forward to the president. (Pending greater elaboration on this by George, it seems just as logical to argue in criticism of MA that if the raw materials of MA are the various parochial concerns of individual bureaucracies, increasing the volume of advocates, as MA would do, would have the net effect of merely increasing the volume of slanted, parochial, unrealistic information and advice. MA advocates need to specify how more parochial advice will lead to the president's getting a more realistic picture.)

With regard to the compatibility of premises, Kaufman (1956) offers us a possible framework for assessing consistency. He gives us a typology of different underlying value premises. Though he does not claim that his typology involves mutually exclusive categories, there is a strong implication that consistency is the absence of any confusion of values. Kaufman (p. 1057) notes that there are three core values underlying administrative theory: representativeness, neutral competence, and executive leadership. Each constitutes a different kind of criterion for evaluating organizations. Multiple advocacy applies all three. In MA, the ultimate policy decision is judged in terms of executive leadership. The advocates are judged by "representativeness," and the special advisor is judged by standards of "neutral competence." Such a scheme, without elaboration by the proponents, must be judged as at least a looming inconsistency. Another looming contradiction is that, as noted in figure 9.5.3, MA seeks to solve both problems of search and of upward communications. It seems that a reasonable argument can be made that solutions for one type of communications problem may not be a solution for the other. In fact, solutions for search, such as soliciting outside advice, might undermine upward communications by alienating those within the organization. Lacking a more detailed explication from MA advocates, it does not seem outlandish to speculate that MA's attempt to eliminate the search problem of conceptual blinders might impede upward inputs, e.g., the special advisor/monitor chides advocates for myopia, etc., with the result being that the advocates are more cautious and leery of advocating.

Relevance can be assessed by speculating about the likelihood that the prescriptions will provide relief for the presumed problem. The presumed problem for MA, as noted in figure 9.5.1, is a bad decision resulting from inadequate information. Lack of debate, etc., causes information shortages. MA is proposed to increase debate and therefore render more information and better policy. There are some problems here. More information may not result in better policy. Depending on the president or the situation, it may simply be ignored. After all, in the MA scheme of things, ultimate authority still rests with the president. Also, executive decision-making is plagued by many problems, of which information shortages are only one type. More information, though solving for problems of incomplete options, may exacerbate other problems such as control. With regard to relevance, a major limitation of the MA scheme is that it does not guard against irrational or deranged decision makers. Certainly, many policy malfunctions can be attributed to the character of the policy maker and not simply the policy process.

With this brief survey for logic, we conclude that multiple advocacy suffers from some definitional gaps, looming inconsistencies, potential negative externalities, and probable irrelevancies.

Empirical Veracity

In an analysis of a proposed framework for problem solving, it is crucial to check the veracity of underlying hypotheses. As numerous policy scientists have noted, the adequacy of an author's prescriptions are only as good as the empirical base on which they are built. Ideally, in the case of MA this would involve a testing of the veracity of all the empirical propositions explicated above (with the exception of those of feasibility that will be considered following this section). But, such an ambitious task is beyond the scope of this survey. What will be done here is a literature review. Relevant literature will be searched in an effort to see what evidence exists in support, or contradiction, of the empirical assumptions of MA. The findings will be presented under two categories: hard data and soft data.

There is very little in the way of hard, experimental data concerning MA assumptions. This may be a function of the general paucity of decision-making research. More likely, it seems attributable to site, task, and situation differences in experimental conditions. No experimental study gives us the decisional context posited by MA: high level, high stakes. Studies taken under other conditions provide an approximation, but in making an inference for MA a big jump must be made.

Most of the hard, experimental research concerns decision-making in small groups under highly variable situations. The results have been anything but conclusive. Some light can be shed on MA assumptions but, as noted above, a giant leap is involved. Much of the group dynamics research substantiates the notion that, generally, groups are superior to individuals in solving problems (Maier, 1963; Allport, 1920; Taylor and Faust, 1952; Perlmutter, 1952; Hall, 1971). In the works of Blau and Scott (1962), "It appears that collaboration with others in problem-solving improves performance quite independently of any other improvements . . ." (p. 118). Or, "The horse that is put together by a committee that understands group dynamics won't turn out to be a camel; it may be a thoroughbred filly fit for the triple crown" (Hall, 1971, p. 88). Though the George prescriptions do not posit group decision-making, these findings are relevant to at least Janis's discussion group. More importantly, these studies are relevant to MA in that, by explaining group superiority in terms of an error-correction mechanism provided by social interaction (Lorge and Soloman, 1955; Marjorie Shaw, 1932), they confirm the major assumption of MA that the interplay of different ideas refines thought. The conclusion that "groups seem assured of a much larger proportion of correct solutions than individuals" (Shaw, 1932, p. 504), however, is not accepted without qualification. For instance, Thorndike (1938) finds that, in doing crossword puzzles, a group is more efficient, but in drawing up a crossword puzzle, individuals are superior. For MA, this seems to suggest that group superiority is highly conditional and therefore cannot be prescribed for all decision situations. Some findings are strongly supportive of Janis. Most notable are Blau and Scott, who declare that cohesive groups will have a natural tendency toward uniformity. Some run counter to MA's assumptions, finding that high cohesive groups are more effective. Dissupportive findings are perhaps overridden by the research findings most relevant to MA. Pelz (1956) sets up what is a test of a major MA assumption: that a more diversified group will lead to more options and thus better performance. Pelz substantiates this assumption. "Heterophily rather than homophily is more associated with efficiency. Results indicate that scientists tend to perform more acceptably when they are closely associated with colleagues having a variety of values, experiences and disciplines" (Pelz, p. 310). Thus, although our acceptance of these studies is limited, especially given their lack of any standard measure of success or effectiveness and lack of equivalent experimental conditions, we can conclude that the few experiments that are relevant to our topics generally confirm major assumptions, qualify others, and contradict or at least render inconclusive a few. *By way of summary, those supported are: (1) collaboration with others provides error correction, (2) cohesion produces uniformity, and (3) interaction with others produces higher performance than unilateral behavior.*

In addition to the experimental data, several analytical or interpretive works based on soft data (case studies, logical suppositions) provide interesting commentary on MA's empirical assumptions. The most noteworthy are those by Page, Wilensky, and Downs. All three provide support for Janis and George. Paige (1968), on the basis of his exhaustive study of the *Korean Decision*, gives a prescription for MA: ". . . decision makers are advised to broaden their understanding of the situation by calling for existing information at variance with the prevailing consensus" (p. 361). Thus, he agrees with the MA theory's assumption that more diversity of information leads to better decisions. Wilensky (1967), in his book of case studies, holds, like George and Janis, that problems in organizational intelligence and search are responsible for bad decisions. Downs (1967) notes with a concurring deduction that "use of redundant information channels increases the probability of obtaining accurate information" (p. 269).

Other major commentary on the empirical assumptions of Janis and George, beyond that provided by these authors themselves, is provided by Thomas, Rourke, Sorensen, Geiger and Hansen, and Thayer. Thomas (1970) supports multiple advocacy by noting "that leadership is heavily dependent on the advice and information that the president receives" (p. 570). Rourke is supportive of George's assumption that bureaucracy functions in a bargaining arena. For Rourke, bureaucrats are constantly struggling and competing and probably would provide an advocacy network (Rourke, 1969). Sorensen presents a contrasting note. He argues that a president's decisions are made less on the basis of information and more on the basis of politics (Sorensen, 1963). Geiger and Hansen concur with Sorensen. "Decision-makers' . . . willingness and ability to seek and utilize particular kinds of information are never determined solely—and in many cases not even mainly—by purely intellectual considerations" (Geiger and Hansen, 1968, p. 330). For MA, the implications of Sorensen and Geiger and Hansen call into question MA's assumption that increasing the flow of information and advice will enhance the prospects for a rational decision. Thayer (1971), with his conclusion that "wider participation in policy processes might lead to improvements in policies themselves" and "let us begin the search for viable revisions," lends support to the major theme of MA (p. 561).

To conclude this section, although MA's assumptions are generally supported by available evidence and commentary, the evidence necessary for a thorough analysis is lacking. Many key propositions are not addressed in general literature. And, given the difficulty of defining "malfunction," "good policy," and "rationality," it is not likely that they will be. Perhaps the best possible test would involve simulation exercises to see if heterophily and diversity lead to a longer list of options. This would be a beginning. That a beginning is needed is suggested by Cameron (1975) in his article on the Ford administration's decision structure. As he notes, Ford proceeded on a highly questionable assumption that numerous advisors with access to the president will lead the president to a wise choice.

Feasibility

Every proposal should be assessed concerning the likelihood of its adoption and the likelihood that it will work as intended. To do this, we will critique the hypotheses concerning feasibility listed above.

1. "MA will be put into operation as a decision mode." Such an assumption cannot be answered with a simple yes or no answer. There reasonably seem to be certain conditions under which MA would be imposed by the president. Those most important are:

a. If he wants it. As Hage and Dewar (1973) point out, leader values are the single strongest predictor of innovation.
b. If an external force demands it.

However, Cyert and March (1963, p. 119) seem to argue strongly against such a model on the grounds that organizations stress short-run considerations and avoid the long-range considerations and the uncertainty that would be associated with the implementation of a MA system. A switch to MA would involve the kind of change most resisted. Also, innovations in policy processes must overcome many formidable barriers, not the least of which is the opposition of entrenched politicos. Given the political overtones of MA, it is reasonable to expect the opposition of those most likely to lose under an MA system.

2. "Bureaucratic politics will provide multiple advocates." The feasibility of this aspect of MA is sustained by voluminous literature on bureaucratic politics (Cleveland, 1956; Long, 1949, 1954; Rourke, 1969; Flash, 1965; Halperin, 1971). This literature upholds the notion that bureaucrats are competitors and that out of the bureaucratic milieu will come numerous advocates arguing for positions that are favored or opposed on the basis of parochial positions concerning goals, stakes, missions, essence, morale, and budgets. Thus, this assumption in MA is probably a feasible one.

3. "A full range of options will result." Serious questions can be raised about the feasibility of this premise. First, not all pertinent information will come forth. For example, as Rourke (1972) notes, bureaucrats will not admit failure. Also, they severely circumscribe options for parochial reasons (p. 42). Or as Halperin and Kanter (1973) note, information is often biased, skewed or slanted (pp. 12, 18, 22). Though this is to be expected, it may still inhibit the range of options. Secondly, the market place might not be genuinely competitive. Some agencies will not have an interest and thus will not mobilize. As Davis (1972) notes, the likelihood that an agency will immerse itself in bureaucratic politics is proportional to its stake in the outcome (pp. 33, 141). Thus, the range of options may be limited due to the fact that marginally concerned bureaus, perhaps with the potential advantage of a fresh slant, will not be heard from. Other considerations that render conflict imperfect for the the purposes of MA are:

- the possibility of compromise, mutual adjustment, and tacit, "anticipatory" bargaining on the part of agencies prior to advocacy, or, along the lines of Blau (1973), the development of informal norms and informal *modus vivendi* worked out among group members.
- only political elites are heard from.
- the executive, by stating a need for information, may give an indication of his preference and thus will engender groupthink.
- bureaucrats, due to common experiences, roles, etc., may share common cultural blinders.
- informal communications may elude advocacy process.
- sunk costs may in actuality preclude certain options from being proposed.
- inbreeding and friendship may cause tunnel vision.
- per Hirchman (1970), certain dissenters may opt to "exit" rather than use "voice."

4. "Resources can be equalized." The feasibility of this aspect is highly suspect. Advocates will always be unequal, always at least with regard to talent, skill, and expertise. Though the basic assumption of multiple advocacy is correct—that ability to proselytize is affected by resources—the goal seems unrealistic. Some actors will always be more favored, valued, and relied on. Certain resource variables (e.g., clientele support) seem beyond the monitor's manipulative abilities.

5. "The special advisor will remain neutral." As Destler (1971-72) notes in his critique of George, it seems unfeasible that any man could be value free. All officials have biases. Cyert and March (1963, p. 122) note two sources of perennial bias in individuals: specialist training and hopes and expectations. It also seems unfeasible to assume that the special assistant will not act, at least unconsciously, to promote the president's interests. On the other hand, it is likely that the special assistant will take the rigid impending position that "we know all of that."

6. "The president will pay attention." Though it is possible that the president will pay attention, it is just as likely that, under certain circumstances, he will ignore advice or at least not request it. Such possible situations might be when:

- the president, due to the pressures of time, cannot meet with everyone.
- a crisis is at hand (Holsti, 1972). The practice usually is for the president to restrict the size of the policy arena.
- the president's personal style is not conducive to debate and choice among alternatives. As Johnson (1975) notes, the advisory network is listened to only when the president wants to listen to it.
- the advocacy of numerous positions may be politically damaging to the president.
- the bureaucracy is perceived by the president as unsympathetic, disloyal, or hostile.
- the presidential span of attention is exceeded. When an information overload occurs, as Sperlich (1969) notes, the president may seek a decisional shortcut.
- a president prefers to be buttressed rather than informed.
- per Downs (1967), during situations of high controversiality, decision-makers may tend to reduce their reliance on information and withdraw inward.

Thus, presidential use of the advocacy system would be highly situational, depending on, among other things, presidential style, the functioning of the advocacy process, and the nature of the issue at hand. It may be, too, that MA will never be used properly. As Halperin (1974) notes, presidential politics—as defined as the generation of a popular image and the construction of coalitions and group appeal—will always constrain the president and, presumably, his search (pp. 63-65).

7. "MA will be employed in all important decisions." As noted above, there are at least two conditions under which it is most difficult to imagine MA being adopted: a crisis situation (Paige, 1963, pp. 286-87; and Downs, 1967) and a decision requiring a short suspense. Two additional points argue against the feasibility of the assumption that MA will be employed in important decisions. One is that, as Cronin (1972), Destler (1972a) and Neustadt (1964) have argued, the president is not really all that powerful. Many "important" decisions are not made by him. Under the George and Janis prescriptions, such decisions would be beyond the reach of MA. The second stems from the concept of incremental policy-making. It is Hilsman's notion that, on many issues, debate does not matter, for there really is not any definite decision point. As he notes,

> Policy is developed as a series of slight modifications. The new policy emerges slowly and haltingly by small and usually tentative steps. Policy is not presented in simple means-ends continuum. This explains inconsistency. (1959, p. 366)

For policy made under these conditions, MA is irrelevant.

Thus, MA's assumptions about feasibility are most suspect. In terms of feasibility, assumptions run from highly improbable to highly conditional. In concluding this section the following several general reservations are added:

- As Paige (1968, p.360) and Cyert and March (1963) note, there is no guarantee that decision premises will be re-examined. Search usually occurs only when there is a problem.
- There is no guarantee that MA, once implemented, would persist. Many things can threaten an organizational restructuring: lack of consistency, loss of support, loss of leadership and skills, stress, crisis, tensions, and unfavorable ratio of psychic costs to benefits.

- As Johnson (1975) notes, MA, if implemented, might succumb to the problems of "competitive" presidential management systems: aggravation of staff competition and high turnover/attrition due to wear and tear on advocates.
- Per Katz and Kahn (1966, p. 225), all social systems, regardless of attempts to correct bias, will function as communication networks with all attendant distortions.
- Per Wilensky (1967, pp. 177-79), regardless of structure, it is the nature of large organizations to suffer from communications and search problems.
- A serious breach in the MA system (prolonged acrimony) may destroy it.
- Some topics may be too complex for effective multiple advocacy.
- How will the president synthesize the outcome of multiple advocacy?

Desirability

In our analysis of MA, a final topic that must be addressed is desirability. In considering any proposal for organizational reform, it is important to consider the extent to which the proposal, if implemented, would have desirable consequences. The definition of "what is desirable" is, of course, a highly relative and contextual matter and cannot be provided by the analyst. What the analyst can do, however, is to specify what might be some probable outcomes of MA, leaving the final judgment of desirability up to the reader. This is what will be done in this section; we will identify some possible negative externalities that may be encountered in the event MA is implemented. This is not intended to be a polemical discussion of the goals of the MA theorists. It is intended to be a specification of certain criticisms, problems, and trade-offs that might be encountered in MA, and thus that should be considered above and beyond the proponent's values in any discussion of MA's desirability.

With regard to MA, there appear to be five broad areas of possible externalities: leadership control, security, overload, manipulation, and presidential impulsiveness. Each constitutes a potential target for specific criticisms.

With regard to control and leadership, as Cronin (1975) notes, MA may harm the president's ability to control the bureaucracy.

> Sometimes . . . the president does not want to hear objective, balanced advice. He may have his own policy preferences and he may be more worried about gaining the cooperation of various agencies than about giving all advocates an equal hearing. (p. 276)

What Cronin is implying here is that the "openness" of the policy arena and the "responsiveness" of the subpresidential bureaucracy to the control of the president may vary inversely. The more advocates are called for, the more vigorously they press their point of view; and the more supporting analyses they make, the more difficult is the process of establishing coordination, cooperation, control, and agreement on objectives once the decision is made. This certainly is Kissinger's perspective. For him, bureaucracy interferes with executive planning and policy implementation (Destler, 1972b, p. 297). In discussing control we should also reference a possible externality noted by Drucker (1966, 1968). Drucker laments executive reliance on staff. To him, "staff for strength" is nonsense. The executive should try to make himself independent of his staff. Though MA theorists would argue that they are trying to decrease executive reliance in general, in fact, under George's proposal, executive reliance on staff for information may be increased. By assigning the special advisor to monitor search, the executive may suffer the distortions of the Haldeman syndrome.

Under security, it must be pointed out that in certain policy situations, secrecy is required. In those situations where security is valued, multiple advocacy may not be desired because of the increased chances of a security compromise.

With regard to overload, it is quite possible that advocacy, by inundating the president, may squander executive attention. The executive may be led in a number of directions. Katz and Kahn (1966) give an unpleasant picture of how executives in a state of information confusion and overload attempt to cope. They argue that the executive possibly will respond by (1) distorting to fit his own biases, (2) ignoring contrary information, or (3) escaping from the task (p. 231). None of these are desired by anyone. It may be that a less perfect scheme operating as "bounded rationality" may be preferable to these potential pathologies.

With regard to manipulation, a potential pathology is noted by Ross (1973) and by Krasner (1972). If MA is implemented, it is possible that leaders could symbolically use it to absolve themselves of responsibility for bad judgments. They would blame the system, not themselves. Also, as Ross notes, decisionmakers may over rely on the advocacy system and not develop the intuition and ability to confront ambiguity—something required of leaders (p. 205).

A final externality, that of impulsiveness, is suggested by Cameron (1975). He notes that proposals for reducing presidential insulation and for increasing the president's information presume that he has the ability to synthesize all that is forwarded to him. However, as Cameron argues, if the president does not possess this knack but, instead, is impulsive, a MA kind of system might very well produce a bad decision. The president may simply leap to the first option he hears. In such instances, "good policy" might better be served by a revision of the domestic Eisenhower network: the presentation of a single option, thrashed out by advisors, to the president for a yes or no.

We can conclude this section by saying that, although, as George and Janis note, MA may be desirable when major directions in policy are set, when the president's advisors are too like-minded or when policy is floundering, some may conclude that MA may not be desirable for reasons of control, security, and leadership. It may also not be desired out of fear of manipulation and impulsiveness.

III. Conclusions

The purpose of this paper, in a larger sense, has been to outline a framework for analyzing proposals for organizational change, reform, and innovation within the presidency. Specifically, it is contended that such prescriptions must be assessed in terms of logic, veracity, feasibility, and desirability. With regard to our specific example of MA, we concluded that major theoretical, empirical, feasibility, and externality problems plague the MA proposals of George and Janis.

Where to now? Should we relegate MA to the same intellectual purgatory that now contains such panaceas as "party government," "nonpartisanship," "politics/administration dichotomy," etc.? "Not yet" is our answer. The questions raised in this paper show the need for more elaboration and greater refinement of the MA model, if MA is to be an effective answer to decision-making problems. Yet, professors George and Janis should be thanked for providing us with schemes which dramatize the problems of search, information, and "option formulation" in decision-making. Moreover, in 1980, Professor George presented us with a much improved prescription for open decision-making that takes into account and benefits from criticisms offered by Destler (1972a) and others. He logically states his problem and then proposes solutions. The solutions are offered with acknowledged caveats, reservations, limitations, and a sophisticated anticipation of criticism. He effectively states the case against vest-pocket decision-making and an arrogance of power that fails to reassess decision premises. Second, Professor George offers us "not a panacea" (p. 204), but a series of reminders and aphorisms to instinctively aid decisionmakers. His proposals are best placed in perspective by considering them not as prescriptions for institutionalized decision-making but as standards by which we may (a) systematically evaluate presidential decision and processes and (b) make reasoned guesses about the likely quality of decisions emitted from those processes. Like Barber's *Presidential Character*, it clues us to potential disorders in the nation's highest office.

In conclusion, perhaps the goals of reformers George and Janis would be better served with "middle range" prescriptions of the type offered by Halperin, Sorensen, and Cyert and March, Halperin (1971), in a subsection entitled "What Every President Should Know," warns the president that "information is distorted" by bureaucratic politics, "options incomplete," freedom to choose options is "circumscribed," and decisions may be "sabotaged" in the implementation process by recalcitrant bureaucrats. Sorensen (1963) advises presidents to be aware of personal biases that may act as blinders. Cyert and March (1963) call attention to the distortions and biases of structure. These kinds of prescriptions, if widely disseminated and coupled with incentives for adoption, might be more effective and more realistic in promoting improvements in decision-making. Such prescriptions have at least three advantages over more utopian schemes. First, they are amenable to empirical research. Because they are more narrow in terms of the range of underlying assumptions, an empirical test is more reasonable than with a more elegant scheme. Second, a middle range prescription allows for situational differences. It does not require a set decision mode for every situation. It allows for the variation in decision strategy. Finally, middle range prescriptions allow us to address decision-making problems other than just search and information. Not being confined to a particular structure, such as the George model, permits recognition of other, noncommunications problems.

References

Allison, Graham T. "Conceptual Models and the Cuban Missile Crisis." *American Political Science Review*, 63 (Sept. 1969), 689-718.

—————. *Essence of Decision: Explaining the Cuban Missile Crisis*, 1971.

—————, and Halperin, Morton H. "Bureaucratic Politics: A Paradigm and Some Policy Implications." *World Politics*, 24 (Spring Supplement, 1972).

Allport, Floyd H. "The Influences of the Group upon Association and Thought." *Journal of Psychology*, 3 (1920), 159-82.

Bauer, Raymond A., and Gergen, Kenneth J., eds. *The Study of Policy Formation*, 1968.

Bennis, W. G. "Beyond Bureaucracy." *American Bureaucracy*. Edited by W. G. Bennis, 1970.

Bion, W. *Experiences in Groups*, 1961.

Blau, Peter M. "Consultation among Colleagues and Informal Norms." *Perspectives on Public Bureaucracy*. Edited by F. A. Kramer, 1973.

—————, and Scott, W.R. *Formal Organizations: A Comparative Approach*, 1962.

Burns, Tom, and Stalker, G. M. *The Management of Innovations*, 1967.

Cameron, Juan. "The Management Problem in Ford's White House." *Fortune*, 92 (July 1975), 74-81, 176.

Campbell, D. T. "Stereotypes and the Perception of Group Differences." *American Psychologist*, 22 (1967), 817-29.

Cartwright, D. "The Nature of Group Cohesiveness." *Group Dynamics: Research and Theory*. 3d ed. Edited by D. Cartwright and A. Zander, 1968.

—————, and Zander A., eds. *Group Dynamics: Research and Theory*. 3d ed. 1968.

Christie, L. S.; Luce, R. D.; and Macy, J., Jr. *Communication and Learning in Task-Oriented Groups*. Technical Report 231, Cambridge, Mass., MIT Research Lab of Electronics, 1952.

Clerk, Joseph Porter, Jr. "The Art of the Memorandum." *Washington Monthly*, 1 (March 1969), 58-62.

Cleveland, Harlan. "Executives in the Political Jungle." *Annals of the American Academy of Political and Social Science*, 399 (Sept. 1956), 37-47.

Cronin, Thomas E. "Everybody Believes in Democracy Until He Gets to the White House: An Example of White House-Departmental Relations." *Law and Commentary Problems*, 35 (Summer 1970).

—————. *The State of the Presidency*, 1975.

—————. "The Textbook Presidency and Political Science." *The American Political Arena*. 3d ed. Edited by J. Fiszman and G. Poschman, 1972.

—————, and Greenberg, Sanford D., eds. *The Presidential Advisory System*, 1969.

Cyert, Richard M., and March, James G. *Behavioral Theory of the Firm*, 1963.

Davis, David Howard. *How the Bureaucracy Makes Foreign Policy*, 1972.

Delbecq, Andre L. "The Management of Decision-Making within the Firm: Three Types of Decision-Making." *Academy of Management Journal*, 10 (Dec. 1967), 329-39.

Destler, I. M. "Can One Man Do?" *Foreign Policy*, No. 5 (Winter 1971-72), 28-40.

—————. "Comment: Multiple Advocacy: Some 'Limits and Costs.'" *American Political Science Review*, 66 (Sept. 1972), 786-90. (a)

—————. *Presidents, Bureaucrats, and Foreign Policy*, 1972. (b)

Deutsch, Morton. "An Experimental Study of the Effects of Cooperation and Competition Upon Group Process." *Human Relations*, 2 (1949), 199-231.

—————. "A Theory of Co-operation and Competition." *Human Relations*, 2 (1949), 129-52.

Downs, Anthony. *Inside Bureaucracy*, 1967.

Drucker, Peter F. *The Age of Discontinuity*, 1968.

—————. *The Effective Executive*, 1966.

—————. *Managing for Results*, 1964.

Eulau, Heinz. "APSA Presidential Address: Skill Revolution and Consultative Commonwealth." *American Political Science Association*, 67 (March 1973), 168-91.

Fenno, Richard F. *The President's Cabinet*, 1959.

Festinger, L. "A Theory of Social Comparison Processes." *Human Relations*, 7 (1954), 117-40.

Flash, Edward S., Jr. *The Politics of Economic Advice and Presidential Leadership*, 1965.

Frederickson, H. G. "Organization Theory and New Public Administration." *Toward a New Public Administration*. Edited by F. Marini, 1971.

Freeman, J. Leiper. "The Bureaucracy in Pressure Politics." *The Annals of the American Academy of Political and Social Science*, 319 (1952), 10-19.

Gawthrop, Louis C. *Administrative Politics and Social Change*, 1971.

———. *Bureaucratic Behavior in the Executive Branch: An Analysis of Organizational Change*, 1969.

Geiger, T., and Hansen, R. D. "The Role of Information in Decision Making on Foreign Aid." *The Study of Policy Formation*. Edited by R. A. Bauer and K. J. Gergen, 1968.

Gelb, L. H. "Today's Lessons from the Pentagon Papers." *Life*, Sept. 17, 1971.

George, Alexander L. "The Case for Multiple Advocacy in Making Foreign Policy." *American Political Science Review*, 66 (Sept. 1972), 751-85.

———. "Rejoinder to 'Comment' by I. M. Destler." *American Political Science Review*, 66 (Sept. 1972), 791-95.

Golembiewski, Robert T. *Men, Management and Morality: Toward a New Organization Ethic*, 1965.

Guetzkow, Harold. "Communications in Organizations." *Handbook of Organizations*. Edited by James March, 1965.

———, and Dill, William R. "Factors in the Organizational Development of Task-Oriented Groups." *Sociometry*, 20 (1957), 175-204.

———, and Simon, Herbert A. "The Impact of Certain Communication Nets Upon Organization and Performance in Task-Oriented Groups." *Management Science*, 1 (1955), 233-50.

Hage, Gerald, and Dewar, Robert. "Elite Values Versus Organizational Structure in Predicting Innovation." *Administrative Science Quarterly*, 18 (Sept. 1973), 279-90.

Halberstam, David. *The Best and the Brightest*, 1972.

Hall, R. H. *Organizations: Structure and Process*, 1971.

Halperin, Morton H. *Bureaucratic Politics and Foreign Policy*, 1974.

———. "Why Bureaucrats Play Games." *Foreign Policy* (May 1971), 70-90.

———, and Kanter, Arnold. "The Bureaucratic Perspective: A Preliminary Framework." *Readings in American Foreign Policy*. Edited by Halperin and Kanter, 1973.

Hammond, Paul Y. "The National Security Council: An Interpretation and Appraisal." *American Political Science Review*, 54 (Dec. 1960), 899-910.

Heinicke, C., and Bales, R. F. "Developmental Trends in the Structure of Small Groups." *Sociometry*, 16 (1953), 7-38.

Hess, Stephen. *Organizing the Presidency*, 1976.

Hilsman, Roger. "The Foreign Policy Consensus: An Interim Research Report." *Journal of Conflict Resolution*, 3 (Dec. 1959), 361-82.

Hirchman, Albert O. *Exit, Voice and Loyalty*, 1970.

Hoffman, R. L. "Conditions for Creative Problem Solving." *Journal of Psychology*, 52 (Oct. 1961), 429-44.

Holsti, K.J. *International Politics: A Framework for Analysis*. 2nd ed., 1972.

Hoopes, Townsend. *The Limits of Intervention*, 1969.

Janis, Irving L. *Victims of Group Think*, 1972 (2d ed. 1982).

Jervis, Robert. "Hypotheses on Misperception." *World Politics*, 26 (April 1968), 454-79.

Johnson, Richard T. "Presidential Style." *Perspectives on the Presidency*. Edited by Aaron Wildavsky, 1975.

Katz, D., and Kahn, R. *The Social Psychology of Organizations*, 1966.

Kaufman, Herbert. "Emerging Conflicts in the Doctrines of Public Administration." *American Political Science Review*, 50 (Dec. 1956), 1057-73.

Kennedy, R. F. *Thirteen Days*, 1969.

Kessel, John H. *The Domestic Presidency: Decision-Making in the White House*, 1975.

Kissinger, Henry. "Domestic Structure and Foreign Policy." *Daedalus*, 95 (Spring 1966), 503-29.

Krasner, Stephen D. "Are Bureaucrats Important?" *Foreign Policy*, 7 (Sept. 1972), 159-79.

Landau, Martin. "Redundancy, Rationality, and the Problem of Duplication and Overlap." *Public Administration Review*, 29 (July-Aug. 1969), 346-58.

Leacocos, John P. "Kissinger's Apparat." *Foreign Policy*, No. 5 (Winter 1971-72).

Lewin, K. "Group Decision and Social Change." *Readings in Social Psychology*. Edited by T. Newcomb and E. Hartley, 1947.

Lindblom, Charles. *The Intelligence of Democracy: Decision-Making Through Mutual Adjustment*, 1965.

———. *The Policy-Making Process*, 1968.

Long, Norton. "Power and Administration." *Public Administration Review*, 9 (1949), 257-64.

———. "Public Policy and Administration: The Goals of Rationality and Responsibility." *Public Administration Review*, 14 (1954), 22-31.

Lorge, Irving, and Soloman, Herbert. "Two Models of Group Behavior in the Solution of Eureka-type Problems." *Psychometrika*, 20 (1955), 139-48.

Maier, N. R. F. *Problem-Solving and Creativity in Individuals and Groups*, 1970.

———. *Problem-Solving Discussions and Conferences: Leadership Methods and Skills*, 1963.

———, and Solem, A. R. "The Contributions of a Discussion Leader to the Quality of Group Thinking." *Human Relations*, 5 (1952), 277-88.

March, James G., and Simon, Herbert A. *Organizations*, 1958.

Mason, Richard O. *Dialectics in Decision-Making: A Study in the Use of Counterplanning and Structured Debate in Management Information Systems.* Ph.D. dissertation, Business Administration, University of California, Berkeley, 1968.

McCurdy, H. G., and Lambert, W. E. "The Efficiency of Small Human Groups in the Solution of Problems Requiring Genuine Cooperation." *Journal of Personnel*, 20 (1952), 478-94.

McDonough, Adrian M. *Information Economics and Management Systems*, 1963.

Met. Kahin, George. "The Pentagon Papers: A Critical Evaluation." *American Political Science Review*, 69 (June 1975), 675-84.

Mulder, Maul. "Communication Structure, Decision Structure and Group Performance." *Sociometry*, 23 (1960), 1-14.

Neustadt, R. E. *Presidential Power: The Politics of Leadership*, 1964.

Paige, G. D. *The Korean Decision*, 1968.

Pateman, Carole. *Participation and Democratic Theory*, 1970.

Pelz, Donald C. "Some Social Factors Related to Performance in a Research Organization." *Administrative Science Quarterly*, 1 (1956), 310-25.

Perlmutter, Howard V., and deMontmollin, Germaine. "Group Learning of Nonsense Syllables." *Journal of Abnormal and Social Psychology*, 42 (1952), 762-69.

Reedy, George E. *The Twilight of the Presidency*, 1970.

Robinson, James A.; Hermann, Charles F.; and Hermann, Margret G. "Search Under Crisis in Political Gaming and Simulation." *Theory and Research in the Causes of War*. Edited by D. Pruitt and R. C. Snyder, 1969.

Ross, Arthur M. "The Data Game." *Inside the System.* 2d ed. Edited by Charles Peters and John Rothchild, 1973.

Rourke, Francis E. *Bureaucracy and Foreign Policy*, 1972.

―――――. *Bureaucracy, Politics and Public Policy*, 1969.

Rowen, Henry S. "Bargaining and Analysis in Government." *The Administrative Process and Democratic Theory*. Edited by Louis C. Gawthrop, 1970.

Schachter, S. *The Psychology of Affiliation*, 1959.

Schick, Allen. "Toward the Cybernetic State." *Public Administration in a Time of Turbulence*. Edited by Dwight Waldo, 1971.

Schubert, Glendon A., Jr. " 'The Public Interest' in Administrative Decision-Making: Theorem, Theosophy, or Theory?" *American Political Science Review*, 51 (June 1957), 346-68.

Selznick, Philip. "The Cooptative Mechanism." *The National Administrative System*. Edited by Dean Yarwood, 1971.

―――――. *Leadership in Administration*, 1957.

Shaw, Marjorie E. "A Comparison of Individuals and Small Groups in the Rational Solution of Complex Problems." *American Journal of Psychology*, 44 (1932), 491-504.

Shaw, Martin. *Group Dynamics*, 1971.

Sorensen, Theodore C. *Decision-Making in the White House*, 1963.

Sperlich, Peter W. "Bargaining and Overload: An Essay on Presidential Power." *The Presidency*. Edited by A. Wildavsky, 1969.

Taylor, Donald W., and Faust, William L. "Twenty Questions." *Journal of Experimental Psychology*, 44 (1952), 360-68.

Thayer, Frederick C. *An End to Hierarchy! An End to Competition!* 1973.

―――――. "Presidential Policy Processes and 'New Administration': A Search for Revised Paradigms." *Public Administration Review*, 31 (Sept./Oct. 1971), 552-56.

Thomas, Norman C., ed. *The Presidency in Contemporary Context*, 1975.

―――――. "Presidential Advice and Information: Policy and Program Formulation." *Law and Contemporary Problems*, 35 (Summer 1970), 540-72.

Thompson, James C. "How Could Vietnam Happen?: An Autopsy." *The Atlantic Monthly* (April 1968), and in *Readings in American Foreign Policy*. Edited by M. Halperin and A. Kanter, 1973.

Thompson, Victor A. "Bureaucracy and Innovation." *Administrative Science Quarterly*, 10 (June 1965), 1-20.

Thorndike, R. L. "On What Type of Task Will a Group Do Well?" *Journal of Abnormal and Social Psychology*, 33 (1938), 409-13.

Torrance, E. Paul. "Some Consequences of Power Differences on Decision-Making in Permanent and Temporary Three-man Groups." *Small Groups*. Edited by A. Paul Hare, et al., 1955.

Tullock, Gordon. *The Politics of Bureaucracy*, 1965.

Voos, Henry. *Organizational Communications*, 1967.

Vroom, Victor H.; Grant, Lester D.; and Cotton, Timothy S. "The Consequences of Social Interaction in Group Problem Solving." *Organizational Behavior and Human Performance*, 4 (Feb. 1969), 77-95.

Wallack, M. A.; Kogan, N.; and Benn, D.J. "Group Influence on Risk-Taking." *Group Dynamics: Research and Theory*. 3d ed., 1968.

Westerfield, H. Bradford. "What Use Are Three Versions of the Pentagon Papers?" *American Political Science Review*, 69 (June 1975), 685-97.

White, Ralph, and Lippitt, Ronald. "Leader Behavior and Member Reaction in Three 'Social Climates.'" *Group Dynamics: Research and Theory*. 3d ed. Edited by D. Cartwright and A. Zander, 1968.

Wilensky, Harold L. *Organizational Intelligence*, 1967.

Wilson, James Q. "Innovations in Organizations: Notes Toward a Theory." *Approaches to Organizational Design*. Edited by James D. Thompson, 1966.

Zaltman, Gerald; Duncan, Robert; and Holbek, Jonny. *Innovations and Organizations*, 1973.

Perspectives on the System

The Reform Agenda 9.6

William Lammers

The following essay places in perspective proposals to alternatively structure the presidency. Lammers focuses attention on the various goals of reformers and some of the tradeoffs that might be encountered.

The American presidency does show significant capacity for change. Both the enactment of many post-Watergate reforms and the impact of President Ford as a distinct contrast to his predecessor dramatized the capacities for change by the mid-1970s. The occupant of the White House can make significant differences in the organizational pattern within the institution, and in the characteristics surrounding at least aspects of the relationships with the press, the federal bureaucracy, Congress, and major interests. Election returns and an indignant electorate revealed, by 1975, a capacity for altering presidential relationships with Congress rather substantially for at least a short-run period.

The rush of reform activity in the wake of the Watergate scandals often seemed to be primarily directed at a reduction in the chances that another president would behave as arrogantly as did Richard Nixon. This was obviously not a modest objective! At the same time, there is a good deal more to effective presidential politics than achieving situations in which the president no longer finds it necessary to proclaim, as did Nixon, that he is not a crook.

Reform Goals

To adequately confront the question of possible reform in presidential politics, it is essential to consider basic goals. Obviously, there cannot be easy agreement on either the goals themselves or the strategies and techniques most suited to the achievement of major goals. Some adjustments in institutions can be made in an effort at avoiding difficult situations in the future but with little sense of partisan advantage and policy preference as they are being enacted. Reform in such areas as the selection of vice-presidents might come in an uncontroversial context. Many other changes, however, are inexorably tied to the nature of the policy outcomes which are preferred by various participants in the political process.

The question of goals in presidential politics reintroduces the issue of American political values. Issues involving democratic politics, policy effectiveness, and political legitimacy are all involved. Concern for democracy requires a concern for the distribution of access to decisionmakers and for the distribution of resources for influencing decisions. Clearly, a concern for democratic politics must also involve an opposition to secretive, manipulative use of executive power. Within the category of democratic concerns, there are good reasons for individuals to differ on the extent to which such values as expanded participation ought to be sought.

The goal of democratic politics may well be challenged more seriously in the next years than in the past by those looking for a more rapid movement toward particular policy goals. Periods of economic difficulty and of declining faith in national achievements can indeed foster greater interest in the abandonment of democratic commitments. It is well worth emphasizing, in the context of these issues in America, that the more autocratic regimes can also have major difficulties in de-

Presidential Politics: Patterns and Prospects (pp. 88-90, 267-71) by William H. Lammers, 1976, New York: Harper & Row Publishers, Inc. Copyright 1976 by William H. Lammers. Reprinted by permission.

veloping effective policies. The demands which changing resource levels place on a system may be impossible to resolve, and the tendencies toward groupthink, executive isolation, and inadequacies in leaders' personalities can produce major problems.[1] At the same time, emerging policy issues can rightly be interpreted as placing a very real strain on the American democratic commitment.

Concern for effective public policy must be basic in efforts at reforming presidential politics. Public confidence in presidential politics is not going to be restored solely by more earnest personalities or different staff patterns. Process concerns and political styles can be important, but electoral orientations are often strongly influenced by the nature of the policies emerging from the operation of presidential politics.

Seeking to define effective policy is obviously a task of potentially limitless proportions. Broadly, it is useful to recognize three views of possible modifications in the effectiveness of public policy. (1) For some, Americans are encouraged to lower expectations and simply declare yesterday's seemingly unsatisfactory results to be the best attainable state of affairs in the future. (2) A second view emphasizes economies of scale and more efficient use of resources. Mass transit systems, school systems with greater effectiveness as well as lower per-pupil costs, and regional health centers are among the policy thrusts which fit this orientation. (3) In another view, the answer to effective policy must now come with redistributive approaches to income and wealth distribution and in alterations in the relationships between business and government. Proposals for major taxes on wealth, various income policy steps, and nationalization of such industries as health services and defense procurement receive attention from this perspective.

More satisfactory policy results from presidential politics are not apt to develop easily from an overwhelming emphasis on just one of the three approaches. Lowered expectations may be forced on Americans at some points, given the greater scarcity of resources which the coming years portend. Yet it seems unnecessary to abandon in total the quest for policies which improve life for Americans through effective use of presidential politics. Economies of scale and more effective use of resources are, in principle, attainable in a variety of policy situations. Furthermore, even with a possible redistributive thrust in public policy there will still be a need for improving the way in which various services are made available for the average American. It also seems apparent that the redistributive issues cannot be ignored. In part, resources held and influence wielded by corporations and the wealthy make it difficult at points for more efficient policies to emerge. Transportation policies with a dependence on highways, resource policies with a dependence on oil, and housing policies influenced by the impact of tax advantages through manipulating tax-loss provisions all show aspects of this problem. In addition, the question of the distribution of wealth contains some possible answers for confronting aspects of the scarcity issue.

Effectiveness in policy relates, in turn, to the question of public confidence in presidential operations. The legitimacy of American political institutions has dropped sharply in recent years, including the presidency. Reform in presidential politics must be concerned with actions which facilitate both greater electoral confidence and also a greater sense of fairness in basic operations. Efforts at tax reform, for example, involve the question of how *fairly* the public judges the government to be operating, and not simply the question of what additional revenue can be generated.

Expanding the democratic dimensions of presidential politics, improving its policy-developing capacities, and increasing public support involve fairly difficult choices. It can be difficult to foster several political values at the same time within a given political system. For example, greater participation in the name of expanded access to the presidency may conflict with the objective of policy-formulation which reacts fast enough to economic conditions to keep employment high. Similarly, the pursuit of greater openness in government can produce situations in which public confidence is further undercut by the information which is revealed. Reform would indeed be a much easier task if goals were never in conflict.

Efforts at moving presidential politics toward various goals are also restricted in that reform tends generally to focus on structural aspects of the presidency. Formal institutional arrangements and requirements *are* important. Requiring a president to release information, or allowing for changes in legislative committee chairmen, for example, may alter not only the prevailing political practices but important policy outcomes as well.

The totality of presidential behavior is also shaped by several other factors, including presidential personality, power relationships, general policy contexts, and electoral expectations. Several of these factors can also be altered, as political resources for influencing presidential selection are altered by restrictions on campaign finance, or as the presidents correctly sense that the electorate is tired of false promises. In several contexts, the future presidency has clearly been altered in likely behavior by the traumas which Richard Nixon encountered. Regardless of the specific thrusts of campaign reform legislation, for example, a president's fund-raiser in the future will be more cautious—perhaps to the point of even avoiding the job. Major aspects of the reform agenda must nonetheless be structural, and they deserve careful attention along with a consideration of ways in which other factors may change or be changed in the evolution of presidential politics.

The Reform Agenda

Responses to the Watergate scandals did produce significant reform activity. Several reform issues emerged on the nation's agenda at the same time. In considering that reform agenda, it is useful to look at presidential selection, presidential information systems, the secrecy questions, policy analysis, modifications in access to policy making activity, the role of Congress, and electoral expectations. In looking at reforms in these areas, it is important to keep in mind the general directions which are being prescribed for modifying presidential politics. First, there must be increased opportunities for policy change without direct presidential leadership, and second, it is essential to reduce opportunities for the manipulative and miscalculating uses of the fait accompli role. Concerns involving not only a more democratic politics but also policy effectiveness and electoral support are related to this thrust in several ways.

The Presidential Dilemma

Presidential politics does ultimately confront Americans with a series of dilemmas. Expansion of the presidency in a quest for coordination and the use of expertise in policy development can easily lead to an isolated president and an expansion in staff power. Access to the presidency can too easily become quite limited. Electoral expectations, at the same time, can lead to an overdependence upon a president who can supposedly orchestrate wise solutions to difficult problems. Inadequate presidential personalities then simply aggravate possibilities for deceitful and manipulative operations.

Yet hoping that a president will return to a uniformly passive role is also inadequate. There are situations in which a president appropriately fills his role by working to close bargaining relationships and by mobilizing support for new policy steps. Simply cutting the president "down to size" and turning the presidency into a museum for visitors would not insure wise policy development during difficult times for the nation.

A perspective for reducing tensions over presidential roles nonetheless does emerge. There *are* important indications that policy alteration can take place without presidential involvement, and these need to be strengthened. In turn, presidents must be restricted from engaging in the more manipulative and secretive policy-making activities. From this perspective, our view of the reform agenda deserves final emphasis.

Changes in the selection process to decrease the likelihood of inadequate presidential personalities in the future can be pursued, through the provision of a better screening process and a more substantial opening of the recruitment process. Presidential information systems can also be strengthened. This is particularly important in the situations where the president must inevitably make some decisions in a fairly closed manner. Reduction in secrecy is in turn essential, so that at least the decisions themselves are not hidden.

Expanded assessment of overall trends and policy impacts in American society is also essential to more adequate policy development. This does *not* mean that more units need be added to the presidential staff. Rather, expanded information must be generated to provide a more adequate general public debate.

Various policy-making activities need to be opened up to the consideration of a wider range of interests and values. Statutory provisions reducing the likelihood of budgetary examination should be reduced, and analytic tools for examining policy consequences expanded. At points, this can happen at "the center," either with a president promoting interest, or a debate focusing on the floor of Congress. Where issues are in central focus, there is no ready ground for arguing that the plans from either president or Congress are superior; a good faith bargaining process is needed between the two institutions, with Congress possessing enough of the information leading to executive plans so that it can respond intelligently.

Much policy making must nonetheless take place away from the center of concern either for the president or for Congress in general. Actions in the federal bureaucracy and in state and local governments will often have significant consequences. An important federal government role should be to increase the chance that these activities will not be dominated by a veto process created by a few congressmen, a few campaign contributors, an inflexible agency, or a few individuals with highly privileged access. Controlling access to policy making activities is a critical role in all federal government operations.

A reduced dependency upon either the president or the presidency for directing policy change does not *necessarily* mean that the political process will become stagnant and resistant to continual evolution of various policies. Groups can develop on their own initiative, agencies can evolve different policies and relationships with their clienteles, and legislative action can modify both programs and levels of funding. Some presidential closing of bargaining processes and some mobilizing can occur and will sometimes be absolutely necessary. Attention must be given to the range of access various segments of the population have to these processes and the nature of the political resources which count. Fortunately, the turn away from the campaign funding practices of the recent past offers some hope that money may be a less important resource in the future.

It was difficult to be overly sanguine or overly certain in viewing presidential politics as the nation undertook the celebration of the two hundredth anniversary of the signing of the Declaration of Independence. The American system, historically, enjoyed very definite advantages in not having to confront very many issues at the same time. Then in the brief period since the early 1960s conflicts and tensions involving race issues, environmental and energy concerns, a lengthy and divisive war, and an economy running into serious difficulty all buffeted presidential politics. American desires for democratic politics, effective policy, and a government warranting and receiving citizen confidence and trust were obviously under considerable stress.

America nonetheless remained dynamic in many respects. A politics of dynamic adjustment, involving less assumed dependence upon the president, more informed bargaining, wider policy-making access, less secrecy, and better policy information seemed to offer reasonable hope. One conclusion was in any event clear: Americans have for too long lived too comfortably under the illusion that all major questions of institutional development have been effectively settled.

Note

1. For a strong statement emphasizing the problems with autocratic regimes in the context of comparative research, see Alexander T. Groth, *Comparative Politics: A Distributive Approach* (New York: Macmillan, 1971), especially chap. 11.

Illustration 9a: Classification of Presidential Reforms by Level and Focus
Norman Thomas

Many proposals have been made for reforming, changing, and restructuring the presidency. The following table by Norman Thomas classifies a variety of proposals by focus and level. This illustration is most helpful in illuminating the variety of reform proposals.

Classification of Presidential Reforms by Level and Focus

Level	Focus: Structural[a]	Focus: Procedural[b]
Systemic[c]	1. Parliamentary system 2. Parliamentary variants 3. Initiative and recall 4. Council of state 5. Cabinet upgrading 6. National planning agency 7. Altered presidential selection 8. Six-year presidential terms 9. Congressional reform 10. Party-system overhaul	1. War Powers Resolution (1973) 2. Budget and Impoundment Control Act (1974) 3. Campaign Finance Act (1974) 4. National planning bill (proposed 1975, 1976) 5. Restriction of executive-privilege claims
Institutional[d]	1. Collegial executive 2. Limited size and function of presidential staff 3. Strengthened presidential planning and evaluation staffs	1. Explicit delegations of presidential functions to staff 2. Requirement of presidential-powers impact statements, specific reports with State of Union message, and annual national-posture statement 3. Multiple advocacy

a. Structural: the way in which the parts and elements of the governmental organization are arranged.
b. Procedural: forms and methods of conducting the business of government.
c. Systemic: having to do with the overall political system in the United States.
d. Institutional: having to do with the established organization of the Presidency.

"Reforming the Presidency: Problems and Prospects" by Norman C. Thomas in *The Presidency Reappraised* 2d ed. (p. 328). Ed. by Thomas E. Cronin and Ruxford G. Tugwell, 1977, New York: Praeger Publishers. Copyright 1977 by Thomas E. Cronin. Reprinted by permission.

Reassessing the Imperial Presidency 9.7

Louis W. Koenig

The American presidency has alternatively been viewed as either too powerful or not powerful enough. Usually, the views one has as to an imperial or imperiled presidency depends on how one's ox is gored. If people feel that a president of their persuasion is likely to further their policy goals, they will applaud presidential power. If the opposite is true and a president opposed or hostile to their persuasion is in office, presidential power will be feared and opposed. The following article by a noted presidential scholar examines the notion of an imperial presidency from an historical perspective, and warns against using the term lightly.

Among the innumerable books published about the American presidency in the nearly two centuries of the office's existence, Arthur M. Schlesinger, Jr.'s *Imperial Presidency* holds a unique place.[1] Published in 1973, the book's title remains part of the American political lexicon. Mention *presidency* in a word association test administered to any number of politicians, civil servants, academics, and others tolerably informed about the office, and the likelihood is that the word *imperial* will figure prominently in the results. Adding to the book's impact are Schlesinger's previous writings and service in a presidential administration, a record in sharp contrast to the theme of his book. His earlier works were laudatory chronicles of the presidencies of Jackson, Franklin Roosevelt, and Kennedy, which, with his service in the latter's presidency, were encouraging to other writers, especially in the 1960s, in building their cases for an activist presidency. *The Imperial Presidency* is a 180-degree turnaround from this previous record.

Writing in 1973, when the unpopularity of the Vietnam War was reaching a crescendo and Richard Nixon's abuses of power were surfacing and straining the credence of shocked citizens, Schlesinger's contention that presidential power had attained a state of extreme aggrandizement seemed justified and aptly timed. In an extended analysis, he argued that Watergate and the Vietnam War were not isolated aberrations but the long-building climaxes of rampant presidential power that had been set in the direction of abuse soon after the office commenced its operations in 1789.

The rock on which the imperial presidency rests is the phenomenon of presidential wars, launched simply by the chief executive's fiat. Innumerable small-scale hostilities were initiated in the nineteenth century; more elaborate conflicts were waged by Tyler, Polk, and above all Lincoln in the Civil War. In the twentieth century such wars were conducted on the scale of the Korean and Vietnam conflicts. The spreading use of executive agreements and ever broadening executive privilege were other ingredients that made foreign policy the principal arena of the imperial presidency. Particularly since World War II, according to Schlesinger, "the image of the president acting by himself in foreign affairs, imposing his own sense of reality and necessity on a waiting government and people became the new orthodoxy."[2] In domestic affairs, the rise of social programs, such as the New Deal and the Great Society, and the expansion of a national economy dominated by interstate business and amenable to control through national regulation, enlarged the imperial presidency's domain.

Certainly after the compounded troubles of Watergate and the Vietnam War, one should not be surprised that the presidency underwent sweeping indictment and search-

---

"Reassessing the 'Imperial Presidency'" by Louis W. Koenig in *The Power to Govern: Assessing Reform in the United States* (pp. 31-44). Ed. by Richard M. Pious, 1981, Vol. 34, No. 2, New York: The Academy of Political Science. Copyright 1981 by The Academy of Political Science. Reprinted by permission.

ing reexamination. Criticism, a common experience of the presidency, is fed by the nation's historic suspicion of executive power and the fear of its susceptibility to abuse, rooted in popular perceptions of George III. The American Revolution was fought against executive power. After the presidency was established, criticism often took on an antimonarchical cast. President Washington, with his taste for fine living and receptivity to deference, was sometimes accused of acting like a king. When Martin Van Buren enhanced the White House grounds by planting trees and improving the landscaping, he was assailed for aping the monarchs of Europe by creating an orangery in the rear of his palace where he might enjoy majestic seclusion.

But throughout its lengthy history the presidency's incumbents have been virtually unanimous in their heartfelt testimony of its inadequacies, which perceives the office as anything but imperial. John Adams exclaimed, after pitching endlessly on the presidency's rough waters: "No! The real fault is, that the president has not influence enough, and is not independent enough." Thomas Jefferson spoke of the office as a "splendid misery," and James A. Garfield, in a brief tenure, for which he sacrificed his life, exclaimed, "My God, what is there in this place that a man should ever want to get in it?" Herbert Hoover, after battling the economic depression with prodigious labor and experiencing unremitting failure, could understandably declare, with nonimperial fervor, "This office is a compound hell."[3]

Scholars and Observers

Scholars and observers who analyzed the presidency in the nineteenth and for most of the twentieth centuries were impressed not that it was exercising too much power, as the imperial thesis contends, but suffered from serious deficiencies of power. In 1885, political scientist Woodrow Wilson argued that Congress was "the dominant, nay, the irresistible, power of the federal system."[4] In the interval between Lincoln and Cleveland, he found the presidency weak and helpless, its power steadily disintegrating.

That acute observer of American society and politics, Alexis de Tocqueville, compared the president's power with the power of the constitutional kings of France. Tocqueville's findings do not support Schlesinger's contention that at this juncture the presidency was already well embarked on the imperial road. Tocqueville thought that the president was highly limited by functioning in a federal system of government, by his modest tenure of four years compared with the monarch's life tenure, and by his responsibility for his actions in contrast to the inviolability of the person of the king declared by French law.[5]

Another distinguished foreign commentator, James Bryce, assessing the presidency near the close of the nineteenth century, while conceding the immense dignity of the president's position and his unrivalled platform "from which to impress his ideas (if he has any) upon the people," felt that a tyrannical president was "hard to imagine." The president, Bryce noted, has no standing army and cannot create one, and Congress can checkmate him by stopping supplies. A more serious problem, Bryce argued, was the lack of great men in the presidency: "The only thing remarkable about them is that being so commonplace they should have climbed so high."[6]

Most twentieth-century commentators have been tolerant of the presidency's power. After leaving the office William Howard Taft, mindful that his former mentor, Theodore Roosevelt, had made extravagant claims of power in his memorable stewardship theory in contrast to his own conservative theory, nonetheless viewed the office's state and future confidently. Taft saw little danger of a tyrannous president who lacked popular support. At least one house of Congress, Taft concluded serenely, would block him. And if the people should support him, Taft also felt, their "good sense" would prevail, if a wayward president exploited their approval.[7]

In 1942 Thomas K. Finletter of the law faculty of the University of Pennsylvania, a special assistant to the secretary of state and a future secretary of the air force, expressed a widely felt sense that the presidency was lacking in power and effectiveness as it approached public problems after World War II.[8] To Finletter, the office's long history displayed not an imperial presidency but a "government of fits and starts," which had become "no longer good enough for our purposes"—the grand-scale adjustment of the nation and the international community, moving from an era of war to an era of peace and reconstruction. Finletter was troubled by the ease with which Congress can thwart a president, even a strong president, who offers creative initiatives for public problems. Only if the two branches worked together harmoniously and constructively, Finletter argued, could government become sufficiently effective, and he offered thoughtful proposals for restructuring relations between Congress and the presidency toward that end. Similarly, Sidney Hyman, writing in 1956, concluded that the presidency alone of the governmental system is structurally organized to be at the center of affairs. The role of Congress is to investigate and criticize, and if the sword of power that the president holds "seems more dangerous, it is simply because our position in the world has become dangerously great. It will not become less so if the Congress allows its individual members to shatter that sword."[9] Other commentators in this era were equally serene and accepting of presidential power. In his widely read work, *The American Presidency*, Harold J. Laski, a British political scientist, contended that the warnings of abuse following the tenure of a strong president were "baseless," and their chief consequence was that they often led to the selection of a successor "who has half-abdicated from the control of policy."[10]

In another classic study bearing the same title, Clinton Rossiter waved off efforts to reduce the president's powers as "ill-considered and ill-starred." In a world of unrest and aggression, in a country over which industrialism has swept in great waves, in a world where active diplomacy is the minimum price of survival, "it is not a lone power but a vacuum of power that men must fear." Urging that the presidency remain unamended and untouched, he concluded that "the strong presidency is the product of events that cannot be undone and of forces that continue to roll."[11]

Although popular presidents like Jackson and the Roosevelts were objects of venomous attack, the office they occupied remained relatively unscathed until its encounter with the Vietnam War and Watergate in the presidencies of Johnson and Nixon. A precursor of Schlesinger's study was George Reedy's influential *Twilight of the Presidency*, published in 1970. A long-time aide of President Johnson, Reedy depicted the president as isolated from reality, living in a euphoric dream of the matchless goodness of his works, shielded by his enormous power and a human wall of sycophants who served as his staff. Other influential voices of the 1970s, stirred by the Vietnam War and Watergate, recommended drastic surgery for the ills of the office. A former senator and presidential candidate, Eugene McCarthy, called for the depersonalization and decentralization of the presidency. Barbara Tuchman, contending that the office had become too complex and extended, a place where an impetuous man might run amok and cause horrendous damage, proposed a six-member executive with a rotating chairman, in the fashion of the Swiss presidency. Political scientist and journalist Max Lerner urged that the president be fettered with a council of state, with half of its members from Congress and the other half drawn from outside of Congress. Schlesinger, it should be noted, opposed any shearing away of presidential power. Rather, to set things aright, institutions with which the presidency deals, such as Congress and the bureaucracy of the executive branch, must be shaken out of their torpor and invigorated to do the job of checking the president, the job they had always been expected to do.

Assessing Congress

Schlesinger depicts Congress as largely compliant, supine, and only occasionally assertive against the president. This perception runs counter to the widely prevailing view of political scientists and historians in their writing on the presidency. If anything, Congress, often spoken of as the most powerful legislative body in history, has been a highly consequential presence. After the dazzling first hundred days of the New Deal, that most imperial of presidents, Franklin Roosevelt, as early as 1934—after only a year in office and seemingly favored with staunch public and congressional support—suffered defeat on three important issues. The Senate rejected the St. Lawrence Seaway Treaty and refused to empower the president to embargo the shipment of arms to countries at war. The American Legion and the Government Employees' Union pushed his solidly Democratic Congress into overriding his veto of increases in veterans' pensions and a restored cut in the federal payrolls. Congress thenceforth seldom allowed Roosevelt to forget its presence as a powerful vetoing body.

Even that spectacular Exhibit A of Schlesinger's imperial presidents, Richard Nixon, who stretched to the farthermost limits claims of executive privilege, impoundments of appropriations, and indulgence in sheer indictable acts, suffered many congressional rebuffs. As the Nixon years illustrate, the claim of imperial power does not necessarily constitute actual power. Time and time again Congress prevailed over Nixon. It ended his once secret war in Cambodia by cutting off funds. His claims of almost limitless powers to impound funds, keep secrets, and abolish programs were rejected by Congress and the courts. His modest program proposals were rebuffed by Congress more frequently than those of any other modern president. Eventually, Nixon's clear impending doom in the impeachment process drove him from the presidency. The imperial thesis underrates Congress and distorts history by portraying it as largely an institution of ineffectuality and slender impact.

In the American system, as Edward S. Corwin put it, the president proposes and Congress disposes. No presidential policy of importance can long endure without funds, and only Congress under the Constitution can provide appropriations. While in many ways the Vietnam War was conducted by the president, it was also a congressional war, supported annually and deliberately by that body's appropriations. At any moment that it chose, Congress could have ended the war by withholding appropriations, but it did not so choose.

In foreign affairs, the Elysian Fields of the imperial presidency, the role of Congress has been far greater than Schlesinger allows. From the beginning of independence to the close of the Civil War, Congress was largely the dominant force, with expansionist legislators often winning out as the United States absorbed great stretches of the North American mainland. In 1812, the expansionist "war hawks" of the House of Representatives, eyeing Canada to the north and the Floridas to the south, compelled a reluctant President Madison to make war on England. Again, expansionists in the House pressed President James Monroe, at the risk of war with Spain, to recognize the new Latin American republics emerging from the disintegrating Spanish empire. And again, the expansionists, unable to muster the two-thirds vote in the Senate required to approve a treaty, annexed Texas in 1845 via a joint resolution, making war with Mexico a certainty.

From the post-Civil War years until the close of the nineteenth century, Congress's influence was stronger in foreign affairs than the president's, and its tenor was decidedly "imperial." Expansionists in Congress, their eyes trained acquisitively on Cuba, agitated for war with Spain. But a nonimperial president, Grover Cleveland, said that if Congress declared war, it must not be assumed that he would wage it. Congress was more successful in annexing Hawaii in 1895, and it subsequently induced a peace-minded president, William McKinley, to follow its guideposts down the road to war with Spain over Cuba. In a joint resolution, in whose drafting McKinley took no part, the president was called on to affirm the right of Cubans to freedom and independence. The resolution was in effect a declaration of war since it directed the president to employ the armed forces to eject Spain from Cuba.

Not until Theodore Roosevelt's adventurism in foreign affairs did the presidency fit the imperial model neatly. Roosevelt "took Panama," intervened freely in the affairs of Latin American countries, and sided with and encouraged France and Japan in their foreign policy ventures. Except when his policies required legislation for their implementation Roosevelt thrived in high-handed independence from Congress.

Not so two other allegedly stellar contributors to the imperial model in the first half of the twentieth century, Woodrow Wilson and Franklin Roosevelt. Acting according to his own well-developed ideas of popular leadership and intent on converting the national government from a negative system of checks and balances into a positive, effective mechanism, Wilson worked elaborately and often in the manner of a British prime minister, which he admired, to elicit Congress's approval and support. A masterful political leader, he scored impressive successes with his New Freedom program of domestic reforms and with foreign policy measures. But after an initial "honeymoon" year of success, congressional opposition grew, as Wilson had anticipated it would. Henry Cabot Lodge, Albert Fall, and other senators demanded armed intervention in Mexico. A Senate filibuster blocked a bill granting the president authority to arm merchant vessels, driving a thoroughly frustrated Wilson into his memorable outburst against "a little group of willful men." American entry into war dispelled the interbranch conflict temporarily, but it resumed when Congress sought to force a war cabinet on the president and raked the War Department with acrimonious attack, while voters spurned Wilson's appeal for a Democratic Congress in 1918. The pendulum of power swung more decisively to Congress when it defeated the Versailles treaty and the president's ardently advocated membership of the United States in the League of Nations.

Franklin Roosevelt, a wizard of politics and the exercise of power, who guided the country through the Great Depression and World War II, was equally a prime candidate for top honors as an imperial president. To be sure, he provided dramatic moments when he seemed to fit the model—uprooting Japanese-Americans from the West Coast in World War II, for example, and when Congress was overdue in renewing price control legislation, threatening to pass the law himself. Fortunately, Congress acquiesced. Roosevelt's more customary stance was a careful nurturing of congressional and public opinion to support the measures necessary for the crisis.

From one perspective, Roosevelt played the role of an imperial president to the hilt, particularly in the crucial interval between the German conquest of France and the attack on Pearl Harbor (June 1940-December 1941). Britain then stood alone, with much of its military resources lost in the frantic escape at Dunkirk, and was threatened with invasion. With congressional and public opinion closely divided between intervention and isolation, Roosevelt acted with audacious initiative, to the point of committing warlike acts. Among other things, fifty "obsolete" but still serviceable destroyers were given Britain in exchange for leases of bases for American forces on British territories in the Western Hemisphere. When Germany occupied Denmark, Roosevelt moved American forces into the Danish territories of Greenland and Iceland. To safeguard arms deliveries to Britain, he provided naval convoys and ordered the shooting of Axis naval craft at sight. Several violent encounters ensued.

But while playing out his imperial role, Roosevelt in speeches and statements was diligently explaining to the public the nature of the peril lurking in the events of Europe, the necessity of alert citizen interest, and the certainty of severe sacrifices. By these attentions Roosevelt fashioned an essential, though imperfect, basis of support for his warlike initiatives.

Likewise, Roosevelt struggled in Congress to secure laws and appropriations to further his policies. The vehicle of continuous large-scale aid to Britain was the Lend Lease Act of 1941, in effect a thoroughly deliberated abandonment by Congress of its foreign policy of neutrality established in previous statutes. Roosevelt also had to secure extension of the Selective Service Act of 1940, which by dint of prodigious administration lobbying, squeezed through the House of Representatives by a single vote. Life was not always imperial for the president.

Cycles of the Presidency

The thesis of the imperial presidency boldly undertakes to interpret all of presidential history and both perceives and explains the office as a force of steadily aggrandizing power. From other extensive writing on the presidency, however, one can extract or build on other theories that undertake to explain the presidency's lengthy historic experience. One theory, for example, represented in various writings about the office, is the cycle theory.[12] It suggests that the impact and effectiveness of the presidency fluctuate. Unlike the imperial theory, which sees the presidency as sustaining a steady linear progression of power, a cyclical overview of the presidency suggests rises and falls in the office's fortunes.

Fluctuation and the cycle effect are produced by many forces. Much of the president's power over foreign and domestic affairs is shared with Congress, but the precise patterns of sharing are often tentative and unclear. Even after nearly two centuries of constitutional practice, they remain largely unpredictable. Power fluctuates because of shifts in public mood and opinion. In foreign affairs, the mood swings between high ideals and costly sacrifice, as during the two World Wars, to an opposite extreme of absorption in domestic affairs, characteristic of the nineteenth century, and even to moods of disillusionment and withdrawal prevailing in the era between the two World Wars and to some extent subsequent to the Vietnam War. Likewise, in domestic affairs, after breasting a flood of Lyndon Johnson's Great Society programs, the public seemed to crave less initiative and proved receptive to the Nixon-Ford-Carter retrenchment.

Other regulators built into the political system ensure that the president's power circumstances will fluctuate. The principle of separation of powers, employed by the founding fathers in constructing the Constitution, both produced the three branches of government and gave rise to a psychology of identity and self-assertion. Congress struggles to maintain its identity. For a time, especially during war, it may acquiesce to the president's initiatives, but sooner or later it will assert itself by contesting, amending, or rejecting what the president puts before it. Congress's identity is thereupon bolstered; unremitting assent erodes it. Likewise, the public mood, whose support the president must elicit if he is to accomplish objectives of any magnitude, is regulated by a limited span of attention. The presidential call for support to further a grand purpose cannot be made too often in a society devoted to private values and whose rewards fall most generously on private achievement.

Another potent variable is the personality of the incumbent, his conception of the presidency's powers, how and to what extent they should be used, and his political skill in using them. In writings on the presidency, classifications of the incumbents are offered on the basis of such factors.

Thomas Finletter, for example, concerned not that the presidency was imperial but that all too often the office hobbled an incumbent's capacity for accomplishment and produced results that failed to meet the needs of the times, noted what he called "the orthodox presidents." This type is characterized by a failure to use "the potential power which the direct election by the people gives him."[13] Taft, for example, a strict constructionist of the Constitution, felt that the president could exercise no authority that was not traceable to some specific grant of power in the Constitution or to an act of Congress. His stance toward Congress was decidedly nonimperial; he made no attempt to lead Congress assertively, as did his predecessor Roosevelt and his successor Wilson. Although important legislation was enacted during his term, much of it was carried over from Roosevelt's tenure, and no amount of straining could detect in Taft's policymaking an imperial flair. Roosevelt, who had his own scheme of classifying presidents and spoke of a Buchanan-Taft school, contended that it was denoted by the attitude that "the president is the servant of Congress rather than of the people.... Most able lawyers who are past middle age take this view."[14]

A contrasting type, Finletter and Roosevelt agree, is the president who excels as a popular leader, exemplified by Washington, Jackson, Lincoln, Wilson, and the Roosevelts. This type flourishes in times of crisis and change—during war or economic depression or when political movements such as populism or progressivism attain their crest. He interprets his powers liberally, is a precedent-maker, and causes the legality of his actions to be challenged. Clearly he is the most eligible type for Schlesinger's imperial category, particularly when he resorts to war-making. But "imperial" is hardly apt to denote this type's other noteworthy contributions in promoting the general welfare through social and economic programs for the body of citizens and responding constructively to the tasks and opportunities of international leadership.

There is also a middle category of presidents suggested by the tenure of Grover Cleveland. Its characteristics mix those of the categories that flank it. At times the president personally is at the forefront; at other times his office. Now he acquiesces to Congress; later he leads or contests it. At one time he summons the nation to advance to some new horizon; at another he is stopped in his tracks or moving backward. As president, he is often defensive or negative, resorting to the veto, shunning issues, halting what predecessors and others have set in motion, and using executive power only to maintain an equilibrium. Eisenhower is a recent illustration of this type.

Whether a given president becomes "imperial" depends mainly on his situation, his times, and the events of his tenure. His chances for reaching that heady clime are slim if he comes into office after a long war and the nation is fed up with conflict. Woe betide Andrew Johnson, succeeding in office that highflier of presidential power, Abraham Lincoln. Eisenhower's electoral success in 1952 was significantly predicated on his promise to end the war in Korea, a nonimperial act and a promise he kept. It was hardly likely that he would then involve the nation in another war, and he did not. He resisted the pressure of his military advisers to dispatch American forces to Vietnam. Similarly, after the termination of the long war in Indochina, Ford and Carter faced a situation in which initiating a further war of any scale was politically out of the question.

Situations, so far as the viability of a genuinely imperial presidency is concerned, vary by kind according to their potential. War, economic depression, and an encompassing political consensus supportive of a large-scale program of economic and social reform, such as Johnson's Great Society, are situations inviting presidential ascendance, a fertile ground for Schlesinger's imperial presidency. Less propitious are situations inviting a presidential administration whose effect is consolidation. Eisenhower's presidency was of this genre, coming on the heels of the tempestuous years of Truman, with war in Korea, hobbling labor-management disputes, an ambitious but abortive Fair Deal program of domestic reforms, and scandals sparked by mink coats and deep freezes. The situation invited a presidency capable of providing equilibrium, defined as avoidance of the conflict and upheaval characterizing the Truman years.

Least promising for the thriving of the imperial presidency is a situation that puts the office in a state of clearly diminished fortunes. Warren Harding's era of "normalcy" after World War I, like the Andrew Johnson administration after Lincoln, who had used the presidency to the hilt, provided fallow ground for the imperial seed.

The Presidency as Democracy-Serving

To single out a presidency and to label certain of its acts as imperial runs the danger that other acts, contributing to the common good, will be overlooked. Theodore Roosevelt's Square Deal, Wilson's New Freedom, and Franklin Roosevelt's New Deal are hardly to be dismissed as merely contributing to the imperial momentum. More memorably, they ameliorated human suffering, improved the lot of the general body of citizens, and responded to the essential needs of groups such as the elderly with social security pensions and blacks with enhanced political rights and economic opportunities. In one perspective, democracy requires benevolence, or a fraternal concern for the well-being of others, manifested in the social and economic programs of modern presidents.

Presidents have been a principal means of access to government and to responsive policymaking for left-out groups. Labor leaders enjoyed an access to Franklin Roosevelt unmatched in earlier presidencies, opening doors to his championship of legislation that enhanced labor's legal rights to organize and engage in collective bargaining, and that enormously enlarged the ranks of organized labor. Lincoln's Emancipation Proclamation dealt slavery its most mortal blows, and in more recent times black rights received high priorities in the presidencies of Kennedy and Johnson. Both placed themselves at the head of the black civil rights movement and employed a variety of presidential resources to promote their purposes. In addition to proposing legislation and resorting to the courts, Kennedy, for example, made public appeals in radio and television addresses. He employed private persuasion with individuals and delegations of southern businessmen, theater owners, and newspaper editors, as well as intensive dialogue with civil rights leaders, to keep the explosive issues within tolerable bounds. Kennedy also employed government contracts, hiring and promotion policies in the civil service, and the expenditure of federal funds, among other things, to clear the way for civil rights advances. In one perspective these accumulated efforts might be seen as contributing cubits of growth to an imperial presidency, but their far weightier importance is their function of democratic benevolence, of providing access to society's benefits and opportunities for a vast group that had for so long been left out.

If democracy is considered from another basic perspective, civil liberties, their observance and support by presidents are underrated by tagging their tenure as imperial. Jefferson was the first popular president, but his leadership was committed to human liberty, to developing public understanding of that concept, and of strengthening its protection. Even in what appear to be the presidency's most imperial moments, such as Lincoln's assertion of power in the Civil War, a moment when the nation's survival was in greatest peril, democracy in its essentials was observed, an achievement that ought not to be lightly regarded. James G. Randall, after close study of Lincoln's presidency, concluded that "no undue advantage was taken of the emergency to force arbitrary rule upon the country or to promote personal ends." Political opposition, Randall noted, continued to air its opinions, and the voters could repudiate their president at the polls if they wanted to. Lincoln's power, however "imperial," remained contingent on popular support.[15]

The contention that there is an imperial presidency largely ignores the office's everyday political functioning in a democratic context. The case for the imperial presidency centers on its incumbents' claims of legal power to make war, keep secrets, impound funds, and the like but treads lightly on the president's standard political tasks of political brokerage and consensus-building. As broker, the president projects an image of the good society and the means of attaining it. He struggles to weave together legislative majorities to enact his vision and to obtain support from interest groups. As Richard Neustadt recounts the process in his study, *Presidential Power*,[16] the president, contrary to the imperial thesis and its implications, has little power of command but has primarily the power to persuade, to influence groups and others in political life to perceive that it is in their interest to do what he asks. To help these respondents see the light, the president holds forth inducements from the store of benefits and advantages his office provides, and he bargains to evoke the desired behavior and metes out punishments and rewards. If he can awaken public opinion and evoke its support, he eases his tasks of persuading and bargaining. This picture of everyday presidential functioning, of one player with limited power among many players, is decidedly more democratic than imperial.

The Age of Television

According to one view, television has been a leading contributor to the rise of the imperial presidency. It has been a mighty force in reducing the strength and function of political parties that have historically mediated between the president and the voters, interpreting each to the other, and providing ties that hold the political structure together. Television presents presidents and other politicians directly to the voters. Certainly, John Kennedy enormously expanded his popularity and image by deftly using television to concentrate attention on his presidency. A president who dominates television can determine the way issues are shaped and focus national attention on what he wants to accomplish. Fred Friendly, a former television producer and now a professor of journalism, after considering television's potential for presidential leadership, exclaimed, "No mighty king, no ambitious emperor, no pope, no prophet ever dreamt of such an awesome pulpit, so potent a magic wand."[17]

But television is by no means the sheer advantage for the presidency it is often hailed to be. If television has enhanced the president's position as the nation's supreme political symbol, it has also done much to establish him as the nation's favorite scapegoat. If things go wrong, a program is maladministered, the Vietnam War drags on, the Soviet Union launches a new thrust, or inflation soars, the president is the readiest object on which to hang blame. Even though his powers for dealing with these occurrences are limited and shared with Congress, the executive branch bureaucracy, interest groups, and private corporate leaders, he is a readily summoned scapegoat.

Following the Vietnam War and Watergate and the burrowing of the notion of an imperial presidency into the national consciousness, television has abounded with reporters who not only follow the journalistic preference for bad news over good news but also frequently moralize over the policies and performances of presidents and their administrations. Since presidential policies, like other public policies, seldom offer clear moral choices and since the implementation of presidential policies is easily snarled by the misadventures of the many human beings on whom their effectuation depends, the president is a ready target.

Television also restricts the president's capacity to lay complicated issues before the public, to explain his proposals of action, and to perform the educative tasks of leadership. Like others in the political system, the president must reckon with television's preference for questions that are not too complicated to treat in approximately one minute and fifteen seconds and its predilection for visual drama as a context for those questions. Presidents, too, must accommodate the imperatives of television and largely abstain from the full-length expositions of issues they were accustomed to rendering on radio but which are rarely viable on television. Like other citizens, the president must capsulize serious questions to be represented in that most prized domain, television's evening news.

Leadership for the 1980s

The notion of an imperial presidency both contributes to a weakening of today's presidency and misstates its true condition. The thesis reinforces the contemporary mood to disparage the presidency, to suspect the motives and statements of the incumbent, and to thrust serious restrictions on the office. In foreign affairs, for example, Congress increasingly limits the president's policy choices. According to a recent count, Congress has used its appropriations power to impose more than seventy "constraints" on the president, such as barring military assistance to Thailand unless authorized by Congress, barring foreign aid from being spent on abortions, and prohibiting direct financing of any assistance to Angola. President Carter subsequently complained that because of congressional restraints, the United States was unable to provide assistance to rebels in Angola fighting Cubans. In the War Powers Act of 1973, Congress made many presidential deployments of the armed forces subject to its veto, although precisely which of the president's actions fall within the resolution remains unclear.

The Senate is increasingly engaged in the negotiation of treaties to the point that at its insistence a treaty may be renegotiated. Often this assertiveness comes not at the advice stage but at the consent stage, adding to the president's difficulties. A vivid illustration of these phenomenon was provided in the final stages of the Panama Canal treaties, when Senate Majority Leader Robert C. Byrd and Minority Leader Howard H. Baker journeyed to Panama and negotiated changes in the treaty with Panama's president.

Congress in its countermoves against a presumed imperial presidency has been anything but the supine body that Schlesinger describes. The mood engendered by the idea of the imperial presidency also affects citizen attitudes, making the public continuously suspicious and disparaging. Any new president becomes eligible for deprecation if he does not quickly produce visible results through leadership initiatives. The apparatus of public opinion polls and interest groups that are better funded, more sophisticated, and more committed to particular issues are increasingly resulting in presidential policymaking by fits and starts. Progress on energy, inflation, unemployment, tax reform, and urban affairs, all have experienced advances and retreats in the Carter years but the cause cannot be explained merely in terms of the president himself and the talents of his aides but as reflecting the ever more deft thrusts of private interests, the disinclination of legislators to follow the president's lead, and the decline of the party as a unifying force.

Ironically, while presidential leadership is being denigrated by cries of "imperial," the demands on it, as the 1980s begin, are fast enlarging. Inflation, the energy shortage, the spread of nuclear weapons capability, and the constant presence of war are survival problems threatening not only American well-being but the well-being of all mankind. The complexity of these issues, the broad canvass of interests that they traverse, and their constant unwinding in new manifestations heighten the demands on leadership.

To make its way, future president leadership must summon a high order of creativity, political dexterity both at home and abroad, and resolute humanism in its orientation. It must experiment and educate; it must be fair-minded in the distribution of burdens and sensitive to avoiding unnecessary hardship. In the certain shifting of fortunes between good days and bad days in policymaking and implementation, the president, above all, must be capable of maintaining public confidence and trust. It will be easier if the clouds of suspicion generated by the notion of an imperial presidency can be dispelled.

Notes

1. Arthur M Schlesinger, Jr., *The Imperial Presidency* (Boston: Houghton Mifflin, 1973).
2. Ibid., 206.
3. Quotations are from Arthur Benson Tourtelot, *The Presidents on the Presidency* (New York: Russell and Russell, 1970).
4. Woodrow Wilson, *Congressional Government* (Cleveland: World, 1956), 31.
5. Phillips Bradley, ed., *Alexis de. Tocqueville: Democracy in America*, vol.1 (New York: Knopf, 1948), 123-25.
6. James Bryce, *The American Commonwealth*, vol. 1 (New York: Macmillan, 1893), 76-78.
7. William Howard Taft, *Our Chief Magistrate and His Powers* (New York: Columbia University Press, 1916), 156-57.
8. Thomas K. Finletter, *Can Representative Government Do the Job?* (New York: Reynal and Hitchcock, 1945), 64.
9. Sidney Hyman, "The Art of the Presidency," *The Annals of the American Academy of Political and Social Science* 307 (September 1956): 9.
10. Harold J. Laski, *The American Presidency* (New York: Harper and Row, 1940), 15.
11. Clinton Rossiter, *The American Presidency* (New York: Harcourt Brace Jovanovich, 1956), 159-60.
12. See, e.g., Norman Small, *Some Presidential Interpretations of the Presidency* (Baltimore: Johns Hopkins University Press, 1930).
13. Finletter, *Can Representative Government Do the Job?* 26.
14. Theodore Roosevelt, *An Autobiography* (New York: Scribners, 1920), 406.
15. E. Pendleton Herring, *Presidential Leadership* (New York: Holt, Rinehart & Winston, 1940), 17.
16. Richard E. Neustadt, *Presidential Power* (New York: Wiley, 1960).
17. Newton N. Minow, John Bartlow Martin, and Lee M. Mitchell, *Presidential Television* (New York: Basic Books, 1973), vii.

To Form a Government 9.8

Lloyd N. Cutler

The following essay written by a Carter administration staffer expresses frustration with the Madisonian system of dispersed power. In it Cutler advocates a form of parliamentary government. Students should be prepared to grapple with proposals to bridge the separation of powers. Specifically, we all should be ready to address the strengths and benefits of existing arrangements, the strengths and

---

"To Form a Government" by Lloyd N. Cutler, Fall 1980, *Foreign Affairs, 59,* pp. 126-44. Copyright 1980 by the Council on Foreign Relations, Inc. Reprinted by permission.

[On May 10, 1940, Winston Churchill was summoned to Buckingham Palace.] His Majesty received me most graciously and bade me sit down. He looked at me searchingly and quizzically for some moments, and then said: "I suppose you don't know why I have sent for you?" Adopting his mood, I replied, "Sir, I simply couldn't imagine why." He laughed and said: "I want to ask you to form a government." I said I would certainly do so.

— Winston S. Churchill
The Gathering Storm (1948)

Our society was one of the first to write a Constitution. This reflected the confident conviction of the Enlightenment that explicit written arrangements could be devised to structure a government that would be neither tyrannical nor impotent in its time, and to allow for future amendment as experience and change might require.

We are all children of this faith in a rational written arrangement for governing. Our faith should encourage us to consider changes in our Constitution—for which the framers explicitly allowed—that would assist us in adjusting to the changes in the world in which the Constitution must function. Yet we tend to resist suggestions that amendments to our existing constitutional framework are needed to govern our portion of the interdependent world society we have become, and to cope with the resulting problems that all contemporary governments must resolve.

A particular shortcoming in need of a remedy is the structural inability of our government to propose, legislate, and administer a balanced program for governing. In parliamentary terms, one might say that under the U.S. Constitution it is not now feasible to "form a government." The separation of powers between the legislative and executive branches, whatever its merits in 1793, has become a structure that almost guarantees stalemate today. As we wonder why we are having such a difficult time making decisions we all know must be made, and projecting our power and leadership, we should reflect on whether this is one big reason.

We elect one presidential candidate over another on the basis of our judgment of the overall program he presents, his ability to carry it out, and his capacity to adapt his program to new developments as they arise. We elected President Carter, whose program included, as one of its most important elements, the successful completion of the SALT II negotiations that his two predecessors had been conducting since 1972. President Carter did complete and sign a SALT II treaty, in June 1979, which he and his cabinet regarded as very much in the national security interest of the United States. Notwithstanding recent events, the president and his cabinet still hold that view—indeed they believe the mounting intensity of our confrontation with the Soviet Union makes it even more important for the two superpowers to adopt and abide by explicit rules as to the size and quality of each side's strategic nuclear arsenal, and as to how each side can verify what the other side is doing.

But because we do not "form a government," it has not been possible for President Carter to carry out this major part of his program.

Of course the constitutional requirement of Senate advice and consent to treaties presents a special situation. The case for the two-thirds rule was much stronger in 1793, when events abroad rarely affected this isolated continent, and when "entangling foreign alliances" were viewed with a skeptical eye. Whether it should be maintained in an age when most treaties deal with such subjects as taxation and trade is open to question. No parliamentary regime anywhere in the world has a similar provision. But in the American case—at least for major issues like SALT—there is merit to the view that treaties should indeed require the careful bipartisan consultation essential to win a two-thirds majority. This is the principle that Woodrow Wilson fatally neglected in 1919. But it has been carefully observed by recent presidents, including President Carter for the Panama Canal treaties and the SALT II treaty. In each of these cases there was a clear prior record of support by previous Republican administrations, and there would surely have been enough votes for fairly rapid ratification if the president could have counted on the total or near-total support of his own party—if, in short, he had truly formed a government, with a legislative majority which takes the responsibility for governing.

Treaties may indeed present special cases, and I do not argue here for any change in the historic two-thirds requirement. But our inability to "form a government" able to ratify SALT II is replicated regularly over the whole range of legislation required to carry out any president's overall program, foreign and domestic. Although the enactment of legislation takes only a simple majority of both houses, that majority is very difficult to achieve. Any part of the president's legislative program may be defeated, or amended into an entirely different measure, so that the legislative record of any presidency may bear little resemblance to the overall program the president wanted to carry out. Energy and the budget provide two current and critical examples. Indeed, SALT II itself could have been presented for approval by a simple majority of each House under existing arms control legislation, but the administration deemed this task even more difficult than achieving a two-thirds vote in the Senate. And this difficulty is of course compounded when the president's party does not even hold the majority of the seats in both houses, as was the case from 1946 to 1948, from 1954 to 1960, and from 1968 to 1976—or almost half the duration of the last seven administrations.

The Constitution does not require or even permit in such a case the holding of a new election, in which those who oppose the president can seek office to carry out their own overall program. Indeed, the opponents of each element of the president's overall program usually have a different makeup from one element to another. They would probably be unable to get together on any overall program of their own, or to obtain the congressional votes to carry it out. As a result the stalemate continues, and because we do not form a government, we have no overall program at all. We cannot fairly hold the president accountable for the success or failure of his overall program, because he lacks the constitutional power to put that program into effect.

Compare this with the structure of parliamentary governments. A parliamentary government may have no written constitution, as in the United Kingdom. Or it may have a written constitution, as in West Germany, Japan, and Ireland, that in other respects—such as an independent judiciary and an entrenched Bill of Rights—closely resembles our own. But while there may be a ceremonial president or, as in Japan, an emperor, the executive consists of those members of the legislature chosen by the elected legislative majority. The majority elects a premier or prime minister from among its number, and he selects other leading members of the majority as the members of his cabinet. The majority as a whole is responsible for forming and conducting the "government." If any key part of its overall program is rejected by the legislature, or if a vote of "no confidence" is carried, the "government" must resign and either a new "government" must be formed out of the existing legislature or a new legislative election must be held. If the program *is* legislated, the public can judge the results, and can decide at the next regular election whether to reelect the majority or turn it out. At all times the voting public knows who is in charge, and whom to hold accountable for success or failure.

Operating under a parliamentary system, Chancellor Helmut Schmidt formed the present West German government with a majority of only four, but he has succeeded in carrying out his overall program these past five years. Last year Mrs. Thatcher won a majority of some thirty to forty in the British Parliament. She has a very radical program, one that can make fundamental changes in the economy, social fabric, and foreign policy of the United Kingdom. There is room for legitimate doubt as to whether her overall program will achieve its objectives and, even if it does, whether it will prove popular enough to reelect her government at the next election. But there is not the slightest doubt that she will be able to legislate her entire program, including any modifications she makes to meet new problems. In a parliamentary system, it is the duty of each majority member of the legislature to vote for each element of the government's program, and the government possesses the means to punish members if they do not. In a very real sense, each member's political and electoral future is tied to the fate of the government his majority has formed. Politically speaking, he lives or dies by whether that government lives or dies.

President Carter's party has a much larger majority percentage in both houses of Congress than Chancellor Schmidt or Mrs. Thatcher. But this comfortable majority does not even begin to assure that President Carter or any other president can rely on that majority to vote for each element of his program. No member of that majority has the constitutional duty or the practical political need to vote for each element of the president's program. Neither the president nor the leaders of the legislative majority have the means to punish him if he does not. In the famous phrase of Joe Jacobs, the fight manager, "it's every man for theirself."

Let me cite one example. In the British House of Commons, just as in our own House, some of the majority leaders are called the whips. In the Commons, the whips do just what their title implies. If the government cares about the pending vote, they "whip" the fellow members of the majority into compliance, under pain of party discipline if a member disobeys. On the most important votes, the leaders invoke what is called a three-line whip, which must be obeyed on pain of resignation or expulsion from the party.

In our House, the majority whip, who happens to be one of our very best Democratic legislators, can himself feel free to leave his Democratic president and the rest of the House Democratic leadership on a crucial vote, if he believes it important to his constituency and his conscience to vote the other way. When he does so, he is not expected or required to resign his leadership post; indeed he is back a few hours later "whipping" his fellow members of the majority to vote with the president and the leadership on some other issue. But all other members are equally free to vote against the president and the leadership when they feel it important to do so. The president and the leaders have a few sticks and carrots they can use to punish or reward, but nothing even approaching the power that Mrs. Thatcher's government or Chancellor Schmidt's government can wield against any errant member of the majority.

I am hardly the first to notice this fault. As Judge Carl McGowan has reminded us, that "young and rising academic star in the field of political science, Woodrow Wilson—happily unaware of what the future held for him in terms of successive domination of, and defeat by, the Congress—despaired in the late 19th century of the weakness of the executive branch vis-à-vis the legislative, so much so that he concluded that a coalescence of the two in the style of English parliamentary government was the only hope."[1]

As Wilson put it, "power and strict accountability for its use are the essential constituents of good government."[2] Our separation of executive and legislative power fractions power and prevents accountability.

In drawing this comparison, I am not blind to the proven weaknesses of parliamentary government, or to the virtues which our forefathers saw in separating the executive from the legislature. In particular, the parliamentary system lacks the ability of a separate and vigilant legislature to investigate and curb the abuse of power by an arbitrary or corrupt executive. Our own recent history has underscored this virtue of separating these two branches.

Moreover, our division of executive from legislative responsibility also means that a great many more voters are represented in positions of power, rather than as mere members of a "loyal opposition." If I am a Democrat in a Republican district, my vote in the presidential election may still give me a proportional impact. And if my party elects a president, I do not feel—as almost half the voters in a parliamentary constituency like Oxford must feel—wholly unrepresented. One result of this division is a sort of a permanent centrism. While this means that no extreme or Thatcher-like program can be legislated, it means also that there are fewer wild swings in the statutory policy.

This is also a virtue of the constitutional division of responsibility. It is perhaps what John Adams had in mind when, at the end of his life, he wrote to his old friend and adversary, Thomas Jefferson, that "checks and balances, Jefferson, . . . are our only Security, for the Progress of Mind, as well as the Security of Body."[3]

But these virtues of separation are not without their costs. I believe these costs have been mounting in the last half-century, and that it is time to examine whether we can reduce the costs of separation without losing its virtues.

During this century, other nations have adopted written constitutions, sometimes with our help, that blend the virtues of our system with those of the parliamentary system. The Irish constitution contains a replica of our Bill of Rights, an independent Supreme Court that can declare acts of the government unconstitutional, a figurehead president, and a parliamentary system. The postwar German and Japanese constitutions, which we helped to draft, are essentially the same. While the Gaullist French constitution contains a Bill of Rights somewhat weaker than ours, it provides for a strong president who can dismiss the legislature and call for new elections. But it also retains the parliamentary system and its blend of executive and legislative power achieved by forming a government out of the elected legislative majority. The president, however, appoints the premier or first minister.

II

We are not about to revise our own Constitution so as to incorporate a true parliamentary system. But we do need to find a way of coming closer to the parliamentary concept of "forming a government," under which the elected majority is able to carry out an overall program, and is held accountable for its success or failure.

There are several reasons why it is far more important in 1980 than it was in 1940, 1900, or 1800 for our government to have the capability to formulate and carry out an overall program.

1. The first reason is that government is now constantly required to make a different kind of choice than usual in the past, a kind for which it is difficult to obtain a broad consensus. That kind of choice, which one may call "allocative," has become the fundamental challenge to government today. As a recent newspaper article put it:

> The domestic programs of the last two decades are no longer seen as broad campaigns to curb pollution or end poverty or improve health care. As these programs have filtered down through an expanding network of regulation, they single out winners and losers. The losers may be workers who blame a lost promotion on equal employment programs; a chemical plant fighting a tough pollution control order; a contractor who bids unsuccessfully for a government contract; or a gas station owner who wants a larger fuel allotment.[4]

This is a way of recognizing that, in giving government great responsibilities, we have forced a series of choices among these responsibilities.

During the second half of this century, our government has adopted a wide variety of national goals. Many of these goals—checking inflation, spurring economic growth, reducing unemployment, protecting our national security, assuring equal opportunity, increasing social security, cleaning up the environment, improving energy efficiency—conflict with one another, and all of them compete for the same resources. There may have been a time when we could simultaneously pursue all of these goals to the utmost. But even in a country as rich as this one, that time is now past. One of the central tasks of modern government is to make wise balancing choices among courses of action that pursue one or more of our many conflicting and competing objectives.

Furthermore, as new economic or social

problems are recognized, a responsible government must *adjust* these priorities. In the case of energy policy, the need to accept realistic oil prices has had to be balanced against the immediate impact of drastic price increases on consumers and affected industries, and on the overall rate of inflation. And to cope with the energy crisis, earlier objectives of policy have had to be accommodated along the way. Reconciling one goal with another is a continuous process. A critical regulatory goal of 1965 (auto safety) had to be reconciled with an equally critical regulatory goal of 1970 (clean air) long before the auto safety goal had been achieved, just as both these critical goals had to be reconciled with 1975's key goal (closing the energy gap) long before either auto safety or clean air had lost their importance. Reconciliation was needed because many auto safety regulations had the effect of increasing vehicle size and weight and therefore increasing gasoline consumption and undesirable emissions, and also because auto emission control devices tend to increase gasoline consumption. Moreover, throughout this fifteen year period, we have had to reconcile all three of these goals with another critical national objective—wage and price stability—when in pursuit of these other goals we make vehicles more costly to purchase and operate.

And now, in 1980, we find our auto industry at a serious competitive disadvantage vis-à-vis Japanese and European imports, making it necessary to limit those regulatory burdens which aggravate the extent of the disadvantage. A responsible government must be able to adapt its programs to achieve the best balance among its conflicting goals as each new development arises.

For balancing choices like these, a kind of political triage, it is almost impossible to achieve a broad consensus. Every group will be against some part of the balance. If the "losers" on each item are given a veto on that part of the balance, a sensible balance cannot be struck.

2. The second reason is that we live in an increasingly interdependent world. What happens in distant places is now just as consequential for our security and our economy as what happens in Seattle or Miami. No one today would use the term "Afghanistanism," as the opposition benches did in the British Parliament a century ago, to deride the government's preoccupation with a war in that distant land. No one would say today, as President Wilson said in 1914, that general European war could not affect us and is no concern of ours. We are now an integral part of a closely interconnected world economic and political system. We have to respond as quickly and decisively to what happens abroad as to what happens within the portion of this world system that is governed under our Constitution.

New problems requiring new adjustments come up even more frequently over the foreign horizon than the domestic one. Consider the rapid succession of events and crises since President Carter took up the relay baton for his leg of the SALT II negotiations back in 1977: the signing of the Egyptian-Israeli peace treaty over Soviet and Arab opposition, the Soviet-Cuban assistance to guerrilla forces in Africa and the Arabian peninsula, the recognition of the People's Republic of China, the final agreement on the SALT II terms and the signing of the treaty in Vienna, the revolution in Iran and the later seizure of our hostages, the military coup in Korea, the Soviet-supported Vietnamese invasion of Kampuchea, our growing dependence on foreign oil from politically undependable sources, the affair of the Soviet brigade in Cuba, the polarization of rightist and leftist elements in Central America, and finally (that is, until the next crisis a month or two from now) the Soviet invasion of Afghanistan and the added threat it poses to the States of Southwest Asia and to the vital oil supplies of Europe, Japan, and the United States.

Each of these portentous events required a prompt reaction and response from our government, including in many cases a decision as to how it would affect our position on the SALT II treaty. The government has to be able to adapt its overall program to deal with each such event as it arises, and it has to be able to execute the adapted program with reasonable dispatch. Many of these adaptations—such as changes in the levels and direction of military and economic assistance—require joint action by the president and the Congress, something that is far from automatic under our system. And when Congress does act, it is prone to impose statutory conditions or prohibitions that fetter the president's policy discretion to negotiate an appropriate assistance package or to adapt it to fit even later developments. The congressional bans on military assistance to Turkey, any form of assistance to the contending forces in Angola, and any aid to Argentina if it did not meet our human rights criteria by a deadline now past, are typical examples.

Indeed, the doubt that Congress will approve a presidential foreign policy initiative has seriously compromised our ability to make binding agreements with nations that "form a government." Given the fate of SALT II and lesser treaties, and the frequent congressional vetoes of other foreign policy actions, other nations now realize that our executive branch commitments are not as binding as theirs, that Congress may block any agreement at all, and that at the very least they must hold something back for a subsequent round of bargaining with the Congress.

3. The third reason is the change in Congress and its relationship to the executive. When the Federalist and Democratic Republican parties held power, a Hamilton or a Gallatin would serve in the cabinet, but they continued to lead rather than report to their party colleagues in the houses of Congress. Even when the locus of congressional leadership shifted from the cabinet to the leaders of Congress itself, in the early nineteenth century, it was a congressional leadership capable of collaboration with the executive. This was true until very recently. The Johnson-Rayburn collaboration with Eisenhower a generation ago is an instructive example. But now Congress itself has changed.

There have been the well-intended democratic reforms of Congress, and the enormous growth of the professional legislative staff. The former ability of the president to sit down with ten or fifteen leaders in each house, and to agree on a program which those leaders could carry through Congress, has virtually disappeared. The committee chairmen and the leaders no longer have the instruments of power that once enabled them to lead. A Lyndon Johnson would have a much harder time getting his way as majority leader today than when he did hold and pull these strings of power in the 1950s. When Senator Mansfield became majority leader in 1961, he changed the practice of awarding committee chairmanships on the basis of seniority. He declared that all senators are created equal. He gave every Democratic senator a major committee assignment and then a subcommittee chairmanship, adding to the sharing of power by reducing the leadership's control.

In the House the seniority system was scrapped. Now the House majority caucus—not the leadership—picks the committee chairmen and the subcommittee chairmen as well. The House parliamentarian has lost the critical power to refer bills to a single committee selected by the Speaker. Now bills like the energy bills go to several committees which then report conflicting versions back to the floor. Now mark-up sessions take place in public; indeed, even the House-Senate joint conference committees, at which differing versions of the same measure are reconciled, must meet and barter in public.

The recent conference committees on the Synthetic Fuels Corporation and the Energy Mobilization Board, for example, were so big and their procedures so cumbersome that they took six months to reach agreement, and then the agreement on the Board was rejected by the House. All this means that there are no longer a few leaders with power who *can* collaborate with the president. Power is further diffused by the growth of legislative staffs, sometimes making it difficult for the members even to collaborate with each other. In the past five years, the Senate alone has hired 700 additional staff members, an average of seven per member.

There is also the decline of party discipline and the decline of the political party itself. Presidential candidates are no longer selected, as Adlai Stevenson was selected, by the leaders or bosses of their party. Who are the party leaders today? There are no such people. The party is no longer the instrument that selects the candidate. Indeed, the party today, as a practical matter, is no more than a neutral open forum that holds the primary or caucus in which candidates for president and for Congress may compete for favor and be elected. The party does not dispense most of the money needed for campaigning, the way the European and Japanese parties do. The candidates raise most of their own money. To the extent that money influences legislative votes, it comes not from a party with a balanced program, but from a variety of single-interest groups.

We now have a great many diverse and highly organized interest groups—not just broad-based agriculture, labor, business, and ethnic groups interested in a wide variety of issues affecting their members. We now have single-issue groups—environmental, consumer, abortion, right to life, pro- and anti-SALT, pro- and anti-nuclear, that stand ready to lobby for their single issue and to reward or punish legislators, both in cash and at the ballot box, according to how they respond on the single issue that is the group's raison d'être. And on many specific foreign policy issues involving particular countries, there are exceptionally strong voting blocs in this wonderful melting pot of a nation that exert a great deal of influence on individual senators and congressmen.

III

It is useful to compare this modern failure of our governmental structure with its earlier classic successes. There can be no structural fault, it might be said, so long as an FDR could put through an entire antidepression program in one hundred days, or an LBJ could enact a broad program for social justice three decades later. These infrequent exceptions, however, confirm the general rule of stalemate.

If we look closely we will find that in this century the system has succeeded only on the rare occasions when there is an unusual event that brings us together and creates substantial consensus throughout the country on the need for a whole new program. FDR had such a consensus in the early days of the New Deal and from Pearl Harbor to the end of World War II. But we tend to forget that in 1937 his court-packing plan was justifiably rejected by Congress—a good point for those who favor complete separation of the executive from the legislature[5]—and that as late as August 1941, when President Roosevelt called on Congress to pass a renewal of the Selective Service Act, passage was gained by a single vote in the House. Lyndon Johnson had such a consensus for both his domestic and his Vietnam initiatives during the first three years after the shock of John Kennedy's assassination brought us together. But it was gone by 1968. Jimmy Carter has had it this past winter and spring for his responses to the events in Iran and Afghanistan and to the belated realization of our need for greater energy self-sufficiency, but he may not hold it for long. Yet the consensus on Afghanistan was marred by the long congressional delay in appropriating the small amounts needed to register nineteen- and twenty-year-olds under the Selective Service Act—a delay that at least blurred the intended impact of this signal to the world of our determination to oppose further Soviet aggression.[6]

When the great crisis and the resulting large consensus are not there—when the country is divided somewhere between 55-45 and 45-55 on each of a wide set of issues, and when the makeup of the majority is different on every issue—it has not been possible for any modern president to "form a government" that could legislate and carry out his overall program.

Yet modern government has to respond promptly to a wide range of new challenges. Its responses cannot be limited to those for which there is a large consensus induced by some great crisis. Modern government also has to work in every presidency, not just in one presidency out of four, when a Wilson, an FDR, or an LBJ comes along. It also has to work for the president's full time in office, as it did not even for Wilson and LBJ. When they needed congressional support for the most important issue of their presidencies, they could not get it.

When the president gets only "half a loaf" of his overall program, this half a loaf is not necessarily better than none, because it may lack the essential quality of balance. And half a loaf leaves both the president and the public in the worst of all possible worlds. The public—and the press—still expect the president to govern. But the president cannot achieve his overall program, and the public cannot fairly blame the president because he does not have the power to legislate and execute his program. Nor can the public fairly blame the individual members of Congress, because the Constitution allows them to disclaim any responsibility for forming a government and hence any accountability for its failures.

Of course the presidency always has been and will continue to be what Theodore Roosevelt called "a bully pulpit"—not a place from which to "bully" in the sense of intimidating the Congress and the public, but in the idiom of TR's day a marvelous place from which to exhort and lift up Congress and the public. All presidents have used the bully pulpit in this way, and this is one reason why the American people continue to revere the office and almost always revere its incumbent. Television has probably amplified the power of the bully pulpit, but it has also shortened the time span of power; few television performers can hold their audiences for four consecutive years. In any event, a bully pulpit, while a glorious thing to have and to employ, is not a government, and it has not been enough to enable any postwar president to "form a government" for his entire term.

Finally, the myth persists that the existing system can be made to work satisfactorily if only the president will take the trouble to consult closely with the Congress. If one looks back at the period between 1947 and 1967 there were indeed remarkable cases, at least in the field of foreign policy, where such consultation worked to great effect, even across party lines. The relationships between Senator Vandenberg and Secretaries Marshall and Acheson, and between Senator George and Secretary Dulles, come readily to mind. But these examples were in an era of strong leadership within the Congress and of unusual national consensus on the overall objectives of foreign policy and the measures needed to carry it out.

Even when these elements have not been present, every president has indeed tried to work with the majority in Congress, and the majority in every Congress has tried to work with the president. Within this past year, when there has been a large consensus in response to the crises in Afghanistan and Iran, a notable achievement has been a daily private briefing of congressional leaders by the secretary of state, and weekly private briefings with all Senate and House members who want to attend—a step that has helped to keep that consensus in being. Another achievement of recent times is the development of the congressional budget process, exemplified by the cooperation between the congressional leadership and the president in framing the 1981 budget.

But even on Iran, Afghanistan, and the budget, the jury is still out on how long the large consensus will hold. And except on the rare issues where there is such a consensus, the structural problems usually prove too difficult to overcome. In each administration, it becomes progressively more difficult to make the present system work effectively on the range of issues, both domestic and foreign, that the United States must now manage even though there is no large consensus.

IV

If we decide we want the capability of forming a government, the only way to do so is to amend the Constitution. Amending the Constitution, of course, is extremely difficult. Since 1793, when the Bill of Rights was added, we have amended the Constitution only sixteen times. Some of these amendments were structural, such as the direct election of senators, votes for women and 18-year-olds, the two-term limit for presidents, and the selection of a successor vice-president. But none has touched the basic separation of executive and legislative powers.

The most one can hope for is a set of modest changes that would make our structure work somewhat more in the manner of a parliamentary system, with somewhat less separation between the executive and the legislature than now exists.

There are several candidate proposals. Here are some of the more interesting ideas:

1. We now vote for a presidential candidate and a vice-presidential candidate as an inseparable team. We could provide that in presidential election years, voters in each congres-

sional district would be required to vote for a trio of candidates, as a team, for president, vice-president, and the House of Representatives. This would tie the political fortunes of the party's presidential and congressional candidates to one another, and provide some incentive for sticking together after they are elected. Such a proposal could be combined with a four-year term for members of the House of Representatives. This would tie the presidential and congressional candidates even more closely, and has the added virtue of providing members with greater protection against the pressures of single-issue political groups. This combination is the brainchild of Congressman Jonathan Bingham of New York, and is now pending before the Congress.

In our bicameral legislature, the logic of the Bingham proposal would suggest that the inseparable trio of candidates for president, vice-president, and member of Congress be expanded to a quintet including the two senators, who would also have the same four-year term. But no one has challenged the gods of the Olympian Senate by advancing such a proposal.

2. Another idea is to permit or require the president to select 50 percent of his cabinet from among the members of his party in the Senate and House, who would retain their seats while serving in the cabinet. This would be only a minor infringement on the constitutional principle of separation of powers, but it would require a change in Article I, Section 6, which provides that "no person holding any office under the United States shall be a member of either house during his continuance in office." It would tend to increase the intimacy between the executive and the legislature, and add to their sense of collective responsibility. The 50-percent test would leave the president adequate room to bring other qualified persons into his cabinet, even though they do not hold elective office.

3. A third intriguing suggestion is to provide the president with the power, to be exercised not more than once in his term, to dissolve Congress and call for new congressional elections. This is the power now vested in the president under the French Constitution. It would provide the opportunity that does not now exist to break an executive-legislative impasse, and to let the public decide whether it wishes to elect senators and congressmen who *will* legislate the president's overall program.

For obvious reasons, the president would invoke such a power only as a last resort, but his potential ability to do so could have a powerful influence on congressional responses to his initiatives. This would of course be a radical and highly controversial proposal, and it involves a number of technical difficulties relating to the timing and conduct of the new election, the staggering of senatorial terms, and similar matters. But it would significantly enhance the president's power to form a government.

On the other hand, the experience of presidents—one recalls Nixon in 1970—who sought to use the mid-term election as a referendum on their programs suggests that any such dissolution and new election would be equally as likely to continue the impasse as to break it. Perhaps any exercise of the power to dissolve Congress should automatically require a new presidential election as well. But even then, the American public might be perverse enough to reelect all the incumbents to the office.

4. Another variant on the same idea is that in addition to empowering the president to call for new congressional elections, we might empower a majority or two-thirds of both houses to call for new presidential elections. This variant has been scathingly attacked in a series of conversations between Professor Charles Black of the Yale Law School and Congressman Bob Eckhardt of Texas, published in 1975, because they think that such a measure would vitally diminish the president's capacity to lead.[7]

5. There are other proposals that deserve consideration. There could be a single six-year presidential term, an idea with many supporters, among them Presidents Eisenhower, Johnson, and Carter, to say nothing of a great many political scientists. (The French constitution provides a seven-year term for the president, but permits reelection.) Of course presidents would like to be elected and then forget about politics and get to the high ground of saving the world. But if first-term presidents did not have the leverage of reelection, we might institutionalize for every presidency the lame duck impotence we now see when a president is not running for reelection.

6. It may be that one combination involving elements of the third, fourth, and fifth proposals would be worthy of further study. It would be roughly as follows:

a. The president, vice-president, senators and congressmen would all be elected for simultaneous six-year terms.
b. On one occasion each term, the president could dissolve Congress and call for new congressional elections for the remainder of the term. If he did so, Congress, by majority vote of both houses within 30 days of the president's action, could call for simultaneous new elections for president and vice-president for the remainder of the term.
c. All state primaries and state conventions for any required mid-term elections would be held 60 days after the first call for new elections. Any required national presidential nominating conventions would be held 30 days later. The national elections would be held 60 days after the state primary elections and state conventions. The entire cycle would take 120 days. The dissolved Congress would be free to remain in session for part or all of this period.
d. Presidents would be allowed to serve only one full six-year term. If a mid-term presidential election is called, the incumbent would be eligible to run and, if reelected, to serve the balance of his six-year term.

Limiting each president to one six-year term would enhance the objectivity and public acceptance of the measures he urges in the national interest. He would not be regarded as a lame duck because of his continuing power to dissolve Congress. Our capacity to "form a government" would be enhanced if the president could break an impasse by calling for a new congressional election and by the power of Congress to respond by calling for a new presidential election.

Six-year terms for senators and congressmen would diminish the power of single-interest groups to veto balanced programs for governing. Because any mid-term elections would have to be held promptly, a single national primary, a shorter campaign cycle, and public financing of congressional campaigns—three reforms with independent virtues of their own—would become a necessity for the mid-term election. Once tried in a mid-term election, they might well be adopted for regular elections as well.

7. One final proposal may be mentioned. It would be possible, through constitutional amendment, to revise the legislative process in the following way. Congress would enact broad mandates first, declaring general policies and directions, leaving the precise allocative choices, within a congressionally approved budget, to the president. All agencies would be responsible to the president. By dividing up tasks among them, and making the difficult choices of fulfilling some congressional directions at the expense of others, the president would fill in the exact choices, the allocative decisions. Then any presidential action would be returned to Congress where it would await a two-house legislative veto. If not so vetoed within a specified period, the action would become law.

If the legislative veto could be overturned by a presidential veto—subject in turn to a two-thirds override—then this proposal would go a long way to enhance the president's ability to "form a government." In any event, it should enable the elected president to carry out the program he ran on, subject to congressional oversight, and end the stalemate over whether to legislate the president's program in the first instance. It would let Congress and the president each do what they have shown they now do best.

Such a resequencing, of course, would turn the present process on its head. But it would bring much closer to reality the persisting myth that it is up to the president to govern—something he now lacks the constitutional power to do.

V

How can these proposals be evaluated? How can better proposals be devised? Above all, how can the public be educated to understand the costs of the present separation between our executive and legislative branches, to weigh these costs against the benefits, and to decide whether a change is needed?

One obvious possibility is the widely feared constitutional convention—something for which the Constitution itself provides—to be called by Congress itself or two-thirds of the states. Jefferson expected one to occur every generation. Conventions are commonplace to revise state constitutions. But Congress has never even legislated the applicable rules for electing and conducting a national constitutional convention, even though more than 30 states have now called for one to adopt an amendment limiting federal taxes and expenditures. Because of the concern generated by this proposal, any idea of a national constitutional convention on the separation of powers is probably a non-starter.

A more practicable first step would be the appointment of a bipartisan presidential commission—perhaps an offshoot of President Carter's first-class Commission on the Eighties—to analyze the issues, compare how other constitutions work, hold public hearings, and make a full report. The presidential commission could include ranking members of the House and Senate, or perhaps Congress could establish a parallel joint commission of its own.

The point of this article is not to persuade the reader of the virtue of any particular amendment. I am far from persuaded myself. But I am convinced of these propositions:

We need to do better than we have in "forming a government" for this country, and this need is becoming more acute.

The structure of our Constitution prevents us from doing significantly better.

It is time to start thinking and debating about whether and how to correct this structural fault.

Notes

1. Carl McGowan, "Congress, Court, and Control of Delegated Power," *Columbia Law Review*, Vol. 77, No. 8 (1977), 1119-20.

2. *Congressional Government: A Study in American Politics* (Boston and New York: Houghton Mifflin, 1913). 284.

3. *The Adams-Jefferson Letters*, Vol. II, Lester J. Cappon, ed. (Chapel Hill: University of North Carolina Press, 1959), 134.

4. Quoted from Carl P. Leubsdorf, "Contemporary Problems Leave U.S. Political System Straining to Cope," reprinted in the *Congressional Record*, October 31, 1979, S15593-94.

5. The mention of this historic example may strike some readers as sharply impairing the general thesis of this article in favor of disciplined party voting in the Congress. But one can readily envisage a category of issues—analogous to mutual defense treaties—where an administration would not be entitled to apply party discipline. (In Britain, for example, votes on such issues as capital punishment have traditionally not been subject to the party whip.) Any measure amending the Constitution or affecting the separation of powers (as the 1937 Court plan did) should probably be exempted, as well as any issue of religious conscience, such as legislation bearing on abortion.

6. Similarly, the belated consensus on energy self-sufficiency did not restrain the Congress from overriding, by one of the largest margins in history, the president's unpopular but necessary oil import fee order.

7. Bob Eckhardt and Charles L. Black, Jr., *The Tides of Power: Conversations on the American Constitution* (New Haven: Yale University Press, 1976).

Conclusion: The Presidency in the 1980s 9.9

Richard M. Pious

With this concluding essay and the important considerations it raises, we come full circle from the first essay concerning the intentions of the framers. If the vision of the framers concerning a popularly controlled government with limits and balance is to continue, then the subject of accountability raised by Pious must be continuously addressed. To serve the spirit of the Constitution, we must

---

The American Presidency (pp. 16-22) by Richard M. Pious, 1979, New York: Basic Books, Inc. Copyright 1979 by Basic Books, Inc. Reprinted by permission.

constantly strive to insure that the presidency is powerful enough to govern but not powerful enough to oppress.

Presidential scholars make poor forecasters. Creators of the office were convinced by the end of the eighteenth century that incumbents would either subvert the Constitution or prove too weak to preserve it. Prior to the Civil War, constitutional lawyers, reacting to the presidencies of Jefferson and Jackson, argued that the office was the chief defect of the governmental system and should be checked by Congress or by a council of state. Few realized that the real danger to the Union would lie in a succession of weak incumbents incapable of uniting the sections to a common purpose. Near the turn of the nineteenth century the public-law scholars in the graduate schools of political science thought that the presidency was evolving into a ceremonial office, and would be displaced by an emerging parliamentary system. Most recently we had political scientists, using case-study and behavioral methods, claiming that incumbents governed in the national interest primarily through their powers of persuasion rather than by command—just at a time when several presidents used veto and impoundment prerogatives for domestic affairs and warmaking powers for their foreign policies.

It is clear that the only certain forecast about the presidency is that no forecast is certain. With this caution in mind I should like to conclude with some words about present trends and possible developments in the next decade.

The Accountability of Power

Presidents are not likely to become popular or party leaders. The mean turnouts of eligible voters will remain low and may decrease in the next several elections. Media techniques used during campaigns raise public expectations, whereas subsequent performances of incumbents in office result in a disillusioned and cynical electorate. The increase in the number of primaries and the changes in party rules leave incumbents vulnerable to intraparty challenges, and midterm policy conventions may embarrass the administration and provide ammunition for partisan opponents. Legislators will remain disassociated from the presidential electoral system, and the White House will be unable to purge dissidents or use the caucuses to impose party discipline.

Presidents will be tempted to appeal to the people. They will emphasize their expertise, their unique "vantage point," and equate their proposals with the national interest. But incumbents are not experts; worse, they are not perceived by legislators as effective politicians, nor by the public as competent managers. Interest groups all challenge the president when he attempts to define a national agenda. The media delight in putting incumbents on the defensive, and relish serving up the evidence of double-talk or double-dealing in the executive branch. The legacy of Watergate is wolfpack journalism, which will confirm the worst fears of the public. The White House will remain in a state of siege, as the normal transactions of the political system are unearthed, magnified, and then distorted by the media. Presidential attempts to control the national agenda seem destined to fail on most issues.

The Locus of Power

Presidents will continue the decentralization of domestic policymaking and program management. Bureau chiefs and program managers will maintain their ties with congressional committees and subcommittees, and with interest and clientele groups. Presidents are not likely to take more than a passing interest in struggles between departments and bureaus, or between state and federal officials, for in most cases their stakes are limited. Executive Office agencies, particularly the Office of Management and Budget and the domestic staff in the White House Office, will continue to participate in departmental business, thus maintaining the appearance, if not the reality, of intense presidential participation in domestic program planning. But the major stakes for the White House will be political and economic rather than programmatic or managerial: to retain some influence in the distributive process to build support in Congress and with state parties; to influence the magnitude and timing of national commitments so that aggregate spending levels do not exceed White House targets.

Presidential domestic priorities will involve management of fiscal and natural resource policymaking. In both areas Congress has traditionally played a major role, and it has created mechanisms in the budget, impoundment, and fiscal processes that require the administration to collaborate with it. There are substantial differences between the two parties in these areas, and a president who could capitalize on these differences might succeed as a legislative leader. But the problem for a Democratic president is that he might be tempted to rely on national agenda politics and so split his party on ideological or sectional lines. For a Republican president the danger is that party differences will be expressed institutionally through the checks and balances system, with an antiadministration majority in Congress dominating policymaking through the new fiscal and budget mechanisms. Split government might produce deadlock, followed by presidential subversion of the spirit or letter of the new mechanisms. It is likely that instead of party government, decentralized policymaking in the executive branch will be matched by autonomous legislative leaders working closely with interest groups to develop policies, which will then pass Congress through transactional methods. That is why prospects that the White House can develop, for example, serious energy and natural resource policies for long-term development without relying on emergency powers are not good.

The Limits of Power

Presidents will not be able to manage foreign relations well. The various foreign policy communities remain at odds with one another and with the White House: Defense wants more funds for advanced weapons systems and opposes concessions in arms limitation negotiations; the CIA remains demoralized as a result of cutbacks in personnel and increased White House supervision; State does not receive the authority it requests to manage foreign policy, and friction between it and the National Security Council staff seems to have become an institutionalized feature of the foreign policy machinery. The situation will not improve, because foreign affairs in the next decade will center on economic negotiations, and both State and the NSC staff remain poorly equipped to deal with these matters. In the resulting vacuum the Treasury, special White House aides, the ambassador to the United Nations, and even the vice-president, all stake out their "turf," or meddle in the business of State and the NSC. There are too many rhetorical flourishes, too many "policies" enunciated in too many speeches—and too little policy, direction, or coherence. Camp David successes remain sweet—and rare.

Presidents will continue to rely on their prerogative powers. Nixon, Ford, and Carter all argued that their powers as commander-in-chief could not be diminished by the War Powers Resolution. Each used constitutional authority to expend the functions of the intelligence community, strengthen secrecy systems, and make commitments to foreign nations. Presidents argue that they cannot be held legally liable by the judiciary for violations of constitutional rights of citizens in national security matters.

But presidents must contend with the "backlash" effects produced by Vietnam and Watergate. Congress has passed laws designed to provide it with more information about executive branch activities. These may require the president to specify the constitutional or legal authority for his actions, or provide Congress or its committees with information. Even when such information is classified or closely held, some committees have arranged to be briefed on a regular basis by administration officials. Each year Congress passes more laws that require briefings or formal reports. It is not clear, however, that presidents will provide timely or complete information to Congress. Nor is it certain that legislators have the time, the interest, or the ability to digest and act upon massive amounts of information that they now require be transmitted to them by the executive branch.

Congress has also legislated action-forcing mechanisms that limit or affect statutory presidential authority. These include requirements for the concurrence of committees or one or both chambers before action may be taken, concurrence if action is to be continued past a specified deadline, "vetoes" of actions already taken, and termination of an existing situation or repeal of presidential authority by concurrent resolution. These systems have not always worked well. Congress sometimes acts perfunctorily and acquiesces in important matters without thorough review of executive action. In other circumstances it uses these mechanisms to dominate the distributive process rather than to make policy. Occasionally the legislature uses these mechanisms as part of the checks and balances system, to require constructive modifications of administration proposals, as in the cases of arms sales to Iran and Saudi Arabia. The constitutionality of some of these mechanisms has been challenged by the White House, especially in circumstances where they seem to infringe on the constitutional prerogatives of the president. It is possible that some committee vetoes and concurrences will be struck down by the courts. Congress might then respond by tying its systems of administrative oversight directly to the appropriations process. What seems certain is that Congress intends to legislate more veto and concurrence systems, especially in national security affairs.

Presidents have at times evaded the letter or spirit of some of the action-forcing systems. Ford worked grudgingly within the impoundment system but tried to overload Congress with trivia. He avoided full compliance with the reporting provisions of the War Powers Resolution. Carter tied various arms sales to nations in the Middle East in a single package, pressuring Congress to approve all components by threatening to withdraw all sales if a single element were disapproved. He canceled the B-1 bomber in a way that evaded the mechanisms of the impoundment process. He did not concede the constitutionality of some of the provisions of the War Powers Resolution. He also questioned the constitutionality of several committee and chamber veto systems.

In the future presidents will continue to oppose such provisions, especially in national security matters. They argue that the government can speak no longer with one voice, since the executive may make promises or commitments that Congress will delay, modify, or refuse to honor. Foreign leaders will charge presidents with bad faith, or will conclude that the White House can neither make nor carry out a foreign policy. These leaders may be tempted to deal directly with members of Congress rather than confine their official representations and negotiations to the Department of State and the president. They will attempt to influence Congress not only by force of argument but, if past history is any guide, by national agenda politics and through transactions or corruption.

Presidents will be tempted to pass the buck and blame Congress for all setbacks in foreign policy. The stage seems set for a replay of the period just prior to World War II, when attempts by Congress to restrict presidential freedom of maneuver—which succeeded all too well—ultimately led the generation that assumed power in the postwar period to conclude that Congress was incapable of sharing power in foreign policymaking. However poorly some presidents have performed in recent years as world leaders, there is little evidence to suggest that Congress, as it presently operates, is in a position to formulate better policies. There is some evidence to suggest that without executive leadership, Congress is likely to blunder terribly in alliance politics. The challenge for Congress is to demonstrate that it can collaborate effectively with the executive in making foreign policy and in managing foreign relations, for if it fails to do so, its use of the new action-forcing mechanisms simply to check the president will leave it discredited, and a backlash will set in against the mechanisms it has created. In major crises the White House is likely to institute some form of prerogative government and disregard provisions of the mechanisms Congress has legislated; such seem to be the lessons of the *Mayaguez* incident and the evacuations in Indochina.

The Uses of Power

Like generals who plan for the next war around the lessons of the last one, presidential scholars have focused attention on the "dirty tricks" of the recent past. Preventing another Watergate by decreasing the size of the White House staff, preventing political police from functioning in the Executive Office, extending public financing of elections, providing for fuller disclosure of lobbying activities, and establishing mechanisms for a special prosecutor to investigate charges of malfeasance involving the White House—these are commendable reforms, and some will probably be instituted. But they do not address the central problem of presidential power: how to make collaborative government work.

Congress must demonstrate that the action-forcing collaborative mechanisms it has created can work in crises, and that they are a viable alternative to prerogative government. Collaboration means more than sharing superintendence of the departments with the executive branch in order to control the distributive process for the benefit of constituents, interest groups, and voting blocs. It involves more than dominating bureaus that administer routine programs. Rather, it involves interactions between the branches that result in important national policies; and it calls for effective use of mechanisms that require the president to inform, consult, and propose, and require Congress to concur, perfect, and if necessary veto presidential initiatives within a limited period of time. Perhaps the most important use of collaborative mechanisms is to keep presidents in a consultative and persuasive frame of mind, which involves a purpose as much psychological as institutional.

Presidents do their part when they invite full and timely consultation within the executive branch, permitting careerists to work closely with political executives in formulating options. They act in the spirit of the system when they give advance notice of their intentions to legislative leaders, provide them with adequate and relevant information, and allow congressional thinking to influence their own deliberations.

Congress does its part when it uses its pooled resources and staffs to obtain its own information and develop its own options. It then can evaluate presidential proposals against alternatives, prior to concurring, perfecting, or vetoing his initiatives. But as yet Congress has not demonstrated that it is prepared to assume a major role in a collaborative system. Incentives for legislators to take the initiative in making policy are lacking. Congress is still not committed to using advanced techniques in the budgetary process. It does not interact early enough with the departments to make a significant impact on overall expenditure levels or on program options. It continues to react, and therefore continues to acquiesce, while making "paper" policies or legislating irresponsible amendments in its budget resolutions. In some policy areas, such as taxation and energy, the committees go their own way; the net result is that the executive controls the resolution of some issues by default, while on other issues the chaotic, decentralized patterns of committee government are maintained.

Americans want presidents to solve problems. But the party system, the legislature, and the subgovernments each deny the White House the political power or legal authority necessary to manage public affairs. Because we emphasize the limits to power rather than the uses of power, incumbents must substitute rhetoric for achievement. In real or manufactured crises they institute forms of prerogative government, and such crises will continue to occur precisely because presidents remain too weak to manage most problems until they get out of hand. Prerogatives are still seen by the White House as the antidote to paralysis.

There are no easy answers to the problems of a presidential office that remains the major destabilizing factor in the political system by oscillating between too little and too much power. Decentralizing responsibility for most domestic programs to subgovernments and the federal system, strengthening collaborative mechanisms for management of the economy and foreign affairs, and setting new and stricter standards for the exercise of prerogative powers in genuine national emergencies—these might be steps toward placing presidential power and accountability in better constitutional balance.